Lecture Notes in Computer Science 12537

More information about this subseries at http://www.springer.com/series/7412

Adrien Bartoli · Andrea Fusiello (Eds.)

Computer Vision –
ECCV 2020 Workshops

Glasgow, UK, August 23–28, 2020
Proceedings, Part III

 Springer

Editors
Adrien Bartoli
University of Clermont Auvergne
Clermont Ferrand, France

Andrea Fusiello
Università degli Studi di Udine
Udine, Italy

ISSN 0302-9743   ISSN 1611-3349 (electronic)
Lecture Notes in Computer Science
ISBN 978-3-030-67069-6   ISBN 978-3-030-67070-2 (eBook)
https://doi.org/10.1007/978-3-030-67070-2

LNCS Sublibrary: SL6 – Image Processing, Computer Vision, Pattern Recognition, and Graphics

This Springer imprint is published by the registered company Springer Nature Switzerland AG
The registered company address is: Gewerbestrasse 11, 6330 Cham, Switzerland

Foreword

Hosting the 2020 European Conference on Computer Vision was certainly an exciting journey. From the 2016 plan to hold it at the Edinburgh International Conference Centre (hosting 1,800 delegates) to the 2018 plan to hold it at Glasgow's Scottish Exhibition Centre (up to 6,000 delegates), we finally ended with moving online because of the COVID-19 outbreak. While possibly having fewer delegates than expected because of the online format, ECCV 2020 still had over 3,100 registered participants.

Although online, the conference delivered most of the activities expected at a face-to-face conference: peer-reviewed papers, industrial exhibitors, demonstrations, and messaging between delegates. As well as the main technical sessions, the conference included a strong program of satellite events, including 16 tutorials and 44 workshops.

On the other hand, the online conference format enabled new conference features. Every paper had an associated teaser video and a longer full presentation video. Along with the papers and slides from the videos, all these materials were available the week before the conference. This allowed delegates to become familiar with the paper content and be ready for the live interaction with the authors during the conference week. The 'live' event consisted of brief presentations by the 'oral' and 'spotlight' authors and industrial sponsors. Question and Answer sessions for all papers were timed to occur twice so delegates from around the world had convenient access to the authors.

As with the 2018 ECCV, authors' draft versions of the papers appeared online with open access, now on both the Computer Vision Foundation (CVF) and the European Computer Vision Association (ECVA) websites. An archival publication arrangement was put in place with the cooperation of Springer. SpringerLink hosts the final version of the papers with further improvements, such as activating reference links and supplementary materials. These two approaches benefit all potential readers: a version available freely for all researchers, and an authoritative and citable version with additional benefits for SpringerLink subscribers. We thank Alfred Hofmann and Aliaksandr Birukou from Springer for helping to negotiate this agreement, which we expect will continue for future versions of ECCV.

August 2020

Vittorio Ferrari
Bob Fisher
Cordelia Schmid
Emanuele Trucco

Preface

Welcome to the workshops proceedings of the 16th European Conference on Computer Vision (ECCV 2020), the first edition held online. We are delighted that the main ECCV 2020 was accompanied by 45 workshops, scheduled on August 23, 2020, and August 28, 2020.

We received 101 valid workshop proposals on diverse computer vision topics and had space for 32 full-day slots, so we had to decline many valuable proposals (the workshops were supposed to be either full-day or half-day long, but the distinction faded away when the full ECCV conference went online). We endeavored to balance among topics, established series, and newcomers. Not all the workshops published their proceedings, or had proceedings at all. These volumes collect the edited papers from 28 out of 45 workshops.

We sincerely thank the ECCV general chairs for trusting us with the responsibility for the workshops, the workshop organizers for their involvement in this event of primary importance in our field, and the workshop presenters and authors.

August 2020

Adrien Bartoli
Andrea Fusiello

Organization

General Chairs

Vittorio Ferrari   Google Research, Switzerland
Bob Fisher   The University of Edinburgh, UK
Cordelia Schmid   Google and Inria, France
Emanuele Trucco   The University of Dundee, UK

Program Chairs

Andrea Vedaldi   University of Oxford, UK
Horst Bischof   Graz University of Technology, Austria
Thomas Brox   University of Freiburg, Germany
Jan-Michael Frahm   The University of North Carolina at Chapel Hill, USA

Industrial Liaison Chairs

Jim Ashe   The University of Edinburgh, UK
Helmut Grabner   Zurich University of Applied Sciences, Switzerland
Diane Larlus   NAVER LABS Europe, France
Cristian Novotny   The University of Edinburgh, UK

Local Arrangement Chairs

Yvan Petillot   Heriot-Watt University, UK
Paul Siebert   The University of Glasgow, UK

Academic Demonstration Chair

Thomas Mensink   Google Research and University of Amsterdam,
    The Netherlands

Poster Chair

Stephen Mckenna   The University of Dundee, UK

Technology Chair

Gerardo Aragon Camarasa   The University of Glasgow, UK

Tutorial Chairs

Carlo Colombo   University of Florence, Italy
Sotirios Tsaftaris   The University of Edinburgh, UK

Publication Chairs

Albert Ali Salah   Utrecht University, The Netherlands
Hamdi Dibeklioglu   Bilkent University, Turkey
Metehan Doyran   Utrecht University, The Netherlands
Henry Howard-Jenkins   University of Oxford, UK
Victor Adrian Prisacariu   University of Oxford, UK
Siyu Tang   ETH Zurich, Switzerland
Gul Varol   University of Oxford, UK

Website Chair

Giovanni Maria Farinella   University of Catania, Italy

Workshops Chairs

Adrien Bartoli   University Clermont Auvergne, France
Andrea Fusiello   University of Udine, Italy

Workshops Organizers

W01 - Adversarial Robustness in the Real World

Adam Kortylewski   Johns Hopkins University, USA
Cihang Xie   Johns Hopkins University, USA
Song Bai   University of Oxford, UK
Zhaowei Cai   UC San Diego, USA
Yingwei Li   Johns Hopkins University, USA
Andrei Barbu   MIT, USA
Wieland Brendel   University of Tübingen, Germany
Nuno Vasconcelos   UC San Diego, USA
Andrea Vedaldi   University of Oxford, UK
Philip H. S. Torr   University of Oxford, UK
Rama Chellappa   University of Maryland, USA
Alan Yuille   Johns Hopkins University, USA

W02 - BioImage Computation

Jan Funke   HHMI Janelia Research Campus, Germany
Dagmar Kainmueller   BIH and MDC Berlin, Germany
Florian Jug   CSBD and MPI-CBG, Germany
Anna Kreshuk   EMBL Heidelberg, Germany

Peter Bajcsy	NIST, USA
Martin Weigert	EPFL, Switzerland
Patrick Bouthemy	Inria, France
Erik Meijering	University New South Wales, Australia

W03 - Egocentric Perception, Interaction and Computing

Michael Wray	University of Bristol, UK
Dima Damen	University of Bristol, UK
Hazel Doughty	University of Bristol, UK
Walterio Mayol-Cuevas	University of Bristol, UK
David Crandall	Indiana University, USA
Kristen Grauman	UT Austin, USA
Giovanni Maria Farinella	University of Catania, Italy
Antonino Furnari	University of Catania, Italy

W04 - Embodied Vision, Actions and Language

Yonatan Bisk	Carnegie Mellon University, USA
Jesse Thomason	University of Washington, USA
Mohit Shridhar	University of Washington, USA
Chris Paxton	NVIDIA, USA
Peter Anderson	Georgia Tech, USA
Roozbeh Mottaghi	Allen Institute for AI, USA
Eric Kolve	Allen Institute for AI, USA

W05 - Eye Gaze in VR, AR, and in the Wild

Hyung Jin Chang	University of Birmingham, UK
Seonwook Park	ETH Zurich, Switzerland
Xucong Zhang	ETH Zurich, Switzerland
Otmar Hilliges	ETH Zurich, Switzerland
Aleš Leonardis	University of Birmingham, UK
Robert Cavin	Facebook Reality Labs, USA
Cristina Palmero	University of Barcelona, Spain
Jixu Chen	Facebook, USA
Alexander Fix	Facebook Reality Labs, USA
Elias Guestrin	Facebook Reality Labs, USA
Oleg Komogortsev	Texas State University, USA
Kapil Krishnakumar	Facebook, USA
Abhishek Sharma	Facebook Reality Labs, USA
Yiru Shen	Facebook Reality Labs, USA
Tarek Hefny	Facebook Reality Labs, USA
Karsten Behrendt	Facebook, USA
Sachin S. Talathi	Facebook Reality Labs, USA

W06 - Holistic Scene Structures for 3D Vision

Zihan Zhou	Penn State University, USA
Yasutaka Furukawa	Simon Fraser University, Canada
Yi Ma	UC Berkeley, USA
Shenghua Gao	ShanghaiTech University, China
Chen Liu	Facebook Reality Labs, USA
Yichao Zhou	UC Berkeley, USA
Linjie Luo	Bytedance Inc., China
Jia Zheng	ShanghaiTech University, China
Junfei Zhang	Kujiale.com, China
Rui Tang	Kujiale.com, China

W07 - Joint COCO and LVIS Recognition Challenge

Alexander Kirillov	Facebook AI Research, USA
Tsung-Yi Lin	Google Research, USA
Yin Cui	Google Research, USA
Matteo Ruggero Ronchi	California Institute of Technology, USA
Agrim Gupta	Stanford University, USA
Ross Girshick	Facebook AI Research, USA
Piotr Dollar	Facebook AI Research, USA

W08 - Object Tracking and Its Many Guises

Achal D. Dave	Carnegie Mellon University, USA
Tarasha Khurana	Carnegie Mellon University, USA
Jonathon Luiten	RWTH Aachen University, Germany
Aljosa Osep	Technical University of Munich, Germany
Pavel Tokmakov	Carnegie Mellon University, USA

W09 - Perception for Autonomous Driving

Li Erran Li	Alexa AI, Amazon, USA
Adrien Gaidon	Toyota Research Institute, USA
Wei-Lun Chao	The Ohio State University, USA
Peter Ondruska	Lyft, UK
Rowan McAllister	UC Berkeley, USA
Larry Jackel	North-C Technologies, USA
Jose M. Alvarez	NVIDIA, USA

W10 - TASK-CV Workshop and VisDA Challenge

Tatiana Tommasi	Politecnico di Torino, Italy
Antonio M. Lopez	CVC and UAB, Spain
David Vazquez	Element AI, Canada
Gabriela Csurka	NAVER LABS Europe, France
Kate Saenko	Boston University, USA
Liang Zheng	The Australian National University, Australia

Xingchao Peng   Boston University, USA
Weijian Deng   The Australian National University, Australia

W11 - Bodily Expressed Emotion Understanding

James Z. Wang   Penn State University, USA
Reginald B. Adams, Jr.   Penn State University, USA
Yelin Kim   Amazon Lab126, USA

W12 - Commands 4 Autonomous Vehicles

Thierry Deruyttere   KU Leuven, Belgium
Simon Vandenhende   KU Leuven, Belgium
Luc Van Gool   KU Leuven, Belgium, and ETH Zurich, Switzerland
Matthew Blaschko   KU Leuven, Belgium
Tinne Tuytelaars   KU Leuven, Belgium
Marie-Francine Moens   KU Leuven, Belgium
Yu Liu   KU Leuven, Belgium
Dusan Grujicic   KU Leuven, Belgium

W13 - Computer VISion for ART Analysis

Alessio Del Bue   Istituto Italiano di Tecnologia, Italy
Sebastiano Vascon   Ca' Foscari University and European Centre for Living
                            Technology, Italy
Peter Bell   Friedrich-Alexander University Erlangen-Nürnberg,
                            Germany
Leonardo L. Impett   EPFL, Switzerland
Stuart James   Istituto Italiano di Tecnologia, Italy

W14 - International Challenge on Compositional and Multimodal Perception

Alec Hodgkinson   Panasonic Corporation, Japan
Yusuke Urakami   Panasonic Corporation, Japan
Kazuki Kozuka   Panasonic Corporation, Japan
Ranjay Krishna   Stanford University, USA
Olga Russakovsky   Princeton University, USA
Juan Carlos Niebles   Stanford University, USA
Jingwei Ji   Stanford University, USA
Li Fei-Fei   Stanford University, USA

W15 - Sign Language Recognition, Translation and Production

Necati Cihan Camgoz   University of Surrey, UK
Richard Bowden   University of Surrey, UK
Andrew Zisserman   University of Oxford, UK
Gul Varol   University of Oxford, UK
Samuel Albanie   University of Oxford, UK

| Kearsy Cormier | University College London, UK |
| Neil Fox | University College London, UK |

W16 - Visual Inductive Priors for Data-Efficient Deep Learning

Jan van Gemert	Delft University of Technology, The Netherlands
Robert-Jan Bruintjes	Delft University of Technology, The Netherlands
Attila Lengyel	Delft University of Technology, The Netherlands
Osman Semih Kayhan	Delft University of Technology, The Netherlands
Marcos Baptista-Ríos	Alcalá University, Spain
Anton van den Hengel	The University of Adelaide, Australia

W17 - Women in Computer Vision

Hilde Kuehne	IBM, USA
Amaia Salvador	Amazon, USA
Ananya Gupta	The University of Manchester, UK
Yana Hasson	Inria, France
Anna Kukleva	Max Planck Institute, Germany
Elizabeth Vargas	Heriot-Watt University, UK
Xin Wang	UC Berkeley, USA
Irene Amerini	Sapienza University of Rome, Italy

W18 - 3D Poses in the Wild Challenge

Gerard Pons-Moll	Max Planck Institute for Informatics, Germany
Angjoo Kanazawa	UC Berkeley, USA
Michael Black	Max Planck Institute for Intelligent Systems, Germany
Aymen Mir	Max Planck Institute for Informatics, Germany

W19 - 4D Vision

Anelia Angelova	Google, USA
Vincent Casser	Waymo, USA
Jürgen Sturm	X, USA
Noah Snavely	Google, USA
Rahul Sukthankar	Google, USA

W20 - Map-Based Localization for Autonomous Driving

Patrick Wenzel	Technical University of Munich, Germany
Niclas Zeller	Artisense, Germany
Nan Yang	Technical University of Munich, Germany
Rui Wang	Technical University of Munich, Germany
Daniel Cremers	Technical University of Munich, Germany

W21 - Multimodal Video Analysis Workshop and Moments in Time Challenge

Dhiraj Joshi	IBM Research AI, USA
Rameswar Panda	IBM Research, USA
Kandan Ramakrishnan	IBM, USA
Rogerio Feris	IBM Research AI, MIT-IBM Watson AI Lab, USA
Rami Ben-Ari	IBM-Research, USA
Danny Gutfreund	IBM, USA
Mathew Monfort	MIT, USA
Hang Zhao	MIT, USA
David Harwath	MIT, USA
Aude Oliva	MIT, USA
Zhicheng Yan	Facebook AI, USA

W22 - Recovering 6D Object Pose

Tomas Hodan	Czech Technical University in Prague, Czech Republic
Martin Sundermeyer	German Aerospace Center, Germany
Rigas Kouskouridas	Scape Technologies, UK
Tae-Kyun Kim	Imperial College London, UK
Jiri Matas	Czech Technical University in Prague, Czech Republic
Carsten Rother	Heidelberg University, Germany
Vincent Lepetit	ENPC ParisTech, France
Ales Leonardis	University of Birmingham, UK
Krzysztof Walas	Poznan University of Technology, Poland
Carsten Steger	Technical University of Munich and MVTec Software GmbH, Germany
Eric Brachmann	Heidelberg University, Germany
Bertram Drost	MVTec Software GmbH, Germany
Juil Sock	Imperial College London, UK

W23 - SHApe Recovery from Partial Textured 3D Scans

Djamila Aouada	University of Luxembourg, Luxembourg
Kseniya Cherenkova	Artec3D and University of Luxembourg, Luxembourg
Alexandre Saint	University of Luxembourg, Luxembourg
David Fofi	University Bourgogne Franche-Comté, France
Gleb Gusev	Artec3D, Luxembourg
Bjorn Ottersten	University of Luxembourg, Luxembourg

W24 - Advances in Image Manipulation Workshop and Challenges

Radu Timofte	ETH Zurich, Switzerland
Andrey Ignatov	ETH Zurich, Switzerland
Kai Zhang	ETH Zurich, Switzerland
Dario Fuoli	ETH Zurich, Switzerland
Martin Danelljan	ETH Zurich, Switzerland
Zhiwu Huang	ETH Zurich, Switzerland

Hannan Lu	Harbin Institute of Technology, China
Wangmeng Zuo	Harbin Institute of Technology, China
Shuhang Gu	The University of Sydney, Australia
Ming-Hsuan Yang	UC Merced and Google, USA
Majed El Helou	EPFL, Switzerland
Ruofan Zhou	EPFL, Switzerland
Sabine Süsstrunk	EPFL, Switzerland
Sanghyun Son	Seoul National University, South Korea
Jaerin Lee	Seoul National University, South Korea
Seungjun Nah	Seoul National University, South Korea
Kyoung Mu Lee	Seoul National University, South Korea
Eli Shechtman	Adobe, USA
Evangelos Ntavelis	ETH Zurich and CSEM, Switzerland
Andres Romero	ETH Zurich, Switzerland
Yawei Li	ETH Zurich, Switzerland
Siavash Bigdeli	CSEM, Switzerland
Pengxu Wei	Sun Yat-sen University, China
Liang Lin	Sun Yat-sen University, China
Ming-Yu Liu	NVIDIA, USA
Roey Mechrez	BeyondMinds and Technion, Israel
Luc Van Gool	KU Leuven, Belgium, and ETH Zurich, Switzerland

W25 - Assistive Computer Vision and Robotics

Marco Leo	National Research Council of Italy, Italy
Giovanni Maria Farinella	University of Catania, Italy
Antonino Furnari	University of Catania, Italy
Gerard Medioni	University of Southern California, USA
Trivedi Mohan	UC San Diego, USA

W26 - Computer Vision for UAVs Workshop and Challenge

Dawei Du	Kitware Inc., USA
Heng Fan	Stony Brook University, USA
Toon Goedemé	KU Leuven, Belgium
Qinghua Hu	Tianjin University, China
Haibin Ling	Stony Brook University, USA
Davide Scaramuzza	University of Zurich, Switzerland
Mubarak Shah	University of Central Florida, USA
Tinne Tuytelaars	KU Leuven, Belgium
Kristof Van Beeck	KU Leuven, Belgium
Longyin Wen	JD Digits, USA
Pengfei Zhu	Tianjin University, China

W27 - Embedded Vision

| Tse-Wei Chen | Canon Inc., Japan |
| Nabil Belbachir | NORCE Norwegian Research Centre AS, Norway |

Stephan Weiss   University of Klagenfurt, Austria
Marius Leordeanu   Politehnica University of Bucharest, Romania

W28 - Learning 3D Representations for Shape and Appearance

Leonidas Guibas   Stanford University, USA
Or Litany   Stanford University, USA
Tanner Schmidt   Facebook Reality Labs, USA
Vincent Sitzmann   Stanford University, USA
Srinath Sridhar   Stanford University, USA
Shubham Tulsiani   Facebook AI Research, USA
Gordon Wetzstein   Stanford University, USA

W29 - Real-World Computer Vision from inputs with Limited Quality and Tiny Object Detection Challenge

Yuqian Zhou   University of Illinois, USA
Zhenjun Han   University of the Chinese Academy of Sciences, China
Yifan Jiang   The University of Texas at Austin, USA
Yunchao Wei   University of Technology Sydney, Australia
Jian Zhao   Institute of North Electronic Equipment, Singapore
Zhangyang Wang   The University of Texas at Austin, USA
Qixiang Ye   University of the Chinese Academy of Sciences, China
Jiaying Liu   Peking University, China
Xuehui Yu   University of the Chinese Academy of Sciences, China
Ding Liu   Bytedance, China
Jie Chen   Peking University, China
Humphrey Shi   University of Oregon, USA

W30 - Robust Vision Challenge 2020

Oliver Zendel   Austrian Institute of Technology, Austria
Hassan Abu Alhaija   Interdisciplinary Center for Scientific Computing
                                 Heidelberg, Germany
Rodrigo Benenson   Google Research, Switzerland
Marius Cordts   Daimler AG, Germany
Angela Dai   Technical University of Munich, Germany
Andreas Geiger   Max Planck Institute for Intelligent Systems
                                 and University of Tübingen, Germany
Niklas Hanselmann   Daimler AG, Germany
Nicolas Jourdan   Daimler AG, Germany
Vladlen Koltun   Intel Labs, USA
Peter Kontschieder   Mapillary Research, Austria
Yubin Kuang   Mapillary AB, Sweden
Alina Kuznetsova   Google Research, Switzerland
Tsung-Yi Lin   Google Brain, USA
Claudio Michaelis   University of Tübingen, Germany
Gerhard Neuhold   Mapillary Research, Austria

Matthias Niessner	Technical University of Munich, Germany
Marc Pollefeys	ETH Zurich and Microsoft, Switzerland
Francesc X. Puig Fernandez	MIT, USA
Rene Ranftl	Intel Labs, USA
Stephan R. Richter	Intel Labs, USA
Carsten Rother	Heidelberg University, Germany
Torsten Sattler	Chalmers University of Technology, Sweden and Czech Technical University in Prague, Czech Republic
Daniel Scharstein	Middlebury College, USA
Hendrik Schilling	rabbitAI, Germany
Nick Schneider	Daimler AG, Germany
Jonas Uhrig	Daimler AG, Germany
Jonas Wulff	Max Planck Institute for Intelligent Systems, Germany
Bolei Zhou	The Chinese University of Hong Kong, China

W31 - The Bright and Dark Sides of Computer Vision: Challenges and Opportunities for Privacy and Security

Mario Fritz	CISPA Helmholtz Center for Information Security, Germany
Apu Kapadia	Indiana University, USA
Jan-Michael Frahm	The University of North Carolina at Chapel Hill, USA
David Crandall	Indiana University, USA
Vitaly Shmatikov	Cornell University, USA

W32 - The Visual Object Tracking Challenge

Matej Kristan	University of Ljubljana, Slovenia
Jiri Matas	Czech Technical University in Prague, Czech Republic
Ales Leonardis	University of Birmingham, UK
Michael Felsberg	Linköping University, Sweden
Roman Pflugfelder	Austrian Institute of Technology, Austria
Joni-Kristian Kamarainen	Tampere University, Finland
Martin Danelljan	ETH Zurich, Switzerland

W33 - Video Turing Test: Toward Human-Level Video Story Understanding

Yu-Jung Heo	Seoul National University, South Korea
Seongho Choi	Seoul National University, South Korea
Kyoung-Woon On	Seoul National University, South Korea
Minsu Lee	Seoul National University, South Korea
Vicente Ordonez	University of Virginia, USA
Leonid Sigal	University of British Columbia, Canada
Chang D. Yoo	KAIST, South Korea
Gunhee Kim	Seoul National University, South Korea
Marcello Pelillo	University of Venice, Italy
Byoung-Tak Zhang	Seoul National University, South Korea

W34 - "Deep Internal Learning": Training with no prior examples

Michal Irani	Weizmann Institute of Science, Israel
Tomer Michaeli	Technion, Israel
Tali Dekel	Google, Israel
Assaf Shocher	Weizmann Institute of Science, Israel
Tamar Rott Shaham	Technion, Israel

W35 - Benchmarking Trajectory Forecasting Models

Alexandre Alahi	EPFL, Switzerland
Lamberto Ballan	University of Padova, Italy
Luigi Palmieri	Bosch, Germany
Andrey Rudenko	Örebro University, Sweden
Pasquale Coscia	University of Padova, Italy

W36 - Beyond mAP: Reassessing the Evaluation of Object Detection

David Hall	Queensland University of Technology, Australia
Niko Suenderhauf	Queensland University of Technology, Australia
Feras Dayoub	Queensland University of Technology, Australia
Gustavo Carneiro	The University of Adelaide, Australia
Chunhua Shen	The University of Adelaide, Australia

W37 - Imbalance Problems in Computer Vision

Sinan Kalkan	Middle East Technical University, Turkey
Emre Akbas	Middle East Technical University, Turkey
Nuno Vasconcelos	UC San Diego, USA
Kemal Oksuz	Middle East Technical University, Turkey
Baris Can Cam	Middle East Technical University, Turkey

W38 - Long-Term Visual Localization under Changing Conditions

Torsten Sattler	Chalmers University of Technology, Sweden, and Czech Technical University in Prague, Czech Republic
Vassileios Balntas	Facebook Reality Labs, USA
Fredrik Kahl	Chalmers University of Technology, Sweden
Krystian Mikolajczyk	Imperial College London, UK
Tomas Pajdla	Czech Technical University in Prague, Czech Republic
Marc Pollefeys	ETH Zurich and Microsoft, Switzerland
Josef Sivic	Inria, France, and Czech Technical University in Prague, Czech Republic
Akihiko Torii	Tokyo Institute of Technology, Japan
Lars Hammarstrand	Chalmers University of Technology, Sweden
Huub Heijnen	Facebook, UK
Maddern Will	Nuro, USA
Johannes L. Schönberger	Microsoft, Switzerland

Pablo Speciale   ETH Zurich, Switzerland
Carl Toft   Chalmers University of Technology, Sweden

W39 - Sensing, Understanding, and Synthesizing Humans

Ziwei Liu   The Chinese University of Hong Kong, China
Sifei Liu   NVIDIA, USA
Xiaolong Wang   UC San Diego, USA
Hang Zhou   The Chinese University of Hong Kong, China
Wayne Wu   SenseTime, China
Chen Change Loy   Nanyang Technological University, Singapore

W40 - Computer Vision Problems in Plant Phenotyping

Hanno Scharr   Forschungszentrum Jülich, Germany
Tony Pridmore   University of Nottingham, UK
Sotirios Tsaftaris   The University of Edinburgh, UK

W41 - Fair Face Recognition and Analysis

Sergio Escalera   CVC and University of Barcelona, Spain
Rama Chellappa   University of Maryland, USA
Eduard Vazquez   Anyvision, UK
Neil Robertson   Queen's University Belfast, UK
Pau Buch-Cardona   CVC, Spain
Tomas Sixta   Anyvision, UK
Julio C. S. Jacques Junior   Universitat Oberta de Catalunya and CVC, Spain

W42 - GigaVision: When Gigapixel Videography Meets Computer Vision

Lu Fang   Tsinghua University, China
Shengjin Wang   Tsinghua University, China
David J. Brady   Duke University, USA
Feng Yang   Google Research, USA

W43 - Instance-Level Recognition

Andre Araujo   Google, USA
Bingyi Cao   Google, USA
Ondrej Chum   Czech Technical University in Prague, Czech Republic
Bohyung Han   Seoul National University, South Korea
Torsten Sattler   Chalmers University of Technology, Sweden
                                   and Czech Technical University in Prague,
                                   Czech Republic
Jack Sim   Google, USA
Giorgos Tolias   Czech Technical University in Prague, Czech Republic
Tobias Weyand   Google, USA

Xu Zhang	Columbia University, USA
Cam Askew	Google, USA
Guangxing Han	Columbia University, USA

W44 - Perception Through Structured Generative Models

Adam W. Harley	Carnegie Mellon University, USA
Katerina Fragkiadaki	Carnegie Mellon University, USA
Shubham Tulsiani	Facebook AI Research, USA

W45 - Self Supervised Learning – What is Next?

Christian Rupprecht	University of Oxford, UK
Yuki M. Asano	University of Oxford, UK
Armand Joulin	Facebook AI Research, USA
Andrea Vedaldi	University of Oxford, UK

Contents – Parts III

W24 - Advances in Image Manipulation Workshop and Challenges

AIM 2020 Challenge on Efficient Super-Resolution: Methods and Results . . . 5
*Kai Zhang, Martin Danelljan, Yawei Li, Radu Timofte, Jie Liu, Jie Tang,
Gangshan Wu, Yu Zhu, Xiangyu He, Wenjie Xu, Chenghua Li,
Cong Leng, Jian Cheng, Guangyang Wu, Wenyi Wang, Xiaohong Liu,
Hengyuan Zhao, Xiangtao Kong, Jingwen He, Yu Qiao, Chao Dong,
Xiaotong Luo, Liang Chen, Jiangtao Zhang, Maitreya Suin,
Kuldeep Purohit, A. N. Rajagopalan, Xiaochuan Li, Zhiqiang Lang,
Jiangtao Nie, Wei Wei, Lei Zhang, Abdul Muqeet, Jiwon Hwang,
Subin Yang, JungHeum Kang, Sung-Ho Bae, Yongwoo Kim, Yanyun Qu,
Geun-Woo Jeon, Jun-Ho Choi, Jun-Hyuk Kim, Jong-Seok Lee,
Steven Marty, Eric Marty, Dongliang Xiong, Siang Chen, Lin Zha,
Jiande Jiang, Xinbo Gao, Wen Lu, Haicheng Wang, Vineeth Bhaskara,
Alex Levinshtein, Stavros Tsogkas, Allan Jepson, Xiangzhen Kong,
Tongtong Zhao, Shanshan Zhao, P. S. Hrishikesh, Densen Puthussery,
C. V. Jiji, Nan Nan, Shuai Liu, Jie Cai, Zibo Meng, Jiaming Ding,
Chiu Man Ho, Xuehui Wang, Qiong Yan, Yuzhi Zhao, Long Chen,
Long Sun, Wenhao Wang, Zhenbing Liu, Rushi Lan,
Rao Muhammad Umer, and Christian Micheloni*

Residual Feature Distillation Network for Lightweight Image
Super-Resolution. 41
Jie Liu, Jie Tang, and Gangshan Wu

Efficient Image Super-Resolution Using Pixel Attention. 56
Hengyuan Zhao, Xiangtao Kong, Jingwen He, Yu Qiao, and Chao Dong

LarvaNet: Hierarchical Super-Resolution via Multi-exit Architecture 73
Geun-Woo Jeon, Jun-Ho Choi, Jun-Hyuk Kim, and Jong-Seok Lee

Efficient Super-Resolution Using MobileNetV3 87
*Haicheng Wang, Vineeth Bhaskara, Alex Levinshtein, Stavros Tsogkas,
and Allan Jepson*

Multi-attention Based Ultra Lightweight Image Super-Resolution 103
*Abdul Muqeet, Jiwon Hwang, Subin Yang, JungHeum Kang,
Yongwoo Kim, and Sung-Ho Bae*

Adaptive Hybrid Composition Based Super-Resolution Network
via Fine-Grained Channel Pruning.   119
  Siang Chen, Kai Huang, Bowen Li, Dongliang Xiong, Haitian Jiang,
  and Luc Claesen

IdleSR: Efficient Super-Resolution Network with Multi-scale IdleBlocks   136
  Dongliang Xiong, Kai Huang, Haitian Jiang, Bowen Li, Siang Chen,
  and Xiaowen Jiang

AIM 2020 Challenge on Learned Image Signal Processing Pipeline.   152
  Andrey Ignatov, Radu Timofte, Zhilu Zhang, Ming Liu, Haolin Wang,
  Wangmeng Zuo, Jiawei Zhang, Ruimao Zhang, Zhanglin Peng,
  Sijie Ren, Linhui Dai, Xiaohong Liu, Chengqi Li, Jun Chen, Yuichi Ito,
  Bhavya Vasudeva, Puneesh Deora, Umapada Pal, Zhenyu Guo, Yu Zhu,
  Tian Liang, Chenghua Li, Cong Leng, Zhihong Pan, Baopu Li,
  Byung-Hoon Kim, Joonyoung Song, Jong Chul Ye, JaeHyun Baek,
  Magauiya Zhussip, Yeskendir Koishekenov, Hwechul Cho Ye, Xin Liu,
  Xueying Hu, Jun Jiang, Jinwei Gu, Kai Li, Pengliang Tan,
  and Bingxin Hou

EEDNet: Enhanced Encoder-Decoder Network for AutoISP   171
  Yu Zhu, Zhenyu Guo, Tian Liang, Xiangyu He, Chenghua Li,
  Cong Leng, Bo Jiang, Yifan Zhang, and Jian Cheng

AWNet: Attentive Wavelet Network for Image ISP   185
  Linhui Dai, Xiaohong Liu, Chengqi Li, and Jun Chen

PyNET-CA: Enhanced PyNET with Channel Attention for End-to-End
Mobile Image Signal Processing   202
  Byung-Hoon Kim, Joonyoung Song, Jong Chul Ye, and JaeHyun Baek

AIM 2020 Challenge on Rendering Realistic Bokeh   213
  Andrey Ignatov, Radu Timofte, Ming Qian, Congyu Qiao, Jiamin Lin,
  Zhenyu Guo, Chenghua Li, Cong Leng, Jian Cheng, Juewen Peng,
  Xianrui Luo, Ke Xian, Zijin Wu, Zhiguo Cao, Densen Puthussery,
  C. V. Jiji, P. S. Hrishikesh, Melvin Kuriakose, Saikat Dutta,
  Sourya Dipta Das, Nisarg A. Shah, Kuldeep Purohit, Praveen Kandula,
  Maitreya Suin, A. N. Rajagopalan, M. B. Saagara, A. L. Minnu,
  A. R. Sanjana, S. Praseeda, Ge Wu, Xueqin Chen, Tengyao Wang,
  Max Zheng, Hulk Wong, and Jay Zou

BGGAN: Bokeh-Glass Generative Adversarial Network for Rendering
Realistic Bokeh. 229
  Ming Qian, Congyu Qiao, Jiamin Lin, Zhenyu Guo, Chenghua Li,
  Cong Leng, and Jian Cheng

Bokeh Rendering from Defocus Estimation 245
  Xianrui Luo, Juewen Peng, Ke Xian, Zijin Wu, and Zhiguo Cao

Human Motion Transfer from Poses in the Wild. 262
  Jian Ren, Menglei Chai, Sergey Tulyakov, Chen Fang, Xiaohui Shen,
  and Jianchao Yang

CA-GAN: Weakly Supervised Color Aware GAN for Controllable
Makeup Transfer. 280
  Robin Kips, Pietro Gori, Matthieu Perrot, and Isabelle Bloch

FamilyGAN: Generating Kin Face Images Using Generative
Adversarial Networks 297
  Raunak Sinha, Mayank Vatsa, and Richa Singh

Genetic-GAN: Synthesizing Images Between Two Domains by Genetic
Crossover. 312
  Ishtiak Zaman and David Crandall

GIA-Net: Global Information Aware Network for Low-Light Imaging. 327
  Zibo Meng, Runsheng Xu, and Chiu Man Ho

Flexible Example-Based Image Enhancement with Task Adaptive Global
Feature Self-guided Network 343
  Dario Kneubuehler, Shuhang Gu, Luc Van Gool, and Radu Timofte

A Benchmark for Burst Color Constancy. 359
  Yanlin Qian, Jani Käpylä, Joni-Kristian Kämäräinen, Samu Koskinen,
  and Jiri Matas

Noise-Aware Merging of High Dynamic Range Image Stacks Without
Camera Calibration 376
  Param Hanji, Fangcheng Zhong, and Rafał K. Mantiuk

AIM 2020 Challenge on Real Image Super-Resolution:
Methods and Results   392
   Pengxu Wei, Hannan Lu, Radu Timofte, Liang Lin, Wangmeng Zuo,
   Zhihong Pan, Baopu Li, Teng Xi, Yanwen Fan, Gang Zhang,
   Jingtuo Liu, Junyu Han, Errui Ding, Tangxin Xie, Liang Cao, Yan Zou,
   Yi Shen, Jialiang Zhang, Yu Jia, Kaihua Cheng, Chenhuan Wu, Yue Lin,
   Cen Liu, Yunbo Peng, Xueyi Zou, Zhipeng Luo, Yuehan Yao, Zhenyu Xu,
   Syed Waqas Zamir, Aditya Arora, Salman Khan, Munawar Hayat,
   Fahad Shahbaz Khan, Keon-Hee Ahn, Jun-Hyuk Kim, Jun-Ho Choi,
   Jong-Seok Lee, Tongtong Zhao, Shanshan Zhao, Yoseob Han,
   Byung-Hoon Kim, JaeHyun Baek, Haoning Wu, Dejia Xu, Bo Zhou,
   Wei Guan, Xiaobo Li, Chen Ye, Hao Li, Haoyu Zhong, Yukai Shi,
   Zhijing Yang, Xiaojun Yang, Haoyu Zhong, Xin Li, Xin Jin, Yaojun Wu,
   Yingxue Pang, Sen Liu, Zhi-Song Liu, Li-Wen Wang, Chu-Tak Li,
   Marie-Paule Cani, Wan-Chi Siu, Yuanbo Zhou, Rao Muhammad Umer,
   Christian Micheloni, Xiaofeng Cong, Rajat Gupta, Keon-Hee Ahn,
   Jun-Hyuk Kim, Jun-Ho Choi, Jong-Seok Lee, Feras Almasri,
   Thomas Vandamme, and Olivier Debeir

Real Image Super Resolution via Heterogeneous Model Ensemble Using
GP-NAS   423
   Zhihong Pan, Baopu Li, Teng Xi, Yanwen Fan, Gang Zhang,
   Jingtuo Liu, Junyu Han, and Errui Ding

Enhanced Adaptive Dense Connection Single Image Super-Resolution.   437
   Tangxin Xie, Jing Li, Yi Shen, Yu Jia, Jialiang Zhang, and Bing Zeng

Self-calibrated Attention Neural Network for Real-World
Super Resolution.   453
   Kaihua Cheng and Chenhuan Wu

FAN: Frequency Aggregation Network for Real Image Super-Resolution. . . .   468
   Yingxue Pang, Xin Li, Xin Jin, Yaojun Wu, Jianzhao Liu, Sen Liu,
   and Zhibo Chen

Deep Cyclic Generative Adversarial Residual Convolutional Networks
for Real Image Super-Resolution.   484
   Rao Muhammad Umer and Christian Micheloni

AIM 2020: Scene Relighting and Illumination Estimation Challenge   499
Majed El Helou, Ruofan Zhou, Sabine Süsstrunk, Radu Timofte,
Mahmoud Afifi, Michael S. Brown, Kele Xu, Hengxing Cai, Yuzhong Liu,
Li-Wen Wang, Zhi-Song Liu, Chu-Tak Li, Sourya Dipta Das,
Nisarg A. Shah, Akashdeep Jassal, Tongtong Zhao, Shanshan Zhao,
Sabari Nathan, M. Parisa Beham, R. Suganya, Qing Wang,
Zhongyun Hu, Xin Huang, Yaning Li, Maitreya Suin, Kuldeep Purohit,
A. N. Rajagopalan, Densen Puthussery, P. S. Hrishikesh,
Melvin Kuriakose, C. V. Jiji, Yu Zhu, Liping Dong, Zhuolong Jiang,
Chenghua Li, Cong Leng, and Jian Cheng

WDRN: A Wavelet Decomposed RelightNet for Image Relighting   519
Densen Puthussery, Hrishikesh Panikkasseril Sethumadhavan,
Melvin Kuriakose, and Jiji Charangatt Victor

SA-AE for Any-to-Any Relighting   535
Zhongyun Hu, Xin Huang, Yaning Li, and Qing Wang

Deep Relighting Networks for Image Light Source Manipulation   550
Li-Wen Wang, Wan-Chi Siu, Zhi-Song Liu, Chu-Tak Li,
and Daniel P. K. Lun

LightNet: Deep Learning Based Illumination Estimation from
Virtual Images   568
Sabari Nathan and M. Parisa Beham

An Ensemble Neural Network for Scene Relighting with Light
Classification   581
Liping Dong, Yu Zhu, Zhuolong Jiang, Xiangyu He, Zhaohui Meng,
Chenghua Li, Cong Leng, and Jian Cheng

Long-Term Human Video Generation of Multiple Futures Using Poses   596
Naoya Fushishita, Antonio Tejero-de-Pablos, Yusuke Mukuta,
and Tatsuya Harada

AgingMapGAN (AMGAN): High-Resolution Controllable Face Aging
with Spatially-Aware Conditional GANs   613
Julien Despois, Frédéric Flament, and Matthieu Perrot

Unconstrained Text Detection in Manga: A New Dataset and Baseline   629
Julián Del Gobbo and Rosana Matuk Herrera

Joint Demosaicking and Denoising for CFA and MSFA Images Using
a Mosaic-Adaptive Dense Residual Network.   647
Zhihong Pan, Baopu Li, Hsuchun Cheng, and Yingze Bao

Gated Texture CNN for Efficient and Configurable Image Denoising   665
Kaito Imai and Takamichi Miyata

Quantized Warping and Residual Temporal Integration for Video
Super-Resolution on Fast Motions.............................. 682
   Konstantinos Karageorgos, Kassiani Zafeirouli,
   Konstantinos Konstantoudakis, Anastasios Dimou, and Petros Daras

Pyramidal Edge-Maps and Attention Based Guided Thermal
Super-Resolution... 698
   Honey Gupta and Kaushik Mitra

AIM 2020 Challenge on Image Extreme Inpainting.................. 716
   Evangelos Ntavelis, Andrés Romero, Siavash Bigdeli, Radu Timofte,
   Zheng Hui, Xiumei Wang, Xinbo Gao, Chajin Shin, Taeoh Kim,
   Hanbin Son, Sangyoun Lee, Chao Li, Fu Li, Dongliang He, Shilei Wen,
   Errui Ding, Mengmeng Bai, Shuchen Li, Yu Zeng, Zhe Lin, Jimei Yang,
   Jianming Zhang, Eli Shechtman, Huchuan Lu, Weijian Zeng,
   Haopeng Ni, Yiyang Cai, Chenghua Li, Dejia Xu, Haoning Wu, Yu Han,
   Uddin S. M. Nadim, Hae Woong Jang, Soikat Hasan Ahmed,
   Jungmin Yoon, Yong Ju Jung, Chu-Tak Li, Zhi-Song Liu, Li-Wen Wang,
   Wan-Chi Siu, Daniel P. K. Lun, Maitreya Suin, Kuldeep Purohit,
   A. N. Rajagopalan, Pratik Narang, Murari Mandal,
   and Pranjal Singh Chauhan

Fast Light-Weight Network for Extreme Image Inpainting Challenge....... 742
   Mengmeng Bai, Shuchen Li, Jianhua Fan, Chenchen Zhou, Li Zuo,
   Jaekeun Na, and MoonSik Jeong

Author Index 759

W24 - Advances in Image Manipulation Workshop and Challenges

W24 - Advances In Image Manipulation Workshop And Challenges

The second edition of the AIM workshop was organized jointly with ECCV 2020. The success of AIM 2020 was contributed by 27 organizers, 67 PC members, 6 sponsors, 300+ authors with submitted papers, 4 invited speakers and thousands of participants in 8 associated challenges. AIM 2020 attracted 94 paper submissions to its two tracks meant for early and regular papers and late and challenge papers. We had 12 submissions of rejected papers from ECCV 2020 and BMVC 2020, out of which 7 were accepted. In total, 60 papers were accepted for publication. Each submission (except the challenge reports) was reviewed on average by three reviewers. The pool of reviewers was comprised from PC members, organizers, and volunteer reviewers. AIM 2020 had 8 associated challenges on: scene relighting and illumination estimation, image extreme inpainting, learned image signal processing pipeline, rendering realistic bokeh, real image super-resolution, efficient super-resolution, video temporal super-resolution, and video extreme super-resolution. The challenges were hosted by the CodaLab platform. From thousands of registered participants, hundreds entered in the final test phases and submitted results, factsheets and codes/executables for reproducibility. 22 teams were awarded certificates from which the top ranking winners received prizes: money or an Nvidia Titan RTX GPU. We are grateful to our sponsors: Huawei, Qualcomm AI Research, MediaTek, Nvidia, Google, CVL/ETH Zurich. AIM 2020 had 4 highly impactful invited talks provided by David Bau (MIT) on "Reflected Light and Doors in the Sky: Rewriting a GAN's Rules", Richard Zhang (Adobe Research) on "Style and Structure Disentanglement for Image Manipulation", Ravi Ramamoorthi (UCSD) on "Light Fields and View Synthesis from Sparse Images: Revisiting Image-Based Rendering", and Peyman Milanfar (Google Research) on "Modern Computational Photography". We would like to express our gratitude to all our colleagues in the community for submitting papers, to our PC members for their support and help with the reviewing process, to all the challenge participants, to CodaLab for hosting our challenges, to the invited speakers for sharing their research, to our sponsors, and last but not least, to the attendees for their active, positive attitude.

This volume contains 44 papers from the workshop. The remaining papers were published in the preceding ECCVW volume, LNCS 12538.

August 2020

Radu Timofte
Andrey Ignatov
Kai Zhang
Dario Fuoli
Martin Danelljan
Zhiwu Huang
Hannan Lu
Wangmeng Zuo
Shuhang Gu
Ming-Hsuan Yang
Majed El Helou
Ruofan Zhou
Sabine Süsstrunk
Sanghyun Son
Jaerin Lee
Seungjun Nah
Kyoung Mu Lee
Eli Shechtman
Evangelos Ntavelis
Andres Romero
Siavash Bigdeli
Pengxu Wei
Liang Lin
Ming-Yu Liu
Roey Mechrez
Luc Van Gool

AIM 2020 Challenge on Efficient Super-Resolution: Methods and Results

Kai Zhang[1]([✉]), Martin Danelljan[1], Yawei Li[1], Radu Timofte[1], Jie Liu[2],
Jie Tang[2], Gangshan Wu[2], Yu Zhu[3], Xiangyu He[3], Wenjie Xu[3], Chenghua Li[3],
Cong Leng[3], Jian Cheng[3], Guangyang Wu[4], Wenyi Wang[4], Xiaohong Liu[5],
Hengyuan Zhao[6], Xiangtao Kong[6], Jingwen He[6], Yu Qiao[6], Chao Dong[6],
Xiaotong Luo[7], Liang Chen[7], Jiangtao Zhang[7], Maitreya Suin[8],
Kuldeep Purohit[8], A. N. Rajagopalan[8], Xiaochuan Li[9], Zhiqiang Lang[10],
Jiangtao Nie[10], Wei Wei[10], Lei Zhang[10], Abdul Muqeet[11], Jiwon Hwang[11],
Subin Yang[11], JungHeum Kang[11], Sung-Ho Bae[11], Yongwoo Kim[12],
Yanyun Qu[7], Geun-Woo Jeon[13], Jun-Ho Choi[13], Jun-Hyuk Kim[13],
Jong-Seok Lee[13], Steven Marty[14], Eric Marty[14], Dongliang Xiong[15],
Siang Chen[15], Lin Zha[16], Jiande Jiang[16], Xinbo Gao[17], Wen Lu[17],
Haicheng Wang[18], Vineeth Bhaskara[18], Alex Levinshtein[18], Stavros Tsogkas[18],
Allan Jepson[18], Xiangzhen Kong[19], Tongtong Zhao[20], Shanshan Zhao[21],
P. S. Hrishikesh[22], Densen Puthussery[22], C. V. Jiji[22], Nan Nan[23], Shuai Liu[23],
Jie Cai[24], Zibo Meng[24], Jiaming Ding[24], Chiu Man Ho[24], Xuehui Wang[25,26],
Qiong Yan[25], Yuzhi Zhao[27], Long Chen[26], Long Sun[28], Wenhao Wang[28],
Zhenbing Liu[28], Rushi Lan[28], Rao Muhammad Umer[29],
and Christian Micheloni[29]

[1] Computer Vision Lab, ETH Zurich, Zürich, Switzerland
{kai.zhang,martin.danelljan,yawei.li,radu.timofte}@vision.ee.ethz.ch
[2] State Key Laboratory for Novel Software Technology, Nanjing University,
Nanjing 210023, China
jieliu@smail.nju.edu.cn
[3] Nanjing Artificial Intelligence Chip Research, Institute of Automation, Chinese
Academy of Sciences (AiRiA); MAICRO, Nanjing, China
zhuyu.cv@gmail.com
[4] University of Electronic Science and Technology of China, Nanjing, China
mulns@outlook.com
[5] McMaster University, Hamilton, Canada
[6] Shenzhen Institutes of Advanced Technology, Chinese Academy of Sciences,
Beijing, China
hy.zhao1@siat.ac.cn
[7] Xiamen University, Xiamen, China
xiaotluo@qq.com, 1806668306@qq.com, 1328937778@qq.com
[8] Indian Institute of Technology Madras, Chennai, India
maitreyasuin21@gmail.com

K. Zhang, M. Danelljan, Y. Li and R. Timofte were the challenge organizers, while the
other authors participated in the challenge.
Appendix A contains the authors' teams and affiliations. AIM webpage: https://data.
vision.ee.ethz.ch/cvl/aim20/

A. Bartoli and A. Fusiello (Eds.): ECCV 2020 Workshops, LNCS 12537, pp. 5–40, 2020.
https://doi.org/10.1007/978-3-030-67070-2_1

[9] Nanjing University of Aeronautics and Astronautics, Nanjing, China
1182784700@qq.com
[10] School of Computer Science, Northwestern Polytechnical University, Xi'an, China
20153031071ang@mail.nwpu.edu.cn
[11] Kyung Hee University, Seoul, Republic of Korea
amuqeet@khu.ac.kr
[12] Sang Myung University, Seoul, Republic of Korea
[13] Yonsei University, Seoul, Republic of Korea
geun-woo.jeon@yonsei.ac.kr
[14] ETH Zurich, Zürich, Switzerland
martyste@student.ethz.ch
[15] Zhejiang University, Hangzhou, China
xiongdl@zju.edu.cn, 11631032@zju.edu.cn
[16] Qingdao Hi-image Technologies Co., Ltd. (Hisense Visual Technology Co., Ltd.),
Shandong, China
zhalin@hisense.com
[17] Xidian University, Xi'an, China
[18] Samsung AI Centre, Toronto, Canada
h.wang1@samsung.com
[19] Wuhan, China
neptune.team.ai@gmail.com
[20] Dalian Maritime University, Dalian, China
yaopuss@126.com
[21] China Everbright Bank Co., Ltd., Beijing, China
[22] College of Engineering, Trivandrum, India
hrishikeshps94@gmail.com
[23] Jinan, China
2829272117@qq.com
[24] InnoPeak Technology, Inc., Palo Alto, USA
caijie0620@mail.com
[25] SenseTime Research, Hong Kong, China
wangxh228@mail2.sysu.edu.cn
[26] Sun Yat-sen University, Guangzhou, China
[27] City University of Hong Kong, Kowloon, Hong Kong
[28] Guilin University of Electronic Technology, Guilin 541004, China
lungsuen@163.com
[29] University of Udine, Udine, Italy
engr.raoumer943@gmail.com

Abstract. This paper reviews the AIM 2020 challenge on efficient single image super-resolution with focus on the proposed solutions and results. The challenge task was to super-resolve an input image with a magnification factor ×4 based on a set of prior examples of low and corresponding high resolution images. The goal is to devise a network that reduces one or several aspects such as runtime, parameter count, FLOPs, activations, and memory consumption while at least maintaining PSNR of MSRRes-Net. The track had 150 registered participants, and 25 teams submitted the final results. They gauge the state-of-the-art in efficient single image super-resolution.

1 Introduction

Single image super-resolution (SR) aims at recovering a high-resolution (HR) image from a single degraded low-resolution (LR) image. Since the dawn of deep learning, this problem has been frequently tackled by researchers from low-level vision community with models based on convolutional neural networks (CNN) [9, 22, 23, 43]. In order to strive towards the ultimate goal of deploying SR models for real-world applications, there exist a number of important research directions. The most popular direction is to improve PSNR or the perceptual quality, based on bicubic degradation assumption [47, 59]. Significant achievements have been made on designing network architectures and training losses for this purpose [23, 50]. However, such bicubic degradation based methods would give rise to poor performance if the real degradation deviates from the assumed one [10]. Hence, another direction is to design a network to handle a more general degradation with varying factors such as blur kernel [61–64]. In practical applications, the blur kernel is usually unknown, thus some researchers attempt to estimate the blur kernel of a given LR image for better reconstruction [3]. Such a strategy has also been successfully applied to the direction of SR with unpaired data [35, 36], where even more general degradation operations are considered. A recently emerging direction is to account for the ill-posed nature of the SR problem by learning stochastic and explorable LR to HR mappings using GAN [2, 37] or Normalizing Flow based [34] approaches. This challenge report focuses on another research direction, namely that of *efficient SR*, which is of crucial importance in order to deploy models on resource-constrained devices.

There are many factors that affect the efficiency of an SR network. Some typical factors are runtime, the number of parameters, and floating point operations (FLOPs). During past few years, several efficient SR works have been proposed based on different techniques, including hand-designed network architectures [9, 18, 22, 65], network pruning [27], filter decomposition [25], network quantization [28, 33], neural architecture search (NAS) [4, 30], and knowledge distillation [15, 55]. Despite of significant achievements, these methods mostly focus on the number of parameters and FLOPs. Recent works on high-level tasks have pointed out that fewer FLOPs does not always indicate better network efficiency, and the number of network activations is instead a more accurate measure of the network efficiency [41]. As a result, efficient SR methods require a thorough analysis from different aspects rather than only from the aspects of parameters and FLOPs.

Jointly with the Advances in Image Manipulation (AIM) 2020 workshop, we organize the AIM Challenge on Efficient Super-Resolution. The task of the challenge is to super-resolve an LR image to an HR image with a magnification factor ×4 by a network that reduces one or several aspects such as runtime, parameters, FLOPs, activations and memory consumption, while at least maintaining PSNR of the baseline model. The challenge aims to seek advanced and novel solutions for efficient SR, to benchmark their efficiency, and identify the general trends.

2   AIM 2020 Efficient Super-Resolution Challenge

This challenge is one of the AIM 2020 associated challenges on: scene relighting and illumination estimation [11], image extreme inpainting [40], learned image signal processing pipeline [19], rendering realistic bokeh [20], real image super-resolution [51], efficient super-resolution [58], video temporal super-resolution [44] and video extreme super-resolution [12]. The objectives of this challenge are: (i) to advance research on efficient SR; (ii) to compare the efficiency of different methods and (iii) to offer an opportunity for academic and industrial attendees to interact and explore collaborations. This section details the challenge itself.

2.1   DIV2K Dataset [1]

Following [1], the DIV2K dataset is adopted, which contains 1,000 DIVerse 2K resolution RGB images. The HR DIV2K is divided into 800 training images, 100 validation images and 100 testing images. The corresponding LR DIV2K in this challenge is the bicubicly downsampled counterpart with a down-scaling factor ×4. The testing HR images are hidden from the participants during the whole challenge.

2.2   MSRResNet Baseline Model

The MSRResNet [50] serves as the reference SR model in this challenge. The aim is to improve its efficiency while maintaining the SR performance. The MSRResNet contains 16 residual blocks and a global identity skip connection is adopted. Specifically, each residual block of MSRResNet consists of two 3×3 convolutional layers with Leaky ReLU activation in the middle and an identity skip connection summed to its output, while the global identity skip connection directly sums the bilinearly interpolated LR image to the output of final convolutional layer. The reference MSRResNet is trained on DIV2K [1], Flickr2K and OST [49] datasets. The quantitative performance and efficiency metrics of MSRResNet are given as follows. (1) The number of parameters is 1,517,571 (1.5M). (2) The average PSNRs on validation and testing sets of DIV2K are 29.00 dB and 28.70 dB, respectively. (3) The average runtime over validation set with PyTorch 1.5.1, CUDA Toolkit 10.2, cuDNN 7.6.2 and a single Titan Xp GPU is 0.110 s. (4) The number of FLOPs for an input of size 256×256 is 166.36G. (5) The number of activations (*i.e.*, elements of all outputs of convolutional layers) for an input of size 256×256 is 292.55M. (5) The maximum GPU memory consumption for an input of size 256×256 is 610M. (6) The number of convolutional layers is 37.

2.3   Competition

The aim of this challenge is to devise a network that reduces one or several aspects such as runtime, parameters, FLOPs, activations and memory consumption while at least maintaining the PSNR of MSRResNet.

Challenge Phases. *(1) Development and validation phase:* The participants had access to the 800 LR/HR training image pairs and 100 LR validation images of the DIV2K dataset. The participants were also provided the reference MSRResNet model from github (https://github.com/znsc/MSRResNet), allowing them to benchmark its runtime on their system, and to adopt it as a baseline if desired. The participants could upload the HR validation results on the evaluation server to measure the PSNR of their model to get immediate feedback. The number of parameters and runtime was computed by the participant. *(2) Testing phase:* In the final test phase, the participants recieved access to the 100 LR testing images. The participants then submitted their super-resolved results to the Codalab evaluation server and e-mailed the code and factsheet to the organizers. The organizers verified and ran the provided code to obtain the final results. Finally, the participants received the final results at the end of the challenge.

Evaluation Protocol. The quantitative evaluation metrics includes validation and testing PSNRs, runtime, number of parameters, number of FLOPs, number of activations, and maximum GPU memory consumed during inference. The PSNR was measured by first discarding the 4-pixel boundary around the images. The runtime is averaged over the 100 LR validation images and the best one among three consecutive trails is selected as the final result. The FLOPs, activations, and memory consumption are evaluated on an input image of size 256×256. Among the above metrics, the runtime is regarded as the most important one. The validation and testing PSNRs should be at least on par with the baseline. A code example for calculating these metrics is available at https://github.com/cszn/KAIR/blob/master/main_challenge_sr.py.

3   Challenge Results

Table 1 reports the final test results and rankings of the teams. The solutions with lower validation PSNR than the MSRResNet baseline are not ranked. In addition, the solutions by lyl, LMSR, CET_CVLab and wozhu teams are not ranked due to the lack of experimental verification by the organizers. The results of the overall first place winner team in AIM 2019 constrained SR challenge [60] are also reported for comparison. The methods evaluated in Table 1 are briefly described in Sect. 4 and the team members are listed in Appendix A.

   According to Table 1, we can have the following observations. First, the NJU_MCG team is the overall first place winner of this challenge, while AiriA_CG and UESTC-MediaLab win the overall second place and overall third place, respectively. Second, NJU_MCG and AiriA_CG produce the best runtime; XPixel is the first place winner for the number of parameters; SC-CVLab, NJU_MCG and MLVC are the top-3 teams that achieve similar performance on FLOPs; NJU_MCG and AiriA_CG are the first two place winners for the number of activations; MLVC achieves the best performance for memory consumption. Third, MLVC and SC-CVLAB are superior in the number of parameters and the number of FLOPs but fail to get a matched runtime. On the other

Table 1. Results of AIM 2020 efficient SR challenge. '*' means the organizers did not verify the results. 'Runtime' is tested on validation datasets, the average image size is 421×421. '#Params' denotes the total number of parameters. 'FLOPs' is the abbreviation for floating point operations. '#Activations' measures the number of elements of all outputs of convolutional layers. 'Memory' represents maximum GPU memory consumption according to the PyTorch function `torch.cuda.max_memory_allocated()`. '#Conv' represents the number of convolutional layers. 'FLOPs', '#Activations', and 'Memory' are tested on an LR image of size 256×256. **This is not a challenge for PSNR improvement. The 'validation/testing PSNR' and '#Conv' are not ranked.**

Team	Author	PSNR [Val.]	PSNR [Test]	Runtime [Val.] [s]	#Params [M]	#FLOPs [G]	#Activations [M]	Memory [M]	#Conv	Extra Data
NJU_MCG	TinyJie	29.04	28.75	$0.037_{(1)}$	$0.433_{(3)}$	$27.10_{(2)}$	$112.03_{(1)}$	$200_{(4)}$	64	Yes
AiriA_CG	Now	29.00	28.70	$0.037_{(1)}$	$0.687_{(10)}$	$44.98_{(9)}$	$118.49_{(2)}$	$168_{(3)}$	33	Yes
UESTC-MediaLab	Mulns	29.01	28.70	$0.060_{(4)}$	$0.461_{(5)}$	$30.06_{(4)}$	$219.61_{(10)}$	$146_{(2)}$	57	Yes
XPixel	zzzhy	29.01	28.70	$0.066_{(6)}$	$0.272_{(1)}$	$32.19_{(6)}$	$270.53_{(12)}$	$311_{(8)}$	121	Yes
HaiYun	Sudo	29.09	28.78	$0.058_{(3)}$	$0.777_{(13)}$	$49.67_{(10)}$	$132.31_{(4)}$	$225_{(5)}$	104	Yes
IPCV_IITM	ms_ipcv	29.10	28.68	$0.064_{(5)}$	$0.761_{(12)}$	$50.85_{(11)}$	$130.41_{(3)}$	$229_{(6)}$	59	Yes
404NotFound	xiaochuanLi	29.01	28.70	$0.073_{(9)}$	$0.599_{(8)}$	$39.36_{(7)}$	$170.06_{(6)}$	$271_{(7)}$	90	Yes
MDISL-lab	ppplang	29.01	28.68	$0.067_{(7)}$	$0.660_{(9)}$	$42.40_{(8)}$	$149.09_{(5)}$	$516_{(12)}$	61	Yes
MLVC	ysb	29.00	28.72	$0.104_{(11)}$	$0.441_{(4)}$	$27.11_{(3)}$	$212.24_{(9)}$	$112_{(1)}$	159	No
XMUlab	SuckChen	29.00	28.77	$0.078_{(10)}$	$0.691_{(11)}$	$53.62_{(12)}$	$184.74_{(7)}$	$468_{(10)}$	72	No
MCML-Yonsei	GWJ	29.01	28.66	$0.070_{(8)}$	$1.289_{(15)}$	$84.43_{(14)}$	$188.74_{(8)}$	$798_{(16)}$	68	Yes
LMSR	martyste	29.00	28.71	$0.081^{*}_{(11)}$	$1.126_{(14)}$	$75.72^{*}_{(14)}$	$158.33^{*}_{(6)}$	$192^{*}_{(4)}$	31*	Yes
ZJUESR2020	BearMaxZJU	29.04	28.74	$0.105_{(12)}$	$0.516_{(6)}$	$54.38_{(13)}$	$225.44_{(11)}$	$594_{(13)}$	42	Yes
SC-CVLAB	chensa	29.01	28.72	0.157	$0.353_{(2)}$	$26.96_{(1)}$	$302.30_{(13)}$	$595_{(15)}$	91	Yes
HiImageTeam	HiImageTeam	29.01	28.68	0.153	$0.530_{(7)}$	$90.11_{(15)}$	$325.05_{(14)}$	$378_{(9)}$	101	Yes
SAMSUNG_TOR_AIC	hcwang	28.98	28.71	0.240	$0.558_{(8)}$	$31.88_{(5)}$	$576.45_{(16)}$	$477_{(11)}$	59	Yes
neptuneai	neptuneai	29.14	28.84	0.217	$1.227_{(14)}$	$147.72_{(16)}$	$535.82_{(15)}$	$597_{(15)}$	45	*
lyl	tongtong	29.44	29.13	*	0.408*	*	*	*	128*	No
CET_CVLab	hrishikeshps	29.00	28.74	5.00	1.378*	*	*	*	*	Yes
wozhu	wozhu	28.98	*	*	0.720*	*	*	*	*	Yes
The following 5 methods are not ranked since their validation/testing PSNRs are not on par with the baseline										
InnoPeak_SR	qiuzhangTiTi	28.93	28.60	0.053	0.361	81.72	145.75	66	35	Yes
Summer	sysu_wxh	28.87	28.54	0.043	0.488	31.82	125.30	227	35	No
Zhang9678	Zhang9678	28.78	28.50	*	0.664*	48.08*	*	*	36*	No
H-ZnCa	suen	28.69	28.42	0.045	0.364	32.01	170.45	299	67	No
MLP_SR	raoumer	27.89	27.77	1.313	0.047	50.66*	351.27*	1064	10*	Yes
Winner AIM19	*IMDN*	29.13	28.78	0.050	0.893	58.53	154.14	120	43	Yes
Baseline	*MSRResNet*	29.00	28.70	0.114	1.517	166.36	292.55	610	37	Yes

Table 2. Spearman rank-order correlation coefficient (SROCC) values of #Params, #FLOPs, #Activations, Memory with respect to runtime.

Metric	#Params	#FLOPs	#Activations	Memory
SROCC	0.1734	0.2397	0.8737	0.6671

hand, although the methods proposed by 404NotFound and MLVC have lower parameters and FLOPs than IMDN, they exhibit a much slower runtime. To analyze such discrepancies, we report the Spearman rank-order correlation coefficient (SROCC) values of the number of parameters, the number of FLOPs, the number of activations, and maximum GPU memory consumption with respect to runtime in Table 2. Note that SROCC is widely used to measure the prediction monotonicity of a metric and a better metric tends to have a higher SROCC. It can be seen from Table 2 that the number of parameters and the number of FLOPs do not correlate well with the runtime. Instead, the number of activations is a better metric. Such a phenomenon has also been reported in [41]. Note that the number of parameters and the number of FLOPs are still important aspects of model efficiency.

3.1 Architectures and Main Ideas

Various techniques are proposed to improve the efficiency of MSRResNet and IMDN. Some typical techniques are given in the following.

1. **Modifying the information multi-distillation block of IMDN.** The overall first place winner NJU_MCG proposed an efficient residual feature distillation block (RFDB) by incorporating shallow residual connection and enhanced spatial attention (ESA) module, using 1×1 convolutions for feature distillation, and reducing the number of channels from 64 to 50. AiRiA_CG proposed to reduce IMDB blocks and adopt converted asymmetric convolution to improve the efficiency. Inspired by IMDB and IdleBlock, ZJUESR2020 proposed multi-scale IdleBlock.

2. **Changing the upsampling block.** Instead of achieve a upscaling factor of 4 via two successive 'PixelShuffle($\times 2$)→Conv→Leaky ReLU' as in MSRRes-Net, XPixel proposed to replace the PixelShuffle layer with nearest neighbor interpolation layer, while most of the other methods, such as NJU_MCG, AiRiA_CG, HaiYun and IPCV_IITM, proposed to directly reconstruct the HR image via a single PixelShuffle($\times 4$) layer.

3. **Adopting global feature aggregation.** In contrast to the local feature aggregation strategy of IMDN, a global feature aggregation strategy which concatenates the features of different blocks is adopted in several teams such as NJU_MCG, Haiyun, IPCV_IITM and 404NotFound. As a typical example, NJU_MCG proposed to concatenate the outputs of 4 RFDB blocks, then use a 1×1 convolutional layer for feature reduction and finally adopt 'Conv3×3→PixelShuffle($\times 4$)' to produce the HR image.

4. **Incorporating attention module.** NJU_MCG proposed to insert enhanced spatial attention module into the RFDB block. Xpixel proposed pixel attention to produce 3D attention maps. MLVC proposed multi-attention block based on enhanced spatial attention (ESA) and cost-efficient attention (CEA).

5. **Reducing the number of parameters by recursive layers.** Zhang9678 proposed to adopt LSTM to reduce parameters, while InnoPeak_SR proposed recursive residual blocks.

6. **Applying network pruning.** SC-CVLAB proposed a fine-grained channel pruning strategy to get a lightweight model from an over-parameterized hybrid composition based SR network.

7. **Replacing the basic residual block of MSRResNet with new block**. Xpixel proposed self-calibrated convolution block with pixel attention. 404NotFound proposed to replace the normal 3 × 3 convolution with Ghost convolution and 1 × 3 convolution. SAMSUNG_TOR_AIC proposed modified MobileNetV3 block.

3.2   Fairness

There are some fair and unfair tricks to improve the validation and testing PSNRs for this challenge. On one hand, using additional training data is fair since the MSRResNet baseline was trained on DIV2K [1], Flickr2K [46] and OST [49] datasets. Most of the teams used the provided DIV2K and additional Flickr2K for training. In addition, using advanced data augmentation strategy during training is also a fair trick. On the other hand, it is unfair to train the model with the validation LR images, validation HR images, and testing LR images. First, training on LR/HR validation images would improve the validation PSNR. Second, it tends to get a PSNR gain if the model is trained on pairs of LR images and their downsampled counterparts. Third, the PSNR can be improved by knowledge distillation technique on validation and testing LR images.

3.3   Conclusions

From the above analysis of different solutions, we can have several conclusions. (i) The proposed methods improve the state-of-the-art for efficient SR. Compared to the first place method IMDN in AIM 2019 constrained SR challenge, NJU_MCG team's method provides a significant gain with respect to the runtime, parameters, FLOPs, and activations. (ii) The number of FLOPs and the number of parameters do not correlate well with network efficiency. In comparison, the number of activations is a more proper metric. (iii) All of the overall top-6 methods employ hand-designed network architecture. The effectiveness of network pruning, knowledge distillation, network quantization and NAS for this efficient SR challenge requires further study. (iv) Future work on efficient SR should take runtime, parameters, FLOPs, and activations into consideration.

4   Challenge Methods and Teams

NJU_MCG

The NJU_MCG proposed **Residual Feature Distillation Network (RFDN)** for fast and lightweight image SR [31]. The proposed RFDN is inspired by two recent works IMDN [18] and RFANet [32]. As shown in Fig. 1(a), the main part of information distillation block (IMDB) is a progressive refinement module (PRM) marked with a gray background. Although PRM achieves prominent improvements, it is not efficient enough and introduces some inflexibility because of the channel splitting operation. The distilled features are generated by 3 × 3 convolution filters that have many redundant parameters. Moreover, the feature refinement pipeline (along the right branch of the PRM) is coupled together with channel splitting operation so that it is hard to use identity connections only for this pipeline. The IMDB-R in Fig. 1(b) solves these problems by replacing the channel splitting operation with two concurrent 3 × 3 convolutions. It is more flexible than the original IMDB. Based on this new architecture, RFDB in Fig. 1(c) uses three 1 × 1 convolutions for feature distillation. Furthermore, it uses the shallow residual block (SRB) in Fig. 1(d) as the feature extractor which can benefit most from the residual learning strategy. For shallow SR models, it is more efficient to use spatial attention than channel attention. So RFDB replaces the CCA layer with the ESA block in RFANet [32].

The proposed RFDN model contains 4 RFDBs, the overall framework follows the pipeline of IMDN, where global feature aggregation is used to augment the final features and the number of feature channels is set to 50. During the training of RFDN, HR patches of size 256 × 256 are randomly cropped from HR images, and the mini-batch size is set to 64. The RFDN model is trained by minimizing L1 loss function with Adam optimizer. The initial learning rate is set to 5×10^{-4} and halved at every 200 epochs. After 1000 epochs, L2 loss is used for fine-tuning with learning rate of 1×10^{-5}. DIV2K and Flickr2K datasets are used for training the RFDN model.

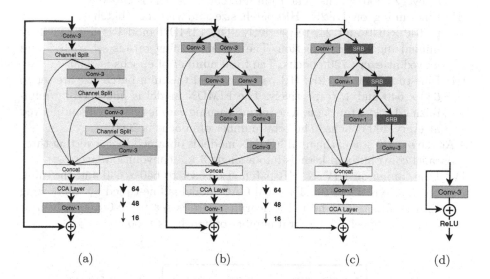

Fig. 1. NJU_MCG Team: (a) IMDB: the original information multi-distillation block. (b) IMDB-R: rethinking of the IMDB. (c) RFDB: residual feature distillation block. (d) SRB: shallow residual block.

AiRiA_CG

The AiRiA_CG team proposed **Faster Information Multi-Distillation Network via Asymmetric Convolution (FIMDN)**. The proposed FIMDN shown in Fig. 2 is modified from IMDN [18] with minor improvements such as less building blocks and converted asymmetric convolution. Different from IMDN, FIMDN only uses 6 CACBs as the building blocks to further accelerate the network. As illustrated in Fig. 3, FIMDN employs four 'Conv-3' layers and retains a part of the information step-by-step. Then the hierarchical features are fused by using a 1×1 convolution layer. In particular, inspired by ACNet [8], FIMDN utilizes the original AC model where 3×3 convolution layer is coupled with parallel $1 \times 3, 3 \times 1$ kernels. After the first training stage, the original AC model is converted into a single standard 3×3 convolution layer. Figure 3 illustrates the fusion process. The training process contains two stages with four steps.

1. At the first stage, the original AC model is equipped with three parallel asymmetric convolutions.
   I. Pre-training on DIV2K+Flickr2K (DF2K). HR patches of size 256×256 are randomly cropped from HR images, and the mini-batch size is set to 64. The original FIMDN model is trained by minimizing L1 loss function with Adam optimizer. The initial learning rate is set to 2e-4 and halved at every 3600 epochs. The total number of epochs is 18000.
   II. Fine-tuning on DF2K. HR patch size and the mini-batch size are set to 640×640 and 24, respectively. The FIMDN model is fine-tuned by minimizing L2 loss function. The initial learning rate is set to 1e-5 and halved at every 720 epochs. The total number of epochs is 3600.
   III. Fine-tuning on DIV2K. HR patch size and the mini-batch size are set to 640×640 and 4, respectively. The FIMDN model is finetuned by minimizing L2 loss function. The initial learning rate is set to 1e-6 and halved at every 400 epochs. The total number of epochs is 2000.
2. At the second stage, the final FIMDN model is obtained by converting three parallel convolutional kernels into a single 3×3 convolution layer.
   IV. Fine-tuning on DIV2K. HR patch size is set to 640×640 and the mini-batch size is set to 24. The final CAC model is fine-tuned by minimizing L2 loss function. The initial learning rate is set to 1e-6 and halved at every 200 epochs. The total number of epochs is 1000.

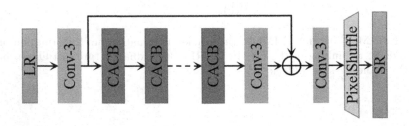

Fig. 2. AiRiA_CG Team: architecture of FIMDN.

UESTC-MediaLab

The UESTC-MediaLab team proposed a novel training strategy which is able to boost the performance of CNNs without extra parameters. The traditional convolution layer can be formulated as $\mathbf{F}_{output} = \mathbf{F}_{input} * \tilde{\mathbf{k}} + \mathbf{b}$. The team decomposed the kernel $\tilde{\mathbf{k}}$ into N kernel bases, $i.e.$, $\tilde{\mathbf{k}} = \sum_i \pi_i \times \mathbf{k}_i$, where $\{\pi_i | i = 1, 2, \ldots, N\}$ are trainable merging weights [25]. The proposed training procedure has multiple stages. At the first stage (denoted as 0-th stage), the model is trained from scratch with the number of kernel bases $N_0 = 3$ in each layer. All kernel bases are initialized randomly with Xavier-Uniform [13], merging weights with $\frac{1}{N_0}$ and bias with zeros. At the t-th ($t \geq 1$) stage, δ_t kernel bases in each layer which are added and randomly initialized, and the merge weights are initialized with $\frac{1}{N_t}$ where $N_t = N_{t-1} + \delta_t$. Each training stage terminates when the validation loss converges. After the training phase, only merged kernels $\tilde{\mathbf{k}}$ and the bias $\mathbf{b}$ are saved. The kernel bases $\mathbf{k}_i$ and merging weights π_i are not necessary in the inference phase. As shown in Fig. 4, the performance increases gradually with the number of kernel bases in Dilut-Net (the network trained with the proposed strategy). The Plain-Net denotes the network using traditional convolutional layers without kernel bases.

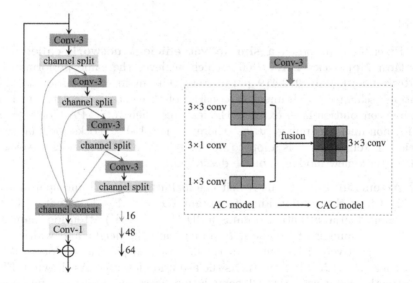

Fig. 3. AiRiA_CG Team: Left: Detailed architecture of FIMDN. "Conv-1" denotes the 1×1 convlution layer. 64, 48, and 16 represent the number of output channels. Right: Details of the asymmetric 3×3 convolution. "CAC" means converted Asymmetric Convolution (CAC).

As for the model structure, the UESTC-MediaLab team modified the structure of IMDN [18] from the following aspects. Firstly, the computing unit 'conv3×3 → LeakyRelu' is replaced by 'gconv3×3 → PRelu → conv1×1', where gconv denotes the group convolution which doubles the number of feature maps. Secondly, adaptive skip-connection is adopted in the model, which parameterizes the connection relationship between the outputs of blocks. Thirdly, the depth and width of the network is modified to achieve a better balance between efficiency and effectiveness.

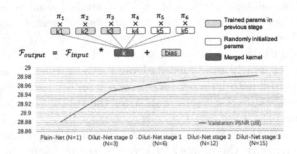

Fig. 4. UESTC-MediaLab Team: kernel dilution and performance of different training stages.

XPixel

The XPixel team proposed **a simple yet efficient network called Pixel Attention Network (PAN)** [66], which achieves the same performance as MSRResNet with only 272,419 parameters. The main contribution is "Pixel Attention" scheme. The framework consists of three stages depicted in Fig. 5. First, one convolution layer extracts the features, then 16 SC-PA blocks are utilized for non-linear mapping, at last there are two U-PA blocks for final reconstruction. Pixel attention is adopted in the SC-PA and U-PA blocks. Next, the details of these new modules will be described.

Pixel Attention. First, let us revisit channel attention [17] and spatial attention [42]. Channel attention aims to obtain 1D ($C \times 1 \times 1$) attention feature vector, while spatial attention obtains a 2D ($1 \times H \times W$) attention map. Note that C is the number of channels, H and W are the height and width of the features, respectively. Different from them, proposed pixel attention is able to generate a 3D ($C \times H \times W$) matrix as the attention features. As shown in Fig. 5, pixel attention only uses a 1×1 convolution layer and a sigmoid function to obtain the attention maps which will then be multiplied with the input features.

SC-PA Block. The main block in the network is called Self-Calibrated convolution with Pixel Attention (SC-PA). Specifically, proposed pixel attention scheme is added to the Self-Calibrated convolution module. Basically, SC-PA is comprised of two branches. Each branch contains a 1×1 convolution layer at the beginning, which will reduce half of the channel number. The upper branch also contains two 3×3 convolution layers, where the first one is equipped with a PA module. This branch transforms X_1 to Y_1. In the second branch, only a single 3×3 convolution layer is used to generate Y_2 since the original information should be maintained. Finally, Y_1 and Y_2 are concatenated into Y_3, which will then be passed to a 1×1 convolution layer. In order to accelerate training, shortcut is used to produce the final output features Y.

U-PA Block. Except for the main blocks, pixel attention is also adopted in the final reconstruction stage. Specifically, proposed U-PA block is added after each upsampling layer. Note that in previous SR networks, a reconstruction stage is basically comprised of upsampling and convolution layers. Besides, plenty of SR networks (e.g.. MSRResNet) use PixelShuffle layer to upsample the features, which is computational expensive. To reduce the computation cost and parameters in the reconstruction stage, Nearest Neighbor interpolation layer is used to replace the PixelShuffle layer and the following convolution layer will reduce the number of channels by half. Moreover, previous works have shown that attention mechanism can effectively improve the performance in SR tasks but few researchers investigate it in the upsampling stage. In this work, the U-PA block is introduced after each upsampling layers. As shown in Fig. 5, the U-PA block consists of a PA layer between two convolution layers. Experiments have been conducted to demonstrate its effectiveness.

Implementation Details. During training, DIV2K and Flickr2K are uesd as training datasets. The HR patch size is set to 256×256. The batch size is set to 32. L1 loss function is adopted with Adam optimizer to train the model. During validation, the model achieves an average PSNR of 29.00 dB on DIV2K validation dataset. The inference time is about 0.0758s per image with a single GTX 1080Ti GPU.

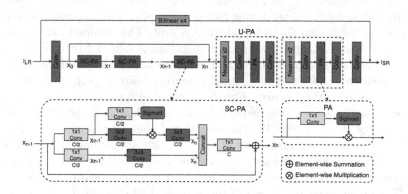

Fig. 5. XPixel Team: the network architecture.

HaiYun

The HaiYun team proposed **a lightweight SR network** (see Fig. 6). Due to the frequent use of residual block (RB) in SR models, they pursue an economical structure to adaptively combine RBs. Inspired by lattice filter bank, a lattice block (LB) is designed where two butterfly structures are applied to combine two RBs. LB has the potential of various linear combinations of two RBs. Each case of LB depends on the combination coefficients which are determined by the attention mechanism. LB favors the lightweight SR model with the reduction of about half amount of the parameters while keeping the similar SR performance. Moreover, a lightweight SR model, *i.e.*, LatticeNet, is proposed, which uses a series of LBs and the backward feature fusion.

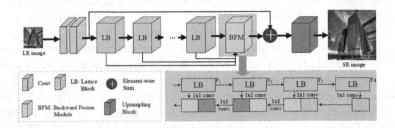

Fig. 6. HaiYun Team: the network architecture.

IPCV_IITM

The IPCV_IITM team proposed to **stack multiple residual blocks for gradual feature refinement**. One 3×3 convolution with 64 output channels is used to extract features from the LR image. Multiple residual blocks are stacked together and at the end all intermediate feature maps are fused by a 1×1 convolution layer. As shown in Fig. 7, residual blocks perform channel split operation on the preceding features, producing two feature splits. One is preserved and the other portion is fed into the next calculation unit. The retained part is used as the refined features. Each convolutional operation is followed by a Leaky ReLU activation function except for the last 1×1 convolution. Two sub-networks are used for predicting spatial and channel attention map to perform feature-wise gating operation on the features. For the purpose of faster inference, the gating function is used in alternating residual blocks as indicated in the figure. Given a feature map of size $C \times H \times W$, the spatial and channel attention module produces $H \times W$ and C dimensional soft gates, which are element-wise multiplied with the feature. The same sub-networks are used for all the residual blocks to reduce the number of parameters. At the end, the gated feature is added to the input. The up-sampler at the end of the network includes one 3×3 convolution and a sub-pixel convolution.

404NotFound

The 404NotFound team proposed **GCSR** which includes three main parts (see Fig. 8). Firstly, the input channels are divided into 2 parts. Ghost convolution and 1×3 convolution are adopted to replace normal convolution. Secondly, a special loss is proposed which consists of L1 loss for low frequency information reconstruction and gradient loss for high-frequency information reconstruction. Thirdly, bicubic upscaling for the LR image is used.

MDISL-lab

The MDISL-lab team proposed **PFSNet**. The main idea is to keep the width of features in an SR network by making full use of a shared feature in every block for efficient SR. In details, the MDISL-lab team found that keeping the width of features is necessary for the high performance of SR networks. And there are many redundancy in feature maps of SR networks. Thus, a series of cheap operations with cheap cost are applied to a shared feature to generate many simple features. These simple features are then concatenated with some normal features at the channel dimension and fed to convolutional layers. In this way, the width of output feature of most convolutional layers could be reduced, thus reducing the computational cost. Meanwhile, the width of input features could still be maintained by the shared feature followed by cheap operations.

The architecture of PFSNet is shown in Fig. 9. First, the Feautre Share Block (FSB) is constructed by several 3×3 convolutional layers, a shared 3×3 convolutional layer, several cheap operations. And a 1×1 convolutional layer is used to reduce the number of feature channels. The $\oplus$ symbol in the figure represents concatenation at channel dimension. All 3×3 convolutional layers output features with 32 channels while the input features of all convolutional layers has 64 channels.

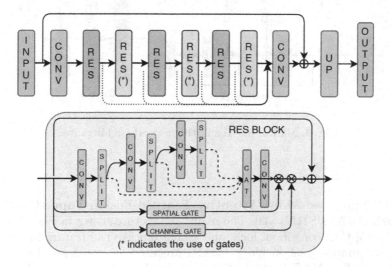

Fig. 7. IPCV_IITM Team: the network architecture.

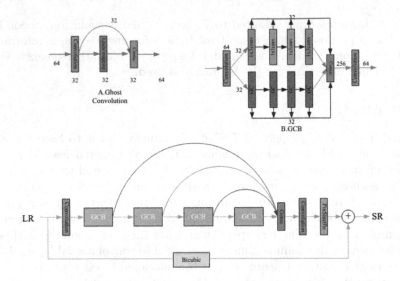

Fig. 8. 404NotFound Team: the network architecture.

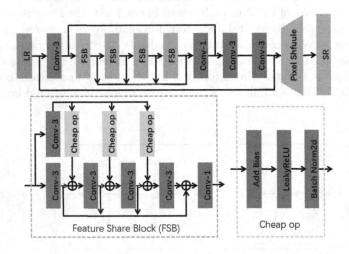

Fig. 9. MDISL-lab Team: the network architecture.

MLVC

The MLVC proposed **Multi-Attentive Feature Fusion Super-Resolution Network (MAFFSRN)** [38]. The main architecture shown in Fig. 10 is based on RDN [65] that consists of local and global blocks. The feature fusion group (FFG) and multi-attention block (MAB) are used as global and local blocks, respectively. The MAB is inspired by enhanced spatial attention (ESA) [32]. MAB introduces another cost-efficient attention mechanism (CEA) [5] to refine the input features. The CEA basically consists of point-wise and depth-wise convolutions. It is incorporated into the MAB block to improve the performance of the network with negligible additional computational cost. Furthermore, it is observed that the original ESA block is computationally expensive due to convolutional group. Thus, the convolutional group is replaced by dilated convolutions with different dilated factors. Lastly, element-wise addition is performed between the output of dilated convolutions to avoid the grid effects [57]. FFG is composed of a stack of MAB which are combined using binarized feature fusion (BFF) [39].

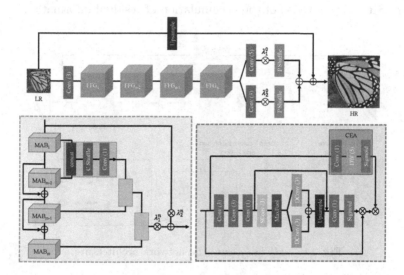

Fig. 10. MLVC Team: the network architecture. The top image represents the whole structure of proposed model, bottom left represents structure of feature fusion group (FFG), and bottom right shows structure of multi-attention block (MAB).

XMUlab

The XMUlab team proposed **PixelShuffle Attention Network**. As shown in Fig. 11, the network contains several gated fusion groups. Each group has 4 residual blocks. Unlike the common use of attention module, PixelShuffle attention Network applies spatial attention and channel attention to the upscaled feature. Gated fusion group gather the output features from previous groups. The channel number in the network is reduced from 64 to 32 compared with other methods, which enables the network goes deeper. The LR image is also concatenated with feature map to extract more information.

MCML-Yonsei

The MCML-Yonsei proposed **LarvaNet: Hierarchical Super-Resolution via Multi-exit Architecture** [21] (see Fig. 12). The main idea of the proposed

LarvaNet is to divide a network into some body modules and to make each body module to generate an output SR image. This is inspired by the fact that MSRResNet is effective for generating residual contents which is added to the image interpolated from the LR image. In their experiment, using interpolation increases PSNR by about 0.2 dB compared to the MSRResNet model without interpolation. Like MSRResNet generates residual contents to be added with a interpolated image, each body module of LarvaNet generates residual contents to be added with the previous modules output image. With this idea, the model can learn features important for SR at early stages, and can generate a more accurate SR image because of the accumulation of residual information.

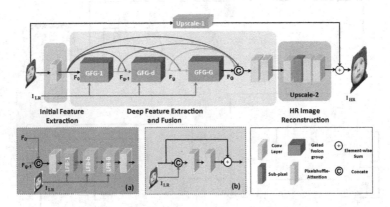

Fig. 11. XMUlab Team: the network architecture.

In order to search for an optimal base architecture, they investigate extensive variations of the baseline MSRResNet model in terms of the numbers of channels and blocks, upsampling methods, interpolation methods, weight initialization methods, and activation functions. Following the results of the investigating experiments, they used a MSRResNet with best settings as base architecture of the multi-exit architecture, LarvaNet. The overall architecture of LarvaNet is illustrated in Fig. 12. Each body module consisting of residual blocks generates features and the previous features are accumulated by skip connection. A sub-module is appended to the body module. It generates an SR output image using features from the body module and interpolated SR image. The tail module takes all the features generated by the body modules and concatenates the features, and generates a final output image. The average of all the losses from the early and final output images is considered as the loss function of training the model.

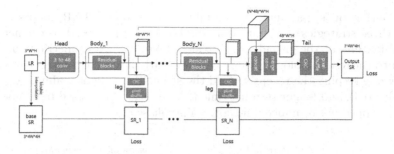

Fig. 12. MCML-Yonsei Team: the network architecture.

LMSR

LMSR adapts the MSRResNet. First, the activation function is replaced by the MTLU [14], which adds complexity to the model, while only making runtime measurements slightly worse. On top of that, the complexity of the upsampling part of the MSRResNet is reduced, by only doubling the numbers of channels before doing a pixel-shuffle compared to quadrupling them as in the baseline model (Fig. 13). In this way, a large number of operations can be reduced. Those convolutions contain the heaviest computations as the spatial resolution has a quadratic influence on the number of operations. Finally, the number of residual blocks is reduced to 13.

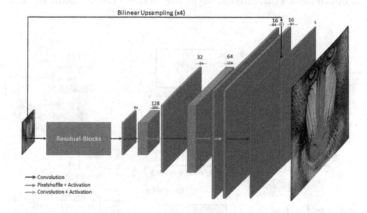

Fig. 13. LMSR Team: the comparison between the lightweight upsampling method (red) and the one of the baseline model. The numbers represent the number of channels in each layer. (Color figure online)

ZJUESR2020

The ZJUESR2020 team proposed **IdleSR** [53] (see Fig. 14). The basic architecture of IdleSR is same to that of NoUCSR [52]. To achieve a better trade-off among performance, parameters, and inference runtime, IdleSR adopts the following three strategies. 1) Multi-scale IdleBlocks are proposed to extract hierarchical features at the granularity of residual block. 2) Asymmetric kernels are applied to the residual blocks, which reduces nearly half of parameters and operations while keeping the receptive field the same. 3) Gradient scaling, larger LR patch size (64), and longer training time (2M iterations) are used to compensate for the dropped performance during training phase.

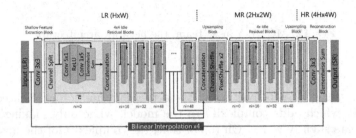

Fig. 14. ZJUESR2020 Team: the network architecture.

Multi-scale IdleBlocks combine the advantage of Information Multi-Distillation Block (IMDB) [18] and IdleBlocks [54]. Figure 15 compares the architecture of the three blocks. Compared to IMDB, multi-scale IdleBlocks can avoid the usage of bottleneck convolution layer and reduce the amount of channel split operations.

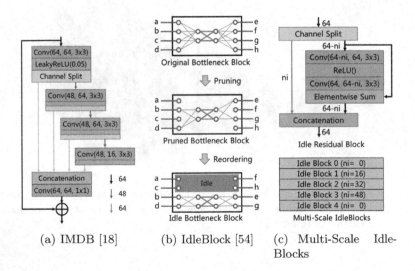

(a) IMDB [18]   (b) IdleBlock [54]   (c) Multi-Scale Idle-Blocks

Fig. 15. ZJUESR2020 Team: the architecture of IMDB, IdleBlock and proposed Multi-Scale IdleBlocks.

SC-CVLAB

The SC-CVLAB team proposed **Adaptive Hybrid Composition Based Super-Resolution Network via Fine-grained Channel Pruning** [6]. Firstly, a hybrid composition based SR neural network (HCSRN) is designed. As shown in Fig. 16(a), the hybrid composition is constructed by three parallel blocks. The element-wise sum operation is conducted for local feature fusion. The whole block adopts residual connection. The asymmetric kernels are adopted. Instead of using 5×1 and 1×5 kernels, kernels with smaller sizes are used to factorize the normal 3×3 convolution into an 3×1 and a 1×3 convolution. To extract different features without significant performance drop, two asymmetric blocks with inverted kernel order is utilized. Another way to reduce model size is reducing the scale of feature. Thus an average pooling followed by "Conv-LeakyReLU-Conv" is utilized, and sub-pixel convolution is used to reconstruct the HR image. Then the proposed HCSRN is constructed based on this hybrid module with progressive upsampling strategy as shown in Fig. 17.

Secondly, the over-parameterized HCSRN is used as the baseline model and channel pruning is applied to it to further reduce model size. The pruning criterion in [56] is utilized. Instead of employing the group pruning strategy [7, 26], the gating function is asserted before and after each convolution. Thus each channel is allowed to be pruned independently. To avoid the misalignment problem between the convolution and the skip connection, the skip connections will not be pruned and the residual addition operation should always be kept. The difference between the proposed fine-grained channel pruning strategy and the previous grouping method is shown in Fig. 16(b). Finally, a pruned lightweight model called adaptive hybrid composition based super-resolution network (AHC-SRN) is obtained.

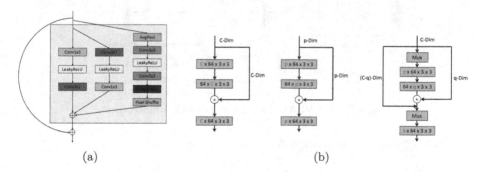

(a)   (b)

Fig. 16. SC-CVLAB Team: (a) the architecture of hybrid composition; (b) an illustration of baseline structure, structure pruned by group strategy, and structure pruned by the proposed fine-grained strategy.

HiImageTeam

The HiImageTeam team proposed **Efficient SR-Net (ESR-Net)** for the challenge. As shown in Fig. 18(a), ESR-Net achieves an upscaling factor of 4 via two successive ×2 subnetworks (ESRB). In order to improve the performance, residual dense network shown in Fig. 18(b) is adopted. L1 loss is used to train ESR-Net.

SAMSUNG_TOR_AIC

The SAMSUNG_TOR_AIC team proposed **SAM_SR_LITE**, a Lightweight MobileNetV3 network for Efficient Super-Resolution [48]. The core of this approach is to use modified MobileNetV3 [16] blocks to design an efficient method for SR. The authors found that for the MobileNetV3 architecture batch normalization layers improved the performance. The architecture takes the LR images as input and consists of N+1 modified MobileNetV3 blocks, with a skip connection (addition) from the output of the first block to the output of the last block. The output of the last block is then upscaled using the two PixelShuffle operations [43] with non-linearities and convolutions. To yield three color channels, a post-processing block containing a depthwise separable convolution and a 1 × 1 convolution layer is applied to the output of the upscaled result. Finally, there is an additional skip connection between the bicubic upsampling of the LR input and the output of the post processing block. Figure 19 provides a overview of the architecture.

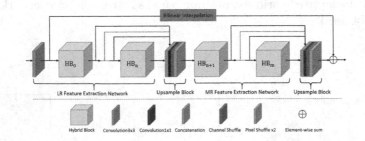

Fig. 17. SC-CVLAB Team: the network architecture.

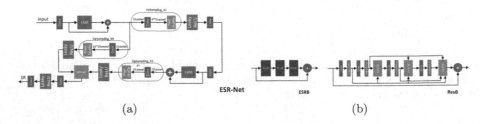

Fig. 18. HiImageTeam Team: (a) the network architecture; (b) the ESR Block and Residual Block.

The hyperparameters include the number of blocks N, the number of feature mapss n_f in each block, and the expansion factor in each block. For the final submission, $N = 16$, $n_f = 72$, and the block expansion factor is 2.

neptuneai

The model is based on the MSRResNet and the basic blocks in MSRResNet is changed to Inverted Residuals Block in MobileNetV2. This architecture is used as backbone network. Then NAS is used to discover the best architecture for lightweight SR tasks. A search space which is composed of several kinds of blocks is designed. The basic blocks for NAS include

1. Inverted Residuals Block with 3 expand ration,
2. Inverted Residuals Block with 6 expand ration,
3. Basic Residual Block,
4. Basic Residual Block with leaky ReLU activation function.

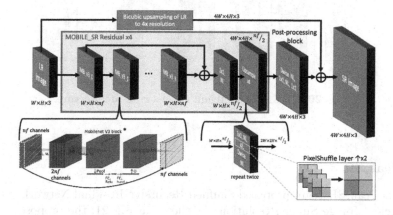

Fig. 19. SAMSUNG_TOR_AIC Team: the network architecture.

lyl

The lyl team proposed **Coarse to Fine network (CFN)** progressive super-resolution reconstruction, which contains a CoarseNet and a FineNet. The FineNet contains a lightweight upsampling module (LUM). There are two characteristics in CFN, *i.e.*, the progressiveness and the merging of the output of the LUM to correct the input in each level. Such progressive cause-and-effect process helps to achieve the principle for image SR. That is, high-level information can guide an LR image to recover a better SR image. In the proposed network, there are three indispensable parts: 1) tying the loss at each level, 2) using LUM and 3) providing feature maps extracted in lower level to ensure the availability of low-level information.

CET_CVLab

The architecture used is inspired by wide activation based network and channel attention network. The network, as shown in Fig. 20, mainly consists of 3 blocks, a feature extraction block, a series of wide activation residual blocks and a set of progressive upsampling blocks (×2). The expansion factor used for wide activation block is six. The depth within the feature extraction blocks and wide activation blocks is 32. The network contains 1.378 million trainable parameters. Charbonnier loss is used for training the network as it captures the edge information better than the mean squared error (MSE) loss.

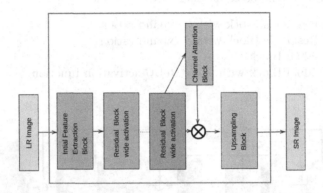

Fig. 20. CET_CVLab Team: the network architecture.

InnoPeak_SR

The InnoPeak_SR team proposed Shuffled Recursive Residual Network (SRRN) for Efficient Image Super-Resolution. As shown in Fig. 21, the proposed SRRN mainly consists of four parts: shallow feature extraction, residual block feature extraction, skip connection module, and upscale reconstruction module. To extract the shallow features, one 3 × 3 convolution layer (pad 1, stride 1, and channel 64) is used, which is followed by one Leaky ReLU layer (slop 0.1). To extract the mid-level and high-level features, 16 weights shared recursive residual blocks are used. The residual block consists of two 3 × 3 convolution layer (pad 1, stride 1, and channel 64). Only the first convolution layer is followed by a Leaky ReLU layer (slop 0.1). Batch Normalization (BN) layers are not used. In this work, one 3 × 3 convolution layer (pad 1, stride 1, and channel 64) and one sub-pixel convolution layer is used as upscaling module and reconstruction module. During the training, HR patches of size 196 × 196 are randomly cropped from HR images, and the mini-batch size is set to 25. The proposed model is trained by minimizing L1 loss function with Adam optimizer.

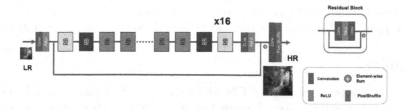

Fig. 21. InnoPeak_SR Team: an illustration of the proposed SRRN. SRRN consists of 16 residual blocks, but only have four different weights. The residual blocks with same color share the same parameter weights.

Summer

The Summer team proposed **AMAF-Net**. The model consists of four parts: 1) Attentive Auxiliary Feature Block (AAF Block) reuses all features of the preceding blocks as the input feature map of the current layer. By applying convolution to the concatenated feature maps, the network learns how to combine the information from different blocks. 2) Global residual connection. The input image are directly upsampled by PixelShuffler, which can be regarded as a part of the output image. It brings the most basic information to the output. 3) Multi-gradients skip connection. The outputs of each block are upsampled by 1×1 convolution and PixelShuffler. The results are also a proportion of the output, which are useful for transmitting different frequency information. Meanwhile, gradients can be propagated from the tail of the network to the head. 4) By using the adaptive weight factor multiple outputs are combined with the learnable parameters, which can adaptively determine the contributions of each blocks. The network architecture is shown in Fig. 22.

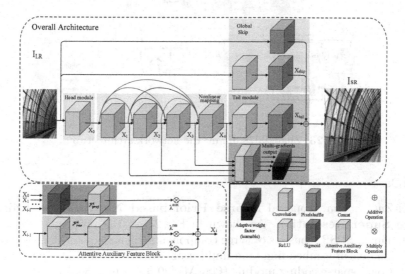

Fig. 22. Summer Team: the network architecture.

L1 loss is used in the training process. To further reduce parameters and FLOPs, the convolution of last two blocks is replaced by 1×1 convolution.

Zhang9678

The Zhang9678 team proposed **LFN** which contains three parts, including shallow feature extraction, deep feature fusion and upsampling. Shallow feature extraction contains a convolutional layer, which is used to map images from image space to feature space. Deep feature fusion contains four DB blocks and one modified convLSTM. The feature map obtained by the shallow feature extraction of the image passes through four consecutive DB modules to obtain feature maps in different depths. LSTM is usually used to process time series data. For time series data, there is a high degree of similarity between the time steps, showing a progressive relationship on the time dimension. The feature maps at different levels are regarded as a kind of pseudo-time series data because they also contain a progressive relationship at different levels and their similarity is also high. Specifically, the hidden state h and cell state c of the initial LSTM are initialized to 0. For each state update, a feature map is selected and sent to the LSTM along with the corresponding h and c. After the operations in the LSTM, the new h and c are obtained. This cycle is repeated for four times in total. The resulting h is concatenated with the shallow features. Then a 1×1 convolution and a 3×3 convolution are appended to get the feature map with 48 channels. Finally, a PixelShuffler is used to get the final SR image (Fig. 23).

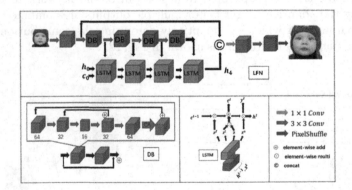

Fig. 23. Zhang9678 Team: the network architecture.

H-ZnCa

The H-ZnCa team proposed **Sparse Prior-based Network for Efficient Image Super-Resolution**. As shown in Fig. 24(a), the proposed lightweight model, named SPSR, consists of three components: high-frequency sparse coding generation, feature embedding, and multi-scale feature extraction. Specifically, a convolutional sparse coding module (CSCM) [29,45] is first performed to obtain the high-frequency spare representation of the input. Then, a feature embedding block (FEB) [49] which consists of a Spatial Feature Transform (SFT) layer and two convolutional layers is designed for spatial-wise feature modulation conditioned on the sparse prior representation. To further enhance the abstract ability of SPSR, a multi-scale feature extraction module (MFEM) with channel split mechanism is proposed to efficiently utilize the hierarchical features. As shown in Fig. 24(b), MFEM contains several convolutions with different dilation factors.

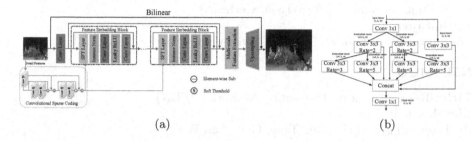

(a)   (b)

Fig. 24. H-ZnCa Team: (a) the architecture of SPSR Network; (b) the multi-scale feature extraction module (MFEM).

MLP_SR

The MLP_SR team proposed a lightweight deep iterative SR learning method (ISRResDNet) that solves the SR task as a sub-solver of image denoising by the residual denoiser networks [24]. It is inspired by powerful image regularization and large-scale optimization techniques used to solve general inverse problems. The proposed iterative SR approach is shown in Fig. 25. The authors unroll the ResDNet [24] into K stages and each stage performs the PGM updates.

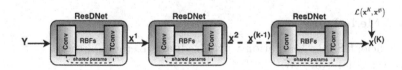

Fig. 25. MLP_SR Team: the architecture of the iterative SR approach ISRResDNet.

Acknowledgements. We thank the AIM 2020 sponsors: HUAWEI, MediaTek, Google, NVIDIA, Qualcomm, and Computer Vision Lab (CVL) ETH Zurich.

A   Teams and Affiliations

AIM2020 Team

Title: AIM 2020 Efficient Super-Resolution Challenge
Members:
Kai Zhang (mailto:kai.zhang@vision.ee.ethz.ch),
Martin Danelljan (martin.danelljan@vision.ee.ethz.ch),
Yawei Li (yawei.li@vision.ee.ethz.ch),
Radu Timofte (radu.timofte@vision.ee.ethz.ch)
Affiliations:
Computer Vision Lab, ETH Zurich, Switzerland

NJU_MCG

Title: Residual Feature Distillation Network (RFDN)
Members: Jie Liu
(jieliu@smail.nju.edu.cn), Jie Tang, Gangshan Wu
Affiliation:
State Key Laboratory for Novel Software Technology, Nanjing University, Nanjing 210023, China

AiRiA_CG

Title: Faster Information Multi-distillation Network via Asymmetric Convolution
Members: Yu Zhu
(zhuyu.cv@gmail.com), Xiangyu He, Wenjie Xu, Chenghua Li, Cong Leng, Jian Cheng
Affiliation:
Nanjing Artificial Intelligence Chip Research, Institute of Automation, Chinese Academy of Sciences (AiRiA); MAICRO

UESTC-MediaLab

Title: Efficient Super-Resolution with Gradually Kernel Dilution
Members: Guangyang Wu[1]
(mulns@outlook.com), Wenyi Wang[1], Xiaohong Liu[2]
Affiliation:
[1] University of Electronic Science and Technology of China
[2] McMaster University

XPixel

Title: Efficient Image Super-Resolution using Pixel Attention
Members: Hengyuan Zhao
(hy.zhao1@siat.ac.cn), Xiangtao Kong, Jingwen He,Yu Qiao, Chao Dong
Affiliation:
Shenzhen Institutes of Advanced Technology, Chinese Academy of Sciences

HaiYun

Title: Lightweight Image Super-resolution with Lattice Block
Members: Xiaotong Luo
(xiaotluo@qq.com), Liang Chen, Jiangtao Zhang
Affiliation:
Xiamen University, China

IPCV_IITM

Title: Lightweight Attentive Residual Network for Image Super-Resolution
Members: Maitreya Suin
(maitreyasuin21@gmail.com), Kuldeep Purohit, A. N. Rajagopalan
Affiliation:
Indian Institute of Technology Madras, India

404NotFound

Title: GCSR
Members: Xiaochuan Li (1182784700@qq.com)
Affiliation:
Nanjing University of Aeronautics and Astronautics, Nanjing, China

MDISL-lab

Title: PFSNet: Partial Features Sharing for More Efficient Super-Resolution
Members: Zhiqiang Lang
(2015303107lang@mail.nwpu.edu.cn), Jiangtao Nie, Wei Wei, Lei Zhang
Affiliation:
School of Computer Science, Northwestern Polytechnical University, China

MLVC

MLVC
Title: Multi Attention Feature Fusion Super-Resolution Network
Members: Abdul Muqeet[1]
(amuqeet@khu.ac.kr), Jiwon Hwang[1], Subin Yang[1], JungHeum Kang[1], Sungho Bae[1], Yongwoo Kim[2]
Affiliation:
[1] Kyung Hee University, Republic of Korea
[2] Sang Myung University, Republic of Korea

XMUlab

Title: Pixelshuffle Attention Network
Members: Liang Chen
(1806668306@qq.com), Jiangtao Zhang, Xiaotong Luo, Yanyun Qu
Affiliation:
Xianmen University

MCML-Yonsei

Title: LarvaNet: Hierarchical Super-Resolution via Internal Output and Loss
Members: Geun-Woo Jeon
(geun-woo.jeon@yonsei.ac.kr), Jun-Ho Choi, Jun-Hyuk Kim, Jong-Seok Lee
Affiliation:
Yonsei University, Republic of Korea

LMSR

Title: LMSR
Members: Steven Marty
(martyste@student.ethz.ch), Eric Marty
Affiliation:
ETH Zurich
ZJUESR2020

Title: IdleSR: Efficient Super-Resolution Network with Multi-Scale IdleBlocks
Members: Dongliang Xiong (xiongdl@zju.edu.cn)
Affiliation: Zhejiang University

SC-CVLAB

Title: Adaptive Hybrid Composition Based Super-Resolution Network via Fine-grained Channel Pruning
Members: Siang Chen (11631032@zju.edu.cn)
Affiliation: Zhejiang University

HiImageTeam

Title: Efficient SR-Net
Members: Lin Zha[1]
(zhalin@hisense.com), Jiande Jiang[1], Xinbo Gao[2], Wen Lu[2]
Affiliation:
[1] Qingdao Hi-image Technologies Co.,Ltd (Hisense Visual Technology Co.,Ltd.)
[2] Xidian University

SAMSUNG_TOR_AIC

Title: Lightweight MobileNetV3 for Efficient Super-Resolution
Members: Haicheng Wang
(h.wang1@samsung.com), Vineeth Bhaskara, Alex Levinshtein, Stavros Tsogkas, Allan Jepson
Affiliation: Samsung AI Centre, Toronto

neptuneai

Title: Lightweight super resolution network with Neural Architecture Search
Members: Xiangzhen Kong (neptune.team.ai@gmail.com)

lyl

Title: Coarse to Fine Pyramid Networks for Progressive Image Super-Resolution
Members: Tongtong Zhao[1]
(yaopuss@126.com), Shanshan Zhao[2]
Affiliation:
[1] Dalian Maritime University
[2] China Everbright Bank Co., Ltd

CET_CVLab

Title: Efficient Single Image Super-resolution using Progressive Wide Activation Net
Members: Hrishikesh P S
(hrishikeshps94@gmail.com), Densen Puthussery, Jiji C V
Affiliation:
College of Engineering, Trivandrum

wozhu

Title: FSSR
Members: Nan Nan
(2829272117@qq.com), Shuai Liu

InnoPeak_SR

Title: Shuffled Recursive Residual Network for Efficient Image Super-Resolution
Members: Jie Cai
(caijie0620@mail.com), Zibo Meng, Jiaming Ding, Chiu Man Ho
Affiliation:
InnoPeak Technology, Inc.

Summer

Title: Adaptively Multi-gradients Auxiliary Feature Learning for Efficient Super-resolution
Members: Xuehui Wang[1,2]
(wangxh228@mail2.sysu.edu.cn), Qiong Yan[1], Yuzhi Zhao[3], Long Chen[2]
Affiliation:
[1] SenseTime Research
[2] Sun Yat-sen University
[3] City University of Hong Kong

Zhang9678

Title: Lightweight super-resolution network using convLSTM fusion features
Members: Jiangtao Zhang
(1328937778@qq.com),
Xiaotong Luo, Liang Chen, Yanyun Qu
Affiliation:
Xianmen University

H-ZnCa

Title: Sparse Prior-based Network for Efficient Image Super-Resolution
Members: Long Sun
(lungsuen@163.com), Wenhao Wang, Zhenbing Liu, Rushi Lan
Affiliation:
Guilin University of Electronic Technology, Guilin 541004, China.

MLP_SR

Title: A Light-weight Deep Iterative Residual Convolutional Network for Super-Resolution
Members: Rao Muhammad Umer
(engr.raoumer943@gmail.com), Christian Micheloni
Affiliation:
University of Udine, Italy

References

1. Agustsson, E., Timofte, R.: NTIRE 2017 challenge on single image super-resolution: dataset and study. In: The IEEE Conference on Computer Vision and Pattern Recognition (CVPR) Workshops, July 2017
2. Bahat, Y., Michaeli, T.: Explorable super resolution. In: IEEE Conference on Computer Vision and Pattern Recognition (2020)
3. Bell-Kligler, S., Shocher, A., Irani, M.: Blind super-resolution kernel estimation using an internal-GAN. In: Advances in Neural Information Processing Systems, pp. 284–293 (2019)
4. Cai, H., Gan, C., Han, S.: Once for all: Train one network and specialize it for efficient deployment. arXiv preprint arXiv:1908.09791 (2019)
5. Cai, Y., et al.: Learning delicate local representations for multi-person pose estimation. arXiv preprint arXiv:2003.04030 (2020)
6. Chen, S., Huang, K., Claesen, L., Li, B., Xiong, D., Jiang, H.: Adaptive hybrid composition based super-resolution network via fine-grained channel pruning. In: Bartoli, A., Fusiello, A. (eds.) ECCV 2020, LNCS 12537, pp. 119–135. Springer, Cham (2020)
7. Ding, X., Ding, G., Guo, Y., Han, J.: Centripetal SGD for pruning very deep convolutional networks with complicated structure. In: Proceedings of the IEEE Conference on Computer Vision and Pattern Recognition, pp. 4943–4953 (2019)
8. Ding, X., Guo, Y., Ding, G., Han, J.: ACNet: strengthening the kernel skeletons for powerful CNN via asymmetric convolution blocks. In: The IEEE International Conference on Computer Vision (ICCV), October 2019
9. Dong, C., Loy, C.C., He, K., Tang, X.: Learning a deep convolutional network for image super-resolution. In: Fleet, D., Pajdla, T., Schiele, B., Tuytelaars, T. (eds.) ECCV 2014. LNCS, vol. 8692, pp. 184–199. Springer, Cham (2014). https://doi.org/10.1007/978-3-319-10593-2_13

10. Efrat, N., Glasner, D., Apartsin, A., Nadler, B., Levin, A.: Accurate blur models vs. image priors in single image super-resolution. In: IEEE International Conference on Computer Vision, pp. 2832–2839 (2013)
11. El Helou, M., et al.: AIM 2020: scene relighting and illumination estimation challenge. In: Bartoli, A., Fusiello, A. (eds.) ECCV 2020, LNCS 12537, pp. 499–518. Springer, Cham (2020)
12. Fuoli, D., et al.: AIM 2020 challenge on video extreme super-resolution: methods and results. In: Bartoli, A., Fusiello, A. (eds.) ECCV 2020, LNCS 1253, pp. xx–yy. Springer, Cham (2020)
13. Glorot, X., Bengio, Y.: Understanding the difficulty of training deep feedforward neural networks. J. Mach. Learn. Res. **9**, 249–256 (2010)
14. Gu, S., Timofte, R., Van Gool, L.: Multi-bin trainable linear unit for fast image restoration networks. arXiv preprint arXiv:1807.11389 (2018)
15. Hinton, G., Vinyals, O., Dean, J.: Distilling the knowledge in a neural network. arXiv preprint arXiv:1503.02531 (2015)
16. Howard, A., et al.: Searching for mobilenetv3. arXiv preprint arXiv:1905.02244 (2019)
17. Hu, J., Shen, L., Sun, G.: Squeeze-and-excitation networks. In: IEEE Conference on Computer Vision and Pattern Recognition, pp. 7132–7141 (2018)
18. Hui, Z., Gao, X., Yang, Y., Wang, X.: Lightweight image super-resolution with information multi-distillation network. In: ACM Multimedia (ACM MM) (2019)
19. Ignatov, A., Timofte, R., et al.: AIM 2020 challenge on learned image signal processing pipeline. In: Bartoli, A., Fusiello, A. (eds.) ECCV 2020, LNCS 12537, pp. 152–170. Springer, Cham (2020)
20. Ignatov, A., Timofte, R., et al.: AIM 2020 challenge on rendering realistic bokeh. In: Bartoli, A., Fusiello, A. (eds.) ECCV 2020, LNCS 12537, pp. 213–228. Springer, Cham (2020)
21. Jeon, G.W., Choi, J.H., Kim, J.H., Lee, J.S.: LarvaNet: Hierarchical super-resolution via multi-exit architecture. In: Bartoli, A., Fusiello, A. (eds.) ECCV 2020, LNCS 12537, pp. 73–86. Springer, Cham (2020)
22. Kim, J., Kwon Lee, J., Mu Lee, K.: Accurate image super-resolution using very deep convolutional networks. In: The IEEE Conference on Computer Vision and Pattern Recognition, June 2016
23. Ledig, C., et al.: Photo-realistic single image super-resolution using a generative adversarial network. In: IEEE Conference on Computer Vision and Pattern Recognition, pp. 4681–4690 (2017)
24. Lefkimmiatis, S.: Universal denoising networks: a novel CNN architecture for image denoising. In: Proceedings of the IEEE Conference on Computer Vision and Pattern Recognition, pp. 3204–3213 (2018)
25. Li, Y., Gu, S., Gool, L.V., Timofte, R.: Learning filter basis for convolutional neural network compression. In: Proceedings of the IEEE International Conference on Computer Vision, pp. 5623–5632 (2019)
26. Li, Y., Gu, S., Mayer, C., Gool, L.V., Timofte, R.: Group sparsity: the hinge between filter pruning and decomposition for network compression. In: Proceedings of the IEEE/CVF Conference on Computer Vision and Pattern Recognition, pp. 8018–8027 (2020)
27. Li, Y., Gu, S., Zhang, K., Van Gool, L., Timofte, R.: DHP: differentiable meta pruning via hypernetworks. arXiv preprint arXiv:2003.13683 (2020)
28. Li, Y., Dong, X., Wang, W.: Additive powers-of-two quantization: an efficient non-uniform discretization for neural networks. In: International Conference on Learning Representations (2019)

29. Liu, D., Wang, Z., Wen, B., Yang, J., Han, W., Huang, T.S.: Robust single image super-resolution via deep networks with sparse prior. IEEE Trans. Image Process. **25**(7), 3194–3207 (2016)
30. Liu, H., Simonyan, K., Yang, Y.: Darts: differentiable architecture search. arXiv preprint arXiv:1806.09055 (2018)
31. Liu, J., Tang, J., Wu, G.: Residual feature distillation network for lightweight image super-resolution. In: Bartoli, A., Fusiello, A. (eds.) ECCV 2020, LNCS 12537, pp. 41–55. Springer, Cham (2020)
32. Liu, J., Zhang, W., Tang, Y., Tang, J., Wu, G.: Residual feature aggregation network for image super-resolution. In: Proceedings of the IEEE/CVF Conference on Computer Vision and Pattern Recognition (CVPR), June 2020
33. Liu, Z., Wu, B., Luo, W., Yang, X., Liu, W., Cheng, K.-T.: Bi-real net: enhancing the performance of 1-bit CNNs with improved representational capability and advanced training algorithm. In: Ferrari, V., Hebert, M., Sminchisescu, C., Weiss, Y. (eds.) ECCV 2018. LNCS, vol. 11219, pp. 747–763. Springer, Cham (2018). https://doi.org/10.1007/978-3-030-01267-0_44
34. Lugmayr, A., Danelljan, M., Van Gool, L., Timofte, R.: SRFlow: learning the super-resolution space with normalizing flow. In: Vedaldi, A., Bischof, H., Brox, T., Frahm, J.-M. (eds.) ECCV 2020. LNCS, vol. 12350, pp. 715–732. Springer, Cham (2020). https://doi.org/10.1007/978-3-030-58558-7_42
35. Lugmayr, A., Danelljan, M., Timofte, R.: Unsupervised learning for real-world super-resolution. In: IEEE International Conference on Computer Vision Workshop, pp. 3408–3416 (2019)
36. Lugmayr, A., Danelljan, M., Timofte, R.: Ntire 2020 challenge on real-world image super-resolution: methods and results. In: IEEE Conference on Computer Vision and Pattern Recognition Workshops, pp. 494–495 (2020)
37. Menon, S., Damian, A., Hu, S., Ravi, N., Rudin, C.: Pulse: self-supervised photo upsampling via latent space exploration of generative models. In: CVPR (2020)
38. Muqeet, A., Hwang, J., Yang, S., Kang, J.H., Kim, Y., Bae, S.H.: Ultra lightweight image super-resolution with multi-attention. In: European Conference on Computer Vision Workshops (2020)
39. Muqeet, A., Iqbal, M.T.B., Bae, S.H.: Hybrid residual attention network for single image super resolution. arXiv preprint arXiv:1907.05514 (2019)
40. Ntavelis, E., et al.: AIM 2020 challenge on image extreme inpainting. In: Bartoli, A., Fusiello, A. (eds.) ECCV 2020, LNCS 12537, pp. 716–741. Springer, Cham (2020)
41. Radosavovic, I., Kosaraju, R.P., Girshick, R., He, K., Dollár, P.: Designing network design spaces. In: IEEE Conference on Computer Vision and Pattern Recognition, pp. 10428–10436 (2020)
42. Roy, A.G., Navab, N., Wachinger, C.: Concurrent spatial and channel 'Squeeze & Excitation' in fully convolutional networks. In: Frangi, A.F., Schnabel, J.A., Davatzikos, C., Alberola-López, C., Fichtinger, G. (eds.) MICCAI 2018. LNCS, vol. 11070, pp. 421–429. Springer, Cham (2018). https://doi.org/10.1007/978-3-030-00928-1_48
43. Shi, W., et al.: Real-time single image and video super-resolution using an efficient sub-pixel convolutional neural network. In: IEEE Conference on Computer Vision and Pattern Recognition, pp. 1874–1883 (2016)
44. Son, S., et al.: AIM 2020 challenge on video temporal super-resolution. In: Bartoli, A., Fusiello, A. (eds.) ECCV 2020, LNCS 1253, pp. xx–yy. Springer, Cham (2020)

45. Sreter, H., Giryes, R.: Learned convolutional sparse coding. In: 2018 IEEE International Conference on Acoustics, Speech and Signal Processing (ICASSP), pp. 2191–2195 (2018)
46. Timofte, R., Agustsson, E., Van Gool, L., Yang, M.H., Zhang, L., et al.: Ntire 2017 challenge on single image super-resolution: methods and results. In: The IEEE Conference on Computer Vision and Pattern Recognition (CVPR) Workshops, July 2017
47. Timofte, R., De Smet, V., Van Gool, L.: A+: Adjusted anchored neighborhood regression for fast super-resolution. In: Cremers, D., Reid, I., Saito, H., Yang, M.H. (eds.) 12th Asian Conference on Computer Vision (2014)
48. Wang, H., Bhaskara, V., Levinshtein, A., Tsogkas, S., Jepson, A.: Efficient super-resolution using mobilenetv3. In: Bartoli, A., Fusiello, A. (eds.) ECCV 2020, LNCS 12537, pp. 87–102. Springer, Cham (2020)
49. Wang, X., Yu, K., Dong, C., Change Loy, C.: Recovering realistic texture in image super-resolution by deep spatial feature transform. In: IEEE Conference on Computer Vision and Pattern Recognition, pp. 606–615 (2018)
50. Wang, X., et al.: ESRGAN: enhanced super-resolution generative adversarial networks. In: Leal-Taixé, L., Roth, S. (eds.) ECCV 2018. LNCS, vol. 11133, pp. 63–79. Springer, Cham (2019). https://doi.org/10.1007/978-3-030-11021-5_5
51. Wei, P., et al.: AIM 2020 challenge on real image super-resolution. In: Bartoli, A., Fusiello, A. (eds.) ECCV 2020, LNCS 1253, pp. xx–yy. Springer, Cham (2020)
52. Xiong, D., Huang, K., Chen, S., Li, B., Jiang, H., Xu, W.: NoUCSR: efficient super-resolution network without upsampling convolution. In: ICCV Workshop (2019)
53. Xiong, D., Huang, K., Jiang, H., Li, B., Chen, S., Jiang, X.: IdleSR: efficient super-resolution network with multi-scale IdleBlocks. In: Bartoli, A., Fusiello, A. (eds.) ECCV 2020, LNCS 12537, pp. 136–151. Springer, Cham (2020)
54. Xu, B., Tulloch, A., Chen, Y., Yang, X., Qiao, L.: Hybrid composition with idle-block: More efficient networks for image recognition. CoRR abs/1911.080609 (2019)
55. Yin, H., et al.: Dreaming to distill: data-free knowledge transfer via deepinversion. In: Proceedings of the IEEE Conference on Computer Vision and Pattern Recognition, pp. 8715–8724 (2020)
56. You, Z., Yan, K., Ye, J., Ma, M., Wang, P.: Gate decorator: global filter pruning method for accelerating deep convolutional neural networks. In: Advances in Neural Information Processing Systems, pp. 2133–2144 (2019)
57. Yu, F., Koltun, V., Funkhouser, T.: Dilated residual networks. In: IEEE Conference on Computer Vision and Pattern Recognition, pp. 472–480 (2017)
58. Zhang, K., et al.: AIM 2020 challenge on efficient super-resolution: Methods and results. In: Bartoli, A., Fusiello, A. (eds.) ECCV 2020, LNCS 12537, pp. 5–40. Springer, Cham (2020)
59. Zhang, K., Gu, S., Timofte, R.: Ntire 2020 challenge on perceptual extreme super-resolution: Methods and results. In: IEEE Conference on Computer Vision and Pattern Recognition Workshops, pp. 492–493 (2020)
60. Zhang, K., Gu, S., Timofte, R., et al.: Aim 2019 challenge on constrained super-resolution: methods and results. In: International Conference on Computer Vision Workshop, pp. 3565–3574 (2019)
61. Zhang, K., Li, Y., Zuo, W., Zhang, L., Van Gool, L., Timofte, R.: Plug-and-play image restoration with deep denoiser prior. arXiv preprint (2020)
62. Zhang, K., Van Gool, L., Timofte, R.: Deep unfolding network for image super-resolution. In: IEEE Conference on Computer Vision and Pattern Recognition, pp. 3217–3226 (2020)

63. Zhang, K., Zuo, W., Gu, S., Zhang, L.: Learning deep CNN denoiser prior for image restoration. In: IEEE conference on Computer Vision and Pattern Recognition, pp. 3929–3938 (2017)

64. Zhang, K., Zuo, W., Zhang, L.: Learning a single convolutional super-resolution network for multiple degradations. In: IEEE Conference on Computer Vision and Pattern Recognition, pp. 3262–3271 (2018)

65. Zhang, Y., Tian, Y., Kong, Y., Zhong, B., Fu, Y.: Residual dense network for image super-resolution. In: Proceedings of the IEEE Conference on Computer Vision and Pattern Recognition, pp. 2472–2481 (2018)

66. Zhao, H., Kong, X., He, J., Qiao, Y., Dong, C.: Efficient image super-resolution using pixel attention. In: In: Bartoli, A., Fusiello, A. (eds.) ECCV 2020, LNCS 12537, pp. 56–72. Springer, Cham (2020)

Residual Feature Distillation Network for Lightweight Image Super-Resolution

Jie Liu, Jie Tang$^{(\boxtimes)}$, and Gangshan Wu

State Key Laboratory for Novel Software Technology, Nanjing University,
Nanjing, China
jieliu@smail.nju.edu.cn, {tangjie,gswu}@nju.edu.cn

Abstract. Recent advances in single image super-resolution (SISR)
explored the power of convolutional neural network (CNN) to achieve
a better performance. Despite the great success of CNN-based methods, it is not easy to apply these methods to edge devices due to the
requirement of heavy computation. To solve this problem, various fast
and lightweight CNN models have been proposed. The information distillation network is one of the state-of-the-art methods, which adopts
the channel splitting operation to extract distilled features. However, it
is not clear enough how this operation helps in the design of efficient
SISR models. In this paper, we propose the feature distillation connection (FDC) that is functionally equivalent to the channel splitting operation while being more lightweight and flexible. Thanks to FDC, we can
rethink the information multi-distillation network (IMDN) and propose
a lightweight and accurate SISR model called residual feature distillation
network (RFDN). RFDN uses multiple feature distillation connections
to learn more discriminative feature representations. We also propose
a shallow residual block (SRB) as the main building block of RFDN
so that the network can benefit most from residual learning while still
being lightweight enough. Extensive experimental results show that the
proposed RFDN achieves a better trade-off against the state-of-the-art
methods in terms of performance and model complexity. Moreover, we
propose an enhanced RFDN (E-RFDN) and won the first place in the
AIM 2020 efficient super-resolution challenge. Code will be available at
https://github.com/njulj/RFDN.

Keywords: Image super-resolution · Computational photography ·
Image processing

1 Introduction

Image super-resolution (SR) is a classic computer vision task to reconstruct a
high-resolution (HR) image from its low-resolution (LR) counterpart. It is an ill-
posed procedure since many HR images can be degraded to the same LR image.
Image SR is a very active research area where many approaches [15,25] have
been proposed to generate the upscaled images. In this paper, we focus on the

© Springer Nature Switzerland AG 2020
A. Bartoli and A. Fusiello (Eds.): ECCV 2020 Workshops, LNCS 12537, pp. 41–55, 2020.
https://doi.org/10.1007/978-3-030-67070-2_2

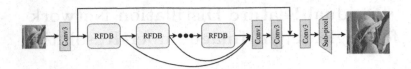

Fig. 1. The architecture of residual feature distillation network (RFDN).

problem of lightweight image SR which is needed in time-sensitive applications such as video streaming.

Recently, various convolutional neural network (CNN) based methods [?][7, 11, 16, 17, 23, 32] have been proposed and achieved prominent performance in image SR. As a pioneering work, Dong *et al.* [4] proposed the super-resolution convolutional neural network (SRCNN), which is a three-layer network to directly model the mapping from LR to HR. Then, Kim *et al.* [12] pushed the depth of SR network to 20 and achieved much better performance than SRCNN, which indicates that the quality of upscaled images can be improved with deeper networks. The EDSR [17] network further proved this by using more than 160 layers. Although deeper networks increase the quality of SR images, they are not suitable for real-world scenarios. It is important to design fast and lightweight CNN models that have a better trade-off between SR quality and model complexity.

To reduce the number of parameters, DRCN [13] and DRRN [22] adopted a recursive network that decreases the number of parameters effectively by parameter sharing. However, it has to increase the depth or the width of the network to compensate for the loss caused by the recursive module. These models reduce the model size at the expense of increased number of operations and inference time. In real-world applications, the number of operations is also an important factor to consider so that the SR model can be performed in real-time. So, it is better to design dedicated networks that are lightweight and efficient enough for real-world scenarios.

To this end, Ahn *et al.* [1] proposed the CARN-M for mobile devices by using a cascading network architecture, but it is at the cost of a large PSNR drop. Hui *et al.* [11] proposed an information distillation network (IDN) that explicitly split the intermediate features into two parts along the channel dimension, one was retained and the other was further processed by succeeding convolution layers. By using this channel splitting strategy, IDN can aggregate current information with partially retained local short-path information and achieve good performance at a modest size. Later, IMDN [10] further improved IDN by designing an information multi-distillation block (IMDB) that extracted features at a granular level. Specifically, the channel splitting strategy was applied multiple times within a IMDB. Each time, one part of the features was retained and another was sent to the next step. IMDN has a good performance in terms of both PSNR and inference time and won the first place in the AIM 2019 constrained image super-resolution challenge [30]. However, the number of parameters of IMDN is more than most of the lightweight SR models (*e.g.* VDSR [12], IDN [11], Mem-Net [23]). There is still room for improvement to be more lightweight.

The key component of both IDN and IMDN is the information distillation mechanism (IDM) that explicitly divides the preceding extracted features into two parts, one is retained and the other is further refined. We argue that the IDM is not efficient enough and it brings some inflexibility in the network design. It is hard to incorporate identity connections with the IDM. In this paper, we will give a more comprehensive analysis of the information distillation mechanism and propose the feature distillation connection (FDC) that is more lightweight and flexible than the IDM. We use IMDN as the baseline model since it makes a good trade-off between the reconstruction quality and the inference speed, which is very suitable for mobile devices. But the IMDN is not lightweight enough and the SR performance can still be further improved. To build a more powerful fast and lightweight SR model, we rethink the architecture of IMDN and propose the residual feature distillation network (RFDN). In comparison with IMDN, our RFDN is much more lightweight by using the feature distillation connections (FDCs). Further more, we propose a shallow residual block (SRB) that uses as the building blocks of RFDN to further improve the SR performance. The SRB consists of one convoltuional layer, an identical connection and an activation unit at the end. It can benefit from the residual learning [8] without introducing extra parameters compared with plain convolutions. It is very easy to incorporate SRB with the feature distillation connection to build a more powerful SR network.

The main contributions of this paper can be summarized as follows:

1. We propose a lightweight residual feature distillation network (RFDN) for fast and accurate image super-resolution, which achieves state-of-the-art SR performance while using much fewer parameters than the competitors.
2. We give a more comprehensive analysis of the information distillation mechanism (IDM) and rethink the IMDN network. Based on these new understandings, we propose the feature distillation connections (FDC) that are more lightweight and flexible than the IDM.
3. We propose the shallow residual block (SRB) that incorporates the identity connection with one convolutional block to further improve the SR performance without introducing any extra parameters.

2   Related Work

Recently, deep learning based models have achieved dramatic improvements in image SR. The pioneering work was done by Dong et al. [4], they first exploited a three-layer convolutional neural network SRCNN to jointly optimize the feature extraction, non-linear mapping and image reconstruction in an end-to-end manner. Then Kim et al. [12] proposed the very deep super-resolution (VDSR) network, which stacked 20 convolutional layers to improve the SR performance. To reduce the model complexity, Kim et al. [13] introduced DRCN that recursively applied the feature extraction layer for 16 times. DRRN [22] improved

DRCN by combining the recursive and residual network schemes to achieve better performance with fewer parameters. Lai *et al.* [14] proposed the laplacian pyramid super-resolution network (LapSRN) to address the speed and accuracy problem by taking the original LR images as input and progressively reconstructing the sub-band residuals of HR images. Tai *et al.* [23] presented the persistent memory network (MemNet) for image restoration task, which tackled the long-term dependency problem in the previous CNN architectures. To reduce the computational cost and increase the testing speed, Shi *et al.* [21] designed an efficient sub-pixel convolution to upscale the resolutions of feature maps at the end of SR mdoels so that most of computation was performed in the low-dimensional feature space. For the same purpose, Dong *et al.* [5] proposed fast SRCNN (FSRCNN), which employed transposed convolution as upsampling layers to accomplish post-upsampling SR. Then Lim *et al.* [17] proposed EDSR and MDSR, which achieved significant improvements by removing unnecessary modules in conventional residual networks. Based on EDSR, Zhang *et al.* proposed the residual dense network (RDN) [34] by introducing dense connections into the residual block. They also proposed the very deep residual attention network (RCAN) [32] and the residual non-local attention network (RNAN) [33]. Dai *et al.* [3] exploited the second-order attention mechanism to adaptively rescale features by considering feature statistics higher than first-order. Guo *et al.* [6] developed a dual regression scheme by introducing an additional constraint such that the mappings can form a closed-loop and LR images can be reconstructed to enhance the performance of SR models.

Despite the great success of CNN-based methods, most of them are not suitable for mobile devices. To solve this problem, Ahn *et al.* [1] proposed the CARN-M model for mobile scenario through a cascading network architecture. Hui *et al.* [11] proposed the information distillation network (IDN) that explicitly divided the preceding extracted features into two parts. Based on IDN, the also proposed the fast and lightweight information multi-distillation network (IMDN) [10] that is the winner solution of the AIM 2019 constrained image super-resolution challenge [30].

3   Method

3.1   Information Multi-distillation Block

As shown in Fig. 2a, the main part of information distillation block (IMDB) [10] is a progressive refinement module (PRM), which is marked with a gray background. The PRM first uses a 3×3 convolution layer to extract input features for multiple subsequent distillation steps. For each step, the channel splitting operation is employed on the preceding features and it divides the input features into two parts. One part is retained and the other part is fed into the next distillation step. Given the input features F_{in}, this procedure can be described

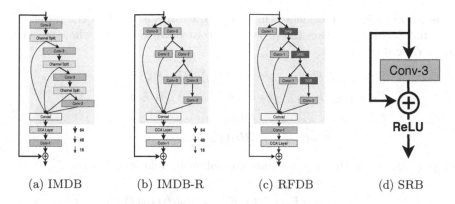

(a) IMDB   (b) IMDB-R   (c) RFDB   (d) SRB

Fig. 2. (a) IMDB: the original information multi-distillation block. (b) IMDB-R: rethinking of the IMDB. (c) RFDB: residual feature distillation block. (d) SRB: shallow residual block.

as

$$
\begin{aligned}
F_{distilled\_1}, F_{coarse\_1} &= Split_1(L_1(F_{in})), \\
F_{distilled\_2}, F_{coarse\_2} &= Split_2(L_2(F_{coarse\_1})), \\
F_{distilled\_3}, F_{coarse\_3} &= Split_3(L_3(F_{coarse\_2})), \\
F_{distilled\_4} &= L_4(F_{coarse\_3})
\end{aligned}
\tag{1}
$$

where L_j denotes the j-th convolution layer (including the activation unit), $Split_j$ denotes the j-th channel splitting operation, $F_{distilled\_j}$ represents the j-th distilled features, and F_{coarse_j} is the j-th coarse features that will be further processed by succeeding layers. Finally, all the distilled features are concatenated together as the output of the PRM.

$$
F_{distilled} = Concat(F_{distilled\_1}, F_{distilled\_2}, F_{distilled\_3}, F_{distilled\_4})
\tag{2}
$$

where $Concat$ represents the concatenation operation along the channel dimension.

3.2   Rethinking the IMDB

Although PRM achieves prominent improvements, it is not efficient enough and introduces some inflexibility because of the channel splitting operation. The distilled features are generated by 3×3 convolution filters that has many redundant parameters. Moreover, the feature refinement pipeline (along the right branch of the PRM) is coupled together with channel splitting operation so that it is hard to use identity connections only for this pipeline. Next, we will rethink the channel splitting operation and give a new equivalent architecture of the PRM to tackle the aforementioned problems.

As depicted in Fig. 2b, the 3×3 convolution followed by a channel splitting layer can be decoupled into two 3×3 convolution layers DL and RL. The layer

DL is responsible for producing the distilled features and RL is the refinement layer that further processes the proceeding coarse features. The whole structure can be described as

$$
\begin{aligned}
F_{distilled\_1}, F_{coarse\_1} &= DL_1(F_{in}), RL_1(F_{in}) \\
F_{distilled\_2}, F_{coarse\_2} &= DL_2(F_{coarse\_1}), RL_2(F_{coarse\_1}), \\
F_{distilled\_3}, F_{coarse\_3} &= DL_3(F_{coarse\_2}), RL_3(F_{coarse\_2}), \\
F_{distilled\_4} &= DL_4(F_{coarse\_3})
\end{aligned}
\tag{3}
$$

Comparing Eq. 1 with Eq. 3, we have the following relationships

$$
\begin{aligned}
DL_1(F_{in}), RL_1(F_{in}) &= Split_1(L_1(F_{in})), \\
DL_2(F_{coarse\_1}), RL_2(F_{coarse\_1}) &= Split_2(L_2(F_{coarse\_1})), \\
DL_3(F_{coarse\_2}), RL_3(F_{coarse\_2}) &= Split_3(L_3(F_{coarse\_2})), \\
DL_4(F_{coarse\_3}) &= L_4(F_{coarse\_3})
\end{aligned}
\tag{4}
$$

The above equations describe that each group of split operation can be viewed as two convolution layers that work concurrently. We call this new architecture IMDB-R, which is more flexible than the original IMDB. It has a clearer view on how the PRM works so that we can get more clues on how to design more efficient SR models.

3.3   Residual Feature Distillation Block

Inspired by the rethinking of IMDB, in this section, we introduce the residual feature distillation block (RFDB) that is more lightweight and powerful than the IMDB. In Fig. 2, we can see that the information distillation operation is actually implemented by a 3×3 convolution that compresses feature channels at a fixed ratio. However, we find that it is more efficient to use the 1×1 convolution for channel reduction as have done in many other CNN models. As depicted in Fig. 2c, the three convolutions on the left are replaced with 1×1 convolutions, which significantly reduces the amount of parameters. The right-most convolution still uses 3×3 kernels. This is because it locates on the main body of the RFDB and it must take the spatial context into account to better refine the features. For clarity, we call these outer connections feature distillation connections (FDC).

Despite aforementioned improvements, we also introduce more fine-grained residual learning into the network. For this purpose, we design a shallow residual block (SRB), as shown in Fig. 2d, which consists of a 3×3 convolution, an identity connection and the activation unit. The SRB can benefit from residual learning without introducing any extra parameters. The original IMDB only contains mid-level residual connections that are too coarse for the network to benefit most from the residual connections. In contrast, our SRB enables deeper residual connections and can better utilize the power of residual learning even with a lightweight shallow SR model. We use the proposed RFDB to build our residual feature distillation network (RFDN) as will be described in the next section.

3.4   Framework

We use the same framework as IMDN [10], as shown in Fig. 1, the residual feature distillation network (RFDN) consists of four parts: the first feature extraction convolution, multiple stacked residua feature distillation blocks (RFDBs), the feature fusion part and the last reconstruction block. Specifically, the initial feature extraction is implemented by a 3×3 convolution to generate coarse features from the input LR image. Given the input x, this procedure can be expressed as

$$F_0 = h(x) \tag{5}$$

where h denotes the coarse feature extraction function and F_0 is the extracted features. The next part of RFDN is multiple RFDBs that are stacked in a chain manner to gradually refine the extracted features. This process can be formulated as

$$F_k = H_k(F_{k-1}), k = 1, \ldots, n \tag{6}$$

where H_k denotes the k-th RFDB function, F_{k-1} and F_k represent the input feature and output feature of the k-th RFDB, respectively. After gradually refined by the RFDBs, all the intermediate features are assembled by a 1×1 convolution layer. Then, a 3×3 convolution layer is used to smooth the aggregated features as follows

$$F_{assemble} = H_{assemble}(Concat(F_1, \ldots, F_n)) \tag{7}$$

where $Concat$ is the concatenation operation along the channel dimension, $H_{asemble}$ denotes the 1×1 convolution followed by a 3×3 convolution, and $F_{assemble}$ is the aggregated features. Finally, the SR images are generated through the reconstruction as follows

$$y = R(F_{assemble} + F_0) \tag{8}$$

where R denotes the reconstruction function and y is the output of the network. The reconstruction process only consists of a 3×3 convolution and a non-parametric sub-pixel operation.

The loss function of our RFDN can be expressed by

$$\mathbb{L}(\theta) = \frac{1}{N} \sum_{i=1}^{N} ||H_{RFDN}(I_i^{LR}) - I_i^{HR}||_1 \tag{9}$$

where H_{RFDN} represents the function of our proposed network, θ indicates the learnable parameters of RFDN and $||.||_1$ is the l_1 norm. I^{LR} and I^{HR} are the input LR images and the corresponding ground-truth HR images, respectively.

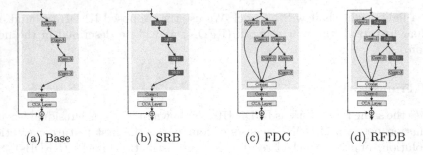

(a) Base   (b) SRB   (c) FDC   (d) RFDB

Fig. 3. The Base block, SRB block, FDC block and RFDB used in ablation study.

4   Experiments

4.1   Datasets and Metrics

Following previous works [1,10,11,17,32], we use the recently popular dataset DIV2K [24] to train our models. The DIV2K dataset contains 800 high-quality RGB training images. For testing, we use five widely used benchmark datasets: Set5 [2], Set14 [27], BSD100 [19], Urban100 [9] and Manga109 [20]. We employ peak signal-to-noise ratio (PSNR) and structural similarity (SSIM) [26] to measure the quality of the super-resolved images. All the values are calculated on the Y channel of the YCbCr channels converted from the RGB channels as with existing works [1,10–12,17,22,32,34].

4.2   Implementation Details

We generate the training LR images by down-sampling HR images with scaling factors (×2, ×3 and ×4) using bicubic interpolation in MATLAB. As of preparing for this paper, the IMDN has not released the training code yet. To reproduce the results that reported in the IMDN paper, we use different training settings from the original paper. More details will be discussed in Sect. 4.5. In this paper, we randomly crop 64 patches of size 64×64 from the LR images as input for each training minibatch. We augment the training data with random horizontal flips and 90 rotations. We train our model with ADAM optimizer by setting $\beta_1 = 0.9$, $\beta_2 = 0.999$, and $\epsilon = 10^{-8}$. The learning rate is initialized as 5×10^{-4} and halved at every 2×10^5 minibatch updates. When training the final models, the ×2 model is trained from scratch. After the model converges, we use it as a pretrained network for other scales. All the models in the ablation study are trained from scratch for saving the training time. We implement two models in this paper, which are named RFDN and RFDN-L. RFDN uses a channel number of 48 while RFDN-L uses a channel number of 52 to ahcieve a better reconstruction quality. We set the number of RFDB to 6 in both RFDN and RFDN-L. The networks are implemented by using PyTorch framework with a NVIDIA 1080Ti GPU.

Table 1. Investigations of FDC and SRB on the benchmark datasets with scale factor of ×4. The best results are highlighted.

Method	Params	Set5	Set14	B100	Urban100	Manga109
Base	652K	32.08/0.8932	28.55/0.7802	27.53/0.7345	26.05/0.7842	30.28/0.9050
SRB	652K	**32.19**/0.8949	28.58/0.7809	27.53/0.7347	26.07/0.7849	30.40/0.9074
FDC	637K	32.18/0.8945	28.58/0.7811	27.55/0.7352	26.09/0.7849	30.47/0.9077
RFDB	637K	32.18/**0.8950**	**28.61/0.7820**	**27.56/0.7356**	**26.10/0.7859**	**30.55/0.9082**

Table 2. Investigations of the distillation rate on the benchmark datasets with scale factor of ×4. The best results are highlighted. ↑ represents rising, ↓ represents falling and ∧ represents rising first and then falling.

Ratio	Params	Set5	Set14	B100	Urban100	Manga109
0.25	523K	**32.18/0.8946**	28.57/0.7811	27.53/0.7348	26.09/0.7851	30.44/0.9071
0.5	544K	32.16/0.8945	28.60/**0.7819**	**27.55/0.7351**	26.10/**0.7858**	30.45/0.9074
0.75	565K	32.15/0.8944	**28.61**/0.7816	27.54/0.7350	**26.12**/0.7853	**30.46/0.9081**
-	-	↓/↓	↑/∧	∧/∧	↑/∧	↑/↑

4.3 Model Analysis

Ablation Study. To evaluate the importance of the proposed feature distillation connection (FDC) and shallow residual block (SRB), we design four blocks that will be stacked as the body part of the SR network (Fig. 1), respectively. The four blocks are depicted in Fig. 3 and the evaluation results are shown in Table 1. Comparing the first two rows of Table 1, we can find that SRB improves the performance (*e.g.* PSNR:**+0.12 dB**, SSIM:**+0.0024** for Manga109) without introducing any extra parameters. We can also observe similar improvements when comparing the last two rows, which indicates the effectiveness of the shallow residual block. By adding FDC, the performance of the base method is improved by a large margin, for example the PSNR of Manga109 improves from 30.28 to 30.47 (**+0.19 dB**). Thanks to FDC and SRB, our RFDB significantly outperforms the base block.

Investigation of Distillation Rate. We investigate the distillation rate of the feature distillation connections in Table 2. Different distillation rates indicate different number of output channels in the feature distillation connections. As shown in the last row of Table 2, when the distillation rate increases, the growth trends of PSNR and SSIM are different on each dataset. Overall, the distillation rate of 0.5 has a good trade-off between SR performance and the number of parameters, which is adopted as the final distillation rate in our RFDN and RFDN-L.

Model Complexity Analysis. Figure 4 depicts the comparison of PSNR *vs.* parameters on Set5 ×4 dataset. The models depicted in Fig. 4 including

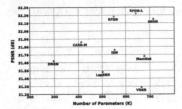 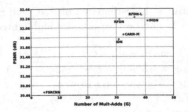

Fig. 4. PSNR *vs*. Parameters.   **Fig. 5.** PSNR *vs*. Mult-Adds.

DRRN [22], LapSRN [14], VDSR [12], MemNet [23], IDN [11], CARN-M [1] and IMDN [10]. When evaluating a lightweight model, the number of model parameters is a key factor to take into account. From Table 3, we can observe that our RFDN achieves comparable or better performance when comparing with the state-of-the-art lightweight models with fewer parameters. As shown in Fig. 4, though IMDN achieves prominent improvements compared with the previous methods, such as MemNet and IDN, it has more parameters than most of the lightweight models. In contrast, our RFDN achieves better performance than VDSR, MemNet, IDN, and IMDN with fewer parameters. When using more feature channels, our RFDN-L achieves even better results than RFDN while maintaining a modest model size. To get a more comprehensive understanding of the model complexity, we also show the comparison of PSNR *vs*. Mult-Adds on Set5 ×4 dataset in Fig. 5. As we can see, our RFDN and RFDN-L achieve higher PSNR than IMDN while using fewer calculations. IMDN won the first place in the parameters and inference tracks of AIM 2019 constrained super-resolution challenge [30], so we compare our RFDN with IMDN in terms of FPS. Our RFDN (44 FPS) has a comparable inference speed with IMDN (49 FPS) while being more accurate and lightweight. Moreover, our method has fewer calculations than IMDN and can save more energy.

4.4   Comparison with State-of-the-Arts

We compare the proposed RFDN with various lightweight SR methods on ×2, ×3 and ×4 scales, including SRCNN [4], FSRCNN [5], VDSR [12], DRCN [13], LapSRN [14], DRRN [22], MemNet [23], IDN [11], SRMDNF [31], CARN [1] and IMDN [10]. Table 3 shows the quantitative comparisons on the five benchmark datasets. We can find that the proposed RFDN can make a better trade-off than IMDN. Our RFDN can achieve comparable or better results with state-of-the-art methods while using 534/541/550K parameters for ×2/×3/×4 SR. By using slightly more parameters, our RFDN-L achieves the best in most quantitative results, especially on large scaling factors.

Table 3. Average PSNR/SSIM for scale factor 2, 3 and 4 on datasets Set5, Set14, BSD100, Urban100, and Manga109. The best and second best results are highlighted in red and blue respectively.

Method	Scale	Params	Set5 PSNR/SSIM	Set14 PSNR/SSIM	BSD100 PSNR/SSIM	Urban100 PSNR/SSIM	Manga109 PSNR/SSIM
Bicubic	x2	-	33.66/0.9299	30.24/0.8688	29.56/0.8431	26.88/0.8403	30.80/0.9339
SRCNN [4]		8K	36.66/0.9542	32.45/0.9067	31.36/0.8879	29.50/0.8946	35.60/0.9663
FSRCNN [5]		13K	37.00/0.9558	32.63/0.9088	31.53/0.8920	29.88/0.9020	36.67/0.9710
VDSR [12]		666K	37.53/0.9587	33.03/0.9124	31.90/0.8960	30.76/0.9140	37.22/0.9750
DRCN [13]		1774K	37.63/0.9588	33.04/0.9118	31.85/0.8942	30.75/0.9133	37.55/0.9732
LapSRN [14]		251K	37.52/0.9591	32.99/0.9124	31.80/0.8952	30.41/0.9103	37.27/0.9740
DRRN [22]		298K	37.74/0.9591	33.23/0.9136	32.05/0.8973	31.23/0.9188	37.88/0.9749
MemNet [23]		678K	37.78/0.9597	33.28/0.9142	32.08/0.8978	31.31/0.9195	37.72/0.9740
IDN [11]		553K	37.83/0.9600	33.30/0.9148	32.08/0.8985	31.27/0.9196	38.01/0.9749
SRMDNF [31]		1511K	37.79/0.9601	33.32/0.9159	32.05/0.8985	31.33/0.9204	38.07/0.9761
CARN [1]		1592K	37.76/0.9590	33.52/0.9166	32.09/0.8978	31.92/0.9256	38.36/0.9765
IMDN [10]		694K	38.00/0.9605	33.63/0.9177	32.19/0.8996	32.17/0.9283	38.88/0.9774
RFDN (Ours)		534K	38.05/0.9606	33.68/0.9184	32.16/0.8994	32.12/0.9278	38.88/0.9773
RFDN-L (Ours)		626K	38.08/0.9606	33.67/0.9190	32.18/0.8996	32.24/0.9290	38.95/0.9773
Bicubic	x3	-	30.39/0.8682	27.55/0.7742	27.21/0.7385	24.46/0.7349	26.95/0.8556
SRCNN [4]		8K	32.75/0.9090	29.30/0.8215	28.41/0.7863	26.24/0.7989	30.48/0.9117
FSRCNN [5]		13K	33.18/0.9140	29.37/0.8240	28.53/0.7910	26.43/0.8080	31.10/0.9210
VDSR [12]		666K	33.66/0.9213	29.77/0.8314	28.82/0.7976	27.14/0.8279	32.01/0.9340
DRCN [13]		1774K	33.82/0.9226	29.76/0.8311	28.80/0.7963	27.15/0.8276	32.24/0.9343
LapSRN [14]		502K	33.81/0.9220	29.79/0.8325	28.82/0.7980	27.07/0.8275	32.21/0.9350
DRRN [22]		298K	34.03/0.9244	29.96/0.8349	28.95/0.8004	27.53/0.8378	32.71/0.9379
MemNet [23]		678K	34.09/0.9248	30.00/0.8350	28.96/0.8001	27.56/0.8376	32.51/0.9369
IDN [11]		553K	34.11/0.9253	29.99/0.8354	28.95/0.8013	27.42/0.8359	32.71/0.9381
SRMDNF [31]		1528K	34.12/0.9254	30.04/0.8382	28.97/0.8025	27.57/0.8398	33.00/0.9403
CARN [1]		1592K	34.29/0.9255	30.29/0.8407	29.06/0.8034	28.06/0.8493	33.50/0.9440
IMDN [10]		703K	34.36/0.9270	30.32/0.8417	29.09/0.8046	28.17/0.8519	33.61/0.9445
RFDN (Ours)		541K	34.41/0.9273	30.34/0.8420	29.09/0.8050	28.21/0.8525	33.67/0.9449
RFDN-L (Ours)		633K	34.47/0.9280	30.35/0.8421	29.11/0.8053	28.32/0.8547	33.78/0.9458
Bicubic	x4	-	28.42/0.8104	26.00/0.7027	25.96/0.6675	23.14/0.6577	24.89/0.7866
SRCNN [4]		8K	30.48/0.8626	27.50/0.7513	26.90/0.7101	24.52/0.7221	27.58/0.8555
FSRCNN [5]		13K	30.72/0.8660	27.61/0.7550	26.98/0.7150	24.62/0.7280	27.90/0.8610
VDSR [12]		666K	31.35/0.8838	28.01/0.7674	27.29/0.7251	25.18/0.7524	28.83/0.8870
DRCN [13]		1774K	31.53/0.8854	28.02/0.7670	27.23/0.7233	25.14/0.7510	28.93/0.8854
LapSRN [14]		502K	31.54/0.8852	28.09/0.7700	27.32/0.7275	25.21/0.7562	29.09/0.8900
DRRN [22]		298K	31.68/0.8888	28.21/0.7720	27.38/0.7284	25.44/0.7638	29.45/0.8946
MemNet [23]		678K	31.74/0.8893	28.26/0.7723	27.40/0.7281	25.50/0.7630	29.42/0.8942
IDN [11]		553K	31.82/0.8903	28.25/0.7730	27.41/0.7297	25.41/0.7632	29.41/0.8942
SRMDNF [31]		1552K	31.96/0.8925	28.35/0.7787	27.49/0.7337	25.68/0.7731	30.09/0.9024
CARN [1]		1592K	32.13/0.8937	28.60/0.7806	27.58/0.7349	26.07/0.7837	30.47/0.9084
IMDN [10]		715K	32.21/0.8948	28.58/0.7811	27.56/0.7353	26.04/0.7838	30.45/0.9075
RFDN (Ours)		550K	32.24/0.8952	28.61/0.7819	27.57/0.7360	26.11/0.7858	30.58/0.9089
RFDN-L (Ours)		643K	32.28/0.8957	28.61/0.7818	27.58/0.7363	26.20/0.7883	30.61/0.9096

Table 4. Performance comparison of RFDN and IMDN under the same experimental settings. Both models are trained from scratch with scaling facotr ×4.

Method	Params	Set5	Set14	B100	Urban100	Manga109
IMDN [10]	715K	32.16/0.8940	28.59/0.7812	27.54/0.7350	26.05/0.7841	30.42/0.9074
RFDN	550K	**32.24/0.8953**	**28.59/0.7814**	**27.54/0.7355**	**26.15/0.7868**	**30.48/0.9080**

4.5   About the Experimental Settings

As described in Sect. 4.2, we use a slightly different experimental setup when training our models. In order to get a clearer insight on the improvements of our RFDN, we train both RFDN and the IMDN [10] from scratch under the same experimental settings. Table 4 shows the performance comparison on the five benchmark datasets. Our RFDN outperforms IMDN on all the datasets in terms of both PSNR and SSIM with much fewer parameters, which proves that the improvements on network design of our RFDN indeed boosts the performance of image SR.

4.6   Enhanced RFDN for AIM20 Challenge

As shown in Table 5, our enhanced RFDN (E-RFDN) won the first place in the AIM 2020 efficient super-resolution challenge [29]. Specifically, we replace the CCA layer in RFDB with the ESA block [18] and we use 4 such enhanced RFDBs (E-RFDBs) in E-RFDN. The number of feature channels in E-RFDN is set to 50 and the feature distillation rate is 0.5. During the training of E-RFDN, HR patches of size 256×256 are randomly cropped from HR images, and the mini-batch size is set to 64. The E-RFDN model is trained by minimizing L1 loss function with Adam optimizer. The initial learning rate is set to 5×10^{-4} and halved at every 200 epochs. After 1000 epochs, L2 loss is used for fine-tuning with learning rate of 1×10^{-5}. DIV2K and Flickr2K datasets are used for training the E-RFDN model. We include the top five methods in Table 5, the "#Activations" measures the number of elements of all outputs of convolutional layers. Compared to the first place method IMDN in AIM 2019 constrained SR challenge [28], our method provides a significant gain with respect to the runtime, parameters, FLOPs, and activations. More details and reuslts can be found in [29].

Table 5. AIM 2020 efficient SR challenge results (we only include the fisrt five methods).

Team	Author	PSNR [test]	Runtime [s]	#Params. [M]	FLOPs [G]	#Activations [M]	Extra Data
NJU_MCG (ours)	TinyJie	28.75	0.037	0.433	27.10	112.03	Yes
AiriA_GG	Now	28.70	0.037	0.687	44.98	118.49	Yes
UESTC-MediaLab	Mulns	28.70	0.060	0.461	30.06	219.61	Yes
XPixel	zzzhy	28.70	0.066	0.272	32.19	270.53	Yes
HaiYun	Sudo	28.78	0.058	0.777	49.67	132.31	Yes
IMDN	zheng222	28.78	0.050	0.893	58.53	154.14	Yes
Baselin	MSRResNet	28.70	0.114	1.517	166.36	292.55	Yes

5   Conclusion

In this paper, we give a comprehensive analysis of the information distillation mechanism for lightweight image super-resolution. Then we rethink the information multi-distillation network (IMDN) and propose the feature distillation connections (FDC) that are much more lightweight and flexible. To further boost the super-resolution performance, we also propose the shallow residual block (SRB) that incorporates the identity connection with one convolutional block. By using the shallow residual blocks and the feature distillation connections, we build the residual feature distillation network (RFDN) for fast and lightweight image super-resolution. Extensive experiments have shown that the proposed method achieves state-of-the-art results both quantitatively and qualitatively. Furthermore, our model has a modest number of parameters and mult-adds such that it can be easily ported to mobile devices.

References

1. Ahn, N., Kang, B., Sohn, K.-A.: Fast, accurate, and lightweight super-resolution with cascading residual network. In: Ferrari, V., Hebert, M., Sminchisescu, C., Weiss, Y. (eds.) ECCV 2018. LNCS, vol. 11214, pp. 256–272. Springer, Cham (2018). https://doi.org/10.1007/978-3-030-01249-6_16
2. Bevilacqua, M., Roumy, A., Guillemot, C., Alberi-Morel, M.: Low-complexity single-image super-resolution based on nonnegative neighbor embedding. In: BMVC, pp. 1–10. BMVA Press (2012)
3. Dai, T., Cai, J., Zhang, Y., Xia, S., Zhang, L.: Second-order attention network for single image super-resolution. In: CVPR, pp. 11065–11074. Computer Vision Foundation/IEEE (2019)
4. Dong, C., Loy, C.C., He, K., Tang, X.: Learning a deep convolutional network for image super-resolution. In: Fleet, D., Pajdla, T., Schiele, B., Tuytelaars, T. (eds.) ECCV 2014. LNCS, vol. 8692, pp. 184–199. Springer, Cham (2014). https://doi.org/10.1007/978-3-319-10593-2_13
5. Dong, C., Loy, C.C., Tang, X.: Accelerating the super-resolution convolutional neural network. In: Leibe, B., Matas, J., Sebe, N., Welling, M. (eds.) ECCV 2016. LNCS, vol. 9906, pp. 391–407. Springer, Cham (2016). https://doi.org/10.1007/978-3-319-46475-6_25

6. Guo, Y., et al.: Closed-loop matters: dual regression networks for single image super-resolution. CoRR abs/2003.07018 (2020)
7. Haris, M., Shakhnarovich, G., Ukita, N.: Deep back-projection networks for super-resolution. In: CVPR, pp. 1664–1673. IEEE Computer Society (2018)
8. He, K., Zhang, X., Ren, S., Sun, J.: Deep residual learning for image recognition. In: CVPR, pp. 770–778. IEEE Computer Society (2016)
9. Huang, J., Singh, A., Ahuja, N.: Single image super-resolution from transformed self-exemplars. In: CVPR, pp. 5197–5206. IEEE Computer Society (2015)
10. Hui, Z., Gao, X., Yang, Y., Wang, X.: Lightweight image super-resolution with information multi-distillation network. In: ACM Multimedia, pp. 2024–2032. ACM (2019)
11. Hui, Z., Wang, X., Gao, X.: Fast and accurate single image super-resolution via information distillation network. In: CVPR, pp. 723–731. IEEE Computer Society (2018)
12. Kim, J., Lee, J.K., Lee, K.M.: Accurate image super-resolution using very deep convolutional networks. In: CVPR, pp. 1646–1654. IEEE Computer Society (2016)
13. Kim, J., Lee, J.K., Lee, K.M.: Deeply-recursive convolutional network for image super-resolution. In: CVPR, pp. 1637–1645. IEEE Computer Society (2016)
14. Lai, W., Huang, J., Ahuja, N., Yang, M.: Deep Laplacian pyramid networks for fast and accurate super-resolution. In: CVPR, pp. 5835–5843. IEEE Computer Society (2017)
15. Ledig, C., et al.: Photo-realistic single image super-resolution using a generative adversarial network. In: CVPR, pp. 105–114. IEEE Computer Society (2017)
16. Li, Z., Yang, J., Liu, Z., Yang, X., Jeon, G., Wu, W.: Feedback network for image super-resolution. In: CVPR, pp. 3867–3876. Computer Vision Foundation/IEEE (2019)
17. Lim, B., Son, S., Kim, H., Nah, S., Lee, K.M.: Enhanced deep residual networks for single image super-resolution. In: CVPR Workshops. pp. 1132–1140. IEEE Computer Society (2017)
18. Liu, J., Zhang, W., Tang, Y., Tang, J., Wu, G.: Residual feature aggregation network for image super-resolution. In: CVPR. pp. 2356–2365. IEEE (2020)
19. Martin, D.R., Fowlkes, C.C., Tal, D., Malik, J.: A database of human segmented natural images and its application to evaluating segmentation algorithms and measuring ecological statistics. In: ICCV, pp. 416–425 (2001)
20. Matsui, Y., et al.: Sketch-based manga retrieval using manga109 dataset. Multimedia Tools Appl. **76**(20), 21811–21838 (2016). https://doi.org/10.1007/s11042-016-4020-z
21. Shi, W., et al.: Real-time single image and video super-resolution using an efficient sub-pixel convolutional neural network. In: CVPR, pp. 1874–1883. IEEE Computer Society (2016)
22. Tai, Y., Yang, J., Liu, X.: Image super-resolution via deep recursive residual network. In: CVPR, pp. 2790–2798. IEEE Computer Society (2017)
23. Tai, Y., Yang, J., Liu, X., Xu, C.: MemNet: a persistent memory network for image restoration. In: ICCV, pp. 4549–4557. IEEE Computer Society (2017)
24. Timofte, R., et al.: NTIRE 2017 challenge on single image super-resolution: methods and results. In: CVPR Workshops, pp. 1110–1121. IEEE Computer Society (2017)
25. Timofte, R., Rothe, R., Gool, L.V.: Seven ways to improve example-based single image super resolution. In: CVPR, pp. 1865–1873. IEEE Computer Society (2016)

26. Wang, Z., Bovik, A.C., Sheikh, H.R., Simoncelli, E.P.: Image quality assessment: from error visibility to structural similarity. IEEE Trans. Image Processing **13**(4), 600–612 (2004)
27. Zeyde, R., Elad, M., Protter, M.: On single image scale-up using sparse-representations. In: Boissonnat, J.-D., et al. (eds.) Curves and Surfaces 2010. LNCS, vol. 6920, pp. 711–730. Springer, Heidelberg (2012). https://doi.org/10.1007/978-3-642-27413-8_47
28. Zhang, K., et al.: Aim 2019 challenge on constrained super-resolution: Methods and results. In: 2019 IEEE/CVF International Conference on Computer Vision Workshop (ICCVW), pp. 3565–3574 (2019)
29. Zhang, K., Danelljan, M., Li, Y., Timofte, R., et al.: AIM 2020 challenge on efficient super-resolution: Methods and results. In: Bartoli, A., Fusiello, A. (eds.) ECCV 2020, LNCS 1253, pp. 5–40 (2020)
30. Zhang, K., et al.: AIM 2019 challenge on constrained super-resolution: methods and results. In: ICCV Workshops, pp. 3565–3574. IEEE (2019)
31. Zhang, K., Zuo, W., Zhang, L.: Learning a single convolutional super-resolution network for multiple degradations. In: CVPR, pp. 3262–3271. IEEE Computer Society (2018)
32. Zhang, Y., Li, K., Li, K., Wang, L., Zhong, B., Fu, Y.: Image super-resolution using very deep residual channel attention networks. In: Ferrari, V., Hebert, M., Sminchisescu, C., Weiss, Y. (eds.) ECCV 2018. LNCS, vol. 11211, pp. 294–310. Springer, Cham (2018). https://doi.org/10.1007/978-3-030-01234-2_18
33. Zhang, Y., Li, K., Li, K., Zhong, B., Fu, Y.: Residual non-local attention networks for image restoration. In: ICLR (Poster). OpenReview.net (2019)
34. Zhang, Y., Tian, Y., Kong, Y., Zhong, B., Fu, Y.: Residual dense network for image super-resolution. In: CVPR, pp. 2472–2481. IEEE Computer Society (2018)

Efficient Image Super-Resolution Using Pixel Attention

Hengyuan Zhao[1,2(✉)], Xiangtao Kong[1,2,3(✉)], Jingwen He[1,2(✉)], Yu Qiao[1,2(✉)], and Chao Dong[1,2(✉)]

[1] ShenZhen Key Lab of Computer Vision and Pattern Recognition, SIAT-SenseTime Joint Lab, Shenzhen Institutes of Advanced Technology, Chinese Academy of Sciences, Beijing, China
{hy.zhao1,xt.kong,jw.he,yu.qiao,chao.dong}@siat.ac.cn
[2] SIAT Branch, Shenzhen Institute of Artificial Intelligence and Robotics for Society, Shenzhen, China
[3] University of Chinese Academy of Sciences, Beijing, China

Abstract. This work aims at designing a lightweight convolutional neural network for image super resolution (SR). With simplicity bare in mind, we construct a pretty concise and effective network with a newly proposed pixel attention scheme. Pixel attention (PA) is similar as channel attention and spatial attention in formulation. The difference is that PA produces 3D attention maps instead of a 1D attention vector or a 2D map. This attention scheme introduces fewer additional parameters but generates better SR results. On the basis of PA, we propose two building blocks for the main branch and the reconstruction branch, respectively. The first one—SC-PA block has the same structure as the Self-Calibrated convolution but with our PA layer. This block is much more efficient than conventional residual/dense blocks, for its two-branch architecture and attention scheme. While the second one—U-PA block combines the nearest-neighbor upsampling, convolution and PA layers. It improves the final reconstruction quality with little parameter cost. Our final model—PAN could achieve similar performance as the lightweight networks—SRResNet and CARN, but with only 272K parameters (17.92% of SRResNet and 17.09% of CARN). The effectiveness of each proposed component is also validated by ablation study. The code is available at https://github.com/zhaohengyuan1/PAN.

Keywords: Super resolution · Deep neural networks

1 Introduction

Image super resolution is a long-standing low-level computer vision problem, which predicts a high-resolution image from a low-resolution observation. In recent years, deep-learning-based methods [4] have dominated this field, and consistently improved the performance. Despite of the fast development, the huge and increasing computation cost has largely restricted their application in

© Springer Nature Switzerland AG 2020
A. Bartoli and A. Fusiello (Eds.): ECCV 2020 Workshops, LNCS 12537, pp. 56–72, 2020.
https://doi.org/10.1007/978-3-030-67070-2_3

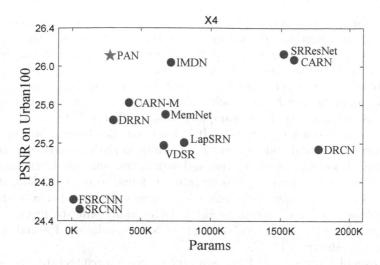

Fig. 1. Performance and Parameters comparison between our PAN and other state-of-the-art lightweight networks on Urban100 dataset for upscaling factor ×4.

real-world usages, such as real-time zooming and interactive editing. To address this issue, the AIM 2020 [6,7,13,14,25,30,38] held the "Efficient Super Resolution" challenge [41], which asked the participants to use fewer computation cost to achieve the same performance as a standard baseline – SRResNet [19]. This challenge could significantly promote the development of light-weight networks. With the goal of minimizing parameters, we propose an extremely simple yet effective model - PAN, which has fewest parameters among all participants. We will introduce our method in this paper. The review of previous studies can be found in the Related Work section. Our main contribution is called pixel attention (PA), which is inspired by channel attention (CA) [10] and spatial attention (SA) [39]. These attention schemes are popular as they can effectively improve the feature representation capacity by a "second order" feature multiplication. By applying a more powerful feature propagation strategy, the network could achieve higher performance with the same computation load (e.g., RCAN [44], CARN [1], PANet [24]). This is a promising direction for network compression. Specifically, as shown in Fig. 3, channel attention pools the previous features to a vector by spatial global pooling, while spatial attention pools the features to a single feature map by channel-wise pooling. We find that these schemes are less effective in SR task, which requires pixel-level evaluation. On the other hand, simply removing the pooling operation could significantly improves the performance. As the features are multiplied in a pixel-wise manor (see Fig. 3), we call this modified attention scheme as pixel attention, and our network as pixel attention network (PAN).

We equip PA in two building blocks, which forms the whole network. The first block is the basic block in the main branch, called Self-Calibrated block with Pixel Attention (SC-PA). Its main structure is the same as the recent

Self-Calibrated Convolutions [21]. As shown in Fig. 2, the convolutions are divided into two portions: the upper one is responsible for higher-level feature manipulation, while the other one is to maintain the original information. We adopt PA in the upper one, and standard convolutions in the other one. The SC-PA block enjoys a very simple structure without complex connections and up/down sampling operations, which are not friendly for hardware acceleration.

The second block is the Upsampling block with Pixel Attention (U-PA), which is in the reconstruction stage. It is based on the observation that previous SR networks mainly adopt similar structures in the reconstruction branch, i.e., deconvolution/pixel-shuffle layers and regular convolutions. Little efforts are devoted in this area. However, this structure is found to be redundant and less effective. To further improve the efficiency, we introduce PA between the convolution layers and use nearest neighbor (NN) upsampling to further reduce parameters. Thus the U-PA block consists of NN, convolution, PA and convolution layers, as shown in Fig. 2.

The overall framework of PAN is pretty simple in architecture, yet is much more effective than previous models. In AIM 2020 challenge, we are ranked 4th in overall ranking, as we are inferior in the number of convolutions and activations. However, our entry contains the fewest parameters – only 272K, which is 161K fewer than the 1st, and 415K fewer than the 2nd. From Fig. 1, we observe that PAN achieves a better trade-off between the reconstruction performance and the model size. To further realize the potential of our method, we try to expand PAN to a larger size. However, it will become hard to train the larger PAN without adding connections in the network. But if we add connections (e.g. dense connections) in PAN, it will dramatically increase the computation, which is not consistent with our goal – efficient SR. We believe that PA is an useful and independent component, which could also benefit other computer vision tasks.

Contributions. The main contributions of this work are threefold:

1. We propose a simple and fundamental attention scheme – pixel attention (PA), which is demonstrated effective in lightweight SR networks.
2. We integrate pixel attention and Self-Calibrated convolution [21] in a new building block – SC-PA, which is efficient and constructive.
3. We employ pixel attention in the reconstruction branch and propose a U-PA block. Note that few studies have investigated attention schemes after upsampling.

2   Related Work

2.1   Efficient CNN for SR

Recently, many deep neural networks [3, 9, 20, 43–45] have been introduced to improve the reconstruction results. However, the huge amount of parameters and the expensive computational cost limit their practice in real applications [1].

To save the computation, Dong et al. [5] directly use the original LR images as input instead of the pre-upsampled ones. This strategy has been widely used in SISR models [5,29,35]. Besides, group convolution [2,8,23], depth-wise separable convolutions [11,33], and self-calibrated convolution [21] have been proposed to accelerate the deep models. Some of these modules have been utilized in SR and shows effectiveness [1,36]. CARN-M [1] uses group convolution for efficient SR and obtains comparable results against computational complexity models. IMDN [12] extracts hierarchical features step-by-step by split operations, and then aggregates them by simply using a 1×1 convolution. It won the first place at Contrained Super-Resolution Challenge in AIM 2019 [42]. In this work, we employ the self-calibrated convolution scheme [21] in our PAN networks for efficient SR.

2.2 Attention Scheme

Attention mechanism has demonstrated great superiority in improving the performance of deep models for computer vision tasks. SE-Net [10] is the first attention method to learn channel information and achieves state-of-the-art performance. Roy et al. [28] uses a 1×1 convolution layer to generate spatial attention features. BAM [26] decomposes 3D attention map inference into channel and spatial attention map. CBAM [39] computes spatial attention using a 2D convolution layer of kernel size $k \times k$, then combines it with channel attention to generate 3D attention map. ECA [34] employs global average pooling (GAP) to generate channel weights by performing a fast 1D convolution of size k. Zhang et al. [44] proposed the residual channel attention network (RCAN) by introducing the channel attention mechanism into a modified residual block for SR. The channel attention mechanism uses global average pooling to extract channel statistics. It can rescale channel-wise features by considering interdependencies among channels to help train a very deep network. Dai et al. [3] proposed the second-order attention network (SAN) by using second-order feature statistics for more discriminative representations.

Obviously, most of the above methods focus on developing complex attention modules to gain better performance. Different from them, our PA aims at learning effective pixel attention with lower computation complexity and generates 3D attention features with a 1×1 convolution layer.

2.3 Reconstruction Methods in SR Networks

Instead of adopting interpolation based upsampling methods at the beginning of network[4,15,31], the learning-based reconstruction methods such as pixel-shuffle [29] generally implement upsampling in the final stage of the network. But in recent works, interpolation based upsampling methods can also be employed in the end of network to obtain good performance [35]. Therefore, the reconstruction module now basically consists of upsampling (interpolation based or learning based) and convolutional layers. Our reconstruction method in PAN adopts interpolation based – nearest neighbor upsampling and convolution layers.

Besides, previous works have shown that attention mechanism can effectively improve the performance in SR tasks but few researchers investigate it in reconstruction stage. Therefore, in this work, our U-PA block based on attention mechanism is adopted in reconstruction stage for better reconstruction.

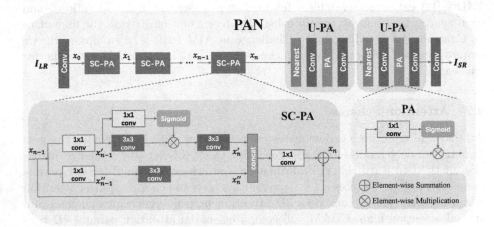

Fig. 2. Network architecture of the proposed PAN.

3 Proposed Method

3.1 Network Architecture

As shown in Fig. 2, the network architecture of our PAN, consists of three modules, namely the feature extraction (FE) module, the nonlinear mapping module with stacked SC-PAs, and the reconstruction module with U-PA blocks.

The LR images are first fed to the FE module that contains a convolution layer for shallow feature extraction. The FE module can be formulated as

$$x_0 = f_{ext}(I_{LR}),\tag{1}$$

where $f_{ext}(\cdot)$ denotes a convolution layer with a 3×3 kernel to extract features from the input LR image I_{LR}, and x_0 is the extracted feature maps. It is worth noting that only one convolution layer is used here for lightweight design.

Then, we use the non-linear mapping module that consists of several stacked SC-PAs to generate new powerful feature representations. We denote the proposed SC-PA as $f_{SCPA}(\cdot)$ given by

$$x_n = f_{SCPA}^n(f_{SCPA}^{n-1}(...f_{SCPA}^0(x_0)...)),\tag{2}$$

where x_n is the output feature map of the nth SC-PA.

At last, we utilize the reconstruction module that contains two U-PA blocks and a convolution layer to upsample the features to the HR size. In addition, we add a global connection path f_{UP}, in which a bilinear interpolation is performed on the input I_{LR}. Finally, we obtain:

$$I_{SR} = f_{rec}(x_n) + f_{up}(I_{LR}),\qquad(3)$$

where $f_{rec}(\cdot)$ is the reconstruction module, and I_{SR} is the final result of the network.

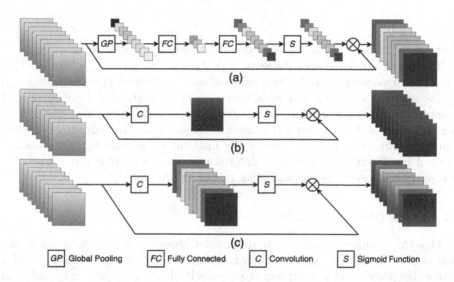

Fig. 3. (a) CA: Channel Attention; (b) SA: Spatial Attention; (c) PA: Pixel Attention.

3.2 Pixel Attention Scheme

First, we revisit channel attention [10] and spatial attention [39]. As shown in Fig. 3, channel attention aims to obtain a 1D ($C \times 1 \times 1$) attention feature vector, while spatial attention obtains a 2D ($1 \times H \times W$) attention map. Note that C is the number of channels, H and W are the height and width of the features, respectively. Different from them, our pixel attention is able to generate a 3D ($C \times H \times W$) matrix as the attention features. In other word, pixel attention generates attention coefficients for all pixels of the feature map. As shown in Fig. 4, pixel attention only uses a 1×1 convolution layer and a sigmoid function to obtain the attention maps which will then be multiplied with the input features.

We denote the input and output feature map as x_{k-1} and x_k, respectively. The PA layer can be computed as

$$x_k = f_{PA}(x_{k-1}) \cdot x_{k-1},\qquad(4)$$

where $f_{PA}(\cdot)$ is a 1×1 convolution layer followed by a sigmoid function.

3.3 SC-PA Block

The nonlinear mapping module contains several stacked Self-Calibrated convolution with Pixel Attention (SC-PA) blocks. Here, we define x_{n-1} and x_n as the input and output of the nth SC-PA block, respectively. As shown in Fig. 2, similarly as SCNet [21], SC-PA block contains two branches, where each branch has a 1×1 convolution layer at the beginning, which is called $f_{split}(\cdot)$. Given input feature x_{n-1}, we have:

$$x_{n-1}' = f'_{split}(x_{n-1}), \tag{5}$$

$$x_{n-1}'' = f''_{split}(x_{n-1}), \tag{6}$$

where x_{n-1}' and x_{n-1}'' only have half of the channel number of x_{n-1}.

The upper branch also contains two 3×3 convolution layers, where the first one is equipped with a pixel attention module. This branch transforms x'_{n-1} to x'_n. We only use a single 3×3 convolution layer to generate x''_n for the purpose of maintaining the original information. Finally, x'_n and x''_n are concatenated and then passed to a 1×1 convolution layer to generate x_n. In order to accelerate training, shortcut is used to produce the final output feature x_n. This block is inspired by SCNet [21]. The main difference is that we employ our PA scheme to replace the pooling and upsampling layer in SCNet [21].

3.4 U-PA Block

Besides the nonlinear mapping module, pixel attention is also adopted in the final reconstruction module. As shown in Fig. 4, the U-PA block consists of a nearest neighbor (NN) upsampling layer and a PA layer between two convolution layers. Note that in previous SR networks, a reconstruction module is basically comprised of upsampling and convolution layers. Moreover, few researchers have investigated the attention mechanism in the upsampling stage. Therefore, in this work, we adopt PA layer in the reconstruction module. Experiments show that introducing PA could significantly improve the final performance with little parameter cost. Besides, we also use the nearest-neighbor interpolation layer as the upsampling layer to further save parameters.

3.5 Discussion

The proposed PAN is specially designed for efficient SR, thus is very concise in network architecture. The building blocks – SC-PA and U-PA are also simple and easy to implement. Nevertheless, when expanding this network to a larger scale, i.e., >50 blocks, the current structure will face the problem of training difficulty. Then we need to add other techniques, like dense connections, to allow successful training. As this is not the focus of this paper, we do not investigate these additional strategies for very deep networks. There is also another limitation for the proposed PA scheme.

We experimentally find that PA is especially useful for small networks. But the effectiveness decreases with the increase of network scales. This is mainly because that PA can improve the expression capacity of convolutions, which could be very important for lightweight networks. In contrast, large-scale networks are highly redundant and their convolutions are not fully utilized, thus the improvement will mainly comes from a better training strategy. We have shown this trend in ablation study.

4 Experiments

In this section, we systematically compare our PAN with state-of-the-art SISR algorithms on five commonly used benchmark datasets. Besides, we conduct ablation study to validate the effectiveness of each proposed component.

4.1 Datasets and Metrics

We use DIV2K and Flickr2K datasets as our training datasets. The LR images are obtained by the bicubic downsampling of HR images. During the testing stage, five standard benchmark datasets, Set5 [2], Set14 [40], B100 [22], Urban100 [11], Manga109 [23], are used for evaluation. The widely used peak signal to noise ratio (PSNR) and the structural similarity index (SSIM) on the Y channel are used as the evaluation metrics.

4.2 Implementation Details

During training, we use DIV2K and Flickr2K to train our PAN. For training SRResNet-PA and RCAN-PA, we only use DIV2K dataset. Data augmentation is also performed on the training set by random rotations of 90°, 180°, 270° and horizontal flips. The HR patch size is set to 256×256, while the minibatch size is 32. L1 loss function [37] is adopted with Adam optimizer [17] for model training. The cosine annealing learning scheme rather than the multi-step scheme is adopted since it has a faster training speed. The initial maximum learning rate is set to $1e-3$ and the minimum learning rate is set to $1e-7$. The period of cosine is $250k$ iterations. The proposed algorithm is implemented under the PyTorch framework [27] on a computer with an NVIDIA GTX 1080Ti GPU.

4.3 Comparison with SRResNet and CARN

PAN is dedicated for the efficient SR challenge[41]. According to the requirements, our aim is to achieve at least the same performance as the SRResNet [19] in the provided validation dataset with lower computational cost. In this section, we mainly compare with SRResNet on the aforementioned five standard benchmark datasets for super resolution ×2, ×3, and ×4. Besides, we select another state-of-the-art network – CARN [1], which is specially designed to be efficient and lightweight.

From Table 1, it is obviously observed that our proposed PAN outperforms CARN on five benchmark datasets for all upscaling factors ×2, ×3, and ×4. Note that the number of parameters in PAN only accounts for less than 1/5 of CARN [1]. As for comparison with SRResNet [19], our proposed PAN could obtain higher PSNR on Manga109 and B100 dataset, but yeilds inferior results on the other three datasets. Specifically, for task ×4, the number of parameters in PAN is only 17.92% of SRResNet [19] and 17.09% of CARN [1], respectively.

Table 1. Comparison of SRResNet, CARN and PAN for upscaling factors ×2, ×3, and ×4. Red/Blue text: best/second-best.

Scale	Method	Params	Mult-Adds	Set5 PSNR	Set14 PSNR	B100 PSNR	Urban100 PSNR	Manga109 PSNR
×2	CARN	1,592K	222.8G	37.76	33.52	32.09	31.92	38.36
	SRResNet	1,370K	341.7G	38.05	33.64	32.22	32.23	38.05
	PAN(Ours)	261K	70.5G	38.00	33.59	32.18	32.01	38.70
×3	CARN	1,592K	118.8G	34.29	30.29	29.06	28.06	33.50
	SRResNet	1,554K	190.2G	34.41	30.36	29.11	28.20	33.54
	PAN(Ours)	261K	39.0G	34.40	30.36	29.11	28.11	33.61
×4	CARN	1,592K	90.9G	32.13	28.60	27.58	26.07	30.47
	SRResNet	1,518K	146.1G	32.17	28.61	27.59	26.12	30.48
	PAN(Ours)	272K	28.2G	32.13	28.61	27.59	26.11	30.51

4.4 Ablation Study

Comparison of Different Attention Schemes. To demonstrate the effectiveness of our PA layer, we use PAN as the basic network, and then replace the 16 SC-PA blocks with 8 residual blocks (RB), 8 residual blocks with channel attention (RB-CA), 8 residual blocks with spatial attention (RB-SA) and 8 residual blocks with pixel attention (RB-PA), respectively. As shown in Fig. 4, the attention module is inserted after the second convolution in the original residual block, which is consistent with other attention schemes.

In Table 2, we compare the number of parameters, Multi-Adds, and the performance in PSNR for all methods. Note that all results are the mean values of PSNR calculated by 328 images on 5 benchmark datasets. Mult-Adds is computed by assuming that the resolution of HR image is 720p. It is observed that RB-CA and RB-PA could improve the PSNR by 0.03 dB and 0.09 dB, respectively, while RB-SA is slightly worse than RB. This indicates that pixel attention is more effective than channel attention and spatial attention.

Table 2. Comparison of the number of parameters, Mult-Adds and mean values of PSNR obtained by Basic RB, RB-CA, RB-SA and RB-PA on five datasets for upscaling factor ×4. We record the results in 5×10^5 iterations.

Attention Type	Params	Mult-Adds	PSNR
RB	272,009	28.16G	27.94 dB
RB-CA	285,379	28.16G	27.97 dB(+0.03 dB)
RB-SA	272,427	28.18G	27.93 dB(−0.01 dB)
RB-PA	285,219	28.90G	28.03 dB(+0.09 dB)

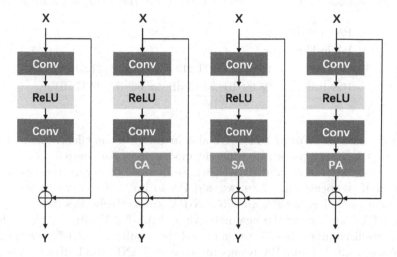

Fig. 4. (a) RB: basic residual block; (b) RB-CA: basic residual block with channel attention; (c) RB-SA: basic residual block with spatial attention; (d) RB-PA: basic residual attention with pixel attention.

The Effectiveness of Self-Calibrated (SC) Block. We validate the effectiveness of the Self-Calibrated (SC) block by comparing SC-PA with RB-PA. Here, we use RB as a baseline. From Table 3, we find that both RB-PA and SC-PA could improve the PSNR on the basis of RB. Furthermore, SC-PA outperforms RB-PA by 0.12 dB and it only requires 410 (1/30 of RB-PA) additional parameters compared with RB. This demonstrates that the Self-Calibrated (SC) block is able to achieve more significant improvement compared with the traditional residual blocks.

The Effectiveness of PA. Here, we show the importance of pixel attention (PA) in the Self-Calibrated (SC) block and Upsampling (U) block. For baseline, we remove all PA in our proposed PAN. As shown in Table 4, we observe that adding pixel attention (PA) in Self-Calibrated (SC) block and Upsampling (U) block could achieve improvement by 0.06 dB.

Table 3. Comparison of the number of parameters and mean values of PSNR obtained by Basic RB, RB-PA and SC-PA on five datasets for upscaling factor ×4. We record the results in 5×10^5 iterations.

Basic Unit	RB	RB-PA	SC-PA
Params Diff	0	+13,210	+410
Mult-Adds	28.16G	28.90G	28.16G
PSNR	27.94 dB	28.03 dB (+0.09 dB)	28.15 dB (+0.21 dB)

Table 4. The effectiveness of PA in SC-PA and U-PA blocks measured on the five benchmark datasets for upscaling factor ×4. We record the PSNR in 5×10^5 iterations.

PA in SC-PA	×	√	×	√
PA in U-PA	×	×	√	√
Params	264,499	271,219	265,699	272,419
PSNR	28.09 dB	28.12 dB	28.08 dB	28.15 dB

The Influence of Model Size. We also investigate the effectiveness of pixel attention (PA) in networks with different model sizes. For comparison, we select two networks, SRResNet and RCAN, whose number of parameters are 1,518K and 15,592K, respectively. Then, we add PA to both of the two networks and name them as SRResNet-PA and RCAN-PA, respectively. Besides, we remove PA from PAN and name the new network as PAN-SC-U. Since training larger network requires more time, here we record the results in 1×10^6 iterations. As we can see from Table 6, PA brings increase in PSNR (0.11 dB) on the basis of PAN-SC-U. However, it seems that PA could degrade the performance of the larger networks (SRResNet-PA and RCAN-PA). For instance, RCAN-PA is worse than RCAN with a 0.06 dB drop in PSNR. The experimental results shows that PA is more effective in lightweight models (Fig. 5).

4.5   Comparison with State-of-the-Art Methods

We compare the proposed PAN with commonly used lightweight SR models for upscaling factor ×2, ×3, and ×4, including SRCNN [4], FSRCNN [5], VDSR [15], DRCN [16], LapSRN [18], DRRN [31], MemNet [32], CARN [1], SRResNet [19] and IMDN [12]. We have also listed the performance of state-of-the-art large SR models – RDN [45], RCAN [44], and SAN [3] for reference.

    Table 5 shows quantitative results in terms of PSNR and SSIM on 5 benchmark datasets obtained by different algorithms. In addition, the number of parameters of compared models is also given. From Table 5, we find that our PAN only has less than 300K parameters but outperforms most of the state-of-the-art methods. Specifically, CARN [1] achieves similar performance as us, but its parameters are close to 1,592K which is about six times of ours. Compared with the baseline – SRResNet, we could achieve higher PSNR on Set14

Table 5. Quantitative results of state-of-the-art SR methods for all upscaling factors ×2, ×3, and ×4. Red/Blue text: best/second-best among all methods except RDN, RCAN, and SAN. Overstriking: our methods.

Method	Params	Set5 PSNR/SSIM	Set14 PSNR/SSIM	B100 PSNR/SSIM	Urban100 PSNR/SSIM	Manga109 PSNR/SSIM
Scale	×2					
SRCNN	57K	36.66/0.9542	32.45/0.9067	31.36/0.8879	29.50/0.8946	35.60/0.9663
FSRCNN	13K	37.00/0.9558	32.63/0.9088	31.53/0.8920	29.88/0.9020	36.67/0.9710
VDSR	666K	37.53/0.9587	33.03/0.9124	31.90/0.8960	30.76/0.9140	37.22/0.9750
DRCN	1,774K	37.63/0.9588	33.04/0.9118	31.85/0.8942	30.75/0.9133	37.55/0.9732
LapSRN	251K	37.52/0.9591	32.99/0.9124	31.80/0.8952	30.41/0.9103	37.27/0.9740
DRRN	298K	37.74/0.9591	33.23/0.9136	32.05/0.8973	31.23/0.9188	37.88/0.9749
MemNet	678K	37.78/0.9597	33.28/0.9142	32.08/0.8978	31.31/0.9195	37.72/0.9740
CARN	1,592K	37.76/0.9590	33.52/0.9166	32.09/0.8978	31.92/0.9256	38.36/0.9765
SRResNet	1,370K	38.05/0.9607	33.64/0.9178	32.22/0.9002	32.23/0.9295	38.05/0.9607
IMDN	694K	38.00/0.9605	33.63/0.9177	32.19/0.8996	32.17/0.9283	38.88/0.9774
PAN	**261K**	38.00/0.9605	33.59/0.9181	32.18/0.8997	32.01/0.9273	38.70/0.9773
RDN	22,123K	38.24/0.9614	34.01/0.9212	32.34/0.9017	32.89/0.9353	39.18/0.9780
RCAN	15,444K	38.27/0.9614	34.12/0.9216	32.41/0.9027	33.34/0.9384	39.44/0.9786
SAN	15,674K	38.31/0.9620	34.07/0.9213	32.42/0.9028	33.10/0.9370	39.32/.09792
Scale	×3					
SRCNN	57K	32.75/0.9090	29.30/0.8215	28.41/0.7863	26.24/0.7989	30.48/0.9117
FSRCNN	13K	33.18/0.9140	29.37/0.8240	28.53/0.7910	26.43/0.8080	31.10/0.9210
VDSR	666K	33.66/0.9213	29.77/0.8314	28.82/0.7976	27.14/0.8279	32.01/0.9340
DRCN	1,774K	33.82/0.9226	29.76/0.8311	28.80/0.7963	27.15/0.8276	32.24/0.9343
LapSRN	502K	33.81/0.9220	29.79/0.8325	28.82/0.7980	27.07/0.8275	32.21/0.9350
DRRN	298K	34.03/0.9244	29.96/0.8349	28.95/0.8004	27.53/0.8378	32.71/0.9379
MemNet	678K	34.09/0.9248	30.00/0.8350	28.96/0.8001	27.56/0.8376	32.51/0.9369
CARN	1,592K	34.29/0.9255	30.29/0.8407	29.06/0.8034	28.06/0.8493	33.50/0.9440
SRResNet	1,554K	34.41/0.9274	30.36/0.8427	29.11/0.8055	28.20/0.8535	33.54/0.9448
IMDN	703K	34.36/0.9270	30.32/0.8417	29.09/0.8046	28.17/0.8519	33.61/0.9445
PAN	**261K**	34.40/0.9271	30.36/0.8423	29.11/0.8050	28.11/0.8511	33.61/0.9448
RDN	22,308K	34.71/0.9296	30.57/0.8468	29.26/0.8093	28.80/0.8653	34.13/0.9484
RCAN	15,629K	34.74/0.9299	30.65/0.8482	29.32/0.8111	29.09/0.8702	34.44/0.9499
SAN	15,859K	34.75/0.9300	30.59/0.8476	29.33/0.8112	28.93/0.8671	34.30/0.9494
Scale	×4					
SRCNN	57K	30.48/0.8628	27.49/0.7503	26.90/0.7101	24.52/0.7221	27.66/0.8505
FSRCNN	12K	30.71/0.8657	27.59/0.7535	26.98/0.7105	24.62/0.7280	27.90/0.8517
VDSR	665K	31.35/0.8838	28.01/0.7674	27.29/0.7251	25.18/0.7524	28.83/0.8809
DRCN	1,774K	31.53/0.8854	28.02/0.7670	27.23/0.7233	25.14/0.7510	28.98/0.8816
LapSRN	813K	31.54/0.8850	29.19/0.7720	27.32/0.7280	25.21/0.7560	29.09/0.8845
DRRN	297K	31.68/0.8888	28.21/0.7720	27.38/0.7284	25.44/0.7638	29.46/0.8960
MemNet	677K	31.74/0.8893	28.26/0.7723	27.40/0.7281	25.50/0.7630	29.42/0.8942
CARN	1,592K	32.13/0.8937	28.60/0.7806	27.58/0.7349	26.07/0.7837	30.47/0.9084
SRResNet	1,518K	32.17/0.8951	28.61/0.7823	27.59/0.7365	26.12/0.7871	30.48/0.9087
IMDN	715K	32.21/0.8948	28.58/0.7811	27.56/0.7353	26.04/0.7838	30.45/0.9075
PAN	**272K**	32.13/0.8948	28.61/0.7822	27.59/0.7363	26.11/0.7854	30.51/0.9095
RDN	22,271K	32.47/0.8990	28.81/0.7871	27.72/0.7419	26.61/0.8028	31.00/0.9151
RCAN	15,592K	32.63/0.9002	28.87/0.7889	27.77/0.7436	26.82/0.8087	31.22/0.9173
SAN	15,822K	32.64/0.9003	28.92/0.7888	27.78/0.7436	26.79/0.8068	31.18/0.9169

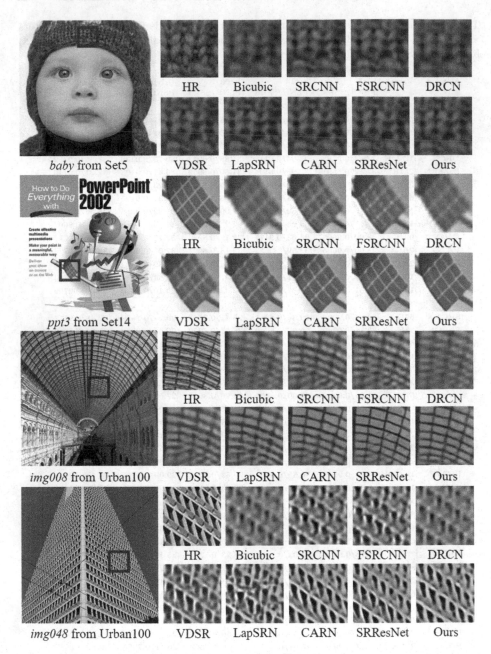

Fig. 5. Visual comparison for upscaling factor ×4.

Table 6. The results of adding PA in different networks. We use the mean values of PSNR obtained on five datasets for upscaling factor ×4. We record the results in 1×10^6 iterations.

Model	Params	Mult-Adds	PSNR
PAN-SC-U	264K	27.1G	28.11 dB
PAN	272K	28.2G	28.22 dB(+0.11 dB)
SRResNet	1,518K	146.1G	28.22 dB
SRResNet-PA	1,584K	149.9G	28.20 dB(−0.02 dB)
RCAN	15,592K	916.9G	28.75 dB
RCAN-PA	16,308K	964.1G	28.69 dB(−0.06 dB)

and Manga109 datasets. We also compare with IMDN, which is the first place of AIM 2019 Challenge on Constrained Super-Resolution and has 715K parameters. It turns out that our proposed PAN outperforms IMDN in terms of PSNR on Set14, B100 and Urban100 datasets.

As for visual comparison, our model is able to reconstruct stripes and line patterns more accurately. For image "ppt3", we observe that most of the compared methods generate noticeable artifacts and blurry effects while our method produces more accurate lines. For the details of the buildings in "img008" and "img048", PAN could achieve reconstruction with less artifacts.

5   Conclusions

In this work, a lightweight convolutional neural network is proposed to achieve image super resolution. In particular, we design a new pixel attention scheme, pixel attention (PA), which contains very few parameters but helps generate better reconstruction results. Besides, two building blocks for the main and reconstruction branches are proposed based on the pixel attention scheme. The SC-PA block for main branch shares similar structure as the Self-Calibrated convolution, while the U-PA block for reconstruction branch adopts the nearest-neighbor upsampling and convolution layers. This framework could improve the SR performance with little parameter cost. Experiments have demonstrated that our final model—PAN could achieve comparable performance with state-of-the-art lightweight networks.

References

1. Ahn, N., Kang, B., Sohn, K.-A.: Fast, accurate, and lightweight super-resolution with cascading residual network. In: Ferrari, V., Hebert, M., Sminchisescu, C., Weiss, Y. (eds.) ECCV 2018. LNCS, vol. 11214, pp. 256–272. Springer, Cham (2018). https://doi.org/10.1007/978-3-030-01249-6_16
2. Bevilacqua, M., Roumy, A., Guillemot, C., Alberi-Morel, M.L.: Low-complexity single-image super-resolution based on nonnegative neighbor embedding (2012)

3. Dai, T., Cai, J., Zhang, Y., Xia, S.T., Zhang, L.: Second-order attention network for single image super-resolution. In: Proceedings of the IEEE Conference on Computer Vision and Pattern Recognition, pp. 11065–11074 (2019)
4. Dong, C., Loy, C.C., He, K., Tang, X.: Image super-resolution using deep convolutional networks. IEEE Trans. Pattern Anal. Mach. Intell. **38**(2), 295–307 (2015)
5. Dong, C., Loy, C.C., Tang, X.: Accelerating the super-resolution convolutional neural network. In: Leibe, B., Matas, J., Sebe, N., Welling, M. (eds.) ECCV 2016. LNCS, vol. 9906, pp. 391–407. Springer, Cham (2016). https://doi.org/10.1007/978-3-319-46475-6_25
6. El Helou, M., Zhou, R., Süsstrunk, S., Timofte, R., et al.: AIM 2020: scene relighting and illumination estimation challenge. In: Bartoli, A., Fusiello, A. (eds.) ECCV 2020, LNCS 12537, pp. 499–518 (2020)
7. Fuoli, D., Huang, Z., Gu, S., Timofte, R., et al.: AIM 2020 challenge on video extreme super-resolution: Methods and results. In: Bartoli, A., Fusiello, A. (eds.) ECCV 2020, LNCS 1253, pp. xx–yy (2020)
8. He, J., Dong, C., Qiao, Y.: Modulating image restoration with continual levels via adaptive feature modification layers. In: The IEEE Conference on Computer Vision and Pattern Recognition (CVPR), June 2019
9. He, J., Dong, C., Qiao, Y.: Multi-dimension modulation for image restoration with dynamic controllable residual learning. arXiv preprint arXiv:1912.05293 (2019)
10. Hu, J., Shen, L., Sun, G.: Squeeze-and-excitation networks. In: Proceedings of the IEEE Conference on Computer Vision and Pattern Recognition, pp. 7132–7141 (2018)
11. Huang, J.B., Singh, A., Ahuja, N.: Single image super-resolution from transformed self-exemplars. In: Proceedings of the IEEE Conference on Computer Vision and Pattern Recognition, pp. 5197–5206 (2015)
12. Hui, Z., Gao, X., Yang, Y., Wang, X.: Lightweight image super-resolution with information multi-distillation network. In: Proceedings of the 27th ACM International Conference on Multimedia, pp. 2024–2032 (2019)
13. Ignatov, A., Timofte, R., et al.: AIM 2020 challenge on learned image signal processing pipeline. In: Bartoli, A., Fusiello, A. (eds.) ECCV 2020, LNCS 12537, pp. 152–170 (2020)
14. Ignatov, A., Timofte, R., et al.: AIM 2020 challenge on rendering realistic bokeh. In: Bartoli, A., Fusiello, A. (eds.) ECCV 2020, LNCS 12537, pp. 213–228 (2020)
15. Kim, J., Kwon Lee, J., Mu Lee, K.: Accurate image super-resolution using very deep convolutional networks. In: Proceedings of the IEEE Conference on Computer Vision and Pattern Recognition, pp. 1646–1654 (2016)
16. Kim, J., Kwon Lee, J., Mu Lee, K.: Deeply-recursive convolutional network for image super-resolution. In: Proceedings of the IEEE Conference on Computer Vision and Pattern Recognition, pp. 1637–1645 (2016)
17. Kingma, D.P., Ba, J.: Adam: a method for stochastic optimization. arXiv preprint arXiv:1412.6980 (2014)
18. Lai, W.S., Huang, J.B., Ahuja, N., Yang, M.H.: Deep Laplacian pyramid networks for fast and accurate super-resolution. In: Proceedings of the IEEE Conference on Computer Vision and Pattern Recognition, pp. 624–632 (2017)
19. Ledig, C., et al.: Photo-realistic single image super-resolution using a generative adversarial network. In: Proceedings of the IEEE Conference on Computer Vision and Pattern Recognition, pp. 4681–4690 (2017)
20. Lim, B., Son, S., Kim, H., Nah, S., Lee, K.M.: Enhanced deep residual networks for single image super-resolution. In: The IEEE Conference on Computer Vision and Pattern Recognition (CVPR) Workshops, July 2017

21. Liu, J.J., Hou, Q., Cheng, M.M., Wang, C., Feng, J.: Improving convolutional networks with self-calibrated convolutions. In: Proceedings of the IEEE/CVF Conference on Computer Vision and Pattern Recognition, pp. 10096–10105 (2020)
22. Martin, D., Fowlkes, C., Tal, D., Malik, J.: A database of human segmented natural images and its application to evaluating segmentation algorithms and measuring ecological statistics. In: Proceedings Eighth IEEE International Conference on Computer Vision, ICCV 2001, vol. 2, pp. 416–423. IEEE (2001)
23. Matsui, Y., et al.: Sketch-based manga retrieval using manga109 dataset. Multimedia Tools Appl. **76**(20), 21811–21838 (2017)
24. Mei, Y., et al.: Pyramid attention networks for image restoration. arXiv preprint arXiv:2004.13824 (2020)
25. Ntavelis, E., Romero, A., Bigdeli, S.A., Timofte, R., et al.: AIM 2020 challenge on image extreme inpainting. In: Bartoli, A., Fusiello, A. (eds.) ECCV 2020, LNCS 12537, pp. 716–741 (2020)
26. Park, J., Woo, S., Lee, J.Y., Kweon, I.S.: Bam: Bottleneck attention module. arXiv preprint arXiv:1807.06514 (2018)
27. Paszke, A., et al.: Automatic differentiation in pytorch (2017)
28. Roy, A.G., Navab, N., Wachinger, C.: Concurrent spatial and channel 'Squeeze & Excitation' in fully convolutional networks. In: Frangi, A.F., Schnabel, J.A., Davatzikos, C., Alberola-López, C., Fichtinger, G. (eds.) MICCAI 2018. LNCS, vol. 11070, pp. 421–429. Springer, Cham (2018). https://doi.org/10.1007/978-3-030-00928-1_48
29. Shi, W., et al.: Real-time single image and video super-resolution using an efficient sub-pixel convolutional neural network. In: Proceedings of the IEEE Conference on Computer Vision and Pattern Recognition, pp. 1874–1883 (2016)
30. Son, S., Lee, J., Nah, S., Timofte, R., Lee, K.M., et al.: AIM 2020 challenge on video temporal super-resolution. In: Bartoli, A., Fusiello, A. (eds.) ECCV 2020, LNCS 1253, pp. xx–yy (2020)
31. Tai, Y., Yang, J., Liu, X.: Image super-resolution via deep recursive residual network. In: Proceedings of the IEEE Conference on Computer Vision and Pattern Recognition, pp. 3147–3155 (2017)
32. Tai, Y., Yang, J., Liu, X., Xu, C.: MemNet: a persistent memory network for image restoration. In: Proceedings of the IEEE International Conference on Computer Vision, pp. 4539–4547 (2017)
33. Timofte, R., Agustsson, E., Van Gool, L., Yang, M.H., Zhang, L.: Ntire 2017 challenge on single image super-resolution: Methods and results. In: Proceedings of the IEEE Conference on Computer Vision and Pattern Recognition Workshops, pp. 114–125 (2017)
34. Wang, Q., Wu, B., Zhu, P., Li, P., Zuo, W., Hu, Q.: ECA-net: efficient channel attention for deep convolutional neural networks. In: Proceedings of the IEEE/CVF Conference on Computer Vision and Pattern Recognition, pp. 11534–11542 (2020)
35. Wang, X., et al.: ESRGAN: enhanced super-resolution generative adversarial networks. In: Leal-Taixé, L., Roth, S. (eds.) ECCV 2018. LNCS, vol. 11133, pp. 63–79. Springer, Cham (2019). https://doi.org/10.1007/978-3-030-11021-5_5
36. Wang, Z., Chen, J., Hoi, S.C.: Deep learning for image super-resolution: a survey. IEEE Trans. Pattern Anal. Mach. Intell. (2020)
37. Wang, Z., Bovik, A.C., Sheikh, H.R., Simoncelli, E.P.: Image quality assessment: from error visibility to structural similarity. IEEE Trans. Image Process. **13**(4), 600–612 (2004)

38. Wei, P., Lu, H., Timofte, R., Lin, L., Zuo, W., et al.: AIM 2020 challenge on real image super-resolution. In: Bartoli, A., Fusiello, A. (eds.) ECCV 2020, LNCS 12537, pp. 392–422 (2020)

39. Woo, S., Park, J., Lee, J.-Y., Kweon, I.S.: CBAM: convolutional block attention module. In: Ferrari, V., Hebert, M., Sminchisescu, C., Weiss, Y. (eds.) ECCV 2018. LNCS, vol. 11211, pp. 3–19. Springer, Cham (2018). https://doi.org/10.1007/978-3-030-01234-2_1

40. Yang, J., Wright, J., Huang, T.S., Ma, Y.: Image super-resolution via sparse representation. IEEE Trans. Image Process. **19**(11), 2861–2873 (2010)

41. Zhang, K., Danelljan, M., Li, Y., Timofte, R., et al.: AIM 2020 challenge on efficient super-resolution: methods and results. In: Bartoli, A., Fusiello, A. (eds.) ECCV 2020, LNCS 12537, pp. 5–40 (2020)

42. Zhang, K., Gu, S., Timofte, R., et al.: Aim 2019 challenge on constrained super-resolution: methods and results. In: IEEE International Conference on Computer Vision Workshops (2019)

43. Zhang, W., Liu, Y., Dong, C., Qiao, Y.: RankSRGAN: generative adversarial networks with ranker for image super-resolution. In: Proceedings of the IEEE International Conference on Computer Vision, pp. 3096–3105 (2019)

44. Zhang, Y., Li, K., Li, K., Wang, L., Zhong, B., Fu, Y.: Image super-resolution using very deep residual channel attention networks. In: Ferrari, V., Hebert, M., Sminchisescu, C., Weiss, Y. (eds.) ECCV 2018. LNCS, vol. 11211, pp. 294–310. Springer, Cham (2018). https://doi.org/10.1007/978-3-030-01234-2_18

45. Zhang, Y., Tian, Y., Kong, Y., Zhong, B., Fu, Y.: Residual dense network for image super-resolution. In: Proceedings of the IEEE Conference on Computer Vision and Pattern Recognition, pp. 2472–2481 (2018)

LarvaNet: Hierarchical Super-Resolution via Multi-exit Architecture

Geun-Woo Jeon[ID], Jun-Ho Choi, Jun-Hyuk Kim, and Jong-Seok Lee[✉][ID]

School of Integrated Technology, Yonsei University, Seoul, Korea
{geun-woo.jeon,idearibosome,junhyuk.kim,jong-seok.lee}@yonsei.ac.kr
http://mcml.yonsei.ac.kr/

Abstract. In recent years, image super-resolution (SR) methods using convolutional neural networks (CNNs) have achieved successful results. Nevertheless, it is often difficult to apply them in resource-constrained environments due to the requirement of heavy computation and huge storage capacity. To address this issue, we propose an efficient network model for SR, called LarvaNet. First, we investigate a number of architectural factors for a baseline model and find optimal settings in terms of performance, number of parameters, and running time. Based on that, we design our model using a multi-exit architecture. Our experiments show that the proposed method achieves state-of-the-art SR performance with a reasonable number of parameters and running time. We also show that the multi-exit architecture of the proposed model allows us to control the trade-off between resource consumption and SR performance by selecting which exit point to be used.

Keywords: Efficient super-resolution · Deep convolutional neural network · Multi-exit architecture

1 Introduction

Single image super-resolution (SR) is a computer vision task to reconstruct a high-resolution (HR) image from a single low-resolution (LR) image. SR is intrinsically difficult because there can be many HR images corresponding to one LR image.

Recently, SR methods based on convolutional neural networks (CNNs) have been proposed with remarkable performance improvement [5,11,18]. The network architectures have become larger and larger, in terms of depth, number of parameters, number of floating point operations (FLOPs), etc., to achieve better performance. For example, the enhanced deep super-resolution network (EDSR) [18] has about 69 layers with about 43M parameters, and the residual channel attention network (RCAN) [33] has up to 400 layers and 16M parameters [9]. These methods have improved the performance of SR, but require huge amounts of resources and long inference time. Therefore, they are not suitable for constrained situations such as mobile applications and video applications. Thus, needs for more efficient and lightweight SR networks have emerged.

© Springer Nature Switzerland AG 2020
A. Bartoli and A. Fusiello (Eds.): ECCV 2020 Workshops, LNCS 12537, pp. 73–86, 2020.
https://doi.org/10.1007/978-3-030-67070-2_4

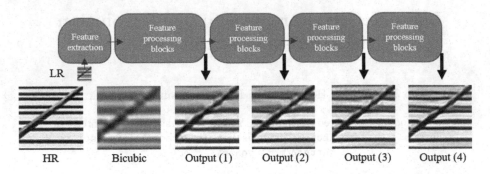

Fig. 1. Illustration of hierarchical SR by the proposed model. Output images are obtained at the three intermediate stages as well as at the final stage. Gradual quality improvement of the output images can be observed. The ground truth HR image and the upsampled version of the LR image by bicubic interpolation are also shown.

To address this issue, a number of approaches such as recursive architectures [12,23] or parameter sharing [24] have been proposed, which reduce the number of parameters. However, the number of operations and inference time are not effectively reduced because of their architectures. After that, efficient SR network structures without recursive operations have been also proposed. Ahn *et al.* propose the cascading residual network (CARN) [2], which uses a cascading mechanism upon a residual SR network. Hui *et al.* propose information distilling structures called information distillation network (IDN) and information multi-distillation network (IMDN) [9,10]. IMDN is the winner of the AIM 2019 Constrained Super-Resolution Challenge [31]. The modified super-resolution residual network (MSRResNet) [27] is the baseline model of the AIM 2020 Efficient Super-Resolution Challenge [30], which has a simple residual architecture but performs considerably efficiently.

Taking a different approach for efficient SR, we propose a network based on a multi-exit architecture [17,25], called LarvaNet (Fig. 1). In this architecture, output images are generated not only at the final stage but also from the intermediate layers of the model. The losses for these early outputs are also considered for model training, so that the model can learn features important for SR at an early stage of the model and the subsequent layers focus on generating residual contents. In order to search for an optimal base architecture, we investigate extensive variations of the baseline MSRResNet model in terms of the numbers of channels and blocks, upsampling methods, interpolation methods, weight initialization methods, and activation functions, based on which our multi-exit architecture is built. Our experimental results demonstrate that the proposed model shows good SR performance with reduced computational complexity. In addition, we show that the multi-exit architecture of the proposed model can implement anytime prediction [7,16,17], which allows us to control the trade-off between resource consumption and SR performance by selecting which exit point to be used.

The remainder of the paper is organized as follows. The following section presents our study on variations of the baseline MSRResNet model. Section 3 details the proposed model architecture. Section 4 shows experimental results and, finally, conclusions are given in Sect. 5.

2 Analysis of Baseline Model

For a deep SR method, there are several architectural factors that can be varied. In this section, we investigate how such factors affect the performance for the baseline MSRResNet model. We evaluate the models with different settings in terms of the running time, FLOPs, and peak signal-to-noise ratio (PSNR) on ×4 SR.

Each model is trained on the DIV2K dataset [1], which contains 800 high-quality training images. The input image patches with a size of 48 × 48 are randomly cropped. The mini-batch size is set to 16. We train the models for 300K steps by the Adam optimizer [13]. The learning rate is initially set to 10^{-4} and halved at 200K steps.

The average running time and PSNR are calculated on the 100 images of the DIV2K validation dataset. PSNR is computed on the RGB channels of the images. We use a PC with a RTX 2080Ti GPU to evaluate the running time. The FLOPs are measured for a 256 × 256 input patch.

2.1 Channels and Blocks

The baseline MSRResNet model has 64 channels and 16 residual blocks. By decreasing the number of channels while increasing the number of residual blocks, it is possible to maintain the number of parameters similar but obtain a deeper model.

As shown in Table 1, the models having reduced numbers of channels and increased numbers of residual blocks take increased running time despite reduced FLOPs. Since the computation of each layer requires the computed output of its previous layer, deeper models consume more computational time than shallower models, even though they can achieve better performance. From these results, we decide to use 48 channels for our model due to the improved PSNR with a similar number of parameters and only slightly increased running time compared to the original baseline model.

2.2 Reduced Upsampling

The upsampling part of the original MSRResNet model for ×4 scaling consists of two convolutional layers that output four times as many channels as the input to the layers (i.e., 64 × 4 = 256), and two PixelShuffle (or sub-pixel) operations [22] to enlarge the spatial dimension with a factor of 2 in each operation. After that, other convolutional layers follow and reduce the number of channels to three

Table 1. Comparison of the MSRResNet models with different numbers of channels and blocks.

#channels	#blocks	#params	Running time	PSNR	FLOPs
64	16	1,518K	0.108 s	28.99 dB	166G
48	32	1,520K	0.140 s	29.04 dB	137G
32	77	1,509K	0.261 s	–	116G

(corresponding to the RGB color components). We observe that the computational cost of this part is considerably expensive and employs a large number of parameters (i.e., 295K parameters). In the modified MSRResNet model with 48 channels and 32 blocks, the number of parameters for the upsampling part is 166K, which is still considerably large.

Table 2. Performance comparison of the MSRResNet models with different hyperparameters and model structures.

Model	#channels	#blocks	#params	Running time	PSNR	FLOPs
MSRResNet	64	16	1,518K	0.108 s	28.99 dB	166G
MSRResNet	48	32	1,520K	0.140 s	29.04 dB	137G
MSRResNet-RU	48	32	1,332K	0.074 s	28.99 dB	87G

To reduce the number of parameters and running time of the upsampling part, we apply a PixelShuffle operation without channel-enlarging convolution. From a feature map having a size of the LR image with 48 channels, the PixelShuffle operation for ×4 scaling leads to a feature map having a size of the HR image with three channels, which has the same form as a super-resolved image. We denote this modified MSRResNet model as MSRResNet-RU. Table 2 shows the evaluation results of the baseline MSRResNet, MSRResNet with 48 channels, and MSRResNet-RU. Thanks to the lightened upsampling part and the increased depth, MSRResNet-RU has significantly reduced running time and a reduced number of parameters, while maintaining the same PSNR as the baseline MSRResNet.

2.3   Interpolation

The baseline MSRResNet model applies the bilinear interpolation to the input image and adds it to the output image. This enables the model to calculate only the residual information and can achieve better performance. This part can be modified by using different interpolation methods. We evaluate three interpolation methods including no interpolation, bilinear interpolation, and bicubic interpolation on MSRResNet-RU with eight blocks.

As shown in Table 3, applying interpolation significantly improves the performance by 0.20 dB of PSNR. This is because interpolation takes charge of low frequency contents, and the network only needs to reconstruct high frequency contents. Similarly, Bahat et al. [3] found that passing the output super-resolved image of a pre-trained SR network into a high pass filter and adding it with an interpolated image can improve PSNR performance without any additional parameters. According to the results in Table 3, the bicubic interpolation is slightly better than the bilinear interpolation as much as 0.01 dB of PSNR. Thus, we use the bicubic interpolation method for the models in the following experiments.

Table 3. Comparison of different interpolation methods.

Model	#channels	#blocks	Interpolation	PSNR (dB)
MSRResNet-RU	48	8	None	28.45
MSRResNet-RU	48	8	Bilinear	28.65
MSRResNet-RU	48	8	Bicubic	28.66

2.4 Weight Initialization

In Pytorch 1.5, the default weight and bias initialization method is based on the Kaiming uniform distribution. However, the baseline MSRResNet employs the Kaiming normal distribution with $\times 0.1$ weight scaling as the weight initialization method and initializes the bias values to zero. We call these two initialization methods as Pytorch initialization and MSRResNet initialization, respectively. We evaluate them on MSRResNet-RU with eight residual blocks.

As shown in Table 4, the MSRResNet initialization shows higher PSNR values by about 0.05 dB than the Pytorch initialization. In the case of the MSRResNet initialization, the output super-resolved image of the model before adding the interpolated image has small values with a small variance, and thus the final output image after the addition is very close to the interpolation image. Therefore, the model with the MSRResNet initialization has a relatively smaller loss value in the beginning of learning, which makes the following learning process more stable. According to this result, we use the MSRResNet initialization in the following experiments.

Table 4. Comparison of different weight initialization methods.

Model	#channels	#blocks	Initialization method	PSNR (dB)
MSRResNet-RU	48	8	Pytorch	28.61
MSRResNet-RU	48	8	MSRResNet	28.66

2.5 Activation Function

The baseline MSRResNet model employs the rectified linear unit (ReLU) as the activation function for residual blocks and Leaky ReLU for the convolutional layers outside the residual blocks. But EDSR-baseline [18], a model whose structure is nearly the same with MSRResNet, employs ReLU for the convolutional layers outside the residual blocks. Considering such variations, we test different activation functions in the residual blocks including ReLU, Leaky ReLU with a negative slope of 0.2, Leaky ReLU with a negative slope of 0.5, linear unit, and ReLU6 [14]. The results are shown in Table 5. It is observed that the ReLU function yields the best performance.

Table 5. Comparison of different activation functions in residual blocks.

Model	#channels	#blocks	Act. function	PSNR (dB)
MSRResNet-RU	48	8	ReLU	28.66
MSRResNet-RU	48	8	Leaky ReLU (0.2)	28.63
MSRResNet-RU	48	8	Leaky ReLU (0.5)	28.56
MSRResNet-RU	48	8	Linear	27.31
MSRResNet-RU	48	8	ReLU6	28.60

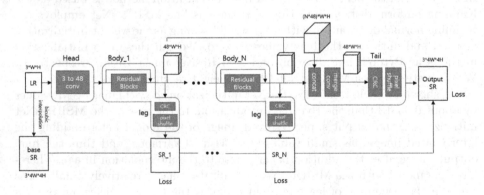

Fig. 2. Overall architecture of the proposed model.

3 Method

We propose a multi-exit architecture for the SR task, called LarvaNet, which uses the MSRResNet-RU described in Sect. 2 as its backbone structure. We group the residual blocks of MSRResNet-RU into parts and make each part produce an early output. Each part is induced to only take care of residual contents to be added with the previous early output. We refer to this procedure as hierarchical SR, which is inspired by the effectiveness of interpolation as shown in Sect. 2.3.

Figure 2 depicts the overall LarvaNet structure. The head module is a feature extraction layer and the body modules are partitions of the residual blocks of MSRResNet-RU employing 48 convolutional channels. A leg module is attached to the very end of each body module. It generates a super-resolved image through a convolution-ReLU-convolution (CRC) layer and a PixelShuffle layer. This makes LarvaNet a multi-exit architecture. A body module's output features need to be converted to the early output by its shallow leg module, thus we can regard the output features as information close to the output image. The output features are added with the next body module's output through skip connection inside the body module, to accumulate useful information. Therefore, the subsequent body modules are expected to only take care of residual contents (i.e., high frequency contents) that are not restored yet. Due to this, LarvaNet can conduct hierarchical SR. The last part, the tail module, concatenates the output features of all body modules, converts them into 48 channels, and performs CRC and PixelShuffle to generate the final super-resolved image. The loss function of LarvaNet is defined as the average of the losses for the outputs from all leg modules and the final output.

To express the LarvaNet implementation formally, let X be the input LR image and Y be the ground truth HR image. The super-resolved image $\hat{Y}$ is written by

$$\hat{Y} = \text{LarvaNet}(X). \tag{1}$$

The detailed structure of LarvaNet is as follows. First, the base super-resolved image is obtained from the bicubic interpolation:

$$\hat{Y}_{base} = bicubic(X). \tag{2}$$

The head module extracts initial feature map F_0 from X:

$$F_0 = head(X). \tag{3}$$

Then, the ith body module ($body_i$) processes the features by using a set of residual blocks (res_i) with a skip connection:

$$F_i = body_i(F_{i-1}) = F_{i-1} + res_i(F_{i-1}) \ (i \in \{1,\ 2,\ \dots,\ n\}), \tag{4}$$

where n is the number of body modules. This can be also written as

$$F_i = F_0 + res_1(F_0) + \cdots + res_i(F_{i-1}), \tag{5}$$

which shows the accumulation of features clearly. The leg module of each body module generates a super-resolved image by adding the base super-resolved image to its output:

$$\hat{Y}_i = \hat{Y}_{base} + leg_i(F_i). \tag{6}$$

The tail module concatenates the outputs of all body modules to produce the final super-resolved image:

$$\hat{Y} = \hat{Y}_{base} + tail(F_1,\ F_2,\ \dots,\ F_n). \tag{7}$$

Thus, the outputs of the leg modules $\hat{Y}_i$ are not used during the inference process but only for training. We use the L1 loss as the loss function, as in many recent studies [2,9,18]. In particular, the loss for LarvaNet is defined as the average value of the L1 losses for $\hat{Y}_1, \hat{Y}_2, \dots, \hat{Y}_n$, and $\hat{Y}$:

$$Loss = \frac{1}{n+1}\Big[\sum_{i=1}^{n} ||Y - \hat{Y}_i||_1 + ||Y - \hat{Y}||_1\Big], \tag{8}$$

where $|| \cdot ||_1$ indicates the l_1 norm. A body module is trained as both a part of a shallow model (by the loss from itself) and a part of deeper models (by the losses from the subsequent modules) at the same time. Therefore, each body module is trained to generate features that are effectively used to reconstruct output HR images.

4 Experiments

4.1 Datasets and Metrics

We train the models on both the DIV2K dataset [1] and the Flickr2K dataset [26]. For evaluation, we use six benchmark datasets: Set5 [4], Set14 [29], BSD100 [20], Urban100 [8], Manga109 [21], and the DIV2K validation dataset. We evaluate the performance of SR using two metrics, PSNR and structure similarity index (SSIM) [28]. PSNR is measured on the RGB channels for the DIV2K validation dataset, and on the Y channel of the YCbCr color space for the other benchmark datasets.

4.2 Implementation Details

We use randomly cropped input patches with a size of 80×80 pixels from the training images. The mini-batch size is set to 32. For data augmentation, we perform random horizontal flips and $90°$ rotation. The proposed model is trained by the AdamW optimizer [19] with $\beta_1 = 0.9$, and $\beta_2 = 0.99$. The initial learning rate is set to 4×10^{-4} and halved at every 50K steps. We use a RTX 2080 Ti GPU for training and evaluation.

4.3 Ablation Study

To investigate effectiveness of the proposed methods, we evaluate three different models, including the baseline MSRResNet, MSRResNet-RU, and LarvaNet. The LarvaNet model has four body modules, each of which has eight residual blocks and a leg module.

Evaluation results in terms of the number of parameters, FLOPs, running time, and PSNR on the DIV2K validation dataset are shown in Table 6. By adjusting the numbers of blocks and channels and applying the reduced upsampling method, MSRResNet-RU can reduce 186K parameters (which is a decrease of 12.26%), 79G FLOPs (which is a decrease of 47.59%), and 0.034s of running time (which is a decrease of 31.48%) with PSNR improvement by 0.11 dB compared to the reported performance of MSRResNet [31]. By additionally adopting the multi-exit architecture, LarvaNet achieves additional PSNR improvement by 0.02 dB with a slightly increased number of parameters by 124K, slightly increased running time by 0.007s, and slightly increased FLOPs by 8G compared to MSRResNet-RU. Note that the MSRResNet-RU in this subsection is trained with different settings from MSRResNet-RU in Sect. 2, therefore the performance on the DIV2K validation dataset is different.

Table 6. Effects of different components including reduced upsampling and multi-exit architecture.

Model	MSRResNet	MSRResNet-RU	LarvaNet
Reduced upsampling	–	✓	✓
Multi-exit	–	–	✓
# channels	64	48	48
# residual blocks	16	32	8 × 4
# parameters (K)	1,518	1,332	1,456
FLOPs (G)	166	87	95
Running time (s)	0.108	0.074	0.081
PSNR (dB)	29.00	29.11	29.13

4.4 Comparison with State-of-the-Art Methods

We compare the proposed LarvaNet with 12 state-of-the-art methods, which are super-resolution convolutional neural network (SRCNN) [5], fast super-resolution convolutional neural network (FSRCNN) [6], very deep super-resolution network (VDSR) [11], deeply-recursive convolutional network (DRCN) [12], Laplacian pyramid super-resolution network (LapSRN) [15], deep recursive residual network (DRRN) [23], very deep persistent memory network (MemNet) [24], IDN [10], super-resolution network for multiple noise-free degradations (SRMDNF) [32], CARN [2], MSRResNet [27], and IMDN [9]. The compared LarvaNet has four body modules, each of which has seven residual blocks.

Table 7 shows quantitative comparisons for ×4 SR. In all cases, the proposed LarvaNet outperforms the state-of-the-art methods with a reasonable number of parameters and quality improvement. Especially on the Urban100 and Manga109 datasets, our model achieves PSNR improvements of 0.09 dB and 0.16 dB compared with the second-ranked method.

Table 7. Quantitative evaluation results of different SR models for ×4 SR. Red and blue colors indicate the best and second best performance, respectively.

Method	#params	Set5 PSNR/SSIM	Set14 PSNR/SSIM	BSD100 PSNR/SSIM	Urban100 PSNR/SSIM	Manga109 PSNR/SSIM
Bicubic	–	28.42/0.8104	26.00/0.7027	25.96/0.6675	23.14/0.6577	24.89/0.7866
SRCNN [5]	8K	30.48/0.8628	27.50/0.7513	26.90/0.7101	24.52/0.7221	27.58/0.8555
FSRCNN [6]	13K	30.72/0.8660	27.61/0.7550	26.98/0.7150	24.62/0.7280	27.90/0.8610
VDSR [11]	666K	31.35/0.8838	28.01/0.7674	27.29/0.7251	25.18/0.7524	28.83/0.8870
DRCN [12]	1,774K	31.53/0.8854	28.02/0.7670	27.23/0.7233	25.14/0.7510	28.93/0.8854
LapSRN [15]	502K	31.54/0.8850	28.19/0.7720	27.32/0.7270	25.21/0.7560	29.09/0.8900
DRRN [23]	298K	31.68/0.8888	28.21/0.7720	27.38/0.7284	25.44/0.7638	29.46/0.8960
MemNet [24]	678K	31.74/0.8893	28.26/0.7723	27.40/0.7281	25.50/0.7630	29.42/0.8942
IDN [10]	553K	31.82/0.8903	28.25/0.7730	27.41/0.7297	25.41/0.7632	29.41/0.8942
SRMDNF [32]	1,552K	31.96/0.8925	28.35/0.7787	27.49/0.7337	25.68/0.7731	30.09/0.9024
CARN [2]	1,592K	32.13/0.8937	28.60/0.7806	27.58/0.7349	26.07/0.7837	30.47/0.9084
IMDN [9]	715K	32.21/0.8948	28.58/0.7811	27.56/0.7353	26.04/0.7838	30.45/0.9075
MSRResNet [27]	1,518K	32.21/0.8954	28.65/0.7828	27.60/0.7367	26.13/0.7873	30.50/0.9090
LarvaNet (ours)	1,290K	32.23/0.8957	28.69/0.7835	27.62/0.7373	26.22/0.7901	30.66/0.9102

Figure 3 shows visual qualitative comparisons on the Urban100 datasets. It can be seen that proposed model reconstructs high frequency contents such as detailed patterns more accurately, which demonstrates the effectiveness of the proposed hierarchical SR method.

4.5   Progressive SR

In LarvaNet, the path from the input to an early exit composes a SR network having a smaller size than the whole LarvaNet model, which is denoted as a submodel. Therefore, from the trained LarvaNet model having four body modules, we can obtain five model alternatives, i.e., four submodels and the whole model. They have different sizes and thus different computational complexities. At the same time, the SR performance in terms of PSNR (or SSIM) also differs among them, i.e., a larger submodel would show better SR performance. This allows LarvaNet to adapt to given computational environments instead of failing to produce an output due to the limitation of resources. We investigate this capability in this section.

Table 8 shows the evaluation results in terms of the number of parameters, FLOPs, running time, and PSNR on the DIV2K validation dataset. As expected, a submodel with more blocks spends more running time, while achieving higher PSNR performance. Figure 4 depicts the relationship between the running time and PSNR of the LarvaNet and the submodels. By selecting an exit point to be used, we can control the trade-off between amount of computational resources and SR performance. For instance, we can still obtain a SR result using Sub-2 with only a half of the amount of computations (i.e., FLOPs) required for the whole model although a PSNR drop of 0.2 dB is inevitable. Therefore, once trained, LarvaNet is adaptable to different constrained environments.

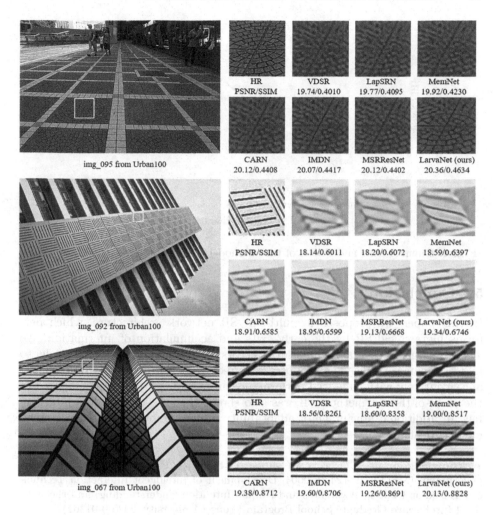

Fig. 3. Visual comparisons of LarvaNet with other methods on ×4 SR.

Table 8. Comparison of the submodels of LarvaNet. Sub-i denotes the ith submodel.

Model	Sub-1	Sub-2	Sub-3	Sub-4	LarvaNet
# residual blocks	7 × 1	7×2	7 × 3	7 × 4	7 × 4
Channel concat	–	–	–	–	✓
# parameters (K)	334	625	916	1,207	1,290
FLOPs (G)	22	41	60	79	84
Running time (s)	0.036	0.051	0.060	0.073	0.075
PSNR (dB)	28.67	28.85	28.97	29.04	29.05

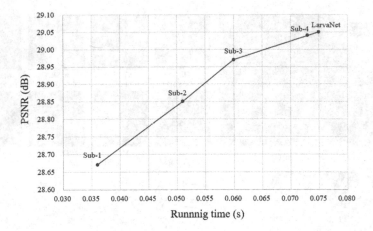

Fig. 4. Running time and PSNR of the submodels and the whole LarvaNet model.

5 Conclusion

In this paper, we proposed a multi-exit SR network architecture, which performs hierarchical SR by the early exits and accumulation of information. We also investigated several architectural factors of our baseline backbone model to find optimum settings. The proposed architecture performs image SR efficiently and accurately with enhanced performance on benchmark datasets compared to the state-of-the-art methods. It was also shown that the proposed architecture has an additional advantage of adaptability under computationallyconstrained environments.

Acknowledgement. This work was supported by the IITP grant funded by the Korea government (MSIT) (R7124-16-0004, Development of Intelligent Interaction Technology Based on Context Awareness and Human Intention Understanding) and the Artificial Intelligence Graduate School Program (Yonsei University, 2020-0-01361).

References

1. Agustsson, E., Timofte, R.: NTIRE 2017 challenge on single image superresolution: dataset and study. In: Proceedings of the IEEE Conference on Computer Vision and Pattern Recognition (CVPR) Workshops, pp. 126–135 (2017)
2. Ahn, N., Kang, B., Sohn, K.-A.: Fast, accurate, and lightweight super-resolution with cascading residual network. In: Ferrari, V., Hebert, M., Sminchisescu, C., Weiss, Y. (eds.) ECCV 2018. LNCS, vol. 11214, pp. 256–272. Springer, Cham (2018). https://doi.org/10.1007/978-3-030-01249-6_16
3. Bahat, Y., Michaeli, T.: Explorable super resolution. In: Proceedings of the IEEE Conference on Computer Vision and Pattern Recognition (CVPR), pp. 2716–2725 (2020)
4. Bevilacqua, M., Roumy, A., Guillemot, C., Morel, M.L.A.: Low-complexity single-image super-resolution based on nonnegative neighbor embedding. In: Proceedings of the British Machine Vision Conference (BMVC) (2012)

5. Dong, C., Loy, C.C., He, K., Tang, X.: Learning a deep convolutional network for image super-resolution. In: Fleet, D., Pajdla, T., Schiele, B., Tuytelaars, T. (eds.) ECCV 2014. LNCS, vol. 8692, pp. 184–199. Springer, Cham (2014). https://doi.org/10.1007/978-3-319-10593-2_13
6. Dong, C., Loy, C.C., Tang, X.: Accelerating the super-resolution convolutional neural network. In: Leibe, B., Matas, J., Sebe, N., Welling, M. (eds.) ECCV 2016. LNCS, vol. 9906, pp. 391–407. Springer, Cham (2016). https://doi.org/10.1007/978-3-319-46475-6_25
7. Huang, G., Chen, D., Li, T., Wu, F., van der Maaten, L., Weinberger, K.Q.: Multi-scale dense networks for resource efficient image classification. In: Proceedings of the International Conference on Learning Representations (ICLR) (2018)
8. Huang, J.B., Singh, A., Ahuja, N.: Single image super-resolution from transformed self-exemplars. In: Proceedings of the IEEE Conference on Computer Vision and Pattern Recognition (CVPR), pp. 5197–5206 (2015)
9. Hui, Z., Gao, X., Yang, Y., Wang, X.: Lightweight image super-resolution with information multi-distillation network. In: Proceedings of the 27th ACM International Conference on Multimedia (MM), pp. 2024–2032 (2019)
10. Hui, Z., Wang, X., Gao, X.: Fast and accurate single image super-resolution via information distillation network. In: Proceedings of the IEEE Conference on Computer Vision and Pattern Recognition (CVPR), pp. 723–731 (2018)
11. Kim, J., Lee, J., Lee, K.: Accurate image super-resolution using very deep convolutional networks. In: Proceedings of the IEEE Conference on Computer Vision and Pattern Recognition (CVPR) (2016)
12. Kim, J., Lee, J., Lee, K.: Deeply-recursive convolutional network for image super-resolution. In: Proceedings of the IEEE Conference on Computer Vision and Pattern Recognition (CVPR), pp. 1637–1645 (2016)
13. Kingma, D., Ba, J.: Adam: a method for stochastic optimization. In: Proceedings of the International Conference on Learning Representations (ICLR) (2015)
14. Krizhevsky, A., Hinton, G.: Convolutional deep belief networks on cifar-10. Unpublished manuscript (2010)
15. Lai, W.S., Huang, J.B., Ahuja, N., Yang, M.H.: Deep Laplacian pyramid networks for fast and accurate super-resolution. In: Proceedings of the IEEE Conference on Computer Vision and Pattern Recognition (CVPR) (2017)
16. Larsson, G., Maire, M., Shakhnarovich, G.: Fractalnet: Ultra-deep neural networks without residuals. In: Proceedings of the International Conference on Learning Representations (ICLR) (2017)
17. Lee, H., Lee, J.: Local critic training of deep neural networks. In: Proceedings of the International Joint Conference on Neural Networks (IJCNN) (2019)
18. Lim, B., Son, S., Kim, H., Nah, S., Lee, K.: Enhanced deep residual networks for single image super-resolution. In: Proceedings of the IEEE Conference on Computer Vision and Pattern Recognition (CVPR) Workshops, pp. 136–144 (2017)
19. Loshchilov, I., Hutter, F.: Decoupled weight decay regularization. In: Proceedings of the International Conference on Learning Representations (ICLR) (2019)
20. Martin, D., Fowlkes, C., Tal, D., Malik, J.: A database of human segmented natural images and its application to evaluating segmentation algorithms and measuring ecological statistics. In: Proceedings of the IEEE International Conference on Computer Vision (ICCV), pp. 416–423 (2001)
21. Matsui, Y., et al.: Sketch-based manga retrieval using manga109 dataset. Multimedia Tools Appl. **76**(20), 21811–21838 (2016). https://doi.org/10.1007/s11042-016-4020-z

22. Shi, W., et al.: Real-time single image and video super-resolution using an efficient sub-pixel convolutional neural network. In: Proceedings of the IEEE Conference on Computer Vision and Pattern Recognition (CVPR), pp. 1874–1883 (2016)
23. Tai, Y., Yang, J., Liu, X.: Image super-resolution via deep recursive residual network. In: Proceedings of the IEEE Conference on Computer Vision and Pattern Recognition (CVPR), pp. 3147–3155 (2017)
24. Tai, Y., Yang, J., Liu, X., Xu, C.: MemNet: a persistent memory network for image restoration. In: Proceedings of the IEEE Conference on Computer Vision and Pattern Recognition (CVPR), pp. 4539–4547 (2017)
25. Teerapittayanon, S., McDanel, B., Kung, H.T.: BranchyNet: Fast inference via early exiting from deep neural networks. In: Proceedings of the International Conference on Pattern Recognition (ICPR), pp. 2464–2469 (2016)
26. Wang, X., Yu, K., Dong, C., Loy, C.C.: Recovering realistic texture in image super-resolution by deep spatial feature transform. In: Proceedings of the IEEE Conference on Computer Vision and Pattern Recognition (CVPR), pp. 606–615 (2018)
27. Wang, X., et al.: ESRGAN: enhanced super-resolution generative adversarial networks. In: Leal-Taixé, L., Roth, S. (eds.) ECCV 2018. LNCS, vol. 11133, pp. 63–79. Springer, Cham (2019). https://doi.org/10.1007/978-3-030-11021-5_5
28. Wang, Z., Bovik, A.C., Sheikh, H.R., Simoncelli, E.P.: Image quality assessment: from error visibility to structural similarity. IEEE Trans. Image Process. **13**(4), 600–612 (2004)
29. Woo, S., Park, J., Lee, J.-Y., Kweon, I.S.: CBAM: convolutional block attention module. In: Ferrari, V., Hebert, M., Sminchisescu, C., Weiss, Y. (eds.) ECCV 2018. LNCS, vol. 11211, pp. 3–19. Springer, Cham (2018). https://doi.org/10.1007/978-3-030-01234-2_1
30. Zhang, K., Danelljan, M., Li, Y., Timofte, R., et al.: AIM 2020 challenge on efficient super-resolution: methods and results. In: Bartoli, A., Fusiello, A. (eds.) ECCV 2020, LNCS 12537, pp. 5–40 (2020)
31. Zhang, K., et al.: AIM 2019 challenge on constrained super-resolution: methods and results. In: Proceedings of the IEEE/CVF International Conference on Computer Vision (ICCV) Workshops, pp. 3565–3574 (2019)
32. Zhang, K., Zuo, W., Zhang, L.: Learning a single convolutional super-resolution network for multiple degradations. In: Proceedings of the IEEE Conference on Computer Vision and Pattern Recognition (CVPR), pp. 3262–3271 (2018)
33. Zhang, Y., Li, K., Li, K., Wang, L., Zhong, B., Fu, Y.: Image super-resolution using very deep residual channel attention networks. In: Ferrari, V., Hebert, M., Sminchisescu, C., Weiss, Y. (eds.) ECCV 2018. LNCS, vol. 11211, pp. 294–310. Springer, Cham (2018). https://doi.org/10.1007/978-3-030-01234-2_18

Efficient Super-Resolution Using MobileNetV3

Haicheng Wang[✉], Vineeth Bhaskara, Alex Levinshtein, Stavros Tsogkas, and Allan Jepson

Samsung AI Centre Toronto, Toronto, Canada
{h.wang1,s.bhaskara,alex.lev,stavros.t,allan.jepson}@samsung.com

Abstract. Deep learning methods for super-resolution (SR) have been dominating in terms of performance in recent years. Such methods can potentially improve the digital zoom capabilities of most modern mobile phones, but are not directly applicable on device, due to hardware constraints. In this work, we adapt MobileNetV3 blocks, shown to work well for classification, detection and segmentation, to the task of super-resolution. The proposed models with the modified MobileNetV3 block are shown to be efficient enough to run on modern mobile phones with an accuracy approaching that of the much heavier, state-of-the-art (SOTA) super-resolution approaches.

Keywords: Super-resolution · Efficient CNN · Mobile digital zoom

1 Introduction

Enhancing the quality of images taken with digital cameras is useful in a broad range of both professional and consumer applications, such as photo editing, or improving the quality of video and image content in TVs and mobile phones, respectively.

One particular form of image enhancement involves taking an image of relatively low starting resolution and "upscaling" it to create an image of higher resolution, allowing us to increase the raw size of the image, while producing fine details. In the context of computer vision and image processing, this task is called *super-resolution* (SR) and has traditionally been tackled in two different ways *Classical* super-resolution algorithms frame SR as an optimization problem, which is solved by minimizing the loss between the low-resolution (LR) input(s) and the projection of the predicted high-resolution (HR) image back to the low-resolution domain, combined with appropriate regularization [11,15,37]. In other works, the input is not a single, but *multiple*, slightly misaligned LR depictions of the same scene, defining a system of linear constraints that produces the underlying HR image, when solved [9,10,20,39]. The common feature of all these methods is that they do not require any training; however, this

---

H. Wang, V. Bhaskara, A. Levinshtein—Equal contribution.

© Springer Nature Switzerland AG 2020
A. Bartoli and A. Fusiello (Eds.): ECCV 2020 Workshops, LNCS 12537, pp. 87–102, 2020.
https://doi.org/10.1007/978-3-030-67070-2_5

advantage is usually offset by slow runtimes due to iterative optimization or kernel approximation schemes, or limited effectiveness for scale factors larger than ×2.

Example-based super-resolution [3,12,13,23], on the other hand, relies on a dataset of corresponding low-resolution (LR) and high-resolution (HR) images (or patches). A model is trained to map a *single* low-resolution input to a high-resolution output, with a specified upscaling factor. Being fast and able to effectively handle higher scale factors (such as ×4 or ×8) are advantages example-based methods enjoy over classical approches; the caveat is that, inferring the ideal LR-to-HR mapping is an ill-posed problem, because there are multiple HR images that may correspond to a LR input[1].

Nevertheless, in the last few years, we have seen an explosion of example-based methods, especially with the proliferation of deep learning models such as CNNs [7,22,34] and GANs [27,41]. These models are quite effective in generating images of high perceptual quality, but they are often cumbersome, having a large number of parameters and increased time and memory footprint.

These requirements become especially limiting for mobile phone applications. Zoom, for instance, remains a challenge for mobile phones, since the manufacturer must satisfy two conflicting specifications: on one hand, high quality optical zoom requires a physically large lens; on the other hand, the phone device itself must remain compact to improve usability and aesthetics. Digital zoom can potentially be the answer, but the low-power CPUs and GPUs that fit inside a phone are not powerful enough to run the heavier, state of the art SR networks, that are designed for desktop computers[2].

Lifting the need for such compromises is the main motivation behind our submission to the AIM 2020 Efficient SR challenge [44]. Our goal is to propose a deep network that performs comparably to powerful, state of the art models, like ESRGAN [41] or RCAN [46], while being efficient enough to run on a mainstream mobile phone device.

There is already a significant body of research on improving the efficiency of deep CNNs for super-resolution. Some works attempt to design and use more lightweight architectures, without compromising performance [6,35,44], while others introduce new modules that improve performance in a cost-effective way [34]. However, it is still questionable whether these models are applicable to mobile applications, because their efficiency is evaluated on desktop GPUs rather than mobile devices, and the output size at test time is usually smaller than that of a typical photo taken with a mobile phone. In classification and segmentation tasks, MobileNet architectures [16,17,33] demonstrate promising performance-efficiency trade-offs. Besides attractive performance in the

---

[1] This is why this task is sometimes called *image hallucination*.

[2] ESRGAN [41] takes 2.69 s on a V100 GPU, and 10.46 GB of memory, to generate a 12MP (3000 × 4000) output – a standard photo size for a mobile camera. Obtaining the same output using mobile phone hardware would be prohibitively slow, or impossible, due to limited memory.

literature, the architectures are also widely adopted as the backbone model for many deep learning applications in computationally constrained environments.

In this work, we adapt the MobileNetV3 [16] architecture design for the SR task, and propose a deep learning method that can achieve good performance while running efficiently on a mobile phone, opening up the possibility for on-device deployment.

We evaluate our approach on 4x super-resolution and show that it approaches the performance of state-of-the-art (SOTA) methods such as ESRGAN and RCAN [41, 46] *while being 40–1000× and 30–1000× more efficient in FLOPs and parameter size respectively.* In addition to achieving a better performance-efficiency trade-off compared to previous methods, we also showcase an "extremely lite" variant of our model. The runtime performance of the latter is fast enough to make direct deployment to mobile devices possible.

2   Related Work

2.1   Deep Learning Models Focusing on Image Quality

Since the seminal work of Dong *et al.* [7], there has been an steadily increasing interest in Single-image Super-Resolution (SISR) using deep neural networks. Network architectures of high representational power [22,27,36,38,41], including models of visual attention [46], have been proposed to improve fidelity. Researchers have also explored various loss objectives [28,32,41] to improve the sharpness of the generated image or make the output more visually pleasing, according to human perception, with tools such as GANs [41] and perceptual losses [21] that have been widely adopted. The caveat, however, is that these trained models have high requirements in terms of memory, processing power, or both, making their direct application to edge devices impossible.

2.2   Efficient Deep Learning Models

To achieve better trade-off between fidelity and efficiency, a separate line of SISR research has been focusing on more cost-aware architecture design. Dong *et al.* [8] speed up their model using an hourglass-shaped CNN architecture. Shi *et al.* [34] and Vu *et al.* [40] develop subpixel and de-subpixel convolution to approach efficient model inference. Ahn *et al.* [2] propose a lighter ResNet architecture with multi-scale cascading connections. Lai *et al.* [25] address the efficiency requirement by progressive reconstruction of the output, using a Laplacian pyramid in the feature branch. Hui *et al.* [19] introduce multiple information distillation blocks, which reduce the computation budget by progressively splitting features into one half that is merged with the output, and another half that is processed further.

Apart from manual architecture adaptation, Neural Architecture Search (NAS) has also been explored for efficient super-resolution. Chu *et al.* [6] employ evolutionary algorithms to get the proper parameters for convolution blocks and connections among blocks. Song *et al.* [35] utilize a similar approach to determine the optimal location of non-linearities and upsampling layers, while also utilizing efficient Residual Dense blocks.

While these models are a step in the right direction, most of them are still not efficient enough to stay within the runtime and memory constraints on a mobile phone. First, the 12MP target output resolution on a typical mobile phone is much larger than the output size used in research benchmarks; and second, even flagship mobile phones possess hardware that is much less capable, compared to desktop GPUs, both in terms of memory capacity, and processing power. Thus, there is a strong incentive to make models that are even more efficient, and lightweight enough for mobile deployment. We achieve this by a network architecture that can bring better trade-off between FLOPs and fidelity performance, especially, when FLOPs are extremely low.

3 Proposed Method

3.1 MobileNet Architecture Overview

MobileNet [16,17,33] is a family of CNN architectures that are specifically designed for deployment on lightweight devices. These architectures have shown promising performance-efficiency trade-offs in computer vision tasks such as classification, detection and segmentation.

Each member of the MobileNet family builds on its predecessors, bringing new design changes that improve performance. MobileNet [17] introduces the depth separable convolution (Fig. 1a) that replaces the standard convolution operation, achieving comparable accuracy performance but with much fewer FLOPs. MobileNetV2 [33](Fig. 1b) proposes inverted residuals, expanding features inside a block so that the representation power of the model can be improved in a cost-effective way. MobileNetV3 [16](Fig. 1c) additionally introduces the squeeze-excitation (SE) attention module and a new activation function (hard-swish), combined with hardware-aware NAS for hyperparameter tuning.

3.2 Efficient Architecture Using Adapted MobileNetV3 Blocks

We use the most recent MobileNetV3 [16] blocks as the basis for our efficient super-resolution model. Our architecture takes a single LR image as input, and passes it through $N + 1$ modified MobileNetV3 blocks, with a skip connection (addition) from the output of the first block to the output of the last block. Contrary to the findings of Lim *et al.* [28], we found the BatchNorm layers within the MobileNetV3 blocks to be beneficial to performance; we discuss this in more detail in Sect. 4.4. The output of the last block is then upscaled using two pixel-shuffle operations [34] with non-linearities and convolutions. To yield three channels, post-processing consisting of a depth-wise separable convolution together with a 1×1 convolution layer, is applied to the output of the upscaling

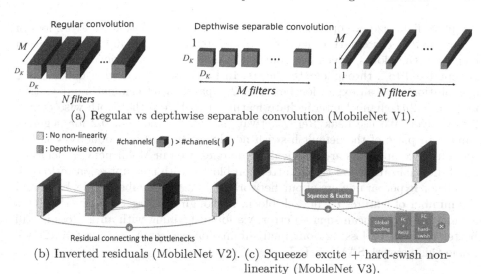

(a) Regular vs depthwise separable convolution (MobileNet V1).

(b) Inverted residuals (MobileNet V2). (c) Squeeze excite + hard-swish non-linearity (MobileNet V3).

Fig. 1. Features introduced in different versions of the MobileNet architecture.

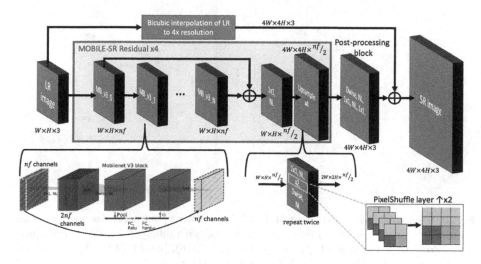

Fig. 2. Method architecture. NL stands for non-linearity, which we set to LeakyReLU with a slope of 0.2 for negative values.

result. Finally, the LR input is bicubically interpolated to the 4x higher resolution and added to the output of the post-processing block using a skip connection. As a result of this skip connection, the main body of the network is tasked with only computing an update to the bicubically interpolated image. Figure 2 provides a visual overview of our architecture.

We modify the MobileNetV3 blocks for SR as follows. Unlike the original MobileNetV3, which performs progressive downsampling to increase the receptive field size, we operate in the original image resolution, to avoid loss of detail, as it is customary in modern SR architectures [8,41,46]. The expansion factor for the blocks, which determines the number of 1×1 convolution filters, is kept fixed to 2 throughout the layers. In Fig. 2, we are showing how a 1×1 convolution with an expansion factor of 2 expands a nf-channel input feature map to a $2nf$-channel intermediate feature map before the depth-wise convolution layer. We use LeakyReLU activations (with a slope of 0.2 for negative values) in place of the default h-swish non-linearity used in MobileNetV3. The remaining components are identical to the ones used in MobilenetV3, including batch normalization and the SE attention blocks, with a compression ratio of 4.

Other hyperparameters of our network include the number of blocks N and the number of features nf in each block. Although the target metric (PSNR) is a function of the mean squared error, we found training with an L1 loss is still better than an L2 loss. For our final submission, we set $N = 16$, $nf = 72$. We name this network SAM_SR_LITE.

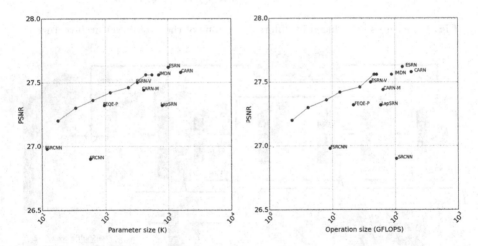

Fig. 3. Comparisons in PSNR-Y on BSD100 dataset w.r.t parameter size and operation count. Dots connected by red lines are our models with different N and nf configurations. From right to left are $(nf, N) = (72, 16)$, $(64, 16)$, $(64, 8)$, $(32, 16)$, $(32, 8)$, $(16, 16)$, $(16, 8)$. Models closer to top left corner are better.

4   Experiments

4.1   Datasets and Implementation Details

Our submitted method (SAM_SR_LITE) was trained on the combined DIV2K (800 images) [1] and FLICKR2K (2680 images) [1] datasets. We use 100×100 low-res image crops, with a batch size of 128, training for a total of 350 K steps. For data augmentation, we use random cropping, flipping and 90° rotations. Learning rate is initialized to 0.005 and halved at steps [100K, 200K, 250K, 300K].

Training is done using the Adam optimizer [24] with parameters $\beta_1 = 0.9$ and $\beta_2 = 0.99$. The model is implemented in PyTorch [30].

The results in Table 1 show that SAM_SR_LITE achieves a validation PSNR of 28.976 dB, which is on par with the baseline method for the AIM 2020 Efficient Super-Resolution challenge, namely, MSRResNet [41,45]. This is despite our model using just 18% of the FLOPs and 37% of the parameters (although, using more activations in total) compared to the baseline model. We measure FLOPs based on a LR image of size 256×256, and the memory reported is the peak memory allocated during inference on the DIV2K validation set. Activation size is the total number of elements among all convolutional layers' output tensors [31]. Note that by this measure, dpeth separable convolutions will have twice the number of activations as full convolutions. In this report, we measure runtime on the DIV2K validation set [1] (having an input size of 421×421, on average), with a NVIDIA RTX 2080 GPU (CUDA 10.1, no cuDNN, PyTorch 1.5.1), unless specified otherwise. We see from Table 1 that, for this environment, the runtime of SAM_SR_LITE is about half the baseline's. Samples of qualitative results can be found in Fig. 4.

Table 1. Comparison of our submitted model SAM_SR_LITE with the baseline method MSRResNet [45]. Our model achieves a performance on par with the baseline while requiring much fewer FLOPs, memory, and parameters.

Model	PSNR-RGB on DIV2K val dataset	PSNR-RGB on DIV2K test dataset	FLOPs	Parameters	Runtime	Activation	Memory
Baseline [45]	29.00	28.70	333.32 G	1517 K	0.336 s	292.55 M	4.37 GB
SAM_SR_LITE	28.98	28.71	58.6 G	558 K	0.169 s	576.45 M	2.56 GB

4.2 Trade-Off Between Quality and Efficiency

We have also experimented with lighter versions of our method, the results are summarized in Table 2 and Fig. 3. In particular, when setting $N = 8$ and $nf = 16$, which we call SAM_SR_XLITE (for eXtremely light), our method has 18K parameters ($\sim$1% of the baseline), and achieves an inference time of $0.03s$ ($\sim$8% of the baseline, using RTX2080), at 2.58G FLOPs ($\sim$0.8% of the baseline), with a validation PSNR of 28.38 dB. Being 0.62 dB below the baseline performance, it was not submitted to the challenge. Nevertheless, we feel this model is of significant interest since it exhibits a large gain in computational efficiency ($\sim$130$\times$ fewer FLOPs than the baseline) at the cost of a performance loss of 0.5 to 1 dB, where 0.5 dB difference is barely noticeable for casual human observers.

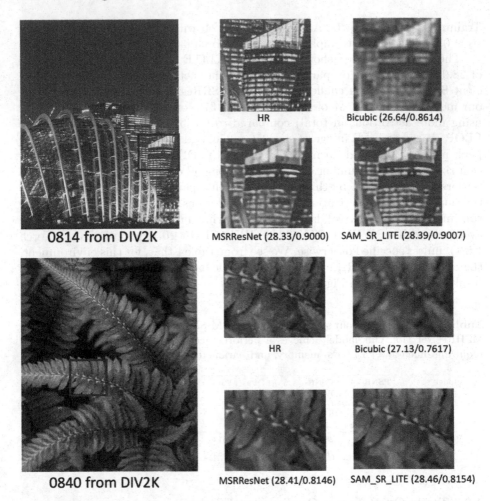

Fig. 4. Qualitative comparison. SAM_SR_LITE outperforms bicubic interpolation and is on-par with MSRResNet [45], while being significantly more efficient than the latter.

4.3   Comparison with Previous Methods

We compare our model with existing models that focus on both efficiency and image quality. We evaluate on Set5 [4], Set14 [43], BSD100 [29] and Urban100 [18], conventionally used as benchmarks for super-resolution, using the PSNR and SSIM [42] metrics computed on only the Y channel of the YCrCb color space. In order to align with test results in the literature, we retrained our models using only DIV2K (without observing any significant differences compared to our models trained on both DIV2K and FLICKR2K). Table 3 shows the results of the comparisons. The SAM_SR_LITE model achieves slightly higher PSNR-Y scores compared with previous methods with roughly similar, or smaller, operation

Table 2. Trade-off between generated image quality and efficiency for proposed model family. Note that the FLOPs and activations are calculated for the 256×256 input. The reported quantitative metrics are PSNR-Y and SSIM-Y, respectively, across different datasets.

nf	N	FLOPs	# Params	Runtime	Activation	Set5 [4]	Set14 [43]	BSD100 [29]	Urban100 [18]
72	16	58.6G	558.54K	0.169 s	576.45M	32.36/0.8968	28.71/0.7826	27.56/0.7363	26.18/0.7881
64	16	47.02G	444.9K	0.142 s	512.75M	32.24/0.8956	28.68/0.7817	27.56/0.7361	26.11/0.7864
64	8	27.84G	233.96K	0.093 s	344.98M	32.09/0.8938	28.54/0.7784	27.46/0.7325	25.86/0.7774
32	16	13.38G	119.28K	0.075 s	257.95M	32.00/0.8924	28.48/0.7768	27.42/0.7319	25.79/0.7758
32	8	8.08G	62.96K	0.051 s	174.06M	31.85/0.8903	28.39/0.7740	27.36/0.7290	25.54/0.7667
16	16	4.16G	33.85K	0.045 s	130.55M	31.75/0.8885	28.30/0.7721	27.30/0.7264	25.42/0.7625
16	8	2.58G	17.98K	0.029 s	88.60M	31.48/0.8843	28.12/0.7675	27.20/0.7226	25.18/0.7526

counts and parameter sizes. Specifically, consider all methods in Table 3 that have fewer than 1M parameters and require less than 100GFLOPs (i.e., the models in the first six rows, up to and including IMDN). We observe that our model has the highest PSNR (including one tie) among these seven methods, providing small PSNR increments of $+0.15\,dB$ (Set5), $+0.13\,dB$ (Set14), $0\,dB$ (BSD100), and $+0.14\,dB$ (Urban100) over the previous best.

Moreover our second model, SAM_SR_XLITE, has less than 5% of the number of parameters and FLOPs as SAM_SR_LITE, and exhibits a loss of at most 1 dB in PSNR performance over the different test sets (specifically, the PSNR difference between the XLITE and LITE models are $-0.88\,dB$ (Set5), $-0.59\,dB$ (Set14), $-0.36\,dB$ (BSD100), and $-1.00\,dB$ (Urban100)). Recall that the difference between these two models is only in two of the hyperparameters, namely the number of blocks, N (16 versus 8), and the number of features per block, nf (72 versus 16). Indeed, we show in Fig. 3 that by selecting different values for these hyperparameters we obtain models that cover a wide range of trade-offs between PSNR performance and computational cost. For current mobile applications, where computational constraints are severe, we are interested in more lightweight models, such as SAM_SR_XLITE (Figs. 5 and 6).

4.4 Ablation Study

We conduct three sets of ablation experiments to investigate the impact of specific components in our architecture design. We first experiment with replacing the batch normalization (BN) and the squeeze and excite modules, each with the identity mapping. A third variation of our model removes the LR to HR bicubically interpolated skip connection.

We observe that batch normalization results in a significant performance improvement for our LITE model (i.e., $+0.44\,dB$ with BN), contrary to [28]. However, batch norm only brings tiny improvement to XLITE model (i.e., $+0.02\,dB$). The skip connection also has a beneficial effect for both LITE ($+0.27\,dB$) and XLITE model ($+0.31\,dB$). This is likely because adding a bicubically interpolated image provides a good baseline for the low-frequency content of the

Table 3. Comparison between our model and efficient models in the literature. Note that the FLOPs are calculated for the 720P (1280 × 720) output. The reported quantitative metrics are PSNR-Y and SSIM-Y, respectively, across different datasets.

Model	FLOPs	# Params	Set5 [4]	Set14 [43]	BSD100 [29]	Urban100 [18]
FSRCNN [8]	9.2G	12K	30.71/0.8657	27.59/0.7535	26.98/0.7150	24.62/0.7280
FEQE-P [40]	11.0G	96K	31.53/0.8824	28.21/0.7714	27.32/0.7273	25.32/0.7583
ESRN-V [35]	41.4G	324K	31.99/0.8919	28.49/0.7779	27.50/0.7331	25.87/0.7782
LapSRN [25]	59.8G	813K	31.54/0.8850	28.19/0.7720	27.32/0.7280	25.21/0.7560
CARN-M [2]	65.0G	677K	31.92/0.8903	28.42/0.7762	27.44/0.7304	25.62/0.7694
IMDN [19]	88.9G	715K	32.21/0.8948	28.58/0.7811	27.56/0.7353	26.04/0.7838
ESRN [35]	132.2G	1,014K	32.26/0.8957	28.63/0.7818	27.62/0.7378	26.24/0.7912
CARN [2]	181.8G	1,592K	32.13/0.8937	28.60/0.7806	27.58/0.7349	26.07/0.7837
RCAN [46]	1839.86G	15.6M	32.63/0.9002	28.87/0.7889	27.77/0.7436	26.82/0.8087
ESRGAN [41]	2068.26G	16.7M	32.60/0.9002	28.88/0.7896	27.76/0.7432	26.73/0.8072
SAM_SR_XLITE	2.2G	18K	31.48/0.8843	28.12/0.7675	27.20/0.7226	25.18/0.7526
SAM_SR_LITE	51.5G	559K	32.36/0.8968	28.71/0.7826	27.56/0.7363	26.18/0.7881

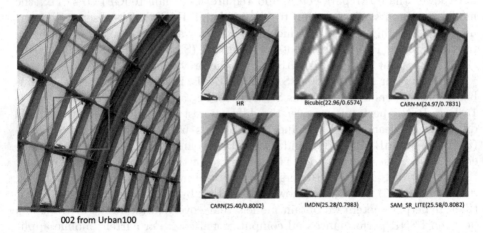

002 from Urban100

Fig. 5. Qualitative comparison on Urban100 [18]. SAM_SR_LITE outperforms other previous methods [2,19] with similar FLOPs and parameter size.

high-resolution image, thereby, allowing the model to focus on adding just the high-frequency details. The SE module is seen to provide a marginal improvement in image quality (+0.01 dB) for both LITE and XLITE model, which may be removed for more lightweight models. See Table 4 for more details.

Moreover, we fuse the batch norm layer to its preceding convolution layer to optimize the inference time without any performance change [26], see Table 4 under SAM_SR_LITE_FUSED. Although it does not improve FLOPs significantly, the fused model improves runtime by around 18%. Note that the fused model was explored after the challenge deadline and was not submitted to the challenge.

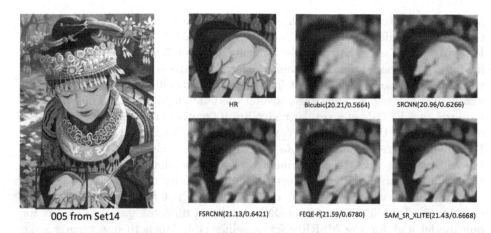

Fig. 6. Qualitative comparison on Set14 [43]. SAM_SR_XLITE outperforms bicubic intepolation, SRCNN [7] and FSRCNN [8] and on par with FEQE-P [40], while being $4-6\times$ smaller in operation size.

Table 4. Ablation study on SAM_SR_LITE and SAM_SR_XLITE. Runtime is measured in the same environment as Table 1. (*The SAM_SR_XLITE has a different validation performance here than the one in Table 2 as it was trained with a smaller input patch size of 64×64.)

Model	PSNR-RGB on DIV2K val dataset	FLOPs	Parameters	Runtime	Memory
SAM_SR_LITE	28.98	58.6G	558K	0.169 s	2.56 GB
w/o batch norm	28.55(−0.44)	57.0G(−1.6G)	546K(−12K)	0.138 s(−0.031 s)	2.50 GB(−0.06 GB)
w/o skip connection	28.71(−0.27)	58.6G(∼0.0G)	558K(0.0K)	0.166 s(−0.003 s)	2.56 GB(∼0.0 GB)
w/o SE	28.97(−0.01)	58.6G(∼0.0G)	393K(−165K)	0.155 s(−0.014 s)	2.56 GB(∼0.0 GB)
SAM_SR_LITE_FUSED	28.98(0.0)	57.0G(−1.6G)	546K(−12K)	0.139 s(−0.030 s)	2.50 GB(−0.06 GB)
SAM_SR_XLITE*	28.35	2.58G	17.98K	0.030 s	0.65 GB
w/o batch norm	28.33(−0.02)	2.4G(−0.18G)	16.54K(−1.44K)	0.027 s(−0.003 s)	0.65 GB(∼0.0 GB)
w/o skip connection	28.04(−0.31)	2.58G(∼0.0G)	17.98K(0.0K)	0.029 s(−0.001 s)	0.65 GB(∼0.0 GB)
w/o SE	28.34(−0.01)	2.56G(−0.02G)	13.88K(−4.1K)	0.028 s(−0.002 s)	0.65 GB(∼0.0 GB)

5   Inference Time

5.1   Disparity Between FLOPs and Runtime

Typically, a lower number of FLOPs implies a faster runtime, when measuring runtime efficiency. However, in our experiments we notice a palpable disparity between the expected runtime performance of our model and the one observed in practice. Results from AIM 2020 organizers indicate that in their environment, the SAM_SR_LITE is approximately two times slower than the baseline [44], while requiring only 18% of the FLOPs. We have two observations regarding this disparity.

Currently, optimized depth-wise convolution operations are not well supported by some deep learning frameworks, including PyTorch [30]. For example, note the open issue in the PyTorch repository [14] showing that the inference run-time of a single depth-wise convolution layer Conv2d(32,32,3,groups=32) is *at best* only $\sim 3\times$ faster than a regular convolution layer Conv2d(32,32,3), despite having a $32\times$ smaller operation count. A fair comparison would be to use depth-wise separable convolutions; that is, depthwise convolutions Conv2d(32,32,3, group=32) followed by pointwise convolutions Conv2d(32,32,1). This operation requires 14% FLOPs of a regular convolution Conv2d(32,32,3), but takes 81% of the inference time for regular convolution (using PyTorch on a V100 GPU). Depthwise separable computations are a key design element of MobileNetV3 blocks, and subsequently, of our model as well. Therefore, any improvement in their efficiency would directly affect the runtime of our model.

In addition, we observed that our model does not fully take advantage of cuDNN [5]. Table 5 shows that cuDNN results in different speed-up factors for our model and for the MSRResNet baseline [45]. Much to our surprise, the challenge [44] organizers measured an even slower inference time using a *better* RTX 2080Ti GPU than our testing machine with a RTX 2080 GPU. In short, the inference time of our model varies from being 20% faster to being over twice slower than the baseline model as a function of software and hardware combination.

For these reasons, we argue that the number of operations (FLOPs) is a better measure for the computational efficiency of our model.

5.2   Activation Size as a Proxy for Runtime

The activation size is first analyzed as a proxy for performance in [31], with the authors reporting a strong correlation of the activation size of convolution layers with runtime. The AIM challenge organizers [44] also find that the activation size has a better ranking correlation with runtime compared to other complexity metrics (FLOPs, parameter size, memory).

We also investigate the correlation between runtime and activation size in our family of models by sampling models with various capacities. We find that for our family of models there is a strong linear correlation between runtime and **all** other complexity metrics (activation size, FLOPs, and parameter size); see Fig. 7. Thus, different from the finding in [31], for our models activation size is no more informative than the other metrics.

Evaluation of model complexity w.r.t. the activation size [44] puts our family of models at a disadvantage. A standard replacement of regular convolution with a depth separable convolution (a depthwise convolution followed by a pointwise convolution) will double the activation measurement, while blocks in MobileNetV3 would have an even larger activation size due to the internal expansion factor. As a result, despite the lower FLOP count, our models may be slower in runtime than models from different families with smaller activation size.

Finally, it is worth noting that, the strong correlation between activation size and runtime on memory-bound accelerators (desktop GPUs and TPUs) [31] may not translate to mobile phone accelerators, which have considerably lower computational resources. Moreover, we believe that optimizing memory (e.g., pre-allocation of activations for a fixed input) for specific applications will reduce the impact of memory on runtime.

5.3 Runtime on Mobile Devices

Since the environment we are targetting for applying our models is the phone, we deploy a slightly modified SAM_SR_XLITE on a Samsung Note 10 to evaluate the runtime on an actual mobile device. We first perform the required conversion of the model from PyTorch to a Snapdragon Neural Processing Engine (SNPE) Deep Learning Container file. It takes our model 1.41 s to generate a 12MP image and 0.8 s for its 8-bit quantized version. Although the model cannot achieve real-time inference on the mobile devices, it is already deployable for many mobile applications such as zooming in mobile camera.

Table 5. Running time under different configurations for SAM_SR_LITE and baseline model. The running time is computed by averaging across 5 rounds per image (after 5 rounds warm-up on the same image).

GPU	CUDA	cuDNN	PyTorch	OS	Running Time-SAM_SR_LITE/baseline	Note
RTX 2080	10.1	Disabled	1.5.1	Ubuntu 16.04	0.2137 s/−(OOM)	Our results
RTX 2080	10.1	7.6.3	1.5.1	Ubuntu 16.04	0.1668 s/0.1240 s	Our results
V100	10.1	Disabled	1.5.1	Ubuntu 16.04	0.1188 s/0.1488 s	Our results
V100	10.1	7.6.3	1.5.1	Ubuntu 16.04	0.0892 s/0.0680 s	Our results
RTX 2080Ti	10.2	7.6.5	1.5.1	Ubuntu	0.240 s/0.114 s	From challenge organizers

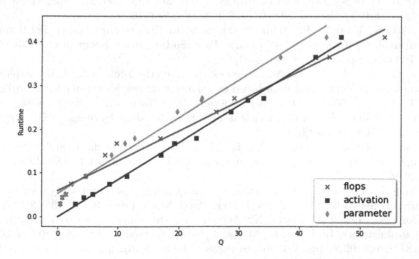

Fig. 7. Correlation between runtime and flops, activation and parameter in the proposed model family. The Q in the x-axis refer to $\frac{flops}{6G}$, $\frac{activation}{30M}$ and $\frac{parameter}{50M}$.

6   Conclusion and Future Work

Motivated by efficient super-resolution models for mobile applications, in this paper, we have proposed a set of efficient architectures that use adapted MobileNetV3 blocks. Our models achieve better trade-off between quality and efficiency than the current state-of-the-art in efficient super-resolution. The smallest of these, namely SAM_SR_XLITE, has an extremely small operation and parameter count, making it possible to be deployed on real mobile applications.

While being orders of magnitude more efficient in parameter size and operation count, the inference time of our models in PyTorch is, currently, less impressive. This is partly due to the limited optimization currently supported by the available software and hardware for deep learning and potentially large activation size. Considering the resource constrained devices as the final running environment of efficient SR models, the runtime on desktop GPUs may not fully reflect the runtime in actual applications. Still, optimizing the implementation of operators on both GPUs and edge devices, specifically depthwise convolutions, is a promising future direction for efficient super-resolution for real-time applications.

References

1. Agustsson, E., Timofte, R.: Ntire 2017 challenge on single image super-resolution: Dataset and study. In: Proceedings of the IEEE Conference on Computer Vision and Pattern Recognition (CVPR) Workshops, July 2017
2. Ahn, N., Kang, B., Sohn, K.-A.: Fast, accurate, and lightweight super-resolution with cascading residual network. In: Ferrari, V., Hebert, M., Sminchisescu, C., Weiss, Y. (eds.) ECCV 2018. LNCS, vol. 11214, pp. 256–272. Springer, Cham (2018). https://doi.org/10.1007/978-3-030-01249-6_16
3. Baker, S., Kanade, T.: Hallucinating faces. In: Proceedings Fourth IEEE International Conference on Automatic Face and Gesture Recognition (Cat. No. PR00580), pp. 83–88. IEEE (2000)
4. Bevilacqua, M., Roumy, A., Guillemot, C., Alberi-Morel, M.L.: Low-complexity single-image super-resolution based on nonnegative neighbor embedding (2012)
5. Chetlur, S., Woolley, C., Vandermersch, P., Cohen, J., Tran, J., Catanzaro, B., Shelhamer, E.: cudnn: Efficient primitives for deep learning. arXiv preprint arXiv:1410.0759 (2014)
6. Chu, X., Zhang, B., Ma, H., Xu, R., Li, J., Li, Q.: Fast, accurate and lightweight super-resolution with neural architecture search. arXiv preprint arXiv:1901.07261 (2019)
7. Dong, C., Loy, C.C., He, K., Tang, X.: Image super-resolution using deep convolutional networks. IEEE Trans. Pattern Anal. Mach. Intell. **38**(2), 295–307 (2015)
8. Dong, C., Loy, C.C., Tang, X.: Accelerating the super-resolution convolutional neural network. In: Leibe, B., Matas, J., Sebe, N., Welling, M. (eds.) ECCV 2016. LNCS, vol. 9906, pp. 391–407. Springer, Cham (2016). https://doi.org/10.1007/978-3-319-46475-6_25
9. Elad, M., Feuer, A.: Restoration of a single superresolution image from several blurred, noisy, and undersampled measured images. IEEE Trans. Image Process. **6**(12), 1646–1658 (1997)

10. Farsiu, S., Elad, M., Milanfar, P.: Multiframe demosaicing and super-resolution of color images. IEEE Trans. Image Process. **15**(1), 141–159 (2005)
11. Farsiu, S., Robinson, M.D., Elad, M., Milanfar, P.: Fast and robust multiframe super resolution. IEEE Trans. Image Process. **13**(10), 1327–1344 (2004)
12. Freeman, W.T., Jones, T.R., Pasztor, E.C.: Example-based super-resolution. IEEE Comput. Graphics Appl. **22**(2), 56–65 (2002)
13. Freeman, W.T., Pasztor, E.C., Carmichael, O.T.: Learning low-level vision. Int. J. Comput. Vision **40**(1), 25–47 (2000)
14. Github: FP32 depthwise convolution is slow in GPU (2020). https://github.com/pytorch/pytorch/issues/18631. Accessed 16 July 2020
15. Gotoh, T., Okutomi, M.: Direct super-resolution and registration using raw CFA images. In: Proceedings of the 2004 IEEE Computer Society Conference on Computer Vision and Pattern Recognition, 2004. CVPR 2004, vol. 2, p. II. IEEE (2004)
16. Howard, A., et al.: Searching for mobilenetv3. In: ICCV (2019)
17. Howard, A.G., et al.: MobileNets: efficient convolutional neural networks for mobile vision applications. arXiv preprint arXiv:1704.04861 (2017)
18. Huang, J.B., Singh, A., Ahuja, N.: Single image super-resolution from transformed self-exemplars. In: Proceedings of the IEEE Conference on Computer Vision and Pattern Recognition, pp. 5197–5206 (2015)
19. Hui, Z., Gao, X., Yang, Y., Wang, X.: Lightweight image super-resolution with information multi-distillation network. In: Proceedings of the 27th ACM International Conference on Multimedia. pp. 2024–2032 (2019)
20. Irani, M., Peleg, S.: Improving resolution by image registration. CVGIP Graphical Models Image Process. **53**(3), 231–239 (1991)
21. Johnson, J., Alahi, A., Fei-Fei, L.: Perceptual losses for real-time style transfer and super-resolution. In: Leibe, B., Matas, J., Sebe, N., Welling, M. (eds.) ECCV 2016. LNCS, vol. 9906, pp. 694–711. Springer, Cham (2016). https://doi.org/10.1007/978-3-319-46475-6_43
22. Kim, J., Kwon Lee, J., Mu Lee, K.: Accurate image super-resolution using very deep convolutional networks. In: Proceedings of the IEEE Conference on Computer Vision and Pattern Recognition, pp. 1646–1654 (2016)
23. Kim, K., Kwon, Y.: Example-based learning for singleimage SR and jpeg artifact removal. MPI-TR, (173) 8 (2008)
24. Kingma, D.P., Ba, J.: Adam: a method for stochastic optimization. arXiv preprint arXiv:1412.6980 (2014)
25. Lai, W.S., Huang, J.B., Ahuja, N., Yang, M.H.: Deep laplacian pyramid networks for fast and accurate super-resolution. In: Proceedings of the IEEE Conference on Computer Vision and Pattern Recognition, pp. 624–632 (2017)
26. Learnml: Speeding up model with fusing batch normalization and convolution (2020). https://learnml.today/speeding-up-model-with-fusing-batch-normalization-and-convolution-3. Accessed 31 July 2020
27. Ledig, C., et al.: Photo-realistic single image super-resolution using a generative adversarial network. In: Proceedings of the IEEE Conference on Computer Vision and Pattern Recognition, pp. 4681–4690 (2017)
28. Lim, B., Son, S., Kim, H., Nah, S., Mu Lee, K.: Enhanced deep residual networks for single image super-resolution. In: CVPRW (2017)
29. Martin, D., Fowlkes, C., Tal, D., Malik, J.: A database of human segmented natural images and its application to evaluating segmentation algorithms and measuring ecological statistics. In: Proceedings Eighth IEEE International Conference on Computer Vision. ICCV 2001, vol. 2, pp. 416–423. IEEE (2001)

30. Paszke, A., et al.: Automatic differentiation in pytorch (2017)
31. Radosavovic, I., Kosaraju, R.P., Girshick, R., He, K., Dollár, P.: Designing network design spaces. In: Proceedings of the IEEE/CVF Conference on Computer Vision and Pattern Recognition, pp. 10428–10436 (2020)
32. Sajjadi, M.S., Scholkopf, B., Hirsch, M.: Enhancenet: single image super-resolution through automated texture synthesis. In: Proceedings of the IEEE International Conference on Computer Vision, pp. 4491–4500 (2017)
33. Sandler, M., Howard, A., Zhu, M., Zhmoginov, A., Chen, L.C.: Mobilenetv 2: inverted residuals and linear bottlenecks. In: Proceedings of the IEEE Conference on Computer Vision and Pattern Recognition, pp. 4510–4520 (2018)
34. Shi, W., et al.: Real-time single image and video super-resolution using an efficient sub-pixel convolutional neural network. In: CVPR (2016)
35. Song, D., Xu, C., Jia, X., Chen, Y., Xu, C., Wang, Y.: Efficient residual dense block search for image super-resolution. In: AAAI, pp. 12007–12014 (2020)
36. Tai, Y., Yang, J., Liu, X., Xu, C.: MemNet: a persistent memory network for image restoration. In: Proceedings of the IEEE International Conference on Computer Vision, pp. 4539–4547 (2017)
37. Takeda, H., Farsiu, S., Milanfar, P.: Robust kernel regression for restoration and reconstruction of images from sparse noisy data. In: 2006 International Conference on Image Processing, pp. 1257–1260. IEEE (2006)
38. Tong, T., Li, G., Liu, X., Gao, Q.: Image super-resolution using dense skip connections. In: Proceedings of the IEEE International Conference on Computer Vision, pp. 4799–4807 (2017)
39. Tsai, R.: Multiframe image restoration and registration. Adv. Comput. Vis. Image Process. **1**, 317–339 (1984)
40. Vu, T., Nguyen, C.V., Pham, T.X., Luu, T.M., Yoo, C.D.: Fast and efficient image quality enhancement via desubpixel convolutional neural networks. In: Leal-Taixé, L., Roth, S. (eds.) ECCV 2018. LNCS, vol. 11133, pp. 243–259. Springer, Cham (2019). https://doi.org/10.1007/978-3-030-11021-5_16
41. Wang, X., Yu, K., Wu, S., Gu, J., Liu, Y., Dong, C., Qiao, Yu., Loy, C.C.: ESR-GAN: enhanced super-resolution generative adversarial networks. In: Leal-Taixé, L., Roth, S. (eds.) ECCV 2018. LNCS, vol. 11133, pp. 63–79. Springer, Cham (2019). https://doi.org/10.1007/978-3-030-11021-5_5
42. Wang, Z., Bovik, A.C., Sheikh, H.R., Simoncelli, E.P.: Image quality assessment: from error visibility to structural similarity. IEEE Trans. Image Process. **13**(4), 600–612 (2004)
43. Zeyde, R., Elad, M., Protter, M.: On single image scale-up using sparse-representations. In: Boissonnat, J.-D., et al. (eds.) Curves and Surfaces 2010. LNCS, vol. 6920, pp. 711–730. Springer, Heidelberg (2012). https://doi.org/10.1007/978-3-642-27413-8_47
44. Zhang, K., Danelljan, M., Li, Y., Timofte, R., et al.: AIM 2020 challenge on efficient super-resolution: methods and results. In: European Conference on Computer Vision Workshops (2020)
45. Zhang, K., et al.: Aim 2019 challenge on constrained super-resolution: methods and results. In: 2019 IEEE/CVF International Conference on Computer Vision Workshop (ICCVW), pp. 3565–3574. IEEE (2019)
46. Zhang, Y., Li, K., Li, K., Wang, L., Zhong, B., Fu, Y.: Image super-resolution using very deep residual channel attention networks. In: Ferrari, V., Hebert, M., Sminchisescu, C., Weiss, Y. (eds.) ECCV 2018. LNCS, vol. 11211, pp. 294–310. Springer, Cham (2018). https://doi.org/10.1007/978-3-030-01234-2_18

Multi-attention Based Ultra Lightweight Image Super-Resolution

Abdul Muqeet[1], Jiwon Hwang[1], Subin Yang[1], JungHeum Kang[1],
Yongwoo Kim[2(✉)], and Sung-Ho Bae[1(✉)]

[1] Department of Computer Science and Engineering,
Kyung Hee University, Yongin, South Korea
{amuqeet,jiwon.hwang,ysb8049,chhkang123,shbae}@khu.ac.kr
[2] Department of System Semiconductor Engineering,
Sangmyung University, Cheonan, South Korea
yongwoo.kim@smu.ac.kr

Abstract. Lightweight image super-resolution (SR) networks have the utmost significance for real-world applications. There are several deep learning based SR methods with remarkable performance, but their memory and computational cost are hindrances in practical usage. To tackle this problem, we propose a Multi-Attentive Feature Fusion Super-Resolution Network (MAFFSRN). MAFFSRN consists of proposed feature fusion groups (FFGs) that serve as a feature extraction block. Each FFG contains a stack of proposed multi-attention blocks (MAB) that are combined in a novel feature fusion structure. Further, the MAB with a cost-efficient attention mechanism (CEA) helps us to refine and extract the features using multiple attention mechanisms. The comprehensive experiments show the superiority of our model over the existing state-of-the-art. We participated in AIM 2020 efficient SR challenge with our MAFFSRN model and won 1st, 3rd, and 4th places in memory usage, floating-point operations (FLOPs) and number of parameters, respectively.

Keywords: Super-Resolution · Feature extraction · Multi-attention · Low-computing resources · Lightweight convolutional neural networks

1 Introduction

This paper focuses on the single image super-resolution (SISR) problem. In SISR we aim to reconstruct a high-resolution (HR) image from a low-resolution (LR) image. We refer super-resolution (SR) as interchangeably with SISR in remaining of the paper. According to [45], SISR problem can be mathematically written as,

$$I_{LR} = (I_{HR} \otimes k) \downarrow_\mathbf{s} + n, \tag{1}$$

© Springer Nature Switzerland AG 2020
A. Bartoli and A. Fusiello (Eds.): ECCV 2020 Workshops, LNCS 12537, pp. 103–118, 2020.
https://doi.org/10.1007/978-3-030-67070-2_6

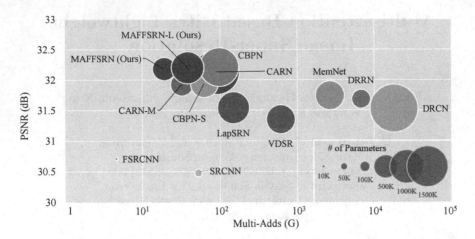

Fig. 1. Performance comparison of existing lightweight methods on Set5 [3] (4×). Multi-adds are calculated on 720p HR image. The results show the superiority of our models among existing methods

where I_{LR} and I_{HR} refer to given input LR and desire HR images. 'k' in Eq. 1) denotes as a blur kernel, $\downarrow_s$ represents a down-scaling operator, and 'n' is a Gaussian noise. By following previous works, we assume that images are down-sampled with bicubic interpolation [2,50].

There are multiple mapping solutions possible from single LR to HR images that make this problem ill-posed. Albeit of its ill-posedness, the deep learning methods like [8,9,21] have shown notable success in this domain. For instance, SRCNN [8] with only three layers outperformed the previous non-deep learning methods. Subsequently, deeper and complex architectures have been proposed to improve the performance of SR methods [2,12,27,48,49]. In spite of their outstanding performance, such methods are impracticable for real-world applications because of their large memory size, number of operations, and parameters.

Numerous lightweight models have been proposed to resolve these issues. CARN [2] introduces a lightweight and efficient cascaded residual network with several residual connections. FALSR [7] employs a network architecture search (NAS) technique rather than manually searching it in SISR domain. CBPN [50] proposed an efficient version of the DBPN network [12] that emphasizes the importance of high-resolution features of LR images. These models were designed to reduce the computational cost, though all of these come with their smaller version of models, such as, CARN-M [2], CBPN-S [50], FALSR-B, and FALSR-C [7]. Hence, it shows that their original models are inadequate for real-world application.

The need of such practical models motivated us to propose a lightweight model called MAFFSRN. Its computation cost is similar to CARN-M, CBPN-S, FALSR-B, FALSR-C [2,7,50], but matches the performance of their corresponding original models. With the comprehensive experiments, we show that our

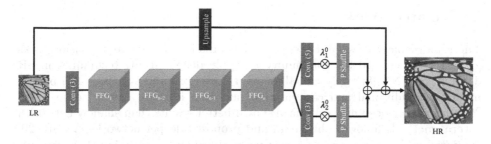

Fig. 2. Our main network architecture (MAFFSRN). It consists of stack of FFG where each FFG has multiple MAB combined with modified BFF. Conv (3) and Conv (5) refer to 3 × 3 and 5 × 5 convolutions, respectively, P Shuffle means pixel shuffle [32]. Each lambda (λ) is trainable scalar parameter. Lastly, we add up-sampled LR image to the reconstructed output

models achieve the best performance on all of the benchmark datasets. Further, we introduce a large model (MAFFSRN-L) to compare performance with heavy state-of-the-art methods. Note that its size still remains smaller than existing efficient models. We show our benchmark results in Fig. 1.

Our model is specifically aimed to minimize the computation cost such as floating point operations (FLOPs) and memory consumption but maximize the network performance. To increase the network performance, we utilize the feature fusion group (FFG) that consists of several multi-attention blocks (MAB). In SR deep network architectures the vital information is vanished during the flow of network [48]. Our method tackles this problem with FFG and MAB and results suggest that they enable us to increase the depth of network with minimal computational cost, consequently increasing the network performance. The next challenge is to minimize the computational cost and memory usage. For this purpose, we propose changes for the enhanced spatial attention (ESA) block [28]. First, we introduce cost-efficient (CEA) block to directly apply attention mechanism on the input features. Second, we replaced the Conv groups of ESA [28] with dilated convolutions to get benefit from the large spatial size. For the feature fusion structure, we found during the experiments that the performance of hierarchical feature fusion (HFF) [26] remains lower than the binarized feature fusion (BFF) [30]. We discuss the details of these experiments in ablations studies. We evaluate our method on benchmark datasets and compare the performance against existing methods.

Our overall contributions are summarized as follows: 1) we introduce a lightweight model consisting of modified BFF, MAB, and CEA modules, that outperforms existing methods. We participated in AIM 2020 SR challenge [44] where our model was ranked 1st in memory consumption, 3rd in FLOPS, and 4th in number of parameters. 2) We provide comprehensive qualitative and quantitative comparison results on the benchmark datasets with multiple scaling factors (×2, ×3, and ×4).

2   Related Work

The remarkable success of deep neural networks in other computer vision tasks [6,13,16] encouraged SR community to apply deep learning techniques in SR domain. SRCNN [8] apply a shallow neural network and surpasses the performance of traditional and conventional non-deep learning based methods. As [37] shows that deep networks have shown better results than shallow networks, several methods followed this trend and proposed deeper networks. VDSR [20] proposed a 20 layers network consisting of global skip-connection that element-wise add the up-sampled LR image to the output reconstructed image. EDSR [27] improved the SRResNet [25], that was based on ResNet architecture [13], by removing the trivial layers or those layers which degrade the performance, such as Batch Normalization [19]. RDN introduced dense connections similar to DenseNet [17] and improved the performance with fewer parameters than EDSR [27]. Certainly, they have improved the image fidelity, such as PSNR or SSIM significantly, however, the constrained real-world environments having low-power computing devices require to focus on other metrics, such as number of parameters, memory consumption, FLOPs, latency time, etc.

Therefore, there is growing interest to build lightweight models that need to be accurate as well. One strategy is to adopt model compression techniques to compress the models [11,15]. In this paper, our focus is to develop a new network architecture to remedy this problem. Hence, we only discuss the previous works that address such issues in SR domain.

The progress of such lightweight architectures started from FSRCNN [9]. It improves the performance of SRCNN [8] by directly applying SR network to LR images rather than up-sampled input. It also decreases the inference time by removing the high-cost up-sampling layers. DRRN [33] utilized recursive layers to reduce the number of parameters while keeping the depth of the network. CARN [2] applied several residual connections and recursive layers to reduce computational cost. FALSR [7] introduced automated neural architecture search (NAS) strategies in SR domain to propose an SR model for constrained environment. CBPN [50] proposed an efficient version of DBPN network [12] by replacing the expensive up- and down- projection modules with pixel shuffle layers. We observed that all these methods focused on trade-off between performance and computation cost that led them to propose another smaller version of their model such as CBPN-S [50], CARN-M [2], FALSR-B [7]. However, our proposed method achieves better or comparable performance as their original models whereas the computational cost remains the same or lower compared to their lightweight versions.

3   Proposed Method

In this section, we describe the details of our proposed architecture. As shown in Fig. 2, our network architecture consists of n FFGs that are stacked in a sequential way. The details of FFG are given Sect. 3.1. We use one convolutional

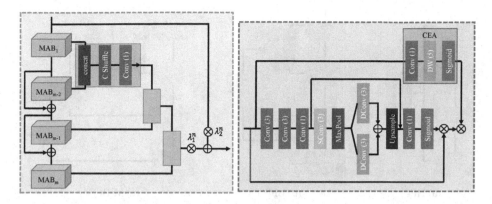

Fig. 3. Left figure shows structure of FFG and right figure shows MAB. 'C Shuffle' refers to channel shuffle, 'SConv' means strided convolution, 'DConv' means dilated convolution and 'DW' means depth-wise convolution. Parenthesis such as (1), (3) and (5) represents 1×1, 3×3, and 5×5 filters, respectively

(Conv) layer before FFGs to extract the shallow features from input LR image. Lastly, we apply couple of Conv layers with different filter sizes to extract multi-scale features that are followed by pixel-shuffle layers [32]. Further, motivated from [38], we add weights (denoted by λ_1^0 and λ_2^0) to both Conv layers to give weightage to the features and carry the weighted features to later layers. Later, the resultant information is element-wise added. Similar to [20], we element-wise add up-sample LR input into the output layer. Note, our overall architecture is primarily based on RDN architecture [49] that consists of local and global blocks.

For the given I_{LR} image, the shallow feature extraction step is given as

$$x_{sfe} = f_{sfe}(I_{LR}),\qquad(2)$$

where f_{sfe} and x_{sfe} represent the 3×3 convolution and the resultant output, respectively. Next, for non-linear mapping or deep feature extraction step, we apply the stack of FFG as follows

$$x_{dfe} = f_{FFG}^n\left(f_{FFG}^{n-1}\left(\ldots f_{FFG}^0\left(x_{sfe}\right)\right)\right),\qquad(3)$$

where f_{FFG}^n and x_{dfe} denote the n_{th} FFG and output of deep feature extraction step, respectively. Lastly, the reconstruction stage is given as

$$I_{SR} = f_{ps}\left(\lambda_1^0 f_5\left(x_{dfe}\right)\right) + f_{ps}\left(\lambda_2^0 f_3\left(x_{dfe}\right)\right) + f_{up}\left(I_{LR}\right),\qquad(4)$$

where the details of notations in Eq. 4 are as follows: I_{SR} represents the desired SR image, f_3 and f_5 denote 3×3 and 5×5 convolutions, respectively, f_{ps} shows pixel-shuffle layer [32], f_{up} represent an up-sampling layer and λ_1^0 and λ_2^0 denote trainable scalar parameters.

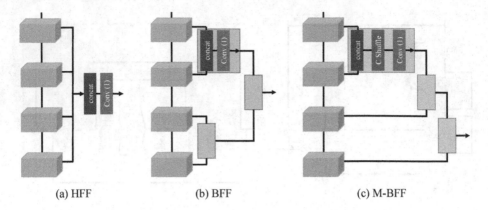

(a) HFF   (b) BFF   (c) M-BFF

Fig. 4. Comparison of different feature fusion structures (1) HFF [26], (2) BFF [30], (3) M-BFF (Ours). In figure 'concat' refers to channel-wise concatenation, 'Conv(1) refers to 1×1 convolution, and 'C Shuffle' shows channel shuffle

3.1   Feature Fusion Group (FFG)

Our proposed FFG has m multi-attention blocks (MAB). The details of MAB are discussed in the next section. The proposed MABs are combined through a modified form of binarized feature fusion (BFF) structure [30]. HFF [26] is another fusion structure that is commonly used though during experiments we found that BFF [30] performs better than HFF [26] (details are discussed in Sect. 4.1). We refer to modified BFF as M-BFF. The comparisons of structures are shown in Fig. 4. In BFF, all the adjacent blocks are separately concatenated like a binary tree structure. In contrast, our M-BFF concatenates the resultant feature block with the next MAB as shown on the left side of Fig. 3. By taking the inspiration from ShuffleNet [47] that applies a channel shuffle method to mix the information among groups, we introduce the channel shuffle to mix the information between concatenated channels followed by a channel reduction layer that reduces the channels to make it equal to the number of input channels. In the end, we element-wise add the input features to the output features. Additionally, the residual connections may contain redundant information, thus to filter desired and useful information we multiply the results with trainable parameters λ_1^n and λ_2^n where n refers to n^{th} FFG.

3.2   Multi-attention Block (MAB)

In this section, we define the details of our proposed residual block, called MAB. [48] has emphasized the importance of channel attention (CA) mechanism. Consequently, many SR methods have focused on attention mechanisms, mainly CA and spatial attention (SA) [22,30,41]. Recently, [28] proposed a combined solution for CA and SA called enhanced spatial attention (ESA). The ESA block reduces the number of channels with 1×1 convolutions and the number of spatial size with strided convolutions. Later, these spatial and channel sizes are increased to match the input size. Lastly, sigmoid operation is applied to get a similar effect as channel attention mechanism [16].

We modify the ESA block to make it more efficient by introducing dilated convolutions with different filter sizes. Further, we element-wise add all output features of dilated convolutions together to minimize the gridding effects [42]. The dilated convolutions not only reduce our memory computations but also increase spatial filter sizes, enabling us to improve the performance. Further, we introduce another cost-efficient attention mechanism (CEA) [4] to refine our input features. The CEA consists of point-wise and depth-wise convolutions. It is incorporated into the MAB block to improve the performance of our network with the negligible additional computational cost. The structure of MAB is presented on the right side of Fig. 3.

4 Experimental Setup

Implementation Details
As we focus on developing a lightweight model, we aim to maximize the performance of existing networks as well as minimize their computational cost. We denote our original model as MAFFSRN. Further, we also introduce our larger model MAFFSRN-L to show that we can enhance the performance of our model depending on the available computing resources.

Our lightweight model MAFFSRN consists of 4 FFGs and 4 MABs whereas, for MAFFSRN-L model, we keep the same number of MABs and increase the FFGs to 8. We reduce the number of channels by a factor of 4 in MAB and set stride $= 3$ to reduce the spatial size. The dilatation factors are set to $D = 1$ and $D = 2$. The values of scale λ are initialized with 0.5. We set the number of filters to 32 for every Conv layer except the last layer. For the last layer, we use 3 filters to reconstruct 3-color images. It can be modified to 1 filter for grayscale images.

Training Settings
We used AdamP optmizer [14] to train our models with initial learning rate 2×10^{-4}. For the data augmentations, we apply standard techniques i.e., images are flipped horizontally or vertically and randomly rotated by 90°, 180° and 270°. The models are trained for 1000 epochs and learning rate is decreased to half after every 200 epochs. We set batch-size to 16 and input patch size to 48×48. We implement our network on PyTorch and train it on NVIDIA RX 2080TI GPU and select the best performance model.

Datasets
We use the high-quality DIV2K [1] dataset for training our models. It consists of LR and HR pairs of 800 training images. The LR images are obtained through bicubic down-sampling. For the evaluation of our models, we use the standard and publicly available benchmark datasets, Set5 [3], Set14 [43], B100 [29], and Urban100 [18] datasets. Set5 [3], Set14 [43], B100 [29] contain animals, people, and natural scenes, while Urban100 [18] consists of urban scenes only.

Evaluation metrics

We measure the performance of reconstructed SR images with PSNR and SSIM [40] by following [20], using luminance or Y-channel of transformed YCbCr color space. We also calculate the number of parameters and multi-adds to compare the computational complexity of proposed models with existing methods.

Table 1. Effects of BFF, M-BFF, and CEA modules. Experiments are performed on Set5 (2×)

BFF	M-BFF	CEA	PSNR/SSIM	Parameters
✗	✗	✗	37.87/0.9601	364K
✓	✗	✗	37.91/0.9602	372K
✗	✓	✗	37.94/0.9602	372K
✗	✗	✓	37.93/0.9603	394K
✗	✓	✓	**37.97/0.9603**	402K

4.1   Ablation Studies

We conduct a series of ablation studies to demonstrate the importance of each proposed module used in our model. For all these experiments, we fully train our MAFFSRN model for 1000 epochs. In the first experiment, we train multiple models with similar settings to show the overall contribution of M-BFF and CEA. Each time we remove one component and test the network performance without that specific module. The results are shown in Table 1. It is noted that the model without M-BFF refers to model with HFF [26] structure that is a common choice for SR methods. Row 2 of Table 1 suggests that M-BFF improves 0.07 dB PSNR with only 8 K additional parameters. Similarly, CEA adds 0.05 dB with 32 K parameters. Lastly, when we combine CEA and M-BFF, our model obtains 0.1 dB PSNR with less than 40 K additional parameters. Note, for the fair comparisons, we add channel shuffle in all three methods.

To demonstrate the importance of channel shuffle in our proposed MAFFSRN, we remove channel shuffle from MAFFSRN and report the results in Table 2. The results clearly indicate that with channel shuffle, we can increase the performance up to 0.04 PSNR.

For further evaluation, we experimented with a different type of Conv layers to show the efficacy of dilated convolutions in MAB. The experimental results in Table 3 suggest that our dilated convolutions perform better results than three convolutions and, surprisingly, methods having 5×5 convolutions are the worst performances. The reason could be the structure of the Conv layers as element-wise addition of 3×3 and 5×5 Conv layers has no significant benefits over dilated convolutions that utilize both layers more effectively.

Table 2. Importance of channel shuffle in MAFFSRN. Experiments are performed on Set5 (2×)

Method	PSNR/SSIM
Without Channel Shuffle	37.93/0.9603
With Channel Shuffle (Ours)	**37.97/0.9603**

Table 3. Evaluation of performance of different Conv layers in MAB. Here 'd' represents dilation factors. Experiments are performed on Set5 (2×) with MAFFSRN

Number of Conv Layers	Details	PSNR/SSIM	Params
2 (ours)	$3 \times 3, 3 \times 3$ (d=2)	**37.97** /0.9603	402394
2	$3 \times 3, 3 \times 3$	37.95/0.9603	402394
3	$3 \times 3, 3 \times 3, 3 \times 3$	37.96/**0.9604**	411738
2	$3 \times 3, 5 \times 5$	37.89/0.9602	418778
2	$5 \times 5, 3 \times 3$	37.92/0.9602	418778

We further experimented to compare the Adam [23] and AdamP [14] in Table 4 and found that AdamP [14] consistently outperforms the Adam[23] optimizer on all of the datasets with a large margin.

Table 4. Performance comparison between Adam [23] and AdamP[14]

Optimizer	Set5 [3] PSNR/SSIM	Set14[43] PSNR/SSIM	B100 [29] PSNR/SSIM	Urban100 [18] PSNR/SSIM
Adam[23]	37.87/0.9601	33.42/0.9165	32.09/0.8987	31.75/0.9245
AdamP[14]	37.97/0.9603	33.49/0.9170	32.14/0.8994	31.96/0.9268

4.2   Comparison with Existing Methods

In this section, we present our quantitatively and qualitatively results and compare their performance with the state-of-the-art methods [2, 5, 7–10, 20, 21, 24, 31, 33, 46, 50] on three up-scaling factors 2×, 3× and 4×. The quantitative results are shown in Table 5. These also include the number of operations (Multi-Adds) and number of parameters to show the model complexity. Multi-Adds are estimated on 720p HR image. The results suggest that our lightweight MAFFSRN model achieves better performance than other methods on multiple datasets and scaling factors. Note that, our lightweight MAFFSRN model shows comparable performance to those models that consume 2× to 3× computing resources.

Table 5. Quantitative comparisons of existing methods on four datasets and three scales 2×, 3×, and 4×. Red/blue/green text: best/second-best/third-best

Scale	Model	Params	Multi-Adds	Set5 PSNR/SSIM	Set14 PSNR/SSIM	B100 PSNR/SSIM	Urban100 PSNR/SSIM
	SRCNN[8]	57K	52.7G	36.66/0.9542	32.42/0.9063	31.36/0.8879	29.50/0.8946
	FSRCNN[9]	12K	6.0G	37.00/0.9558	32.63/0.9088	31.53/0.8920	29.88/0.9020
	VDSR[20]	665K	612.6G	37.53/0.9587	33.03/0.9124	31.90/0.8960	30.76/0.9140
	DRCN[21]	1,774K	17,974.3G	37.63/0.9588	33.04/0.9118	31.85/0.8942	30.75/0.9133
	CNF[31]	337K	311.0G	37.66/0.9590	33.38/0.9136	31.91/0.8962	-
2	LapSRN[24]	813K	29.9G	37.52/0.9590	33.08/0.9130	31.80/0.8950	30.41/0.9100
	DRRN[33]	297K	6,796.9G	37.74/0.9591	33.23/0.9136	32.05/0.8973	31.23/0.9188
	BTSRN[10]	410K	207.7G	37.75/-	33.20/-	32.05/-	31.63/-
	MemNet[33]	677K	2,662.4G	37.78/0.9597	33.28/0.9142	32.08/0.8978	31.31/0.9195
	SelNet [5]	974K	225.7G	37.89/0.9598	33.61/0.9160	32.08/0.8984	-
	FALSR-A[7]	1,021K	234.7G	37.82/0.9595	33.55/0.9168	32.12/0.8987	31.93/0.9256
	FALSR-B[7]	326K	74.7G	37.61/0.9585	33.29/0.9143	31.97/0.8967	31.28/0.9191
	FALSR-C[7]	408K	93.7G	37.66/0.9586	33.26/0.9140	31.96/0.8965	31.24/0.9187
	SRMDNF[46]			37.79/0.9601	33.32/0.9159	32.05/0.8985	31.33/0.9204
	CARN [2]	1,592K	222.8G	37.76/0.9590	33.52/0.9166	32.09/0.8978	31.92/0.9256
	CARN-M [2]	412K	91.2G	37.53/0.9583	33.26/0.9141	31.92/0.8960	31.23/0.9193
	CBPN-S[50]	430K	101.5G	37.69/0.9583	33.36/0.9147	32.02/0.8972	31.55/0.9217
	CBPN[50]	1,036K	240.7G	37.90/0.9590	33.60/0.9171	32.17/0.8989	32.14/0.9279
	MAFFSRN (ours)	402K	77.2G	37.97/0.9603	33.49/0.9170	32.14/0.8994	31.96/0.9268
	MAFFSRN-L (ours)	790K	154.4G	38.07/0.9607	33.59/0.9177	32.23/0.9005	32.38/0.9308
	SRCNN[8]	57K	52.7G	32.75/0.9090	29.28/0.8209	28.41/0.7863	26.24/0.7989
	FSRCNN[9]	12K	5.0G	33.16/0.9140	29.43/0.8242	28.53/0.7910	26.43/0.8080
	VDSR[20]	665K	612.6G	33.66/0.9213	29.77/0.8314	28.82/0.7976	27.14/0.8279
	DRCN[21]	1,774K	17,974.3G	33.82/0.9226	29.76/0.8311	28.80/0.7963	27.15/0.8276
	CNF[31]	337K	311.0G	33.74/0.9226	29.90/0.8322	28.82/0.7980	-
3	DRRN[33]	297K	6,796.9G	34.03/0.9244	29.96/0.8349	28.95/0.8004	27.53/0.8378
	BTSRN[10]	410K	176.2G	34.03/-	29.90/-	28.97/-	27.75/-
	MemNet[34]	677K	2,662.4G	34.09/0.9248	30.00/0.8350	28.96/0.8001	27.56/0.8376
	SelNet[5]	1,159K	120.0G	34.27/0.9257	30.30/0.8399	28.97/0.8025	-
	SRMDNF[46]	-	-	34.12/0.9254	30.04/0.8382	28.97/0.8025	27.57/0.8398
	CARN [2]	1,592K	118.8G	34.29/0.9255	30.29/0.8407	29.06/0.8034	28.06/0.8493
	CARN-M [2]	412K	46.1G	33.99/0.9236	30.08/0.8367	28.91/0.8000	27.55/0.8385
	MAFFSRN (ours)	418K	34.2G	34.32/0.9269	30.35/0.8429	29.09/0.8052	28.13/0.8521
	MAFFSRN-L (ours)	807K	68.5G	34.45/0.9277	30.40/0.8432	29.13/0.8061	28.26/0.8552
	SRCNN[8]	57K	52.7G	30.48/0.8628	27.49/0.7503	26.90/0.7101	24.52/0.7221
	FSRCNN[9]	12K	4.6G	30.71/0.8657	27.59/0.7535	26.98/0.7150	24.62/0.7280
	VDSR[20]	665K	612.6G	31.35/0.8838	28.01/0.7674	27.29/0.7251	25.18/0.7524
	DRCN[21]	1,774K	17,974.3G	31.53/0.8854	28.02/0.7670	27.23/0.7233	25.14/0.7510
	CNF[31]	337K	311.0G	31.55/0.8856	28.15/0.7680	27.32/0.7253	-
	LapSRN[24]	813K	149.4G	31.54/0.8850	28.19/0.7720	27.32/0.7280	25.21/0.7560
4	DRRN[33]	297K	6,796.9G	31.68/0.8888	28.21/0.7720	27.38/0.7284	25.44/0.7638
	BTSRN [10]	410K	165.2G	31.85/-	28.20/-	27.47/-	25.74/-
	MemNet[33]	677K	2,662.4G	31.74/0.8893	28.26/0.7723	27.40/0.7281	25.50/0.7630
	SelNet[5]	1,417K	83.1G	32.00/0.8931	28.49/0.7783	27.44/0.7325	-
	SRDenseNet [36]	2,015K	389.9G	32.02/0.8934	28.50/0.7782	27.53/0.7337	26.05/0.7819
	SRMDNF[46]	-	-	31.96/0.8925	28.35/0.7787	27.49/0.7337	25.68/0.7731
	CARN [2]	1,592K	90.9G	32.13/0.8937	28.60/0.7806	27.58/0.7349	26.07/0.7837
	CARN-M [2]	412K	32.5G	31.92/0.8903	28.42/0.7762	27.44/0.7304	25.62/0.7694
	CBPN-S[50]	592K	63.1G	31.93/0.8908	28.50/0.7785	27.50/0.7324	25.85/0.7772
	CBPN[50]	1,197K	97.9G	32.21/0.8944	28.63/0.7813	27.58/0.7356	26.14/0.7869
	MAFFSRN (ours)	441K	19.3G	32.18/0.8948	28.58/0.7812	27.57/0.7361	26.04/0.7848
	MAFFSRN-L (ours)	830K	38.6G	32.20/0.8953	28.62/0.7822	27.59/0.7370	26.16/0.7887

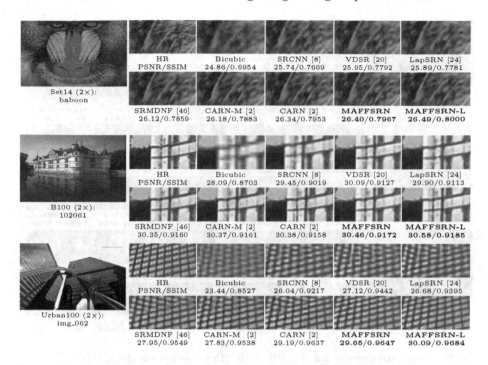

Fig. 5. Visual comparison for 2× SR with other models on Set14, B100, Urban10 dataset. The best results are **highlighted**

Furthermore, to demonstrate the superiority of our model, we compare the performance (PSNR) and computational cost (Multi-Adds) of our models with the existing models in Fig. 1. It is evident from figure that our methods outperform the existing networks in both complexity and PSNR. It is worth to note that our MAFFSRN model even consists of fewer Multi-Adds than SRCNN [8] which is a shallow neural network with 3-layers.

We present our qualitative results in Fig. 5 and Fig. 6. In Fig. 5, it can be seen from output results that the hairs of 'baboon' moustache are accurately reconstructed whereas other methods show blurry results. The similar effects can be seen in other images of Fig. 5 where our methods demonstrate superior results. The results also include PSNR to show the qualitative results. Furthermore, our method continues to show improved results in even larger scale 4×. Overall, our methods have shown improved results as compared to existing methods.

5   AIM2020 Efficient SR Challenge

Our model is developed to participate in the AIM 2020 efficient SR challenge [44]. This competition targets to develop a practicable SR method that can be utilized in a constrained environment. The aim was to maintain the PSNR of MSResNet [39] on DIV2K [35] validation set while decreasing its computational

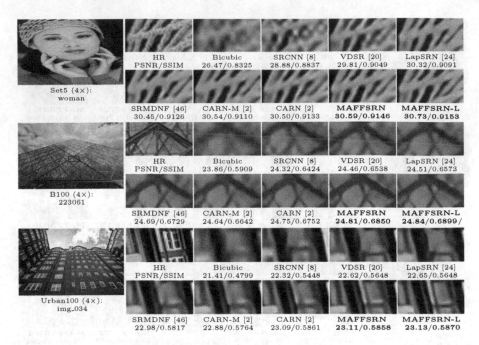

Fig. 6. Visual comparison for 4× SR with other models on Set5, B100, Urban10 dataset. The best results are **highlighted**

Table 6. Performance comparison of each entry in the AIM2020 efficient SR challenge. The number in the parenthesis denotes the rank

Method	Memory [MB]	FLOPs [G]	Parameters [M]
MAFFSRN	112(1)	27.11(3)	0.441(4)
Participant 1	146(2)	30.06(4)	0.461(5)
Participant 2	168(3)	44.98(9)	0.687(11)
Participant 3	200(4)	27.10(2)	0.433(3)
Participant 4	225(5)	49.67(10)	0.777(14)
Participant 5	229(6)	50.85(11)	0.761(13)
Baseline	610	166.36	1.517

cost. We submitted our MAFFSRN model to this challenge and won 1st in Memory computations, 3rd in FLOPs, 4th in number of parameters.

We present the results in Fig. 7 and Table 6. Figure 7 shows the normalized scores on the y-axis and final participants on the x-axis. It also indicates that our proposed MAFFSRN model is a lightweight model among all participants. Similarly, we show the performance of top participants in Table 6 sorted by memory computations. Note that memory computations are tested with Pytorch code *torch.cuda.max_memory_allocated()* and FLOPs are calculated with an input image 256 × 256.

6 Limitation and Future Work

In spite of having reduced computational cost (memory consumption, FLOPs, number of parameters), the runtime of the proposed method on the 100 valida-tion images of DIV2K dataset [35] is 0.104 s per image[1]. The estimated runtime is averaged over 100 images. We assume it is a consequence of more layers in our networks than other efficient architectures. Nevertheless, the proposed method is ultra lightweight, and its memory-efficient modules can assist future researchers in the advancement of efficient SR architectures that have lower runtime and reduced memory consumption.

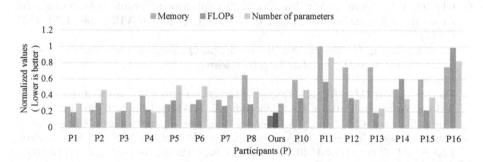

Fig. 7. Computational cost of all participants. Normalized values are shown on the x-axis whereas participants are shown on the y-axis. The results are shown in dark colors (ours) and light colors (other participants)

7 Conclusion

This work introduces a lightweight SR method for a constrained environment called MAFFSRN. We show with the several quantitative and qualitative experi-ments that MAFFSRN outperforms other existing lightweight models in terms of both performance and computational cost. Further, we present ablation studies to show the contributions of each proposed module.

Acknowledgement. This research was supported by Basic Science Research Program through the National Research Foundation of Korea (NRF) funded by the Ministry of Science, ICT & Future Planning (2018R1C1B3008159). Also, this research was a result of a study on the "HPC Support" Project, supported by the 'Ministry of Science and ICT' and NIPA.

---

[1] it is reported in [44].

References

1. Agustsson, E., Timofte, R.: Ntire 2017 challenge on single image super-resolution: Dataset and study. In: Proceedings Computer Vision and Pattern Recognition (CVPR) Workshops, pp. 126–135 (2017)
2. Ahn, N., Kang, B., Sohn, K.A.: Fast, accurate, and lightweight super-resolution with cascading residual network. In: Proceedings European Conference on Computer Vision (ECCV), pp. 252–268 (2018)
3. Bevilacqua, M., Roumy, A., Guillemot, C., Alberi-Morel, M.: Low-complexity single-image super-resolution based on nonnegative neighbor embedding. In: Proceedings British Machine Vision Conference (BMVC), pp. 1–10 (2012)
4. Cai, Y., et al.: Learning delicate local representations for multi-person pose estimation. arXiv preprint arXiv:2003.04030 (2020)
5. Choi, J.S., Kim, M.: A deep convolutional neural network with selection units for super-resolution. In: Proceedings Computer Vision and Pattern Recognition (CVPR) Workshops, pp. 154–160 (2017)
6. Chollet, F.: Xception: deep learning with depthwise separable convolutions. In: Proceedings Computer Vision and Pattern Recognition (CVPR), pp. 1251–1258 (2017)
7. Chu, X., Zhang, B., Ma, H., Xu, R., Li, J., Li, Q.: Fast, accurate and lightweight super-resolution with neural architecture search. arXiv preprint arXiv:1901.07261 (2019)
8. Dong, C., Loy, C.C., He, K., Tang, X.: Image super-resolution using deep convolutional networks. Pattern Anal. Mach. Intell. (PAMI) **38**(2), 295–307 (2015)
9. Dong, C., Loy, C.C., Tang, X.: Accelerating the super-resolution convolutional neural network. In: Leibe, B., Matas, J., Sebe, N., Welling, M. (eds.) ECCV 2016. LNCS, vol. 9906, pp. 391–407. Springer, Cham (2016). https://doi.org/10.1007/978-3-319-46475-6_25
10. Fan, Y., et al.: Balanced two-stage residual networks for image super-resolution. In: Proceedings Computer Vision and Pattern Recognition (CVPR) Workshops, pp. 161–168 (2017)
11. Han, S., Mao, H., Dally, W.J.: Deep compression: compressing deep neural networks with pruning, trained quantization and huffman coding. arXiv preprint arXiv:1510.00149 (2015)
12. Haris, M., Shakhnarovich, G., Ukita, N.: Deep back-projection networks for super-resolution. In: Proceedings Computer Vision and Pattern Recognition (CVPR) (2018)
13. He, K., Zhang, X., Ren, S., Sun, J.: Deep residual learning for image recognition. In: Proceedings Computer Vision and Pattern Recognition (CVPR), pp. 770–778 (2016)
14. Heo, B., et al.: Slowing down the weight norm increase in momentum-based optimizers. arXiv preprint arXiv:2006.08217 (2020)
15. Hinton, G., Vinyals, O., Dean, J.: Distilling the knowledge in a neural network. arXiv preprint arXiv:1503.02531 (2015)
16. Hu, J., Shen, L., Sun, G.: Squeeze-and-excitation networks. In: Proceedings Computer Vision and Pattern Recognition (CVPR), pp. 7132–7141 (2018)
17. Huang, G., Liu, Z., Van Der Maaten, L., Weinberger, K.Q.: Densely connected convolutional networks. In: Proceedings Computer Vision and Pattern Recognition (CVPR), pp. 4700–4708 (2017)

18. Huang, J.B., Singh, A., Ahuja, N.: Single image super-resolution from transformed self-exemplars. In: Proceedings Computer Vision and Pattern Recognition (CVPR), pp. 5197–5206 (2015)
19. Ioffe, S., Szegedy, C.: Batch normalization: accelerating deep network training by reducing internal covariate shift. arXiv preprint arXiv:1502.03167 (2015)
20. Kim, J., Lee, J.K., Lee, K.M.: Accurate image super-resolution using very deep convolutional networks. In: CVPR, June 2016
21. Kim, J., Lee, J.K., Lee, K.M.: Deeply-recursive convolutional network for image super-resolution. In: CVPR, June 2016
22. Kim, J.H., Choi, J.H., Cheon, M., Lee, J.S.: Ram: residual attention module for single image super-resolution. arXiv preprint arXiv:1811.12043 (2018)
23. Kingma, D.P., Ba, J.: Adam: a method for stochastic optimization. arXiv preprint arXiv:1412.6980 (2014)
24. Lai, W.S., Huang, J.B., Ahuja, N., Yang, M.H.: Deep laplacian pyramid networks for fast and accurate super-resolution. In: CVPR (2017)
25. Ledig, C., et al.: Photo-realistic single image super-resolution using a generative adversarial network. In: Proceedings Computer Vision and Pattern Recognition (CVPR), pp. 4681–4690 (2017)
26. Li, J., Fang, F., Mei, K., Zhang, G.: Multi-scale residual network for image super-resolution. In: Proceedings European Conference on Computer Vision (ECCV), pp. 517–532, September 2018
27. Lim, B., Son, S., Kim, H., Nah, S., Lee, K.M.: Enhanced deep residual networks for single image super-resolution. In: Proceedings Computer Vision and Pattern Recognition (CVPR) Workshops, July 2017
28. Liu, J., Zhang, W., Tang, Y., Tang, J., Wu, G.: Residual feature aggregation network for image super-resolution. In: Proceedings Computer Vision and Pattern Recognition (CVPR), pp. 2359–2368 (2020)
29. Martin, D., Fowlkes, C., Tal, D., Malik, J.: A database of human segmented natural images and its application to evaluating segmentation algorithms and measuring ecological statistics. In: Proc. International Conference on Computer Vision (ICCV), vol. 2, pp. 416–423. IEEE (2001)
30. Muqeet, A., Iqbal, M.T.B., Bae, S.H.: Hybrid residual attention network for single image super resolution. arXiv preprint arXiv:1907.05514 (2019)
31. Ren, H., El-Khamy, M., Lee, J.: Image super resolution based on fusing multiple convolution neural networks. In: Proceedings Computer Vision and Pattern Recognition (CVPR) Workshops, pp. 54–61 (2017)
32. Shi, W., et al.: Real-time single image and video super-resolution using an efficient sub-pixel convolutional neural network. In: Proceedings Computer Vision and Pattern Recognition (CVPR), pp. 1874–1883 (2016)
33. Tai, Y., Yang, J., Liu, X.: Image super-resolution via deep recursive residual network. In: Proceedings Computer Vision and Pattern Recognition (CVPR) (2017)
34. Tai, Y., Yang, J., Liu, X., Xu, C.: Memnet: A persistent memory network for image restoration. In: Proceedings International Conference on Computer Vision (ICCV) (2017)
35. Timofte, R., Agustsson, E., Van Gool, L., Yang, M.H., Zhang, L.: Ntire 2017 challenge on single image super-resolution: Methods and results. In: Proceedings Computer Vision and Pattern Recognition (CVPR) Workshops, pp. 114–125 (2017)
36. Tong, T., Li, G., Liu, X., Gao, Q.: Image super-resolution using dense skip connections. In: Proceedings International Conference on Computer Vision (ICCV), pp. 4799–4807 (2017)

37. Urban, G., et al.: Do deep convolutional nets really need to be deep and convolutional? arXiv preprint arXiv:1603.05691 (2016)
38. Wang, C., Li, Z., Shi, J.: Lightweight image super-resolution with adaptive weighted learning network. arXiv preprint arXiv:1904.02358 (2019)
39. Wang, X., et al.: Esrgan: Enhanced super-resolution generative adversarial networks. In: Proceedings European Conference on Computer Vision (ECCV) (2018)
40. Wang, Z., Bovik, A.C., Sheikh, H.R., Simoncelli, E.P., et al.: Image quality assessment: from error visibility to structural similarity. IEEE Trans. Image Process. **13**(4), 600–612 (2004)
41. Woo, S., Park, J., Lee, J.Y., So Kweon, I.: Cbam: convolutional block attention module. In: Proceedings European Conference on Computer Vision (ECCV), pp. 3–19 (2018)
42. Yu, F., Koltun, V., Funkhouser, T.: Dilated residual networks. In: Proceedings Computer Vision and Pattern Recognition (CVPR), pp. 472–480 (2017)
43. Zeyde, R., Elad, M., Protter, M.: On single image scale-up using sparse-representations. In: Boissonnat, J.-D., Chenin, P., Cohen, A., Gout, C., Lyche, T., Mazure, M.-L., Schumaker, L. (eds.) Curves and Surfaces 2010. LNCS, vol. 6920, pp. 711–730. Springer, Heidelberg (2012). https://doi.org/10.1007/978-3-642-27413-8_47
44. Zhang, K., Danelljan, M., Li, Y., Timofte, R., et al.: Aim 2020 challenge on efficient super-resolution: methods and results. In: European Conference on Computer Vision Workshops (2020)
45. Zhang, K., Gool, L.V., Timofte, R.: Deep unfolding network for image super-resolution. In: Proceedings Computer Vision and Pattern Recognition (CVPR), pp. 3217–3226 (2020)
46. Zhang, K., Zuo, W., Zhang, L.: Learning a single convolutional super-resolution network for multiple degradations. In: Proceedings Computer Vision and Pattern Recognition (CVPR), pp. 3262–3271 (2018)
47. Zhang, X., Zhou, X., Lin, M., Sun, J.: Shufflenet: an extremely efficient convolutional neural network for mobile devices. In: Proceedings Computer Vision and Pattern Recognition (CVPR), pp. 6848–6856 (2018)
48. Zhang, Y., Li, K., Li, K., Wang, L., Zhong, B., Fu, Y.: Image super-resolution using very deep residual channel attention networks. In: Proceedings European Conference on Computer Vision (ECCV), pp. 286–301 (2018)
49. Zhang, Y., Tian, Y., Kong, Y., Zhong, B., Fu, Y.: Residual dense network for image super-resolution. In: Proceedings Computer Vision and Pattern Recognition (CVPR) (2018)
50. Zhu, F., Zhao, Q.: Efficient single image super-resolution via hybrid residual feature learning with compact back-projection network. In: Proceedings of the IEEE International Conference on Computer Vision Workshops (2019)

Adaptive Hybrid Composition Based Super-Resolution Network via Fine-Grained Channel Pruning

Siang Chen[1], Kai Huang[1(✉)], Bowen Li[1], Dongliang Xiong[1], Haitian Jiang[1], and Luc Claesen[2]

[1] Zhejiang University, Hangzhou, China
11631032@zju.edu.cn, huangk@zju.edu.cn, 11631033@zju.edu.cn,
xiongdl@zju.edu.cn, jianghaitian@zju.edu.cn
[2] Hasselt University, 3590 Diepenbeek, Belgium
luc.claesen@uhasselt.be

Abstract. In recent years, remarkable progress has been made in single image super-resolution due to the powerful representation capabilities of deep neural networks. However, the superior performance is at the expense of excessive computation costs, limiting the SR application in resource-constrained devices. To address this problem, we firstly propose a hybrid composition block (HCB), which contains asymmetric and shrinked spatial convolution in parallel. Secondly, we build our baseline model based on cascaded HCB with a progressive upsampling method. Besides, feature fusion method is developed which concatenates all of the previous feature maps of HCB. Thirdly, to solve the misalignment problem in pruning residual networks, we propose a fine-grained channel pruning that allows adaptive connections to fully skip the residual block, and any unimportant channel between convolutions can be pruned independently. Finally, we present an adaptive hybrid composition based super-resolution network (AHCSRN) by pruning the baseline model. Extensive experiments demonstrate that the proposed method can achieve better performance than state-of-the-art SR models with ultra-low parameters and Flops.

Keywords: Single image super-resolution · Efficient model · Channel pruning

1 Introduction

Single image super-resolution (SISR) is a classic computer vision task that reconstructs a high-resolution (HR) image from its degraded low-resolution (LR) version. It has broad applications in photo editing, medical imaging and object detection. Although numerous methods have been proposed for SISR [32,34], it is still an active and challenging task as an ill-posed problem.

© Springer Nature Switzerland AG 2020
A. Bartoli and A. Fusiello (Eds.): ECCV 2020 Workshops, LNCS 12537, pp. 119–135, 2020.
https://doi.org/10.1007/978-3-030-67070-2_7

Recently, deep learning based methods have shown superior performance compared with previous example-based methods. After [4] first developed a convolutional neural network (CNN) to establish a mapping between LR and HR images, various networks have been proposed to boost the overall performance of image super-resolution. However, the significant improvement always comes at the expense of a large amount of parameters and high computation cost, which is not suitable to be deployed on resource-limited devices.

To tackle this problem, a natural idea is designing light-weight neural networks [18]. For example, FSRCNN [5] and ESPCN [28] reduce model size by building shallow network models, [2] and [28] utilize squeeze and group operations to construct efficient super-resolution blocks. Another trend is to use recursive operators or parameter sharing strategy, such as DRCN [20], DRRN [30].

In addition to designing efficient networks, compressing pre-trained deep neural networks is also helpful in deriving the optimal architectures. Pruning is an effective method to reduce the redundancy in networks by removing those unimportant individual neurons with negligible performance degradation. While doing this reduces the theoretical size of the model, it does not result in real computation cost or memory footprint reduction unless special hardware and software are designed. Therefore, channel pruning [16,25,38] is proposed to implement real speed up and memory footprint reduction on general hardware (CPU/GPU) by removing the whole filters in networks. While this compression method has shown state-of-the-art accuracy on image classification problems, channel pruning has rarely been investigated for the efficient image super-resolution task. In addition, residual learning has been widely employed by SR models, which ease the task by learning only the residuals between input and output images, and alleviate the vanishing problem as well. However, pruning residual networks is challenging due to the constraints induced by the cross layer connections. Recent works [3,8,39] propose to assign channels connected by skip connections in the same group and prune them simultaneously, while solving the constraint problem, the pruning ratio on these troublesome filters is limited.

In this paper, we firstly propose a hybrid composition based super-resolution neural network (HCSRN). To leverage the efficiency of different kernel size and resolution, we design a hybrid composition block (HCB) which contains asymmetric convolution and shrinked spatial convolution, and then construct HCSRN based on HCB via a progressive upsampling method. Secondly, we take HCSRN as our baseline model and apply pruning on it to further reduce parameters and FLOPs. To solve the constraint that the pruning problem encounters when pruning residual blocks, we propose a novel fine-grained channel pruning strategy that allows any channel to be pruned independently, which breaks the monotonous design constraint in residual neural networks. Finally, we obtain an efficient pruned model called AHCSRN based on adaptive hybrid composition blocks with different weights for asymmetric convolution and shrinked spatial convolution blocks, as well as adaptive local feature fusion connections. Extensive experiments show that the proposed AHCSRN can achieve better performance with ultra-low parameters and FLOPs compared to state-of-the-art methods.

In summary, the main contributions of this paper are as follows:

1) We propose HCSRN for image super-resolution, a basic neural network based on the hybrid composition modules (HCB), thanks to the efficient compositions in hybrid modules, our HSRN achieves high performance on SR task with a modest number of parameters.

2) We propose the adaptive hybrid composition based super-resolution network (AHCSRN) with ultra-low parameters and FLOPs while still keeping high performance. By applying fine-grained channel pruning (FCP) on HCSRN, we not only reduce channels, but also derive adaptive hybrid modules with different weights on asymmetric and shrinked spatial convolutions. Moreover, the proposed FCP avoids the misalignment problem for pruning residual networks, and results in a novel efficient residual architecture.

3) Experimental results show that the proposed lightweight AHCSRN achieves superior performance than the state-of-the-art methods with ultra-low parameters and computation cost.

2   Related Work

2.1   Deep Learning Based Super-Resolution

Convolutional Neural Network (CNN) has shown great success in image super-resolution. [4] firstly employ CNN with tree layers (SRCNN) to learn the SR task, which achieves superior performance than previous example-based methods [6,7,33,35]. After that, various improved algorithms have been proposed. [19] explore a deeper network named VDSR with 20 convolution layers, which show noticeable progress than SRCNN. [24] utilize residual network to ease the training of deep networks and make the neural network go deeper which is denoted as EDSR. RCAN [42] even built an SR network with more than 400 layers with channel attention mechanisms to further improve performance. However, with the networks going deeper, the number of parameters and Flops are also dramatically increasing, which limits the real-world applications on resource-constrained devices. Therefore, there is an urgent need to design light-weight SR networks.

FSRCNN [5] reduces the computation cost of SRCNN by removing the preprocessing bicubic interpolation and upscales the image at the end of the network. DRRN [30], MemNet [31] share parameters through recursive mechanism to avoid introducing new parameters while improving the reconstruction quality. [2] propose a cascading residual network (CARN) to learn the LR-HR mapping more efficiently. Recently, [17] propose a light-weight information multi-distillation network by constructing the cascaded information multi-distillation blocks, which shows a better tradeoff between computation cost and performance. And [36] design an architecture that makes full use of the features by adaptive weighted residual connections.

2.2   Channel Pruning

Model pruning is a predominant approach in learning compressed light-weight neural networks by removing unimportant neurons. Early works [9,10] propose to remove individual weight values, despite the deep compression of parameters, such pruning strategy results in non-structured sparsity in the network, and practical runtime acceleration cannot be achieved unless special custom software and hardware are designed. Therefore recent works focus more on filter pruning (a.k.a. channel pruning) which is a universal technique that can be applied to various types of CNN models, and benefits from inference speedup and memory saving as well. Some leverage heuristic metric to evaluate the importance such as the magnitude of filters [13], the average percentage of zero activations [15], and the geometric median criterion [14]. Some methods add a regularization function such as L_1 [26], Group LASSO [37] to the loss function to induce sparsity. However, due to the cross layer connections in residual neural networks, methods for pruning plain networks such as VGG and AlexNet cannot be applied directly. To address the misalignment problem of feature maps in the shortcut connection, several solutions have been proposed. [12] only prune internal channels layers in residual blocks. [26] place a channel selection layer before the first convolution in each residual block to mask out insignificant channels, and leave the last convolution layer unpruned, which only works for pre-activation networks. [22] use a mixed block connectivity to avoid redundant computation. Recently, [3,8,39] propose to assign the layers connected by pure skip connections into the same group, thus the filters in the same group can be pruned simultaneously. However, although the above methods avoid the misalignment problem, pruning ratios on these troublesome filters are still limited, which results in non-optimal neural network structures.

3 Approach

3.1 Compression Flow

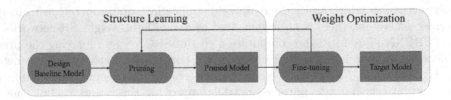

Fig. 1. The overall flow to obtain the light-weight model.

The goal of efficient super-resolution challenge [40] in the 2020 ECCV AIM workshop is to devise a network that reduces one or several aspects such as runtime, parameters, FLOPs, activations, and depth while at least maintaining PSNR of MSRResNet. Directly applying pruning on MSRResNet to reduce model size is not a reasonable choice, because the performance of the pruned model will be lower than the baseline model especially when the pruning ratio is large. Therefore, as shown in Fig. 1 we should firstly design a larger but more efficient baseline model before pruning, then employ the pruning method to compress the model to get a better tradeoff between performance and model size. To reduce the model size as much as possible while keeping the performance higher than MSRResNet during validation, we utilize an iterative pruning and fine-tuning strategy to get the final model.

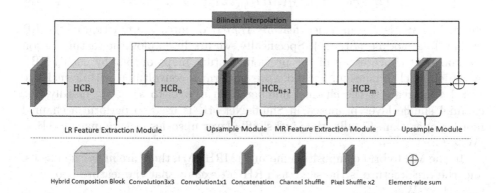

Fig. 2. The architecture of hybrid composition based super-resolution neural network (HCSRN)

3.2 Architecture of HCSRN

In this section, we describe our proposed baseline model, a hybrid composition based super-resolution neural network (HCSRN) in detail. Figure 2 shows the architecture of HCSRN. We employ the progressive upsampling strategy that decomposes the image space in HCSRN into low-resolution (LR, H × W), middle-resolution (MR, 2H × 2W) and high resolution (HR, 4H × 4W), which is divided by two upsampling modules. HCSRN consists of five modules, namely the feature extraction module, the LR hybrid composition module, the first upsampling module, the MR hybrid composition module and the second upsampling module.

The feature extraction module is a convolution layer with kernel size of 3×3, which can be formulated as

$$LHBF_0 = f_{FE}(I_{LR}) \tag{1}$$

where I_{LR} is the input LR image, f_{FE} denotes the feature extraction function, and $LHBF_0$ is the output feature map from the first convolution layer.

In the LR hybrid composition module (LRHCM), there are n numbers of the proposed sequential hybrid composition blocks (HCB), the function can be expressed as

$$LHBF_i = f_{LHB_i}(LHBF_{i-1}) \tag{2}$$

where i is 1,2,...,n, $LHBF_i$ is the output of ith hybrid block, f_{LHB_i} denotes the corresponding function, of which the details will be described in Sect. 3.3.

For the upsampling module, assume the input feature size to be H × W × C, and scaling factor to be s^2, the first upsampling module reshapes the image size to be sH × sW × C.

$$MHBF_0 = f_{LRUM}(LHBF_1, LHBF_2, ..., LHBF_n) \tag{3}$$

where $MHBF_0$ is the upscaled feature, f_{LRUM} denotes the function of the LR upsampling module (LRUM). Specifically, we firstly employ the feature fusion method that concates all of the previous feature maps output by each LHBF in the channel dimension. Secondly, we perform a convoltuion with kernel size 1 × 1 that reduces the channel number from n × C to s^2 × C. Thirdly, the channel shuffle layer proposed in ShuffleNet [41] is used to perform a channel reorder operation. Finally, the pixel shuffle layer upscales feature maps to sH × sW × C.

In the MR hybrid composition module (MRHCM), there are m hybrid blocks, and the architecture is the same as LRHCM except that the feature map is of size sH × sW × C.

$$MHBF_i = f_{MHB_i}(MHBF_{i-1}) \tag{4}$$

where i is 1, 2,...,m.

To further compress the model size, instead of upsampling feature maps and follows a reconstruction module that reshapes the image to the final HR size, our MR upsampling module (MRUM) upscales features of size sH × sW × C to the final HR image size directly. In addition, we apply the global residual learning and bilinear upsampling operator, the output of the HCSRN is the element-wise sum of MRUM's output and the interpolated image.

$$I_{SR} = f_{MRUM}(MHBF_1, MHBF_2, ..., MHBF_m) + f_{Bilinear}(I_{LR}) \tag{5}$$

where f_{MRUM} and $f_{Bilinear}$ are the function of the MR upsampling module and bilinear upsampling operator respectively, and I_{SR} denotes the output of HCSRN.

3.3 Basic Hybrid Block

As depicted in Fig. 3, our hybrid composition block is constructed by three parallel blocks, of which the element-wise sum operation is utilized for local feature fusion. The whole block adopts the residual connection. The main idea of this module is extracting useful features by different efficient blocks.

One of the methods to depress the computation of networks is reducing the kernel size of convolutions. We adopt the same idea as [29] that employ the asymmetric kernel. However, instead of using 5×1 and 1×5 kernels, we aggressively use smaller kernel size that factorizes the normal 3×3 Conv into an 3×1 Conv followed by a 1×3 Conv, thus the parameters and operations decrease

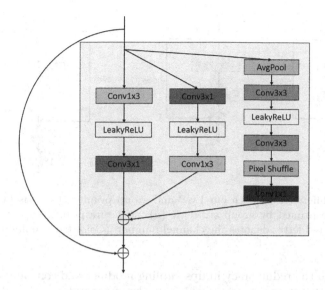

Fig. 3. The architecture of our proposed hybrid composition block (HCB).

dramatically from $O(3^2)$ to $O(2\times3)$. To extract different features without significant performance drop, two asymmetric blocks with inversed kernel orders are utilized.

Another way is reducing the scale of features. Assume the input feature is of size $H \times W \times C$, an average pooling layer with kernel size 2×2 is firstly adopted to shrink the feature from $H \times W \times C$ to $(H/2) \times (W/2) \times C$. Then we use the same sequential Conv-LeakyRuLU-Conv structure to extract features. In order to do element-wise sum operations with the other two parallel blocks, sub-pixel convolution is used for reconstructing the high-resolution image of size $H \times W \times (C/4)$ due to its efficiency. Finally, a convolution with kernel 1×1 is adopted to expand the channel number back to C. While reducing the computation cost, scaling the feature also expands the receptive field to obtain more context information, which is helpful to extract different features for local fusion.

3.4 Fine-Grained Channel Pruning

Although the efficient blocks in HCB provide different features for local fusion, it's hard to determine the weights for these features manually especially when the model size is limited. In addition, which are the most important features that the upsampling module needs remains a question. Therefore, we utilize pruning method to remove those channels that contribute little to the quality of the reconstruction image.

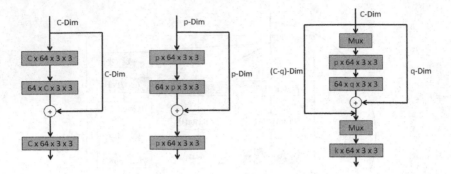

Fig. 4. The difference between our FCP and group pruning. **(a)**: baseline structure. **(b)**: structure pruned by group strategy. **(c)**: structure pruned by our fine-grained strategy. The red letter denotes the channel number. (Color figure online)

We reduce the redundancy in upsampling modules and convolutions in HCB by asserting the gating function, which can be expressed as

$$g(\alpha) = \begin{cases} 0, & IS(\alpha) < T \\ \alpha, & otherwise \end{cases} \qquad (6)$$

where α is a scaling factor that multiplied on each channel, $IS(\alpha)$ denotes the importance score of each channel, T is the global score threshold that depends on the pruning ratio. For the importance criterion, we utilize the algorithm in [27,39] that estimate the change in loss function caused by setting α to zero, which can be easily computed during back-propagation.

The difference between our fine-grained channel pruning strategy and the previous grouping method is shown in Fig. 4. Grouping method assigns the channels connected by the skip connection into a group, and importance scores for channels in the same group are accumulated which makes these troublesome filters harder to be pruned. Instead of only considering the output channel of each convolution, we try to assert the gating function before and after each convolution, and allow each channel to be pruned independently. To avoid the misalignment problem between the convolution and the skip connection, we do not prune the skip connections. Figure 5(a) shows the possible structures pruned by our proposed FCP. For representational simplicity, we only show structures of one path, while the condition is the same for pruning the other two paths and the upsampling module. Note that since there is no difference for pruning channels inner residual blocks between FCP and other methods, these channels are not considered in Fig. 5(a).

1) Only prune the input channel of the first convolution in residual blocks. As shown in Fig. 5(b), channel 0 will totally skip Resblock$_l$, and directly perform the element-wise operation with the output channel of Resblock$_l$.

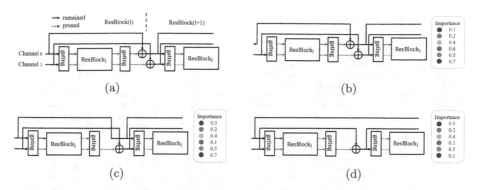

Fig. 5. Illustration of possible architectures pruned and reconstructed by FCP in channel-wise view, the dotted lines denote pruned channels. (**a**): structure before pruning. (**b**): only prune input channel. (**c**): only prune output channel. (**d**): prune both input and output channels

2) Only prune the output channel of the last convolution in residual blocks. As shown in Fig. 5(c), the output channel 0 of Resblock$_l$ is removed, however, we do not prune the input channel 0 of Resblock$_{l+1}$, previous channel 0 will bypass the element-wise operation and become the input of Resblock$_{l+1}$.

3) Prune both input and output channels. Figure 5(d) shows the condition, although the channel 0 between Resblock$_l$ and Resblock$_{l+1}$ is removed, the input channel 0 of Resblock$_l$ will bypass these two blocks and flow into Resblock$_{l+2}$, which leverages the full use of residual information.

4   Experiments

4.1   Datasets and Metric

We use the DIV2K [1] and Flicker2K datasets [32] as our training set, which contains 800 and 2650 high-resolution images respectively. The HR images are cropped into small images with size 480 × 480 and we downscale the HR images using bicubic interpolation to produce LR images. The LR patches with size of 96 × 96 are randomly cropped from LR images as the input of our model. Data augmentation is performed on the training set, such as random rotations of 90°, 180°, 270° and horizontal flips. For evaluation, we use five standard benchmark datasets: Set5, Set14, BSD100, Urban100 and Manga109. We evaluate the performance of the SR images using the peak signal-to-noise ratio(PSNR) and structure similarity index (SSIM). The results are calculated on Y channel of transformed YCbCr space, and the scaling factor is ×4 in all our experiments.

4.2   Implementation Details

Training Baseline Model. In all our experiments, we set the number of LR HCB (n) and MR HCB (m) to be 12 and 4 respectively. The model is trained

Table 1. Quantitative results of evaluated methods for ×4 SR

Method	Params	Flops	Set5 PSNR/SSIM	Set14 PSNR/SSIM	BSD100 PSNR/SSIM	Urban PSNR/SSIM	Manga109 PSNR/SSIM
Bicubic	-	-	28.42/0.8104	26.00/0.7027	25.96/0.6675	23.14/0.6577	24.89/0.7866
D-DBPN [11]	10426K	5925.3G	32.47/0.8980	28.82/0.7860	27.72/0.7400	26.38/0.7946	30.91/0.9137
RCAN [42]	15592K	1042.4	32.63/0.9002	28.87/0.7889	27.77/0.7436	26.82/0.8087	31.22/0.9173
SRCNN [4]	57K	59.9G	30.48/0.8628	27.50/0.7513	26.90/0.7101	24.52/0.7221	27.58/0.8555
FSRCNN [5]	13K	5.2G	30.72/0.8660	27.61/0.7550	26.98/0.7150	24.62/0.7280	27.90/0.8610
VDSR [19]	668K	43.8G	31.35/0.8838	28.01/0.7674	27.29/0.7251	25.18/0.7524	28.83/0.8870
LapSRN [21]	818K	172.3G	31.54/0.8852	28.09/0.7700	27.32/0.7275	25.21/0.7562	29.09/0.8900
DRRN [30]	302K	19.8G	31.68/0.8888	28.21/0.7720	27.38/0.7284	25.44/0.7638	29.45/0.8946
MemNet [31]	677K	709.4G	31.74/0.8893	28.26/0.7723	27.40/0.7281	25.50/0.7630	29.42/0.8942
EDSR [24]	1518K	130.2G	32.09/0.8938	28.58/0.7813	27.57/0.7357	26.04/0.7849	30.35/0.9067
CARN [2]	1592K	103.6G	32.13/0.8937	28.60/0.7806	27.58/0.7349	26.04/0.7838	30.45/0.9073
IMDN [17]	715K	46.7G	32.21/0.8948	28.58/0.7811	27.56/0.7353	26.04/0.7838	30.45/0.9075
MSRResNet	1517K	166.7G	32.19/0.8943	28.64/0.7821	27.58/0.7356	26.12/0.7864	30.49/0.9079
HCSRN (Ours)	2216K	147.2G	32.43/0.8967	28.83/0.7867	27.71/0.7402	26.56/0.7999	31.10/0.9146
AHCSRN1 (Ours)	487K	36.7G	32.24/0.8949	28.70/0.7834	27.62/0.7371	26.23/0.7897	30.72/0.9105
AHCSRN2 (Ours)	354K	27.3G	32.18/0.8942	28.65/0.7824	27.59/0.7360	26.12/0.7860	30.58/0.9087

by L1 loss with cyclic cosine annealing schedule. The restart learning rate is set to 2×10^{-4}, while the minimum learning rate is 10^{-7}. Optimizer is configured as ADAM with $\beta_1 = 0.9$, $\beta_2 = 0.99$. Note that when training with multiple GPUs, we multiply the learning rate and mini-batch size with the number of GPUs. For example, when using 4 GPUs, the restart and minimum learning rate should be modified to 8×10^{-4} and 4×10^{-7}. If not stated otherwise, all the configurations are described in the 4 GPUs condition in the following. The mini-batch is set to 64 and we train 500000 iterations totally with 8 cosine annealing cycles (each cycle 62500 iterations).

Pruning. We employ an iterative pruning and finetuning strategy. The importance scores of channels are estimated every 800 iterations, and 2% of total channels are pruned away each time. After performing 10 times of such pruning, we finetune the model by 8000 iterations to recover the performance with learning rate linearly decreasing from 8×10^{-4} to 4×10^{-7}. When the compression ratio meets the requirement, we finetune the model for another 250000 iterations with 4 cosine annealing cycles, learning rate is set to the same as training baseline model.

4.3   Comparison with State-of-the-arts

Table 1 shows the results of our baseline HCSRN, pruned model AHCSRN and other state-of-the-art SR models. For calculating Flops and parameters, we utilize the open-source tool THOP[1], and input image is of size $1 \times 3 \times 256 \times 256$.

Firstly, we compare our proposed models with the performance-oriented models. Although D-DBPN and RCAN achieve very high performance, the superior PSNR and SSIM are at the expanse of increased network depth and additional blocks, which result in too much computation costs. We notice that our baseline model HCSRN has similar performance with D-DBPN, worse than D-DBPN on Set5 and BSD100 but better on Set14, Urban100 and Manag109, however,

---

[1] https://github.com/youzhonghui/pytorch-OpCounter.

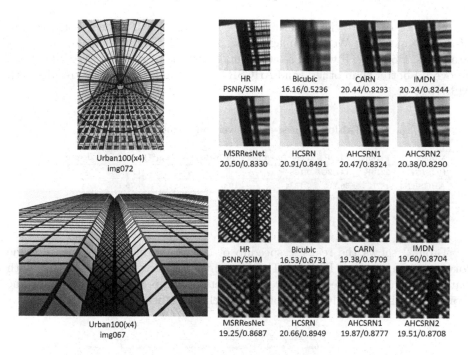

Fig. 6. Visual comparisons of HCSRN/AHCSRN with other SR methods.

the parameters of D-DBPN is nearly 4.7 times of HCSRN, and the Flops is even 40.25 times of HCSRN. Therefore, the quantitative results show that our baseline model HCSRN archives better tradeoff among parameters, Flops and fidelity.

Secondly, we compare our pruned models with other light-weight methods. We show two variants of the pruned model (AHCSRN1 and AHCSRN2) of different pruning ratio. LapSRN also adopts the progressive upsampling strategy, which increases the computation cost in HR image space, therefore LapSRN has fewer parameters but more Flops than MSRResNet. In spite of employing progressive upsampling strategy, AHCSRN eliminates unnecessary computation in HR space by combining efficient blocks and pruning together, thus parameters and Flops of AHCSRN1 are both much less than MSRResNet while the performance is even higher. SRCNN, VDSR, CARN and DRRN have fewer parameters and Flops than MSRResNet, but these lightweight models all sacrifice performance to achieve such computation reduction. IMDN keeps the similar PSNR and SSIM as MSRResNet, and can reduce the parameters and Flops to 715K and 46.7G respectively. Our AHCSRN is even more efficient than IMDN, AHCSRN1 has much higher performance than IMDN with fewer parameters and Flops, the more lightweight version AHCSRN2 performs little worse on Set5, but much better on Other four test datasets than IMDN. These experiment results validate the effect of pruning on HCSRN, and show that AHCSRN is more efficient than other state-of-the-art light-weight SR models.

Then we compare the visual results of HCSRN/AHCSRN with other state-of-the-art methods. We take images '067' and '072' from Urban100 dataset as examples, from Fig. 6 we can see that image details of HCSRN, AHCSRN1 are recovered better than others, and AHCSRN2 has similar qualitative results with MSRResNet.

Table 2. Speed-up analysis on pruned models

Model	Params	FLOPs	Time (ms/img)	Realistic speed-up(%)	Theoretical speed-up(%)
HCSRN	2216K	147.2G	0.1659	–	–
AHCSRN1	487K	36.7G	0.1334	19.6	75.1
AHCSRN2	354K	27.3G	0.1180	28.9	81.5

Table 2 shows the realistic speedup of our prune model. We measure the forward time with one RTX2028Ti GPU on the DIV2K validation dataset with batch size set to 1. The gap between theoretical and realistic models may come from the limitation of IO delay, buffer switch and efficiency of BLAS libraries.

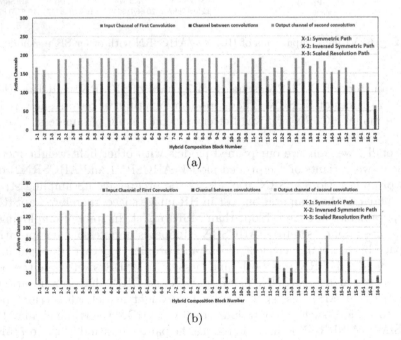

Fig. 7. Channel number allocation of pruned model AHCSRN with parameters of **(a)**: 1503K. **(b)**: 354K.

Figure 7(a) and 7(b) shows the architecture of AHCSRN with 1503K and 534K parameters respectively. Apparently, the three parallel paths in hybrid composition block have different weights in different layers, the shrinked spatial convolution paths always have the smallest channel numbers while the other two paths have similar weights. However, as the pruning ratio goes deeper, we can see that in some layers such as layer 8/10/11 in Fig. 7(b), the channel number in the inversed symmetric path is 0 and the shrinked spatial path is more important. In addition, channel numbers between each residual convolutions are also different, which validates the effectiveness of our proposed FCP.

Table 3. Quantitative results of evaluated methods for x4 SR

Method	Params	FLOPs	Set5 PSNR/SSIM	Set14 PSNR/SSIM	B100 PSNR/SSIM	Manga109 PSNR/SSIM
Bicubic	–	–	28.63/0.8138	26.21/0.7087	26.04/0.6719	25.07/0.7904
EDSR	43090K	2894.5G	32.46/0.8968	28.80/0.7876	27.71/0.7420	31.02/0.9148
MSRResNet	1517K	146.0G	32.22/0.8952	28.63/0.7826	27.59/0.7357	30.48/0.9089
CARN	1592K	90.8G	32.13/0.8937	28.60/0.7806	27.58/0.7349	30.45/0.9073
Li et al. [23]	861K	78.69G	32.03/0.8931	28.54/0.7803	27.53/0.7346	30.23/0.9056
FPGM [14]	859K	83.94G	31.95/0.8917	28.48/0.7790	27.48/0.7332	30.03/0.9033
GBN [39]	863K	75.76G	32.09/0.8944	28.58/0.7815	27.56/0.7356	30.36/0.9075
Ours (60%)	973K	90.29G	32.18/0.8947	28.61/0.7823	27.58/0.7362	30.44/0.9084
Ours (50%)	799K	75.73G	32.15/0.8946	28.58/0.7816	27.57/0.7358	30.40/0.9080

4.4 Ablation Study of FCP

To validate the effect of our proposed fine-grained channel pruning, we compare with other state-of-the-art pruning methods on MSRResNet. Table 3 shows the quantitative results, FCP can reduce more parameters and FLOPs while maintaining higher PSNR and SSIM on all datasets than other approaches. Specifically, we can achieve nearly 64% parameters and 62% computation cost of the baseline MSRResNet with negligible performance drop, and SSIM on dataset BSD100 can be even better than the original model. GBN adopts the same pruning criterion and applies group pruning strategy, but our 50% pruned model has less computation costs while the performance is higher. These results show that our FCP can compress the model size into a smaller one while still keeping high performance (Fig. 8).

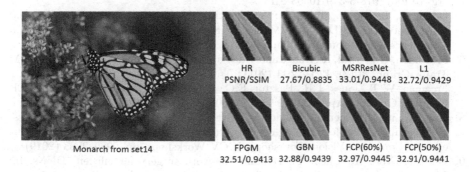

Fig. 8. Visual results of different pruning methods.

5   Conclusions

In summary, we propose an adaptive hybrid composition based super-resolution network called AHCSRN for SISR. We take two steps to design an efficient super-resolution network with the resource constraints: 1) Design a baseline model and 2) Apply channel pruning. To leverage the efficiency of different kernel size and feature scale, we firstly propose a hybrid composition block which contains asymmetric convolution and shrinked spatial convolution blocks. And we construct our baseline model with cascaded hybrid block via a progressive upsampling method. Secondly, we propose a fine-grained channel pruning method to solve the misalignment problem in pruning residual networks, and apply it to our baseline model to get the AHCSRN. Extensive experiments have shown that the proposed method can achieve a better tradeoff between performance and computation costs than state-of-the-art models, and the proposed AHCSRN has the same performance as MSRRResNet with ultra-low parameters and Flops.

Acknowledgement. This work is supported by the National Key R&D Program of China (2020YFB0906000, 2020YFB0906001).

References

1. Agustsson, E., Timofte, R.: Ntire 2017 challenge on single image super-resolution: dataset and study. In: Proceedings of the IEEE Conference on Computer Vision and Pattern Recognition Workshops, pp. 126–135 (2017)
2. Ahn, N., Kang, B., Sohn, K.-A.: Fast, accurate, and lightweight super-resolution with cascading residual network. In: Ferrari, V., Hebert, M., Sminchisescu, C., Weiss, Y. (eds.) ECCV 2018. LNCS, vol. 11214, pp. 256–272. Springer, Cham (2018). https://doi.org/10.1007/978-3-030-01249-6_16
3. Ding, X., Ding, G., Guo, Y., Han, J.: Centripetal SGD for pruning very deep convolutional networks with complicated structure. In: Conference on Computer Vision and Pattern Recognition, CVPR, pp. 4943–4953 (2019)
4. Dong, C., Loy, C.C., He, K., Tang, X.: Learning a deep convolutional network for image super-resolution. In: Fleet, D., Pajdla, T., Schiele, B., Tuytelaars, T. (eds.) ECCV 2014. LNCS, vol. 8692, pp. 184–199. Springer, Cham (2014). https://doi.org/10.1007/978-3-319-10593-2_13
5. Dong, C., Loy, C.C., Tang, X.: Accelerating the super-resolution convolutional neural network. In: Leibe, B., Matas, J., Sebe, N., Welling, M. (eds.) European Conference on Computer Vision, ECCV
6. Freedman, G., Fattal, R.: Image and video upscaling from local self-examples. ACM Trans. Graph. **30**(2), 12:1–12:11 (2011)
7. Freeman, W.T., Jones, T.R., Pasztor, E.C.: Example-based super-resolution. IEEE Comput. Graphics Appl. **22**(2), 56–65 (2002)
8. Gao, S., Liu, X., Chien, L., Zhang, W., Alvarez, J.M.: VACL: variance-aware cross-layer regularization for pruning deep residual networks. In: International Conference on Computer Vision Workshops, ICCV Workshops, pp. 2980–2988 (2019)
9. Guo, Y., Yao, A., Chen, Y.: Dynamic network surgery for efficient DNNs. In: Lee, D.D., Sugiyama, M., von Luxburg, U., Guyon, I., Garnett, R. (eds.) Annual Conference on Neural Information Processing, NeurIPS, pp. 1379–1387 (2016)

10. Han, S., Pool, J., Tran, J., Dally, W.J.: Learning both weights and connections for efficient neural networks. CoRR abs/1506.02626 (2015)
11. Haris, M., Shakhnarovich, G., Ukita, N.: Deep back-projection networks for super-resolution. In: Conference on Computer Vision and Pattern Recognition, CVPR, pp. 1664–1673 (2018)
12. He, K., Zhang, X., Ren, S., Sun, J.: Deep residual learning for image recognition. In: Conference on Computer Vision and Pattern Recognition, CVPR, pp. 770–778 (2016)
13. He, Y., Kang, G., Dong, X., Fu, Y., Yang, Y.: Soft filter pruning for accelerating deep convolutional neural networks. In: Lang, J. (ed.) International Joint Conference on Artificial Intelligence, IJCAI, pp. 2234–2240 (2018)
14. He, Y., Liu, P., Wang, Z., Hu, Z., Yang, Y.: Filter pruning via geometric median for deep convolutional neural networks acceleration. In: Conference on Computer Vision and Pattern Recognition, CVPR, pp. 4340–4349 (2019)
15. Hu, H., Peng, R., Tai, Y., Tang, C.: Network trimming: a data-driven neuron pruning approach towards efficient deep architectures. CoRR abs/1607.03250 (2016)
16. Huang, Q., Zhou, S.K., You, S., Neumann, U.: Learning to prune filters in convolutional neural networks. In: Winter Conference on Applications of Computer Vision, WACV, pp. 709–718 (2018)
17. Hui, Z., Gao, X., Yang, Y., Wang, X.: Lightweight image super-resolution with information multi-distillation network. In: Amsaleg, L., Huet, B., Larson, M.A., Gravier, G., Hung, H., Ngo, C., Ooi, W.T. (eds.) International Conference on Multimedia, MM, pp. 2024–2032 (2019)
18. Ignatov, A., et al.: Pirm challenge on perceptual image enhancement on smartphones: report. In: Proceedings of the European Conference on Computer Vision (ECCV) (2018)
19. Kim, J., Lee, J.K., Lee, K.M.: Accurate image super-resolution using very deep convolutional networks. In: Conference on Computer Vision and Pattern Recognition, CVPR, pp. 1646–1654 (2016)
20. Kim, J., Lee, J.K., Lee, K.M.: Deeply-recursive convolutional network for image super-resolution. In: Conference on Computer Vision and Pattern Recognition, CVPR, pp. 1637–1645 (2016)
21. Lai, W., Huang, J., Ahuja, N., Yang, M.: Deep laplacian pyramid networks for fast and accurate super-resolution. In: Conference on Computer Vision and Pattern Recognition, CVPR, pp. 5835–5843 (2017)
22. Lemaire, C., Achkar, A., Jodoin, P.: Structured pruning of neural networks with budget-aware regularization. In: Conference on Computer Vision and Pattern Recognition, CVPR, pp. 9108–9116 (2019)
23. Li, H., Kadav, A., Durdanovic, I., Samet, H., Graf, H.P.: Pruning filters for efficient convnets. In: International Conference on Learning Representations, ICLR (2017)
24. Lim, B., Son, S., Kim, H., Nah, S., Lee, K.M.: Enhanced deep residual networks for single image super-resolution. In: Conference on Computer Vision and Pattern Recognition Workshops, CVPR Workshops, pp. 1132–1140 (2017)
25. Lin, S., Ji, R., Li, Y., Wu, Y., Huang, F., Zhang, B.: Accelerating convolutional networks via global & dynamic filter pruning. In: Lang, J. (ed.) International Joint Conference on Artificial Intelligence, IJCAI, pp. 2425–2432 (2018)
26. Liu, Z., Li, J., Shen, Z., Huang, G., Yan, S., Zhang, C.: Learning efficient convolutional networks through network slimming. In: International Conference on Computer Vision, ICCV, pp. 2755–2763 (2017)

27. Molchanov, P., Mallya, A., Tyree, S., Frosio, I., Kautz, J.: Importance estimation for neural network pruning. In: Conference on Computer Vision and Pattern Recognition, CVPR, pp. 11264–11272 (2019)
28. Shi, W., et al.: Real-time single image and video super-resolution using an efficient sub-pixel convolutional neural network. In: Conference on Computer Vision and Pattern Recognition, CVPR, pp. 1874–1883 (2016)
29. Szegedy, C., Vanhoucke, V., Ioffe, S., Shlens, J., Wojna, Z.: Rethinking the inception architecture for computer vision. In: Conference on Computer Vision and Pattern Recognition, CVPR, pp. 2818–2826 (2016)
30. Tai, Y., Yang, J., Liu, X.: Image super-resolution via deep recursive residual network. In: Conference on Computer Vision and Pattern Recognition, CVPR, pp. 2790–2798 (2017)
31. Tai, Y., Yang, J., Liu, X., Xu, C.: Memnet: a persistent memory network for image restoration. In: International Conference on Computer Vision, ICCV. pp. 4549–4557 (2017)
32. Timofte, R., Agustsson, E., Van Gool, L., Yang, M.H., Zhang, L., et al.: Ntire 2017 challenge on single image super-resolution: Methods and results. In: The IEEE Conference on Computer Vision and Pattern Recognition (CVPR) Workshops, July 2017
33. Timofte, R., De Smet, V., Van Gool, L.: A+: adjusted anchored neighborhood regression for fast super-resolution. In: Cremers, D., Reid, I., Saito, H., Yang, M.-H. (eds.) ACCV 2014. LNCS, vol. 9006, pp. 111–126. Springer, Cham (2015). https://doi.org/10.1007/978-3-319-16817-3_8
34. Timofte, R., Gu, S., Wu, J., Van Gool, L.: Ntire 2018 challenge on single image super-resolution: Methods and results. In: Proceedings of the IEEE Conference on Computer Vision and Pattern Recognition Workshops, pp. 852–863 (2018)
35. Timofte, R., Smet, V.D., Gool, L.V.: Anchored neighborhood regression for fast example-based super-resolution. In: International Conference on Computer Vision, ICCV, pp. 1920–1927 (2013)
36. Wang, C., Li, Z., Shi, J.: Lightweight image super-resolution with adaptive weighted learning network. CoRR abs/1904.02358 (2019)
37. Wen, W., Wu, C., Wang, Y., Chen, Y., Li, H.: Learning structured sparsity in deep neural networks. In: Lee, D.D., Sugiyama, M., von Luxburg, U., Guyon, I., Garnett, R. (eds.) Annual Conference on Neural Information Processing Systems, NeurIPS, pp. 2074–2082 (2016)
38. Ye, J., Lu, X., Lin, Z., Wang, J.Z.: Rethinking the smaller-norm-less-informative assumption in channel pruning of convolution layers. In: International Conference on Learning Representations, ICLR (2018)
39. You, Z., Yan, K., Ye, J., Ma, M., Wang, P.: Gate decorator: global filter pruning method for accelerating deep convolutional neural networks. In: Wallach, H.M., Larochelle, H., Beygelzimer, A., d'Alché-Buc, F., Fox, E.B., Garnett, R. (eds.) Annual Conference on Neural Information Processing, NeurIPS, pp. 2130–2141 (2019)
40. Zhang, K., Danelljan, M., Li, Y., Timofte, R., et al.: AIM 2020 challenge on efficient super-resolution: methods and results. In: European Conference on Computer Vision Workshops (2020)

41. Zhang, X., Zhou, X., Lin, M., Sun, J.: Shufflenet: an extremely efficient convolutional neural network for mobile devices. In: Conference on Computer Vision and Pattern Recognition, CVPR, pp. 6848–6856 (2018)
42. Zhang, Y., Li, K., Li, K., Wang, L., Zhong, B., Fu, Y.: Image super-resolution using very deep residual channel attention networks. In: Ferrari, V., Hebert, M., Sminchisescu, C., Weiss, Y. (eds.) ECCV 2018. LNCS, vol. 11211, pp. 294–310. Springer, Cham (2018). https://doi.org/10.1007/978-3-030-01234-2_18

IdleSR: Efficient Super-Resolution Network with Multi-scale IdleBlocks

Dongliang Xiong[ID], Kai Huang[(✉) ID], Haitian Jiang[ID], Bowen Li[ID],
Siang Chen[ID], and Xiaowen Jiang[ID]

Zhejiang University, Hangzhou, China
{xiongdl,rockets,jianghaitian,11631033,11631032,xiaowen_jiang}@zju.edu.cn

Abstract. In recent years, deep learning approaches have achieved impressive results in single image super-resolution (SISR). However, most of these models require high computational and memory resources beyond the capability of most mobile and embedded devices. How to significantly reduce the number of operations and parameters while maintaining the performance is a meaningful and challenging problem. To address this problem, we propose an efficient super-resolution network with multi-scale IdleBlocks called IdleSR. Firstly, inspired by information multi-distillation blocks and hybrid composition of IdleBlocks, we construct efficient multi-scale IdleBlocks at the granularity of residual block. Secondly, we replace two 3×3 kernels in residual blocks by a 5×1 kernel and a 1×5 kernel, decreasing parameters and operations dramatically. Thirdly, we use gradient scaling, large input patch size and extra data during training phase to compensate dropped performance. The experiments show that IdleSR can achieve a much better trade-off among parameter, runtime and performance than start-of-the-art methods.

Keywords: Image super-resolution · Compact model · Multi-scale IdleBlock · Gradient scaling

1 Introduction

Single image super-resolution (SISR) aims at reconstructing a visually high-resolution (HR) image given its low-resolution (LR) counterpart. It is inherently ill-posed because any LR input can be degraded from multiple HR images. Ever since the success of SRCNN [7], deep neural networks become the mainstream approaches to learn the complex non-linear mapping between LR and HR image pairs. Thanks to the powerful feature representation capability and end-to-end training paradigm, deep learning approaches can achieve superior performance than traditional interpolation-based and example-based methods.

Earlier deep learning approaches, like SRResNet [22], EDSR [23], RDN [49], RCAN [48], and EBRN [28], focused on training deeper or wider networks

© Springer Nature Switzerland AG 2020
A. Bartoli and A. Fusiello (Eds.): ECCV 2020 Workshops, LNCS 12537, pp. 136–151, 2020.
https://doi.org/10.1007/978-3-030-67070-2_8

to achieve state-of-the-art performance, without considering the increase of parameters and computation complexity. Skip connections (residual or dense) are often used to alleviate gradient vanishing problem. EDSR, the winner of NTIRE2017 [33] competition, has about 43M parameters, 69 layers and 256 filters per layer; RCAN, the deepest SR model, has 16M parameters, up to 415 layers and 64 filters per layer. Due to high requirement of computational and memory resources, these approaches are not suitable for most mobile and embedded devices. The resource-constrained devices demand for lightweight but efficient models that pursue higher SISR performance while constraining available memory and inference time in a certain range.

Model compression techniques [6] are widely used for memory saving and compute acceleration, and can be classified into five categories: 1) compact model; 2) knowledge distillation; 3) tensor decomposition; 4) data quantization and 5) network pruning. However, most existing works for efficient SISR models, like IDN [18], CARN-M [2], IMDN [17], and NoUCSR [38], only focused on the design of compact model, and seldom combined different techniques for the joint-way compression. The simplified version of IMDN won the constrained super-resolution competition of AIM2019 [46]. From the perspective of model compression techniques, there is still large room for improvement in term of SISR model efficiency.

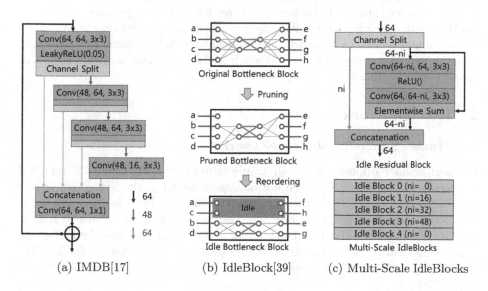

(a) IMDB[17]   (b) IdleBlock[39]   (c) Multi-Scale IdleBlocks

Fig. 1. Architecture of IMDB, IdleBlock and proposed Multi-Scale IdleBlocks

In this paper, we propose an efficient super-resolution network with multi-scale IdleBlocks called IdleSR. Firstly, the structure of multi-scale IdleBlocks is inspired by information multi-distillation block (IMDB) [17] and hybrid composition of IdleBlocks [39]. As shown in Fig. 1(a), IMDB extracts input features by the 3×3 convolution layer, and splits the preceding features into two parts: one is retained as the refined feature, and the other is further processed. The last 1×1 convolution layer aggregates the concatenated refined features. The hierarchical refined features contributes a lot to the efficiency of IMDB. Figure 1(b) shows the architecture of IdleBlock for image recognition, which naturally prunes connections within the block. Xu et al. [39] suggested that leveraging the pruned computation budget from IdleBlock to make the network deeper with hybrid composition is more efficient than various state-of-the-art neural architecture search methods for small models. So we combine the advantages of IMDB and IdleBlock, and propose multi-scale IdleBlocks for efficient super-resolution. Secondly, we replace two 3×3 convolution in multi-scale IdleBlocks by a 1×5 convolution followed by a 5×1 convolution, dramatically reducing the number of parameters and operations. To keep same receptive field with less computation cost, InceptionV3 [31] suggests that any $n \times n$ convolution can be replaced by a $1 \times n$ convolution followed by a $n \times 1$ convolution. Finally, we apply gradient scaling, large input patch size, extra data, and more iterations during training phase to compensate dropped performance. Gradient scaling is originally designed for large batch training [40,41], and successfully applied to quantization-aware training [9]. We find that gradient scaling can improve the performance of SISR models like MSRResNet [35] and IdleSR. Therefore, IdleSR achieves good results in the efficient super-resolution competition of AIM2020[45].

In summary, our contributions are three-fold: (1) We propose multi-scale IdleBlocks that combine the advantages of IMDB and IdleBlock; (2) We apply the asymmetric kernel into residual blocks, which can keep same receptive field with much less parameters; and (3) we introduce gradient scaling method to image super-resolution.

2   Related Work

2.1   Image Super-Resolution Networks

For performance-oriented image super-resolution networks, EDSR[23] removed unnecessary modules (e.g., batch normalization layer) in the SRResNet [22] to improve performance. RDN [49] can extract abundant local features via dense connected convolutional layers and achieve comparable performance to EDSR. Further, Zhang et al. introduced residual in residual structure and channel attention mechanism to train the very deep residual attention network RCAN [48]. EBRN [28] restored information of different frequencies by modules of different complexity.

For efficient image super-resolution networks, Hui et al. developed information distillation network (IDN) [18] and information multi-distillation network (IMDN) [17] for better exploiting hierarchical features. The features in IDN are distilled by only one step, while the features in IMDN are distilled by multiple steps. CARN-M [2] boosted the performance with cascading residual network, and combined the efficient residual block and the recursive network scheme for efficient super-resolution. NoUCSR [38] replaced the parameter- and computation-intensive upsampling convolution by concatenation and channel shuffle. Gu et al. [10] proposed the multi-bin trainable linear unit (MTLU) to increase the non-linear modeling capacity. Ma et al. [25] introduced network binarization approach for SR methods, and binarized the convolution filters in only residual blocks. Yu et al. [43] demonstrated that with same parameters and computational budgets, models with wider features before ReLU activation have significantly better performance for image super-resolution. Song et al. [30] proposed an efficient residual dense block search algorithm for lightweight and accurate super-resolution networks.

2.2 Compact Model

From the perspective of convolution kernels with identical receptive field, the principle of using the 3×3 kernel is widely adopted in modern CNNs. InceptionV3 [31] factorizes an $n \times n$ into an $n \times 1$ convolution followed by a $1 \times n$ convolution, reducing the parameters and operations dramatically from $O(n^2)$ to $O(2n)$. Dilated convolution [42] uses irregular kernels with holes to enlarge receptive field, and can generate multi-scale contextual information by using different dilation factors. Deformable convolution [5] augments the spatial sampling locations of kernels with additional learned task-specific offsets, and greatly enhance the transformation modeling capability. From the perspective of network architecture, the shortcut connection (residual [13] or dense [15]) is an effective and elegant way to address the gradient vanishing problem. Group convolution [37] is often used to alleviate the convolution overhead and depthwise convolution is an extreme case of group convolution. However, simply stacking group convolutions can't fuse information from different channel groups, weakening the network expressive power. Depthwise-separable convolution [4] consists of a depthwise convolution and a pointwise convolution, and can sufficiently decouple spatial and channel correlations. Therefore, depthwise-separable convolution has become a popular component for compact CNNs such as MobileNet [14] and ShuffleNet [47]. Xu et al. [39] combined compact model with network pruning, and developed IdleBlock that naturally prunes connections within the block.

3 Method

3.1 Architecture of IdleSR

In constrained super-resolution competition of AIM2019 [46], NoUCSR [38] achieves a good tradeoff among performance, parameters, and inference runtime. NoUCSR just replaces the computation- and parameter-intensive upsampling convolution layer, and has no modification to residual block. Therefore, we select NoUCSR as the basic architecture of IdleSR, and develop the efficient residual block.

Figure 2 shows the architecture of IdleSR. Let the size of input low-resolution image be $H \times W \times C$. IdleSR employs the progressive upsampling method, and

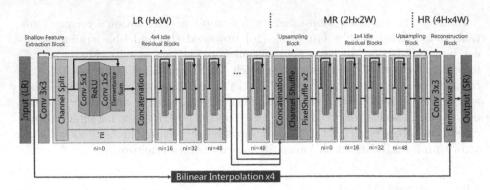

Fig. 2. Architecture of proposed IdleSR.

divides the image space into three stages: LR($H \times W$), MR($2H \times 2W$) and HR($4H \times 4W$). Using progressive upsampling method can boost the performance at the cost of increased computation. Therefore, we should simplify the architecture in MR or HR space as much as possible. IdleSR consists of shallow feature extraction block (SfeBlk), 16 idle residual blocks in LR space (LRResBlk), first upsampling block (UpsBlk1), 4 idle residual blocks in MR space (MRResBlk), second upsampling block (UpsBlk2) and reconstruction block in HR space (RecBlk).

Let's denote I_{LR} and I_{SR} as the input and output of IdleSR. IdleSR employs the global residual learning, and uses the bilinear interpolation to upsample the input image I_{LR}.

$$I_{BI} = f_{Bilinear}(I_{LR}) \tag{1}$$

where $f_{Bilinear}(\cdot)$ denotes the bilinear interpolation and I_{BI} is the upsampled image.

Like RCAN [48], we only use one convolution layer without non-linear activation to extract the shallow feature LF_0 from the input LR image.

$$LR_0 = f_{SFE}(I_{LR}) \tag{2}$$

where $f_{SFE}(\cdot)$ denotes the shallow feature extraction block.

In LRResBlk, there are 4×4 sequential idle residual blocks for deep feature extraction.

$$LF_i = f_{LRB_i}(LF_{i-1}) \tag{3}$$

where i is 1,2,...,16, and $f_{LRB_i}(\cdot)$ denotes the i-th idle residual blocks in LR space.

UpsBlk1 consists of a concatenation layer, a channel shuffle layer and a pixelshuffle [29] layer with scale factor x2. Since UpsBlk1 has no upsampling convolution layer, it needs four deep features with size $H \times W \times C$ in LR space as input and generates an upscaled feature MF_0 with $2H \times 2W \times C$ in MR space.

$$MF_0 = f_{UP1}(LF_4, LF_8, LF_{12}, LF_{16}) \tag{4}$$

where f_{UP1} is the function of UpsBlk1.

To save computation cost, MRResBlk has only 4 sequential idle residual blocks for deep features extraction in MR space.

$$MF_i = f_{MRB_i}(MF_{i-1}) \tag{5}$$

where i is 1,2,3 and 4, and $f_{MRB_i}(\cdot)$ denotes the i-th idle residual blocks in MR space.

UpsBlk2 has a channel shuffle layer and a pixelshuffle layer with scale factor x2.

$$HF_0 = f_{UP2}(MF_4) \tag{6}$$

where f_{UP2} is the function of UpsBlk2, and HF_0 is the upscaled feature in HR space.

RecBlk has only one convolution layer to reconstruct upscale feature HF_0. The output of IdleSR is the elementwise sum of reconstructed residual and the interpolated image.

$$I_{SR} = f_{REC}(MF_4) + I_{BI} = f_{IdleSR}(I_{LR}) \tag{7}$$

where f_{REC} and f_{IdleSR} denotes the function of RecBlk and IdleSR.

IdleSR is optimized with common-used L_1 loss function. Given a training set $\{I_{LR}^i, I_{HR}^i\}_{i=1}^N$ containing N LR-HR pairs, the goal of training IdleSR is to minimize the L_1 loss function

$$L(\theta) = \frac{1}{N} \sum_{i=1}^{N} \|f_{IdleSR}(I_{LR}^i) - I_{HR}^i\|_1, \tag{8}$$

where θ denotes the parameters of IdleSR.

3.2   Multi-scale IdleBlocks

As shown in Fig. 1(c), the input of idle residual block is divided into two parts along the channel dimension: one part is bypassed, and the other part is processed by original residual block. The residual block consists of two convolution layers, a ReLU layer and an elementwise sum layer. The output feature of residual block and the bypassed input feature are concatenated along the channel dimension.

$$OF_{0:ni-1} = IF_{0:ni-1}, \tag{9}$$

$$OF_{ni:nf-1} = IF_{ni:nf-1} + W_2 * \delta(W_1 * IF_{ni:nf-1}) \tag{10}$$

where IF and OF denotes input feature and output feature respectively, W_1 and W_2 denote two convolution layers in residual block, δ means the non-linear activation of ReLU, $i : j$ means that from i-th channel to j-th channel, ni is the number of bypassed channels, and nf is the number of input and output feature channels.

In IdleSR, nf is fixed at 64, while ni is set to $16 \times [(i-1)\%4]$ for the i-th multi-scale IdleBlock. So multi-scale IdleBlocks consist of 4 sequential idle residual blocks with ni increasing from 0 to 48. IMDB [17] extracts input features by the convolution layer and fuses multiple distilled features by a 1×1 convolution layer. While in multi-scale IdleBlocks, hierarchical features are extracted by idle residual block. The idle residual block with $ni = 0$ can fuse multiple distilled features, so there is no need for additional 1×1 convolution layer. Compared to IMDB, multi-scale IdleBlocks can achieve similar performance with lower parameters and faster inference runtime.

Table 1. Comparison of Residual Blocks with Identical Receptive Field

Type	Factorization	Receptive field	Parameters	Normalized
Original	C3 × 3, C3 × 3	5 × 5	18	1
Asymmetric	C1 × 5, C5 × 1	5 × 5	10	0.56

To reduce the parameter further, we introduce the asymmetric kernel into the idle residual block. In Fig. 1(c), the residual block has two convolution layers with kernel 3×3, while in Fig. 2, the residual block consists of a 5×1 convolution layer and a 1×5 convolution layer. The comparison of these two architecture is shown in Table 1. We can find that they have same depth and receptive field. However, the residual block with asymmetric kernels has much less parameters, nearly a half of that in original residual block. The experiments show that the performance drop by using asymmetric kernel is acceptable.

3.3 Gradient Scaling

Gradient scaling is originally designed for large batch training [40][41], and successfully applied to quantization-aware training [9]. You et al. have implemented gradient scaling method into two optimizers: LARS [40] for SGD optimizer, and LAMB [41] for Adam [20] optimizer. We observe that LARS can improve the performance of MSRResNet, but LAMB harms the performance of MSRResNet. The reason is that LARS is designed for large batch training of convolutional networks on ImageNet, while LAMB is designed to accelerate training of attention models like BERT. Image super-resolution is more similar to the former scenario. In this paper, we implement gradient scaling on AdamW [24] optimizer, and get a new optimizer called AdamGS.

As shown in Algorithm 1, the magnitude of original gradient is scaled to the corresponding weight norm and the gradient scaling step is performed before the

---

Algorithm 1. AdamGS: Modified AdamW Optimizer with Gradient Scaling

---

Input: learning rate $\alpha = 0.001$, $\beta_1 = 0.9$, $\beta_2 = 0.999$, $\epsilon = 10^{-8}$, weight decay $\lambda \in \mathbb{R}$
Initialize: time step $t \leftarrow 0$, parameter vector $\theta_{t=0} \in \mathbb{R}^n$, first moment vector
  $m_{t=0} \leftarrow 0$, second moment vector $v_{t=0} \leftarrow 0$, scheduler multiplier $\eta_{t=0} \in \mathbb{R}$
Repeat:
  $t \leftarrow t + 1$
  $g_t \leftarrow \nabla L_t(\theta_{t-1}, Batch_t)$ $\triangleright$ Compute Gradient
  $\hat{g}_t \leftarrow \frac{\|\theta_{t-1}\|}{\|g_t\|} g_t$ $\triangleright$ Gradient Scaling
  $m_t \leftarrow \beta_1 m_{t-1} + (1 - \beta_1)\hat{g}_t$
  $v_t \leftarrow \beta_2 v_{t-1} + (1 - \beta_2)\hat{g}_t^2$
  $\hat{m}_t \leftarrow m_t/(1 - \beta_1^t)$
  $\hat{v}_t \leftarrow v_t/(1 - \beta_2^t)$
  $r_t \leftarrow \hat{m}_t/(\sqrt{\hat{v}_t} + \epsilon)$
  $\eta_t \leftarrow SetScheduleMultiplier(t)$ $\triangleright$ Learning Rate Scheduling
  $\theta_t \leftarrow \theta_{t-1} - \eta_t(\alpha r_t + \lambda\theta_{t-1})$
Until: stopping criterion is met
Return: optimized parameters θ_t

---

update of moment vector. Like LARS, AdamGS has two advantages: 1) it uses a separate learning rate for each layer, and not for each weight, which leads to better stability, and 2) the magnitude of the weight update is controlled with respect to the weight norm for better control of training speed.

4   Experiments

4.1   Datasets and Metrics

The proposed network is trained with DIV2K [1], Flickr2K [23] and OST [34]. DIV2K and Flickr2K contain 800 and 2650 high-quality RGB training images respectively. The HR images are cropped into small images with size $480 \times 480 \times 3$ by step 240, and corresponding LR images are generated by performing a bicubic operation. The input patch with size 64×64 is randomly cropped from small LR images and the batch size is set to 64. For data augmentation, we perform randomly 90 degree rotation, horizontal flip and vertical flip. We use AdamGS with $\beta_1 = 0.9$, $\beta_2 = 0.99$, $\epsilon = 10^{-8}$, and weight decay $\lambda = 0.01$. The learning rate is initialized as 2×10^{-4}, and scheduled by the consine learning rate decay scheduler with restarts. The minimum learning rate is 1×10^{-7} and the restart period is 250K iterations. For all convolution layers, the weights and biases are initialized by He initialization [12] and rescaled by 0.1. The total training time is 2M iterations and the validation is performed every 5K iterations. The performance of SR results is evaluated by two common-used metrics, peak signal-to-noise (PSNR) and structure similarity index (SSIM) [36]. We select the checkpoint with best PSNR on DIV2K validation dataset as the final model. For testing, we use five standard benchmark datasets: Set5 [3], Set14 [44], B100 [26], Urban100 [16] and Manga109 [27]. To compared with previous SR methods, the

SR performance is evaluated with metrics PSNR and SSIM on Y channel of transformed YCbCr space.

4.2 Compare with Start-of-The-Art Methods

We compare proposed IdleSR with Bicubic, baseline MSRResNet and 13 start-of-the-art SR methods: 1) performance-oriented models: SRCNN [7], VDSR [19], MemNet [32], EDSR [23], D-DBPN [11], RCAN [48], and EBRN [28]; and 2) efficiency-oriented models: FSRCNN [8], LapSRN [21], CARN-M [2], CARN [2], IMDN [17], and NoUCSR [38].

Table 2. Quantitative results of evaluated methods for ×4 SR.

Model	Set 5 PSNR/SSIM	Set14 PSNR/SSIM	B100 PSNR/SSIM	Urban100 PSNR/SSIM	Manga109 PSNR/SSIM
Bicubic	28.42/0.8104	26.00/0.7027	25.96/0.6675	23.14/0.6577	24.89/0.7866
SRCNN[7]	30.48/0.8628	27.49/0.7503	26.90/0.7101	24.52/0.7221	27.58/0.8555
VDSR[19]	31.35/0.8838	28.01/0.7674	27.29/0.7251	25.18/0.7524	28.83/0.8870
MemNet[32]	31.74/0.8893	28.26/0.7723	27.40/0.7281	25.50/0.7630	29.42/0.8942
EDSR[23]	32.46/0.8968	28.80/0.7876	27.71/0.7420	26.64/0.8033	31.02/0.9148
D-DBPN[11]	32.47/0.8980	28.82/0.7860	27.72/0.7400	26.38/0.7946	30.91/0.9137
RCAN[48]	32.63/0.9002	28.87/0.7889	27.77/0.7436	26.82/0.8087	31.22/0.9173
EBRN[28]	32.79/0.9032	29.01/0.7903	27.85/0.7464	27.03/0.8114	31.53/0.9198
FSRCNN[8]	30.71/0.8657	27.59/0.7535	26.98/0.7150	24.62/0.7280	27.90/0.8610
LapSRN[21]	31.54/0.8850	28.19/0.7720	27.32/0.7280	25.21/0.7560	29.09/0.8900
CARN-M[2]	31.92/0.8903	28.42/0.7762	27.44/0.7304	25.63/0.7688	29.83/0.8992
CARN[2]	32.13/0.8937	28.60/0.7806	27.58/0.7349	26.07/0.7837	30.45/0.9073
IMDN[17]	32.21/0.8948	28.58/0.7811	27.56/0.7353	26.04/0.7838	30.45/0.9075
NoUCSR[38]	32.15/0.8936	28.64/0.7824	27.57/0.7356	26.15/0.7871	30.57/0.9087
MSRResNet	32.19/0.8943	28.64/0.7821	27.58/0.7356	26.12/0.7864	30.49/0.9079
IdleSR	32.26/0.8962	28.67/0.7836	27.62/0.7374	26.18/0.7885	30.61/0.9101

Quantitative Results. Table 2 shows the PSNR and SSIM scores of evaluated methods for x4 SR. Firstly, EDSR makes a significant breakthrough in term of SR performance among performance-oriented models. After EDSR, nearly all SR models employ the residual block without BatchNormalization layers to boost the performance. Although the baseline MSRResNet and proposed IdleSR have lower performance than EDSR, their performance is still much higher than early models like LapSRN and MemNet. Secondly, large and complex SR models like D-DBPN, RCAN, and EBRN have much better performance than IdleSR, but they usually have large number of parameters and operations. Thirdly, proposed IdleSR has superior performance than all efficiency-oriented models. CARN uses group convolution and depthwise convolution to make residual blocks efficient. IMDN improves representation capability by extracting hierarchical features.

Existing efficiency-oriented models use 3 × 3 kernels by default, while proposed IdleSR uses asymmetric kernels (1 × 5 and 5 × 1) to reduce parameters and operations. Moreover, IdleSR also employs the multi-scale features in the granularity of residual blocks. So IdleSR can achieve better performance with less parameters.

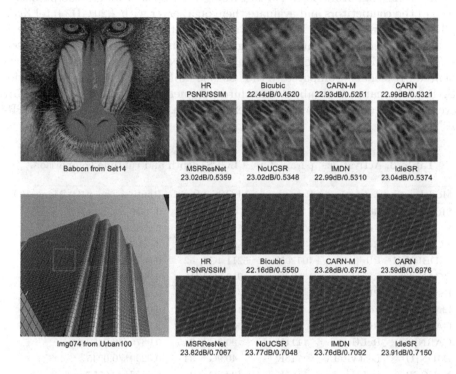

Fig. 3. Qualitative results of evaluated methods for ×4 SR.

Qualitative Results. Figure 3 shows the qualitative results of Bicubic, CARN, MSRResNet, NoUCSR and IdleSR. The two test images are "baboon" from Set14 and "img074" from Urban100. We select a region with high-frequency details to compare. It's clear that all CNN-based SR models have better visual performance than Bicubic. However, It's hard to determine which CNN-based SR model has better visual performance. Higher PSNR and SSIM does not mean higher visual quality.

Other Results. Table 3 shows the activations, parameters, FLOPS, depth, and runtime of evaluated SR methods. For activations, most of evaluated SR models use ReLU as activation function. Parameter ReLU (PReLU) [12] and LeakyReLU can be used to enhance the non-linearity of activations. For parameters and FLOPS, early SR models like SRCNN, VDSR use interpolated low-resolution images as input, leading to high computation cost; while recent SR models use original low-resolution images as input and upscale the intermediate features at the end, reducing FLOPS significantly. EDSR, D-DBPN and RCAN have large number of parameters and FLOPS, not suitable for embedded devices. The network depth here is defined as the number of convolution or deconvolution layers with $m \times n$ kernels, where $m \times n > 1$. Most efficient SR models have the depth in range from 30 to 50. Regarding the runtime, we use the published codes of the competitors and evaluate them on a server with 2.20 GHz Intel Xeon CPU E5-2650 v4, 128 GB RAM and a Nvidia TitanXP GPU card. In table 3, we list the average runtime per image on Urban100 and Manga109 dataset. Performance-oriented SR models have higher average runtime than efficiency-oriented SR models. Compared to the baseline MSRResNet, IdleSR has superior PSNR performance with about one-third parameters and FLOPS, nearly 45% lower average runtime. Therefore, IdleSR is more efficient than baseline MSR-ResNet.

Table 3. Activations, parameters, FLOPS, depth and runtime comparison.

Model	Activations	Parameters	FLOPS	Depth	Runtime urban100/Manga109
SRCNN[7]	ReLU	57K	52.7G	3	0.0226 s/0.0281 s
VDSR[19]	ReLU	665K	612.6G	20	0.1533 s/0.1915 s
EDSR[23]	ReLU	43090K	2894.5G	69	0.5207 s/0.6437 s
D-DBPN[11]	PReLU	10426K	5211.4G	52	0.6629 s/0.8179 s
RCAN[48]	ReLU	15592K	916.8G	415	0.2916 s/0.3416 s
FSRCNN[8]	PReLU	12K	4.6G	8	0.0023 s/0.0026 s
LapSRN[21]	LeakyReLU	814K	149.4G	27	0.0730 s/0.0898 s
CARN-M[2]	ReLU	294K	32.4G	25	0.0320 s/0.0389 s
CARN[2]	ReLU	1111K	90.8G	34	0.0375 s/0.0452 s
IMDN[17]	LeakyReLU	715K	40.9G	34	0.0209 s/0.0245 s
NoUCSR[38]	ReLU	1185K	120.6G	34	0.0456 s/0.0557 s
MSRResNet	ReLU	1517K	146.0G	37	0.0484 s/0.0597 s
IdleSR	ReLU	516K	47.7G	42	0.0280 s/0.0338 s

4.3   Ablation Study

The Benefit of Multi-Scale IdleBlock. Here we compare the efficiency of common-used residual block (ResBlk), information multi-distillation block (IMDB) and multi-scale IdleBlock (MSIB). To make the comparison fair, we use DIV2K as training and validation dataset, select AdamGS as the optimizer and set the LR image patch size to 32. The total training time is 1M iterations and the kernel size is 3×3. Meanwhile, we construct a simple network called CompareSR to compare the efficiency of different residual blocks. The network structure of CompareSR is shown in Fig. 4, the number of filters nf is set to 64, and nb is the number of residual blocks. The type of residual block can be configured as common-used residual block (ResBlk), information multi-distillation block

(IMDB) and multi-scale IdleBlock (MSIB). The number of bypassed channels ni in the i-th multi-scale IdleBlock is set to $(i\%4) \times (nf/4)$, where $i = 0, 1, ..., nb-1$. The number of ResBlk, IMDB and MSIB is set to 16, 8 and 17 respectively.

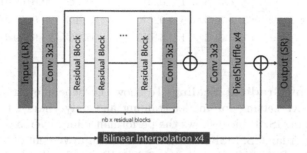

Fig. 4. The network structure of CompareSR.

Table 4 shows the efficiency of three evaluated residual blocks. The PSNR metric is evaluated on the RGB space, and the average runtime per image is for DIV2K validation dataset. CompareSR-IMDB and CompareSR-MSIB have similar amount of parameters and operations, and they also have nearly same PSNR performance. The runtime of CompareSR-MSIB is about 3.5% less than that of Compare-IMDB. This is because MSIB extracts hierarchical features at the granularity of residual block, not convolution layers. Therefore, MSIB has similar efficiency to IMDB.

Table 4. Efficiency comparison of different residual blocks.

Block Type	nb	Kernel Size	Parameters	FLOPS	Depth	DIV2K	
						RunTime	PSNR
ResBlk[23]	16	$3 \times 3, 3 \times 3$	1248K	71.7G	35	0.0738 s	29.0022 dB
IMDB[17]	8	$3 \times 3, 3 \times 3$	893K	51.4G	35	0.0655 s	28.9759 dB
MSIB	17	$3 \times 3, 3 \times 3$	879K	50.5G	37	0.0632 s	28.9746 dB

The Benefit of Asymmetric Kernel Table 5 shows the results when using asymmetric and symmetric kernels on MSRResNet and IdleSR. The asymmetric kernel can provide the same receptive field as the symmetric kernel, and can reduce the amount of parameters and operations by nearly 45%. The performance of MSRResNet and IdleSR drop about 0.0191dB and 0.0462dB respectively. Since IdleSR has low amount of parameters, IdleSR can benefit a lot when replacing asymmetric kernel to symmetric kernel. Compared to reduced model size, the performance drop is still acceptable. Therefore, using assymmetric kernel can improve the efficiency of residual block.

Table 5. The benefit of asymmetric kernel.

Model	Kernel	Parameters	FLOPS	PSNR
MSRResNet	$3 \times 3, 3 \times 3$	1517K	146.0G	29.0352 dB
	$1 \times 5, 5 \times 1$	1034K	118.2G	29.0161 dB
IdleSR	$3 \times 3, 3 \times 3$	925K	85.4G	29.0061 dB
	$1 \times 5, 5 \times 1$	516K	47.7G	28.9599 dB

The Benefit of Gradient Scaling To show the benefit of gradient scaling, we use the above setting for model training and only change the optimizer: AdamW or AdamGS. Table 6 shows the performance improvement when replacing AdamW by AdamGS. MSResNet has a PSNR improvement of 0.0360dB, and IdleSR also has a PSNR improvement of 0.0206dB. The gradient scaling can balance the training speed of each layer by using a separate learning rate for each layer. Our experiments show that gradient scaling is also beneficial to the SR models like MSRResNet and IdleSR.

Table 6. The benefit of gradient scaling.

Model	Optimizer	PSNR	Model	Optimizer	PSNR
MSRResNet	AdamW	28.9992 dB	IdleSR	AdamW	28.9393 dB
	AdamGS	29.0352 dB		AdamGS	28.9599 dB

The Configurations of IdleSR Table 7 shows the results of IdleSR at various configurations. By increasing the total training time from 1M iterations to 2M iterations, the performance of IdleSR is improved from 29.0103dB to 29.0360dB. The LR patch size and extra data have significant influence on performance, improving PSNR by about 0.0504dB. Using gradient scaling also has a PSNR improvement of 0.0206dB. The multi-scale IdleBlock and asymmetric kernel can reduce the amount of parameters dramatically at the cost of acceptable performance drop. The performance drop caused by asymmetric kernel and multi-scale IdleBlock is about 0.0462dB and 0.0632dB respectively. The experiments show that both network architecture and training strategies are important to the network efficiency.

Table 7. The performance of IdleSR with different configurations.

Configurations						Param	PSNR
Block	Kernel	Optimizer	PatchSize	Iterations	Extra Data	(K)	(dB)
MSIB	1 × 5, 5 × 1	AdamGS	64	2M	1	516	29.0360
MSIB	1 × 5, 5 × 1	AdamGS	64	1M	1	516	29.0103
MSIB	1 × 5, 5 × 1	AdamGS	32	1M	0	516	28.9599
MSIB	1 × 5, 5 × 1	AdamW	32	1M	0	516	28.9393
MSIB	3 × 3, 3 × 3	AdamGS	32	1M	0	925	29.0061
ResBlk	3 × 3, 3 × 3	AdamGS	32	1M	0	1479	29.0693

5 Conclusions

In this paper, we propose an efficient network with multi-scale IdleBlocks called IdleSR for single image super-resolution. We construct multi-scale IdleBlocks to extract hierarchical feature step-by-step at the granularity of residual block. To make IdleSR more efficient, we apply asymmetric kernels to residual blocks, reducing the amount of parameters and operations significantly. To compensate the dropped performance, we introduce the gradient scaling trick for large batch training to image super-resolution, and find that gradient scaling is beneficial to SR models like MSRResNet and IdleSR. Numerous experiments have shown that the proposed method achieves a better tradeoff among various factors, including visual quality, the amount of parameters and operations, and inference time.

Acknowledgement. This work is supported by the National Key R&D Program of China (2020YFB0906000, 2020YFB0906001).

References

1. Agustsson, E., Timofte, R.: Ntire 2017 challenge on single image super-resolution: dataset and study. In: CVPR Workshop (2017)
2. Ahn, N., Kang, B., Sohn, K.A.: Fast, accurate, and lightweight super-resolution with cascading residual network. In: ECCV (2018)
3. Bevilacqua, M., Roumy, A., Guilemot, C., Alberi-Morel, M.L.: Low-complexity single-image super-resolution based on nonnegative neighbor embedding. In: BMVC (2012)
4. Chollet, F.: Xception: deep learning with depthwise separable convolutions. In: CVPR (2017)
5. Dai, J., Qi, H., Xiong, Y., Li, Y., Zhang, G., Hu, H., Wei, Y.: Deformable convolutional networks. In: ICCV (2017)
6. Deng, L., Li, G., Han, S., Shi, L., Xie, Y.: Model compression and hardware acceleration for neural networks: a comprehensive survey. Process. IEEE **108**(4), 485–532 (2020)
7. Dong, C., Loy, C.C., He, K., Tang, X.: Learning a deep convolutional network for image super-resolution. In: ECCV (2014)

8. Dong, C., Loy, C.C., Tang, X.: Accelerating the super-resolution convolutional neural network. In: ECCV (2016)
9. Esser, S.K., McKinstry, J.L., Bablani, D., Appuswamy, R., Modha, D.S.: Learned step size quantization. In: ICLR (2020)
10. Gu, S., Li, W., Gool, L.V., Timofte, R.: Fast image restoration with multi-bin trainable linear units. In: ICCV (2019)
11. Haris, M., Shakhnarovich, G., Ukita, N.: Deep back-projection networks for super-resolution. In: CVPR (2018)
12. He, K., Zhang, X., Ren, S., Sun, J.: Delving deep into rectifiers: surpassing human-level performance on imagenet classification. In: ICCV (2015)
13. He, K., Zhang, X., Ren, S., Sun, J.: Deep residual learning for image recognition. In: CVPR (2016)
14. Howard, A.G., et al.: Mobilenets: efficient convolutional neural networks for mobile vision applications. CoRR abs/1704.04861 (2017)
15. Huang, G., Liu, Z., van der Maaten, L., Weinberger, K.Q.: Densely connected convolutional networks. In: CVPR (2017)
16. Huang, J., Singh, A., Ahuja, N.: Single image super-resolution from transformed self-exemplars. In: CVPR (2015)
17. Hui, Z., Gao, X., Yang, Y., Wang, X.: Lightweight image super-resolution with information multi-distillation network. In: ACM MM (2019)
18. Hui, Z., Wang, X., Gao, X.: Fast and accurate single image super-resolution via information distillation network. In: CVPR (2018)
19. Kim, J., Lee, J.K., Lee, K.M.: Accurate image super-resolution using very deep convolutional networks. In: CVPR (2016)
20. Kingma, D.P., Ba, J.L.: Adam: a method for stochastic optimization. In: ICLR (2015)
21. Lai, W., Huang, J., Ahuja, N., Yang, M.H.: Deep laplacian pyramid networks for fast and accurate super-resolution. In: CVPR (2017)
22. Ledig, C., Theis, L., Huszár, F., Caballero, J., Cunningham, A., et al.: Photo-realistic single image super-resolution using a generative adversarial network. In: CVPR (2017)
23. Lim, B., Son, S., Kim, H., Nah, S., Lee, K.M.: Enhanced deep residual networks for single image super-resolution. In: CVPR Workshop (2017)
24. Loshchilov, I., Hutter, F.: Decoupled weight decay regularization. In: ICLR (2019)
25. Ma, Y., Xiong, H., Hu, Z., Ma, L.: Efficient super-resolution using binarized neural network. In: CVPR Workshop (2019)
26. Martin, D.R., Fowlkes, C.C., Tal, D., Malik, J.: A database of human segmented natural images and its application to evaluating segmentation algorithms and measuring ecological statistics. In: ICCV (2001)
27. Matsui, Y., et al.: Sketch-based manga retrieval using manga109 dataset. Multimedia Tools Appl. 76, 21811–21838 (2017)
28. Qiu, Y., Wang, R., Tao, D., Cheng, J.: Embedded block residual network: a recursive restoration model for single-image super-resolution. In: ICCV (2019)
29. Shi, W., et al.: Real-time single image and video super-resolution using an efficient sub-pixel convolutional neural network. In: CVPR (2016)
30. Song, D., Xu, C., Jia, X., Chen, Y., Xu, C., Wang, Y.: Efficient residual dense block search for image super-resolution. In: AAAI (2020)
31. Szegedy, C., Vanhoucke, V., Ioffe, S., Shlens, J.: Rethinking the inception architecture for computer vision. In: CVPR (2016)
32. Tai, Y., Yang, J., Liu, X., Xu, C.: Memnet: a persistent memory network for image restoration. In: ICCV (2017)

33. Timofte, R., Agustsson, E., Gool, L.V., Yang, M.H., Zhang, L., et al.: Ntire 2017 challenge on single image super-resolution: methods and results. In: CVPR Workshop (2017)
34. Wang, X., Yu, K., Dong, C., Loy, C.C.: Recovering realistic texture in image super-resolution by deep spatial feature transform. In: CVPR (2018)
35. Wang, X., et al.: Esrgan: enhanced super-resolution generative adversarial networks. In: ECCV Workshop (2018)
36. Wang, Z., Bovik, A.C., Sheikh, H.R., Simoncelli, E.P.: Image quality assessment: from error visibility to structural similarity. IEEE Trans. Image Process. **13**(4), 600–612 (2004)
37. Xie, S., Girshick, R.B., Dollár, P., Tu, Z., He, K.: Aggregated residual transformations for deep neural networks. In: CVPR (2017)
38. Xiong, D., Huang, K., Chen, S., Li, B., Jiang, H., Xu, W.: Noucsr: efficient super-resolution network without up sampling convolution. In: ICCV Workshop (2019)
39. Xu, B., Tulloch, A., Chen, Y., Yang, X., Qiao, L.: Hybrid composition with idle-block: more efficient networks for image recognition. CoRR abs/1911.080609 (2019)
40. You, Y., Gitman, I., Ginsburg, B.: Large batch training of convolutional networks. CoRR abs/1708.03888 (2017)
41. You, Y., Li, J., Reddi, S., Hseu, J., Kumar, S., Bhojanapalli, S., et al.: Large batch optimization for deep learning: training bert in 76 minutes. In: ICLR (2020)
42. Yu, F., Koltun, V.: Multi-scale context aggregation by dilated convolutions. In: ICLR (2016)
43. Yu, J., Fan, Y., Huang, T.: Wide activation for efficient image and video super-resolution. In: BMVC (2019)
44. Zeyde, R., Elad, M., Protter, M.: On single image scale-up using sparse-representations. In: Curves and Surfaces (2010)
45. Zhang, K., Danelljan, M., Li, Y., Timofte, R., et al.: Aim 2020 challenge on efficient super-resolution: methods and results. In: European Conference on Computer Vision Workshops (2020)
46. Zhang, K., Gu, S., Timofte, R., Hui, Z., Wang, X., et al.: Aim 2019 challenge on constrained super-resolution: methods and results. In: ICCV Workshop (2019)
47. Zhang, X., Zhou, X., Lin, M., Sun, J.: Shufflenet: an extremely efficient convolutional neural network for mobile devices. In: CVPR (2018)
48. Zhang, Y., Li, K., Li, K., Wang, L., Zhong, B., Fu, Y.: Image super-resolution using very deep residual channel attention networks. In: ECCV (2018)
49. Zhang, Y., Tian, Y., Kong, Y., Zhong, B., Fu, Y.: Residual dense network for image super-resolution. In: CVPR (2018)

AIM 2020 Challenge on Learned Image Signal Processing Pipeline

Andrey Ignatov[1]([⊠]), Radu Timofte[1], Zhilu Zhang[2], Ming Liu[2], Haolin Wang[2],
Wangmeng Zuo[2], Jiawei Zhang[3], Ruimao Zhang[3], Zhanglin Peng[3], Sijie Ren[3],
Linhui Dai[4], Xiaohong Liu[4], Chengqi Li[4], Jun Chen[4], Yuichi Ito[5],
Bhavya Vasudeva[6], Puneesh Deora[6], Umapada Pal[6], Zhenyu Guo[7], Yu Zhu[7],
Tian Liang[7], Chenghua Li[7], Cong Leng[7], Zhihong Pan[8], Baopu Li[8],
Byung-Hoon Kim[9], Joonyoung Song[9], Jong Chul Ye[9], JaeHyun Baek[10],
Magauiya Zhussip[11], Yeskendir Koishekenov[12], Hwechul Cho Ye[11], Xin Liu[13],
Xueying Hu[13], Jun Jiang[13], Jinwei Gu[13], Kai Li[14], Pengliang Tan[14],
and Bingxin Hou[15]

[1] Computer Vision Lab, ETH Zurich, Zurich, Switzerland
{andrey,radu.timofte}@vision.ee.ethz.ch
[2] Harbin Institute of Technology, Harbin, China
cszlzhang@outlook.com
[3] SenseTime, Hong Kong, China
[4] McMaster University, Hamilton, Canada
dai15@mcmaster.ca
[5] Vermilion Vision, Abbeville, USA
yito@vermilionvision.net
[6] CVPR Unit, ISI Kolkata, Kolkata, India
bhavyavasudeva10@gmail.com
[7] Nanjing Artificial Intelligence Chip Research, Institute of Automation Chinese
Academy of Sciences (AiRiA), MAICRO, Nanjing, China
guozhenyu2019@ia.ac.cn
[8] Baidu Research, Sunnyvale, USA
zhihongpan@baidu.com
[9] Korea Advanced Institute of Science and Technology (KAIST), Daejeon, Korea
egyptdj@kaist.ac.kr
[10] Amazon Web Services, Seattle, South Korea
[11] ST Unitas AI Research (STAIR), Narashino, South Korea
magauiya173@gmail.com
[12] Allganize, Oakland, USA
[13] SenseBrain, New York City, USA
liuxin@sensebrain.site
[14] Beijing University of Posts and Telecommunications, Beijing, China
492071523@qq.com
[15] Santa Clara University, Santa Clara, USA
houbingxin@gmail.com

A. Ignatov and R. Timofte ({andrey,radu.timofte}@vision.ee.ethz.ch, ETH Zurich) are
the challenge organizers, while the other authors participated in the challenge.
The Appendix A contains the authors' teams and affiliations.
AIM 2020 webpage: https://data.vision.ee.ethz.ch/cvl/aim20/.

Abstract. This paper reviews the second AIM learned ISP challenge and provides the description of the proposed solutions and results. The participating teams were solving a real-world RAW-to-RGB mapping problem, where to goal was to map the original low-quality RAW images captured by the Huawei P20 device to the same photos obtained with the Canon 5D DSLR camera. The considered task embraced a number of complex computer vision subtasks, such as image demosaicing, denoising, white balancing, color and contrast correction, demoireing, etc. The target metric used in this challenge combined fidelity scores (PSNR and SSIM) with solutions' perceptual results measured in a user study. The proposed solutions significantly improved the baseline results, defining the state-of-the-art for practical image signal processing pipeline modeling.

1 Introduction

Recently, the advent of deep learning, end-to-end learning paradigms, adversarial learning and the continuous improvements in memory and computational hardware led to tremendous advances in a number of research fields including computer vision, graphics, and computational photography. Particularly, the image restoration, enhancement and manipulation topics have witnessed an increased interest from the researchers, which resulted in an explosion of works defining and proposing novel solutions to improve different image quality aspects [2–5,11,12,32,39], including its resolution, blur, noise, color rendition, perceptual quality, etc. One of the most important real-world problems is the restoration and enhancement of the low-quality images recorded by compact camera sensors available in portable mobile devices [7,15,18,20,21] that are the prime source of media recordings nowadays. In 2017, the first works were proposed to deal with a comprehensive image enhancement [15,16]. They were followed by a large number of subsequent papers that have significantly improved the baseline results [14,27,34,37,40]. The PIRM challenge on perceptual image enhancement on smartphones [21], the NTIRE 2019 challenge on image enhancement [17] that were working with a diverse DPED dataset [15] and several other

Huawei P20 RAW - Visualized   Huawei P20 ISP   Canon 5D Mark IV

Fig. 1. Example set of images from the collected Zurich RAW to RGB dataset. From left to right: original RAW image visualized with a simple ISP script, RGB image obtained with P20's built-in ISP system, and Canon 5D Mark IV target photo.

NTIRE and AIM challenges were instrumental for producing a large number of efficient solutions and for further development in this field.

The AIM 2020 challenge on learned image signal processing pipeline is a step forward in benchmarking example-based single image enhancement. Same as the first RAW to RGB mapping challenge [19], it is targeted at processing and enhancing RAW photos obtained with small mobile camera sensors. AIM 2020 challenge uses a large-scale Zurich RAW to RGB (ZRR) dataset [24] consisting of RAW photos captured with the Huawei P20 mobile camera and the Canon 5D DSLR, and is taking into account both quantitative and qualitative visual results of the proposed solutions. In the next sections we describe the challenge and the corresponding dataset, present and discuss the results and describe the proposed methods.

This challenge is one of the AIM 2020 associated challenges on: scene relighting and illumination estimation [9], image extreme inpainting [33], learned image signal processing pipeline [22], rendering realistic bokeh [23], real image super-resolution [41], efficient super-resolution [42], video temporal super-resolution [36] and video extreme super-resolution [10].

2   AIM 2020 Challenge on Learned Image Signal Processing Pipeline

One of the biggest challenges in the RAW-to-RGB mapping task is to get high-quality real data that can be used for training deep models. To tackle this problem, we are using a large-scale ZRR dataset [24] dataset consisting of 20 thousand photos that was collected using Huawei P20 smartphone capturing RAW photos and a professional high-end Canon 5D Mark IV camera with Canon EF 24mm f/1.4L fast lens. RAW data was read from P20's 12.3 MP Sony Exmor IMX380 Bayer camera sensor – though this phone has a second 20 MP monochrome camera, it is only used by Huawei's internal ISP system, and the corresponding images cannot be retrieved with any public camera API. The photos were captured in automatic mode, and default settings were used throughout the whole collection procedure. The data was collected over several weeks in a variety of places and in various illumination and weather conditions. An example set of captured images is shown in Fig. 1.

Since the captured RAW–RGB image pairs are not perfectly aligned, we first performed their matching using the same procedure as in [15]. The images were first aligned globally using SIFT keypoints and RANSAC algorithm. Then, smaller patches of size 448×448 were extracted from the preliminary matched images using a non-overlapping sliding window. Two windows were moving in parallel along the two images from each RAW-RGB pair, and the position of the window on DSLR image was additionally adjusted with small shifts and rotations to maximize the cross-correlation between the observed patches. Patches with cross-correlation less than 0.9 were not included into the dataset to avoid large displacements. This procedure resulted in 48043 RAW-RGB image pairs (of size $448 \times 448 \times 1$ and $448 \times 448 \times 3$, respectively) that were later used for training/validation (46.8K) and testing (1.2K) the models. RAW image patches were additionally reshaped into the size of $224 \times 224 \times 4$, where the four channels correspond to the four colors of the RGBG Bayer filer. It should be mentioned that all alignment operations were performed only on RGB DSLR images, therefore RAW photos from Huawei P20 remained unmodified, containing the same values as were obtained from the camera sensor.

2.1 Tracks and Competitions

The challenge consists of the following phases:

i *development:* the participants get access to the data;
ii *validation:* the participants have the opportunity to validate their solutions on the server and compare the results on the validation leaderboard;
iii *test:* the participants submit their final results, models, and factsheets.

All submitted solutions were evaluated based on three measures:

- PSNR measuring fidelity score,
- SSIM, a proxy for perceptual score,
- MOS scores measured in the user study for explicit image quality assessment.

The AIM 2020 learned ISP pipeline challenge consists of two tracks. In the first "Fidelity" track, the target is to obtain an output image with the highest pixel fidelity to the ground truth as measured by PSNR and SSIM metrics. Since SSIM and PSNR scores are not reflecting many aspects of real image quality, in the second, "Perceptual" track, we are evaluating the solutions based on their Mean Opinion Scores (MOS). For this, we conduct a user study evaluating the visual results of all proposed methods. The users were asked to rate the quality of each submitted solution (based on 42 full resolution enhanced test images) by selecting one of five quality levels (5 - comparable image quality, 4 - slightly worse, 3 - notably worse, 2 - poor image quality, 1 - completely corrupted image) for each method result in comparison with the original Canon images. The expressed preferences were averaged per each test image and then per each method to obtain the final MOS.

3   Challenge Results

The Track 1 of the challenge attracted more than 110 registered participants and the Track 2 more than 80. However, only 11 teams provided results in the final phase together with factsheets and codes for reproducibility. Table 1 summarizes the final test phase challenge results in terms of PSNR, SSIM and MOS scores for each submitted solution in the two tracks in addition to self-reported hardware/software configurations and runtimes. Short descriptions of the proposed solutions are provided in Sect. 4, and the team details (contact email, members and affiliations) are listed in Appendix A.

Table 1. AIM 2020 learned ISP pipeline challenge results and final rankings. The results are sorted based on the MOS scores.

Team	Author	Framework	Hardware, GPU	Runtime, s	PSNR↑	SSIM↑	PSNR↑	SSIM↑	MOS↑
			Factsheet Info		Track 1: Fidelity		Track 2: Perceptual		
MW-ISPNet	zhangzhilu	PyTorch	4 × GeForce GTX 1080 Ti	∼1	21.91	0.7842	21.57	0.7770	**4.7**
MacAI	itb202d	PyTorch	2 × GeForce RTX 2080 Ti	0.83	21.86	0.7807	21.86	0.7807	4.5
Vermilion Vision	wataridori2010	TensorFlow	GeForce RTX 2080 Ti	0.062	21.40	0.7834	21.40	0.7834	4.2
Eureka	bhavya_vasudeva	Keras (TF)	4 × GeForce GTX 1080 Ti	0.078	21.18	0.7794	21.18	0.7794	4.1
Airia_CG	mo_ming	PyTorch	8 × Nvidia TITAN Xp	-	**22.26**	**0.7913**	21.01	0.7691	4
Baidu	zhihongp	PyTorch	GeForce GTX 2080 Ti	1.2	21.91	0.7829	**21.91**	0.7829	4
skyb	egyptdj	PyTorch	Nvidia Tesla V100	0.2	21.93	0.7865	21.73	**0.7891**	3.8
STAIR	dark_lim1ess	PyTorch	4 × GeForce GTX 1080	0.59	21.57	0.7846	21.57	0.7846	3.5
Sensebrainer	acehu	PyTorch	4 × Nvidia Tesla V100	0.075	21.14	0.7729	21.14	0.7729	3.2
bupt-mtc206	TheClearwind	PyTorch	GeForce GTX 1080 Ti	0.03	20.19	0.7622	20.19	0.7622	2.4
BingSoda	houbingxin	PyTorch	Nvidia TITAN RTX	0.04	20.14	0.7438	20.14	0.7438	2.2

3.1 Architectures and Main Ideas

All the proposed methods are relying on end-to-end deep learning-based solutions. The majority of submitted models have a multi-scale encoder-decoder architecture and are processing the images at several scales. This allows to introduce global image manipulations and to increase the training speed/decrease GPU RAM consumption as all heavy image processing is done on images of low resolution. Additionally, many challenge participants used channel-attention RCAN [43] modules and various residual connections as well as discrete wavelet transform layers instead of the standard pooling ones to prevent the information loss. The majority of teams were using the MSE, $L1$, SSIM, VGG-based and color-based loss functions, while GAN loss was considered by only one team. Almost all participants are using Adam optimizer [26] to train deep learning models and PyTorch framework to implement and train the networks.

3.2 Performance

Quality. Team Airia_CG achieves the best fidelity with the best PSNR and SSIM scores in Track 1, while team MW-ISPNet is the winner of the Track 2, achieving the best perceptual quality measured by Mean Opinion Scores (MOS) through a user study.

Airia_CG, MW-ISPNet and skyb are the only teams that submitted different solutions to the two tracks. Second to MW-ISPNet's 22.26dB PSNR, there are four teams with similar results in the range of [21.86–21.93]. We also note that there is a good correlation between PSNR/SSIM scores and the perceptual ranking: the poorest perceptual quality is achieved by solutions that have the lowest PSNR and SSIM scores. Notable exceptions are the solutions proposed by Eureka and Airia_CG for track 2 with good perceptual quality but poor PSNR. MacAI provides a solution with a good balance between fidelity (21.86dB PSNR) and perceptual quality (4.5 MOS, second only to MW-ISPNet).

Runtime. The best fidelity and the best perceptual quality winning solutions are also among the more computational demanding in this challenge. MW-ISPNet reports around 1 s per image crop. At the same time, order of magnitude faster solutions rank at the bottom in both tracks.

3.3   Discussion

The AIM 2020 challenge on learned image signal processing (ISP) pipeline promoted a novel direction of research aiming at replacing the current tedious and expensive handcrafted ISP solutions with data-driven learned ones capable to surpass them in terms of image quality. For this purpose, the participants were asked to map the smartphone camera RAW images not to the RGB outputs produced by a commercial handcrafted ISP but to the higher quality images captured with a high-end DSLR camera. The challenge employed the ZRR dataset [24] containing paired and aligned photos captured with the Huawei P20 smartphone and Canon 5D Mark IV DSLR camera. Many of the proposed approaches significantly improved over the original RAW images in perceptual quality in the direction of the DSLR quality target. The challenge through the proposed solutions defines the state-of-the-art for the practical learned ISP *aka* RAW to RGB image mapping task.

4   Challenge Methods and Teams

This section describes solutions submitted by all teams participating in the final stage of the AIM 2020 challenge on learned ISP pipeline.

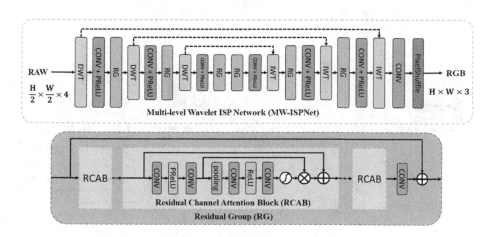

Fig. 2. MW-ISPNet multi-level wavelet network.

4.1   MW-ISPNet

Team MW-ISPNet proposed a U-Net based multi-level wavelet ISP network (MW-ISPNet) illustrated in Fig. 2 that takes advantage of the MWCNN [28] and RCAN [43] architectures. In each U-Net level of this model, a residual group (RG) composed of 20 residual channel attention blocks (RCAB) is embedded. The standard downsampling and upsampling operations are replaced with a discrete wavelet transform based (DWT) decomposition to minimize the information loss in these layers.

The model is trained with a combination of the L_1, SSIM and VGG-based loss functions using the Adam algorithm. In the fidelity track, the authors used an additional MW-ISPNet model trained on the SIDD [1] dataset to perform raw image denoising, which outputs were passed to the main MW-ISPNet model. In the perceptual track, the authors added an adversarial loss following the LSGAN [30] paper to improve the perceptual quality of the produced images. Finally, the authors used a self-ensemble method averaging the eight outputs from the same model that is taking flipped and rotated images as an input.

4.2   MacAI

Team MacAI presented the AWNet model [8] (Fig. 3) utilizing the attention mechanism and wavelet transform and consisting of three blocks: lateral block,

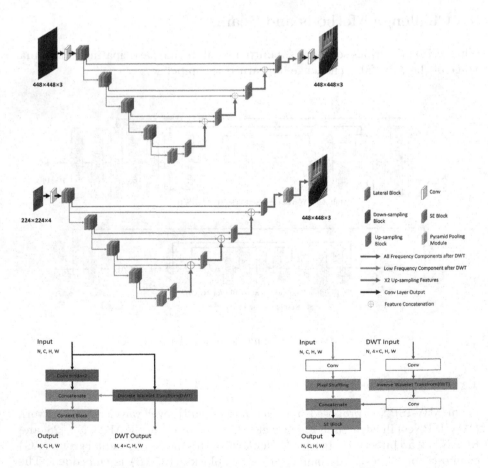

Fig. 3. AWNet model proposed by team MacAI.

upsampling and downsampling blocks. The lateral block consists of several residual dense blocks (RDB) and a global context block (GCB) [6]. Same as the previous team, the authors used the discrete wavelet transform (DWT) instead of the pooling layers to preserve the low-frequency information, though they additionally used the standard downscaling convolutional and pixel shuffle layers in parallel with the DWT layers to get a richer set of learned features. Finally, the authors trained one additional model that is taking a simple demosaiced raw image as an input (instead of the four Bayer channels), and combined the outputs of both models to produce the final image.

The model was trained with a combination of the Charbonnier, SSIM and VGG-based loss functions. The parameters of the model were optimized using the Adam algorithm with the initial learning rate of $1e-4$ halved every 10 epochs. A self-ensemble method averaging the eight outputs from the same model was used.

4.3 Vermilion Vision

Vermilion Vision based their solution on Scale-Recurrent Networks [38]. The architecture of the proposed model is shown in Fig. 4: it consists of 4 scales (though only two scales are shown here), *tanh* activation function is used after the last layer to achieve a better tone-mapping effect. The authors used demosaiced (with a conventional DDFAPD algorithm) images as an input to their model, and the network was trained to minimize the standard MSE loss function. To get the final results, the authors were additionally averaging the outputs of the best 3 models.

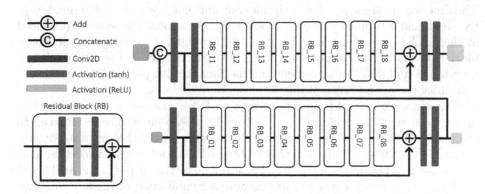

Fig. 4. Vermilion Vision model architecture based on the Scale-recurrent Networks [38].

4.4   Eureka

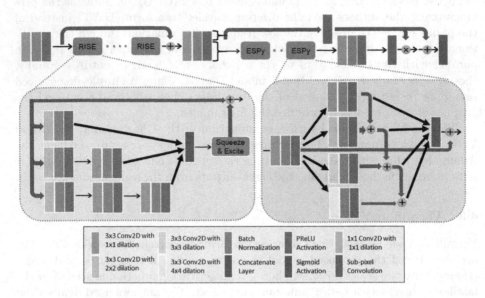

Fig. 5. Network architecture with RISE and ESPy modules proposed by team Eureka.

The solution proposed by Eureka (Fig. 5) is using a residual inception module with squeeze and excite (RISE) module and an efficient spatial pyramid (ESPy) module. The first one has three parallel paths for convolutional layers with different receptive fields and is primarily focused on low-level operations. The features produced in this module are concatenated and passed through a squeeze block and excite block that controls the importance/weight of each channel. The second module is targeted at high-level enhancement and has four parallel paths with dilated convolutional layers and different dilation rates to cover larger image areas.

The output obtained from the sequence of RISE modules is divided into two parts: the first 12 channels are passed through the sub-pixel convolution layer to obtain the RGB channels, and the other channels are passed through the sequence of the ESPy modules. The final output is obtained as a linear regression of the aforementioned RGB channels, which weights are given by the output of the final ESPy module. The network is trained to minimize a combination of the following five losses: the mean absolute error (MAE), color loss (measured as the cosine distance between the RGB vectors), SSIM, VGG-based and exposure fusion [31] loss. The parameters of the model are optimized using the Adam algorithm for 400 epochs.

4.5   Airia_CG

Team Airia_CG used two different approaches in this challenge. In the Perceptual track, it proposed a Progressive U-Net (PU-Net) architecture (Fig. 6, bottom) that is essentially a U-Net model augmented with Contrast-Aware Channel Attention modules [13], switchable normalization layers [29] and pixel shuffle layers for upsampling the images. The authors have additionally cleaned the provided ZRR dataset by removing all blurred photos, and used the obtained image subset for training the model.

In the fidelity track, the authors used an ensemble of six different models: the PU-Net model described above, PyNET [24] and four EEDNets [44] (Fig. 6, top) with slightly different architectures: EEDNetv1 uses simple copy and crop rather than RRDB modules compared to EEDNetv2, and EEDNetv4 adds a contrast-aware channel attention module after the RRDB module. The considered ensemble was able to improve the PSNR on the validation dataset by 0.61dB compared to its best single model.

4.6   Baidu Research Vision

Baidu team based their solution on a mosaic-adaptive dense residual network (Fig. 7). A mosaic stride convolution layer at the beginning of the model is used to extract mosaic-adaptive shallow features. The model is enhanced with

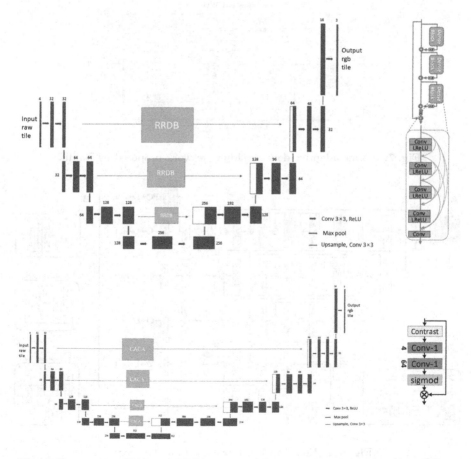

Fig. 6. Progressive U-Net and EEDNetv2 architectures proposed by Airia_CG.

additional channel-attention modules as in RCAN [43]. The network was trained with a combination of the L_1 and SSIM loss functions, a self-assemble strategy was additionally used for generating the final results.

4.7   Skyb

Skyb presented a PyNet-CA model [25] (Fig. 8) that adds several enhancements on top of the standard PyNET [24] architecture. In particular, the authors added RCAN style channel attention [43] on top of the outputs from multi-convolutional layers. Besides that, some instance normalization ops were

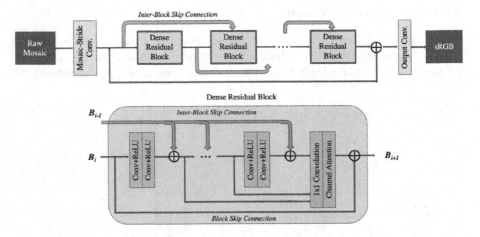

Fig. 7. Mosaic-adaptive dense residual network proposed by Baidu.

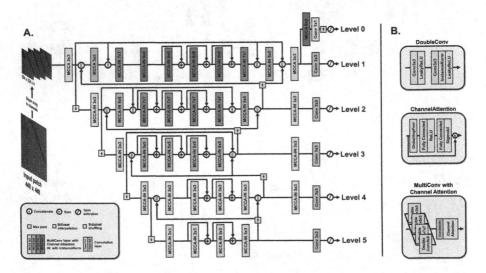

Fig. 8. PyNet-CA model proposed by team Skyb.

removed, an additional multi-convolutional layer was used for upscaling the final image, and a different one-cycle learning rate policy [35] was used for training each level of the model. The network was trained with a combination of the MSE, VGG-based and SSIM loss function taken in different combinations depending on the track and PyNET level, a self-ensemble strategy was additionally applied for producing the final outputs.

4.8   STAIR

STAIR used the RRGNet model presented in Fig. 9 for restoring RGB images. The network utilizes a combination of spatial attention (SA) and channel attention (CA) blocks enhanced with residual connections between CNN modules. The model was trained to minimize L_1 loss, its parameters were optimized using the Adam algorithm for 30 epochs, a self-ensemble strategy was additionally applied for producing the final outputs.

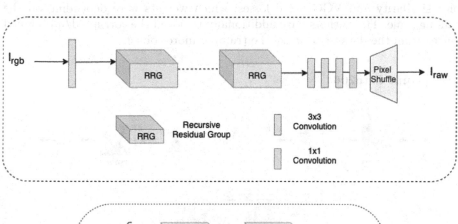

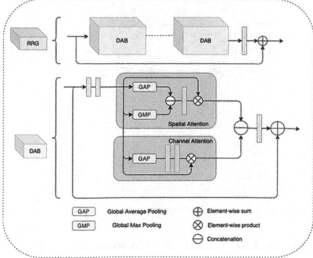

Fig. 9. RRGNet model used by team STAIR.

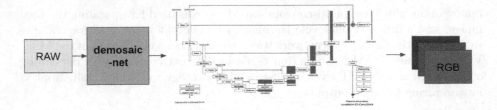

Fig. 10. A Multiscaled U-Net architecture proposed by SenseBrainer.

4.9   SenseBrainer

SenseBrainer proposed a Multiscaled U-Net model displayed in Fig. 10 for the considered task. The authors first processed raw images with the Demosaic-Net to produce RGB images reconstructed without color correction. Multiscaled U-Net was then trained to restore image colors with a combination of the MSE, color similarity and VGG-based losses, which weights were depending on the training scale. The authors have additionally removed the corrupted/misaligned images from the dataset to make the training more robust.

4.10   Bupt-Mtc206

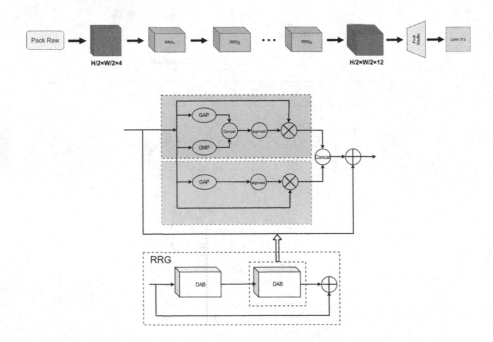

Fig. 11. RRGNet model used by team Bupt-mtc206.

Similarly to team STAIR, the authors tried to apply the RRGNet model (Fig. 11) to the considered problem. Due to a hardware problem, the authors were not able to run their solution on full-resolution images, therefore they had to use the stitching method in their final submission.

4.11 BingSoda

Team BingSoda presented a Pixel-Wise Color Distance (PWCD) model illustrated in Fig. 12. The model was using the LAB color space instead of the RGB one, and was trained to minimize the CIELAB color difference between the predicted and target images.

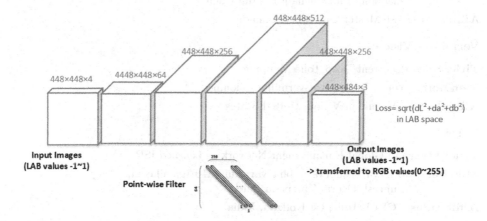

Fig. 12. PWCD model proposed by team BingSoda.

Acknowledgments. We thank the AIM 2020 sponsors: Huawei, MediaTek, Qualcomm, NVIDIA, Google and Computer Vision Lab/ETH Zürich.

A   Appendix 1: Teams and affiliations

AIM 2020 Learned ISP Challenge Team

Title: AIM 2020 Challenge on Learned Image Signal Processing Pipeline

Members: Andrey Ignatov – andrey@vision.ee.ethz.ch,
               Radu Timofte – radu.timofte@vision.ee.ethz.ch

Affiliations: Computer Vision Lab, ETH Zurich, Switzerland

MW-ISPNet

Title: Multi-level Wavelet ISP Network

Members: Zhilu Zhang [1] – cszlzhang@outlook.com,
         Ming Liu [1], Haolin Wang [1], Wangmeng Zuo [1]
         Jiawei Zhang [2], Ruimao Zhang [2], Zhanglin Peng [2], Sijie Ren [2]

Affiliations: [1] – Harbin Institute of Technology, China
         [2] – SenseTime, China

MacAI

Title: Attentive Wavelet Network for Image ISP [8]

Members: Linhui Dai – dail5@mcmaster.ca,
         Xiaohong Liu, Chengqi Li, Jun Chen

Affiliations: McMaster University, Canada

Vermilion Vision

Title: Scale Recurrent Deep Tone Mapping

Members: Yuichi Ito – yito@vermilionvision.net,

Affiliations: Vermilion Vision, United States

Eureka

Title: Local and Global Enhancement Network as Learned ISP

Members: Bhavya Vasudeva – bhavyavasudeva10@gmail.com,
         Puneesh Deora, Umapada Pal

Affiliations: CVPR Unit, ISI Kolkata, India

Airia_CG

Title 1: EEDNet: Enhanced Encoder-Decoder Network

Title 2: PUNet: Progressive U-Net via Contrast-aware Channel Attention

Members: Zhenyu Guo – guozhenyu2019@ia.ac.cn,
         Yu Zhu, Tian Liang, Chenghua Li, Cong Leng

Affiliations: Nanjing Artificial Intelligence Chip Research, Institute of Automation
         Chinese Academy of Sciences (AiRiA), MAICRO, China

Baidu Research Vision

Title: Learned Smartphone ISP using Mosaic-Adaptive Dense Residual Network

Members: Zhihong Pan – zhihongpan@baidu.com,
         Baopu Li

Affiliations: Baidu Research, United States

Skyb

Title: PyNet-CA: Enhanced PyNet with Channel Attention for Mobile ISP

Members: Byung-Hoon Kim [1] – egyptdj@kaist.ac.kr,
         Joonyoung Song [1], Jong Chul Ye [1], JaeHyun Baek [2]

Affiliations: [1] – Korea Advanced Institute of Science and Technology (KAIST),
[2] – Amazon Web Services, South Korea

STAIR

Title: Recursive Residual Group Network for Image Mapping

Members: Magauiya Zhussip [1] – magauiya173@gmail.com,
Yeskendir Koishekenov [2], Hwechul Cho Ye [1]

Affiliations: [1] – ST Unitas AI Research (STAIR), South Korea
[2] – Allganize, South Korea

SenseBrainer

Title: Multiscaled UNet

Members: Xin Liu – liuxin@sensebrain.site,
Xueying Hu, Jun Jiang, Jinwei Gu

Affiliations: SenseBrain, United States

Bupt-mtc206

Title: RRGNet for Smartphone ISP

Members: Kai Li – 492071523@qq.com,
Pengliang Tan

Affiliations: Beijing University of Posts and Telecommunications, China

BingSoda

Title: Pixel-Wise Color Distance (PWCD model)

Members: Bingxin Hou – houbingxin@gmail.com,

Affiliations: Santa Clara University, United States

References

1. Abdelhamed, A., Lin, S., Brown, M.S.: A high-quality denoising dataset for smartphone cameras. In: Proceedings of the IEEE Conference on Computer Vision and Pattern Recognition. pp. 1692–1700 (2018)
2. Abdelhamed, A., Timofte, R., Brown, M.S., et al.: Ntire 2019 challenge on real image denoising: Methods and results. In: The IEEE Conference on Computer Vision and Pattern Recognition (CVPR) Workshops (2019)
3. Ancuti, C.O., Ancuti, C., Timofte, R., et al.: Ntire 2019 challenge on image dehazing: methods and results. In: The IEEE/CVF Conference on Computer Vision and Pattern Recognition (CVPR) Workshops (2019)
4. Blau, Y., Mechrez, R., Timofte, R., Michaeli, T., Zelnik-Manor, L.: The 2018 pirm challenge on perceptual image super-resolution. In: The European Conference on Computer Vision (ECCV) Workshops (2018)
5. Cai, J., Gu, S., Timofte, R., Zhang, L., et al.: Ntire 2019 challenge on real image super-resolution: methods and results. In: The IEEE Conference on Computer Vision and Pattern Recognition (CVPR) Workshops (2019)

6. Cao, Y., Xu, J., Lin, S., Wei, F., Hu, H.: Gcnet: Non-local networks meet squeeze-excitation networks and beyond. In: Proceedings of the IEEE International Conference on Computer Vision Workshops (2019)
7. Chen, Y.S., Wang, Y.C., Kao, M.H., Chuang, Y.Y.: Deep photo enhancer: unpaired learning for image enhancement from photographs with gans. In: The IEEE Conference on Computer Vision and Pattern Recognition (CVPR) (2018)
8. Dai, L., Liu, X., Li, C., Chen, J.: AWNet: attentive wavelet network for image isp. In: European Conference on Computer Vision Workshops (2020)
9. El Helou, M., Zhou, R., Süsstrunk, S., Timofte, R., et al.: AIM 2020: Scene relighting and illumination estimation challenge. In: European Conference on Computer Vision Workshops (2020)
10. Fuoli, D., Huang, Z., Gu, S., Timofte, R., et al.: AIM 2020 challenge on video extreme super-resolution: methods and results. In: European Conference on Computer Vision Workshops (2020)
11. Gu, S., Timofte, R.: A brief review of image denoising algorithms and beyond. In: Escalera, S., Ayache, S., Wan, J., Madadi, M., Guclu, U., Baro, X., (eds.) Inpainting and Denoising Challenges. The Springer Series on Challenges in Machine Learning. Springer, Cham (2019) https://doi.org/10.1007/978-3-030-25614-2_1
12. Gu, S., Timofte, R., Zhang, R., et al.: Ntire 2019 challenge on image colorization: report. In: The IEEE Conference on Computer Vision and Pattern Recognition (CVPR) Workshops (2019)
13. Hui, Z., Gao, X., Yang, Y., Wang, X.: Lightweight image super-resolution with information multi-distillation network. In: Proceedings of the 27th ACM International Conference on Multimedia. pp. 2024–2032 (2019)
14. Hui, Z., Wang, X., Deng, L., Gao, X.: Perception-preserving convolutional networks for image enhancement on smartphones. In: European Conference on Computer Vision Workshops (2018)
15. Ignatov, A., Kobyshev, N., Timofte, R., Vanhoey, K., Van Gool, L.: Dslr-quality photos on mobile devices with deep convolutional networks. In: the IEEE International Conference on Computer Vision (ICCV) (2017)
16. Ignatov, A., Kobyshev, N., Timofte, R., Vanhoey, K., Van Gool, L.: Wespe: weakly supervised photo enhancer for digital cameras. arXiv preprint arXiv:1709.01118 (2017)
17. Ignatov, A., Timofte, R.: Ntire 2019 challenge on image enhancement: methods and results. In: Proceedings of the IEEE Conference on Computer Vision and Pattern Recognition Workshops (2019)
18. Ignatov, A.,et al.: Ai benchmark: Running deep neural networks on android smartphones. In: Proceedings of the European Conference on Computer Vision (ECCV) (2018)
19. Ignatov, A., et al.: Aim 2019 challenge on raw to rgb mapping: Methods and results. In: 2019 IEEE/CVF International Conference on Computer Vision Workshop (ICCVW). pp. 3584–3590. IEEE (2019)
20. Ignatov, A., et al.: Ai benchmark: All about deep learning on smartphones in 2019. In: 2019 IEEE/CVF International Conference on Computer Vision Workshop (ICCVW). pp. 3617–3635. IEEE (2019)
21. Ignatov, A., Timofte, R., et al.: Pirm challenge on perceptual image enhancement on smartphones: Report. In: European Conference on Computer Vision Workshops (2018)
22. Ignatov, A., Timofte, R., et al.: AIM 2020 challenge on learned image signal processing pipeline. In: European Conference on Computer Vision Workshops (2020)

23. Ignatov, A., Timofte, R., et al.: AIM 2020 challenge on rendering realistic bokeh. In: European Conference on Computer Vision Workshops (2020)
24. Ignatov, A., Van Gool, L., Timofte, R.: Replacing mobile camera isp with a single deep learning model. In: Proceedings of the IEEE/CVF Conference on Computer Vision and Pattern Recognition Workshops. pp. 536–537 (2020)
25. Kim, B.H., Song, J., Ye, J.C., Baek, J.: PyNET-CA: enhanced PyNET with channel attention for end-to-end mobile image signal processing. In: European Conference on Computer Vision Workshops (2020)
26. Kingma, D.P., Ba, J.: Adam: A method for stochastic optimization. arXiv preprint arXiv:1412.6980 (2014)
27. Liu, H., Navarrete Michelini, P., Zhu, D.: Deep networks for image to image translation with mux and demux layers. In: European Conference on Computer Vision Workshops (2018)
28. Liu, P., Zhang, H., Zhang, K., Lin, L., Zuo, W.: Multi-level wavelet-cnn for image restoration. In: Proceedings of the IEEE Conference on Computer Vision and Pattern Recognition Workshops. pp. 773–782 (2018)
29. Luo, P., Ren, J., Peng, Z., Zhang, R., Li, J.: Differentiable learning-to-normalize via switchable normalization. arXiv preprint arXiv:1806.10779 (2018)
30. Mao, X., Li, Q., Xie, H., Lau, R.Y., Wang, Z., Paul Smolley, S.: Least squares generative adversarial networks. In: Proceedings of the IEEE International Conference on Computer Vision. pp. 2794–2802 (2017)
31. Mertens, T., Kautz, J., Van Reeth, F.: Exposure fusion: A simple and practical alternative to high dynamic range photography. In: Computer graphics forum. vol. 28, pp. 161–171. Wiley Online Library (2009)
32. Nah, S., et al.: Ntire 2019 challenge on video deblurring and super-resolution: dataset and study. In: The IEEE Conference on Computer Vision and Pattern Recognition (CVPR) Workshops (2019)
33. Ntavelis, E., Romero, A., Bigdeli, S.A., Timofte, R., et al.: AIM 2020 challenge on image extreme inpainting. In: European Conference on Computer Vision Workshops (2020)
34. Pengfei, Z., et al.: Range scaling global u-net for perceptual image enhancement on mobile devices. In: European Conference on Computer Vision Workshops (2018)
35. Smith, L.N., Topin, N.: Super-convergence: Very fast training of neural networks using large learning rates. In: Artificial Intelligence and Machine Learning for Multi-Domain Operations Applications. vol. 11006, p. 1100612. International Society for Optics and Photonics (2019)
36. Son, S., Lee, J., Nah, S., Timofte, R., Lee, K.M., et al.: AIM 2020 challenge on video temporal super-resolution. In: European Conference on Computer Vision Workshops (2020)
37. de Stoutz, E., Ignatov, A., Kobyshev, N., Timofte, R., Van Gool, L.: Fast perceptual image enhancement. In: European Conference on Computer Vision Workshops (2018)
38. Tao, X., Gao, H., Shen, X., Wang, J., Jia, J.: Scale-recurrent network for deep image deblurring. In: Proceedings of the IEEE Conference on Computer Vision and Pattern Recognition. pp. 8174–8182 (2018)
39. Timofte, R., Gu, S., Wu, J., Van Gool, L.: Ntire 2018 challenge on single image super-resolution: Methods and results. In: The IEEE Conference on Computer Vision and Pattern Recognition (CVPR) Workshops (2018)
40. Van Vu, T., Van Nguyen, C., Pham, T.X., Liu, T.M., Youu, C.D.: Fast and efficient image quality enhancement via desubpixel convolutional neural networks. In: European Conference on Computer Vision Workshops (2018)

41. Wei, P., Lu, H., Timofte, R., Lin, L., Zuo, W., et al.: AIM 2020 challenge on real image super-resolution. In: European Conference on Computer Vision Workshops (2020)
42. Zhang, K., Danelljan, M., Li, Y., Timofte, R., et al.: AIM 2020 challenge on efficient super-resolution: Methods and results. In: European Conference on Computer Vision Workshops (2020)
43. Zhang, Y., Li, K., Li, K., Wang, L., Zhong, B., Fu, Y.: Image super-resolution using very deep residual channel attention networks. In: Proceedings of the European Conference on Computer Vision (ECCV). pp. 286–301 (2018)
44. Zhu, Y., et al.: EEDNet: enhanced encoder-decoder network for autoisp. In: European Conference on Computer Vision Workshops (2020)

EEDNet: Enhanced Encoder-Decoder Network for AutoISP

Yu Zhu[1], Zhenyu Guo[2,3], Tian Liang[2,3], Xiangyu He[2], Chenghua Li[2,4(✉)],
Cong Leng[2,4], Bo Jiang[1], Yifan Zhang[2,4], and Jian Cheng[2,4(✉)]

[1] School of Computer Science and Technology, Anhui University, Hefei 230601, China
zhuyu.cv@gmail.com
[2] Institute of Automation, Chinese Academy of Sciences, Beijing 100190, China
{xiangyu.he,jcheng}@nlpr.ia.ac.cn,
lichenghua2014@ia.ac.cn
[3] School of Artificial Intelligence, University of Chinese Academy of Sciences,
Beijing 100049, China
[4] Nanjing Artificial Intelligence Chip Research, Institute of Automation,
Chinese Academy of Sciences (AiRiA), Nanjing, China

Abstract. Image Signal Processor (ISP) plays a core rule in camera systems. However, ISP tuning is highly complicated and requires professional skills and advanced imaging experiences. To skip the painful ISP tuning process, we introduce EEDNet in this paper, which directly transforms an image in the raw space to an image in the sRGB space (RAW-to-RGB). Data-driven RAW-to-RGB mapping is a grand new low-level vision task. In this work, we propose a hypothesis of the receptive field that large receptive field (LRF) is essential in high-level computer vision tasks, but not crucial in low-level pixel-to-pixel tasks. Besides, we present a ClipL1 loss, which simultaneously considers easy examples and outliers during the optimization process. Benefiting from the LRF hypothesis and ClipL1 loss, EEDNet can generate high-quality pictures with more details. Our method achieves promising results on Zurich RAW2RGB (ZRR) dataset and won the first place in AIM2020 ISP challenging.

Keywords: ISP · RAW-to-RGB · LRF hypothesis · ClipL1

1 Introduction

Image Signal Processor (ISP) is a specialized digital signal processor for reconstructing RGB images from raw Bayer images. In conventional camera pipelines, whether smartphones or DSLR cameras, complex and confidential hardware processes are employed to perform image signal processing. Meanwhile, ISP tuning is highly complicated where professional skills and advanced imaging experiences are indispensable. It consists of various processing steps including denoising, white balancing, exposure correction, demosaicing, colour transform, gamma

---

Y. Zhu, Z. Guo, T. Liang, X. He—Equal Contribution

encoding and so on. While every step with independent task-specific loss function in conventional ISP is performed sequentially, residual error accumulates at the same time [17]. To correct these stepwise accumulated errors, tedious parameter tuning process should be employed at the later stages.

More concretely, many of the conventional methods use hand-crafted heuristics-based approaches to derive the solution at each step in the image signal processor pipeline, thus leaving oceans of parameters to be tuned in corresponding to complicated and volatile environments in the real world. Besides, the sequentially performed various ISP process using modular-based algorithms will result in cumulative errors at every step. A small change in parameter configuration may lead to different reconstructed RGB images.

Meanwhile, smartphones have gradually become a part of daily life. High-quality photos, along with the continuous improvement of mobile phone cameras, have gone from the privilege of professional camera to something that ordinary people can easily access. Heavy image signal processing systems are embedded in phones, promoting the quality of photos. However, due to the limited hardware resources of mobile cameras, there may always be a big gap between phone and professional cameras. How to make the picture quality of the mobile phone camera as close as possible to the professional one has become our concern. It's known that a well adjusted ISP can bring competitive quality to the images taken by smartphones. Nevertheless, the design of ISP and the adjustment of internal module parameters are not very simple. For camera or smartphone manufacturers, ISP is regarded as a core competency. In light of this, we conduct EEDNet to evade the painful ISP tuning process and narrow the gaps between various smartphone cameras generated by different ISP pipelines. EEDNet uses a unified loss function to optimize the entire processing involved in an ISP pipeline in an end-to-end optimization setting.

Each module in traditional ISP can neither control the output of other modules nor recover the signal loss of previous modules. The idea that using a convolutional neural network (CNN) to replace the hardware-based ISP is supported by the fact that CNN can compensate for the information loss of input images, which is more reliable than the traditional ISP, and can effectively break through the hardware limitation. Andrey et al. [9] pioneered the application of CNN to replace the camera ISP of smartphones and proposed the RAW-to-RGB dataset with PyNET network.

In this paper, we show that deep neural networks with Large Receptive Fields (LRF) are not required in this task. In contrast to the popular design in object detection [12,18] and semantic segmentation [4], which emphasize semantic information, we assume that low-level image processing tasks such as RAW-to-RGB could pay more attention to local structures. To further verify our hypothesis, we conduct extended experiments on SIDD+ [1]. The results show that U-Net [19] without LRF can also obtain promising results.

Our main contributions can be summarized as follows:

- We prove that the RAW-to-RGB task does not require LRF in the encoder-decoder structure. Furthermore, we verify our hypothesis on the SIDD+ task.

- We propose ClipL1 loss, which eliminates the effect of easy examples and outliers during training.
- We present EEDNet with a desirable receptive filed configuration, which outperforms PyNET.

2 Related Work

In this section, we briefly review and discuss the work about image signal processing in two parts, i.e., convolution neural network for low-level vision tasks and previous works using deep learning techniques to learn the ISP pipeline.

2.1 CNN for Low-Level Vision

During the recent years, the deep learning techniques have been widely used in low-level vision tasks, including removing moire patterns [20,25], denoising [26,27], super-resolution [6,23], high dynamic range expansion [14,24], deblur [15,21] and bokeh [7,16]. CNNs have been popular solutions to various single imaging tasks. Sun et al. proposed a deep CNN to remove moire artefacts in a photo taken of screens [20] with the non-linear multiresolution analysis of the moire photos and created a large-scale benchmark dataset for this task. FFD-Net [27] is an excellent work in denoising tasks that can handle a wide range of noise levels with a tunable noise level map as the input. The super-resolution tasks possess remembrances with image signal processing tasks. Especially the Residual-in-Residual Dense Block, which is of higher capacity and easier to train, introduced in ESRGAN [23] is verified effective in our enhanced U-Net for the ISP task. ExpandNet [14] is a three branches convolution neural network, combining local, medium level and global feature information, and it avoids the use of upsampling layers to improve image quality when generating HDR content from LDR content. Tao et al. proposed an efficient and effective network [21] for the image deblurring task, which restores the sharp image of different resolutions in a pyramid. [7] presents a large-scale bokeh dataset consisting of 5K shallow wide depth-of-field image pairs and uses PyNet to deal with this task.

2.2 ISP Designing

CNNs, have not only shown significant advantages in low-level vision tasks but also widely used in high-level tasks, such as object detection, segmentation [4,13]. Therefore, it is highly conceivable to apply CNNs to reconstruct high-quality, full-colour images from image signals(such as RAW Bayer pattern). However, despite these successes in various vision tasks, little work has been conducted on the ISP pipeline learning. Deep Camera [17] analyzed the reason why traditional ISP pipeline may be tough to tune and developed a fully convolutional network for performing ISP pipeline. Andrey et al. [9] proposed RAW-to-RGB data set and the end-to-end PyNET to conduct the ISP task for the first time. It undoubtedly shows the potential of CNN for image processing as a substitution of hardware modules, even the most sophisticated ISP. CameraNet [11]

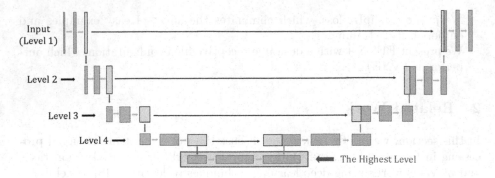

Fig. 1. Five level U-Net [19] with an additional upsample layer added to the top of UNet.

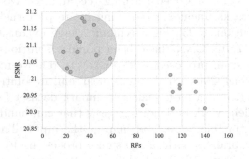

Fig. 2. Receptive Fields of the highest level layers in different encoder decoder networks and its corresponding fidelity.

categorized the ISP pipeline into two weakly correlated parts, restoration and enhancement, and proposed a two-stage network to account for the two independent operations. In this paper, we proposed a simple but effective EEDNet to achieve better performance both in PSNR and visual effect.

3   Analysis of Receptive Field

Before introducing the network, we briefly review the definition of receptive field. Receptive fields are defined portion of space or spatial construct containing units that provide input to a set of units within a corresponding layer [2]. We hypothesize that Large Receptive Field (LRF) is required by high-level image understanding tasks, while it is not strongly related to low-level image processing tasks. In this section, comprehensive experiments are conducted to demonstrate that RF is one of the critical factors in the RAW-to-RGB task.

Without loss of generality, we define the encoder's bottom-up RF calculation formula as follow:

$$\mathcal{F}_n = (\mathcal{F}_{n-1}) + ((k_n - 1) * \prod_{i=1}^{n-1} s_i) \tag{1}$$

$\mathcal{F}_n$ and $\mathcal{F}_{n-1}$ represent the required RF of nth layer and the known RF of n-1th layer whose initial value is 1. k_n stands for the nth layer's kernel size. s_n is the stride of layer i.

In our experiments, we take modified U-Net [19] as a baseline and adjust the receptive field of the highest level (as shown in the bottom red box in Fig. 1) by four factors: the number of downsampling operations, the size of the filters, the depth of each level, and the dilation rate.

– For downsampling, we gradually remove the `max_pooling` layer from top to bottom. Besides, the convolutional layers after the removed pooling layer will also be deprecated, which is for ensuring that the PSNR improvement is not obtained by increasing the computations.
– For kernel size, we randomly select several low-level convolutional layers and change its kernel size from 1×1 to 9×9 (with a step size of 2) without changing the architecture.
– For the number of convolutional layers in each level, we randomly remove some convolutional layers belonging to the highest level. At the same time, we add corresponding layers at lower levels to guarantee approximately the same computing cost.
– For dilated convolution, we randomly select one normal convolutional layer in the encoder and replace it with different dilated convolutional layers.

The results are shown in Fig. 2. In conclusion, for the highest level, the RF should not be too large, and there is a rough scale of favourable RF configuration (preferably between 10 and 60). This phenomenon is related to those operations that shrink the receptive field, such as adopting convolution with small kernel sizes and cutting the downsampling. If not, the fidelity will be drastically changed.

4   Proposed EEDNet

In this section, we introduce EEDNet inspired by UNet [19] and RF hypothesis. Besides, to make EEDNet focus more on the significant changes of pixels in the RGB domain, we propose Channel Attention Residual Dense Block (CA-RDB) block and ClipL1 loss.

4.1   Network Design

According to the LRF hypothesis, LRF may make the network architecture suboptimal. To avoid this problem, we design EEDNet with only three downsampling layers to obtain an appropriate receptive field. Besides, the RAW to RGB

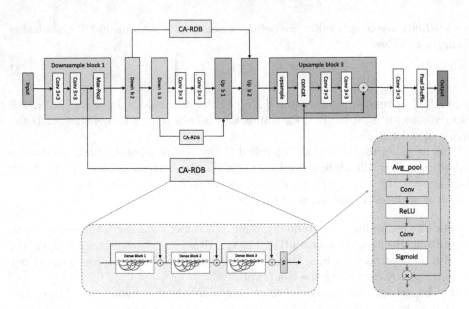

Fig. 3. Overall structure of EEDNet.

task generally involves both global and local image corrections. Layers belonging to different levels should have different sensitivity to both high-level properties, such as brightness or white balance, and low-level features, like textures and edges. In light of this, we apply Channel Attention Residual Dense Block (CA-RDB) block to skip connections, shown in Fig. 3. The idea that adding Channel attention [5] after RDBs is heuristical for making the skip connection focus on useful information.

For low-level tasks, especially pixel-to-pixel, the information of each pixel of each sample is very important. Therefore, Batch Normalization [10] considering the content of all pictures in a batch may result in the loss of unique details of each sample. Similarly, for algorithms like Layer Normalization (LN) [3] that need to consider correlations across channels, the difference between different channels may be ignored. RAW to RGB task is similar to style transfer, which means models should focus on the uniqueness of each sample since the generated images depend on the corresponding input images. In this case, Instance Normalization (IN) [22] becomes an ideal choice. Furthermore, for obtaining more effective statistical information, we adopt SN, which combines the characteristics of BN, LN and IN. In Sect. 5.4, we verify that SN is more effective than IN. LeakyReLU is applied after each convolutional layer, except for the last layer. Besides, we use the nearest neighbour interpolation for upsampling to avoid time-consuming deconvolutions.

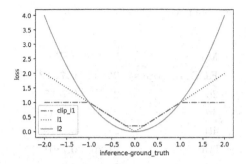

Fig. 4. Loss comparison between L1 loss, L2 loss and ClipL1 loss

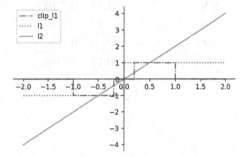

Fig. 5. Gradient comparison between L1 loss, L2 loss and ClipL1 loss. The x axis is the residual value between prediction and ground truth image, and the y axis is the gradient value

4.2   ClipL1 Loss

ClipL1 Loss is inspired by [12], which is designed to address class imbalance in object detection. As easy examples can overwhelm training and lead to degenerated models, we propose a ClipL1 Loss with only a small modification to the original L1 Loss:

$$\mathcal{L}_{ClipL1}(x,y) = \begin{cases} c_{min}, & \text{if } |x-y| < c_{min} \\ |x-y|, & \text{if } c_{min} < |x-y| < c_{max} \\ c_{max}, & \text{if } |x-y| > c_{max} \end{cases} \tag{2}$$

where x is the reconstructed RGB image by our network, and y represents the ground truth RGB image from canon ISP. c_{min} and c_{max} are thresholds for clipping easy samples and outliers. Figure 4 shows the comparison between L1 Loss, L2 Loss and ClipL1 loss. As shown above, we regard every pixel in an image as one sample, and reset it to the threshold if it is out of the range. The gradient comparison between different losses is shown in Fig. 5.

Table 1. The test set results of AIM 2020 Learned Smartphone ISP Challenge Track 1 - Fidelity.

Models	PSNR	SSIM
EEDNet(ours)	**22.26**	**0.7913**
2nd	21.92	0.7865
3rd	21.91	0.7842
4th	21.90	0.7829
5th	21.86	0.7807
6th	21.56	0.7846
7th	21.40	0.7834
8th	21.17	0.7794
9th	21.14	0.7729
10th	20.19	0.7622
11th	20.13	0.7438

5   Experiments

5.1   Dataset

We use Zurich RAW to RGB dataset in experiments, which is supplied by AIM2020 Learned Smartphone ISP Challenge [8]. The data set consists of 48403 RAW-RGB image pairs. The input RAW images were captured by the Huawei P20 smartphone and the Canon 5D Mark IV camera was adopted to collect ground truth RGB images. The scenarios in the data set are mainly streets, sky, trees and lawn. The training data set consists of image patch pairs. The test data set in Track1 are also raw image patches, while in Track2 it is made up of full-resolution RAW images. However, part of the ground truth RGB patches in training data set are of low quality with various defects. For example, most of the images with grass are fuzzy, and some images with sky are overexposed. To build a reliable model to reconstruct RGB images from the RAW pattern, we manually washed the dataset. After that, there are about 22437 image pairs left.

5.2   Implementation Details

Training Process. Our method is implemented in PyTorch 1.5.0 and trained on 8 NVIDIA RTX 2080 Ti GPUs(11G). The negative slope of Leaky ReLU is 0.2 in our EEDNet. The initial learning rate is 10^{-3} and step at 33th and 46th epoch with $\frac{1}{10}$ of the former value. We trained the networks using the Adam optimizer with $\beta_1 = 0.9$ and $\beta_2 = 0.999$. We train the EEDNet with a mini-batch size of 48. In each training batch, we apply random geometric transformations of 90°, 180° rotations, horizontal and vertical flipping. We train EEDNet for 50 epochs with ClipL1 loss, and it takes about 2.5 h. c_{min} and c_{max} are respectively set to $\frac{1}{255}$ and 1 in our experiments. Note that since ClipL1 loss only focuses on changes within a certain range, it will be sub-optimal when the network trained with other losses.

Testing Process. For Track1, we trained 5 models with the same setting for ensembling. They are, respectively, 4 levels U-Net with Leaky ReLU and SN (called Modified U-Net) trained with mean square error (MSE), Modified U-Net trained with L1, Modified U-Net trained with ClipL1, EEDNet trained with MSE + 0.8∗MS-SSIM, EEDNet trained with ClipL1. Yet for Track2, We only took the output full-resolution images of EEDNet trained with ClipL1 as the final submitted results.

5.3 Results

The competition results of Track1 is shown as Table 1. We have got the first place. Our best single model achieves 21.63 dB on the development set. The submitted ensemble model reaches 22.26 dB on the test set. And part of the full resolutoin images are presented in Fig. 6. We still achieved state-of-the-art results. Our processed images have softer lighting, rich colours and no overexposure, compared to PyNET [9].

5.4 Ablation Studies

In order to study the effects of each component in the proposed EEDNet, we gradually modify the baseline UNet [19] and compare their differences. The overall visual comparison is illustrated in Fig. 7. Each column represents a model with its configurations shown at the top. For more clarity, we select the full resolution images processed by our EEDNet and put it in the 1st column. In the 2nd to 4th columns, we first compare the effects of BN, IN, and SN. It can be seen that UNet with SN has the best effect. Besides, based on the LRF hypothesis in Sect. 3, we remove a downsampling layer of UNet and the convolutional layers belonging to the highest level. The 5th column shows the results of the model, which is significantly better than the model on the left. All the above models are supervised by the L1 loss function. In the 7th column, we use the proposed CLipL1 to train our EEDNet and it shows the superiority over other models.

5.5 Smartphone-Image-Denoising Results

To further verifying our LRF hypothesis, we conduct extended experiments on the SIDD+ task [1]. First of all, the U-Net [19] is modified by removing one downsampling layer and its corresponding upsampling layer for decreasing the RF of the highest level, as U-Net*. For a fair comparison, we trained both models without data augmentation under the same conditions.

In this pair of experiments, U-Net and modified U-Net* are supervised with $L1$ loss, and optimized by Adam algorithm. On real image denoising rawRGB data set, we train the pair models with 4000 epochs and batch size of 2, where

Huawei_RAW   Huawei_ISP   Canon_ISP/GT   PyNET   EEDNet(ours)

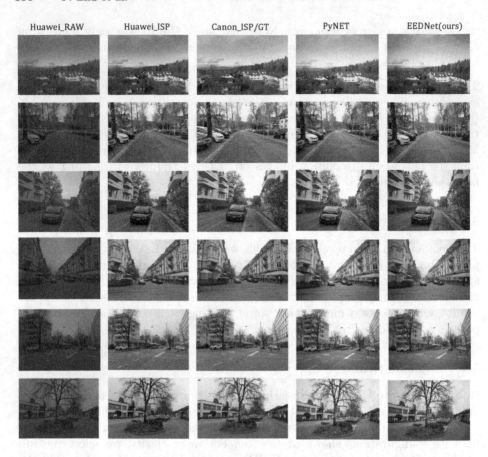

Fig. 6. Comparison of different ISPs. The Canon output photo in the middle is the ground truth of the RAW-to-RGB task. Especially, for the first row, the photos processed by our AutoISP aremore colorful compared with PyNET [9] and closer to the Cannon camera's output. (Color figure online)

the learning rate is 10^{-4} and step to 10^{-5} at epoch 1500. On sRGB data set, we train the model for 1200 epochs and batch size 48, where the learning rate is 3×10^{-4} for the first 10 epochs, and then 3×10^{-5} until training process finished. The experiments are performed on RTX 2080 Ti.

The results are shown in Table 2. For the left rawRGB task, it is obvious that U-Net* performs better than U-Net in terms of PSNR. Since the SSIM is already high, there is not much improvement. However, for the right sRGB task, the PSNR and SSIM of U-Net* are all conspicuously higher than U-Net. Therefore, our LRF hypothesis can be applied to the SIDD+ task no matter what the colour space.

	1st	2nd	3rd	4th	5th	6th	7th
BN	√	-	-	-	-	-	
IN	-	√	-	-	-	-	
SN	-	-	√	√	√	√	
4-levles	-	-	-	√	√	√	
CA_RDB	-	-	-	-	√	√	
ClipL1	-	-	-	-	-	√	

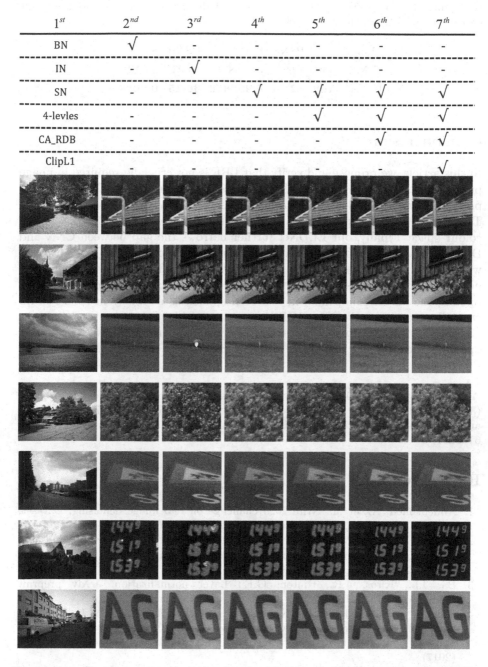

Fig. 7. Overall visual comparisons for showing the effects of each component in EED-Net. Each column represents a model with its configurations in the top.

Table 2. Comparison of U-net with different receptive field. $\mathcal{F}_h$ represents the RF of the highest level in U-Net or U-Net*. The left of the vertical line presents the result on the rawRGB task. The right is on sRGB task.

Models	$\mathcal{F}_h$	PSNR	SSIM	PSNR	SSIM
U-Net	140	52.29	0.995871	35.93	0.9052
U-Net*	**108**	**52.33**	**0.995878**	**36.15**	**0.9086**

6   Conclusion

In this article, we propose and verify that LRF is not crucially required in image processing tasks, especially the RAW-to-RGB task and the SIDD task. This preknowledge will undoubtedly benefit other basic image processing research. Then, ClipL1 Loss is proposed to enhance the sensitivity of EEDNet to RGB colour space. Finally, our EEDNet further narrows the gap between CNN and DSLR's ISP, making CNN more likely to replace ISP on smartphones. Although we can get considerable results on the RAW-to-RGB data set, it should be noticed that the data set is relatively small, and the scenes are not productive, making the model suboptimal in real scenes, such as at night. In future work, we will expand the RAW-to-RGB data set, enriching its scenes and discover an effective solution to solve white balance. At the same time, we will further optimize the EEDNet and diminish its computations to be applied to mobile phones.

Acknowledgements. This work was supported by the Advance Research Program (31511130301); National Key Research and Development Program (2017YFF0209806), and National Natural Science Foundation of China (No. 61906193; No. 61906195; No. 61702510).

References

1. Abdelhamed, A., et al.: Ntire 2020 challenge on real image denoising: Dataset, methods and results. arXiv preprint arXiv:2005.04117 (2020)
2. Araujo, A., Norris, W., Sim, J.: Computing receptive fields of convolutional neural networks. Distill (2019). https://doi.org/10.23915/distill.00021, https://distill.pub/2019/computing-receptive-fields
3. Ba, J.L., Kiros, J.R., Hinton, G.E.: Layer normalization. arXiv preprint arXiv:1607.06450 (2016)
4. Chen, L.C., Papandreou, G., Kokkinos, I., Murphy, K., Yuille, A.L.: Deeplab: Semantic image segmentation with deep convolutional nets, atrous convolution, and fully connected crfs. IEEE Trans. Pattern Anal. Mach. Intell. **40**(4), 834–848 (2017)
5. Chen, L., Zhang, H., Xiao, J., Nie, L., Shao, J., Liu, W., Chua, T.S.: Sca-cnn: Spatial and channel-wise attention in convolutional networks for image captioning. In: Proceedings of the IEEE Conference on Computer Vision and Pattern Recognition. pp. 5659–5667 (2017)

6. Fan, Y., Yu, J., Liu, D., Huang, T.S.: Scale-wise convolution for image restoration (2019)
7. Ignatov, A., Patel, J., Timofte, R.: Rendering natural camera bokeh effect with deep learning. In: Proceedings of the IEEE/CVF Conference on Computer Vision and Pattern Recognition (CVPR) Workshops (June 2020)
8. Ignatov, A., Timofte, R., et al.: AIM 2020 challenge on learned image signal processing pipeline. In: European Conference on Computer Vision Workshops (2020)
9. Ignatov, A., Van Gool, L., Timofte, R.: Replacing mobile camera isp with a single deep learning model. arXiv preprint arXiv:2002.05509 (2020)
10. Ioffe, S., Szegedy, C.: Batch normalization: Accelerating deep network training by reducing internal covariate shift. arXiv preprint arXiv:1502.03167 (2015)
11. Liang, Z., Cai, J., Cao, Z., Zhang, L.: Cameranet: A two-stage framework for effective camera isp learning (2019)
12. Lin, T.Y., Goyal, P., Girshick, R., He, K., Dollár, P.: Focal loss for dense object detection. In: Proceedings of the IEEE International Conference on Computer Vision. pp. 2980–2988 (2017)
13. Long, J., Shelhamer, E., Darrell, T.: Fully convolutional networks for semantic segmentation. In: Proceedings of the IEEE Conference on Computer Vision and Pattern Recognition. pp. 3431–3440 (2015)
14. Marnerides, D., Bashford-Rogers, T., Hatchett, J., Debattista, K.: Expandnet: A deep convolutional neural network for high dynamic range expansion from low dynamic range content. Comput. Graph. Forum **37**(2), 37–49 (2017)
15. Nah, S., Son, S., Timofte, R., Lee, K.M.: Ntire 2020 challenge on image and video deblurring. In: Proceedings of the IEEE/CVF Conference on Computer Vision and Pattern Recognition (CVPR) Workshops (2020)
16. Purohit, K., Suin, M., Kandula, P., Ambasamudram, R.: Depth-guided dense dynamic filtering network for bokeh effect rendering. In: 2019 IEEE/CVF International Conference on Computer Vision Workshop (ICCVW). pp. 3417–3426 (2019)
17. Ratnasingam, S.: Deep camera: A fully convolutional neural network for image signal processing. In: Proceedings of the IEEE/CVF International Conference on Computer Vision (ICCV) Workshops (2019)
18. Ren, S., He, K., Girshick, R., Sun, J.: Faster r-cnn: Towards real-time object detection with region proposal networks. In: Advances in Neural Information Processing Systems. pp. 91–99 (2015)
19. Ronneberger, O., Fischer, P., Brox, T.: U-net: convolutional networks for biomedical image segmentation. In: Navab, N., Hornegger, J., Wells, W.M., Frangi, A.F. (eds.) MICCAI 2015. LNCS, vol. 9351, pp. 234–241. Springer, Cham (2015). https://doi.org/10.1007/978-3-319-24574-4_28
20. Sun, Y., Yu, Y., Wang, W.: Moiré photo restoration using multiresolution convolutional neural networks. IEEE Trans. Image Process. **27**(8), 4160–4172 (2018)
21. Tao, X., Gao, H., Shen, X., Wang, J., Jia, J.: Scale-recurrent network for deep image deblurring. In: Proceedings of the IEEE Conference on Computer Vision and Pattern Recognition (CVPR) (2018)
22. Ulyanov, D., Vedaldi, A., Lempitsky, V.: Instance normalization: The missing ingredient for fast stylization. arXiv preprint arXiv:1607.08022 (2016)
23. Wang, X., et al.: Esrgan: Enhanced super-resolution generative adversarial networks. In: Proceedings of the European Conference on Computer Vision (ECCV) Workshops (2018)
24. Yan, Q., et al.: Deep hdr imaging via a non-local network. IEEE Trans. Image Process. **29**, 4308–4322 (2020)

25. Yuan, S., et al.: Aim 2019 challenge on image demoireing: Methods and results. In: 2019 IEEE/CVF International Conference on Computer Vision Workshop (ICCVW). pp. 3534–3545 (2019)
26. Zhang, K., Zuo, W., Chen, Y., Meng, D., Zhang, L.: Beyond a gaussian denoiser: Residual learning of deep cnn for image denoising. IEEE Trans. Image Process. **26**(7), 3142–3155 (2017)
27. Zhang, K., Zuo, W., Zhang, L.: Ffdnet: Toward a fast and flexible solution for cnn-based image denoising. IEEE Trans. Image Process. **27**(9), 4608–4622 (2018)

AWNet: Attentive Wavelet Network
for Image ISP

Linhui Dai$^{(\boxtimes)}$, Xiaohong Liu , Chengqi Li , and Jun Chen

McMaster University, Hamilton, ON, Canada
{dai15,liux173,lic222,chenjun}@mcmaster.ca

Abstract. As the revolutionary improvement being made on the performance of smartphones over the last decade, mobile photography becomes one of the most common practices among the majority of smartphone users. However, due to the limited size of camera sensors on phone, the photographed image is still visually distinct to the one taken by the digital single-lens reflex (DSLR) camera. To narrow this performance gap, one is to redesign the camera image signal processor (ISP) to improve the image quality. Owing to the rapid rise of deep learning, recent works resort to the deep convolutional neural network (CNN) to develop a sophisticated data-driven ISP that directly maps the phone-captured image to the DSLR-captured one. In this paper, we introduce a novel network that utilizes the attention mechanism and wavelet transform, dubbed AWNet, to tackle this learnable image ISP problem. By adding the wavelet transform, our proposed method enables us to restore favorable image details from RAW information and achieve a larger receptive field while remaining high efficiency in terms of computational cost. The global context block is adopted in our method to learn the non-local color mapping for the generation of appealing RGB images. More importantly, this block alleviates the influence of image misalignment occurred on the provided dataset. Experimental results indicate the advances of our design in both qualitative and quantitative measurements. The source code is available at https://github.com/Charlie0215/AWNet-Attentive-Wavelet-Network-for-Image-ISP.

Keywords: Image ISP · Discrete wavelet transform · Multi-scale CNN

1 Introduction

Traditional image ISP is a critical processing unit that maps RAW images from the camera sensor to RGB images in order to accommodate the human visual system (HVS). For this purpose, a series of sub-processing units are leveraged

L. Dai and X. Liu—Contributed equally.

Electronic supplementary material The online version of this chapter (https://doi.org/10.1007/978-3-030-67070-2_11) contains supplementary material, which is available to authorized users.

© Springer Nature Switzerland AG 2020
A. Bartoli and A. Fusiello (Eds.): ECCV 2020 Workshops, LNCS 12537, pp. 185–201, 2020.
https://doi.org/10.1007/978-3-030-67070-2_11

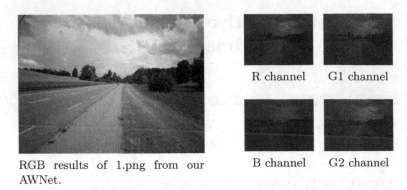

RGB results of 1.png from our AWNet.   B channel   G2 channel

Fig. 1. Visualization of each channel in the RAW image and the corresponding RGB image reconstructed by AWNet. Zoom-in for better views. (Color figure online)

in order to tackle the different artifacts from photo-capturing devices, including, among others, the color shifts, signal noises, and moire effects. However, tuning each sub-processing unit requires legions of efforts from imagery experts.

Nowadays, mobile devices have been equipped with high-resolution cameras to serve the incremental need for mobile photography. However, due to the compact space, the hardware is limited with respect to the quality of the optics and the pixel numbers. Moreover, the time of exposure is relatively short due to the instability of hand-holding. Therefore, a mobile specific ISP has to compensate for these limitations as well.

Recently, deep learning (DL) based methods have achieved considerable success on various image enhancement tasks, including image denoising [1,39], image demosaicing [10], and super-resolution [15,18,22,35]. Different from traditional image processing algorithms that commonly require prior knowledge of natural image statistics, data-driven methods can implicitly learn such information. Due to this fact, the DL-based method becomes a good fit for mapping problems [5,37,42]. In here, learning image ISP can be regarded as an image-to-image translation problem, which can be well-addressed by the DL-based method. In ZRR dataset from [14], the RAW images can be decomposed into 4 channels, which are red (R), green (G1), blue (B) and green (G2) from the Bayer pattern, as shown in Fig. 1. Remark that 2 of 4 channels record the radiance information from green sensors. Therefore, additional operations such as demosaicing and color correction are needed to tackle the RAW images as compared to RGB images. Moreover, due to the nature of the Bayer filter, the size of these 4 channels is down-sampled by the factor of two. In order to make the size of prediction and ground truth images consistent, an up-sampling operation is required. This can be regarded as a restoration problem, where the recovery of high-frequency information should be taken into consideration. In our observation, the misalignment between the DSLR and mobile photographed image pairs is severe even though the authors have adopted the SIFT [21] and RANSAC [33] algorithms to mitigate this effect. It is worth mentioning that the minor misalignment between the input RAW image and ground-truth RGB image would cause a significant performance drop.

To tackle the aforementioned problems, we introduce a novel trainable pipeline that utilizes the attention mechanism and wavelet transform. More specifically, the input of our proposed methods is a combination of a RAW image and its demosaiced counterpart as a complement, where the two-branch design is aimed at emphasizing the different training tasks, namely, noise removal and detail restoration on RAW model and the color mapping on the demosaiced model; the discrete wavelet transform (DWT) is adopted to restore fine context details from RAW images while reserving the informativeness in features during training; as for the color correction and tone mapping, the res-dense connection and attention mechanism are utilized to encourage the network putting effort on the focused areas.

In summary, our main contributions are:

1) Exploring the effectiveness of wavelet transform and non-local attention mechanism in image ISP pipeline.
2) A two-branch design to take a raw image and its demosaiced counterpart that endows our proposed method the ability to translate the RAW image to the RGB image.
3) A lightweight and fully convolutional encoder-decoder design that is time-efficient and flexible on different input sizes.

2   Related Works

In this section, we provide a brief review of the traditional image ISP methods, some representative RAW to RGB mapping algorithms, and the existing learnable imaging pipelines.

2.1   Traditional Image ISP Pipeline

Traditional ISP pipeline encompasses multiple image signal operations, including, among others, denoising, demosaicing, white balancing, color correction, gamma correction, and tone mapping. Due to the nature of the image sensor, the existence of noise in RAW images is inevitable. Therefore, some operations are [1,8,39] proposed to remove the noise and improve the signal-to-noise ratio. The demosaicing operation interpolates the single-channel raw image with repeated mosaic patterns into multi-channel color images [10]. White balancing corrects the color by shifting illuminations of RGB channels to make the image more perceptually accepted [7]. Color correction adjust the image value by a correction matrix [17,28]. Tone mapping shrinks the histogram of image values to enhance image details [26,38]. Note that all sub-processing units in the traditional image ISP pipeline require human effort to manually adjust the final result.

2.2   RAW Data Usage in Low-Level Image Restoration

The advantages of applying RAW data on low-level vision tasks have been explored by different works in the field of image restoration. For instance, [5] uses dark RAW image and bright color image pairs to restore dark images from images with long exposure. In this case, the radiance information that retained by raw data contributes to the restoration of image illumination. [37] takes advantage of rich radiance information from unprocessed camera data to restore high frequency details and improve their network performance on super-resolution tasks. Their experiment reveals that using raw data as a substitute for camera processed data is beneficial on single image super-resolution tasks. Lately, [14,29] adopt unprocessed image data to enhance mobile camera imaging. Since RAW data avoids the information loss introduced by quantization in ISP, it is favorable for a neural network to restore the delicate image details. Inspired by [14], our work makes use of the RAW data to train our network for a learnable ISP pipeline. Instead of only taking RAW images as the input, we adopt the combination of the input data formats from [14] and [29] to encourage our network to learn different sub-tasks of image ISP, for example, noise removal, color mapping, and detail restoration.

2.3   Deep Learning Based Image ISP Pipeline

Since CNN has achieved the promising performance on plenty of low-level vision tasks [11,15,18,30,35], it is intuitive to leverage it for the learning of camera ISP. [29] collects RAW low-lit images from Samsung S7 phone, and uses a neural network to improve image brightness and remove noise on demosaiced RGB images from a simple ISP pipeline. [27] generates synthetic RAW images from JPEG ones and applies RAW-to-RGB mapping to restore the original RGB images. Moreover, some previous works in AIM 2019 RAW to RGB Mapping Challenge have achieved appealing results. For example, [32] considers using the stacked U-Nets to produce a pipeline in a coarse-to-fine manner. [24] adopts a multi-scale training strategy that recovers the image details while remaining the global perceptual acceptance. The most recent work [14] tries to narrow the visual quality gap between the mobile and DSLR color images by directly translating mobile RAW images to DSLR color ones, where RAW images are captured by Huawei P20 phone and color ones are from Canon 5D Mark IV. Nonetheless, all previous learnable ISP methods only focus on the general mapping problem without mentioning other artifacts from the training dataset. For example, without additional operation, the misalignment between the DSLR and mobile image pairs can cause severe degradation on estimated outputs. In our work, we apply the global context block combined with the res-dense block that learns the global color mapping to tackle misaligned image features. The added blocks enable our network to outperform the current state-of-the-art method proposed by [14].

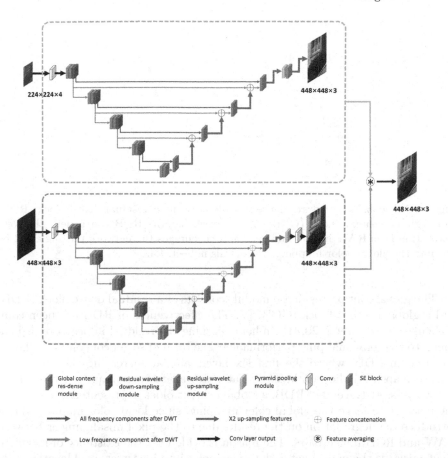

Fig. 2. The main architecture of the proposed AWNet. The top and bottom ones are the RAW and demosaiced models, respectively. We take the average of both outputs from these two models to obtain the final prediction.

3 Proposed Methods

We describe the proposed method and training strategy in this section. First, the overall network architecture (shown in Fig. 2) and details of each network module are demonstrated, and then the sense of this design is illustrated. In the end, the loss functions adopted in training is introduced.

3.1 Network Structure

The proposed AWNet employs a U-Net resembled structure and consolidates the architecture by three main modules, namely global context res-dense module, residual wavelet up-sampling module, and residual wavelet down-sampling module (see Fig. 3 and Fig. 4).

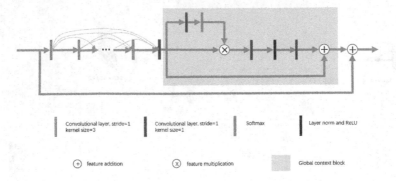

Fig. 3. Our global context res-dense module contains a residual dense block (RDB) and a global context block (GCB). We observe that the RDB can benefit the color restoration from RAW images and the GCB encourages the network putting effort on learning the global color mapping. See details in Sect. 4.4.

The global context res-dense module consists of a residual dense block (RDB) and a global context block (GCB) [3]. The effectiveness of RDB has been comprehensively examined [20, 41]. In here, learning the residual information is beneficial to the color-mapping performance. The total of seven convolutional layers are used in RDB, where the first six layers aim at increasing the number of feature maps and the last layer concatenates all feature maps generated from these layers. At the end of RDB, a global context block is presented to encourage the network to learn the global color mapping, since local color mapping might introduce the degradation on the results due to the pixel misalignment between RAW and RGB image pairs. The reason is evident as the existence of misalignment misleads the neural network to map color into incorrect pixel locations. By considering that the convolutional kernel only covers the local information of an image, [34] proposed a non-local attention mechanism. This work can realize the dependency between long-distance pixels so that the value at a query point can be calculated by the weighted sum of the features of all positions on the input feature. However, heavy computation is required, especially when the feature map has a large size (e.g., the full resolution input image from ZRR dataset). By experiments, [3] claims that the attention map obtained from different query points has minor differences. Therefore, they propose a lightweight global context block (GCB) that simplifies the non-local module and combines with the global context framework and the SE block [12]. The GCB encourages the network to learn key information spatial-wise and channel-wise while effectively reduce the computation complexity. These characteristics are exactly what we look for in this RAW-to-RGB mapping problem.

For up-sampling and down-sampling, we borrow the idea from the discrete wavelet transform (DWT), since the nature of DWT decomposes the input feature maps into the high-frequency and low-frequency components, in which the low-frequency one can be served as the result from average pooling (further discussion can be found in Sect. 3.3). As shown in Fig. 4, we use the low-frequency

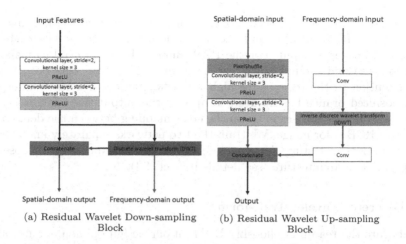

(a) Residual Wavelet Down-sampling Block   (b) Residual Wavelet Up-sampling Block

Fig. 4. Illustration of our up-sampling and down-sampling modules in Fig. 2. The residual design enables our model to operate in frequency-domain and spatial-domain that facilitates the learning of abundant features in up-sampling and down-sampling blocks.

component as part of our down-sampling feature maps and connect the high-frequency part to the up-sampling block for image recovery (i.e., inverse DWT). However, the feature maps produced by frequency-domain operation might be lack of spatial correlation. Therefore, an additional spatial convolutional layer is adopted to downsample the feature map with learned kernels. Similarly, a pixel-shuffle operation along with a spatial convolutional layer is employed for up-sampling as the complement to the IDWT. The combination of frequency-domain and spatial-domain operations facilitates the learning of abundant features in up-sampling and down-sampling blocks. At the end of the proposed method, we use a Pyramid Pooling block [6] to further enlarge the receptive field.

3.2 Two-Branch Network

By consolidating the encoder-decoder structure with previously mentioned modules, our network is able to surpass the state-of-the-art when trained on the RAW images. However, using multiple neural networks to train on different low-level vision tasks is a more effective way to learn image ISP. One of the reasons is that feeding distinct data to different network branches can provide abundant information during training. Recently, the two-stream design has been successfully applied in various computer vision tasks, especially in video field. Note that fusing the information from different formats of input (e.g., optical flow and image frames) can significantly improve the network performance. Inspired by [4,9], we build AWNet based on the idea of two-branch architecture to facilitate network performance on different low-level imaging tasks by utilizing different inputs. Our two-branch design contains two encoder-decoder models, namely the

RAW model and the demosaiced model. In here, the RAW model is trained on $224 \times 224 \times 4$ RAW images, and the demosaiced branch takes $448 \times 448 \times 3$ demosaiced images as input. For the RAW model, there is a need to make the prediction size and ground truth size consistent. Therefore, this branch pays more attention to the recovery of high frequency details. For its counterpart, the demosaiced branch has no need to upscale the output size for consistency. Instead, this branch focuses more on the color mapping between the demosaiced image and RGB color image. We train the two networks separately and average their predictions at testing. As expected, a great performance boost is observed by applying this architecture (see details in Sect. 4.3).

3.3 Discrete Wavelet Transform

To elaborate the reason of choosing DWT in our design opinion, we introduce the connection between DWT and traditional pooling operation. In 2D discrete wavelet transform, there are four filters, i.e., f_{LL}, f_{LH}, f_{HL}, and f_{HH}, can be used to decomposed an image [23]. By convolving with each filter, a full-size image x is split into 4 sub-bands, i.e., x_{LL}, x_{LH}, x_{HL}, and x_{HH}. Due to the nature of DWT, we can express x_{LL} as $(f_{LL} \circledast x) \downarrow_2$ (the expressions of x_{LH}, x_{HL}, and x_{HH} are similar), where $\circledast$ represents convolutional operation and $\downarrow_2$ indicates down-sampling by the scale factor of 2. According to the bi-orthogonal property, the original image x can be restored by IDWT, i.e., $x = IDWT(x_{LL}, x_{LH}, x_{HL}, x_{HH})$. Therefore, the down-sampling and up-sampling operations of DWT can be considered as lossless. In addition, inspired by [19], the wavelet transform can be employed to replace the traditional pooling operation that usually causes information loss. We define the mathematical format to further elaborate the connection between DWT and pooling operation. For example, in Haar DWT, $f_{LL} = \left(\begin{smallmatrix} 1 & 1 \\ 1 & 1 \end{smallmatrix} \right)$. Thus, the (m, n)-th value of x_{LL} after 2D Haar wavelet transform can be defined as

$$x_{LL}(m,n) = x(2m-1, 2n-1) + x(2m-1, 2n) + x(2m, 2n-1) + x(2m, 2n). \quad (1)$$

Moreover, by defining x_p to be the feature map after p-level of average pooling, the (m, n)-th value of x_p can be expressed as

$$x_p(m,n) = 0.25 \times (x_{p-1}(2m-1, 2n-1) + x_{p-1}(2m-1, 2n) \\ + x_{p-1}(2m, 2n-1) + x_{p-1}(2m, 2n)). \quad (2)$$

As we can see, Eq. (2) is highly correlated with Eq. (1). By taking four subbands into account, pooling operation discards all the high-frequency components and only makes use of low-frequency part. Therefore, the information loss in traditional pooling operation is severe. To alleviate this problem, we design our up-sampling and down-sampling modules in the way that uses both wavelet transform and convolutional operation to manage scaling. By doing that, our network can learn from both spatial and frequency information. Our experiments reveal the superior performance of this design (see details in Sect. 4.4).

3.4 Loss Function

In this section, we introduce our three loss functions and the multi-scale loss strategy. We denote I as the target RGB image and $\tilde{I}$ as the predicted result from our method.

Pixel Loss. We adopt the Charbonnier [2,40] loss as an approximate L_1 term for our loss function to better handle outliers and improve the performance. From previous experiments, we realize that Charbonnier loss can efficiently improve the performance on the signal-to-noise ratio of reconstructed images. In addition, Charbonnier loss has been applied in multiple image reconstruction tasks and outperforms the traditional L_2 penalty [40]. The Charbonnier penalty function is defined as:

$$L_{char} = \sqrt{(\tilde{I} - I)^2 + \epsilon^2}, \tag{3}$$

where we set ϵ to $1e - 3$. Note that using only the pixel loss on RAW-to-RGB mapping results in blurry images as reported in [32]. Thus, we redeem this problem by adding other feature loss functions.

Perceptual Loss. To deal with the pixel misalignment problem from ZRR dataset, we also employ perceptual loss. The loss function is defined as

$$L_P = L_{MSE}(F(\tilde{I}) - F(I)), \tag{4}$$

where F denotes the pretrained VGG-19 network, $\tilde{I}$ and I represent the predicted image and ground truth, respectively. As misaligned images are processed by the pretrained VGG network, the resulting downsampled feature maps have fewer variants in terms of the misalignment. Therefore, adding a L_2 term on such feature maps is beneficial for the network to recognize the global information and minimize the perceptual difference between the reconstructed image and the ground truth image.

SSIM Loss. We also employ the structural similarity (SSIM) loss L_{SSIM} [36] that is aiming to reconstruct the RGB images by enhancing on structural similarity index. The resulting images are more perceptually accepted than the predictions without applying SSIM loss. Note that the loss function can be defined as:

$$L_{SSIM} = 1 - F_{SSIM}(\tilde{I} - I), \tag{5}$$

where F denotes the function of calculating structural similarity index.

Multi-scale Loss Function. Inspired by [25], we apply supervision on outputs from different decoder layers to refine reconstructed images of different sizes. For each scale level, we focus on different restoration aspects, thus different loss combinations are applied. In our RAW model, there are 5 up-sampling operations, which form feature maps in 6 different scales, named as scale 1–6 from small to large. Similarly, there are 5 different scales presented in the demosaiced model and we name those as scales 1–5.

1) Scale 1–2 process feature maps that are down-scaled by a factor of 16 and 32. The feature maps at this scale contain less context information compare with ground truth. Thus, we mainly focus on global color and tone mapping. These layers are supervised only by Charbonnier loss, which can be written as:

$$L_{1,2} = L_{char}. \tag{6}$$

2) Scale 3–4 are computed on feature maps with down-scaled factors of 4 and 8; since these features are smaller as compared to the size of ground truth yet contain richer information than the scale 1–2, we apply a loss combination that incorporates perceptual and Charbonnier losses to perform global mapping while remaining the perceptual acceptance. The loss function of these layers is defined as:

$$L_{3,4} = L_{char} + 0.25 \times L_P. \tag{7}$$

3) In scale 5–6, the size of feature maps is close or equal to the original one, thus we are able to pay more attention to the recovery of image context in addition to the color mapping. We choose a more comprehensive loss combination at this level, which can be shown as:

$$L_{5,6} = L_{char} + 0.25 \times L_P + 0.05 \times L_{SSIM}. \tag{8}$$

Note that we manually choose the coefficients of different loss terms. The total loss function can be expressed as:

$$L_{total} = \sum_{n=1}^{k} L_n, \tag{9}$$

where k is equal to 5 and 6 for demosaiced model and RAW model, respectively.

4   Experiments

We conduct comprehensive experiments to demonstrate that the proposed method performs favorable against the baseline model [14] in terms of quantitative and qualitative comparisons on ZRR dataset.

4.1   Datasets

To enhance smartphone images, the Zurich dataset from AIM 2020 Learned Smartphone ISP Challenge [14] provides 48043 RAW-RGB image pairs (of size $448 \times 448 \times 1$ and $448 \times 448 \times 3$, respectively). The training data has been divided into 46,839 image pairs for training and 1,204 ones for testing. In addition, 168 full resolution image pairs are used for perceptual validation. For data preprocessing and augmentation, we normalize the input data and perform vertical and horizontal flipping.

4.2   Training Details

Our model is trained on PyTorch framework with Intel i7, 32 GB of RAM, and two NVIDIA RTX2080 Ti GPUs. The batch size is set to 6 and 2 for the RAW model and the demosaiced model, respectively. Except for that, our two models share the same training strategy. We employ Adam optimizer [16] with $\beta_1 = 0.9, \beta_2 = 0.999$ and set the initial learning rate as 1×10^{-4}. We decrease the learning rate by half in every 10 epochs and train for 50 epochs in total.

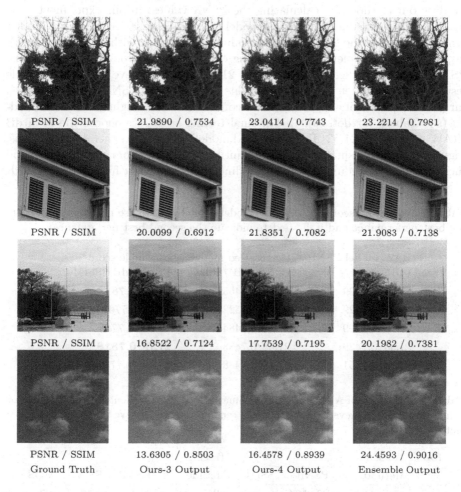

Fig. 5. PSNR/SSIM and visual comparisons of reconstructed images from different network models. Ours-3 and Ours-4 denote our demosaiced and RAW models, respectively. Zoom-in for better views.

4.3   Ensemble Strategy

Inspired by [31], we applied a self-ensemble mechanism during the validation and testing stage of AIM2020 Learned Smartphone ISP Challenge. Specifically, we use ensembles comprised of 8 variants (original, rotated 90°, rotated 180°, rotated 270°, rotated 90° & flipped, rotated 180° & flipped, and rotated 270° & flipped ones). After that, we average out the ensemble outputs and obtain our final result. To evaluate the benefit of ensembles, we apply our method to the validation dataset (without ground truth) during the development stage to validate our methods by calculating the PSNR values. In our experiments, the non-ensembles version of the RAW model and the demosaiced model in Track 1 achieves 21.55 dB and 21.68 dB on the validation dataset (without ground truth), respectively. Subsequently, by averaging out the results from both models, the PSNR can be significantly boosted to 21.97 dB. To achieve optimal ensemble result, for each model, we prepare weights with different PSNR scores, and then carry out experiments to test different combinations of weights across two models (see Table 1 for details). At the final testing stage, we choose the 21.36 dB (RAW model) and 21.52 dB (demosaiced model) weights to generate predictions. Figure 5 shows the qualitative and quantitative results from these models and their ensemble outcomes (tested on offline validation data from provided ZRR

Table 1. Validation scores by different model ensembles. We use bold text to indicate the best performance and italic text to indicate the second best performance.

RAW model PSNR (dB)/SSIM	Demosaiced model PSNR (dB)/SSIM	Ensemble score PSNR (dB)/SSIM
21.36/0.7429	21.30/0.7455	21.60/**0.7818**
21.36/0.7429	21.38/0.7522	21.92/0.7761
21.36/0.7429	21.52/0.7484	*21.95/0.7788*
21.36/0.7429	21.58/0.7488	21.79/**0.7818**
21.38/0.7451	21.58/0.7488	**21.97**/0.7784

Table 2. The result of AIM2020 Learned Smartphone ISP Challenge for the two tracks. Our method can achieve high MOS while remaining competetive in PSNR and SSIM metrics.

Rank	Track 1			Track 2			
	Method	PSNR	SSIM	Method	PSNR	SSIM	MOS
1	Airia_CG	22.2574	0.7913	MW-ISPNet	21.574	0.777	4.7
2	skyb	21.9263	0.7865	**AWNet**	**21.861**	**0.7807**	**4.5**
3	MW-ISPNet	21.9149	0.7842	Baidu	21.9089	0.7829	4.0
4	Baidu	21.9089	0.7829	skyb	21.734	0.7891	3.8
5	**AWNet**	**21.8610**	**0.7807**	STAIR	21.569	0.7846	3.5

dataset). Table 2 shows the result of AIM2020 Learned Smartphone ISP Challenge [13] for the two tracks. We are ranked in the 5th and 2nd place in track 1 and 2, respectively.

4.4   Performance Comparisons and Ablation Studies

We conduct an experiment by first comparing it with other state-of-the-arts to demonstrate the superior performance of our method. After that, we provide solid justification for the effectiveness of wavelet transform and global context blocks. Our proposed method is tested on offline validation data that is provided during the development stage. We choose some popular network architectures from different computer vision tasks, including UNet and RCAN, for comparisons. The qualitative comparisons can be seen from Table 3, and Fig. 6 shows the qualitative comparison between our method and other state-of-the-arts. As we can see, both U-Net and RCAN have some color mapping artifacts, which manifests the incapability of mapping color into RGB space correctly in a pixel-

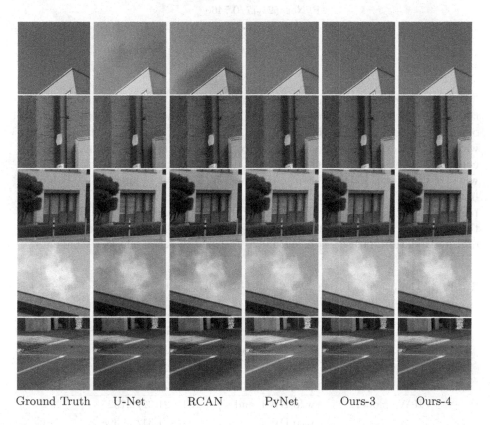

Ground Truth   U-Net   RCAN   PyNet   Ours-3   Ours-4

Fig. 6. Qualitative comparisons of reconstructed images from different networks. Ours-3 and Ours-4 denote our demosaiced and RAW models, respectively. Zoom-in for better views.

to-pixel manner. For example, in the first row of Fig. 6, the color of the sky is inaccurately predicted. Although the PyNet performs better in the color mapping aspect, it tends to obscure the image details. This artifact is obvious in the second, the third, and the last row of images. Beneficial from DWT and GCB blocks, the proposed method remedies these artifacts, which present in other state-of-the-arts. Moreover, the RAW model provides more fine image details whereas the demosaiced model has a better matching in color space; this reveals the effectiveness of our design.

Table 3. Quantitative results from different models. Both of our proposed models outperform the state-of-the-arts. Ours-3 and Ours-4 indicate our demosaiced and RAW models, respectively.

Models	PSNR (dB)/SSIM
U-Net	21.01/**0.7520**
RCAN	20.85/0.7510
PyNet	21.17/0.7460
Ours-3	**21.58**/0.7488
Ours-4	21.38/0.7451

To validate that the wavelet transform and GCB blocks enable to improve the output performance, two corresponding experiments are conducted. The first one is to remove wavelet transform and GCB blocks (see Fig. 4) from residual wavelet up-sampling module, residual wavelet down-sampling module, and global context res-dense module; the another one is to restore GCB blocks and leave wavelet transform blocks absent. As shown in Table 4, by adding GCB blocks, both of our models can be boosted by 0.1 dB in terms of PSNR metric. The performance can be further improved by 0.2 dB while adding DWT block. Note that all these variants are trained in the same way as before and tested on the offline validation dataset from AIM2020 Learned Smartphone ISP Challenge.

Table 4. The benefit of using DWT and GCB blocks is evident. Both of our models can receive approximate 0.3 dB gains.

Model	Operation	PSNR (dB)\SSIM
Demosaiced model	w/o DWT and w/o GCB	21.13/0.7398
	w/o DWT	21.22/0.7421
	Proposed model	**21.38/0.7451**
RAW model	w/o DWT and w/o GCB	21.22/0.7325
	w/o DWT	21.31/0.7398
	Proposed model	**21.58/0.7488**

Our qualitative and quantitative results validate superiority of our two-branch design as well as the effectiveness of wavelet transform block and attention mechanism, in the application of learning RAW-to-RGB color mapping.

5 Conclusion

In this paper, we propose a novel two-branch network structure, named AWNet, which can effectively enhance the smartphone images. We embed wavelet transform blocks into the scaling modules associated with convolutional operations that enable our network to learn from both the spatial and frequency domains. In addition, the presence of GCB blocks improves the robustness of our network to deal with the misalignments that occurred in the ZRR dataset. Our work can shed some light on the application of wavelet transform in image ISP problem. As for future work, our network is able to tackle other low-level imaging tasks, such as image denoising and super-resolution.

References

1. Abdelhamed, A., Afifi, M., Timofte, R., Brown, M.S.: NTIRE 2020 challenge on real image denoising: dataset, methods and results. In: Proceedings of the IEEE Conference on Computer Vision and Pattern Recognition Workshops, pp. 496–497 (2020)
2. Bruhn, A., Weickert, J., Schnörr, C.: Lucas/Kanade meets Horn/Schunck: combining local and global optic flow methods. Int. J. Comput. Vision **61**(3), 211–231 (2005). https://doi.org/10.1023/B:VISI.0000045324.43199.43
3. Cao, Y., Xu, J., Lin, S., Wei, F., Hu, H.: GCNet: non-local networks meet squeeze-excitation networks and beyond. In: Proceedings of the IEEE International Conference on Computer Vision Workshops (2019)
4. Carreira, J., Zisserman, A.: Quo vadis, action recognition? A new model and the kinetics dataset. In: Proceedings of the IEEE Conference on Computer Vision and Pattern Recognition, pp. 6299–6308 (2017)
5. Chen, C., Chen, Q., Xu, J., Koltun, V.: Learning to see in the dark. In: Proceedings of the IEEE Conference on Computer Vision and Pattern Recognition, pp. 3291–3300 (2018)
6. Chen, L.C., Zhu, Y., Papandreou, G., Schroff, F., Adam, H.: Encoder-decoder with atrous separable convolution for semantic image segmentation. In: Proceedings of the IEEE European Conference on Computer Vision, pp. 801–818 (2018)
7. Cheng, D., Price, B., Cohen, S., Brown, M.S.: Beyond white: ground truth colors for color constancy correction. In: Proceedings of the IEEE International Conference on Computer Vision, pp. 298–306 (2015)
8. Dabov, K., Foi, A., Katkovnik, V., Egiazarian, K.: Image denoising by sparse 3-D transform-domain collaborative filtering. IEEE Trans. Image Process. **16**(8), 2080–2095 (2007)
9. Feichtenhofer, C., Pinz, A., Zisserman, A.: Convolutional two-stream network fusion for video action recognition. In: Proceedings of the IEEE European Conference on Computer Vision, pp. 1933–1941 (2016)
10. Gharbi, M., Chaurasia, G., Paris, S., Durand, F.: Deep joint demosaicking and denoising. ACM Trans. Graph. (TOG) **35**(6), 1–12 (2016)

11. He, B., Wang, C., Shi, B., Duan, L.Y.: Mop moire patterns using MopNet. In: Proceedings of the IEEE International Conference on Computer Vision, pp. 2424–2432 (2019)
12. Hu, J., Shen, L., Sun, G.: Squeeze-and-excitation networks. In: Proceedings of the IEEE Conference on Computer Vision and Pattern Recognition, pp. 7132–7141 (2018)
13. Ignatov, A., Timofte, R., et al.: AIM 2020 challenge on learned image signal processing pipeline. In: Bartoli, A., Fusiello, A. (eds.) ECCV 2020. LNCS, vol. 12537, pp. 152–170. Springer, Cham (2020)
14. Ignatov, A., Van Gool, L., Timofte, R.: Replacing mobile camera ISP with a single deep learning model. In: Proceedings of the IEEE Conference on Computer Vision and Pattern Recognition Workshops, pp. 536–537 (2020)
15. Kim, J., Kwon Lee, J., Mu Lee, K.: Accurate image super-resolution using very deep convolutional networks. In: Proceedings of the IEEE Conference on Computer Vision and Pattern Recognition, pp. 1646–1654 (2016)
16. Kingma, D.P., Ba, J.: Adam: a method for stochastic optimization. arXiv preprint arXiv:1412.6980 (2014)
17. Kwok, N.M., Shi, H., Ha, Q.P., Fang, G., Chen, S., Jia, X.: Simultaneous image color correction and enhancement using particle swarm optimization. Eng. Appl. Artif. Intell. **26**(10), 2356–2371 (2013)
18. Ledig, C., et al.: Photo-realistic single image super-resolution using a generative adversarial network. In: Proceedings of the IEEE Conference on Computer Vision and Pattern Recognition, pp. 4681–4690 (2017)
19. Liu, P., Zhang, H., Zhang, K., Lin, L., Zuo, W.: Multi-level wavelet-CNN for image restoration. In: Proceedings of the IEEE Conference on Computer Vision and Pattern Recognition Workshops, pp. 773–782 (2018)
20. Liu, X., Ma, Y., Shi, Z., Chen, J.: GridDehazeNet: attention-based multi-scale network for image dehazing. In: Proceedings of the IEEE International Conference on Computer Vision, pp. 7314–7323 (2019)
21. Lowe, D.G.: Distinctive image features from scale-invariant keypoints. Int. J. Comput. Vis. **60**(2), 91–110 (2004). https://doi.org/10.1023/B:VISI.0000029664.99615.94
22. Lugmayr, A., Danelljan, M., Timofte, R.: NTIRE 2020 challenge on real-world image super-resolution: methods and results. In: Proceedings of the IEEE Conference on Computer Vision and Pattern Recognition Workshops, pp. 494–495 (2020)
23. Mallat, S.G.: A theory for multiresolution signal decomposition: the wavelet representation. IEEE Trans. Pattern Anal. Mach. Intell. **11**(7), 674–693 (1989)
24. Mei, K., Li, J., Zhang, J., Wu, H., Li, J., Huang, R.: Higher-resolution network for image demosaicing and enhancing. In: Proceedings of the IEEE International Conference on Computer Vision Workshops, pp. 3441–3448. IEEE (2019)
25. Qian, R., Tan, R.T., Yang, W., Su, J., Liu, J.: Attentive generative adversarial network for raindrop removal from a single image. In: Proceedings of the IEEE Conference on Computer Vision and Pattern Recognition, pp. 2482–2491 (2018)
26. Rana, A., Singh, P., Valenzise, G., Dufaux, F., Komodakis, N., Smolic, A.: Deep tone mapping operator for high dynamic range images. IEEE Trans. Image Process. **29**, 1285–1298 (2019)
27. Ratnasingam, S.: Deep camera: a fully convolutional neural network for image signal processing. In: Proceedings of the IEEE International Conference on Computer Vision Workshops (2019)
28. Rizzi, A., Gatta, C., Marini, D.: A new algorithm for unsupervised global and local color correction. Pattern Recogn. Lett. **24**(11), 1663–1677 (2003)

29. Schwartz, E., Giryes, R., Bronstein, A.M.: DeepISP: toward learning an end-to-end image processing pipeline. IEEE Trans. Image Process. **28**(2), 912–923 (2018)
30. Tao, X., Gao, H., Shen, X., Wang, J., Jia, J.: Scale-recurrent network for deep image deblurring. In: Proceedings of the IEEE Conference on Computer Vision and Pattern Recognition, pp. 8174–8182 (2018)
31. Timofte, R., Rothe, R., Van Gool, L.: Seven ways to improve example-based single image super resolution. In: Proceedings of the IEEE Conference on Computer Vision and Pattern Recognition, pp. 1865–1873 (2016)
32. Uhm, K.H., Kim, S.W., Ji, S.W., Cho, S.J., Hong, J.P., Ko, S.J.: W-Net: two-stage U-Net with misaligned data for raw-to-RGB mapping. In: Proceedings of the IEEE International Conference on Computer Vision Workshop, pp. 3636–3642. IEEE (2019)
33. Vedaldi, A., Fulkerson, B.: VLFeat: an open and portable library of computer vision algorithms. In: Proceedings of the 18th ACM International Conference on Multimedia, pp. 1469–1472 (2010)
34. Wang, X., Girshick, R., Gupta, A., He, K.: Non-local neural networks. In: Proceedings of the IEEE Conference on Computer Vision and Pattern Recognition, pp. 7794–7803 (2018)
35. Wang, X., Chan, K.C., Yu, K., Dong, C., Change Loy, C.: EDVR: video restoration with enhanced deformable convolutional networks. In: Proceedings of the IEEE Conference on Computer Vision and Pattern Recognition Workshops (2019)
36. Wang, Z., Simoncelli, E.P., Bovik, A.C.: Multiscale structural similarity for image quality assessment. In: The Thrity-Seventh Asilomar Conference on Signals, Systems & Computers, vol. 2, pp. 1398–1402. IEEE (2003)
37. Xu, X., Ma, Y., Sun, W.: Towards real scene super-resolution with raw images. In: Proceedings of the IEEE Conference on Computer Vision and Pattern Recognition, pp. 1723–1731 (2019)
38. Yuan, L., Sun, J.: Automatic exposure correction of consumer photographs. In: Fitzgibbon, A., Lazebnik, S., Perona, P., Sato, Y., Schmid, C. (eds.) ECCV 2012. LNCS, vol. 7575, pp. 771–785. Springer, Heidelberg (2012). https://doi.org/10.1007/978-3-642-33765-9_55
39. Zhang, K., Zuo, W., Chen, Y., Meng, D., Zhang, L.: Beyond a Gaussian denoiser: residual learning of deep CNN for image denoising. IEEE Trans. Image Process. **26**(7), 3142–3155 (2017)
40. Zhang, Y., Li, K., Li, K., Wang, L., Zhong, B., Fu, Y.: Image super-resolution using very deep residual channel attention networks. In: Proceedings of the IEEE European Conference on Computer Vision. pp. 286–301 (2018)
41. Zhang, Y., Tian, Y., Kong, Y., Zhong, B., Fu, Y.: Residual dense network for image super-resolution. In: Proceedings of the IEEE Conference on Computer Vision and Pattern Recognition, pp. 2472–2481 (2018)
42. Zhu, J.Y., Park, T., Isola, P., Efros, A.A.: Unpaired image-to-image translation using cycle-consistent adversarial networks. In: Proceedings of the IEEE International Conference on Computer Vision, pp. 2223–2232 (2017)

PyNET-CA: Enhanced PyNET with Channel Attention for End-to-End Mobile Image Signal Processing

Byung-Hoon Kim[1], Joonyoung Song[1], Jong Chul Ye[1(✉)],
and JaeHyun Baek[2]

[1] Korea Advanced Institute of Science and Technology, Daejeon, South Korea
{egyptdj,songjy18,jong.ye}@kaist.ac.kr
[2] Amazon Web Services, Seoul, South Korea
jakemraz100@gmail.com

Abstract. Reconstructing RGB image from RAW data obtained with a mobile device is related to a number of image signal processing (ISP) tasks, such as demosaicing, denoising, etc. Deep neural networks have shown promising results over hand-crafted ISP algorithms on solving these tasks separately, or even replacing the whole reconstruction process with one model. Here, we propose PyNET-CA, an end-to-end mobile ISP deep learning algorithm for RAW to RGB reconstruction. The model enhances PyNET, a recently proposed state-of-the-art model for mobile ISP, and improve its performance with channel attention and subpixel reconstruction module. We demonstrate the performance of the proposed method with comparative experiments and results from the AIM 2020 learned smartphone ISP challenge. The source code of our implementation is available at https://github.com/egyptdj/skyb-aim2020-public.

Keywords: RAW to RGB · Mobile image signal processing · Image reconstruction · Deep learning

1 Introduction

Reconstructing RGB image from the RAW data obtained with a mobile device is a topic of growing interest. The data acquired from the image sensors of mobile devices require several image signal processing (ISP) steps to solve a number of low-level computer vision problems, such as demosaicing, denoising, color correction, etc. Hand-crafted ISP algorithms depend on the prior knowledge about the data acquisition process or degradation principles. Softwares of the mobile device implement these algorithms to process the RAW data sequentially, solving each tasks step by step to reconstruct the RGB image presented to the user [5].

Deep neural networks, specifically the convolutional neural networks (CNNs), have recently shown promising results over hand-crafted ISP algorithms. There

© Springer Nature Switzerland AG 2020
A. Bartoli and A. Fusiello (Eds.): ECCV 2020 Workshops, LNCS 12537, pp. 202–212, 2020.
https://doi.org/10.1007/978-3-030-67070-2_12

(a) RAW   (b) Proposed   (c) Canon 5D Mark IV

Fig. 1. Reconstructed RGB image from RAW data with the proposed method. (a) Input RAW image (visualised). (b) Reconstructed RGB image with proposed method. (c) Target image taken with Canon 5D Mark IV.

also have been attempts to not just replace each ISP algorithm with deep neural networks, but to reconstruct RGB images from the RAW data by training a single end-to-end deep learning reconstruction model. However, one of the difficulties in training an end-to-end reconstruction model over separately processing the RAW data is that the prior knowledge about the data is not directly incorporated into the model. For example, it is important to take both global (e.g. luminance, color balance) and local features (e.g. fine-grained textures, edge structures) of the image into account during the reconstruction process, which is not explicitly present in the input RAW data.

We consider a recently proposed end-to-end RAW to RGB reconstruction model PyNET [7], which is basically a CNN designed to exploit both global and local features of the input data. Despite the fact that the PyNET achieves state-of-the-art performance in RAW to RGB reconstruction, there exists some drawbacks in the model architecture and the training process that can be further improved. In this paper, we address these issues and propose PyNET-CA, an enhanced PyNET with channel attention to improve the performance and reduce the training time. We demonstrate the performance of the proposed model by a number of comparative experiments, and report the results of participating the AIM 2020 learned smartphone ISP challenge.

2   Related Work

Since the introduction of the SRCNN [3] which solves the single image super-resolution (SISR) problem with a CNN, a large variety of neural network based image reconstruction and enhancement methods have been proposed. Deep learning for SISR has rapidly grown with deeper network architectures [8], and better modules [10,20]. Models that employ the channel attention mechanism have also shown to improve the performance of image enhancement tasks [19]. Although these development of network architectures do improve the quantiative quality of the enhanced images, it does not necessarily mean that the enhanced images are perceptually of good quality. Generative adversarial network (GAN) based SISR models, such as SRGAN [9] and ESRGAN [17], are introduced to address this issue, and enhances the images in a photo-realistic way. Enhancing the image to both quantitatively accurate and perceptually realistic within the perception-distortion tradeoff [1] is now an important issue in image enhancement tasks [2].

Along with the development of neural networks for image enhancement tasks, there have also been attempts to train an end-to-end deep learning model for RAW to RGB reconstruction. One of the earliest model was proposed by [5] which is based on a CNN with composite loss function and adversarial training scheme. The DeepISP [13] also is based on the CNN structure, and addresses the issue of global and local feature priors with a two-stage approach. The W-Net is another model with the two-stage approach proposed by [16], which stacks two U-Net [12] structure with channel attention module. The SalGAN [21] employs the U-Net structure as the generator of the adversarial training scheme and incorporates spatial attention scheme into the loss function. The HERN [11] modifies the channel attention module of the residual in residual module of [19] to construct a dual-path network and incorporates global feature information with a separate full-image encoder. One of the most recent model is PyNET [7], a CNN with inverted pyramidal structure. The PyNET achieves state-of-the-art result on the RAW to RGB reconstruction task, owing to the model architecture that can account for both global and local features of the image [7].

3 Proposed Method

3.1 Network Architecture

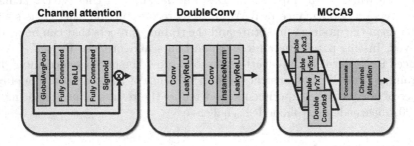

Fig. 2. Basic modules of the proposed model

Basic Modules. First, we define some of the modules that constitute the PyNET-CA model (Fig. 2). The channel attention module (CA) of PyNET-CA follows from [19]. Global average pooling is first applied to the height and width dimension of the features to output a vector with length corresponding to the number of input channels. The pooled vector is linearly mapped, passed through the nonlinear ReLU activation, and is again linearly mapped to match the number of input channels. The length of output features after the first linear mapping is determined by the reduction ratio r, which reduces the number of channels by $\frac{1}{r}$ of the input channels. The final features are squashed to range $[0, 1]$ by the sigmoid function, and are multiplied element-wise with the channels of the input to account for the level of attention for each channels.

The DoubleConv module is defined as two sequential operations of 2D convolution followed by a LeakyReLU activation. The kernels of the two convolution layers have the same shape, which is one of 3×3, 5×5, 7×7, 9×9. The input image or feature to the DoubleConv module is reflect-padded before the convolution to match the size of the output feature. Unlike the original PyNET [7], we apply instance normalisation after only the second convolution layer where needed.

The MultiConv channel attention (MCCA) module is the basic building block of our model. It comprise concatenating the features from the DoubleConv modules and a channel attention module. We specify four types of MCCA (MCCA3, MCCA5, MCCA7, MCCA9) based on the kernel size of the DoubleConv module. The MCCA3 module has only one 3×3 DoubleConv module, while the MCCA5 module concatenates the output of 3×3 and 5×5 DoubleConv module, and so forth. Lastly, channel attention is applied to the concatenated features from the DoubleConv modules. The reduction ratio r of the channel attention module is set to 1, 2, 3, 4 for MCCA3, MCCA5, MCCA7, MCCA9, respectively.

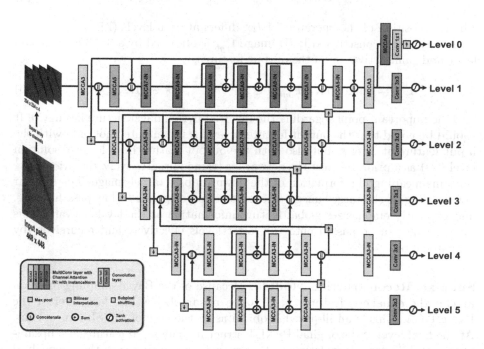

Fig. 3. Schematic illustration of the PyNET-CA model.

Inverted Pyramidal Structure. To account for both the global and local features of the image, PyNET-CA has an inverted pyramidal structure as in Fig. 3. Given a RAW image with Bayer pattern $\mathbf{I}_{raw} \in \mathbb{R}^{H \times W}$, Bayer sampling function f_{Bayer} is first applied to obtain

$$\hat{\mathbf{I}}_{raw} = f_{Bayer}(\mathbf{I}_{raw}) \in \mathbb{R}^{\frac{H}{2} \times \frac{W}{2} \times 4}. \tag{1}$$

At each levels, the images are downscaled by 2×2 max pooling followed by the MCCA3 module to serve as the input feature F_{in}^k at level k,

$$F_{in}^1 = \text{MCCA3}(\hat{\mathbf{I}}_{raw}), \tag{2}$$

$$F_{in}^{k+1} = \text{MCCA3}(\text{MaxPool2}(F_{in}^k)), \quad k \in \{1, 2, 3, 4\}. \tag{3}$$

We denote the set of operations at each level k that process the input feature F_{in}^k as function H^k. The function H^k is composed of a number of MCCA modules along with residual connections, within-level and between-level skip connections to compute the output feature F_{out}^k,

$$F_{out}^5 = H^5(F_{in}^5) \tag{4}$$

$$F_{out}^k = H^k(F_{in}^k, F_{out}^{k+1}), \quad k \in \{1, 2, 3, 4\}. \tag{5}$$

The composition of the operators of H^k differs at each levels (Fig. 3).

Lastly, the reconstructed RGB image $\hat{\mathbf{I}}_{rgb}^k$ is obtained by a 3×3 convolution layer and tanh activation of the output features,

$$\hat{\mathbf{I}}_{rgb}^k = \tanh(\text{Conv3}(F_{out}^k)) \in \mathbb{R}^{\frac{H}{2^k} \times \frac{W}{2^k} \times 3}, \quad k \in \{1, 2, 3, 4, 5\}. \tag{6}$$

One important point regarding the inverted pyramidal structure lies in (5). It should be noted that the output feature at level k is computed not only with the input feature at level k, but also with the output feature from lower-resolution level $k+1$ as a prior. Because the network is trained progressively, the prior F_{out}^{k+1} contains meaningful information of the downsampled target image. The bilinear downscaling of the target image at each level corresponds to low-pass filtering, and explicitly emphasizes global feature information as the levels elevate. This information can be passed onto the lower levels effectively and recursively by concatenation.

Subpixel Reconstruction Module. Because of the Bayer sampling function in (1), the enhanced features need to be upsampled at the last level of the PyNET-CA. This is an ill-posed problem as in the case of the SISR problems. At the final level of the original PyNET structure, enhanced features are upsampled with bilinear interpolation or transposed convolution, and then convolved with a 3×3 kernel convolution layer to output the final image. However, bilinear interpolation or transposed convolution can cause blurring or checkerboard artifacts in the upsampled image. Furthermore, reconstructing final image with the convolution layer after upsampling the image is computationally inefficient.

For computational efficiency and better image quality, the proposed PyNET-CA upsamples the image with the MCCA9 module, followed by 1×1 convolution layer and upsamples the features by subpixel shuffling [14] at the final level of the model,

$$\hat{\mathbf{I}}_{rgb} = \tanh(\mathrm{SubpixelShuffle}(\mathrm{Conv1}(\mathrm{MCCA9}(F_{out}^1)))) \in \mathbb{R}^{H \times W \times 3}. \qquad (7)$$

We denote the RGB reconstruction module (7) as the subpixel reconstruction module (SRM).

3.2 Network Training

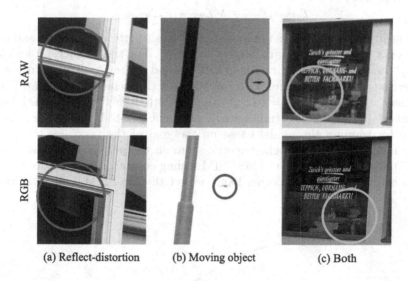

(a) Reflect-distortion   (b) Moving object   (c) Both

Fig. 4. Exemplar images from the ZRR dataset with pixel-level mismatch between the RAW and RGB image pairs. The mismatch is due to (a) angular distortion of the reflection, (b) rapidly moving object, (c) reflect-distortion of the rapidly moving object (both).

Dataset. For training the network, we used the Zurich RAW to RGB (ZRR) dataset. One important fact about the dataset is that it consists of a RANSAC [4] aligned pair of RAW and RGB images, taken separately from a smartphone (Huawei P20) and a DSLR camera (Canon 5D Mark IV), respectively. Considering the collection process, the dataset is prone to significant pixel-level mismatch between the RAW and RGB image pairs if the object is moving or if the object has large area of reflection (see Fig. 4). We screened out the images with large area of reflection (e.g. on cars, on windows) or moving objects (e.g. people, animal, vehicles on the road). There were 1,679 out of 46,839 (3.58%) training image pairs excluded from this screening, leaving out 45,160 image pairs for training the model. For testing, we used 1,204 image pairs provided by the AIM 2020 challenge organizers without excluding any image pairs. All RAW and RGB images were 448×448 cropped patches, and were casted into single precision floating point data centered and scaled to the range $[-1, 1]$ to stabilise the training.

Progressive Training. The PyNET-CA model is progressively trained from the level with the lowest resolution. The target image $\mathbf{I}_{rgb}$ is downsampled with bilinear interpolation to match the resolution of the reconstructed images $\hat{\mathbf{I}}_{rgb}^k$ at each level. The loss function used for training the PyNET-CA is a linear combination of the mean squared error (MSE) loss, the perceptual loss using one VGG layer `relu5_4`, and the multi-scale structural similarity index measure (MS-SSIM) loss,

$$\mathcal{L} = \lambda_1 \mathcal{L}_{\text{MSE}} + \lambda_2 \mathcal{L}_{\text{VGG}} + \lambda_3 \mathcal{L}_{\text{MS-SSIM}}.$$

Basically the MSE loss is minimised at all levels with λ_1 set to 1.0, and other coefficients were adjusted with respect to the λ_1. For training level 5 and level 4, only the MSE loss is minimised, with λ_2 and λ_3 set to 0.0. From level 3, the perceptual loss is minimised to account for the perceptual similarity with coefficient $\lambda_2 = 0.01$, $\lambda_3 = 0.0$. At the last 0th level, the MS-SSIM loss is maximised (i.e., negatively minimised). Different MS-SSIM scaling coefficient is used for training the model based on the goal of the task. For the fidelity task, which is to achieve highest metric score on the peak signal-to-noise ratio (PSNR) and the MS-SSIM, the MS-SSIM scaling coefficient λ_3 is set to 0.01. For the perceptual task, on the other hand, we set the MS-SSIM scaling coefficient to 0.1.

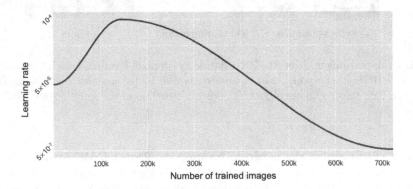

Fig. 5. One-cycle policy of the learning rate for training the PyNET-CA.

One-Cycle Policy of the Learning Rate. The PyNET requires a long training time, especially at the high-resolution levels. To address this issue and hasten convergence, we employ the one-cycle policy of the learning rate for training the PyNET-CA [15]. At each levels, the learning rate starts with 5.0×10^{-5}, reaches the maximum learning rate 1.0×10^{-4} at the early 20% of the training, and gradually decays to 5.0×10^{-7} by the end of the training as in Fig. 5. We train the model for 16 epochs per level, which is around 68% decrement of the training epochs at the last level compared to [7].

4 Experiment

4.1 Comparative Studies

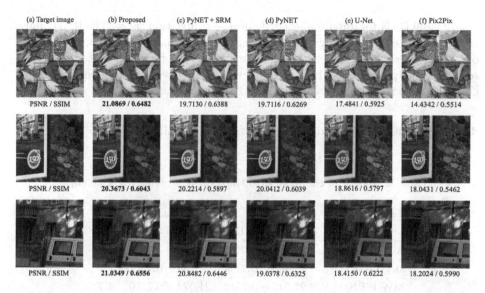

Fig. 6. Reconstruction result from the comparative experiments. (a) The target RGB image. (b) Reconstructed RGB image with the proposed PyNET-CA. (c)–(f) Reconstructed images from ablation studies and benchmark models.

We demonstrate the effectiveness of the proposed method by comparative studies (Table 1, Fig. 6). First, we performed ablation studies to evaluate the performance with and without the modules of the PyNET-CA. The performance of the PyNET-CA degrades if the channel attention at the MCCA module is removed, and further degrades without the SRM (7). In the case of the PyNET-CA without both modules, the model architecture corresponds to the architecture of the original PyNET, network training scheme being the only difference from [7]. From the ablation studies, it can be shown that the PyNET model is enhanced in its performance with the channel attention module and the SRM upsampling.

Second, we compare the PyNET-CA model with two benchmark models, the U-Net [12], and the Pix2Pix [22]. The U-Net is a encoder-decoder CNN with skip connections, applied to many image reconstruction tasks. Although the local features of the output images were relatively well recovered, the global features such as luminance or color balance were easily lost. The Pix2Pix is a

Table 1. Comparative study of the proposed method.

Model	CA	SRM	PSNR	SSIM
PyNET-CA (proposed)	✓	✓	**21.5022**	**0.7438**
PyNET + SRM		✓	21.4126	0.7375
PyNET			21.2071	0.7367
U-Net			20.5057	0.7297
Pix2Pix			20.4502	0.7196

conditional GAN for unpaired image-to-image translation tasks. The RGB image is reconstructed with the generator, taking RAW image as the condition. The output images were perceptually more realistic than fully supervised methods, retaining sharp edges with high-frequency details. However, the model could not correctly reconstruct the color of the RGB images in many cases.

4.2   AIM 2020 Learned Smartphone ISP Challenge

Table 2. Result of the AIM 2020 learned smartphone ISP challenge

Team	Fidelity		Perceptual		
	PSNR	SSIM	PSNR	SSIM	MOS
Airia_CG	**22.257**	**0.7913**	21.011	0.7729	4.0
skyb (ours)	**21.926**	**0.7865**	21.734	**0.7891**	3.8
MW-ISPNet	21.915	0.7842	21.574	0.7770	**4.7**
Baidu	21.909	0.7829	**21.909**	0.7829	4.0
MacAI	21.861	0.7807	**21.861**	0.7807	**4.5**
STAIR	21.569	0.7846	21.569	**0.7846**	3.5
Vermilion Vision	21.403	0.7834	21.403	0.7834	4.2
Eureka	21.179	0.7794	21.179	0.7794	4.1
Sensebrainer	21.144	0.7729	21.144	0.7729	3.2
bupt-mtc206	20.192	0.7622	-	-	-
BingSoda	20.138	0.7438	20.138	0.7438	2.2

We report the results from the AIM 2020 learned smartphone ISP challenge [6]. There were two separate tracks which we both participated in. The goal of the first track was to achieve highest fidelity in terms of the PSNR and the SSIM, while the goal of the second track was to reconstruct RGB images with the best perceptual quality. In the second track, the perceptual quality was evaluated by the mean opinion score (MOS). To find the best model with low generalisation error, we used the provided 1,204 images for validating the model during training. We early stopped the training with highest PSNR value on the validation dataset to participate in the fidelity track. For the perceptual track, we trained the last level for 32 epochs, and early stopped the training with lowest learned perceptual image patch similarity (LPIPS) [18] value on the validation dataset. All models were implemented with PyTorch 1.5.0 and were trained with four NVIDIA V100 GPUs with 16 GB memory each. We applied 8x self-ensemble of 90° rotation and horizontal/vertical flip during test time. We have ranked 2nd place for both the PSNR and the SSIM on the fidelity track, and 1st place for the SSIM on the perceptual track as reported in Table 2. The challenge results demonstrate the exceptional performance of the proposed method.

5 Conclusion

We propose PyNET-CA, an end-to-end deep learning model for RAW to RGB image reconstruction. The model enhances the PyNET structure to improve its performance and reduce training time. Comparative experiments and results from the AIM 2020 challenge demonstrate the exceptional performance of the proposed model.

Acknowledgement. This work was supported byInstitute of Information & Communications Technology Planning & Evaluation (IITP) grant funded by the Korea government (MSIT) [2016-0-00562(R0124-16-0002), Emotional Intelligence Technology to Infer Human Emotion and Carry on Dialogue Accordingly].

References

1. Blau, Y., Michaeli, T.: The perception-distortion tradeoff. In: Proceedings of the IEEE Conference on Computer Vision and Pattern Recognition, pp. 6228–6237 (2018)
2. Deng, X., Yang, R., Xu, M., Dragotti, P.L.: Wavelet domain style transfer for an effective perception-distortion tradeoff in single image super-resolution. In: Proceedings of the IEEE International Conference on Computer Vision, pp. 3076–3085 (2019)
3. Dong, C., Loy, C.C., He, K., Tang, X.: Image super-resolution using deep convolutional networks. IEEE Trans. Pattern Anal. Mach. Intell. **38**(2), 295–307 (2015)
4. Fischler, M.A., Bolles, R.C.: Random sample consensus: a paradigm for model fitting with applications to image analysis and automated cartography. Commun. ACM **24**(6), 381–395 (1981)
5. Ignatov, A., Kobyshev, N., Timofte, R., Vanhoey, K., Van Gool, L.: DSLR-quality photos on mobile devices with deep convolutional networks. In: Proceedings of the IEEE International Conference on Computer Vision, pp. 3277–3285 (2017)
6. Ignatov, A., Timofte, R., et al.: AIM 2020 challenge on learned image signal processing pipeline. In: European Conference on Computer Vision Workshops (2020)
7. Ignatov, A., Van Gool, L., Timofte, R.: Replacing mobile camera ISP with a single deep learning model. In: Proceedings of the IEEE/CVF Conference on Computer Vision and Pattern Recognition Workshops, pp. 536–537 (2020)

8. Kim, J., Kwon Lee, J., Mu Lee, K.: Accurate image super-resolution using very deep convolutional networks. In: Proceedings of the IEEE Conference on Computer Vision and Pattern Recognition, pp. 1646–1654 (2016)
9. Ledig, C., et al.: Photo-realistic single image super-resolution using a generative adversarial network. In: Proceedings of the IEEE Conference on Computer Vision and Pattern Recognition, pp. 4681–4690 (2017)
10. Lim, B., Son, S., Kim, H., Nah, S., Mu Lee, K.: Enhanced deep residual networks for single image super-resolution. In: Proceedings of the IEEE Conference on Computer Vision and Pattern Recognition Workshops, pp. 136–144 (2017)
11. Mei, K., Li, J., Zhang, J., Wu, H., Li, J., Huang, R.: Higher-resolution network for image demosaicing and enhancing. In: 2019 IEEE/CVF International Conference on Computer Vision Workshop (ICCVW), pp. 3441–3448. IEEE (2019)
12. Ronneberger, O., Fischer, P., Brox, T.: U-Net: convolutional networks for biomedical image segmentation. In: Navab, N., Hornegger, J., Wells, W.M., Frangi, A.F. (eds.) MICCAI 2015. LNCS, vol. 9351, pp. 234–241. Springer, Cham (2015). https://doi.org/10.1007/978-3-319-24574-4_28
13. Schwartz, E., Giryes, R., Bronstein, A.M.: Deepisp: toward learning an end-to-end image processing pipeline. IEEE Trans. Image Process. **28**(2), 912–923 (2018)
14. Shi, W., et al.: Real-time single image and video super-resolution using an efficient sub-pixel convolutional neural network. In: Proceedings of the IEEE Conference on Computer Vision and Pattern Recognition, pp. 1874–1883 (2016)
15. Smith, L.N., Topin, N.: Super-convergence: very fast training of neural networks using large learning rates. In: Artificial Intelligence and Machine Learning for Multi-Domain Operations Applications, vol. 11006, p. 1100612. International Society for Optics and Photonics (2019)
16. Uhm, K.H., Kim, S.W., Ji, S.W., Cho, S.J., Hong, J.P., Ko, S.J.: W-Net: two-stage U-Net with misaligned data for raw-to-RGB mapping. In: 2019 IEEE/CVF International Conference on Computer Vision Workshop (ICCVW), pp. 3636–3642. IEEE (2019)
17. Wang, X., et al.: Esrgan: enhanced super-resolution generative adversarial networks. In: Proceedings of the European Conference on Computer Vision (ECCV) (2018)
18. Zhang, R., Isola, P., Efros, A.A., Shechtman, E., Wang, O.: The unreasonable effectiveness of deep features as a perceptual metric. In: Proceedings of the IEEE Conference on Computer Vision and Pattern Recognition, pp. 586–595 (2018)
19. Zhang, Y., Li, K., Li, K., Wang, L., Zhong, B., Fu, Y.: Image super-resolution using very deep residual channel attention networks. In: Proceedings of the European Conference on Computer Vision (ECCV), pp. 286–301 (2018)
20. Zhang, Y., Tian, Y., Kong, Y., Zhong, B., Fu, Y.: Residual dense network for image super-resolution. In: Proceedings of the IEEE Conference on Computer Vision and Pattern Recognition, pp. 2472–2481 (2018)
21. Zhao, Y., et al.: Saliency map-aided generative adversarial network for raw to RGB mapping. In: 2019 IEEE/CVF International Conference on Computer Vision Workshop (ICCVW), pp. 3449–3457. IEEE (2019)
22. Zhu, J.Y., Park, T., Isola, P., Efros, A.A.: Unpaired image-to-image translation using cycle-consistent adversarial networks. In: Proceedings of the IEEE International Conference on Computer Vision, pp. 2223–2232 (2017)

AIM 2020 Challenge on Rendering Realistic Bokeh

Andrey Ignatov[1(✉)], Radu Timofte[1], Ming Qian[2], Congyu Qiao[2], Jiamin Lin[2],
Zhenyu Guo[2], Chenghua Li[2], Cong Leng[2], Jian Cheng[2], Juewen Peng[3],
Xianrui Luo[3], Ke Xian[3], Zijin Wu[3], Zhiguo Cao[3], Densen Puthussery[4],
C. V. Jiji[4], P. S. Hrishikesh[4], Melvin Kuriakose[4], Saikat Dutta[5,6,7],
Sourya Dipta Das[5,6,7], Nisarg A. Shah[5,6,7], Kuldeep Purohit[5],
Praveen Kandula[5], Maitreya Suin[5], A. N. Rajagopalan[5], M. B. Saagara[4],
A. L. Minnu[4], A. R. Sanjana[4], S. Praseeda[4], Ge Wu[8], Xueqin Chen[8],
Tengyao Wang[8], Max Zheng[8], Hulk Wong[8], and Jay Zou[8]

[1] Computer Vision Lab, ETH Zurich, Zürich, Switzerland
{andrey,radu.timofte}@vision.ee.ethz.ch
[2] Nanjing Artificial Intelligence Chip Research, Institute of Automation,
Chinese Academy of Sciences (AiRiA), MAICRO, Beijing, China
20181223053@nuist.edu.cn
[3] Huazhong University of Science and Technology, Wuhan, China
im.pengjw@gmail.com
[4] College of Engineering Trivandrum, Trivandrum, India
puthusserydensen@gmail.com, {hrishikeshps,saagara}@cet.ac.in,
ar.sanjanaar@gmail.com
[5] Indian Institute of Technology Madras, Chennai, India
cs18s016@smail.iitm.ac.in, kuldeeppurohit3@gmail.com
[6] Jadavpur University, Kolkata, India
[7] Indian Institute of Technology Jodhpur, Jodhpur, India
[8] Beijing, China
1047670389@qq.com, 1843639867@qq.com

Abstract. This paper reviews the second AIM realistic bokeh effect rendering challenge and provides the description of the proposed solutions and results. The participating teams were solving a real-world bokeh simulation problem, where the goal was to learn a realistic shallow focus technique using a large-scale EBB! bokeh dataset consisting of 5K shallow/wide depth-of-field image pairs captured using the Canon 7D DSLR camera. The participants had to render bokeh effect based on only one single frame without any additional data from other cameras or sensors. The target metric used in this challenge combined the runtime and the perceptual quality of the solutions measured in the user study. To ensure the efficiency of the submitted models, we measured their runtime on standard desktop CPUs as well as were running the models on smartphone GPUs. The proposed solutions significantly improved the baseline results, defining the state-of-the-art for practical bokeh effect rendering problem.

A. Ignatov and R. Timofte are the challenge organizers, while the other authors participated in the challenge.
The Appendix A contains the authors' teams and affiliations.
AIM 2020 webpage: https://data.vision.ee.ethz.ch/cvl/aim20/

1   Introduction

The advances in image manipulation tasks are impressive. In particular, the image manipulation related to portable devices such as smartphone cameras has recently faced an interest boost from the research community to match the users' demands. Multiple novel solutions were proposed in the literature for various tasks, such as image quality enhancement [1,12,17,35], style transfer [8,22,27], learning of an image signal processor (ISP) [20], photo segmentation and blurring [2,4,33,36], etc. Moreover, modern mobile devices got powerful GPUs and NPUs that are well suitable for running the proposed deep learning models [15,16].

Rendering an automatic bokeh effect has been one of the most popular topics over past few years, with many solutions that are now included within the majority of smartphone camera applications. In 2014, a seminal work on portrait segmentation [9] was published, and substantial improvements in segmentation accuracy were reported in many subsequent papers [33,38]. Wadhwa *et al.* [36] provided a detailed description of the synthetic depth-of-field rendering method found in the Google Pixel phones and inspired further development in this field.

The AIM 2020 challenge on rendering realistic bokeh builds upon the success of the previous AIM 2019 challenge [14], and advances the benchmarking of example-based single image bokeh effect rendering by introducing two tracks with evaluation on several recent-generation desktop CPUs and smartphone GPUs. The AIM 2020 challenge uses the large-scale EBB! [13] dataset consisting of photo pairs with shallow and wide depth-of-field captured using the Canon 70D DSLR camera. Quantitative and qualitative visual results as well as the inference time and efficiency are used for ranking the proposed solutions. The challenge, the corresponding dataset, the results and the proposed methods are described and discussed in the next sections.

This challenge is one of the AIM 2020 associated challenges on: scene relighting and illumination estimation [6], image extreme inpainting [29], learned image signal processing pipeline [18], rendering realistic bokeh [19], real image super-resolution [37], efficient super-resolution [40], video temporal super-resolution [34] and video extreme super-resolution [7].

2   AIM 2020 Challenge on Realistic Bokeh

The objectives of the AIM 2020 challenge on rendering realistic bokeh effect is to promote realistic settings as defined by the *EBB!* Bokeh dataset, to push the state-of-the-art in synthetic shallow depth-of-field rendering, and to ensure that the final solutions are efficient enough to run both on desktop and mobile hardware.

Fig. 1. Sample wide and shallow depth-of-field image pairs from the EBB! dataset.

2.1 *Everything is Better with Bokeh!* Dataset

One of the biggest challenges in the bokeh rendering task is to get high-quality real data that can be used for training deep models. To tackle this problem, we used a large-scale *Everything is Better with Bokeh!* (EBB!) dataset presented in [13] that is containing more than 10 thousand images collected in the wild during several months. By controlling the aperture size of the lens, images with shallow and wide depth-of-field were taken. In each photo pair, the first image was captured with a narrow aperture (f/16) that results in a normal sharp photo, whereas the second one was shot using the highest aperture (f/1.8) leading to a strong bokeh effect. The photos were taken during the daytime in a wide variety of places and in various illumination and weather conditions. The photos were captured in automatic mode, the default settings were used throughout the entire collection procedure. An example set of collected images is presented in Fig. 1.

The captured image pairs are not aligned exactly, therefore they were first matched using SIFT keypoints and RANSAC method same as in [12]. The resulting images were then cropped to their intersection part and downscaled so that their final height is equal to 1024 pixels. From the resulting 10 thousand images, 200 image pairs were reserved for testing, while the other 4.8 thousand photo pairs can be used for training and validation.

2.2 Tracks and Competitions

The challenge consists of the following phases:

 i *development:* the participants get access to the data;
 ii *validation:* the participants have the opportunity to validate their solutions on the server and compare the results on the validation leaderboard;
iii *test:* the participants submit their final results, models, and factsheets.

All submitted solutions were evaluated based on the following measures:

– PSNR measuring fidelity score,
– SSIM, a proxy for perceptual score,
– The runtime of the submitted models on desktop CPUs and mobile GPUs,
– MOS scores measured in the user study for explicit image quality assessment.

The AIM 2020 challenge on realistic bokeh consists of two tracks. In the first "CPU" track, the target was to produce a model which runtime is optimized for standard desktop CPUs. In the second, "Smartphone GPU" track, the goal was to develop a TensorFlow Lite [25] compatible solution that was tested on several mobile GPUs using a publicly available[1] *AI Benchmark* application [16] and an OpenCL-based TFLite GPU delegate [5]. During the development and validation phases, the quantitative performance of the solutions was measured by PSNR and SSIM metric. Since SSIM and PSNR scores are not reflecting many aspects of real quality of the resulted images, during the final test phase we evaluated the solutions based on their Mean Opinion Scores (MOS). For this, we conducted a user study evaluating the visual results of all proposed methods. The users were asked to rate the quality of each submitted solution by selecting one of the five quality levels (5 - comparable perceptual quality, 4 - slightly worse, 3 - notably worse, 2 - poor perceptual quality, 1 - completely corrupted image) for each method result in comparison with the original Canon images exhibiting bokeh effect. The expressed preferences were averaged per each test image and then per each method to obtain the final MOS.

3   Challenge Results

The Track 1 of the challenge attracted more than 110 registered participants and the Track 2 more than 80. However, only 9 teams provided results in the final phase together with factsheets and codes for reproducibility. Tables 1 and 2 summarize the final challenge results in terms of PSNR, SSIM and MOS scores for each submitted solution in addition to self-reported hardware/software configurations and runtimes. Short descriptions of the proposed solutions are provided in Sect. 4, and the team details (contact email, members and affiliations) are listed in Appendix A.

---

[1] http://ai-benchmark.com.

Table 1. AIM 2020 realistic bokeh rendering challenge, CPU Track: results and final rankings. The results are sorted based on the MOS scores. * - These teams submitted solutions that are using pre-computed depth maps and therefore were excluded from the final evaluation phase.

Team	Author	Factsheet Info		Track 1: Desktop CPU			
		Framework	Training Hardware, GPU	Avg. Runtime, s	PSNR↑	SSIM↑	MOS↑
Airia-bokeh	MingQian	TensorFlow	Nvidia TITAN RTX	5.52	23.58	0.8770	**4.2**
AIA-Smart	JuewenPeng	PyTorch	GeForce GTX 1080	1.71	23.56	0.8829	3.8
CET_SP	memelvin99	TensorFlow	Nvidia Tesla P100	1.17	21.91	0.8201	3.3
CET_CVLab	Densen	TensorFlow	Nvidia Tesla P100	1.17	23.05	0.8591	3.2
Team Horizon	tensorcat	PyTorch	GeForce GTX 1080 Ti	19.27	23.27	0.8818	3.2
IPCV_IITM	ms_ipcv	PyTorch	NVIDIA Titan X	27.24	**23.77**	**0.8866**	2.5
CET21_CV	SaagaraMB	TensorFlow	Nvidia Tesla P100	**0.74**	22.80	0.8628	1.3
CET_ECE	Sanjana.A.R	TensorFlow	Nvidia Tesla P100	**0.74**	22.85	0.8629	1.2
xuehuapiaopiao-team	xuehuapiaopiao	TensorFlow	GeForce GTX 1080 Ti	-	22.98	0.8758	- *
Terminator	Max_zheng	TensorFlow	GeForce GTX 1080 Ti	-	23.04	0.8756	- *

Table 2. AIM 2020 realistic bokeh rendering challenge, GPU Track: results and final rankings. The results are sorted based on the MOS scores. The model submitted by the Team Horizon was unable to run on mobile GPUs due to NCHW channel order that is currently not supported by the TensorFlow Lite GPU delegate.

Team	Author	Factsheet Info		Track 2: Smartphone GPU			
		Framework	Training Hardware, GPU	Avg. Runtime, s	PSNR↑	SSIM↑	MOS↑
Airia-bokeh	MingQian	TensorFlow	Nvidia TITAN RTX	**1.52**	**23.58**	0.8770	**4.2**
AIA-Smart	JuewenPeng	PyTorch	GeForce GTX 1080	15.2	22.94	**0.8842**	4.0
CET_CVLab	Densen	TensorFlow	Nvidia Tesla P100	2.75	23.05	0.8591	3.2
Team Horizon	tensorcat	PyTorch	GeForce GTX 1080 Ti	- *	23.27	0.8818	3.2

3.1   Architectures and Main Ideas

All the proposed methods are relying on end-to-end deep learning-based solutions. Almost all submitted models have a multi-scale encoder-decoder architecture and are processing the images at several scales. This allows to achieve a significantly faster runtime as all heavy image processing is done on images of low resolution, as well as adds the possibility of introducing heavy global image manipulations. The majority of teams were using the $L1$, SSIM/MS-SSIM, VGG-based, Sobel and Charbonnier loss functions, while team Airia-bokeh demonstrated that a proper adversarial loss can significantly boost the quality of the resulting bokeh effect. Almost all teams were using the Adam optimizer [23] to train deep learning models and TensorFlow or PyTorch frameworks to implement and train the networks.

3.2 Performance

Quality. Airia-bokeh is the winner of the AIM 2020 challenge on rendering realistic bokeh. Airia-bokeh ranks the best in perceptual quality in both track 1 and track 2 with the same solution (deep model). Only one team – AIA-Smart, – submitted different models/solutions for the two tracks of the challenge. Surprisingly, the solution submitted for evaluation on smartphone GPU (Track 2) obtained better SSIM and MOS results than the one for CPU (Track 1). They are coming second to Airia-bokeh in the MOS score while reporting the best SSIM (0.8842) in Track 2. As expected, the perceptual ranking according to the MOS does not strongly correlate with the fidelity measures such as PSNR and SSIM. In particular, IPCV_IITM team ranks first in terms of SSIM and PSNR but only sixth in terms of perceptual quality (Track 1). Interestingly, the CET_SP team has the lowest fidelity (PSNR) and SSIM results, though comes third in perceptual quality (MOS).

Runtime. The measured average runtimes of the proposed solutions on standard Nvidia GPU cards (CPU Track 1) vary from 0.7 s to more than 27 s per single image. The fastest solutions (~0.7 s) are also among the worst performing in perceptual ranking, while the top fidelity method proposed by IPCV_IITM requires 27 s, and the top perceptual methods of Airia-bokeh and of AIA-Smart require 5.52 s and 1.71 s, respectively. When it comes to the solutions proposed in Track 2 evaluated on smartphone GPUs, the best perceptual quality solution of Airia-bokch is also with the lowest inference time, 1.52 s. We conclude that the proposed solutions do not meet the requirements for real-time applications on the current generation of smartphones, thus all processing should be done in the background after the image is obtained/captured.

3.3 Discussion

With the AIM 2020 challenge, we went further compared to the previously held challenges and aimed at solutions meant to run efficiently on desktop and smartphone hardware. The challenge employed the EBB! [13], a novel large dataset containing paired and aligned low- and high-aperture photos captured with a high-end Canon 70D DSLR camera. Several of the proposed approaches produced results with good perceptual quality and runtime suitable for on-device image processing. These methods are gauging the state-of-the-art for the practical bokeh synthesis task learned from pairs of real exemplars.

4 Challenge Methods and Teams

This section describes solutions submitted by all teams participating in the final stage of the AIM 2020 realistic bokeh rendering challenge.

4.1   Airia-Bokeh

Team Airia-bokeh proposed a Bokeh-Glass Network (BG-Net) [31] model for rendering realistic bokeh that is illustrated in Fig. 2. The model consists of two stacked U-Net based networks that were first trained separately using a combination of the L_1 and SSIM losses (with weights 0.5 and 1, respectively). During the second stage, two PatchGAN [42] discriminators with different receptive fields were added to improve the quality of the produced images. The generator and the discriminator were trained together using the WGAN-GP algorithm with a batch size of 1. The authors have additionally enhanced the EBB! dataset by removing some image pairs that did not correspond in color or were not in focus.

4.2   AIA-Smart

The solution of AIA-Smart team is based on defocus map estimation [28]. The proposed architecture consists of 4 modules (Fig. 3): defocus estimation, radiance, rendering and upsampling modules. Defocus estimation module is used to predict a defocus map, which works as a guidance for defocus rendering. Radiance module calculates the weight map used for estimating the weight of each pixel in the rendering process. In the rendering module, the low resolution bokeh result can be obtained with the input of the radiance map, weight map and defocus map using the refocusing pipeline proposed in [3]. In the upsampling module, the low resolution bokeh result and the high resolution original image are combined to generate the final full-resolution bokeh image.

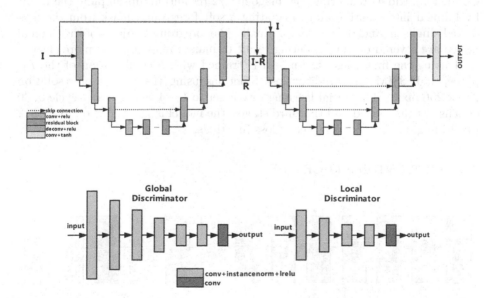

Fig. 2. Bokeh-Glass Network network (top) and PatchGAN-based discriminators (bottom) proposed by Airia-bokeh team.

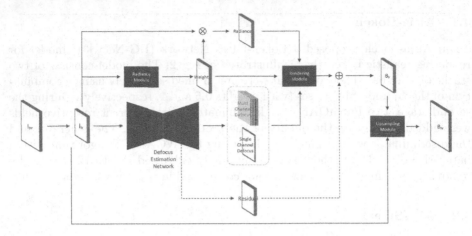

Fig. 3. AIA-Smart network consisting of the defocus estimation, radiance, rendering and upsampling modules.

The training of the network can be divided into 4 stages: 1) predicting the layered defocus maps and render the bokeh result on 1/4 of the original resolution, 2) rendering bokeh effect at 1/2 resolution while using the pretrained network from the first stage to refine the details around foreground boundaries, 3) replacing the multi-channel classification layer with a single-channel regression layer in the defocus estimation module to generate the pleasing'Circle of Confusion', and 4) rendering the image at 1/2 resolution, upsampling the result by bilinear interpolation and calculating a soft foreground mask from the predicted single-channel defocus map. Finally, the foreground objects of the original image are covered on the rendering result to make the foreground more clear.

During the first stage, the model is trained with a combination of the L_1, perceptual, SSIM and gradient loss functions using the images of resolution 256×256 pixels. The initial learning rate is set to $1e-4$ with a decay-cycle of 30 epochs. At the second and the third stages, the model is fine-tuned on 512×512 pixel images using the same set of loss functions.

4.3　CET_CVLab and CET_SP

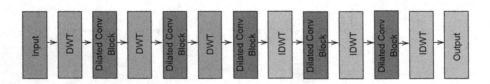

Fig. 4. Dilated Wavelet CNN model used by CET_CVLab and CET_SP teams.

Both CET_CVLab and CET_SP teams used the same U-Net based Dilated Wavelet CNN model (Fig. 4) for generating bokeh images. In this network, the standard downsampling and upsampling operations are replaced with a discrete wavelet transform based (DWT) decomposition to minimize the information loss in these layers. The proposed methodology is computationally efficient and is based on the multi-level wavelet-CNN (MWCNN) proposed in [26].

CET_SP trained the model with a combination of the Charbonnier and perceptual VGG loss, while CET_CVLab additionally used Sobel and Grayscale (L_1 distance between the grayscale images) loss functions. Both models were optimized using the Adam algorithm with a batch size of 10 for 600 and 500 epoch, respectively.

4.4   Team Horizon

The authors proposed an encoder-decoder based model shown in Fig. 5 that is trained at several scales. At each level, the encoder-decoder module is producing the weight maps that are used together with the input image by the bokeh generation module to render the bokeh image. Generated weight maps and bokeh images are then upscaled and concatenated with the input image in the next level, while the upscaled encoded features are added to the corresponding encoded features used in the next level. The model is trained with a combination of the MS-SSIM and SSIM loss functions.

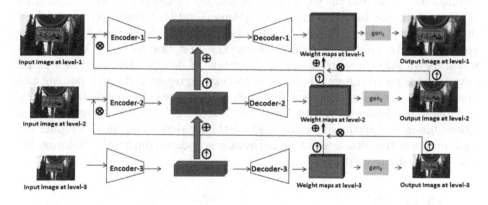

Fig. 5. A multiscale encoder-decoder based model proposed by Team Horizon.

4.5   IPCV_IITM

The authors proposed a depth-guided dynamic filtering dense network for rendering shallow depth-of-field (Fig. 6). At the onset, the network uses a space-to-depth module that divides each input channel into a number of blocks concatenated along the channel dimension. The output of this layer is concatenated with

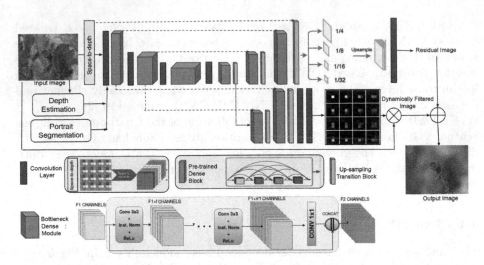

Fig. 6. Depth-guided Dynamic Filtering Dense Network proposed by IPCV_IITM.

the outputs of the pre-trained depth estimation [24] and salient object segmentation [10] networks to achieve more accurate rendering results. The resulting feature maps are passed to a U-net [32] based encoder consisting of densely connected modules. The first dense-block contains 12 densely-connected layers, the second block – 16, and the third one – 24 densely-connected layers. The weights of each block are initialized using the DenseNet-121 network [11] trained on the ImageNet dataset. The decoder has two difference branches which outputs are summed to produce the final result. The first branch has a U-net architecture with skip-connections and also consists of densely connected blocks. Its output is enhanced through multi-scale context aggregation through pooling and upsampling at 4 scales. The second branch uses the idea of dynamic filtering [21] and generates dynamic blurring filters conditioned on the encoded feature map. These filters are produced locally and on-the-fly depending on the input, the parameters of the filter-generating network are updated during the training. We refer to [30] for more details.

4.6   CET21_CV

CET21_CV proposed a modified U-Net model depicted in Fig. 7. Compared to the original U-Net implementation, the authors replaced the max-pooling downsampling operation with a strided convolution layer, and the feature maps from shortcut connections are concatenated before applying the activation functions in the decoder module. *Leaky ReLU* activations are used in the convolutional layers, and the entire model is trained to minimize the mean absolute error loss using the Adam algorithm.

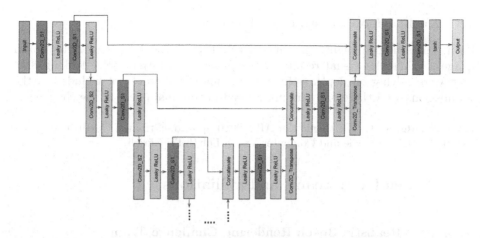

Fig. 7. A modified U-Net model used by CET21_CV team.

4.7 CET_ECE

The model architecture proposed by CET_ECE team was inspired from the wide activation [39] and channel attention [41] based networks. The proposed network (Fig. 8) is generally consisting of 2 block types: a feature extraction block and a series of wide activation residual blocks. To reduce the model complexity and information loss, a space-to-depth layer with a scale factor of 4 is used before the initial feature extraction block, and a depth-to-space operation is used as the last layer of the network. The Charbonnier loss function is used for training the network as it better captures the edge information compared to the MSE loss.

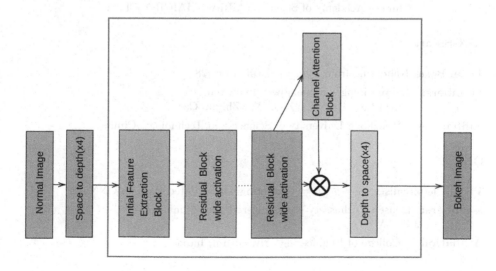

Fig. 8. CET_ECE's network architecture.

4.8   Xuehuapiaopiao-Team and Terminator

Both teams used a slightly modified PyNET [13] model for generating bokeh images. While the visual results of the proposed solutions were looking fine, they were relying on depth estimation modules that were not included in the submissions, and therefore were not ranked in the final phase of the challenge.

Acknowledgment. We thank the AIM 2020 sponsors: Huawei, MediaTek, Qualcomm, NVIDIA, Google and Computer Vision Lab/ETH Zürich.

A   Appendix 1: Teams and affiliations

AIM 2020 Realistic Bokeh Rendering Challenge Team

Title: AIM 2020 Challenge on Rendering Realistic Bokeh

Members: Andrey Ignatov – andrey@vision.ee.ethz.ch,
             Radu Timofte – radu.timofte@vision.ee.ethz.ch

Affiliations: Computer Vision Lab, ETH Zurich, Switzerland

Airia-bokeh

Title: BGNet: Bokeh-Glass Network for Rendering Realistic Bokeh

Members: Ming Qian – 20181223053@nuist.edu.cn,
             Congyu Qiao, Jiamin Lin, Zhenyu Guo, Chenghua Li,
             Cong Leng, Jian Cheng

Affiliations: Nanjing Artificial Intelligence Chip Research, Institute of Automation Chinese Academy of Sciences (AiRiA), MAICRO, China

AIA-Smart

Title: Bokeh Rendering from Defocus Estimation [28]

Members: Juewen Peng – im.pengjw@gmail.com,
             Xianrui Luo, Ke Xian, Zijin Wu, Zhiguo Cao

Affiliations: Huazhong University of Science and Technology, China

CET_CVLab

Title: Photorealistic Bokeh Effect Rendering with Dilated Wavelet CNN

Members: Densen Puthussery – puthusserydensen@gmail.com,
             Jiji C V

Affiliations: College of Engineering Trivandrum, India

CET_SP

Title: Bokeh Effect using VGG based Wavelet CNN
Members: Hrishikesh P S – hrishikeshps@cet.ac.in,
      Melvin Kuriakose
Affiliations: College of Engineering Trivandrum, India

Team Horizon

Title: Deep Multi-scale Hierarchical Network for Bokeh Effect Rendering
Members: Saikat Dutta – cs18s016@smail.iitm.ac.in,
      Sourya Dipta Das, Nisarg A. Shah
Affiliations: Indian Institute of Technology Madras, India
      Jadavpur University, India
      Indian Institute of Technology Jodhpur, India

IPCV_IITM

Title: Dense Dynamic Filtering Network for Rendering Synthetic Depth-of-Field Effect
Members: Kuldeep Purohit – kuldeeppurohit3@gmail.com,
      Praveen Kandula, Maitreya Suin, A. N. Rajagopalan
Affiliations: Indian Institute of Technology Madras, India

CET21_CV

Title: Synthetic Bokeh Effect with Modified UNet
Members: Saagara M B – saagara@cet.ac.in,
      Minnu A L
Affiliations: College of Engineering Trivandrum, India

CET_ECE

Title: Bokeh Effect Rendering with Deep Convolutional Neural Network
Members: Sanjana A R – ar.sanjanaar@gmail.com,
      Praseeda S
Affiliations: College of Engineering Trivandrum, India

Xuehuapiaopiao-team

Title: Multi-scale Bokeh Rendering Network
Members: Ge Wu – 1047670389@qq.com,
      Xueqin Chen, Tengyao Wang
Affiliations: None

Terminator

Title: Simulating Realistic Bokeh Rendering with an Improved Dataset and Robust Network

Members: Max Zheng – 1843639867@qq.com,
          Hulk Wong, Jay Zou
Affiliations: None

References

1. Ancuti, C.O., Ancuti, C., Timofte, R., et al.: Ntire 2019 challenge on image dehazing: Methods and results. In: The IEEE/CVF Conference on Computer Vision and Pattern Recognition (CVPR) Workshops (2019)
2. Badrinarayanan, V., Kendall, A., Cipolla, R.: SegNet: a deep convolutional encoder-decoder architecture for image segmentation. IEEE Trans. Pattern Anal. Mach. Intell. **39**(12), 2481–2495 (2017)
3. Busam, B., Hog, M., McDonagh, S., Slabaugh, G.: SteReFo: efficient image refocusing with stereo vision. In: Proceedings of the IEEE International Conference on Computer Vision Workshops (2019)
4. Chen, L.C., Papandreou, G., Kokkinos, I., Murphy, K., Yuille, A.L.: DeepLab: Semantic image segmentation with deep convolutional nets, ATROUS convolution, and fully connected CRFs. IEEE Trans. Pattern Anal. Mach. Intell. **40**(4), 834–848 (2017)
5. delegate, T.L.G. https://www.tensorflow.org/lite/performance/gpu
6. El Helou, M., et al.: AIM 2020: scene relighting and illumination estimation challenge. In: Bartoli, A., Fusiello, A. (eds.) ECCV 2020, LNCS 12537, pp. 499–518. Springer, Cham (2020)
7. Fuoli, D., et al.: AIM 2020 challenge on video extreme super-resolution: Methods and results. In: Bartoli, A., Fusiello, A. (eds.) ECCV 2020, LNCS 12538, pp. 57–81. Springer, Cham (2020)
8. Gatys, L.A., Ecker, A.S., Bethge, M.: Image style transfer using convolutional neural networks. In: Proceedings of the IEEE Conference on Computer Vision and Pattern Recognition, pp. 2414–2423 (2016)
9. L.B. in the new Google Camera app. https://ai.googleblog.com/2014/04/lens-blur-in-new-google-camera-app.html
10. Hou, Q., Cheng, M.M., Hu, X., Borji, A., Tu, Z., Torr, P.H.: Deeply supervised salient object detection with short connections. In: Proceedings of the IEEE Conference on Computer Vision and Pattern Recognition, pp. 3203–3212 (2017)
11. Huang, G., Liu, Z., Van Der Maaten, L., Weinberger, K.Q.: Densely connected convolutional networks. In: Proceedings of the IEEE Conference on Computer Vision and Pattern Recognition, pp. 4700–4708 (2017)
12. Ignatov, A., Kobyshev, N., Timofte, R., Vanhoey, K., Van Gool, L.: DSLR-quality photos on mobile devices with deep convolutional networks. In: the IEEE International Conference on Computer Vision (ICCV) (2017)
13. Ignatov, A., Patel, J., Timofte, R.: Rendering natural camera bokeh effect with deep learning. In: Proceedings of the IEEE/CVF Conference on Computer Vision and Pattern Recognition Workshops, pp. 418–419 (2020)

14. Ignatov, A., et al.: AIM 2019 challenge on bokeh effect synthesis: methods and results. In: 2019 IEEE/CVF International Conference on Computer Vision Workshop (ICCVW), pp. 3591–3598. IEEE (2019)

15. Ignatov, A., et al.: AI Benchmark: running deep neural networks on android smartphones. In: Leal-Taixé, L., Roth, S. (eds.) ECCV 2018. LNCS, vol. 11133, pp. 288–314. Springer, Cham (2019). https://doi.org/10.1007/978-3-030-11021-5_19

16. Ignatov, A., et al.: AI Benchmark: all about deep learning on smartphones in 2019. In: 2019 IEEE/CVF International Conference on Computer Vision Workshop (ICCVW), pp. 3617–3635. IEEE (2019)

17. Ignatov, A., Timofte, R., et al.: PIRM challenge on perceptual image enhancement on smartphones: report. In: European Conference on Computer Vision Workshops (2018)

18. Ignatov, A., Timofte, R., et al.: AIM 2020 challenge on learned image signal processing pipeline. In: Bartoli, A., Fusiello, A. (eds.) ECCV 2020, LNCS 12537, pp. 152–170. Springer, Cham (2020)

19. Ignatov, A., Timofte, R., et al.: AIM 2020 challenge on rendering realistic bokeh. In: Bartoli, A., Fusiello, A. (eds.) ECCV 2020, LNCS 12537, pp. 213–228. Springer, Cham (2020)

20. Ignatov, A., Van Gool, L., Timofte, R.: Replacing mobile camera ISP with a single deep learning model. In: Proceedings of the IEEE/CVF Conference on Computer Vision and Pattern Recognition Workshops, pp. 536–537 (2020)

21. Jia, X., De Brabandere, B., Tuytelaars, T., Gool, L.V.: Dynamic filter networks. In: Advances in Neural Information Processing Systems, pp. 667–675 (2016)

22. Johnson, J., Alahi, A., Fei-Fei, L.: Perceptual losses for real-time style transfer and super-resolution. In: Leibe, B., Matas, J., Sebe, N., Welling, M. (eds.) ECCV 2016. LNCS, vol. 9906, pp. 694–711. Springer, Cham (2016). https://doi.org/10.1007/978-3-319-46475-6_43

23. Kingma, D.P., Ba, J.: Adam: a method for stochastic optimization. arXiv preprint arXiv:1412.6980 (2014)

24. Li, Z., Snavely, N.: Megadepth: learning single-view depth prediction from internet photos. In: Proceedings of the IEEE Conference on Computer Vision and Pattern Recognition, pp. 2041–2050 (2018)

25. Lite, T.: https://www.tensorflow.org/lite

26. Liu, P., Zhang, H., Zhang, K., Lin, L., Zuo, W.: Multi-level wavelet-CNN for image restoration. In: Proceedings of the IEEE Conference on Computer Vision and Pattern Recognition Workshops, pp. 773–782 (2018)

27. Luan, F., Paris, S., Shechtman, E., Bala, K.: Deep photo style transfer. In: Proceedings of the IEEE Conference on Computer Vision and Pattern Recognition, pp. 4990–4998 (2017)

28. Luo, X., Peng, J., Xian, K., Wu, Z., Cao, Z.: Bokeh rendering from defocus estimation. In: Bartoli, A., Fusiello, A. (eds.) ECCV 2020, LNCS 12537, pp. 245–261. Springer, Cham (2020)

29. Ntavelis, E., et al.: AIM 2020 challenge on image extreme inpainting. In: Bartoli, A., Fusiello, A. (eds.) ECCV 2020, LNCS 12537, pp. 716–741. Springer, Cham (2020)

30. Purohit, K., Suin, M., Kandula, P., Ambasamudram, R.: Depth-guided dense dynamic filtering network for bokeh effect rendering. In: 2019 IEEE/CVF International Conference on Computer Vision Workshop (ICCVW), pp. 3417–3426. IEEE (2019)

31. Qian, M., Qiao, C., Lin, J., Guo, Z., Li, C., Leng, C., Cheng, J.: Bggan: Bokeh-glass generative adversarial network for rendering realistic bokeh. In: Bartoli, A., Fusiello, A. (eds.) ECCV 2020, LNCS 12537, pp. 229–244. Springer, Cham (2020)
32. Ronneberger, O., Fischer, P., Brox, T.: U-Net: convolutional networks for biomedical image segmentation. In: Navab, N., Hornegger, J., Wells, W.M., Frangi, A.F. (eds.) MICCAI 2015. LNCS, vol. 9351, pp. 234–241. Springer, Cham (2015). https://doi.org/10.1007/978-3-319-24574-4_28
33. Shen, X., et al.: Automatic portrait segmentation for image stylization. In: Computer Graphics Forum, vol. 35, pp. 93–102. Wiley Online Library (2016)
34. Son, S., Lee, J., Nah, S., Timofte, R., Lee, K.M., et al.: AIM 2020 challenge on video temporal super-resolution. In: European Conference on Computer Vision Workshops (2020)
35. Timofte, R., Gu, S., Wu, J., Van Gool, L.: Ntire 2018 challenge on single image super-resolution: methods and results. In: The IEEE Conference on Computer Vision and Pattern Recognition (CVPR) Workshops, June 2018
36. Wadhwa, N., Garg, R., Jacobs, D.E., Feldman, B.E., Kanazawa, N., Carroll, R., Movshovitz-Attias, Y., Barron, J.T., Pritch, Y., Levoy, M.: Synthetic depth-of-field with a single-camera mobile phone. ACM Trans. Graphics (TOG) **37**(4), 64 (2018)
37. Wei, P., Lu, H., Timofte, R., Lin, L., Zuo, W., et al.: AIM 2020 challenge on real image super-resolution: methods and results. In: Bartoli, A., Fusiello, A. (eds.) ECCV 2020, LNCS 12537, pp. 392–422. Springer, Cham (2020)
38. Xu, N., Price, B., Cohen, S., Huang, T.: Deep image matting. In: Proceedings of the IEEE Conference on Computer Vision and Pattern Recognition, pp. 2970–2979 (2017)
39. Yu, J., et al.: Wide activation for efficient and accurate image super-resolution. arXiv preprint arXiv:1808.08718 (2018)
40. Zhang, K., et al.: AIM 2020 challenge on efficient super-resolution: methods and results. In: Bartoli, A., Fusiello, A. (eds.) ECCV 2020, LNCS 12537, pp. 5–40. Springer, Cham (2020)
41. Zhang, Y., Li, K., Li, K., Wang, L., Zhong, B., Fu, Y.: Image super-resolution using very deep residual channel attention networks. In: Ferrari, V., Hebert, M., Sminchisescu, C., Weiss, Y. (eds.) ECCV 2018. LNCS, vol. 11211, pp. 294–310. Springer, Cham (2018). https://doi.org/10.1007/978-3-030-01234-2_18
42. Zhu, J.Y., Park, T., Isola, P., Efros, A.A.: Unpaired image-to-image translation using cycle-consistent adversarial networks. In: Proceedings of the IEEE International Conference on Computer Vision, pp. 2223–2232 (2017)

BGGAN: Bokeh-Glass Generative Adversarial Network for Rendering Realistic Bokeh

Ming Qian[1], Congyu Qiao[2], Jiamin Lin[3], Zhenyu Guo[4,5], Chenghua Li[4,6(✉)], Cong Leng[4,6], and Jian Cheng[4,6(✉)]

[1] Nanjing University of Information Science and Technology, Nanjing, China
mingqian@nuist.edu.cn
[2] Southeast University, Nanjing, China
cyqiao@njust.edu.cn
[3] Nanjing University of Science and Technology, Nanjing, China
linjiamin@njust.edu.cn
[4] Institute of Automation, Chinese Academy of Sciences, Beijing 100190, China
lichenghua2014@ia.ac.cn
[5] School of Artificial Intelligence, University of Chinese Academy of Sciences, Beijing 100049, China
guozhenyu2019@ia.ac.cn
[6] Nanjing Artificial Intelligence Chip Research, Institute of Automation, Chinese Academy of Sciences (AiRiA), Nanjing, China
lengcong@airia.cn, jcheng@nlpr.ia.ac.cn

Abstract. A photo captured with bokeh effect often means objects in focus are sharp while the out-of-focus areas are all blurred. DSLR can easily render this kind of effect naturally. However, due to the limitation of sensors, smartphones cannot capture images with depth-of-field effects directly. In this paper, we propose a novel generator called Glass-Net, which generates bokeh images not relying on complex hardware. Meanwhile, the GAN-based method and perceptual loss are combined for rendering a realistic bokeh effect in the stage of finetuning the model. Moreover, Instance Normalization(IN) is reimplemented in our network, which ensures our tflite model with IN can be accelerated on smartphone GPU. Experiments show that our method is able to render a high-quality bokeh effect and process one 1024×1536 pixel image in $1.9\,\mathrm{s}$ on all smartphone chipsets. This approach ranked First in AIM 2020 Rendering Realistic Bokeh Challenge Track 1 & Track 2.

Keywords: Bokeh · Depth-of-field · Smartphone GPU · GAN

1 Introduction

In photography, bokeh is considered one of the most important aesthetic standard when we need to blur the out-of-focus parts of an image produced by a

---

M. Qian—The work was done when Ming Qian was an intern at AiRiA.

A. Bartoli and A. Fusiello (Eds.): ECCV 2020 Workshops, LNCS 12537, pp. 229–244, 2020.
https://doi.org/10.1007/978-3-030-67070-2_14

camera lens. It occurs in the scene which lies outside the depth of field. Photographers sometimes deliberately adopt a shallow focus technique to create images with prominent out-of-focus regions [2] when using an SLR with a wide aperture lens. However, we can hardly take a picture with a bokeh effect using a smartphone with a monocular camera, because it is difficult to equip the little smartphone with too many sensors. Hence, it is an excellent way to render a synthetic bokeh effect on mobile devices at the level of software.

Synthetic bokeh effect rendering has developed for several years. Early works related to it only focus on portrait photos [19, 20, 23]. They usually segment the person from the image by using the semantic segmentation method and then blur the rest areas. The disadvantages of these methods are very obvious. Their datasets do not cover the images in a wide scene which are very necessary for most photographers.

In recent years smartphones have adopted various hardware to promote the realization of synthetic bokeh effect rendering. A method is described in detail on how to render a bokeh effect in Google Pixel devices [22]. In this work, they synthesize depth map by using the dual-pixel autofocus system. Plus, iPhone 7+ employs the dual-lens to estimate the depth of the scene. But these methods rely on special or expensive hardware, and these approaches may not suitable for low-end smartphone market. In fact, it is better for the bokeh effect to be rendered directly from a shooted image.

EBB! dataset [8] released by AIM 2020 Bokeh Effect Rendering Challenge [10] makes it possible for us to explore some new methods about Bokeh. The dataset pays more attention to synthetic bokeh effect rendering in wide scenes. In this dataset, objects in the depth-of-field area are not only portraits but also other objects, such as road signs, vehicles, flowers, and so on. It brings many challenges but more possibilities to render the bokeh effect. Many methods [3, 9, 17] have been proposed experimented on EBB! Dataset. Most of these methods are based on some priori knowledge including salient region detection and depth estimation method. In [3], they propose a method based on the depth estimation method megaDepth [15], which is a well-known algorithm for its outstanding performance of depth estimation on a single image. Then they design an efficient algorithm to blur the regions out-of-focus by Gaussian blur kernel. A DDDF architecture is proposed in [17], which uses both salient region segmentation [7] and depth estimation [15] as its priori knowledge. Aside from these, PyNET method [8] also employs the depth map produced by MegaDepth. Furthermore, they point out that depth maps can help improve the visual results despite the prior cannot increase $PSNR$ and $SSIM$, which are commonly used as quantitative indicators. From the methods mentioned above, we conclude that adding some priori knowledge like a salient region detection map or depth estimation map can improve the visual effect of the final generated image to some degree. But from another angle, those methods are relied on the priors heavily, meaning that when the priors do not work in some scenes, the final synthetic image will result in unknown problems. Plus, the pre-process of these prior methods is also time-consuming. Whenever we want to inference a new picture on our device, these models should run at first.

Generative Adversarial Networks (GANs) [4] are well known for the ability to preserve texture details in an image, generate a more realistic image, and fool people in perception. Recent years has witnessed that a large number of image-to-image translation tasks are completed by GANs, such as image deblurring [13], image super-resolution [16], style transferring [12], product photo generation [1] and so on. These works inspire us to consider bokeh as a subtask of image-to-image translation.

In this paper, we describe a novel approach to the bokeh problem, which is different from the existing algorithms that rely on various priori knowledge. We don't need the assistance of any other pre-trained models or datasets. What we need for training are only pairs of narrow-aperture images and shallow depth-of-field images. This strategy shortens the inference time compared with the methods which are based on priori knowledge. In addition, we employ a GAN-based method for finetuning our model, which turns out to be effective to improve the quality of visual effect in our work. To the best of our knowledge, we are the first to introduce the GAN method to image synthetic bokeh effect rendering. Finally, the proposed approach is independent of hardware devices and can perform efficient synthetic bokeh effect rendering on various devices.

Our main contributions are:

1) The first GAN-based method solves the synthetic bokeh effect rendering problem, and the visual effect has been greatly improved: the spot effect similar to that of large aperture SLR and the gradual blurring effect has been obtained.
2) Compared with the baseline, a novel generator architecture not only keeps the accuracy but also significantly improves the speed.
3) IN is re-realized by GPU supported ops on tflite, that ensures our tflite model with IN can be accelerated on smartphone GPU, and process one 1024×1536 pixel image less than $1.9\,s$ on all smartphone chipsets.

2   Proposed Method

We take Glass-Net and Multi-receptive-field Discriminator to construct our BGGAN. Glass-Net is an end-to-end network that takes an image as an input and produces the result with bokeh effect. Multi-receptive-field Discriminator refines the images generated by Glass-Net to make the final outputs cater to human perception. In addition, we use operators supported by TensorFlow Lite framework to reimplement IN to make sure all our model operators to compute on smartphone GPU.

2.1   Glass-Net

The generator is given a name Glass-Net for the network's shape is similar to a pair of glasses. The Glass-Net is a two-stage network. Glass-Net is illustrated in

232   M. Qian et al.

Fig. 1. In the first stage, the network learns the mapping from the image without
bokeh to the residual of the input image and ground truth. The relationship
between input image I, ground truth O, and residual R can be represented as
$R = I - O$, so we assume $I - R$ as the rough bokeh result. Therefore, the second
stage of Glass-Net plays the role of refining rough bokeh results to generate
realistic bokeh effects.

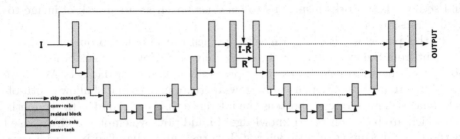

Fig. 1. Demonstration for Glass-Net

In Fig. 1, we can find that the first stage of the network and the second stage
of the network have the almost same structure. Both of them adopt the encoder-
decoder structure. The encoder blocks consist of three down-sampling layers
implemented by convolution with stride 2. We use 9 residual blocks [6] to transform features obtained from encoder blocks and each residual block sequentially
connects conv/ReLU/instancenorm/conv/ReLU layers. In addition, there is an
additional connection between the input and the output of the residual block.
The feature maps transformed by residual blocks are sent to decoder blocks.
Decoder blocks are implemented by three transposed convolutional layers with
stride 2. Convolutional layers of encoder blocks and transposed convolutional
layers of decoder blocks are all activated by ReLU. The output layers of the
two-stage Glass-Net are realized by convolution with stride 1 followed by tanh.
Skip-connections are applied between the convolutional layer and its mirrored
transposed convolutional layer to compensate the details of the output image
and the operation of skip connection is concatenation on the channel. This kind
of connection is also used by U-Net [18] structure. Experiments proved that skip
connections can convey high-frequency information so that the in-focus areas of
output images will not be blurred. The number of basic channels in the first
stage is 16 while the number is 32 in the second stage. The maximum number
of channels in the first stage is 128 and the number of stage two is 256.

2.2 Multi-receptive-field Discriminator

To generate more realistic bokeh images, WGAN-GP [5] is used as a significant
strategy in our network. Figure 2 illustrates the schematic diagram of Multi-
receptive-field Discriminator. An additional gradient penalty in the loss function

enables the finetuning process more stable and easier to produce results with higher perceptual quality.

Besides, the PatchGAN [11] idea proposed by Isola *et al.* inspires us in building the discriminator, which supervises the differences between the generated image and the ground truth on patches of size 70 × 70. In fact, the size of the patches which the discriminator operates on coincides with that of the discriminator's receptive field. And by modifying the depth of PatchGAN discriminator, we can enable the network to pay attention to different sizes of patch details around the same pixel. Correspondingly, our generator will also improve its own performance on some details to counteract the discriminator. Therefore, we decide to apply combined PatchGAN discriminators with different receptive fields as a multi-receptive-field discriminator in the structure of the adversarial part.

The loss function is also important for finetuning the Glass-Net. Aside from L_1 reconstruction loss and negative SSIM loss L_{SSIM}, the perceptual loss which computes the Euclidean loss on the feature maps the relu5_4 layer layer of the VGG19 L_{VGG} and the adversarial loss L_{adv} for the Glass-Net generator will also be optimized in this stage. The perceptual loss is as follow:

$$L_{VGG} = \frac{1}{HWC} \sum_{i=1}^{H} \sum_{j=1}^{W} \sum_{k=1}^{C} \|F(G(I)_{i,j,k}) - F(C_{i,j,k})\|_1 , \tag{1}$$

where $F(\cdot)$ denotes feature maps of the 34-th layer of the VGG network which is pre-trained on ImageNet, $G(I_{i,j})$ denotes the image Glass-Net produces and C denotes the ground truth.

And the adversarial loss for the Glass-Net generator can be expressed as:

$$L_{adv} = -\frac{1}{HW} \sum_{i=1}^{H} \sum_{j=1}^{W} D(G(I)_{i,j}) \tag{2}$$

where $D(\cdot)$ denotes the output of the discriminator.

We incorporate the four loss functions into a hybrid loss L_{hybrid} for finetuning our generator Glass-Net with appropriate weights. The hybrid loss is defined as

$$L_{hybrid} = 0.5 \times L_1 + 0.05 \times L_{SSIM} + 0.1 \times L_{VGG} + L_{adv} \tag{3}$$

L_{adv} is endowed with a larger factor because we want GAN to play a leading role in the optimizing progress. Compared to the perceptual loss in PyNET, we enhance the effect of L_{VGG} and weaken L_{SSIM}, which contributes to reducing the disorder of out-of-focus areas.

2.3 Reimplemented Instance Normalization

Instance Normalization (IN) [21] is an effective trick for image-to-image translation tasks. If we remove IN from Glass-Net, the generated images will not be as attractive as the images produced by BGGAN with IN. In [8], they discussed the

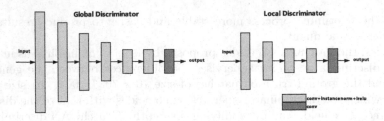

Fig. 2. Demostration for multi-receptive-field discriminator

original implemented IN are still not supported adequately by the TensorFlow Lite framework, thus using IN will increase the inference time and memory consumption due to additional CPU-GPU synchronization. To solve this problem, we use operators supported by tflite framework to reimplement IN to make sure all our model ops compute on smartphone GPU.

To begin with, we should find out which operator cannot be accelerated by tflite framework on smartphone GPUs. As we know, IN is defined as follow:

$$y_{tijk} = \frac{x_{tijk} - \mu_{ti}}{\sqrt{\sigma_{ti}^2 + \epsilon}} \tag{4}$$

$$\mu_{ti} = \frac{1}{HW} \sum_{i=1}^{H} \sum_{j=1}^{W} x_{tijk} \tag{5}$$

$$\sigma_{ti}^2 = \frac{1}{HW} \sum_{i=1}^{H} \sum_{j=1}^{W} (x_{tijk} - \mu_{ti})^2 \tag{6}$$

The challenge of the IN's implementation is computing μ_{ti} and σ_{ti}. Usually, both of them can be worked out through the operation 'tf.nn.moment' in the program code. Alternatively, We can use the command 'tf.reduce_mean' to compute μ_{ti} first and calculate σ_{ti} later with μ_{ti}. However, according to the guidelines of Tflite, 'tf.nn.moment' and 'tf.reduce_mean' with the parameter 'axis' are not supported on smartphone GPU. Different from the common method, we ingeniously adopt 'tf.nn.avg_pool2d' to calculate μ_{ti} due to the constant size of the feature maps at each layer.

3   Experiments

3.1   Dataset

EBB! dataset [8] was released by AIM 2020 Bokeh Effect Rendering Challenge. The dataset consists 5K shallow/wide depth-of-field image pairs. 4600 image pairs are training dataset, the number of validation data and test data are 200 respectively. In each photo pair, the image without bokeh effect is captured with a narrow aperture (f/16), while the corresponding bokeh image is shot using the highest aperture (f/1.8). The photos are captured in a variety of places with automatic mode. Though the dataset has kinds of scenes, we find that EBB! dataset has some poor-aligned image pairs. So we manually clean the train data of EBB! dataset to 4464 images as to make sure our model learn a better mapping from the original image to bokeh image.

3.2 Training Details

TensorFlow is used to implement our algorithm. All experiments run on the server with NVIDIA TITAN RTX and Intel Xeon Gold 5220 CPU. In training, we randomly cropped the images to 1408×1024 sized patches as inputs. The batch size was set to 1 limited by memory, and the number of epochs was set to 60 in two training stages. In order to accelerate the convergence of the model, we apply a two-stage training strategy. For the first training stage, we use L1 loss combined with SSIM loss to train the network roughly. And in the second stage, we joint L1 loss, Adversarial loss, perceptual loss, and SSIM loss to finetune the network. The learning rate of the discriminator and generator in the two training stages are both set to $1e-4$. In addition, we adopt Adam as optimizer for training. It's noted that β_1 and β_2 are set to 0 and 0.9 for Adam.

3.3 Quantitative Evaluation

Our model is proposed to participate in AIM 2020 Bokeh Effect challenge which encourages participants to provide a solution to generate bokeh effect in bokeh-free images. At the beginning of the competition, the results of us are compared with the methods proposed by other teams to test quantitatively on the common metrics $PSNR$, $SSIM$ only for reference. Then, the organizer conducts a user study in which all users evaluate each method by selecting one of the five quality levels(0 - mostly different from the ground truth, 5 - almost identical). The scores are then averaged per each approach to obtain the final Mean Option Scores MOS, which is more convincing than $PSNR$ and $SSIM$. Also, in order to further increase the persuasiveness, PyNet [8] and two excellent methods [3,9] in AIM 2019 Bokeh Effect challenge are used for contrast. Table 1 shows the results. Evaluated on the test dataset, the $PSNR$ of our proposed method ranks second and the MOS ranks first.

3.4 Qualitative Evaluation

We analyzed qualitatively by comparing our results with PyNET [8] and the method proposed by Dutta et al. [3]. And some visual results are shown in Fig. 3. It should be highlighted that we did not certain the Megadepth pretrained model used by PyNET, so we can only choose the official pretrained weights downloaded from MegaDepth. It was introduced in the official website that the pretrained weights have well-down generalization ability to completely unknown scenes. And the method of Dutta et al. is reproduced by us with the same Megadepth weights mentioned above.

Fig. 3. From left to right: input images, results of Dutta et al., results of PyNET, our results. Some pictures show that the method of Dutta et al. and PyNET fail to separate front scenes from back scenes due to bad depth maps obtained from Megadepth.

It's easy to find that BGGAN generates the most natural bokeh effect among the three approaches. The objects of interest in the bokeh images produced by

Table 1. The results on the EBB! test subset obtained with different solutions.

Team/method	PSNR	SSIM	MOS
Dutta et al. [3]	22.14	0.8778	-
xuehuapiaopiao-team	22.97	0.8758	4.1
Terminator	23.04	0.8756	4.1
CET_CVLab	23.05	0.8591	3.2
Team Horizon	23.27	0.8818	3.2
PyNET [8]	23.28	0.8780	4.1
Zheng et al. [9]	23.44	0.8874	-
AIA-Smart	23.55	0.8829	3.8
IPCV_IITM	23.77	0.8866	2.5
Ours	23.58	0.8770	**4.2**

our network are clear while the other two results are a bit fuzzy. What's more, our network can separate front scenes from back scenes well while the other two solutions can't do so. This is because PyNET and the approach of Dutta et al. rely on the depth map generated by Megadepth very much. Once depth maps cannot provide accurate depth information, the results produced by the two methods will become unattractive. Our full test results will be released on github.com/qianmingduowan/AIM2020-bokeh-BGNet.

3.5   Ablation Study and Analysis

Effect of IN. To verify the effectiveness of IN concerning the improvement in visual quality, we compare three variants of the generator: Glass-Net with IN, Glass-Net without Normalization, Glass-Net with batch normalization (BN) are investigated. Besides, we maintain the same training strategy and the same structure of the discriminator to ensure the effectiveness of the ablation study. We show our results in Fig. 4. From the illustration, we can find that generator with BN has the poorest Visual result. A possible explanation is that BN considers more about the characteristics of the whole training dataset rather than individual characteristics. In contrast, Glass-Net without Normalization performs better than the model with BN. Glass-Net with IN has the best performance in qualitative research.

Effect of Discriminator. To prove the effectiveness of our discriminator, we conduct the comparative experiment between the results of Glass-Net with the discriminator and the model without it at the stage of finetuning. Correspondingly, the loss function of Glass-Net without the discriminator does not possess L_{adv} and is defined as:

$$L_{hybrid} = 0.5 \times L_1 + 0.05 \times L_{SSIM} + 0.1 \times L_{VGG} \qquad (7)$$

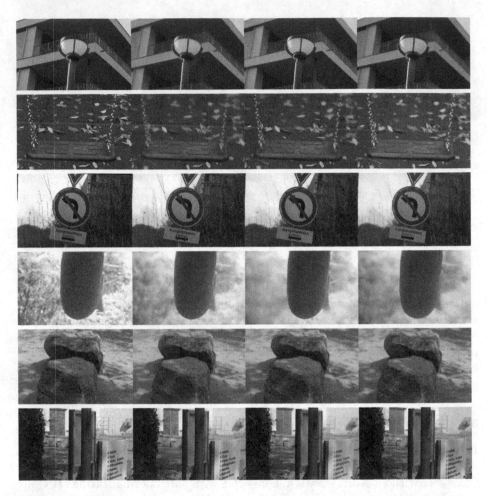

Fig. 4. Effects of different normalization. From left to right: original image, results of BGGAN with batch normalization,results of BGGAN without normalization, results of BGGAN with IN.

Then the two model are trained respectively and some visual results are shown in Fig. 5. By comparison, we can find out two obvious improvements in perceptual quality. The first thing that should be highlighted is that some out-of-focus areas of an image become tidier and the artifacts disappear completely. The well-distributed blur effect makes the whole image look more pleasing. Also, it should be noted that the model with the discriminator has a greater ability to segment the DoF area in photos. On the one hand, some areas in focus which Glass-Net mistakes for the out-of-focus areas are segmented correctly by the model with the discriminator. On the other hand, the boundaries between the in and out of focus areas are rendered much better.

Fig. 5. Comparison between the results of Glass-Net with the discriminator and the model without it. For the single photo from left to right: the input image, the result of Glass-Net without the discriminator and the result of Glass-Net with the discriminator.

3.6   Evaluation on the Photos Taken by the Smartphone

To prove that the BGGAN is also effective in real scenarios, we take some photos of different scenes by iPhone SE2 and Samsung S9, and the photos are processed by BGGAN to get the bokeh effect. The images taken by smartphones and bokeh images processed by our network are shown in Fig. 8 and Fig. 7. From the samples below, we can find that even in real-world scenes, BGGAN can render realistic bokeh well, which proves our network has a strong generalization ability.

Table 2. Average processing time for resolution 1024×1536 pixel obtained on several mainstream high-end mobile SoCs. In each case, the model was running directly on the corresponding GPU with OpenCL-based TensorFlow Lite GPU delegate [14].

Mobile Chipset	Exynos 9820	Kirin 980	Snapdragon 845	Snapdragon 855
GPU Model	Mali-G76	Mali-G76	Adreno 630	Adreno 640
CET_CVLab	2.0	3.0	3.0	3.4
PyNET with original IN	17.3	13.4	-	-
BGGAN with original IN	7.8	6.4	-	-
BGGAN with Reimplemented IN	1.5	1.4	1.5	1.8

Fig. 6. Some failure results.

Fig. 7. Images taken by Samsung S9 are on the left, and bokeh images processed by BGGAN are on the right.

3.7 The Latency on Mobile Devices

Last, Table 2 was presented to validate the reimplemented IN on smartphone GPU which were obtained with the PRO Mode of the AI Benchmark application [9]. Our reimplemented IN can run on all kinds of SoCs of different smartphones, while the original IN only works on Exynos 9820 and Kirin 980. The reason why the original IN cannot run on Snapdragon 855 and Snapdragon 845 is that some operations in it are not supported to be accelerated by the TensorFlow Lite framework and are computed on the CPU, which results in the increase of the

Fig. 8. Images taken by iPhone SE2 are on the left, and bokeh images processed by BGGAN are on the right.

inference time and the great consumption memory due to additional CPU-GPU synchronization. In Table 2, we compare the average running time of processing one single image of 1024×1536 pixel, which indicates that our reimplemented IN is suitable for TensorFlow Lite framework and is of sufficient practical value. Our method was able to process one 1024×1536 pixel photo in less than 1.9 s on all chipsets.

4   Conclusions

In this paper, we put forward a novel approach for the realistic bokeh effect rendering task. The proposed architecture BGGAN is the first GAN-based method to solve the problem of synthetic bokeh effect rendering. Experiments show that our approach enhances visual effects greatly compared with previous methods. In the end, we use the operators supported by tflite framework to reimplement IN to make sure that our full solution can run completely on smartphone GPU rather than partly on smartphone CPU. Thanks to the reimplemented IN, our method was able to process one 1024×1536 pixel photo in less than 1.9 s on all chipsets. This approach ranked First in AIM 2020 Rendering Realistic Bokeh Challenge Track 1 & Track 2. We conclude that our method is an effective solution for the realistic bokeh effect rendering task. However, our method also has a number of limitations: BGGAN still does not work well when the color of the objects in depth-of-field is similar to that of the surrounding background. And it also happens when the scene of the whole picture is complex. The examples of visual results are represented in Fig. 6. The probable reason for this phenomenon is that the model has not learned enough depth information. But if we take some priori knowledge such as MegaDepth, it will lead to another problem: the increase of reference time. So this is a trade-off. In the future, we can make efforts in this direction. Considering that in the stage of model designing there are no good means to quantify the improvement of visual effects by the model, we can only score the picture one by one through the naked eye. How to quantify the improvement of visual quality is an essential research direction.

Acknowledgements. This work was supported by the Advance Research Program (31511130301); National Key Research and Development Program (2017YFF0209806), and National Natural Science Foundation of China (No. 61906193; No. 61906195; No. 61702510).

References

1. Bousmalis, K., Silberman, N., Dohan, D., Erhan, D., Krishnan, D.: Unsupervised pixel-level domain adaptation with generative adversarial networks. In: Proceedings of the IEEE Conference on Computer Vision and Pattern Recognition, pp. 3722–3731 (2017)
2. Davis, H.: Practical Artistry: Light & Exposure for Digital Photographers. O'Reilly Media, Inc., Sebastopol (2008)

3. Dutta, S.: Depth-aware blending of smoothed images for bokeh effect generation. arXiv preprint arXiv:2005.14214 (2020)
4. Goodfellow, I., et al.: Generative adversarial nets. In: Advances in Neural Information Processing Systems, pp. 2672–2680 (2014)
5. Gulrajani, I., Ahmed, F., Arjovsky, M., Dumoulin, V., Courville, A.C.: Improved training of Wasserstein GANs. In: Advances in Neural Information Processing Systems, pp. 5767–5777 (2017)
6. He, K., Zhang, X., Ren, S., Sun, J.: Deep residual learning for image recognition. In: Conference on Computer Vision and Pattern Recognition, pp. 770–778. IEEE (2016)
7. Hou, Q., Cheng, M.M., Hu, X., Borji, A., Tu, Z., Torr, P.H.: Deeply supervised salient object detection with short connections. In: Proceedings of the IEEE Conference on Computer Vision and Pattern Recognition, pp. 3203–3212 (2017)
8. Ignatov, A., Patel, J., Timofte, R.: Rendering natural camera bokeh effect with deep learning. In: Proceedings of the IEEE/CVF Conference on Computer Vision and Pattern Recognition Workshops, pp. 418–419 (2020)
9. Ignatov, A., et al.: Aim 2019 challenge on bokeh effect synthesis: methods and results. In: 2019 IEEE/CVF International Conference on Computer Vision Workshop (ICCVW), pp. 3591–3598. IEEE (2019)
10. Ignatov, A., Timofte, R., et al.: AIM 2020 challenge on rendering realistic bokeh. In: European Conference on Computer Vision Workshops (2020)
11. Isola, P., Zhu, J.Y., Zhou, T., Efros, A.A.: Image-to-image translation with conditional adversarial networks. In: Proceedings of the IEEE Conference on Computer Vision and Pattern Recognition, pp. 1125–1134 (2017)
12. Karras, T., Laine, S., Aittala, M., Hellsten, J., Lehtinen, J., Aila, T.: Analyzing and improving the image quality of StyleGAN. In: Proceedings of the IEEE/CVF Conference on Computer Vision and Pattern Recognition, pp. 8110–8119 (2020)
13. Kupyn, O., Budzan, V., Mykhailych, M., Mishkin, D., Matas, J.: DeblurGAN: blind motion deblurring using conditional adversarial networks. In: Proceedings of the IEEE Conference on Computer Vision and Pattern Recognition, pp. 8183–8192 (2018)
14. Lee, J., et al.: On-device neural net inference with mobile GPUs. arXiv preprint arXiv:1907.01989 (2019)
15. Li, Z., Snavely, N.: MegaDepth: learning single-view depth prediction from internet photos. In: Proceedings of the IEEE Conference on Computer Vision and Pattern Recognition, pp. 2041–2050 (2018)
16. Ma, C., Rao, Y., Cheng, Y., Chen, C., Lu, J., Zhou, J.: Structure-preserving super resolution with gradient guidance. In: Proceedings of the IEEE/CVF Conference on Computer Vision and Pattern Recognition, pp. 7769–7778 (2020)
17. Purohit, K., Suin, M., Kandula, P., Ambasamudram, R.: Depth-guided dense dynamic filtering network for bokeh effect rendering. In: 2019 IEEE/CVF International Conference on Computer Vision Workshop (ICCVW), pp. 3417–3426. IEEE (2019)
18. Ronneberger, O., Fischer, P., Brox, T.: U-Net: convolutional networks for biomedical image segmentation. In: Navab, N., Hornegger, J., Wells, W.M., Frangi, A.F. (eds.) MICCAI 2015. LNCS, vol. 9351, pp. 234–241. Springer, Cham (2015). https://doi.org/10.1007/978-3-319-24574-4_28
19. Shen, X., et al.: Automatic portrait segmentation for image stylization. In: Computer Graphics Forum, vol. 35, pp. 93–102. Wiley Online Library (2016)

20. Shen, X., Tao, X., Gao, H., Zhou, C., Jia, J.: Deep automatic portrait matting. In: Leibe, B., Matas, J., Sebe, N., Welling, M. (eds.) ECCV 2016. LNCS, vol. 9905, pp. 92–107. Springer, Cham (2016). https://doi.org/10.1007/978-3-319-46448-0_6
21. Ulyanov, D., Vedaldi, A., Lempitsky, V.: Instance normalization: the missing ingredient for fast stylization. arXiv preprint arXiv:1607.08022 (2016)
22. Wadhwa, N., et al.: Synthetic depth-of-field with a single-camera mobile phone. ACM Trans. Graph. (TOG) **37**(4), 1–13 (2018)
23. Zhu, B., Chen, Y., Wang, J., Liu, S., Zhang, B., Tang, M.: Fast deep matting for portrait animation on mobile phone. In: Proceedings of the 25th ACM International Conference on Multimedia, pp. 297–305 (2017)

Bokeh Rendering from Defocus Estimation

Xianrui Luo🆔, Juewen Peng🆔, Ke Xian$^{(\boxtimes)}$🆔, Zijin Wu🆔, and Zhiguo Cao🆔

School of Artificial Intelligence and Automation,
Huazhong University of Science and Technology, Wuhan 430074, China
{xianruiluo,juewenpeng,kexian,zjwuzijin,zgcao}@hust.edu.cn

Abstract. In this paper, we study realistic bokeh rendering from a single all-in-focus image. Existing computational bokeh rendering methods generate bokeh effects by adding a simple flat background blur. As a result, the rendering results are different from the real bokeh on DSLR cameras. To address this issue, we propose a multi-stage network to learn shallow depth-of-field from a single bokeh-free image. In particular, our network consists of four modules: defocus estimation, radiance, rendering, and upsampling. The four modules are trained on different sizes to learn global features as well as local details around the boundaries of in-focus objects. Experimental results show that our approach is capable of rendering a pleasing distinctive bokeh effect in complex scenes.

Keywords: Bokeh rendering · Defocus estimation · Radiance · Upsampling

1 Introduction

Realistic bokeh effect, *a.k.a.* shallow depth-of-field, is an important feature in photography. It is often rendered from a digital single-lens reflex camera (DSLR) with a wide aperture by maneuver operations, however, the cost of time and money makes this process unfriendly to non-professionals. It is expected that we are able to produce bokeh effect from a single image with narrow aperture without the expensive hardware of DSLR cameras.

In this work, we propose a multi-stage network to learn bokeh synthesis by means of defocus estimation only supervised by bokeh images (Fig. 1). We employ an effective monocular depth estimation model as the basis of defocus estimation model, however we make modifications at the end of the fully convolutional network at the first stage because it has difficulty in learning without the ground truth of defocus maps. The modified output is changed from single-channel to multi-channel and it represents a group of probabilistic defocus maps for different blur amount. The final result is a combination of layered bokeh

---

X. Luo, J. Peng—Equal contributions.

© Springer Nature Switzerland AG 2020
A. Bartoli and A. Fusiello (Eds.): ECCV 2020 Workshops, LNCS 12537, pp. 245–261, 2020.
https://doi.org/10.1007/978-3-030-67070-2_15

Original Image   Defocus Map   Weight Map   Rendered Bokeh

Fig. 1. Given a single narrow aperture image, our algorithm estimates the corresponding defocus map using a network based on depth estimation, and a weight map from radiance module which demonstrates the brightness relationship between pixels is predicted. This network was trained only under the supervision of bokeh images with a wider aperture size.

blurred by kernels with different radius. We change the output back to a single-channel defocus map at the third stage.

Furthermore, we apply a simple radiance module to learn the relationship between the intensity of pixels in a single image, because we aim to produce the Circle of Confusion (CoC), which is crucial for the aesthetic quality of shallow depth-of-field effects. Distinctive CoC only appears when the intensity of pixel is much higher than any other pixels, which means the real value of the pixels are only available in High Dynamic Range (HDR). Since we process bokeh-free images under Low Dynamic Range, we predict weight maps to highlight the pixels with high intensity.

To train our network in a multi-stage manner, low resolution images of 1/4 the original size are used for input for the first stage to obtain global information, and at the second stage the model gets the upsampled features from the first stage and use high resolution images of 1/2 resolution to refine the details around edges. For stage 3, in order to present the CoC effect distinctively, the output of last layer is changed to a single-channel defocus map, which is further divided into layers and rendered on the guidance of Proportional relationship between blur radius and value within the map. For the last upsampling stage, first bilinear interpolation is used on rendered bokeh, then we adopt mask from predicted single-channel defocus map to make the in-focus objects clearer.

In summary, our main contributions are:

(1) We propose an autofocus model for bokeh rendering from monocular images with narrow aperture.
(2) We utilize defocus estimation and radiance estimation to predict blur amount and the intensity relationship among pixels in each image.
(3) A multi-stage training scheme using a combination of low resolution and high resolution images to acquire global features as well as preserving the details around boundaries.

2   Related Work

2.1   Defocus Estimation

Defocus maps can be applied in various tasks such as image deblurring [45], blur magnification [1] and depth estimation [24,28]. Defocus maps estimation can be categorized into two types of methods. The first category is region-based, and the other one is edge-based.

Region based methods use image patches to estimate the defocus amount in a straightforward manner. There are works [28,29] that focus on detecting and estimating defocus map from images that have small blur amount. Yan *et al.* [43] apply a regression neural network to predict the blur type and its parameters. Tang *et al.* [34] use log averaged spectrum residual to obtain a coarse defocus map and refine it iteratively by exploiting the relevance of similar neighbor regions.

As for Edge-based methods, Zhuo *et al.* [47] introduce a typical method to use the ratio of the gradients of original and blurred images at edge points to produce a sparse map, and Laplacian matting [20] is used for interpolation with the input image as guidance. Park *et al.* [25] introduce various hand-crafted features and a deep convolutional neural network is applied to learn deep features and produce defocus map from multi-scale image patches under the guidance of edge-preserved images. However, sometimes the value in homogeneous areas is inconsistent. Xu *et al.* [42] propose a metric based on the connection between the metric rank of a defocused patch and the amount of blur at edges, then a sparse defocus map is reconstructed from ranks of local patches in gradient domain. There are also approaches to exploit the frequency information of image edges for defocus estimation, using spectrum contrast [33] or sub-band decomposition[3].

2.2 Monocular Depth Estimation

Monocular depth estimation is an important area which has potential in various tasks. Eigen *et al.* [7] propose a multi-scale deep neural network based on AlexNet [18] and extend the work [6] by replacing AlexNet with a deeper VGG16 [31] to increase accuracy. At present, the commonly used method to obtain the depth is from kinect infrared sensor (NYU Depth V2 [30]) or Lidar (KITTI [8]). But in reality, it is not always easy to obtain the depth value corresponding to the scene. So unsupervised methods are purposed, using stereo matching [10] or left-right consistency loss [9]. Apart from depth maps as ground truth, shallow depth-of-field images can also be used as supervision [32]. Recently, internet photos [22,39,40], which are promising sources of supervision, have attracted more and more attention. The models trained on this kind of data have shown great generalization in complex scenes. Videos from YouTube are also used as a data source to train the network [21], which can estimate dense depth maps when both the human and the camera are moving. Lasinger *et al.* [19] proposed a 3D movie dataset and apply joint training of multiple datasets initiated with the structure of [39] to improve the generalization of the model and make it suitable for a variety of scenarios.

2.3 Shallow Depth-of-Field

Bokeh rendering can be applied in the task of autofocus, and it is suitable for images [12] and videos [46]. The existing lens blur methods can be divided into object space methods and image space methods. Among object space methods [11,26,44], ray tracing methods [26,44] can accurately reproduce the ray integration performed in the camera body. However, this requires large time cost, which is computationally difficult to solve. This has prompted the search for a method to produce blur directly in the image domain. The blur kernel can be produced as a scatter [17] or a cluster [27] operation. There are methods that allow users to control focus parameters and blur amount [2,36]. Wang *et al.* [36] propose a multi-stage model to combine real data and synthetic data to generate a generalized shallow depth of field synthesis effect from a single picture. Wadhwa *et al.* [35] focus on the shallow depth of field effect of the mobile phone, segmenting portrait and the objects on the human body to improve bokeh effect, and dual-pixel (DP) sensors are applied to predict depth maps. A blending scheme of depth-based bokeh rendering [2,5,46] is proposed to generate shallow depth-of-field effects based on composition of images blurred by different kernels. Ignatov *et al.* [13] present a large-scale bokeh dataset and purpose a multi-level network to gradually learn low-level details from lower levels and refines the results on higher resolution.

3   Proposed Method

Rendering bokeh effect from an all-in-focus image is a complicated task which requires obtaining the global information and manipulating the image in low level. The intuitive process usually contains three steps: (i) Monocular depth estimation. (ii) Focal plane detection or saliency detection. (iii) Bokeh rendering on out-of-focus regions. We simplify this process and combine the first two steps into one, which termed as defocus estimation. The defocus map can be written as:

$$D = |d - d_f| \tag{1}$$

where d is the disparity map and d_f denotes the disparity of focal plane. Further, the blur radius R in rendering process can be directly calculated from defocus map:

$$R = K \cdot D \tag{2}$$

where $\cdot$ is used for the entrywise Hadamard product, K is a constant determined by camera parameters. While the real optical rendering in DSLR camera is based on scene radiance [23] instead of image intensity, we propose the radiance module and expect to simulate this transformation. Besides, as we render the image at low resolution, we utilize a simple and efficient strategy to upsample the rendering result and ensure the refocused object is clear. In summary, our model is made up of 4 modules: defocus estimation, radiance, rendering, and upsampling. The pipeline is shown in Fig. 2. In the following, we will describe the details of each module.

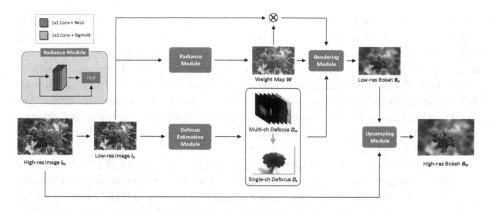

Fig. 2. Pipeline of our proposed method. We first predict defocus map and weight map from the input image of low resolution. Then the bokeh image can be obtained with two predicted maps and pre-defined blur kernels. Finally, we utilize upsampling module to restore the bokeh result to original size.

3.1   Defocus Estimation

Defocus estimation belongs to dense prediction task. Therefore, we use the state-of-the-art U-Net architecture [39] proposed in the field of monocular depth estimation for our defocus estimation network. To accelerate the speed of inference, we utilize ResNeXt50 [41] pre-trained on ImageNet [4] as backbone. In spite of the fact that the architecture performs well in depth estimation, we observe that the network is hard to train when utilizing the single-channel defocus map to render the image directly, so we replace the last single-channel regression layer in original architecture with multi-channel classification layer at training stage 1 and 2. At stage 3, we switch back to the original regression layer. In order to make training process more stable, we also fix most parameters of the pre-trained network and just train the last several layers.

With the defocus estimation network $f_\theta(\cdot)$, the defocus map predicted in different stages can be written as:

$$\text{Stage 1,2:}\quad D_m = f_{\theta_m}(I)$$
$$\text{Stage 3:}\quad D_s = f_{\theta_s}(I) \tag{3}$$

where D_s is the single-channel defocus map in the range of 0 to 1. D_m is the multi-channel defocus map which is normalized by softmax function, so it can also be considered as a probabilistic map. The channels of D_m is set to 6, specifically.

3.2   Radiance

Digital cameras generally have two color rendering strategies: the photofinishing model and the slide or photographic reproduction model. In photofinishing model, imaging pipeline is different in terms of shooting scenes. The photographic reproduction, using the fixed color rendering, is suitable for most amateur photographers. In this paper, we suppose all of the images are captured in the second mode and the radiance of each pixel only depends on its RGB values. However, as the transformation from image intensity to scene radiance is always nonlinear, it is difficult to establish formulas for forward and inverse transformations. We achieve the similar result by giving pixels different weights in rendering process according to their RGB values. As shown in Fig. 2, we use a simple network to calculate this weight map.

In addition, we observe that the bright pixels whose R, G or B value is very close to the upper bound, i.e., 255 are supposed to have more exaggerated weights as their actual energies are much higher than other pixels in HDR. Therefore, we deal with these pixels separately and give them much larger weights manually.

$$W = M_b \cdot \alpha I^\beta + (1 - M_b) \cdot g_\theta(I) \tag{4}$$

where image I is normalized to 0–1. $g_\theta(I)$ generates the initial weight map from input image. M_b is a mask which denotes whether R, G or B value of each pixel is more than a threshold. The threshold is set to 0.99 in this paper. α and β are two hyperparameters. α controls the maximum weight of bright pixels and β adjusts the degree of difference among RGB color channels. We set α to 3 and β to 5. From the experiment, one can see that this operation leads to the HDR effect in final bokeh result.

3.3   Bokeh Rendering

Physically motivated refocusing pipeline proposed in SteReFo [2] is able to mimic the real rendering process efficiently. The core idea is to decompose the scene into different depth layers and composite them back together after blurring each layer with pre-defined blur kernels. We leverage this rendering method and make some appropriate modifications on it. (i) We design a soft disk blur kernel K_s instead of hard disk blur kernel K_h which is discretized by 0 or 1. The formula of two kernels can be described as:

$$K_h(x, y, r) = \begin{cases} 0 & (r^2 - x^2 - y^2 < 0) \\ 1 & (r^2 - x^2 - y^2 \geq 0) \end{cases} \tag{5}$$

$$K_s(x, y, r) = \frac{1}{2} + \frac{1}{2}\tanh\left(\frac{1}{4}(r^2 - x^2 - y^2) + \frac{1}{2}\right) \tag{6}$$

The comparison of two kernels with various kernel sizes are shown in Fig. 3. One can see that the soft kernel looks more like a disk, especially for small kernel size, which will create a more natural CoC effect. (ii) The interval of pre-defined kernel sizes are not set to the same due to the fact that the blur amounts of bokeh images are unbalanced. Specifically, the kernel sizes for different stages are listed in Table 1 where size 1 can be viewed as no blur. (iii) To render more

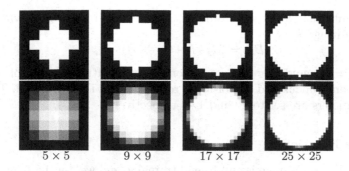

$$5 \times 5 \qquad 9 \times 9 \qquad 17 \times 17 \qquad 25 \times 25$$

Fig. 3. Visualizations of disk blur kernels with different kernel sizes. The first row is the results of the hard kernel. The second row is the results of the soft kernel designed in this paper.

Table 1. Kernel sizes of different stages.

Stage	1	2	3
Kernel sizes	1, 5, 11, 19, 27, 35	1, 9, 21, 37, 53, 69	1, 3, 5, 7, 11, 15, 19, 23, 27, 33, 39, 45, 53, 61, 69

realistic bokeh effect, we give weights calculated by radiance module to different pixels. For each pixel, the weighted blurring process can be formulated as:

$$B_i = \frac{K(r_i) * (W_i \cdot I_i)}{K(r_i) * W_i} \tag{7}$$

where B_i is the bokeh result of pixel i, W_i are the weights of surrounding pixels I_i within the range of blurring kernel $K(r_i)$. While the blurring operations to each pixel is completely linear, we can extend above process to the whole image.

$$B = \frac{\text{blur\_func}(W \cdot I, D)}{\text{blur\_func}(W, D)} \tag{8}$$

where blur_func is the refocusing pipeline [2] which has been modified as mentioned above. It should be noted that for stage 1 and 2, the defocus map D_m has multi-channel, so there is no need to discretize the defocus map again in rendering process.

3.4 Upsampling

Super-resolution or any other learning based methods [36,37] can be employed to increase the resolution of bokeh result. However, these approaches tend to destroy the CoC effect produced at stage 3. As a result, we calculate a soft mask M_s from predicted single-channel defocus map, and render the final result

B_{hr} by combining the bokeh result B_{lr} upsampled from stage 3 with original all-in-focus image I.

$$B_{hr} = M_s \cdot I + (1 - M_s) \cdot B_{lr} \tag{9}$$

where $M_s = \text{sigmoid}(\eta\,(\tau - D_s))$. η controls the softness degree of transition part between in-focus and out-of-focus regions and τ is a threshold. These two hyperparameters are set to 20 and 1/8, respectively.

3.5   Loss Functions

The network of each stage is end-to-end trainable and we use the same losses for all stages.

$$L_{total} = L_{l_1}(B, B_{gt}) + L_{vgg}(B, B_{gt}) + L_{ssim}(B, B_{gt}) + 0.1 \cdot L_{grad}(D) \tag{10}$$

where L_{l_1} is the L1 loss. L_{vgg} is the perceptual loss which is based on pre-trained VGG19 [16]. L_{ssim} is the structural similarity (SSIM) loss [38]. L_{grad} is the pyramid gradient loss used to constrain the defocus map to be locally smooth, especially in the areas with consistent colors. However, the formula is a little different between the multi-channel defocus map D_m predicted at stage 1, 2 and single-channel defocus map D_s predicted at stage 3.

$$L_{grad}(D_m) = \frac{1}{S}\frac{1}{C}\sum_{i=1}^{S}\sum_{j=1}^{C}\left(\left\|\partial_x D_m^{i,j}\right\|_1 \cdot e^{-\left|\partial_x I^i\right|} + \left\|\partial_y D_m^{i,j}\right\|_1 \cdot e^{-\left|\partial_y I^i\right|} \right) \tag{11}$$

$$L_{grad}(D_s) = \frac{1}{S}\sum_{i=1}^{S}\left(\left\|\partial_x D_m^i\right\|_1 \cdot e^{-\left|\partial_x I^i\right|} + \left\|\partial_y D_m^i\right\|_1 \cdot e^{-\left|\partial_y I^i\right|} \right) \tag{12}$$

where C is the channel numbers of D_m. S denotes the different scales of the defocus map or image and is set to 4.

4   Experiments

In this section, we first introduce the details about our experimental setting. Then we evaluate the quantitative and qualitative performance of our method on a large-scale bokeh dataset EBB! Finally, we conduct an ablation study to analyse the influence of different factors on the bokeh results.

4.1   Experimental Setup

Our method uses standard PyTorch packages, and is implemented on a single Nvidia GTX 1080 GPU, 251 GB RAM and Intel Xeon Processor. *Everything is Better with Bokeh!* (EBB!) [13] is a large-scale dataset consisting of 4694 aligned wide/shallow depth-of-field image pairs captured using the Canon 7D DSLR with 50 mm f/1.8 lenses. We divide it into a train set with 4224 pairs and a validation set with 470 pairs which is termed as Val470. The training process is made up of three stages. At stage 1, the model is trained on the resolution of 256 × 256. Initial learning rate used is 1e−4 with a decay-cycle of 30 epochs. At stage 2, the model is fine-tuned on 512 × 512. At stage 3, we replace the multi-channel classification layer with single-channel regression layer in defocus estimation module and train the whole network with most parameters fixed. In addition, for the CPU task of AIM 2020 Rendering Realistic Bokeh Challenge, we only apply the first stage with a residual module for bokeh synthesis.

4.2   Quantitative and Qualitative Evaluation

Quantitative Results. Our model is initially proposed to participate in the AIM 2020 Rendering Realistic Bokeh Challenge [15] and our solution is the runner-up of all methods. The purpose of this challenge is to achieve shallow depth-of-field with the best perceptual quality similar to the ground truth as measured by the Mean Opinion Score (MOS). Table 2 and Table 3 shows the performance of our model. It is worth mentioning that our runtime on GPU is calculated by the speed of TFLite model instead of PyTorch. The average runtime of our PyTorch model on GPU is 0.055 s.

Table 2. Quantitative results of our method from the CPU track of AIM 2020 Rendering Realistic Bokeh Challenge. The results are sorted based on the MOS scores.

Track1: CPU				
Team	MOS↑	PSNR↑	SSIM↑	Avg. runtime (s)
Airia-bokeh	**4.2**	23.58	0.8770	5.52
AIA-Smart	3.8	23.56	0.8829	1.71
CET_SP	3.3	21.91	0.8201	1.17
CET_CVLab	3.2	23.05	0.8591	1.17
Team Horizon	3.2	23.27	0.8818	19.27
IPCV_IITM	2.5	**23.77**	**0.8866**	27.24
CET21_CV	1.3	22.80	0.8628	**0.74**
CET_ECE	1.2	22.85	0.8629	**0.74**

Table 3. Quantitative results of our method from the GPU track of AIM 2020 Rendering Realistic Bokeh Challenge. The results are sorted based on the MOS scores.

Track2: GPU				
Team	MOS↑	PSNR↑	SSIM↑	Runtime (s)
Airia-bokeh	**4.2**	23.58	0.8770	**1.52**
AIA-Smart	3.8	**23.94**	**0.8842**	15.2
CET_CVLab	3.2	23.05	0.8591	2.75

Qualitative Results. In this section, first we present a sample visual result of our solution consisting of intermediate outputs, then we compare our method to the current state-of-the-art solutions [13,14] that were trained and tuned specifically for bokeh rendering. The sample result, which contains a defocus map and a weight map, is shown in Fig. 4, and the visual results of all methods are shown in Fig. 5. As shown in Fig. 5, our method produces a distinctive CoC effect and achieves better quality around the boundaries between in and out-of-focus regions.

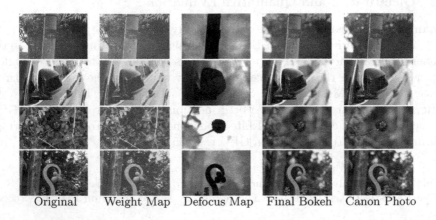

Original   Weight Map   Defocus Map   Final Bokeh   Canon Photo

Fig. 4. Visual results obtained with the proposed method. Best zoomed on screen.

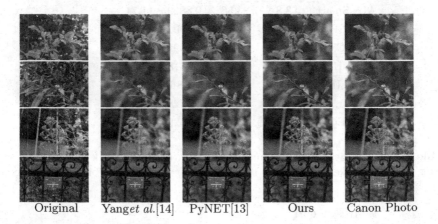

Original   Yang et al.[14]   PyNET[13]   Ours   Canon Photo

Fig. 5. Visual results obtained with three different methods. From left to right: the original narrow aperture image, Yang et al. [14], PyNET [13], our solution and the target Canon photo.

4.3   Ablation Study

As mentioned above, our model consists of different components and is trained in a multi-stage manner with the combination of different losses and various blur kernels. Therefore, we do an ablation study to compare different settings, and demonstrate the effectiveness and superiority of our method. To simplify the verification, we only do the experiments at stage 1 unless otherwise specified.

Combination of Losses. As shown in Table 4, we obtain the best result when all of the losses are used. Besides, we visualize some examples of predicted defocus maps with different combinations of losses in Fig. 6 to verify the effect of each loss. One can see that the predicted defocus maps become more delicate on in-focus regions and smoother on out-of-focus regions by adding loss function gradually. Note that the displayed defocus maps are overlaid by different probabilistic layers produced at stage 1.

Table 4. Quantitative results of stage 1 training with different losses on Val470.

	L_{l1}	$L_{l1} + L_{ssim}$	$L_{l1} + L_{ssim} + L_{vgg}$	L_{total}
PSNR	23.4028	23.4021	23.4306	**23.4495**
SSIM	0.8638	0.8664	0.8665	**0.8668**

Settings of Blur Kernels. The number and size of the blur kernel is largely determined by experience. On the one hand, too many kernels will slow down the running speed while too few kernels will cause the certain limitation. On the other hand, the maximum kernel size is supposed to be consistent with the maximum blur amount in real scene. However, we observe that the defocus map corresponding to the large scale blur is really hard to be learnt as the blur amount varies greatly among the images and most of them are less blurry. In consequence, we do some experiments on the settings of blur kernels for stage 1 and stage 3. we ignore stage 2 because it is similar to stage 1. We compare the different numbers and maximum sizes of blur kernels for stage 1 in Table 5 and Table 6. For stage 3, to generate a smooth bokeh result, the kernel size should be set continuously. We adopt two sampling strategies, i.e., growing sampling and uniform sampling. The growing sampling is the way we mentioned in Sect. 3.3. For uniform sampling, the interval of kernel sizes is set to 4 from beginning to end. The comparison between two strategies is shown in Table 7. The above analysis process can help us set the pre-defined blur kernel better.

Radiance Module. As shown in Table 8, models with radiance module achieve better results. The weight maps obtained from radiance module are able to demonstrate scene radiance, which is more suitable for bokeh rendering than

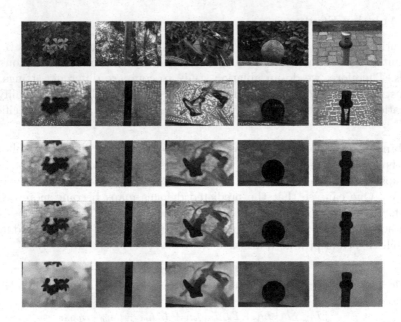

Fig. 6. Visualization of defocus maps predicted at stage 1. The first row is all-in-focus image. The second row to the last row present the predicted defocus maps training with L_{l1}, $L_{l1}+L_{ssim}$, $L_{l1}+L_{ssim}+L_{vgg}$ and L_{total}, respectively.

Table 5. Quantitative results of stage 1 with different numbers of blur kernels on Val470.

Kernel sizes	1, 7, 19, 35	1, 5, 11, 19, 27, 35	1, 5, 9, 13, 17, 23, 29, 35
PSNR	23.3879	**23.4495**	23.4368
SSIM	0.8647	**0.8668**	**0.8668**

Table 6. Quantitative results of stage 1 with different maximum sizes of blur kernels on Val470.

Kernel sizes	1, 5, 9, 13, 19, 25	1, 5, 11, 19, 27, 35	1, 7, 15, 25, 35, 45
PSNR	23.4156	**23.4495**	23.4004
SSIM	0.8659	**0.8668**	0.8651

Table 7. Quantitative results of stage 3 with different sampling strategies on Val470.

Sampling strategy	Growing	Uniform
PSNR	**23.6776**	23.6757
SSIM	**0.8815**	0.8814

Table 8. Quantitative results of stage 1 with or without radiance module

	w/radiance	w/o radiance
PSNR	**23.4495**	23.2756
SSIM	**0.8668**	0.8649

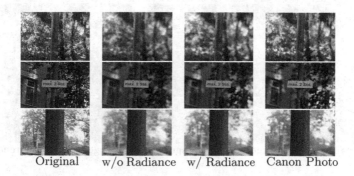

Original   w/o Radiance   w/ Radiance   Canon Photo

Fig. 7. Qualitative results of inference stage with and without radiance module.

Table 9. Quantitative results of different stages on Val470.

Stage	1	2	3	Inference
PSNR	23.4495	**23.7480**	23.6776	23.6262
SSIM	0.8668	**0.8821**	0.8815	0.8798
Runtime (s)	**0.030**	0.039	0.054	0.055

image intensity. To further prove this, we show some examples of final inference stage in Fig. 7.

Training Stages. The training process is made up of three stages. At stage 1, predicting multi-channel defocus map at 1/4 resolution is beneficial for the network to learn global features, At stage 2, we predict defocus map at 1/2 resolution to preserve more details around foreground boundaries. To produce more prominent CoC effect, we change the defocus map from multi-channel to single-channel at stage 3. At inference stage, as we render the image at 1/2 resolution, a simple upsampling strategy is utilized to ensure the clarity of the refocused object. We prove these points in Fig. 8. We also list the quantitative result of different stages in Table 9. Although the PSNR and SSIM of stage 3 is slightly lower than those of stage 2, the layer effect of CoC on out-of-focus regions is more pleasing and realistic. In addition, we observe that the indicators decrease again at inference stage while obtaining better visual quality.

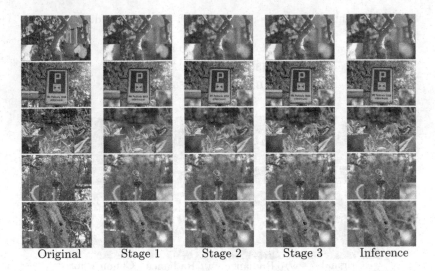

Original   Stage 1   Stage 2   Stage 3   Inference

Fig. 8. Qualitatively results of different stages

5   Conclusion

We have presented an effective way to train neural network to predict a shallow depth-of-field image from a single narrow aperture image. By introducing defocus estimation within our network using only bokeh images as supervision, we train our multi-stage network to produce results from multi-channel probabilistic defocus maps to single-channel defocus maps, improving aesthetic quality of synthesized bokeh. Our model also consists of a radiance module which transforms image intensity into scene radiance, rendering bokeh in a physics-based manner. We significantly enhance the quality of bokeh images by applying the above model. Exhaustive visualizations and ablation studies are presented to validate the modules and demonstrate their effects on the performance of our proposed network. In the future we can explore using dynamic filters for selection of kernels and modify the defocus estimation model to learn single-channel defocus maps without trained parameters, eventually decreasing training time.

Acknowledgements. This work was supported in part by the National Natural Science Foundation of China (Grant No. U1913602).

References

1. Bae, S., Durand, F.: Defocus magnification. In: Computer Graphics Forum, vol. 26, pp. 571–579. Wiley (2007)
2. Busam, B., Hog, M., McDonagh, S., Slabaugh, G.: SteReFo: efficient image refocusing with stereo vision. In: Proceedings of the IEEE International Conference on Computer Vision Workshops (2019)

3. Chakrabarti, A., Zickler, T., Freeman, W.T.: Analyzing spatially-varying blur. In: 2010 IEEE Computer Society Conference on Computer Vision and Pattern Recognition, pp. 2512–2519. IEEE (2010)
4. Deng, J., Dong, W., Socher, R., Li, L.J., Li, K., Fei-Fei, L.: ImageNet: a large-scale hierarchical image database. In: 2009 IEEE Conference on Computer Vision and Pattern Recognition, pp. 248–255. IEEE (2009)
5. Dutta, S.: Depth-aware blending of smoothed images for bokeh effect generation. arXiv preprint arXiv:2005.14214 (2020)
6. Eigen, D., Fergus, R.: Predicting depth, surface normals and semantic labels with a common multi-scale convolutional architecture. In: Proceedings of the IEEE International Conference on Computer Vision, pp. 2650–2658 (2015)
7. Eigen, D., Puhrsch, C., Fergus, R.: Depth map prediction from a single image using a multi-scale deep network. In: Advances in Neural Information Processing Systems, pp. 2366–2374 (2014)
8. Geiger, A., Lenz, P., Stiller, C., Urtasun, R.: Vision meets robotics: the KITTI dataset. Int. J. Robot. Res. **32**(11), 1231–1237 (2013)
9. Godard, C., Mac Aodha, O., Brostow, G.J.: Unsupervised monocular depth estimation with left-right consistency. In: Proceedings of the IEEE Conference on Computer Vision and Pattern Recognition, pp. 270–279 (2017)
10. Guo, X., Li, H., Yi, S., Ren, J., Wang, X.: Learning monocular depth by distilling cross-domain stereo networks. In: Proceedings of the European Conference on Computer Vision (ECCV), pp. 484–500 (2018)
11. Haeberli, P., Akeley, K.: The accumulation buffer: hardware support for high-quality rendering. ACM SIGGRAPH Comput. Graph. **24**(4), 309–318 (1990)
12. Herrmann, C., et al.: Learning to autofocus. In: Proceedings of the IEEE/CVF Conference on Computer Vision and Pattern Recognition, pp. 2230–2239 (2020)
13. Ignatov, A., Patel, J., Timofte, R.: Rendering natural camera bokeh effect with deep learning. In: Proceedings of the IEEE/CVF Conference on Computer Vision and Pattern Recognition Workshops, pp. 418–419 (2020)
14. Ignatov, A., et al.: Aim 2019 challenge on bokeh effect synthesis: methods and results. In: 2019 IEEE/CVF International Conference on Computer Vision Workshop (ICCVW), pp. 3591–3598. IEEE (2019)
15. Ignatov, A., Timofte, R., et al.: AIM 2020 challenge on rendering realistic bokeh. In: Bartoli, A., Fusiello, A. (eds.) ECCV 2020. LNCS, vol. 12537, pp. 213–228. Springer, Cham (2020)
16. Johnson, J., Alahi, A., Fei-Fei, L.: Perceptual losses for real-time style transfer and super-resolution. In: Leibe, B., Matas, J., Sebe, N., Welling, M. (eds.) ECCV 2016. LNCS, vol. 9906, pp. 694–711. Springer, Cham (2016). https://doi.org/10.1007/978-3-319-46475-6_43
17. Krivánek, J., Zara, J., Bouatouch, K.: Fast depth of field rendering with surface splatting. In: 2003 Proceedings Computer Graphics International, pp. 196–201. IEEE (2003)
18. Krizhevsky, A., Sutskever, I., Hinton, G.E.: ImageNet classification with deep convolutional neural networks. In: Advances in Neural Information Processing Systems, pp. 1097–1105 (2012)
19. Lasinger, K., Ranftl, R., Schindler, K., Koltun, V.: Towards robust monocular depth estimation: mixing datasets for zero-shot cross-dataset transfer. arXiv preprint arXiv:1907.01341 (2019)
20. Levin, A., Lischinski, D., Weiss, Y.: A closed-form solution to natural image matting. IEEE Trans. Pattern Anal. Mach. Intell. **30**(2), 228–242 (2007)

21. Li, Z., et al.: Learning the depths of moving people by watching frozen people. In: Proceedings of the IEEE Conference on Computer Vision and Pattern Recognition, pp. 4521–4530 (2019)
22. Li, Z., Snavely, N.: MegaDepth: learning single-view depth prediction from internet photos. In: Proceedings of the IEEE Conference on Computer Vision and Pattern Recognition, pp. 2041–2050 (2018)
23. Lin, H., Kim, S.J., Süsstrunk, S., Brown, M.S.: Revisiting radiometric calibration for color computer vision. In: 2011 International Conference on Computer Vision, pp. 129–136. IEEE (2011)
24. Lin, J., Ji, X., Xu, W., Dai, Q.: Absolute depth estimation from a single defocused image. IEEE Trans. Image Process. **22**(11), 4545–4550 (2013)
25. Park, J., Tai, Y.W., Cho, D., So Kweon, I.: A unified approach of multi-scale deep and hand-crafted features for defocus estimation. In: Proceedings of the IEEE Conference on Computer Vision and Pattern Recognition, pp. 1736–1745 (2017)
26. Pharr, M., Jakob, W., Humphreys, G.: Physically Based Rendering: From Theory to Implementation. Morgan Kaufmann, Burlington (2016)
27. Robison, A., Shirley, P.: Image space gathering. In: 2009 Proceedings of the Conference on High Performance Graphics, pp. 91–98 (2009)
28. Shi, J., Tao, X., Xu, L., Jia, J.: Break ames room illusion: depth from general single images. ACM Trans. Graph. (TOG) **34**(6), 1–11 (2015)
29. Shi, J., Xu, L., Jia, J.: Just noticeable defocus blur detection and estimation. In: Proceedings of the IEEE Conference on Computer Vision and Pattern Recognition, pp. 657–665 (2015)
30. Silberman, N., Hoiem, D., Kohli, P., Fergus, R.: Indoor segmentation and support inference from RGBD images. In: Fitzgibbon, A., Lazebnik, S., Perona, P., Sato, Y., Schmid, C. (eds.) ECCV 2012. LNCS, vol. 7576, pp. 746–760. Springer, Heidelberg (2012). https://doi.org/10.1007/978-3-642-33715-4_54
31. Simonyan, K., Zisserman, A.: Very deep convolutional networks for large-scale image recognition. arXiv preprint arXiv:1409.1556 (2014)
32. Srinivasan, P.P., Garg, R., Wadhwa, N., Ng, R., Barron, J.T.: Aperture supervision for monocular depth estimation. In: Proceedings of the IEEE Conference on Computer Vision and Pattern Recognition, pp. 6393–6401 (2018)
33. Tang, C., Hou, C., Song, Z.: Defocus map estimation from a single image via spectrum contrast. Opt. Lett. **38**(10), 1706–1708 (2013)
34. Tang, C., Wu, J., Hou, Y., Wang, P., Li, W.: A spectral and spatial approach of coarse-to-fine blurred image region detection. IEEE Sig. Process. Lett. **23**(11), 1652–1656 (2016)
35. Wadhwa, N., et al.: Synthetic depth-of-field with a single-camera mobile phone. ACM Trans. Graph. (TOG) **37**(4), 1–13 (2018)
36. Wang, L., et al.: DeepLens: shallow depth of field from a single image. arXiv preprint arXiv:1810.08100 (2018)
37. Wang, X., et al.: ESRGAN: enhanced super-resolution generative adversarial networks. In: Leal-Taixé, L., Roth, S. (eds.) ECCV 2018. LNCS, vol. 11133, pp. 63–79. Springer, Cham (2019). https://doi.org/10.1007/978-3-030-11021-5_5
38. Wang, Z., Bovik, A.C., Sheikh, H.R., Simoncelli, E.P.: Image quality assessment: from error visibility to structural similarity. IEEE Trans. Image Process. **13**(4), 600–612 (2004)
39. Xian, K., et al.: Monocular relative depth perception with web stereo data supervision. In: Proceedings of the IEEE Conference on Computer Vision and Pattern Recognition, pp. 311–320 (2018)

40. Xian, K., Zhang, J., Wang, O., Mai, L., Lin, Z., Cao, Z.: Structure-guided ranking loss for single image depth prediction. In: The IEEE/CVF Conference on Computer Vision and Pattern Recognition (CVPR), June 2020
41. Xie, S., Girshick, R., Dollár, P., Tu, Z., He, K.: Aggregated residual transformations for deep neural networks. In: Proceedings of the IEEE Conference on Computer Vision and Pattern Recognition, pp. 1492–1500 (2017)
42. Xu, G., Quan, Y., Ji, H.: Estimating defocus blur via rank of local patches. In: Proceedings of the IEEE International Conference on Computer Vision, pp. 5371–5379 (2017)
43. Yan, R., Shao, L.: Blind image blur estimation via deep learning. IEEE Trans. Image Process. **25**(4), 1910–1921 (2016)
44. Yang, Y., Lin, H., Yu, Z., Paris, S., Yu, J.: Virtual DSLR: high quality dynamic depth-of-field synthesis on mobile platforms. Electron. Imaging **2016**(18), 1–9 (2016)
45. Zhang, X., Wang, R., Jiang, X., Wang, W., Gao, W.: Spatially variant defocus blur map estimation and deblurring from a single image. J. Vis. Commun. Image Represent. **35**, 257–264 (2016)
46. Zhang, X., Matzen, K., Nguyen, V., Yao, D., Zhang, Y., Ng, R.: Synthetic defocus and look-ahead autofocus for casual videography. arXiv preprint arXiv:1905.06326 (2019)
47. Zhuo, S., Sim, T.: Defocus map estimation from a single image. Pattern Recogn. **44**(9), 1852–1858 (2011)

Human Motion Transfer from Poses in the Wild

Jian Ren[1]([✉]), Menglei Chai[1], Sergey Tulyakov[1], Chen Fang[2], Xiaohui Shen[2], and Jianchao Yang[2]

[1] Snap Inc., Santa Monica, USA
jian.ren0905@rutgers.edu
[2] ByteDance Inc., Beijing, China

Abstract. In this paper, we tackle the problem of human motion transfer, where we synthesize novel motion video for a target person that imitates the movement from a reference video. It is a video-to-video translation task in which the estimated poses are used to bridge two domains. Despite substantial progress on the topic, there exist several problems with the previous methods. First, there is a domain gap between training and testing pose sequences–the model is tested on poses it has not seen during training, such as difficult dancing moves. Furthermore, pose detection errors are inevitable, making the job of the generator harder. Finally, generating realistic pixels from sparse poses is challenging in a single step. To address these challenges, we introduce a novel pose-to-video translation framework for generating high-quality videos that are temporally coherent even for in-the-wild pose sequences unseen during training. We propose a pose augmentation method to minimize the training-test gap, a unified paired and unpaired learning strategy to improve the robustness to detection errors, and two-stage network architecture to achieve superior texture quality. To further boost research on the topic, we build two human motion datasets. Finally, we show the superiority of our approach over the state-of-the-art studies through extensive experiments and evaluations on different datasets.

1 Introduction

Video synthesis receives growing attention from research and industrial communities due to a wide range of applications. Among them, human motion retargeting saw significant progress, showing that by utilizing up-to-date deep neural network design and training techniques, approximate human motion can be transferred from one video to another. Such methods make it possible to generate a personalized dancing video of a subject not having any dancing experience. For example, one can animate themselves by using a ballerina video; or generate motion synchronized videos from multiple persons to be used for fake video detection [8].

Similarly to the Everybody Dance Now work [8] and other video-to-video translation works [49,58], our method requires a training video of a person performing a variety of motions. An off-the-shelf body pose detector [7] is used

© Springer Nature Switzerland AG 2020
A. Bartoli and A. Fusiello (Eds.): ECCV 2020 Workshops, LNCS 12537, pp. 262–279, 2020.
https://doi.org/10.1007/978-3-030-67070-2_16

Fig. 1. Application of our method. We generate images of the target subject (left) and output foreground content only, allowing them to be easily blended with a new background (right).

to parse pose skeleton and represent it as multi-channel pose maps to feed our network. Then, instead of focusing on generating the entire frame, as previous methods do [8,49], we argue that using the foreground only (e.g., the person) improves performance and increases the number of possible applications (Fig. 1). Furthermore, focusing on foreground saves network capacity and computation time and costs, and allows the generated foreground to be easily reused on a new background. Generating the entire frame limits the side movements of the generated person as the situation when the person leaves the known background region is not handled by traditional methods. We, therefore, focus on the foreground only. For the application of changing background, further limitations of generating the whole frame, such as introducing extra background region and missing body limbs, are presented in Fig. 2.

Despite substantial progress, state-of-the-art human motion retargeting methods are still far from perfect, with several questions remain open. How to generalize to arbitrary in-the-wild reference motions, including extreme poses not seen during training? How to achieve robust results against possible pose detection errors? How to obtain realistic texture details while keeping temporal consistency and smoothness of the video? These challenging issues prevent us from crossing the realism gap and achieving higher visual fidelity. To answer these questions and tackle the human motion translation problem, we need a more robust method that generalizes well across different pose domains, produces high fidelity texture details, and features temporal consistency at the same time. In this work, we attempt to answer these questions by proposing a novel two-stage pose-to-video translation network employing a unified paired and unpaired learning framework.

Pose estimation networks often fail on in-the-wild input frames (Fig. 4), so that mismatching body parts appear. Moreover, for some poses, especially in the in-the-wild scenarios, several keypoints can be missed. To tackle these issues and in order to enrich the variance in the input, enhancing the robustness of the network to keypoint detector errors, we propose a body pose augmentation method. Specifically, we drop out random pose channels and resize lengths of certain body parts. Furthermore, we observe that direct synthesis of realistic textures from sparse pose representation is often challenging (see Fig. 5 for

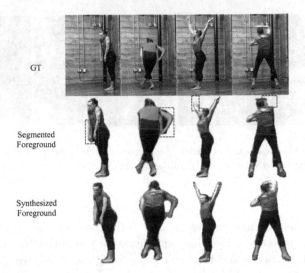

Fig. 2. Comparison of the segmented and synthesized foreground for the validation images. Top row: four ground-truth (GT) images; middle row: the segmented foreground from GT images using a state-of-the-art segmentation network [10]; last row: the synthesized foreground using our methods. The segmented foreground images introduce extra background regions (left two columns) and miss parts of right arms (right two columns), as indicated by red boxes, while our methods can generate intact body images with less background region.

examples), we propose a refinement network to refine textures from images that are obtained from a pose-to-image translation network. Finally, there exists a gap between training and testing poses; in-the-wild poses during testing will be substantially different from the training poses sequences extracted from the person itself. This limitation is by design, and we would like to handle poses that the reference person is not able to do themselves, including difficult dancing moves. To bridge the gap, we introduce unpaired learning into the paired training pipeline improving the generalization of the system. To make unpaired learning feasible, we collect a large-scale single-person activities (SPA) dataset and use the dataset as the source of in-the-wild input to the training pipeline, leveraging it along with the supervised paired training branch by adopting the carefully designed combination of discriminators.

With our method, we can generate superior results featuring texture realism, motion smoothness and robustness to poses never seen during training. We extensively evaluate our system by conducting comparisons with state-of-the-art human motion retargeting techniques by reporting quantitative and qualitative metrics on three different datasets. The results support that our method significantly outperforms existing works by obtaining better numerical scores and achieving higher visual fidelity.

In summary, our major contributions are three-fold:

- We propose a pose-to-video translation framework to generate high fidelity videos for unseen in-the-wild poses by minimizing the domain gaps between testing and training pose sequences.
- We conduct extensive experiments and evaluations, both quantitatively and qualitatively, which demonstrate the significant advantage over state-of-the-art methods with superior result quality and generalization ability on unseen input poses. When presented with the results generated by our method vs. the ground truth examples, the users are often unable to tell which is real, preferring our method in 48.1% of cases.
- We collect two datasets: a high-quality indoor human video dataset containing all training sequences of the target persons used in this paper, recorded in front of a green backdrop screen, and a single-person activities dataset including large-scale in-the-wild pose sequences that are used during both training and evaluation.

2 Related Work

Image-to-Image Translation. With the recent development in conditional GANs [34], various inputs, including but not limited to classification categories [35] and images [27], can be utilized to condition high fidelity image synthesis, besides noise in previous works [11,36]. Image-to-image translation [21] uses paired training data to transfer an image from one domain to another and introduces an encoder-decoder architecture with skip connections. The architecture and training methods have been widely adopted in follow-up work. After that, pix2pixHD [50] further proposes a multi-scale generator and discriminator structure with residual-blocks to synthesize high-resolution photo-realistic images. However, obtaining paired data may still be prohibitively difficult for some tasks. Unsupervised image-to-image translation methods are presented to focus on minimizing domain gaps using unpaired image data [54,59]. Nevertheless, compared with single images, video translation is usually more challenging since temporal consistency should also be considered as one vital factor besides image quality that impacts the final result quality.

Video-to-Video Translation. Early efforts on non-conditional video synthesis typically convert a latent code into low-resolution short video frames via a recurrent neural network [37,42,45]. These methods often suffer from low-quality results, similar to the works on future frames prediction, that also use adversarial training and image reconstruction losses [12,16,46,47]. To generate photo-realistic videos and allow more fine-grain controls, the conditional video generation methods have shown great potential recently by using a sequence of conditioning inputs [9,17,20,49], such as semantic segmentation maps [49]. A further group of work attempts to perform video-to-video translation requiring only a few images for the reference person. Despite substantial progress achieved recently [18,28,38,52,55], the generated human motion results are far from being realistic [26,48]. Our work also falls into the scope of video-to-video translation, specifically focusing on the pose to video translation for unseen in-the-wild poses.

Human Motion Transfer. Synthesizing novel views for human face and body has been studied extensively [5,6,13,14,23,25,29,30,33,56]. Some methods transfer facial expressions with parametric face models [3,41]. Extending such method to animating bodies is not trivial. Similar to the face re-animation method of Kim et al. [24], human body motion transfer can be achieved by adopting image generation neural networks. Villegas et al. [43,44] use pose to predict future frames to synthesize a new human video. Ma et al. [31,32] use a reference image to synthesize novel view given a target pose. Siarohin et al. [39] improve the approach by proposing a deformable network architecture. Balakrishnan et al. [4] segment human body parts according to the target pose and use a spatial transformation sub-module to synthesize unseen poses. Instead of predicting future frames or generating single frames from an input pose, we focus on high fidelity personalized video generation, where a network is specifically trained for each target person.

Discussion. Our focus is to synthesize personalized videos given arbitrary reference pose sequences, utilizing training videos for the target subject. We borrow the basic problem formulation from existing literature on pose to image generation [1,8,49,58]. However, compared with Everybody Dance Now (EDN) [8], Video-to-Video Synthesis (vid2vid) [49], and Zhou et al. [58], besides different methods on enforcing temporal coherence, we also adopt a two-stage translation and refinement network to improve generation texture quality, and propose a novel unified learning framework incorporating both paired and unpaired training examples to help the network generalize better on unseen in-the-wild poses. We demonstrate the clear advantage of our methods over EDN [8] and vid2vid [49] in experiments.

3   Method

Given a source pose sequence $\{p_1, p_2, \ldots, p_T\}$, our goal is to generate a photo-realistic human video sequence $\{f_1, f_2, \ldots, f_T\}$ of the target person performing a sequence of motions provided by the input sequence of poses.

To train the method, for each subject, we record a set of video clips, covering common body poses and motions. We then parse the human pose skeleton from each video frame so that the paired training data is formed. Each pair includes a pose skeleton and the corresponding ground-truth image. In the setting of conditional GAN [34], a pose-to-image translation network can be used to synthesize a body video from input poses.

However, for such a challenging task, there are a few critical issues that prevent the baseline framework from working well in most general cases:

- There exist multiple domain gaps between the training and in-the-wild poses, including different recording devices/environments, subject identities, and motion styles. Direct inference on in-the-wild poses using networks

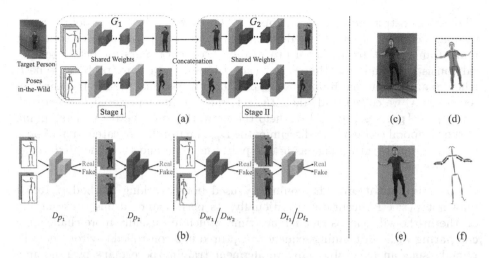

Fig. 3. Pipeline and data augmentation. (a) Our architecture consists of a Pose2Video network (Stage I) and a texture refinement network (Stage II). The top branch represents paired learning, and the lower one indicates unpaired learning. (b) Three types of discriminator: D_p is the single frame discriminator for paired training, which is conditioned on the input to its corresponding stage (pose maps for D_{p1} and Stage I output for D_{p2}); D_w is the unpaired single frame discriminator, always conditioned on the input pose maps; D_t is the temporal discriminator accepts stacked generated continuous frames. (c) One example frame captured in front of the green screen. (d) Extract the pose skeleton and remove the background, the pose information is further used to calculate the cropping region around the person. (e) Crop foreground and fill background with solid green color. (f) Perform data augmentation on the poses, such as elongating or shortening arms as indicated by arrows. (Color figure online)

trained purely with paired supervision will produce notably degraded results (Table 4);
- State-of-the-art pose detection methods often lose track of important body key-points (top row in Fig. 4b) or mispredict (top row in Fig. 4c). Such noisy inputs make the generation even harder;
- A single-stage pose-to-image translation network tends to focus more on mapping the input pose to a rough spatial body image layout. Its limited capability is usually not sufficient to achieve high local visual realism at the same time, especially on dynamic texture details of body and clothes.

We detail our solutions to these problems in the next sections.

3.1 Pose2Video Network

As the first stage, the Pose2Video network performs pose-to-video translation, as shown in Fig. 3a (G_1 in Stage I). We encode the tracked skeleton with n_s parts, such as arms and legs, into an input pose map with exactly n_s channels by drawing a line segment of each part at its corresponding map channel.

The network structure follows pix2pixHD [50]. However, instead of doing image-to-image translation at the single-frame level, we adapt the network to accept multi-frame input to further utilize training sequence pairs for better temporal consistency and smoothness. For each training data pair $(\mathbf{p}_t, \mathbf{f}_t)$ at time t, where $\mathbf{p}$ and $\mathbf{f}$ represent input pose maps and corresponding ground-truth frames respectively, we collect and stack $2K + 1$ frames centered around t as network input $\tilde{\mathbf{p}} \equiv \{\mathbf{p}_{t-K}, \ldots, \mathbf{p}_{t+K}\}$, to help the network gain a better understanding of the temporal context. For discriminator D_{p_1}, we use the concatenation of pose and the ground-truth image as a true pair, and pose and the generated image as a false pair.

Pose Augmentation. The commonly used body tracking method [7,15,53] may not perfectly accurate. Additionally, its performance drops substantially on the in-the-wild videos at inference time, which are usually more challenging comparing with our training sequences captured in a controlled environment. To remedy such an inevitable gap, we augment training pose maps by randomly dropping some input channels, perturb the location of joints keypoints, and elongate or shorten body part lengths in some channels, such as an example in Fig. 3f, so that both lengths and location of body limbs can be randomly changed during training.

3.2 Texture Refinement Network

Our Pose2Video network can already generate video output conditioned by the input pose sequence. However, to tackle the challenging problem of photo-realistic human video generation, it is often difficult for the network to directly synthesize realistic texture from sparse pose in a single stage. Therefore, we concatenate an additional texture refinement network after Pose2Video, as shown in Fig. 3 (G_2 in Stage II), to further refine the local texture details based on the rough output from the first stage. The texture refinement network also follows the setting of condition GAN where the inputs for generator G_2 are adjacent $2K + 1$ frames of Pose2Video RGB outputs $\tilde{G}_1(\tilde{\mathbf{p}})$, where $\tilde{G}_1(\tilde{\mathbf{p}}) \equiv \{G_1(\tilde{\mathbf{p}}_{t-K}), \ldots, G_1(\tilde{\mathbf{p}}_{t+K})\}$. For discriminator D_{p_2}, the concatenated $\tilde{G}_1(\tilde{\mathbf{p}})$ and a ground-truth image is treated as true pair, and $\tilde{G}_1(\tilde{\mathbf{p}})$ and a generated image is false pair.

3.3 Unified Paired and Unpaired Learning

Even with our pose augmentation method, the paired poses extracted from the recorded training data may still have limited coverage over the vast human motion space, given that users may probably want to test challenging motion sequences at inference time such as ballet and hip-hop moves. Furthermore, in-the-wild videos with complex background and occlusions also tend to raise the difficulty of pose estimation comparing to our chroma-keyed training sequences. In light of these, we propose to not only use augmented pairs of training data but also introduce unpaired learning with in-the-wild poses to boost the generalization ability and robustness.

We unify paired and unpaired training branches by swapping inputs and learning objectives while sharing weights of the target networks, as shown in Fig. 3a. In what follows, we introduce learning strategies of both paired and unpaired training branches respectively and conclude with the full training objective.

Notation. Stage I and II share similar network structures and learning objectives. For the purpose of simplification, we use the same notation system to elaborate the training strategies for both stages within a single framework. Besides the paired pose map $\mathbf{p}_t$ and ground-truth frame $\mathbf{f}_t$ that are consistent across the paper, we also uniformly denote the corresponding input and generator of each network stage as $\mathbf{x}_t$ and G, where $\mathbf{x}_t \equiv \tilde{\mathbf{p}}$ and $G \equiv G_1$ for the Pose2Video network (Stage I), and $\mathbf{x}_t \equiv \tilde{G}_1(\tilde{\mathbf{p}})$ and $G \equiv G_2$ for the refinement network (Stage II).

Paired Learning. In the paired learning branch, the existence of ground-truth images allows us to enforce paired supervision on the network output. Instead of using low-level pixel objectives such as L1 reconstruction loss, we measure the perceptual similarity loss [22] $\mathcal{L}_{vgg}(G(\mathbf{x}_t), \mathbf{f}_t)$ with VGG19 network [40] between the network output and the corresponding ground-truth, to let the network gain a better semantic understanding and avoid blurriness caused by imperfect pose-image pairing and non-deterministic texture details regarding the pose.

We also use a single-frame discriminator D_p conditioned on the input pose to enforce natural result and proper pose correspondences:

$$\mathcal{L}_{D_p} = \mathbb{E}_{\mathbf{x},\mathbf{f}}[\log D_p(\mathbf{x}_t, \mathbf{f}_t)] + \mathbb{E}_{\mathbf{x}}[\log(1 - D_p(\mathbf{x}_t, G(\tilde{\mathbf{x}}_t)))], \tag{1}$$

where $\tilde{\mathbf{x}} \equiv \{\mathbf{x}_{t-K}, \ldots, \mathbf{x}_{t+K}\}$ is the temporal stacking of adjacent $2K+1$ frames centered around t, as described in the Pose2Video Network section.

To achieve more stable GAN training, we also adopted the discriminator feature matching loss [50] $\mathcal{L}_{f_p}(G, D_p)$.

Besides single-frame quality, the generated sequences should also be temporally consistent and retain plausible motion quality. Therefore, we use an additional unconditioned temporal discriminator D_t to tell whether a continuous subset of M result frames is realistic or not in the temporal domain:

$$\mathcal{L}_{D_t} = \mathbb{E}_{\mathbf{f}}[\log D_t(\mathbf{f}_t^{t+M-1})] + \mathbb{E}_{\mathbf{x}}[\log(1 - D_t(G(\tilde{\mathbf{x}})_t^{t+M-1})], \tag{2}$$

where $G(\tilde{\mathbf{x}})_t^{t+M-1}$ stands for stacking M frames of generator outputs $\{G(\tilde{\mathbf{x}}_t), \ldots, G(\tilde{\mathbf{x}}_{t+M-1})\}$. We also use a feature matching loss $\mathcal{L}_{f_t}(G, D_t)$ for D_t.

Unpaired Learning. During unpaired learning, instead of using recorded paired data, we randomly feed the network with body pose inputs extracted from video sequences with different subjects. Incorporating these in-the-wild inputs helps bridge the pose domain gap and increase network robustness against unseen inputs. Without paired ground-truth supervision, we perform unpaired training based on network models that share weights with paired training and solely adopt a single-frame discriminator D_w similar to that introduced in the paired learning section. Different from D_p, those positive examples do not share the same condition $\mathbf{p}_t$ as the negative ones, but randomly draw pairs $(\mathbf{p}'_t, \mathbf{f}'_t)$ from recorded sequences used in paired learning:

$$\mathcal{L}_{D_w} = \mathbb{E}_{\mathbf{p},\mathbf{f}}[\log D_w(\mathbf{p}'_t, \mathbf{f}'_t)] + \mathbb{E}_{\mathbf{x},\mathbf{p}}[\log(1 - D_w(\mathbf{p}_t, G(\tilde{\mathbf{x}}_t)))]. \tag{3}$$

Full Objective. We train our networks with a two-stage training strategy that we first train the Pose2Video network G_1 by optimizing D_{p1}, D_{t_1}, and D_{w_1}, and then fix the weights in G_1 and train the refinement network G_2 by optimizing D_{p_2}, D_{t_2}, and D_{w_2}. The overall loss functions for both training stages are similarly defined as:

$$\begin{aligned} \min_G(\max_{D_p}\mathcal{L}_{D_p}(G, D_p) + \max_{D_t}\mathcal{L}_{D_t}(G, D_t) + \max_{D_w}\mathcal{L}_{D_w}(G, D_w)) \\ + \lambda_{vgg}\mathcal{L}_{vgg}(G) + \lambda_{fm}(\mathcal{L}_{f_p}(G, D_p) + \mathcal{L}_{f_t}(G, D_t)). \end{aligned} \tag{4}$$

4 Experiments

In this section, we conduct both quantitative and qualitative experiments to demonstrate the advantages of our method, especially on challenging poses.

4.1 Experiment Setup

Data Preparation. We use three datasets to perform validation. The first one is released with the Everybody Dance Now (EDN) paper [8]. The dataset includes videos of five subjects. We follow the training and validation strategy in [8] to perform experiments. To facilitate the following presentation, we denote the validation videos from EDN as **EDN-Vali**.

For the second dataset, we collected videos containing four subjects. All videos are filmed in an indoor environment with the subject standing in front of a backdrop green-screen (as an example frame shown in Fig. 3(c)) to help isolate the foreground and achieve better segmentation quality. An iPhone fixed on a tripod is used to shoot the videos. During the process, all subjects are asked to either perform slow random moves or follow simple online dancing videos (these guidance videos are not used in either training or validation). On average, we collect 22 minutes video for each target person. We split all videos of each subject into training and validation sets with a ratio of 17 : 3. We denote the validation set as **Target-Vali**.

We process these captured data by first applying an off-the-shelf pose detection networks [7] to get estimated body poses. Then we perform chroma-key composition to mask out the target person and change the background to a solid green color. Finally, we crop each frame with the smallest rectangle that encloses the target person, as shown in Fig. 3(e).

Besides the two datasets for paired learning, we create a large-scale single-person activities dataset (**SPA**) for unpaired learning and validation. To make SPA suitable for poses-to-video generation, we collect 1,060 single-person activity videos and make sure that all these videos catch the whole human body, and each video only includes one person. The average duration of each video is about 10 seconds and we extract frames at 30 FPS, giving 315,000 frames in total. The body poses of each SPA video are detected for training and inference uses. Additionally, we randomly take out 64 videos from SPA as a validation dataset, denoted as **SPA-Vali**, to verify model performance on unseen in-the-wild poses. The average duration of SPA-Vali videos is about 17 seconds. Compared with the other two validation datasets, SPA-Vali is more challenging.

Implementation Details. We adopt the multi-scale generator and discriminator architecture and apply the progressive training schedule. We first train a model for 128×256 and then upsample to 256×512. We set $K = 2$ for input pose maps $\tilde{p}$, and $M = 3$ in Eq. 2. The hyper-parameters in Eq. 4 are set as $\lambda_{fm} = 10$ and $\lambda_{vgg} = 10$. We use the initial learning rate as 0.0002 and gradually decrease it.

Evaluation Metrics. We numerically evaluate the generated videos with both objective analysis and subjective user studies.

– **Objective Metrics.** We adopt the three widely-used objective metrics to assess the result quality: SSIM (Structural Similarity) [51] index to measure the perceived image quality degradation between both synthesized and real frames; LPIPS (Learned Perceptual Image Patch Similarity) [57] to measure the perceptual similarity between generated and real images; and FID (Fréchet Inception Distance) [19] to measure the distribution distance.
– **Subjective Scores.** We also conduct user studies to analyze the video quality regarding real human perception. The experiments are performed using the Amazon Mechanical Turk (AMT) platform. We design two settings for users to compare video quality: 1) Pairwise comparison: we show workers pairs of videos with exactly the same motion but from two different sources (including ground-truth, results of our method, or results of state-of-the-art methods), and ask them to choose the more realistic one. The two videos are shown side-by-side and their orders are randomly chosen; 2) Single-video evaluation: we only show workers a single video and ask them whether this video looks real to them. Workers can only choose a video as real or not.

4.2 Comparison Results

Both EDN [8] and vid2vid [49] are state-of-the-art methods on human body motion transfer and have achieved significantly better results compared with

Table 1. Objective compar-isons on the EDN-Vali dataset.

	SSIM ↑	LPIPS ↓
EDN	0.838	0.050
Ours w/ BG	0.948	0.027
Ours segmented FG	0.959	0.031
Ours w/o BG	**0.976**	**0.015**

Table 2. Objective compar-isons on the Target-Vali dataset.

	SSIM ↑	FID ↓
Vid2vid	0.9518	7.5214
Ours	0.9666	5.9453

Table 3. User study on paired comparison. Each user is presented with a pair of videos generated by different methods and asked to pick the relatively better one.

	Target-Vali	SPA-Vali
Vid2vid/ours	29.2%/**70.8%**	9.7%/**90.3%**
Vid2vid/GT	36.2%/**63.8%**	-
Ours/GT	48.1%/**51.9%**	-

Table 4. User study on single video evaluation. Each user is presented with a single video and asked to choose if it is real.

	Target-Vali	SPA-Vali
Vid2vid	42.3%	25.7%
Ours	71.4%	**44.5%**
GT	**85.1%**	-

existing image-based human body generation methods [4,50]. In the following sections, we compare our method with the two studies and show both qualitative and quantitative results.

Comparison with EDN [8]. We use the data collected by EDN to train our models, and then validate the models on EDN-Vali dataset. We conduct three experimental settings: 1) **ours w/ BG:** similarly to EDN, we use original images with background for training and validation; 2) **ours segmented FG:** similarly to EDN, we use original images to train the networks, but apply a segmentation network [10] on the generated images to get foreground region; 3) **ours w/o BG:** we apply a segmentation network on the training data and only use the segmented foreground to train our model, so the synthesized results only contain foreground. Following EDN, we run the experiments for five subjects and report the averaged results. The results in Table 1 show that our method outperforms EDN significantly as we achieve much higher SSIM and much lower LPIPS. We also notice that using the foreground region for training performs better than using a whole frame as the networks can focus on synthesizing only the foreground part. Although the foreground region can be obtained by segmenting the generated image, the image quality is inferior to the foreground that is synthesized directly, supporting that it is beneficial to remove the background prior to training.

Comparison with Vid2vid [49]. In their original article, vid2vid extracts human poses with both OpenPose [7] and DensePose [2]. However, DensePose detects human body shapes together with skeleton poses. The shape information encodes the identity of the reference subject, which can cause difficulty preserving the target identity during inference. In order to have a fair comparison, we implement their method using the same pose generation and augmentation methods as ours.

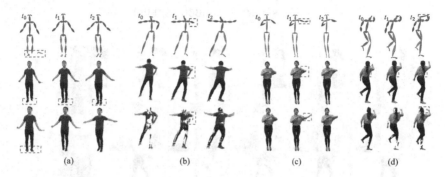

Fig. 4. Visual comparisons with vid2vid [49]. Each of these four sequences contains three consecutive frames, with the first row shows the input skeletons, the seconds row shows our results, and the third row shows the results by vid2vid. We emphasis the incorrect pose regions with red dashed box, and the corresponding results generated by our method and vid2vid with green and blue boxes respectively. (Color figure online)

Quantitative Evaluations. We list the average SSIM and FID metrics in Table 2, evaluated on our Target-Vali dataset in which we have access to ground-truth. Compared with vid2vid [49], we achieve noticeably higher scores on SSIM and lower scores on FID, which proves that our method can synthesize results with better objective quality.

We also present user study results, with both pair-wise comparison and single-video evaluation settings shown in Table 3 and Table 4. From the pair-wise comparison result, we can see that 70.8% and 90.3% users prefer our results to those by vid2vid on Target-Vali and SPA-Vali datasets respectively. Also, users demonstrate very close preferences between our results and the ground-truth (48.1% vs. 51.9%), which shows that our results are somehow comparable to the real videos. As for the single-video evaluation, we show the number of percentage videos that are rated as real videos by users. We can notice our method achieves better scores than vid2vid on both datasets as well. As expected, both methods receive lower scores on SPA-Vali compared with Target-Valid since SPA contains more challenging poses. However, our method continues to perform substantially better than vid2vid, demonstrating superior generalization.

Table 5. Ablation analysis on our method. Our full method (PL-UL-Stage2) achieves significantly better results comparing with other alternatives.

	SSIM ↑	FID ↓
PL-Stage1	0.9611	8.0105
PL-Stage1-DA	0.9633	7.1197
PL-Stage1-DA-F	0.9651	6.5701
PL-Stage2	0.9655	6.2046
PL-UL-Stage2	**0.9666**	**5.9453**

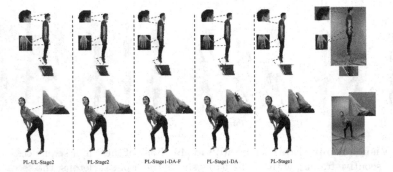

Fig. 5. Qualitative ablation study results. The result generated by our full method is shown on the leftmost, four results generated by alternative strategies shown in the middle with key components gradually removed at each step, and the ground-truth shown on the rightmost. We also show some zoom-in insets to better visualize the differences.

Qualitative Evaluations. For visual comparison, we randomly selected pose sequences from SPA-Vali and generate motion transfer results with both our method and vid2vid in Fig. 4. The results confirm that our approach generated more realistic results in cases when the pose detector fails to reliably find the keypoints. For example, in top row of Fig. 4a, the left foot is incorrectly detached from the leg in the first frame. However, our method is still capable of generating the foot in the right position with consistent orientation, while vid2vid generates an unnatural dot at the wrong location, misled by the input pose. In Fig. 4b, the right lower arm is entirely missing in the second frame. Our method successfully predicts the missing arm utilizing the adjacent frames, achieving significantly better results than vid2vid. In Fig. 4c, the position of the left lower arm in the second frame is inconsistent with its neighbors. Our method again generates consistent results while vid2vid generates an extra arm at that frame. In Fig. 4d, the detected face key-points are unnaturally stretched in the third frame. In contrast to the broken head result by vid2vid, our method still manages to generate intact head and hair with consistent direction. Besides robustness, it is worth noticing that vid2vid often produce less satisfactory

(a) Single frame results.   (b) Consecutive frame results.

Fig. 6. Motion transfer results. Both (a) single and (b) consecutive frames results are shown here. In each example, the first row shows the reference video, and the other rows show the transferred results on two different target persons.

foreground masks, which leads to internal holes or missing parts as shown in Fig. 4b and Fig. 4d. As can be seen, our method consistently produces complete and accurate foreground boundaries.

4.3 Ablation Analysis

We perform ablation studies to identify which of the contributions are responsible for superior quality. We report the following experiments: 1) **PL-Stage1**: as the baseline, we adopt a single-stage Pose2Video network without unpaired learning and pose augmentation, and stack the input poses as $\{\mathbf{p}_{t-K}, \ldots, \mathbf{p}_t\}$, which follows the settings of existing methods [8,49]; 2) **PL-Stage1-DA**: we add pose augmentation to PL-Stage1; 3) **PL-Stage1-DA-F**: based on PL-Stage1-DA, we change input poses to $\{\mathbf{p}_{t-K}, \ldots, \mathbf{p}_{t+K}\}$; 4) **PL-Stage2**: we add the second refinement stage to PL-Stage1-DA-F, but still without unpaired learning; 5) **PL-UL-Stage2**: our full method, with unpaired learning used on both stages.

Table 5 summarizes the quantitative ablation analysis results. We can see that by incrementally introducing these key components, both SSIM and FID metrics gradually improve supporting that for photorealistic human motion retargeting all the proposed contributions are essential. We also present visual results for ablation analysis in Fig. 5. By zooming in certain areas, we can clearly find that comparing with the baseline, our full method is able to produce better mask boundaries, fewer artifacts, and richer and sharper texture details.

4.4 Qualitative Results

More motion transfer examples generated by our method are shown in Fig. 6, including results for both uniformly sampled single frames and consecutive frame sequences. These various results demonstrate that our method can generate high-fidelity results on various subjects from challenging body pose sequences.

5 Conclusions

We introduced a novel approach for video human motion transfer. The network contains two stages with one sub-network for pose-to-image translation and another for image-to-image translation. The network is trained by stacked continuous frames to achieve temporally consistent results. We also incorporate a unified paired and unpaired learning strategy and a pose augmentation method during training to help the network generalize well on unseen in-the-wild poses. Our experiments support that all the proposed contributions are essential for obtaining realistic human motion retargteting. To further boost research on the topic, we collected two datasets containing human motion videos. The first dataset is used for training personalized models, while the second one for unpaired learning and evaluation.

References

1. Aberman, K., Shi, M., Liao, J., Liscbinski, D., Chen, B., Cohen-Or, D.: Deep video-based performance cloning. In: Computer Graphics Forum, vol. 38, pp. 219–233. Wiley Online Library (2019)
2. Alp Güler, R., Neverova, N., Kokkinos, I.: Densepose: dense human pose estimation in the wild. In: Proceedings of the IEEE Conference on Computer Vision and Pattern Recognition, pp. 7297–7306 (2018)
3. Averbuch-Elor, H., Cohen-Or, D., Kopf, J., Cohen, M.F.: Bringing portraits to life. ACM Trans. Graph. **36**(6), 196 (2017). Proceeding of SIGGRAPH Asia 2017
4. Balakrishnan, G., Zhao, A., Dalca, A.V., Durand, F., Guttag, J.: Synthesizing images of humans in unseen poses. In: Proceedings of the IEEE Conference on Computer Vision and Pattern Recognition, pp. 8340–8348 (2018)
5. Bansal, A., Ma, S., Ramanan, D., Sheikh, Y.: Recycle-GAN: unsupervised video retargeting. In: Proceedings of the European Conference on Computer Vision (ECCV), pp. 119–135 (2018)
6. de Bem, R., Ghosh, A., Ajanthan, T., Miksik, O., Siddharth, N., Torr, P.: A semi-supervised deep generative model for human body analysis. In: Proceedings of the European Conference on Computer Vision (ECCV) (2018)
7. Cao, Z., Hidalgo, G., Simon, T., Wei, S.E., Sheikh, Y.: Openpose: real-time multi-person 2D pose estimation using part affinity fields. arXiv preprint arXiv:1812.08008 (2018)
8. Chan, C., Ginosar, S., Zhou, T., Efros, A.A.: Everybody dance now. In: Proceedings of the IEEE International Conference on Computer Vision, pp. 5933–5942 (2019)
9. Chen, D., Liao, J., Yuan, L., Yu, N., Hua, G.: Coherent online video style transfer. In: Proceedings of the IEEE International Conference on Computer Vision, pp. 1105–1114 (2017)
10. Chen, L.C., Zhu, Y., Papandreou, G., Schroff, F., Adam, H.: Encoder-decoder with atrous separable convolution for semantic image segmentation. In: ECCV (2018)
11. Denton, E.L., Chintala, S., Fergus, R., et al.: Deep generative image models using alaplacian pyramid of adversarial networks. In: Advances in Neural Information Processing Systems, pp. 1486–1494 (2015)
12. Denton, E.L., et al.: Unsupervised learning of disentangled representations from video. In: Advances in Neural Information Processing Systems, pp. 4414–4423 (2017)

13. Esser, P., Haux, J., Ommer, B.: Unsupervised robust disentangling of latent characteristics for image synthesis. In: Proceedings of the IEEE International Conference on Computer Vision, pp. 2699–2709 (2019)
14. Esser, P., Sutter, E., Ommer, B.: A variational u-net for conditional appearance and shape generation. In: Proceedings of the IEEE Conference on Computer Vision and Pattern Recognition, pp. 8857–8866 (2018)
15. Fang, H.S., Xie, S., Tai, Y.W., Lu, C.: Rmpe: regional multi-person pose estimation. In: Proceedings of the IEEE International Conference on Computer Vision, pp. 2334–2343 (2017)
16. Finn, C., Goodfellow, I., Levine, S.: Unsupervised learning for physical interaction through video prediction. In: Advances in Neural Information Processing Systems, pp. 64–72 (2016)
17. Gafni, O., Wolf, L., Taigman, Y.: Vid2game: controllable characters extracted from real-world videos. arXiv preprint arXiv:1904.08379 (2019)
18. Ha, S., Kersner, M., Kim, B., Seo, S., Kim, D.: Marionette: few-shot face reenactment preserving identity of unseen targets. arXiv preprint arXiv:1911.08139 (2019)
19. Heusel, M., Ramsauer, H., Unterthiner, T., Nessler, B., Hochreiter, S.: GANs trained by a two time-scale update rule converge to a local nash equilibrium. In: Advances in Neural Information Processing Systems, pp. 6626–6637 (2017)
20. Huang, H., et al.: Real-time neural style transfer for videos. In: Proceedings of the IEEE Conference on Computer Vision and Pattern Recognition, pp. 783–791 (2017)
21. Isola, P., Zhu, J.Y., Zhou, T., Efros, A.A.: Image-to-image translation with conditional adversarial networks. In: Proceedings of the IEEE Conference on Computer Vision and Pattern Recognition, pp. 1125–1134 (2017)
22. Johnson, J., Alahi, A., Fei-Fei, L.: Perceptual losses for real-time style transfer and super-resolution. In: Leibe, B., Matas, J., Sebe, N., Welling, M. (eds.) ECCV 2016. LNCS, vol. 9906, pp. 694–711. Springer, Cham (2016). https://doi.org/10.1007/978-3-319-46475-6_43
23. Joo, D., Kim, D., Kim, J.: Generating a fusion image: one's identity and another's shape. In: Proceedings of the IEEE Conference on Computer Vision and Pattern Recognition, pp. 1635–1643 (2018)
24. Kim, H., et al.: Deep video portraits. ACM Trans. Graph. (TOG) 37(4), 163 (2018)
25. Kim, Y., Nam, S., Cho, I., Kim, S.J.: Unsupervised keypoint learning for guiding class-conditional video prediction. In: Advances in Neural Information Processing Systems, pp. 3809–3819 (2019)
26. Lee, J., Ramanan, D., Girdhar, R.: Metapix: few-shot video retargeting. arXiv preprint arXiv:1910.04742 (2019)
27. Liu, M.Y., Breuel, T., Kautz, J.: Unsupervised image-to-image translation networks. In: Advances in Neural Information Processing Systems, pp. 700–708 (2017)
28. Liu, M.Y., et al.: Few-shot unsupervised image-to-image translation. In: Proceedings of the IEEE International Conference on Computer Vision, pp. 10551–10560 (2019)
29. Liu, W., Piao, Z., Min, J., Luo, W., Ma, L., Gao, S.: Liquid warping GAN: a unified framework for human motion imitation, appearance transfer and novel view synthesis. In: Proceedings of the IEEE International Conference on Computer Vision, pp. 5904–5913 (2019)
30. Lorenz, D., Bereska, L., Milbich, T., Ommer, B.: Unsupervised part-based disentangling of object shape and appearance. In: Proceedings of the IEEE Conference on Computer Vision and Pattern Recognition, pp. 10955–10964 (2019)

31. Ma, L., Jia, X., Sun, Q., Schiele, B., Tuytelaars, T., Van Gool, L.: Pose guided person image generation. In: Advances in Neural Information Processing Systems, pp. 406–416 (2017)
32. Ma, L., Sun, Q., Georgoulis, S., Van Gool, L., Schiele, B., Fritz, M.: Disentangled person image generation. In: Proceedings of the IEEE Conference on Computer Vision and Pattern Recognition, pp. 99–108 (2018)
33. Martin-Brualla, R., et al.: Lookingood: enhancing performance capture with real-time neural re-rendering. arXiv preprint arXiv:1811.05029 (2018)
34. Mirza, M., Osindero, S.: Conditional generative adversarial nets. arXiv preprint arXiv:1411.1784 (2014)
35. Odena, A., Olah, C., Shlens, J.: Conditional image synthesis with auxiliary classifier GANs. In: Proceedings of the 34th International Conference on Machine Learning, vol. 70, pp. 2642–2651. JMLR.org (2017)
36. Radford, A., Metz, L., Chintala, S.: Unsupervised representation learning with deep convolutional generative adversarial networks. arXiv preprint arXiv:1511.06434 (2015)
37. Saito, M., Matsumoto, E., Saito, S.: Temporal generative adversarial nets with singular value clipping. In: Proceedings of the IEEE International Conference on Computer Vision, pp. 2830–2839 (2017)
38. Siarohin, A., Lathuilière, S., Tulyakov, S., Ricci, E., Sebe, N.: First order motion model for image animation. In: Conference on Neural Information Processing Systems (NeurIPS), December 2019
39. Siarohin, A., Sangineto, E., Lathuilière, S., Sebe, N.: Deformable GANs for pose-based human image generation. In: Proceedings of the IEEE Conference on Computer Vision and Pattern Recognition, pp. 3408–3416 (2018)
40. Simonyan, K., Zisserman, A.: Very deep convolutional networks for large-scale image recognition. arXiv preprint arXiv:1409.1556 (2014)
41. Thies, J., Zollhofer, M., Stamminger, M., Theobalt, C., Nießner, M.: Face2face: real-time face capture and reenactment of RGB videos. In: Proceedings of the IEEE Conference on Computer Vision and Pattern Recognition, pp. 2387–2395 (2016)
42. Tulyakov, S., Liu, M.Y., Yang, X., Kautz, J.: Mocogan: decomposing motion and content for video generation. In: Proceedings of the IEEE Conference on Computer Vision and Pattern Recognition, pp. 1526–1535 (2018)
43. Villegas, R., Yang, J., Ceylan, D., Lee, H.: Neural kinematic networks for unsupervised motion retargetting. In: Proceedings of the IEEE Conference on Computer Vision and Pattern Recognition, pp. 8639–8648 (2018)
44. Villegas, R., Yang, J., Zou, Y., Sohn, S., Lin, X., Lee, H.: Learning to generate long-term future via hierarchical prediction. In: Proceedings of the 34th International Conference on Machine Learning, vol. 70, pp. 3560–3569. JMLR.org (2017)
45. Vondrick, C., Pirsiavash, H., Torralba, A.: Generating videos with scene dynamics. In: Advances in Neural Information Processing Systems, pp. 613–621 (2016)
46. Walker, J., Doersch, C., Gupta, A., Hebert, M.: An uncertain future: forecasting from static images using variational autoencoders. In: Leibe, B., Matas, J., Sebe, N., Welling, M. (eds.) ECCV 2016. LNCS, vol. 9911, pp. 835–851. Springer, Cham (2016). https://doi.org/10.1007/978-3-319-46478-7_51
47. Walker, J., Marino, K., Gupta, A., Hebert, M.: The pose knows: video forecasting by generating pose futures. In: Proceedings of the IEEE International Conference on Computer Vision, pp. 3332–3341 (2017)

48. Wang, T.C., Liu, M.Y., Tao, A., Liu, G., Kautz, J., Catanzaro, B.: Few-shot video-to-video synthesis. In: Advances in Neural Information Processing Systems (NeurIPS) (2019)

49. Wang, T.C., et al.: Video-to-video synthesis. In: Advances in Neural Information Processing Systems (NeurIPS) (2018)

50. Wang, T.C., Liu, M.Y., Zhu, J.Y., Tao, A., Kautz, J., Catanzaro, B.: High-resolution image synthesis and semantic manipulation with conditional GANs. In: Proceedings of the IEEE Conference on Computer Vision and Pattern Recognition (2018)

51. Wang, Z., Bovik, A.C., Sheikh, H.R., Simoncelli, E.P., et al.: Image quality assessment: from error visibility to structural similarity. IEEE Trans. Image Process. **13**(4), 600–612 (2004)

52. Wiles, O., Sophia Koepke, A., Zisserman, A.: X2face: a network for controlling face generation using images, audio, and pose codes. In: Proceedings of the European Conference on Computer Vision (ECCV), pp. 670–686 (2018)

53. Xiu, Y., Li, J., Wang, H., Fang, Y., Lu, C.: Pose flow: efficient online pose tracking. arXiv preprint arXiv:1802.00977 (2018)

54. Yi, Z., Zhang, H., Tan, P., Gong, M.: Dualgan: unsupervised dual learning for image-to-image translation. In: Proceedings of the IEEE International Conference on Computer Vision, pp. 2849–2857 (2017)

55. Zakharov, E., Shysheya, A., Burkov, E., Lempitsky, V.: Few-shot adversarial learning of realistic neural talking head models. In: Proceedings of the IEEE International Conference on Computer Vision, pp. 9459–9468 (2019)

56. Zanfir, M., Popa, A.I., Zanfir, A., Sminchisescu, C.: Human appearance transfer. In: Proceedings of the IEEE Conference on Computer Vision and Pattern Recognition, pp. 5391–5399 (2018)

57. Zhang, R., Isola, P., Efros, A.A., Shechtman, E., Wang, O.: The unreasonable effectiveness of deep features as a perceptual metric. In: Proceedings of the IEEE Conference on Computer Vision and Pattern Recognition, pp. 586–595 (2018)

58. Zhou, Y., Wang, Z., Fang, C., Bui, T., Berg, T.L.: Dance dance generation: motion transfer for internet videos. arXiv preprint arXiv:1904.00129 (2019)

59. Zhu, J.Y., Park, T., Isola, P., Efros, A.A.: Unpaired image-to-image translation using cycle-consistent adversarial networks. In: Proceedings of the IEEE International Conference on Computer Vision, pp. 2223–2232 (2017)

CA-GAN: Weakly Supervised Color Aware GAN for Controllable Makeup Transfer

Robin Kips[1,2]([✉]), Pietro Gori[2], Matthieu Perrot[1], and Isabelle Bloch[2]

[1] L'Oréal Research and Innovation, Clichy, France
robin.kips@loreal.com
[2] LTCI, Télécom Paris, Institut Polytechnique de Paris, Paris, France

Abstract. While existing makeup style transfer models perform an image synthesis whose results cannot be explicitly controlled, the ability to modify makeup color continuously is a desirable property for virtual try-on applications. We propose a new formulation for the makeup style transfer task, with the objective to learn a color controllable makeup style synthesis. We introduce CA-GAN, a generative model that learns to modify the color of specific objects (e.g. lips or eyes) in the image to an arbitrary target color while preserving background. Since color labels are rare and costly to acquire, our method leverages weakly supervised learning for conditional GANs. This enables to learn a controllable synthesis of complex objects, and only requires a weak proxy of the image attribute that we desire to modify. Finally, we present for the first time a quantitative analysis of makeup style transfer and color control performance.

Keywords: Image synthesis · GANs · Weakly supervised learning · Makeup style transfer

1 Introduction

The development of online cosmetic purchase has led to a growing interest in makeup virtual try-on technologies. Based on image filtering [32] or physical modeling of skin and makeup optical properties [25], makeup can be virtually applied to a source portrait image. Furthermore, thanks to the development of real-time facial landmark tracking [19], consumers can now try new cosmetics directly from their smartphone using Augmented Reality (AR) applications [29,30]. However, conventional makeup rendering models often fail to take into account complex appearance effects such as specular highlights. In addition, makeup is applied on face pixels according to an estimated segmentation mask. This can lead to large failures for images with extreme facial poses, which are common when trying cosmetics such as lipsticks.

Electronic supplementary material The online version of this chapter (https://doi.org/10.1007/978-3-030-67070-2_17) contains supplementary material, which is available to authorized users.

© Springer Nature Switzerland AG 2020
A. Bartoli and A. Fusiello (Eds.): ECCV 2020 Workshops, LNCS 12537, pp. 280–296, 2020.
https://doi.org/10.1007/978-3-030-67070-2_17

More recently, the development of style transfer and image-to-image translation based on neural networks has led to new advances in the domain of makeup synthesis. The task of makeup style transfer, which consists in extracting makeup style from a reference portrait image, and applying it to the target image of a different person, has been widely studied [3,4,12,26,27,33]. In contrast to standard augmented reality, such methods can implicitly model and transfer more complex makeup in a realist manner. Yet, makeup style transfer models suffer from a lack of control as the generated makeup style cannot be modified by the user to explore different cosmetic shades. Consequently, the obtained rendering cannot be transformed to simulate another close makeup shade or a target cosmetic product. Furthermore, the ability to try various shades is an indispensable characteristic expected by consumers in virtual try-on applications.

In this paper, we propose to develop a makeup style transfer method in which the user can have fine control over the color of the synthesized makeup. Our main contributions can be summarized as follows:

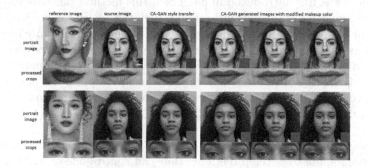

Fig. 1. Our CA-GAN model performs a color controllable makeup style transfer. The makeup color is explicitly estimated from the reference image and passed to the generator. Represented at the bottom right corner of each image, the makeup color can be modified to explore makeup style and reach the desired result.

- We propose CA-GAN, a color aware conditional gan that can modify the color of specific objects in the image to an arbitrary target color. This model is based on the use of a color regression loss combined with a novel background consistency loss that preserves the color attributes of non-targeted objects.
- To remove the need for costly color labeled data, we introduce weakly supervised learning for GAN based controllable synthesis. This method enables to learn a controllable synthesis of complex objects, and only requires a weak proxy of the image attribute that we desire to modify.
- We share a novel makeup dataset, the *social media* dataset[1] 9K images, with largely increased variability in skin tones, facial poses, and makeup color.

---

[1] Available upon demand at *contact.ia@rd.loreal.com*.

- For the first time, we introduce a quantitative analysis of color accuracy and makeup style transfer performance for lipsticks cosmetics using ground-truth images and demonstrate that our model outperforms state of the art.

2   Related Work

In this section, we review related work on image synthesis and makeup style transfer. We first review GAN based methods for image-to-image translation that is the starting point of our approach. Then, we describe recent advances in controllable image-to-image synthesis using GANs. Finally, we present existing popular approaches for makeup style transfer.

GANs for Image-to-Image Translation. GAN based methods are at the origin of a large variety of recent success in image synthesis and image-to-image-translation tasks. The idea of adversarial training of a discriminator and a generator model was first introduced in [9]. Then, this method was extended in [16] to image-to-image translation with conditional GANs. However, this method requires the use of pixel aligned image pairs for training, which is rare in practice. To overcome this limitation, the cycle consistency loss was introduced in [37], allowing to train GAN for image-to-image translation from unpaired images. The use of GAN for solving image-to-image translation problems has later been extended to many different applications such as image completion [15], super-resolution [24] or video frame interpolation [17].

Controllable Image Synthesis with GANs. In the field of GANs, efforts have recently been made to develop methods that can control one or more *attributes* of the generated images. A first research direction gathers works that attempt to implicitly control the model outputs in an unsupervised manner, through operations in the latent space. Among them, InfoGAN [5] aims to learn interpretable representations in the latent space based on information regularization. Furthermore, StyleGAN [18] is an architecture that leverages AdaIn layers [14] to implicitly diversify and control the style of generated images at different scales. More recently, an unsupervised method was proposed in [34] to identify directions in a GAN model latent space that are semantically meaningful. However, while these methods introduce a meaningful modification of the generated images, they have no control over which attributes are edited. Hence, the meaning of each modified attribute is described *a posteriori* by the researchers while observing empirically the induced modification ("zoom", "orientation", "gender", etc.) On the other hand, other studies attempt to provide explicit control of the generated images through supervised methods that leverage image labels. For instance, the method in [23] achieves continuous control along a specific class attribute by using adversarial training in the latent space. Besides, the StarGAN architecture in [6] extends image-to-image translation to multiple class domains. This provides control over multiple attributes simultaneously, each being encoded as a discrete class. Later, in [7], inspired by the success of

StyleGAN [18], the StarGAN architecture was improved using a style vector to enforce diversity of generated images within each target classes domain. However, it cannot be directly extended to continuous attributes. While some studies attempt to modify color attributes, they only provide control on discrete color categories [6] (e.g. "blond hair", "dark hair"), or on the intensity of a discrete color class [23]. Other synthesis methods are based on sketch conditions, that might contain color information as in [31]. However, in practice, such conditions can be complex for non-artist users and are not adapted to consumer-level applications. To the best of our knowledge, there is no existing method that enables high-level color control to an arbitrary shade in the continuous color space.

Makeup Style Transfer. The task of makeup style transfer has drawn interest throughout the evolution of computer vision methods. Traditional image processing methods such as image analogy [13] were first applied to this problem in [33]. Other early methods, such as in [12], propose to decompose an image into face structure, skin and color layers and transfer information between corresponding layers of different images. Later, neural networks based style transfer [8] were used for makeup images [27]. However, such a method requires aligned faces and similar skin tones in source and target images. Inspired by recent successes in GANs, makeup style transfer was formulated in [3] as an asymmetric domain translation problem. The authors of this work jointly trained a makeup transfer and makeup removal network using a conditional GAN approach. In a later work, BeautyGAN [26] improved this GAN based approach by introducing a makeup instance-level transfer in addition to the makeup domain transfer. This is ensured through makeup segmentation and histogram matching between the source and the reference image. Furthermore, in [10], makeup style transfer models were extended from processing local lips and eyes patches to the entire region of the face by using multiple overlapping discriminators. Such an improvement allows accurately transferring extreme makeup styles.

However, existing methods suffer from several limitations. First, the makeup extracted from the reference image is represented implicitly. It is therefore impossible to associate the synthesized makeup style with an existing cosmetic product that could be recommended to obtain that look. Furthermore, once the makeup style has been transferred, the generated image cannot be modified to explore other makeup shades. Prior studies [4, 27, 36] attempted to propose makeup style transfer methods that are controllable, but only in terms of transfer intensity.

3 Problem Formulation

We propose a new formulation for the makeup style transfer problem, where the objective is to learn a color controllable makeup style synthesis. Hence, we propose to train a generator G to generate a makeup style of an arbitrary target color c from source image x. Furthermore, in order to perform makeup style transfer from reference image y to source image x we also need to train a discriminator D_{color} to estimate the makeup color c^y from y. Equation 1 describes the objective of color controllable makeup style transfer, where c^y belongs to a continuous three-dimensional color space:

$$G(x, c^y) = G(x, D_{color}(y)) \qquad (1)$$

With this new objective, the makeup color is transferred from the reference to the source image, and at the same time, explicitly controlled to reach the desired result. Furthermore, the estimated makeup color can be used to compute a correspondence with existing cosmetics products that can be recommended.

In contrast to other studies, we do not decompose between before and after makeup image domains. Indeed, in practice consumers desire to virtually try new shades without removing their current makeup. For this reason, it is desirable to train a model that can generate makeup style from portrait images with or without makeup. Furthermore, we consider that makeup style can be decomposed as lipstick, eye makeup, and foundation. We address the first and consider the second as the eye shadow. However, since foundation is close to skin color, we consider it as part of the source image content rather than makeup style, and propose to enforce its preservation in the makeup transfer.

4   CA-GAN: Color Aware GAN

To solve this problem, we introduce the novel CA-GAN architecture, a color aware generative adversarial network that learns to modify the color of specific objects to an arbitrary target color. Our proposed model is not specific to makeup images and could be trained on any object category that can be described by a single color. Furthermore, the CA-GAN model does not require images with color labels since it can be trained in a weakly supervised manner. While the architecture of our model is close to existing popular methods, we introduce new losses for both generator and discriminator that are critical for accurate color control (see Sect. 4.3).

4.1   Weakly Supervised Color Features

Since our objective is to learn to modify the color of an object in the image to an arbitrary color, we need color values to support the training of our generator. However, most available datasets do not contain labels on objects color. Furthermore, labeling the apparent color value of an object in an image is a tedious task that is highly subjective. On the other hand, GAN based models require a large amount of data to be trained. To overcome this difficulty, we introduce a method to train our model in a weakly supervised manner. Instead of using manually annotated color labels, we propose to use a weak proxy for the target object color attributes that can be obtained without supervision. In particular, in the case of makeup, we build on the assumption that makeup is generally localized on specific regions of the face, which can be approximately estimated for each image using traditional face processing methods. We denote by $C_m(x)$ our weak makeup colors feature extractor, illustrated in Fig. 2. This weak estimator consists in first estimating the position of facial landmarks using the popular *dlib* library [20] and then computing the median pixel in a fixed region defined from landmarks position, for lips and eye shadow. Similarly, we also use $C_s(x)$, a weak skin color model to compute the skin color in each image, using the inverse makeup segmentation mask. Skin color will be used to ensure background color consistency when processing local crops.

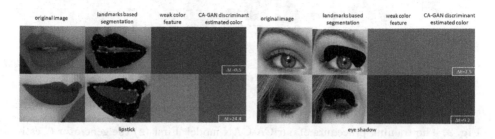

Fig. 2. Example on test images of $C_m(x)$ the weak makeup extractor versus $D_{color}(x)$ our learned color discriminator module. Estimated facial landmarks are represented as red dots. While the two models agree on many images (top row), our learnt model seems superior in case of disagreement (bottom row).

This color feature extractor is *weak* in the sense that it produces a noisy estimate of a makeup color. The landmarks estimation often fails for complex poses, and the median color estimation does not take into account shading effects nor occlusion, as illustrated in Fig. 2. Furthermore, the spatial information on which $C_m(x)$ relies only captures a simplified information of the makeup style, in particular for eye makeup. For this reason, we avoid to use $C_m(x)$ to directly control the generator output, and instead use it as a weak supervisor for $D_{color}(x)$ learned color discriminant module. By leveraging the noisy signal of $C_m(x)$ over a large amount of data, $D_{color}(x)$ learns a better representation for the attribute of interest, and outperforms $C_m(x)$ as discussed in Sect. 5.3.

4.2 CA-GAN Architecture

Our CA-GAN model consists of two different networks, a generator and a discriminator, that are jointly trained. To achieve a higher resolution in the generated images, the model only processes crops of the region of interest. Besides, we train two independent CA-GAN models to process lips and eyes images.

Generator. Our generator takes as input a source image together with a target color and outputs an estimated image. Its architecture is described in detail in Table 1 of the supplementary material. As in StarGAN [6] the input condition is concatenated as an additional channel of the source image. The residual blocks that we use consist of two convolutional layers with 4×4 kernels and a skip connection. Similarly to [3], the generator outputs a pixel difference that is added to the source image in order to obtain the generated image.

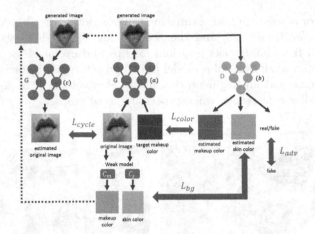

Fig. 3. The training procedure of our CA-GAN model. First (a) the generator G estimates an image from a source image and a target makeup color. Secondly (b) the discriminator D estimates the makeup color, skin color and a real/fake classification from the generated image, used to compute the color regression loss L_{color}, background consistency loss L_{bg} and adversarial loss L_{adv}, respectively. Thirdly (c), the source image is reconstructed from the generated one using the makeup color as target. The reconstruction is used to compute the cycle consistency loss L_{cycle}.

Discriminator. As described in Table 1 of the supplementary material, our discriminator network is a fully convolutional neural network, similar to Patch-GAN [16], with multi-task output branches. The discriminator network simultaneously estimates makeup color, skin color, and classifies the image as real or fake, as illustrated in Fig. 3.

4.3 CA-GAN Objective Function

In this section, we introduce the loss functions that are the key components of our novel CA-GAN model. The training procedure is summarized in Fig. 3.

Color Regression Loss. The color regression loss ensures that the makeup color in the generated image is close to the target color condition passed to the generator. During training, for each image x_i among the n training examples, a target color c_i is randomly sampled at each epoch among existing colors in the training set. The color regression loss computes a color distance between a target color c_i and $D_{color}(G(x_i, c_i))$, the color of the generated image as estimated by the makeup color branch of the discriminator. As a color regression loss, we propose to use $mse - lab$, the mean squared error in the CIE $L^*a^*b^*$ space. Introduced for neural networks in [22], the $mse - lab$ loss inherits from the perceptual properties of the color distance *CIE ΔE^* 1976* [28] which is key for color estimation problems. The color regression loss is described in Eqs. 2 and 3 for the discriminator and the generator respectively, where D_{color} is the makeup color regression output of the discriminator, and $c_i^{x_i} = C_m(x_i)$ the color label for image x_i obtained using our weak model:

$$L_{color}^D = \frac{1}{n} \sum_{i=1}^{n} \|c_i^{x_i} - D_{color}(x_i)\|^2 \tag{2}$$

$$L_{color}^G = \frac{1}{n} \sum_{i=1}^{n} \|c_i - D_{color}(G(x_i, c_i))\|^2 \tag{3}$$

Adversarial Loss. As in any GAN problem, we use an adversarial loss whose objective is to make generated images indistinguishable from real images. In particular, we use the Wasserstein GAN loss [2] and more specifically the one from [11] with gradient penalty. Our used adversarial loss is described in Eq. 4 for the discriminator and Eq. 5 for the generator, where D_{proba} is the realism classification output of the discriminator and $\lambda_{gp} \, gp(D)$ the weighted gradient penalty term computed on D:

$$L_{adv}^D = \frac{1}{n} \sum_{i=1}^{n} D_{proba}(G(x_i, c_i)) - \frac{1}{n} \sum_{i=1}^{n} D_{proba}(x_i) + \lambda_{gp} \, gp(D) \tag{4}$$

$$L_{adv}^G = -\frac{1}{n} \sum_{i=1}^{n} D_{proba}(G(x_i, c_i)) \tag{5}$$

Cycle Consistency Loss. Since we are learning image-to-image translation from unpaired images, we need an additional loss to ensure that we will not modify undesired content in the source image. Consequently, we employ a cycle consistency loss described in Eq. 6, where we compute a perceptual distance between x_i and its reconstruction $\hat{x}_i = G(G(x_i, c_i), c_i^{x_i})$. As a perceptual distance, we choose $MSSIM$, the multiscale structural similarity loss introduced by [35], leading to:

$$L_{cycle} = 1 - MSSIM(x_i, \hat{x}_i) \tag{6}$$

Background Consistency Loss. Since the generator is only processing local crops of the image, we need to ensure that the background color stays consistent with the rest of the image. Besides, if the background color is modified by the generator, the adversarial loss and the cycle consistency loss will not be able to penalize this change as it might lead to a realistic image and modify color in the same direction as the target color. Thus, we propose a background consistency loss that penalizes the color modification of the background. In the case of makeup color, the background color is represented by the skin color on the source image. Equations 7 and 8 describe background consistency for the discriminator and the generator, respectively, where D_{bg} is the background color estimation output of the discriminator and $b_i^{x_i} = C_s(x_i)$ the extracted background color of the image x_i:

$$L_{bg}^D = \frac{1}{n} \sum_{i=1}^{n} \|b_i^{x_i} - D_{bg}(x_i)\|^2 \tag{7}$$

$$L_{bg}^G = \frac{1}{n} \sum_{i=1}^{n} \|D_{bg}(x_i) - D_{bg}(G(x_i, c_i))\|^2 \tag{8}$$

Total Objective Functions. Finally, to combine all the loss functions, we propose to use weighting factors for each loss of the generator. Indeed, some factors such as the cycle consistency loss and the reconstruction loss must be balanced as they penalize opposite transformations. Equations 9 and 10 describe the total objective functions of the discriminator and the generator, where λ_{color}, λ_{bg} and λ_{cycle} are weighting factors for each generator loss that are set experimentally:

$$L_D = L_{adv}^D + L_{color}^D + L_{bg}^D \tag{9}$$

$$L_G = L_{adv}^G + \lambda_{color}\, L_{color}^G + \lambda_{bg}\, L_{bg}^G + \lambda_{cycle}\, L_{cycle} \tag{10}$$

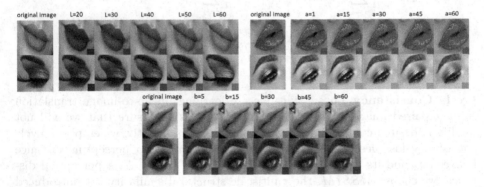

Fig. 4. Modification of makeup color along each dimension of the $CIEL^*a^*b^*$ color space, using images from our social media dataset. The color patch on the bottom-right of each image illustrates the target color passed to the model. Our approach generalizes to lips and eyes images with various makeup textures and facial poses.

5   Experiments

5.1   Data

Since our model does not require images before and after makeup to be trained, we are not restricted to the conventional makeup style transfer datasets such as the MT dataset [26]. Instead, we collected a database of 5000 social media images from makeup influencers. Compared to MT, this dataset contains a larger variety of skin tones, facial poses, and makeup color, with 1591 shades of 294 different cosmetics products. Since these images are unpaired and unlabeled, they are used to train our model using our proposed weakly supervised approach. We will refer to this database as the social media dataset. Furthermore, for model evaluation purposes, we collected a more controlled database focusing on the lipstick category. Therefore, we gathered images of 100 panelists with a range of 80 different lipsticks with various shades and finish. For each panelist, we collected images without makeup, and with three different lipsticks drawn from the 80 possible shades. This dataset will be referred to as the lipstick dataset.

5.2   Implementation

Our CA-GAN model is implemented using the Tensorflow [1] deep learning framework. The generator and discriminator are jointly trained on 90% of our social media dataset, with lips and eyes crops of size 128 by 128 pixels. The weighting factors of the generator loss are set to $\lambda_{gp} = 10$, $\lambda_{color} = 10$, $\lambda_{bkg} = 5$, $\lambda_{cycle} = 200$. We train our model over 200 epochs using the adam optimizer [21] with a learning rate of 10^{-3} for the discriminator and 3.10^{-3} for the generator. Finally, we train separated CA-GAN models for processing lips and eyes images, as well as a joint model trained on both categories. As illustrated in Sect. 5.4 and the supplementary material, separated models slightly overperform the joint model, and are thus used for the image results presented in this study.

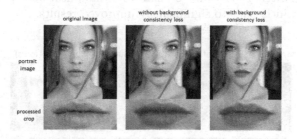

Fig. 5. Our background consistency loss improves the preservation of the skin color in the modified image, which is essential at the portrait scale.

5.3   Qualitative Evaluation

Color Controllable Makeup Synthesis. First, we use images from our social media dataset that are unseen during training and modify their makeup color independently in each dimension of the $CIE\ L^*a^*b^*$ color space. This experiment intends to illustrate the performance of our model with complex poses and makeup textures, and the results are displayed in Fig. 4. In addition, we generate portrait images typically encountered in augmented reality tasks using our lipstick dataset, visible in Fig. 1. For both experiments, it can be observed that the synthesized images reach well the target color while preserving their realistic appearance. Our approach generalizes well for both lips and eye images, with various skin colors, makeup colors, and textures. In particular, for images of eyes without makeup, eye shadow seemed to be synthesized on an average position around the eye, as visible in Fig. 1. Furthermore, our model implicitly learns to only modify the makeup color attributes, preserving other dimensions such as shine or eye color, as it can be observed in Fig. 4. Such results are usually obtained through complex image filtering techniques and would need a specific treatment depending on each object category. Additional generated images and videos[2] are presented in the supplementary material, illustrating performance on various skin tones, poses, and illuminants.

Skin Color Preservation. Even though our model only processes a local crop of the image, the color of skin pixels is preserved, and the crop modification is not easily perceivable at the portrait scale, as seen in Fig. 1. For this reason, we do not need to use Poisson blending to insert the processed crop in the final image as used in [3,4], which speeds up computations and avoids using a segmentation of the lips or eyes region. As an ablation study, we train a CA-GAN model without using the proposed background consistency loss. As observed in Fig. 5, skin pixels are also modified in the generated image. Even though these changes might look realistic at the patch level and thus are not penalized by the adversarial loss, they are not acceptable at the portrait image level. Using our background consistency loss however, skin color modification is penalized by the discriminator, which leads to significantly improved results.

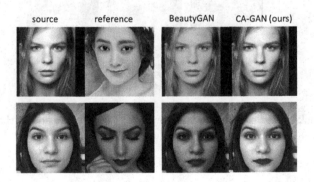

Fig. 6. Our model shows makeup style transfer performances that are equivalent to state of the art models, while obtaining better preservation of the skin color of the source subject. More results are presented in the supplementary material.

---

[2] Also accessible at https://robinkips.github.io/CA-GAN/.

Makeup Style Transfer. We use our lipstick dataset as typical source images, and perform makeup style transfer from reference images drawn from the MT dataset, as illustrated in Fig. 1. In addition to obtaining a realistic generated image, the makeup style can be edited to explore other makeup styles in a continuous color space. Furthermore, our model also estimates the makeup color which can be used to recommend existing cosmetics that can be used in practice to achieve a similar result. Moreover, we compared our results on the style transfer tasks against other popular models for which the code is available. To perform style transfer with our CA-GAN model, we estimate the makeup color in the reference image using the color regression branch of the discriminator, and generate a synthetic makeup image using the generator. The obtained results can be observed in Fig. 6. We compared our model against BeautyGAN [26] which is a state of the art method for conventional makeup style transfer. Our model transfers makeup color with equivalent performance. Furthermore, while BeautyGAN tends to transfer the skin color together with the makeup style, our model obtains better preservation of the original skin tone of the source subject, which is a desirable property for virtual try-on applications.

Weak vs Learned Color Estimator. While the weak color estimator $C_m(x)$ used for weak supervision is fixed, the learnt color extractor in the discriminant $D_{color}(x)$ leverages a large dataset. Hence, even if $C_m(x)$ has high variance and largely fails for some images, $D_{color}(x)$ learns a more robust color estimator. To illustrate this idea, we computed on test images the color difference between estimates of the weak model and the corresponding learned discriminant, as illustrated in Fig. 7. Even if the two models agree for most images, large differences occur in some cases. In practice, we found that in most large difference cases, the weak estimator was failing due to poor facial landmark localization, occlusion, or complex appearance with shading and specularities (see Fig. 2 and supplementary material). The difference is even larger for the eye shadow region in which appearance is more complex due to hair and eyelash occlusion. This reinforces the interest of weakly supervised learning for GAN based model, since improved color estimation will improve the generator control and in turn the style transfer accuracy.

5.4   Quantitative Evaluation

In this section, we focus on the evaluation of the model on lips images. Indeed, while there is no existing approach for eye makeup segmentation, that might be on a larger region than the eyelid, it is possible to segment the lips makeup region for our experiments using face parsing models.

Color Accuracy Evaluation. First, we evaluate the ability of our CA-GAN model to generate makeup images that are close to the chosen color target. For this experiment, illustrated in the supplementary material, we use the 500 test images from our social media dataset. First, we choose a set of 50 representative

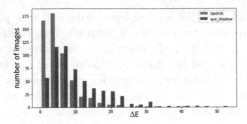

Fig. 7. Color difference between weak color features and learnt discriminant. Large differences between the two models are generally due to failure of the weak feature extractor.

lipstick shades by computing the centroids of a k-means clustering of the lipstick colors in our training data. Then, for each test sample, we generate an image with each representative lipstick color as target. Finally, using a lips segmentation algorithm we estimate the median color of lips to compute a color distance to the model target. We also estimate the difference between the color of the skin before and after image synthesis to control its preservation. The results of these experiments are reported in Table 1. The ablation study confirms that the use of the *lab − mse* for color loss largely increases the color accuracy of our model. Furthermore, our novel background consistency loss helps the generator to disentangle skin and lips color, which leads to significantly improved lipstick color accuracy and skin color preservation.

Table 1. The ablation study demonstrates that our color regression loss and background consistency loss significantly increase the makeup color synthesis accuracy and skin color preservation.

Model	Color loss	Background consistency loss	Training images	Lips color accuracy (ΔE mean)	Skin color preservation (ΔE mean)
CA-GAN	rgb-mse	no	lips	25.82	19.49
CA-GAN	lab-mse	no	lips	9.62	10.18
CA-GAN	lab-mse	yes	lips	**6.80**	**6.05**
CA-GAN	lab-mse	yes	eyes and lips	7.78	8.76

Style Transfer Performance Evaluation. For the first time, we introduce a quantitative evaluation of model performance on the makeup style transfer task, as illustrated in Fig. 8. We use our collected lipstick dataset that contains images of multiple panelists wearing the same lipstick shade. Thus, it is possible to construct ground-truth triplets with a reference portrait, a source portrait, and the associated ground-truth image with the reference makeup. The style transfer accuracy is then computed using the MSSIM similarity [35] as a measure of a perceptual distance. Furthermore, to avoid lighting bias, we select the ground-truth among several images of the same panelist, using the most similar skin color compared to the source image. We perform this experiment on 300 image triplets with 100 different panelists and 80 different lipstick shades. The results of this experiment are reported in Table 2. The ablation study confirms that our color regression loss and background consistency loss significantly improve the style transfer performance. Furthermore, we observe that our model outperforms BeautyGAN by a significant margin. This is expected given the ability of our model to preserve the skin color in the source image.

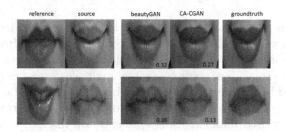

Fig. 8. The style transfer performance is evaluated using triplets of lips images. The makeup is extracted from the reference image and transferred to the source image of a different panelist. We use a ground-truth image of the source panelist with the same lipstick to compute a style transfer performance. The computed perceptual distance $1 - MSSIM$ is given at the bottom right of each generated image.

Table 2. A quantitative evaluation of the style transfer performance using style transfer image triplets.

Model	Color loss	Background consistancy loss	Training images	L1	1 - MSSIM
BeautyGAN [26]	-	-	-	0.124	0.371
CA-GAN	rgb-mse	no	lips	0.231	0.698
CA-GAN	lab-mse	no	lips	0.097	0.313
CA-GAN	lab-mse	yes	lips	**0.085**	**0.283**
CA-GAN	lab-mse	yes	eyes and lips	0.087	0.312

6   Conclusion and Future Work

In this paper, we introduced CA-GAN, a generative model that learns to modify the color of objects in an image to an arbitrary target color. This model is based on the combined use of a color regression loss with a novel background consistency loss that learns to preserve the color of non-target objects in the image. Furthermore, CA-GAN can be trained on unlabeled images using a weakly supervised approach based on a noisy proxy of the attribute of interest. Using this architecture on makeup images of eyes and lips we show that we can perform makeup synthesis and makeup style transfer that are controllable in a continuous color space. For the first time, we introduce a quantitative analysis of makeup style transfer and color control performance. Our results show that our model can accurately modify makeup color, while outperforming conventional models such as [26] in makeup style transfer realism. Since our CA-GAN model does not require labeled images, it could be directly applied to other object categories for which it is possible to compute pixel color statistics, such as hair, garments, cars, or animals.

Finally, we emphasize some perspectives for future work. First, we represent eyes and lips makeup by three-dimensional color coordinates. However, extreme makeup can be composed of multiple different cosmetics, in particular for the eye shadow category. To achieve color control on multiple cosmetics simultaneously, our model should be extended with a spatial information condition in addition to our current color condition. However, while our model can currently be trained in a weakly supervised manner, using segmentation masks to carry the spatial information would require to have annotated images. Moreover, the representation of cosmetics could also be completed using a shine representation. While the current model objective is to learn to modify color only, without affecting the other image attributes such as shine and specularities, using a shine score as an additional generator condition would make it possible to simulate mat and shine cosmetics with more accuracy.

References

1. Abadi, M., et al.: Tensorflow: a system for large-scale machine learning. In: Operating Systems Design and Implementation, pp. 265–283 (2016)
2. Arjovsky, M., Chintala, S., Bottou, L.: Wasserstein generative adversarial networks. In: International Conference on Machine Learning, pp. 214–223 (2017)
3. Chang, H., Lu, J., Yu, F., Finkelstein, A.: Pairedcyclegan: asymmetric style transfer for applying and removing makeup. In: Computer Vision and Pattern Recognition, pp. 40–48 (2018)
4. Chen, H.J., Hui, K.M., Wang, S.Y., Tsao, L.W., Shuai, H.H., Cheng, W.H.: Beautyglow: on-demand makeup transfer framework with reversible generative network. In: Computer Vision and Pattern Recognition, pp. 10042–10050 (2019)
5. Chen, X., Duan, Y., Houthooft, R., Schulman, J., Sutskever, I., Abbeel, P.: Infogan: interpretable representation learning by information maximizing generative adversarial nets. In: Advances in Neural Information Processing Systems, pp. 2172–2180 (2016)
6. Choi, Y., Choi, M., Kim, M., Ha, J.W., Kim, S., Choo, J.: Stargan: unified generative adversarial networks for multi-domain image-to-image translation. In: Conference on Computer Vision and Pattern Recognition, pp. 8789–8797 (2018)

7. Choi, Y., Uh, Y., Yoo, J., Ha, J.W.: Stargan v2: diverse image synthesis for multiple domains. In: Conference on Computer Vision and Pattern Recognition, pp. 8188–8197 (2020)
8. Gatys, L.A., Ecker, A.S., Bethge, M.: Image style transfer using convolutional neural networks. In: Computer Vision and Pattern Recognition, pp. 2414–2423 (2016)
9. Goodfellow, I., et al.: Generative adversarial nets. In: Advances in Neural Information Processing Systems, pp. 2672–2680 (2014)
10. Gu, Q., Wang, G., Chiu, M.T., Tai, Y.W., Tang, C.K.: Ladn: local adversarial disentangling network for facial makeup and de-makeup. In: International Conference on Computer Vision, pp. 10481–10490 (2019)
11. Gulrajani, I., Ahmed, F., Arjovsky, M., Dumoulin, V., Courville, A.C.: Improved training of Wasserstein GANs. In: Advances in Neural Information Processing Systems, pp. 5767–5777 (2017)
12. Guo, D., Sim, T.: Digital face makeup by example. In: Computer Vision and Pattern Recognition, pp. 73–79. IEEE (2009)
13. Hertzmann, A., Jacobs, C.E., Oliver, N., Curless, B., Salesin, D.H.: Image analogies. In: Computer Graphics And Interactive Techniques, pp. 327–340 (2001)
14. Huang, X., Belongie, S.: Arbitrary style transfer in real-time with adaptive instance normalization. In: International Conference on Computer Vision, pp. 1501–1510 (2017)
15. Iizuka, S., Simo-Serra, E., Ishikawa, H.: Globally and locally consistent image completion. ACM Trans. Graph. 36(4), 1–14 (2017)
16. Isola, P., Zhu, J.Y., Zhou, T., Efros, A.A.: Image-to-image translation with conditional adversarial networks. In: Computer Vision and Pattern Recognition, pp. 1125–1134 (2017)
17. Jiang, H., Sun, D., Jampani, V., Yang, M.H., Learned-Miller, E., Kautz, J.: Super slomo: high quality estimation of multiple intermediate frames for video interpolation. In: Conference on Computer Vision and Pattern Recognition, pp. 9000–9008 (2018)
18. Karras, T., Laine, S., Aila, T.: A style-based generator architecture for generative adversarial networks. In: Computer Vision and Pattern Recognition, pp. 4401–4410 (2019)
19. Kazemi, V., Sullivan, J.: One millisecond face alignment with an ensemble of regression trees. In: Conference on Computer Vision and Pattern Recognition, pp. 1867–1874 (2014)
20. King, D.E.: Dlib-ml: a machine learning toolkit. J. Mach. Learn. Res. 10(Jul), 1755–1758 (2009)
21. Kingma, D.P., Ba, J.: Adam: a method for stochastic optimization. In: International Conference for Learning Representations (2015)
22. Kips, R., Tran, L., Malherbe, E., Perrot, M.: Beyond color correction: skin color estimation in the wild through deep learning. Electron. Imaging (2020)
23. Lample, G., Zeghidour, N., Usunier, N., Bordes, A., Denoyer, L., Ranzato, M.: Fader networks: manipulating images by sliding attributes. In: Advances in Neural Information Processing Systems, pp. 5967–5976 (2017)
24. Ledig, C., et al.: Photo-realistic single image super-resolution using a generative adversarial network. In: Conference on Computer Vision and Pattern Recognition, pp. 4681–4690 (2017)
25. Li, C., Zhou, K., Lin, S.: Simulating makeup through physics-based manipulation of intrinsic image layers. In: Conference on Computer Vision and Pattern Recognition, pp. 4621–4629 (2015)

26. Li, T., et al.: Beautygan: instance-level facial makeup transfer with deep generative adversarial network. In: International Conference on Multimedia, pp. 645–653 (2018)
27. Liu, S., Ou, X., Qian, R., Wang, W., Cao, X.: Makeup like a superstar: deep localized makeup transfer network. In: IJCAI (2016)
28. McLaren, K.: XIII-The development of the CIE 1976 (L* a* b*) uniform colour space and colour-difference formula. J. Soc. Dyers Colour. **92**(9), 338–341 (1976)
29. Modiface Inc: Modiface - augmented reality. http://modiface.com/. Accessed 24 Feb 2020
30. Perfect Corp.: Perfect corp. - virtual makeup. https://www.perfectcorp.com/business/products/virtual-makeup. Accessed 24 Feb 2020
31. Portenier, T., Hu, Q., Szabo, A., Bigdeli, S.A., Favaro, P., Zwicker, M.: Faceshop: deep sketch-based face image editing. ACM Trans. Graph. **37**(4) (2018)
32. Sokal, K., Kazakou, S., Kibalchich, I., Zhdanovich, M.: High-quality AR lipstick simulation via image filtering techniques. In: CVPR Workshop on Computer Vision for Augmented and Virtual Reality (2019)
33. Tong, W.S., Tang, C.K., Brown, M.S., Xu, Y.Q.: Example-based cosmetic transfer. In: Pacific Conference on Computer Graphics and Applications, pp. 211–218 (2007)
34. Voynov, A., Babenko, A.: Unsupervised discovery of interpretable directions in the GAN latent space. arXiv preprint arXiv:2002.03754 (2020)
35. Wang, Z., Simoncelli, E.P., Bovik, A.C.: Multiscale structural similarity for image quality assessment. In: Thirty-Seventh Asilomar Conference on Signals, Systems & Computers, vol. 2, pp. 1398–1402 (2003)
36. Zhang, H., Chen, W., He, H., Jin, Y.: Disentangled makeup transfer with generative adversarial network. arXiv preprint arXiv:1907.01144 (2019)
37. Zhu, J.Y., Park, T., Isola, P., Efros, A.A.: Unpaired image-to-image translation using cycle-consistent adversarial networks. In: International Conference on Computer Vision, October 2017

FamilyGAN: Generating Kin Face Images Using Generative Adversarial Networks

Raunak Sinha[1], Mayank Vatsa[2], and Richa Singh[2(✉)]

[1] IIIT-Delhi, New Delhi, India
raunak15075@iiitd.ac.in
[2] IIT Jodhpur, Jodhpur, India
{mvatsa,richa}@iitj.ac.in

Abstract. Automatic kinship verification using face images involves analyzing features and computing similarities between two input images to establish kin-relationship. It has gained significant interest from the research community and several approaches including deep learning architectures are proposed. One of the law enforcement applications of kinship analysis involves predicting the kin image given an input image. In other words, the question posed here is: "given an input image, can we generate a kin-image?" This paper attempts to generate kin-images using Generative Adversarial Learning for multiple kin-relations. The proposed FamilyGAN model incorporates three information, kin-gender, kinship loss, and reconstruction loss, in a GAN model to generate kin images. FamilyGAN is the first model capable of generating kin-images for multiple relations such as parent-child and siblings from a single model. On the WVU Kinship Video database, the proposed model shows very promising results for generating kin images. Experimental results show 71.34% kinship verification accuracy using the images generated via FamilyGAN.

Keywords: Kinship · Image generation · Generative adversarial networks · Deep learning

1 Introduction

The prevalent discourse on kinship facial-analysis is determining if two individuals are related (kins) through given face images. This analysis extends to predict the possible relation between given individuals such as father-daughter, mother-son, and mother-daughter. Such relations are ascertained through leveraging and understanding common facial features [6, 7, 15]. In this research, we are exploring the scantly addressed question related to kinship analysis and predicting looks of possible kin of an individual (Fig. 1).

For cases of missing persons and long-lost relatives where kin-images were not available to compare, a possible kin-image can potentially assist in speeding

© Springer Nature Switzerland AG 2020
A. Bartoli and A. Fusiello (Eds.): ECCV 2020 Workshops, LNCS 12537, pp. 297–311, 2020.
https://doi.org/10.1007/978-3-030-67070-2_18

Fig. 1. Relation samples from WVU Kinship Video Database. FamilyGAN is learning to generate kin face images by understanding the facial heredity hierarchy in such relations and applying appropriate transforms.

Fig. 2. Sisters separated at birth (https://abcnews.go.com/GMA/ Family/adopted-woman-searches-long-lost-sister-learn-shes/story? id=56230030).

Fig. 3. Suspects for the Boston Bombing (https://en.wikipedia.org/wiki/ Boston_Marathon_bombing). The two individuals were later identified to be brothers.

the search[1],[2]. For a recent case of long-lost sisters at Greenwood, USA[3] (Fig. 2), where sisters were separated at birth, "probable kin-image" could assist this search. Kinship verification can help investigations such as Boston Bombing[4] (Fig. 3). With initial images of suspects, kinship verification could have helped them to ascertain relations and conduct targeted search for suspects, but what if the images of one of the brothers was missing. Kinship image generation can help synthesize possible family members.

We are keen on understanding the hierarchy of facial features amongst relations. Fabricating possible face image of kin given only the face image of a person requires capturing and reproducing dominant transforms observed in different relations. Applying an appropriate transform for different individuals is essential in the creation of images that can possibly be the face images of kins. Kin feature heredity varies extremely with a single family e.g. feature heredity between a mother-daughter is different than mother-son. This feature heredity also varies amongst different families as genetic matter shared between two pairs

---

[1] https://abcnews.go.com/Lifestyle/long-lost-brothers-discover-college-disbelief/ story?id=51918769.

[2] https://www.mirror.co.uk/3am/celebrity-news/rochelle-humes-reunites-long-lost-14977068.

[3] https://abcnews.go.com/GMA/Family/adopted-woman-searches-long-lost-sister-learn-shes/story?id=56230030.

[4] https://en.wikipedia.org/wiki/Boston_Marathon_bombing.

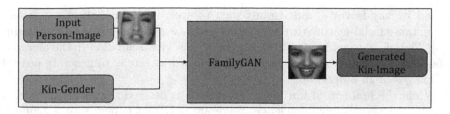

Fig. 4. Conceptualizing kin image generation task. FamilyGAN takes image of a person and kin-gender as input to generate possible kin image as output.

of mother-daughter is highly conditional. Such large variations make it hard to observe global patterns for fabricating kin images. While generating possible kin images extreme emphasis is required on physical features and type of relation for suitable transforms.

We formulate FamilyGAN to address the complex problem of kinship image generation. FamilyGAN is successful in learning intricate feature heredity and administering apposite feature transforms to generate the possible image of kin with just the input image of a person and the relation to be generated (Fig. 1). FamilyGAN is simultaneously trained to identify and verify kin relations between the given individuals as a by-product of learning to generate kin images. The research contributions are as followed:

– The proposed FamilyGAN model learns and understands kin feature heredity. The model is capable of administering learned feature transforms on the image of an individual to generate a possible face image of kin. The kin image is generated under the conditioning of kin gender (Fig. 4).
– We propose a novel optimization and loss for learning how to generate kin-images.
– We perform both qualitative and quantitative evaluation of kin face images generated by FamilyGAN on the WVU Kinship Video Dataset [14]. For quantitative evaluation we use two approaches: (i) evaluation using state-of-the-art kinship verification algorithms and (ii) face recognition algorithms.

2   Related Work

The problem statement of kin-image generation observes its foundation from the problem of kinship verification [19] and image generation. Kinship verification is determining if two individuals are related based on evidence of common physical features. Given the images of two individuals, kinship verification leverages the facial features of two individuals to answer the question - are the two individuals related (kins) or not. This binary classification can be further extended to multi-class classification, predicting the kin relation between given individuals such as father-daughter, mother-son, and mother-daughter [6,7,15]. The human face is formed by key features and regions such as eyes, nose, lips, cheeks, and face-shape, these facial-features are contingent on the genetic makeup of an individual [4,5]. Therefore, to understand the kinship hierarchy we can discern the hierarchy in facial features amongst kin and use the learned hierarchy to generate possible kin images of an individual.

While the problem of kin image generation is derived from kinship verification, to the best of our knowledge, there are only two papers that attempt to generate possible kin images of a given individual. Ozkan *et al.* [17] use a cycle consistent GAN (CycleGAN) framework [22] to generate images of children by analysing images of parents. Their work is limited to generating images of children and do not model other kin-relations. Similarly Ghatas *et al.* [8] takes both parents (father and mother) as input and pass the concatenated information through a kin-feature predictor network. The predicted features act as input to a PGGAN [11] network for generating images of children for a given age.

3   Proposed FamilyGAN Model

GANs are generative networks that rely on adversarial training for learning an underlying distribution and generating new members of the learned distribution. These models can transform noise or alter input data to generate realistic-looking samples [9,16,18]. Various GAN architectures exist to model different kinds of distributions and problem statements, such as Deep Convolutions GANs (DCGANs) [18], WGAN [1], Conditional GANs (CGAN) [16], CycleGAN [22], Pix2Pix [10], and StarGAN [2].

The proposed FamilyGAN captures key kin-feature hierarchies using the proposed loss function. Three key components are driving the learning for achieving the desired transformations. The new formulated loss function (Eq. 3, Eq. 4) learns adversarial sample generation and kinship verification in cohesion. Learning features through kinship verification improves the training of the generator for this specific task. Furthermore, conditioning the generator on kin-gender and additionally conditioning the discriminator on kinship verification samples is not present in the current literature for a kin-image generation. Finally, constricting the generator with an additional reconstruction loss helps the generator learn better transforms as this drives the generator to maintain the facial-integrity of generated samples. This ensures that the generated images resemble naturally occurring human faces.

3.1   FamilyGAN Model

FamilyGAN learns to perform facial feature transformation observing underlying kin hierarchy. The transformations learned are kin-gender specific, where the model explicitly learns appropriate kin transformations for female kin relations and male kin relations. This is achieved by conditioning the generator on kin-gender. Kin feature hierarchy is dependent on kin relation and gender relations. Kins with same-gender relations (such as father-son, mother-daughter) have a

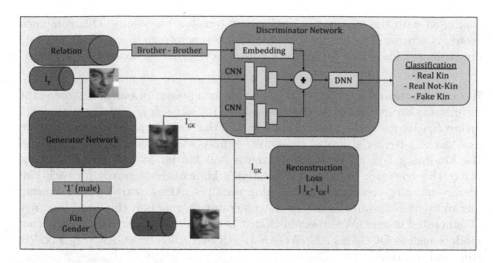

Fig. 5. Architecture of FamilyGAN model. Generator takes image person I_P and Kin-Gender as input and generates kin-image I_{GK}. Reconstruction loss between I_{GK} and I_K (real-kin) guides training. The discriminator takes I_P, I_{GK} and kin-relation as input to calculate an adversarial loss and also for kinship verification. Both these losses steer model training.

higher correlation of physical features [21]. Thus, we are focusing on generating images of the same kin-gender so that FamilyGAN learns strong discriminating features for each kin-gender.

3.2 Generator

The generator of FamilyGAN is tasked with fooling the discriminator by generating realistic face images of individuals that can be their kin relative. Not only is the generator producing images that should look like samples from the given data space, but it is also additionally focused on generating faces that follow a particular kinship hierarchy for facial features. The generator needs to learn both these aspects to fool the FamilyGAN discriminator in believing that the generated kin-image is the actual kin of an individual. One of the prime novelties of FamilyGAN is to incorporate the notion of facial-feature hierarchy in a GAN framework.

Kin-Gender. Input to the generator is the images of an individual I_P and kin-gender label vector R (0 for female kin and 1 for male kin). A convolutional neural network with residual connections is used to extract latent features from I_P. We use residual connections to counter the degradation problem because of network depth. These connections ensure the flow of information to deeper layers, without any non-linear activation on residual connections the information flows freely during both forward and backward pass. The learned features are combined with the kin-gender label vector (one-hot encoding). This combined vector is processed by deconvolution layers to generate an image of appropriate dimensions. This is how we generate kin-images I_{GK} conditioned on kin-gender.

Reconstruction Loss. Another important component of our generator is the reconstruction loss between the generated kin-image I_{GK} and the actual kin image I_K. We use mean squared error to find this loss. By adding reconstruction loss to the adversarial loss of generator, FamilyGAN governs the generation of the kin-image I_{GK} to be closer to the actual kin image I_K. This constraint drives the generator to learn the underlying kin feature hierarchy for each kin-pair, generating more probable looking relatives. Along with learning kinship hierarchy, the kinship loss forces the generator to maintain the facial integrity of generated images. We observed that it is difficult to preserve this with other models such as DCGANs [18], WGAN [1], CGAN [16], CycleGAN [22], Pix2Pix [10], and StarGAN [2].

$$L_G = E_{K \sim p-K}, E_{z \sim p-P}[log(1 - D(G(z|K)|I_P, I_{GK/K}, R))] \tag{1}$$

$$L_{G'} = L_G + \lambda ||I_K - I_{GK}||_2^2 \tag{2}$$

Equation 1 captures the real vs fake loss for the generated kin image, this is similar to the standard optimization for generator networks. Kin-image generation is conditioned over kin-gender K. The generator is optimized over Eq. 2. Reconstruction loss is added to the loss of the generator as an auxiliary loss.

3.3   Discriminator

We construct a 3-class classification objective for our discriminator function. Given a pair of kin-images with their corresponding kin-relations, the discriminator determines the appropriate class, classes being: {[real + true kin], [real + false kin], [fakegenerated + true kin]}. FamilyGAN is optimized for only a 3-class classification as the {[fake − false kin]} class does not fit into our objective of generating realistic samples that follow pertinent kin feature hierarchy. The proposed loss captures notions of both kinship-verification and adversarial training. Kinship-verification is learned through a tradeoff between {[real − true kin]} and {[real − false kin]}. Concomitantly, the discriminator learns to distinguish real images from fake by training on both real images of kin I_K (from database) and fake kin images I_{GK} (from the generator) in an adversarial setting. Deep CNN extracts latent feature from given image input, CNNs can extract the information while keeping the spatial information of image intact.

During fakeness detection, the discriminator is concerned only with predicting if the input facial image is real or fabricated. At this stage, the discriminator is concerned with determining the closeness of generated samples and the actual data along with validating kinship-relations through kinship verification. While training the discriminator for learning kinship feature hierarchy both actual-positive-pairs (image-of-person I_P, actual-image-of-kin I_K) and generated-positive-pairs (image-of-person I_P, generated-image-of-kin I_{GK}) along with negative-actual-pairs are processed. The discriminator also takes kin-relation (father-son, daughter-mother, sister-sister, and brother-brother) as input. The discriminator processes the image-pair along with the kin-relation to determine if the image-pair are valid kins or not (the pair has to be related by the given kin-relation).

As training progresses the discriminator becomes smarter at detecting minute details between real and fake images making the discriminator more powerful. Now, as the discriminator becomes more powerful it guides the generator better and in turn, trains the generator for more realistic looking images. In addition to the real-fake discrimination, incorporating kinship verification in the optimization function of the discriminator makes the discriminator learn kinship feature hierarchy while learning to detect fakeness. We propose a new discriminator loss function in Eq. 3. The discriminator classifies input pair as x, the decision is conditioned on image of person I_P, generated kin-image I_{GK}/real kin-image I_K and kin-relation R. To learn the decision boundary Cross-Entropy loss is calculated for the predictions. c is the number of classes (3), $y_{x,c}$ is 1 if x equals c otherwise 0.

$$L_D = -\Sigma_{c=1}^3 y_{x,c} log(\mathbb{P}(D(x|I_{GK}, I_P, R)))$$ (3)

Combined loss equation for GAN model is:

$$min_G max_D (L_{G'} - L_D)$$ (4)

3.4 Model Training

The generator and discriminator of FamilyGAN are trained in tandem. The generator is dependent on the discriminator's ability to understand how far generated samples are from real kin. In turn, the discriminator becomes more capable in distinguishing minute difference as the generator becomes powerful. The FamilyGAN discriminator, in a combined fashion, finds out fake images as well as performing kinship verification for a given pair of images and their gender-relation.

The discriminator has two separate training steps. To optimally learn kinship-features through verification, the discriminator is initially trained over a data-set of both positive and negative kin-pairs. During this phase boundary between the [real]+[true kin] and [real]+[false kin] are learned. This lets FamilyGAN focus on learning optimal facial kinship features for guiding generation. For the second phase, the discriminator is retrained on only positive kin-pairs from the real-data as well as generated kin-images. During this step, the discriminator is being trained contemporaneously with the generator. Through this step the discriminator learns to optimize decision boundary for [real]+[true kin] and [fake]+[true kin].

To learn the kinship feature hierarchy transforms, we experimented with using the actual kin relations classes (for example father-son, mother-daughter) as conditional input to the generator. Such generation would provide more nuanced control concerning the kin feature transform, but FamilyGAN was not able to converge with such conditioning. The facial feature hierarchy follows some ubiquitous patterns amongst the same gender but the feature hierarchy may not be similar for all pairs, e.g. different mother-daughter pairs observe different feature transforms dependent on their gene. Such conditioning on gender separates the learning space, as it does not have to learn more constricted feature transforms based on kin-relations that may not follow generic patterns. Nuances for feature transforms are dependent on the input face image of the individual. FamilyGAN relies mainly on three key components, which are:

- The novel loss function (Eq. 4) learns to optimize FamilyGAN jointly over kinship verification and kinship generation. This provides more supervision.
- Conditioning the generator on kin-gender as the feature hierarchy is more readily observed amongst kin-gender relations as compared to specific kin relations (e.g. father-son, mother-daughter), so the model can capture kin-gender transforms better.
- Inspired from autoencoders, a reconstruction loss is used to maintain the facial features of generated images. This constricts the generation of kin that looks like the true kin.

3.5   Implementation Details

True (real) positive and negative samples are randomly shuffled in the training dataset. Fake positive kin samples are generated by conditioning the generator on the input image of the person and conditioning of kin-gender for each pair. Adam optimizer is used for both the discriminator and generator loss.

The generator of FamilyGAN combines input image I_K and the kin-relation by a simple addition operation and passed through a series of convolution and deconvolution blocks to generate kin-images. Each convolution (downsampling) block consists of a convolution layer, instance normalization, ReLU activation, and residual connection. Whereas, the deconvolution (upsampling) blocks consist of a transposed convolution layer, ReLU activation, and instance normalization. The output of the generator is passed to the discriminator and also used to determine reconstruction loss.

For the FamilyGAN discriminator, each convolutional block consists of a convolutional layer, LeakyReLu activation, and Dropout layer. Inputs to the discriminator are passed to four such convolutional blocks before propagating them through a deep neural network for classification. The three inputs to the discriminator are processed separately before combining them for further propagation (Fig. 5). Two separate CNN networks process image of input-person I_P and image of kin I_{GK}/I_K. An embedding layer is used to transform the relation vector. A simple concatenation of extracted latent-feature vectors is then passed forward for processing.

4   Experimental Analysis

To evaluate the performance of the proposed FamilyGAN approach, we have used WVU Kinship Video database [13]. This section first briefly presents the database and protocol followed by the results.

4.1   WVU Kinship Video Database

This dataset contains video clips of individuals and kin-relationship information for positive and negative kin pair. The pairs have been divided between testing and training. For each individual, image frames are extracted from the video footage. Positive kin-pairs have the correct kin relations, whereas negative kin-pairs have false kin relations mentioned.

- 141 positive, 141 negative kin sets (videos) for training
- 214 positive, 214 negative kin sets (videos) for testing

There are seven types of kin-pair relations in the dataset mother-daughter, mother-son, father-daughter, father-son, brother-brother, sister-sister, and brother-sister. The database has majorly same gender kin cases, i.e. mother-daughter (21.28%), father-son (21.28%), brother-brother (11.34%), and sister-sister (13.47%). For cross-gender cases, the total cases are around 32%, i.e. mother-son (7.80%), father-daughter (16.31%), and brother-sister (8.52%). The Several image frames for each individual are extracted and filtered, the total number of positive pairs possible is 33,965,699. We find limited data for cross gender relations, such as mother-son and brother-sister [14].

The dataset contains extreme pose variations and that makes the underlying data distribution highly complex to learn. For pruning pose variance, we use pose estimation. For each individual, we choose 50 facial images (after pose estimation) providing 2,500 image pairs for each kin set. We construct positive and negative kin pairs through the same process, to ensure uniformity and avoid unwanted bias. Both sets of kin pair (negative and positive) are necessary for proper optimization of the loss function. We follow the same procedure for generating test kin image pairs from 214 positive and negative testing kin sets.

The final processed training dataset consists of 462,500 kin pairs (both positive and negative kins). The dataset provides meta-data of the kin relation for each pair. Kin type is crucial for training the discriminator to predict kin class correctly (kinship verification). Introducing kin verification loss in the overall loss function of the discriminator allows it to be more partitioned in learning latent features described in Sect. 3.4. We create additional kin-gender labels that we input to the generator. The generation of kin images is conditioned on the kin-gender, where female genders such as mother-daughter or sister-sister are given a label 0 while male genders such as father-son or brother-brother are given a label 1.

4.2 Results

Evaluating models for kin-image generation is a challenge. Kin-image datasets are not comprehensive in multiple regards. When generating kin images in an unconstrained environment, the generated image may belong to a certain point of time to the actual-kin-pair image. Additionally, when generating kin-images, a person may have multiple possibilities of kins based on different feature transforms. For example, a person may have 3 sisters and the evaluation dataset may contain samples of only 2. What happens if the kin-image generated resembles the third sister? To address these concern we propose two evaluation techniques. First, understanding the closeness in features of generated kin with input and real kin through a Siamese framework for kinship classification. Secondly, we evaluate generated kin-images through a state-of-the-art kinship verification model. Such a model is adept at understanding underlying notions of kinship relations in a

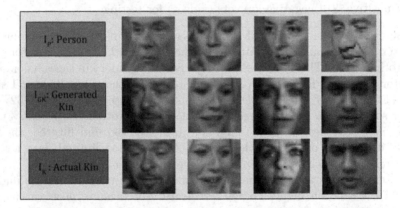

Fig. 6. Kin-samples generated from the training set, using the proposed FamilyGAN.

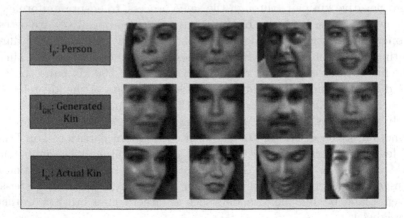

Fig. 7. Kin samples generated from the unseen (testing) set, using the proposed FamilyGAN.

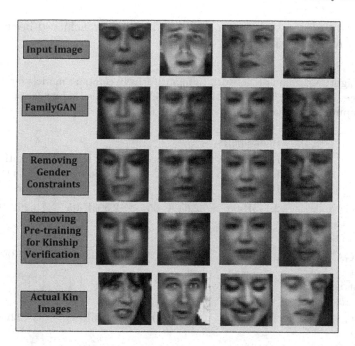

Fig. 8. Comparing effects of various FamilyGAN components for generating kin images on unseen (testing) data.

given dataset and has fewer chances of giving a false positive. So we don't need to generate an image that is exactly similar to the real-kin pair for establishing that FamilyGAN is successfully generating kin-images. Furthermore, we provide with qualitative analysis of FamilyGAN and an ablative study it's various components.

Qualitative Analysis of Kin Image Generation. FamilyGAN successfully learns the facial feature hierarchy transforms. Transforms learned are used to generate possible kin images for a given individual. The generation is controlled through kin-gender as conditional input to the generator, this lets the generator use an appropriate transform for different kin-gender. The generation is dependent on the input image distribution, so each generated kin is dependent on the initial facial features of the input person. The dependence on the input image allows FamilyGAN to generate unique possible kin images, this dependence also enables FamilyGAN to generate realistic kin-image for previously unseen individuals (Fig. 7). Figure 6 shows that the generator is learning the correct feature transforms during training and is able to model the observable kin feature hierarchy.

FamilyGAN drives the generator to produce such close results by including the reconstruction loss while training the model. From Fig. 6 and Fig. 7 we see that the network not only is able to learn the facial-feature transform but is also able to learn the pose variance in images. This again is achieved because of the addition of reconstruction loss.

Table 1. LightCNN-Siamese network to quantitatively compare models for generation of kin-images. Reported values are the average-MSE between latent-feature representation of inputs to the siamese network for the testing data.

Model	Image pairs			
	Real-Kin & Input (True Pairs)	Generated-Kin & Input	Real-Kin & Generated-Kin	Negative pairs (False Pairs)
FamilyGAN without Gender Constraints	2.775E-05	2.649E-05	2.503E-05	3.29E-05
FamilyGAN without Reconstruction Loss	2.564E-05	2.497E-05	2.460E-05	3.013E-05
FamilyGAN without pre-training for kinship verification	3.008E-05	2.954E-05	2.786E-05	3.722E-05
Proposed FamilyGAN	**2.478E-05**	**2.463E-05**	**2.334E-05**	**2.892E-05**

A fascinating observation from Fig. 6 is that the generated kin-images have slight variations to the actual kin-images, which shows that the generator is not simply replicating actual kin images during training but learning sensible and generic kin feature transforms. Figure 8 shows that FamilyGAN learns kinship feature hierarchy in detail for each kin-gender. Specific feature transforms for different facial features are learned. As FamilyGAN learns kin-gender based feature transforms for each kin-pair, the transforms learned are generic to the kin-gender which makes the model useful to generate possible kin images even if the input person was not seen before. Not only are hierarchical relations in facial features learned, but are also learned for skin tone, hair type, hair color, eyebrow shape, and eye color.

To demonstrate the feasibility of FamilyGAN we show the result of kin generation for unseen samples from the testing data (Fig. 7). Generated kin images for unseen samples have facial features resembling the input person. The possible kin images show resemblance to the actual kin image but are closer to the input individuals. This happens because FamilyGAN is learning generic but specific for a kin-gender, making the transformations are not specific to any single kin pair. This allows FamilyGAN to generate more likely kin images for any unseen input. The resemblance between generated and actual kin shows that learned transforms capture the notion of kin hierarchy. In Sect. 4.2 we determine experiment and discuss result for a quantitative evaluation of generated kin images.

Quantitative Analysis of LightCNN-Siamese Kin Image Distance. To evaluate the generated images with rigor, we formulate an experiment that can quantify how similar are the generated kin-images I_{GK} to both input person I_P and real-kin I_K. The following quantitative experiment is performed to evaluate the similarity. We train a LightCNN [20] based siamese network [3,12] to capture the closeness of true kin-pairs (I_P and I_K) in terms of facial features. To achieve this, we optimize the MSE-distance between the true image of the person and real-kin image from the training set. The distance between latent-feature representations from the two networks is a quantitative benchmark for kinship similarity. The distance between input person I_P and generated kin I_{GK} is now calculated to gauge the performance of the generator. We additionally find the distance between the generated kin I_{GK} and real-kin I_K to evaluate the closeness.

The distances for testing protocols are determined, the results are summarised in Table 1. We can see that proposed FamilyGAN outperforms other models and has the least distance between the input person and generated kin. We observe comparable distance between 'real-kin & input person (True)' and 'generated-kin & input person', which indicates that FamilyGAN is aware the appropriate feature transform that should be applied given the context. Additionally, the distance between 'real-kin & generated-kin' is the least amongst comparable pairs showing that the generated-kin is close to the real-kin in the embedding space.

This effectively shows us that FamilyGAN can learn and apply suitable kinship feature transforms such that the generated kin images are close to the true kin as well as input in terms of feature hierarchy. The power and utility of FamilyGAN can be observed by the images generated for unseen (testing) samples. Though the model has not seen the images before it can apply appropriate transform based on features and maintain kinship feature hierarchy.

Kinship Verification Performance. Using the experimental protocol (frame-based) defined in Kohli et al. [14], we performed kinship verification experiments. We generated 3674 kin images of real subjects using FamilyGAN and computed the kinship verification accuracies (i.e. "positive pairs between real (input) - generated kin"). For these input images, we have real kin images that are used to compute verification accuracy of "real to real kinship positive pairs". Using Supervised Mixed Norm Autoencoder for kinship verification approach [14], we computed the positive pair accuracy and observed that for "real (input) to real kinship positive pairs", it is 74.06% whereas, for "real (input) to generated kin positive pairs", the accuracy is 71.34%. This experiment shows that the proposed FamilyGAN is able to generate images useful for automatic analysis as well.

5   Conclusion

Learning to generate kin face images by understanding the nuances of kinship facial feature as well as heredity patterns and when to apply appropriate transforms is an arduous task. FamilyGAN is a novel model that attempts to capture these complex feature hierarchy and govern the generation of possible kin face images. FamilyGAN conditions the generation of kin face images on kin-gender (Sect. 3.2) and the input face image of the person. The generative dexterity of FamilyGAN is analyzed qualitatively and quantitatively to show that the generated images are closely related to input face image of person and the real-kin face image in terms of facial features. FamilyGAN is adept at applying felicitous facial features transform to maintain kin feature hierarchy while observing relation (kin-gender) constraints. As a future work, we plan to extend the model to include kin-relation as well, to enable generating kin-images of different gender relations, such as father-daughter and mother-son.

References

1. Arjovsky, M., Chintala, S., Bottou, L.: Wasserstein GAN. arXiv preprint arXiv:1701.07875 (2017)
2. Choi, Y., Choi, M., Kim, M., Ha, J.W., Kim, S., Choo, J.: Stargan: unified generative adversarial networks for multi-domain image-to-image translation. arXiv preprint arXiv:1711.09020 (2017)
3. Chopra, S., Hadsell, R., LeCun, Y., et al.: Learning a similarity metric discriminatively, with application to face verification. CVPR 1, 539–546 (2005)
4. Cole, J.B., et al.: Human facial shape and size heritability and genetic correlations. Genetics 205(2), 967–978 (2017)
5. Crouch, D.J., et al.: Genetics of the human face: identification of large-effect single gene variants. Proc. Nat. Acad. Sci. 115(4), E676–E685 (2018)
6. Dahan, E., Keller, Y.: Selfkin: self adjusted deep model for kinship verification. arXiv preprint arXiv:1809.08493 (2018)
7. Fang, R., Tang, K.D., Snavely, N., Chen, T.: Towards computational models of kinship verification. In: 2010 17th IEEE International Conference on Image Processing (ICIP), pp. 1577–1580. IEEE (2010)
8. Ghatas, F.S., Hemayed, E.E.: GANKIN: generating kin faces using disentangled GAN. SN Appl. Sci. 2(2), 1–10 (2020)
9. Goodfellow, I., et al.: Generative adversarial nets. In: Advances in Neural Information Processing Systems, pp. 2672–2680 (2014)
10. Isola, P., Zhu, J.Y., Zhou, T., Efros, A.A.: Image-to-image translation with conditional adversarial networks. In: Proceedings of the IEEE Conference on Computer Vision and Pattern Recognition, pp. 1125–1134 (2017)
11. Karras, T., Aila, T., Laine, S., Lehtinen, J.: Progressive growing of GANs for improved quality, stability, and variation. arXiv preprint arXiv:1710.10196 (2017)
12. Koch, G., Zemel, R., Salakhutdinov, R.: Siamese neural networks for one-shot image recognition. In: ICML Deep Learning Workshop, vol. 2 (2015)
13. Kohli, N., Vatsa, M., Singh, R., Noore, A., Majumdar, A.: Hierarchical representation learning for kinship verification. IEEE Trans. Image Process. 26(1), 289–302 (2016)

14. Kohli, N., Yadav, D., Vatsa, M., Singh, R., Noore, A.: Supervised mixed norm autoencoder for kinship verification in unconstrained videos. IEEE Trans. Image Process. **28**(3), 1329–1341 (2018)

15. Lu, J., et al.: Kinship verification in the wild: The first kinship verification competition. In: 2014 IEEE International Joint Conference on Biometrics (IJCB), pp. 1–6. IEEE (2014)

16. Mirza, M., Osindero, S.: Conditional generative adversarial nets. arXiv preprint arXiv:1411.1784 (2014)

17. Ozkan, S., Ozkan, A.: Kinshipgan: synthesizing of kinship faces from family photos by regularizing a deep face network. In: 2018 25th IEEE International Conference on Image Processing (ICIP), pp. 2142–2146. IEEE (2018)

18. Radford, A., Metz, L., Chintala, S.: Unsupervised representation learning with deep convolutional generative adversarial networks. arXiv preprint arXiv:1511.06434 (2015)

19. Wang, W., You, S., Karaoglu, S., Gevers, T.: Kinship identification through joint learning using kinship verification ensemble. arXiv preprint arXiv:2004.06382 (2020)

20. Wu, X., He, R., Sun, Z., Tan, T.: A light CNN for deep face representation with noisy labels. IEEE Trans. Inf. Forensics Secur. **13**(11), 2884–2896 (2018)

21. Xia, S., Shao, M., Luo, J., Fu, Y.: Understanding kin relationships in a photo. IEEE Trans. Multimedia **14**(4), 1046–1056 (2012)

22. Zhu, J.Y., Park, T., Isola, P., Efros, A.A.: Unpaired image-to-image translation using cycle-consistent adversarial networks. In: Proceedings of the IEEE International Conference on Computer Vision, pp. 2223–2232 (2017)

Genetic-GAN: Synthesizing Images Between Two Domains by Genetic Crossover

Ishtiak Zaman[✉] and David Crandall[✉]

Indiana University Bloomington, Bloomington, USA
izaman@iu.edu, djcran@indiana.edu

Abstract. Synthesizing an interpolated image between two real images can be achieved by a simple interpolation on the latent space of the images, so that the resulting image inherits features from both. The task becomes more difficult when two images are in different domains, because an interpolated image whose latent representation lies near the middle of two distant input images may not be realistic and may end up in either domain. In this paper, we present a novel technique called Genetic-GAN that solves a novel problem of synthesizing a set of images that inherit features from both of the domains, while at the same time allowing control of which domain the resulting images fall into. We experiment on human face images using female and male genders as two different domains. We show that our method can take two images with very different attributes and synthesize images between them, and can perform domain transformations.

Keywords: Image to image translation · Unsupervised learning · Genetic crossover · Generative adversarial network

1 Introduction

Although we often think of objects as belonging to neatly-defined, independent, discrete categories, many objects in the real world are actually combinations of different things: classroom desks are combinations of tables and chairs, motorcycles are combinations of cars and bikes, tablets are combinations of computers and smartphones, etc. In fact, in the biological world, almost all living things are combinations of earlier organisms because of evolution and reproduction.

Creating synthetic combinations of visual objects is thus an interesting task for computer vision. A straightforward approach would be to obtain a latent encoding of two source images, perform interpolation between them, and then generate a hybrid image through a decoder that converts the encoding back to an image. However, one of the many issues with this approach is that all the combinations of latent codes within the latent space may not represent high-quality images. This is especially true when two input images are far away in the latent space, such as from two different domains. For example, human facial

© Springer Nature Switzerland AG 2020
A. Bartoli and A. Fusiello (Eds.): ECCV 2020 Workshops, LNCS 12537, pp. 312–326, 2020.
https://doi.org/10.1007/978-3-030-67070-2_19

images of different genders or hair styles may yield distant latent codes, and as a result, the interpolated latent code may generate a highly unrealistic combination image. This approach also does not provide a way to control attributes of the combined image or which domain it will fall into.

In this paper, we consider the problem of producing synthetic images that are combinations of two input images, where both the relative weighting of the two input images can be specified, and the domain of the output can also be fixed. To do this, we train our model with multiple possible latent codes between the two input codes to make the latent space more uniform. We also separate the domain-specific attributes from the latent space, which allows the latent space to learn general features of the images, and then train separate decoders to generate images for different domains.

Although our technique could be employed on any domains, we apply it (and describe it) on a fun, intuitive task: combining visual features of two input faces ("parents") into an output face ("offspring") within a particular age range and gender. Figure 1 shows an example. We cheekily call the model Genetic-GAN.[1]

Irrespective of the offspring's gender, they can inherit facial features more from the mother or more from the father or equally from both. In addition to crossover, Genetic-GAN is able to do domain transformation tasks such as gender and age transformation in an unsupervised manner. Our contribution involves keeping the domain-invariant latent space and channelling the domain-based information to two streams of decoder networks instead. To produce meaningful latent codes, we use our discriminator network to train on both the parent encoding and the offspring encoding with the help of a Dynamic Switching Module. To enhance domain-based attributes of the offspring, we train our discriminator network to recognize opposite domains (genders) from the real dataset as fake images, which forces the generator to avoid generating images characteristic of the other domain (more on Sect. 4.1). We achieve this without using supervised image to image mapping. We evaluate our image synthesis techniques both qualitatively and quantitatively in a human observer study.

2   Related Work

Our work is related to many others in image synthesis using GANs. The groundbreaking work on GANs [4] inspired many other image synthesis techniques that map a vector to a realistic synthetic image. Conditional GANs [5] introduced the idea of using an image as input; we use conditional GANs in this paper to provide a pair of source ("parent") images as input. Our work is also related to domain translation. For example, pix2pixHD [12] gave state-of-the art results with supervised data, but in our problem, we do not have ground truth (actual "offspring" examples). CycleGAN [14] introduced domain translation with unpaired images.

---

[1] We use parent, children, and genetic analogies because they are particularly intuitive, but we do not claim that our technique is a faithful model of biological genetic recombination or that it can be used to actually predict what a couple's child will look like. For simplicity, we also consider only male and female genders.

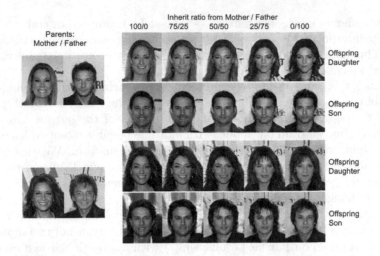

Fig. 1. Result of Genetic-GAN, showing sets of daughter and son offsprings that inherit characteristics from both their mothers and fathers. The top and bottom rows show the female and male offspring, respectively. They inherit different ratios of features from the mother and father (specifically either 100/0, 75/25, 50/50, 25/75, or 0/100). A split of 100/0 implies that the offspring inherits all characteristics from the mother and none from the father, while a split of 50/50 implies equal influence of both.

StarGAN [2] can transform multiple attributes at once, but requires ground truth attributes during training. Moreover, both CycleGAN and StarGAN work best on texture transformation while keeping an object's structure intact, which makes it hard for them to perform transformations such as changing length of hair. UNIT [9] uses a variational-autoencoder with a shared latent space that can translate both structure and texture at the same time. Our work similarly employs an encoder-decoder framework with shared latent space, but with the added functionality of latent space crossover.

Although there has been much work on image-to-image translation, there have not been many papers that can perform image interpolation between two images. DNA-Net [3] synthesizes a child image from two parent images, but requires supervised parent-child triplets and cannot control interpolation based on inheritance splits between parents. TransGaGa [13] can do geometric and appearance interpolation, but input faces must be very similar. StyleGAN [6] is the state-of-the-art in image generation, and can transform human facial attributes with high quality. With truncation trick [6], StyleGAN can also perform interpolation between faces, but there is a common "average" face of the whole dataset, which means that the middle of the interpolation converges to that common mean face for any set of inputs (Fig. 2). Thus, StyleGAN cannot produce a 50/50 split interpolation between two images that inherits 50% from both. Our objective is to synthesize a set of offspring that inherits different proportions from the parents.

To our knowledge, this paper presents the first method that can take two images (e.g, one female, one male) with very different attributes and combine over their latent codes, producing sets of "offspring" in different domains (e.g., genders). With the set of the offspring latent codes, we can generate separate streams of output (e.g., for female and male) because of our invariant latent space and by including the domain-specific characteristics into the decoders.

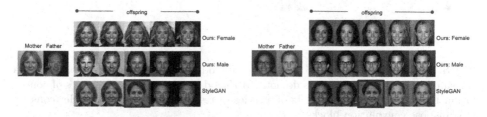

Fig. 2. Comparison with StyleGAN. StyleGAN interpolates through a mean face (in red border) regardless of the inputs, and thus the mean face does not inherit attributes from the parents. (Color figure online)

3   Method

This section presents our proposed Genetic-GAN method in detail. The technique consists of an Encoder-Decoder, Crossover Module, Discriminator Model, Dynamic Switching, and Siamese Network.

3.1   Encoder-Decoder Based Generator

The generator is based on an encoder-decoder architecture (Fig. 3(a)). The encoder takes an image as input and generates the latent code, while the decoder takes the latent code and generates an image. The encoder is composed of the encoding part followed by the translation part, while the decoder is a translation part followed by a decoding part (Fig. 3(b)). We follow the same encoder-translation-decoder design as pix2pixHD [12].

The last residual block of the encoder (that outputs the latent vector z) does not have an activation function. We use a KL-Loss with zero mean and unit variance to make sure that the latent space is evenly distributed.

For the reconstruction loss, we compare $Parent_f$ with $Dec_f(Enc(Parent_f))$ and $Parent_m$ with $Dec_m(Enc(Parent_m))$, and as the cycle consistancy loss, we compare $Parent_f$ with $Dec_f(Enc(Dec_m(Enc(Parent_f))))$ and $Parent_m$ with $Dec_m(Enc(Dec_f(Enc(Parent_m))))$. We set hyper-parameters for the reconstruction loss and the cycle loss such that the reconstructed image looks similar to the original image but is not exactly the same. This is because even when a female (or male) offspring inherits 100% from their mother (or father), we still would not want the female (or male) offspring to look exactly like the mother (or father), but to look similar and younger (more discussion in Sect. 4.1).

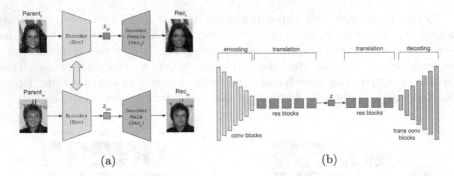

(a)   (b)

Fig. 3. Generator Architecture. (a) Both the Encoder for $Parent_f$ and $Parent_m$ shares the same weight, while decoders do not. (b) Encoder part consists of a series of convolution blocks, Translation consists of a series of residual blocks, and Decoder consists of transpose convolution blocks [12].

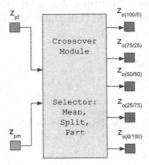

Fig. 4. Crossover generates five offspring latent vectors from two parent latent vectors.

3.2 Crossover Module

The parent latent codes do not directly go to the decoders. Instead, we perform crossover with the parent latent codes z_{pf} and z_{pm} that generate offspring latent vectors using the Crossover Module (Fig. 4). Here, $z_{o(ratio_f/ratio_m)}$ denotes the offspring latent code that inherits $ratio_f$ from z_{pf} and $ratio_m$ from z_{pm}, while $ratio_f + ratio_m = 100$.

We tried three different techniques for performing crossover:

- **Mean:** We take the weighted average of the two parent latent vectors,

$$crossover('mean', z_{pf}, z_{pm})$$
$$= \forall_{r=\{100,75,50,25,0\}} \{z_{pf} \times r/100.0 + z_{pm} \times (1.0 - r/100.0)\}.$$

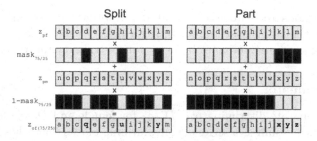

Fig. 5. Sample crossover between z_{pf} and z_{pm} with 'Spilt' and 'Part' methods when $ratio_f : ratio_m = 100 : 75$.

- **Split**: We alternatively take part from z_{pf} and z_{pm} as determined by $ratio_f$ and $ratio_m$ (Fig. 5). We define a binary vector $mask_{r_f/r_m} \in [0,1]^{|z_{pf}|}$ with length equal to z_{pf} or z_{pm},

$$mask^i_{r_f/r_m} = \begin{cases} 1, & r_f = 100 \\ 0, & r_m = 100 \\ 1, & r_f \geq r_m \text{ and } i \bmod \left(\frac{r_f}{r_m} + 1\right) \neq \frac{r_f}{r_m} \\ 1, & r_f < r_m \text{ and } i \bmod \left(\frac{r_m}{r_f} + 1\right) = \frac{r_m}{r_f} \\ 0, & \text{otherwise.} \end{cases}$$

and then we perform crossover,

$$crossover('split', z_{pf}, z_{pm})$$
$$= \forall_{r=\{100,75,50,25,0\}} \{z_{pf} \times mask_{r/(100-r)} + z_{pm} \times (1- \ mask_{r/(100-r)})\}.$$

- **Part**: This is similar to 'Split' except that we divide z_{pf} and z_{pm} into two parts as determined by $ratio_f$ and $ratio_m$ (Fig. 5) and perform crossover over them. Again, $mask_{r_f/r_m} \in [0,1]^{|z_{pf}|}$,

$$mask^i_{r_f/r_m} = \begin{cases} 1, & i \leq |z_{pf}| \times \frac{r_f}{r_f+r_m} \\ 0, & \text{otherwise,} \end{cases}$$

and then we perform crossover as with Split.

We have 5 latent points $\forall_{r=\{100,75,50,25,0\}} \{z_{o(r/(100-r))}\}$ that are the output of the crossover module (right side of Fig. 4). Considering all the 5 latent points as a set z_o where $z_o = \forall_{r=\{100,75,50,25,0\}} \{z_{o(r/(100-r))}\}$, we pass all the offspring latent points z_o through the decoder followed by the discriminator (as described in Sect. 3.3). If we were to only pass z_{pf} and z_{pm} but not z_o, the image resulting from z_o would not have meaningful outcomes for different modes because the placement of z_o over the latent space is different for different modes.

We trained our networks using each of the three crossover methods, and we found that they give very similar results (more in Sect. 4.3). We tried different crossover methods to demonstrate that our approach on training the middle points makes the latent space uniform, regardless of the crossover method. But the same crossover method must be used during training and testing.

3.3   Discriminator

We use two separate discriminators, $Disc_f$ for female and $Disc_m$ for male. The discriminators are built as a series of convolutional blocks that takes input images and outputs patches, similar to PatchGAN [5]. We calculate adversarial loss from the discriminators as LSGAN [11] (more in Sect. 3.5). We pass images from the dataset as *real* and offspring images as *fake* to the discriminators, so that the encoder-decoder-based generator learns to generate realistic images. We also train the discriminators to differentiate between female and male images by passing real male images to $Disc_f$ as *fake* and real female images to $Disc_m$ as *fake*. This encourages Dec_f and Dec_m to produce faces that appear to be of the correct gender. By applying this additional step, we overcome some of the challenges in gender-based domain translation, such as being able to translate from a bald, bearded male to a long-haired female with no facial hair (more in Sect. 4.1).

3.4   Dynamic Switching

During training, for each pair of inputs $Parent_f$ and $Parent_m$, we generate 5 pairs of offspring images from $Dec_f(z_o)$ and $Dec_m(z_o)$, where

$$z_o = \forall_{r=\{100,75,50,25,0\}}\{z_{o(r/(100-r))}\},$$

as shown in Fig. 6. We train the discriminators with real images from the dataset and fake images as the offspring images. To balance the discriminators on the number of real and fake images, we only allow one pair of offspring images out of every five pairs by using the Dynamic Switching Module. For each iteration, the module switches to the next branch, $next\_branch = (current\_branch+1) \bmod 5$, and allows the discriminators to train on the same number of real and fake images. Without the dynamic switching module, there would have been five times more fake images than real images in each iteration of the training.

3.5   Loss Functions

Given two input images, $Parent_f$ and $Parent_m$, we generate $z_{pf} = Enc(Parent_f)$ and $z_{pm} = Enc(Parent_m)$. We use crossover to generate $z_o = crossover(z_{pf}, z_{pm})$, which is a set of five latent vectors $\forall_{r=\{100,75,50,25,0\}}\{z_{o(r/(100-r))}\}$. Finally, for the set of latent vectors z_o, we generate the offspring images,

$$OS_f = \forall_{r=\{100,75,50,25,0\}}OS_{f(r/(100-r))}$$
$$= \forall_{r=\{100,75,50,25,0\}}Dec_f(z_{o(r/(100-r))}),$$

and

$$OS_m = \forall_{r=\{100,75,50,25,0\}} OS_{m(r/(100-r))}$$
$$= \forall_{r=\{100,75,50,25,0\}} Dec_m(z_{o(r/(100-r))}).$$

We apply the following four loss functions.

Kullback–Leibler Loss: We use KL-loss based on VAE reparameterization [7] with zero mean and unit variance over $z_p = \{z_{pf}, z_{pm}\}$ to regularize the latent vectors on the latent space,

$$Loss_{KL} = mean(z_p)^2 + std(z_p) - \log(std(z_p)),$$

where *mean* and *std* represent mean and standard deviation, respectively.

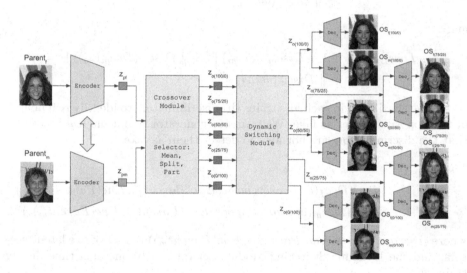

Fig. 6. Genetic-GAN Architecture. We generate 10 output images derived from 2 input images.

Reconstruction Loss: $OS_{f(100/0)}$ and $OS_{m(0/100)}$ inherit 100% from $Parent_f$ and $Parent_m$, respectively. Thus the reconstruction loss for these two pairs is,

$$Loss_{Rec} = \| Parent_f - OS_{f(100/0)} \|_1 + \| Parent_m - OS_{m(0/100)} \|_1 .$$

Cycle Consistency Loss: We also use a cycle consistency loss to overcome the mode collapse problem [14] and to produce high quality output,

$$Loss_{Cyc} = \| Parent_f - Dec_f(Enc(OS_{m(100/0)})) \|_1$$
$$+ \| Parent_m - Dec_m(Enc(OS_{f(0/100)})) \|_1 .$$

We do not strictly enforce the reconstruction or the cycle consistency losses so that offspring do not look exactly like the parents, but do have very similar appearances (more in Sect. 3.6).

Adversarial Loss. We have two separate discriminators, $Disc_f$ and $Disc_m$, for female and male, respectively, that learn to distinguish between real images from the dataset (outputs as 1) and fake images as the offspring (outputs as 0). We train our discriminators in three steps and apply an adversarial loss based on LSGAN [11]. If $data_f$ and $data_m$ are real instances of female and male instances, respectfully, from the dataset,

$$Loss_{Disc_f} = \| 1 - Disc_f(data_f) \|^2 + \| Disc_f(Dec_f(z_o)) \|^2 \\ + \| Disc_f(data_m) \|^2,$$

and

$$Loss_{Disc_m} = \| 1 - Disc_m(data_m) \|^2 + \| Disc_m(Dec_m(z_o)) \|^2 \\ + \| Disc_m(data_f) \|^2,$$

where the third term in each loss trains the discriminators to identify real images of the opposite gender as fake. We train our generator to output *real* images so that the discriminators are not able to detect them as *fake*,

$$Loss_{Adv} \\ = \| 1 - Disc_f(Dec_f(crossover(mode, Enc(Parent_f), Enc(Parent_m)))) \|^2 \\ + \| 1 - Disc_m(Dec_m(crossover(mode, Enc(Parent_f), Enc(Parent_m)))) \|^2,$$

where $crossover(mode, Enc(Parent_f), Enc(Parent_m))$ is a set of five latent vectors, and the Dynamic Switching Module activates only one at a time during training.

3.6   Model Objective

To train Enc, Dec_f and Dec_m jointly, our final objective is the sum of all losses,

$$Loss = \lambda_{KL} \times Loss_{KL} + \lambda_{Rec} \times Loss_{Rec} + \lambda_{Cyc} \times Loss_{Cyc} + \lambda_{Adv} \times Loss_{Adv},$$

where λ hyper-parameters determine the weight of each of the losses.

We use $\lambda_{KL} = 1.0$, $\lambda_{Rec} = 2.0$, $\lambda_{Cyc} = 2.0$, and $\lambda_{Adv} = 4.0$.

4   Experiments

To evaluate our technique, we ran experiments with the celebA dataset [10] with full size images of 218×178. We used the *gender* attribute for separating female and male images, the *id* attribute to group images by the same person to train

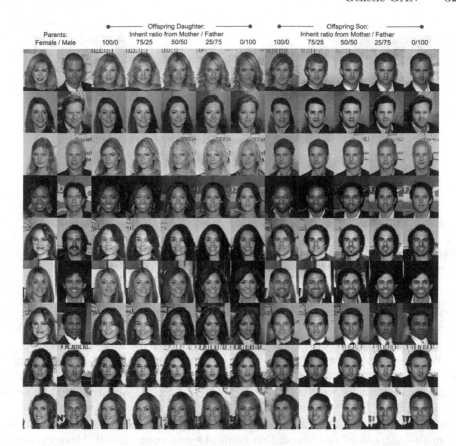

Fig. 7. Results from our Genetic-GAN. Each row has two parent inputs and ten off-spring outputs.

a Siamese network (Sect. 4.5), and the *young* attribute to select offspring-like faces (more on *young* attribute in Sect. 4.1). Our main objective is to produce synthetic offspring images from two parent images. We show sample results from our model on Fig. 7. Qualitatively, we observed that our model can generate synthetic offspring images from parents with very different appearances.

4.1 Gender and Age Translation

By accomplishing the objective of offspring generation while inheriting charac-teristics from the parents, our model also achieves the tasks of gender and age translation. In Fig. 6 we see that $OS_{f(0/100)}$ is a female offspring that inherits 100% from $Parent_m$, and $OS_{m(100/0)}$ is a male offspring that inherits 100% from $Parent_f$. This case is similar to domain translation between genders.

Some more examples of gender translation are presented in Fig. 8. The figure shows faces with typically-masculine features such as facial hair and receding hairline being transformed into more typically female features such as smoother

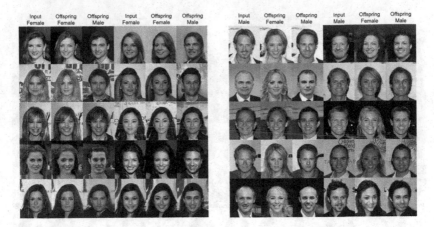

Fig. 8. For each input, our technique produces an output with the opposite gender and a younger age.

skin and long hair, and vice-versa. As mentioned above, we tune the hyper-parameters of our loss functions such that even if an offspring inherits 100% from one parent, they will still not look exactly the same as the parent.

We use the *young* attribute from the celebA dataset to select images to train the discriminators, which encourages the generators to produce younger looking images. From Fig. 7 we see that $OS_{f(100/0)}$ is a female offspring that inherits 100% from the $Parent_f$, and $OS_{m(0/100)}$ is a male offspring that inherits 100% from the $Parent_m$. Thus the $Parent_f \rightarrow OS_{f(100/0)}$ and $Parent_m \rightarrow OS_{m(0/100)}$ serve the purpose of age translation from older to younger self. More examples of age translation are presented in Fig. 8.

4.2   Relation to Human Genetics

Our technique is learned in a data-driven way, and obviously can only capture visual features and is not intended to model human genetics. Nevertheless, it is interesting to draw an analogy to human genetics. The human genome has 23 pairs of chromosomes, the first 22 of which are responsible for characteristics and the last pair for gender; typically XX represents female while XY represents male. In our project, the Encoder and the Crossover Module together create latent codes that represent the characteristics of the offspring but not the gender. And the Decoders turn the latent code either into a female (as an XX) or into a male (as an XY). As shown in Fig. 9, for every input in the first column, we obtain a female and male offspring that inherits 100% of the input parent. Although both offspring contain the exact same latent code, they appear as different genders after the Dec_f and Dec_m apply the gender-based attributes to them (i.e. applying XX or XY chromosome).

Similar to crossover in human reproduction, we apply crossover between the two parent latent codes. With the Crossover Module, we also control the relative

Fig. 9. Examples when both offspring inherit 100% from the input on the left. In (a), (d), and (e) the male offspring inherits the facial hair from the parent which stays recessive in the female offspring despite having the exact same latent code. Similar results for declining hairline in (c), (g), and (h). In (b) and (f) the offspring get mutated by not inheriting the glasses, as glasses are not necessary to determining gender.

ratio of attributes inherited from each of the two parents. Moreover, in Fig. 9 we see that the male offspring sometimes shows signs of facial hair and receding hairline inherited from the parent, but the female offspring does not show these signs, despite having the exact same latent code, a concept similar to recessive genes in human genetics. We also observe mutation in the offspring (Fig. 9).

4.3   Quantitative Evaluation

We evaluated 20,000 synthetic images generated by each of our three crossover modes and compared their PSNR and SSIM scores, as shown in Table 1. We observe that the three crossover modes give similar results. We trained on the 5 middle points to make the latent space uniform, and all the crossover methods are able to make the latent space uniform to the same extent. In this table, we compare the offspring with the parent to generate the PSNR and SSIM scores. Due to the structural dissimilarity between the parents and offspring, we obtain lower SSIM value for all modes.

Table 1. Comparison between crossover modes.

	Crossover mode		
	Mean	Split	Part
PSNR	14.31	14.55	14.38
SSIM	0.43	0.44	0.45

We also evaluated the quality of the synthetic images by training a gender classifier on just the synthetic images produced by our system, and then testing the classifier on real data. We generated 20,000 synthetic images and trained a simple Alexnet [8]-based binary classifier to perform classification on gender. This model gives 87% accuracy on the original celebA dataset, suggesting that the synthetic images are quite realistic.

4.4   Human Observer Evaluation

Of course, the true measure of success of an image synthesis technique is in how the images appear to human observers. We conducted four human observer studies on Amazon Mechanical Turk [1] to evaluate four properties of our technique: (1) how often the model produces offspring that are recognized by AMT users as the target gender, (2) how often the offspring of the model appear to be similar to parents, (3) how well the model produces offspring with a given ratio of the parents, and (4) how the model compares to a baseline (StarGAN).

Gender. First, we presented each AMT user with a single synthetic offspring image, and asked them to identify the gender of the face. Of the 196 trials, 182 (92.9%) were identified as the gender intended by the model, which suggests that our technique reliably produces faces that appear to be of the specified gender to human observers.

Offspring Similarity to Parents. Second, AMT users were presented with images of two parents, and then asked to identify the offspring from one of three possible faces (all of which were generated by our algorithm but only one of which corresponded to the given parents). Of the 192 trials, 119 (61.98%) were correct. Given that random guessing would produce 33.3% accuracy, this result suggests that our technique generally produces realistic-looking offspring images, given a pair of parents.

Accurate Combinations of Parents. Third, we evaluate how well our model can control how much of the similarity comes from each parent. Each AMT user was shown images of two parents and an offspring from them produced by our algorithm. The offspring was generated according to an inheritance ratio chosen randomly from a set of three possibilities (50%–50% from each, or higher ratio from the first image, or higher ratio from the second image), and the user was asked to choose among the three possibilities. Of the 196 trials, 109 (55.6%) were correct, compared to random guessing of 33.3%.

Comparison to StarGAN. Fourth, we compared our gender transformation result with StarGAN [2]. While StarGAN can successfully transform a face to the opposite gender, the face it produces is very similar. In contrast, we are able to properly add or remove gender specific-features (Fig. 10). We presented pairs of synthetic images to AMT users, one produced by our technique and one produced by StarGAN, and asked them to choose the more realistic image. Out of 221 trials, 184 (83.2%) chose ours.

4.5   Evaluation of Loss Functions and Ablation Study

To evaluate the relative importance of our four types of loss function (KL loss, Rec loss, Cyc loss, and Adv loss), we run experiments in which we disable one

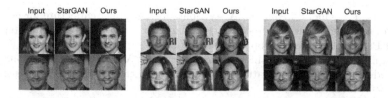

Fig. 10. Comparison with StarGAN on gender transformation.

type of loss at a time. However, we found that either the training becomes unstable (when disabling the KL loss), we get unrealistic faces (when disabling Adv loss), or we experience mode collapse [14] (when disabling Rec or Cyc loss). We set our loss hyper-parameters as described on Sect. 3.6 to produce stable and high-quality results.

We also tried ignoring the *young* attributes, which gave us the same PSNR scores as in Table 1. But without using the attribute, we get output images with a look of similar age as the inputs.

We also tried to incorporate an additional Siamese loss, where we pre-train a Siamese network that learns similarity between images with supervised data pairs, and use that network as a loss function between parent and offspring pairs. However, our experiments did not find any qualitative or quantitative advantage with this extra loss included.

5   Conclusions

To summarize, Genetic-GAN is able to take two images from two domains and do crossover between them with multiple ratios to synthesize two streams of images interpolated between them. Our future goal is to incorporate more complex and multiple domains at the same time.

References

1. Buhrmester, M.D., Kwang, T.N., Gosling, S.D.: Amazon's mechanical turk. Perspect. Psychol. Sci. **6**, 3–5 (2011)
2. Choi, Y., Choi, M., Kim, M., Ha, J.W., Kim, S., Choo, J.: Stargan: unified generative adversarial networks for multi-domain image-to-image translation. In: Proceedings of the IEEE Conference on Computer Vision and Pattern Recognition, pp. 8789–8797 (2018)
3. Gao, P., et al.: What will your child look like? DNA-net: age and gender aware kin face synthesizer. arXiv preprint arXiv:1911.07014 (2019)
4. Goodfellow, I., et al.: Generative adversarial nets. In: Advances in Neural Information Processing Systems, pp. 2672–2680 (2014)
5. Isola, P., Zhu, J.Y., Zhou, T., Efros, A.A.: Image-to-image translation with conditional adversarial networks. In: Proceedings of the IEEE Conference on Computer Vision and Pattern Recognition, pp. 1125–1134 (2017)

6. Karras, T., Laine, S., Aila, T.: A style-based generator architecture for generative adversarial networks. In: Proceedings of the IEEE Conference on Computer Vision and Pattern Recognition, pp. 4401–4410 (2019)
7. Kingma, D.P., Welling, M.: Stochastic gradient VB and the variational auto-encoder. In: Second International Conference on Learning Representations, ICLR, vol. 19 (2014)
8. Krizhevsky, A., Sutskever, I., Hinton, G.E.: Imagenet classification with deep convolutional neural networks. In: Advances in Neural Information Processing Systems, pp. 1097–1105 (2012)
9. Liu, M.Y., Breuel, T., Kautz, J.: Unsupervised image-to-image translation networks. In: Advances in Neural Information Processing Systems, pp. 700–708 (2017)
10. Liu, Z., Luo, P., Wang, X., Tang, X.: Deep learning face attributes in the wild. In: Proceedings of International Conference on Computer Vision (ICCV), December 2015
11. Mao, X., Li, Q., Xie, H., Lau, R.Y., Wang, Z., Paul Smolley, S.: Least squares generative adversarial networks. In: Proceedings of the IEEE International Conference on Computer Vision, pp. 2794–2802 (2017)
12. Wang, T.C., Liu, M.Y., Zhu, J.Y., Tao, A., Kautz, J., Catanzaro, B.: pix2pixhd: high-resolution image synthesis and semantic manipulation with conditional GANs (2018)
13. Wu, W., Cao, K., Li, C., Qian, C., Loy, C.C.: Transgaga: geometry-aware unsupervised image-to-image translation. In: Proceedings of the IEEE Conference on Computer Vision and Pattern Recognition, pp. 8012–8021 (2019)
14. Zhu, J.Y., Park, T., Isola, P., Efros, A.A.: Unpaired image-to-image translation using cycle-consistent adversarial networks. In: Proceedings of the IEEE International Conference on Computer Vision, pp. 2223–2232 (2017)

GIA-Net: Global Information Aware Network for Low-Light Imaging

Zibo Meng[1]([✉]) [iD], Runsheng Xu[2], and Chiu Man Ho[1]

[1] InnoPeak Technology, Palo Alto, CA 94043, USA
{zibo.meng,chiuman}@innopeaktech.com
[2] Mercedes-Benz R&D North America, Sunnyvale, CA 94085, USA
derrickxu1994@gmail.com

Abstract. It is extremely challenging to acquire perceptually plausible images under low-light conditions due to low SNR. Most recently, U-Nets have shown promising results for low-light imaging. However, vanilla U-Nets generate images with artifacts such as color inconsistency due to the lack of global color information. In this paper, we propose a global information aware (GIA) module, which is capable of extracting and integrating the global information into the network to improve the performance of low-light imaging. The GIA module can be inserted into a vanilla U-Net with negligible extra learnable parameters or computational cost. Moreover, a GIA-Net is constructed, trained and evaluated on a large scale real-world low-light imaging dataset. Experimental results show that the proposed GIA-Net outperforms the state-of-the-art methods in terms of four metrics, including deep metrics that measure perceptual similarities. Extensive ablation studies have been conducted to verify the effectiveness of the proposed GIA-Net for low-light imaging by utilizing global information.

1 Introduction

Taking photos with good perceptual quality under low illumination conditions is extremely challenging due to low signal-to-noise ratio (SNR) [2]. One common practice to improve the low-light image quality is to extend the exposure time. However, this can easily introduce motion blur due to camera shake or object movements and it is not always applicable in real life. In the past decade, extensive studies have been conducted for imaging under low-light conditions including denoising techniques [4,8,12,17,21,23,27] which aim at removing noises introduced in the acquired low-light images, and image enhancement techniques [5,9,16,18,20] which are developed for improving the perceptual quality of digital images.

Most recently, deep convolutional neural networks [2,26] have shown promise for imaging under low-light conditions. Specifically, Chen *et al.* developed a framework based on a U-Net using ℓ_1 loss function as the objective function. Following Chen's work, Zamir *et al.* [26] proposed a new joint loss function to train the U-Net with the same architecture as in [2] for low-light imaging.

© Springer Nature Switzerland AG 2020
A. Bartoli and A. Fusiello (Eds.): ECCV 2020 Workshops, LNCS 12537, pp. 327–342, 2020.
https://doi.org/10.1007/978-3-030-67070-2_20

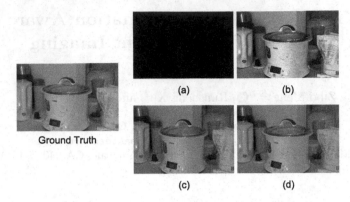

Ground Truth

(a)

(b)

(c)

(d)

Fig. 1. An illustration of low-light imaging. (a) A short-exposed RAW input taken from the SONY subset of the SID dataset [2] with an exposure time of 0.04 s; (b) The RGB image produced by applying traditional image signal processing pipeline to the short exposed raw image given in (a). Note that the brightness has been increased for better representation; (c) The RGB image produced using the state-of-the-art approach [2]. Note that severe artifacts, such as color inconsistency, can be spotted in the resulting image; (d) The output of the proposed GIA-Net, where the color of the image is consistent everywhere because of the introduction of global information.

Although inspiring results have been presented in those work, both of the proposed methods produced severe artifacts, such as color inconsistency, due to the lack of global information in the network. For example, as illustrated in Fig. 1, Fig. 1(a) gives a short-exposed RAW input taken from the SONY subset of the SID dataset [2] with an exposure time of 0.04s; Fig. 1 (b) depicts the output image produced by applying traditional digital signal processing pipeline to the short exposed image (a). Note the high noise level and color distortion; Fig. 1 (c) shows the output image produced using the state-of-the-art approach [2]. Note the color inconsistency in the output image because of the lack of the global information in the U-Net employed.

To overcome the shortcomings of the vanilla U-Nets for low-light imaging, in this work, we develop a framework for imaging under extremely low-light conditions in an end-to-end fashion with global color information integrated. Specifically, we propose a global information-aware (GIA) module for low-light imaging, which is capable of extracting global information, together with the pixel-level features, to improve the perceptual qualities for low-light image enhancement. Furthermore, we insert the proposed GIA module into a vanilla U-Net to construct a GIA-Net. As illustrated in Fig. 1 (d), the output of our GIA-Net gives consistent color compared with Fig. 1 (c) produced by [2]. The GIA-Net can be trained in an end-to-end fashion with a joint loss function. **The code for training and testing, as well as the trained models will be publicly available.**

Our main contributions are threefold:

We propose a GIA module to extract and integrate global information into U-Nets;

We design a GIA-Net with the proposed GIA module integrated, and demonstrated its effectiveness for low-light imaging;

We conduct extensive ablation study to demonstrate the effectiveness of the proposed GIA-Net for low-light imaging.

2 Related Work

Image processing and enhancement have been extensively studied in the past decades which are discussed in the following sections.

2.1 Image Denoising

Image denoising has been widely studied in low-level vision field.

Single image denoising, such as total variation denoising [23] and 3D transform-domain filtering (BM3D) [4] for image denoising, is often based on analytical priors such as image smoothness, sparsity, low rank, or self-similarity to recover the image signals from noisy images. In the past few years, because of their extraordinary performance in other computer vision applications, deep convolutional neural networks (CNNs) have been emerging for image denoising [1,27,28]. While remarkable improvement has been achieved, those methods are generally developed and evaluated on synthetic data and do not generalize well to real images. Most recently, while elf-guided network [7,14] has been proposed and shown promise for image enhancement, its performance might degrade for low-light images since it directly uses the highly noisy images as input for every level.

Burst denoising performs denoising on burst of noisy images captured sequentially using the same device from the same scene [10,15]. Those approaches generally first register all the frames to a common reference, and then perform denoising by robust averaging [19]. In addition, a set of approaches is using a burst of images taken at the same time to perform denoising. Although these methods typically yield good performance, they are elaborately and computationally expensive. Moreover, image alignment algorithms become unreliable under extremely low-light conditions, resulting in ghosting effects in the final image.

2.2 Low-Light Image Enhancement

A number of techniques have been developed for image enhancement, such as histogram equalization, and gamma correction. Recently, more advanced approaches have been proposed to deal with the enhancement of low-light images [3,5,6,9,16,18,20] . However, these models share a strong assumption where the input image has clean representation without any noise. Thus, a separate denoising step should be employed beforehand for low-light image enhancement. One particular method that is related to our approach is the "learning to see in the dark" model (SID) [2] where an encoder-decoder CNN is employed to perform denoising, as well as image enhancement at the same time. In a follow-up work [26], a joint loss function, i.e. ℓ_1, MS-SSIM [25], and perceptual loss [13], is proposed to improve the quality of the generated images. However, since the global information is not considered in both of the work, severe artifacts such as color inconsistency can be observed in the output images.

Most of the current approaches perform image denoising and enhancement separately, which is time and computationally costly. Moreover, although SID [2] performed image denoising and enhancement jointly and achieved promising results, it failed to consider the global information which is crucial for color consistency in the output images. In this work, we propose to perform low-light image denoising and enhancement in a single shot with the integration of the global context. This makes the network to be aware of the global context/color information to better generate the final output.

3   Methodology

In this section, we firstly present some analyses on drawbacks of applying vanilla U-Nets on low-light imaging as proposed in [2, 26]. Then, we introduce a global information aware (GIA) module to deal with the drawbacks and insert the proposed GIA module into a U-Net for low-light imaging.

3.1   Analysis on Vanilla U-Nets

U-Nets have been widely adopted for image-to-image translation and have been demonstrated to be effective for semantic segmentation. However, vanilla U-Nets have some drawbacks for low-light imaging. For example, as illustrated in Fig. 1 (c), color inconsistency can be observed in the generated result using a vanilla U-Net [2] due to the lack of global color information. Specifically, the effective receptive size of the network used in [2] is around 224, while the input image of the network is 2832×4240 for images in Sony dataset. Thus, we develope a global information aware (GIA) module which can be inserted into a U-Net to extract and utilize the global information for low-light imaging.

3.2   Global Information Aware Module

The above-mentioned analysis motivates us to design a global information extraction module, i.e. GIA module, to extract and include the global information into the network to enable better performance for low-light imaging.

One natural choice is dilated convolutonal operation, which is widely adopted in deep convolutional neural networks for expanding the receptive field size. However, dilated convolutional operations ignore the local information and do not

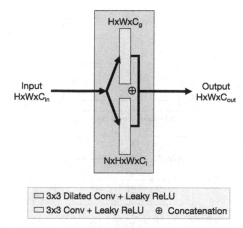

Fig. 2. An illustration of the seeing wider (SW) block, where the input will be fed into a vanilla convoluitonal layer, which is responsible to extract the local information, and a dilated convolutional layer, which is responsible to extract contextual information in a wider range. The outputs are concatenated as the final output of the SW block.

fully use all the information in the neighborhood. An alternative design is to use a combination of dilated convolutional operation and the vanilla convolutional operation. Specifically, as illustrated in Fig. 2, we design a see-wider (SW) module to enable the network to see both local fine details and wider contextual information. In a SW block, the input with a shape of $H \times W \times C_{in}$ will be separately fed into a vanilla convolutional layer with an output of a shape of $H \times W \times C_l$ and a dilated convolutional layer with an output of a shape of $H \times W \times C_g$. The outputs of the two layers are concatenated as the output of the SW block. Although the proposed SW block can integrate the local information with information extracted with a larger receptive field size, the design has three potential problems. First, the size of the input of the network can be arbitrarily large, while the receptive field size is fixed once the network is designed and trained. Second, another hyper-parameter, i.e. the dilate rate, is introduced, which needs extra effort to tune to achieve optimal performance. Third, the numbers of dilated convolutional kernel and the regular convolutional kernel require to be determined through extensive experimental search.

In this paper, we propose a simple yet effective module, i.e. a global information aware (GIA) module, to extract the global color information, which is further integrated with the pixel-level feature maps into the network for low-light imaging.

As depicted in Fig. 3, a GIA module consists of a stack of operations with the shapes of feature maps after each operation specified. Particularly, given an input feature map, i.e. **X**, with a size of H × W × C, a down-sampling function $f_1(\mathbf{X})$ is employed to extract the global information producing a feature map with a size of 1 × 1 × C. Then, an up-sampling function $f_2(X_1)$ is utilized to upscale the down-sampled feature map which is processed by a 1 × 1 convlutional

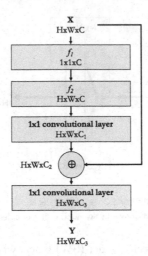

Fig. 3. An illustration of a global information aware (GIA) module. A GIA module consists of a stack of operations with the shapes of feature maps after each operation specified.

layer to shrink the number of channels, yielding a feature map with a size of $H \times W \times C_1$. Then a function f_3 is employed to combine the input feature map (encoding local information) and $\mathbf{X}$ (encoding the global information) to produce an output feature map, i.e. $\mathbf{Y}$, with a size of $H \times W \times C_2$. The designed GIA module is easy to be implemented and introduces negligible learnable parameters or computational cost.

3.3   Global Information Aware Network

To illustrate the effectiveness of the proposed GIA module, we insert the GIA module into the bottleneck of a vanilla U-Net, denoted as GIA-Net, to perform low-light imaging. Specifically, as illustrated in Fig. 4, the base network is a U-Net consisting of 18 convolutional layers, represented by the blue bars. The proposed GIA module integrated in the bottleneck denoted by the yellow block. During inference, an input image firstly goes through a set of downsampling stages to extract abstract features, as well as to reduce the spatial resolution. In the bottleneck, the proposed GIA module is responsible for extracting the global information which is combined with the input feature map. Then, the feature map will go through a set of upscaling stages. In the upscaling stage, the input layer is firstly upscaled and then concatenated with the layer of the same resolution from the downsampling stage, indicated by the directed arrow which can effectively preserve the details in an image. More formally, given an input raw image, I, the GIA-Net is employed to learn a mapping, $\hat{I} = f(I : w)$, to produce the output RGB image, where w is a set of learnable parameters of the network.

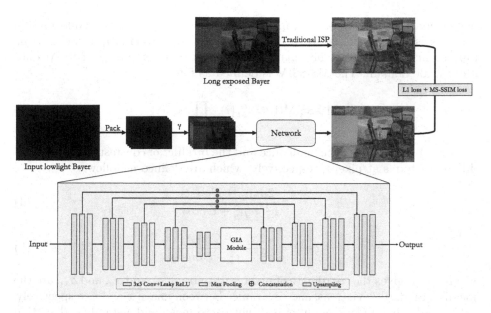

Fig. 4. An illustration of the global information aware network (GIA-Net), where the base network is a vanilla U-Net with the proposed GIA module inserted into the bottleneck.

3.4   Joint Loss Function

We follow paper [30] to use a joint guidance of ℓ_1 loss plus MS-SSIM loss. The joint loss function has the following form:

$$\mathcal{L} = \gamma \mathcal{L}^{\ell_1}(I, \hat{I}) + (1 - \gamma)\mathcal{L}^{MS-SSIM}(I, \hat{I}) \tag{1}$$

where $\gamma \in [0, 1]$ is the weight to balance the two terms.

Pixel Level Constraint: The ℓ_1 loss function calculates the difference between the ground truth image and long exposure image with the output produced by the proposed network with the corresponding short-exposed image as input. The ℓ_1 loss function is defined as follows:

$$\mathcal{L}^{\ell_1} = \frac{1}{N}\sum_{p=1}^{N}(I_p, \hat{I}_p) \tag{2}$$

where p is the pixel location and N gives the total number of pixels.

Structural Similarity Constraint: Although ℓ_1 loss is widely used for image reconstruction and has been proven effective, it is reported to produce blurry results. In this work, the multiscale structural similarity index (MS-SSIM) is widely used in measuring the structural similarities of two images. SSIM is a perception-based metric which captures the similarities in structural information (i.e. pixels spatially close to each other are highly correlated), as well as the illuminance and contrast information. MS-SSIM is an extension of SSIM onto multi-scale domain. The MS-SSIM is defined as follows:

$$\text{MS-SSIM}(i) = l_M^\alpha(i) \cdot \prod_{j=1}^{M} cs_j^{\beta_j}(i) \tag{3}$$

where $l(i)$ and $cs(i)$ are the luminance and the product of contrast and structural difference terms at pixel i, respectively, which are defined as follows:

$$l(i) = \frac{2\mu_x\mu_y + Const_1}{\mu_x^2 + \mu_y^2 + Const_1} \tag{4}$$

$$cs(i) = \frac{2\sigma_{xy} + Const_2}{\sigma_x^2 + \sigma_y^2 + Const_2} \tag{5}$$

where (x, y) gives the coordinate of pixel i; μ_x and μ_y, σ_x and σ_y, and σ_{xy} are the means, standard deviations, and covariance between image x and y, respectively, calculated using a Gaussian filter, G_g, with zero mean and a standard deviation σ_g; M is the number of levels to perform SSIM; and α and β_j for $j = i, ..., M$ are set to 1. $Const_1$ and $Const_2$ are small constant numbers [25].

The MS-SSIM is a scalar between 0 and 1, the larger the better. Thus, the final loss function used to optimize the network is given as follows:

$$\mathcal{L}^{MS-SSIM} = 1 - \text{MS-SSIM} \tag{6}$$

Table 1. Quantitative comparison between the proposed GIA-Net and the state-of-the-art methods in terms of PSNR (higher is better), SSIM (higher is better), PieAPP (lower is better), and LPIPS (lower is better). The numbers are obtained by taking the average on Sony and Fuji subsets respectively. *For SID-Net, we retrained the networks using the code provided by the author of SID-Net and report the yielded numbers. Note that the numbers in the original paper is given in the parenthesis.

	Sony				Fuji			
	PSNR	SSIM	PieAPP	LPIPS	PSNR	SSIM	PieAPP	LPIPS
DnCNN [27]	27.79	0.738	1.678	0.538	26.23	0.687	1.935	0.583
RID-Net [1]	28.51	0.755	1.577	0.459	26.75	0.694	1.915	0.578
SID-Net [2]*	28.52 (28.88)	0.786 (0.787)	1.532	0.420	26.71 (26.61)	0.707 (0.680)	1.902	0.562
SGN [7]	29.06	–	–	–	27.41	–	–	–
SE-UNet [11]	29.36	0.768	1.542	0.433	27.78	0.708	1.787	0.533
Zamir et al. [26]	29.43	–	1.511	0.443	27.63	–	1.763	**0.476**
GIA-Net	**29.72**	**0.795**	**1.425**	**0.404**	**28.15**	**0.722**	**1.739**	0.519

4   Experimental Results

4.1   Database

To enable the development of low-light imaging approaches with real-world images, Chen et al. [2] constructed a large scale dataset, i.e. See-in-the-Dark (SID) dataset. Specifically, two subsets were collected using two different sensors, i.e. Sony α7S II with a Bayer color filter array with a resolution of 4240×2832, and a Fuji X-T2 with an X-Trans CFA with a resolution of 6000×4000. There are 5,094 short-exposure RAW input images with corresponding long-exposure reference images collected under both indoor and outdoor scenarios containing only static objects. The images were collected under an environment of 0.2 to 5 lux and 0.03 to 0.3 lux for outdoor and indoor scenes, respectively. The short exposure images were taken with an exposure time of 1/30, 1/25 or 1/10 s and the long exposure images were taken with an exposure time of 10 s.

To the best of our knowledge, the SID dataset is the first and only dataset available to develop data-driven digital image processing solutions under extreme low-light conditions. Thus, in this work, we trained and evaluated our proposed method on the SID dataset [2].

4.2   Implementation Details

Preprocessing. There are two subsets in SID dataset constructed using two different sensors, respectively. The raw images are packed into 4 channels for Sony images with a Bayer filter array, and into 9 channels for Fuji images with an X-Trans filter array. A camera-specific black level is subtracted from the packed images. The result is then normalized into [0,1]. The normalized signal is multiplied with an amplification factor to match the brightness of its corresponding long exposure image, which is employed as input to the network.

Training. We trained two separate networks for the two subsets. For fair comparison, the base U-Net adopted the same architecture in SID-Net. Each network takes a short-exposed image preprocessed as mentioned above and yields an output image. The joint loss function, i.e. Eq. 1, between the output and the corresponding long-exposed image, is used to guide the training process. γ in Eq. 1 is set to 0.84 following the settings in [30]. Adam is employed with an initial learning rate of 0.1 for 2,000 epochs. The learning rate is decayed by a factor of 0.1 and used to train the network for another 2,000 epochs. For the GIA module, f_1 is global pooling, f_2 is bilinear interpolation, and f_3 is concatenation in our experiments.

Data Augmentation. Following the settings in SID [2], we randomly crop a patch with random flipping and transpose as the input for training the network. Moreover, to help the GIA-Net to better capture the global information from inputs with different spatial resolutions, different from the practice in [2,26] using patches of the same size, we propose to cropped patches with different sizes for training the network. Specifically, for each iteration, we randomly crop a patch with a size of $(a \times b) \times (a \times b)$ as input, where $a = 32$ and $b \in [16, 32]$.

4.3   Quantitative Results

In this work, we compare our proposed approach with several state-of-the-art methods, including DnCNN [27], RID-Net [1], SID-Net [2], SGN [7], SE-UNet, and Zamir's method [26]. Note that, SE-UNet is constructed by inserting an squeeze-and-excitation (SE) module [11] into the bottleneck of the same U-Net we employed. The results for RID-Net [1], and DnCNN [27] are generated by retraining the models on SID dataset.

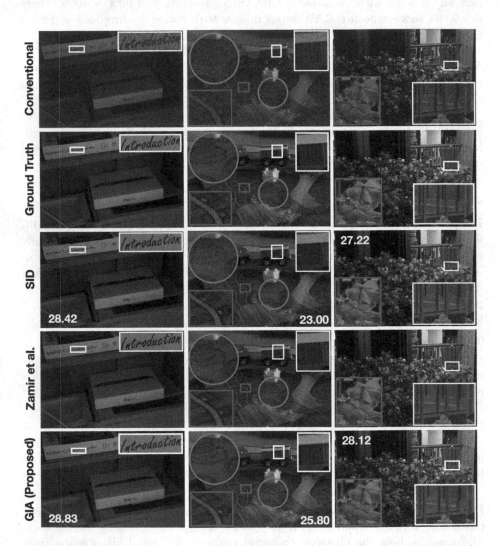

Fig. 5. Quantitative comparison with state-of-the-art methods. Rows 1–5 give the results generated by conventional pipeline, the ground truth, SID-Net [2], Zamir's approach [26] and the proposed GIA-Net. (Color figure online)

We evaluate our method with the widely used PSNR and SSIM [24] following [2]. In addition, two recently proposed learning-based metrics, i.e. PieAPP [22] and LPIPS [29], which are designed to measure the perceptual similarities between an image pair, are adopted to demonstrate the effectiveness of the proposed method. The quantitative results are obtained by taking the average of the metrics on all the testing images in Sony and Fuji subset in SID dataset, which are given in Table 1. Since the PieAPP and LPIPS values are not given in [2], we retrained the model using the code provided by the authors and reported the results in the table. Note that the numbers reported in the original paper are given in parenthesis. The SSIM values are omitted for Zamir's method since they are not provided in the original paper. For SGN [7], since only PSNR values are given in the original paper, we list them in the table for comparison.

On the Fuji subset, the proposed GIA-Net outperforms all the methods in comparison for all the metrics except the LPIPS compared with Zamir's method. The reason is because LPIPS and Zamir et al. both employed the same pretrained VGG network to calculate the perceptual loss. On the Sony dataset, our method outperforms the state-of-the-art methods significantly in terms of all the metrics employed including the LPIPS compared with Zamir's approach, which have demonstrated the effectiveness of the proposed GIA-Net for low-light imaging with exceptional perceptual quality. Note that, although the SE-module is operation in a similar way with GIA-module by applying global average pooling, it is not as effective as the GIA module in terms of integrating the global information into the network for low-light image enhancement.

4.4   Qualitative Results

Figure 5 gives the quantitative comparison with the state-of-the-art methods, where rows 1–5 provide the images generated by the conventional image pipeline, the ground truth, SID-Net, Zamir's method, and the proposed GIA-Net, respectively. Since the code or the result images were not released in [26], to perform qualitative comparison with the state-of-the-arts, we took the Fig. 5 in [26] and extended it by adding the ground truth images and the results produced by our proposed GIA-Net. The qualitative results measured by PSNR are shown on the images (the values are omitted for Zamir's method since they are not provided). Note that the zoomed-in areas are directly adopted from [26] except the region highlighted by the orange circle in the middle column, where GIA-Net achieves better performance compared with SID and comparable performance compared with Zamir's approach in terms of detail reconstruction in the areas highlighted by the white and green rectangles. More importantly, the proposed GIA-Net produces better color representation compared with the other two approaches. For example, the area highlighted by the orange circle in the second column is green, as shown in the groundtruth image. However, SID-Net and Zamir's method failed to restore the green color, while the proposed GIA-Net successfully captured the green color thanks to the integration of the global color information. In addition, in the third column, the flowers highlighted in the image generated by GIA-Net has the same color with those in the ground truth image, which has

further demonstrated the effectiveness of introducing global information into the
network for low-light imaging.

4.5   Ablation Study

Importance of Global Information
To validate the importance of extracting and exploiting the global information
for low-light imaging, we compare the performance of the proposed GIA-Net
with the following models: (1) the original SID-Net; (2) a network with all the
convolutional layers replaced by dilated convolutional layers with dilated rate
as 2, denoted as SID-dilated, which has larger receptive field size than SID-
Net while the local information is not well utilized; (3) a network constructed
by replacing all the convolutional layers with the SW block, denoted as SW-
Net, which utilizes both local information and wider contextual information as
receptive field size gradually increases; (4) a vanilla U-Net trained using ℓ_1 loss
with GIA module inserted into the bottleneck, denoted as GIA-ℓ_1. For SW-Net,
we set $C_l = C_g = C_{in}/2$ in SW block using a dilate rate of 2 as illustrated in
Fig. 2. Note that SID-dilated, SW-Net and GIA-ℓ_1 are proposed in this work.
The experimental results are reported in Table 2. The proposed GIA-ℓ_1 achieves
the best performance thanks to the utilization of global information extracted
by the integrated GIA module. More importantly, on Fuji subset, although SID-
dilated fails to outperform SID-Net in terms of PSNR and SSIM, it achieves
better performance measured by PieAPP and LPIPS, which illustrates that the
global information is crucial for generating images with good perceptual quality.

Table 2. Performance comparison using SID-Net [2], SID-dilated, SW-Net, and GIA-
ℓ_1.

	Sony				Fuji			
	PSNR	SSIM	PieAPP	LPIPS	PSNR	SSIM	PieAPP	LPIPS
SID-Net [2]	28.52	0.786	1.532	0.420	26.71	0.707	1.902	0.562
SID-dilated	28.62	0.780	1.583	0.417	26.61	0.695	1.759	**0.536**
SW-Net	28.89	0.787	1.508	0.417	27.05	0.708	1.872	0.548
GIA-ℓ_1	**29.45**	**0.790**	1.449	**0.410**	**27.48**	**0.711**	1.819	0.548

Figure 6 gives some qualitative results, where (a), (b), (c), (d) give results
produced by SID-Net, SID-dilated, SW-Net, and the GIA-Net with only ℓ_1 loss
and the PSNR values are reported on the images. Severe color artifacts can be
spotted on the image produced by SID-Net due to the lack of global color information. Although the perceptual quality is much better in the image generated
by SID-dilated, it becomes blurry because the dilated convolutions do not fully
use all the pixels in the local neighborhood. In the image yielded by SW-Net,
both the color and details are somehow well restored. However, the dilation rate

and the C_l, C_g require extensive experiments to tune to achieve optimal results. The image produced by the proposed GIA-Net gives good perceptual quality with fine details, demonstrating the effectiveness of the proposed GIA module to extract and integrate the global information into the network for low-light imaging.

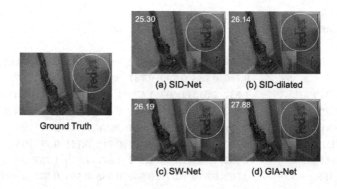

Fig. 6. A comparison of the results produced by different models.

Model Analysis. To better understand the proposed model, we conducted controlled experiments to evaluate how much each component contribute to the final performance. We compare the models with or without ℓ_1 loss, MS-SSIM, GIA, and data augmentation. Besides, to validate the performance does not come from the depth increase, i.e. two more convolutional layers are introduced in to the network by GIA module, we also conduct an experiment using a network with two convolutional layers added to the bottleneck of SID-Net. The results can be found in Table 3.

Depth increase does bring improvements to the final performance, e.g. 28.76 (model 2) v.s. 28.52 (model 1) measured in PSNR on Sony subset. However, the major performance gain is from the integration of the proposed GIA moduel as indicated by the comparison between model 2 and model 6, e.g. 28.76 (model 2) v.s. 29.45 (model 6) measured in PSNR on Sony subset.

Importance of GIA module is emphasized by the comparison between the models without GIA modules (i.e. model 1, 3, 4, 5) with their counterparts using GIA modules (i.e. model 6, 7, 8, 9). More importantly, without using GIA module in the network, all the other techniques, i.e. using MS-SSIM loss (model 3), data augmentation (model 4), and both (model 5), yield similar performance with the original SID-Net. In contrast, the models with GIA modules integrated can benefit from using MS-SSIM loss and data augmentation.

Computational cost introduced by the GIA module Table 4 gives the comparison of the number of parameters and FLOPs of the proposed GIA-Net,

Table 3. Performance comparison between models with different component choices on the SID datasets.

No.	SID-Net based models					GIA-Net based models			
	1	2	3	4	5	6	7	8	9
ℓ_1 loss	√	√	√	√	√	√	√	√	√
GIA module						√	√	√	√
MS-SSIM loss			√		√		√		√
Data augmentation				√	√			√	√
Additional 2 conv. layers		√							
Sony PSNR	28.52	28.76	28.62	28.57	28.73	29.45	29.62	29.65	**29.72**
SSIM	0.786	0.788	0.790	0.787	0.790	0.790	0.793	0.791	**0.795**
PieAPP	1.532	1.513	1.507	1.539	1.494	1.449	1.445	1.425	**1.425**
LPIPS	0.420	0.416	0.415	0.419	0.414	0.410	0.409	0.408	**0.404**
Fuji PSNR	26.71	26.70	26.69	26.64	26.76	27.48	27.74	28.06	**28.15**
SSIM	0.707	0.706	0.711	0.706	0.712	0.711	0.717	0.713	**0.722**
PieAPP	1.902	1.853	1.833	1.882	1.877	1.819	1.757	1.765	**1.739**
LPIPS	0.562	0.550	0.527	0.551	0.535	0.548	0.531	0.540	**0.519**

relative to the SID-Net [2] processing an image from Sony subset with a resolution of 4240 × 2832. The proposed GIA-Net achieves much better performance in terms of all the metrics employed than SID-Net (e.g. according to Table 1, 29.72 v.s. 28.52 measured in PSNR on Sony subset) with negligible extra computational cost (0.008× increase in FLOPs).

Table 4. Comparison of numbers of params and FLOPs between SID-Net [2] and GIA-Net processing an input image from Sony dataset with a resolution of 4240 × 2832. The numbers of parameters and FLOPs are relative to the SID-Net (7.76M and 1112.92B).

Model	Params	FLOPs
SID-Net	1×	1×
GIA-Net	1.07×	1.008×

5 Conclusion

Taking images with good perceptual quality is challenging due to low SNR under extremely low-light conditions. Most recently, deep U-Nets have show promising results on low-light imaging. However, vanilla U-Nets suffer from color distortion due to the lack of global information. In this paper, we propose a GIA module which can be inserted into a vanilla U-Net to extract and integrate global information into the network to improve the perceptual quality of the generated image for low-light imaging. The experimental results on a public dataset have demonstrated the effectiveness of the proposed approach. In the future, we plan to explore the possibilities of applying it in a multi-scale fashion to better extract the color information to further improve the performance for low-light imaging. Also, we would like to explore the possibilities to apply the proposed GIA module to other computer vision applications, such as image segmentation and image deblurring.

References

1. Anwar, S., Barnes, N.: Real image denoising with feature attention. In: Proceedings of International Conference on Computer Vision (ICCV), pp. 3155–3164 (2019)
2. Chen, C., Chen, Q., Xu, J., Koltun, V.: Learning to see in the dark. In: Proceedings of IEEE Conference on Computer Vision and Pattern Recognition (CVPR), pp. 3291–3300 (2018)
3. Chen, Y.S., Wang, Y.C., Kao, M.H., Chuang, Y.Y.: Deep photo enhancer: unpaired learning for image enhancement from photographs with GANs. In: Proceedings IEEE Conference on Computer Vision and Pattern Recognition (CVPR), pp. 6306–6314 (2018)
4. Dabov, K., Foi, A., Katkovnik, V., Egiazarian, K.: Image denoising by sparse 3-D transform-domain collaborative filtering. IEEE Trans. Image Process. $16(8)$, 2080–2095 (2007)
5. Dong, X., et al.: Fast efficient algorithm for enhancement of low lighting video. In: Proceedings of International Conference on Multimedia and Expo (ICME), pp. 1–6. IEEE (2011)
6. Gharbi, M., Chen, J., Barron, J.T., Hasinoff, S.W., Durand, F.: Deep bilateral learning for real-time image enhancement. ACM Trans. Graph. $36(4)$, 1–12 (2017)
7. Gu, S., Li, Y., Gool, L.V., Timofte, R.: Self-guided network for fast image denoising. In: Proceedings of IEEE Conference on Computer Vision and Pattern Recognition (CVPR), pp. 2511–2520 (2019)
8. Gu, S., Zhang, L., Zuo, W., Feng, X.: Weighted nuclear norm minimization with application to image denoising. In: Proceedings of IEEE Conference on Computer Vision and Pattern Recognition (CVPR), pp. 2862–2869 (2014)
9. Guo, X., Li, Y., Ling, H.: Lime: low-light image enhancement via illumination map estimation. IEEE Trans. Image Process. $26(2)$, 982–993 (2017)
10. Hasinoff, S.W., et al.: Burst photography for high dynamic range and low-light imaging on mobile cameras. ACM Trans. Graph. $35(6)$, 192 (2016)
11. Hu, J., Shen, L., Sun, G.: Squeeze-and-excitation networks. In: Proceedings of IEEE Conference on Computer Vision and Pattern Recognition (CVPR), pp. 7132–7141 (2018)
12. Jain, V., Seung, S.: Natural image denoising with convolutional networks. In: Proceedings of Advances in Neural Information Processing Systems (NIPS), pp. 769–776 (2009)
13. Johnson, J., Alahi, A., Fei-Fei, L.: Perceptual losses for real-time style transfer and super-resolution. In: Leibe, B., Matas, J., Sebe, N., Welling, M. (eds.) ECCV 2016. LNCS, vol. 9906, pp. 694–711. Springer, Cham (2016). https://doi.org/10.1007/978-3-319-46475-6_43

14. Kneubuehler, D., Gu, S., Gool, L.V., Timofte, R.: Flexible example-based image enhancement with task adaptive global feature self-guided network. arXiv preprint arXiv:2005.06654 (2020)
15. Liu, Z., Yuan, L., Tang, X., Uyttendaele, M., Sun, J.: Fast burst images denoising. ACM Trans. Graph. **33**(6), 232 (2014)
16. Loza, A., Bull, D.R., Hill, P.R., Achim, A.M.: Automatic contrast enhancement of low-light images based on local statistics of wavelet coefficients. Digit. Signal Proc. **23**(6), 1856–1866 (2013)
17. Mairal, J., Bach, F.R., Ponce, J., Sapiro, G., Zisserman, A.: Non-local sparse models for image restoration. In: Proceedings of International Conference on Computer Vision (ICCV), vol. 29, pp. 54–62. Citeseer (2009)
18. Malm, H., Oskarsson, M., Warrant, E., Clarberg, P., Hasselgren, J., Lejdfors, C.: Adaptive enhancement and noise reduction in very low light-level video. In: Proceedings of International Conference on Computer Vision (ICCV), pp. 1–8. IEEE (2007)
19. Mildenhall, B., Barron, J.T., Chen, J., Sharlet, D., Ng, R., Carroll, R.: Burst denoising with kernel prediction networks. In: Proceedings of IEEE Conference on Computer Vision and Pattern Recognition (CVPR), pp. 2502–2510 (2018)
20. Park, S., Yu, S., Moon, B., Ko, S., Paik, J.: Low-light image enhancement using variational optimization-based retinex model. IEEE Trans. Consum. Electron. **63**(2), 178–184 (2017)
21. Portilla, J., Strela, V., Wainwright, M.J., Simoncelli, E.P.: Image denoising using scale mixtures of gaussians in the wavelet domain. IEEE Trans. Image Process. **12**(11), 1338–1351 (2003)
22. Prashnani, E., Cai, H., Mostofi, Y., Sen, P.: Pieapp: perceptual image-error assessment through pairwise preference. In: Proceedings of IEEE Conference on Computer Vision and Pattern Recognition (CVPR), pp. 1808–1817 (2018)
23. Rudin, L.I., Osher, S., Fatemi, E.: Nonlinear total variation based noise removal algorithms. Physica D **60**(1–4), 259–268 (1992)
24. Wang, Z., Bovik, A.C., Sheikh, H.R., Simoncelli, E.P., et al.: Image quality assessment: from error visibility to structural similarity. IEEE Trans. Image Process. **13**(4), 600–612 (2004)
25. Wang, Z., Simoncelli, E.P., Bovik, A.C.: Multiscale structural similarity for image quality assessment. In: Asilomar Conference on Signals, Systems & Computers, vol. 2, pp. 1398–1402. IEEE (2003)
26. Zamir, S.W., Arora, A., Khan, S., Khan, F.S., Shao, L.: Learning digital camera pipeline for extreme low-light imaging. arXiv preprint arXiv:1904.05939 (2019)
27. Zhang, K., Zuo, W., Chen, Y., Meng, D., Zhang, L.: Beyond a gaussian denoiser: residual learning of deep CNN for image denoising. IEEE Trans. Image Process. **26**(7), 3142–3155 (2017)
28. Zhang, K., Zuo, W., Zhang, L.: FFDNet: toward a fast and flexible solution for CNN-based image denoising. IEEE Trans. Image Process. **27**(9), 4608–4622 (2018)
29. Zhang, R., Isola, P., Efros, A.A., Shechtman, E., Wang, O.: The unreasonable effectiveness of deep features as a perceptual metric. In: Proceedings of IEEE Conference on Computer Vision and Pattern Recognition (CVPR), pp. 586–595 (2018)
30. Zhao, H., Gallo, O., Frosio, I., Kautz, J.: Loss functions for image restoration with neural networks. IEEE Trans. Comput. Imaging **3**(1), 47–57 (2016)

Flexible Example-Based Image Enhancement with Task Adaptive Global Feature Self-guided Network

Dario Kneubuehler$^{(\boxtimes)}$, Shuhang Gu, Luc Van Gool, and Radu Timofte

Computer Vision Lab, ETH Zurich, Zurich, Switzerland
dario.kneubuehler@vision.ee.ethz.ch

Abstract. We propose the first practical multitask image enhancement network, that is able to learn one-to-many and many-to-one image mappings. We show that our model outperforms the current state of the art in learning a single enhancement mapping, while having significantly fewer parameters than its competitors. Furthermore, the model achieves even higher performance on learning multiple mappings simultaneously, by taking advantage of shared representations. Our network is based on the recently proposed SGN architecture, with modifications targeted at incorporating global features and style adaption. Finally, we present an unpaired learning method for multitask image enhancement, that is based on generative adversarial networks (GANs).

1 Introduction

Digital images are omnipresent in today's society, with a wide scope of applications ranging from posting snapshots taken with smartphones on social media, to high profile fashion shoots and photojournalism. Current image enhancement software provides tools to locally and globally adjust images to one's liking, yet the use of such tools requires a considerable amount of time and the results highly depend on the user's skills. Automating this work through the use of algorithms remains a challenging task to this day. In this paper, we study the problem of automatic image enhancement through deep neural networks (DNN). Image enhancement comprises a wide set of different image processing tasks ranging from image denoising, super resolution to illumination adjustment. We focus on the task of example-based image enhancement, which aims to enhance a group of low-quality images to the quality of another group of high quality images. Early image enhancement works [2,6,17] mainly focused on contrast enhancement and illumination estimation using algorithmic models and traditional machine learning methods. Recently, the success of deep neural networks (DNN) on other computer vision tasks triggered the study of DNN-based image

Electronic supplementary material The online version of this chapter (https://doi.org/10.1007/978-3-030-67070-2_21) contains supplementary material, which is available to authorized users.

A. Bartoli and A. Fusiello (Eds.): ECCV 2020 Workshops, LNCS 12537, pp. 343–358, 2020.
https://doi.org/10.1007/978-3-030-67070-2_21

enhancement approaches. Compared with traditional heuristic or prior based approaches, DNN methods that directly learn a mapping function from the low quality image to high quality image, have achieved promising enhancement performance. Despite their impressive performance, current DNN-based methods are limited by the following three issues.

Network Architecture. Compared with classical image restoration tasks such as image denoising and super-resolution, the image illumination enhancement tasks requires global adjustment of the input and thus a very large receptive field is inevitable. Although several network architectures have been proposed for this task, better architectures are necessary to achieve a better trade-off between performance and efficiency.

Limited Flexibility. The working scenarios of enhancement algorithms are very complex, which requires the enhancement network to be highly flexible. On the one hand, low quality images produced by different devices, or by the same device in different environmental conditions have distinct characteristics. The poor generalization of existing DNN-based algorithms requires us to train different networks for different types of degradation, which is highly impractical. On the other hand, image enhancement is a highly subjective task, for the same input image, different people might favor different enhancement results. Adapting to the preference of different customers is very important.

Training Data. Enhancement algorithms need to adjust images globally and locally. In order to learn a global illumination mapping a large number of training samples is required to provide image-level supervision. However, the acquisition of paired data for image enhancement is laborious and costly. In [3], Bychkovsky et al. provide a dataset with 5000 raw input images and corresponding professionally retouched versions, that is well suited for use with supervised machine learning methods. However, 5000 pairs of images are far from enough to train a good enhancement network. In [12], Ignatov et al. collected weakly paired data from different devices, e.g., cell phones and DSLR camera. However, the authors only provide roughly aligned patches (100×100px) which significantly limits the valid receptive field of an enhancement network in the training phase.

In this paper, we propose a novel network architecture to address all the issues above. To efficiently exploit large scale contextual information, we modify the recently proposed self-guided network [9] by adding multiple modification targeted at incorporating global features. Specifically, we follow the top-down strategy of SGN and incorporate large scale contextual information at an early stage to guide the following processing steps, by adding a global feature branch on top of it. Besides incorporating global information via the global feature branch, we constantly incorporate image scale information using instance normalization (IN) layers on all levels of the network. Concretely, for handling different enhancement tasks with a compact model, we switch the instance normalization layers with adaptive instance normalization Layers (AdaIN) and add a small auxiliary network that transforms the latent input. Using this scheme we train the network for different tasks and only allow the AdaIN layers to be task-specific. Another advantage of such a multi-task learning strategy lies in a data augmentation perspective. As the network is able to take advantage of shared feature representations and leverage training data from multiple tasks, our method achieves better results on both the many-to-one mapping and one-to-many mapping cases. In summary, our main contributions are:

- We propose a novel SGN [9] based deep neural network architecture that outperforms its competitors by a large margin on the task of supervised image to image mapping, while requiring considerably fewer parameters.
- We show that by using multitask learning to learn multiple mappings simultaneously, we can take advantage of shared representations which yields even higher performance compared to learning one-to-one mappings separately.
- For the supervised and unsupervised settings, we conduct experiments for both, one-to-many and many-to-one mappings. The experimental results validate the effectiveness of multi-task learning for image enhancement.

2   Related Work

Image enhancement is a classical computer vision problem. While initial research in the field was based on algorithms that rely on heuristic rules, such as histogram equalization and retinex-based methods, recent research has shifted to learning based methods. Specially, as a powerful tool for image to image mapping, deep neural networks (DNNs) have achieved great success in image enhancement. Previous works have investigated different aspects of DNN-based image enhancement. One category of studies aims to investigate better network for capture the mapping function between input and target image. Yan et al. [18] trained a multilayer feed forward neural network to capture the mapping function between two groups of images. Lore et al. [14] used an autoencoder based network to tackle low-light image enhancement. Gharbi et al. [7] presented a bilateral learning approach that is optimized for real time performance on smartphones. Chen et al. [4] augmented the U-Net approach [15] with a global branch to better capture the global information. Wang et al. [16] presented a supervised learning method for improving underexposed photos that relies on an intermediate illumination mapping. Another category of research attempts to push image enhancement toward real application scenarios. To improve the quality of cell phone images, Ignatov et al. [12] collected images with different devices and roughly aligned image patches for training enhancement network. However, as accurate image registration is a challenging problem, Ignatov et al. [12] only provide image patches for training, which greatly limited the capacity of network to leverage global information. To enhance images for real applications, unsupervised learning approaches have been proposed. Deng et al. [5] used adversarial learning for aesthetic-driven image enhancement with weak supervision. Chen et al. [4] proposed a deep photo enhancer which relies on a two-way generative adversarial network (GAN) architecture.

While some of the recently proposed models show impressive results for supervised and weakly supervised image enhancement, none of them is able to learn more than a single deterministic mapping function. However, users of enhancement software are known for having different aesthetic preferences, that cannot be satisfied with a single mapping function. This limitation is also non-ideal from the perspective of neural network training, since a lot more data would be available if the models were able to learn multiple tasks simultaneously. The next logical step is to introduce multi-task learning into image enhancement and provide the user with high level controls that can satisfy multiple stylistic preferences.

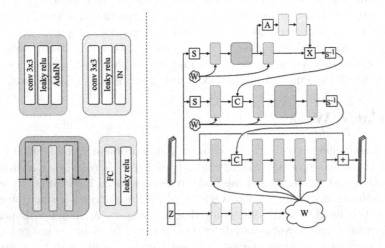

Fig. 1. Architecture of MT-GSGN network. The latent vector z is mapped to a intermediate latent space w, which is used as input to the adaptive instance normalization layers (AdaIn). For GSGN no mapping network is used and AdaIn layers are replaced with instance normalization (IN) layers. S stands for the shuffling operation, S^{-1} for the inverse shuffling operation, and C for concatenation. A denotes global average pooling. Residual blocks, convolutional blocks and fully connected blocks, have purple, green and orange color coding respectively. (Color figure online)

3   Proposed Method

In this section, we introduce our Global feature Self-Guided Network (GSGN) model and how it can be extend to the multi-tasks version, *i.e.* MT-GSGN. First, we briefly review the network architecture of the original SGN model. Then, we introduce modifications targeted at solving the illumination enhancement problem. Lastly, we present how the task-specific global feature branch can be utilized, and propose the flexible MT-GSGN method.

3.1   Brief Introduction to SGN [9]

Gu *et al.* [9] proposed the Self-Guided Network (SGN) to more efficiently incorporate large scale contextual information for image denoising. In order to have an overview of the image content from large receptive field, the SGN method adopts a top-down guidance strategy. Specifically, shuffling operations are adopted to generate multi-resolution inputs, and SGN firstly processes the top-branch and gradually propagates the features extracted at low spatial resolution to higher resolution sub-networks. With the effective self-guided mechanism, the SGN [9] has achieved state-of-the-art denoising performance.

3.2   Global Feature Self-guided Network (GSGN)

As SGN has been shown to be an effective network architecture for incorporating large scale contextual information, we adopt it to solve the image illumination enhancement task, for which a large receptive field is even more essential. Although the receptive field of SGN is much larger than the other denoising networks, it is still insufficient for the illumination enhancement task. Furthermore, SGN has a considerable number of parameters, training it with the limited number of samples in the enhancement datasets might lead to over-fitting during training or unused networks capacity. In order to adapt the network to the enhancement task, we introduce the Global feature Self-Guided Network (GSGN). The architecture of the proposed GSGN is shown in Fig. 1. GSGN differs from SGN in the following aspects.

Global Feature Incorporation. We incorporate global features by using global average pooling in the top most branch of GSGN, followed by two fully connected layers. These global features are then multiplied with the output feature maps on the same branch. In contrast to the global feature scheme used in [4], our approach works for arbitrary size input images.

Less Parameters. In order to reduce the number of parameters, we reduce the number of levels from 3 to 2 and reduce the number of channels in the higher level sub-networks by a factor of two. At the same time we increase the number of feature maps in the base level sub-network by a factor of two.

Constantly Incorporating Global Information. In spite of incorporating the global information in an early stage of the network, we employ instance normalization (IN) layers after the activation functions of convolutional layers. While instance normalization is mostly used as a means for stabilizing training, we use it to learn global features in all levels of the network. Each instance normalization layer has two parameters for each channel. These parameters operate on the whole feature map of a single image and therefore act as global features.

With the above modifications we obtain a relatively lightweight GSGN model with only 339k parameters. In Sect. 5.1, we provide an ablation study to validate our design choices.

3.3 Flexible Image Enhancement with Task Adaptive GSGN

To enable task adaptive learning, GSGN is augmented with an additional mapping network that consists of multiple fully connected layers with leaky relu activation functions, similar to the technique used in [13]. The number of fully connected layers was empirically set to 3. The mapping networks takes a latent vector z as input, which encodes the desired style to be learned, and maps it to a intermediate latent space w. This transformed latent vector is then used as the input to adaptive instance normalization [11] layers that are inserted after the convolution layers. Furthermore, an additional fully connected layer is used before each adaptive instance normalization layer to match the dimension of w to the dimension of the relevant feature map.

3.4 Unsupervised Flexible Enhancement with Task Adaptive GSGN

To show the suitability of our Task Adaptive GSGN for unsupervised learning, we use the popular CycleGAN architecture [20], and add an addition network that provides a conditional loss based on the task. A illustration of our unpaired training setup is shown in Fig. 2. In general, the setup can be described as a two player game where player one, called the generator G tries to conditionally produce fake samples X_t' given a prior sample X_s. Player two, called the critic D tries to evaluate how close the fake samples X_t' are to the real samples X_t. In our case X_s are image samples from the source distribution, while X_t are high quality samples from the target distribution and X_t' is the estimated enhanced version of the input image.

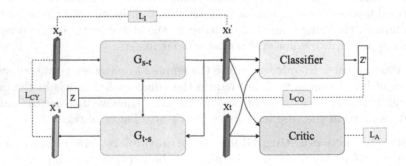

Fig. 2. Two way GAN training setup used for learning one-to-many mappings with unpaired data. Note that for simplicity only the cycle loss from X_s to X_s'' is displayed, while the second cycle from X_t to X_t'' is omitted

In addition to the generator $G_{s\to t}$ that maps samples from the source domain to the target domain, a CycleGAN architecture uses an additional generator $G_{t\to s}$ that maps samples from the target domain back to the source domain. Using these mappings, we define two cyclic mappings between the domains: 1)

$X_s \rightarrow X_t' \rightarrow X_s''$ and 2) $X_t \rightarrow X_s' \rightarrow X_t''$. Since both $G_{s \rightarrow t}$ and $G_{t \rightarrow s}$ are optimized using the same loss function, we only use the term G in reference for both networks.

Adversarial Loss. We use a version of the WGAN-GP loss [10], where a critic is used instead of a discriminator. In contrast to loss functions based on the original GAN formulation [8], the output of the network is not feed through a sigmoid function but used directly to approximate the wasserstein distance between two probability distributions. In order for this to work the network needs to be constrained to a 1-Lipschitz function. This is achieved by putting a penalty on the gradients of the critic during training. The gradient penalty λ is computed by evaluating the gradients of linearly interpolated samples $\hat{y}$ between X_t and X_t':

$$\lambda = max(0, ||\nabla \mathbb{D}(\hat{y})||_2 - 1). \tag{1}$$

While, the loss functions for the critic D amounts to:

$$L_D = (D(X_t) - D(X_t'))\lambda w, \tag{2}$$

where w is a hyper-parameter used to control the amplitude of the gradient penalty λ. The adversarial loss for the generator G can be computed as:

$$L_A = D(X_t'). \tag{3}$$

Cycle Loss. To ensure cycle consistency of the mappings between distributions, we impose a cycle loss between X_s and X_s'' as well as between X_t and X_t''. Defined as:

$$L_{CY} = MSE(X_s, X_s'') + MSE(X_t, X_t'') \tag{4}$$

Illumination Invariant Identity Loss. The use of identity losses between the source and target images is common in CycleGAN setups, to ensure that the content of the processed image is similar to the input image. However, since the change in illumination between input and output is large for the image enhancement task, traditional MSE and MAE pixel based losses result in high identity losses for target mapping. Because illumination enhancement results in a shift of the mean pixel values, a simple measure to mitigate this problem is to substract the mean over the pixel values of each image before computing the identity loss. Using the this definition, the identity loss can be stated as follows:

$$L_I = MSE\left(X_s - \mu(X_s), X_t' - \mu(X_t)\right) + MSE\left(X_t - \mu(X_t), X_s' - \mu(X_s')\right), \tag{5}$$

where μ is the arithmetic mean function, applied over all the pixel values of an image.

Conditional Loss. For the one-to-many case, we use an additional network C that acts as a classifier on the images produced and provides a loss based on reconstructing the latent vector z from the generated image. Therefore we define the conditional loss:

$$L_{CO} = -\left(z \log(C(X_t')) + (1 - z) \log(1 - C(X_t'))\right). \tag{6}$$

The network C is optimized using the same loss function but computed over X_t instead of X_t'.

Total Loss. The total loss for the Generator network G amounts to:

$$L_G = L_{CY}w_{CY} + L_I w_I + L_A w_A + L_{CO}w_{CO} \tag{7}$$

where w_{CY}, w_I, w_A, and w_{CO} are weights to balance the contribution of the different losses to the total generator loss.

4   Experimental Setup

4.1   Datasets

MIT5K [3]. The dataset is composed of 5,000 high resolution images that are retouched by five experts performing global and local adjustments. We follow the experimental setting of [4] and use 2,250 images and their retouched adaptations for training the supervised models. The test set contains 500 images. The remaining 2,250 images are reserved for the target domain in the unsupervised setting. For the multitask experiments data of all five experts is used, thus increasing the amount of train and test images to 11,250 and 2,500, respectively.

DPED [12]. DPED contains paired data of scenes captures with three smartphone cameras, *i.e.*, iPhone 3GS, BlackBerry Passport and Sony Xperia Z, and a professional quality DSLR, Cannon 70D. In total the dataset contains 22K full resolution photos. To get paired samples suited for supervised training, the authors generated aligned patches of 100×100 pixels. There are 139K, 160K and 162K training patches for BlackBerry, iPhone and Sony smartphones respectively. Correspondingly, there are 2.4K, 4.4K and 2.5K test patches.

Flickr Multi-style. To test our approach on a dataset in the wild, we created a small multi class dataset. There are three style classes. *1) Normal*, which consists of a subset of 600 images from the MIT5K dataset. *2) Sunset*, which consists of 600 images with the tag sunset that are collected from Flickr and selected according to Flickr's interestness score. *3) HDR*, which is a subset of 594 of the HDR-Flickr dataset from [4] that are also collected using the Flickr API. Some visual examples of the constructed dataset can be found in Fig. 3.

| Normal | HDR | Sunset |

Fig. 3. Visual examples of the images in different subset of the constructed Flickr dataset.

4.2   Performance Measures

In our experiments we use the standard Peak Signal to Noise Ratio (PSNR) and Structural Similarity Index (SSIM) to measure the fidelity of the enhanced images towards the ground truth/target reference images. Complementary we use LPIPS [19], a learned perceptual metric meant to approximate the human perceptual similarity judgements.

4.3   Implementation Details

We use the TensorFlow framework for all experiments. For the supervised experiments on the MIT5K dataset [3], we follow the setup used in [4]. This includes using the exact train and test split, in order to get comparable results. The size of the input layer is fixed at 512×512 pixels during training. Images are resized for the longer edge to equal 512 pixels prior to training. To match the input of the network the images are zero padded. In all supervised experiments we use the following cost function, which maximizes the PSNR: $L_G = -log_{10}(MSE(I_s, I_t))$. The models are trained for 100k iterations with batch size 4 and learning rate 1e-4 on MIT5K dataset, while on DPED dataset the models are trained for 150k iterations with batch size 50 and learning rate 1e–4.

5   Results on Supervised Image Enhancement

In this section, we evaluate our method for supervised image enhancement. For more visual results we refer to the supplementary material.

5.1   Single Task Enhancement

To justify our design choices as well as to compare with other state-of-the-art approaches, we firstly conduct experiments on the supervised single task enhancement setting. We follow the experimental setting of [4] and train different models to approximate the retouched results by expert C in the MIT5K dataset [3].

Concretely, we compare the proposed GSGN network with the original 2 level SGN [9], denoted by SGN2; and the SGN2 with reduced number filter channel numbers, denoted by GSGN w/o global feat. & instance normalization; SGN2 with reduced number filter channel numbers and global feature branch, denoted by GSGN w/o instance normalization; and our final GSGN model. In addition to our ablation study, we also compare GSGN with three recently proposed architectures that were designed for this task. The comparison methods include DPED [12], DPE [4] and UPEDIE [16]. DPED [12] uses a fully convolutional ResNet for image enhancement. DPE [4] used U-Net [15] as a backbone and augmented it with global features. UPEDIE [16] adopts an alternative approach by learning an illumination map from an encoder network. Table 1 shows the average PSNR and SSIM of the different approaches, evaluated on the 500 test

Table 1. Comparison between state-of-the-art and our GSGN with different configurations on MIT5K dataset (Expert C). We refer the reader to the latest **corrected** version of the UPEDIE paper [16].

Method	PSNR	SSIM	Para.
DPED [12]	21.76	0.871	401k
DPE [4]	23.80	0.900	5019k
UPEDIE [16]	23.04	0.893	–
SGN2	20.98	0.863	769k
GSGN w/o global feat. & IN	21.19	0.865	325k
GSGN w/o IN	23.74	0.900	338k
GSGN (Ours)	**24.16**	**0.905**	339k

images of the MIT5K dataset. Figure 4 shows visual results of the proposed GSGN network. For the results reported in [4] we were not able to reproduce their high PSNR and SSIM, to be fair we still use the original numbers they claim in the paper. The results show, that our network not only outperforms its competitors by at least 0.36 dB, but also uses considerably less parameters to achieve these results. The results in Table 1 validate the effectiveness of the proposed GSGN architecture. GSGN achieved higher PSNR and SSIM while using fewer parameters than current state-of-the-art methods.

5.2 Multi-task Enhancement: One-to-Many

The fact that the Adobe MIT-5K dataset contains five retouched versions of each input image, makes it ideally suited to be used as a base for multitask learning in a supervised one-to-many setting. In order to demonstrate the feasibility of our task adaptive GSGN model, we train models to capture all five input to output mappings of the MIT5K dataset simultaneously. We consider the following three experimental settings. Results are found in Table 2.

Single Task Models. We train our GSGN model on the task of learning all input to output mappings separately for all five experts A to E in a traditional one-to-one setting. The averaged PSNR over all five experiments is 23.97 dB. It is worth noting that there is quite a large difference of up to 3.82 dB PSNR between the different experts. This gives interesting insights into the dataset. On one side this could mean that certain experts were more consistent when applying the mapping. On the other hand, this could also indicate that some experts used more complex adjustments than others, which made it harder for the network to learn these mappings.

Single Model for All Tasks. The GSGN model is trained on data of all five task simultaneously in a traditional one-to-many setting but without a constant latent embedding so it can not explicitly discriminate between the different tasks. This

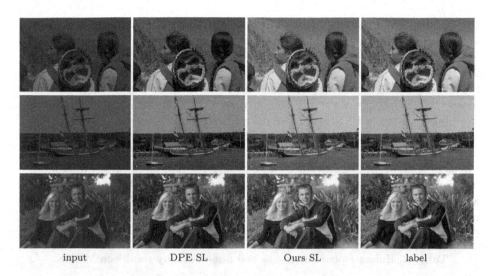

input   DPE SL   Ours SL   label

Fig. 4. Visual comparison of learned supervised mappings of our GSGN network against the DPE [4] method on the test set of the MIT5K dataset.

input   learned A   learned B   learned C   learned D   learned E

expert A   expert B   expert C   expert D   expert E

Fig. 5. Comparison of learned supervised mappings by our MT-GSGN model and corresponding expert labels.

effectively increases the amount of training data by a factor of five. However, the network is only able to learn a average mapping and cannot take the specific style of each expert into account. While performance gains come from being trained on larger amounts of data, the lack of being able to differentiate between the different experts causes the performance to decrease, this results in a lower average PSNR of 23.30 dB.

Multi-tasking with a Task Adaptive Model. We use our task adaptive GSGN model to learn all five tasks simultaneously, in a one-to-many setting. This combines the advantages of the previous two settings. The resulting model reaches the highest average PSNR of 24.32 dB and also outperforms the other settings in terms of SSIM, MSSIM and LPIPS [19]. This not only shows that the model is able to efficiently use the labels to learn multiple mappings simultaneously, but also that by taking advantage of the larger amounts of data available in a multitask setting, the model is able to outperform models that were trained for a single task. Figure 5 shows visual results of the MT-GSGN model and the corresponding expert labels.

Table 2. Enhancement one-to-one and **one-to-many** results on MIT5K.

Tasks	Methods								
	Task-specific models			Single model for all tasks			Multi-tasking (MT-GSGN)		
	PSNR	SSIM	LPIPS	PSNR	SSIM	LPIPS	PSNR	SSIM	LPIPS
Supervised enhancement									
Raw → A	22.30	0.876	0.0743	21.28	0.862	0.080	22.51	0.879	0.072
Raw → B	26.12	0.949	0.0443	25.48	0.939	0.049	26.53	0.952	0.043
Raw → C	24.16	0.905	0.0610	23.71	0.896	0.069	24.44	0.904	0.063
Raw → D	23.02	0.903	0.0621	23.14	0.905	0.063	23.27	0.906	0.060
Raw → E	24.23	0.924	0.0571	22.92	0.911	0.067	24.86	0.928	0.055
Avg.	23.97	0.911	0.0598	23.30	0.903	0.066	**24.32**	**0.914**	**0.059**
Unsupervised enhancement									
Raw → A	18.95	0.771	0.212	16.63	0.705	0.289	19.99	0.824	0.123
Raw → B	20.49	0.840	0.204	18.23	0.809	0.255	22.30	0.908	0.097
Raw → C	19.16	0.779	0.228	16.76	0.707	0.304	20.81	0.839	0.120
Raw → D	17.92	0.767	0.246	16.46	0.743	0.287	20.36	0.866	0.111
Raw → E	17.75	0.758	0.271	16.03	0.730	0.311	19.89	0.859	0.124
Avg.	18.85	0.783	0.232	16.82	0.739	0.289	**20.67**	**0.859**	**0.115**

5.3   Multi-task Enhancement: Many-to-One

We further validate our model on a many-to-one multi-task mapping on DPED [12] dataset and train models to enhance the images from the iPhone, Sony and Blackberry cameras to the DSLR camera domain. We follow the same three step approach described in the previous section, and compare the average performance of the single task model against the multi-task model. It is worth noting that in this case a weighted average is needed because the number of images in the training sets for each phone is different.

Table 3. Enhancement one-to-one and **many-to-one** results on DPED.

Method	Supervised			Unsupervised		
	PSNR	SSIM	LPIPS	PSNR	SSIM	LPIPS
Iphone	22.94	0.819	0.142	19.47	0.648	0.264
Sony	24.46	0.877	0.103	23.21	0.821	0.142
Blackberry	23.18	0.842	0.108	19.44	0.640	0.225
Weighted avg.	23.41	**0.841**	**0.122**	20.48	0.640	0.225
Single Model (all)	23.35	0.836	0.129	20.22	0.685	0.238
Multi-tasking	**23.69**	0.839	0.128	**20.69**	**0.749**	**0.209**

Table 3 shows the evaluation results for this experiment. In this case the multi-task model outperforms its single task counterparts, in terms of PSNR, but not in terms of SSIM and LPIPS. This is likely due to the fact that the model is trained to optimize PSNR but training patches coming from different sources can never be perfectly aligned due to nonlinear distortions coming from different lenses and sensors, as well as perspective distortions. The authors of [12] note that there could be shift of up to 5 pixels between source and target images. This makes the problem formulation ill posed for supervised learning and suggests that this dataset is better suited for weakly supervised learning methods.

6   Results on Unsupervised Image Enhancement

Implementation Details. As described in Sect. 3, we follow a two cycle GAN approach inspired by [1], where an additional conditional loss is used to provide task specific gradients during training. A discriminator architecture similar to the one described in [4] is used. We train the critic 30 times more than the generator for the MIT5K and Flickr Multi-style datasets and 40 times more often for the DPED dataset.

Multi-task Enhancement: One-to-Many. We evaluate our model on MIT5K dataset, using our weakly supervised GAN architecture. Analog to the supervised experiments, we perform the same three experimental settings. Table 2 shows the validation results. Our multi-task learning approach with task adaptive GSGN again outperforms, our GSGN network by taking advantage of shared feature representations.

Multi-task Enhancement: Many-to-One. We validate the proposed algorithm on the many-to-one task on the DPED dataset. In contrast to the one-to-many setting, this setting does not require a conditional loss on the generated images, which simplifies the training. Table 3 shows the evaluation results.

(a)   (b)   (c)   (d)   (e)   (f)

Fig. 6. Visual examples of enhanced images from MT-GSGN trained on the Flickr dataset. (a) Input, (b) Normal, (c) Interpolation between HDR and Sunset, (d) HDR, (e) Sunset, (f) Interpolation between Normal and HDR. We refer to Sect. 6 for details.

Flickr Multi-style Dataset. Finally, we evaluate our MT-GSGN model on a dataset on the wild. For this purpose we train it on our Flickr dataset on the task of learning a one-to-many mapping with three styles to learn, normal, sunset and hdr. Figure 6 shows visual examples of the learned mappings. Note that the model is also able to interpolate between styles, even though it was not explicitly trained for this task. Figure 7 shows a visual comparison of the learned mappings against the state of the art. For more visual results we refer to the supplementary material.

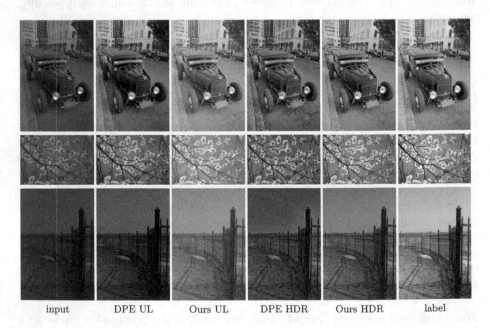

input   DPE UL   Ours UL   DPE HDR   Ours HDR   label

Fig. 7. Visual comparison of learned unsupervised mappings by our Task Adaptive GSGN model trained on the small Flickr Multi-style dataset, against the DPE [4] method. Note that our model learns both mappings in a single training while DPE requires separate networks and multiple trainings.

7   Conclusion

In this paper, we have investigated and proposed a flexible example-based image enhancement method, that uses a task adaptive global feature self-guided network. First, we proposed a novel network architecture capable to outperform existing methods on the task of supervised image to image mapping while requiring much fewer parameters. Second, we demonstrated that by using multi-task learning we benefit from shared representation and achieve higher performance compared to learning one to one mappings separately. Third, for both supervised and unsupervised settings our experimental results validate the effectiveness of our multi-task learning for image enhancement in one-to-many and many-to-one settings. To the best of our knowledge this is the first successful work in applying multi task learning to the challenging image enhancement problem.

Acknowledgements. This work was partly supported by ETH Zurich General Fund (OK), by a Huawei project and by Amazon AWS and Nvidia grants.

References

1. Almahairi, A., Rajeswar, S., Sordoni, A., Bachman, P., Courville, A.: Augmented cyclegan: learning many-to-many mappings from unpaired data. arXiv preprint arXiv:1802.10151 (2018)
2. Aubry, M., Paris, S., Hasinoff, S.W., Kautz, J., Durand, F.: Fast local Laplacian filters: theory and applications. ACM Trans. Graph. (TOG) **33**(5), 167 (2014)
3. Bychkovsky, V., Paris, S., Chan, E., Durand, F.: Learning photographic global tonal adjustment with a database of input/output image pairs. In: CVPR 2011, pp. 97–104. IEEE (2011)
4. Chen, Y.S., Wang, Y.C., Kao, M.H., Chuang, Y.Y.: Deep photo enhancer: Unpaired learning for image enhancement from photographs with gans. In: Proceedings of the IEEE Conference on Computer Vision and Pattern Recognition, pp. 6306–6314 (2018)
5. Deng, Y., Loy, C.C., Tang, X.: Aesthetic-driven image enhancement by adversarial learning. In: Proceedings of the 26th ACM International Conference on Multimedia, pp. 870–878 (2018)
6. Farbman, Z., Fattal, R., Lischinski, D., Szeliski, R.: Edge-preserving decompositions for multi-scale tone and detail manipulation. ACM Trans. Graph. (TOG) **27**(3), 1–10 (2008)
7. Gharbi, M., Chen, J., Barron, J.T., Hasinoff, S.W., Durand, F.: Deep bilateral learning for real-time image enhancement. ACM Trans. Graph. (TOG) **36**(4), 118 (2017)
8. Goodfellow, I., et al.: Generative adversarial nets. In: Advances in Neural Information Processing Systems, pp. 2672–2680 (2014)
9. Gu, S., Li, Y., Gool, L.V., Timofte, R.: Self-guided network for fast image denoising. In: Proceedings of the IEEE International Conference on Computer Vision, pp. 2511–2520 (2019)
10. Gulrajani, I., Ahmed, F., Arjovsky, M., Dumoulin, V., Courville, A.C.: Improved training of wasserstein gans. In: Advances in Neural Information Processing Systems, pp. 5767–5777 (2017)

11. Huang, X., Belongie, S.: Arbitrary style transfer in real-time with adaptive instance normalization. In: Proceedings of the IEEE International Conference on Computer Vision, pp. 1501–1510 (2017)
12. Ignatov, A., Kobyshev, N., Timofte, R., Vanhoey, K., Van Gool, L.: Dslr-quality photos on mobile devices with deep convolutional networks. In: Proceedings of the IEEE International Conference on Computer Vision, pp. 3277–3285 (2017)
13. Karras, T., Laine, S., Aila, T.: A style-based generator architecture for generative adversarial networks. In: Proceedings of the IEEE Conference on Computer Vision and Pattern Recognition, pp. 4401–4410 (2019)
14. Lore, K.G., Akintayo, A., Sarkar, S.: Llnet: a deep autoencoder approach to natural low-light image enhancement. Pattern Recogn. **61**, 650–662 (2017)
15. Ronneberger, O., Fischer, P., Brox, T.: U-Net: convolutional networks for biomedical image segmentation. In: Navab, N., Hornegger, J., Wells, W.M., Frangi, A.F. (eds.) MICCAI 2015. LNCS, vol. 9351, pp. 234–241. Springer, Cham (2015). https://doi.org/10.1007/978-3-319-24574-4_28
16. Wang, R., Zhang, Q., Fu, C.W., Shen, X., Zheng, W.S., Jia, J.: Underexposed photo enhancement using deep illumination estimation. In: Proceedings of the IEEE Conference on Computer Vision and Pattern Recognition, pp. 6849–6857 (2019)
17. Wang, S., Zheng, J., Hu, H.M., Li, B.: Naturalness preserved enhancement algorithm for non-uniform illumination images. IEEE Trans. Image Process. **22**(9), 3538–3548 (2013)
18. Yan, Z., Zhang, H., Wang, B., Paris, S., Yu, Y.: Automatic photo adjustment using deep neural networks. ACM Trans. Graph. (TOG) **35**(2), 1–15 (2016)
19. Zhang, R., Isola, P., Efros, A.A., Shechtman, E., Wang, O.: The unreasonable effectiveness of deep features as a perceptual metric. In: Proceedings of the IEEE Conference on Computer Vision and Pattern Recognition, pp. 586–595 (2018)
20. Zhu, J.Y., Park, T., Isola, P., Efros, A.A.: Unpaired image-to-image translation using cycle-consistent adversarial networks. In: Proceedings of the IEEE International Conference on Computer Vision, pp. 2223–2232 (2017)

A Benchmark for Burst Color Constancy

Yanlin Qian[1,2,3(✉)], Jani Käpylä[1], Joni-Kristian Kämäräinen[1],
Samu Koskinen[2], and Jiri Matas[3]

[1] Computing Sciences, Tampere University, Tampere, Finland
yanlin.qian@tuni.fi
[2] Huawei, Shenzhen, China
[3] Center for Machine Perception, Czech Technical University in Prague,
Prague, Czechia

Abstract. Burst Color Constancy (CC) is a recently proposed approach
that challenges the conventional single-frame color constancy. The conventional approach is to use a single frame - shot frame - to estimate
the scene illumination color. In burst CC, multiple frames from the view
finder sequence are used to estimate the color of the shot frame. However,
there are no realistic large-scale color constancy datasets with sequence
input for method evaluation. In this work, a new such CC benchmark
is introduced. The benchmark comprises of (1) 600 real-world sequences
recorded with a high-resolution mobile phone camera, (2) a fixed train-
test split which ensures consistent evaluation, and (3) a baseline method
which achieves high accuracy in the new benchmark and the dataset
used in previous works. Results for more than 20 well-known color constancy methods including the recent state-of-the-arts are reported in our
experiments.

1 Introduction

The human visual system perceives colors of objects independently of the incident illumination. This ability to perceive the colors in varying conditions as
the scene is viewed under a white light is known as color constancy (CC) [1].
To achieve this property, computational color constancy algorithms are used in
Image Signal Processor (ISP) pipelines of digital cameras to provide an estimate
of the color of the illumination of the captured scene.

The existing color constancy algorithms can be mainly classified into two
categories: 1) static methods and 2) learning-based methods. Gijsenji *et al.* [2]
defined a third class, gamut-based methods, in their survey. Since the gamut
methods often require training examples to define a target gamut [3] we include
them to the learning-based category. *Static methods* do not rely on training

---

Y. Qian and J. Käpylä—Equal contribution.

Electronic supplementary material The online version of this chapter (https://
doi.org/10.1007/978-3-030-67070-2_22) contains supplementary material, which is
available to authorized users.

A. Bartoli and A. Fusiello (Eds.): ECCV 2020 Workshops, LNCS 12537, pp. 359–375, 2020.
https://doi.org/10.1007/978-3-030-67070-2_22

data, but are based on assumed statistical or physical properties of the image formation. For instance, Gray-world [4] relates the averaged pixel values to the global illumination and Gray pixel [5] and its extension [6] identify achromatic pixels using the properties of the lambertian model or dichromatic reflection model to reveal illumination, respectively. *Learning-based methods* learn to map input image features to the illumination estimate. Learning-based methods can operate in the chroma space (Corrected moments [1] and Convolutional CC [7]) or in the spatial space full of rich semantic information (FC4 [8]). Static methods are easier to implement on commodity ISP hardware, but the recent advantages in the mobile CPUs and GPUs have made it intriguing to investigate whether the better performing learning-based methods can replace static methods.

The above computational color constancy methods estimate the illumination color from a single frame - referred to as the "shot frame" in our work. However, recently Qian *et al.* [9] proposed an alternative and extensible approach where **multiple frames preceding the shot frame are also used in the global illumination estimation on the shot frame** - an approach that can be termed as *burst color constancy* or multi-frame color constancy. They proposed a recurrent network architecture based on AlexNet semantic features and recursive network module for sequential processing. The experiments were conducted on the SFU Gray Ball dataset [10] that is captured with a video camera where a calibration target is visible in every frame. Qian *et al.* demonstrated superior accuracy for the temporal multi-frame setting vs. the conventional single-frame setting, but it is unclear to which extend the SFU Gray Ball video clips are related to real use cases of customer photography. SFU Gray Ball consists of 15 sequences, the sequences are captured over long time duration and physically distant locations, and the frame resolution is low (240×320). Moreover, the ground truth visible in every frame can convey unintentional cues to deep net methods even if masked.

Our work makes the following contributions:

- We release a **burst color constancy (BCC) benchmark**. The dataset consists of 600 sequences of varying length (from 3 to 17 frames). The dataset covers indoor and outdoor scenes with varying weather and daylight conditions, and is till now the largest realistic image-sequence dataset.
- We make a **benchmark analysis** with over 20 statistical and learning-based single and the existing temporal methods, using a fixed train-test setting.
- We propose a strong **burst color constancy baseline**, termed as BCC-Net, that achieves state-of-the-art results on the new dataset and the previously used SFU Gray Ball, with fast inference speed and light memory footprint.

BCC-benchmark and BCC-Net will be made publicly available as an open-source project, to facilitate fair comparison and development of novel color constancy ideas. We also provide wrapper functionality for experimenting with other datasets such as the NUS dataset [11] and include implementations of the recent methods such as FC4 [8] and C4 [9].

2   Related Work

Conventional color constancy (CC) refers to the algorithms that estimate the illuminant color from an image. Gijsenji *et al.* [2] provide a comprehensive survey of the contemporary methods and divide them under three categories: i) static, ii) gamut-based and iii) learning-based methods. The static methods do not require training data. Well-known static methods and commonly used baselines are Gray-world [4] and General Gray-world (inc. multiple variants) [12]. More recent static methods are Gray Pixel [5] and Grayness Index [6]. The static methods are inferior in the single dataset setting where training and test images are drawn from the same dataset, but outperform learning-based methods in the cross-dataset evaluations [6]. In Gijsenji's taxonomy the gamut-based methods operate in the color spaces and thus omit the spatial domain information. A strong baseline is Gamut Mapping [3]. In our work, we assign the gamut-based methods to the learning-based methods if they use training data such as [3]. More recent methods operating in the colour spaces are Corrected moments [1], Convolutional CC [7] and its Fast Fourier implementation (FFCC) [13]. The most recent learning-based methods are based on deep architectures that use pre-trained backbone networks to extract rich semantic features: FC4 [8] and C4 [14]. We include the mentioned methods to our experiments since they report top-performing results for various single-frame datasets. There also exists a list of works exploring spatial illumination, however it is out of scope and not discussed in this paper.

Burst (multi-frame) color constancy has received much less attention than the single-frame CC. Attention has been paid on several special cases. For example, Yang *et al.* [15] extract illuminant color from two distinct frames of a scene that contains specular surfaces (highlights). Prinet *et al.* [16] propose a probabilistic and more robust version of the Yang *et al.* method. Wang *et al.* [17] compute color constancy for video input. In their approach existing CC methods can be used and illuminant is estimated from multiple frames of a same scene where scene boundaries are automatically detected. Yoo *et al.* [18] propose a color constancy algorithm for AC bulb illuminated (indoor) scenes using a high-speed camera and Qian *et al.* [19] for a pair of images with and without flash. However, the seminal work of temporal color constancy is Qian *et al.* [9] who proposed a burst CC algorithm using semantic AlexNet features and a Long Short Term Memory (LSTM) recurrent neural network to process sequential input frames. Qian *et al.* method and the dataset used in their experiments are included to our experiments.

Public datasets are available for the evaluation of single-frame color constancy methods, for example, Gehler-Shi Color Checker [20,21], SFU Gray Ball [10] and NUS [11].[1] SFU Gray Ball is collected with a video camera and is therefore suitable for multi-frame color constancy experiments [9]. However, the SFU

---

[1] See http://colorconstancy.com for download links of datasets and methods.

Gray Ball has very low resolution (240 × 320), contains only 15 sequences, and its capture procedure does not correspond to the behavior of the consumer still photography. Yoo *et al.* [18] have published the dataset of 80 sequences used in their experiments, but their sequences were specifically designed for AC bulb illumination experiments and high-speed capturing. Prinet *et al.* [16] released a small dataset of 11 sequences used in their video color constancy experiments. In summary, the existing multi-frame color constancy datasets are **small and ill-suited for generic consumer still photography color constancy studies**. Therefore we introduce a new dataset of 600 sequences captured with a rooted mobile phone that makes the multi-frame capture invisible to the mobile phone user and therefore better resembles the typical behavior of consumer still photography.

3   Dataset

The proposed BCC dataset was collected by several volunteering students who captured the shots in their daily life. They were not instructed but guided to take photographs whenever they wish. Students were given a Huawei P30 Pro mobile phone which is one of the high-end models and was rooted and re-programmed to automatically start storing raw sensor images when the camera application was launched. The sensor images were linked to the shot frames using the date and time tags of the files.

3.1   Image Capture

The rooted phone saves the raw data as unprocessed 16-bit 3648 × 2736 Bayer pattern images. Mobile phone camera ISP and memory I/O limit the viewfinder capture to 3–5 fps, but this way we were able to integrate the viewfinder frame capture to the normal photo mode without users noticing it.

To resolve the illuminant color ground truth the shot frame scenes need to be captured with a color calibration target installed into the scene. For example, in the Gehler-Shi dataset there is a Macbeth color checker calibration target visible in the images. In the SFU Gray Ball dataset a gray ball calibration target is mounted in front of the video camera to capture per-frame annotation and is therefore visible in all captured frames. In our dataset we wanted to annotate only the shot frame and avoid using visible targets since they may unintentionally convey information to the learning-based methods even if they are masked in the training and testing sets. We need to mention that, differing from SFU Gray Ball providing per-frame annotation, in the proposed dataset only the shot frames is annotated, assuming real illumination variation is unknown depending on agnostic use scenario.

Similar to SFU Gray Ball we used a gray surface calibration target, Spyder-Cube (Fig. 1), which is put into the shot scene instantly after the shot.[2] The

---

[2] The target is always at the image center so that color shading has minimal effect on the ground truth.

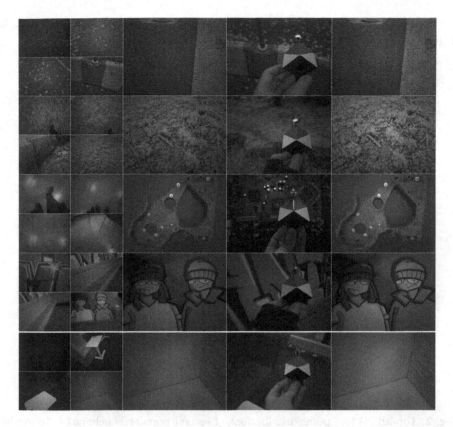

Fig. 1. Examples of 5 frame sequences in the collected BCC dataset. From each sequence there are (left-to-right): 4 viewfinder frames, the shot frame, the calibration target frame and the color corrected shot frame. Note that sensor specific color correction is not applied, only color constancy. Gamma correction (2.2) is applied for better visualization.

students were instructed to take one shot of the calibration target in the location which was the main target or location in their photograph. The captured sequences contain 3–17 frames depending on the viewfinder duration (Fig. 1). The SpyderCube object contains two neutral 18% gray surfaces, from which the one that better reflects the casting illumination was annotated and used to compute the ground truth illumination color. The ground truth was verified by manually checking all sequences using the ground truth color correction. In total, 600 sequences were recorded and verified during different times of day, in various indoor and outdoor locations and in various weathers during the time period of October 2019 to January 2020.

In the dataset project page we also provide linear demosaiced images in the PNG format with the pixel values normalized to $[0, 255]$, with a black level of zero and with no saturated pixels. The format correspond to that of Gehler-Shi dataset which is a popular evaluation set in color constancy literature. The black level of the specific camera sensor and device is 256 and the saturation level is at 4095. The final RGB images are of the resolution 1824 × 1368.

3.2   Dataset Statistics and Performance Metrics

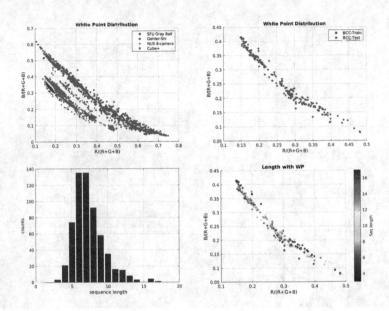

Fig. 2. Top-left: White point distributions of several popular benchmarks. Top-right: White point distribution of our new dataset. Bottom-left: Histogram of sequence lengths of BCC. Bottom-right: Correlation between sequence chromaticity (white points) and the sequence length.

We profile the distributions of ground truth chromaticity values of several mainstream color constancy benchmarks (Gehler-Shi, NUS 8-camera, Cube+ and SFU Gray Ball datasets) in the top-left inset of Fig. 2, while we show that of the new Burst Color Constancy dataset (BCC benchmark) in the top-right position. Our chromacity distributions are similar to the popular Gehler-Shi, NUS and Cube+ datasets.[3] The small spatial shifts between the datasets are mainly due to different sensor spectrum sensibility functions used in the datasets.

In the bottom left of Fig. 2 we draw the histogram of sequence lengths in the BCC benchmark. The mean length is 7.3, median 7.0 and mode is 8.5. The bottom-right inset of Fig. 2 shows the correlation coefficient between the sequence lengths and the ground truth vectors, which indicates that there is no clear correlation between the sequence length and the global illumination.

---

[3] Note that SFU Gray Ball distribution is larger than others since the data was captured with a high-end Sony VX-2000 video camera that has separate sensors for each color channel and therefore less spectral cross-talk and better channel separation.

The main performance measure in our work is the *angular error* which is used in the prior works [9,13]. The angular error ε is computed from the estimated tri-stimulus (RGB) illumination vector $\hat{c}$ and the ground truth vector c_{gt} as

$$\varepsilon_{\hat{c},c_{gt}} = \arccos\left(\frac{\hat{c} \cdot c_{gt}}{\| \hat{c} \| \| c_{gt} \|}\right) , \tag{1}$$

where $\cdot$ denotes the inner product between the two vectors and $\|\|$ is the Euclidean norm. As overall performance measures we report *mean, median* and *trimean*. Tukey's trimean is a measure of a probability distribution's location defined as a weighted average of the distribution's median and its two quartiles. In addition, we report the top quartile (25%), the worst quartile (worst 25%) and the 95% percentile numbers.

4 Methods

4.1 Extensions of Single-Frame Methods

The conventional single-frame methods are designed to estimate the illuminant color from a single image - the shot frame. However, it is straightforward to extend the single-frame methods to the multi-frame setting. A single-frame method is executed on every frame and the per frame estimates are combined using a suitable statistical tool such as the *moving average*. In the following we introduce temporal extensions of the SoTA statistical and learning-based methods.

Temporal Grayness Index (T.GI): Qian *et al.* [6] proposed a substantial extension of the Gray Pixel method of Yang *et al.* [5]. They introduced *Grayness Index (GI)* that provides a spatial grayness map of the input image and the pixels of the highest gray index are selected for the illumination estimation. In the temporal extension of GI, T.GI, all frames over the time are combined to form a multi-frame GI map from which the best pixels are selected.

Temporal Fast Fourier Color Constancy (T.FFCC): We use the official temporal smoothing implementation released by the author of FFCC [13]. It is based on a simplified Kalman filter with a simplified transition model, no control model and varying observation noise. The current estimate (modeled as an isotropic Gaussian) is smoothed by multiplying with last observed estimate. For more details, we refer to the temporal smoothing section in [13].

4.2 Burst Color Constancy Network

In the following, we propose a strong baseline for burst color constancy. The baseline is a deep network architecture (BCC-Net) inspired by the RCC-Net in [9], but with the following significant improvements: 1) a more powerful backbone network for the semantic feature extraction, 2) 2D LSTM that provides

Input: $I_1,,,I_{len}$ Input: $\hat{I}_1,,,\hat{I}_{len}$

Backbone-3-512   Backbone-3-512
2DLSTM-512-128 2DLSTM-512-128
concatenation
MaxPool2d
Conv-256-64
Sigmoid
Conv-64-3
Sigmoid

Output: **y**

Fig. 3. The architecture of BCC-Net. "LayerName-x-y" denotes a 2D layer of y filters of the size $x \times x$ where the layer is either a standard convolution layer, a backbone network (e.g. SqueezeNet) or a 2D LSTM. "len" denotes the length of the input sequence where the shot frame is I_{len}. From the shot frame, a pseudo sequence of the same length is generated using the procedure in [9]. **y** is the illumination color vector after the last sigmoid layer.

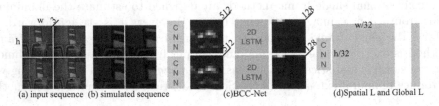

(a) input sequence (b) simulated sequence   (c)BCC-Net   (d)Spatial L and Global L

Fig. 4. An overview of the BCC-Net processing pipeline: (a) input frame sequence; (b) a pseudo zoom-out sequence generated from the last (shot) frame; (c) from the both sequences the backbone network extracts 512-channel semantic features that are recursively processed by the 2D LSTMs that output 128-channel features; (d) LSTM outputs are concatenated channel-wise and processed by a 1×1 convolution filter that produces a spatial illumination map. The global illumination vector **y** is calculated by average pooling.

more effective spatial recurrent information and 3) support for variable length sequences. The overall architecture is described in Fig. 3. BCC-Net adopts the two CNN+LSTM branch structure from RCC-Net. The first branch, the temporal branch, processes the image sequence, and the second branch, the shot frame branch, processes a pseudo zoom-out sequence in the shot frame. In BCC-Net the both branches are based on a novel 2D LSTM that produces spatio-temporal information which are merged into a single RGB vector at the end of the processing pipeline.

The backbone feature extraction network of RCC-Net (VGG-Net or AlexNet) is replaced with SqueezeNet [22] in BCC-Net. In a recent architecture for computational color constancy, FC4 [8], the SqueezeNet [22] was found superior and this was verified by our experiments (see Sect. 5.3). Following [8], we keep all layers up to the last convolution layer of SqueezeNet which outputs a 512-channel 2D feature map. Similar to [8], considering different signal dynamics of raw images and ImageNet images, we perform a gamma correction on raw images before passing it to SqueezeNet.

The second improvement is to adopt a 2D LSTM to temporally process sequences and learn a 2D spatial-temporal illumination feature map. We refer to the ordinary LSTM used by RCC-Net as "1DLSTM" due to the fact that its memory cells and the hidden states are encoded as 1D vectors. Although several 1DLSTMs can be stacked to learn more complex sequence-to-sequence mapping, the nature of 1DLSTM hinders its representative power for spatial information. 2DLSTM, introduced in [23], extends 1DLSTM to 2D space by using convolutional structures in both input-to-state and state-to-state transitions. Combining these changes, we have an end-to-end deep network which predicts spatial illumination. To get the global estimate vector, averaging (or more advanced manipulation, *e.g.* confidence weighted averaging in [8]) is applied.

BCC-Net provides native support to varying-length input. This is implemented by the dynamic computational graph feature supported in PyTorch. In contrast, RCC-Net supports only a pre-defined and fixed length sequences (3 or 5 frames in the original paper). With Nvidia GTX 1080ti the processing speed of BCC-Net is 6 ms per frame (only the network operations).

For better understanding of the network parameters we present the brief equations implemented in the BCC-Net architecture. For simplicity, the equations are given only for one branch, but the both branches share the similar stages. Given an input sequence $\{I_1, \ldots, I_{len}\}$ and the SqueezeNet backbone F_s BCC-Net proceeds as

Initialize the hidden state H_0 and the memory cell C_0 of 2D-LSTM

$$
\begin{aligned}
&\textit{for t in range(1,len)}: \\
&\quad \mathcal{X}_t = F_s(I_t) \\
&\quad i_t = \sigma(W_{xi} * \mathcal{X}_t + W_{hi} * \mathcal{H}_{t-1} + W_{ci} \circ \mathcal{C}_{t-1} + b_i) \\
&\quad f_t = \sigma(W_{xf} * \mathcal{X}_t + W_{hf} * \mathcal{H}_{t-1} + W_{cf} \circ \mathcal{C}_{t-1} + b_f) \qquad (2) \\
&\quad \mathcal{C}_t = f_t \circ \mathcal{C}_{t-1} + i_t \circ \tanh(W_{xc} * \mathcal{X}_t + W_{hc} * \mathcal{H}_{t-1} + b_c) \\
&\quad o_t = \sigma(W_{xo} * \mathcal{X}_t + W_{ho} * \mathcal{H}_{t-1} + W_{co} \circ \mathcal{C}_t + b_o) \\
&\quad \mathcal{H}_t = o_t \circ \tanh(\mathcal{C}_t) \\
&L = F_r(\mathcal{H}_t)
\end{aligned}
$$

where i_t, f_t, o_t are 3D tensors and refer to the input, forget, and output gates of 2D-LSTM. W_{mn} denotes the conv kernel of Gate n for Data m, where $n \in \{i, f, o\}$ and $m \in \{x, h, c\}$. "$*$" denotes convolution and "$\circ$" Hadamard product. 2D-LSTM has two parameters: the convolution kernel size K (a larger value corresponds to faster illumination variations) and the output channel size H of the convolution filter (corresponds to hidden channels of 1D-LSTM). Ablation study of the both parameters is provided in Sect. 5. Figure 4 visualizes the workings of the BCC-Net pipeline.

Table 1. Method comparison with the BCC-benchmark. Performance metrics are based on the angular error (Sect. 3.2). The best results are bolded and the second best underlined.

Method	Mean	Med.	Tri.	B25%	W25%	95% Quant.
Single-frame static						
White-Patch [25]	11.20	10.42	10.87	1.87	21.48	26.20
Gray-World [4]	6.45	4.74	5.19	1.19	14.74	22.78
Shades-of-Grey (p = 4) [26]	5.50	3.20	3.70	0.85	13.92	21.86
General Grey-World (p = 1 ,σ = 9) [12]	6.44	4.76	5.24	1.18	14.75	22.83
1st-order Grey-Edge (p = 1, σ = 9) [12]	5.46	4.09	4.25	1.01	12.84	21.06
2nd-order Grey-Edge (p = 1, σ = 9) [12]	5.10	3.62	3.85	1.00	12.00	20.48
PCA (Dark+Bright) [11]	5.45	3.00	3.68	0.96	13.78	22.93
Grayness Index (GI) [6]	4.99	2.68	3.10	0.71	13.22	24.12
Temporal extensions						
T.GI	4.73	2.96	3.39	0.82	11.38	17.42
Single-frame learning-based						
Pixel-based Gamut (σ = 4) [3]	6.90	5.53	6.20	1.18	14.72	19.19
Edge-based Gamut (σ = 3) [3]	8.69	7.58	8.12	2.00	17.16	20.54
Intersection-based Gamut (σ = 4) [3]	8.46	7.94	7.85	2.03	16.60	20.80
Natural Images Statistics [27]	5.63	6.89	5.88	1.41	14.61	22.20
LSRS [28]	6.61	4.92	5.52	1.67	13.90	21.37
Exemplar-based Colour Constancy [29]	5.24	3.88	4.21	1.38	11.58	19.82
color-by-correlation [30]	4.94	2.69	3.21	0.61	13.19	15.93
Corrected-Moments [1]	4.70	3.96	4.10	1.12	9.66	11.83
Chakrabarti *et al.* 2015 [31] Empirical	4.26	2.60	2.82	0.51	11.07	16.43
Regression (SVR) [32]	4.00	3.09	3.45	1.36	7.81	11.07
Bayesian [20]	4.25	2.86	3.16	0.93	9.97	16.27
Random Forest [33]	3.76	2.66	2.94	0.74	8.54	13.14
AlexNet-FC^4 [8]	3.10	2.12	2.35	0.85	6.78	8.21
SqueezeNet-FC^4 [8]	2.84	2.10	2.23	0.74	6.39	7.83
C4 (3 stage) [14]	2.37	1.60	1.76	0.57	5.58	<u>6.85</u>
FFCC(model Q) [13]	<u>2.33</u>	<u>1.37</u>	<u>1.60</u>	<u>0.49</u>	5.84	10.97
Temporal extensions						
T.FFCC	3.35	1.70	1.99	0.51	9.06	17.41
Temporal						
Prinet *et al.* [16]	7.51	6.94	6.97	1.63	14.96	20.70
RCC-Net [9]	2.74	2.23	2.39	0.75	<u>5.51</u>	8.21
Our (BCC-Net)	**1.99**	**1.21**	**1.46**	**0.30**	**4.84**	**6.34**

Training: In all experiments we use the following settings. The optimizer is *RMSprop* [24] with the learning rate $3e^{-5}$ and the batch size 1. The network was trained for 2,000 epochs. For data augmentation, images were randomly rotated from $-30°$ to $+30°$ and randomly cropped to the size $[0.8, 1.0]$ of the shorter size. Each patch was horizontally flipped with the probability 0.5. The SqueezeNet backbone was initialized with the weights pretrained on ImageNet.

5   Experiments

We run a large number of well-known methods on the new BCC Benchmark and report their accuracy in Sect. 5.1. In Sect. 5.2 we verify good performance of the new baseline method (BCC-Net) with the previously used SFU Gray Ball dataset. In Sect. 5.3 we provide ablation study of the main components and parameters of BCC-Net.

5.1   Method Comparison on BCC-benchmark

The results for various single-frame static and learning-based methods (see the related work section), their temporal extensions (Sect. 4.1), the current temporal state-of-the-art (RCC-Net) [9] and our temporal baseline (Sect. 4.2) are shown in Table 1. The results demonstrate that the recent deep learning based methods (FC^4 and C4) and the convolutional CC (FFCC) are clearly superior to the conventional static and learning-based methods. These methods improve the performance over the whole error distribution, i.e. both the easy and difficult test samples. On our dataset the previous temporal state-of-the-art, RCC-Net [9], is slightly inferior to the best single-frame methods C4 and FFCC.

The temporal extension of GI [6], T.GI, improves its results. On the contrary, T.FFCC, referred to as "temporal smoothing" in [13], is inferior to its single-frame version. The Kalman filter extension of FFCC provides smoother change of the illuminant estimates over the frames, but the accuracy is worse than the non-smoothed estimates. We also test Prinet et al. [16] and it achieves 7.51 mean error due to its assumption that the illumination remains constant over time.

The proposed BCC-Net (Model G in Table 3) obtains the best performance on all error measures and improves performance on both easy and difficult cases. As compared to the previous state-of-the-art, RCC-Net, the performance improvement is over 35% in the mean error and and 43% in the median error. Considering the fact that end-users are more sensitive to large estimation errors [11] and $\leq 3.0°$ is generally considered as the sufficient accuracy, then W25% error of the BCC-Net (4.84) is closest to the practical use among all tested methods.

In Fig. 5 are examples of color-corrected images with various methods. The first two examples demonstrate easy cases from outdoors where all methods perform comparably well. The third and fourth examples represent typical view finder sequences toward a target which itself does not provide visually-rich clue for inferring the illumination color. In these sequences the two temporal methods, RCC-Net and BCC-Net, provide the best results since they effectively exploit cues from the view finder frames. The last example is a difficult case where the shot frame is a closeup of a tinted fabric material which can be of any plausible color. For the fifth sequence only the proposed BCC-Net provides an accurate estimate.

5.2   Method Comparison on SFU Gray Ball

To validate the findings in the previous experiment with the new BCC-benchmark, we replicated the experiments in Qian et al. [9], using their metrics (the mean, median, 95% percentile and maximum errors) and the SFU Gray Ball dataset. The results are collected to Table 2 (cf. Table 1 in [9]).

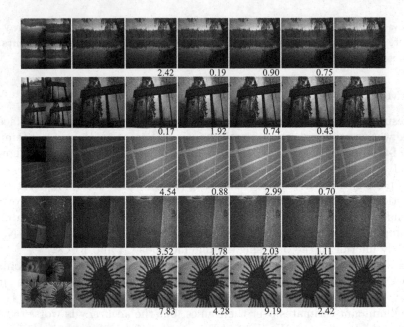

Fig. 5. Color corrected BCC examples and their angular errors (left-to-right): 1) four view finder frames; 2) the shot frame; 3) FC^4 [8]; 4) RCC-Net [9]; 5) FFCC [13]; 6) the proposed BCC-Net; 7) ground truth correction.

On the temporal version of the SFU Gray Ball dataset, the proposed BCC-Net again outperforms the RCC-Net [9], with a clear margin. The difference of these two methods is particularly evident on the hardest cases as BCC-Net obtains more than 40% lower error on the both 95% percentile and the maximum error metrics.

5.3   Ablation Study

Results with different components and parameter settings of BCC-Net are given in Table 3 and briefly discussed below.

Does LSTM help? The 1-branch BCC-Net (Model B in Table 3) without the LSTM module becomes equivalent to SqueezeNet-FC^4 in Table 1. However, with the LSTM module, for example the mean error is 11% lower than SqueezeNet-FC^4 which can be explained only by the temporal information carried in the LSTM memory cell. Additionally, Fig. 6 shows the t-SNE visualization [36] of how LSTM representation is more discriminative than that of SqueezeNet backbone in our BCC-Net. t-SNE is used to visualize high-dimensional feature data. For each of the four selected samples shown in the right-hand-side of Fig. 6, SqueezeNet backbone and 2D-LSTM output deep representations. The representations are of the dimensions of (h,w,512) and (h,w,128), respectively, where

Table 2. Method comparison with the SFU Gray Ball dataset (non-linear). The numbers for other methods are copied from the original papers and [9].

Method	Mean	Med.	W5%	Max
Single-frame static				
Gray-World [4]	7.9	7.0	–	48.1
General Grey-World (p = 1 (0), σ = 9) [12]	6.1	5.3	–	41.2
1st-order Grey-Edge (p = 1, σ = 9) [12]	5.9	4.7	–	41.2
Gray Pixel [5]	6.2	4.6	20.8	33.3
Shades-of-Gray [26]	6.1	5.2	–	41.2
Single-frame learning-based				
Pixel-based Gamut (σ = 5) [3]	7.1	5.8	–	41.9
Edge-based Gamut (σ = 3) [3]	6.8	5.8	–	40.3
Intersection-based Gamut (σ = 9) [3]	6.9	5.8	–	41.9
Inverse-Intensity Chromaticity Space [34]	6.6	5.6	–	76.2
Random Forest [33]	6.1	4.8	13.1	30.6
LSRS [28]	6.0	5.1	–	–
Natural Images Statistics [27]	5.2	3.9	–	44.5
Exemplar-based Colour Constancy [29]	4.4	3.4	–	45.6
ColorCat [35]	4.2	3.2	–	43.7
Temporal				
Prinet *et al.* [16]	5.4	4.6	–	–
Wang *et al.* [17]	5.4	4.1	–	26.8
RCC-Net [9]	<u>4.0</u>	<u>2.9</u>	<u>12.2</u>	<u>25.2</u>
Our (BCC-Net)	**2.8**	**2.3**	**7.1**	**13.9**

where h is the height, w width and 512 (or 128) the number of the feature channels. Contrast to the SqueezeNet backbone, LSTM exploits spatio-temporal information over multiple frames and provides features which better represent the different illuminations.

Backbone network: The Model A in Table 3 is the baseline as this configuration corresponds to RCC-Net in [9]. The effect of using SqueezeNet instead of AlexNet backbone is evident between the models A and C. The results with SqueezeNet are superior to the results with AlexNet and the memory footprint of SqueezeNet is substantially smaller making it more practical for mobile devices. Intriguingly, a single-branch BCC-Net without the pseudo sequence branch (Model B) also performs better than the RCC-Net baseline (Model A) and thus verifies superior performance of SqueezeNet for color constancy. By comparing Model B and Model C it is clear that the two branch design provides better performance than a single branch by a clear margin (the mean error is reduced by 12.7%).

Table 3. Ablation study of BCC-Net with various different configurations. The default values for the number of LSTM channels is H = 128 and for the convolutional kernel size K = 5.

	BCC Configuration	Mean	Med.	Tri.	B25%	W25%	95%	Mem. (MB)
A	2branch,AlexNet,1D-LSTM	2.74	2.23	2.39	0.75	5.51	8.21	20.4
B	1branch,SqueezeNet,1D-LSTM	2.52	1.77	2.04	0.52	5.65	6.58	3.3
C	2branch,SqueezeNet,1D-LSTM	2.20	1.55	1.65	0.43	5.05	6.18	6.6
D	2branch,SqueezeNet,2D-LSTM,len1	3.27	3.46	3.32	2.07	4.44	4.80	68.8
E	2branch,SqueezeNet,2D-LSTM,len5	2.50	1.78	1.99	0.53	5.65	6.94	68.8
F	2branch,SqueezeNet,2D-LSTM(H = 64)	2.17	1.59	1.68	0.40	5.00	6.72	33.3
G	2branch,SqueezeNet,2D-LSTM,(H = 128)	1.99	1.21	1.46	0.30	4.84	6.34	68.8
H	2branch,SqueezeNet,2D-LSTM,(H = 512)	2.06	1.09	1.40	0.30	5.19	7.65	476.1
I	2branch,SqueezeNet,2D-LSTM(K = 1)	2.01	1.42	1.58	0.34	4.65	5.48	11.0
J	2branch,SqueezeNet,2D-LSTM(K = 7)	2.08	1.43	1.60	0.35	4.83	5.83	131.0

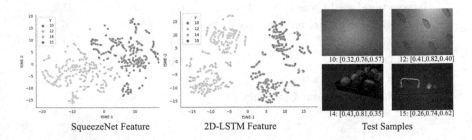

SqueezeNet Feature   2D-LSTM Feature   Test Samples

Fig. 6. t-SNE visualizations of SqueezeNet and 2D-LSTM feature maps in the BCC-Net architecture. Colors represents different illuminations in the shot frames of the sequences #10, #12, #14 and #15 (on the right). Dots represent feature vectors (512 for SqueezeNet and 128 for 2D-LSTM) at different spatial locations of the shot frames. (Color figure online)

1D vs. 2D LSTM: Model G is the main model reported in Table 1. The same configuration but with 1D LSTMs is Model C. By comparing the performances of C and G it is obvious that 2D LSTMs provide better performance and achieve state-of-the-art in the BCC and SFU Gray Ball benchmarks. BCC-Net baseline (Model G) is a fully 2D convolutional architecture that is the best found architecture for illuminant estimation in temporal color constancy.

Dimensionality of LSTM Hidden Channels: Three different sizes of the LSTM hidden channels, $H = \{64, 128, 512\}$, where tested (Models F, G and H, respectively). For H = 64 (Model F) the LSTM underfits and for H = 512 the network starts to overfit thus making H = 128 a good trade-off between training error and model generalization.

Kernel Size of 2D LSTM: The kernel size defines the amount of spatial correlations retained by the 2D LSTM. Kernel size K = 1 means that the neighbor pixels do not affect to the LSTM inference. Different kernel sizes were tested (Models G, I an J) and the best results were achieved with K = 5.

Varying-Length Input: One significant difference to the previous state-of-the-art (RCC-Net) [9] is that BCC-Net allows an arbitrary number of input frames before the shot frame. We experimented on two fixed lengths, 1 (only the shot frame) and 5, and the arbitrary length (Models D, E and G, respectively). The single-frame results are the worst, five frames is the second best, and arbitrary length achieves the best performance and is the most convenient for the end-user cases where the length of a view finder sequence is unknown.

Memory Footprint: From the perspective of deploying the deep net into a GPU/NPU-supported consumer mobile platform, we profiled the memory footprints of all BCC-Net variants in Table 3. The model C, combining SqueezeNet and 1D-LSTM, obtains a good balance between accuracy and memory print (6.6 MB). The best-performing variant G occupies memory of 68.8 MB, due to the larger dimensionality of hidden LSTM channels and the 2D LSTM structure.

6 Conclusions

Our work introduces BCC-benchmark, by far, the largest burst color constancy dataset of high resolution images. More than 20 popular methods were evaluated on the dataset including the recent state-of-the-arts. As a new baseline method, we proposed BCC-Net which is an end-to-end learnable deep and recurrent neural network architecture. BCC-Net achieves state-of-the-art results on our BCC-benchmark and SFU Gray Ball used in the previous works on video CC. In doing so we present the technique how to combine SqueezeNet and 2D-LSTM to capture spatial-temporal variations in a video. We present multiple variants of BCC-Net including ones with small memory consumption and therefore suitable for mobile devices.

References

1. Finlayson, G.D.: Corrected-moment illuminant estimation. In: ICCV, pp. 1904–1911 (2013)
2. Gijsenij, A., Gevers, T., Van De Weijer, J.: Computational color constancy: survey and experiments. TIP **20**(9), 2475–2489 (2011)
3. Gijsenij, A., Gevers, T., Van De Weijer, J.: Generalized gamut mapping using image derivative structures for color constancy. IJCV **86**(2–3), 127–139 (2010). https://doi.org/10.1007/s11263-008-0171-3
4. Buchsbaum, G.: A spatial processor model for object colour perception. J. Franklin Inst. **310**(1), 1–26 (1980)
5. Yang, K.F., Gao, S.B., Li, Y.J.: Efficient illuminant estimation for color constancy using grey pixels. In: CVPR (2015)
6. Qian, Y., Kamarainen, J.K., Nikkanen, J., Matas, J.: On finding gray pixels. In: The IEEE Conference on Computer Vision and Pattern Recognition (CVPR) (2019)
7. Barron, J.T.: Convolutional color constancy. In: ICCV (2015)
8. Hu, Y., Wang, B., Lin, S.: FC4: fully convolutional color constancy with confidence-weighted pooling. In: CVPR (2017)

9. Qian, Y., Chen, K., Kämäräinen, J., Nikkanen, J., Matas, J.: Recurrent color constancy. In: ICCV (2017)
10. Ciurea, F., Funt, B.: A large image database for color constancy research. In: Color Imaging Conference (CIC) (2003)
11. Cheng, D., Prasad, D.K., Brown, M.S.: Illuminant estimation for color constancy: why spatial-domain methods work and the role of the color distribution. JOSA A 31(5), 1049–1058 (2014)
12. Van De Weijer, J., Schmid, C., Verbeek, J.: Using high-level visual information for color constancy. In: ICCV (2007)
13. Barron, J.T., Tsai, Y.T.: Fast fourier color constancy. In: CVPR (2017)
14. Yu, H., Chen, K., Wang, K., Qian, Y., Zhang, Z., Jia, K.: Cascading convolutional color constancy. In: AAAI Conference on Artificial Intelligence (2020)
15. Yang, Q., Wang, S., Ahuja, N., Yang, R.: A uniform framework for estimating illumination chromaticity, correspondence, and specular reflection. TIP 20(1), 53–63 (2011)
16. Prinet, V., Lischinski, D., Werman, M.: Illuminant chromaticity from image sequences. In: ICCV (2013)
17. Wang, N., Funt, B., Lang, C., Xu, D.: Video-based illumination estimation. In: Schettini, R., Tominaga, S., Trémeau, A. (eds.) CCIW 2011. LNCS, vol. 6626, pp. 188–198. Springer, Heidelberg (2011). https://doi.org/10.1007/978-3-642-20404-3_15
18. Yoo, J.S., Kim, J.O.: Dichromatic model based temporal color constancy for AC light sources. In: Proceedings of the IEEE Conference on Computer Vision and Pattern Recognition, pp. 12329–12338 (2019)
19. Qian, Y., Yan, S., Kamarainen, J.K., Matas, J.: Flash lightens gray pixels. In: ICIP (2019)
20. Gehler, P.V., Rother, C., Blake, A., Minka, T., Sharp, T.: Bayesian color constancy revisited. In: CVPR (2008)
21. Shi, L., Funt, B.: Re-processed version of the gehler color constancy dataset of 568 images (2010). Accessed from http://www.cs.sfu.ca/~colour/data/
22. Iandola, F.N., Han, S., Moskewicz, M.W., Ashraf, K., Dally, W.J., Keutzer, K.: Squeezenet: alexnet-level accuracy with 50x fewer parameters and < 0.5 MB model size. arXiv preprint arXiv:1602.07360 (2016)
23. Xingjian, S., Chen, Z., Wang, H., Yeung, D.Y., Wong, W.K., Woo, W.C.: Convolutional LSTM network: a machine learning approach for precipitation nowcasting. In: Advances in Neural Information Processing Systems, pp. 802–810 (2015)
24. Tieleman, T., Hinton, G.E.: Lecture 6.5-rmsprop: divide the gradient by a running average of its recent magnitude. In: Coursera Lecture slides (2012). https://www.coursera.org/learn/neural-networks
25. Land, E.H., McCann, J.J.: Lightness and retinex theory. Josa 61(1), 1–11 (1971)
26. Finlayson, G.D., Trezzi, E.: Shades of gray and colour constancy. In: Color Imaging Conference (CIC) (2004)
27. Gijsenij, A., Gevers, T.: Color constancy using natural image statistics and scene semantics. TPAMI 33(4), 687–698 (2011)
28. Gao, S., Han, W., Yang, K., Li, C., Li, Y.: Efficient color constancy with local surface reflectance statistics. In: Fleet, D., Pajdla, T., Schiele, B., Tuytelaars, T. (eds.) ECCV 2014. LNCS, vol. 8690, pp. 158–173. Springer, Cham (2014). https://doi.org/10.1007/978-3-319-10605-2_11
29. Joze, H.R.V., Drew, M.S.: Exemplar-based color constancy and multiple illumination. TPAMI 36(5), 860–873 (2014)

30. Finlayson, G.D., Hordley, S.D., Hubel, P.M.: Color by correlation: a simple, unifying framework for color constancy. TPAMI **23**(11), 1209–1221 (2001)
31. Chakrabarti, A.: Color constancy by learning to predict chromaticity from luminance. In: NIPS (2015)
32. Funt, B., Xiong, W.: Estimating illumination chromaticity via support vector regression. In: Color Imaging Conference (CIC) (2004)
33. Cheng, D., Price, B., Cohen, S., Brown, M.S.: Effective learning-based illuminant estimation using simple features. In: CVPR (2015)
34. Tan, R.T., Ikeuchi, K., Nishino, K.: Color constancy through inverse-intensity chromaticity space. In: Ikeuchi, K., Miyazaki, D. (eds.) Digitally Archiving Cultural Objects, pp. 323–351. Springer, Boston (2008). https://doi.org/10.1007/978-0-387-75807-16
35. Banić, N., Lončarić, S.: Color cat: Remembering colors for illumination estimation. IEEE Signal Process. Lett. **22**(6), 651–655 (2014)
36. Maaten, L.V.D., Hinton, G.: Visualizing data using t-SNE. J. Mach. Learn. Res. **9**, 2579–2605 (2008)

Noise-Aware Merging of High Dynamic Range Image Stacks Without Camera Calibration

Param Hanji[✉], Fangcheng Zhong, and Rafał K. Mantiuk

Department of Computer Science and Technology, University of Cambridge,
Cambridge, UK
{pmh64,fz261,rkm38}@cam.ac.uk

Abstract. A near-optimal reconstruction of the radiance of a High
Dynamic Range scene from an exposure stack can be obtained by modeling the camera noise distribution. The latent radiance is then estimated using Maximum Likelihood Estimation. But this requires a well-
calibrated noise model of the camera, which is difficult to obtain in practice. We show that an unbiased estimation of comparable variance can be
obtained with a simpler Poisson noise estimator, which does not require
the knowledge of camera-specific noise parameters. We demonstrate this
empirically for four different cameras, ranging from a smartphone camera
to a full-frame mirrorless camera. Our experimental results are consistent
for simulated as well as real images, and across different camera settings.

Keywords: High dynamic range reconstruction · Exposure stacks ·
Camera noise · Computational photography

1 Introduction

The dynamic range of a scene may far exceed the range of light intensities that
a standard digital sensor can capture. The conventional way of capturing all the
information for such a High Dynamic Range (HDR) scene is with a stack of
images taken with different exposure times. These are later combined in post-
processing as part of the digital pipeline [2,9,10,12,19,24]. The probabilistic
photon registration and electronic processing in the camera will result in some
variation in the values recorded in each pixel, which manifests as noise in images.
Any method attempting to accurately estimate the scene radiance from multiple images strives to increase the dynamic range while simultaneously reducing
such noise. In this paper, we provide a comprehensive analysis of how noise in
images affects the performance of several scene radiance estimators [8,10,12].
This work is restricted to static and well-aligned images and we do not consider
the problems of pixel alignment and deghosting [14,25].

Electronic supplementary material The online version of this chapter (https://
doi.org/10.1007/978-3-030-67070-2_23) contains supplementary material, which is
available to authorized users.

ⓒ Springer Nature Switzerland AG 2020
A. Bartoli and A. Fusiello (Eds.): ECCV 2020 Workshops, LNCS 12537, pp. 376–391, 2020.
https://doi.org/10.1007/978-3-030-67070-2_23

It has been shown that, under the assumption of a normal distribution, Maximum Likelihood Estimation (MLE) provides near-optimal estimates of the true radiance values [2]. However, it does not offer a closed-form solution and running non-linear solvers on large images is impractical. For this reason, MLE is typically approximated with an iterative Expectation Maximization (EM) algorithm [10]. We show that such a solver does not always converge to the correct MLE solution and thus, may introduce an error in estimation. Another limitation of MLE is that it is highly sensitive to the correct calibration of noise parameters [2]. Motivated by these observations, we derive a much simpler, analytical estimator based on the Poisson nature of photon noise that is independent of camera-specific noise parameters and can, therefore, be used with any camera without requiring prior knowledge of its noise characteristic.

Starting with a multi-source noise model [1,12], we describe a calibration procedure to determine camera-specific noise model parameters. For experimentation, we generated synthetic HDR stacks using physically accurate simulations with the noise parameters of real cameras. We rely on such simulations to compare the empirical biases and standard deviations of different estimators for the scene radiance.

The main contributions of this paper are:

- A simple yet practical camera noise model, fitted for several cameras with both large (full-frame) and small (smartphone) sensors.
- A recommendation to use an estimator based on the Poisson nature of photon noise, which performs as well as near-optimal MLE estimators for the usable dynamic range.
- An empirical validation showing that estimating the sensor noise characteristic is unnecessary when merging HDR images in a noise-aware manner.
- An extended analysis showing that the recommended estimator is robust to high camera noise and is a suitable choice for low-light HDR photography.

2   Related Work

Early HDR reconstruction methods [3,8,19,21,22] focused on inverting the Camera Response Function (CRF). This is because camera manufacturers did not historically provide access to unprocessed and uncompressed RAW images. Most estimators proposed were weighted averages of the linearized pixel values, where the weights were functions of the inverse and the derivative of the CRF. Debevec and Malik proposed a hat-shaped function that assigns higher weights to linearized pixels near the middle of the intensity range [8]. All these methods do not account for camera noise and therefore provide sub-optimal estimations of HDR pixel values. We refer the reader to chapter three of the book *HDR Video* for a detailed discussion on *Stack-Based Algorithms for HDR Capture and Reconstruction* [9].

The first HDR estimation method that used a noise model was proposed by Tsin et al. [24]. They proposed to combine images with weights equal to the ratios of the respective exposure times and standard deviations, measured directly from the images. In a later work, Granados et al. [10] showed that Tsin et al.'s method was sub-optimal under a compound-normal noise assumption as pixels near the saturation point were given smaller than ideal weights despite having the highest signal-to-noise ratio (SNR). Debevec and Malik's hat-shaped weighting function [8] also suffers from this limitation of under-weighting pixels close to the saturation point. Kirk and Anderson [15] proposed an MLE based weighting scheme using a simple noise model. This was later extended to a more complete model that incorporated noise from several sources by Hasinoff et al. [12]. Granados et al. [10] noted that the true MLE-based estimator does not have an analytical solution and used the EM algorithm for a more accurate estimation than other similar works.

Aguerrebere et al. [2] compared the previously mentioned HDR reconstruction methods and analyzed how far each of their variances were from the theoretical Cramér–Rao Lower Bound (CRLB). They concluded that the variance of MLE-based estimators, such as that of Granados et al. [10], were close to the CRLB but the estimation could be easily affected by errors in noise parameter calibration. In this paper, we show that a comparable performance can be achieved by a simpler estimator without the need for camera calibration.

3   Image Formation Pipeline

We begin this section by explaining the capturing process, highlighting the probabilistic nature of camera noise. A more comprehensive description can be found elsewhere [1, 7, 16], but we include this overview for completeness. After introducing the sensor noise model, we describe the calibration procedure to estimate camera-specific noise model parameters.

3.1   Sensor Model

Photons from a scene are captured by the camera lens and pass through a Color Filter Array (CFA), before being focused on an imaging sensor such as a Charged Coupled Device (CCD) or Complementary Metal Oxide Semiconductor (CMOS) sensor as depicted in Fig. 1. When exposed for a fixed interval, the imaging sensor converts some incident photons to electrons. The number of electrons is proportional to the number of registered photons. These electrons accumulate to yield a voltage, which is processed by ana-

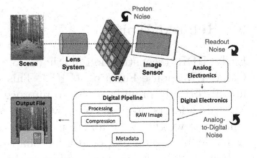

Fig. 1. The illustration of an image formation pipeline that converts photons from a scene into images. Variance in pixel values arises from the noise added at different stages (marked in red). (Color figure online)

log electronics. The next operation performed is amplification of the voltage based on the camera gain. The exposure time and gain are determined by the user-controllable shutter speed and ISO settings. Finally an Analog-to-Digital Converter (ADC) digitizes the signal into discrete pixel intensities. Modern digital cameras provide access to this uncompressed, minimally processed data directly from the electronic imaging sensor in the form of RAW images.

3.2 Noise Model

RAW values are inaccurate measurements of the unknown scene radiance due to the potential saturation of the sensor and the addition of noise at various stages of the pipeline (Fig. 1). To correctly reconstruct a scene in a noise-optimal manner, we model the probabilistic nature of noise in RAW images.

The process of photon registration by the sensor inherently follows a Poisson distribution [13]. This leads to photon noise and is the first source of noise in our model. The other contributions to noise are signal-independent. Because the signal is amplified by some *gain* before reaching the ADC, the signal-independent noise is typically split into pre-amplifier and post-amplifier components [12]. Readout noise captures the voltage fluctuations while accumulating electrons and is amplified along with the signal. The last component, analog-to-digital noise, is added after amplification and is attributed to the quantization error. Digital sensors also exhibit fixed-pattern noise due to photo-response and dark-current non-uniformity [1]. These sources of noise, however, are easy to compensate for as they are fixed for every sensor and are often removed by camera firmware from RAW images. We do not model fixed-pattern noise as it was not present in the images captured by our cameras. Other random sources of noise, such as temperature-dependent dark-current shot noise [7], are accommodated in the signal-independent components. Moreover, previous works [10,12] indicate that a simple, statistical noise model is sufficient for the problem of HDR radiance estimation.

Let the image be taken with an exposure time t and gain g, and let $Y(p)$ be a random variable representing the final recorded value of the unknown scene radiance $\phi(p)$ at pixel p. The different sources of noise depicted in Fig. 1 motivate the decomposition of this random variable into a sum of three independent random variables. The first random variable is sampled from a Poisson distribution with a parameter equal to the number of incoming photons; the other two are sampled from zero-mean normal distributions. The first normally distributed component accounts for readout noise and has a standard deviation equal to σ_{read} and the second component, parameterized by σ_{adc}, captures amplifier and quantization noise. Assuming that the pixel is not saturated,

$$Y(p) \sim \mathrm{Pois}(\phi(p)\,t)\,g\,k_c + \mathcal{N}(0, \sigma_{\mathrm{read}})\,g\,k_c + \mathcal{N}(0, \sigma_{\mathrm{adc}})\,k_c. \tag{1}$$

Each color channel has a different quantum efficiency for photon-to-electron conversion due to differences in the sensitivity of the sensor across the light spectrum. This is accounted for by the color coefficient k_c where $c \in \{r, g, b\}$. Gain affects the Poisson random variable and the first normal random variable,

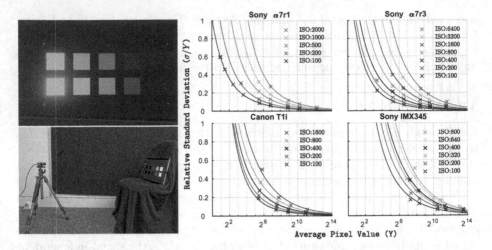

Fig. 2. The calibration target (top-left) and capture setup (bottom-left) used to measure the variance of sensor noise, and the corresponding fitted noise models for the green channel of different cameras (right). Relative standard deviation is plotted against the average pixel value recorded on a logarithmic scale. We control gain by changing ISO (different lines in each plot) since our noise equation (Eq. 2) models how the variance of a pixel changes with gain. The *crosses* represent measurements and the *lines* are the model predictions. The RAW pixel values of all the cameras sensors have been scaled to 14-bit values to enable the comparison of different sensors. (Color figure online)

while the k_c is a multiplier on all three terms. The expected value and variance of $Y(p)$ can be written as:

$$
\begin{aligned}
E[Y(p)] &= \phi(p)\,t\,g\,k_c \\
\mathrm{var}(Y(p)) &= \phi(p)\,t\,g^2\,k_c^2 + \sigma_{\mathrm{read}}^2\,g^2\,k_c^2 + \sigma_{\mathrm{adc}}^2\,k_c^2 \\
&= \underbrace{E[Y(p)]\,g\,k_c}_{\text{photon noise}} + \underbrace{\sigma_{\mathrm{read}}^2\,g^2\,k_c^2 + \sigma_{\mathrm{adc}}^2\,k_c^2}_{\text{static noise}}.
\end{aligned}
\tag{2}
$$

Notice that the variance can be conveniently represented as a function of the expected value. We refer to the signal-independent component of the variance as static noise. Static noise is the same for all pixels of an image. When the radiance of the scene is close to zero, static noise can result in the underestimation of the true radiance, effectively making some pixel values negative. Camera manufacturers typically add an offset, called black-level, to ensure that RAW pixel values are positive. In all our experiments we subtract black level to operate on the actual measurements.

3.3   Noise Parameter Estimation

Let us consider Eq. 2, the noise model, and how to estimate its camera specific parameters. Rather than measuring the noise added from various sources individually, we use a calibration target shown in the top-left image of Fig. 2. This

Table 1. Noise parameters fitted for the tested cameras

Camera	Sensor Size (mm)	Pitch (μm)	Color Coefficients			σ_read	σ_adc
			k_r	k_g	k_b		
Sony α7r1	35.9 × 24	4.86	0.327	0.33	0.32	0.7	0.04
Sony α7r3	35.6 × 23.8	4.5	0.422	0.384	0.389	0.705	3.028
Canon T1i	22.3 × 14.9	4.69	1.363	1.183	1.153	0.928	5.005
Sony IMX345	8.27 × 5.51	1.4	0.303	0.313	0.321	1.063	2.373

is constructed by overlaying a uniform light source (a light box) with Neutral Density (ND) filters of different transmittance values so that each square region emits a different radiance. The variance of pixels within each captured square provides an empirical measure of noise for a specific value of radiance.

We extracted several data points (RAW pixel mean and standard deviation pairs) and plotted them using crosses in Fig. 2. The mean of a large number of pixels contained within each square is used as a substitute for the expected value to fit Eq. 2. To minimize the error in the expected value of the RAW pixel intensity of each square, we computed the average of all pixels within each square from a set of five images captured using the same settings. We captured several such sets starting with a base ISO of 100 and an appropriate shutter speed such that none of the pixels were saturated. We assume that ISO 100 corresponds to the gain of 1. To capture subsequent sets of images, we doubled the ISO and halved the shutter speed every time to maintain the same mean intensity and to use the complete dynamic range of the camera sensor. The number of image sets varied from camera to camera and was typically between five and seven.

We then used a nonlinear solver [17] to estimate the 5 parameters of the noise model from Eq. 2. Very noisy samples with SNR less than one were excluded to ensure convergence. The fit for different cameras, shown in Fig. 2, demonstrates that the model can well explain the noise found in the tested cameras. Each plot shows the measured relative noise against recorded digital intensity, as well as fitted noise model for the green channel. Please refer to the supplementary material to view similar plots for the red and blue channels and also the individual contribution of each component of noise. For a better comparison, the digital values from each camera were rescaled such that the maximum pixel value of every image was set to $2^{14}-1$. This is the largest bit-rate registered among all our cameras. Estimated parameters for our calibrated cameras are given in Table 1. Images with synthetic noise, generated using Eq. 1 can be found in the supplementary material.

A few interesting observations can be made about the measured cameras. If we define the dynamic range as the ratio between the largest registered value and the smallest value whose SNR is 1 (corresponding to $\sigma/Y = 1$ in the plots in Fig. 2), we notice that the dynamic range differs substantially between the sensors. But it should be noted that these sensors differ in their pixel pitches and resolutions (see Table 1). Hence, the effective amount of noise in images from the different sensors can vary even more when rescaled to the same resolution. The dynamic range of every sensor is also reduced with increased gain (ISO).

3.4　Digital Pipeline

The RAW image from the sensor passes through the digital Image Signal Processing (ISP) pipeline starting with black-level subtraction, followed by demosaicing, denoising, tone-mapping and compression [6]. Most of these stages perform nonlinear operations and alter the original readings significantly. Any attempt to recover the scene radiance should thus omit these digital operations. Working with RAW values is preferable as they are linearly related to the scene radiance. The only step needed is black-level subtraction to ensure this linear relationship between radiance and pixel values.

4　HDR Radiance Estimation

In this section, we formulate the problem of estimating radiance values from a number of noisy sensor measurements. We use upper case letters to represent random variables and lower case letters to represent their observed values. Given a stack of RAW images $i = 1, 2, \ldots, N$, let $y_i(p)$ represent the RAW value of pixel p and image i captured using a corresponding exposure time t_i and gain g_i. To compensate for the differences in exposure time and gain, and to bring all exposures in the stack to the same scale, we represent their relative radiance as:

$$X_i(p) = \frac{Y_i(p)}{t_i \, g_i \, k_c} ,\tag{3}$$

such that each $x_i(p)$ is an observation of the true value $\phi(p)$. The expected value of $X_i(p)$ is thus $\phi(p)$ and its variance is obtained by scaling Eq. 2:

$$\sigma_i^2(p) = \frac{\text{var}(Y_i(p))}{t_i^2 \, g_i^2 \, k_c^2} = \frac{\phi_i(p)}{t_i} + \frac{\sigma_{\text{read}}^2}{t_i^2} + \frac{\sigma_{\text{adc}}^2}{t_i^2 \, g_i^2} .\tag{4}$$

All the estimators considered in this section assume that the images in the stack are perfectly aligned. This can be achieved by a global homography-based alignment [23] or a local alignment based on optical flow [4,18,26].

Uniform Estimator. The simplest estimator is the arithmetic mean of all the available samples and is referred to as the *Uniform* estimator. This is obviously a poor estimator as pixel values from different images in the stack are sampled from different distributions and have different SNRs.

Hat-shaped Estimator. The widely-used weighting scheme proposed by Debevec and Malik [8] assigns higher weights to image pixel values in the middle of the intensity range. The weights are functions of tone-mapped pixel values that pass through the whole pipeline. Let the smallest and largest intensities that can be recorded by a particular sensor be $y_{\min}$ and $y_{\max}$ respectively. Approximating the CRF by the gamma function, the weights are equal to

$$
w_i(p) = \begin{cases} y_i(p)^{1/\gamma} - y_{\min}^{1/\gamma} + \epsilon, & y_i(p)^{1/\gamma} \le \dfrac{y_{\min}^{1/\gamma} + y_{\max}^{1/\gamma}}{2} \\[2ex] y_{\max}^{1/\gamma} - y_i(p)^{1/\gamma} + \epsilon, & y_i(p)^{1/\gamma} > \dfrac{y_{\min}^{1/\gamma} + y_{\max}^{1/\gamma}}{2}, \end{cases} \tag{5}
$$

where $\epsilon = 10^{-10}$ is a small constant added to ensure that the weights are strictly positive and prevent division by zero. γ is generally set to 2.2. Pixels with values close to the noise floor or the saturation point are assigned lower weights. The weights are applied to the linearized pixel values to obtain the *Hat-shaped* estimator:

$$
\hat{\phi}_{\text{hat}}(p) = \frac{\sum_{i=1}^{N} w_i(p)\, x_i(p)}{\sum_{i=1}^{N} w_i(p)}. \tag{6}
$$

4.1 Maximum Likelihood Estimation

Given the probabilistic image formation model described by Eq. 1, the best estimators are based on MLE, which has been shown to be near-optimal for this problem [2]. The problem is that the Probability Density Function (PDF) of each $X_i(p)$ is a convolution of the three independent density or mass functions, and does not have a close-form expression.

Variance-Weighted Estimator. The noise-based estimator introduced in [15] and extended in [12] assumes that the Poisson component of each $X_i(p)$ can be approximated by a normal distribution. Equation 1 then simplifies to the sum of three normally distributed random variables, which is also normally distributed. The log-likelihood function to be maximized simplifies to:

$$
\ln \mathcal{L}_{\mathcal{N}}(\phi(p)) = \sum_{i=1}^{N} \ln \frac{1}{\sqrt{2\pi\,\sigma_i^2(p)}} + \sum_{i=1}^{N} \frac{-(x_i(p) - \phi(p))^2}{2\,\sigma_i^2(p)}. \tag{7}
$$

where $\sigma_i^2(p)$ is the variance of $X_i(p)$ from Eq. 4. When $\sigma_i^2(p)$ and $\phi(p)$ are independent, the MLE has a simple form:

$$
\hat{\phi}_{\text{var}}(p) = \frac{\sum_{i=1}^{N} \frac{x_i(p)}{\sigma_i^2(p)}}{\sum_{i=1}^{N} \frac{1}{\sigma_i^2(p)}}. \tag{8}
$$

The problem is that $\sigma_i^2(p)$ and $\phi(p)$ are not independent as $\sigma_i^2(p)$ is a function of $\phi(p)$ due to photon noise (refer to Eq. 4). This requires another simplifying assumption, that $\sigma_i^2(p)$ can be estimated using a single observation $y_i(p)$. However, when $E[Y_i(p)]$ is approximated by $y_i(p)$, the variance computed using Eq. 4, can be zero or negative. This may happen because $y_i(p)$ can be negative and larger in magnitude than the static noise. In our implementation, the weights $\frac{1}{\sigma_i^2(p)}$ are replaced in such instances with a small value of $\epsilon = 10^{-10}$.

Iterative Expectation Maximization (EM). A simple method that produces a computationally efficient MLE solution for Eq. 7 is the EM algorithm. In this iterative approach, proposed by Granados et al. [10], $\phi(p)$ is initialized as the mean of $y_i(p)$. Then variances for every exposure are calculated according to Eq. 4 and a better estimate of $\phi(p)$ is found using the new variances according to Eq. 8. The alternating procedure is repeated until converge.

Full MLE. The MLE for Eq. 7 can be estimated without making any additional assumptions using a non-linear optimization method. Although this is the most accurate estimator, running such a solver for each pixel is too computationally expensive to be used in practice. We include this estimator to show how close other estimator are to the true MLE solution.

Normal Photon Noise Estimator (NPNE). Equation 7 has an analytical solution if we assume that the variance is only due to photon noise and there is no static noise. Such a simplification is justified because the overall noise is dominated by the photon noise component for the usable range of $\phi(p)$. Setting static noise to zero and maximizing Eq. 7 yields the estimator:

$$\hat{\phi}_{\mathrm{npne}}(p) = \frac{\sqrt{\sum_{i=1}^{N} x_i^2(p)\, t_i \cdot \sum_{i=1}^{N} t_i + N^2} - N}{\sum_{i=1}^{N} t_i}. \tag{9}$$

Poisson Photon Noise Estimator (PPNE). Setting static noise to zero also enables us to simplify the PDF of each $X_i(p)$ and derive an estimator that maximizes the likelihood without the normal approximation to the Poisson distribution. This means that the random variables are sampled from:

$$X_i(p) \sim \frac{\mathrm{Pois}(\phi(p)\, t_i)}{t_i}. \tag{10}$$

And the new log-likelihood function to be maximized is:

$$\ln \mathcal{L}_{\mathrm{Pois}}(\phi(p)) = \sum_{i=1}^{N} x_i t_i \ln \phi t_i - \sum_{i=1}^{N} \phi t_i - \sum_{i=1}^{N} \ln(x_i t_i)!. \tag{11}$$

The last sum does not depend on $\phi(p)$ and can safely be ignored. The resulting Poisson Estimator takes on the simple form:

$$\hat{\phi}_{\mathrm{ppne}}(p) = \frac{\sum_{i=1}^{N} x_i(p)\, t_i}{\sum_{i=1}^{N} t_i} \tag{12}$$

Such an estimator is a classical choice in the imaging industry [2]. Here, we demonstrated how it can be derived from the assumption of Poisson noise. Additionally, in the supplementary material, we employ the *Lehmann-Scheffe theorem* to show that *PPNE* is the unique Minimum Variance Unbiased Estimator (MVUE) under the assumption of zero static noise. This is an important

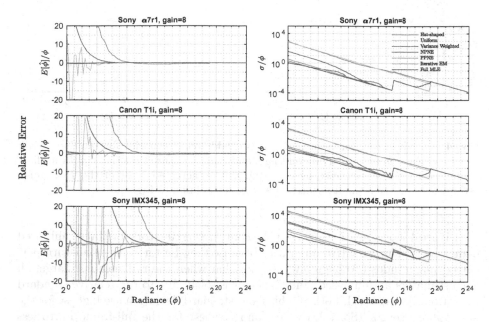

Fig. 3. Monte Carlo simulation results: relative errors of the different estimators (*color lines*) for logarithmically spaced values of the ground truth scene radiance, ϕ (*x-axis*). The errors arise due to non-zero biases (left column of plots) and non-zero standard deviations (right column of plots). The simulation was performed for three exposures, spaced five stops apart.

result, since estimators produced by MLE are generally not guaranteed to be unbiased or to have the minimum variance.

Estimators and Noise Parameters. An advantage of *NPNE* and *PPNE* estimators that ignore static noise is that they do not require knowledge of the noise parameters to provide accurate estimates. Equations 9 and 12 are functions of $x_i(p)$, which depends only on the parameter k_c. And, since k_c is the same for all exposures, it is effectively a constant multiplier, which does not affect relative radiance values.

5 Comparison of Estimators—Simulation

We empirically compare the calibration-independent estimators, *NPNE* and *PPNE*, to the classical *Uniform* and *Hat-shaped* estimators [8] and state-of-the-art MLE-based estimators, *Variance-weighted* [12] and *Iterative EM* [2,10]. We rely on Monte Carlo (MC) methods and simulate 10,000 HDR exposure stacks. Each stack consists of three exposures separated by five stops in exposure time and a constant gain of 8. Starting with 100 logarithmically-spaced ground truth values of radiance, spanning a dynamic range of 24 stops, we simulated the probabilistic camera capture process described in Sect. 3.2. Our noisy samples were generated using the parameters of calibrated cameras from Table 1.

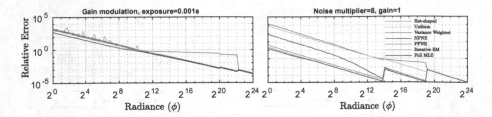

Fig. 4. Relative errors of estimators for two additional scenarios for the Sony α7r3: using a stack of images with different gain and same exposure time (left) and the effect of increasing the static noise by 8$\times$ (right). The increased error of the *Hat-shaped* estimator is due to a small negative bias (see left column of Fig. 3).

Figure 3 shows relative errors of the compared estimators for three calibrated cameras. We show relative quantities because they better correspond with perceived magnitudes (Weber's law). Notice that when the radiance ϕ is large, all the estimators are unbiased, and the error is solely due to the relative standard deviation. As expected, both the bias and standard deviation are highest for the smartphone sensor (Sony IMX345), and smallest for the full-frame mirrorless camera (Sony α7r3). The sawtooth patterns visible in the standard deviation plots are due to the three exposures: the highest five stops are captured only in images with the shortest exposure time and, therefore, the error drops at $\phi \approx 2^{19}$ and $\phi \approx 2^{14}$ when data from the second and third images become available.

The results in Fig. 3 confirm that the estimators that do not account for noise (*Uniform* and *Hat-shaped*) result in the highest bias and the highest amount of noise. The bias of the *Uniform* estimator appears unstable at low radiance values because the estimate is dominated by noise. The popular *Variance-weighted* estimator performs reasonably well for the high quality sensor (Sony α7r3) but results in a noisy estimate with a negative bias for the two other sensors. The negative bias is due to clamping of weights since variances can not be negative. As expected, the *Full MLE* achieves the best performance. It is, however, much more computationally expensive. Notice that, the *Iterative EM* estimator does not converge to the same solution as the *Full MLE* for lower radiance values.

The most interesting results are seen for the two estimators that account only for photon noise. The estimator that assumes photon noise is normally distributed (*NPNE*) introduces a positive bias and results in a higher standard deviation than the estimator that assumes Poisson photon noise distribution (*PPNE*). Overall, the error of the *PPNE* is comparable with that of the *Iterative EM* estimator, which is the best estimator used in practical applications. The relative standard deviation of noise is only marginally higher than that of the *Iterative EM* but only for very low pixel values. However, it has a major advantage over the *Iterative EM* as it does not require knowledge of the noise parameters. Therefore, it can be used with any camera without prior calibration, as long as the camera noise characteristic can be well explained by our model (Eq. 1).

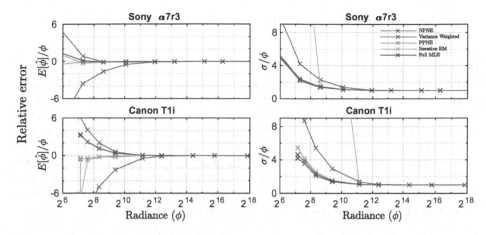

Fig. 5. Results for real images: observed relative biases and standard deviations for the green channel of two cameras. The sudden increase in standard deviation at $\phi \approx 2^{11}$ for the *Iterative EM* estimator in the top-right plot is due to the non-convergence of the EM algorithm for low inputs.

5.1   Gain Modulation

An alternate acquisition strategy for capturing HDR scenes is modulating gain while maintaining the same exposure time and consistent motion blur across images [11]. A detailed analysis of the increase in dynamic range and SNR with the number of images captured for different strategies is presented in the supplementary material. Here, we compare the estimators on a stack of gain modulated captures. The plots on the left of Fig. 4 indicate that the performance of most estimators is very similar, except for the better performance of *Full MLE* for low radiance and failure of the *Hat-shaped* estimator for medium radiance values.

5.2   Robustness to Noise

We validated the performance of the estimators for exposure stacks captured with increased camera noise. The noise in input image stacks was artificially increased by amplifying the contribution of static noise $2\times, 4\times$ and $8\times$ the measured value for the Sony α7r3 sensor. See the right side of Fig. 4 for the simulation with $8\times$ static noise and the supplementary for other multipliers. These additional MC simulations, confirm that the relative performance of *PPNE* does not noticeably degrade with noise. Its relative error is very similar to the calibration-sensitive *Iterative EM* estimator even when the input is very noisy. Since the proportion of static noise is much greater in low-luminance conditions, these results indicate that *PPNE* is suitable for low-light HDR photography.

6   Comparison of Estimators — Real Images

To make sure that our simulation results are not the outcome of wrong assumptions about camera noise, we measured the errors of different estimators on real data using a stack of images of our calibration target (see Fig. 2-left). The stack is composed of images captured with different exposure times and gains as described in Sect. 3.3. The reference radiance ϕ was calculated as the average of all pixels in each square of the target. Figure 5 shows the error, due to bias and standard deviation, of the HDR estimations for our calibrated cameras. Here we see a similar pattern as in Fig. 3, where the standard deviation of the *Variance-weighted* estimator is much higher than other MLE-based estimators and it has a large negative bias at low radiance. The performance of the analytical *PPNE* is very similar to that of the *Iterative EM* and the *Full MLE*.

(a) Hat-shaped   (b) NPNE   (c) Variance-weighted   (d) Iterative EM   (e) PPNE

Fig. 6. HDR reconstructions of outdoor scenes, "Trees" and "House", using different estimators given exposure stacks of three images captured by the Sony α7r3 at ISO 6400 and gamma-encoded for visualization ($\gamma = 2.2$). The positive bias of the *Hat-shaped* estimator and *NPNE* as well as the negative bias of the *Variance-weighted* estimator are visible in the dark regions. The images produced by the iterative EM estimator and *PPNE* are almost identical. Refer to the supplementary for the "Cottage" and "Street" scenes. In all the scenes, the shortest exposure times were deliberately set to a small value to produce noisy images and test the robustness of the estimators.

6.1   Qualitative and Quantitative Comparison on Complex Images

Next, we show visual differences in HDR images due to the choice of the estimator in challenging conditions. We captured several scenes with three exposure times, spaced two stops apart. The images are processed with different estimators

Table 2. The reconstruction error for images in Fig. 6 and Fig. 4 in the supplementary. The error is computed using HDR image quality metrics: PU-PSNR, PU-SSIM [5] and HDR-VDP-3 [20] (v3.0.6, Q-values). For all the metrics, a higher value denotes higher quality. In each column, the highest value has a gold background, the second-best has a silver background and the third has a bronze background. Overall, *PPNE* is the second-best estimator and it is narrowly outperformed by the calibration-sensitive *EM* estimator.

Estimator	PU-PSNR				PU-SSIM				HDR-VDP-3			
	House	Trees	Cottage	Street	House	Trees	Cottage	Street	House	Trees	Cottage	Street
Hat-shaped	20.266	13.241	18.516	9.019	0.636	0.489	0.51	0.302	5.719	5.39	5.013	4.638
Var-weighted	16.412	18.191	22.476	13.267	0.624	0.497	0.578	0.512	6.049	5.946	5.846	5.581
NPNE	24.326	17.451	13.588	13.331	0.681	0.543	0.374	0.289	6.027	6.114	5.391	5.304
PPNE	24.428	18.876	22.336	13.361	0.72	0.538	0.607	0.432	6.255	6.253	5.904	5.802
EM	24.922	18.339	23.059	13.962	0.72	0.52	0.614	0.524	6.273	6.37	5.983	5.928

and show substantial differences, as depicted in Fig. 6. The *Hat-shaped* weights resulted in a noisy image with a positive bias (Fig. 6a) in dark regions. *NPNE* substantially reduced the amount of noise but still produced the bias (Fig. 6b). The *Variance-weighted* estimator produced a noisier image than *NPNE* (Fig. 6c) and also introduced a negative bias. This made some pixel values darker than they should be, resulting in an accidental increase in contrast. Merged images of *PPNE* (Fig. 6d) and the *EM* estimator (Fig. 6e) show the least amount of noise and smallest bias. For additional indoor and outdoor scenes, please refer to the supplementary material. Apart from the independence to noise-parameters, another advantage over the *Iterative EM* estimator is the reduced computation time of *PPNE* due to its analytical form. This does not make much of a difference for the simple logarithmic gradient, but is important for high-resolution images captured by a DSLR.

Finally, we report quality scores for three HDR image quality metrics in Table 2. The test images were obtained from three exposures, captured at high ISO setting and merged with each estimator while the reference images were obtained by merging five exposures with the *EM* estimator (the most accurate). The results confirm the findings of other experiments; *PPNE* produces results that are only marginally worse than those of *EM*, even though *EM* was used to generate the reference images.

7   Conclusions

Although the state-of-the-art HDR reconstruction methods advocate using MLE solvers that require accurate camera parameters, we demonstrate that they provide little advantage over the simple Poisson noise estimator, which does not require camera noise calibration. We show that the Poisson noise estimator is unbiased and its standard deviation is only marginally higher that of the near-optimal MLE solution for very low pixel values. Such a difference is unlikely to be noticed in complex images. For a simplified noise model, the Poisson estimator is provably MVUE. Furthermore, we show how each estimator can be derived making different simplifying assumptions about the camera noise model, and we illustrate the relative errors of the estimators using gain modulation and under increased static noise. In all our experiments, the Poisson noise estimator was consistently among the best performing estimators.

Acknowledgement. We would like to thank Minjung Kim and Maryam Azimi for their advice on the paper. This project has received funding from the European Research Council (ERC) under the European Union's Horizon 2020 research and innovation programme (grant agreement N° 725253–EyeCode).

References

1. Aguerrebere, C., Delon, J., Gousseau, Y., Musé, P.: Study of the digital camera acquisition process and statistical modeling of the sensor raw data. Technical report August 2013
2. Aguerrebere, C., Delon, J., Gousseau, Y., Musé, P.: Best Algorithms for HDR Image Generation. A Study of Performance Bounds. SIAM J. Imaging Sci. **7**(1), 1–34 (2014)
3. Akyüz, A.O., Reinhard, E.: Noise reduction in high dynamic range imaging. J. Vis. Commun. Image Representation **18**(5), 366–376 (2007)
4. Anderson, R., et al.: Jump: virtual reality video. ACM Trans. Graph. (TOG) **35**(6), 1–13 (2016)
5. Aydın, T.O., Mantiuk, R., Seidel, H.P.: Extending quality metrics to full dynamic range images. In: Human Vision and Electronic Imaging XIII, pp. 6806–10. Proceedings of SPIE, San Jose, USA, January 2008
6. Buckler, M., Jayasuriya, S., Sampson, A.: Reconfiguring the imaging pipeline for computer vision. In: Proceedings of the IEEE Conference on Computer Vision and Pattern Recognition, pp. 975–984, May 2017
7. Costantini, R., Susstrunk, S.: Virtual sensor design. In: Sensors and Camera Systems for Scientific, Industrial, and Digital Photography Applications V. vol. 5301, pp. 408–419. International Society for Optics and Photonics (2004)
8. Debevec, P.E., Malik, J.: Recovering high dynamic range radiance maps from photographs. In: Proceedings of SIGGRAPH 1997, pp. 369–378. ACM Press, Los Angeles, CA. USA (1997)
9. Gallo, O., Sen, P.: Stack-Based Algorithms for HDR Capture and Reconstruction. In: High Dynamic Range Video, pp. 85–119. Elsevier (2016)
10. Granados, M., Ajdin, B., Wand, M., Theobalt, C., Seidel, H.P., Lensch, H.P.: Optimal HDR reconstruction with linear digital cameras. In: 2010 IEEE Computer Society Conference on Computer Vision and Pattern Recognition, pp. 215–222. IEEE (2010)
11. Hajisharif, S., Kronander, J., Unger, J.: Adaptive dualiso hdr reconstruction. EURASIP J. Image Video Process. **2015**(1), 41 (2015)
12. Hasinoff, S., Durand, F., Freeman, W.: Noise-optimal capture for high dynamic range photography. In: CVPR, pp. 553–560. IEEE (2010)
13. Healey, G., Kondepudy, R.: Radiometric CCD camera calibration and noise estimation. IEEE Trans. Pattern Anal. Machine Intell. **16**(3), 267–276 (1994)

14. Karaduzovic-Hadziabdic, K., Telalovic, J.H., Mantiuk, R.: Expert evaluation of deghosting algorithms for multi-exposure high dynamic range imaging. In: Second International Conference and SME Workshop on HDR Imaging, pp. 1–4. Citeseer (2014)

15. Kirk, K., Andersen, H.J.: Noise characterization of weighting schemes for combination of multiple exposures. In: BMVC, vol. 3, pp. 1129–1138. Citeseer (2006)

16. Konnik, M., Welsh, J.: High-level numerical simulations of noise in CCD and CMOS photosensors: review and tutorial (2014)

17. Lagarias, J.C., Reeds, J.A., Wright, M.H., Wright, P.E.: Convergence properties of the nelder-mead simplex method in low dimensions. SIAM J. Optimization $9(1)$, 112–147 (1998)

18. Liu, C., et al.: Beyond pixels: exploring new representations and applications for motion analysis. Ph.D. thesis, Massachusetts Institute of Technology (2009)

19. Mann, S., Picard, R.: Being "undigital" with digital cameras: extending dynamic range by combining differently exposed pictures. In: Proceedings IS&T 48th Annual Conference, pp. 442–428 (1995)

20. Mantiuk, R., Kim, K.J., Rempel, A.G., Heidrich, W.: Hdr-vdp-2: a calibrated visual metric for visibility and quality predictions in all luminance conditions. ACM Trans. Graph. (TOG) $30(4)$, 1–14 (2011)

21. Mitsunaga, T., Nayar, S.K.: Radiometric self calibration. In: Proceedings. 1999 IEEE Computer Society Conference on Computer Vision and Pattern Recognition (Cat. No PR00149), vol. 1, pp. 374–380. IEEE (1999)

22. Robertson, M.A., Borman, S., Stevenson, R.L.: Estimation-theoretic approach to dynamic range enhancement using multiple exposures. J. Electron. Imag. $12(2)$, 219–229 (2003)

23. Tomaszewska, A., Mantiuk, R.: Image registration for multi-exposure high dynamic range image acquisition (2007)

24. Tsin, Y., Ramesh, V., Kanade, T.: Statistical calibration of CCD imaging process. In: Proceedings Eighth IEEE International Conference on Computer Vision. ICCV 2001, vol. 1, pp. 480–487. IEEE (2001)

25. Tursun, O.T., Akyüz, A.O., Erdem, A., Erdem, E.: The state of the art in hdr deghosting: a survey and evaluation. In: Computer Graphics Forum. vol. 34, pp. 683–707. Wiley Online Library (2015)

26. Zimmer, H., Bruhn, A., Weickert, J.: Optic flow in harmony. Int. J. Comput. Vis. $93(3)$, 368–388 (2011)

AIM 2020 Challenge on Real Image Super-Resolution: Methods and Results

Pengxu Wei[1]([✉]), Hannan Lu[2], Radu Timofte[3], Liang Lin[1], Wangmeng Zuo[2],
Zhihong Pan[4], Baopu Li[4], Teng Xi[5], Yanwen Fan[5], Gang Zhang[5],
Jingtuo Liu[5], Junyu Han[5], Errui Ding[5], Tangxin Xie[6], Liang Cao[6], Yan Zou[6],
Yi Shen[6], Jialiang Zhang[6], Yu Jia[6], Kaihua Cheng[7], Chenhuan Wu[7], Yue Lin[8],
Cen Liu[8], Yunbo Peng[9], Xueyi Zou[10], Zhipeng Luo[11], Yuehan Yao[11],
Zhenyu Xu[11], Syed Waqas Zamir[12], Aditya Arora[12], Salman Khan[12],
Munawar Hayat[12], Fahad Shahbaz Khan[12], Keon-Hee Ahn[13], Jun-Hyuk Kim[13],
Jun-Ho Choi[13], Jong-Seok Lee[13], Tongtong Zhao[14], Shanshan Zhao[14],
Yoseob Han[15], Byung-Hoon Kim[16], JaeHyun Baek[17], Haoning Wu[18],
Dejia Xu[19], Bo Zhou[19], Wei Guan[20], Xiaobo Li[20], Chen Ye[20], Hao Li[21],
Haoyu Zhong[21], Yukai Shi[21], Zhijing Yang[21], Xiaojun Yang[21], Haoyu Zhong[21],
Xin Li[22], Xin Jin[22], Yaojun Wu[22], Yingxue Pang[22], Sen Liu[22], Zhi-Song Liu[23],
Li-Wen Wang[24], Chu-Tak Li[24], Marie-Paule Cani[24], Wan-Chi Siu[24],
Yuanbo Zhou[25], Rao Muhammad Umer[26], Christian Micheloni[26],
Xiaofeng Cong[26], Rajat Gupta[27], Keon-Hee Ahn[28], Jun-Hyuk Kim[28],
Jun-Ho Choi[28], Jong-Seok Lee[28], Feras Almasri[29], Thomas Vandamme[29],
and Olivier Debeir[29]

[1] Sun Yat-sen University, Guangzhou, China
weipx3@mail.sysu.edu.cn
[2] Harbin Institute of Technology University, Harbin, China
[3] Computer Vision Lab, ETH Zurich, Zurich, Switzerland
[4] Baidu Research, Silicon Valley, USA
[5] Department of Computer Vision Technology (VIS), Baidu Incorporation,
Silicon Valley, USA
[6] China Electronic Technology Cyber Security Co., Ltd., Beijing, China
[7] Guangdong OPPO Mobile Telecommunications Corp., Ltd., Dongguan, China
[8] NetEase Games AI Lab, Beijing, China
[9] Noah's Ark Lab Huawei, Beijing, China
[10] DeepBlue Technology (Shanghai) Co., Ltd., Shanghai, China
[11] Inception Institute of Artificial Intelligence (IIAI), Beijing, China
[12] Yonsei University, Seodaemun-gu, South Korea
[13] Dalian Maritime Univerity, Dalian, China
[14] Loa Alamos National Laboratory (LANL), New Mexico, USA
[15] Korea Advanced Institute of Science and Technology (KAIST),
Daejeon, South Korea
[16] Amazon Web Services (AWS), Seattle, USA
[17] Peking University, Beijing, China

(P. Wei, H. Lu, R. Timofte, L. Lin, W. Zuo—Challenge organizers and the other others
participated in the challenge. Appendix A contains the authors's teams and affiliations.
AIM webpage: https://data.vision.ee.ethz.ch/cvl/aim20/)

A. Bartoli and A. Fusiello (Eds.): ECCV 2020 Workshops, LNCS 12537, pp. 392–422, 2020.
https://doi.org/10.1007/978-3-030-67070-2_24

[18] Jiangnan University, Jiangnan, China
[19] Karlsruher Institut fuer Technologie, Karlsruher, Germany
[20] Tongji University, Tongji, China
[21] Guangdong University of Technology, Tongji, China
[22] University of Science and Technology of China, Hefei, China
[23] LIX - Computer science laboratory at the Ecole polytechnique [Palaiseau],
Palaiseau, France
[24] Center of Multimedia Signal Processing, The Hong Kong Polytechnic University,
Hong Kong, China
[25] Fuzhou University, Fuzhou, Fujian, China
[26] University of Udine, Udine, Italy
[27] Indian Institute of Technology, Khargapur, India
[28] National University of Defense Technology, Changsha, China
[29] LISA Department, Universie Libre de Bruxelles, Brussels, Belgium

Abstract. This paper introduces the real image Super-Resolution (SR) challenge that was part of the Advances in Image Manipulation (AIM) workshop, held in conjunction with ECCV 2020. This challenge involves three tracks to super-resolve an input image for ×2, ×3 and ×4 scaling factors, respectively. The goal is to attract more attention to realistic image degradation for the SR task, which is much more complicated and challenging, and contributes to real-world image super-resolution applications. 452 participants were registered for three tracks in total, and 24 teams submitted their results. They gauge the state-of-the-art approaches for real image SR in terms of PSNR and SSIM.

1 Introduction

Single image super-resolution (SR) reconstructs high-resolution (HR) images from low-resolution (LR) counterparts with image quality degradations [12,44]. Instead of imposing higher requirements on hardware devices and sensors, it could be applicable to many practical scenarios, such as video surveillance, satellite, medical imaging, *etc.* As a fundamental res earch topic, SR has attracted a long-standing and considerable attention in computer vision community.

With the emergence of deep learning, convolutional neural network (CNN) based SR methods (*e.g.*, SRCNN [8], SRGAN [18], EDSR [20], ESRGAN [38] and RCAN [51]) inherit the powerful capacity of deep learning and have achieved remarkable performance improvements. Nevertheless, so far, the remarkable progress of SR is mainly driven by the supervised learning of models from LR images and their HR counterparts. While the bicubic downsampling is usually adopted to simulate the LR images, the learned deep SR model performs much less effective for real-world SR applications since the image degradation in real-world is much more complicated.

To mitigate this issue, several real SR datasets have been recently built, City 100 [5] and SR-RAW [50]. The images in City100 were captured for the printed postcards in the indoor environment, which are limited in capturing the complicated image and degradation characteristics of natural scenes. The images in SR-RAW were collected in the real world and a contextual bilateral loss was proposed to address the misalignment problem in the dataset. Besides, Cai *et al.* [4] released another real image SR dataset, named RealSR, which was captured from two DSLR cameras. They proposed the LP-KPN method in a Laplacian pyramid framework. Considering the complex image degradation across different scenes and devices, a large-scale diverse real SR dataset, named DRealSR [40], was released to further promote the research on real-world image SR. Images of DRealSR were captured by five different DSLR cameras and posed more challenging image degradation. In [40], the proposed component divide-and-conquer model (CDC) built a baseline, hourglass SR network (HGSR), in a stacked architecture, explored different reconstruction difficulties in terms of three low-level image components inspired by corner point detection, *i.e*, the flat, edges and corner points, and trained the model with a mediate supervision strategy. Besides, its proposed gradient-weighted (GW) loss also drives the model to adapt learning objectives to the reconstruction difficulties of three image components and has a flexibility of the application to any SR model.

Jointly with the Advances in Image Manipulation (AIM) 2020 workshop, we organize the AIM Challenge on Real-world Image Super-Resolution. Specifically, this challenge concerns the real-world SISR, which poses two challenging issues [40]: (1) more complex degradation against bicubic downsampling, and (2) diverse degradation processes among devices, aiming to learn a generic model to super-resolve LR images captured in practical scenarios. To achieve this goal, paired LR and HR images are captured by various DSLR cameras and provided for training. They are randomly selected from the DRealSR dataset. Images for training, validation and testing are captured in the same way with the same set of cameras. The setting is similar to that from the NTIRE 2019 challenge on real image super-resolution [3] employing RealSR dataset [4], and is different from the AIM 2019 [25] and NTIRE 2020 [24] challenges on real-world super-resolution where no LR-HR pairs are available for training, therefore an unsupervised setting defined in [23].

This challenge is one of the AIM 2020 associated challenges on: scene relighting and illumination estimation [10], image extreme inpainting [27], learned image signal processing pipeline [15], rendering realistic bokeh [16], real image super-resolution [39], efficient super-resolution [49], video temporal super-resolution [32] and video extreme super-resolution [11].

Table 1. Details of the dataset for the challenge

Scale	Split	Type	Number	Size (LR)	Evaluation
×2	Train	Cropped patches	19,000	380 × 380	PSNR (on RGB channels), SSIM
	Validation	Aligned images	20	~2000 × 3000	
	Test	Aligned images	60		
×3	Train	Cropped patches	19,000	272 × 272	
	Validation	Aligned images	20	~1300 × 2000	
	Test	Aligned images	60		
×4	Train	Cropped patches	19,000	192 × 192	
	Validation	Aligned images	20	~1000 × 1250	
	Test	Aligned images	60		

2   AIM 2020 Challenge on Real Image Super-Resolution

The objectives of the AIM 2020 challenge on real image super-resolution challenge are: (i) to further explore the researches on real image SR; (ii) to fully evaluate different SR approaches on different scale factors; (iii) to offer an opportunity of communications between academic and industrial participants.

2.1   DRealSR Dataset

DRealSR[1] [40] is a large-scale real-world image super-resolution. Only half of images in DRealSR are randomly selected for this challenge. These images are captured from five DSLR cameras (i.e., Canon, Sony, Nikon, Olympus and Panasonic) in natural scenes and cover indoor and outdoor scenes avoiding moving objects, e.g., advertising posters, plants, offices, buildings, etc. These HR-LR image pairs are aligned. To get access to the training and validation data and submit SR results, the registration on Codalab[2] is required. Details of the dataset in this challenge are given in Table 1.

2.2   Track and Competition

Tracks. The challenge uses the newly released DRealSR dataset and has three tracks corresponding to ×2, ×3, ×4 upscaling factors. The aim is to obtain a network design or solution capable to produce high-quality results with the best fidelity to the reference ground truth.

Challenge Phases. *(1) Development phase:* HR images from DRealSR have 4000 × 6000 pixels on average. For the convenience of model training, images are cropped into patches. For ×2 scale factor, LR image patches are 380 × 380; for ×3 scale factor, LR image patches are 272 × 272; for ×4 scale factor, LR image

---

[1] The dataset is publicly available at https://github.com/xiezw5/Component-Divide-and-Conquer-for-Real-World-Image-Super-Resolution.
[2] https://competitions.codalab.org.

patches are 192×192. *(2) Testing Phase:* In the final test phase, participants have access to LR images for three tracks, submit their SR results to Codalab evaluation server and email their codes and factsheets to the organizers. The organizers checked all the SR results and the provided codes to obtain the final results.

Evaluation Protocol. The evaluation includes the comparison of the super-resolved images with the reference ground truth images. We use the standard peak signal to noise ratio (PSNR) and, complementary, the structural similarity (SSIM) index as often employed in the literature. PSNR and SSIM implementations are found in most of the image processing toolboxes. For each dataset, we report the average results (i.e. $PSNR_{avg}$ and $SSIM_{avg}$) over all the processed images belonging to it and employ for ranking the weighted value of normalized $PSNR_{avg}$ and $SSIM_{avg}$, which is defined as follows,

$$PSNR_{avg}/50 + (SSIM_{avg} - 0.4)/0.6. \tag{1}$$

3   Challenge Results

There are 174, 128 and 168 registered participants for three tracks, respectively. In total, 24 teams submitted their super-resolution results; 10, 2 and 11 teams submitted results of one, two and three tracks, respectively. Among those submitted results of one track, seven teams are for $\times 4$ scale factor. Details of final testing results are provided in Table 2. It mainly reports the final evaluation results and model training details.

As for the evaluation metric of weighted score claimed in Sect. 2.2, the leading entries for Track 1, 2 and 3 are all from team Baidu. For Track 1 and 2, the CETC-CSKT and the OPPO_CAMERA team win the second and the third places, respectively. For Track 3, ALONG and CETC-CSKT win the second and the third places, respectively. Among those solutions for the challenge, some interesting trends can be observed as follows.

Network Architecture. All the teams utilize deep neural networks for super-resolution. The architecture of the deep network will greatly affect the performance of super-resolution images. Several teams, *e.g.*, TeamInception, construct a network with the residual structure to reduce the difficulty of optimization, While OPPO_CAMERA connected the input to the output with a trainable convolution layer. CETC-CSKT further proposed to pre-train the trainable layer in the skip branch in advance. Several teams, such as DeepBlueAI and SR-IM applied channel attention module in their network, while several others like TeamInception and Noah_TerminalVision employ both spatial attention and channel attention on the feature level.

Data Augmentation. Most solutions conduct the data augmentation by randomly flipping and rotating images by $90°$. The newly proposed CutBlur method was employed by ALONG and OPPO_CAMERA and performance improvements are reported by these teams.

Table 2. Evaluation results in the final testing phase. "Score" indicates the weighted score (Eq. 1), *i.e.*, the evaluation metric for the challenge. For "Ensemble", "model" and "self" indicate the model ensemble and the self-ensemble, respectively. "/" indicates that those items are not provided by participants. We also provide results of "EDSR*" for comparison with the same challenge dataset.

Team	PSNR	SSIM	Score	Ensemble	ExtraData	Loss
				Track1 ($\times 2$)		
Baidu	**33.446**	**0.927**	**0.7736**	Model+Self	False	L_1 + SSIM
CETC-CSKT	33.314	0.925	0.7702	Model+Self	False	L_1
OPPO_CAMERA	33.309	0.924	0.7699	Model+Self	False	L_1 + SSIM + MS-SSIM
AiAiR	33.263	0.924	0.7695	Model+Self	True	Clip L_1
TeamInception	33.232	0.924	0.7690	Model+Self	True	L_1 + MS-SSIM + VGG
Noah_TerminalVision	33.289	0.923	0.7686	Self	False	adaptive robust loss
DeepBlueAI	33.177	0.924	0.7681	Self	False	/
ALONG	33.098	0.924	0.7674	Self	False	L_1 + L_2
LISA-ULB	32.987	0.923	0.7659	/	False	L_1 + SSIM
lyl	32.937	0.921	0.7635	/	False	L_1
GDUT-SL	32.973	0.920	0.7634	Model	False	L_1
MCML-Yonsei	32.903	0.919	0.7612	None	False	L_1
Kailos	32.708	0.920	0.7601	Self	False	L_1 + wavelet loss
qwq	31.640	0.913	0.7436	None	False	L_1 + SSIM
debut_kele	31.236	0.889	0.7196	None	True	/
EDSR*	31.220	0.889	0.7194	/	/	/
RRDN_IITKGP	29.851	0.845	0.6696	None	True	/
				Track2 ($\times 3$)		
Baidu	**30.950**	**0.876**	**0.7063**	Model+Self	False	L_1 + SSIM
CETC-CSKT	30.765	0.871	0.7005	Model+Self	False	L_1
OPPO_CAMERA	30.537	0.870	0.6966	Model+Self	False	L_1 + SSIM + MS-SSIM
Noah_TerminalVision	30.564	0.866	0.6941	Self	False	adaptive robust loss
MCML-Yonsei	30.477	0.866	0.6931	Self	False	L_1
TeamInception	30.418	0.866	0.6928	Model+Self	True	L_1 + MS-SSIM + VGG
ALONG	30.375	0.866	0.6922	Self	False	L_1 + L_2
DeepBlueAI	30.302	0.867	0.6918	Self	False	/
lyl	30.365	0.864	0.6905	/	False	L_1
Kailos	30.130	0.866	0.6900	Self	False	L_1 + wavelet loss
qwq	29.266	0.852	0.6694	None	False	L_1 + SSIM
EDSR*	28.763	0.821	0.6383	/	/	/
anonymous	18.190	0.825	0.5357	/	False	/
				Track3 ($\times 4$)		
Baidu	**31.396**	**0.875**	**0.7099**	Model+Self	False	L_1 + SSIM
ALONG	31.237	0.874	0.7075	Self	False	L_1 + L_2
CETC-CSKT	31.123	0.874	0.7066	Model+Self	False	L_1
SR-IM	31.174	0.873	0.7057	Self	False	/
DeepBlueAI	30.964	0.874	0.7044	Self	False	/
JNSR	30.999	0.872	0.7035	Model+Self	True	/
OPPO_CAMERA	30.86	0.874	0.7033	Model+Self	False	L_1 + SSIM + MS-SSIM
Kailos	30.866	0.873	0.7032	Self	False	L_1 + wavelet loss
SR_DLu	30.605	0.866	0.6944	Self	False	/
Noah_TerminalVision	30.587	0.866	0.6944	Self	False	adaptive robust loss
Webbzhou	30.417	0.867	0.6936	None	False	/
TeamInception	30.347	0.868	0.6935	Model+Self	True	L_1 + MS-SSIM + VGG
lyl	30.319	0.866	0.6911	/	False	L_1
MCML-Yonsei	30.420	0.864	0.6906	Self	False	L_1
MoonCloud	30.283	0.864	0.6898	Model + Self	True	/
qwq	29.588	0.855	0.6748	None	False	L_1 + SSIM
SrDance	29.595	0.852	0.6729	/	True	MAE+VGG+GAN loss
MLP_SR	28.619	0.831	0.6457	Self	True	GAN,TV,L_1,SSIM,MS-SSIM,Cycle
EDSR*	28.212	0.824	0.6356	/	/	/
RRDN_IITKGP	27.971	0.809	0.6201	None	True	/
congxiaofeng	26.392	0.826	0.6187	None	False	L_1

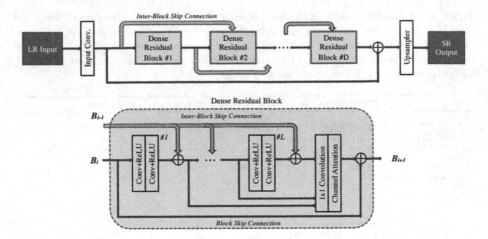

Fig. 1. The dense residual network architecture of the Baidu team for image Super-Resolution

Ensemble Strategy. Most solutions adopted self-ensemble ×8. Some solutions also performed model-ensemble by fusing results from models with different training parameter, or even of different architectures.

Platform. All the teams except one team using Tensorflow utilized PyTorch to conduct their experiments.

4   Challenge Methods and Teams

Baidu
The Baidu team proposed to apply Neural Architecture Search (NAS) approach selecting variations of their previous dense residual model as well as RCAN model [28]. In order to accelerate the searching process, Gaussian Process based Neural Architecture Search (GP-NAS) was applied as in [19]. Specifically, given the hyper-parameters of GP-NAS, they are capable of predicting the performance of any architectures in the search space effectively. Then, the NAS process is converted to hyper-parameters estimation. By mutual information maximization, the Baidu team can efficiently sample networks. Accordingly, based on the performances of sampled networks, the posterior distribution of hyper-parameters can be gradually and efficiently updated. Based on the estimated hyper-parameters, the architecture with the best performance can be obtained.

The backbone model of the proposed method is a deep dense residual network originally developed for raw image demosaicing and denoising. As depicted in Fig. 1, in addition to the shallow feature convolution at the front and the upsampler at the end, the proposed network consists of a total depth of D dense residual blocks (DRB). The input convolution layer converts the 3-channel LR input to a total of F-channel shallow features. For the middle DRB blocks, each one

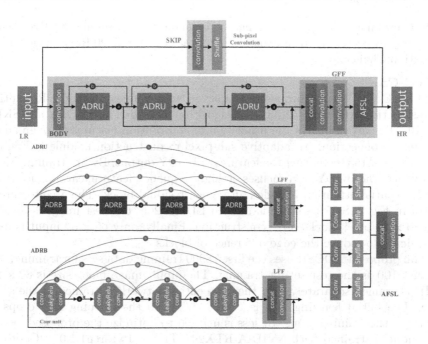

Fig. 2. Framework of Adaptive Dense Connection Super Resolution reconstruction (ADCSR) for the CETC-CSKT team

includes L stages of double layers of convolution and the outputs of all L stages are concatenated together before convoluted from $F \times L$ to F channels. An additional channel-attention layers are included at the end of each block, similar to RCAN [51]. There are two types of skip connections included in each block, the block skip connection (BSC) and inter-block skip connection (IBSC). The BSC is the shortcut between input and output of block B_i, while IBSC includes two shortcuts from the input of block B_{i-1} to the two stages inside block B_i, respectively. The various skip connections, especially IBSC, are included to combine features with a large range of receptive fields. The last block is an enhanced upsampler that transforms all F-channel LR features to the estimated 3-channel SR image. This dense residual network has three main hyper-parameters: F is the number of feature channels, D is the number of DRB layers and L is the number of stages for each DRB. All these three hyper-parameters construct the search space for NAS.

During training, a 120×120 patch is randomly cropped and augmented with flipping and transposing from each training image for each epoch. A mixed loss of L_1 and multi-scale structural similarity (MS-SSIM) is taken for training. For the experiment, the new model candidate search scheme using GP-NAS was implemented in PaddlePaddle [26] and the final-training of searched models were conducted using PyTorch. A multi-level ensemble scheme is proposed in testing, including self-ensemble for patches, as well as patch-ensemble and model-ensemble for full-size images. The proposed method is validated to be highly effective, generating impressive testing results on all three tracks of AIM2020 Real Image Super-resolution Challenge.

CETC-CSKT

The CETC-CSKT team proposed Adaptive Dense Connection Super Resolution reconstruction(ADCSR) [42,43]. The algorithm is divided into BODY and SKIP. The BODY part improves the utilization of convolution features through adaptive dense connection. An adaptive sub-pixel reconstruction module (AFSC) is also proposed to reconstruct the features of BODY output. By pre-training SKIP in advance, the BODY part focuses on high-frequency feature learning. for track 1 (×2), spatial attention is added after each residual block. The architecture is shown in Fig. 2. Self-ensemble is used in EDSR [20]. The test image is divided into 80 × 80 pixel blocks for reconstruction. Finally, only 60 × 60 input is used for splicing to reduce the edge difference of blocks.

The proposed ADCSR uses the first 18900 training data sets for training, and the last 100 as the test set for training. The input image block size is 80 × 80. SKIP is trained separately, and then the entire network is trained at the same time. The initial learning rate is 1×10^{-4}. When the learning rate drops to 5×10^{-7}, the training stops. L_1 loss is utilized to optimize the proposed model. The model is trained with NVIDIA RTX2080Ti * 4. Pytorch1.1.0 + Cuda10.0 + cudnn7.5.0 is selected as the deep learning environment.

OPPO_CAMERA

The OPPO_CAMERA team proposed Self-Calibrated Attention Neural Network for Real-World Super Resolution [6]. As shown in Fig. 3, the proposed model is constituted of four integral components, *i.e.*, feature extraction, residual in residual deep feature extraction, upsampling and reconstruction. It employs the same residual structure and dense connections to DRLN [1]. A longer skip connection is also added to connect the input to the output with a trainable parameter, which can greatly reduces the difficulty of optimization and thus, the network would pay more attention to the learning of the high frequency parts in images. As shown in Fig. 4, three Basic Residual Block (BRB) forms a Large Residual Block (LRB) with dense connection. Self-Calibration convolution (SCC) [22], shown at top of Fig. 4, is adopted as a basic unit in order to expand receptive field. Unlike conventional convolution, SCC enables each point in space to have interactive information from nearby regions and channels. Dense connections are established between the Self-Calibration convolution block (SCCB), each densely connected residual block has three SCCB. To incorporate channel information efficiently, an attention block with multi-scale feature integration is added in every basic residual block as DRLN [1]. For the network optimization, L_1 loss function was introduced as pixel-wise loss. In order to improve the fidelity, SSIM and MS-SSIM loss were also used as structure loss. With pixel loss and structure loss, the total loss is formulated as follows,

$$\mathcal{L}_{total} = \mathcal{L}^{L_1} + 0.2 \cdot \mathcal{L}^{MS-SSIM} + 0.2 \cdot \mathcal{L}^{SSIM}$$

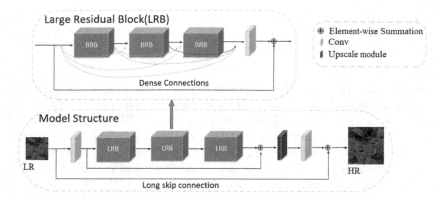

Fig. 3. The detailed network architecture of the proposed network for the OPPO_CAMERA team

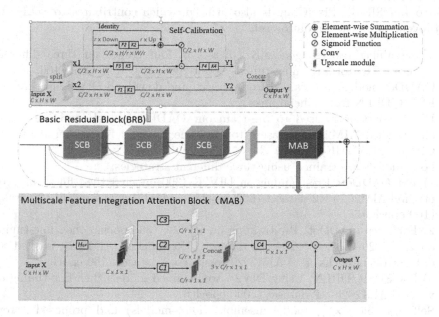

Fig. 4. The proposed BRB and MAB for the OPPO_CAMERA team. The top of the figure shows the basic convolution structure of the proposed network with the dense connection. The middle of the figure shows the basic residual block. The bottom of the figure presents the channel attention mechanism of the network.

For the training, the proposed method splits the training data randomly into two parts, *i.e.*, training set and validation set, with the ratio of 18500:500. Considering its significant improvement in the Real World SR task, CutBlur [45] is applied to augment training images. Self-ensemble and Parameter-fusion strategy would obviously improve the fidelity index(PSNR and SSIM), and meanwhile, less noise in result images. The strategy of self-ensembles (×8) was used as explained in RCAN [52], and all the corresponding parameters of last 3 models are fused to derive a fused model G_{fused}, as described in [30]. Experiments are conducted with Tesla V100 GPU.

AiAiR

The AiAiR team proposes that orientation-aware convolutions meet dual path enhancement network (OADDet). Their method consists of four basic models (model ensemble): OADDet, Deep-OADDet, original EDSR [21] and original DRLN [1]. The core modules of OADDet, illustrated in Fig. 5, are borrowed from DDet [31], Inception [33] and OANet [9] with minor improvements, such as less attention modules, removing skip connections and replacing ReLU with LeakyReLU. Overall architectures are similar to DDet [31]. It is found that redundant attention modules will damage the performance and slow down the training process. Therefore, attention modules are only applied to the last few blocks of the backbone network and the last layer of the shallow network. Similar to RealSR [4], PixelConv is also utilized, which contributes to ∼0.15 dB improvement on the validation set.

- The training process generally consists of four stages on three different datasets. The total training time is about 2000 GPU hours on V100.
- OADDet models are trained from scratch and download DIV2K pre-trained EDSR/DRLN from official links.
- DIV2K dataset is used to pre-train our OADDet models and use manually washed AIM2020 datasets to fine-tune all models (further details in GitHub README).
- Four models are trained using three different strategies:
  1) For OADDet: Pre-training on DIV2K (300 epochs) then fine-tuning on original AIM2020 ×2 dataset (600 epochs) and AIM2020 washed ×2 dataset (100 epochs).
  2) For Deep-OADDet: Pre-training on DIV2K (30 epochs) then fine-tuning on AIM2020 washed ×2 + ×3 dataset (350 epochs), AIM2020 washed ×2 dataset (350 epochs) and AIM2020 washed ×2 dataset (100 epochs).
  3) For EDSR/DRLN: Using DIV2K well-trained models then fine-tuning on washed AIM2020 ×2 dataset (1000 epochs).
- Self-ensemble (×8), model-ensemble (four models) and proposed "crop-ensemble" are conducted (further details in GitHub README Reproduce ×2 test dataset results).
- OADDet enjoys a more stable and faster training process than OANet, which introduces too many attention modules at the early stage of the networks. DDet proposes to use dynamic PixelConv with kernelsize = 5,7,9; however, it is proved that kernelsize = 3,5,7 works better during training and testing time.

TeamInception

The TeamInception team proposes learning Enriched Features for Real Image Restoration and Enhancement. MIRNet, recently introduced in [47], is utilized

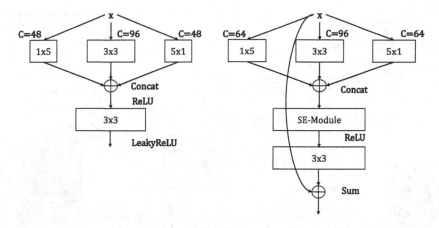

Fig. 5. OADDet and Deep-OADDet for the AiAiR team.

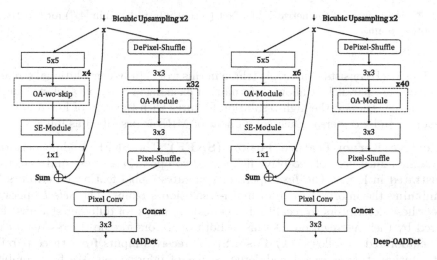

Fig. 6. Overall architectures of OADDet and Deep-OADDet for the AiAiR team.

with the collective goals of maintaining spatially-precise high-resolution representations through the entire network and receiving strong contextual information from the low-resolution representations. In Fig. 7. MIRNet[3] has a multi-scale residual block (MRB) containing several key elements: **(a)** parallel multi-resolution convolution streams for extracting (fine-to-coarse) semantically-richer and (coarse-to-fine) spatially-precise feature representations, **(b)** information exchange across multi-resolution streams, **(c)** attention-based aggregation of features arriving from multiple streams, and **(d)** dual-attention units to capture contextual information in both spatial and channel dimensions.

---

[3] The code is publicly available at https://github.com/swz30/MIRNet.

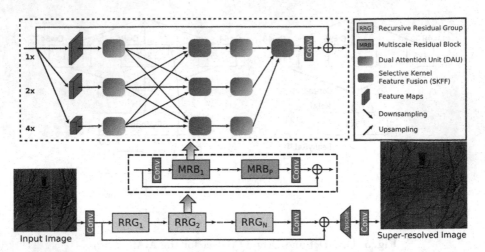

Fig. 7. Framework of the network MIRNet (recently introduced in [47]) for the Team-Inception team.

The MRB consists of multiple (three in this work) fully-convolutional streams connected in parallel. It allows information exchange across parallel streams in order to consolidate the high-resolution features with the help of low-resolution features, and vice versa. Each component of MRB is described as follows.

Selective Kernel Feature Fusion (SKFF). The SKFF module performs dynamic adjustment of receptive fields via two operations –*Fuse* and *Select*, as illustrated in Fig. 8. The *fuse* operator generates global feature descriptors by combining the information from multi-resolution streams. The *select* operator uses these descriptors to recalibrate the feature maps (of different streams) followed by their aggregation. Details of both operators for the three-stream case are elaborated as follows. **(1) Fuse:** SKFF receives inputs from three parallel convolution streams carrying different scales of information. We first combine these multi-scale features using an element-wise sum as: $\mathbf{L} = \mathbf{L}_1 + \mathbf{L}_2 + \mathbf{L}_3$. We then apply global average pooling (GAP) across the spatial dimension of $\mathbf{L} \in \mathbb{R}^{H \times W \times C}$ to compute channel-wise statistics $\mathbf{s} \in \mathbb{R}^{1 \times 1 \times C}$. Next, a channel-downscaling convolution layer is used to generate a compact feature representation $\mathbf{z} \in \mathbb{R}^{1 \times 1 \times r}$, where $r = \frac{C}{8}$ for our experiments. Finally, the feature vector $\mathbf{z}$ passes through three parallel channel-upscaling convolution layers (one for each resolution stream) and provides us with three feature descriptors $\mathbf{v}_1, \mathbf{v}_2$ and $\mathbf{v}_3$, each with dimensions $1 \times 1 \times C$. **(2) Select:** this operator applies the softmax function to $\mathbf{v}_1, \mathbf{v}_2$ and $\mathbf{v}_3$, yielding attention activations $\mathbf{s}_1, \mathbf{s}_2$ and $\mathbf{s}_3$ that we use to adaptively recalibrate multi-scale feature maps $\mathbf{L}_1, \mathbf{L}_2$ and $\mathbf{L}_3$, respectively. The overall process of feature recalibration and aggregation is defined as: $\mathbf{U} = \mathbf{s}_1 \cdot \mathbf{L}_1 + \mathbf{s}_2 \cdot \mathbf{L}_2 + \mathbf{s}_3 \cdot \mathbf{L}_3$. Note that the SKFF uses $\sim 6\times$ fewer parameters than aggregation with the concatenation but generates more favorable results.

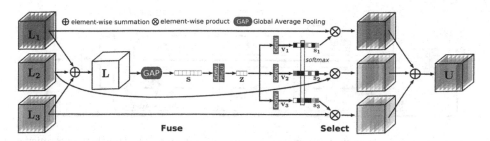

Fig. 8. Schematic for selective kernel feature fusion (SKFF) for the TeamInception team. It operates on features from multiple convolutional.

Dual Attention Unit (DAU). While the SKFF block fuses information across multi-resolution branches, we also need a mechanism to share information within a feature tensor, both along the spatial and the channel dimensions. The dual attention unit (DAU) is proposed to extract features in the convolutional streams. The schematic of DAU is shown in Fig. 9. The DAU suppresses less useful features and only allows more informative ones to pass further. This feature recalibration is achieved by using channel attention [14] and spatial attention [41] mechanisms. **(1) Channel attention (CA)** branch exploits the inter-channel relationships of the convolutional feature maps by applying *squeeze* and *excitation* operations [14]. Given a feature map $\mathbf{M} \in \mathbb{R}^{H \times W \times C}$, the squeeze operation applies global average pooling across spatial dimensions to encode global context, thus yielding a feature descriptor $\mathbf{d} \in \mathbb{R}^{1 \times 1 \times C}$. The excitation operator passes $\mathbf{d}$ through two convolutional layers followed by the sigmoid gating and generates activations $\hat{\mathbf{d}} \in \mathbb{R}^{1 \times 1 \times C}$. Finally, the output of CA branch is obtained by rescaling $\mathbf{M}$ with the activations $\hat{\mathbf{d}}$. **(2) Spatial attention (SA)** branch is designed to exploit the inter-spatial dependencies of convolutional features. The goal of SA is to generate a spatial attention map and use it to recalibrate the incoming features $\mathbf{M}$. To generate the spatial attention map, the SA branch first independently applies global average pooling and max pooling operations on features $\mathbf{M}$ along the channel dimensions and concatenates the outputs to form a feature map $\mathbf{f} \in \mathbb{R}^{H \times W \times 2}$. The map $\mathbf{f}$ is passed through a convolution and sigmoid activation to obtain the spatial attention map $\hat{\mathbf{f}} \in \mathbb{R}^{H \times W \times 1}$, which is used to rescale $\mathbf{M}$.

For training, L_1, multi-scale SSIM and VGG loss functions are considered in the model, defined as follows

$$\mathcal{L}_f = \alpha \mathcal{L}_1(\hat{\mathbf{y}}, \mathbf{y}) + \beta \mathcal{L}_{\text{MS-SSIM}}(\hat{\mathbf{y}}, \mathbf{y}) + \gamma \mathcal{L}_{\text{VGG}}(\hat{\mathbf{y}}, \mathbf{y}) \qquad (2)$$

$\mathcal{L}_{\text{VGG}}$ uses the features of *conv2* layer after ReLU in the pre-trained VGG-16 network. Three RRGs are utilized, each of which contains 2 MRBs. MRB consists of 3 parallel streams with channel dimensions of $64, 128, 256$ at resolutions $1, \frac{1}{2}, \frac{1}{4}$, respectively. Each stream has 2 DAUs. Patches with the size of 128×128 are cropped. Horizontal and vertical flips are employed for data augmentation. The model is trained from scratch with the Adam optimizer ($\beta_1 = 0.9$, and $\beta_2 = 0.999$) for 7×10^5 iterations. The initial learning rate is 2×10^{-4} and the batch

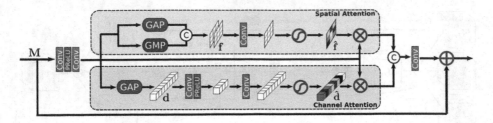

Fig. 9. Dual attention unit incorporating spatial and channel attention mechanisms for the TeamInception team.

size is 16. The cosine annealing strategy is employed to steadily decrease the learning rate from the initial value to 10^{-6} during training.

At inference time, the self-ensemble strategy [2] is employed. For each test image, a set of following 8 images are created: original, flipped, rotated 90°, rotated 180°, rotated 270°, 90° & flipped, 180° & flipped, and 270° & flipped. Next, these transformed images are passed through our model and obtain super-resolved outputs. Then we undo the transformations and perform averaging to obtain the final image. To fuse results, three different variants of the proposed networks are trained with different loss functions (Eq. 2): **(1)** only the first term, **(2)** the first two terms (i.e., $\alpha\mathcal{L}_1 + \beta\mathcal{L}_{\text{MS-SSIM}}$), and **(3)** all the terms. For the variant 2, $\alpha = 0.16$ and $\beta = 0.84$; for the variant 3, $\alpha = 0.01$ and $\beta = 0.84$, $\gamma = 0.15$.

Given an image, the generated self-ensembled results with each of these three networks are averaged to obtain the final image. Results with self-ensemble strategy and fusion are reported in Table 3. With 4 Tesla-V100 GPUs, it takes ~3 days to train the network. The time required to process a test image of size 3780×5780 is 2 s (single method), 30 s (self-ensemble) and 87 s (fusion).

Noah_TerminalVision

The Noah_TerminalVision team proposed Super Resolution with weakly-paired data using an Adaptive Robust Loss. The network is based on RRDBNet with 23 Residual in Residual Denseblocks. Only training pairs with a high PSNR score were used for training. To further alleviate the bad effect of miss-alignment of training data, the adaptive robust loss function proposed by Jon Barron was used. For track 3, it additionally used a spatial attention module and an efficient channel attention module. The spatial attention module is borrowed from EDVR [37] and the efficient attention module is borrowed from ECA-Net [36]. Considering that the training data are not perfectly aligned, Adaptive Robust Loss Function [2] for super resolution tasks is utilized to solve the weakly-paired training problem. The self-ensemble strategy is to run inference on the combination of the 90/180/270-degree rotated images of the original/flipped input and then to average the results.

Only training pairs with a high PSNR score (29) were used for training. The learning rate is 2e−4, the patch size of inputs is 80×80 and the batchsize is 4. CosineAnnealingLR_Restart learning rate scheme is employed and the restart

Table 3. Results of validation set for the scale factor ×4 for the TeamInception team. Comparison of using single method (SM), self-ensemble (SE) and Fusion (F) on validation set.

	$\mathcal{L}_1$	$\mathcal{L}_1 + \mathcal{L}_{\text{MS-SSIM}}$	$\mathcal{L}_1 + \mathcal{L}_{\text{MS-SSIM}} + \mathcal{L}_{\text{VGG}}$	PSNR
SM	✓			29.72
SM		✓		29.83
SM			✓	29.89
SM + F	✓	✓	✓	30.08
SE + F	✓	✓	✓	30.25

period is 250,000 steps. For each input, due to GPU memory constraint, images are tested patch-wisely. The crop window is of size 120 × 120, and a stride of 110 × 110 was used to collect patches.

DeepBlueAI

The DeepBlueAI team proposed a solution based on RCAN [51], which was implemented with PyTorch. In each RG, the RCAB number is 20, G = 10 and C = 128 in the RIR structure. The model is trained from scratch, which costs about 4 days with 4 × 32G Tesla V100 GPU. For training, all the training images are augmented by random horizontal flips and 90 rotations. In each training batch, LR color patches with the size of 64 × 64 are extracted as inputs. The initial leaning rate is set to 2.0×10^{-4} and learning rate of each parameter group use a cosine annealing schedule with total 1.0×10^5 iterations and without restart. For testing, each low resolution image is flipped and rotated to generate seven augmented inputs; with the trained RCAN model, the corresponding super-resolved images are generated. An inverse transform is applied to those output images to get the original geometry. The transformed outputs are averaged all together to yield the self-ensemble result.

ALONG

The ALONG team proposed Dual Path Network with high frequency guided for real-world image Super-Resolution. The proposed method follows the main structure of RCAN [51] and utilizes the guild filter to decompose the detail layer and to restore high-frequency details. As illustrated in Fig. 10, a lot of share-source skip connections in the original feature extraction path with channel attention. Due to share-source skip connections, the abundant low-frequency information can be bypassed and facilitate to train deeper network. Compared with the previous simulated datasets, the image degradation process for real SR is much more complicated. Low-resolution images lose more high-frequency information and look blurry. Inspired by other image deblurring tasks [37,54,55], a pre-deblur module is used before the residual groups to pre-process blurry inputs and improve super-resolution accuracy. Specifically, the input image is first down-sampled with strided convolution layers; then the upsampling layer at the end will resize the features back to the original input resolution. The

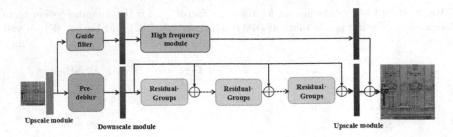

Fig. 10. RCAN for the Real Image Super-Resolution (RCANv2) for the ALONG team.

proposed dual path network restores fine details by decomposing the input image and focusing on the detail layers. An additional branch focuses on the high-frequency reconstruction. The input LR image is decomposed into the detail layer using the guided filter, an edge-preserving low-pass filter [13]. Then a high-frequency module is adopted on the detail layer, so the output result can focus on restoring high-frequency details.

Besides, a variety of data augmentation strategies are combined to achieve competitive results in different tracks, including Cutout [7], CutMix [46], Mixup [48], CutMixup, RGB permutation, Blend. In addition, inspired by [45], CutBlur, unlike Cutout, can utilize the entire image information while it enjoys the regularization effect due to the varied samples of random HR ratios and locations. The experimental results also show that a reasonable combination of data enhancement can improve the model performance without additional computation cost in the test phase. The model is trained with 8 2080Ti, 11G memory each GPU. Pseudo ensemble is also employed. The inputs are flipped/rotated and the HR results are aligned and averaged for enhanced prediction.

LISA-ULB

The LISA-ULB team proposed VCycles BackProjection networks generation two (VCBPv2), which utilized an iterative error correcting feedback mechanism to guide the reconstruction of the final SR output. As shown in Fig. 11, the proposed network is composed of an outer loop of 10 cycles and an inner loop of 3 cycles. The input of the proposed VCBPv2 is the LR image and the upsampled counterpart. The upsample and downsample modules iteratively transform features between high- and low-resolution space as residual for error correction. The decoder in the end reconstructs the corrected feature to SR image.

The model is trained using AdamW optimizer with learning rate of 1×10^{-4} and halved at every 400 epochs, then the training is followed by SGDM optimizer. Equally weighted ℓ_1 and SSIM loss is adopted for training.

lyl

The lyl team proposed a coarse to fine network for progressive super-resolution. As shown in Fig. 12, based on the Laplacian pyramid framework, the proposed model takes an LR image as input and progressively predicts residual images at $S_1, S_2...S_n$ levels. S is the scale factor, $S = S_1 \times S_2... \times S_n$, where $n = log_2^S$.

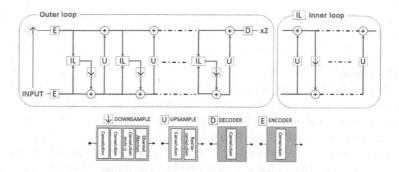

Fig. 11. The architecture of the proposed network by the LISA-ULB team.

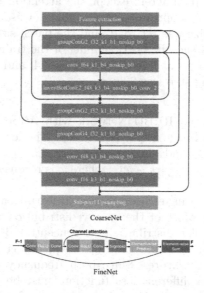

Fig. 12. The architecture of the proposed network by the lyl team.

ℓ_1 was adopted to optimize the proposed network. Each level of the proposed CFN was supervised by different scales of HR images.

GDUT-SL

The GDUT-SL team used the RRDBNet of ESRGAN [38] to perform super-resolution. Typical RRDB block has 3 Dense blocks, which including 5 Conv layers with Leaky-ReLU and remove BN layers. The RRDB number was set to 23. Two UpConv layer is used for upsampling. Different from ESRGAN, the GDUT-SL team replaced the activation function with ReLU to obtain better PSNR results.

Residual scaling and smaller initialization were adopted to facilitate training a deep architecture. In training phase, the mini-batch size was set to 16, with image size of 96 × 96. 20 promising models were selected for model-ensemble.

MCML-Yonsei

As shown in Fig. 13, the MCML-Yonsei team proposed an attention based multi-scale deep residual network based on MDSR [20], which shares most of the parameters across different scales. In order to utilize various features in each real image adaptively, the MCML-Yonsei team added an attention module in the existing Resblock. As shown in Fig. 14, the attention module is based on MAMNet [17] where the global variance pooling was replaced with total variation pooling.

They initialized all parameters except the attention module with the pre-trained MDSR, which was optimized for bicubic downsampling based training data. The mini-batch size was set to 16 and the patch size was set to 48. They subtracted the mean of each R, G, B channel of the train set for data normalization. The learning rate was initially set to $1e - 4$, and it decayed at the 15k steps. The total training step was 20k.

kailos

The kailos team proposed RRBD Network with Attention mechanism using Wavelet loss for Single Image Super-Resolution. The loss function consisted of conventional L_1 loss $\mathcal{L}_{L_1}$ and novel wavelet loss $\mathcal{L}_{wavelet}$. The conventional L_1 loss $\mathcal{L}_{L_1}$ is given as $\mathcal{L}_{L_1} = \sum | x - y |_1$, where x is reconstructed image and y is ground truth image.

A wavelet transform can separate the signal features along the low and high frequency components. Most of the energy distribution in the signal, such as global structure and color distribution, is concentrated in the low frequency components. On the other hand, the high frequency components include signal patterns and image textures. Since both frequency components have different characteristics, a different loss function must be applied to each component. Therefore, the proposed novel wavelet loss $\mathcal{L}_{wavelet}$ is the sum of L_1 loss for high frequency components and L_2 loss for low frequency components given as $\mathcal{L}_{high} = \sum_{i=1}^{N} | \Psi_H^i(x) - \Psi_H^i(y) |_1$, $\mathcal{L}_{low} = \sum_{i=1}^{N} \| \Psi_L^i(x) - \Psi_L^i(y) \|_2^2$, and $\mathcal{L}_{wavelet} = \mathcal{L}_{low} + \mathcal{L}_{high}$, where N denotes the stage of wavelet transform and Ψ_H and Ψ_L are high and low frequency decomposition filters, respectively.

In the experiment, N is 2 and Haar wavelet filters are used as wavelet decomposition filters. Therefore, a total loss is defined by $\mathcal{L}_{total} = \mathcal{L}_{L_1} + \lambda \, \mathcal{L}_{wavelet}$, where λ denotes the regularization parameter and $\lambda = 1$ was used in the proposed method. Figure 16 shows an overview of the proposed method. Adam optimizer was used in training process, and the size of image patch was the quarter size of training data.

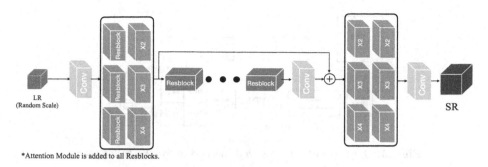

Fig. 13. Overview of the network for the MCML-Yonsei team.

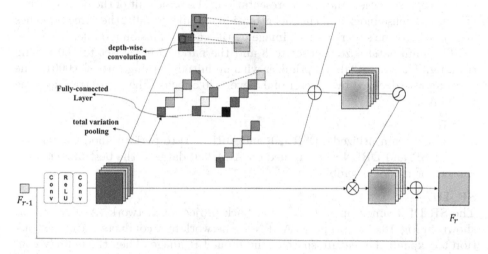

Fig. 14. Resblock with attention module for the MCML-Yonsei team.

qwq

The qwq team proposed a Multi-Scale Network based on RCAN [51]. As shown in Fig[1], the multi-scale mechanism was integrated into the base block of RCAN in order to enlarge the receptive field. Dual Loss was adopted for training. Mix-Corrupt augmentation was conducted, for it allowed the network to learn from robust SR results from different degradations, which is specially designed for the real-world scenario.

RRDN_IITKGP

The RRDN_IITKGP used a GAN based Residual in Residual Dense Network [38], where the model is pre-trained on other dataset and evaluated on the challenge dataset.

SR-IM

The SR-IM team proposed frequency-aware network [29], as shown in Fig. 17. A hierarchical feature extractor (HFE) is utilized to extract the high representation,

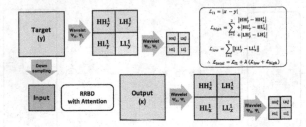

Fig. 15. Overview of the proposed method of for the kailos team.

middle representation and low representation. The basic unit of the body consists of residual dense block and channel attention module. Finally, the three branches are fused into one super-resolved image by the gate and fusion module.

The mini-batch size was set to 8 and the patch size was set to 160 during training. They used Adam optimizer with an initial learning rate of 0.0001. The learning rate decayed by a factor of 0.5 every 30 epochs. The entire training time is about 48 h.

JNSR

The JNSR team utilized EDSR [20] and DRLN [1] to perform model ensemble. The EDSR and DRLN were trained on AIM2020 dataset, the best models were chosen for model ensemble.

SR_DL

The SR_DL team proposed attention back projection network (ABPN++), as shown in Fig. 18. The proposed ABPN++ network first conducts feature extraction to expand the feature space of the input LR image. Then the densely connected enhanced down- and up-sampling back projection blocks perform up- and down-sampling the feature maps. The Cross-scale Attention Block (CAB) takes the outputs from down-sampling back projection blocks to compute the cross-correlation for feature fusion. Finally, the Refined Back Projection Block works as a final refinement that estimates the feature residuals between input LR and predicted LR images for update. The complete network includes 10 down- and up-sampling back projection block, 2 feature extraction blocks and 1 refined back projection block. Each back projection block is made of 5 convolutional layers. The kernel number is 32 for all convolution and deconvolution layers. For down- and up-sampling convolution layer, the kernel size is 6, stride is 4 and padding is 1.

The mini-batch size was set to 16 and the LR patch size was set to 48 during training. The learning rate is fixed to 1e-4 for all layers for 2×10^5 iterations in total as the first stage. Then the batch size increases to 32 for 1×10^5 iterations as fine-tuning.

Webbzhou

The Webbzhou team fine-tuned the pre-trained RRDB [38] on the challenge dataset.

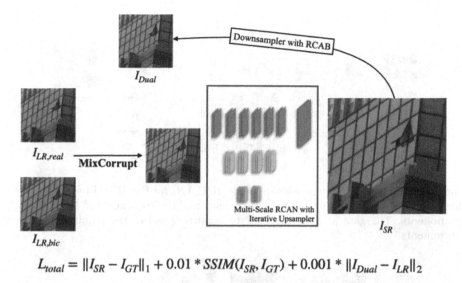

$$L_{total} = \|I_{SR} - I_{GT}\|_1 + 0.01 * SSIM(I_{SR}, I_{GT}) + 0.001 * \|I_{Dual} - I_{LR}\|_2$$

Fig. 16. The total learning diagram of for the qwq team. In upsample network, they used features from 0.25×, 1×, 2× and 4×(HR) five scales.

MoonCloud

The MoonCloud team utilized RCAN [51] for the challenge. Totally 6 models were used for model ensemble. Three of them were trained on challenge dataset with scale of 4. The other three were trained on the challenge dataset with scale of 3, which were fine-tuned on the dataset with scale of 4 after. The final outputs were obtained by averaging the outputs of these six models.

SrDance

The SrDance team utilized RRDB [38]. A new training strategy was adopted for model optimization. The model was firstly pre-trained on DIV2K dataset. Then they trained their model by randomly picking one image in dataset and randomly crop a few 40 × 40 patches, which is alike stochastic gradient descent. Second, when model stepped, they trained on 10 pics, one 40 × 40 patch from each picture and fed to the model.

MLP_SR

The MLP_SR team proposed Deep Cyclic Generative Adversarial Residual Convolutional Networks for Real Image Super-Resolution [35], as shown in Fig. 19. The SR generator [34] network G_{SR} was trained in a GAN framework by using the LR (**y**) images with their corresponding HR images with pixel-wise supervision in the clean HR target domain (**x**), while maintaining the cyclic consistency between the LR and HR domain.

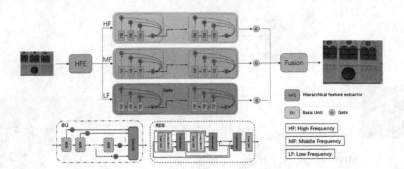

Fig. 17. Structure of Frequency-aware Network (FAN) for the SR-IM team. There are three branches, representing the high frequency, middle frequency and low frequency components. The gate attention is used to adaptively select the required frequency components.

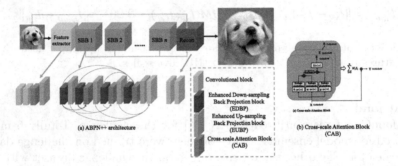

Fig. 18. (a): ABPN++: Attention based Back Projection Network for image super-resolution. (b): the proposed Cross-scale Attention Block by the SR_DL team.

congxiaofeng

The congxiaofeng team proposed RDB-P SRNet, which contains several residual-dense blocks with pixel shuffle for upsampling. The network was inspired by RDN [53].

debut_kele

The debut_kele team proposed Enhanced Deep Residual Networks for real image super-resolution.

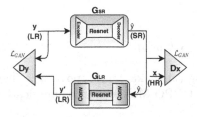

Fig. 19. Illustration of the structure of SR approach setup proposed by the MLP_SR team.

Acknowledgements. We thank the AIM 2020 sponsors: Huawei, MediaTek, NVIDIA, Qualcomm AI Research, Google and Computer Vision Lab (CVL) ETH Zurich.

A. Teams and Affiliations

AIM2020 team
Title: AIM 2020 Challenge on Real Image Super-Resolution
Members:
Pengxu Wei[1] (weipx3@mail.sysu.edu.cn),
Hannan Lu[2] (hannanlu@hit.edu.cn),
Radu Timofte[3] (radu.timofte@vision.ee.ethz.ch),
Liang Lin[1] (linliang@ieee.org),
Wangmeng Zuo[2] (cswmzuo@gmail.com)
Affiliations:
[1] Sun Yat-sen University, China
[2] Harbin Institute of Technology University, China
[3] Computer Vision Lab, ETH Zurich, Switzerland

Baidu
Title: Real Image Super Resolution via Heterogeneous Model Ensemble using GP-NAS
Members: Zhihong Pan[1] (zhihongpan@baidu.com), Baopu Li[1] Teng Xi[2], Yanwen Fan[2], Gang Zhang[2], Jingtuo Liu[2], Junyu Han[2], Errui Ding[2]
Affiliation:
[1] Baidu Research (USA)
[2] Department of Computer Vision Technology (VIS), Baidu Incorporation

CETC-CSKT
Title: Adaptive dense connection super resolution reconstruction
Members: Tangxin Xie (xxh96@outlook.com), Yi Shen, Jialiang Zhang, Yu Jia, Liang Cao, Yan Zou
Affiliation: China Electronic Technology Cyber Security Co., Ltd.

OPPO_CAMERA
Title: Self-Calibrated Attention Neural Network for Real-World Super Resolution
Members: Kaihua Cheng (chengkaihua@oppo.com), Chenhuan Wu
Affiliation: Guangdong OPPO Mobile Telecommunications Corp., Ltd.

ALONG
Title: Dual Path Network with High Frequency Guided for Real World Image Super-Resolution
Members: Yue Lin (gzlinyue@corp.netease.com), Cen Liu, Yunbo Peng
Affiliation: NetEase Games AI Lab

Noah_TerminalVision
Title: Super Resolution with weakly-paired data using an Adaptive Robust Loss
Members: Xueyi Zou (zouxueyi@huawei.com),
Affiliation: Noah's Ark Lab, Huawei

DeepBlueAI
Title: A solution based on RCAN
Members: Zhipeng Luo, Yuehan Yao (yaoyh@deepblueai.com), Zhenyu Xu
Affiliation: DeepBlue Technology (Shanghai) Co., Ltd

TeamInception
Title: Learning Enriched Features for Real Image Restoration and Enhancement
Members: Syed Waqas Zamir (waqas.zamir@inceptioniai.org), Aditya Arora, Salman Khan, Munawar Hayat, Fahad Shahbaz Khan
Affiliation: Inception Institute of Artificial Intelligence (IIAI)

MCML-Yonsei
Title: Multi-scale Dynamic Residual Network Using Total Variation for Real Image Super-Resolution
Members: Keon-Hee Ahn (khahn196@gmail.com), Jun-Hyuk Kim, Jun-Ho Choi, Jong-Seok Lee
Affiliation: Yonsei University

lyl
Title: Coarse to Fine Pyramid Networks for Progressive image super-resolution
Members: Tongtong Zhao (daitoutiere@gmail.com), Shanshan Zhao
Affiliation: Dalian Maritime Univerity

kailos
Title: RRDB Network with Attention mechanism using Wavelet loss for Single Image Super-Resolution

Members: Yoseob Han[1] (yoseobhan@lanl.gov), Byung-Hoon Kim[2], JaeHyun Baek[3]
Affiliation:
[1] Loa Alamos National Laboratory (LANL)
[2] Korea Advanced Institute of Science and Technology (KAIST)
[3] Amazon Web Services (AWS)

qwq
Title: Dual Learning for SR using Multi-Scale Network
Members: Haoning Wu, Dejia Xu *Affiliation:* Peking University

AiAiR
Title: OADDet: Orientation-aware Convolutions Meet Dual Path Enhancement Network
Members: Bo Zhou[1] (1826356001@qq.com),
Haodong Yu[2] (haodong.yu@outlook.com)
Affiliation:
[1] Jiangnan University
[2] Karlsruher Institut fuer Technologie

JNSR
Title: Dual Path Enhancement Network
Members: Bo Zhou (jeasonzhou1@gmail.com)
Affiliation: Jiangnan University

SrDance
Title: Training Strategy Optimization
Members: Wei Guan (missanswer@163.com), Xiaobo Li, Chen Ye
Affiliation: Tongji University

GDUT-SL
Title: Ensemble of RRDB for Image Restoration
Members: Hao Li (2111903004@mail2.gdut.edu.cn), Haoyu Zhong, Yukai Shi, Zhijing Yang, Xiaojun Yang
Affiliation: Guangdong University of Technology

MoonCloud
Title: Mixed Residual Channel Attention
Members: Haoyu Zhong (hy0421@outlook.com), Yukai Shi, Xiaojun Yang, Zhijing Yang,
Affiliation: Guangdong University of Technology,

SR-IM
Title: FAN: Frequency-aware network for image super-resolution

Members: Xin Li (`lixin666@mail.ustc.edu.cn`), Xin Jin, Yaojun Wu, Yingxue Pang, Sen Liu
Affiliation: University of Science and Technology of China

SR_DL

Title: ABPN++: Attention based Back Projection Network for image super-resolution
Members: Zhi-Song Liu[1], Li-Wen Wang[2], Chu-Tak Li[2], Marie-Paule Cani[1], Wan-Chi Siu[2]
Affiliation:
[1] LIX - Computer science laboratory at the Ecole polytechnique [Palaiseau]
[2] Center of Multimedia Signal Processing, The Hong Kong Polytechnic University

Webbzhou

Title: RRDB for Real World Super-Resolution
Members: Yuanbo Zhou (`webbozhou@gmail.com`),
Affiliation: Fuzhou University, Fujian Province, China

MLP SR

Title: Deep Cyclic Generative Adversarial Residual Convolutional Networks for Real Image Super-Resolution
Members: Rao Muhammad Umer (`engr.raoumer943@gmail.com`), Christian Micheloni
Affiliation: University Of Udine, Italy

congxiaofeng

Title: RDB-P SRNet: Residual-dense block with pixel shuffle
Members: Xiaofeng Cong (`1752808219@qq.com`)
Affiliation: (Not provided)

RRDN_IITKGP

Title: A GAN based Residual in Residual Dense Network
Members: Rajat Gupta (`rajatgba2021@email.iimcal.ac.in`)
Affiliation: Indian Institute of Technology

debut_kele

Title: Self-supervised Learning for Pretext Training
Members: Kele Xu (`kelele.xu@gmail.com`), Hengxing Cai, Yuzhong Liu
Affiliation: National University of Defense Technology

Team-24
Title: VCBPv2 - VCycles Backprojection Upscaling Network
Members: Feras Almasri, Thomas Vandamme, Olivier Debeir
Affiliation: Universié Libre de Bruxelles, LISA department

References

1. Anwar, S., Barnes, N.: Densely residual laplacian super-resolution. arXiv preprint arXiv:1906.12021 (2019)
2. Barron, J.T.: A general and adaptive robust loss function. In: Proceedings of the IEEE Conference on Computer Vision and Pattern Recognition, pp. 4331–4339 (2019)
3. Cai, J., Gu, S., Timofte, R., Zhang, L.: Ntire 2019 challenge on real image super-resolution: methods and results. In: Proceedings of the IEEE/CVF Conference on Computer Vision and Pattern Recognition (CVPR) Workshops, June 2019
4. Cai, J., Zeng, H., Yong, H., Cao, Z., Zhang, L.: Toward real-world single image super-resolution: a new benchmark and a new model. In: International Conference on Computer Vision (2019)
5. Chen, C., Xiong, Z., Tian, X., Zha, Z., Wu, F.: Camera lens super-resolution. In: IEEE Conference on Computer Vision and Pattern Recognition. pp. 1652–1660 (2019)
6. Cheng, K., Wu, C.: Self-calibrated attention neural network for real-world super resolution. In: European Conference on Computer Vision Workshops (2020)
7. DeVries, T., Taylor, G.W.: Improved regularization of convolutional neural networks with cutout. arXiv preprint arXiv:1708.04552 (2017)
8. Dong, C., Loy, C.C., He, K., Tang, X.: Learning a deep convolutional network for image super-resolution. In: European Conference on Computer Vision, pp. 184–199 (2014)
9. Du, C., et al.: Orientation-aware deep neural network for real image super-resolution. In: Proceedings of the IEEE Conference on Computer Vision and Pattern Recognition (CVPR) Workshops, June 2019
10. El Helou, M., Zhou, R., Süsstrunk, S., Timofte, R., et al.: AIM 2020: scene relighting and illumination estimation challenge. In: European Conference on Computer Vision Workshops (2020)
11. Fuoli, D., Huang, Z., Gu, S., Timofte, R., et al.: AIM 2020 challenge on video extreme super-resolution: Methods and results. In: European Conference on Computer Vision Workshops (2020)
12. Glasner, D., Bagon, S., Irani, M.: Super-resolution from a single image. In: 2009 IEEE 12th International Conference on Computer Vision, pp. 349–356 (2009)
13. He, K., Sun, J., Tang, X.: Guided image filtering. IEEE Trans. Pattern Anal. Machine Intell. **35**(6), 1397–1409 (2012)
14. Hu, J., Shen, L., Sun, G.: Squeeze-and-excitation networks. In: CVPR (2018)
15. Ignatov, A., Timofte, R., et al.: AIM 2020 challenge on learned image signal processing pipeline. In: European Conference on Computer Vision Workshops (2020)
16. Ignatov, A., Timofte, R., et al.: AIM 2020 challenge on rendering realistic bokeh. In: European Conference on Computer Vision Workshops (2020)
17. Kim, J.H., Choi, J.H., Cheon, M., Lee, J.S.: Mamnet: multi-path adaptive modulation network for image super-resolution. Neurocomputing **402**, 38–49 (2020)

18. Ledig, C., et al.: Photo-realistic single image super-resolution using a generative adversarial network. In: IEEE Conference on Computer Vision and Pattern Recognition, pp. 105–114 (2017)

19. Li, Z., Xi, T., Deng, J., Zhang, G., Wen, S., He, R.: Gp-nas: gaussian process based neural architecture search. In: Proceedings of the IEEE Conference on Computer Vision and Pattern Recognition (CVPR), June 2020

20. Lim, B., Son, S., Kim, H., Nah, S., Lee, K.M.: Enhanced deep residual networks for single image super-resolution. In: IEEE Conference on Computer Vision and Pattern Recognition Workshops, pp. 1132–1140 (2017)

21. Lim, B., Son, S., Kim, H., Nah, S., Lee, K.M.: Enhanced deep residual networks for single image super-resolution. In: IEEE Conference on Computer Vision and Pattern Recognition (CVPR) Workshops (2017)

22. Liu, J.J., Hou, Q., Cheng, M.M., Wang, C., Feng, J.: Improving convolutional networks with self-calibrated convolutions. In: Proceedings of the IEEE Conference on Computer Vision and Pattern Recognition, pp. 10096–10105 (2020)

23. Lugmayr, A., Danelljan, M., Timofte, R.: Unsupervised learning for real-world super-resolution. In: 2019 IEEE/CVF International Conference on Computer Vision Workshop (ICCVW), pp. 3408–3416. IEEE (2019)

24. Lugmayr, A., Danelljan, M., Timofte, R.: Ntire 2020 challenge on real-world image super-resolution: methods and results. In: Proceedings of the IEEE/CVF Conference on Computer Vision and Pattern Recognition (CVPR) Workshops, June 2020

25. Lugmayr, A., et al.: Aim 2019 challenge on real-world image super-resolution: methods and results. In: 2019 IEEE/CVF International Conference on Computer Vision Workshop (ICCVW), pp. 3575–3583. IEEE (2019)

26. Ma, Y., Yu, D., Wu, T., Wang, H.: Paddlepaddle: an open-source deep learning platform from industrial practice. Front. Data Comput. 1(1), 105–115 (2019)

27. Ntavelis, E., Romero, A., Bigdeli, S.A., Timofte, R., et al.: AIM 2020 challenge on image extreme inpainting. In: European Conference on Computer Vision Workshops (2020)

28. Pan, Z., Li, B., Xi, T., Fan, Y., Zhang, G., Liu, J., Han, J., Ding, E.: Real image super resolution via heterogeneous model ensemble using gp-nas. In: European Conference on Computer Vision Workshop (2020)

29. Pang, Y., Li, X., Jin, X., Wu, Y., Liu, J., Liu, S., Chen, Z.: FAN: frequency aggregation network for real image super-resolution. In: European Conference on Computer Vision Workshops (2020)

30. Shang, T., Dai, Q., Zhu, S., Yang, T., Guo, Y.: Perceptual extreme super-resolution network with receptive field block. In: Proceedings of the IEEE/CVF Conference on Computer Vision and Pattern Recognition Workshops, pp. 440–441 (2020)

31. Shi, Y., Zhong, H., Yang, Z., Yang, X., Lin, L.: Ddet: Dual-path dynamic enhancement network for real-world image super-resolution. arXiv preprint arXiv:2002.11079 (2020)

32. Son, S., Lee, J., Nah, S., Timofte, R., Lee, K.M., et al.: AIM 2020 challenge on video temporal super-resolution. In: European Conference on Computer Vision Workshops (2020)

33. Szegedy, C., et al.: Going deeper with convolutions. In: IEEE Conference on Computer Vision and Pattern Recognition (CVPR) (2015)

34. Umer, R.M., Foresti, G.L., Micheloni, C.: Deep generative adversarial residual convolutional networks for real-world super-resolution, pp. 1769–1777 (2020)

35. Umer, R.M., Micheloni, C.: Deep cyclic generative adversarial residual convolutional networks for real image super-resolution. In: European Conference on Computer Vision Workshops (2020)

36. Wang, Q., Wu, B., Zhu, P., Li, P., Zuo, W., Hu, Q.: Eca-net: efficient channel attention for deep convolutional neural networks. In: Proceedings of the IEEE Conference on Computer Vision and Pattern Recognition, pp. 11534–11542 (2020)

37. Wang, X., Chan, K.C., Yu, K., Dong, C., Change Loy, C.: Edvr: video restoration with enhanced deformable convolutional networks. In: Proceedings of the IEEE Conference on Computer Vision and Pattern Recognition Workshops (2019)

38. Wang, X., et al.: Esrgan: enhanced super-resolution generative adversarial networks. In: Proceedings of the European Conference on Computer Vision (2018)

39. Wei, P., Lu, H., Timofte, R., Lin, L., Zuo, W., et al.: AIM 2020 challenge on real image super-resolution. In: European Conference on Computer Vision Workshops (2020)

40. Wei, P., Xie, Z., Lu, H., Zhan, Z., Ye, Q., Zuo, W., Lin, L.: Component divide-and-conquer for real-world image super-resolution. In: European Conference on Computer Vision (2020)

41. Woo, S., Park, J., Lee, J.Y., So Kweon, I.: CBAM: Convolutional block attention module. In: ECCV (2018)

42. Xie, T., Li, J., Shen, Y., Jia, Y., Zhang, J., Zeng, B.: Enhanced adaptive dense connection single image super-resolution. In: European Conference on Computer Vision Workshops (2020)

43. Xie, T., Yang, X., Jia, Y., Zhu, C., Xiaochuan, L.: Adaptive densely connected single image super-resolution. In: 2019 IEEE/CVF International Conference on Computer Vision Workshop (ICCVW), pp. 3432–3440. IEEE (2019)

44. Yang, J., Wright, J., Huang, T.S., Ma, Y.: Image super-resolution via sparse representation. IEEE Trans. Image Process. **19**(11), 2861–2873 (2010)

45. Yoo, J., Ahn, N., Sohn, K.A.: Rethinking data augmentation for image super-resolution: a comprehensive analysis and a new strategy. In: Proceedings of the IEEE Conference on Computer Vision and Pattern Recognition, pp. 8375–8384 (2020)

46. Yun, S., Han, D., Oh, S.J., Chun, S., Choe, J., Yoo, Y.: Cutmix: regularization strategy to train strong classifiers with localizable features. In: Proceedings of the IEEE International Conference on Computer Vision, pp. 6023–6032 (2019)

47. Zamir, S.W., Arora, A., Khan, S., Hayat, M., Khan, F.S., Yang, M.H., Shao, L.: Learning enriched features for real image restoration and enhancement. In: ECCV (2020)

48. Zhang, H., Cisse, M., Dauphin, Y.N., Lopez-Paz, D.: mixup: Beyond empirical risk minimization. arXiv preprint arXiv:1710.09412 (2017)

49. Zhang, K., Danelljan, M., Li, Y., Timofte, R., et al.: AIM 2020 challenge on efficient super-resolution: methods and results. In: European Conference on Computer Vision Workshops (2020)

50. Zhang, X., Chen, Q., Ng, R., Koltun, V.: Zoom to learn, learn to zoom. In: Proceedings of the IEEE Conference on Computer Vision and Pattern Recognition, pp. 3762–3770 (2019)

51. Zhang, Y., Li, K., Li, K., Wang, L., Zhong, B., Fu, Y.: Image super-resolution using very deep residual channel attention networks. In: Proceedings of the European Conference on Computer Vision, pp. 286–301 (2018)

52. Zhang, Y., Li, K., Li, K., Wang, L., Zhong, B., Fu, Y.: Image super-resolution using very deep residual channel attention networks. In: Proceedings of the European Conference on Computer Vision (ECCV), pp. 286–301 (2018)

53. Zhang, Y., Tian, Y., Kong, Y., Zhong, B., Fu, Y.: Residual dense network for image super-resolution. In: Proceedings of the IEEE International Conference on Computer Vision (2018)

54. Zhou, S., Zhang, J., Pan, J., Xie, H., Zuo, W., Ren, J.: Spatio-temporal filter adaptive network for video deblurring. In: Proceedings of the IEEE International Conference on Computer Vision, pp. 2482–2491 (2019)
55. Zhou, S., Zhang, J., Zuo, W., Xie, H., Pan, J., Ren, J.S.: Davanet: stereo deblurring with view aggregation. In: Proceedings of the IEEE Conference on Computer Vision and Pattern Recognition, pp. 10996–11005 (2019)

Real Image Super Resolution via Heterogeneous Model Ensemble Using GP-NAS

Zhihong Pan[1(✉)], Baopu Li[1], Teng Xi[2], Yanwen Fan[2], Gang Zhang[2],
Jingtuo Liu[2], Junyu Han[2], and Errui Ding[2]

[1] Baidu Research, Baidu Inc., Sunnyvale, USA
{zhihongpan,baopuli}@baidu.com

[2] Department of Computer Vision Technology (VIS), Baidu Inc., Beijing, China
{xiteng01,fanyanwen,zhanggang03,liujingtuo,hanjunyu,dingerrui}@baidu.com

Abstract. With advancement in deep neural network (DNN), recent
state-of-the-art (SOTA) image super-resolution (SR) methods have
achieved impressive performance using deep residual network with dense
skip connections. While these models perform well on benchmark dataset
where low-resolution (LR) images are constructed from high-resolution
(HR) references with known blur kernel, real image SR is more challenging when both images in the LR-HR pair are collected from real cameras.
Based on existing dense residual networks, a Gaussian process based neural architecture search (GP-NAS) scheme is utilized to find candidate network architectures using a large search space by varying the number of
dense residual blocks, the block size and the number of features. A suite of
heterogeneous models with diverse network structure and hyperparameter are selected for model-ensemble to achieve outstanding performance in
real image SR. The proposed method won the first place in all three tracks
of the AIM 2020 Real Image Super-Resolution Challenge.

Keywords: Single image super resolution · Dense residual network ·
Neural architecture search

1 Introduction

Image super-resolution (SR) refers the process to recover high-resolution (HR)
images from low-resolution (LR) inputs. It is an important image processing
technique to enhance image quality which subsequently helps to improve higher-
level computer vision tasks [3,8]. Over the years, many classical SR methods have
been proposed to successfully use various levels of features like statistics [24],
edges [26,27] and patches [28,31] to restore HR images from LR inputs. While
there are also methods developed for SR using multiple frames [10], the scope
of introduction here is limited to single image super-resolution (SISR).

More recently, the powerful deep learning techniques have led to developments of many deep learning based SR models [4,12,14,17,33,34]. These deep

© Springer Nature Switzerland AG 2020
A. Bartoli and A. Fusiello (Eds.): ECCV 2020 Workshops, LNCS 12537, pp. 423–436, 2020.
https://doi.org/10.1007/978-3-030-67070-2_25

learning models commonly rely on a large set of synthetic training image pairs, where the LR input is downsampled from the HR reference image using bicubic interpolation with antialiasing filters. Common image quality metrics used to assess performance of these SR models include peak signal-to-noise ratio (PSNR) and the structural similarity index (SSIM) [35], both emphasizing image restoration fidelity by comparing to the HR reference. This may lead to SR results of high PSNR values but lack of HR details perceptually. Lately, a new metric LPIPS [32] is proposed to apply image features extracted from pretrained AlexNet [13] to compare two images. The smaller LPIPS is, the closer the generated SR image is to the HR reference perceptually. With advancements in Generative Adversarial Nets (GAN) [5], SR models trained using GAN [9,21,29] have achieved the best performance of image perceptual quality as compared to LPIPS.

In the past few years, neural architecture search (NAS) that aims to find the optimal network structure has received a lot of attention [18,19,36,37]. It effectively boosts the SOTA in many typical computer vision problems such as image classification [20], object detection [16], segmentation [1] and so on. Most recently, some researches also begin to apply NAS for image SR problems [2,7,25] with impressive results using efficient SR models.

In general, the SR problem is ill-posed as there are multiple HR images corresponding to a single LR image even when the LR image is constructed from the HR reference using bicubic interpolation without added noise. This ambiguity increases when the blur kernel and noise statistics of the LR are not known, and is even more prominent in real image SR problems where the LR image is not constructed from the HR reference. With the increased uncertainty, it is common to see different deep learning SR models lead to different versions of the restored HR images for a single LR image, especially when the network architectures are quite different. To achieve the best performance of the real image SR problem set forth by the AIM 2020 challenge [30], a new fusion scheme is proposed in this study to generate the final SR output using multi-level ensemble from a suite of heterogeneous deep learning models that are obtained by applying NAS approach. The main contributions of the proposed method include:

- A Gaussian Process based NAS (GP-NAS) is first utilized for super-resolution with specially designed search space, which can efficiently search and obtain the key architecture related parameters and can yield multiple candidate models.
- A multi-level ensemble scheme is proposed in testing, including self-ensemble for patches, as well as patch-ensemble and model-ensemble for full-size images.
- The proposed method was applied for the AIM 2020 Real Image Super-Resolution Challenge [30] and won the first place in all three tracks (upscaling factors of ×2, ×3 and ×4) with a comfortable margin in both PSNR and SSIM.

2   Related Works

Deep Learning for Single Image Super-Resolution. As the first success-ful application, Dong *et al.* [4] proposed a deep CNN model for end-to-end LR to HR mapping and showed that the training of the neural network is equiva-lent to global optimization of traditional sparse-coding-based SR methods. Kim *et al.*[12] designed a deeply recursive neural network to raise SR performance without increasing parameters for additional convolutions. Ledig *et al.*[14] were the first to use GAN for SR, introducing a perceptual loss function to generate photo-realistic SR images from LR inputs. Inspired by other SR models using deep residual networks [11,12], Lim *et al.*[17] simplified the network structure by removing BN layers and optimized the training process to achieve the best restoration fidelity at that time. Zhang *et al.*first applied dense skip-connections [34] and later channel attention module [33] in deep residual network for fur-ther advancing of SOTA. Most recently, Guo *et al.*[6] proposed a dual-regression method by adding a second downsampling model and corresponding loss to make sure the restored SR image can best match the LR input after downsampled by the co-trained secondary model.

NAS for Single Image Super-Resolution. As the first attempt to apply NAS for SR, Chu *et al.*[2] made use of an elastic search method on both micro and macro level with a hybrid controller that profits from evolutionary compu-tation and reinforcement learning (RL), achieving comparable performance of PSNR with light model. Based on different types of residual blocks and evolu-tionary algorithm, Song *et al.*[25] proposed a search method for better and more efficient network for image SR. Guo *et al.*[7] put forward a novel hierarchical NAS approach that considers both the cell-level and network-level design based on a RL controller. While all the three works are promising at searching for effi-cient SR models where resources like model size or FLOPS are limited, they are not able to achieve the high PSNR or SSIM values comparing to other SOTA methods using manually designed residual networks with dense skip connections. Aiming at AIM 2020 challenge that does not take model efficiency in consider-ation, we mainly concentrate on the macro level structure design for a better network structure that can achieve the best SR performance in terms of PSNR and SSIM. Moreover, instead of using RL or evolutionary based search method that tend to be very time consuming, we apply GP-NAS approach to search the key network structure parameters such as the number of dense residual block, the block size and the number of features.

3   Problem Formulation

Learning based image SR methods often rely on a large number of image pairs, including low-res image $\mathbf{I}_{LR}$ and reference high-res $\mathbf{I}_{HR}$. For real image SR, as shown in Eq. 1, $\mathbf{I}_{LR}$ could be modeled from $\mathbf{I}_{HR}$ using three steps: convolution with a kernel $\mathbf{k}$, downsampling $D_s(\cdot)$ and addition of noise $\mathbf{n}$.

$$\mathbf{I}_{LR} = D_s(\mathbf{I}_{HR} * \mathbf{k}) + \mathbf{n} \tag{1}$$

The goal of image SR is to reverse this process, finding the matching $\mathbf{I}_{HR}$ from a known $\mathbf{I}_{LR}$. This problem is challenging as there are many versions of $\mathbf{I}_{HR}$ that could generate the same $\mathbf{I}_{LR}$ following the process in Eq. 1, even when the kernel $\mathbf{k}$ is known and there is no noise $\mathbf{n}$. Learning based SR model $f(\cdot)$ use a total of n image pairs to minimize the average error as in Eq. 2. It is common that only $\mathbf{I}_{HR}^i$ is a real image and the corresponding $\mathbf{I}_{LR}^i$ is constructed from $\mathbf{I}_{HR}^i$ following the process described in Eq. 1.

$$\arg\min_f \sum \|f(\mathbf{I}_{LR}^i) - \mathbf{I}_{HR}^i\|, i \in \{1, 2, \cdots, n\} \tag{2}$$

In the case that both $\mathbf{I}_{HR}$ and $\mathbf{I}_{LR}$ are real images collected separately, the relationship between the image pair is much more complicated. To get a digital image $\mathbf{I}$ from an object $\mathbf{O}$, there are three transformations included in general as shown in Eq. 3. The optical transformation $\mathbb{O}(\cdot)$ refers to the process of photons reflected from the object passing through the lens of the camera. Optical characteristics of the lens like modulation transfer function (MTF) and lens settings like aperture are key variables here. The second transformation $\mathbb{D}(\cdot)$ refers to the analog to digital converter (ADC) that turns photons to digital numbers, where the noise is introduced. The last one $\mathbb{I}(\cdot)$ refers to the image signal processor (ISP) which transforms noisy raw images to end result of sRGB images. This step is the most complicated of three, including multiple processes like denoising and color balancing at both global and local levels.

$$\mathbf{I} = \mathbb{I}(\mathbb{D}(\mathbb{O}(\mathbf{O}))) \tag{3}$$

As each of the three transformations could be different for HR and LR images, the relationship between $\mathbf{I}_{LR}$ and $\mathbf{I}_{HR}$ can be illustrated as in Eqs. 4–6 where they are linked indirectly by the downsampling of $\mathbf{O}_{HR}$ to $\mathbf{O}_{LR}$ using $D_s(\cdot)$. With all these added variations, the real image SR becomes more challenging. For example, $\mathbf{I}_{HR}$ is more clear in general compared to $\mathbf{I}_{LR}$. But for background objects at a further distance, they could be more blurry in $\mathbf{I}_{HR}$ if its lens has a smaller f-number which lead to smaller depth-of-field. The motivation to use heterogeneous model ensemble is based on the observation that different model could lead to optimization results biased towards different variation factors even when using the same set of training image pairs.

$$\mathbf{I}_{LR} = \mathbb{I}_{LR}(\mathbb{D}_{LR}(\mathbb{O}_{LR}(\mathbf{O}_{LR}))) \tag{4}$$

$$\mathbf{I}_{HR} = \mathbb{I}_{HR}(\mathbb{D}_{HR}(\mathbb{O}_{HR}(\mathbf{O}_{HR}))) \tag{5}$$

$$\mathbf{O}_{LR} = D_s(\mathbf{O}_{HR}) \tag{6}$$

4   Proposed Real Image SR Method

The proposed real image SR method using dense residual network, GP-NAS and heterogeneous model ensemble is explained in this section. First, the primary dense residual network and the search space of different hyperparameters are introduced. Then, method to find heterogeneous models using GP-NAS is explained, followed by the multi-level ensemble that is used to generate full-size SR images for the AIM 2020 challenge [30].

4.1   Dense Residual Network (DRN)

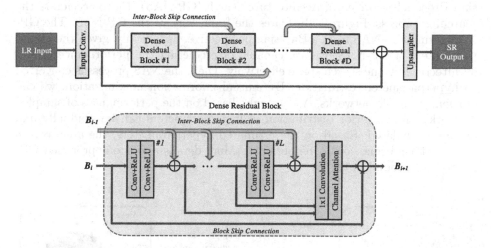

Fig. 1. The deep dense residual network architecture for image super resolution.

The backbone model of the proposed method is a deep dense residual network originally developed for raw image demosaicking and denoising. As depicted in Fig. 1, in addition to the shallow feature convolution at the front and the upsampler at the end, the proposed network consists of a total depth of D dense residual blocks (DRB). The input convolution layer converts the 3-channel LR input to a total of F-channel shallow features. For the middle DRB blocks, each one includes L stages of double layers of convolution and the outputs of all L stages are concatenated together before convoluted from $F \times L$ to F channels. An additional channel-attention layer is included at the end of each block, similar to RCAN [33]. There are two types of skip connections included in each block, the block skip connection (BSC) and inter-block skip connection (IBSC). The BSC is the shortcut between input and output of block B_i, while the IBSC includes two shortcuts from the input of block B_{i-1} to the two stages inside block B_i respectively. The various skip connections, especially IBSC, are included to combine features with a large range of receptive fields. The last block is an enhanced upsampler that transforms all F-channel LR features to the estimated 3-channel SR image. This dense residual network has three main hyperparameters: F is the number of feature channels, D is the number of DRB layers and L is the number of stages for each DRB. All these three hyperparameters will greatly affect the performance of SR. Previous efforts mainly use professional expertise or experience to choose them based on, which is laborious. To overcome this issue, we apply NAS to search for the optimal network structure, which will be elaborated in the subsequent subsection.

4.2   Gaussian Process Based Neural Architecture Search

Since most NAS methods are still time consuming, we had proposed Gaussian Process based Neural Architecture Search (GP-NAS) [15] to accelerate the searching process. Figure 2 illustrates the framework of the GP-NAS. The GP-NAS formulates NAS from a Bayesian perspective. Specifically, given the hyperparameters of GP-NAS, we are capable of predicting the performance of any architectures in the search space effectively. Then, the NAS process is converted to hyperparameters estimation. By mutual information maximization, we can efficiently sample networks. Accordingly, based on the performances of sampled networks, the posterior distribution of hyperparameters can be gradually and efficiently updated. Based on the estimated hyperparameters, the architecture with best performance can be obtained. More details about our proposed GP-NAS can be found in [15].

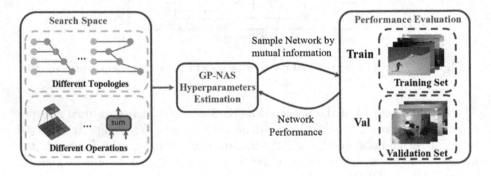

Fig. 2. The framework of the GP-NAS.

4.3   Multi-level Ensemble

Targeting for the AIM 2020 challenge [30], where the test images are much larger than the training patches, a multi-level ensemble scheme is designed to achieve optimal image restoration quality. First, for model-ensemble, the input LR image is processed by a suite of heterogeneous models separately and the output HR images are averaged to get the final output. Additionally, each full size LR input is cropped to patches, with each has an overlapping buffer with neighboring patches. A patch-ensemble method is then used to blend all restored HR patches together, using different weights for each pixel which are correlated to the distance between the patch center and corresponding pixels. The most commonly used self-ensemble is also applied by flipping and/or transposing the input patch before restoration.

5 Experimental Results

The AIM 2020 challenge [30] aims to find a generic model to super-resolve LR images captured in practical scenarios. To achieve this goal, paired LR and HR images were taken by various DSLR cameras. However, images used for training, validation and testing are captured in the same way with the same set of cameras, so the transformation processes described in Eqs. 4–6 are not changed among images of the same upscaling factor, meaning the learned transformation from training data is expected to achieve similar results on the validation and test images. For this new real image SR dataset, a total of 19,000 LR-HR pairs are available for model training for each of the ×2, ×3 and ×4 upscaling factors. The LR image resolutions are 380×380 for ×3, 272×272 for ×2 and 194×194 for ×4 respectively.

For our experiments of each upscaling factor, 600 of the 19,000 pairs are reserved for validation while the remaining ones are used for training. Note that any LR-HR pairs that are not perfectly aligned, those with normalized cross-correlation (NCC) less than 0.99, were excluded from both training and validation. For each epoch, a 120×120 patch is randomly cropped and augmented with flipping and transposing from each training image. A mixed loss of $L1$ and multi-scale structural similarity (MS-SSIM) is taken for training. For the experiment, the new model candidate search scheme using GP-NAS was implemented in PaddlePaddle [22] and the final-training of searched models were conducted using PyTorch [23].

Table 1. Quantitative results of single-model and model-ensemble methods. Best results are in bold and the ranks in each category are superscripted.

	Upscaling ×2		Upscaling ×3		Upscaling ×4	
	PSNR	SSIM	PSNR	SSIM	PSNR	SSIM
DRN*	32.51^1	0.9209^1	31.07^1	0.8796^1	30.26^3	0.8401^3
RCAN*	32.31^3	0.9188^3	30.97^3	0.8787^3	30.31^2	0.8403^1
RCAN	32.40^2	0.9200^2	31.01^2	0.8792^2	30.32^1	0.8402^1
DRN*+RCAN*	32.56^2	0.9210^2	31.21^2	0.8811^3	30.47^3	0.8423^1
RCAN*+RCAN	32.49^3	0.9204^3	31.17^3	0.8807^3	30.48^1	0.8421^3
DRN*+RCAN	32.62^1	0.9215^1	31.24^1	0.8814^1	30.48^1	0.8423^1
3-Model Ensemble	**32.63**	**0.9218**	**31.28**	**0.8822**	**30.55**	**0.8435**

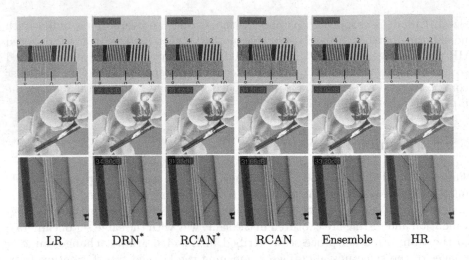

LR   DRN*   RCAN*   RCAN   Ensemble   HR

Fig. 3. Visual and quantitative comparison of ×2 SR results.

5.1   Ablation Study

Ablation studies were conducted to examine the effectiveness of the proposed heterogeneous model ensemble. Three models were trained for all three upscaling factors. DRN* is the selected DRN model using GP-NAS where $F = 128, D = 18, L = 3$. RCAN* is the GP-NAS selected variation of RCAN [33] with 128 features, 5 residual groups and 10 residual blocks in each group. And RCAN uses the original settings in [33] with 64 features, 10 residual groups and 20 residual blocks per group.

As shown in Table 1, the average performances of three individual models are very close. In general, DRN* is the best with RCAN as the close second. In comparison, results from model ensemble is always better than the individual models of the ensemble no matter it is a 2-model ensemble or 3-model one. Overall, the best results are always from the 3-model ensemble. One thing interesting to note is, out of three 2-model ensemble results, the one combining RCAN and RCAN* is consistently worse than others. It could be explained that, for heterogeneous model ensemble, differences in network architecture is more beneficial than differences in hyperparameters of the same network architecture.

Some image examples are shown in Figs. 3, 4 and 5, where PSNR values of SR results are also annotated for quantitative comparison too. For small upscaling factor ×2 as in Fig. 3, there is no big difference among SR results visually. In the top example, individual SR models are all able to super-resolve the fine line features which are blurred in the LR input. By combining the models together, the ensemble result has higher PSNR than individual ones. But the other two examples show that the ensemble PSNR is lower than the best individual one. For the middle one, RCAN* seems to be the outlier comparing with the other two. Removing outlier before averaging would have increased the performance

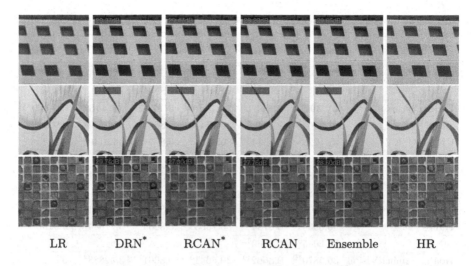

LR   DRN*   RCAN*   RCAN   Ensemble   HR

Fig. 4. Visual and quantitative comparison of ×3 SR results.

of ensemble. However, the outlier DRN* in the bottom example is the most accurate and removing it would lead to worse ensemble result.

Visual difference starts to stand out more in ×3 examples as represented in Fig. 4. For the first example on the top, all three individual models are able to super-resolve the small dot pattern which are blurred in LR input, but each is slightly different in details. By combining the models together, the ensemble result has higher PSNR than individual ones. The middle example also show ensemble result is higher than all individual ones and the visual difference are around the feather-like structures, showing different color and contrast. The

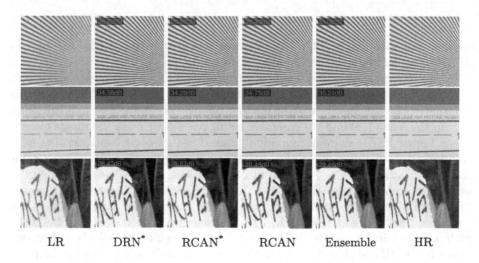

LR   DRN*   RCAN*   RCAN   Ensemble   HR

Fig. 5. Visual and quantitative comparison of ×4 SR results.

Table 2. Quantitative results of all three tracks for the AIM 2020 Real Image Super-Resolution Challenge [30]. The superscript number indicates ranking of each metric.

	Upscaling ×4		Upscaling ×3		Upscaling ×2	
	PSNR	SSIM	PSNR	PSNR	PSNR	SSIM
Baidu (ours)	**31.3960**[1]	**0.8751**[1]	**30.9496**[1]	**0.8762**[1]	**33.4460**[1]	**0.9270**[1]
ALONG	31.2369[2]	0.8742[3]	30.3745[5]	0.8661[6]	33.0982[8]	0.9238[6]
CETC-CSKT	31.1226[4]	0.8744[2]	30.7651[2]	0.8714[2]	33.3140[2]	0.9245[2]
SR-IM	31.1735[3]	0.8728[7]	–	–	–	–
DeepBlueAI	30.9638[6]	0.8737[4]	30.3017[7]	0.8665[4]	33.1771[7]	0.9236[7]
JNSR	30.9988[5]	0.8722[8]	–	–	–	–
OPPO_CAMERA	30.8603[8]	0.8736[5]	30.5373[4]	0.8695[3]	33.3091[3]	0.9242[4]
Kailos	30.8659[7]	0.8734[6]	30.1303[8]	0.8664[5]	32.7084[12]	0.9196[11]
SR_DL	30.6045[9]	0.8660[12]	–	–	–	–
Noah_TerminalVision	30.5870[10]	0.8662[11]	30.5641[3]	0.8661[7]	33.2888[4]	0.9228[8]
Webbzhou	30.4174[12]	0.8673[10]	–	–	–	–
TeamInception	30.3465[13]	0.8681[9]	–	–	33.2322[6]	0.9240[5]
lyl	30.3191[14]	0.8655[13]	30.3654[6]	0.8642[8]	32.9368[10]	0.9210[9]
MCML-Yonsei	30.4201[11]	0.8637[15]	–	–	32.9032[11]	0.9186[12]
MoonCloud	30.2827[15]	0.8644[14]	–	–	–	–
qwq	29.5878[17]	0.8547[16]	29.2656[9]	0.8521[9]	31.64[13]	0.9126[13]
SrDance	29.5952[16]	0.8523[17]	–	–	–	–
MLP_SR	28.6185[18]	0.8314[18]	–	–	–	–
RRDN_IITKGP	27.9708[19]	0.8085[20]	–	–	29.8506[14]	0.8453[14]
congxiaofeng	26.3915[20]	0.8258[19]	–	–	–	–
AiAiR	–	–	18.1903[10]	0.8245[10]	33.2633[5]	0.9243[3]
GDUT-SL	–	–	–	–	32.9725[9]	0.9204[10]

bottom example shows DRN* has sharper image than the other two and its PSNR is higher than the ensemble as a result.

More interesting visual differences are observed in ×4 examples as shown in Fig. 5. For the first two examples, individual models resolve the blurred details differently, like the lines near right bottom right corner in the first and the small text in the second. While the ensemble result doesn't increase the image clarity, it has higher PSNR than all individual ones. The last one is worth noting as it demonstrates the difference in the optical transformation $\mathbb{O}(\cdot)$ for different cameras as explained in Sect. 3. The front object in HR image is clearer comparing to LR due to higher spatial resolution, but its background plant is more blurry than the LR counterpart, probably because the camera used for HR images has a smaller depth-of-field. The individual SR models handle this quite differently, with DRN* mimics the depth-of-field of the LR camera while the other two closer to the HR version. The ensemble method results in a significant increase in PSNR comparing to individual ones.

5.2   AIM 2020 Challenge Results [30]

To generate the full-size SR images for the AIM 2020 challenge, all three models from the ablation study were used for all three upscaling tracks. For ×4 track, a double regression model [6] was also trained to include in the model ensemble. Each full-size LR test images were cropped to 120×120 patches and self-ensemble (×8) was applied. The cropping window was slided at 60-pixel spacing and the overlapping patches were average using weights correlated with the distance between the patch center and each pixel. With ensemble applied to all three levels, the generated full-size images were submitted to the challenge and won the first place at all three tracks. As shown in Table 2, both our PSNR and SSIM values lead the second place with a comfortable margin.

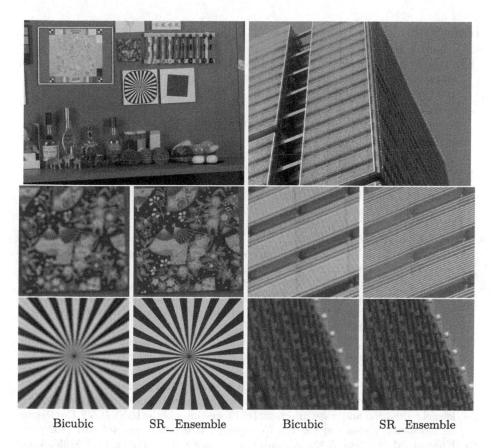

Bicubic   SR_Ensemble   Bicubic   SR_Ensemble

Fig. 6. Examples of full-size test images from the AIM 2020 challenge (×4).

One set of representative ×4 images are shown in the Fig. 6. The full-size SR output are located at the top, with selected areas zoomed in to compare with bicubic interpolation results.

6   Conclusions

In this paper, based on the models searched via GP-NAS, we have introduced a new heterogeneous model ensemble method for real image super resolution. Since network architecture greatly affects the results of SR, we first apply GP-NAS approach to search the key factors such as the number of residual network block, block size and the number of features in our network structure. Then, different models selected using GP-NAS are fused together to boost the performance of SR. Combined with patch-ensemble and self-ensemble, the proposed new scheme is validated to be highly effective, generating impressive testing results on all three tracks ($\times 2$, $\times 3$ and $\times 4$) of the AIM 2020 challenge [30] in terms of both PSNR and SSIM.

References

1. Chen, L.C., Papandreou, G., Kokkinos, I., Murphy, K., Yuille, A.L.: DeepLab: semantic image segmentation with deep convolutional nets, atrous convolution, and fully connected CRFs. TPAMI **40**(4), 834–848 (2017)
2. Chu, X., Zhang, B., Ma, H., Xu, R., Li, J., Li, Q.: Fast, accurate and lightweight super-resolution with neural architecture search. arXiv preprint arXiv:1901.07261 (2019)
3. Dai, D., Wang, Y., Chen, Y., Van Gool, L.: Is image super-resolution helpful for other vision tasks? In: 2016 IEEE Winter Conference on Applications of Computer Vision (WACV), pp. 1–9. IEEE (2016)
4. Dong, C., Loy, C.C., He, K., Tang, X.: Learning a deep convolutional network for image super-resolution. In: Fleet, D., Pajdla, T., Schiele, B., Tuytelaars, T. (eds.) ECCV 2014. LNCS, vol. 8692, pp. 184–199. Springer, Cham (2014). https://doi.org/10.1007/978-3-319-10593-2_13
5. Goodfellow, I., et al.: Generative adversarial nets. In: Advances in Neural Information Processing Systems, pp. 2672–2680 (2014)
6. Guo, Y., Chen, J., Wang, J., Chen, Q., Cao, J., Deng, Z., Xu, Y., Tan, M.: Closed-loop matters: Dual regression networks for single image super-resolution. In: Proceedings of the IEEE/CVF Conference on Computer Vision and Pattern Recognition, pp. 5407–5416 (2020)
7. Guo, Y., Luo, Y., He, Z., Huang, J., Chen, J.: Hierarchical neural architecture search for single image super-resolution. arXiv preprint arXiv:2003.04619 (2020)
8. Haris, M., Shakhnarovich, G., Ukita, N.: Task-driven super resolution: Object detection in low-resolution images. arXiv preprint arXiv:1803.11316 (2018)
9. Ji, X., Cao, Y., Tai, Y., Wang, C., Li, J., Huang, F.: Real-world super-resolution via kernel estimation and noise injection. In: Proceedings of the IEEE/CVF Conference on Computer Vision and Pattern Recognition Workshops, pp. 466–467 (2020)
10. Khattab, M.M., Zeki, A.M., Alwan, A.A., Badawy, A.S., Thota, L.S.: Multi-frame super-resolution: a survey. In: 2018 IEEE International Conference on Computational Intelligence and Computing Research (ICCIC), pp. 1–8. IEEE (2018)
11. Kim, J., Kwon Lee, J., Mu Lee, K.: Accurate image super-resolution using very deep convolutional networks. In: Proceedings of the IEEE Conference on Computer Vision and Pattern Recognition, pp. 1646–1654 (2016)

12. Kim, J., Kwon Lee, J., Mu Lee, K.: Deeply-recursive convolutional network for image super-resolution. In: Proceedings of the IEEE Conference on Computer Vision and Pattern Recognition, pp. 1637–1645 (2016)

13. Krizhevsky, A., Sutskever, I., Hinton, G.E.: ImageNet classification with deep convolutional neural networks. In: Advances in Neural Information Processing Systems, pp. 1097–1105 (2012)

14. Ledig, C., et al.: Photo-realistic single image super-resolution using a generative adversarial network. In: Proceedings of the IEEE Conference on Computer Vision and Pattern Recognition, pp. 4681–4690 (2017)

15. Li, Z., Xi, T., Deng, J., Zhang, G., Wen, S., He, R.: GP-NAS: gaussian process based neural architecture search. In: CVPR, pp. 11933–11942 (2020)

16. Liang, F., Lin, C., Guo, R., Sun, M., Wu, W., Yan, J., Ouyang, W.: Computation reallocation for object detection. In: International Conference on Learning Representations (2020), https://openreview.net/forum?id=SkxLFaNKwB

17. Lim, B., Son, S., Kim, H., Nah, S., Mu Lee, K.: Enhanced deep residual networks for single image super-resolution. In: Proceedings of the IEEE Conference on Computer Vision and Pattern Recognition Workshops, pp. 136–144 (2017)

18. Liu, C., et al.: Progressive neural architecture search. In: ECCV, pp. 19–34 (2018)

19. Liu, H., Simonyan, K., Vinyals, O., Fernando, C., Kavukcuoglu, K.: Hierarchical representations for efficient architecture search. arXiv preprint arXiv:1711.00436 (2017)

20. Liu, H., Simonyan, K., Yang, Y.: DARTS: Differentiable architecture search. arXiv preprint arXiv:1806.09055 (2018)

21. Ma, C., Rao, Y., Cheng, Y., Chen, C., Lu, J., Zhou, J.: Structure-preserving super resolution with gradient guidance. In: Proceedings of the IEEE/CVF Conference on Computer Vision and Pattern Recognition, pp. 7769–7778 (2020)

22. Ma, Y., Yu, D., Wu, T., Wang, H.: PaddlePaddle: an open-source deep learning platform from industrial practice. Front. Data Domput. 1(1), 105–115 (2019)

23. Paszke, A., et al.: Pytorch: an imperative style, high-performance deep learning library. In: Wallach, H., Larochelle, H., Beygelzimer, A., d'Alché-Buc, F., Fox, E., Garnett, R. (eds.) Advances in Neural Information Processing Systems 32, pp. 8024–8035. Curran Associates, Inc. (2019), http://papers.neurips.cc/paper/9015-pytorch-an-imperative-style-high-performance-deep-learning-library.pdf

24. Pickup, L.C., Capel, D.P., Roberts, S.J., Zisserman, A.: Bayesian methods for image super-resolution. Comput. J. 52(1), 101–113 (2009)

25. Song, D., Xu, C., Jia, X., Chen, Y., Xu, C., Wang, Y.: Efficient residual dense block search for image super-resolution. In: AAAI, pp. 12007–12014 (2020)

26. Sun, J., Xu, Z., Shum, H.Y.: Image super-resolution using gradient profile prior. In: 2008 IEEE Conference on Computer Vision and Pattern Recognition, pp. 1–8. IEEE (2008)

27. Tai, Y.W., Liu, S., Brown, M.S., Lin, S.: Super resolution using edge prior and single image detail synthesis. In: 2010 IEEE Computer Society Conference on Computer Vision and Pattern Recognition, pp. 2400–2407. IEEE (2010)

28. Wang, Q., Tang, X., Shum, H.: Patch based blind image super resolution. In: Tenth IEEE International Conference on Computer Vision (ICCV 2005), vol. 1, vol. 1, pp. 709–716. IEEE (2005)

29. Wang, X., et al.: ESRGAN: Enhanced super-resolution generative adversarial networks. In: Proceedings of the European Conference on Computer Vision (ECCV), pp. 63–79 (2018)

30. Wei, P., Lu, H., Timofte, R., Lin, L., Zuo, W., et al.: AIM 2020 challenge on real image super-resolution. In: European Conference on Computer Vision Workshops (2020)
31. Yang, J., Wright, J., Huang, T., Ma, Y.: Image super-resolution as sparse representation of raw image patches. In: 2008 IEEE Conference on Computer Vision and Pattern Recognition, pp. 1–8. IEEE (2008)
32. Zhang, R., Isola, P., Efros, A.A., Shechtman, E., Wang, O.: The unreasonable effectiveness of deep features as a perceptual metric. In: Proceedings of the IEEE Conference on Computer Vision and Pattern Recognition, pp. 586–595 (2018)
33. Zhang, Y., Li, K., Li, K., Wang, L., Zhong, B., Fu, Y.: Image super-resolution using very deep residual channel attention networks. In: Proceedings of the European Conference on Computer Vision (ECCV), pp. 286–301 (2018)
34. Zhang, Y., Tian, Y., Kong, Y., Zhong, B., Fu, Y.: Residual dense network for image super-resolution. In: Proceedings of the IEEE Conference on Computer Vision and Pattern Recognition, pp. 2472–2481 (2018)
35. Zhou Wang, A. C. Bovik, H.R.S., Simoncelli, E.P.: Image quality assessment: from error visibility to structural similarity. IEEE Trans. Image Process. 13(4), 600–612 (2004)
36. Zoph, B., Le, Q.V.: Neural architecture search with reinforcement learning. arXiv preprint arXiv:1611.01578 (2016)
37. Zoph, B., Vasudevan, V., Shlens, J., Le, Q.V.: Learning transferable architectures for scalable image recognition. In: CVPR, pp. 8697–8710 (2018)

Enhanced Adaptive Dense Connection Single Image Super-Resolution

Tangxin Xie$^{(\boxtimes)}$ (ID), Jing Li, Yi Shen, Yu Jia, Jialiang Zhang, and Bing Zeng

China Electronic Technology Cyber Security Co., Ltd., Chengdu, China
xxh96@outlook.com

Abstract. Increasing model size often results in improved performance on super-resolution reconstruction. However, at some point large model cannot SR huge images due to GPU/TPU memory limitations. In this paper, to address this problem, we present Block-Reconstruction(BR) strategy to improve the reconstruction quality of large images, which lower memory consumption. Meanwhile, we propose an enhanced adaptive dense connection super resolution reconstruction network(EDCSR) that has 89M parameters. In AIM2020 Real Image Super-Resolution Challenge, we won the second place in Track 1 and Track 2, and the third place in Track 3.

Keywords: SISR · Dense connection · Sub-pixel reconstruction · Convolutional neural network · Deep learning

1 Introduction

The task of single image super-resolution (SISR) is to map a degraded low-resolution (LR) image to a visually high-resolution (HR) image. Many deep Convolution Neural Networks (CNN) based methods for SISR have been proposed in recent years, due to the fast development of deep learning.

The SR networks proposed at the beginning were trained with bicubic interpolation as a downsampling method. Dong et al. introduced the super-resolution reconstruction convolutional neural network (SRCNN) [3], which is the first SR algorithm based on convolutional networks. However, similar to [23], SRCNN used LR image with bicubic interpolation as the input of the model.

FSRCNN [4], ESPCN [18] reduced the computational cost by using the original LR image directly as the input of the SR network. In general, the deeper the network, the better the performance.

Kim et al. made great progress by increasing the network depth in VDSR and DRCN [10]. But very deep networks often have gradients disappearing and exploding problems. Therefore residual connections and dense connections were introduced into SISR, such as SRResNet [12], EDSR [13], RDN [30]. Besides, WDSR [25] introduced a wide activation convolution to obtain better performance with less computation. AWSRN [14] proposed an adaptive weight network to control the weight of convolution and skip connections adaptively. The main

© Springer Nature Switzerland AG 2020
A. Bartoli and A. Fusiello (Eds.): ECCV 2020 Workshops, LNCS 12537, pp. 437–452, 2020.
https://doi.org/10.1007/978-3-030-67070-2_26

network of ADCSR [21] was composed of adaptive dense connection, which won the AIM 19 Extreme Super Resolution Challenge: track 1.

In the above work, the image degradation model is built based on bicubic degradation. Obviously it is not consistent with the real scenarios. In the super-resolution reconstruction problem of real images, there are two challenges, one is more complex degradation than bicubic downsampling, another is diverse degradation differences among devices. Therefore, there have been many studies on real scenarios SR in the past two years. [2,20,28] all generated training data by shooting real image pairs. [7,22,26] improved the reconstruction quality of blurry images by blur kernel estimation, where the blur kernels were unknown.

The AIM2020 real image SR is a challenge for a real degraded scene, which chooses paired real scenarios image pairs as the training data directly [19]. Based on the ADCSR [21] architecture, the contributions of our paper are as follows:

(1) We have improved ADCSR to obtain better performance;
(2) We propose a Block-Reconstruction(BR) method, which can reduce the memory usage sufficiently during reconstruction. Besides, BR can improve the performance of reconstruction results, with computation increased by 78% and more test time;
(3) For AIM2020 Real Image Super-Resolution Challenge [19], we not only remove misaligned images but also take the advantage of data augmentation method-CutBlur. Finally we won the second place of track 1($\times$2), track 2($\times$3), and the third place of track 3($\times$4).

2   Related Works

Many traditional machine learning algorithms have been developed and achieved significant improvements in terms of SR task in recent years. These algorithms includes interpolation-based methods [15,27,31], reconstruction-based methods [9,16,17] and learning-based methods [5,6,23]. The latest SR algorithms has better reconstruction performance than traditional SR algorithms, with constructing a data-driven deep learning model to obtain the details required in the reconstruction process.

After Dong et al. [3] proposed SRCNN for SR task, the SR method based on deep learning began to replace the corresponding traditional algorithm. In 2015, Kim et al. [10] introduced a SR method using very deep convolutional neural networks (VDSR), with 20 convolutional layers. It indicated that using deeper networks may achieve better performance on PSNR and image quality. EDSR [13] further confirmed this claim with the number of convolutional layers increased nearly four times that of VDSR [10]. The reconstruction effect was substantially improved in EDSR [13] by removing the batch normalization layer and adding ReLU activation. Furthermore, RCAN [29] added a channel attention residual block with more than four hundred convolutional layers to the residual block, so that an RIR (Residual in Residual) structure was formed.

Subsequently, Kim et al. [11] proposed a deep recursive convolutional network (DRCN) based on VDSR [10], in which the same convolutional layer was applied multiple times. By doing so, the parameter amount remained unchanged during the recursive process, which proved that recursive connection is effective in improving the performance of reconstruction. FSRCNN [14] network was more complex than SRCNN [3] with more network parameters. However, FSRCNN improved performance and reconstruction quality in real scenarios significantly, due to adopting the original LR image as input to learn feature maps directly. ESPCN [18], introduced in 2016, also used the original LR image directly as input, which operated on images and videos in real scenarios. The model also proposed sub-pixel convolution for up-sampling to obtain significant performance improvement.

Inspired by generative adversarial neural networks, Ledig et al. proposed a super-resolution reconstruction model (SRGAN) based on generative adversarial networks (GAN) [12]. And SRGAN had significant advantages in perceptual quality measurement. In 2018, Zhang Yulun et al. proposed RDN [30] inspired by dense connections [8], which combined jump connections and dense connections to integrate local and global features. Yu et al. won the championship in the NTIRE 2018 real image SISR challenge and proposed WDSR [25], where the number of convolutional channels was increased before the activation function but reduced after the activation function. WDSR showed that improving network performance without changing the parameters is possible. Based on WDSR and RDN, Xie proposed ADCSR, which enhances network performance through adaptive dense connections.

Recently, some attention-based models are also proposed to further improve the SR performance. Zhang et al. proposed the residual channel attention network (RCAN) by introducing the channel attention mechanism into a modified residual block for image SR. The channel attention mechanism uses global average pooling to extract channel statistics which are called first-order statistics. On the contrary, Dai et al. proposed the second-order attention network (SAN) to explore more powerful feature expression by using second-order feature statistics. Liu et al. [14] proposed a novel residual feature aggregation (RFA) framework to extract more effective feature and also proposed an enhanced spatial attention (ESA) block to make residual features more concentrated for key spatial content.

Due to the difficulty of collecting HR-LR pairs, non-blind SISR approaches usually adopt a simulated image degradation for training and testing, e.g., bicubic downsampling. These above algorithms often do not work well for real images. Therefore, researchers began to consider real image SR by generating real datasets or using blind reconstruction methods. Zhang K et al. proposed a degradation model that is more suitable for real applications[26]. For blur kernel estimation in blind image super-resolution, Gu et al. proposed Iterative Kernel Correction (IKC)[7]. Xu et al. proposed a new pipeline to generate realistic training data by simulating the imaging process of digital cameras[22]. Zhang X et al. obtained the official HRLR image pair through the camera's optical zoom, and built the SR-RAW dataset for SR[28]. Chen C et al. captured the image pair with cellphones[2]. Pengxu Wei built a larger and more challenging real SR dataset with five DSLR cameras[20]. A new data augmentation method-CutBlur [24] was proposed, which cuts a low-resolution patch and pastes it to the corresponding high-resolution image region and vice versa. By doing so, the model can improve the performance across various scenarios.

3   Our Model

In the AIM2020 Real Image Super-Resolution Challenge [19], we used two different models to participate in three race tracks: we used ADCSR [21] to participate in the ×3 track and ×4 track, and the improved ADCSR to participate in the ×2 track, which is called EDCSR in this paper.

3.1   Network Architecture

Figure 1 displayed the architecture of EDCSR and ADCSR [21]. Similar to ADCSR, EDCSR is also composed of two parts: SKIP and BODY. SKIP is a simple minits convolution, while BODY includes a feature extraction layer, multiple ADRU (adaptive, dense residual unit), GFF (global feature fusion layer) [30] and AFSL (adaptive feature sub-pixel reconstruction layer), where each ADRU is composed of four ADRB. It is worth emphasizing that the convolutional unit of ADCSR and EDCSR are different. EDCSR adds the enhanced spatial attention (ESA) block [14] to wide active convolution.

SKIP is a single or multiple sub-pixel convolution with a convolution kernel size of 5, SKIP of ×2 and ×3 is a single layer, and ×4 scale model is obtained by using ×2 sub-pixel convolution repeatedly.

$$HR_{SKIP} = f_{sub-conv5}(I_{LR}) \tag{1}$$

where HR_{SKIP} represents the output of SKIP, I_{LR} denotes the input LR image and $f_{sub-conv5}$ represents the sub-pixel convolution, which convolution kernel is of a size 5.

In the BODY, first we use a convolutional layer to extract the shallow features from LR image.

$$F_f = f_{conv3}(I_{LR}) \tag{2}$$

Second, we use several ADRU to extract the deep features. There are four ADRB (adaptive dense residual blocks) through adaptive dense connections in each ADRU. The features are merged by the LFF (Local Feature Fusion Layer) and combined with a skip connection as the output of the ADRU. Each ADRB combines four convolutional units by the same adaptive dense connection structure as ADRU. For ADRB, the convolutional units adopt a convolutional structure. Similar to WDSR [25], ADRB includes two layers of wide active convolution and one layer of leakyrelu. Futhermore, we add the enhanced spatial attention (ESA) block [14] to EDSCR. We will describe in detail in the next section.

After that, we fuse features by LFF, which combined with a skip connection as the output of the ADRB. GFF fuses the outputs of multiple ADRU by means of concatenation and convolution. The kth ADRU is expressed as:

$$F_{ADRUk} = b_k x + a_k f_{ADRUk}(x) \tag{3}$$

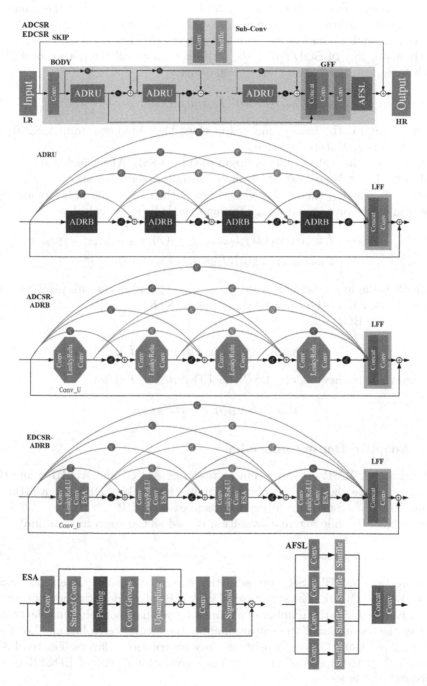

Fig. 1. The architecture of adaptive densely connected super-resolution (ADCSR [21]) and our proposed enhanced adaptive densely connected super-resolution(EDCSR)

Where x is the input feature map of the kth ADRU, which is of the same size as the output feature map of the feature extraction layer, and $f_{ADRUk}(x)$ is the kth ADRU, both a_k and b_k are adaptive parameters that can be trained.

The third part of BODY uses the GEF to combine all the output of ADRU, which fuses features by two convolutional layers.

$$F_{GFF} = f_{conv3}(f_{conv1}(concat(f_{ADRU1}, f_{ADRU2}, \cdots, F_{ADRUn}))) \qquad (4)$$

where $concat()$ is the feature merge function. The difference from ADCSR [21] is that we merge feature before a_k.

After that, the feature map is upsampled by AFSL. AFSL includes four sub-pixel convolution branches, which use convolution kernel of size 3, 5, 7, and 9 respectively. Finally, the combined features of the concatenated layers are used to obtain the reconstructed image through single-layer convolution.

$$F_{AFSL} = f_{conv1}(concat(f_{sub-conv3\_ \times S}(x), f_{sub-conv5\_ \times S}(x),$$
$$f_{sub-conv7\_ \times S}(x), f_{sub-conv9\_ \times S}(x))) \qquad (5)$$

Where S is the magnification scale, $f_{sub-convK\_ \times S}(x)$ is the sub-pixel convolution with the size of the convolution kernel is $[K, K, 3 \times S^2]$.

The whole BODY is:

$$HR_{BODY} = F_{AFSL}(F_{GFF}(F_f(LR))) \qquad (6)$$

The whole framework of ADSCR or EDCSR is as follows:

$$HR = HR_{BODY} + HR_{SKIP} \qquad (7)$$

3.2   Adaptive Dense Connection

EDCSR and ADCSR [21] have almost the same ADRU and ADRB connection structure, where the four convolutional units that make ADRB are a little different. There are four convolutional units in each ADRB.

For ADCSR, wide active convolution is used as the convolutional unit.

$$f_{conv-unit} = f_{conv3}(Leakyrelu(f_{conv3}(x))) \qquad (8)$$

Moreover, for EDCSR, we add the enhanced spatial attention (ESA) block [14] to ADCSR. The structure of ESA is illustrated as the bottom part of Fig. 1. ESA reduces the number of channels by the first convolutional layer, and reduces the resolution of the feature map by the second convolutional layer and pooling layer. Conv Groups consists of three convolutional layers. The resolution is restored by the upsampling layer. The convolutional unit of EDCSR can be expressed as follows:

$$f_{conv-unit} = f_{ESA}(f_{conv3}(Leakyrelu(f_{conv3}(x)))) \qquad (9)$$

In order to achieve adaptive learning of the weights of dense connections in ADRB, a_B are added after every convolutional unit, and b_B are added to each dense jump connection. Both a_B and b_B are the weight parameters.

$$Y_1 = f_{conv-unit1}(X_1)$$
$$X_2 = a_B^{12} \times Y_1 + b_B^{01} \times X_1$$
$$Y_2 = f_{conv-unit2}(X_2)$$
$$X_3 = a_B^{23} \times Y_2 + b_B^{12} \times Y_1 + b_B^{02} \times X_1$$
$$Y_3 = f_{conv-unit3}(X_3)$$
$$X_4 = a_B^{34} \times Y_3 + b_B^{23} \times Y_2 + b_B^{13} \times Y_1 + b_B^{03} \times X_1 \quad (10)$$
$$Y_4 = f_{conv-unit4}(X_4)$$
$$f_{ADRB} = f_{conv1}(concat(a_B^{45} \times Y_4, b_B^{34} \times Y_3,$$
$$b_B^{24} \times Y_2, b_B^{14} \times Y_1 b_B^{04} \times X_1)) + X_1$$

Where $f_{conv-unitk}$ is the kth convolutional unit, X_k and Y_k are the input and output of the convolutional unit respectively, X_1 is the input of the ADRB. a_B^{mn} and b_B^{mn} are the adaptive parameters between the mth convolutional unit and the nth convolutional unit. The position 0 is the ADRB input position, and the position 5 represents the LFF position of ADRB, $f_{conv1}(concat())$ is the LEF.

ADRU includes 4 adaptive densely connected ADRB blocks and LFF, and the connection mode is completely the same as ADRB, so the mathematical expression of ADRU is similar to ADRB:

$$Y_1 = f_{ADRB1}(X_1)$$
$$X_2 = a_U^{12} \times Y_1 + b_U^{01} \times X_1$$
$$Y_2 = f_{ADRB2}(X_2)$$
$$X_3 = a_U^{23} \times Y_2 + b_U^{12} \times Y_1 + b_U^{02} \times X_1$$
$$Y_3 = f_{ADRB3}(X_3)$$
$$X_4 = a_U^{34} \times Y_3 + b_U^{23} \times Y_2 + b_U^{13} \times Y_1 + b_U^{03} \times X_1 \quad (11)$$
$$Y_4 = f_{ADRB4}(X_4)$$
$$f_{ADRU} = f_{conv1}(concat(a_U^{45} \times Y_4, b_U^{34} \times Y_3,$$
$$b_U^{24} \times Y_2, b_U^{14} \times Y_1, b_U^{04} \times X_1)) + X_1$$

Similarly, X_k and Y_k are the input and output of the kth ADRB, a_U^{mn} and a_U^{mn} are the adaptive parameters between the mth ADRB and the nth ADRB, position 0 is the input position of ADRU, and position 5 represents the LFF of ADRU position, $f_{conv1}(concat())$ is the LEF.

4   Experiments

4.1   Block-Reconstruction

It is difficult to reconstruct high-resolution images with large models due to GPU/TPU memory limitations. In this paper, we take the advantage of Block-Reconstruction(BR) to resolve this problem. First, we decompose LR image into different blocks LR_p, then we reconstruct high-resolution blocks SR_p from these blocks LR_p, finally we stitch these SR_p into the whole reconstructed SR image.

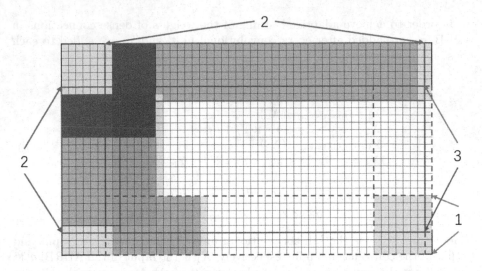

Fig. 2. The stitching preceduce of block-reconstruction

Only the central part of SR_p is taken out during the stitching procedure, because SR image is stitched. By doing so, the effect of distortion on SR image is reduced naturally, which caused by the edges of these blocks. The details of the stitching procedure are displayed in Fig. 2. The 4 corner blocks are reconstructed firstly, then the remainder part of 4 edge blocks are reconstructed, finally the central block is reconstructed. Except for the edge part of the whole SR image, 1/8 of the edge of each block is removed. The reconstructed part later will cover the previous reconstructed part if the reconstructed images partially overlap. The utilization rate of SR_p is approximately 56%, which means that will increase computation by 78%. Since LR_p can be set to a size of tens of pixels, Block-Reconstruction can effectively reduce the memory usage.

In Table 1, we compare the result of Block-Reconstruction from the result of ADCSRS [21] on the benchmark datasets. When LR image has small resolution, which is nearly of the same size as the patch used during training, there is little difference between the reconstruction result of LR image and the result of Block-Reconstruction, which may even lead to poor performance.

However, in this challenge, the Block-Reconstruction(BR) method boosts the performance substantially, due to the size of images in the test dataset and the patch size used during training are quite different. The closer the size of LR_p is to the patch size used during training, the more the performance improves. Table 2 gives the compared results of PSNR and SSIM with different LR_p size, using the same testing model on ValidationLR_×4 dataset. It can be found that as the LR_p size gets smaller and smaller, PSNR increases significantly. When the LR_p size is 56, PSNR increases by 0.121dB.

Table 1. Performance comparison of ADCSRS [21] with different LR_p size on the benchmark datasets(PSNR(dB)/SSIM). "LR" means using the whole LR image as input, while "320", "160", "80" represent the different LR_p size

Dataset	Set5	Set14	Urban100
Size	128×128	256×256	512×384
LR	38.27/0.9616	34.28/0.9237	33.27/0.9385
320	–/–	–/–	33.25/0.9383
160	–/–	34.26/0.9236	33.27/0.9384
80	38.27/0.9616	34.27/0.9237	33.23/0.9381

Table 2. Performance comparison of ADCSR with different LR_p size on ValidationLR_×4 dataset. "LR" means using the whole LR image as input

LR_p size	LR	640	320	160	80	56
PSNR(dB)	30.466	30.468	30.468	30.497	30.567	30.589
PSNR(+)	–	+0.002	+0.002	+0.031	+0.099	+0.121
SSIM	0.86194	0.86192	0.86195	0.86210	0.86233	0.86214
SSIM(+)	–	−0.00002	+0.00001	+0.00016	+0.00039	+0.00020

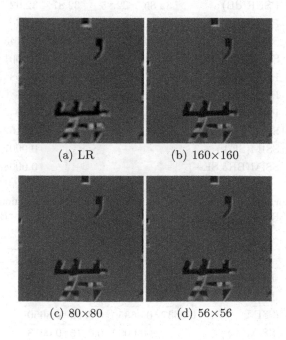

(a) LR   (b) 160×160

(c) 80×80   (d) 56×56

Fig. 3. Comparison of stitching edge with different LR_p size

PSNR increases but SSIM slightly decreases when the LR_p size is 640. As the LR_p size decreases, the quality of SR images increases, and SSIM increases too. However, when the LR_p size decreases to 56, SSIM reduces significantly, and we can clearly see the stitching edge in SR image. Figure 3 shows us the edge comparison of the reconstructed image with different block sizes. When the size is 160, the block edge is almost invisible in the whole image. However, in the reconstructed image with blocks of 80 and 56, we see some stitched edges, and the stitched edge in the image with the block of 56 is relatively obvious.

Compared with EDSR's Self-Ensemble(SE) method [13], Block-Reconstruction has 178% of computation, while Self-Ensemble has 800%. Table 3 and Table 4 show quantitative comparisons for EDCSR and ADCSR. As diaplayed in Table 2 and Table 3, the improvement of PSNR using Block-Reconstruction is comparable to that of Self-Ensemble, but SSIM has a slight improvement. In Table 4, although the improvement of block reconstruction is reduced, it is proved that the two methods can be superimposed without affecting each other to obtain a higher-quality reconstructed image, but the computation will reach 1424%.

Table 3. Performance comparison of EDCSR Block-Reconstruction(BR) on ValidationLR_×2 dataset

	LR_p Size	640	320	160	80	56
BR	PSNR(dB)	32.85	32.85	32.87	32.92	32.96
	PSNR(BR+)	–	0	0.02	0.07	0.11
	SSIM	0.9144	0.9143	0.9144	0.9145	0.9145
	SSIM(BR+)	–	−0.0001	0	0.0001	0.0001
BR& SE	PSNR(dB)	–	–	–	32.98	33.01
	PSNR(SE+)	–	–	–	0.06	0.06
	PSNR(BR& SE+)	–	–	–	0.13	0.16
	SSIM	–	–	–	0.9152	0.9151
	SSIM(SE+)	–	–	–	0.0007	0.0006
	SSIM(BR&SE+)	–	–	–	0.0008	0.0007

Table 4. Performance comparison between Block-Reconstruction and Self-Ensemble(SE). "LR" means using the whole LR image as input. "BR" means LR_p size is set to 80

	LR	BR	SE	BR&SE
PSNR(dB)	30.719	30.733	30.804	30.818
PSNR(+)	–	0.014	0.085	0.099
SSIM	0.8637	0.8635	0.8652	0.8650
SSIM(+)	–	−0.0002	0.0015	0.0013
Computation	100%	178%	800%	1424%

4.2   Implementation Details

In this section, we will give specific implementation details. For both ADCSR and EDCSR, 6 ADRU are included. In the convolutional unit of ADRB, the number of convolutional channels is set to 128 and 384 respectively. In SKIP, the convolutional channel for the sub-pixel convolutional layer is 5. The convolution kernel size of the LFF in BODY is 1. The two convolution kernel sizes of GFF are 1 and 3. In AFSL, the convolution kernels are 3, 5, 7 and 9. All other convolution kernel sizes are set to 3. There are 4 ADRU in BODY. The number of output channels in feature extraction layer, convolutional unit, LFF, and GFF are 128, and the 4 sub-pixel convolutions and the final output in AFSL are 3. The stride size is 1 throughout the network while using Leakyrelu as the activation function. Finally, the number of model parameters reached 89M.

4.3   Training Settings

We train our model on the 19000 Real Image pairs provided by the AIM Challenge [19], with CutBlur [24] as a data augmentation method. Before training, we firstly downsample HR image by bicubic interpolation to the LR size, and then remove the image pairs with too large MSE(unaligned image pair). Futhermore, we exclude the last 100 images from training for validation.

For ADCSR($\times$4) and EDCSR($\times$2), the patch size of the input LR is set to 80×80. At first, we train SKIP separately, and then we train the whole network at the same time. The initial learning rate is set to 1×10^{-4}, and finally, when the learning rate drops to 5×10^{-7} the training stops. We implemented our model using Pytorch1.1.0+Cuda10.0+cudnn7.5.0 framework as the deep learning environment with 4 NVIDIA 2080Ti GPU.

4.4   Results with Real Image

Table 5. Performance comparison on ValidationLR_$\times$4

Model	Bicubic	EDSR	RCAN	EDSR	RCAN	DRLN	ADCSR	ADCSR_S80+
Train data	–	Bicu	Bicu	Real	Real	Real	Real	Real
PSNR(dB)	28.14	28.22	28.20	29.98	30.25	30.53	30.72	30.82
SSIM	0.8128	0.8153	0.8150	0.8519	0.8605	0.8632	0.8637	0.8650

Table 5 and Table 6 show the results of the competition validation dataset of the submitted scheme. In Table 5, we compare our method with several state-of-the-art SR methods, including EDSR [13], RCAN [29], DRLN [1]. "S80+" represents that we divide the blocks into 80 $\times$ 80 for reconstruction and use Self-Ensemble [13] at the same time. On the $\times$4 track, a combination of Block-Reconstruction and Self-Ensemble achieved higher PSNR and SSIM. In addition to ADCSR, thanks to WCH for providing experimental results of other models.

Table 6. Performance comparison on ValidationLR_×2

Model	ADCSR_S80	EDCSR_S80	EDCSR_S80+	EDCSR_S56+
PSNR(dB)	32.87	32.92	32.98	33.01
SSIM	0.9147	0.9145	0.9152	0.9151

Because of the too large size of LR, we only did Block-Reconstruction experiment on ValidationLR_×2. In the case of the same block size of 80×80, EDCSR has obtained better performance than ADCSR. Although EDCSR_S56+ achieved the best performance, the final image we submitted still adopted the EDCSR_S80+ method.

In Fig. 4, we illustrated the visual comparisons of the models in Table 5. It can be seen that DRLN [1] obtained good performance when using the same training dataset as ADCSR. Futhermore, ADCSR reconstructed a clearer texture, and the subjective effect of the image was better.

4.5   AIM2020 REAL IMAGE Challenge

We proposed EDCSR to participate this challenge [19], which concerns the real image SR. This challege poses not only more complex degradation than bicubic downsampling but also diverse degradation differences among devices. This challenge provides paired LR and HR real images for traing. Each track provides 20 large-size LR images for verification and 60 large-size LR images for final testing. Finally, we used EDCSR to participate in track 1: × 2, and ADCSR to participate in track 2:×3, track3:×4. Because the results of the model in the validation set ValidationLR_×3 were not good, we used the ×4 model to reconstruct the final test set of ×3, and then downsampled to ×3 scale. The top 5 results of the final test set are shown in Table 7.

Table 7. The top 5 results of the final test set [19]

Track	track1:×2		track2:×3		track3:×4	
Ranking	Team	PSNR/SSIM	Team	PSNR/SSIM	Team	PSNR/SSIM
1	Baidu	33.45/0.9270	Baidu	30.95/0.8762	Baidu	31.40/0.8751
2	Ours	33.31/0.9245	Ours	30.77/0.8714	ALONG	31.24/0.8742
3	OPPO	33.31/0.9242	OPPO	30.54/0.8695	Ours	31.12/0.8744
4	AiAiR	33.26/0.9242	Noah	30.56/0.8661	SR-IM	31.17/0.8728
5	Inception	33.23/0.9240	MCML	30.48/0.8660	DeepBlueAI	30.96/0.8737

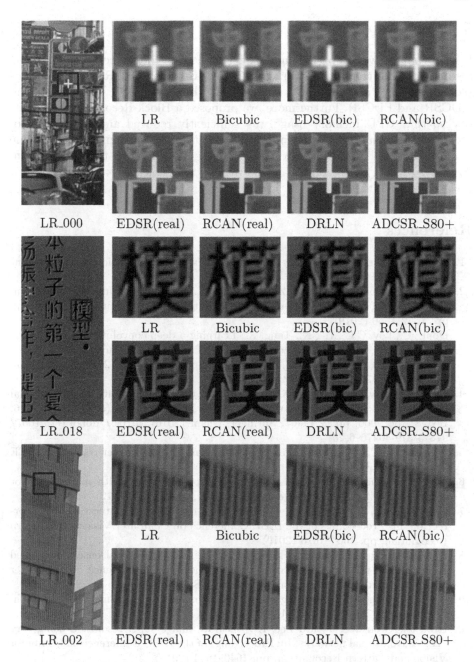

Fig. 4. Qualitative comparison of the models in Table 5

5   Conclusions

In this paper, we proposed an enhanced adaptive dense connection super-resolution reconstruction network (EDCSR) based on ADCSR. Meanwhile, we participated in the three tracks of the AIM20 Real Image SR Challenge, using ADCSR and EDCSR. Furthermore, we proposed a Block-Reconstruction strategy so that GPU memory usage was sufficiently reduced and the quality of reconstructed images was also improved. By using Self-Ensemble at the same time, we boosted the performance and got a higher ranking in this competition. Anyway, we won the second place of track 1: × 2, track 2: ×3, and the third place of track 3: ×4.

References

1. Anwar, S., Barnes, N.: Densely residual laplacian super-resolution. arXiv preprint arXiv:1906.12021 (2019)
2. Chen, C., Xiong, Z., Tian, X., Zha, Z.J., Wu, F.: Camera lens super-resolution. In: Proceedings of the IEEE Conference on Computer Vision and Pattern Recognition, pp. 1652–1660 (2019)
3. Dong, C., Loy, C.C., He, K., Tang, X.: Learning a deep convolutional network for image super-resolution. In: Fleet, D., Pajdla, T., Schiele, B., Tuytelaars, T. (eds.) ECCV 2014. LNCS, vol. 8692, pp. 184–199. Springer, Cham (2014). https://doi.org/10.1007/978-3-319-10593-2_13
4. Dong, C., Loy, C.C., Tang, X.: Accelerating the super-resolution convolutional neural network. In: Leibe, B., Matas, J., Sebe, N., Welling, M. (eds.) ECCV 2016. LNCS, vol. 9906, pp. 391–407. Springer, Cham (2016). https://doi.org/10.1007/978-3-319-46475-6_25
5. Freeman, W.T., Jones, T.R., Pasztor, E.C.: Example-based super-resolution. IEEE Comput. Graphics Appl. **22**(2), 56–65 (2002)
6. Gao, X., Zhang, K., Tao, D., Li, X.: Image super-resolution with sparse neighbor embedding. IEEE Trans. Image Process. **21**(7), 3194–3205 (2012)
7. Gu, J., Lu, H., Zuo, W., Dong, C.: Blind super-resolution with iterative kernel correction. In: Proceedings of the IEEE Conference on Computer Vision and Pattern Recognition, pp. 1604–1613 (2019)
8. Huang, G., Liu, Z., Van Der Maaten, L., Weinberger, K.Q.: Densely connected convolutional networks. In: Proceedings of the IEEE Conference on Computer Vision and Pattern Recognition, pp. 4700–4708 (2017)
9. Irani, M., Peleg, S.: Improving resolution by image registration. CVGIP: Graph. Models Image Proc. **53**(3), 231–239 (1991)
10. Kim, J., Kwon Lee, J., Mu Lee, K.: Accurate image super-resolution using very deep convolutional networks. In: Proceedings of the IEEE Conference on Computer Vision and Pattern Recognition, pp. 1646–1654 (2016)
11. Kim, J., Kwon Lee, J., Mu Lee, K.: Deeply-recursive convolutional network for image super-resolution. In: Proceedings of the IEEE Conference on Computer Vision and Pattern Recognition, pp. 1637–1645 (2016)
12. Ledig, C., et al.: Photo-realistic single image super-resolution using a generative adversarial network. In: Proceedings of the IEEE Conference on Computer Vision and Pattern Recognition, pp. 4681–4690 (2017)

13. Lim, B., Son, S., Kim, H., Nah, S., Mu Lee, K.: Enhanced deep residual networks for single image super-resolution. In: Proceedings of the IEEE Conference on Computer Vision and Pattern Recognition Workshops, pp. 136–144 (2017)

14. Liu, J., Zhang, W., Tang, Y., Tang, J., Wu, G.: Residual feature aggregation network for image super-resolution. In: Proceedings of the IEEE/CVF Conference on Computer Vision and Pattern Recognition, pp. 2359–2368 (2020)

15. Liu, X., Zhao, D., Xiong, R., Ma, S., Gao, W., Sun, H.: Image interpolation via regularized local linear regression. IEEE Trans. Image Process. 20(12), 3455–3469 (2011)

16. Patti, A.J., Sezan, M.I., Tekalp, A.M.: Superresolution video reconstruction with arbitrary sampling lattices and nonzero aperture time. IEEE Trans. Image Process. 6(8), 1064–1076 (1997)

17. Schultz, R.R., Stevenson, R.L.: Extraction of high-resolution frames from video sequences. IEEE Trans. Image Process. 5(6), 996–1011 (1996)

18. Shi, W., et al.: Real-time single image and video super-resolution using an efficient sub-pixel convolutional neural network. In: Proceedings of the IEEE Conference on Computer Vision and Pattern Recognition, pp. 1874–1883 (2016)

19. Wei, P., Lu, H., Timofte, R., Lin, L., Zuo, W., et al.: AIM 2020 challenge on real image super-resolution. In: European Conference on Computer Vision Workshops (2020)

20. Wei, P., et al.: Component divide-and-conquer for real-world image super-resolution (2020)

21. Xie, T., Yang, X., Jia, Y., Zhu, C., Xiaochuan, L.: Adaptive densely connected single image super-resolution. In: 2019 IEEE/CVF International Conference on Computer Vision Workshop (ICCVW), pp. 3432–3440. IEEE (2019)

22. Xu, X., Ma, Y., Sun, W.: Towards real scene super-resolution with raw images. In: Proceedings of the IEEE Conference on Computer Vision and Pattern Recognition, pp. 1723–1731 (2019)

23. Yang, S., Wang, M., Chen, Y., Sun, Y.: Single-image super-resolution reconstruction via learned geometric dictionaries and clustered sparse coding. IEEE Trans. Image Process. 21(9), 4016–4028 (2012)

24. Yoo, J., Ahn, N., Sohn, K.A.: Rethinking data augmentation for image super-resolution: A comprehensive analysis and a new strategy. In: Proceedings of the IEEE/CVF Conference on Computer Vision and Pattern Recognition, pp. 8375–8384 (2020)

25. Yu, J., et al.: Wide activation for efficient and accurate image super-resolution. arXiv preprint arXiv:1808.08718 (2018)

26. Zhang, K., Zuo, W., Zhang, L.: Deep plug-and-play super-resolution for arbitrary blur kernels. In: Proceedings of the IEEE Conference on Computer Vision and Pattern Recognition, pp. 1671–1681 (2019)

27. Zhang, X., Wu, X.: Image interpolation by adaptive 2-d autoregressive modeling and soft-decision estimation. IEEE Trans. Image Process. 17(6), 887–896 (2008)

28. Zhang, X., Chen, Q., Ng, R., Koltun, V.: Zoom to learn, learn to zoom. In: Proceedings of the IEEE Conference on Computer Vision and Pattern Recognition, pp. 3762–3770 (2019)

29. Zhang, Y., Li, K., Li, K., Wang, L., Zhong, B., Fu, Y.: Image super-resolution using very deep residual channel attention networks. In: Proceedings of the European Conference on Computer Vision (ECCV), pp. 286–301 (2018)

30. Zhang, Y., Tian, Y., Kong, Y., Zhong, B., Fu, Y.: Residual dense network for image super-resolution. In: Proceedings of the IEEE Conference on Computer Vision and Pattern Recognition, pp. 2472–2481 (2018)
31. Zhou, F., Yang, W., Liao, Q.: Interpolation-based image super-resolution using multisurface fitting. IEEE Trans. Image Process. **21**(7), 3312–3318 (2012)

Self-calibrated Attention Neural Network for Real-World Super Resolution

Kaihua Cheng[1(✉)] and Chenhuan Wu[1,2]

[1] OPPO, Dongguan, China
chengkaihuha@oppo.com
[2] Nanjing University of Aeronautics and Astronautics, Nanjing, China
wch1996@nuaa.edu.cn

Abstract. Single Image Super-Resolution in practical scenarios is quite challenging, because of more complex degradation than bicubic downsampling and diverse degradation differences among devices. To solve this problem, we develop a novel super resolution network with large receptive field called **SCA-SR**. The contributions mainly contain the following four points. First, we introduce self-calibrated convolutions to low-level vision task for the first time to significantly enlarge the receptive field of SR model. Second, Cutblur methods are used to improve the generalization of model. Third, long skip connection was used in model design to improve the convergence of deep model structure. Fourth, we use both self-ensemble and model-ensemble to improve the robustness of model and reduce the noise introduced by individual model. According to the preliminary results of AIM 2020 Real Image Super-Resolution Challenge, our solution ranks third in both ×2 and ×3 tracks.

Keywords: Real-world image super-resolution · Receptive field · Self-calibrated convolutions · Data augmentation

1 Introduction

Single Image Super Resolution (SISR) [7,9,29] is the process of recovering a High Resolution(HR) image from a given Low Resolution(LR) image. An image may have a "lower resolution" due to a smaller spatial resolution(i.e. size) or due to a result of degradation(such as blurring). The relationship between LR and HR image can be described by the following equation:

$$I_x = \mathcal{D}(I_y; \delta) \tag{1}$$

where I_x is the degraded image or LR image, whereas I_y is the corresponding HR image. $\mathcal{D}$ is the degradation mapping function while δ is the parameters of the degradation process. The degradation mapping often include blurring, downsampling and nosie jamming. Solving (1) is an extremely ill-posed problem since there are always multiple HR images corresponding to a single LR image.

© Springer Nature Switzerland AG 2020
A. Bartoli and A. Fusiello (Eds.): ECCV 2020 Workshops, LNCS 12537, pp. 453–467, 2020.
https://doi.org/10.1007/978-3-030-67070-2_27

In literature, a variety of classical SR methods have been proposed, these algorithms are mainly divided into three categories: interpolation-based methods, reconstruction-based methods and learning-based methods. Interploation-based SISR methods excel in speed and simple logic, such as bicubic interpolation [12] and Lanczos resampling [6], but suffer from accuracy shortcomings and always bring the loss of image details. Reconstruction-based SR methods [4,21,26,34] often take advantage of the prior knowledge of the unidentified HR image to resolve the SR problem, which always result in flexible and sharp details. On the other hand, the performance of many reconstruction-based methods degrades dramatically as the scale factor increases, and high time-consuming is another drawback of these methods.

As machine learning has made great achievements in other applications, learning-based SR methods also attracted much attention owning to their outstanding performance as well as low time-consuming. These methods usually utilize machine learning algorithms to synthesize a HR image based on learning patch pairs of LR and HR images, such as Markov random field methods [7], anchored regressors [28,29], random forest methods [23], learned filters methods [22,29] and sparse coding methods [35].

Most recent SR algorithms [10,11,20,32,37] often rely on data-driven deep learning models to reconstruct richer details for accurate super-resolution. These methods can be classified into learning-based SR methods as a new and powerful branch. The first deep learning based SISR method called SRCNN was introduced by Dong et al. in ECCV 2014 [5]. SRCNN consists of only three convolution layers, but it outperformed the previous non-deep approaches [28,29]. Very Deep Super Resolution (VDSR) [13] goes much deeper to achieved higher accuracy. Both SRCNN and VDSR apply bicubic upsampling at the input stage and deal with the feature maps at the same scale as output, which is less efficient because upscaled LR image does not have more information than LR image but would take more computation cost. Shi et al. proposed Efficient Sub-Pixel Convolution Neural Network(ESPCN) [25] to make SRCNN more efficient. ESPCN deals with the feature maps at LR resolution and upsampling is carried out afterwards, which makes the total amount of computation much smaller than SRCNN. In 2017 Lim et al. developed a more advanced network called EDSR [17] and won the first NTIRE 2017 single image super-resolution challenge [1,27]. They started from SRResNet [16] and optimized it for achieving further accuracy.

More recently, a lot of attention-based SR models have shown significant improvements for SR [19,30,38]. The previously discussed network designs consider all spatial locations and channels to have equal importance for the SR. In several cases, it helps to selectively attend to only a few features at a given layer. Attention-based models allow this flexibility and consider that not all the features are essential for super-resolution. Zhang et al. [39] proposed residual channel attention networks(RCAN) that exploits channel attention mechanism acts as a selective attention over channel maps. Densely Residual Laplacian Attention Network(DRLN) [2] was developed to improve channel attention module to multi-scale Laplacian attention. Residual Non-local Attention networks(RNAN) [40] have gone further on the attention mechanism, which use Non-Local block to model pixel-wise attention in image SR.

AIM 2020 Real Image Super-Resolution Challenge [31], that is, the task of super-resolving (increasing the resolution) of a real input image by a desired factor using a training set of low and corresponding aligned high resolution real images captured in pairs by DSLR cameras. This is the second challenge of this kind after the NTIRE 2019 challenge [3]. The AIM 2020 challenge has three tracks corresponding to ×2, ×3, ×4 upscaling factors. The aim is to obtain a network design/solution capable to produce high quality results with the best fidelity to the reference ground truth. As discussed before, there are two difficulties in this challenge, more complex degradation than bicubic downsampling and diverse degradation differences among devices, so we need to develop a generic model to super-resolve LR images captured in practical scenarios.

In this work, we used densely connected residual blocks and a Laplacian attention for accurate image super-resolution just like DRLN [2]. In each residual block, self-calibrated convolutions [18] were used to replace traditional convolution to enlarge receptive field of total model because a large receptive field is essential for image SR. To train a more generic model, we use CutBlur [36] to augment the training data. Finally in the testing phase, model parameter fusion and self-ensemble were used to improve the robustness and stablity of the model to different test images.

2   Related Work

Attention-Based Networks. For image super-resolution, attention-based SR networks have shown significant improvements on image fidelity. Attention is arguably one of the most powerful concepts in the deep learning field nowadays. It is based on a common-sensical intuition that we "attend to" a certain part when processing a large amount of information. For low-level vision tasks(e.g., image SR), "certain part" often refer to channel dimension or spatial dimension or mixing them. Zhang et al. [39] proposed residual channel attention networks(RCAN) that exploits channel attention mechanism, which was first investigation on the effect of attention for low-level vision task. Densely Residual Laplacian Attention Network(DRLN) [2] was developed to improve channel attention module to multi-scale Laplacian attention. Residual Non-local Attention Networks(RNAN) [40] have gone further on the attention mechanism, which use Non-Local block to model pixel-wise attention in image SR.

Self-calibrated Convolutions. A large receptive field is essential for image SR. Before RCAN [39], large receptive field can only be achieved by deep stacks of convolutional operations [8,15]. RCAN [39] can get global receptive field by channel attention mechanism, but the spatial informations will be totally lossed due to the global pooling. RNAN [40] used non-local operations to achieve global receptive field with only a few layers and no spatial information loss. Though it brings perforamnce boost, the huge computation overhead is unacceptable and worst of all, the computation cost will exponential grow with image resolution. Benefiting from heterogeneous convolutions and between-filter communication, self-calibrated convolutions [18] was proved to significantly enlarge receptive field for many high-level tasks. Better yet, the self-calibrated convolutions is generic and can be easily replace traditional convolution without computation cost overhead. So, for the first time in low-level task, we use self-calibrated convolutions as basic module in network.

Data Augmentation. Because diverse degradation differences among devices, so there would be big variance of distribution among training and test data supplied by AIM2020 [31]. Thus, model generalization is crucial for the final fidelity scores. Data Augmentation(DA) is an effective way to improve model generalization, and using rotation and flipping is the traditional approach. Yoo et al. [36] proposed CutBlur, a novel DA method developed specifically for low level vision tasks. CutBlur can reduce unrealistic distortions by regularizing a model to learn not only "how" but also "where" to apply the super-resolution to a given image.

3   Self-calibrated Attention Neural Network for Real-World Super Resolution

The real image super resolution aim to super-resolving LR images captured in practical scenarios. Larger receptive field and model generalization are keys for model design. A proven effective module self-calibrated convolutions [18] was introduced to replace traditional convolution structure to enlarge receptive field. Cutblur [36] was used as data augmentation method for a more generic model. Based on these design principle, we proposed a novel Super-Resolution Network based on self-calibrated convolutions named SCA-SR.

3.1   Basic Network Architecture

We first upsample input image I_{LR} to $\hat{I}_{LR}$ by corresponding upscale factor using nearest interpolation because Cutblur requires to match the resolution of I_{LR} and I_{HR}. As shown in Fig. 1, SCA-SR is constituted of four integral components: feature extraction, residual in residual deep feature extraction, upsampling and reconstruction. We use the same residual structure and dense connections as DRLN [2]. Inspired by VDSR, global residual learning is adopted to improve the convergence of SCA-SR. A longer skip connection was added to connect the input to the output with a trainable parameter, so that our network only needs to focus on the high frequency part of the image. Therefore, the reconstructed image I_{SR} can be represented by the following formula, where I_l, I_h respectively represent the low-frequency and high-frequency parts of the image and α is a trainable parameter.

$$I_{SR} = \alpha I_l + I_h \tag{2}$$

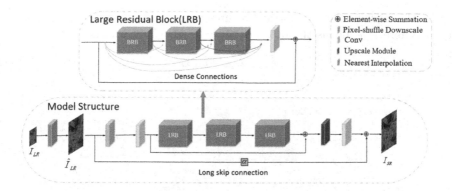

Fig. 1. The detailed network architecture of the proposed network

The first convolution layer with 3×3 kernel size is used for feature extraction, which can be formulated as Eq. 3. Where f_{conv} denotes the first convolution function for the upscaled LR image $\hat{I}_{LR}$.

$$x_{conv} = f_{conv}(\hat{I}_{LR}) \tag{3}$$

Our model is mainly composed of 20 Large Residual Block (LRBs). Define the function of nth LRB as f_{LRB}^n. The output of residual block can be given by following formula.

$$x_{LRB}^n = f_{LRB}^n(f_{LRB}^{n-1}(...(f_{LRB}^0(x_{conv}))...)) \tag{4}$$

Each LRB module consists of 3 Basic Residual Block (BRB) (as shown in Fig. 2) modules with dense connections. The output of BRB can be formulated as following equation.

$$x_{BRB}^n = f_{BRB}^n([x_{BRB}^0, ..., x_{BRB}^{n-1}]) \tag{5}$$

where x_{BRB}^n, f_{BRB}^n is the output and function of the nth BRB.

Further more, Self-calibrated Convolutions (SCC), as shown at top of Fig. 2) was adopted as basic unit of BRB in order to expand receptive field. We will cover SCC in more detail in the next section. Similarly, the BRB is also composed of three SCC with dense connections. The output of SCC can be formulated as equation (6). Where f_{SCC}^n means the function of SCC and x_{SCC}^n means the output of nth SCC.

$$x_{SCC}^n = f_{SCC}^n([x_{SCC}^0, ..., x_{SCC}^{n-1}]) \tag{6}$$

After being processed by the SCC, the feature map is forward into the Laplacian Attention Block (LAB) as DRLN [2] described in each BRB.

In the upscaling phase, Sub-pixel Convolution [25] is used as the upsampling method. The output x_{LRB} of last LRB is fed into the upsampling module to obtain the high frequency portion of image I_{SR} which can be formulated as Eq. 7. Where f_{sub}^n means the function of Sub-pixel Convolution.

$$I_h = f_{sub}^n(x_{LRB})$$ (7)

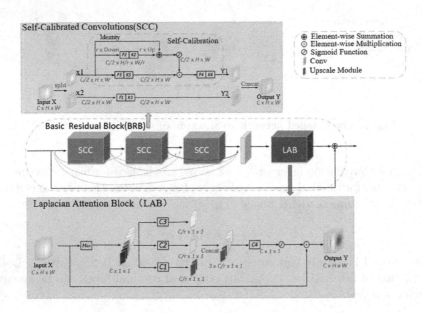

Fig. 2. The top of figure shows the basic convolution structure of SCA-SR with dense connection. The middle of the figure shows our basic residual block. The bottom of figure presents the channel attention mechanism of our network.

3.2 Self-calibrated Convolutions

Self-calibrated Convolutions(SCC) has been proven to perform well in high-level vision tasks. For real world super resolution task, SCC can not only extract multi-scale feature information, but also increase the receptive field. A lot of research [24, 33] shows that multi-scale feature is particularly useful for restoring image details. But this usually requires a large number of convolution kernels with different sizes, such as 3×3, 5×5, 7×7. Obviously, this method is difficult to be applied, considering the rapid increase of computation. So SCC was introduced into the task of our image super resolution.

As shown in Fig. 2, the input feature is divided into two parts by different convolution, represented by X_1 and X_2. Unlike other attention mechanisms that collect global context information, X_1 is only down sampled r times by average pooling. As a result, SCC only considers the context around each spatial location, avoiding some redundant information from irrelevant regions to some extent. The pooling process can be represented by the following equation.

$$T_1 = Avgpool_r(X_1)$$ (8)

In addition, the features X_2 and T_1 are transformed by convolution, which enables us to obtain two spatial features of different scales: one is the original scale space with the same resolution as the input, and the other is the smaller potential space after downsampling. Since the pooled low-scale features incorporate more information and bigger receptive field, these features can be used to guide the feature transformation under the original scale. The feature transformation on T_1 is represented by the following equation.

$$X_1' = Up(F_2(T_1)) = Up(T_1 * K_2) \tag{9}$$

where Up is a bilinear interpolation operator that maps the intermediate references from the small scale space to the original feature space. K_i is the filter of conventional 2D convolutional layer F_i.

The calibration operation can be formulated as following equation.

$$Y_1' = F_3(X_1) \cdot \sigma(X_1 + X_1') \tag{10}$$

where $F_3(X_1) = X_1 * K_3$, σ is the sigmoid function, and $\cdot$ denotes element-wise multiplication. X_1' is used as residuals to form the weights for calibration. The final output after calibration can be written as follows.

$$Y_1 = F_4(Y_1') = Y_1' * K_4 \tag{11}$$

In the work of RCAN, attention mechanisms have been shown to play a very positive role in super-resolution tasks. SCC can be thought of as a complement to the attention mechanism. To use channel information efficiently, LAB and SCC are combined to get more accurate weights for the features of different channels.

3.3   Loss Function

For image super-resolution task, the loss function is usually limited to l_1, l_2 and perceptual loss. Perceptual loss usually used in conjunction with GAN. Theoretically, l_2 loss is the ideal loss function with high PSNR score. But in the specific application, the quality of super-resolution image still depends on the convergence performance of the loss function. l_2 loss is vulnerable to outliers, so l_1 loss function was introduced as pixel loss for our network optimization. Pixel loss is defined as:

$$L_{pix} = \frac{1}{N} \sum_{i=1}^{N} \|I_{SR}^i - I_{HR}^i\| \tag{12}$$

In order to improve the image fidelity, SSIM and MS_SSIM loss were also used as structure losses, as in the following equations:

$$L_{ssim} = \frac{1}{N} \sum_{i=1}^{N} 1 - SSIM(I_{SR}^i, I_{HR}^i) \tag{13}$$

$$L_{ms\_ssim} = \frac{1}{N} \sum_{i=1}^{N} 1 - MS\_SSIM(I_{SR}^i, I_{HR}^i) \tag{14}$$

With pixel loss and structure loss, we can formulate the total loss shown as following equation.

$$L_{total} = L_{pix} + 0.2 L_{ms\_ssim} + 0.2 L_{ssim} \tag{15}$$

3.4   Model Ensemble

To further improve the performance and robustness of SCA-SR, we introduce self-ensemble strategy similar to [17]. Besides, we also adopted the same model ensemble strategy as RFB-ESRGAN [24]. The final model is ensemble of 5 models with the best PSNR and SSIM performance among all recorded models in training stage. The parameters of the best 5 models are averaged to form the ensemble model $M_{Ensemble}$, whose parameters are:

$$\theta_M^{Ensemble} = \frac{1}{N} \sum_{i=1}^{N} \theta_M^i \tag{16}$$

where $\theta_M^{Ensemble}$ represents the parameters of $M_{Ensemble}$. We find that the integration strategy brought more significant benefits as the upsampling scale increased (see Table 3), But on the contrary, too many models for ensemble has a negative impact on the image fidelity. The number of models for ensemble is finally limited to five.

4   Experiment

4.1   Training Details

For AIM 2020 Real Image Super-Resolution Challenge [31], there are three tracks corresponding to ×2, ×3, ×4 upscaling factors. The mini-batch size is 64. The spatial size of cropped HR patch is 192×192(for ×4 upscale), 144×144(for ×3 upscale) and 96×96(for ×2 upscale), and the spatial size of corresponding input LR image for all upscaling fators is 48×48. Because CutBlur requires to match the resolution of LR and HR patch, nearest neighbour interpolation was first used to upscale LR to HR resolution. So actually, for all upscaling factors, LR and HR patch has the same spatial resolution.

To optimize the model, We use Adam [14] with the default parameters of $\beta_1 = 0.9$, $\beta_2 = 0.999$, and $\epsilon = 10^{-8}$. The learning rate is fixed to 2×1^{-4} originally and then decreased to half after every 7×10^4. The total number of iterations T is 42×10^4. We implement SCA-SR with Pytorch framework and train them using Tesla V100 GPUs. There are 72.28M, 72.48M and 72.45M parameters in ×2, ×3 and ×4 models respectively, and it cost 0.34s, 0.46s, 0.40s using one Tesla V100 GPU processing per image with 128×128 pixels for ×2, ×3 and ×4 models.

4.2   Data

AIM 2020 Real Image Super-Resolution Challenge [31] has provided a new real image SR dataset for training. For each tracks($\times 2$, $\times 3$, $\times 4$), there are 19,000 LR-HR image pairs for training. The resolution of HR image is 776×776(for $\times 4$ upscale), 816×816(for $\times 3$ upscale) and 760×760(for $\times 2$ upscale), and the corresponding resolution of LR image is 194×194, 272×272 and 380×380. We use 18,500 pairs for trainging and the rest 500 pairs for validation.

SCA-SR are trained with RGB channels. CutBlur [36] method was used for data augmentation. The result models are evaluated on Test Data (60 LR images) provided by AIM 2020 Real Image Super-Resolution Challenge.

4.3   Qualitative Results

We compared the completed training model with EDSR, RCAN and DRLN on validation set provided by AIM2020. As shown in Table 1, SCA-SR has a huge advantage over real data sets. SCA-SR maintains the authenticity of the reconstructed image. In addition, benefiting from loss function that takes SSIM and MS_SSIM into account, our images are not over-smooth and structures are kept clear.

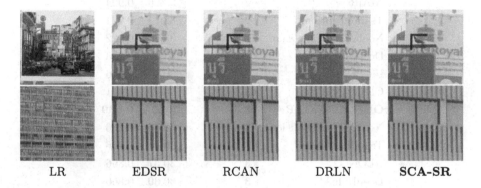

| LR | EDSR | RCAN | DRLN | SCA-SR |

Fig. 3. Qualitative results of SCA-SR. It produces more clear textures, e.g., text images, building structure.

As shown in Fig. 3, SCA-SR has restored the texture of the images well. The text in the image of first row be displayed clearly, and building structure in the image of second row has sharper edges.

We present the top 7 results from the AIM 2020 Real World Super-Resolution Challenge in Table 2. In the challenges of upscale factor $\times 2$ and $\times 3$, we both rank third, and we rank seventh in upscale factor $\times 4$.

Table 1. The PSNR and SSIM results on 93 validation images same as CDC [32] with upscale factor 4

Method	PSNR	SSIM
BICUBIC	30.56	0.820
SRResNet	31.63	0.847
ESRGAN	31.92	0.857
EDSR	32.03	0.855
RCAN	31.85	0.857
DRLN	32.84	0.858
CDC	32.42	**0.861**
SCA-SR	**32.91**	0.859

Table 2. Results of AIM2020 real world super resolution challenge

Team	Upscale factor	PSNR	SSIM
Baidu	×2	33.44	0.927
CETC-CSKT	×2	33.31	0.924
OPPO_CAMERA	×2	**33.30**	**0.924**
AiAiR	×2	33.26	0.924
TeamInception	×2	33.23	0.924
Noah_TerminalVision	×2	33.28	0.922
DeepBlueAI	×2	33.17	0.923
Baidu	×3	30.94	0.876
CETC-CSKT	×3	30.76	0.871
OPPO_CAMERA	×3	**30.53**	**0.869**
Noah_TerminalVision	×3	30.56	0.866
TeamInception	×3	30.41	0.866
ALONG	×3	30.37	0.866
DeepBlueAI	×3	30.30	0.866
Baidu	×4	31.39	0.875
ALONG	×4	31.23	0.874
CETC-CSKT	×4	31.12	0.874
SR-IM	×4	31.17	0.872
DeepBlueAI	×4	30.96	0.873
JNSR	×4	30.99	0.872
OPPO_CAMERA	×4	**30.86**	**0.873**

4.4   Ablation Study

We conducted five experiments which shown in Table 4 to investigate the effects of following four components: ensemble strategy, CutBlur, long skip connection and self-calibrated convolutions.

Ensemble Strategy. To demonstrate the effect of our ensemble strategy, we compare the SR results with ensemble and without ensemble strategy in Table 3. It can be observed that the gain of PSNR and SSIM becomes more obvious as the upscale factor increases. For large upscale factors, the super resolution image is usually accompanied by more noise. The ensemble strategy proves that it can suppress noise well and keep the image details sharp and clear.

Table 3. PSNR and SSIM under different upscale factor

Upscale factor	Without ensemble		With ensemble	
	PSNR	SSIM	PSNR	SSIM
× 2	32.99	0.916	33.01	0.916
× 3	32.17	0.915	32.27	0.916
× 4	30.62	0.863	30.64	0.866

CutBlur. The benefits of CutBlur have been demonstrated in great detail by Yoo et al. [36]. We have also done a similar comparison experiment, and the results of experiment 3 and experiment 4 show that PSNR are significantly improved on real world images.

Long Skip Connection. In recent years, global residual structure is rarely seen in the super resolution tasks because it is more efficient extracting features directly from LR image than upscaled LR. But we can see significant improvements with CutBlur [36] data augmentation in SR tasks which requires the same resolution of LR and HR images. Under this premise, global residual connection was needed to ensure the convergence of SCA-SR. When we removed the long skip connection from experiment 2, there was a huge drop in the model's performance. Compared second image of experiment 2 and 4 in Fig. 4, we can observe that the texture of buildings becomes blurred without long skip connection.

Self-calibrated Convolutions. Self-calibrated Convolutions(SCC) is the first time to be applied to a low-level vision task. In order to prove the effect of SCC, we remove all the SCC in the model so the residual group structure in experiment 1 is just like DRLN [2]. We find that networks with SCC would perform better than those without SCC comparing the results of experiment 1 and experiment 5. We can observe that PSNR score with SCC was improved from 30.52 dB to 30.64 dB.

Table 4. PSNR and SSIM comparisons for showing the effects of each component in SCA-SR

	1	2	3	4	5
Ensemble	✓	✗	✗	✗	✓
Cutblur	✓	✓	✗	✓	✓
Long Skip Connection	✓	✗	✓	✓	✓
SCC	✗	✓	✓	✓	✓
PSNR/SSIM	30.52/0.863	30.01/0.853	30.39/0.863	30.62/0.863	30.64/0.866

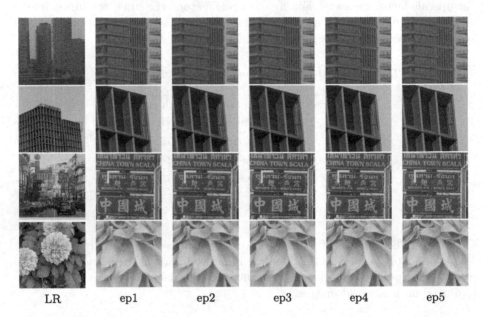

LR   ep1   ep2   ep3   ep4   ep5

Fig. 4. Overall visual comparisons for showing the effects of each component in SCA-SR, ep means experiment

5 Conclusion

We proposed SCA-SR model to the real world images super-resolution. To improve the model generalization, Curblur was used to augment training data. Besides, various components have been adopted to improve the performance of super-resolution. Specifically, the long skip connection helps SCA-SR converging to good results even with very deep structure. Meanwhile, it enables SCA-SR to ignore the low-frequency content which is less relevant to the SR task and focus on the image details. Furthermore, self-calibrated convolutions increases the receptive field of the network and provides multi-scale information, improving the performance of the super-resolution. Extensive experiments and comparisons on AIM2020 Real Image Super-Resolution Challenge [31] prove the effectiveness of our proposed network.

References

1. Agustsson, E., Timofte, R.: Ntire 2017 challenge on single image super-resolution: dataset and study. In: Proceedings of the IEEE Conference on Computer Vision and Pattern Recognition Workshops, pp. 126–135 (2017)
2. Anwar, S., Barnes, N.: Densely residual laplacian super-resolution. arXiv preprint arXiv:1906.12021 (2019)
3. Cai, J., Gu, S., Timofte, R., Zhang, L.: Ntire 2019 challenge on real image super-resolution: methods and results. In: Proceedings of the IEEE Conference on Computer Vision and Pattern Recognition Workshops (2019)
4. Dai, S., Han, M., Xu, W., Wu, Y., Gong, Y., Katsaggelos, A.K.: Softcuts: a soft edge smoothness prior for color image super-resolution. IEEE Trans. Image Process. **18**(5), 969–981 (2009)
5. Dong, C., Loy, C.C., He, K., Tang, X.: Learning a deep convolutional network for image super-resolution. In: Fleet, D., Pajdla, T., Schiele, B., Tuytelaars, T. (eds.) ECCV 2014. LNCS, vol. 8692, pp. 184–199. Springer, Cham (2014). https://doi.org/10.1007/978-3-319-10593-2_13
6. Duchon, C.E.: Lanczos filtering in one and two dimensions. J. Appl. Meteorol. **18**(8), 1016–1022 (1979)
7. Freeman, W.T., Jones, T.R., Pasztor, E.C.: Example-based super-resolution. IEEE Comput. Graphics Appl. **22**(2), 56–65 (2002)
8. Fukushima, K., Miyake, S.: Neocognitron: a self-organizing neural network model for a mechanism of visual pattern recognition. In: Amari, S., Arbib, M.A. (eds.) Competition and Cooperation in Neural Nets, pp. 267–285. Springer, Berlin (1982)
9. Glasner, D., Bagon, S., Irani, M.: Super-resolution from a single image. In: 2009 IEEE 12th International Conference on Computer Vision, pp. 349–356. IEEE (2009)
10. Guo, Y., et al.: Closed-loop matters: Dual regression networks for single image super-resolution. In: Proceedings of the IEEE/CVF Conference on Computer Vision and Pattern Recognition, pp. 5407–5416 (2020)
11. Ji, X., Cao, Y., Tai, Y., Wang, C., Li, J., Huang, F.: Real-world super-resolution via kernel estimation and noise injection. In: Proceedings of the IEEE/CVF Conference on Computer Vision and Pattern Recognition Workshops, pp. 466–467 (2020)
12. Keys, R.: Cubic convolution interpolation for digital image processing. IEEE Trans. Acoustics, Speech, and Signal Proces. **29**(6), 1153–1160 (1981)
13. Kim, J., Kwon Lee, J., Mu Lee, K.: Accurate image super-resolution using very deep convolutional networks. In: Proceedings of the IEEE Conference on Computer Vision and Pattern Recognition, pp. 1646–1654 (2016)
14. Kingma, D.P., Ba, J.: Adam: A method for stochastic optimization. arXiv preprint arXiv:1412.6980 (2014)
15. LeCun, Y., et al.: Backpropagation applied to handwritten zip code recognition. Neural Comput. **1**(4), 541–551 (1989)
16. Ledig, C., et al.: Photo-realistic single image super-resolution using a generative adversarial network. In: Proceedings of the IEEE Conference on Computer Vision and Pattern Recognition, pp. 4681–4690 (2017)
17. Lim, B., Son, S., Kim, H., Nah, S., Mu Lee, K.: Enhanced deep residual networks for single image super-resolution. In: Proceedings of the IEEE Conference on Computer Vision and Pattern Recognition Workshops, pp. 136–144 (2017)
18. Liu, J.J., Hou, Q., Cheng, M.M., Wang, C., Feng, J.: Improving convolutional networks with self-calibrated convolutions. In: Proceedings of the IEEE/CVF Conference on Computer Vision and Pattern Recognition, pp. 10096–10105 (2020)

19. Lugmayr, A., et al.: Aim 2019 challenge on real-world image super-resolution: methods and results. In: 2019 IEEE/CVF International Conference on Computer Vision Workshop (ICCVW), pp. 3575–3583. IEEE (2019)
20. Ma, C., Rao, Y., Cheng, Y., Chen, C., Lu, J., Zhou, J.: Structure-preserving super resolution with gradient guidance. In: Proceedings of the IEEE/CVF Conference on Computer Vision and Pattern Recognition, pp. 7769–7778 (2020)
21. Marquina, A., Osher, S.J.: Image super-resolution by tv-regularization and bregman iteration. J. Sci. Comput. **37**(3), 367–382 (2008)
22. Romano, Y., Isidoro, J., Milanfar, P.: Raisr: rapid and accurate image super resolution. IEEE Trans. Comput. Imaging **3**(1), 110–125 (2016)
23. Schulter, S., Leistner, C., Bischof, H.: Fast and accurate image upscaling with super-resolution forests. In: Proceedings of the IEEE Conference on Computer Vision and Pattern Recognition, pp. 3791–3799 (2015)
24. Shang, T., Dai, Q., Zhu, S., Yang, T., Guo, Y.: Perceptual extreme super-resolution network with receptive field block. In: Proceedings of the IEEE/CVF Conference on Computer Vision and Pattern Recognition Workshops, pp. 440–441 (2020)
25. Shi, W., et al.: Real-time single image and video super-resolution using an efficient sub-pixel convolutional neural network. In: Proceedings of the IEEE Conference on Computer Vision and Pattern Recognition, pp. 1874–1883 (2016)
26. Sun, J., Xu, Z., Shum, H.Y.: Image super-resolution using gradient profile prior. In: 2008 IEEE Conference on Computer Vision and Pattern Recognition, pp. 1–8. IEEE (2008)
27. Timofte, R., Agustsson, E., Van Gool, L., Yang, M.H., Zhang, L.: Ntire 2017 challenge on single image super-resolution: methods and results. In: Proceedings of the IEEE Conference on Computer Vision and Pattern Recognition Workshops, pp. 114–125 (2017)
28. Timofte, R., De Smet, V., Van Gool, L.: Anchored neighborhood regression for fast example-based super-resolution. In: Proceedings of the IEEE International Conference on Computer Vision, pp. 1920–1927 (2013)
29. Timofte, R., De Smet, V., Van Gool, L.: A+: adjusted anchored neighborhood regression for fast super-resolution. In: Cremers, D., Reid, I., Saito, H., Yang, M.-H. (eds.) ACCV 2014. LNCS, vol. 9006, pp. 111–126. Springer, Cham (2015). https://doi.org/10.1007/978-3-319-16817-3_8
30. Timofte, R., Gu, S., Wu, J., Van Gool, L.: Ntire 2018 challenge on single image super-resolution: methods and results. In: Proceedings of the IEEE Conference on Computer Vision and Pattern Recognition Workshops, pp. 852–863 (2018)
31. Wei, P., Lu, H., Timofte, R., Lin, L., Zuo, W., et al.: AIM 2020 challenge on real image super-resolution. In: European Conference on Computer Vision Workshops (2020)
32. Wei, P., et al.: Component divide-and-conquer for real-world image super-resolution. arXiv preprint arXiv:2008.01928 (2020)
33. Wu, H., et al.: Multi-grained attention networks for single image super-resolution. IEEE Trans. Circuits Syst. Video Technol. (2020)
34. Yan, Q., Xu, Y., Yang, X., Nguyen, T.Q.: Single image superresolution based on gradient profile sharpness. IEEE Trans. Image Process. **24**(10), 3187–3202 (2015)
35. Yang, J., Wright, J., Huang, T.S., Ma, Y.: Image super-resolution via sparse representation. IEEE Trans. Image Process. **19**(11), 2861–2873 (2010)
36. Yoo, J., Ahn, N., Sohn, K.A.: Rethinking data augmentation for image super-resolution: a comprehensive analysis and a new strategy. In: Proceedings of the IEEE/CVF Conference on Computer Vision and Pattern Recognition, pp. 8375–8384 (2020)

37. Zhang, K., Gool, L.V., Timofte, R.: Deep unfolding network for image super-resolution. In: Proceedings of the IEEE/CVF Conference on Computer Vision and Pattern Recognition, pp. 3217–3226 (2020)
38. Zhang, K., Gu, S., Timofte, R.: Ntire 2020 challenge on perceptual extreme super-resolution: methods and results. In: Proceedings of the IEEE/CVF Conference on Computer Vision and Pattern Recognition Workshops, pp. 492–493 (2020)
39. Zhang, Y., Li, K., Li, K., Wang, L., Zhong, B., Fu, Y.: Image super-resolution using very deep residual channel attention networks. In: Proceedings of the European Conference on Computer Vision (ECCV), pp. 286–301 (2018)
40. Zhang, Y., Li, K., Li, K., Zhong, B., Fu, Y.: Residual non-local attention networks for image restoration. arXiv preprint arXiv:1903.10082 (2019)

FAN: Frequency Aggregation Network for Real Image Super-Resolution

Yingxue Pang, Xin Li, Xin Jin, Yaojun Wu, Jianzhao Liu, Sen Liu, and Zhibo Chen[✉]

CAS Key Laboratory of Technology in Geo-Spatial Information Processing and Application System, University of Science and Technology of China, Hefei 230027, China
{pangyx,lixin666,jinxustc,yaojunwu,jianzhao}@mail.ustc.edu.cn, elsen@iat.ustc.edu.cn, chenzhibo@ustc.edu.cn

Abstract. Single image super-resolution (SISR) aims to recover the high-resolution (HR) image from its low-resolution (LR) input image. With the development of deep learning, SISR has achieved great progress. However, It is still a challenge to restore the real-world LR image with complicated authentic degradations. Therefore, we propose FAN, a frequency aggregation network, to address the real-world image super-resolu-tion problem. Specifically, we extract different frequencies of the LR image and pass them to a channel attention-grouped residual dense network (CA-GRDB) individually to output corresponding feature maps. And then aggregating these residual dense feature maps adaptively to recover the HR image with enhanced details and textures. We conduct extensive experiments quantitatively and qualitatively to verify that our FAN performs well on the real image super-resolution task of AIM 2020 challenge. According to the released final results, our team SR-IM achieves the fourth place on the X4 track with PSNR of 31.1735 and SSIM of 0.8728.

Keywords: Frequency aggregation network (FAN) · Real image super-resoltion (RealSR) · AIM 2020 challenge

1 Introduction

Single image super-resolution (SISR) task aims to recover the high-resolution (HR) image from its low-resolution (LR) input image, where the LR image is acquired by applying some downsamping settings to the HR image. Whether the early traditional methods like [2,8] or recent methods [6,15,19,27], SISR has drawn more and more attention because of its wide range of application, such as medical image[11], surveillance [36] and security [10]. With the development of convectional neural networks (CNN) and several high quality super-resolution datasets, Recent models [6,15,16,19,20,27] have achieved remarkable success

---

Y. Pang, X. Li—The first two authors contributed equally to this work.

© Springer Nature Switzerland AG 2020
A. Bartoli and A. Fusiello (Eds.): ECCV 2020 Workshops, LNCS 12537, pp. 468–483, 2020.
https://doi.org/10.1007/978-3-030-67070-2_28

in SISR task. A well-designed CNN can effectively capture the non-linear mapping and automatically learn the mapping function based on various high-quality super-resolution dataset. However, these models can perform well on the "clean" standard benchmarks, and they often fail to be applied in real-world scenarios. They cannot handle the real-world image super-resolution problem with complicated degradation processes, as shown in Fig. 1.

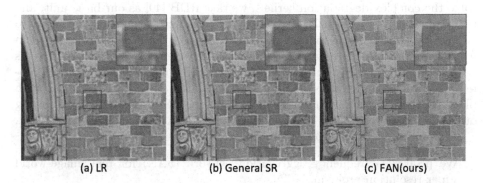

(a) LR   (b) General SR   (c) FAN(ours)

Fig. 1. Examples of SISR cannot be generalized to RealSR. (a) Real low-resolution image, which is captured by low quality DSLR camera. (b) Processed by general SR model EDSR. (c) Processed by our FAN.

Therefore, the real-world image super-resolution (RealSR) has attracted more and more attention. Different from the general SISR, the purpose of RealSR is to learn a general model to restore LR image captured under practical scenarios to high-resolution. This model focuses on solving the degradation problem that is more complex than bicubic downsampling. The paired LR and HR images are captured by various DSLR cameras. The diverse degradation differences among devices can be expressed as Eq. 1

$$I_{HR} = (I * k_{HR}) + n_{HR},$$
$$I_{LR} = (I * k_{LR})\downarrow_s + n_{LR}, \tag{1}$$

where k_{LR} and k_{HR} represent degradation kernel of high quality and low quality DSLR cameras respectively. $\downarrow_s$ denotes the multiple of downsampling. n_{HR} and n_{LR} are additive noise. I represents the real world image. I_{HR} and I_{LR} are the image pairs collected with high-quality and low-quality DSLR cameras respectively. RealSR recovers the I_{HR} from I_{LR}, which more satisfies the needs of industrial applications. According to Eq. 1, we can get the I_{LR} from I_{HR} as Eq. 2.

$$I_{LR} = (I_{HR} * k_{HR}^{-1} * k_{LR})\downarrow_s + n_{LR} - (n_{HR} * k_{HR}^{-1} * k_{LR})\downarrow_s. \tag{2}$$

From the above equation, we can find that the RealSR is more complicated than general SISR. When the degradation of high-quality DSLR camera is small, the Eq. 2 will be degraded to general SISR problem.

In this paper, we propose a frequency aggregation network (FAN) for complex real-world image super-resolution problem. Specifically, we extracted the low-frequency, middle-frequency and high-frequency of LR image with multi-scale representation. Then we utilize different branches to restore the corresponding frequency components of LR and aggregate them adaptively with channel attention mechanism to generate the HR image. From different frequency components, our framework can be more robust to solving different distortions. In order to solve the complex degradation kernels, we take RDB [40] as our basic unit, and redesign GRDB [17] into CA-GRDB by introducing a channel mechanism to adaptively aggregate the representations of different receptive fields, which can further improve the representation ability of the network. Extensive experiments have validated the effectiveness of our FAN for real image super-resolution problem. According to the released final results, our team SR-IM achieves the fourth place on the X4 track with PSNR of 31.1735 and SSIM of 0.8728 by applying our FAN on the real image super-resolution task of AIM 2020 challenge [34, 35].

Our contributions can be summarized as follows:

- We propose a frequency aggregation network (FAN) for real image-world super-resolution problem.
- We redesign the novel CA-GRDB module by introducing a channel attention mechanism to further improve the representation ability of network.
- According to the released final results, our team SR-IM achieves the forth place on the X4 track with PSNR of 31.1735 and SSIM of 0.8728 on the real-world image super-resolution task of AIM 2020 challenge [34].

2   Related Works

2.1   Single Image Super-Resolution

Dong et al. proposed the SRCNN [6,7] which can be roughly seen as the first SISR work based on CNN. They adopted an end-to-end supervised learning model to restore the HR images with its corresponding bicubic downsamping LR images. Compared to traditional methods [2,8], they reconstructed high-quality HR images with clearer details and higher metric scores. SRCNN proves the effectiveness of CNN in solving SISR problem and inspires plenty of works to be proposed to improve the qualitative and quantitative results. Kim et al. [18] proposed DRCN in which they designed a deeper recursive layer with the receptive field of 41 to demonstrate their performance in common benchmarks. But methods extended by SRCNN [18,30] usually utilize the pre-defined unsamping operator which increases unnecessary computational cost and lead to reconstruction artifacts in some cases. To tackle this problem, LapSRN [19] constructed a set of cascaded sub-networks to progressively predicts the sub-band high frequency residuals. It replaced the pre-defined upsampling with the learned transposed convolutional layers to remove the undesired artifacts and reduce the computational cost.

Considered the methods mentioned above, we still have the difficulty to recover the HR image with more high-frequency details when using larger unsampling factors. Since those methods focus to optimize the pixel loss and ignore the image quality, the results often lack high-frequency details or fail to maintain the perceptual fidelity compared to its high-resolution "ground truth". Ledig et al. [21] proposed SRGAN, the first SISR work which utilized Generative Adversarial Network(GAN), to solve the problem. They combine a perceptual loss, an adversarial loss and a content loss to infer HR images for 4x upsampling factors and show hugely significant gains in perceptual quality. Wang et al. [32] proposed ESRGAN which is an enhanced version by reconsidering the entire SRGAN and modifing it in network architecture, adversarial loss and perceptual loss. And ESRGAN brings the subjective state-of-the-art algorithm to SR. Zhang et al. [37] proposed RankSRGAN to introduce a ranker to learn the behavior of perceptual metrics and address the indifferentiable perceptual metrics problem.

Unlike previous feed-forward approaches, Haris et al. [13] introduced the back-projection into the reconstruction process of SISR. They showed that combining the up and down sampling, along with error feedbacks, encourages to get better results. Then, it seems to be a new trend to exploite the attention mechanism which can adaptively process visual information and focus on salient areas. RCAN [38] was proposed to apply the channel attention to capture the dependencies among channels. RNAN [39] utilized the local and non-local attention modules to get feature representation and dependencies. Similarly, SAN [5] also incorporated the non-local attention mechanism to capture long-range spatial contextual information. In addition, multi-pass methods also prove its effectiveness in SISR in recent work [4,12,22,28]. Within it, different paths may perform different operations to extract corresponding feature maps. By fusing these feature maps coming from each path, the whole network provides better modelling capabilities and generalization. We hence get inspired to construct our three-path aggregation network to capture different frequency infromation of LR images. And we demonstrate that our method performs well on the AIM 2020 challenge, came the fourth place on the X4 track with PSNR of 31.1735 and SSIM of 0.8728.

2.2 Real-World Image Super-Resolution

The SISR methods mentioned above usually utilize the clean and ideal datasets which mostly adopt simple and uniform degradation (e.g. bicubic downsampling) to construct LR images from HR images without any distracting artifacts (e.g. sensor noise, image compression, non-ideal PSF, etc.). However, since the degradation in real world images is more complicated, SISR models inevitably fail in real-world image super-resolution with limited application and generalization.

To overcome the problem, several real-world super-resolution challenges [25,26] have been hold to attract more participants to come up their solutions. Cai et al. [1] build a real-world single super-resolution dataset where paired LR-HR images on the same scene are captured by adjusting the focal length of a digital camera.

Shocher et al. [29] proposed ZSSR , the first unsupervised CNN-based SR method, to train a small image-specific CNN at test time by expoliting the internal recurrence information of the image. Fritsche et al. [9] proposed DSGAN to generate LR-HR pairs with similar natural image characteristics. Ji et al. [14] proposed a new degradation framework with various blur kernels and noise injections to solve the realistic image super-resolution problem. However, in this work, we propose FAN to extract the different frequency components of the LR image and then aggregate them to recover the HR image with more high frequency details.

3   Method

In this section, we will illustrate the overall architecture of our FAN and explain each component in detail, including hierarchical feature extractor (HFE), the main body with three branches and fusion module.

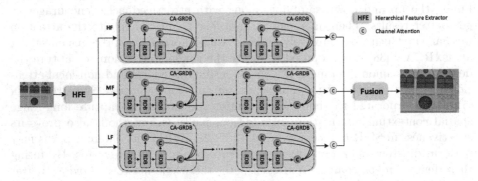

Fig. 2. The proposed network architecture: FAN

3.1   Overall Structure of FAN

Our end-to-end frequency aggregation network (FAN) is shown in Fig. 2. We first extract different frequency components of the LR image through the hierarchical feature extractor (HFE), and then pass them to each branch to obtain corresponding feature map. FAN contains three branches with same structure to process high-frequency component (HF), middle-frequency component (MF) and low-frequency component (LF) respectively. Followed three branches, FAN utilizes the fusion module to recover the HR image with enhanced details and textures from three residual dense feature maps.

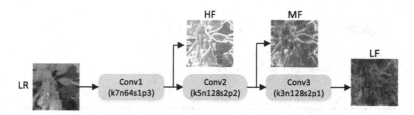

Fig. 3. Hierarchical feature extractor (HFE) with corresponding kernel size (k), number of feature maps (n), stride (s) and padding size (p) for each convolutional layer.

3.2   Hierarchical Feature Extractor

Method [3] has proved that features extracted by different scale factors can capture different frequency information of the image. Inspired by it, we design the hierarchical feature extractor (FHE), which is shown in Fig. 3, to progressively extract different frequency components. Specifically, we gradually input the LR image into three convolutional layers and output the hierarchical feature maps in each layer. As [3] claimed, the larger feature map size is, the higher frequency component it contains. Therefore, we design the first convolutional layer (Conv1) with form of $k7n64s1p3$ to output the same size feature map (HF) as the LR image. The remaining two (Conv2 and Conv3) with forms of $k5n128s2p2$ and $k3n128s2p1$ produce the feature maps (MF and LF) which have half and quarter size of the input LR image. We indicate the convolutional layer by corresponding kernel size (k), number of feature maps (n), stride (s) and padding size (p). Among three frequency components, LF contains the low-level frequency of LR image with roughly structure and HF represents the high-level frequency with fine-grained details such as edges and textures. MF indicates the intermediate value between them. The entire frequency component extraction process can also be defined as Eq. 3.

$$HF = Conv1(I_{LR}), MF = Conv2(HF), LF = Conv3(MF) \qquad (3)$$

3.3   Main Body: Three Branches

Since the degradation of DSLR camera is complex and contains multiple distortions such as blur and noise, we need to improve the network representation ability. After HFE, we hence propose the main body with three same branches to handle each frequency feature map separately. Inspired by [38] and [17], we introduce channel attention mechanism into the grouped residual dense block (GRDB) termed as CA-GRDB to adaptively aggregate those residual dense blocks (RDBs) [40] with different attention weights. We cascade four CA-GRDBs in each branch where each CA-GRDB consists of three RDBs, resulting 12 RDBs of each branch shown in Fig. 2.

Then the specific structure of CA-GRDB and RDB is shown in Fig. 4. In CA-GRDB, we cascade three RDBs and apply channel attention after each RDB.

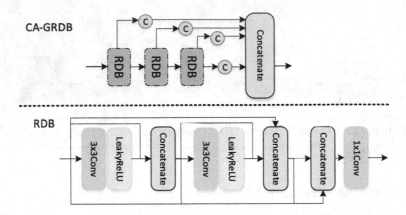

Fig. 4. Components of CA-GRDB and RDB, where C denotes channel attention module from [38] and the convolutional layers in RDB are from [17].

Then the feature maps from channel attention are concatenated together as fusing operation. As for the RDB, we replace ReLU with LeakyReLU to avoid dying ReLU problem [24]. And each RDB is constructed by 8 layers with the form 3x3 Conv-LeakyReLU-Concat via dense connection and residual connection.

3.4 Fusion Module

The fusion module is shown in Fig. 5. Like [31] claimed, Non-Local module (NL) tends to capture the long-term dependencies of features to compensate the lost information due to the local neighborhood filtering in convolutional layers. To fuse the features of different branches, we utilize non-local attention and convolution layer to further capture the correlation between different frequency features. Then we exploit pixel-shuffle layer used in [23] and convolutional layer twice to upsample the frequency feature to the original image size, which is the generated HR image. Notice that we employ 2x upsampling operation using pixel-shuffle layer and we detail each convlutional layer with corresponding kernel size (k), number of feature maps (n), stride (s) and padding size (p) in Fig. 5.

3.5 Loss Functions

We first employ pixel-wise $L1$ loss to measure the reconstruction error and then exploit MSE loss to fine tune our model. And the overall loss function can be represented as follows,

$$\mathcal{L}_{\text{ALL}} = \mathcal{L}_{\text{L1}} + \mathcal{L}_{\text{MSE}} \tag{4}$$

4   Experiments

In this section, we will illustrate the RealSR dataset and evaluation metrics used in our experiments. And we will describe the implementation details of our training and testing. We compare our FAN with seven state-of-the-art methods qualitatively and quantitatively. To further verify the effectiveness of our each FAN module, We also conduct several ablation studies.

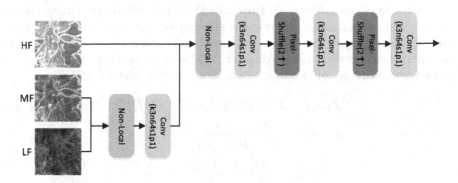

Fig. 5. Fusion module, which integrate non-local attention [31], pixel-shuffle layer [23] and convolution layer to capture the correlation between different frequency features. Each convolutional layer is denoted with corresponding kernel size(k), number of feature maps(n), stride(s) and padding size (p). (2 ↑) means 2x upsampling operation using pixel-shuffle layer.

4.1   Dataset

We train our FAN model based on 19,000 LR-HR pairs of training images provided by AIM 2020 Real Image Super-Resolution Challenge-Track3, where the paired LR-HR images are captured by various camera in practical scenarios. In addition, the validation dataset contains 20 pairs of images. Although the test dataset provides 60 pairs of LR-HR images, the HR images are not available in the test stage. Therefore, we test our FAN model on validation dataset and compare with other state-of-the-art methods in this work. According to the released final results, we achieved the fourth place on the X4 track with PSNR of 31.1735 and SSIM of 0.8728 on test dataset.

4.2   Evaluation Metrics

(1) **Peak Signal-to-Noise Ratio (PSNR)**: PSNR is one of the most widely used full-reference quality metrics. It measures the ratio between the maximum possible value (power) of a signal and the power of distorting noise that affects

the quality of its representation. In other words, PSNR metric reflects the intensity differences between the real HR image and the recovered HR image. A higher PSNR score means that the intensity of two images is more close. Mathematically, it is high related to MSE loss mentioned above:

$$PSNR = 10log_{10}(\frac{R^2}{MSE}) \tag{5}$$

where R^2 denotes the maximum fluctuation in the input image data type.

(2) **The Structural SIMilarity Index (SSIM)** [33]: SSIM evaluate the image quality based on luminance, contrast and structure from the perspective of image formation. We apply it to compute the perceptual distance between the real HR image and the recovered image. A higher SSIM score means that the luminance, contrast and structure of two images are more similar. Mathematically,

$$\mathcal{L}_{SSIM} = [l(\hat{I}, I)^\alpha \cdot [c(\hat{I}, I)]^\beta \cdot [s(\hat{I}, I)]^\gamma$$

$$l(\hat{I}, I)^\alpha = \frac{2\mu_{\hat{I}}\mu_I + C_1}{\mu_{\hat{I}}^2 + \mu_I^2 + C_1}$$

$$c(\hat{I}, I)]^\beta = \frac{2\sigma_{\hat{I}}\sigma_I + C_2}{\sigma_2^2 + \sigma_{\hat{I}}^2 + C_2} \tag{6}$$

$$s(\hat{I}, I)]^\gamma = \frac{\sigma_{\hat{I}I} + C_3}{\sigma_{\hat{I}}\sigma_I + C_3}$$

where $\mu_{\hat{I}}$, $\mu_I, \sigma_{\hat{I}}, \sigma_I$ denote mean and standard deviation of the image $\hat{I}_{HR}$, I_{HR} respectively. C_1, C_2, C_3 are three constants to avoid instability. α, β, γ are hyper-parameters to control the relative importance.

4.3   Implementation Details

Our FAN is implemented based on PyTorch framework with four NVIDIA 1080Ti GPUs. To avoid undesirable over-fitting behaviors due to the limited data, we use data augmentation in the process of training such as randomly cropping, flipping and rotation. The number of mini-batches was set as 8. We use Adam optimizer with a initial learning rate of 0.0001 which will decay by a factor 0.5 every 30 epochs. We spent almost 48 h to train our FAN model.

For testing, we first crop the LR image into several 196×196 small patches and then fed them into our FAN model to obtain the HR patches. Finally we convert those patches into a complete HR image. Our model requires 0.19 s on a single NVIDIA 1080-Ti GPU with an LR image of 196×196 for testing. And we all use the 130 epochs.

4.4   Comparison with the State-of-the-Art Methods

We compare our FAN model with seven state-of-the-art methods in same test settings. The first one is a traditional method, i.e, bicubic upsampling. And the others are CNN-based methods which are retrained on the RealSR x4 dataset for fairness. DBPN [13] exploits iterative up and downsampling layers to self-correct features at each stage by error feedback mechanism. EDSR [23] modifies the conventional residual networks by removing some unnecessary modules and get significant performance improvement. RCAN [38] proposes the channel attention to capture the dependencies among deep residual feature maps. RDN [40] conducts a novel residual dense network to extract feature maps. SAN [5] incorporates the non-local attention mechanism to capture long-range spatial contextual information. VDSR [18] extends the depth of neural network which highly improves the accuracy.

Table 1. Quantitative results on RealSR x4 dataset. We compare our FAN with the state-of-the-art methods in terms of PSNR and SSIM.

Method	VDSR	EDSR	RDN	DBPN	RCAN	SAN	FAN(ours)	FAN+
PSNR	28.966	29.522	29.790	29.305	30.002	30.112	**30.598**	**30.719**
SSIM	0.8322	0.8444	0.8486	0.8388	0.8529	0.8557	**0.8603**	**0.8621**

Table 1 shows the comparisons of our FAN with the previous methods on RealSR x4 dataset. Compared to other methods, our FAN with self-ensemble ($\times 8$) termed as **FAN+** containing flipping ($\times 4$) and rotation ($\times 4$). FAN+ both performs the best scores in PSNR and SSIM, leading to a 0.607 dB and a 0.0064 dB increase respectively compared with SAN [5]. Even without self-ensemble, termed as **FAN(ours)**, can also achieve 0.486 dB and 0.0046 dB increase.

The qualitatively comparison is shown in Fig. 6. The traditional bicubic upsamping produces the most blurry results. And compared with the other cnn-based methods, our FAN model can generate sharper and clearer HR images without obvious artifacts or distortions which are caused by the enlarged DSLR camera lens in the RealSR dataset. For example, the building fences and leaf veins are more clearer and not anamorphic. All in all, our FAN model can solve the RealSR problem well while the previous SISR methods can not generalize to this problem.

4.5   Ablation Study

To further demonstrate the effectiveness of our each module, we conduct several ablation studies to investigate the influence of the multi-frequency branches, channel attention for CA-GRDB, non-local module, channel attention mechanism and the number of RDBs in our FAN.The subjective performance comparisons in ablation study are shown in Fig. 7.

Fig. 6. The performance comparison of our FAN with the state-of-the-art methods performed on RealSR x4 dataset. The state-of-the-art methods are bicubic upsampling, DBPN [13], EDSR [23], RCAN [38], RDN [40], SAN [5] and VDSR [18] respectively.

Dataset. Since the ground truth HR images of validation dataset are not released, we randomly split the training dataset into two parts by the ratio 7:3 for training and testing respectively. Notice that this dataset setting is only for ablation study.

Multi-frequency Branches. We set the number of branches from 1 to 4 to figure out the effects of different branches, denoted as FAN-1, FAN-2, FAN-3, FAN-4 shown in Table 2. with the number of branches increasing, we can observe the improvement of performance in general. However, the gain gets smaller and

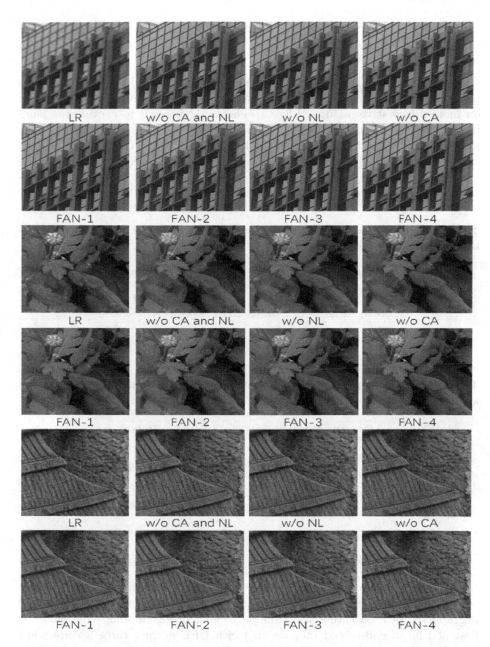

Fig. 7. The subjective performance comparisons in ablation studies of FAN.

the number of parameters increase significantly when the number of branches is more than 3. Therefore, we select 3 as a trade-off to balance the complexity of network and performance.

Channel Attention(CA) and Non-local Module(NL). We exploit CA to model the feature inter-dependencies, which enforces our model to concentrate on more informative features. Like [31] claimed, NL tends to capture the long-term dependencies of features to compensate the lost information due to the local neighborhood filtering in convolutional layers. From Table 3, we can see that whether removing CA (w/o CA) or removing NL (w/o NL) results in the drop of performance. At the same time, adding CA and NL both would achieve best performance while the number of parameters only has slightly increasing.

Table 2. Comparisons between different number of branches in FAN. Tested on partitioned dataset, which is different from validation dataset.

Branches	FAN-1	FAN-2	FAN-3	FAN-4
Parameters (MB)	5.81	27.95	50.30	72.74
PSNR (dB)	28.5210	28.8029	28.9464	28.9598
SSIM	0.8153	0.8194	0.8231	0.8233

Table 3. Ablation study on different combinations of channel attention and non-local attention. Tested on partitioned dataset.

CA	NL	Parameters(MB)	PSNR(dB)	SSIM
✓	✓	50.30	28.9464	0.8231
×	✓	50.28	28.8073	0.8195
✓	×	50.12	28.7931	0.8194
×	×	50.10	28.7571	0.8190

5 Conclusions

In this paper, we proposed FAN, a frequency aggregation network, to solve the real-world image super-resolution problem which suffers from more complicated degradation process rather than simple bicubic downsampling. Our model is designed in an end-to-end manner, in which HFE extract three feature maps contained different frequency information firstly. And then pass them into CA-GRDB module independently to output corresponding residual dense feature map in each frequency. Finally, we apply fusion module to integrate them to recover the HR image. We validate the effectiveness of our FAN in RealSR Dataset with extensive experiments. In addition, our model performs well on the AIM 2020 challenge which came the fourth place on the X4 track with PSNR of 31.1735 and SSIM of 0.8728.

Acknowledgement. This work was supported in part by NSFC under Grant U1908209, 61632001 and the National Key Research and Development Program of China 2018AAA0101400.

References

1. Cai, J., Zeng, H., Yong, H., Cao, Z., Zhang, L.: Toward real-world single image super-resolution: a new benchmark and a new model. In: Proceedings of the IEEE International Conference on Computer Vision, pp. 3086–3095 (2019)
2. Chang, H., Yeung, D.Y., Xiong, Y.: Super-resolution through neighbor embedding. In: Proceedings of the 2004 IEEE Computer Society Conference on Computer Vision and Pattern Recognition, 2004. CVPR 2004, vol. 1, pp. I, IEEE (2004)
3. Chen, Y., et al.: Drop an octave: Reducing spatial redundancy in convolutional neural networks with octave convolution. In: Proceedings of the IEEE International Conference on Computer Vision, pp. 3435–3444 (2019)
4. Dahl, R., Norouzi, M., Shlens, J.: Pixel recursive super resolution. In: Proceedings of the IEEE International Conference on Computer Vision, pp. 5439–5448 (2017)
5. Dai, T., Cai, J., Zhang, Y., Xia, S.T., Zhang, L.: Second-order attention network for single image super-resolution. In: Proceedings of the IEEE Conference on Computer Vision and Pattern Recognition, pp. 11065–11074 (2019)
6. Dong, C., Loy, C.C., He, K., Tang, X.: Learning a deep convolutional network for image super-resolution. In: Fleet, D., Pajdla, T., Schiele, B., Tuytelaars, T. (eds.) ECCV 2014. LNCS, vol. 8692, pp. 184–199. Springer, Cham (2014). https://doi.org/10.1007/978-3-319-10593-2_13
7. Dong, C., Loy, C.C., Tang, X.: Accelerating the super-resolution convolutional neural network. In: Leibe, B., Matas, J., Sebe, N., Welling, M. (eds.) ECCV 2016. LNCS, vol. 9906, pp. 391–407. Springer, Cham (2016). https://doi.org/10.1007/978-3-319-46475-6_25
8. Freeman, W.T., Jones, T.R., Pasztor, E.C.: Example-based super-resolution. IEEE Comput. Soc. Press **22**(2), 56–65 (2002)
9. Fritsche, M., Gu, S., Timofte, R.: Frequency separation for real-world super-resolution. In: 2019 IEEE/CVF International Conference on Computer Vision Workshop (ICCVW), pp. 3599–3608. IEEE (2019)
10. Gohshi, S.: Real-time super resolution algorithm for security cameras. In: 2015 12th International Joint Conference on e-Business and Telecommunications (ICETE), vol. 5, pp. 92–97. IEEE (2015)
11. Greenspan, H.: Super-resolution in medical imaging. Comput. J. **52**(1), 43–63 (2009)
12. Han, W., Chang, S., Liu, D., Yu, M., Witbrock, M., Huang, T.S.: Image super-resolution via dual-state recurrent networks. In: Proceedings of the IEEE Conference on Computer Vision and Pattern Recognition, pp. 1654–1663 (2018)
13. Haris, M., Shakhnarovich, G., Ukita, N.: Deep back-projection networks for super-resolution. In: Proceedings of the IEEE Conference on Computer Vision and Pattern Recognition, pp. 1664–1673 (2018)
14. Ji, X., Cao, Y., Tai, Y., Wang, C., Li, J., Huang, F.: Real-world super-resolution via kernel estimation and noise injection. In: Proceedings of the IEEE/CVF Conference on Computer Vision and Pattern Recognition Workshops, pp. 466–467 (2020)

15. Johnson, J., Alahi, A., Fei-Fei, L.: Perceptual losses for real-time style transfer and super-resolution. In: Leibe, B., Matas, J., Sebe, N., Welling, M. (eds.) ECCV 2016. LNCS, vol. 9906, pp. 694–711. Springer, Cham (2016). https://doi.org/10.1007/978-3-319-46475-6_43

16. Kalarot, R., Li, T., Porikli, F.: Component attention guided face super-resolution network: Cagface. In: The IEEE Winter Conference on Applications of Computer Vision, pp. 370–380 (2020)

17. Kim, D.W., Ryun Chung, J., Jung, S.W.: GRDN: grouped residual dense network for real image denoising and GAN-based real-world noise modeling. In: Proceedings of the IEEE Conference on Computer Vision and Pattern Recognition Workshops (2019)

18. Kim, J., Lee, J.K., Lee, K.M.: Deeply-recursive convolutional network for image super-resolution. In: Proceedings of the IEEE Conference on Computer Vision and Pattern Recognition (CVPR) (June 2016)

19. Lai, W.S., Huang, J.B., Ahuja, N., Yang, M.H.: Deep laplacian pyramid networks for fast and accurate super-resolution. In: Proceedings of the IEEE Conference on Computer Vision and Pattern Recognition (CVPR) (July 2017)

20. Lan, R., et al.: Cascading and enhanced residual networks for accurate single-image super-resolution. IEEE Trans. Cybern. **51**(1), 115–125 (2020)

21. Ledig, C., et al.: Photo-realistic single image super-resolution using a generative adversarial network. In: Proceedings of the IEEE Conference on Computer Vision and Pattern Recognition, pp. 4681–4690 (2017)

22. Li, J., Fang, F., Mei, K., Zhang, G.: Multi-scale residual network for image super-resolution. In: Proceedings of the European Conference on Computer Vision (ECCV), pp. 517–532 (2018)

23. Lim, B., Son, S., Kim, H., Nah, S., Lee, K.M.: Enhanced deep residual networks for single image super-resolution (2017)

24. Lu, L., Shin, Y., Su, Y., Karniadakis, G.E.: Dying relu and initialization: Theory and numerical examples (2019)

25. Lugmayr, A., Danelljan, M., Timofte, R.: Ntire 2020 challenge on real-world image super-resolution: Methods and results. In: Proceedings of the IEEE/CVF Conference on Computer Vision and Pattern Recognition Workshops, pp. 494–495 (2020)

26. Lugmayr, A., et al.: Aim 2019 challenge on real-world image super-resolution: Methods and results. In: 2019 IEEE/CVF International Conference on Computer Vision Workshop (ICCVW), pp. 3575–3583. IEEE (2019)

27. Maeda, S.: Unpaired image super-resolution using pseudo-supervision. In: IEEE/CVF Conference on Computer Vision and Pattern Recognition (CVPR) (June 2020)

28. Ren, H., El-Khamy, M., Lee, J.: Image super resolution based on fusing multiple convolution neural networks. In: Proceedings of the IEEE Conference on Computer Vision and Pattern Recognition Workshops, pp. 54–61 (2017)

29. Shocher, A., Cohen, N., Irani, M.: "zero-shot" super-resolution using deep internal learning. In: Proceedings of the IEEE Conference on Computer Vision and Pattern Recognition, pp. 3118–3126 (2018)

30. Tai, Y., Yang, J., Liu, X.: Image super-resolution via deep recursive residual network. In: Proceedings of the IEEE Conference on Computer Vision and Pattern Recognition, pp. 3147–3155 (2017)

31. Wang, X., Girshick, R., Gupta, A., He, K.: Non-local neural networks. In: Proceedings of the IEEE Conference on Computer Vision and Pattern Recognition (CVPR) (June 2018)

32. Wang, X., et al.: Esrgan: enhanced super-resolution generative adversarial networks. In: Proceedings of the European Conference on Computer Vision (ECCV) (2018)
33. Wang, Z., Bovik, A.C., Sheikh, H.R., Simoncelli, E.P.: Image quality assessment: from error visibility to structural similarity. IEEE Trans. Image Process. **13**(4), 600–612 (2004)
34. Wei, P., et al.: Aim 2020 challenge on real image super-resolution: methods and results (2020)
35. Wei, P., Lu, H., Timofte, R., Lin, L., Zuo, W., et al.: AIM 2020 challenge on real image super-resolution. In: European Conference on Computer Vision Workshops (2020)
36. Zhang, L., Zhang, H., Shen, H., Li, P.: A super-resolution reconstruction algorithm for surveillance images. Signal Process. **90**(3), 848–859 (2010)
37. Zhang, W., Liu, Y., Dong, C., Qiao, Y.: Ranksrgan: generative adversarial networks with ranker for image super-resolution. In: Proceedings of the IEEE International Conference on Computer Vision, pp. 3096–3105 (2019)
38. Zhang, Y., Li, K., Li, K., Wang, L., Zhong, B., Fu, Y.: Image super-resolution using very deep residual channel attention networks. In: Proceedings of the European Conference on Computer Vision (ECCV), pp. 286–301 (2018)
39. Zhang, Y., Li, K., Li, K., Zhong, B., Fu, Y.: Residual non-local attention networks for image restoration. arXiv preprint arXiv:1903.10082 (2019)
40. Zhang, Y., Tian, Y., Kong, Y., Zhong, B., Fu, Y.: Residual dense network for image super-resolution. In: Proceedings of the IEEE Conference on Computer Vision and Pattern Recognition, pp. 2472–2481 (2018)

Deep Cyclic Generative Adversarial Residual Convolutional Networks for Real Image Super-Resolution

Rao Muhammad Umer[✉] and Christian Micheloni

University of Udine, Udine, Italy
engr.raoumer943@gmail.com, christian.micheloni@uniud.it

Abstract. Recent deep learning based single image super-resolution (SISR) methods mostly train their models in a clean data domain where the low-resolution (LR) and the high-resolution (HR) images come from noise-free settings (same domain) due to the bicubic down-sampling assumption. However, such degradation process is not available in real-world settings. We consider a deep cyclic network structure to maintain the domain consistency between the LR and HR data distributions, which is inspired by the recent success of CycleGAN in the image-to-image translation applications. We propose the Super-Resolution Residual Cyclic Generative Adversarial Network (SRResCycGAN) by training with a generative adversarial network (GAN) framework for the LR to HR domain translation in an end-to-end manner. We demonstrate our proposed approach in the quantitative and qualitative experiments that generalize well to the real image super-resolution and it is easy to deploy for the mobile/embedded devices. In addition, our SR results on the AIM 2020 Real Image SR Challenge datasets demonstrate that the proposed SR approach achieves comparable results as the other state-of-art methods.

Keywords: Real image super-resolution · Cyclic GAN · Image restoration · Convex optimization · Deep convolutional neural networks

1 Introduction

The goal of the single image super-resolution (SISR) is to recover the high-resolution (HR) image from its low-resolution (LR) counterpart. SISR problem is a fundamental low-level vision and image processing problem with various practical applications in satellite imaging, medical imaging, astronomy, microscopy imaging, seismology, remote sensing, surveillance, biometric, image compression, etc. Usually, the SISR is described as a linear forward observation model [18] by the following image degradation process[1]:

$$\mathbf{y} = \mathbf{H} * \tilde{\mathbf{x}} + \eta, \tag{1}$$

---

[1] Our code and trained models are publicly available at https://github.com/RaoUmer/SRResCycGAN.

© Springer Nature Switzerland AG 2020
A. Bartoli and A. Fusiello (Eds.): ECCV 2020 Workshops, LNCS 12537, pp. 484–498, 2020.
https://doi.org/10.1007/978-3-030-67070-2_29

Fig. 1. The super-resolution results at the ×4 upscaling factor of the state-of-art–ESRGAN, the proposed SRResCycGAN+ with respect to the ground-truth images. SRResCycGAN+ has successfully remove the visible artifacts, while the ESRGAN has still artifacts due to data bias between the training and testing images.

where **y** is an observed LR image, **H** is a *down-sampling operator* (usually bicubic) that convolves with an HR image $\tilde{x}$ and resizes it by a scaling factor s, and η is considered as an additive white Gaussian noise with standard deviation σ. However, in real-world settings, η also accounts for all possible errors during the image acquisition process that include inherent sensor noise, stochastic noise, compression artifacts, and the possible mismatch between the forward observation model and the camera device. The operator **H** is usually ill-conditioned or singular due to the presence of unknown noise (η) that makes the SISR a highly ill-posed nature of inverse problems. Since, due to the ill-posed nature, there are many possible solutions, regularization is required to select the most plausible ones.

Recently, numerous works have been addressed on the task of SISR that are based on deep CNNs for their powerful feature representation capabilities either on PSNR values [8,12,13,25–28] or on visual quality [9,22]. These SR methods mostly rely on the known degradation operators such as bicubic (*i.e.* noise-free) with paired LR and HR images (same clean domain) in the supervised training, while other methods do not follow the image observation (physical) model (refers to Eq. (1)). In the real-world settings, the input LR images suffer from different kinds of degradation or LR is different from the HR domain. Under such circumstances, these SR methods often fail to produce convincing SR results. In Fig. 1, we show the results of the state-of-art deep learning method–ESRGAN with the noisy input image. The ESRGAN degraded SR result is due to the difference of training and testing data domains. The detailed analysis of the deep learning-based SR models on the real-world data can be found in the recent literature [5,15].

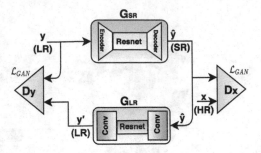

Fig. 2. Visualizes the structure of the our proposed SR approach setup. We trained the network $\mathbf{G}_{SR}$ in a GAN framework, where our goal is to map images from the LR $(\mathbf{y})$ to the HR $(\mathbf{x})$, while maintaining the domain consistency between the LR and HR images.

In this work, we propose a SR learning method (SRResCycGAN) that overcomes the challenges of real image super-resolution. It is inspired by Cycle-GAN [30] structure which maintains the domain consistency between the LR and HR domain. It is also inspired by powerful image regularization and large-scale optimization techniques to solve general inverse problems in the past. The scheme of our proposed real image SR approach setup is shown in Fig. 2. The $\mathbf{G}_{SR}$ network takes the input LR image and produces the SR output with the supervision of the SR discriminator network $\mathbf{D_x}$. For the domain consistency between the LR and HR, the $\mathbf{G}_{LR}$ network reconstructs the LR image from the SR output with the supervision of the LR discriminator network $\mathbf{D_y}$.

We evaluate our proposed SR method on multiple datasets with synthetic and natural image corruptions. We use the Real-World Super-resolution (RWSR) dataset [17] to show the effectiveness of our method through quantitative and qualitative experiments. Finally, we also participated in the AIM2020 Real Image Super-resolution Challenge [24] for the Track-3 ($\times$4 upscaling) associated with the ECCV 2020 workshops. Table 2 shows the final testset SR results for the track-3 of our method (**MLP_SR**) with others as well as the visual comparison in the Fig. 4 and Fig. 5.

2   Related Work

2.1   Image Super-Resolution Methods

Recently, numerous works have addressed the task of SISR using deep CNNs for their powerful feature representation capabilities. A preliminary CNN-based method to solve SISR is a super-resolution convolutional network with three layers (SRCNN) [3]. Kim *et al.* [8] proposed a very deep SR (VDSR) network with residual learning approach. The efficient subpixel convolutional network (ESPCNN) [19] was proposed to take bicubicly LR input and introduced an efficient subpixel convolution layer to upscale the LR feature maps to HR images at the end of the network. Lim *et al.* [13] proposed an enhanced deep SR (EDSR) network by taking advantage of the residual learning. Zhang *et al.* [26] proposed iterative residual convolutional network (IRCNN) to solve SISR problem by using a plug-and-play framework. Zhang *et al.* [27] proposed a deep CNN-based super-resolution with multiple degradation (SRMD). Yaoman *et al.* [12] proposed a feedback network (SRFBN) based on feedback connections and recurrent neural network-like structure. Zhang *et al.* [28] proposed a deep plug-and-play Super-Resolution method for arbitrary blur kernels by following the multiple degradation. In [21], the authors proposed SRWDNet to solve the joint deblurring and super-resolution task by following the realistic degradation. These methods mostly rely on the PSNR-based metric by optimizing the $\mathcal{L}_1/\mathcal{L}_2$ losses with blurry results in a supervised way, while they do not preserve the visual quality with respect to human perception. Moreover, the above-mentioned methods are deeper or wider CNN networks to learn non-linear mapping from LR to HR with a large number of training samples, while neglecting the real-world settings.

2.2   Real Image Super-Resolution Methods

For the perception SR task, a preliminary attempt was made by Ledig *et al.* [9] who proposed the SRGAN method to produce perceptually more pleasant results. To further enhance the performance of the SRGAN, Wang *et al.* [22] proposed the ESRGAN model to achieve the state-of-art perceptual performance. Despite their success, the previously mentioned methods are trained with HR/LR image pairs on the bicubic down-sampling *i.e.* noise-free and thus they have limited performance in the real-world settings. More recently, Lugmayr *et al.* [15] proposed a benchmark protocol for the real-wold image corruptions and introduced the real-world challenge series [16] that described the effects of bicubic downsampling and separate degradation learning for super-resolution. Later on, Fritsche *et al.* [5] proposed the DSGAN to learn degradation by training the network in an unsupervised way and modified the ESRGAN structure as the ESRGAN-FS to further enhance the performance in the real-world settings. Recently, the authors proposed the SRResCGAN [18] to solve real-world SR problem, which is inspired by a physical image formation model. However, the above methods still suffer unpleasant artifacts (see the Fig. 3 and the Table 1). Our approach takes into account the real-world settings by greatly increasing its applicability in practical scenarios.

3   Proposed Method

3.1   Problem Formulation

By referencing to the Eq. (1), the recovery of $\mathbf{x}$ from $\mathbf{y}$ mostly relies on the variational approach for combining the observation and prior knowledge, and is given by the following objective function:

$$\mathbf{J}(\mathbf{x}) = \arg\min_{\mathbf{x}} \frac{1}{2}\|\mathbf{y} - \mathbf{H} * \mathbf{x}\|_2^2 + \lambda\mathcal{R}(\mathbf{x}), \tag{2}$$

where $\frac{1}{2}\|\mathbf{y} - \mathbf{H} * \mathbf{x}\|_2^2$ is the data fidelity (also known as log-likelihood) term that measures the proximity of the solution to the observations, $\mathcal{R}(\mathbf{x})$ is the regularization term that is associated with image priors, and λ is the trade-off parameter that governs the compromise between the data fidelity and the regularizer term. Interestingly, the variational approach has a direct link to the Bayesian approach and the derived solutions can be described either as penalized maximum likelihood or as maximum a posteriori (MAP) estimates [2,4]. Thanks to the recent advances of deep learning, the regularizer (*i.e.* $\mathcal{R}(\mathbf{x})$) is employed by the SRResCGAN [18] generator structure that has powerful image priors capabilities.

3.2 SR Learning Model

The proposed Real Image SR approach setup is shown in the Fig. 2. The SR generator network $\mathbf{G}_{SR}$ borrowed from the SRResCGAN [18] is trained in a GAN [6] framework by using the LR ($\mathbf{y}$) images with their corresponding HR images with pixel-wise supervision in the clean HR target domain ($\mathbf{x}$), while maintaining the domain consistency between the LR and HR images. In the next coming Sects. 3.3, 3.4, and 3.5, we present the details of the network architectures, network losses, and training descriptions for the proposed SR setup.

3.3 Network Architectures

SR Generator ($\mathbf{G_{SR}}$): We use the SR generator $\mathbf{G_{SR}}$ network which is basically an *Encoder-Resnet-Decoder* like structure as done SRResCGAN [18]. In the $\mathbf{G_{SR}}$ network, both *Encoder* and *Decoder* layers have 64 convolutional feature maps of 5×5 kernel size with $C \times H \times W$ tensors, where C is the number of channels of the input image. Inside the *Encoder*, LR image is upsampled by the Bicubic kernel with *Upsample* layer, where the choice of the upsampling kernel is arbitrary. *Resnet* consists of 5 residual blocks with two Pre-activation *Conv* layers, each of 64 feature maps with kernel support 3×3, and the pre-activation is the parametrized rectified linear unit (PReLU) with 64 output feature channels. The trainable projection layer [10] inside the *Decoder* computes the proximal map with the estimated noise standard deviation σ and handles the data fidelity and prior terms. The noise realization is estimated in the intermediate *Resnet* that is sandwiched between *Encoder* and *Decoder*. The estimated residual image after *Decoder* is subtracted from the LR input image. Finally, the clipping layer incorporates our prior knowledge about the valid range of image intensities and enforces the pixel values of the reconstructed image to lie in the range $[0, 255]$. The reflection padding is also used before all the *Conv* layers to ensure slowly varying changes at the boundaries of the input images.

SR Discriminator ($\mathbf{D_x}$): The SR discriminator network is trained to discriminate the real HR images from the fake HR images generated by the $\mathbf{G_{SR}}$. The raw discriminator network contains 10 convolutional layers with kernels support

3×3 and 4×4 of increasing feature maps from 64 to 512 followed by Batch Norm (BN) and leaky ReLU as do in SRGAN [9].

LR Generator ($\mathbf{G_{LR}}$): We adapt the similar architecture as does in [25] for the down-sampling which is basically a *Conv-Resnet-Conv* like structure. We use 6 residual blocks in the *Resnet* with 3 convolutional layers at the head and tail *Conv*, while the stride is set to 2 in the second and third head *Conv* layers for the down-sampling purpose.

LR Discriminator ($\mathbf{D_y}$): The LR discriminator network consists of a three-layer convolutional network that operates on the patch level as do in Patch-GAN [7,11]. All the *Conv* layers have 5×5 kernel support with feature maps from 64 to 256 and also applied the Batch Norm and Leaky ReLU (LReLU) activation after each *Conv* layer except the last *Conv* layer that maps 256 to 1 features.

3.4 Network Losses

To learn the image super-resolution, we train the proposed SRResCycGAN network with the following loss functions:

$$\mathcal{L}_{G_{SR}} = \mathcal{L}_{\text{per}} + \mathcal{L}_{\text{GAN}} + \mathcal{L}_{tv} + 10 \cdot \mathcal{L}_1 + 10 \cdot \mathcal{L}_{\text{cyc}} \tag{3}$$

where, these losses are defined as follows:

Perceptual loss ($\mathcal{L}_{\text{per}}$): It focuses on the perceptual quality of the output image and is defined as:

$$\mathcal{L}_{\text{per}} = \frac{1}{N}\sum_{i}^{N} \mathcal{L}_{\text{VGG}} = \frac{1}{N}\sum_{i}^{N} \|\phi(\mathbf{G}_{SR}(\mathbf{y}_i)) - \phi(\mathbf{x}_i)\|_1 \tag{4}$$

where, ϕ is the feature extracted from the pretrained VGG-19 network at the same depth as ESRGAN [22].

Texture loss ($\mathcal{L}_{\text{GAN}}$): It focuses on the high frequencies of the output image and it is defined as:

$$\mathbf{D_x}(\mathbf{x}, \hat{\mathbf{y}})(C) = \sigma(C(\mathbf{x}) - \mathbb{E}[C(\hat{\mathbf{y}})]) \tag{5}$$

Here, C is the raw discriminator output and σ is the sigmoid function. By using the relativistic discriminator [22], we have:

$$\begin{aligned}
\mathcal{L}_{\text{GAN}} = \mathcal{L}_{\text{RaGAN}} = &- \mathbb{E}_{\mathbf{x}}\left[\log\left(1 - \mathbf{D_x}(\mathbf{x}, \mathbf{G}_{SR}(\mathbf{y}))\right)\right] \\
&- \mathbb{E}_{\hat{\mathbf{y}}}\left[\log\left(\mathbf{D_x}(\mathbf{G}_{SR}(\mathbf{y}), \mathbf{x})\right)\right]
\end{aligned} \tag{6}$$

where, $\mathbb{E}_{\mathbf{x}}$ and $\mathbb{E}_{\hat{\mathbf{y}}}$ represent the operations of taking average for all real ($\mathbf{x}$) and fake ($\hat{\mathbf{y}}$) data in the mini-batches respectively.

Content loss ($\mathcal{L}_1$): It is defined as:

$$\mathcal{L}_1 = \frac{1}{N} \sum_i^N \|\mathbf{G}_{SR}(\mathbf{y}_i) - \mathbf{x}_i\|_1 \tag{7}$$

where, N represents the size of mini-batch.

TV (total-variation) loss ($\mathcal{L}_{tv}$): It focuses to minimize the gradient discrepancy and produces sharpness in the output SR image and it is defined as:

$$\mathcal{L}_{tv} = \frac{1}{N} \sum_i^N (\|\nabla_h \mathbf{G}_{SR}(\mathbf{y}_i) - \nabla_h(\mathbf{x}_i)\|_1 + \|\nabla_v \mathbf{G}_{SR}(\mathbf{y}_i) - \nabla_v(\mathbf{x}_i)\|_1) \tag{8}$$

Here, ∇_h and ∇_v denote the horizontal and vertical gradients of the images.

Cyclic loss ($\mathcal{L}_{cyc}$): It focuses to maintain the cyclic consistency between LR and HR domain and it is defined as:

$$\mathcal{L}_{cyc} = \frac{1}{N} \sum_i^N \|\mathbf{G}_{LR}(\mathbf{G}_{SR}(\mathbf{y}_i)) - \mathbf{y}_i\|_1 \tag{9}$$

3.5 Training Description

At the training phase, we set the input LR patches size as 32×32 with their corresponding HR patches. We train the network in an end-to-end manner for 51000 training iterations with a batch size of 16 using Adam optimizer with parameters $\beta_1 = 0.9$, $\beta_2 = 0.999$, and $\epsilon = 10^{-8}$ without weight decay for generators ($\mathbf{G_{SR}}$ & $\mathbf{G_{LR}}$) and discriminators ($\mathbf{D_x}$ & $\mathbf{D_y}$) to minimize the loss in Eq. (3). The learning rate is initially set to 10^{-4} and then multiplies by 0.5 after 5K, 10K, 20K, and 30K iterations. The projection layer parameter σ is estimated according to [14] from the input LR image.

4 Experiments

4.1 Training Data

We use the source domain data ($\tilde{\mathbf{y}}$: 2650 HR images) that are corrupted with two known degradation, e.g., sensor noise, compression artifacts as well as unknown degradation, and target domain data ($\mathbf{x}$: 800 clean HR images from the DIV2K [1]) provided in the NTIRE2020 Real-World Super-resolution (RWSR) Challenge [17] for the track-1. We use the source and target domain data for training the $\mathbf{G_{SR}}$ network under the different degradation scenarios. The LR data ($\mathbf{y}$) with similar corruption as in the source domain is generated from the down-sample GAN network (DSGAN) [5] with their corresponding HR target domain ($\mathbf{x}$) images. Furthermore, we use the training data (*i.e.* $\mathbf{y}$: 19000 LR images, $\mathbf{x}$: 19000 HR images) provided in the AIM2020 Real Image SR Challenge [24] for the track-3 ($\times 4$ upscaling) for training the SRResCycGAN (refer to the Sect. 4.5).

Table 1. The ×4 SR quantitative results comparison of our method with others over the DIV2K validation-set (100 images). Top section: SR results comparison with added sensor noise ($\sigma = 8$) and compression artifacts (*quality* = 30) in the validation-set. Middle section: SR results with the unknown corruptions (e.g., sensor noise, compression artifacts, etc.) in the validation-set provided in the RWSR challenge series [16,17]. Bottom section: SR results with the real image corruptions in the validation-set and testset provided in the AIM 2020 Real Image SR challenge [24] for the track-3. The arrows indicate if high ↑ or low ↓ values are desired. The best performance is shown in italic and the second best performance is shown in bold.

SR methods	#Params	Sensor noise ($\sigma = 8$)			Compression artifacts ($q = 30$)		
		PSNR↑	SSIM↑	LPIPS↓	PSNR↑	SSIM↑	LPIPS↓
EDSR [13]	43M	24.48	0.53	0.6800	23.75	0.62	0.5400
ESRGAN [22]	16.7M	17.39	0.19	0.9400	22.43	0.58	0.5300
ESRGAN-FT [15]	16.7M	22.42	0.55	0.3645	22.80	0.57	*0.3729*
ESRGAN-FS [5]	16.7M	22.52	0.52	*0.3300*	20.39	0.50	**0.4200**
SRResCGAN [18]	380K	25.46	0.67	**0.3604**	23.34	0.59	0.4431
SRResCycGAN (ours)	380K	**25.98**	**0.70**	0.4167	**23.96**	**0.63**	0.4841
SRResCycGAN+ (ours)	380K	*26.27*	*0.72*	0.4542	*24.05*	*0.64*	0.5192
Unknown corruptions [17]							
SRResCGAN [18]	380K	25.05	0.67	*0.3357*			
SRResCycGAN (ours)	380K	**26.13**	**0.71**	**0.3911**			
SRResCycGAN+ (ours)	380K	*26.39*	*0.73*	0.4245			
Real image corruptions [24]							
SRResCycGAN (ours, valset)	380K	28.6239	0.8250	–			
SRResCycGAN (ours, testset)	380K	28.6185	0.8314	–			

4.2 Technical Details

We implemented our method in the Pytorch. The experiments are performed under Windows 10 with i7-8750H CPU with 16GB RAM and on the NVIDIA RTX-2070 GPU with 8GB memory. It takes about 25 h to train the network. The run time per image (on the GPU) is 4.54 s at the AIM2020 Real Image SR testset. In order to further enhance the fidelity, we use a self-ensemble strategy [20] (denoted as SRResCycGAN+) at the test time, where the LR inputs are flipped/rotated and the SR results are aligned and averaged for enhanced prediction.

4.3 Evaluation Metrics

We evaluate the trained model under the Peak Signal-to-Noise Ratio (PSNR), Structural Similarity (SSIM), and LPIPS [29] metrics. The PSNR and SSIM are distortion-based measures that correlate poorly with actual perceived similarity, while LPIPS better correlates with human perception than the distortion-based/handcrafted measures. As LPIPS is based on the features of pretrained neural networks, so we use it for the quantitative evaluation with features of AlexNet [29]. The quantitative SR results are evaluated on the *RGB* color space.

4.4   Comparison with the State-of-art Methods

We compare our method with other state-of-art SR methods including EDSR [13], ESRGAN [22], ESRGAN-FT [15], ESRGAN-FS [5], and SRResC-GAN [18], whose source codes are available online. The two degradation settings (*i.e.* sensor noise, JPEG compression) have been considered under the same experimental situations for all methods. We run all the original source codes and trained models by the default parameters settings for the comparison. The EDSR is trained without the perceptual loss (only $\mathcal{L}_1$) by a deep SR residual network using the bicubic supervision. The ESRGAN is trained with the $\mathcal{L}_{perceptual}$, $\mathcal{L}_{GAN}$, and $\mathcal{L}_1$ by a deep SR network using the bicubic supervision. The ESRGAN-FT and ESRGAN-FS apply the same SR architecture and perceptual losses as in the ESRGAN using the two known degradation supervision. The SRResCGAN is trained with the similar losses combination as done in the ESRGAN using the two known degradation supervision. We train the proposed SRResCycGAN with the similar losses combination as done in the ESRGAN and SRResCGAN with the additional cyclic loss by using the bicubic supervision.

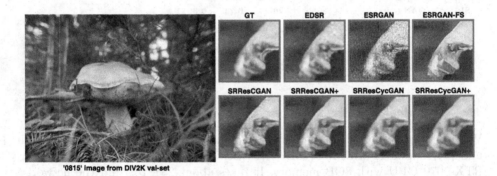

Fig. 3. Visual comparison of our method with the other state-of-art methods on the DIV2K validation set at the ×4 super-resolution.

Table 1 shows the quantitative results comparison of our method over the DIV2K validation-set (100 images) with two known degradation (*i.e.* sensor noise, JPEG compression), the unknown degradation in the NTIRE2020 Real-World SR challenge series [17], and the validation-set and testset in the AIM2020 Real Image SR Challenge [24]. Our method results outperform in terms of PSNR and SSIM compared to the other methods, while in the case of LPIPS, we have comparable results with others. In the case of the sensor noise ($\sigma = 8$) and JPEG compression ($q = 30$) in the top section of the Table 1, the ESRGAN has the worst performance in terms of the PSNR, SSIM, and LPIPS among all methods. Its also depicts the visual quality in Fig. 4. The EDSR has better performance to the noisy input, but it produces more blurry results. These are due to the domain distribution difference by the bicubic down-sampling during training phase. The ESRGAN-FT and ESRGAN-FS have much better performance due to overcoming the domain distribution shift problem, but they have still visible artifacts. The SRResCGAN has better robustness to the noisy input, but still has lower the PSNR and SSIM due to lacking the domain consistency problem. The proposed method has successfully overcome the challenge of the domain distribution shift in both degradation settings, which depicts in the both quantitative and qualitative results. In the middle section of the Table 1, for the unknown degradation in the NTIRE2020 Real-World SR challenge [17], the SRResCycGAN has much better the PSNR/SSIM improvment, while the LPIPS is also comparable with the SRResCGAN. In the bottom section of the Table 1, we also report the validation-set and testset SR results in the AIM2020 Real Image SR Challenge [24] for the track-3. Despite that, the parameters of the proposed $\mathbf{G}_{SR}$ network are much less, which makes it suitable for deployment in mobile/embedded devices where memory storage and CPU power are limited as well as good image reconstruction quality.

Regarding the visual quality, Fig. 4 shows the qualitative comparison of our method with other SR methods at the ×4 upscaling factor on the validation-

Table 2. Final testset results for the real image SR (×4) challenge Track-3 [24]. The table contains ours (**MLP_SR**) with other methods that are ranked in the challenge. The participating methods are ranked according to their weighted score of the PSNR and SSIM given in the AIM 2020 real image SR challenge [24].

Team name	PSNR↑	SSIM↑	Weighed_score↑
Baidu	31.3960	0.8751	0.7099(1)
ALONG	31.2369	0.8742	0.7076(2)
CETC-CSKT	31.1226	0.8744	0.7066(3)
SR-IM	31.1735	0.8728	0.7057
DeepBlueAI	30.9638	0.8737	0.7044
JNSR	30.9988	0.8722	0.7035
OPPO_CAMERA	30.8603	0.8736	0.7033
Kailos	30.8659	0.8734	0.7031
SR_DL	30.6045	0.8660	0.6944
Noah_TerminalVision	30.5870	0.8662	0.6944
Webbzhou	30.4174	0.8673	0.6936
TeamInception	30.3465	0.8681	0.6935
IyI	30.3191	0.8655	0.6911
MCML-Yonsei	30.4201	0.8637	0.6906
MoonCloud	30.2827	0.8644	0.6898
Qwq	29.5878	0.8547	0.6748
SrDance	29.5952	0.8523	0.6729
MLP_SR	28.6185	0.8314	0.6457
RRDN_IITKGP	27.9708	0.8085	0.6201
congxiaofeng	26.3915	0.8258	0.6187

set [17]. In contrast to the existing state-of-art methods, our proposed method produces the excellent SR results that are reflected in the PSNR/SSIM values, as well as the visual quality of the reconstructed images with almost no visible corruptions.

4.5   The AIM 2020 Real Image SR Challenge (×4)

We participated in the AIM2020 Real Image Super-Resolution Challenge [24] for the track-3 (×4 upscaling) associated with the ECCV 2020 workshops. The goal of this challenge is to learn a generic model to super-resolve LR images captured in practical scenarios for more complex degradation than the bicubic down-sampling. In that regard, we propose the SRResCycGAN to super-resolve the LR images with the real-world settings. We use the pretrained model $\mathbf{G_{SR}}$ taken from the SRResCGAN [18] (excellent perceptual quality) and further fine-tune it on the training data provided in the AIM 2020 Real Image SR challenge with the proposed SR scheme as shown in the Fig. 2 by using the following training losses:

$$\mathcal{L}_{G_{SR}} = \mathcal{L}_{\text{GAN}} + \mathcal{L}_{tv} + 10 \cdot \mathcal{L}_1 + \mathcal{L}_{ssim} + \mathcal{L}_{msssim} + 10 \cdot \mathcal{L}_{\text{cyc}} \qquad (10)$$

Since the final ranking is based on the weighted score of the PSNR and SSIM given in this challenge, we adopt the above losses combination where we neglect

Fig. 4. Visual comparison of our method with the other state-of-art methods on the AIM 2020 Real Image SR (track-3) validation set at the ×4 super-resolution.

the $\mathcal{L}_{per}$ and use the $\mathcal{L}_{ssim}$ and $\mathcal{L}_{msssim}$ (refers to the Eq. (3)) whose incorporate the structure similarity [23] as well as the variations of image resolution and viewing conditions for the output image. Table 2 provides the final ×4 SR testset results for the track-3 of our method (**MLP_SR**) with others participants. We also provide the visual comparison of our method with the state-of-art methods on the track-3 validation-set and testset in the Fig. 4 and Fig. 5. Our method produces sharp images without any visible corruptions and achieves comparable visual results with the other methods.

Table 3. This table reports the quantitative results of our method over the DIV2K validation set (100 images) with unknown degradation for our ablation study. The arrows indicate if high ↑ or low ↓ values are desired.

SR method	Cyclic path	Network structure	PSNR↑	SSIM↑	LPIPS↓
SRResCycGAN	×	$y \rightarrow G_{SR} \rightarrow \hat{y}$	25.05	0.67	**0.3357**
SRResCycGAN	✓	$y \rightarrow G_{SR} \rightarrow \hat{y} \rightarrow G_{LR} \rightarrow y'$	26.13	0.71	0.3911
SRResCycGAN+	✓	$y \rightarrow G_{SR} \rightarrow \hat{y} \rightarrow G_{LR} \rightarrow y'$	**26.39**	**0.73**	0.4245

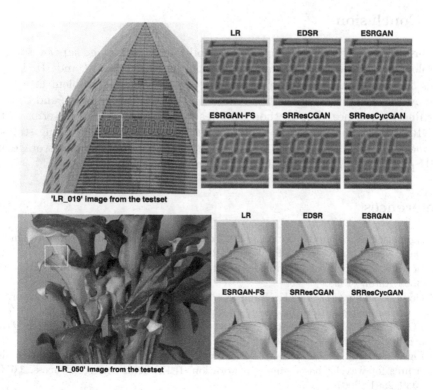

Fig. 5. Visual comparison of our method with the other state-of-art methods on the AIM 2020 Real Image SR (track-3) test set at the ×4 super-resolution.

4.6 Ablation Study

For our ablation study, we design two variants of the proposed network structure with cyclic path or not. The first network structure (*i.e.* $y \rightarrow G_{SR} \rightarrow \hat{y}$) takes the LR input to the G_{SR} and produces the SR output by the supervision of the SR discriminator network D_x without the cyclic path (G_{LR} & D_y) as shown in the Fig. 2. Correspondingly, we minimize the total loss in the Eq. (3) without the $\mathcal{L}_{cyc}$. The second network structure (*i.e.* $y \rightarrow G_{SR} \rightarrow \hat{y} \rightarrow G_{LR} \rightarrow y'$) takes the LR input to the G_{SR} and produces the SR output by the supervision of the SR discriminator network D_x. After that, the SR output fed into the G_{LR} and reconstructs the LR output by the supervision of the LR discriminator network D_y, refers to the Fig. 2. Accordingly, we minimize the the total loss in the Eq. (3). Table 3 shows the quantitative results of our method over the DIV2K validation-set [17] with the unknown degradation. We found that in the presence of the cyclic path, we get the significant improvement of the PSNR/SSIM *i.e.* $+1.34/ + 0.06$ to the first variant. It suggests that the cyclic structure gives the benefits to handle complex degradation such as noise, blurring, compression artifacts, etc., while the other structure lacks this due to the domain difference between LR and HR.

5 Conclusion

We proposed a deep SRResCycGAN method for the real image super-resolution problem by handling the domain consistency between the LR and HR images with the CycleGAN. The proposed method solves the SR problem in a GAN framework by minimizing the loss function with the discriminative and residual learning approaches. Our method achieves excellent SR results in terms of the PSNR/SSIM values as well as visual quality compared to the existing state-of-art methods. The SR network is easy to deploy for limited memory storage and CPU power requirements for the mobile/embedded environment.

References

1. Agustsson, E., Timofte, R.: Ntire 2017 challenge on single image super-resolution: Dataset and study. In: CVPRW, pp. 126–135 (2017)
2. Bertero, M., Boccacci, P.: Introduction to Inverse Problems in Imaging. CRC Press, Boca Raton (1998)
3. Dong, C., Loy, C.C., He, K., Tang, X.: Learning a deep convolutional network for image super-resolution. In: Fleet, D., Pajdla, T., Schiele, B., Tuytelaars, T. (eds.) ECCV 2014. LNCS, vol. 8692, pp. 184–199. Springer, Cham (2014). https://doi.org/10.1007/978-3-319-10593-2_13
4. Figueiredo, M., Bioucas-Dias, J.M., Nowak, R.D.: Majorization-minimization algorithms for wavelet-based image restoration. IEEE Trans. Image Process. **16**(12), 2980–2991 (2007)
5. Fritsche, M., Gu, S., Timofte, R.: Frequency separation for real-world super-resolution. ICCV workshops (2019)

6. Goodfellow, I., et al.: Generative adversarial nets. In: Advances in Neural Information Processing Systems (NIPS), pp. 2672–2680 (2014)

7. Isola, P., Zhu, J.Y., Zhou, T., Efros, A.A.: Image-to-image translation with conditional adversarial networks. In: CVPR, pp. 1125–1134 (2017)

8. Kim, J., Lee, J.K., Lee, K.M.: Accurate image super-resolution using very deep convolutional networks. In: CVPR, pp. 1646–1654 (2016)

9. Ledig, C., et al.: Photo-realistic single image super-resolution using a generative adversarial network. In: Proceedings of the IEEE Conference on Computer Vision and Pattern Recognition (CVPR), pp. 4681–4690 (2017)

10. Lefkimmiatis, S.: Universal denoising networks: a novel cnn architecture for image denoising. In: CVPR, pp. 3204–3213 (2018)

11. Li, C., Wand, M.: Precomputed real-time texture synthesis with markovian generative adversarial networks. In: Leibe, B., Matas, J., Sebe, N., Welling, M. (eds.) ECCV 2016. LNCS, vol. 9907, pp. 702–716. Springer, Cham (2016). https://doi.org/10.1007/978-3-319-46487-9_43

12. Li, Y., Yang, J., Liu, Z., Yang, X., Jeon, G., Wu, W.: Feedback network for image super-resolution. In: CVPR (2019)

13. Lim, B., Son, S., Kim, H., Nah, S., Lee, K.M.: Enhanced deep residual networks for single image super-resolution. In: CVPRW, pp. 1132–1140 (2017)

14. Liu, X., Tanaka, M., Okutomi, M.: Single-image noise level estimation for blind denoising. IEEE Trans. Image Process. (TIP) **22**(12), 5226–5237 (2013)

15. Lugmayr, A., Danelljan, M., Timofte, R.: Unsupervised learning for real-world super-resolution. In: ICCV workshops (2019)

16. Lugmayr, A., Danelljan, M., Timofte, R., et al.: Aim 2019 challenge on real-world image super-resolution: Methods and results. In: ICCV Workshops (2019)

17. Lugmayr, A., Danelljan, M., Timofte, R., et al.: Ntire 2020 challenge on real-world image super-resolution: methods and results. In: CVPR Workshops (2020)

18. Muhammad Umer, R., Luca Foresti, G., Micheloni, C.: Deep generative adversarial residual convolutional networks for real-world super-resolution. In: Proceedings of the IEEE/CVF Conference on Computer Vision and Pattern Recognition Workshops, pp. 438–439 (2020)

19. Shi, W., et al.: Real-time single image and video super-resolution using an efficient sub-pixel convolutional neural network. IEEE Conference on Computer Vision and Pattern Recognition (CVPR), pp. 1874–1883 (2016)

20. Timofte, R., Rothe, R., Van Gool, L.: Seven ways to improve example-based single image super resolution. In: CVPR, pp. 1865–1873 (2016)

21. Umer, R.M., Foresti, G.L., Micheloni, C.: Deep super-resolution network for single image super-resolution with realistic degradations. In: ICDSC, pp. 21:1–21:7 (September 2019)

22. Wang, X., et al.: ESRGAN: Enhanced super-resolution generative adversarial networks. In: Proceedings of the European Conference on Computer Vision (ECCV) (2018)

23. Wang, Z., Bovik, A.C., Sheikh, H.R., Simoncelli, E.P.: Image quality assessment: from error visibility to structural similarity. IEEE Trans. Image Process. **13**, 600–612 (2004)

24. Wei, P., et al.: Aim 2020 challenge on real image super-resolution: methods and results (2020)

25. Yuan, Y., Liu, S., Zhang, J., Zhang, Y., Dong, C., Lin, L.: Unsupervised image super-resolution using cycle-in-cycle generative adversarial networks. In: Proceedings of the IEEE Conference on Computer Vision and Pattern Recognition Workshops, pp. 701–710 (2018)

26. Zhang, K., Zuo, W., Gu, S., Zhang, L.: Learning deep CNN denoiser prior for image restoration. IEEE Conference on Computer Vision and Pattern Recognition (CVPR), pp. 2808–2817 (2017)
27. Zhang, K., Zuo, W., Zhang, L.: Learning a single convolutional super-resolution network for multiple degradations. IEEE Conference on Computer Vision and Pattern Recognition (CVPR), pp. 3262–3271 (2018)
28. Zhang, K., Zuo, W., Zhang, L.: Deep plug-and-play super-resolution for arbitrary blur kernels. In: Proceedings of the IEEE Conference on Computer Vision and Pattern Recognition (CVPR), pp. 1671–1681 (2019)
29. Zhang, R., Isola, P., Efros, A.A., Shechtman, E., Wang, O.: The unreasonable effectiveness of deep features as a perceptual metric. In: IEEE Conference on Computer Vision and Pattern Recognition (CVPR), pp. 586–595 (2018)
30. Zhu, J.Y., Park, T., Isola, P., Efros, A.A.: Unpaired image-to-image translation using cycle-consistent adversarial networks. In: Proceedings of the IEEE International Conference on Computer Vision, pp. 2223–2232 (2017)

AIM 2020: Scene Relighting and Illumination Estimation Challenge

Majed El Helou[1]([⊠]), Ruofan Zhou[1], Sabine Süsstrunk[1], Radu Timofte[2],
Mahmoud Afifi[3], Michael S. Brown[3], Kele Xu[4], Hengxing Cai[4], Yuzhong Liu[4],
Li-Wen Wang[5], Zhi-Song Liu[5,6], Chu-Tak Li[5], Sourya Dipta Das[7],
Nisarg A. Shah[8], Akashdeep Jassal[9], Tongtong Zhao[10], Shanshan Zhao[11],
Sabari Nathan[12], M. Parisa Beham[13], R. Suganya[14], Qing Wang[15],
Zhongyun Hu[15], Xin Huang[15], Yaning Li[15], Maitreya Suin[16],
Kuldeep Purohit[16], A. N. Rajagopalan[16], Densen Puthussery[17],
P. S. Hrishikesh[17], Melvin Kuriakose[17], C. V. Jiji[17], Yu Zhu[18], Liping Dong[18],
Zhuolong Jiang[18], Chenghua Li[18], Cong Leng[18], and Jian Cheng[18]

[1] EPFL, Lausanne, Switzerland
{majed.elhelou,ruofan.zhou,sabine.susstrunk}@epfl.ch
[2] ETHZ, Zrich, Switzerland
radu.timofte@vision.ee.ethz.ch
[3] EECS, York University, Toronto, ON, Canada
mafifi@eecs.yorku.ca
[4] National University of Defense Technology, Changsha, China
kelele.xu@gmail.com
[5] Department of Electronic and Information Engineering, The Hong Kong
Polytechnic University, Hong Kong, China
liwen.wang@connect.polyu.hk
[6] CS laboratory at the Ecole Polytechnique, Palaiseau, France
[7] Jadavpur University, Kolkata, India
dipta.juetce@gmail.com
[8] Indian Institute of Technology, Jodhpur, India
[9] Punjab Engineering College (PEC), Chandigarh, India
[10] Dalian Maritime University, Dalian, China
daitoutiere@gmail.com
[11] China Everbright Bank, Beijing, China
[12] Couger Inc, Tokyo, Japan
sabarinathantce@gmail.com
[13] Sethu Institute of Technology,, Virudhunagar, India
[14] Thiagarajar College of Engineering, Virudhunagar, India

M. El Helou, R. Zhou, S. Süsstrunk, and R. Timofte are the challenge organizers, and
the other authors are challenge participants.
Appendix A lists all the teams and affiliations.
https://github.com/majedelhelou/VIDIT.

Electronic supplementary material The online version of this chapter (https://
doi.org/10.1007/978-3-030-67070-2_30) contains supplementary material, which is
available to authorized users.

[15] Computer Vision and Computational Photography Group, School of Computer
Science, Northwestern Polytechnical University, Xi'an, China
zy_h@mail.nwpu.edu.cn
[16] Indian Institute of Technology Madras, Chennai, India
maitreyasuin21@gmail.com
[17] College of Engineering, Trivandrum, India
puthusserydensen@gmail.com
[18] Nanjing Artificial Intelligence Chip Research, Institute of Automation, Chinese
Academy of Sciences (AiRiA); MAICRO, Beijing, China
zhuyu.cv@gmail.com

Abstract. We review the AIM 2020 challenge on virtual image relighting and illumination estimation. This paper presents the novel VIDIT dataset used in the challenge and the different proposed solutions and final evaluation results over the 3 challenge tracks. The first track considered one-to-one relighting; the objective was to relight an input photo of a scene with a different color temperature and illuminant orientation (i.e., light source position). The goal of the second track was to estimate illumination settings, namely the color temperature and orientation, from a given image. Lastly, the third track dealt with any-to-any relighting, thus a generalization of the first track. The target color temperature and orientation, rather than being pre-determined, are instead given by a guide image. Participants were allowed to make use of their track 1 and 2 solutions for track 3. The tracks had 94, 52, and 56 registered participants, respectively, leading to 20 confirmed submissions in the final competition stage.

Keywords: Image relighting · Illumination estimation · Style transfer

1 Introduction

Deep image relighting has multiple applications both in research and in practice, and is recently witnessing increased interest. A single-image relighting method would allow aesthetic enhancement applications, such as photo montage of images taken under different illuminations, and illumination retouching without human expert work. Very importantly, in computer vision research image relighting can be leveraged for data augmentation, enabling the trained methods to be robust to changes in light source position or color temperature. It could also serve for domain adaptation, by normalizing input images to a unique set of illumination settings that the down-stream computer vision method was trained on. The relighting task contains multiple sub-tasks, namely, illumination estimation and manipulation, shadow removal or practically inpainting for hardly lit areas, and geometric understanding for shadow recasting. The combination of these tasks makes relighting very challenging.

Recently, datasets limited to interior scenes [33], underexposed images enhanced by professionals [48], and rendered images with randomized light directions [54] have been proposed, but none serve the benchmarking needs for image relighting, namely, having all $M \times N$ combinations of M scenes and N illumination settings. Further datasets are used in the literature on style transfer or intrinsic image decomposition. For instance, IIW [6] and SAW [27] contain human-labeled reflectance and shading annotations, and BigTime [29] contains time-lapse data of scenes illuminated under varying light conditions. Multiple methods are recently being developed for relighting [12,34,42], and the prior literature on intrinsic images, which disentangle surface reflectance from lighting, is rich [5,6,18,39,44,51], notably for applications such as relighting [7] and normalization [32].

The aim of this challenge, and of the novel dataset **Virtual Image Dataset for Illumination Transfer** (VIDIT), is to gauge the current state-of-the-art for image relighting. The virtual dataset provides a well-controlled setup to provide full-reference evaluation, which is ideal for benchmarking purposes, and is an important step towards real-image relighting. Such virtual datasets have proven useful in multiple applications to augment even the training datasets containing real images, for instance the vKitti data [9]. There could be differences relative to real images such as the distribution of textures that can vary from man-made to natural scenes [8,45], the specifics of the capturing device like chromatic aberrations [15,31,58], or the presence of multiple light sources. VIDIT itself is described in the following section. The goal of the challenge is thus to provide a benchmark on this dataset for future research on image relighting.

This challenge is one of the AIM 2020 associated challenges on: scene relighting and illumination estimation [17], image extreme inpainting [36], learned image signal processing pipeline [24], rendering realistic bokeh [25], real image super-resolution [50], efficient super-resolution [56], video temporal super-resolution [41] and video extreme super-resolution [19].

2   Scene Relighting and Illumination Estimation Challenge

2.1   Dataset

The challenge, whose 3 tracks are described in the following section, is based on a novel dataset: VIDIT [16]. VIDIT contains 300 virtual scenes used for training, where every scene is captured 40 times in total: from 8 equally-spaced azimuthal angles, each lit with 5 different illuminants. Every image is 1024×1024, but the images are downsampled by a factor of 2, with bicubic interpolation over 4×4 windows, to ease computations for track 3. The dataset is publicly available (https://github.com/majedelhelou/VIDIT).

2.2   Tracks and Competition

Track 1: One-to-one Relighting

Description: the relighting task is pre-determined and fixed for all validation and test samples. In other words, the objective is to manipulate an input image from one pre-defined set of illumination settings (namely, North, 6500K) to another pre-defined set (East, 4500K). The images are in 1024×1024 resolution, both input and output, and nothing other than the input image is provided.

Evaluation Protocol: We evaluate the results using the PSNR and SSIM [49] metrics, and the self-reported run-times and implementation details are also provided. For the final ranking, we define a Mean Perceptual Score (MPS) as the average of the normalized SSIM and LPIPS [57] scores, themselves averaged across the entire test set of each submission

$$0.5 \cdot (S + (1 - L)), \tag{1}$$

where S is the SSIM score, and L is the LPIPS score. We note that normalizing S and $(1 - L)$, by dividing them respectively by their maximum values across all the track's submissions, before averaging the two does not affect the final ranking. We thus do not do this normalization, which also makes it simpler for external comparisons.

Track 2: Illumination Settings Estimation

Description: the goal of this track is to estimate, from a single input image, the illumination settings that were used in rendering it. Given the input image, the output should estimate the color temperature of the illuminant as well as the orientation, i.e. the position of the light source. The input images are also 1024×1024 and no other input is given than the 2D image.

Evaluation Protocol: The evaluation of track 2 is based on the accuracy of predictions following this formula for the loss

$$\sqrt{\sum_{i=0}^{N-1} \left(\frac{|\hat{\phi}_i - \phi_i| mod 180}{180} \right)^2 + (\hat{T}_i - T_i)^2} \tag{2}$$

where $\hat{\phi}_i$ is the predicted angle (0–360) for test sample i and ϕ_i is the ground-truth value for that sample. $\hat{T}_i$ is the temperature prediction for test sample i and T_i is the ground-truth value for that sample. T_i takes values equal to $[0, 0.25, 0.5, 0.75, 1]$, which correspond to the color temperature values [2500K, 3500K, 4500K, 5500K, 6500K].

Track 3: Any-to-any Relighting

Description: this track is a generalization of the first track. The objective is to relight an input image (both color temperature and light source position manipulation) from any arbitrary illumination settings to any arbitrary illumination settings. The latter settings are dictated by a second input guide image, as in style transfer applications. The participants were allowed to make use of their solutions to the first two tracks to develop a solution for this track. The images are in 512×512 resolution to ease computations, as this track is very challenging.

Evaluation Protocol: We carry out a similar evaluation as for track 1. As the inputs are pairs of possible test images, they cover a larger span of candidate options. For that reason, we double the number of data samples in the validation and test sets for this track.

Challenge Phases for all Tracks. (1) Development: registered teams were given access to the training input and target data, as well as the input validation set data. An online validation server with a leader board provided automated feedback for the submitted image results on the validation set, which was made up of 45 images for tracks 1 and 2, and 90 image pairs for track 3; (2) Testing: registered teams were given access to the input test sets, which are of the same size as the validation ones, and could submit their test results to a private test server. For a submission to be accepted, open-source code and a fact sheet detailing the implemented method needed to be submitted along with the test results. Test results were kept hidden from participating teams, to avoid any chances of test over-fitting, and were only revealed at the end of the challenge.

3   Challenge Results

The results of all three tracks are collected in Tables 1, 2, and 3, respectively. The top solutions are described in the following sections, and the remainder is in the supplementary material.

Table 1. AIM 2020 Image Relighting Challenge Track 1 (One-to-one relighting) results. The MPS, used to determine the final ranking, is computed following Eq. (1). *CET_CVLab and CET_SP are merged into one, due to large similarity between the proposed solutions. We also note that normalizing SSIM and (1-LPIPS) scores by the maximum in the track, for computing the MPS, does not affect the ranking.

Team	Author	MPS ↑	SSIM ↑	LPIPS ↓	PSNR ↑	Run-time	Platform	GPU
CET_SP*	hrishikeshps	0.6452 (-)	0.6310 (2)	0.3405 (1)	17.0717 (2)	0.03s	Tensorflow	P100
CET_CVLab	Densen	0.6451 (1)	0.6362 (1)	0.3460 (3)	16.8927 (6)	0.03s	Tensorflow	P100
lyl	tongtong	0.6436 (2)	0.6301 (3)	0.3430 (2)	16.6801 (8)	13s	PyTorch	V100
YorkU	mafifi	0.6216 (3)	0.6091 (4)	0.3659 (5)	16.8196 (7)	6s	PyTorch	1080TI
IPCV_IITM	ms_icpv	0.5897 (4)	0.5298 (7)	0.3505 (4)	17.0594 (3)	0.04s	PyTorch	Titan X
DeepRelight	leven	0.5892 (5)	0.5928 (6)	0.4144 (7)	17.4252 (1)	0.5s	PyTorch	2080TI
Withdrawn	tomanut	0.5603 (6)	0.5236 (8)	0.4029 (6)	16.5136 (9)	0.01s	PyTorch	2080TI
Hertz	souryadipta	0.5339 (7)	0.5666 (6)	0.4989 (8)	16.9234 (4)	0.006s	PyTorch	1080TI
Image Lab	sabarinathan	0.3746 (8)	0.3769 (9)	0.6278 (9)	16.8949 (5)	0.12s	Tensorflow	1080TI
input image	–	0.6438	0.6288	0.3412	16.2796			

Table 2. AIM 2020 Image Relighting Challenge Track 2 (Illumination settings estimation) results. The loss is computed based on the angle and color temperature predictions, following Eq. (2), and is used to determine the final ranking.

Team	Author	Loss ↓	AngLoss ↓	TempLoss ↓	Run-time	Platform	GPU
AiRiA_CG	Airia_CG	0.0875 (1)	0.0722 (3)	0.0153 (1)	0.03s	PyTorch	Titan Xp
YorkU	mafifi	0.0887 (2)	0.0639 (2)	0.0248 (2)	0.95s	MATLAB	1080TI
Image Lab	sabarinathan	0.0984 (3)	0.0513 (1)	0.0471 (5)	0.02s	Tensorflow	1080TI
debut_kele	debut_kele	0.1431 (4)	0.1125 (4)	0.0306 (3)			
RGETH	Georgechogovadze	0.1708 (5)	0.1347 (5)	0.0361 (4)	0.026s	PyTorch	
random guess	–	0.5987	0.3729	0.2257			

Table 3. AIM 2020 Image Relighting Challenge Track 3 (Any-to-any relighting) results. The MPS, used to determine the final ranking, is computed following Eq. (1). We also note that normalizing SSIM and (1-LPIPS) scores by the maximum in the track, for computing the MPS, does not affect the ranking.

Team	Author	MPS ↑	SSIM ↑	LPIPS ↓	PSNR ↑	Run-time	Platform	GPU
NPU-CVPG	walden	0.6484 (1)	0.6353 (1)	0.3386 (3)	18.5436 (2)	0.15s	PyTorch	1080TI
YorkU	mafifi	0.6428 (2)	0.6195 (2)	0.3338 (2)	18.2384 (4)	6s	PyTorch	1080TI
IPCV_IITM	ms_icpv	0.6424 (3)	0.6042 (3)	0.3194 (1)	19.3559 (1)	0.3s	PyTorch	Titan X
lyl	tongtong	0.6213 (4)	0.5881 (4)	0.3455 (4)	17.6314 (5)	13s	PyTorch	V100
AiRiA_CG	Airia_CG	0.5258 (5)	0.4451 (5)	0.3936 (5)	18.3493 (3)		PyTorch	Titan Xp
RGETH	Georgechogovadze	0.3465 (6)	0.4123 (6)	0.7192 (6)	10.4483 (6)	0.0289s	PyTorch	
Input image	–	0.6750	0.6603	0.3103	17.9391			

Visual results of some top submissions along with input and ground-truth images for track 1 are shown in Fig. 1. We notice that most of the outputs generate the relit image with the correct color temperature, however, the shadows are harder to estimate. For instance, lyl and YorkU suffer from shadow removal. Both CET_SP and CET_CVLab tend to remove the unnecessary shadows, although not perfectly, which underlines the difficulty of the shadow-relighting sub-task. We show visual results of some submissions to track 3 in Fig. 2. Among the top 3 submissions, only NPU-CVPG is able to successfully relight the bottom-right part and produce the closest color temperature to the ground-truth.

4   Track 1 Methods

4.1   CET_CVLab: Wavelet Decomposed RelightNet (WDRN)

The architecture of the proposed Wavelet Decomposed RelightNet (WDRN) [37] is shown in Fig. 3. The network structure used is similar to that of an encoder-decoder U-Net. The downsampling operation used in the contraction path is a discrete wavelet transform (DWT) based decomposition instead of a downsampling convolution or pooling. Similarly, in the expansion path, the inverse discrete wavelet transform (IDWT) is used instead of an upsampling convolution.

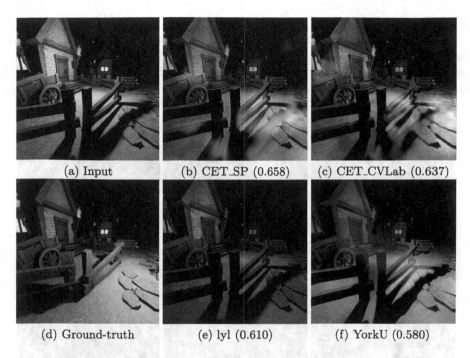

(a) Input   (b) CET_SP (0.658)   (c) CET_CVLab (0.637)

(d) Ground-truth   (e) lyl (0.610)   (f) YorkU (0.580)

Fig. 1. Sample visual results from top submissions in track 1, with MPS scores. We observe that relighting previous shadows is the most difficult sub-task.

In the wavelet based decomposition, the information from all channels is combined in the downsampling process such that there is minimal information loss when compared to that of a convolutional subsampling. For the given task, it can be deduced that the network must learn to re-calibrate the illumination gradient within the image. To this end, the network should be able to establish the relation between distant pixels. The proposed WDRN can achieve a high receptive field and hence establish this relation with the multi-scale wavelet decomposition. Also, this methodology is computationally efficient and is inspired by the multi-level wavelet-CNN (MWCNN) proposed by Liu *et al.* [30]. The training loss used in this work is a weighted sum of the SSIM loss, MAE loss and a *gray loss* (the gray loss term is used in the CET_SP submission, and omitted in that of CET_CVLab). Gray loss is the $\ell 1$ distance between the grayscale version of the restored image and that of the ground-truth image.

4.2 lyl: Coarse-to-Fine Relighting Net (CFRN)

The proposed Coarse-to-Fine Relighting Net (CFRN) is illustrated in Fig. 4. The solution consists of two networks: (1) progressive coarse network and (2) a network merging the output of the coarse network, with channel attention, to correct the input in each level. Such a progressive process helps to achieve the principle for image relighting: high-level information is a good guide to obtain a better relit image. In the proposed method, there are three indispensable parts; (1) tying the loss at each level (2) using the FineNet structure and (3) providing a lower-level extracted feature input to ensure the availability of low-level information. To make full use of the training data, the team augments data in three ways; (1) scaling: randomly downscaling between [0.5,1.0], (2) rotation:

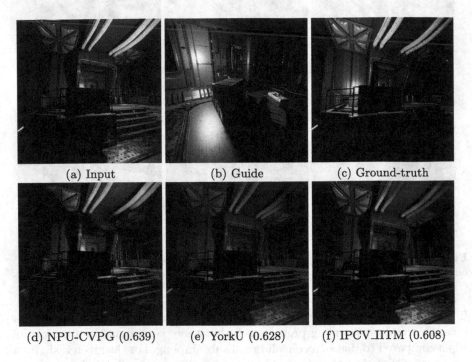

(a) Input   (b) Guide   (c) Ground-truth

(d) NPU-CVPG (0.639)   (e) YorkU (0.628)   (f) IPCV_IITM (0.608)

Fig. 2. Sample visual results from top submissions in track 3, with MPS scores.

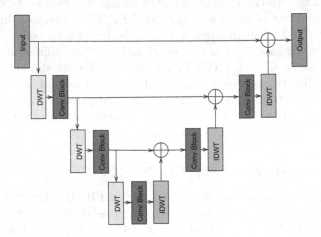

Fig. 3. Architecture of the Wavelet Decomposed RelightNet (WDRN).

randomly rotating the image by 90, 180, and 270 degrees, and (3) flipping: randomly flipping images horizontally or vertically with equal probability.

4.3 YorkU: Norm-Relighting-U-Net (NRUNet)

The method adopts a U-Net architecture [38] as the main backbone of the proposed framework. The solution consists of two networks: (1) the normalization network, which is responsible for producing uniformly-lit white-balanced images, and (2) the relighting network, which performs the one-to-one image relighting. An instance normalization [46] is applied after each stage in the encoder of the normalization network, while batch normalization is used for the encoder of the relighting network. The relighting network is fed the input image and the latent representations of the uniformly-lit image produced by the normalization network. The team uses the white-balance augmenter in [2] to augment the training data. To produce the ground-truth of the normalization network, the team uses the training data provided for tracks 2 and 3, which include a set

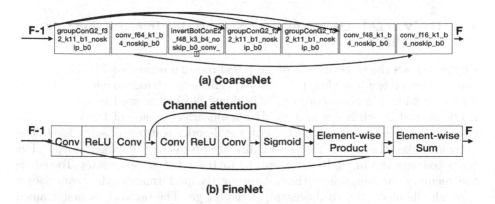

Fig. 4. Architecture diagram of the Coarse-to-Fine Relighting Net (CFRN).

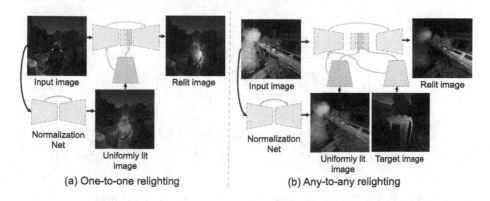

Fig. 5. Overview of YorkU team's NRUNet framework.

of images taken from each scene under different lighting directions. The team exploits their solution for the illumination settings estimation task (see Sect. 5.2) to predict the target scene settings for the one-to-one mapping. Hence, the team increases the number of training images by including the training images provided for tracks 2 and 3. The team pre-trains the normalization network then fixes its weights and the entire framework is jointly trained. The training uses the Adam optimizer [26] with $\ell 1$ loss. At inference, the team processes a resized version of the input image, then a guided up-sampling [10] is applied to obtain the full-resolution image. The team ensembles the final results by utilizing their one-to-any framework (more details on the one-to-any framework in Sect. 6.2). To relight the image using the one-to-any framework, the team randomly selects six images with the predicted illumination settings of the current track to use them as targets. This procedure generates six relit images that are used along with the result image produced by the one-to-one framework to generate the final result. Figure 5-(a) shows an overview of the proposed one-to-one mapping framework. The source code for the three tracks is available at https://github. com/mahmoudnafifi/image_relighting.

4.4   IPCV_IITM: Deep Residual Network for Image Relighting (DRNIR)

Figure 6 shows the structure of the proposed residual network with skip connections, based on the hourglass network [59]. The network has an encoder-decoder structure with skip connections [23]. Residual blocks are used in the skip connections, and Batch-Norm and ReLU non-linearity in each of the blocks. The encoder features are concatenated with the decoder features of same level. The network takes the input image and directly produces the target image. The team converts the input RGB images to LAB for better processing. To reduce the memory consumption without harming the performance, the team uses a pixel-shuffle block [40] to downsample the image. The network is first trained using the $\ell 1$ loss, then fine-tuned with the MSE loss. Note that experiments with adversarial loss did not lead to stable training. The learning rate of the Adam

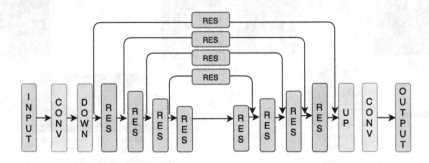

Fig. 6. Diagram illustration of the DRNIR network architecture.

optimizer is 0.0001 with a decay cycle of 200 epochs, and a 512×512 patch size for training. Data augmentation is used to make the network more robust.

4.5   Other Submitted Solutions

The DeepRelight team addresses the one-to-one relighting task by recovering the structure information of the scene, target illumination information, and renders the output with a GAN strategy [47]. Another solution makes use of two pairs of encoder-decoder networks, such that the encoding and decoding are illumination specific, and the learning is also supervised with discriminators. Transforming an image becomes equivalent to encoding it with the first encoder and decoding it with the second. Hertz tackle the problem using a multi-scale hierarchical network, the image is encoded at multiple resolutions and feature information is transferred from lower to higher levels to obtain the final transformation. Lastly, Image Lab [35] build on the multilevel hyper vision net [14], adding convolution block attention [52] in their skip connections. Further details of each of these submitted solutions can be found in the supplementary material.

5   Track 2 Methods

5.1   AiRiA_CG: Dual Path Ensemble Network (DPENet)

The proposed DPENet has two sub-networks, one for angle prediction and one for temperature classification [13]. The full DPENet is shown in Fig. 7. ResNeXt-101_32×4d [53] is adopted for the angle prediction sub-network. The temperature classification sub-network is based on ResNet-50 [20]. The two sub-networks are pre-trained on ImageNet [11]. The solution adopts random flipping and random rotation for data augmentation.

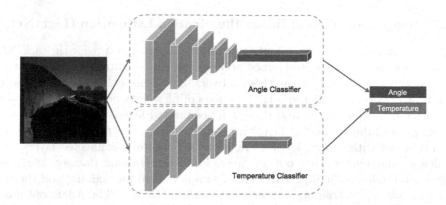

Fig. 7. The structure of Dual Path Ensemble Network (DPENet).

5.2   YorkU: Illuminant-ResNet (I-ResNet)

The team treats the task as two independent classification tasks; (1) illuminant temperature classification and (2) illuminant angle classification. The team adopts the ResNet-18 model [20] trained on ImageNet [11]. The last fully-connected layer is replaced with a new layer with n neurons, where n is the number of output classes for each task. The Adam optimizer [26] is used with cross entropy loss. For angle classification, the team applies the white-balance augmenter proposed in [2] to augment the training data. For temperature classification, the team follows previous work [1,3,4] that uses image histogram features instead of the 2D input image. Specifically, the team feeds the network with 2D RGB-uv projected histogram features [1,3], instead of the original training images. This histogram-based training, rather than image-based, improves the model's generalization. Figure 8 shows an overview of the team's solution, including the white-balance augmentation process.

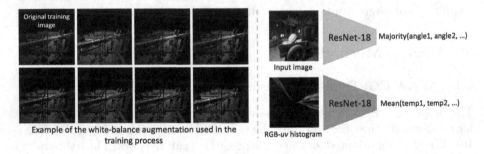

Fig. 8. Overview of the YorkU solution, with the white-balance augmentation [2].

5.3   Image Lab: Virtual Image Illumination Estimation (LightNet)

As shown in Fig. 9, the team adopts a Densenet [22] architecture for the task. The team trains ten different pre-trained networks and also creates a custom network with selective blocks [28]. From these networks, the Densnet121 network achieves the best performance. DenseNet121 consists of fifty-eight dense blocks, followed by three transition blocks and three fully-connected layers. The global average pooling and fully connected layers are removed from the pre-trained network, and replaced with a new global average pooling and fully connected layers with a degree and temperature output layer. From the training dataset, the team creates a random splitting, with 67% of samples taken for training and the rest for validation. The training images are normalized to [0,1]. The Adam optimizer with a learning rate decaying from 0.001 to 0.00001 over 500 epochs is used for training the model with the categorical loss. Attention layers [52] were tested in the development phase but did not yield any improvement.

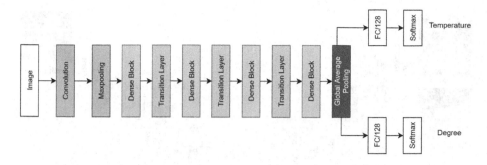

Fig. 9. Overview of the LightNet model's architecture.

5.4   Other Submitted Solution

The debut_kele team proposes to use a single EfficientNet [43] backbone, pre-trained on ImageNet. Further details of this submitted solution can be found in the supplementary material.

6   Track 3 Methods

6.1   NPU-CVPG: Self-Attention AutoEncoder (SA-AE)

As shown in Fig. 10, the team presents the novel Self-Attention AutoEncoder (SA-AE) [21] model for generating a relit image from a source image to match the illumination settings of a guide image. In order to reduce the learning difficulty, the team adopts an implicit scene representation [59] learned by the encoder to render the relit images using the decoder. Based on the learned scene representation, an illumination estimation network is designed as a classier to predict the illumination settings of the guide image. A lighting-to-feature network is also designed to recover the corresponding implicit scene representation from the illumination settings, similar to the inverse of the illumination estimation process. In addition, a self-attention [55] mechanism is introduced in the decoder to focus on the rendering of the regions requiring relighting in the source images.

6.2   YorkU: Norm-Relighting-U-Net (NRUNet)

As for the one-to-one mapping proposed (Sect. 4.3), the U-Net architecture [38] is used as the main backbone of the any-to-any relighting framework, and two networks are used for normalization and relighting, as shown in Fig. 5-(b). The relighting network is fed the input image, the latent representation of the guide image and the uniformly lit image produced by the normalization network. The team uses the white-balance augmentation [2] on the training data for the normalization network. The team trains two frameworks; one framework on 256×256 random patches and one on 256 × 256 resized images. The final result is generated by taking the mean of the two relit images and applying a guided up-sampling [10].

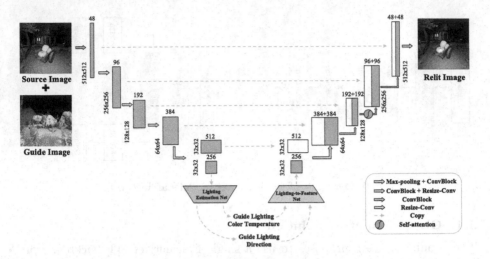

Fig. 10. Overview of the proposed SA-AE network.

6.3 IPCV_IITM: Deep Residual Network for Image Relighting (DRNIR)

Figure 11 shows the structure of the proposed residual network with skip connections, based on the hourglass network [59]. The network has an encoder-decoder structure similar to [23]. The team also uses residual blocks in the skip connections. The encoder features are concatenated with the decoder features of the same level. Along with the input image, the network is given a guide image that is used in two places. First, both the input and the guide image are concatenated. Second, the team adds a separate loss to match the illumination properties between the guide image and the predicted image. A separate network predicts the illumination settings of an image, and is trained with the provided ground-truth labels. The team passes both the guide image and the predicted image through the network and minimizes the distance between intermediate feature representations. The feature representation of the guide image is further concatenated with the encoder output and fed to the decoder. The team converts the input RGB images to LAB for better processing. To reduce memory consumption, pixel-shuffle blocks [40] are used as in track 1.

6.4 lyl: Coarse-to-Fine Relighting Net (CFRN)

The proposed Coarse-to-Fine Relighting Net (CFRN) is shown in Fig. 4, as in track 1. Training is divided in two stages: incomplete training and full training. During an incomplete training, the fine network is trained with a batch size of 16 for 200 epochs. The Adam optimizer ($\beta_1 = 0.9, \beta_2 = 0.999$) is used to minimize the $\ell 1$ loss between the generated relit images and the ground-truth. The learning rate is initialized to 10^4 and kept unchanged. After the incomplete training with

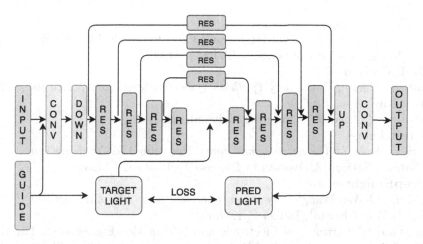

Fig. 11. Network architecture of the DRNIR method.

the fine network, the whole CFRN is fully trained. In each full training batch, the team randomly samples 64 patches for 20k epochs.

6.5 Other Submitted Solution

The AiRiA_CG team proposes a creative solution consisting of a dual encoder and single decoder [13]. The input image is encoded, and so is the target image. However, the encoder of the target image is mirrored to match the decoder of the input image latent representation, and the feature layers of the former are thus transferred, layer by layer, to the decoder of the latter. This allows the illumination information to be transferred from the guide image to the input image during the decoding process. Further details of this submitted solution can be found in the supplementary material.

Acknowledgements. We thank all AIM 2020 sponsors: Huawei, MediaTek, NVIDIA, Qualcomm, Google and CVL, ETH Zurich (https://data.vision.ee.ethz.ch/cvl/aim20/). We also note that all tracks were supported by the CodaLab infrastructure (https://competitions.codalab.org).

A   Teams and Affiliations

AIM challenge organizers
Members: Majed El Helou, Ruofan Zhou, Sabine Süsstrunk (*{majed.elhelou, ruofan.zhou,sabine.susstrunk}@epfl.ch*, EPFL, Switzerland), and Radu Timofte (*radu.timofte@vision.ee.ethz.ch*, ETH Zürich, Switzerland).

– AiRiA_CG –
Members: Yu Zhu(*zhuyu.cv@gmail.com*), Liping Dong, Zhuolong Jiang,

Chenghua Li, Cong Leng, Jian Cheng
Affiliation: Nanjing Artificial Intelligence Chip Research, Institute of Automation, Chinese Academy of Sciences (AiRiA); MAICRO.
– **CET_CVLab** –
Members: Densen Puthussery (*puthusserydensen@gmail.com*), Hrishikesh P S, Melvin Kuriakose, Jiji C V
Affiliation: College of Engineering, Trivandrum, India.
– **debut_kele** –
Members: Kele Xu (*kelele.xu@gmail.com*), Hengxing Cai, Yuzhong Liu
Affiliation: National University of Defense Technology, China.
– **DeepRelight** –
Members: Li-Wen Wang[1] (*liwen.wang@connect.polyu.hk*), Zhi-Song Liu[1,2], Chu-Tak Li[1], Wan-Chi Siu[1], Daniel P. K. Lun[1]
Affiliation: [1]Department of Electronic and Information Engineering, The Hong Kong Polytechnic University, [2]CS laboratory at the Ecole Polytechnique (Palaiseau).
– **Hertz** –
Members: Sourya Dipta Das[1] (*dipta.juetce@gmail.com*), Nisarg A. Shah[2], Akashdeep Jassal[3]
Affiliation: [1]Jadavpur University, Kolkata, India, [2]Indian Institute of Technology Jodhpur, India, [3]Punjab Engineering College (PEC), Chandigarh, India.
– **Image Lab** –
Members: Sabari Nathan[1] (*sabarinathantce@gmail.com*), M.Parisa Beham[2], R.Suganya[3]
Affiliation: [1]Couger Inc, Tokyo, Japan, [2]Sethu Institute of Technology, India, [3]Thiagarajar College of Engineering, India.
– **IPCV_IITM** –
Members: Maitreya Suin (*maitreyasuin21@gmail.com*), Kuldeep Purohit, A. N. Rajagopalan
Affiliation: Indian Institute of Technology Madras, India.
– **lyl** –
Members: Tongtong Zhao[1] (*daitoutiere@gmail.com*), Shanshan Zhao[2]
Affiliation: [1]Dalian Maritime University,[2] China Everbright Bank.
– **NPU-CVPG** –
Members: Zhongyun Hu (*zy_h@mail.nwpu.edu.cn*), Xin Huang, Yaning Li, Qing Wang
Affiliation: Computer Vision and Computational Photography Group, School of Computer Science, Northwestern Polytechnical University.
– **RGETH** –
Members: George Chogovadze (*chogeorg@student.ethz.ch*), Rémi Pautrat
Affiliation: ETH Zurich, Switzerland.
– **YorkU** –
Members: Mahmoud Afifi (*mafifi@eecs.yorku.ca*), Michael S. Brown
Affiliation: EECS, York University, Toronto, ON, Canada.

References

1. Afifi, M., Brown, M.S.: Sensor-independent illumination estimation for DNN models. In: British Machine Vision Conference (BMVC), p. 11 (2019)
2. Afifi, M., Brown, M.S.: What else can fool deep learning? addressing color constancy errors on deep neural network performance. In: IEEE International Conference on Computer Vision (ICCV), pp. 243–252 (2019)
3. Afifi, M., Price, B., Cohen, S., Brown, M.S.: When color constancy goes wrong: correcting improperly white-balanced images. In: IEEE Conference on Computer Vision and Pattern Recognition (CVPR), pp. 1535–1544 (2019)
4. Barron, J.T.: Convolutional color constancy. In: IEEE International Conference on Computer Vision (ICCV), pp. 379–387 (2015)
5. Barron, J.T., Malik, J.: Color constancy, intrinsic images, and shape estimation. In: European Conference on Computer Vision (ECCV), pp. 57–70 (2012)
6. Bell, S., Bala, K., Snavely, N.: Intrinsic images in the wild. ACM Trans. Graph. (TOG) **33**(4), 159 (2014)
7. Bousseau, A., Paris, S., Durand, F.: User-assisted intrinsic images. In: ACM SIGGRAPH Asia, pp. 1–10 (2009)
8. Burton, G.J., Moorhead, I.R.: Color and spatial structure in natural scenes. Appl. Opt. **26**(1), 157–170 (1987)
9. Cabon, Y., Murray, N., Humenberger, M.: Virtual kitti 2. arXiv preprint arXiv:2001.10773 (2020)
10. Chen, J., Adams, A., Wadhwa, N., Hasinoff, S.W.: Bilateral guided upsampling. ACM Trans. Graph. (TOG) **35**(6), 1–8 (2016)
11. Deng, J., Dong, W., Socher, R., Li, L.J., Li, K., Fei-Fei, L.: ImageNet: a large-scale hierarchical image database. In: IEEE Conference on Computer Vision and Pattern Recognition (CVPR), pp. 248–255 (2009)
12. Dherse, A.P., Everaert, M.N., Gwizdała, J.J.: Scene relighting with illumination estimation in the latent space on an encoder-decoder scheme. arXiv preprint arXiv:2006.02333 (2020)
13. Dong, L., Jiang, Z., Li, C.: An ensemble neural network for scene relighting with light classification. In: Proceedings of the European Conference on Computer Vision Workshops (ECCVW) (2020)
14. D. Sabarinathan, Beham, M., Roomi, S.: Moire image restoration using multi level hyper vision net. Image and Video Processing arXiv:2004.08541 (2020)
15. El Helou, M., Dümbgen, F., Süsstrunk, S.: AAM: an assessment metric of axial chromatic aberration. In: IEEE International Conference on Image Processing (ICIP), pp. 2486–2490 (2018)
16. El Helou, M., Zhou, R., Barthas, J., Süsstrunk, S.: VIDIT: virtual image dataset for illumination transfer. arXiv preprint arXiv:2005.05460 (2020)
17. El Helou, M., et al.: AIM 2020: scene relighting and illumination estimation challenge. In: European Conference on Computer Vision Workshops (2020)
18. Finlayson, G.D., Drew, M.S., Lu, C.: Intrinsic images by entropy minimization. In: European Conference on Computer Vision (ECCV), pp. 582–595 (2004)
19. Fuoli, D., et al.: AIM 2020 challenge on video extreme super-resolution: methods and results. In: European Conference on Computer Vision Workshops (2020)
20. He, K., Zhang, X., Ren, S., Sun, J.: Deep residual learning for image recognition. In: IEEE Conference on Computer Vision and Pattern Recognition (CVPR)., pp. 770–778 (2016)

21. Hu, Z., Huang, X., Li, Y., Wang, Q.: SA-AE for any-to-any relighting. In: Proceedings of the European Conference on Computer Vision Workshops (ECCVW) (2020)
22. Huang, G., Liu, Z., Van Der Maaten, L., Weinberger, K.Q.: Densely connected convolutional networks. In: IEEE Conference on Computer Vision and Pattern Recognition (CVPR), pp. 2261–2269 (2017)
23. Huang, G., Liu, Z., Van Der Maaten, L., Weinberger, K.Q.: Densely connected convolutional networks. In: IEEE Conference on Computer Vision and Pattern Recognition (CVPR), pp. 4700–4708 (2017)
24. Ignatov, A., et al.: AIM 2020 challenge on learned image signal processing pipeline. In: European Conference on Computer Vision Workshops (2020)
25. Ignatov, A., et al.: AIM 2020 challenge on rendering realistic bokeh. In: European Conference on Computer Vision Workshops (2020)
26. Kingma, D.P., Ba, J.: Adam: a method for stochastic optimization. arXiv preprint arXiv:1412.6980 (2014)
27. Kovacs, B., Bell, S., Snavely, N., Bala, K.: Shading annotations in the wild. In: IEEE Conference on Computer Vision and Pattern Recognition (CVPR), pp. 6998–7007 (2017)
28. Li, X., Wang, W., Hu, X., Yang, J.: Selective kernel networks. In: IEEE Conference on Computer Vision and Pattern Recognition (CVPR), pp. 510–519 (2019)
29. Li, Z., Snavely, N.: Learning intrinsic image decomposition from watching the world. In: IEEE Conference on Computer Vision and Pattern Recognition (CVPR), pp. 9039–9048 (2018)
30. Liu, P., Zhang, H., Zhang, K., Lin, L., Zuo, W.: Multi-level wavelet-CNN for image restoration. In: IEEE Conference on Computer Vision and Pattern Recognition (CVPR) Workshops, pp. 773–782 (2018)
31. Llanos, B., Yang, Y.H.: Simultaneous demosaicing and chromatic aberration correction through spectral reconstruction. In: IEEE Conference on Computer and Robot Vision (CRV), pp. 17–24 (2020)
32. Matsushita, Y., Nishino, K., Ikeuchi, K., Sakauchi, M.: Illumination normalization with time-dependent intrinsic images for video surveillance. Trans. Pattern Anal. Mach. Intell. 26(10), 1336–1347 (2004)
33. Murmann, L., Gharbi, M., Aittala, M., Durand, F.: A dataset of multi-illumination images in the wild. In: IEEE International Conference on Computer Vision (ICCV), pp. 4080–4089 (2019)
34. Nagano, K., et al.: Deep face normalization. ACM Trans. Graph. (TOG) 38(6), 183 (2019)
35. Nathan, D.S., Beham, M.P.: LightNet: deep learning based illumination estimation from virtual images. In: European Conference on Computer Vision Workshops (2020)
36. Ntavelis, E., et al.: AIM 2020 challenge on image extreme inpainting. In: European Conference on Computer Vision Workshops (2020)
37. Puthussery, D., P S, H., Kuriakose, M., C V., J.: WDRN: a wavelet decomposed relightnet for image relighting. In: European Conference on Computer Vision Workshops (2020)
38. Ronneberger, O., Fischer, P., Brox, T.: U-Net: convolutional networks for biomedical image segmentation. In: Navab, N., Hornegger, J., Wells, W.M., Frangi, A.F. (eds.) MICCAI 2015. LNCS, vol. 9351, pp. 234–241. Springer, Cham (2015). https://doi.org/10.1007/978-3-319-24574-4_28

39. Shen, J., Yang, X., Jia, Y., Li, X.: Intrinsic images using optimization. In: IEEE Conference on Computer Vision and Pattern Recognition (CVPR), pp. 3481–3487 (2011)
40. Shi, W., et al.: Real-time single image and video super-resolution using an efficient sub-pixel convolutional neural network. In: IEEE Conference on Computer Vision and Pattern Recognition (CVPR), pp. 1874–1883 (2016)
41. Son, S., et al.: AIM 2020 challenge on video temporal super-resolution. In: European Conference on Computer Vision Workshops (2020)
42. Sun, T., et al.: Single image portrait relighting. ACM Trans. Graph. (TOG) **38**(4), 79 (2019)
43. Tan, M., Le, Q.V.: Efficientnet: rethinking model scaling for convolutional neural networks. arXiv preprint arXiv:1905.11946 (2019)
44. Tappen, M.F., Freeman, W.T., Adelson, E.H.: Recovering intrinsic images from a single image. In: Advances in Neural Information Processing Systems, pp. 1367–1374 (2003)
45. Torralba, A., Oliva, A.: Statistics of natural image categories. Netw. Comput. Neural Syst. **14**(3), 391–412 (2003)
46. Ulyanov, D., Vedaldi, A., Lempitsky, V.: Instance normalization: the missing ingredient for fast stylization. arXiv preprint arXiv:1607.08022 (2016)
47. Wang, L.W., Siu, W.C., Liu, Z.S., Li, C.T., Lun, D.P.: Deep relighting networks for image light source manipulation. In: Proceedings of the European Conference on Computer Vision Workshops (ECCVW) (2020)
48. Wang, R., Zhang, Q., Fu, C.W., Shen, X., Zheng, W.S., Jia, J.: Underexposed photo enhancement using deep illumination estimation. In: IEEE Conference on Computer Vision and Pattern Recognition (CVPR), pp. 6849–6857 (2019)
49. Wang, Z., Bovik, A.C., Sheikh, H.R., Simoncelli, E.P.: Image quality assessment: from error visibility to structural similarity. IEEE Trans. Image Process. **13**(4), 600–612 (2004)
50. Wei, P., et al.: AIM 2020 challenge on real image super-resolution. In: European Conference on Computer Vision Workshops (2020)
51. Weiss, Y.: Deriving intrinsic images from image sequences. In: IEEE International Conference on Computer Vision (ICCV), vol. 2, pp. 68–75 (2001)
52. Woo, S., Park, J., Lee, J.Y., Kweon, I.S.: CBAM convolutional block attention module. In: Proceedings of the European Conference on Computer Vision (ECCV), pp. 1–17 (2018)
53. Xie, S., Girshick, R., Dollár, P., Tu, Z., He, K.: Aggregated residual transformations for deep neural networks. In: IEEE Conference on Computer Vision and Pattern Recognition (CVPR), pp. 1492–1500 (2017)
54. Xu, Z., Sunkavalli, K., Hadap, S., Ramamoorthi, R.: Deep image-based relighting from optimal sparse samples. ACM Trans. Graph. (TOG) **37**(4), 126 (2018)
55. Zhang, H., Goodfellow, I., Metaxas, D., Odena, A.: Self-attention generative adversarial networks. In: International Conference on Machine Learning (ICML), pp. 7354–7363 (2019)
56. Zhang, K., et al.: AIM 2020 challenge on efficient super-resolution: methods and results. In: European Conference on Computer Vision Workshops (2020)

57. Zhang, R., Isola, P., Efros, A.A., Shechtman, E., Wang, O.: The unreasonable effectiveness of deep features as a perceptual metric. In: IEEE Conference on Computer Vision and Pattern Recognition (CVPR), pp. 586–595 (2018)
58. Zhao, J., Hou, Y., Liu, Z., Xie, H., Liu, S.: Modified color CCD moiré method and its application in optical distortion correction. Precis. Eng. **65**, 279–286 (2020)
59. Zhou, H., Hadap, S., Sunkavalli, K., Jacobs, D.W.: Deep single-image portrait relighting. In: IEEE International Conference on Computer Vision (ICCV), pp. 7194–7202 (2019)

WDRN: A Wavelet Decomposed RelightNet for Image Relighting

Densen Puthussery[ID], Hrishikesh Panikkasseril Sethumadhavan[✉][ID],
Melvin Kuriakose, and Jiji Charangatt Victor[ID]

College of Engineering, Trivandrum, India
{puthusserydenson,hrishikeshps,memelvin,jijicv}@cet.ac.in

Abstract. The task of recalibrating the illumination settings in an image to a target configuration is known as relighting. Relighting techniques have potential applications in digital photography, gaming industry and in augmented reality. In this paper, we address the one-to-one relighting problem where an image at a target illumination settings is predicted given an input image with specific illumination conditions. To this end, we propose a wavelet decomposed RelightNet called WDRN which is a novel encoder-decoder network employing wavelet based decomposition followed by convolution layers under a muti-resolution framework. We also propose a novel loss function called gray loss that ensures efficient learning of gradient in illumination along different directions of the ground truth image giving rise to visually superior relit images. The proposed solution won the first position in the relighting challenge event in advances in image manipulation (AIM) 2020 workshop which proves its effectiveness measured in terms of a Mean Perceptual Score which in turn is measured using SSIM and a Learned Perceptual Image Patch Similarity score.

Keywords: Gray loss · Illumination · Relighting · Wavelet

1 Introduction

par The task of recalibrating the illumination settings of an acquired image is widely known as image relighting. Relighting is an emerging technology owing to its applications in augmented reality (AR) and also in casual digital photography. Relighting enabled AR can bring about great changes in the way one perceives digital experiences like online shopping, online teaching, etc. For example, one may wish to visualize whether furniture to be purchased online is suitable for the room. Since the ambient lighting conditions like the direction of illumination, brightness, color temperature etc. may vary from user to user, adaptability to the same is required in the AR visualization tool. Such adaptability can be realized by integrating relighting techniques in the online platform using the AR tool. In

D. Puthussery and P.S. Hrishikesh—Equal contribution.

A. Bartoli and A. Fusiello (Eds.): ECCV 2020 Workshops, LNCS 12537, pp. 519–534, 2020.
https://doi.org/10.1007/978-3-030-67070-2_31

first and third person gaming, the ambient lighting of a scene is highly dynamic and changes with time of the day, viewpoint of the avatar etc. There is a scope for using relighting techniques to quickly render the scene graphics to drive the gameplay with higher number of frames per second. Figure 1 shows a simple case of relighting where the appearance of the scene is changed drastically when the illuminant is positioned at different azimuthal angles.

    (a) South-West   (b) West   (c) North   (d) East

Fig. 1. An example of scene relighting for a change in illuminant position. It can be observed that the shadows caste in a, b, c and d are quite different from each other owing to the different relative position of objects and illuminant in each case. Also, the gradient in brightness is different in each case since the region in the scene proximal to the light source is different.

In digital photography, relighting techniques are used to enhance the perceptual quality of an image. In natural images of outdoor scenes, it is often difficult to control the illumination. Diverse factors affect natural illuminance like time of the day, weather, clouds, objects in the vicinity etc. Due to these and other factors, it is common that outdoor images are poorly lit. Many modern cameras offer the flexibility to control the image lighting by adjusting the shutter speed, aperture, ISO sensitivity etc. However, such tweaks usually require professional expertise and are prone to degradation like blur, grains etc.

The outdoor images usually have uniform illumination in daytime as sunlight is far-field and heavily scattered. However, indoor images usually have a non-uniform illumination as the objects close to the light source are considerably lit in contrast to the ones far away. The location, directionality and properties of illuminant dictate the appearance of natural indoor images. The formation of shadows and general gradient of illumination are controlled by the location of illuminants in the room.

Additionally, the nature of object shadow like its size, position etc. varies with the location of the light source. Similarly, the illumination pattern produced by a directional source is quite different from that of an omni-directional light source. Besides, the properties of illuminant like its color temperature, spectral power distribution etc. affect the visual quality of an indoor image. The above factors hold true even for outdoor images when natural lighting is not present. Although indoor photography is flexible, as we have a control on these factors, it is only feasible on a professional scale, like in a digital studio. In a home environment and in casual photography, the location and type of illuminant are mostly fixed and there is little control on these aspects. Relighting finds its applications in areas like these where one would like to change the illumination setting of an image without putting much physical effort or using specialized tools.

Another area of image manipulation which necessitates relighting is digital image montaging. In image montaging, a certain portion of an image is replaced with a crop taken from a different image. Multiple images can also be fused in a similar manner to generate a montage. For seamless and visually appealing results in a montage, the illumination in images being combined must be same. Since the images used for montaging are usually unrelated, their illumination setting could be different. In this scenario, relighting techniques can be employed to translate the images into the final illumination setting and then apply montaging for superior results.

In this work, we address a special case of the relighting problem where we describe the solution we proposed as part of the challenge event on one-to-one relighting in Advances in Image Manipulation (AIM) 2020 workshop [6]. The task of the challenge was to develop a solution that recalibrates the illumination setting of an input scene to a given target setting. To this end, a deep convolutional neural network (CNN) that efficiently learns the illumination setting of the target domain is proposed. The contributions of the proposed work are:

- A wavelet decomposed encoder-decoder network to solve the relighting problem that can effectively translate an image from a source illumination setting to a target setting.
- A novel training loss term called gray loss that drives the network to learn the illumination gradient in target domain images.
- Introduced pixel shuffler operations in wavelet based encoder-decoder network for fast training and inference.

Rest of the paper is organized as follows: In Sect. 2 we review related works and in Sect. 3 we describe the proposed methodology. Section 4 details our experiments, Sect. 5 presents our result analysis and in Sect. 6 we describe our ablation studies. Finally, Sect. 7 concludes the work.

2 Related Work

Here we first review the image enhancement techniques, both using conventional and deep learning approaches where the enhanced image is obtained through some form of illumination adjustment. Further, we discuss some of the recently proposed relighting techniques using deep networks.

2.1 Image Enhancement

Conventional Methods. Smartphones and casual photography using these devices have brought an increased demand for methods based on various image manipulation techniques like photo enhancement. Image enhancement is one of the fundamental problems in the field of computer vision starting with methods like histogram equalisation for contrast enhancement. Retinex theory of color vision [10] by Edwin H Land inspired many methods like [7,19] that considers images as the pixel-wise product of reflectance and illumination. These works treat image enhancement problem as an illumination estimation problem, where the illumination component is used to enhance the input images. These works were only able to generate very inferior results because of the high non-linearity across the channels and the spatial sensitivity of colour in the image.

Deep Learning Based Methods. Most of the recent works on photo enhancement is learning based and the first dataset used for the purpose was MIT-Adobe FiveK [1] introduced by Bychkovsky *et al.* The dataset contains five sets of 5000 input-output pairs. Each set is a retouched (using Adobe Lightroom) version of the same input image by different professionals. The work was used to address general tone adjustment rather than enhancing an underexposed image.

Lore *et al.* [12] proposed an auto-encoder architecture for denoising and brightening the low-light images. Many Generative Adversarial Network (GAN) based networks were also developed for image enhancement. Chen *et al.* [2] proposed a method that uses a two-way GAN architecture. The network transforms the input image to an enhanced image with characteristics of a reference image. Ignatov *et al.* [8], proposed weakly supervised (no exact image pair) GAN based network that enhances images that are taken using mobile phones to DSLR quality images. The network used DPED dataset [9] along with many other unpaired HD images.

Wang proposed a learning based method [16] that enhanced under exposed images using end-to-end CNN based model. The network used an encoder-decoder architecture, where the encoder was used to extract the local features like contrast, detail sharpness, shadow, highlight etc. and global features such as color distribution, average brightness and scene category. For driving the network to learn illumination mapping from under-exposed to the enhanced images, they use three loss functions, smoothness loss on the illumination and color and reconstruction loss on the enhanced image. The network was trained on a novel dataset with 3000 under-exposed images and its ground truth.

2.2   Image Relighting

Most of the above mentioned methods cannot remove or change the illumination setting of an input image; it can only modify the effects of the existing illumination. When it comes to image relighting rather than the overall enhancement, the work focuses on predicting a target illumination setting (light direction and colour temperature) from an input with a different illumination setting.

One-to-one relighting can be considered as a special case of image relighting, where the task is to manipulate an input image that was captured under certain illumination settings (light source position, direction and color temperature) to make it look like it was taken under different settings.

Debevec *et al.* proposed a technique [3] for rendering the human face images from varying viewpoints and direction of illumination, similar to the problem addressed in our work. Here, they collected images of human face from different viewpoints under diverse direction of illumination. A reflectance function of the skin was modeled to estimate the image when the target viewpoint is different from the input. Their network was able to give considerable performance but it required hundreds of images with the stationary subject under a controlled illumination setting. Hence, they were unable to provide a solution for single RGB image for an unknown object in an unconstrained environment as in one-to-one relighting problem.

Xu *et al.* proposed a CNN based method [18] to relight a scene under a new illumination based on five images captured under pre-defined illumination setting. Unlike exploiting similarity in a single light transport function as in [3] they try to estimate a non-linear function that generalises the estimation of the above mentioned problem using deep learning based training. Along with three channels (RGB) of the five fused images, they also add two extra channels along with the image, which are 2D coordinates of the light source direction. This method still requires five sparse samples of the same scene in order to predict the scene from a novel light setting.

Indirectly addressing this problem, Sun *et al.* proposed a CNN based approach [15] to relight portrait images that were taken on mobile cameras into user defined illumination setting. They also used a encoder-decoder architecture where the input illumination is predicted and the required illumination of the target is injected at the bottleneck layer between the encoder and the decoder. The work was able to develop a function that can predict diverse illumination but their work was limited to portrait images of human faces.

The proposed method uses wavelet based end-to-end CNN architecture inspired from Multi-level Wavelet-CNN (MWCNN) [11] by Liu *et al.* to learn a mapping function that relights a scene without modeling for the geometry or the reflectance. MWCNN is a fully convolutional encoder-decoder network that was proposed as a general methodology for image restoration. The winners of NTIRE 2020 Challenge on image demoireing [20] used a method inspired from MWCNN which shows its competence. In this work, to relight an input image to a given target illumination settings, we propose a deep convolutional network using wavelet decomposition followed by convolution layers at various scales utilizing novel loss functions.

3   Proposed Method

3.1   Problem Formulation

Under the assumption of a distant illumination source, the scene to be relit under a target direction can be formulated from the light transport function $\lambda(i, \theta)$ and the incident source illuminations from direction θ as:

$$Y_i = \int \lambda(i, \theta) I(\theta) d\theta \qquad (1)$$

where $I(\theta)$ is the radiance of the incident illumination from direction θ and i is the target image pixel. In a fundamental relighting problem, given multiple images of the scene acquired under varying θ, $\lambda(i, \theta)$ can be estimated and then image corresponding to a new value of θ can be rendered [18].

The problem that we discuss in this paper is slightly different, where we describe the solution proposed as part of the one-to-one relighting challenge at Advances in Image Manipulation (AIM) 2020 workshop [6]. The task of the challenge was to develop a solution that recalibrates the illumination setting of an input scene to a target setting. The illumination setting in the challenge refers to two aspects - position and color temperature of the light source. Thus for the given problem, the input image is characterized by a fixed light source direction θ_1 and a fixed color temperature T_1 while the target image is characterized by a different direction θ_2 and color temperature T_2. We employ a deep convolutional neural network (CNN) to learn the complex function $F(\theta_1, \theta_2, T_1, T_2)$ which can render the given scene into the new settings θ_2, T_2.

3.2   Proposed Wavelet Decomposed RelightNet (WDRN)

Overview. The proposed method uses a multi-level encoder-decoder based network that processes the image at different spatial resolutions. The encoder section is used to extract the local features like contrast, sharpness, shadow and global features such as color distribution, brightness, and semantic information. The encoder learns the illumination mapping of the input based on the extracted features. The decoder reconstructs the relit images from the encoder output by progressively upsampling the feature maps to the resolution of the target image.

Also, feature information from the encoder level is forwarded into the decoder level that operates at the same spatial resolution. The information in the decoder is the image context and the forwarded information is the local and global features. By fusing local and contextual information, the target illumination setting is injected into the input image within the decoder. The detailed description of the encoder and decoder sub-net is given in the following sub-sections.

The network is termed Wavelet Decomposed RelightNet (WDRN) because it employs wavelet decomposition to process the image at different scales within the encoder-decoder architecture. WDRN is inspired by the work of multi-level wavelet CNN (MWCNN) for image restoration proposed by Liu *et al.* [11]. The ability of wavelet transform to obtain a large receptive field without information loss or gridding effect was shown in their work. Figure 2 depicts the proposed WDRN architecture for relighting.

Encoder Sub-net. The eage has a fixed illuminati ncoder sub-net operates at three different image scales or spatial resolutions and hence is a multi-level network. In each level, the input feature map is decomposed into four sub-bands using discrete wavelet transform (DWT) based subsampling followed by a convolution block for feature extraction. Here, 2D Haar wavelet has been used for decomposing the input to its sub-bands since it is the simplest of its kind. Other

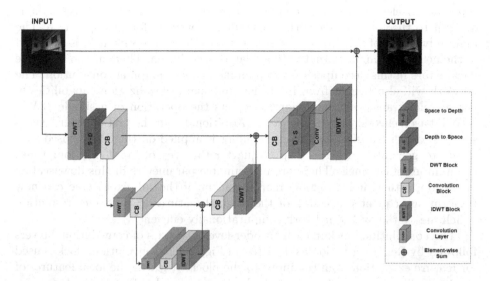

Fig. 2. The proposed WDRN architecture. There are 3 different processing levels in the network. The subsampling and interpolation are done using DWT and IDWT respectively. The operation of a simple DWT-IDWT based encoder-decoder network is depicted in Fig. 3. Convolution blocks are used for feature extraction at each level and the block is expanded in Fig. 4

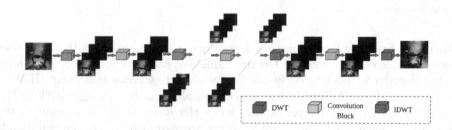

Fig. 3. The operation of a simple DWT-IDWT based encoder-decoder network. Here the input is subsampled and divided into 4 sub-bands and these sub-bands are further processed using convolution block. The same step is repeated in the subsequent levels of the encoder. In the decoder, based on these feature maps information the relit image is reconstructed into required spatial resolution.

Fig. 4. Convolution block contains a series of convolutions and ReLU activations that are stacked in sequence. The number of these conv-ReLU blocks varies in different encoder and decoder levels.

types of wavelets can also be employed here on a trial and error basis as it is difficult to theoretically prove the most suitable wavelet for this operation. The main advantage of this processing step is that a high receptive field is obtained in the network, similar to that with a dilated convolution. There are no trainable parameters in this decomposition step unlike in a subsampling convolution. The network will also benefit from frequency and spatial localization capabilities of the wavelet transformation. Figure 3 depicts the operation of a simple DWT-IDWT based encoder-decoder network. Additionally, in the first encoder level, a space-to-depth transform with pixel shuffler is applied on the decomposed subbands to generate a feature map of quarter the area of input and four times the number of channels. There are no trainable parameters in this downscaling operation, rather, it is a simple rearrangement of the subpixels. One can now perform subsequent processing of the original features at a smaller resolution which makes the overall network computationally efficient.

The convolution block in each encoder level is a series of convolutional layers followed by ReLU activation as depicted in Fig. 4. The convolution block is used for feature extraction from the input to the block. It learns the local features of the image like contrast, sharpness, shadow etc. and global features such as color distribution, brightness, and semantic information. The number of convolutional layers and filters are different for each level of the encoder. In level one, there are four convolution layer with 16 filters in each layer. Similarly, in level two there are four convolution layers with 6 filters. In level three there are seven convolution layers each with 256 filters. In the contraction path of the encoder, the filter size is progressively increased to obtain a rich representation of lower scale features.

Decoder Sub-net. Similar to the encoder, the expansion path sub-net or decoder is also multi-level and has three different scales of operation. Each level in the decoder is constituted by an inverse discrete wavelet transform (IDWT) based interpolation followed by a convolution block for feature aggregation. The feature output of third level of encoder is the input to the first level in the decoder. In each level, the input features are assumed to be four sub-bands of a wavelet decomposition. With this assumption, the IDWT is computed on the input feature set to interpolate the features to twice their spatial resolution and a quarter of the total input channels. The features in the expansion path represent the contextual information of the image. Since the local and global features are present in different encoder level outputs, these features can be carried forward to the decoder. This is achieved by directly adding the interpolated decoder features with the encoder level outputs with the same spatial resolution in an element-wise manner. This output feature set is then processed through a convolutional block to gradually inject the target domain illumination setting.

Similar to encoder, the convolution block in a decoder level is constituted by convolutional layers followed by ReLU activations. Convolution block in Level one of the decoder has four convolution layers of 64 filters each. In level two, there are four convolution layers of 16 filters each. At the output of the second level, a depth-to-space transform with pixel shuffler is employed which serves as the inverse operation of space-to-depth at the input. The third level is constituted only of a single IDWT operation. The last IDWT interpolation generates a three channel feature map which is added to the input image to generate the relit image of target illumination settings. As the last IDWT operation should produce a 3-channel image, the total number of channels at the input of level three IDWT should be 12. Since the output of depth-to-space transform has 16 channels, a convolution layer with 12 filters is placed after it to adjust the depth in subsequent layers.

In general, for efficient illumination recalibration, the network should be able to establish the relationship between distant pixels. This can be realised by using highly dilated convolutions. But for large dilation factors, two adjacent pixels in the predicted feature map are calculated from the completely non-overlapping input feature set and hence leads to spatial information leakage and poor localization in the encoder levels. The proposed WDRN can achieve a high receptive field without this information loss. Moreover, in contrast with MWCNN, the training losses used in WDRN is tailored for the relighting problem. The details of the novel gray loss that we propose for perceptually superior results in relight problem and other losses that we used are detailed in the next section.

3.3 Loss Functions

Network is trained based on three empirically weighted loss functions as shown in Eq. 2.

$$L_{total} = \alpha L_{MAE} + \beta L_{SSIM} + \gamma L_{gray} \tag{2}$$

The MAE loss is the mean absolute error or the L_1 distance between the ground-truth and the predicted images. It is incorporated to generate high fidelity relit images. Mean squared error (MSE) loss was avoided because of the smoothening effect it introduced in our generated images. The MAE is given by:

$$L_{MAE} = \frac{1}{W \times H \times C} \sum_{i=0}^{W-1} \sum_{j=0}^{H-1} \sum_{k=0}^{C-1} \left| Y_{i,j,k} - \hat{Y}_{i,j,k} \right| \tag{3}$$

where, W, H and C are the width, height and number of channels of the output, Y is the ground truth image and $\hat{Y}$ is the predicted image. The structural similarity (SSIM) [17] between two images is a measure of their perceptual difference as SSIM incorporates contrast and luminance masking. A high dynamic range can reveal more details in both poorly and heavily lit regions in an image. Optimising for SSIM loss helps the network to render visually appealing images with better dynamic range. SSIM loss is formulated as:

$$L_{SSIM} = 1 - SSIM(Y, \hat{Y}) \tag{4}$$

Gray Loss. In relighting problems where the objective is to change the general direction of lighting, the network should be able to recalibrate the gradients in illumination within the image. The objects closer to the target illuminant position should be heavily lit while the ones far away should be poorly lit. The MAE loss and SSIM loss can optimize for the general texture of the image, but not the gradients in illumination. Hence the enhancements like shadow recasting are poorly learned. A novel loss term called gray loss is hence proposed that can overcome these limitations. The proposed gray loss is the L_1 distance between blurred versions of the grayscale components of the relit and ground truth images. The texture details are smoothened out when the images are blurred, leaving behind the illumination information. Since much details are not present in the blurred image, this information is constituted by the general direction of illumination gradients. Thus gray loss ensures that the gradient in illumination along different directions of the ground truth image is learned by the network and generate visually superior results. Gray loss is formulated as:

$$L_{gray} = \frac{1}{W \times H} \sum_{i=0}^{W-1} \sum_{j=0}^{H-1} \left| (\psi(Y))_{i,j} - (\psi(\hat{Y}))_{i,j} \right| \tag{5}$$

where $\psi(.)$ is the Gaussian blur function used to smoothen the images.

4   Experiments

4.1   Dataset

The dataset used in the experiments is the Virtual Image Dataset for Illumination Transfer (VIDIT) [5]. The dataset contains 390 different scenes which is captured at 40 different illumination settings (8 azimuthal angles and five different colour temperatures 2500K, 4500K etc.) with a total of 15,600 images. We participated in track 1 - one-to-one relighting in AIM 2020 challenge for Scene Relighting and Illumination Estimation. For the experiments as part of the challenge, we used 390 image pairs from the dataset, where the input image has a fixed illumination setting $\theta_1 =$ North, $T_1 = 6500$K and the target is set at a different illumination setting $\theta_2 =$ East, $T_2 = 4500$K. All the training images are of fixed size $1024 \times 1024 \times 3$. Out of the 390 image pairs, 300 image pairs were used for training, 45 for validation and 45 for testing.

4.2   Training

The network was trained on mini-batches of size 10. The model was trained for 150 epochs and employed Adam optimiser with $\beta_1 = 0.9$ and $\beta_2 = 0.99$. The initial learning rate was $1e^{-4}$ which was then decayed by a factor of 0.5 after every 100 epochs. The training was done on $1\times$ Tesla P100 GPU card with 16 GiB memory. The proposed network has 6.4 million trainable parameters. Training process took 2 h and testing time per image was 0.03 s. The various training accuracy and loss plots are shown in Fig. 5. It can be inferred from the accuracy plot that the network overfits at around 60 epochs.

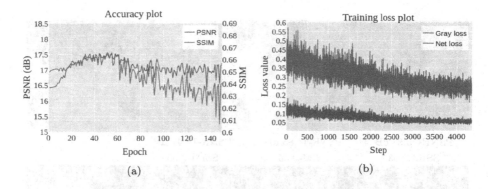

Fig. 5. Plots for (a) Accuracy (b) Training losses

4.3 Evaluation Metrics

In addition to the standard evaluation metrics like peak signal to noise ratio (PSNR) and SSIM, the performance of the proposed WDRN is evaluated using rather new perceptual metrics like Learned Perceptual Image Patch Similarity (LPIPS) [21] and mean perceptual score (MPS). Mean Perceptual Score (MPS) [6] is the average of the normalized SSIM [17] and LPIPS score as shown in Eq. 6

$$MPS = 0.5(S + (1 - L)) \tag{6}$$

where S is the average SSIM score on the test set, and L is the average LPIPS score on the test set.

5 Result Analysis

Figure 6 shows relit examples corresponding to four input images from VIDIT validation set for one-to-one relighting problem using the proposed WDRN trained with and without gray loss. For certain cases, the input images have better PSNR and/or SSIM than the relit images although the latter is perceptually closer to the ground truth. As evident from the figure, the position of the illuminant θ_2 and the color temperature T_2 of the target image is predicted with considerable visual similarity with the WDRN architecture. However, WDRN failed to inpaint information in the shadows that should have been uncovered with the change in illuminant position. Similarly, WDRN failed to recast the shadows in the target domain image. These two issues can be assumed to be the biggest challenges in relighting problem. Although WDRN trained with and without gray loss have comparable performance in terms of quantitative metrics, they differ to a certain extent visually. While WDRN with gray loss inpainted some information in shadowy areas in rows 1 and 4 of the figure, WDRN without gray loss failed to do so. Similarly, WDRN without gray loss inpainted information in unwanted regions in rows 2 and 4 of the figure, thereby having an incorrect representation of the target domain image.

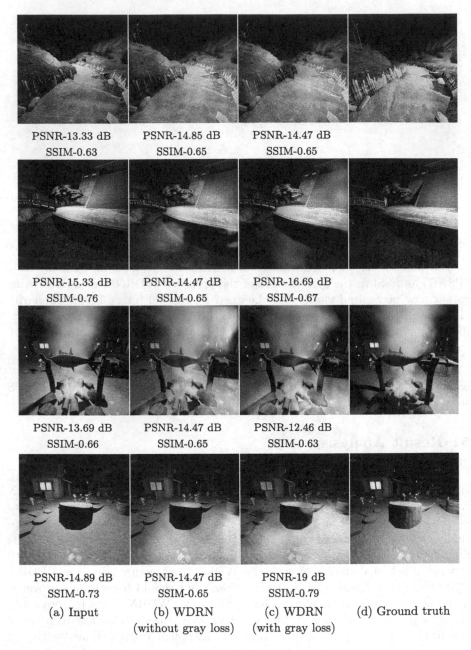

PSNR-13.33 dB PSNR-14.85 dB PSNR-14.47 dB
SSIM-0.63   SSIM-0.65   SSIM-0.65

PSNR-15.33 dB PSNR-14.47 dB PSNR-16.69 dB
SSIM-0.76   SSIM-0.65   SSIM-0.67

PSNR-13.69 dB PSNR-14.47 dB PSNR-12.46 dB
SSIM-0.66   SSIM-0.65   SSIM-0.63

PSNR-14.89 dB PSNR-14.47 dB PSNR-19 dB
SSIM-0.73   SSIM-0.65   SSIM-0.79

(a) Input   (b) WDRN   (c) WDRN   (d) Ground truth
               (without gray loss) (with gray loss)

Fig. 6. Sample results with the proposed method on the validation set of VIDIT. From the visual inspection of Fig. a, b, c and d, it is evident that the proposed WDRN architecture is able to capture the colour temperature of the target domain to a large extent. Although WDRN trained with and without gray loss have comparable performance in terms of quantitative metrics, the former has superior visual quality.

Table 1. Performance comparison of WDRN with competing entries in scene relighting and illumination estimation challenge, track-1 one-to-one relighting at AIM 2020 workshop. The MPS, used to determine the final ranking, is computed following Eq. (6).

Team	MPS	SSIM	LPIPS	PSNR	Run-time
Our method (with gray loss)	**0.6452** (1)	**0.6310** (2)	**0.3405** (1)	**17.0717** (2)	**0.03 s**
Our method (without gray loss)	**0.6451** (2)	**0.6362** (1)	**0.3460** (3)	**16.8927** (6)	**0.03 s**
Team 2	0.6436 (3)	0.6301 (3)	0.3430 (2)	16.6801 (8)	13 s
Team 3	0.6216 (4)	0.6091 (4)	0.3659 (5)	16.8196 (7)	6 s
Team 4	0.5897 (5)	0.5298 (7)	0.3505 (4)	17.0594 (3)	0.04 s
Team 5	0.5892 (6)	0.5928 (6)	0.4144 (7)	17.4252 (1)	0.5 s
Team 6	0.5603 (7)	0.5236 (8)	0.4029 (6)	16.5136 (9)	0.01 s
Team 7	0.5339 (8)	0.5666 (6)	0.4989 (8)	16.9234 (4)	0.006 s
Team 8	0.3746 (9)	0.3769 (9)	0.6278 (9)	16.8949 (5)	0.12 s

Table 1 shows the performance comparison of the proposed WDRN with other competing entries in one-to-one relighting challenge of AIM 2020 workshop. We proposed two variants of WDRN in the competition - one trained with gray loss and the other without it. Both variants were able to achieve better MPS than other methodologies. While the method with gray loss obtained the highest MPS of 0.6452, the one without it obtained highest score in SSIM and 2nd second highest MPS score of 0.6451. Organizers merged both the methods as the architecture followed was same even though the loss functions used were different. Additionally, owing to the network lightness, runtime of WDRN is considerably lower than the immediate runner-ups.

As future work, the proposed WDRN network can be modified to address the related problems like any-to-any relighting, under-exposure correction etc. In any-to-any relighting, WDRN may be modified to feature an additional encoder to which a guide image from the target domain can be given as an additional input and the illumination properties of the guide image can be injected into the input image in the encoder section itself. Another way to realise this is to modify WDRN to have additional scalar inputs corresponding to the target illumination settings and integrate them into encoder in a manner demonstrated in [18].

6   Ablation Studies

6.1   Wavelet Domain Network

To find out the effectiveness of wavelet decomposition approach, an ablation study was conducted using a 3-level encoder-decoder network. In the equivalent pixel domain network, wavelet decomposition was replaced with convolutional downsampling with a stride of two. Similarly, wavelet interpolation has been replaced with transposed convolution with an upscale factor of two. The results of the experiment on validation set of VIDIT is reported in Table 2. It is conclusive that wavelet domain network obtained superior performance in terms of all evaluation metrics of the experiment which proves its effectiveness.

Table 2. Ablation study of wavelet domain network

Domain	MPS	SSIM	LPIPS	PSNR
Pixel	0.6918	0.6619	0.2783	17.3934
Wavelet	**0.6935**	**0.6642**	**0.2771**	**17.4539**

6.2   Wavelet Decomposition Levels

To investigate the effect of various levels of wavelet decomposition, an extensive ablation study have been carried out. Experiments were conducted with two, three and four levels of wavelet decomposition in the encoder-decoder architecture. The model training was limited to 60 iterations to avoid the risk of overfitting. Table 3 shows the comparison of the performance obtained with different decomposition levels on the validation set of VIDIT dataset. Notably, the 3-level decomposed network shows superior performance in terms of perceptual metrics like SSIM and LPIPS while the 4-level network achieves highest PSNR.

Table 3. Ablation study of wavelet decomposition levels

Decomposition level	MPS	SSIM	LPIPS	PSNR
2 level	0.6842	0.6486	0.28	17.0962
3 level	**0.6935**	**0.6642**	**0.2771**	17.4539
4 level	0.6908	0.661	0.2792	**17.5586**

7   Conclusions

In this paper we proposed a novel multi-resolution encoder-decoder network employing wavelet based decomposition called wavelet decomposed RelightNet to address one-to-one image relighting problem. Additionally, a novel gray loss term tailored for the problem resulted in visually superior relit images. The experimental results have proved the effectiveness of the proposed WDRN both qualitatively and in terms of various quantitative parameters. The proposed WDRN can be modified to address other related problems like any-to-any relighting, under-exposure correction etc.

Acknowledgements. We gratefully acknowledge the support of NVIDIA PSG Cluster and Trivandrum Engineering Science and Technology Research Park (TrEST) in providing the computational resource to conduct this research.

References

1. Bychkovsky, V., Paris, S., Chan, E., Durand, F.: Learning photographic global tonal adjustment with a database of input/output image pairs. In: CVPR 2011, pp. 97–104 (2011)
2. Chen, Y., Wang, Y., Kao, M., Chuang, Y.: Deep photo enhancer: unpaired learning for image enhancement from photographs with GANs. In: 2018 IEEE/CVF Conference on Computer Vision and Pattern Recognition, pp. 6306–6314 (2018)
3. Debevec, P., Hawkins, T., Tchou, C., Duiker, H.P., Sarokin, W., Sagar, M.: Acquiring the reflectance field of a human face. In: Proceedings of the 27th Annual Conference on Computer Graphics and Interactive Techniques, SIGGRAPH 2000, pp. 145–156. ACM Press/Addison-Wesley Publishing Co., USA (2000). https://doi.org/10.1145/344779.344855
4. Dherse, A.P., Everaert, M.N., Gwizdała, J.J.: Scene relighting with illumination estimation in the latent space on an encoder-decoder scheme (2020)
5. El Helou, M., Zhou, R., Barthas, J., Süsstrunk, S.: VIDIT: virtual image dataset for illumination transfer. arXiv preprint arXiv:2005.05460 (2020)
6. El Helou, M., Zhou, R., Süsstrunk, S., Timofte, R., et al.: AIM 2020: Scene relighting and illumination estimation challenge. In: Bartoli, A., Fusiello, A. (eds.) ECCV 2020 Workshops. LNCS, vol. 12537, pp. 499–518 (2020)
7. Guo, X., Li, Y., Ling, H.: LIME: low-light image enhancement via illumination map estimation. IEEE Trans. Image Process. 26(2), 982–993 (2017)
8. Ignatov, A., Kobyshev, N., Timofte, R., Vanhoey, K., Gool, L.V.: WESPE: weakly supervised photo enhancer for digital cameras. CoRR abs/1709.01118 (2017). http://arxiv.org/abs/1709.01118
9. Ignatov, A., Kobyshev, N., Vanhoey, K., Timofte, R., Gool, L.V.: DSLR-quality photos on mobile devices with deep convolutional networks. CoRR abs/1704.02470 (2017). http://arxiv.org/abs/1704.02470
10. Land, E.H.: The retinex. Am. Sci. 52(2), 247–264 (1964)
11. Liu, P., Zhang, H., Zhang, K., Lin, L., Zuo, W.: Multi-level wavelet-CNN for image restoration. CoRR abs/1805.07071 (2018). http://arxiv.org/abs/1805.07071
12. Lore, K.G., Akintayo, A., Sarkar, S.: LLNet: a deep autoencoder approach to natural low-light image enhancement. CoRR abs/1511.03995 (2015). http://arxiv.org/abs/1511.03995
13. Matusik, W., Loper, M., Pfister, H.: Progressively-refined reflectance functions from natural illumination. In: Rendering Techniques (2004)
14. Reddy, D., Ramamoorthi, R., Curless, B.: Frequency-space decomposition and acquisition of light transport under spatially varying illumination. In: Fitzgibbon, A., Lazebnik, S., Perona, P., Sato, Y., Schmid, C. (eds.) ECCV 2012. LNCS, vol. 7577, pp. 596–610. Springer, Heidelberg (2012). https://doi.org/10.1007/978-3-642-33783-3_43
15. Sun, T., et al.: Single image portrait relighting. CoRR abs/1905.00824 (2019). http://arxiv.org/abs/1905.00824
16. Wang, R., Zhang, Q., Fu, C., Shen, X., Zheng, W., Jia, J.: Underexposed photo enhancement using deep illumination estimation. In: 2019 IEEE/CVF Conference on Computer Vision and Pattern Recognition (CVPR), pp. 6842–6850 (2019)
17. Wang, Z., Bovik, A.C., Sheikh, H.R., Simoncelli, E.P.: Image quality assessment: from error visibility to structural similarity. IEEE TIP 13(4), 600–612 (2004)
18. Xu, Z., Sunkavalli, K., Hadap, S., Ramamoorthi, R.: Deep image-based relighting from optimal sparse samples. ACM Trans. Graph. 37(4) (2018). https://doi.org/10.1145/3197517.3201313

19. Ying, Z., Li, G., Ren, Y., Wang, R., Wang, W.: A new low-light image enhancement algorithm using camera response model. In: 2017 IEEE International Conference on Computer Vision Workshops (ICCVW), pp. 3015–3022 (2017)
20. Yuan, S., Timofte, R., Leonardis, A., Slabaugh, G.: NTIRE 2020 challenge on image demoireing: methods and results. In: Proceedings of the IEEE/CVF Conference on Computer Vision and Pattern Recognition (CVPR) Workshops, June 2020
21. Zhang, R., Isola, P., Efros, A.A., Shechtman, E., Wang, O.: The unreasonable effectiveness of deep features as a perceptual metric. In: CVPR, pp. 586–595 (2018)

SA-AE for Any-to-Any Relighting

Zhongyun Hu[ID], Xin Huang[ID], Yaning Li[ID], and Qing Wang[(✉)][ID]

School of Computer Science, Northwestern Polytechnical University,
Xi'an 710072, China
{zy_h,hx0817,liyn}@mail.nwpu.edu.cn,qwang@nwpu.edu.cn

Abstract. In this paper, we present a novel automatic model Self-Attention AutoEncoder (SA-AE) for generating a relit image from a source image to match the illumination setting of a guide image, which is called any-to-any relighting. In order to reduce the difficulty of learning, we adopt an implicit scene representation learned by the encoder to render the relit image using the decoder. Based on the learned scene representation, a lighting estimation network is designed as a classification task to predict the illumination settings from the guide images. Also, a lighting-to-feature network is well designed to recover the corresponding implicit scene representation from the illumination settings, which is the inverse process of the lighting estimation network. In addition, a self-attention mechanism is introduced in the autoencoder to focus on the re-rendering of the relighting-related regions in the source images. Extensive experiments on the VIDIT dataset show that the proposed approach achieved the 1st place in terms of MPS and the 1st place in terms of SSIM in the AIM 2020 Any-to-any Relighting Challenge.

Keywords: Any-to-any relighting · Lighting estimation ·
Deep learning · Autoencoder · Self-attention mechanism

1 Introduction

The goal of this paper is to re-render a source image with a certain illumination setting to match the illumination setting of another guide image. As shown in Fig. 1, the input is a source image of a complex scene and a guide image under a novel lighting, and the output is a relit image of the complex scene under the novel lighting (Fig. 1c). Figure 1d is a relit image generated by the proposed approach. This task is important for a range of applications in augmented reality, visual effects, and production visualization. For example, any-to-any relighting can be used to enhance the underexposed images using an adequate and suitable lighting.

In the past few years, physically-based relighting methods [11,15,17,21] are proposed to explicitly estimate the geometry, reflectance, and lighting of the scene and then re-render this scene using the novel illumination setting. However, this is an ill-posed problem: these scene factors interact in complex ways to form images and multiple combinations of these factors may produce the same image

© Springer Nature Switzerland AG 2020
A. Bartoli and A. Fusiello (Eds.): ECCV 2020 Workshops, LNCS 12537, pp. 535–549, 2020.
https://doi.org/10.1007/978-3-030-67070-2_32

Source image   Guide image   Ground-truth   Relit image

Fig. 1. An example of any-to-any relighting. In the upper left corner of the guide image, the red arrow and number indicate the direction and color temperature of the light source, respectively. (Color figure online)

[13]. Thus, such approaches have often focused on restricted settings—objects from a specific class (i.e. faces and human bodies). But they are still limited to what is expressible by their estimated physical model, such as a micro-facet SVBRDF model and spherical Gaussian lighting.

In contrast, some other recent approaches [22,24,29] do not have any explicit inverse rendering step for estimating scene properties. Instead, they trained a single neural network to directly render relit images from an implicit scene representation in the latent space. For example, Zhou et al. [29] proposed an hourglass network to capture and consolidate information across all scales of the image for the portrait relighting task. But for any-to-any relighting, the key is how to recast and remove the shadow with a target lighting. Except for the lighting color temperature, most regions of the source image do not need shadow recasting or removal.

In this paper, we propose a self-attention module based autoencoder for any-to-any relighting. Armed with the self-attention module, the relighting-related regions will be carefully distinguished by the autoencoder. Inspired by [22,24,29], in order to reduce the difficulty of learning, we adopt an implicit scene representation learned by the encoder to render the relit images using the decoder. Considering the fact that regressing the exact values is more difficult than the classification, a lighting estimation network is designed as a classification task to predict the lighting settings from the implicit scene representation. Also, a lighting-to-feature network is well designed to recover the corresponding implicit scene representation. In addition, a resize-conv is utilized to replace the transposed-conv to avoid the checkerboard artifacts.

The main contributions of this paper are summarized as follows:

1) We propose a novel automatic model SA-AE for generating a relit image from a source image and a guide image, which is called any-to-any relighting [7]. In addition, a self-attention mechanism is introduced in the autoencoder to focus on the re-rendering of the relighting-related regions in the source images.
2) We tested our proposed method on the VIDIT dataset [7]. Extensive experiments show that the proposed method can achieve the highest MPS (based on the SSIM, LPIPS scores) in the AIM 2020 Any-to-any Relighting Challenge [8].

2   Related Work

Any-to-any relighting can be seen as a special case of image-based relighting, and also relates to inverse rendering.

2.1   Image-Based Relighting

Debevec et al. [6] proposed to relight the scene by densely sampling the light transport function using thousands of images. Furthermore, the coherence of the light transport function [16,19,20] is utilized to relight the scene using fewer samples. However, these approaches still require hundreds of images, and this acquisition process is very time-consuming. In addition, special acquisition systems need to be designed to simulate the desired illumination. Driven by the success of deep learning, Xu et al. [24] used a non-linear CNN-based representation that exploits correlations in light transport across scenes to relight the scene with only five images. But Sun et al. [22] and Zhou et al. [29] argued that the utility is usually limited due to requirements of multiple images of the scene under controlled or known illuminations, two deep neural networks with similar structure are proposed to relight the face using a single RGB image of a portrait taken in an unconstrained environment. Different from the face with the symmetric structure or single objects of a specific class, the VIDIT dataset [7] contains complex indoor and outdoor scenes. Besides, not all regions of the image are equally important in contributing to the relighting, only the task-related regions are of concern. In this paper, an attention mechanism is introduced to make the network focus on the relighting-related regions.

2.2   Inverse Rendering

Inverse rendering is to estimate the illumination, reflectance properties, and geometry from observed appearance (i.e. one or more images). Once these scene properties are all estimated, relighting can be viewed as a natural extension of inverse rendering, which is performed by the physically based rendering (PBR) pipeline. Traditional inverse rendering [1–4] is usually to jointly optimize the scene properties to achieve the set of values that best explain the observed image. For example, Barron et al. [4] used a complex combination of generic priors to recover shape, albedo, and illumination in an optimization-based framework. In the past few years, researchers have concentrated on data-driven approaches for learning priors instead of handcrafted priors. Sengupta et al. [21] presented a residual block-based architecture SfSNet to disentangle normal and albedo into separate subspaces. Yu et al. [25] used multiview stereo supervision to train an hourglass-based neural network with skip connections to predict normal and albedo from a single image. Although such approaches have an explicit physically meaningful representation, they are sometimes limited to what is expressible by their estimated physical model. In contrast, we utilize an implicit learning-based scene representation to render the target image, which will greatly reduce the difficulty of learning.

3   Method

3.1   Problem Formulation

Given an image I and its corresponding illumination setting L, we formulate the general relighting problem as follows,

$$\phi_1 : I \to \left(Z^i, Z^l\right), \psi_1 : \left(Z^i, Z^l\right) \to \hat{I} \tag{1}$$

$$\phi_2 : Z^l \to L, \psi_2 : L \to \hat{Z}^l \tag{2}$$

$$\hat{\phi}_1, \hat{\psi}_1, \hat{\phi}_2, \hat{\psi}_2 = \underset{\phi_1, \psi_1, \phi_2, \psi_2}{\arg\min} \left\| I - (\psi_1 \circ \phi_1)\, I \right\| + \left\| Z^l - (\psi_2 \circ \phi_2)\, Z^l \right\| \tag{3}$$

where Z^i (Z^l) is the implicit representation of the intrinsic property (lighting setting) of the scene, ϕ_1 and ψ_1 are the encoder and decoder for the input image I respectively, ϕ_2 and ψ_2 are the encoder and decoder for the Z^l respectively. In particular, based on the above general relighting problem formulation, any-to-any relighting can be done as shown in the Fig. 2. A source image I_S and a guide image I_G are both fed into the encoder ϕ_1 to get their own Z^i and Z^l. The $\hat{Z}^l$, which is reconstructed by the encoder ϕ_2 and the decoder ψ_2, and the Z^i are concatenated and fed into the decoder ψ_1 to obtain the relit image I_R. Compared with common style transfer [10], the advantage of this design is that the source image can be relighted with a user-controlled illumination setting even if the guide image is missing (more details in Fig. 7 and Fig. 8).

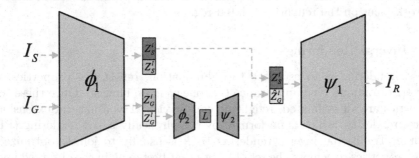

Fig. 2. Schematic diagram.

We model both the encoder ϕ and the decoder ψ as a convolutional neural network. The details of the network architecture are described in Sect. 3.2. We train the network on the VIDIT dataset.

3.2   Network Architecture

As shown in Fig. 3, our proposed SA-AE consists of four parts, which are a scene encoder ϕ_1, a scene decoder ψ_1, a lighting estimation network ϕ_2, and a lighting-to-feature network ψ_2. The scene representation Z in the latent space can be

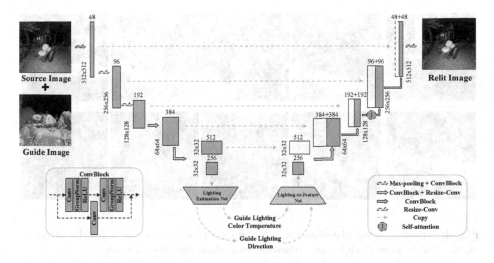

Fig. 3. An overview of the proposed SA-AE.

divided into a lighting-dependent representation Z^l and an intrinsic property-dependent representation Z^i, as discussed in Sect. 3.1. In the scene encoder ϕ_1, Z^l and Z^i are obtained through five ConvBlocks and four max-pooling layers that gradually decrease the spatial resolution and increase the number of channels by a factor 2. In the lighting-to-feature network ψ_2, the lighting directions and color temperatures, which both are represented as one-hot vectors in our work, are processed by two fully connected layers to output a 256-dimensional lighting-dependent feature vector $\hat{Z}^l$. The combination of the two disentangled implicit representation ($\hat{Z}^l$ and Z^i) is then fed into the scene decoder ψ_1 to get the relit image. The scene decoder ψ_1 consists of four ConvBlocks and four Resize-convs that gradually increase the spatial resolution and decrease the number of channels by a factor 2, which is the inverse process of the scene encoder ϕ_1.

As a result, the relit image can be rendered from the lighting-dependent representation of the guide image and the intrinsic property-dependent representation of the source image. Note that the intrinsic property-dependent representation of the source image can be directly obtained by feeding the source image into the scene encoder. But for the lighting-dependent representation of the guide image, a lighting estimation network that consists of two fully connected layers is designed to acquire the illumination setting of the guide image, and then the guide illumination setting is fed into a lighting-to-feature network to recover the corresponding lighting-dependent representation.

Self-attention Mechanism. Recent works [23,26] suggest that the self-attention mechanism helps with modeling long-range, multi-level dependencies across image regions. For any-to-any relighting, the key is how to recast and remove the shadow in the source image with a guide lighting. But recent deep

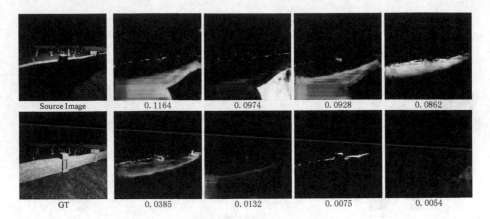

Fig. 4. Attention map visualization. The four columns on the right are the attention maps. The numbers below each attention map show the attention scores.

learning-based relighting approaches [22,29] only focused on extracting and fusing feature maps of different scales, they ignore that the importance of different regions in the source images is different. Therefore, a self-attention mechanism is introduced to focus on the re-rendering of the relighting-related regions in the source images. For feature maps $\mathbf{x}$, the calculation of the corresponding self-attention feature maps $\mathbf{y}$ can be divided into two steps. Firstly, the attention map $\beta_{j,i}$, which indicates the extent to which the model attends to the ith location when synthesizing the jth region, is defined as follows,

$$\beta_{j,i} = \frac{\exp\left((\mathbf{W}_f\mathbf{x}_i)^T(\mathbf{W}_g\mathbf{x}_j)\right)}{\sum_{i=1}^{N}\exp\left((\mathbf{W}_f\mathbf{x}_i)^T(\mathbf{W}_g\mathbf{x}_j)\right)} \tag{4}$$

where $\mathbf{W}_f$ and $\mathbf{W}_g$ are the learned weight matrices. Then the self-attention feature map $\mathbf{y}_j$ is calculated as follows,

$$\mathbf{y}_j = \mathbf{W}_v\left(\sum_{i=1}^{N}\beta_{j,i}\mathbf{W}_h\mathbf{x}_i\right) \tag{5}$$

where $\mathbf{W}_v$ and $\mathbf{W}_h$ are the learned weight matrices. See Sect. 4.2 for more details.

Resize-Conv. Due to the checkerboard artifacts caused by the transposed-conv overlap and random initialization, resize-conv [18] is utilized to replace the common transposed-conv for upsampling. Resize-conv first upscales the low-resolution feature maps using bilinear interpolation and then employs a standard convolutional layer with a kernel size 3×3.

3.3   Supervision for Training SA-AE

In our work, lighting estimation and relighting are seen as a classification task and a regression task respectively. Because the direction and color temperature are two different properties of the light source, we apply the cross-entropy loss function H to supervise the learning of the lighting estimation network:

$$L_c = H\left(p_{temp}, q_{temp}\right) + H\left(p_{dir}, q_{dir}\right) \tag{6}$$

Where p_{temp} and p_{dir} are the expected color temperature and lighting direction respectively, q_{temp} and q_{dir} are the actual color temperature and lighting direction respectively. For the relighting task, a MSE loss is used to supervise the proposed SA-AE, which gives a relatively high weight to large errors and helps the network to pay more attention to relighting-related regions. Inspired by [28], the loss function $SSIM$ is used to make the network learn to produce visually pleasing images. In addition, we also minimize the difference between the gradients of the relit image and Ground-truth to reduce noise effects. Thus, the loss for the relighting task is defined as:

$$L_r = \lambda_1 \left\| \hat{I} - I \right\|_2 + \lambda_2 \left\| Grad\left(\hat{I}\right) - Grad\left(I\right) \right\|_1 + \lambda_3 \left(1 - SSIM\left(\hat{I}, I\right)\right) \tag{7}$$

Where $Grad$ is a function to calculate the gradient of the image, and λ is the weight coefficient. Finally, the total loss is a linear combination of the lighting estimation loss and the relighting loss:

$$L_{total} = L_c + L_r \tag{8}$$

4   Experimental Results

4.1   Training Details

We conduct our experiments using Pytorch on 8 NVIDIA GTX1080Ti GPUs. The parameters of the network are initialized using Kaiming uniform initialization [9]. We optimize the parameters by the Adam optimizer [12] with learning rate $= 1e-4$, betas $= (0.9, 0.999)$. Consequently, the batch size is set to be 16 to maximize GPU memory utilization. Except that the weight λ_3 is set to 0.1, the other weights are all set to 1.

4.2   Model Analysis

Attention Maps Visualization. As discussed in Sect. 3.2, a self-attention module is introduced to focus on the re-rendering of the relighting-related regions in the source images, which gives a high weight to the regions that need shadow removal and recasting. We sum the attention scores of each attention map and sort them from largest to smallest, and the first eight attention maps with high attention scores are visualized in Fig. 4. In addition, the attention scores of the other attention maps are almost 0. It suggests that the relighting-related regions in the source images are well distinguished by the proposed SA-AE.

Fig. 5. Transposed-conv v.s. Resize-conv

Resize-conv v.s. Transposed-conv. In our initial experiment, transposed convolution was used for upsampling. However, it can be seen from the left image in Fig. 5 that a large number of checkerboard artifacts appear in the generated images. Thus, resize convolution is used to replace the transposed convolution for upsampling. The right image in Fig. 5 shows a pleasant visual effect.

4.3   Quantitative Evaluation

Challenge Results. A Mean Perceptual Score [7] (MPS) is defined as the average of the normalized SSIM and LPIPS [27] scores to determine the final ranking in the AIM2020 Relighting Challenge,

$$MPS = 0.5 \cdot (S + (1 - L)) \tag{9}$$

where S is the SSIM score, and L is the LPIPS score. The any-to-any relighting track of the AIM 2020 Challenge had 56 participants, with 6 finalists submitting results for the test stage. Table 1 shows that our results obtained the **1st place** in terms of MPS based on the perceptual quality, which verifies the effectiveness of our proposed model. Our result also achieved 18.54 dB on the test set, which is 0.81 dB lower than the 3nd method and 0.30 dB higher than the 2nd method. Note that our model takes 0.15 s on average to process 512 512 images used in the test phase.

Table 1. AIM 2020 Image Relighting Challenge Track 3 (Any-to-any relighting) results on the test set.

Rank	Method	MPS	SSIM	LPIPS	PSNR	Run-time	GPU
1	Ours	**0.6484 (1)**	**0.6353 (1)**	0.3386 (3)	18.5436 (2)	0.15 s	1080TI
2	the 2nd method	0.6428 (2)	0.6195 (2)	0.3338 (2)	18.2384 (4)	6 s	1080TI
3	the 3rd method	0.6424 (3)	0.6042 (3)	**0.3194 (1)**	**19.3559 (1)**	0.3 s	Titan X
4	the 4th method	0.6213 (4)	0.5881 (4)	0.3455 (4)	17.6314 (5)	13 s	
5	the 5th method	0.5258 (5)	0.4451 (5)	0.3936 (5)	18.3493 (3)		Titan Xp
6	the 6th method	0.3465 (6)	0.4123 (6)	0.7192 (6)	10.4483 (6)	0.0289 s	

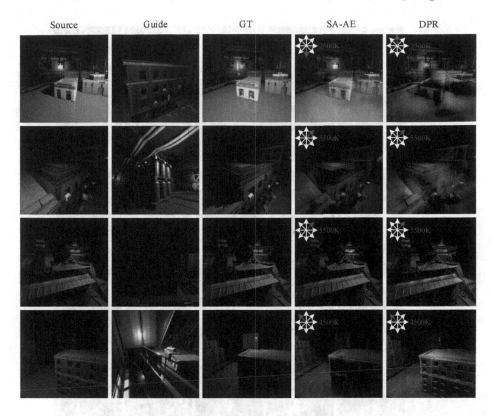

Fig. 6. Visual comparison of different approaches on the validation set.

Comparison to DPR [29]. We compared a deep single-image portrait relighting method DPR to our method on the validation set. Note that the VIDIT dataset only provides 8 different azimuthal angles of the light sources and the corresponding zenith angles of the light sources are unknown. Therefore, a spherical harmonics lighting, which is used to represent the illumination of the environment in DPR, can't be directly applied to the VIDIT dataset. For a fair comparison, we modified their lighting estimation network and loss functions to ours in order to train the DPR on the VIDIT dataset, while the others remain unchanged. Table 2 shows that our method outperforms the DPR in terms of SSIM and PSNR.

4.4   Qualitative Evaluation

Comparison to DPR. Figure 6 shows the qualitative results of DPR and the proposed SA-AE. In the upper left corner of the relit images, the red arrows and numbers indicate the direction and color temperature of the light source, respectively. In the first row, we can see that the predicted light direction by our method is consistent with the actual light direction of the guide image, while the

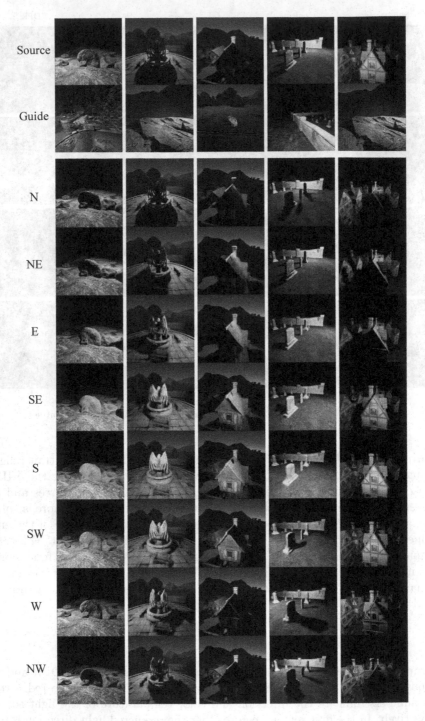

Fig. 7. More relit images with 8 different azimuth angles of the light source.

DPR predicted a completely opposite direction. This may be due to the overall darkness of the guide image, which interferes with the prediction of the DPR. In the third row, although both methods predicted the color temperature of the guide image as 5500K, the relit image generated by the DPR still looks like warm colors. Similarly, in the last row, both methods predicted the direction of the guide image as northwest, but the front of the building is still very bright in the relit image relighted by the DPR, which implies that the DPR doesn't perform recasting shadow very well. In contrast, our method correctly casts the shadow to the front of the building.

Table 2. Quantitative comparison of our method to DPR on the validation set.

Method	PSNR	SSIM
DPR [29]	16.4079	0.5238
SA-AE	**18.0695**	**0.6480**

A User-controlled Relighting. As discussed in Sect. 3.1, even if a guide image is missing, we can still perform relighting according to user demands. As illustrated in Fig. 7, the eight rows of images at the bottom are relighted using 8 different light source directions and the light color temperature of the guide image. As the direction of the light source moves, the shadows caused by the scene geometry are removed and recasted very well. Figure 8 also demonstrated that the five rows of images at the bottom are relighted using 5 different light color temperatures and the light source direction of the guide image. When the light color temperature keeps increasing, the relit images generated by our method changes from warm colors to cool colors gradually.

4.5   Limitations and Future Work

Although our method won the first place in the competition, Table 1 indicates that SSIM, LPIPS, and PSNR of different approaches on the test set are still very low compared to other similar image manipulation tasks [5,14], which means that any-to-any relighting is a very challenging task. As far as our proposed SA-AE is concerned, there are still several problems. First, Fig. 9(a) shows that the shadow is not completely recasted on the locomotive, mainly because of the wrong perception of the scene structure. More geometric information about the scene (i.e. depth maps or normal maps) can be provided in the future to improve shadow recasting. Second, the relit regions where the shadows are removed often lose texture details, as shown in Fig. 9(b). A flow vector can be used to select

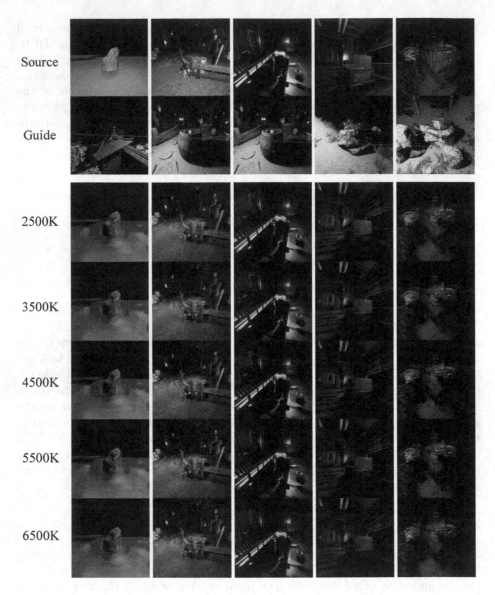

Fig. 8. More relit images with 5 different color temperatures of the light source.

similar textures from adjacent regions to fill in the region where shadow needs to be removed. Third, what we call halo artifacts often appears in the relit images, and imposing more penalties on the region of halo artifacts is one of the potential solutions in the future.

| Source | Guide | GT | SA-AE |

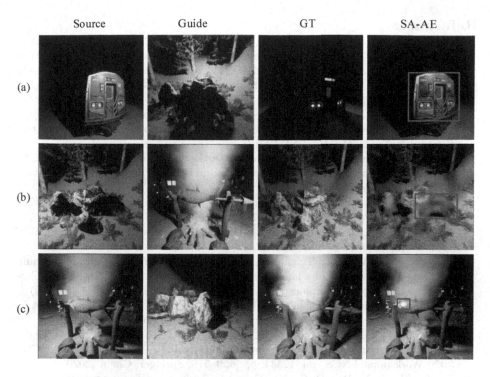

(a)

(b)

(c)

Fig. 9. Failure cases.

5 Conclusions

In this paper, we have presented a novel automatic model SA-AE for any-to-any relighting. A U-shape convolutional neural network-based autoencoder is well designed to learn an implicit scene representation to reduce the difficulty of the learning. In order to focus on the re-rendering of the relighting-related regions in the source images, an attention mechanism is also introduced into autoencoder. In addition, a lighting estimation network and a lighting-to-feature network, which are inverse processes of each other, are proposed to clearly control the relighting of the source image with a given illumination setting. The experiments show that the proposed SA-AE achieved the 1st place in terms of MPS and the 1st place in terms of SSIM in the AIM 2020 Any-to-any Relighting Challenge.

Acknowledgements. This work is supported by NSFC under Grant 61531014.

References

1. Barron, J.T., Malik, J.: Color constancy, intrinsic images, and shape estimation. In: Fitzgibbon, A., Lazebnik, S., Perona, P., Sato, Y., Schmid, C. (eds.) ECCV 2012. LNCS, vol. 7575, pp. 57–70. Springer, Heidelberg (2012). https://doi.org/10.1007/978-3-642-33765-9_5
2. Barron, J.T., Malik, J.: Shape, albedo, and illumination from a single image of an unknown object. In: 2012 IEEE Conference on Computer Vision and Pattern Recognition, pp. 334–341. IEEE (2012)
3. Barron, J.T., Malik, J.: Intrinsic scene properties from a single RGB-D image. In: Proceedings of the IEEE Conference on Computer Vision and Pattern Recognition, pp. 17–24 (2013)
4. Barron, J.T., Malik, J.: Shape, illumination, and reflectance from shading. IEEE Trans. Pattern Anal. Mach. Intell. **37**(8), 1670–1687 (2014)
5. Bau, D., et al.: Semantic photo manipulation with a generative image prior. ACM Trans. Graph. (TOG) **38**(4), 1–11 (2019)
6. Debevec, P., Hawkins, T., Tchou, C., Duiker, H.P., Sarokin, W., Sagar, M.: Acquiring the reflectance field of a human face. In: Proceedings of the 27th Annual Conference on Computer Graphics and Interactive Techniques, pp. 145–156 (2000)
7. El Helou, M., Zhou, R., Johan, B., Süsstrunk, S.: VIDIT: virtual image dataset for illumination transfer. arXiv preprint arXiv:2005.05460 (2020)
8. El Helou, M., Zhou, R., Süsstrunk, S., Timofte, R., et al.: AIM 2020: scene relighting and illumination estimation challenge. In: Bartoli, A., Fusiello, A. (eds.) ECCV 2020 Workshops. LNCS, vol. 12537, pp. 499–518. Springer, Cham (2020)
9. He, K., Zhang, X., Ren, S., Sun, J.: Delving deep into rectifiers: surpassing human-level performance on ImageNet classification. In: Proceedings of the IEEE International Conference on Computer Vision, pp. 1026–1034 (2015)
10. Johnson, J., Alahi, A., Fei-Fei, L.: Perceptual losses for real-time style transfer and super-resolution. In: Leibe, B., Matas, J., Sebe, N., Welling, M. (eds.) ECCV 2016. LNCS, vol. 9906, pp. 694–711. Springer, Cham (2016). https://doi.org/10.1007/978-3-319-46475-6_43
11. Kanamori, Y., Endo, Y.: Relighting humans: occlusion-aware inverse rendering for full-body human images. ACM Trans. Graph. (TOG) **37**(6), 1–11 (2018)
12. Kingma, D.P., Ba, J.: Adam: a method for stochastic optimization. arXiv preprint arXiv:1412.6980 (2014)
13. Knill, D.C., Richards, W.: Perception as Bayesian inference. Chapter The Perception of Shading and Reflectance. Cambridge University Press, New York (1996)
14. Ledig, C., et al.: Photo-realistic single image super-resolution using a generative adversarial network. In: Proceedings of the IEEE Conference on Computer Vision and Pattern Recognition, pp. 4681–4690 (2017)
15. Li, Z., Shafiei, M., Ramamoorthi, R., Sunkavalli, K., Chandraker, M.: Inverse rendering for complex indoor scenes: shape, spatially-varying lighting and SVBRDF from a single image. In: Proceedings of the IEEE/CVF Conference on Computer Vision and Pattern Recognition, pp. 2475–2484 (2020)
16. Matusik, W., Loper, M., Pfister, H.: Progressively-refined reflectance functions from natural illumination. In: Rendering Techniques, pp. 299–308 (2004)
17. Nestmeyer, T., Lalonde, J.F., Matthews, I., Lehrmann, A.: Learning physics-guided face relighting under directional light. In: Proceedings of the IEEE/CVF Conference on Computer Vision and Pattern Recognition, pp. 5124–5133 (2020)

18. Odena, A., Dumoulin, V., Olah, C.: Deconvolution and checkerboard artifacts. Distill **1**(10), e3 (2016)

19. Peers, P., et al.: Compressive light transport sensing. ACM Trans. Graph. (TOG) **28**(1), 1–18 (2009)

20. Reddy, D., Ramamoorthi, R., Curless, B.: Frequency-space decomposition and acquisition of light transport under spatially varying illumination. In: Fitzgibbon, A., Lazebnik, S., Perona, P., Sato, Y., Schmid, C. (eds.) ECCV 2012. LNCS, vol. 7577, pp. 596–610. Springer, Heidelberg (2012). https://doi.org/10.1007/978-3-642-33783-3_43

21. Sengupta, S., Kanazawa, A., Castillo, C.D., Jacobs, D.W.: SfSNET: learning shape, reflectance and illuminance of faces 'in the wild'. In: Proceedings of the IEEE Conference on Computer Vision and Pattern Recognition, pp. 6296–6305 (2018)

22. Sun, T., et al.: Single image portrait relighting. ACM Trans. Graph. **38**(4), 79:1–79:12 (2019)

23. Vaswani, A., et al.: Attention is all you need. In: Advances in Neural Information Processing Systems, pp. 5998–6008 (2017)

24. Xu, Z., Sunkavalli, K., Hadap, S., Ramamoorthi, R.: Deep image-based relighting from optimal sparse samples. ACM Trans. Graph. (TOG) **37**(4), 1–13 (2018)

25. Yu, Y., Smith, W.A.: InverseRenderNet: learning single image inverse rendering. In: Proceedings of the IEEE Conference on Computer Vision and Pattern Recognition, pp. 3155–3164 (2019)

26. Zhang, H., Goodfellow, I., Metaxas, D., Odena, A.: Self-attention generative adversarial networks. In: International Conference on Machine Learning, pp. 7354–7363 (2019)

27. Zhang, R., Isola, P., Efros, A.A., Shechtman, E., Wang, O.: The unreasonable effectiveness of deep features as a perceptual metric. In: Proceedings of the IEEE Conference on Computer Vision and Pattern Recognition, pp. 586–595 (2018)

28. Zhao, H., Gallo, O., Frosio, I., Kautz, J.: Loss functions for image restoration with neural networks. IEEE Trans. Comput. Imag. **3**(1), 47–57 (2016)

29. Zhou, H., Hadap, S., Sunkavalli, K., Jacobs, D.W.: Deep single-image portrait relighting. In: Proceedings of the IEEE International Conference on Computer Vision, pp. 7194–7202 (2019)

Deep Relighting Networks for Image Light Source Manipulation

Li-Wen Wang[1], Wan-Chi Siu[1]([✉]), Zhi-Song Liu[2], Chu-Tak Li[1], and Daniel P. K. Lun[1]

[1] The Hong Kong Polytechnic University, Hung Hom, Hong Kong
enwcsiu@polyu.edu.hk
[2] LIX, Ecole Polytechnique, CNRS, IP Paris, Palaiseau, France

Abstract. Manipulating the light source of given images is an interesting task and useful in various applications, including photography and cinematography. Existing methods usually require additional information like the geometric structure of the scene, which may not be available for most images. In this paper, we formulate the single image relighting task and propose a novel Deep Relighting Network (DRN) with three parts: 1) scene reconversion, which aims to reveal the primary scene structure through a deep auto-encoder network, 2) shadow prior estimation, to predict light effect from the new light direction through adversarial learning, and 3) re-renderer, to combine the primary structure with the reconstructed shadow view to form the required estimation under the target light source. Experiments show that the proposed method outperforms other possible methods, both qualitatively and quantitatively. Specifically, the proposed DRN has achieved the best PSNR in the "AIM2020 - Any to one relighting challenge" of the 2020 ECCV conference.

Keywords: Image relighting · Back-projection theory · Deep learning

1 Introduction

Image is a popular information carrier in this information era, which is intuitive and easy to understand. The rapid development of display devices stimulates people's demand for high-quality pictures. The visual appearance of the images is highly related to the illumination, which is vital in various applications, like photography and cinematography. Inappropriate illumination usually causes various visual degradation problems, like undesired shadows and distorted colours. However, the light source (like sunlight) is difficult to control, or sometimes unchangeable (for captured images), which increases the difficulty of producing satisfying images. The ways to produce the effect of light source on captured images becomes a hi-tech topic which has attracted considerable attention, because it offers opportunities to retouch the illuminations of the captured images.

Some approaches have been proposed that aim to mitigate the degradation caused by improper illuminations. For example, histogram equalization (HE) [38] rearranges the intensity to obey uniform distribution, which increases the

© Springer Nature Switzerland AG 2020
A. Bartoli and A. Fusiello (Eds.): ECCV 2020 Workshops, LNCS 12537, pp. 550–567, 2020.
https://doi.org/10.1007/978-3-030-67070-2_33

(2500K, E)	(3500K, N)	(4500K, NW)	(5500K, S)	(6500K, SW)	(4500K, E)
		(a)			(b)

Fig. 1. An example of the "any to one" relighting task. The 2500K, 3500K, ... are the color temperatures, and the E, N, ... are the light directions. Images in (a) are the inputs with any light settings, and (b) is target out with a specific light setting.

discernment of the low-contrast regions. It balances the illumination of the whole image that manipulates the global light condition. Methods [3,37] in the high-dynamic-range (HDR) field improve the image quality by increasing the dynamic range of the low-contrast regions. The HDR methods can be regarded as a refinement of local contrast but lacks adjustment of the global light. Retinex-based methods [30,36] separate the images as the combination of illumination and reflectance, where the reflectance stores the inherent content of the scene that is unchangeable in different illumination conditions. By refining the illumination, it can improve the visual quality of the images. Low-light image enhancement methods [16,33] amend the visibility of the dark environment that enlighten the whole image. Shadow removal [14,19] is a popular topic in the field of image processing that aims to eliminate the shadow effects caused by the light sources, but cannot simulate the shadows for target light sources. Adjusting the light source provides a flexible and natural way for illumination-based image enhancement. Although considerable research has been devoted to refine the illumination, less effect is being made to study from the view of manipulating the light sources. In other words, changing the illumination by controlling the light source is still in its fancy stage. Literature in relighting field mainly focuses on specific applications, like portrait relighting [27,32,41]. These methods require prior information (like face landmarks, geometric priors) that cannot be implemented in general scenes.

Convolutional Neural Network (CNN) recently has attracted notable attention due to its powerful learning capacity. It can digest extensive training data and extract discriminative representations with the support of powerful computational resource. CNN has shown significant advantages in various tasks, like image classification [18,31], semantic segmentation [28,39], super-resolution[9,24], place recognition [1,20], etc. CNNs with the deep structure are difficult to train because parameters of the shallow layers are often under gradient vanishing and exploding risks. Residual learning [11] mitigates the optimizing difficulty by adding a shortcut connection among each processing block. With the assistance of the normalization layers, the gradient can flow from the deep to shallow layers steadily, which dramatically increases the training efficiency of the deep network. The deeper structure usually means more trainable parameters that bring in more powerful learning capacities, which makes it possible to handle more challenging tasks, like single image relighting.

The image relighting method in this paper focuses on manipulating the position and color temperature of the light source based on our powerful deep CNN architecture. It not only can adjust the dominant hue, but can also recast the shadows of the given images. As shown in Fig. 1, we focus on a specific "any to one" relighting task [5], for which the input is under arbitrary light sources (any direction or color temperature, see Fig. 1(a)), and the objective is to estimate the image under this specific light source (direction: E, color temperature: 4500K, see Fig. 1(b)). The proposed method can be generalized for other light-related tasks. Let us highlight the novelty of our proposed approach.

- Instead of directly mapping the input image to the target light condition, we formulate the relighting task in three parts: scene reconversion, light effects estimation and re-rendering process.
- To preserve more information of the down- and up-sampling processes, we insert the back-projection theory to the auto-encoder structure, which benefits the scene reconversion and light-effect estimation.
- The light effect is difficult to measure, which increases the training difficult. We use the adversarial learning strategy that is implemented by a new shadow-region discriminator, which gives guidance to the training process.

2   Related Works

Back-Projection (BP) Theory. BP theory is popular in the field of single-image super-resolution [10,21,22]. Instead of directly learning the mapping from the input to the target, the BP-based methods iteratively digest the residuals and refine the estimations. It gives more focus on the weakness (i.e., the residuals) that appears at the learning process, which significantly improves the efficiency of the deep CNN architectures.

Recent work on low-light image enhancement [33] extends the BP theory to the light-domain-transfer tasks. It assumes the low-light (LL) and normal-light (NL) images locate at the LL and NL domains separately. Firstly, a lightening operator predicts the NL estimation from the LL input. Then, a darkening operator maps the NL estimation back to the LL domain (LL estimation). In the LL domain, the difference (LL residual) between LL input and LL estimation can be found that indicates the weakness of the two transferring operators (lightening and darkening). Afterwards, the LL residual is mapped back to the NL domain (NL residual) through another lightening operator. The NL residual then refines the NL estimation for a better output. Mathematically, the enlightening process can be written as:

$$\hat{N} = \lambda_2 L_1(L) + L_2(D(L_1(L)) - \lambda_1 L) \tag{1}$$

where L and $\hat{N} \in \mathbb{R}^{H \times W \times 3}$ denote the LL input image and NL estimation separately. The terms H, W and 3 represent the height, width and RGB channels respectively. The symbols L_1 and L_2 are two lightening operators to enlighten the LL image and LL residual individually. The symbol D is the darkening operator that maps the NL estimation to the LL domain. Two weighting coefficients λ_1 and $\lambda_2 \in \mathbb{R}$ are used to balance the residual calculation and final refinement.

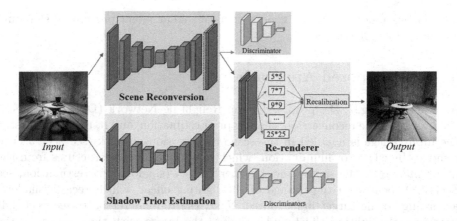

Fig. 2. Architecture of the proposed method

Adversarial Learning. Transferring an image to a corresponding output image is often formed as a pixel-wised regressing task of which the loss function (like L1- or L2-norm loss) indicates the average error for all pixels. This type of loss functions neglects the cross-correlation among the pixels, which easily distorts the perceptual structure and causes blur outputs. A large number of research works have done on quantitative measures of the perceptual similarity among images, like Structure SIMilarity (SSIM) [35], Learned Perceptual Image Patch Similarity (LPIPS) [40], Gram matrix [7], etc. However, the perceptual evaluation basically varies from different visual tasks and is difficult to formulate.

The Generative Adversarial Networks (GANs) [8,15,26] provide a novel solution that embeds the perceptual measurement into the process of adversarial learning. Each GAN consists of a generator and a discriminator. The discriminator aims to find latent perceptual structure inside the target images, which then guides the training of the generator. Subsequently, the generator provides sub-optimal estimations that will work as negative samples for the training process of the discriminator. With the grouped negative and positive (target images) samples, the discriminator conducts a binary classification task, which measures the latent perceptual difference between the two types of samples. The overall training process is shown as:

$$\min_G \max_D V(D, G) = \mathbb{E}_{\mathbf{Y}}[log D(\mathbf{Y})] + \mathbb{E}_{\mathbf{X}}[log(1 - D(G(\mathbf{X})))] \qquad (2)$$

where D and G denote the discriminator and generator separately. The terms $\mathbf{X}$ and $\mathbf{Y}$ represent the input and target images respectively. In the training process, the generator and discriminator play a two-player minimax game. The discriminator learns to distinguish the estimated images $G(\mathbf{X})$ from the target ones $\mathbf{Y}$. The generator aims to minimize the difference between the estimated $G(\mathbf{X})$ and target images $\mathbf{Y}$. The training process follows the adversarial learning strategies, where the latent distribution inside the target images is increasingly learned and used. Finally, the training will reach a dynamic balance, where the estimations produced by the generator have similar latent perceptual structure as the real target images.

3 The Proposed Approach

As shown in Fig. 2, the proposed Deep Relighting Network (DRN) consists of three parts: scene reconversion, shadow prior estimation, and re-renderer. Firstly, the input image is handled in the scene reconversion network (see Sect. 3.2) to remove the effects of illumination, which extracts inherent structures from the input image. At the same time, another branch (shadow prior estimation, see Sect. 3.3) focuses on the change of the lighting effect, which recasts shadows according to the target light source. Next, the re-renderer part (see Sect. 3.4) perceives the lighting effect and re-paints the image with the support of the structure information. Both the scene reconversion and shadow prior estimation networks have a similar deep auto-encoder structure that is an enhanced variation of the "Pix2Pix" network [15]. The details of the three components are presented below.

3.1 Assumption of Relighting

Any-to-one Single image relighting is a challenging low-level vision task that aims to re-paint the input image $\mathbf{X} \in \mathbb{R}^{H \times W \times 3}$ (under any light source Φ) with the target light source Ψ. Inspired by the Retinex theory [30,36], we assume that images can be decomposed into two components, where structure $\mathbf{S}$ is the inherent scene information of the image that is unchangeable under different light conditions. Let us define a lighting operation $L_\Phi(\cdot)$, which provides global illumination and causes the shadow effects for the scene $\mathbf{S}$ under the light source Φ. The input image can be written as:

$$\mathbf{X} = L_\Phi(\mathbf{S}) \tag{3}$$

To re-paint the image $\mathbf{X}$ with another light source Ψ, it firstly needs to remove the lighting effect $L_\Phi^{-1}(\cdot)$, i.e., reconverting the structure information $\mathbf{S}$ from the input image $\mathbf{X}$. Then, with the target light operation $L_\Psi(\cdot)$, the image $\mathbf{Y}$ with the target light source can be obtained through:

$$\mathbf{Y} = L_{\dot{\Psi}}(L_\Phi^{-1}(\mathbf{X})) \tag{4}$$

The key part of the reconversion process $L_\Phi^{-1}(\cdot)$ is to eliminate the shadows, while the lighting operation $L_\Psi(\cdot)$ is to paint new shadows for the target light source. However, the geometric information is unavailable in the single image relighting task, which dramatically increases the difficulty of constructing the lighting operation $L_\Psi(\cdot)$. Hence, instead of finding the lighting operation $L_\Psi(\cdot)$ directly, the proposed method aims to find a transferring operation $L_{(\Phi \to \Psi)}(\mathbf{X})$ that migrate the light effects (mainly the shadows) from the input to the target, which significantly reduces the difficulty of re-painting the shadows. Finally, a re-rendering process $P(\cdot)$ is used to combine the scene structure and light effects. The whole process can be formulated as:

$$\hat{Y} = P(L_\Phi^{-1}(\mathbf{X}), L_{(\Phi \to \Psi)}(\mathbf{X})) \tag{5}$$

3.2 Scene Reconversion

The objective of the scene reconversion is to extract the inherent structure information from the image so that the lighting effects can be removed. As shown in Fig. 3, the network adopts the auto-encoder [23] structure with a skip connection to transfer the shallow features to the end. Firstly, the input image is down-sampled (acted by the "DBP" in the figure) four times to find the discriminative features (codes) for the scene. The channels are doubled after each down-sampling process to preserve information as much as possible. The features have large receptive fields, which contain much global information that benefits illumination estimation and manipulation. We design a similar auto-encoder structure as the Pix2Pix method [15], where nine residual blocks [11] ("ResBlocks" in the figure) act to remove the light effects. Next, four blocks up-sample (acted by the "UBP" in the figure) the feature map back to the original size, which is then enriched by the shallow features from the skip connection. The feature map is further aggregated with a feature selection process that is acted by a convolutional layer, which reduces the channels from 64 to 32 (the top-right "Conv." (gray rectangle) as shown in Fig. 3). The feature is then sent to the following re-renderer process.

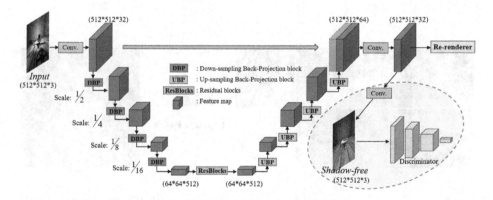

Fig. 3. Structure of the scene reconversion network. The structures in the green circle are removed after the training phase. (Color figure online)

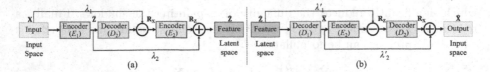

Fig. 4. Structure of the Down-sampling Back-Projection (DBP, as shown in (a)) and Up-sampling Back-Projection (UBP, as shown in (b)) blocks.

Back-Projection Block. Instead of solely down-sampling the features with the pooling or stride-convolution process, we adopt the back-projection block that remedies the lost information through residuals. As shown in Fig. 4, the Down-sampling Back-Projection (DBP) and Up-sampling Back-Projection (UBP) blocks consist of encoding and decoding operations that map the information between the input and latent spaces. To take the DBP block for example, it firstly maps the input ($\mathbf{X}$) to latent space ($\overline{\mathbf{Z}}$) through an encoding process (E_1, acted by a stride convolution layer with filter size of 3×3, stride of 2, padding of 1). Then, a decoder (D_2, acted by a deconvolution layer with filter size of 4×4, stride of 2 and padding of 1) maps it back to the input space ($\hat{\mathbf{X}}$) to calculate the difference (residual, $\mathbf{R_X} = \mathbf{X} - \hat{\mathbf{X}}$). The residual is encoded (E_2, acted by a stride convolution layer with filter size of 3×3, stride of 2 and padding of 1) to the latent space $\mathbf{R_Z}$ to remedy the latent code ($\hat{\mathbf{Z}} = \overline{\mathbf{Z}} + \mathbf{R_Z}$). Mathematically, the DBP and UBP (similarly, see Fig. 4(b)) can be written as:

$$\hat{\mathbf{Z}} = \lambda_2 E_1(\mathbf{X}) + E_2(D_2(E_1(\mathbf{X})) - \lambda_1 \mathbf{X}) \tag{6}$$

$$\hat{\mathbf{X}} = \lambda_2 D_1(\hat{\mathbf{Z}}) + D_2(E_2(D_1(\hat{\mathbf{Z}})) - \lambda_1 \hat{\mathbf{Z}}) \tag{7}$$

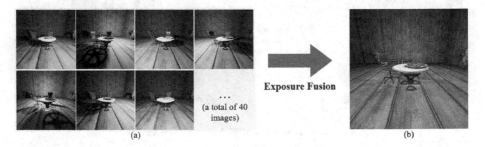

Fig. 5. An example of exposure fusion process (images with ID "239" of the VIDIT dataset [12]). The fourty images in (a) are captured under eight different light directions and five color temperatures of the same scene. The fusion result is shown in (b). (Color figure online)

Semi-supervised Reconversion. The objective of scene reconversion is to remove the light effect from the input image and construct the inherent structures. However, the ground-truth inherent structure is difficult to define because we have only the observed images. Instead of fully-supervising the network by well-defined ground-truths, it learns to estimate corresponding shadow-free images which might contain redundant information from the inherent structure.

Exposure fusion methods [4,25] are widely used to improve the dynamic range of the images captured in uneven light conditions. It takes several images with different exposures, and merges them to an image with better visibility. The Virtual Image Dataset for Illumination Transfer (VIDIT) dataset [12] contains images from 390 scenes. Each scene is captured 40 times with eight different light directions and five color temperatures. Different light directions cast the shadows at different positions, which makes it possible to build shadow-free images by selecting non-shadow pixels. The same selection strategy [25] is adopted to build shadow-free images as implemented by the OpenCV package [2]: 1) Pixels that are too dark (underexposure) or too bright (overexposure) are given small weights. 2) Pixels with high saturation (standard deviation of RGB channels) are usually under good illumination that are given large weights. 3) Edges and textures usually contain more information and are considered more important. Figure 5 gives an example of exposure fusion. Images in Fig. 5(a) are captured under different light direction and color temperatures. It is obvious that these images contain shadows caused by the point-source light. After using the exposure fusion method (as shown in Fig. 5(b)), one shadow-free image is obtained where the scene structure is obvious. The method is then used at the VIDIT dataset [12] to generate shadow-free targets for all scenes.

Adversarial Learning. To train the scene reconversion network, a shadow-free image is formed via a convolutional layer (denoted as "Conv." in the green circle of Fig. 3), which transfers the latency structure back to the image space. However, the shadows cause holes in the input image. To fill the holes with good perceptual consistency, a discriminator is attached to assist the training of the scene reconversion network. We adopt the same discriminator structure as [15] that stacks four stride-convolution layers which hierarchically extract the global representations. During the training process, the discriminator is assigned to distinguish the estimation (of the scene reconversion network) from the ground-truth shadow-free images. At the beginning, the estimation lacks structure information. The discriminator notices the weakness and makes classification based on it. At the same time, the scene reconversion network is assigned to fake the discriminator, i.e., to equip the estimation with similar structure correlation as the target shadow-free images. Mathematically, the adversarial learning is:

$$\mathcal{L}_{cGAN}(G, D) = \mathbb{E}_{(\mathbf{X}, \mathbf{Y}_{sf})}[log D(\mathbf{X}, \mathbf{Y}_{sf})] + \mathbb{E}_{\mathbf{X}}[log(1 - D(\mathbf{X}, G(\mathbf{X})))] \tag{8}$$

where the generator G aims to minimize the loss $\mathcal{L}_{cGAN}(G, D)$, i.e., $G^* = arg\min_G \max_D \mathcal{L}_{cGAN}(G, D)$. The discriminator D tries to maximize the loss $\mathcal{L}_{cGAN}(G, D)$. The term $cGAN$ indicates it is a conditional GAN structure that

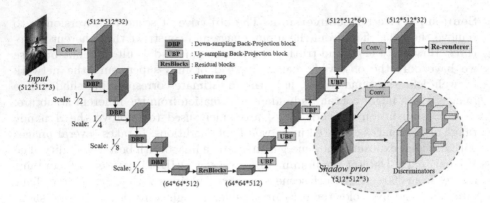

Fig. 6. Structure of the shadow prior estimation network. The structures in the red circle are removed after the training phase. (Color figure online)

the discriminator has the input image $\mathbf{X}$ as prior information. Considering the estimated scene structure should be close to the ground-truth shadow-free target $\mathbf{Y}_{sf}$, the conventional L1-norm loss is used to measure the per-pixel error of the estimation. The objective for the scene reconversion network is defined as:

$$G^* = \lambda \mathbb{E}_{(\mathbf{X},\mathbf{Y}_{sf})}[||\mathbf{Y}_{sf} - G(\mathbf{X})||] + arg \min_G \max_D \mathcal{L}_{cGAN}(G,D) \qquad (9)$$

where the term λ balances the L1-norm and the adversarial losses.

3.3   Shadow Prior Estimation

Different light sources cause different light effects which produce for example, different shadows and color temperatures. To produce the light effects from the target light source, we design a shadow prior estimation network with the architecture as shown in Fig. 6. The network adopts a similar structure as the scene reconversion network (as shown in Fig. 3). Specifically, there are three major modifications: 1) This shadow prior estimation network discards the skip connection, because the network gives more focus on the global light effect. The skip connection brings the local features to the output directly, which makes the network lazy to learn the global change. 2) It has another discriminator that focuses on the shadow regions. 3) The ground-truth target is the image under the target light source. Mathematically, the objective of the shadow prior estimation network can be described as follows:

$$G^* = \lambda \mathbb{E}_{\mathbf{X},\mathbf{Y}}[||\mathbf{Y} - G(\mathbf{X})||] + arg \min_G \max_D \mathcal{L}_{cGAN}(G,D) \qquad (10)$$

$$+ arg \min_G \max_{D_{shad}} \mathcal{L}_{cGAN}(G, D_{shad}) \qquad (11)$$

where D_{shad} denotes the shadow-region discriminator (details will be illustrated below), and the term $\mathbf{Y}$ denotes the image under the target light source.

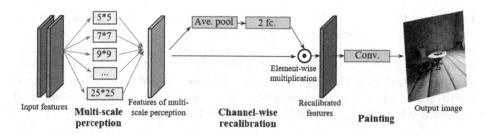

Fig. 7. Structure of the re-renderer. The inputs are two feature maps that come from the scene reconversion and shadow prior networks separately. The rectangles and cubes represent operations and feature maps respectively.

Shadow-Region Discriminator. The shadow-region discriminator adopts the same structure as [15] that stacks four stride-convolution layers, which gradually extracts the global feature representations. To focus on the shadow regions, the estimation is firstly rectified to give focus to the low-intensity (dark, usually the shadows) regions through $z = min(\alpha, x)$, where the symbol x denotes the estimated pixel intensity. The term z represents the rectified value that will be inputted to the discriminator. The term α is a pre-defined threshold for the sensitivity of the shadows (empirically, it is set to $0.059 = 15/255$).

3.4 Re-rendering

After the processing of the scene reconversion and shadow prior estimation networks, the estimated scene structure and light effects will be fused together to produce the relighted output. As shown in Fig. 7, the re-renderer consists of three parts: multi-scale perception, channel-wise recalibration and painting process. Both global and local information are essential for light source manipulation because global information benefits the shadow and illumination consistency, and local information enhances the details. To utilize the information of different perception scales, we propose a novel multi-scale perception block that uses filters with different perceptive sizes (e.g., filter size of 3×3, 5×5, ...), which extracts rich features for the following process.

After processing the multi-scale perception, features with different spatial perception are merged into a single feature map, where each channel stores a type of spatial pattern. However, different patterns may have different importance for the re-rendering process. As designed in [13,33], a recalibration process is designed to investigate the weights for different patterns, which selects the key features for the following painting process. Finally, a convolutional layer (with the filter size of 7×7, padding of 3, stride of 1 and a tanh activation function) paints the estimation from the feature space to the image space.

Loss Function. The loss function designed for the re-renderer consists of per-pixel reconstruction error and perceptual difference. The reconstruction error is measured by the wildly-used L1-norm loss. The perceptual similarity is calculated as [17] based on the features extracted from the VGG-19 network. The network is pre-trained with ImageNet dataset for image classification. The extracted features have discriminative power for visual comparison, so that they are used to measure the perceptual similarity. The loss function is defined as:

$$\mathcal{L}(\mathbf{Y}, \hat{\mathbf{Y}}) = ||\mathbf{Y} - \hat{\mathbf{Y}}|| + \lambda ||feat(\mathbf{Y}) - feat(\hat{\mathbf{Y}})|| \tag{12}$$

where $\mathbf{Y}$ and $\hat{\mathbf{Y}}$ denote the ground-truth target and estimated images respectively. The term $feat(\cdot)$ is the feature maps extracted from the VGG-19 network. The symbol λ is a balanced coefficient and was set to 0.01 in our experiments.

4   Experiments

4.1   Implementation Details

VIDIT Dataset. The Virtual Image Dataset for Illumination Transfer (VIDIT) [12] contains 390 virtual scenes with different scene contents (for example, metal, wood, etc.), where there are 300 scenes for training, 45 scenes for validation and 45 scenes for testing separately. The scenes are rendered by a powerful game engine (Unreal Engine 4 [6]) to get high-resolution images. The objective of the VIDIT dataset is for illumination manipulation. Each scene is rendered with eight light directions and five color temperatures, which results in forty images with the resolution of 1024 * 1024. As we mentioned in Sect. 3.2, the exposure fusion method was used to generate shadow-free images for the scenes, which brings us 300 shadow-free images (work as ground-truth target) to guide the training of the scene reconversion network. We participated the *"AIM Image Relighting Challenge - Track 1: any to one"* [5]. The objective is that, given an image under any types of illuminations, the method should give the estimation under a specific light source (color temperature is 4500k and light direction is from East). We used all possible pairs from the 300 training scenes to train the network, and the provided validation dataset (45 scenes) for evaluation.

Training Process. Limited by the GPU memory and computational power, our three sub-networks (scene reconversion, shadow prior estimation and re-renderer) were trained separately. Firstly, we trained the scene reconstruction network by using the paired inputs and shadow-free targets through the designed loss functions. Similarly, we trained the shadow prior estimation network with paired input and target images. Next, we fixed the scene reconstruction and shadow prior estimation networks and removed their last convolution layer and the discriminators (the green circle in Fig. 5 and the pink circle in Fig. 6). Finally, the re-renderer network was trained with the designed loss functions. All training images were resized from 1024 * 1024 to 512 * 512, and the mini-batch size was set to six. We used the Adam optimization method with the momentum of 0.5 and learning rate of 0.0001. The networks were randomly initialized as [34]. As we mentioned, the scene reconstruction and shadow prior estimation networks were firstly trained independently, where each network was trained for 20 epochs. Then, the two networks were fixed, and the re-renderer network was also trained for 20 epochs. All experiments were conducted through PyTorch [29] on a PC with two NVIDIA GTX2080Ti GPUs. Codes have been released at https:// github.com/WangLiwen1994/DeepRelight.

4.2 Analysis of the Proposed Method

There are no evaluation methods for light source measurement, which makes it difficult to evaluate the performance of different methods. Because we have the ground-truth images under the target light condition, and we believe the estimation should be close to these ground-truth targets. Hence, the Peak Signal-to-Noise Ratio (PSNR) and Structure SIMilarity (SSIM) [35] are adopted to measure the similarity between the estimation and the ground-truth, where a larger value means better performance. To measure the perceptive quality, we use the Learned Perceptual Image Patch Similarity (LPIPS) [40], in which a smaller value means more perceptual similarity.

Pix2pix [15] has shown great success in the image-to-image translation tasks, like background removal, pose transfer, etc. The method is a conditional GAN structure that is trained through the adversarial strategy. The relighting problem can be regarded as an image-to-image translation task that translates the light source to the target settings. Because light source manipulation is a new topic, few methods are available for comparison. Therefore, the Pix2Pix can be considered as the baseline model to present the efficiency of the proposed method. The Pix2Pix method is based on an auto-encoder structure where the input image is firstly down-sampled four times (scale is reduced to 1/16), and then processed by nine residual blocks. Finally, a set of deconvolutional layers is used to up-sample the image back to the original size and the estimation is formed. Table 1 gives a comparison among different structures, where ShadAdv and BPAE are two variations of the Pxi2Pix network. The baseline method (Pix2Pix) achieves 16.28 dB in PSNR, 0.553 in SSIM and 0.482 in LPIPS. The performance of other structures (ShadAdv, BPAE, and the proposed DRN) will be discussed below.

Effect of the Shadow-Region Discriminator. Let us enhance the baseline, Pix2Pix, by adding the proposed shadow-region discriminator (as introduced in Sect. 3.3) to it, and entitled it as "ShadAdv". Compared with the original Pix2Pix method, the "ShadAdv" gives more focus on the appearance of the shadow regions. In other words, the shadow discriminator can provide better guidance for recasting the shadows of the target light source. With more accurate shadows, the PSNR is increased by 0.84 ($= 17.12 - 16.28$) dB, and the perceptive quality is improved by 0.042 ($= 0.482 - 0.440$) in terms of LPIPS.

Table 1. Comparison among different structures

Method	ShadAdv	Structure	Stages	PSNR	SSIM	LPIPS
Pix2Pix [15]	No	Auto-Encoder	One	16.28	0.553	0.482
ShadAdv	Yes	Auto-Encoder	One	17.12	0.569	0.440
BPAE	Yes	Back-Pojection	One	17.22	0.573	0.439
DRN (proposed)	Yes	Back-Pojection	Two	**17.59**	**0.596**	**0.440**

Effect of the Back-Projection (BP) Block. The "Pix2Pix" and "ShadAdv" methods are based on the auto-encoder structure. As we have mentioned, it down- and up-samples the image through stacked convolutional and deconvolutional layers. The "BPAE" method is an enhanced version of the auto-encoder, where the down- and up-sampling processes are done by the DBP and UBP blocks (as illustrated in Fig. 4). The BP blocks are based on the back-projection theory, which remedies the lost information in the down- and up-sampling processes. Compared with the auto-encoder structure (used in "ShadAdv"), the "BPAE" method extracts more informative features, which enriches the structure of the estimation and increases the SSIM from 0.569 to 0.573.

Effect of the Relighting Assumption. As defined in Sect. 3.1, we regard the *any-to-one* relighting task as a two-stage problem, where the first stage finds the scene structure $L_\Phi^{-1}(\mathbf{X})$ and light effect $L_{(\Phi \to \Psi)}(\mathbf{X})$ from the input image $\mathbf{X}$. The second stage paints $P(\cdot)$ the estimation $\hat{\mathbf{Y}}$ under the target light source. As shown in Table 1, the "Pix2Pix", "ShadAdv" and "BPAE" methods learns the mapping to the target light condition directly. The "DRN" is the proposed method that is based on our relighting assumption. It is clear that the proposed method achieves the best reconstruction with the highest PSNR (17.59 dB) and SSIM (0.596) scores, and comparable visual similarity (0.440 of LPIPS). These suggest the effects of the proposed relighting assumption.

4.3 Comparison with Other Approaches

Single image relighting is a new topic in the field of image processing. As we have mentioned, few methods are publicly available for our comparison. Besides comparing with the baseline method (Pix2Pix [15]), we have also made comparisons with other representative methods. U-Net [23] is a popular CNN structure that was initially designed for biomedical image segmentation. It consists of down- (encoder) and up-sampling (decoder) paths to form an auto-encoder structure, where several short-connections transmit the information from the encoder to the decoder part directly. Retinex-Net [36] was designed to enlighten the low-light images based on the Retinex theory. It firstly decomposes the low-light image into the reluctance and illumination elements, and then an adjustment sub-network refines the illumination to enlighten the input images. We retrained

Table 2. Comparison among different approaches

Methods	PSNR	SSIM	LPIPS
U-Net [23]	16.72	0.616	0.441
Retinex-Net [36]	12.28	0.162	0.657
Pix2Pix [15]	16.28	0.553	0.482
DRN (proposed)	**17.59**	**0.596**	**0.440**

the methods with their desired settings at the VIDIT [12] training dataset, and the comparison was made using the VIDIT validation dataset.

Table 2 shows the results of different approaches. Benefiting from the short-connections, the U-Net method preserves much information of the inputs, which achieves good SSIM performance. However, the short-connections preserve too much structure (detailed) information which makes the network lazy to change the light source that limits its PSNR score. The Retinex-Net method can find the inherent scene structure but fails in manipulating the light source. The proposed DRN method is able to manipulate the light source, and shows superior performance (with the best PSNR of 17.59 dB and the LPIPS score of 0.440) compared with all other methods. Also, we made use of the proposed DRN network to join the competition "AIM2020 Image Relighting Challenge - Track 1: any to one" and have achieved the best PSNR score in the final testing phase.

Visual Comparison. Figure 8 gives a visual comparison among different methods. As shown in the first row of Fig. 8(a) that the Retinex-Net method [36] fails to change the color temperature where the hue of the estimation is significantly different from the others. Although U-Net [23] produces correct color temperature for the target light source, it fails to manipulate the light direction (see the arrows in Fig. 8(a)). The Pix2Pix [15] can produce the correct light direction but brings in many artifacts (see the red rectangle area), which decreases the perceptual quality. The proposed method gives correct estimation for the light direction and color temperature with a good perceptual quality.

A challenging case is shown in Fig. 8(b), where the input image is nearly all black (see the top-left image of the figure). For better visualization, we provide a binary mask to show the illuminated and shadow regions (see the 2nd row of the figure). The U-Net [23] fails to enlighten the building with the new light source (the yellow circle in Fig. 8(b)). Pix2Pix [15] brings many artifacts that cause inconsistency shadows (the green circle in Fig. 8(b)). Benefited from our shadow-region discriminator, the proposed DRN enlightens the building and recasts the shadows for the new light source (the blue and red encircled regions, as shown in Fig. 8(b)), which suggests superior performance as compared to all other approaches. However, the structure of the center building is completely lost (the pixels are all zero) in the input image, which makes the relighting difficult. It can be seen from the figure that the proposed method attempts to recover the color and shape of the wall, but fails to construct the detailed structures.

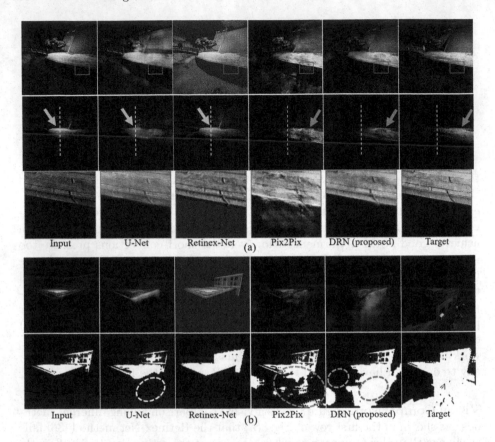

Fig. 8. Visual comparison among different approaches (zoom in for better view). Images in the 2nd row of (a) are the results after gamma correction to highlight the light effects and the arrows indicate the light directions. The 2nd row of (b) contains the binary mask for illuminated and shadow regions. (Color figure online)

Limited by the time and the training data, the network is designed to focus on the global light effects and lacks investigation for more advanced topics, like inpainting the building. In the future, we will continue our work and would like to invite others to work on these challenging relighting cases.

5   Conclusion

In this paper, we have introduced our proposed Deep Relighting Network (DRN) that achieves excellent performance in single image relighting task. We formulate the image relighting as three parts: scene reconversion, shadow prior estimation and re-rendering. We embed the back-projection theory into auto-encoder structure that significantly improves the capacity of the deep network. Benefited from adversarial learning, the proposed DRN can recast the shadows and estimate the required image from the target light source, which confirms our formulation of separating the scene and shadow structures. It is useful and can be generalized to many light-related tasks, for example, cases with dual or blind light sources, reference-based image relighting (i.e., produce images with any light source settings). Experimental results show that the proposed DRN network outperforms all other methods. Also, it obtained the best PSNR in the competition "AIM2020 Image Relighting Challenge - Track 1: any to one" of the 2020 ECCV conference.

References

1. Anoosheh, A., Sattler, T., Timofte, R., Pollefeys, M., Gool, L.V.: Night-to-day image translation for retrieval-based localization. In: 2019 International Conference on Robotics and Automation (ICRA) (2019). https://doi.org/10.1109/icra.2019.8794387
2. Bradski, G.: The OpenCV library. Dr. Dobb's J. Softw. Tools **25**, 120–125 (2000)
3. Debevec, P.E., Malik, J.: Recovering high dynamic range radiance maps from photographs. In: Proceedings of the 24th Annual Conference on Computer Graphics and Interactive Techniques, SIGGRAPH 1997, pp. 369–378. ACM Press/Addison-Wesley Publishing Co., USA (1997). https://doi.org/10.1145/258734.258884
4. Debevec, P.E., Malik, J.: Recovering high dynamic range radiance maps from photographs. In: ACM SIGGRAPH 2008 Classes, pp. 1–10 (2008)
5. El Helou, M., Zhou, R., Süsstrunk, S., Timofte, R., et al.: AIM 2020: scene relighting and illumination estimation challenge. In: Bartoli, A., Fusiello, A. (eds.) ECCV 2020 Workshops. LNCS, vol. 12537, pp. 499–518. Springer, Cham (2020)
6. Epic Games, Inc.: Unreal Engine — The most powerful real-time 3D creation platform. https://www.unrealengine.com/en-US/
7. Gatys, L.A., Ecker, A.S., Bethge, M.: A neural algorithm of artistic style. arXiv preprint arXiv:1508.06576 (2015)
8. Goodfellow, I., et al.: Generative adversarial nets. In: Advances in Neural Information Processing Systems, pp. 2672–2680 (2014)
9. Gu, S., et al.: AIM 2019 challenge on image extreme super-resolution: methods and results. In: 2019 IEEE/CVF International Conference on Computer Vision Workshop (ICCVW), pp. 3556–3564 (2019)
10. Haris, M., Shakhnarovich, G., Ukita, N.: Deep back-projection networks for super-resolution. In: Proceedings of the IEEE Conference on Computer Vision and Pattern Recognition, pp. 1664–1673 (2018)
11. He, K., Zhang, X., Ren, S., Sun, J.: Deep residual learning for image recognition. In: Proceedings of the IEEE Conference on Computer Vision and Pattern Recognition, pp. 770–778 (2016)
12. Helou, M.E., Zhou, R., Barthas, J., Süsstrunk, S.: VIDIT: virtual image dataset for illumination transfer. arXiv preprint arXiv:2005.05460 (2020)
13. Hu, J., Shen, L., Sun, G.: Squeeze-and-excitation networks. In: Proceedings of the IEEE Conference on Computer Vision and Pattern Recognition, pp. 7132–7141 (2018)
14. Hu, X., Zhu, L., Fu, C., Qin, J., Heng, P.: Direction-aware spatial context features for shadow detection. In: 2018 IEEE/CVF Conference on Computer Vision and Pattern Recognition, pp. 7454–7462 (2018)

15. Isola, P., Zhu, J.Y., Zhou, T., Efros, A.A.: Image-to-image translation with conditional adversarial networks. In: Proceedings of the IEEE Conference on Computer Vision and Pattern Recognition, pp. 1125–1134 (2017)
16. Jiang, Y., et al.: EnlightenGAN: deep light enhancement without paired supervision. ArXiv abs/1906.06972 (2019)
17. Johnson, J., Alahi, A., Fei-Fei, L.: Perceptual losses for real-time style transfer and super-resolution. In: Leibe, B., Matas, J., Sebe, N., Welling, M. (eds.) ECCV 2016. LNCS, vol. 9906, pp. 694–711. Springer, Cham (2016). https://doi.org/10.1007/978-3-319-46475-6_43
18. Krizhevsky, A., Sutskever, I., Hinton, G.E.: ImageNet classification with deep convolutional neural networks. In: Advances in Neural Information Processing Systems, pp. 1097–1105 (2012)
19. Le, H., Samaras, D.: Shadow removal via shadow image decomposition. In: 2019 IEEE/CVF International Conference on Computer Vision (ICCV), pp. 8577–8586 (2019)
20. Li, C.T., Siu, W.C.: Fast monocular visual place recognition for non-uniform vehicle speed and varying lighting environment. IEEE Trans. Intel. Transp. Sys., 1–18 (2020)
21. Liu, Z.S., Wang, L.W., Li, C.T., Siu, W.C.: Hierarchical back projection network for image super-resolution. In: The Conference on Computer Vision and Pattern Recognition Workshop (CVPRW) (2019)
22. Liu, Z.S., Wang, L.W., Li, C.T., Siu, W.C.: Image super-resolution via attention based back projection networks. In: IEEE International Conference on Computer Vision Workshop (ICCVW) (2019)
23. Long, J., Shelhamer, E., Darrell, T.: Fully convolutional networks for semantic segmentation. In: Proceedings of the IEEE Conference on Computer Vision and Pattern Recognition, pp. 3431–3440 (2015)
24. Lugmayr, A., Danelljan, M., Timofte, R.: NTIRE 2020 challenge on real-world image super-resolution: Methods and results. In: Proceedings of the IEEE/CVF Conference on Computer Vision and Pattern Recognition (CVPR) Workshops, June 2020
25. Mertens, T., Kautz, J., Van Reeth, F.: Exposure fusion: a simple and practical alternative to high dynamic range photography. In: Computer Graphics Forum, vol. 28, pp. 161–171. Wiley Online Library (2009)
26. Mirza, M., Osindero, S.: Conditional generative adversarial nets. arXiv preprint arXiv:1411.1784 (2014)
27. Nestmeyer, T., Lalonde, J.F., Matthews, I., Lehrmann, A.M.: Learning physics-guided face relighting under directional light. arXiv: Computer Vision and Pattern Recognition (2020)
28. Noh, H., Hong, S., Han, B.: Learning deconvolution network for semantic segmentation. In: Proceedings of the IEEE International Conference on Computer Vision (ICCV), December 2015
29. Paszke, A., et al.: PyTorch: an imperative style, high-performance deep learning library. In: Advances in Neural Information Processing Systems, pp. 8026–8037 (2019)
30. Rahman, Z.u., Jobson, D.J., Woodell, G.A.: Retinex processing for automatic image enhancement. J. Electron. Imag. 13(1), 100–111 (2004)
31. Simonyan, K., Zisserman, A.: Very deep convolutional networks for large-scale image recognition. arXiv preprint arXiv:1409.1556 (2014)
32. Sun, T., et al.: Single image portrait relighting. ACM Trans. Graph. (TOG) 38, 1–12 (2019). https://doi.org/10.1145/3306346.3323008

33. Wang, L.W., Liu, Z.S., Siu, W.C., Lun, D.P.: Lightening network for low-light image enhancement. IEEE Trans. Image Process. **29**, 7984–7996 (2020). https://doi.org/10.1109/TIP.2020.3008396

34. Wang, T.C., Liu, M.Y., Zhu, J.Y., Tao, A., Kautz, J., Catanzaro, B.: High-resolution image synthesis and semantic manipulation with conditional GANs. In: Proceedings of the IEEE Conference on Computer Vision and Pattern Recognition (2018)

35. Wang, Z., Bovik, A.C., Sheikh, H.R., Simoncelli, E.P.: Image quality assessment: from error visibility to structural similarity. IEEE Trans. Image Process. **13**(4), 600–612 (2004)

36. Wei, C., Wang, W., Yang, W., Liu, J.: Deep retinex decomposition for low-light enhancement. ArXiv abs/1808.04560 (2018)

37. Wu, S., Xu, J., Tai, Y.-W., Tang, C.-K.: Deep high dynamic range imaging with large foreground motions. In: Ferrari, V., Hebert, M., Sminchisescu, C., Weiss, Y. (eds.) ECCV 2018. LNCS, vol. 11206, pp. 120–135. Springer, Cham (2018). https://doi.org/10.1007/978-3-030-01216-8_8

38. Yadav, G., Maheshwari, S., Agarwal, A.: Contrast limited adaptive histogram equalization based enhancement for real time video system. In: 2014 International Conference on Advances in Computing, Communications and Informatics (ICACCI), pp. 2392–2397 (2014)

39. Yu, C., Gao, C., Wang, J., Yu, G., Shen, C., Sang, N.: BiseNet V2: bilateral network with guided aggregation for real-time semantic segmentation. arXiv preprint arXiv:2004.02147 (2020)

40. Zhang, R., Isola, P., Efros, A.A., Shechtman, E., Wang, O.: The unreasonable effectiveness of deep features as a perceptual metric. In: Proceedings of the IEEE Conference on Computer Vision and Pattern Recognition (2018)

41. Zhou, H., Hadap, S., Sunkavalli, K., Jacobs, D.W.: Deep single-image portrait relighting. In: Proceedings of the IEEE/CVF International Conference on Computer Vision (ICCV) (2019)

LightNet: Deep Learning Based Illumination Estimation from Virtual Images

Sabari Nathan[1(✉)] and M. Parisa Beham[2]

[1] Couger Inc., Tokyo, Japan
sabarinathantce@gmail.com
[2] Sethu Institute of Technology, Virudhunagar, India

Abstract. In the era of virtual reality (VR), estimating illumination with lighting direction and lighting virtual objects has been a challenging problem. In VR, poor estimation of illumination and lighting direction makes any virtual objects into unrealistic. The inaccurate estimation of lighting can also cause strong artifacts in relighting of the virtual images. Inspired by these issues, the main objective of this paper is to enrich visual rationality of single image by providing accurate assessments of real illumination and lighting direction. We proposed a LightNet architecture by modelling Denseset121 network to estimate the light direction and color temperature level in any virtual reality images. We present quantitative results on VIDIT dataset to evaluate the performance and achieved good results in all the performance metrics. The experimental results proved that the proposed model is robust and provides a good level of accuracy in estimating illumination and lighting direction.

Keywords: Augmented reality · Illumination estimation · Lighting direction · Virtual images · Densenet · Deep learning

1 Introduction

Augmented reality incorporates digital content and images onto the real world. Interpreting virtual objects into real scenes has been widely used in smart city development and planning, art design, animation and film production [17]. The appearance of things in a scene depends on their illumination and lighting direction. This illumination and their direction is not often taken into account in augmented reality, which makes any virtual object look unrealistic. The perfection of virtual objects and their consistency against actual scene are determined by the lighting effects. Predicting light sources offers a way of automatically locating the precise positions of light sources in a photograph. It can be used to render virtual objects and insert artificial or real objects in the image by illuminating them under the same lighting conditions. Lighting virtual objects with proper illumination and correct orientation is a major focus in computer

© Springer Nature Switzerland AG 2020
A. Bartoli and A. Fusiello (Eds.): ECCV 2020 Workshops, LNCS 12537, pp. 568–580, 2020.
https://doi.org/10.1007/978-3-030-67070-2_34

graphics domain. However, the estimation of real illumination from one image of the scene is a challenging problem, especially if the light sources are not directly visible in the image. Figure 1 shows the challenges in estimating the illumination level and light direction in virtual reality images. From the virtual images shown, one can able to estimate the light direction properly but difficult to estimate the lighting temperature.

Fig. 1. Challenges in estimating the illumination level and direction in virtual reality images

Previous research showed that if no priors are used in light source estimation from a single image, it is an ill-conditioned problem [23]. In this paper, our approach is based on an assumption that prior data about illumination and its direction can be learned from a large set of virtual images with known light sources. This learned information can be trained in a deep learning network which is used to estimate lighting levels in a virtual reality scene which was not previously trained. The proposed network can succeed sufficient generality to estimate illumination in various scenes. By maintaining the convergence of training with incrementing network layers and to avoid a vanishing gradients problem, our network has been customized using dense blocks with 121 convolutional layers [9]. In a virtual reality scenario, changing camera orientations cause problems for illumination estimation by a convolutional network. This is because of high dimensionality and complexity of input if a network should handle separate camera orientations in real world.

This work presents the abilities of deep learning network for illumination and light direction estimation in virtual reality by integrating the presented method into a real-time AR rendering system. We also evaluate the results of our method and compare them with the results of a state-of-the-art networks for illumination estimation. Our results indicate that a deep neural network can be used to estimate light sources on scenes which have not been previously seen in the training process.

The main contributions of this paper can be summarized as follows:

1. A novel LightNet architecture for the estimation of illumination and lighting direction in virtual images.

2. Evaluation of the proposed architecture on challenging VIDIT dataset.
3. Comprehensive experiments are conducted and shown the excellence of the proposed method to the baseline methods.
4. Achieve good experimental results in terms of accuracy, F1 score and loss.

2 Related Works

Augmented reality (AR) become more popular in the past decade due to benchmark achievements in computer vision and computer graphics. Several methods were proposed and developed to estimate the illumination conditions in virtual objects in an AR system [11]. In the literature, image processing algorithms have been used to detect the illumination level, and light direction in virtual images [4,11,24]. Jachnik et al. [11], developed an algorithm for real-time surface light-field extract from a single hand-held camera for capturing dense illumination information from specular surfaces. In their work, the light-field is divided into diffuse and specular components where the specular component can be used for environment map estimation. Since the intensity of the shadow is measured as a brute-force approach, computational cost of this method is more. Xing et al. [22] proposed an approach to render virtual objects into a sample image of an outdoor scene by simulating the illumination and the shadow casting between virtual objects and actual scenes. Arief et al. [10] proposed a method for real-time illumination direction estimation for mobile virtual reality systems using analysis of shadows created by a reference object. This method could predict the direction of a single light source in a controlled condition with better accuracy. In this method, the major drawback is that the estimation takes around 15 s. In spite of the good results, these image processing algorithms are not capable of running in a real-time devices due to their high computational cost. Special hardware approaches were also dealt in the literature to generate a 3D reconstruction of the scene. In this method, illumination can be estimated by knowing the position of the objects and the light sources. Gruber et al. [16] developed a method for real-time illumination estimation and picture realistic rendering in virtual reality. Rohmer et al. [20] proposed a differential illumination method to obtain a constant illumination of the inserted virtual objects on mobile devices. Multiple HDR video cameras have been used in a predetermined scenario. Recent work on lighting level estimation decomposed the RGB-D input into albedo and shading fields in order to elaborate the scene [12].

Boom et al. [1] developed a first hybrid CPU-GPU based method for estimating a light source position in a scene recorded by an RGB-D camera. The image and depth information from the Kinect is used to estimate a light position in a scene that appears realistic enough for augmented reality purposes. Chen et al. [21], proposed an illumination estimation method which estimate coarse scene geometry and intrinsic components including shading image and reflectance image. Then they used sparse radiance map of the scene to illuminate virtual objects by using the estimated sparse radiance map.

Success of deep learning network approach paves the way for better enhancement in the field of virtual reality. In the light source estimation by neural networks, the space of light directions is discretized into the set of N classes and the network classifies an image as one of these classes [2]. Previous research also proved that dominant light direction can be directly regressed from an input image by a neural network [7]. In [15], Kan and Kafumann proposed an approach based on a similar deep learning method aiming at higher complexity of a scene, temporal coherence and direct application of the network to an augmented reality scenario. Elizondo et al. [7] presents a novel neural network-based approach for recovering light source direction in relation to the viewpoint direction of a graphical image in noisy environments. The estimated light source direction can be used for the generation of 3D images from 2D ones. Frahm et al. [8] presents an approach which exploits a two camera system, the TV camera captures the video for the augmentation while the fish-eye camera observes the upper hemisphere to track the light sources. Thus the virtual objects are rendered by direct lighting. Soulier et al. [13] present a low-cost approach to detect the direction of the environment illumination, allowing the illumination of virtual objects according to the real light of the ambient, improving the integration of the scene.

Compared to the literature works, our proposed LightNet (Densenet121) architecture preserves information that is added to the network. Densenet layers are very narrow adding only a small set of feature-maps and keep the remaining feature maps unaffected, finally the classifier classify based on all feature-maps in the network. In contrast to ResNets [25], the features have been combined by concatenation. Besides better parameter efficiency, major advantage of densenet is that their enhanced flow of data and gradients throughout the network which makes them easy to train. Each layer has direct access to the gradients leading to an implicit deep supervision [25]. Further, it is also proved that dense connections have a regularizing effect, which reduces over fitting on tasks with smaller training set sizes. Thus our proposed architecture achieves excellent performance in estimating illumination and lighting direction.

3   LightNet: Illumination and Light Direction Estimation

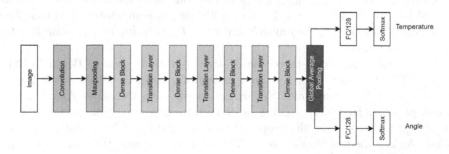

Fig. 2. Overall Block diagram of the proposed LightNet architecture

Our proposed method for estimating illumination and lighting direction uses a deep convolutional network to learn a connection between the input image and a dominant light direction. This network needs to be trained only once on a variety of augmented reality scenes, and then, it can be applied in a new scene. The proposed architecture for illumination estimation was unified into a virtual reality rendering context and evaluated on several real scenes which were not used during training. The overall block diagram of the proposed architecture is shown in Fig. 2 which mainly consist of a Dense network (Densenet) architecture [9]. The Densenet has also a superior property that it alleviates the vanishing gradient and reuses the extracted features properly. The detailed architecture of the Densenet block is shown in Fig. 3. It is provided with the simple connectivity pattern to confirm maximum data flow among layers in the network, where all the layers are connected directly with each other. Each layer in the network gets additional inputs from all the previous layers and directs the feature maps to all the subsequent layers thus preserved the feed-forward nature of the Densenet architecture.

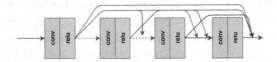

Fig. 3. Dense block

The proposed network includes N layers, each of which implements a nonlinear transformation $T_n(*)$. Here n indicates the layer and denote the output of the n_{th} layer as x_n. Also different connectivity pattern is introduced in densenet that direct connections from any layer is directed to all subsequent layers. Accordingly, the nth layer obtains the feature-maps of all preceding layers, $x_0, x_1, x_2, \ldots x_{n-1}$ as input:

$$x_n = T_n([x_0, x_1, x_2, ..., x_{n-1}]) \tag{1}$$

where $[x_0, x_1, x_2, \ldots x_{n-1}]$ refers to the concatenation of the feature-maps formed in layers $0, 1, 2, \ldots n - 1$. To simplify the implementation and to reduce the computational cost, the multiple inputs of $T_n(*)$ in Eq. (1) are concatenated into a single tensor.

Our network performs three consecutive operations such as Batch Normalization (BN) followed by a Rectified linear units (ReLU) and a 3×3 Convolution (Conv) function. Since the size of feature-maps changes concatenation is not possible. However, because of down-sampling operation, which changes the size of feature-maps, the proposed network is divided into multiple densely allied blocks called as dense blocks. The transition layers, the connecting lines between the dense blocks will perform convolution and pooling operation. In our experimentation, the transition layers contain a batch normalization and a 1×1 convolutional layer followed by a 2×2 average pooling layer. To decrease the number of input feature maps, bottleneck layers are involved in the network before each 3×3 convolution and thus reduce the computational cost. Our

Densenet architecture consists of 58 dense blocks, followed by three transition blocks and three fully-connected layers. Totally our proposed LightNet architecture consist of 121 layers. We replaced the global average pooling and fully connected layers from the pre-trained network with new global average pooling and fully connected layers along with two output layers for lighting angle and temperature estimation. The model is trained with two softmax outputs. One output layer with 8×1 consider for lighting angle prediction and another output layer with 5×1 consider for temperature prediction. The model loss was updated by sum of temperature and lighting angle categorical cross-entropy function.

4   Evaluation and Results

4.1   Dataset

For experimentation and evaluation, we used novel Virtual Image Dataset for Illumination Transfer (VIDIT) dataset [5] for illumination estimation. VIDIT is used for the lighting estimation challenge in the AIM workshop, ECCV 2020 [6]. VIDIT comprises of 390 various unreal engine scenes, each captured with 40 illumination settings. The illumination settings are captured in all the combinations of 5 color temperatures (2500K, 3500K, 4500K, 5500K and 6500K) and 8 light directions (N, NE, E, SE, S, SW, W, NW). Resolution of each original image is 1024×1024. For evaluation all the images are normalized from 0 to 1 scale using mean-max normalization method. An example of virtual images from VIDIT dataset is shown in Fig. 4. First column of the Fig. 4 represents all the light directions for 2500k color temperature. Similarly, 2nd, 3rd, 4th and 5th columns of that figure represents 3500K, 4500K, 5500K and 6500K color temperature respectively.

4.2   Training Data

VIDIT illumination estimation dataset consists of 11999 images. From the whole dataset, we randomly split 67% of images for training and 33% for validation. Adam optimizer is learned at the rate from 0.001 to 0.00001 with 500 epochs to train the proposed model. The proposed architecture has been evaluated for temperature and lighting direction estimation on the set of test images, which are not learned by the network in the training process. Performance evaluation in terms of accuracy has been computed for color temperature and lighting direction is based on the Eq. (2) as given below.

$$Accuracy(\%) = \frac{No.\,of\,correct\,predictions}{Total\,number\,of\,predictions} \times 100 \qquad (2)$$

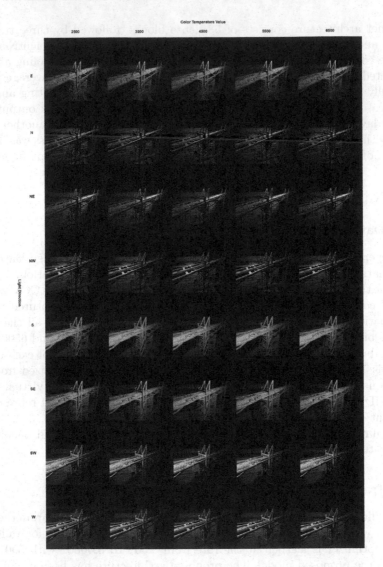

Fig. 4. An example of virtual images from VIDIT dataset. First Column: Images shown for 8 light directions (From top to bottom: E, N, NE, NW, S, SE, SW and W) for 2500k color temperature 2nd column: 8 light directions for 3500k color temperature. 3^d column: 8 light directions for 4500k color temperature. 4th column: 8 light directions for 5500k color temperature. 5th column: 8 light directions for 6500k color temperature.

The model loss was updated by sum of temperature and lighting angle categorical cross-entropy function. The temperature and angle categorical loss is defined as follows:

$$Temperature_{CLoss} = -\sum_{i=1}^{N} T_i log \hat{T}_i \qquad (3)$$

$$Angle_{CLoss} = -\sum_{i=1}^{N} \phi_i log \hat{\phi}_i \tag{4}$$

where i refers to all N test samples, ϕ_i are angle values $[0, 360]$ $\hat{\phi}_i$ indicates the predicted angle value, T_i is the color temperature value and $\hat{T}_i$ is the predicted color temperature value. The color temperature values 2500K, 3500K, 4500K, 5500K and 6500K, in short are takes the values of 0, 0.25, 0.5, 0.75 and 1 respectively.

The performance evaluation of the proposed LightNet model is based on the accuracy of the predictions following this formula for a loss metric:

$$Loss_M = \sqrt{\sum_{i=0}^{N-1} \left(\frac{|\hat{\phi}_i - \phi_i| mod 180}{180} \right)^2 + (\hat{T}_i - T_i)^2} \tag{5}$$

For higher accuracy the loss, $Loss_M$ should be lower.

4.3   Experimental Results

The proposed model is evaluated by estimating the illumination and light directions of VIDIT dataset. Table 1 shows the results of the proposed method on training, validation, development and testing set. The performance metrics such as Temperature loss, Angle loss and Loss metric have been computed as described in Eq. (3), Eq. (4) and Eq. (5) respectively and are tabulated in Table 1.

Table 1. Results of the proposed method on VIDIT - Illumination estimation dataset

Type	Image count	$Loss_M$	Angle loss	Temp loss
Training	8000	0.000315	0.00028906	2.6875e−05
Validation	3999	0.07378	0.071142	0.00264
Development	45	0.0974	0.0597	0.0377
Test	45	0.0984	0.0513	0.0471

In the testing phase, the proposed LightNet model achieved overall loss, angle loss and temperature loss as 0.0984, 0.0513 and 0.0471 respectively. To prove the superior performance of the proposed network, evaluation has also been done with 11 different benchmark baseline models which are listed in Table 2. Compared to the results of the baseline models, our proposed LightNet architecture was outperformed in estimating the illumination level and lighting direction. Performance of the light direction accuracy, temperature accuracy and loss value are considered for comparison with all the models. From the table it is inferred that our Densenet121 model provided better results compared to other benchmark

Table 2. Performance comparison of the proposed Densenet121 model with other benchmark models. T_{AA} -Training Angle Accuracy, T_{TA} -Training Temperature Accuracy, T_{Loss_M} -Training Loss Metric, V_{DA} -Validation Angle Accuracy, V_{TA} -Validation Temperature Accuracy, V_{Loss_M} -Validation Loss Metric

Model type	T_{AA}	T_{TA}	T_{loss_M}	V_{DA}	V_{TA}	V_{Loss_M}
DenseNet-169	99.725	99.7625	0.000492812	79.769	82.14	**0.061512**
DenseNet-201	99.912	99.93	0.000324	78.46961	85.096274	0.0622824
Xception [3]	97.625	95.925	0.00826	75.5188	73.2933	0.08175
MobileNetV2 [19]	99.3125	97.675	0.0024743	68.54	77.779	0.102825
Resnet50 [14]	99.975	99.9375	**2.84E−05**	73.49337	83.14578	0.085773
EfficientNetB0 [18]	98.15	96.2	0.005799	67.866	78.769	0.0952894
EfficientNetB1	99.175	98.25	0.00342593	72.568	80.5701	0.08677
EfficientNetB2	94.975	87.05	0.021672	65.616	75.393	0.11652
EfficientNetB3	99.5625	97.05	0.002173	74.793	77.469	0.0838
EfficientNetB4	99.45	97.35	0.002149	74.89	80.6201	0.077486
EfficientNetB5	99.45	98.2625	0.0020628	77.844	83.795	0.06732
DenseNet-121	99.9375	99.7875	0.000315	76.069	84.2460	0.07378

models. Similarly, Table 3 shows the experimental results of all the existing network models for the development phase data. Table 3 also shows the performance comparison of the proposed Densenet121 model with other baseline models. From the table, it is inferred that our proposed model provided results on par with Resnet 50 and DenseNet-169. Even though the Resnet-50 and Densenet-169 models produced low loss value on training and validation data, these models failed to perform well on development data. It is also observed that, EfficientNetB5 model has a higher loss than DenseNet-121 despite having a larger accuracy in the angle and color temperature estimation. This is because the loss function computation is different from the accuracy calculation. Here we calculate the loss value based on root sum squared analysis as described in Eq. (5). Based on that metrics, the loss value, temperature loss and angle loss of EfficientNetB5 was 0.1065, 0.02733 and 0.07916 respectively. Thus despite of the accuracy, the loss value of the EfficientNetB5 was high because of high temperature loss and angle loss.

To prove the efficacy of the proposed LightNet architecture, we also measured the performance metrics such as Precision, Recall and F1 score values. Table 4 lists the above performance metrics values on development data for the light directions 0, 45, 90, 135, 180, 225, 270 and 315. From the table it is observed that for 90 angle light direction, our method achieved maximum of one in all the three metrics. Likewise, Table 5 shows the performance on development data for various color temperature values. It is observed that, for 0.25 temperature, our method attained higher value of precision, recall and F1 score as 0.8, 0.5 and 0.62 respectively. The experimental results overall indicate that the proposed model achieves higher accuracy on light direction and illumination estimation than the compared baseline methods on challenging dataset.

Table 3. Comparison of experimental Results of Development phase data with benchmark models

Model type	Angle accuracy	Temperature accuracy	Loss$_M$
DenseNet-169	66.67	42.223	0.159
DenseNet-201	66.67	42.224	0.16389
Xception	64.445	42.223	0.19827
MobileNetV2	51.112	46.667	0.2456
Resnet50	57.78	44.45	1.91E−01
EfficientNetB0	64.445	40	0.2123
EfficientNetB1	68.89	42.23	0.1899
EfficientNetB2	64.445	42.23	0.160778
EfficientNetB3	71.12	37.75	0.16988
EfficientNetB4	68.889	46.667	0.16678
EfficientNetB5	77.77	51.11	0.1065
DenseNet-121	75.556	42.223	**0.09744**

Table 4. Evaluation of performance metrics of light direction on development data. I_{count} represents the class wise image count.

Angle	Precision	Recall	F1-Score	I_{count}
0	0.62	1	0.77	5
45	1	0.8	0.89	5
90	1	1	1	4
135	1	0.5	0.67	4
180	0.71	0.83	0.77	6
225	0.71	0.71	0.71	7
270	0.6	0.5	0.55	6
315	0.75	0.75	0.75	8

Light Direction is South
West Degree
and Temperature is 0.25

Light Direction is East
Degree
and Temperature is 0.25

Light Direction is North
West Degree
and Temperature is 0.25

Fig. 5. Sample Images of development set

Table 5. Evaluation of performance metrics of color temperature on development data

Temperature	Precision	Recall	F1-Score	I_{count}
2500	0	0	0	13
3500	0.8	0.5	0.62	8
4500	0.33	0.6	0.43	5
5500	0	0	0	15
6500	0	0	0	4

From the Fig. 5 it is understood that the light direction can be estimated accurately compared to color temperature estimation which is still an unsolvable issue in the field of virtual reality. As an extension, along with the training features, the depth information can also be added to estimate the color temperature accurately. It is also observed that for all kind of images our method estimates illumination and light direction which is visually acceptable and comparable. Moreover, the results show that the proposed LightNet model can estimate illumination and light direction in virtual reality images which were not learnt in a training set.

Computational complexity: In the proposed method, the training parameters of the model are 7,219,981 and the model size is 29.66 MB. Finally, we measured the computation time of our method. During training and testing, the run time consumed per image with the size of $224 \times 224 \times 3$ is 0.019979 s. For training the other baseline models, same loss function and optimization was trained with 100 epochs. The proposed network was trained and tested with the Intel Core i7 processor, GTX 1080 GPU, 8 GB RAM in Keras.

5 Conclusions

Factual illumination of virtual objects inserted in real scenes is one of the important challenges of a virtual reality system. This paper presented a novel LightNet architecture using Densenet121 for estimating illumination and lighting direction in virtual images. Our model is trained with two softmax outputs for color temperature and lighting direction prediction. The proposed architecture is evaluated on challenging VIDIT-illumination estimation dataset. Our experimental results, overall proved that our method achieves higher accuracy, F1 score and minimal loss on estimated light direction and illumination than the compared state-of-the-art methods. Our proposed model have also submitted to the AIM 2020 challenge [6] and secured top position among the participants. In that we used the ImageNet pre-trained weights and obtained the result in terms of loss as 0.0984. Future direction of the present work should focus on the estimation of dynamic illumination as well as intensity of light sources to adjust the illumination even more realistic in virtual reality scenes. Also, an attention-based classifier network can be created to train the model inclusive of depth information with the input to increase the overall accuracy.

References

1. Boom, B.J., Orts-Escolano, S., Ning, X.X., McDonagh, S., Sandilands, P., Fisher, R.B.: Interactive light source position estimation for augmented reality with an RGB-D camera. Computer Animation and Virtual Worlds (2017). https://doi.org/10.1002/cav.1686,e1686cav.1686
2. Marques, B.A., Drumond, R.R., Vasconcelos, C.N., Clua, E.: Deep light source estimation for mixed reality. In: Proceedings of the 13th International Joint Conference on Computer Vision, Imaging and Computer Graphics Theory and Applications - Volume 1 GRAPP, pp. 303–311. INSTICC, SciTePress (2018). https://doi.org/10.5220/0006724303030311
3. Chollet, F.: Xception: deep learning with depthwise separable convolutions. In: 2017 IEEE Conference on Computer Vision and Pattern Recognition (CVPR), pp. 1800–1807 (2017)
4. Clements, M., Zakhor, A.: Interactive shadow analysis for camera heading in outdoor images. In: 2014 IEEE International Conference on Image Processing (ICIP), pp. 3367–3371 (2014)
5. El Helou, M., Zhou, R., Barthas, J., Sstrunk, S.: VIDIT: virtual image dataset for illumination transfer. arXiv preprint (2020). arXiv:2005.05460
6. El Helou, M., Zhou, R., Süsstrunk, S., Timofte, R., et al.: AIM 2020: scene relighting and illumination estimation challenge. In: Bartoli, A., Fusiello, A. (eds.) ECCV 2020 Workshops. LNCS, vol. 12537, pp. 499–518. Springer, Cham (2020)
7. Elizondo, D.A., Zhou, S.M., Chrysostomou, C.: Light source detection for digital images in noisy scenes: a neural network approach. Neural Comput. Appl. **28**, 899–909 (2017)
8. Frahm, J.M., Koeser, K., Grest, D., Koch, R.: Markerless augmented reality with light source estimation for direct illumination. In: The 2nd IEE European Conference on Visual Media Production, CVMP 2005, pp. 211–220 (2005)
9. Huang, G., Liu, Z., Van Der Maaten, L., Weinberger, K.Q.: Densely connected convolutional networks. In: 2017 IEEE Conference on Computer Vision and Pattern Recognition (CVPR), pp. 2261–2269 (2017)
10. Arief, I., McCallum, S., Hardeberg, J.Y.: Realtime estimation of illumination direction for augmented reality on mobile devices. In: Color and Imaging Conference 2012. Society for Imaging Science and Technology, pp. 111–116 (2012)
11. Jachnik, J., Newcombe, R.A., Davison, A.J.: Real-time surface light-field capture for augmentation of planar specular surfaces. In: 2012 IEEE International Symposium on Mixed and Augmented Reality (ISMAR), pp. 91–97 (2012)
12. Barron, J.T., Malik, J.: Intrinsic scene properties from a single RGB-D image. In: 2013 IEEE Conference on Computer Vision and Pattern Recognition, pp. 17–24 (2013)
13. Soulier, K.E., M., Larrea, M.L.: Real-time estimation of illumination direction for augmented reality with low-cost sensors. In: Conference: XXII Congreso Argentino de Ciencias de la Computación (CACIC 2016) (2016)
14. He, K., Zhang, X., Ren, S., Sun, J.: Deep residual learning for image recognition. In: 2016 IEEE Conference on Computer Vision and Pattern Recognition (CVPR), pp. 770–778 (2016)
15. Kán, P., Kafumann, H.: DeepLight: light source estimation for augmented reality using deep learning. Vis. Comput. **2019**(35), 873–883 (2019)
16. Gruber, L., Langlotz, T., Sen, P., Höherer, T., Schmalstieg, D.: Efficient and robust radiance transfer for probeless photorealistic augmented reality. In: 2014 IEEE Virtual Reality (VR), pp. 15–20 (2014)

17. Martînez, H., Laukkanen, S.: Towards an augmented reality guiding system for assisted indoor remote vehicle navigation. EAI Endorsed Trans. Indus. Netw. Intell. Syst. **2**(2) (2015). https://doi.org/10.4108/inis.2.2.e3
18. Tan, M., Le, Q.V.: EfficientNet: rethinking model scaling for convolutional neural networks. In: ICML (2019). arXiv:1905.11946v3
19. Sandler, M., Howard, A., Zhu, M., Zhmoginov, A., Chen, L.: MobileNetV 2: inverted residuals and linear bottlenecks. In: 2018 IEEE/CVF Conference on Computer Vision and Pattern Recognition, pp. 4510–4520 (2018)
20. Rohmer, K., Büschel, W., Dachselt, R., Grosch, T.: Interactive near-field illumination for photorealistic augmented reality on mobile devices. In: 2014 IEEE International Symposium on Mixed and Augmented Reality (ISMAR), pp. 29–38 (2014)
21. Chen, X., Wang, K., Jin, X.: Single image based illumination estimation for lighting virtual object in real scene. In: 12th International Conference on Computer-Aided Design and Computer Graphics, pp. 450–455 (2011)
22. Xing, G., Zhou, X., Peng, Q., Liu ,Y., Qin, X.: Lighting simulation of augmented outdoor scene based on a legacy photograph. Comput. Graph. Forum, 101–110 (2013). https://doi.org/10.1111/cgf.12217. https://onlinelibrary.wiley.com/doi/abs/10.1111/cgf.12217
23. Dong, Y., Chen, G.: Appearance from-motion: recovering spatially varying surface reflectance under unknown lighting. ACM Trans. Graph. (2014). https://doi.org/10.1145/2661229.2661283
24. Liu, Y., Granier, X.: Online tracking of outdoor lighting variations for augmented reality with moving cameras. IEEE Trans. Vis. Comput. Graph. **18**, 573–580 (2012)
25. Zhou, H., Hadap, S., Sunkavalli, K., Jacobs, D.W.: Deep single-image portrait relighting. In: Proceedings of the IEEE/CVF International Conference on Computer Vision (ICCV), October 2019

An Ensemble Neural Network for Scene Relighting with Light Classification

Liping Dong[1], Yu Zhu[2], Zhuolong Jiang[3], Xiangyu He[4], Zhaohui Meng[1],
Chenghua Li[4,5(✉)], Cong Leng[4,5], and Jian Cheng[4,5(✉)]

[1] College of Computer and Information, Hohai University, Nanjing, China
[2] School of Computer Science and Technology, Anhui University, Hefei, China
[3] Jiangnan University, Wuxi, China
[4] Institute of Automation, Chinese Academy of Sciences, Beijing 100190, China
[5] Nanjing Artificial Intelligence Chip Research, Institute of Automation, Chinese
Academy of Sciences (AiRiA), Beijing, China
lichenghua2014@ia.ac.cn,jcheng@nlpr.ia.ac.cn

Abstract. Illumination is a very important environmental condition.
Objects in different illumination environments will present different light
and shadow effects. Different kinds of illumination sources will cause different brightness and colors on the surface of the object. The conversion
of illumination in two pictures is an interesting and challenging new task,
which will be useful in the fields of photography and computer graphics.
To solve this problem, we propose a novel solution with three stages: illumination classification, One-to-One Relighting, and Any-to-Any Relighting. Our solution can accurately classify the illumination condition of the
input image and can change the direction of the illumination source from
any direction to another. We evaluate our methods on VIDIT, a rendered
dataset of artificial scenes. The proposed solution produces good results
under different light conditions.

Keywords: Illumination estimation · Scene relighting · Convolutional
neural network

1 Introduction

Under different illumination conditions, the luminance of the object and the
degree of the shadow may be different. Also, when processing photographs, the
object's information recorded by the camera is different. The illumination plays
a very vital role in photography. Professional photographers should spend a lot
of time getting perfect illumination conditions for their work even though they
have professional equipment to provide different illumination conditions for the
shooting target. For ordinary people, this is impossible because they can not
get professional props easily. However, the demand for professional photography

---

L. Dong, Y. Zhu, Z. Jiang and X. He—Equal contribution.

© Springer Nature Switzerland AG 2020
A. Bartoli and A. Fusiello (Eds.): ECCV 2020 Workshops, LNCS 12537, pp. 581–595, 2020.
https://doi.org/10.1007/978-3-030-67070-2_35

is increasing. It will be meaningful and valuable for solving the problems of relighting.

Our relighting task can be divided into two sub-tasks generally. One has the same scene but two different illuminations, the other one is two different scenes with two different illuminations. For VIDIT [7] dataset, we use has 300 different virtual scenes, each scene contains 5 different color temperatures and 8 different illumination directions. Our object is to design an automatic tool that can transform the illumination between two images. There are already some successful systems reset the illumination of scene [18, 24] but they require a 3D model of the scene to determine the current shadows and to cast shadows from the new light direction. However, because of the limitations of experimental objects and application scenarios, those systems can not be applied to this task. We hope to build a general method for 2D images.

In this work, we start from the relatively simple illumination classification task then apply the pre-trained classification models to the challenging Any-to-Any relighting task. The high-level features of pre-trained networks prove to have content-independent illumination representations, which alleviates the reconstruction of target images. For One-to-One relighting, we also conduct the pre-training strategy where the encoder-decoder is pre-trained in an unsupervised manner. The main contributions are as follow:

- We prove that the illumination settings estimation problem can be well-solved by classification networks. The pre-trained models further facilitate the downstream relighting tasks. Our method wins first place in the AIM2020 illumination settings estimation challenge.
- We propose to combine a mirrored pre-trained encoder into the decoder of an auto-encoder architecture, stage by stage, for the Any-to-Any illumination transfer.
- We present a two-stage training strategy for the One-to-One relighting problem, which contributes to better visualization results than the plain encoder-decoder baseline.

2   Related Works

Image relighting in complex scenes is growing more popular lately and it can be regarded as a form of style transfer specific to illumination (i.e., illumination is an attribute of the given image). The content image and a style (i.e., illumination) reference image setting also shares the same idea as neural style transfer. Therefore, we briefly review the relevant style transfer works and recent relighting methods.

Style Transfer. Liu et al. [13] make a shared-latent space assumption where a hypothesized image in the source domain can be mapped to the target domain of images and the generated images can also be mapped back to the source domain by the same method, which proves that the shared-latent space constraints imply cycle-consistency. This method can produce good results for objects involving less geometry and shadows.

Huang et al. [9] propose a multimodal unsupervised image to the image transformation framework, which generates multiple images of different styles from a single image. It splits the image into content and style parts, the transformation from source domain image to target domain image only needs to combine the content part of the source domain with the style part of the target domain. This method is also suitable for fewer shadows and geometric scenes. Zhu et al. [25] propose a method for transforming source domain to target domain without paired data by learning the mapping between the source domain and target domain and mapping the target domain back to the source domain, also considering the cyclic consistency loss. Isola et al. [10] present a general solution for Image-to-Image Translation based on CGAN.

Image Scene Relighting. Sun et al. [20] and Dherse et al. [1] implement three different light estimation network structure models, which are respectively: IlluminationPredicter, Envmap and Envmap+scene. IlluminationPredicter model estimates the direction of light and color temperature of the input in a numerical way. Envmap model is used to estimate the input environment illumination, also including the direction of light and color temperature. Envmap+scene model estimates the input figure based on environmental illumination, which can also be used to predict the content of the input. Each model has its advantages.

For the light source from any direction to the specified 8 directions and 5 color temperature arbitrary conversion problem in the same scene, Gafton et al. [3] propose a referable method based on pix2pix [20] framework, this method first uses a light direction classifier to identify the direction of the light source in an image and then use the relighting networks consist of 8 neural networks to change the direction and color temperature.

Portrait Relighting. Sun et al. [20] present a portrait relighting system based on U-Net. This technique can transform the illumination of a single input portrait image under an unlimited environment map into the related image under any given environment map. Zhou et al. [24] also implement facial relighting based on Unet. This method uses traditional graphic methods to generate ground-truth data and proposes better facial features and illumination information. Nestmeyer [17] decomposes the image into intrinsic components based on a diffuse physics equation.

3   Illumination Settings Estimation

The purpose of illumination estimation is to recognize the light conditions in the image. Each image in VIDIT contains 8 directions and 5 color temperatures, which means that each scene has 40 illumination conditions. It is intuitive to regard the estimation task as a classification problem and solving the illumination classification problem can alleviate the following relighting task.

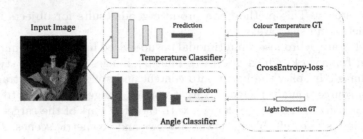

Fig. 1. Main structure of the illumination setting estimation

3.1 Proposed Method

Network Design. Our solution consists of two classification networks: direction classification model and color temperature classification model, as shown in Fig. 1. The ensembled direction classification model consists of ResNext101 [22], ResNext_50_32x4d [22] and ResNext101_32x8d [22], responsible for the classification of 8 light directions. The ensembled color temperature classification model is the combination of ResNet50 [5] and ResNext50_32x4d [22], responsible for the classification of 5 color temperatures.

Since the size of the training dataset is insufficient for 40 classification tasks, and the color temperature and direction belong to different modalities, we separate the classifiers into the illumination direction (8 categories) and color temperature (5 classes). In our experiments, we notice that the color temperature is easier to classify than the angle, hence the direction classification branch is much heavier than the temperature classification model.

Loss Function. Since the artificial scenes in VIDIT are relatively simpler than ImageNet [19] and the training dataset is easy to overfit for large models such as ResNet family [5, 22], it is initutive to use ImageNet pre-trained classification models to fine-tune on these tasks. We use the common setting

$$\mathcal{L}_{CrossEntropy} = -\sum_{c=1}^{M} \hat{y}_c \log(y_c) \tag{1}$$

as the learning object, where $\hat{y}$ is the prediction and y is the ground-truth label.

4 Relighting

By utilizing the results of light classification, we can further explore the relighting task. This task can be further divided into two sub-tasks: One-to-One Relighting and Any-to-Any Relighting. One-to-One means that we only need to transform one illumination in the same scene into another illumination. Any-to-Any means we need to transform any kind of illumination in different scenes to another scene. To this end, we propose two models: ReLighting Network (RLNet) and Fused Dual Path Network (FDPNet).

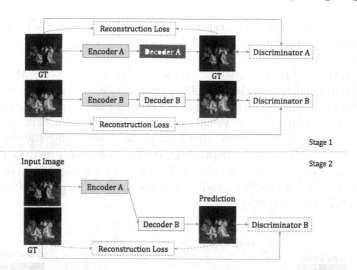

Fig. 2. RLNet two-stage training for One-to-One relighting task. Stage-1 serves as an auto-encoder pre-training to learn data codings in an unsupervised manner. Stage-2 further fine-tunes the deployment model using ground-truth images. "Discriminator" refers to minimizing the Pearson divergence proposed in [16]

4.1 One-to-One Relighting

Network Design. Due to the similarity between style transfer and relighting, we propose ReLighting Network (RLnet) inspired by the style transfer framework UNIT [14], shown in Fig. 2. We extend the unsupervised UNIT structure to the supervised light transfer task. The encoder contains two stride convolution layers as downsampling followed by four DRDB blocks [21] and the decoder has four DRDB blocks with two upsampling layers. For DRDB blocks, when the dilation rate at a high-level becomes larger, the input sampling will become sparse, which will limit the representation capacity since some local information has been lost. Besides the long-distance information may not always contribute to better local constructions. In light of this, we chose 1, 2, 5 as the dilation rates used in each DRDB block as shown in Fig. 3. We apply Switchable Normalization [15] and PReLU [4] after the convolution in each convolution block.

In our two-stage training process, we first train encoder-decoder A and B separately, i.e., encoder-decoder A, B generates reconstructed input images parallelly. The first stage serves as an auto-encoder mechanism. In the second step, we use pre-trained encoder A and decoder B to produce the predicted image.

Loss Function. We use a combination of three different loss functions in the optimization process to consider both local and global reconstructions:

$$\mathcal{L} = \underbrace{||\hat{I} - I||_1 + \eta \cdot (1 - \text{SSIM}(\hat{I}, I))}_{\text{local}} + \underbrace{\lambda \cdot (\text{VGG}(\hat{I}, I) + \text{LsGAN}(\hat{I}, I))}_{\text{global}} \quad (2)$$

where $\| \cdot \|_1$ means absolute error namely L1 Loss, $\hat{I}$, I stands for the predicted image and target image separately, where SSIM$(.,.)$ is Structural Similarity Index (SSIM) used to measure the structural similarity between two images. The larger the SSIM value, the more similar of two images. When the two images are exactly the same, the value of SSIM will be 1. VGG$(.,.)$ is a kind of perceptual loss [11] used to measure the similarity between predicted image features and target image features. As the visual effects are important for this task, we introduce a perceptual loss coupled with LSGAN loss (we follow the same training setting as [16]). The VGG16 network is fine-tuned on the previous 40 illumination classification task instead of ImageNet pre-training to produce task-relevant supervisions. To balance the local and global losses, we emprically set η to 0.2 and λ to 0.1 in our experiments.

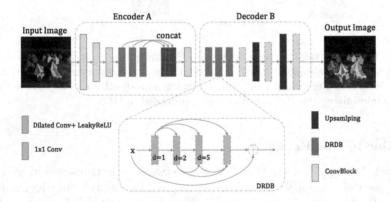

Fig. 3. The encoder-decoder structure in ReLighting Network (RLNet)

4.2   Any-to-Any Relighting

Network Design. The Fused Dual Path Network (FDPNet) consists of three modules: an illumination encoder (i.e., guidance encoder), a content encoder, and the final decoder. The illumination encoder is to extract illumination information. The content encoder captures image content information. The decoder's feature map at each stage contains three parts: hidden features of guidance encoder and content encoder, and the upsampled features from previous layers. The encoding layers are convolution layers with a stride of 2, while the decoding layers consist of upsample layers and standard 3×3 convolution layers. Each convolutional layer is followed by a DRDB block in decoding layers. The output of the last decoder layer is connected to a pixel shuffle layer to produce the final result. The guidance encoder then estimates the illumination of the input image and injects the generated illumination information map into the bottleneck. All convolutional layers in the decoder are followed by Switchable Normalization [15] and LeakyReLU [23]. The channel numbers are doubled at each layer from 32 to 512 during encoding and halved from 512 to 32 during decoding.

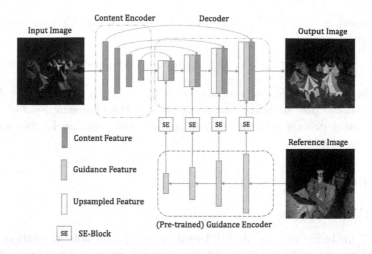

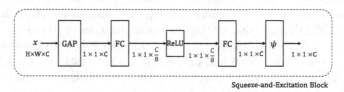

Fig. 4. Main Structure of Fused Dual Path Network (FDPNet), the solution to Any-to-Any relighting task. "Guidance Encoder" is pre-trained on the illumination classification task

Fig. 5. Squeeze-and-Excitation block [8]. "GAP" refers to the Global-Average-Pooling. $\psi(\cdot)$ is the nonlinear activation function. In this work, we use *sigmoid* to normalize the output to $[0, 1]$

For the illumination encoder, we use pre-trained classification models as shown in Fig. 4. Considering the network size and running time, we did not choose the ensembled network used in the previous section. In this case, we use ResNext50 [22] as the guidance encoder. For the content encoder, we first train a complete generative network by reconstructing the input image itself. In the final training phase, we jointly train the whole network in a supervised manner. To ensure the training stability and consistency between the illumination information extracted from the reference image and the prediction, we freeze both encoders to only fine-tune the decoder. Besides, the feature maps from the guidance encoder pass through an SE attention block [8], which is to extract effective illumination information and filter out redundant content information. The structure of the SE block is shown in Fig. 5. The basic module in FDPNet is also DRDB block [21]. Since the illumination information is widely distributed in a large area, networks require a large receptive field to receive extensive illumination information. Hence, DRDB with several dilation convolutions is an ideal choice.

Loss Function. For FDPnet, the loss function is simpler than One-to-One relighting:

$$\mathcal{L} = ||\hat{I} - I||_1 + \eta \cdot (1 - \text{SSIM}(\hat{I}, I)) \qquad (3)$$

where η is set to 0.2. Since this task is much harder than One-to-One relighting, we find that the discriminator can easily classify the fake samples and do harm to the training process. Hence, we only conduct the common L1 loss and SSIM in our experiments.

5   Experiments

5.1   VIDIT Dataset

VIDIT [7] includes in total 390 different scenes (train 300, validation 45, test 45). Each scene has 40 conditions of illumination settings. The illumination settings are combined with 5 color temperatures (2500K, 3500K, 4500K, 5500K and 6500K) and 8 light directions (N, NE, E, SE, S, SW, W, NW). The scenes are obtained from a variety of different virtual environments, which are scaled into a uniform reference space before running the illumination rendering process. In the AIM-2020 illumination setting estimation challenge, there are 12000 pictures (300 scenes). In the One-to-One relighting challenge, we have 600 pictures (input 300, ground-truth 300) and in the Any-to-Any track, we have 12000 (300 scenes, resized to 512×512) images. We randomly choose 120 pictures as the illumination estimation validation set and 5 pictures as the relighting validation set.

5.2   Illumination Estimation

To distinguish different light directions and color temperatures, we consider it as a classification problem. Our model consists of two parts: temperature classifier and direction classifier. This setting is motivated by the fact that the dataset contains eight directions and five color temperatures, in a total of 40. Using a single model to classify 40 categories is harder than the prediction of separate directions and color temperatures.

Implementation Details. For temperature classification, we set the learning rate as 1e−4, batch size as 64, and warm-up iters as 300. Learning rate changes at 33th and 46th epoch. They were both trained with 50 epochs. For angle classification, we set the learning rate as 5e−5 and batch size as 32. The learning rate changes at 66th and 92th epoch with a warm-up of 1000 iterations. We resize input images to 448×448. We conduct all experiments (including training and testing) on 8 Titan XP 12G GPUs. The DRAM size is 256 GB. The deep learning framework is PyTorch with 8 GPUs parallel training. The total training time is about 80 GPU hours on Titan XP. The inference speed is about 30 ms per image.

Table 1. Ablation study on the illumination settings estimation task

Model	Data Aug	Ensemble	Val-loss	Test-loss
ResNext50	–	–	0.1153	–
ResNext50	✓	–	0.0861	–
ResNext50/101+ResNet50	✓	✓	**0.0514**	**0.0875**

Table 2. Illumination settings estimation results on the *test* set

Rank	Team	Test-loss	AngLoss	TempLoss
1st	Ours	**0.0875**	0.0722	**0.0153**
2nd	YorkU	0.0887	0.0639	0.0248
3rd	Image Lab	0.0984	**0.0513**	0.0471
4th	debut_kele	0.1431	0.1125	0.0306
5th	RGETH	0.1708	0.1347	0.0361

In Table 1, we perform ablation experiments on data augmentation (i.e., the standard PyTorch transform settings) and model ensemble. It is shown that the validation error achieves 55% relative improvements over baseline methods by utilizing both data augmentation and model ensemble. We report the final *test* set results [2] in Table 2. Our method wins first place in AIM2020 illumination settings estimation challenge.

5.3 One-to-One Relighting

Implementation Details. In this experiment, we use ADAM [12] optimizer for training. The learning rate is 0.0001 and momentums are set to 0.9 and 0.999. The number of training iterations is 100K. We halve the learning rate every 15K iterations. Due to the limited GPU memory size, we set the batch size as 1.

To verify the effect of the proposed two-stage training strategy, we conduct ablation studies on the *val* set. The results are shown in Table 3. We further evaluate the contributions of GAN loss and the standard content-independent loss to the visualization results. Figure 8 shows that the GAN loss and perceptual loss lead to better visualization results, though the PSNR is much worse than only using L_1 + SSIM. We further visualize the results generated by the best settings under different metrics in Fig. 6. It is shown that LPIPS and MPS[1] are consistent with the human visual system. PSNR works poorly in relighting tasks due to the existence of abnormal samples (e.g., extremely dark scenes shown in Fig. 7).

---

[1] Mean Perceptual Score (MPS): the official evaluation protocol used in the AIM2020 relighting challenge. MPS = $0.5 \cdot$ (SSIM + (1 − LPIPS)).

5.4   Any-to-Any Relighting

Implementation Details. We still use ADAM [12] solver to optimize the weights of the network with $\beta_1 = 0.9$, $\beta_2 = 0.999$, and a learning rate of 0.0001. The mini-batch size is 8. We train decoder on the VIDIT [7] dataset for 100 epochs and report the results on the *val* set, listed in Table 5. Our scheme achieves similar performances as top-ranking methods.

Table 3. Ablation study on the One-to-One image relighting task. We report the results on the *val* set. The two-stage training strategy significantly contributes to higher performances. Since One-to-One is a special case of Any-to-Any relighting, we use FDPNet as a baseline method. "RLNet+FDPNet" refers to model ensemble. Due to the space limit, we only list Top-3 results to make a comparison

Model/Team	Loss	Two-stage	PSNR↑	SSIM↑	LPIPS↓	MPS↑
RLNet	L_1+SSIM+VGG+GAN	–	15.96	0.5298	0.3872	0.5713
RLNet	L_1+SSIM+VGG+GAN	✓	15.95	0.5827	0.3183	**0.6322**
RLNet	L_1+SSIM	✓	16.40	**0.5998**	0.3525	0.6237
RLNet	VGG+GAN	✓	15.86	0.4804	0.3494	0.5655
FDPNet	L_1	–	13.59	0.3251	0.4156	0.4548
FDPNet	SSIM	–	16.46	0.5031	**0.2873**	0.6079
FDPNet	L_1+SSIM	–	**17.21**	0.4425	0.2915	0.5755
leven[1st]	–	–	17.60	0.6198	–	–
souryadipta[2nd]	–	–	17.58	0.5934	–	–
hrishikeshps[3rd]	–	–	17.34	0.6542	–	–
RLNet+FDPNet[6th]	L_1+SSIM+VGG+GAN	✓	17.14	0.6132	0.2764	0.6684

Table 4. Ablation study on the Any-to-Any image relighting task. We report the results on the *val* set. SE module contributes to about +0.06 MPS points. The pre-trained guidance encoder also matters for both subjective and objective evaluations

Model	Pre-train	PSNR↑	SSIM↑	LPIPS↓	MPS↑
FDPNet	✓	17.97	0.4843	**0.2509**	0.6157
FDPNet+SE [8]	–	17.39	0.3862	0.2656	0.5603
FDPNet+SE [8]	✓	18.07	**0.5994**	0.2524	**0.6735**
FDPNet+CGD [6]	✓	**18.14**	0.5241	0.2578	0.6332

To fully evaluate the effectiveness of SE blocks shown in Fig. 4, we conduct an ablation study around the use of SE blocks for the feature combination. Table 4 shows that applying SE blocks to skip connections notably improves the performance. Compact global descriptor (CGD [6]) is another lightweight channel attention mechanism. The experiment results show that using the attention technique to extract useful information from the guidance encoder is generally

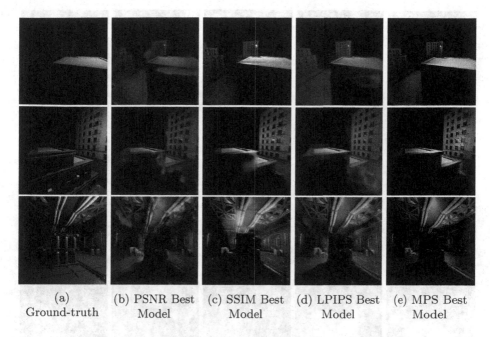

| (a) | (b) PSNR Best | (c) SSIM Best | (d) LPIPS Best | (e) MPS Best |
| Ground-truth | Model | Model | Model | Model |

Fig. 6. Visualization comparisons between the best results under different metrics. PSNR is inconsistent with Human Visual System (HVS)

Table 5. Comparison with other leading methods on the Any-to-Any image relighting *val/test* set. Red colour indicates the best result. Blue colour is the second best result. Due to the space limit, we only list the Top-5 methods

	Team	walden	mafifi	leven	ms_ipcv	tongtong	Ours
val	PSNR↑	18.07	17.96	16.54	18.84	14.41	18.07
val	SSIM↑	0.6480	0.6209	0.6105	0.6053	0.1601	0.5994
test	PSNR↑	18.54	18.24	–	19.36	17.63	18.35
test	SSIM↑	0.6353	0.6195	–	0.6042	0.5881	0.4451
test	Final Rank	1st	2nd	–	3rd	4th	5th

Fig. 7. Extremely dark scences in One-to-One image relighting. PSNR is dominated by the large black area

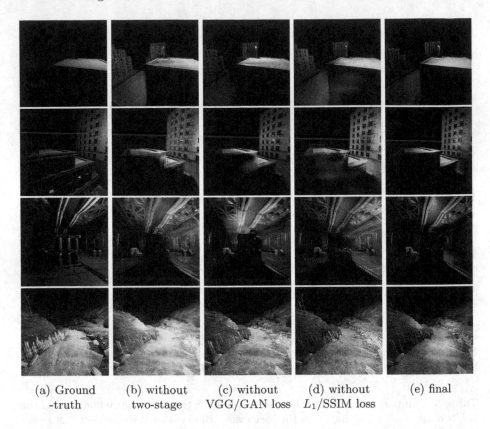

<table>
<tr><td>(a) Ground
-truth</td><td>(b) without
two-stage</td><td>(c) without
VGG/GAN loss</td><td>(d) without
L_1/SSIM loss</td><td>(e) final</td></tr>
</table>

Fig. 8. Illustrations of the effect of two-stage training and different loss functions on the One-to-One *val* set. We visualize the outputs of RLNet

effective. We further make qualitative analysis to SE blocks, illustrated in Fig. 9. Compared with Fig. 9b (without SE), Fig. 9c (with SE) makes the generated images more natural with more accurate light direction estimation. The pretrained guidance encoder also leads to superior performances than training from scratch, which proves the interaction between illumination settings estimation and relighting tasks.

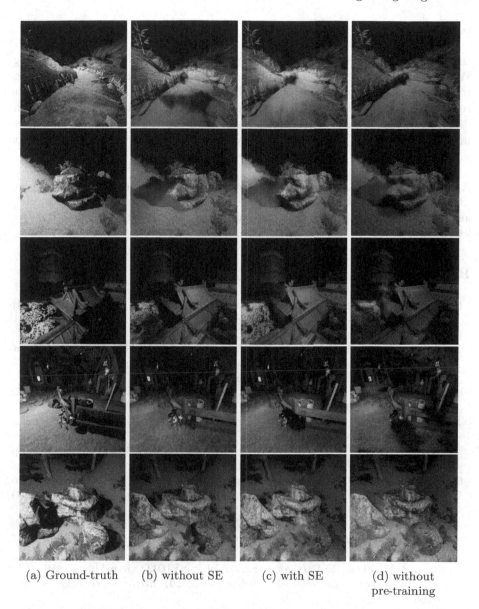

(a) Ground-truth   (b) without SE   (c) with SE   (d) without pre-training

Fig. 9. Illustrations of the effect of SE module and pre-trained guidance encoder on the Any-to-Any *val* set. We visualize the outputs of FDPNet. SE module contributes to more natural and realistic results with fewer artifacts

6   Conclusions

In this paper, we propose a solution to implement the scene image relighting. We use the neural network to classify the light direction and the color temperature. After solving the classification problem, we propose RLNet for One-to-One relighting, which enables changing the light from any direction to a given light direction. Finally, based on the well-trained illumination estimation model, we implement the transformation from any light condition to any light condition via FDPNet.

Acknowledgements. This work was supported by the Advance Research Program (31511130301); National Key Research and Development Program (2017YFF0209806), and National Natural Science Foundation of China (No. 61906193; No. 61906195; No. 61702510).

References

1. Dherse, A.P., Everaert, M., Gwizdala, J.J.: Scene relighting with illumination estimation in the latent space on an encoder-decoder scheme. ArXiv abs/2006.02333 (2020)
2. El Helou, M., Zhou, R., Süsstrunk, S., Timofte, R., et al.: AIM 2020: scene relighting and illumination estimation challenge. In: Bartoli, A., Fusiello, A. (eds.) ECCV 2020 Workshops. LNCS, vol. 12537, pp. 499–518. Springer, Cham (2020)
3. Gafton, P., Maraz, E.: 2D image relighting with image-to-image translation. ArXiv abs/2006.07816 (2020)
4. He, K., Zhang, X., Ren, S., Sun, J.: Delving deep into rectifiers: surpassing human-level performance on ImageNet classification. In: 2015 IEEE International Conference on Computer Vision, ICCV 2015, Santiago, Chile, 7–13 December 2015, pp. 1026–1034 (2015). https://doi.org/10.1109/ICCV.2015.123
5. He, K., Zhang, X., Ren, S., Sun, J.: Deep residual learning for image recognition. In: 2016 IEEE Conference on Computer Vision and Pattern Recognition (CVPR), pp. 770–778 (2016)
6. He, X., Cheng, K., Chen, Q., Hu, Q., Wang, P., Cheng, J.: Compact global descriptor for neural networks. CoRR abs/1907.09665 (2019). http://arxiv.org/abs/1907.09665
7. Helou, M.E., Zhou, R., Barthas, J., Süsstrunk, S.: VIDIT: virtual image dataset for illumination transfer. CoRR abs/2005.05460 (2020). https://arxiv.org/abs/2005.05460
8. Hu, J., Shen, L., Sun, G.: Squeeze-and-excitation networks. In: Proceedings of the IEEE Conference on Computer Vision and Pattern Recognition (CVPR), June 2018
9. Huang, X., Liu, M.Y., Belongie, S.J., Kautz, J.: Multimodal unsupervised image-to-image translation. ArXiv abs/1804.04732 (2018)
10. Isola, P., Zhu, J.Y., Zhou, T., Efros, A.A.: Image-to-image translation with conditional adversarial networks. In: 2017 IEEE Conference on Computer Vision and Pattern Recognition (CVPR), pp. 5967–5976 (2017)
11. Johnson, J., Alahi, A., Fei-Fei, L.: Perceptual losses for real-time style transfer and super-resolution. ArXiv abs/1603.08155 (2016)

12. Kingma, D.P., Ba, J.: Adam: a method for stochastic optimization. CoRR abs/1412.6980 (2015)
13. Liu, M.Y., Breuel, T., Kautz, J.: Unsupervised image-to-image translation networks. ArXiv abs/1703.00848 (2017)
14. Liu, M., Breuel, T., Kautz, J.: Unsupervised image-to-image translation networks. In: Advances in Neural Information Processing Systems 30: Annual Conference on Neural Information Processing Systems 2017, Long Beach, CA, USA, 4–9 December 2017, pp. 700–708 (2017). http://papers.nips.cc/paper/6672-unsupervised-image-to-image-translation-networks
15. Luo, P., Ren, J., Peng, Z., Zhang, R., Li, J.: Differentiable learning-to-normalize via switchable normalization. In: 7th International Conference on Learning Representations, ICLR 2019, New Orleans, LA, USA, 6–9 May 2019 (2019). https://openreview.net/forum?id=ryggIs0cYQ
16. Mao, X., Li, Q., Xie, H., Lau, R.Y.K., Wang, Z., Smolley, S.P.: Least squares generative adversarial networks. In: IEEE International Conference on Computer Vision, ICCV 2017, Venice, Italy, 22–29 October 2017, pp. 2813–2821 (2017). https://doi.org/10.1109/ICCV.2017.304
17. Nestmeyer, T., Lalonde, J.F., Matthews, I., Lehrmann, A.M.: Learning physics-guided face relighting under directional light. arXiv: Computer Vision and Pattern Recognition (2020)
18. Philip, J., Gharbi, M., Zhou, T., Efros, A.A., Drettakis, G.: Multi-view relighting using a geometry-aware network. ACM Trans. Graph. (TOG) 38, 1–14 (2019)
19. Russakovsky, O., et al.: ImageNet large scale visual recognition challenge. Int. J. Comput. Vis. 115(3), 211–252 (2015). https://doi.org/10.1007/s11263-015-0816-y
20. Sun, T., et al.: Single image portrait relighting. ACM Trans. Graph. (TOG) 38, 1–12 (2019)
21. Wang, P., et al.: Understanding convolution for semantic segmentation. In: 2018 IEEE Winter Conference on Applications of Computer Vision (WACV), pp. 1451–1460 (2018)
22. Xie, S., Girshick, R.B., Dollár, P., Tu, Z., He, K.: Aggregated residual transformations for deep neural networks. In: 2017 IEEE Conference on Computer Vision and Pattern Recognition (CVPR), pp. 5987–5995 (2017)
23. Xu, B., Wang, N., Chen, T., Li, M.: Empirical evaluation of rectified activations in convolutional network. CoRR abs/1505.00853 (2015). http://arxiv.org/abs/1505.00853
24. Zhou, H., Hadap, S., Sunkavalli, K., Jacobs, D.W.: Deep single-image portrait relighting. In: 2019 IEEE/CVF International Conference on Computer Vision (ICCV), pp. 7193–7201 (2019)
25. Zhu, J.Y., Park, T., Isola, P., Efros, A.A.: Unpaired image-to-image translation using cycle-consistent adversarial networks. In: 2017 IEEE International Conference on Computer Vision (ICCV), pp. 2242–2251 (2017)

Long-Term Human Video Generation
of Multiple Futures Using Poses

Naoya Fushishita[1]([⊠]), Antonio Tejero-de-Pablos[1], Yusuke Mukuta[1,2],
and Tatsuya Harada[1,2]

[1] The University of Tokyo, Tokyo, Japan
{fushishita,antonio-t,mukuta,harada}mi.t.u-tokyo.ac.jp
[2] RIKEN, Tokyo, Japan

Abstract. Generating future video from an input video is a useful task
for applications such as content creation and autonomous agents. Especially, prediction of human video is highly important. While most previous works predict a single future, multiple futures with different behavior
can potentially occur. Moreover, if the predicted future is too short (e.g.,
less than one second), it may not be fully usable by a human or other
systems. In this paper, we propose a novel method for future human
pose prediction capable of predicting multiple long-term futures. This
makes the predictions more suitable for real applications. After predicting future human motion, we generate future videos based on predicted
poses. First, from an input human video, we generate sequences of future
human poses (i.e., the image coordinates of their body-joints) via adversarial learning. Adversarial learning suffers from mode collapse, which
makes it difficult to generate a variety of multiple poses. We solve this
problem by utilizing two additional inputs to the generator to make the
outputs diverse, namely, a latent code (to reflect various behaviors) and
an attraction point (to reflect various trajectories). In addition, we generate long-term future human poses using a novel approach based on
unidimensional convolutional neural networks. Last, we generate an output video based on the generated poses for visualization. We evaluate
the generated future poses and videos using three criteria (i.e., realism,
diversity and accuracy), and show that our proposed method outperforms other state-of-the-art works.

Keywords: Future video prediction · Long-term video generation ·
Human pose prediction · Generative adversarial network

1 Introduction

Future video generation is a very challenging task that has been tackled consistently in the recent years [20,23,32,34], and has applications in different fields

Electronic supplementary material The online version of this chapter (https://
doi.org/10.1007/978-3-030-67070-2_36) contains supplementary material, which is
available to authorized users.

ⓒ Springer Nature Switzerland AG 2020
A. Bartoli and A. Fusiello (Eds.): ECCV 2020 Workshops, LNCS 12537, pp. 596–612, 2020.
https://doi.org/10.1007/978-3-030-67070-2_36

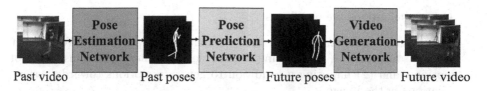

Fig. 1. Overview of the proposed method. First, human pose in the input video is estimated. From this, multiple plausible human poses are predicted for a long-term near-future. Finally, the future video based on the predicted poses is generated.

(e.g., content creation, autonomous agents, sports analysis). On the one hand, video generation allows for a high-level human interpretability of the predictions. On the other hand, predicting the immediate future from an observed scene is challenging, since several requirements have to be met. Firstly, since sometimes future is uncertain, there is a range of multiple plausible events that may occur. Thus, future prediction methods that predict a single future [4,12,22,32] may not be versatile enough, since only one possibility of many is considered. Instead, a more realistic setting would involve predicting a variety of plausible futures, as multiple situations can be considered. Secondly, if the predicted future video is too short, the method would not be realistically usable due to lack of content. For example, if we were to handle a possible dangerous situation predicted in a future video, the predicted time span should be long enough to be able to react in advance. Thus, relatively long predictions are desirable.

This paper proposes a novel method for video generation of multiple futures from a given input video. Since in many applications (e.g., autonomous agents, sports analysis) prediction of human behaviour is critical, we focus on prediction of human video. As many prior works [5,32,34,36] did, we generate future human videos based on human pose sequences. First, we estimate the human motion in the input human video. Then, we predict the multiple futures of their movement. Here, the predicted future is long-term (about two to four times longer than short-term future prediction [23,34]). Finally, after predicting the human behavior, we generate the video representing the predicted future. The overall pipeline is in Fig. 1.

In order to predict future human motion, many methods model pose sequences by using Recurrent Neural Networks (RNNs) [10,12,22,32,34]. However, RNNs suffer from the problem of vanishing gradients and error accumulations, which hamper the learning of long data sequences. So, for long-term pose generation, we use unidimensional convolutional neural networks (1D CNNs) instead of RNNs. We generate predictions of plausible future poses via generative adversarial learning. However, adversarial learning suffers from mode collapse, in which only a few or a single data are generated. We introduce a latent code [7] representing different actions to be able to generate multiple poses. Also, we include a location condition on the generated poses, so human motion is attracted towards different points of the image.

Our contributions are as follows.

- We propose a novel method for future human video prediction. We predict multiple futures by (1) imposing a condition to generate various types of motions, and (2) imposing a condition to generate motions towards various locations in the image.
- In order to handle long-term future prediction of human behavior, we propose a novel approach for generating human pose sequences using unidimensional convolutional networks.
- We provide extensive evaluation of the proposed method to validate our results, and a comparison with state-of-the-art works.

2   Related Work

2.1   Generative Adversarial Networks

Generative Adversarial Networks (GAN) [11] is a generative model in which a discriminator is trained to classify between fake data produced by a generator or real data, while the generator is trained to fool the discriminator. While the output of GAN is generated from latent noise and cannot be controlled, Conditional GAN (CGAN) [24] includes an input condition like class label that conditions the generated data. InfoGAN [7] unsupervisedly models the relationships between the latent code and the generated images by maximizing the mutual information between them. This allows to apply variations to the generated images without requiring an input label. However, these networks suffer from mode collapse, that is, the model ends up generating only a single or a few predominant data.

2.2   Automatic Video Generation

GANs are also used for video generation tasks. Vondrick et al. [33] proposed VGAN, which generates a foreground video, a background image, and a mask video to merge them. In order to improve coherence in motion and appearance, Ohnishi et al. [26] proposed Flow and Texture GAN, which generates optical flow first and then the appearance of the video in a hierarchical architecture. Instead of generating a video from a random latent noise, Mathieu et al. [23] approached the task of generating a video as a continuation of a video input as a condition. Later, Lee et al. [20] generated multiple future videos from the same input video.

2.3   Human Pose Prediction

Human pose prediction aims to generate plausible future human behavior from a human behavior input such as coordinates or angles of human joints. Although many prior works approached this task [2,30,35], recent developments in deep learning provided an improvement in the results. Fragkiadaki et al. [10] proposed the Encoder-Recurrent-Decoder model to predict future human poses, which consists of a long short-term memory (LSTM, a kind of RNN) [14], an encoder and a decoder. Similarly, Bütepage et al. [4] predicted future human poses using an autoencoder-like model. Gui et al. [12] proposed a method for future human pose prediction based on adversarial networks with a gated recurrent unit (GRU, a kind of RNN) [8]. While many previous works employ RNNs, these suffer from the vanishing gradients problem: the longer the path between two elements, the worse forward and backward signal propagation [16,31]. Also, small errors in the output of the RNN are propagated, and accumulated when generating long sequences. This makes them unsuitable for learning long-term pose sequences.

2.4 Future Video Generation Using Human Pose

One of the most successful approaches for generating human video is by using a human pose input. Yan et al. [36] generated future video from an input frame and a given sequence of future human poses. Villegas et al. [32] first predicted future human poses as body-joint coordinates using an LSTM and then generated video frame by frame based on generated poses. This approach succeeded in generating long-term videos, but cannot generate multiple futures because the output of an LSTM does not vary for the same input. Cai et al. [5] proposed an adversarial network that generates human pose sequences from latent noise and an action class label, and a network that generates video from the generated poses. This model can be extended to generate a future pose sequence given a past pose sequence, but cannot generate a variety of multiple futures. Also, using an action class label is unsuitable for future prediction, since the action class of the input movement is not available. Walker et al. [34] combined an LSTM and a variational autoencoder (VAE) [18] to generate multiple human poses from a pose sequence input, and then generate a video using 3D convolutional neural networks. The VAE allows generating multiple human poses, which are then fed to the LSTM to predict a sequence of future poses. However, this approach is unsuitable for long-term future prediction because errors in the LSTM will be accumulated exponentially.

In this paper, we propose a method for long-term video prediction of multiple futures. In order to generate long-term near-future sequences, we leverage unidimensional convolutional neural networks, which allow generating sequences without suffering from the vanishing gradients and error propagation problems. Then, we encourage our network to generate of a variety of multiple futures by using two conditions; a latent code that induces a type of motion, and an attraction point that induces motion towards a location in the image.

3 Methodology

Figure 1 shows an overview of our method, which consists of three networks that are trained independently. First, our pose estimation network provides the human pose in a given input video. Then, our pose prediction network generates future human pose sequences that are smooth, varied and long. Finally, our video generation network generates future video corresponding to the generated poses. Since the predicted human poses have a comparatively long duration, and represent a variety of multiple futures, the videos generated using the predicted poses show the same characteristics.

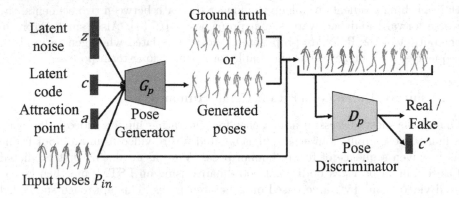

Fig. 2. Overview of our pose prediction network. The pose generator (G_p) generates a future pose sequence from an input pose sequence given as condition. Then, the pose discriminator (D_p) tries to discriminate whether the pose sequence is real (i.e., ground-truth) or fake (i.e., generated). D_p also estimates the latent code c given the generated pose sequence. We use 1D CNN for both G_p and D_p. We are able to generate multiple pose sequences by varying the latent code c and the attraction point a randomly.

3.1   Pose Estimation Network

Our pose estimation network estimates the position of the body joints of the human in the video in image coordinates (xy coordinates). Several networks have been proposed in the past [6,25]; we use OpenPose [6], which has been widely utilized in a variety of related applications. However, OpenPose is applied to each individual frame and sometimes provides inaccurate estimations (e.g., missing joints). In order to correct this, we leverage sequential information and introduce an autoencoder-like network that takes the entire pose sequence estimated by OpenPose as input. This network consists of an encoder and a decoder, which consist of two fully connected layers each, and calibrates the input joints to be natural as a sequence. We use the OpenPose network pretrained with the COCO 2016 keypoints challenge dataset [21]. Thus, only the encoder and the decoder are trained using a dataset with annotations of human joint coordinates (see Sec. 4.1), by minimizing the mean squared error between estimated coordinates and those of the ground truth.

3.2   Pose Prediction Network

Our pose prediction network takes our estimated poses as input and generates future pose sequences. Our generated pose sequences are smoothly connected to the input poses, they have a long-term duration, and represent a variety of multiple futures.

Figure 2 shows an overview of our pose prediction network. A more detailed figure is available in the Sec. A.1 of the supplementary material. It consists of two modules: a pose generator (G_p) and a pose discriminator (D_p). Let $p_t \in \mathbf{R}^{2N}$ be the human pose at time step t. Here, N is the number of joints that compose the pose, and p_t is a vector containing the xy coordinates of N joints at time step t. The input of G_p is a latent noise z, the input poses from a T frames-long video $P_{in} = (p_0, p_1, ..., p_{T-1})$, a latent code $c \in \mathbf{R}^C$, and an attraction point $a \in \mathbf{R}^2$ (c and a are explained later). The output of G_p is a sequence of T' future human poses $\hat{P}_{gen} = (\hat{p}_T, \hat{p}_{T+1}, ..., \hat{p}_{T+T'-1})$ that follow P_{in}.

The structure of the network is based on CGAN [24]; the input poses are included as a condition to G_p and D_p. We use unidimensional convolutional neural networks (1D CNNs) in our generator and discriminator. Although many previous works [10,12,22,32,34] used RNNs (i.e., LSTM and GRU) for predicting future human pose sequences, 1D CNNs have advantages over RNNs. While RNNs output poses one after another, 1D CNNs output an entire pose sequence at once. This frees 1D CNNs from the problem of error accumulation. Furthermore, 1D CNNs can model distant time relationships without being as sensitive as RNNs to the problem of vanishing gradients. Whereas RNNs need $\mathcal{O}(t)$ steps to predict an element separated t frames from the input, 1D CNNs with a stride width of s need only $\mathcal{O}(\log_s t)$ layers. Since the problem of vanishing gradients gets worse with the number of steps/layers, 1D CNNs seem more suitable to model long-term relationships. In image generation with a 2D CNN [17,27], an image is regarded as a three-dimensional entity $\in \mathbf{R}^{H \times W \times 3}$ and convoluted in height and width direction using a two dimensional filter. In our generation task with a 1D CNN, we regard a pose sequence as a two-dimensional entity $P \in \mathbf{R}^{T \times 2N}$ (each row is an individual pose p) and convolute it in the height (time) direction with a one-dimensional filter.

CGAN suffers from mode collapse, that is, the generator fails to adequately cover the space of possible predictions and instead generates one or a few prominent modes, ignoring the latent noise. Thus, only modifying the latent noise z is not enough to generate multiple varied pose sequences. To tackle this problem, our method includes two additional inputs to the generator, namely the latent code c and the attraction point a. Both are randomly initialized during training, and then used during testing for pose generation from different combinations of c and a. InfoGAN [7] models the relationship between the latent code c and the generated data $G(z, c)$ in an unsupervised way, by maximizing the mutual information between them. Since human actions can be categorized to some extent (e.g., "walking" or "sitting"), we aimed at establishing a correspondence between such action categories and the latent code, and thus, we represent c as a one-hot vector. Note that the pose sequences are not paired with any ground-truth action category label.

The attraction point a represents the xy coordinates of a point in the image space, and is used to train G_p to generate poses constrained to move towards the attraction point. This allows our method to generate multiple varied pose sequences depending on a, which in turn is chosen randomly.

Training. During training, G_p tries to fool the discriminator D_p by generating plausible future pose sequences, while D_p tries to classify whether the pose sequences are real or generated. The objective function for adversarial learning between G_p and D_p is as follows:

$$\mathcal{L}_{adv} = \mathbb{E}_{P_{gt}}[\log D_p(P_{gt}|P_{in})] + \mathbb{E}_{z,c,a}[\log(1 - D_p(G_p(z,c,a|P_{in})|P_{in}))] \\ + \lambda_{gp}\mathbb{E}_P[(\|\nabla_P D_p(P|P_{in})\|_2 - 1)^2],$$

(1)

where P_{in} is the input pose sequence and P_{gt} is ground truth for the predicted pose sequence. We utilize the same gradient penalty as in WGAN-GP [13].

Since it is difficult to directly maximize the mutual information between c and generated data, we introduce an auxiliary probability distribution $Q(c|x)$ and minimize the following function:

$$\mathcal{L}_c = -\sum_{i=1}^{C} c_i \ln Q(c'|G_p(z,c,a|P_{in}))_i.$$

(2)

Here, C is the number of categories. As in [7], Q is implemented by adding two linear layers to the convolutional layers of D_p. As depicted in Fig. 2, D_p also outputs the probability c' of the latent code c given the pose generated by G_p.

Our generator G_p is trained to minimize the distance between the generated poses and the attraction point a. More concretely, it minimizes the distance between a and the generated coordinate of the waist joint at future frame t': $\hat{p}_{T+t',waist}$. The objective function is:

$$\mathcal{L}_a = \frac{1}{T'}\sum_{t'=0}^{T'-1} \|a - \hat{p}_{T+t',waist}\|_2^2.$$

(3)

In addition, in order to generate smoother pose sequences, we introduce a loss that reduces sudden speed changes between adjacent poses as follows:

$$\mathcal{L}_{diff} = \frac{1}{T'-2} \times \sum_{t'=0}^{T'-3} \|(\hat{p}_{T+t'+2} - \hat{p}_{T+t'+1}) - (\hat{p}_{T+t'+1} - \hat{p}_{T+t'})\|_2^2.$$

(4)

In summary, the overall objective function is:

$$\min_{G_p,Q} \max_{D_p}(\mathcal{L}_{adv} + \lambda_c\mathcal{L}_c + \lambda_a\mathcal{L}_a + \lambda_{diff}\mathcal{L}_{diff}),$$

(5)

where λs are coefficients to weight the contribution of each loss.

Implementation. In our implementation, T (the length in frames of the input pose sequences) is 16 and T' (the length in frames of the output pose sequences) is 128. C (the number of categories of the latent code c) is 15. These categories correspond to the action classes of the H3.6M dataset [15], which we used for the experiments. G_p consists of an encoder to encode the input pose sequence and a decoder that generates the predicted pose sequence. The encoder consists of three unidimensional convolutional layers (1D CNN) and the decoder consists of one linear layer and six unidimensional convolutional layers. D_p consists of four unidimensional convolutional layers and, one linear layer to model the *real/fake* output and two linear layers to model the c' output. We show the details of these network architectures in the Sec. A.1 of the supplementary material. We set $\lambda_{gp} = 10$, $\lambda_c = 2.5$, $\lambda_a = 2.5$ and $\lambda_{diff} = 50$.

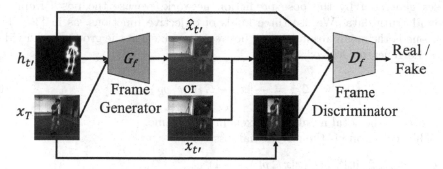

Fig. 3. Overview of our video generation network. Each future frame $\hat{x}_{t'}$ is generated from the last frame of the input video x_T and the generated future pose $h_{t'}$. Input images to the discriminator are masked to show only the area around the predicted poses, so that the discriminator can focus on the human.

3.3 Video Generation Network

Figure 3 shows an overview of our video generation network. Our video generation network generates future frames with respect to a past frame and our predicted future pose sequence, following an adversarial approach. We use an architecture based on [36]. It generates a single future frame from two inputs, namely the last frame of the input video x_T and a generated future pose $p_{t'}$. The final video is obtained by repeating this for all T' future frames. Not generating the whole video directly at once [33,34] but generating each frame individually [32,36] increases the image quality.

Before being input to the video generation network, the human pose coordinates generated by the pose prediction network $p_{t'}$ are transformed into a different representation $h_{t'}$. $h_{t'}$ consists of $N + 1$ channels with the same height and width as the input video frames. It is built by concatenating a heatmap of N channels, in which each channel represents the position of each joint using a Gaussian distribution centered in the xy coordinates generated by G_p, and one channel containing a skeleton that joins those joints. Thus, for a future frame

t', the frame generator G_f takes the last input RGB frame x_T and the predicted future pose $h_{t'}$. Our G_f follows the U-Net architecture [28]. Inputs x_T and $h_{t'}$ are concatenated in the channel direction. G_f encodes the image with $3 + N + 1$ channels and decodes it into the future frame $\hat{x}_{t'}$. Then, our frame discriminator D_f takes the input image x_T, the heatmap of the generated future pose $h_{t'}$, and either the real future frame $x_{t'}$ or the generated future frame $\hat{x}_{t'}$ and discriminates whether future frame is real or fake (i.e., generated). Since generating a realistic human is more difficult than generating the background, D_f should focus on the foreground human. Therefore, we mask D_f input images to show only the area where the human appears, delimited by the outermost joint coordinates (Fig. 3).

Training. When training our video generation network, instead of using the poses generated by the pose prediction network, we use the poses from the ground truth data. We use three kinds of objective functions, as in [36]. The first one is the mean absolute error between the pixels in the ground truth video and the generated video:

$$\mathcal{L}_{L_1} = \frac{1}{M} \| x_{t'} - G_f(x_T, p_{t'}) \|_1, \tag{6}$$

where M is the total number of pixels in each frame.

The second one is the adversarial loss:

$$\mathcal{L}_{adv} = \lambda_{gp} \mathbb{E}_x [(\| \nabla_x D_f(x | x_T, p_{t'}) \|_2 - 1)^2]$$
$$+ \mathbb{E}_{x_{t'}, x_T, p_{t'}} [\log D_f(x_{t'} | x_T, p_{t'})] + \mathbb{E}_{x_T, p_{t'}} [\log(1 - D_f(G_f(x_T, p_{t'}) | x_T, p_{t'}))]. \tag{7}$$

We utilize the gradient penalty of WGAN-GP [13].

Lastly, the triplet loss [29] ensures proper continuity among video frames. Triplet loss addresses three images (i.e., an anchor, a positive and a negative) and minimizes the distance between an anchor and a positive and maximizes the distance between an anchor and a negative. In a video, the L2 distance of adjacent frames should be smaller than that of distant frames. Therefore, when the anchor is $\hat{x}_{t'}$, we set $\hat{x}_{t'+1}$ as positive and $\hat{x}_{t'+5}$ as negative. The concrete objective function is:

$$\mathcal{L}_{tri} = \frac{1}{M} [\| \hat{x}_{t'} - \hat{x}_{t'+1} \|_2^2 - \| \hat{x}_{t'} - \hat{x}_{t'+5} \|_2^2 + \alpha]_+, \tag{8}$$

where α is a margin that is enforced between positive and negative pairs.

In summary, the overall objective function is:

$$\min_{G_f} \max_{D_f} (\mathcal{L}_{L_1} + \lambda_{adv} \mathcal{L}_{adv} + \lambda_{tri} \mathcal{L}_{tri}), \tag{9}$$

where λs are coefficients to weight the contribution of each loss.

Implementation. G_f consists of an encoder and a decoder, which are connected with skip connections. Both the encoder and the decoder consist of eight convolutional layers each. D_f consists of three parallel convolutional layers, which convolute $h_{t'}$, x_T, and $x_{t'}$ or $\hat{x}_{t'}$ respectively, followed by four convolutional layers. We show the details of these network architectures in the Sec. A.2 of the supplementary material. We set $\lambda_{gp} = 10$, $\lambda_{adv} = 0.001$ and $\lambda_{tri} = 10$.

4   Experiments

Evaluating generated video is not straightforward, and normally a single metric is insufficient. While video quality should be evaluated, the diversity of the generated futures is also an important criterion in our method. Furthermore, among all the predicted futures, some of them should be similar to the ground truth. Following the evaluation in [20], we evaluate generated poses and videos from three criteria: realism, diversity and accuracy.

4.1   Dataset

We use the Human3.6M [15] dataset to train and evaluate our entire pipeline. Videos in this dataset show 11 actors showing different behavior (e.g., *walking, sitting*). All frames are annotated with the real and image coordinates of 32 body joint positions accurately measured via motion capture. We use 720 videos corresponding to subjects 1, 5, 6, 7, 8 and 9 as train data and 120 videos of subject number 11 as test data.

We preprocess the videos in the following manner. In order to enlarge actors, videos are cropped by using the outermost poses in the entire sequence, and then resized into 128×128 patches. Since Human3.6M videos have a high frame rate, motion between adjacent frames is small. Therefore, we subsample the video uniformly by taking one every four frames. We apply two kinds of data augmentation. One is horizontal video flipping. The other is padding frames with black pixels, and randomly cropping patches of size 128×128 containing the human. Since our method masks the human of the input image to the discriminator (see Sect. 3.3), this augmentation is not harmful for our method. We use 14 joints out of the 32 provided: *head, neck, right shoulder, right elbow, right wrist, left shoulder, left elbow, left wrist, right waist, right knee, right foot, left waist, left knee and left foot*. In all experiments, an input of 16 frames long is used to generate future videos of 128 frames long generated as a continuation of the input.

4.2   Comparison with the Related Work

To the best of our knowledge, there is no other work on long-term multiple future video generation, so we compare the performance of our method with two state-of-the-art works in future video generation using human poses. One focuses on generating long-term future video, and the other focuses in generating multiple futures. On the one hand, [32] predicts long-term future poses by using an LSTM and then generates the video frame by frame. This method avoids error propagation in long sequences since the predicted poses are not input back, but is not capable of generating multiple futures. On the other hand, [34] predicts multiple future poses by using an LSTM and a VAE, and then generates the entire video using a 3D CNN. This method does not seem to be suitable for generating long-term future video, since the predicted poses are repeatedly input back to the LSTM, which causes errors to accumulate.

4.3   Realism of the Generated Futures

In this experiment, we evaluate the realism of generated futures via a user study on Amazon Mechanical Turk. We show workers a pair of future poses or a pair

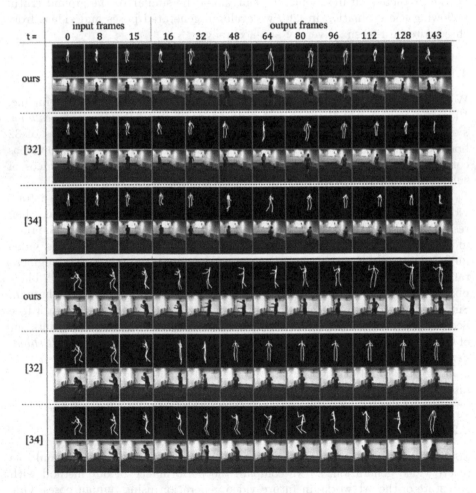

Fig. 4. Examples of generated poses and frames. Input frames are marked in green and generated frames are marked in red. (Color figure online)

of future videos generated by our proposed method and [32] or [34], and workers select the one that looks more realistic. 1200 pairs of poses/videos each were evaluated by 120 workers.

Table 1. Evaluation results regarding the realism of our generated futures: Percentage of workers that preferred futures generated by our method vs. those of previous works. Values in brackets represent the p-values of the binomial test.

	vs. [32]	vs. [34]
Pose	61.3 (1.98×10^{-15})	56.2 (1.08×10^{-5})
Video	53.4 (9.67×10^{-3})	56.3 (8.29×10^{-6})

Table 1 shows the experimental results. We outperformed both [32] and [34] in terms of the realism of the generated poses and videos. Table 1 suggests superiority of our pose prediction network, which leverages a unidimensional CNN to predict long-term poses.

Our generated poses were preferred over those from [32]. As we can see in Fig. 4, the pose sequences generated by [32] contain less motion: In the upper example, the person does not move their legs despite they move forward, and in the lower example, the generated pose sequence has almost no movements. Moreover, the connection between input poses and generated poses is not smooth in [32]. On the other hand, the difference between generated videos is smaller. Both, [32] and our method, generate a future frame from the input frame x_T and a future pose $p_{t'}$; however, the larger the difference between $p_{t'}$ and p_T is, the harder generating a realistic frame is. Thus, because the generated poses in [32] are rather motionless (the difference between $p_{t'}$ and p_T is small), they can easily generate future videos with a realistic appearance. Nevertheless, in spite of generating a variety of motions, our videos are preferred for realism.

Also, users preferred our poses and videos to those of [34]. Since [34] generates poses one after another using LSTM, errors accumulate and poses tend to gradually deform. Our method does not have such consistency problem because we generate a pose sequence at once via 1D CNN. Also, the videos generated by [34] using 3D CNN tend to be blurry compared to those of [32] and ours. This is because we generate the video frames one by one for each pose, whereas [34] generates the video at once.

4.4 Diversity of the Generated Futures

We evaluated the diversity of the predicted futures by calculating the distance between futures generated from the same input video as in [20,37]. The distance becomes larger as the generated futures show more variety. We generate 100 future samples from the same input video, and calculate the distances between all distinct pairs.

We calculate the distance between two future poses as the mean squared error (MSE) of the xy-coordinates of their 14 joints. We use two kind of coordinates systems for this evaluation: One is the absolute coordinates (i.e., image coordinates) and the other is the relative coordinates (i.e., local coordinates with respect to the pose itself). In the relative coordinates, we subtract the coordinates of the right waist joint from all the coordinates. Besides, we calculate the distance between two future videos as the cosine distance of the feature vectors from VGG16 (pretrained by ImageNet [9]) as in [20]. This distance is calculated as the average of the five cosine distances between the feature vectors of each of the five pooling layers of VGG16.

Our method is able to generate multiple futures by leveraging a latent code c and an attraction point a. To determine the contribution of each one, we did an ablation study evaluating the diversity of the generated videos using four configurations: with c and a, with c and without a, without c and with a, without c and a. Also, we compare the results with the multiple futures generated by [34]. Since [32] cannot generate diverse futures, it is not included in this evaluation.

Table 2. Evaluation about the diversity of generated poses and videos.

Method	Pose(absolute)(MSE)	Pose(relative)(MSE)	Video(Cosine)
[34]	0.0181	0.0104	0.1447
w/o c, w/o a	0.0102	0.0062	0.2231
w/o c, w/ a	**0.0556**	0.0162	0.3430
w/ c, w/o a	0.0244	0.0143	0.2848
w/ c, w/ a	0.0523	**0.0192**	**0.3445**

Table 2 shows the obtained results. Disabling both the latent code c and the attraction point a leads to mode collapse, and the variety worsens. Thus, the average pose distance between two samples in our method is smaller than that of [34]. On the other hand, enabling either c or a leads to a greater distance between samples. Since enabling only a encourages the generated human pose to move to a further location in the image, this configuration leads to the largest distance for poses in absolute coordinates. However, in the case of distances for poses in relative coordinates and distances for videos, enabling both a and c achieves the higher diversity. This proves the efficacy of our attraction point a and latent code c to generate multiple future poses.

The qualitative results of our evaluation of diversity are included in the Sec. B.1 of the supplementary materials.

4.5 Accuracy of the Generated Futures

Since this research targets a variety of possible futures, generating futures far from the ground truth is encouraged. However, it would be desirable that at least some futures among the generated are close to the ground truth. Hence, we generate 100 future poses and videos from the same input video, and measure the distance between the ground truth and the sample closest to the ground truth, as in [20,34]. Selecting a "best" future is out of the scope of this paper.

Similarity between poses is calculated using the MSE of the image coordinates of the joints (lower is better). Similarity between videos is calculated as the cosine similarity of the feature vectors of VGG 16, and the peak signal-to-noise ratio (PSNR). We compare the accuracy of the four combinations of adding the latent code c and the attraction point a, and the methods in [32] and [34].

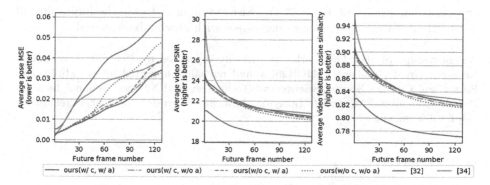

Fig. 5. Comparison of the similarity between the generated futures (poses and videos) and the ground truth.

Figure 5 shows the similarity metrics between the ground truth and the pose/video among the generated one hundred with the highest similarity to the ground truth. With respect to the pose accuracy, using c and a allows for a wider variety of generated poses, thus, there is a higher chance that futures resembling the ground truth are generated. The results suggest that our two additional inputs are effective for not only generating multiple futures but also generating accurate futures. With respect to the video accuracy, although our method outperforms [34] in terms of both accuracy of poses and realism of videos, the video accuracy is slightly lower. The reason is that [34] generates videos that, despite of being blurry, their pixel values are closer to the ground truth. This resembles the phenomenon in which blurred images generated with a pixel-wise loss function (e.g., MSE) tend to have lower MSE with ground truth than sharp images generated using adversarial loss or perceptual loss [1,19]. We found that our video accuracy improves by combining our pose prediction network and [34]'s video generation network, although the video quality becomes blurry.

A further analysis is included in the supplementary material (Sec. B.2).

5   Conclusions and Future Work

In this work, we present a novel method for generating long-term future videos of multiple futures from an input human video using a hierarchical approach:

first predicting future human poses and then generating the future video. We propose a novel network to predict long-term future human pose sequences by using unidimensional convolutional neural network in adversarial training. Also, we propose two additional inputs that allow predicting a variety of multiple futures: a latent code and an attraction point. Finally, videos generated with our predicted poses are also long and multiple. Experimental results on the realism, diversity, and accuracy of the generated poses and videos show the superiority of the proposed method over the state-of-the-art.

As our future work, since our method generates videos frame by frame, videos with a higher resolution could be generated by leveraging the latest image generation techniques using GAN [3,17]. Also, we plan to tackle the limitations of our method; for example, generating videos with moving background.

Acknowledgements. This work was partially supported by JST AIP Acceleration Research Grant Number JPMJCR20U3, and partially supported by the Ministry of Education, Culture, Sports, Science and Technology (MEXT) as "Seminal Issue on Post-K Computer." We thank Takayuki Hara, Sho Inayoshi, and Kohei Uehara for helpful discussions.

References

1. Blau, Y., Michaeli, T.: The perception-distortion tradeoff. In: Computer Vision and Pattern Recognition (2018)
2. Brand, M., Hertzmann, A.: Style machines. In: ACM International Conference on Computer Graphics and Interactive Techniques (2000)
3. Brock, A., Donahue, J., Simonyan, K.: Large scale GAN training for high fidelity natural image synthesis. In: International Conference on Learning Representations (2019)
4. Bütepage, J., Black, M.J., Kragic, D., Kjellström, H.: Deep representation learning for human motion prediction and classification. In: Computer Vision and Pattern Recognition (2017)
5. Cai, H., Bai, C., Tai, Y.-W., Tang, C.-K.: Deep video generation, prediction and completion of human action sequences. In: Ferrari, V., Hebert, M., Sminchisescu, C., Weiss, Y. (eds.) ECCV 2018. LNCS, vol. 11206, pp. 374–390. Springer, Cham (2018). https://doi.org/10.1007/978-3-030-01216-8_23
6. Cao, Z., Simon, T., Wei, S.E., Sheikh, Y.: Realtime multi-person 2D pose estimation using part affinity fields. In: Computer Vision and Pattern Recognition (2017)
7. Chen, X., Duan, Y., Houthooft, R., Schulman, J., Sutskever, I., Abbeel, P.: InfoGAN: interpretable representation learning by information maximizing generative adversarial nets. In: Neural Information Processing Systems (2016)
8. Cho, K., et al.: Learning phrase representations using RNN encoder-decoder for statistical machine translation. In: Empirical Methods in Natural Language Processing (2014)
9. Deng, J., Dong, W., Socher, R., Li, L.J., Li, K., Fei-Fei, L.: ImageNet: a large-scale hierarchical image database. In: Computer Vision and Pattern Recognition (2009)
10. Fragkiadaki, K., Levine, S., Felsen, P., Malik, J.: Recurrent network models for human dynamics. In: International Conference on Computer Vision (2015)

11. Goodfellow, I., et al.: Generative adversarial nets. In: Neural Information Processing Systems (2014)
12. Gui, L.-Y., Wang, Y.-X., Liang, X., Moura, J.M.F.: Adversarial geometry-aware human motion prediction. In: Ferrari, V., Hebert, M., Sminchisescu, C., Weiss, Y. (eds.) ECCV 2018. LNCS, vol. 11208, pp. 823–842. Springer, Cham (2018). https://doi.org/10.1007/978-3-030-01225-0_48
13. Gulrajani, I., Ahmed, F., Arjovsky, M., Dumoulin, V., Courville, A.C.: Improved training of wasserstein GANs. In: Neural Information Processing Systems (2017)
14. Hochreiter, S., Schmidhuber, J.: Long short-term memory. Neural Comput. 9(8), 1735–1780 (1997)
15. Ionescu, C., Papava, D., Olaru, V., Sminchisescu, C.: Human3.6m: large scale datasets and predictive methods for 3D human sensing in natural environments. Trans. Pattern Anal. Mach. Intell. 36(7), 1325–1339 (2014)
16. Kalchbrenner, N., Espeholt, L., Simonyan, K., van den Oord, A., Graves, A., Kavukcuoglu, K.: Neural machine translation in linear time. arXiv preprint arXiv:1610.10099 (2016)
17. Karras, T., Laine, S., Aila, T.: A style-based generator architecture for generative adversarial networks. In: Computer Vision and Pattern Recognition (2019)
18. Kingma, D.P., Welling, M.: Auto-encoding variational Bayes. In: International Conference on Learning Representations (2014)
19. Ledig, C., et al.: Photo-realistic single image super-resolution using a generative adversarial network. In: Computer Vision and Pattern Recognition (2017)
20. Lee, A.X., Zhang, R., Ebert, F., Abbeel, P., Finn, C., Levine, S.: Stochastic adversarial video prediction. arXiv preprint arXiv:1804.01523 (2018)
21. Lin, T.-Y., et al.: Microsoft COCO: common objects in context. In: Fleet, D., Pajdla, T., Schiele, B., Tuytelaars, T. (eds.) ECCV 2014. LNCS, vol. 8693, pp. 740–755. Springer, Cham (2014). https://doi.org/10.1007/978-3-319-10602-1_48
22. Martinez, J., Black, M.J., Romero, J.: On human motion prediction using recurrent neural networks. In: Computer Vision and Pattern Recognition (2017)
23. Mathieu, M., Couprie, C., LeCun, Y.: Deep multi-scale video prediction beyond mean square error. In: International Conference on Learning Representations (2016)
24. Mirza, M., Osindero, S.: Conditional generative adversarial nets. arXiv preprint arXiv:1411.1784 (2014)
25. Newell, A., Yang, K., Deng, J.: Stacked hourglass networks for human pose estimation. In: Leibe, B., Matas, J., Sebe, N., Welling, M. (eds.) ECCV 2016. LNCS, vol. 9912, pp. 483–499. Springer, Cham (2016). https://doi.org/10.1007/978-3-319-46484-8_29
26. Ohnishi, K., Yamamoto, S., Ushiku, Y., Harada, T.: Hierarchical video generation from orthogonal information: optical flow and texture. In: Proceedings of the Thirty-Second AAAI Conference on Artificial Intelligence (2018)
27. Radford, A., Metz, L., Chintala, S.: Unsupervised representation learning with deep convolutional generative adversarial networks. In: International Conference on Learning Representations (2016)
28. Ronneberger, O., Fischer, P., Brox, T.: U-net: convolutional networks for biomedical image segmentation. In: Medical Image Computing and Computer-Assisted Intervention (2015)
29. Schroff, F., Kalenichenko, D., Philbin, J.: Facenet: a unified embedding for face recognition and clustering. In: Computer Vision and Pattern Recognition (2015)
30. Taylor, G.W., Hinton, G.E., Roweis, S.T.: Modeling human motion using binary latent variables. In: Neural Information Processing Systems (2007)

31. Vaswani, A., et al.: Attention is all you need. In: Neural Information Processing Systems (2015)
32. Villegas, R., Yang, J., Zou, Y., Sohn, S., Lin, X., Lee, H.: Learning to generate long-term future via hierarchical prediction. In: International Conference on Machine Learning (2017)
33. Vondrick, C., Pirsiavash, H., Torralba, A.: Generating videos with scene dynamics. In: Neural Information Processing Systems (2016)
34. Walker, J., Marino, K., Gupta, A., Hebert, M.: The pose knows: video forecasting by generating pose futures. In: International Conference on Computer Vision (2017)
35. Wang, J.M., Fleet, D.J., Hertzmann, A.: Gaussian process dynamical models for human motion. Trans. Pattern Anal. Mach. Intell. **30**(2), 283–298 (2008)
36. Yan, Y., Xu, J., Ni, B., Zhang, W., Yang, X.: Skeleton-aided articulated motion generation. In: ACM International Conference on Multimedia (2017)
37. Zhu, J.Y., et al.: Toward multimodal image-to-image translation. In: Neural Information Processing Systems (2017)

AgingMapGAN (AMGAN): High-Resolution Controllable Face Aging with Spatially-Aware Conditional GANs

Julien Despois$^{(\boxtimes)}$, Frédéric Flament, and Matthieu Perrot

L'Oréal Research & Innovation, Saint-Ouen, France
Julien.despois@rd.loreal.com

Abstract. Existing approaches and datasets for face aging produce results skewed towards the mean, with individual variations and expression wrinkles often invisible or overlooked in favor of global patterns such as the fattening of the face. Moreover, they offer little to no control over the way the faces are aged and can difficultly be scaled to large images, thus preventing their usage in many real-world applications. To address these limitations, we present an approach to change the appearance of a high-resolution image using ethnicity-specific aging information and weak spatial supervision to guide the aging process. We demonstrate the advantage of our proposed method in terms of quality, control, and how it can be used on high-definition images while limiting the computational overhead.

Keywords: Conditional GANs · Face aging · High-resolution

1 Introduction

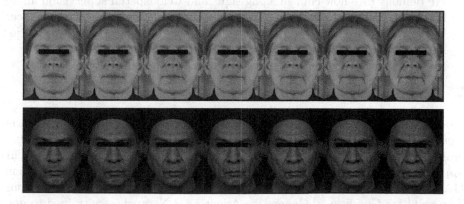

Fig. 1. High-resolution faces aged in a continuous manner with our approach

Electronic supplementary material The online version of this chapter (https://doi.org/10.1007/978-3-030-67070-2_37) contains supplementary material, which is available to authorized users.

Face aging is an image synthesis task in which a reference image must be transformed to give the impression of a person of different age while preserving the identity and key facial features of the subject. When done correctly, this process can be used in various domains, from predicting the future appearance of a missing person to entertainment and educational uses. We focus on achieving high-resolution face aging, as it is a required step towards capturing the fine details of aging (fine lines, pigmentation, etc.). In recent years, Generative Adversarial Networks [14] have allowed a learning-based approach for this task. The results, however, often lack in quality and only provide limited aging options. Popular models such as StarGAN [10] fail to produce convincing results without additional tweaks and modifications. This partially stems from the choice of reducing aging to one's real or apparent age [1]. Also, current approaches treat aging as a step-wise process, splitting age in bins (30–40, 40–50, 50+, etc.) [2,16,30,32,34].

In reality, aging is a continuous process that can take many forms depending on genetic factors such as facial features and phenotype, as well as lifestyle choices (smoking, hydration, sun damage, etc.) or behavior. Notably, expression wrinkles are promoted by habitual facial expressions and can be prominent on the forehead, upper lip, or at the corner of the eyes (crow's feet). In addition, aging is subjective as it depends on the cultural background of the person assessing the age. These factors call for a more fine-grained approach to face aging.

In this paper, we aim to obtain high-resolution face aging results by creating a model capable of individually transforming the local aging signs. Our contributions are as follows:

- We show that a curated high-resolution dataset in association with a combination of novel and existing techniques produces detailed state-of-the-art aging results.
- We demonstrate how clinical aging signs and weak spatial supervision allows fine-grained control over the aging process of the different parts of the face.
- We introduce a patch-based approach to enable inference on high-resolution images while keeping the computational cost of training the model low.

2   Related Work

Conditional Generative Adversarial Networks. Generative Adversarial Networks [14] leverage the principle of an adversarial loss to force samples generated by a generative model to be indistinguishable from real samples. This approach led to impressive results, especially in the domain of image generation. GANs can be extended to generate images based on one or several conditions. The resulting Conditional Generative Adversarial Networks are trained to generate images that satisfy both the realism and condition criteria.

Unpaired Image-to-Image Translation. Conditional GANs are a powerful tool for image-to-image translation[18] tasks, where an input image is given to the model to synthesize a transformed image. StarGAN [10] introduced a way to use an additional condition to specify the desired transformation to be applied. They propose to feed the input condition to the generator in the form of feature maps [10] concatenated to the input image, but new approaches use more complex mechanisms such as AdaIN [20] or its 2D extension SPADE [23] to give the generator the condition in a more optimal manner. Where previous techniques required pixel-aligned training images in the different domains, recent works such as CycleGAN [36] and StarGAN [10] introduced a cycle-consistency loss to enable unpaired training between discrete domains. This has been extended in [24] to allow translation between continuous domains.

Face Aging. To age a face from a single picture, traditional approaches use training data of either one [2,16,29,32,34,35] or multiple images [27,30] of the same person, along with the age of the person when the picture was taken. The use of longitudinal data, with multiple photos of the same person, offers less flexibility as it creates a heavy time-dependent constraint on the dataset collection.

The age is usually binned into discrete age groups (20–30, 30–40, 40–50, 50+, etc.) [2,16,32,34], which frames the problem more simply, but limits the control over the aging process and doesn't allow the training to leverage the ordered nature of the groups. [29,35] address this limitation by considering age as a continuous value. However, aging isn't objective because different skin types age differently, and different populations look for different signs of aging. Focusing on the apparent age as the guide for aging thus freezes the subjective point of view. Such approaches cannot be tailored to a population's perspective without requiring additional age estimation data from their point of view.

To improve the quality and level of details of the generated images, [34] use the attention mechanism from [24] in the generator. The generated samples are, however, low-definition images which are too coarse for real-world applications. Working at this scale hides some difficulties of generating realistic images, such as skin texture, fine lines, and the overall sharpness of the details.

3   Proposed Approach

3.1   Problem Formulation

In this work, our goal is to use single unpaired images to train a model able to generate realistic high-definition (1024 × 1024) aged faces, with continuous control over the fine-grained aging signs to create smooth transformations between the original and transformed images. This is a more intuitive approach, as aging is a continuous process and age group bins do not explicitly enforce a logical order.

We propose the use of ethnicity-specific skin atlases [4–7,13] to incorporate the variety of clinical aging signs. These atlases define numerous clinical signs such as the wrinkles underneath the eye, the ptosis of the lower part of the face, the density of pigmentary spots on the cheeks, etc. Each sign is linked to a specific zone on the face and scored on a standardized scale. Using these labels in addition to the age make for a more complete representation of aging, and allows transforming images with various combination of clinical signs and scores.

The aging target is passed to the network in the form of an aging map (Fig. 2). To do so, we compute facial landmarks and define the relevant zone for each aging sign. Each zone (e.g. forehead) is then filled with the score value of the corresponding sign (e.g. forehead wrinkles). We use the apparent age to fill in the blanks where the clinical signs are not defined. Finally, we coarsely mask the background of the image.

Treating the whole image at once would be ideal, but training a model with 1024×1024 images requires large computational resources. Our approach allows us to train the model by patch, using only part of the image during training, and the corresponding part of the aging map. Patch-based training reduces the context (i.e. global information) for the task but also reduces the computational resources required to process high-resolution images in large batches, as recommended in [8]. We leverage this to use a large batch size on small patches of 128×128, 256×256 or 512×512 pixels.

The major drawback of the patch-based training is that small patches can look similar (e.g. forehead and cheek) yet must be aged differently (e.g. respectively horizontal and vertical wrinkles). To avoid "mean" wrinkles on these ambiguous zones, we give the generator two patches coming respectively from a horizontal and a vertical gradient location map (▮ ▮). This allows the model to know the position of the patch in order to differentiate between potentially ambiguous zones.

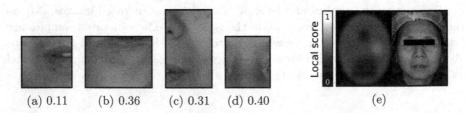

(a) 0.11   (b) 0.36   (c) 0.31   (d) 0.40   (e)

Fig. 2. Aging sign zones (a–d) and their associated scores used to construct the aging map (e). The brightness of each pixel represents the normalized score of the localized clinical sign (wrinkles at the corner of the lips (a), underneath the eye wrinkles (b), nasolabial fold wrinkles (c), inter-ocular wrinkles (d), etc.) or the age where no sign is defined

3.2   AMGAN - Network Architectures

We base our training process on the StarGAN [10] framework. Our generator is a fully convolutional encoder-decoder derived from [11] with SPADE [23] residual blocks in the decoder to incorporate the aging and location maps. This allows the model to leverage the spatial information present in the aging map, and use it at multiple scales in the decoder. To avoid learning unnecessary details, we use the attention mechanism from [24] to force the generator to transform the image only where needed. The discriminator is a modified version of [10], and produces the outputs for the WGAN [3] objective (given for an image i and aging map a in Eq. 1), the estimation of the coordinates of the patch, and the low-resolution estimation of the aging map. Figure 3 and Fig. 4 present the patch-based training workflow.

$$\mathcal{L}_{WGAN} = \mathbb{E}_i[D(i)] - \mathbb{E}_{i,a}[D(G(i,a))] \tag{1}$$

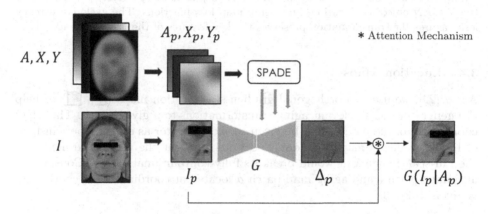

Fig. 3. Generator of our proposed patch-based training. We begin by cropping a patch from the image I, aging map A, and location maps X and Y. The generator transforms the image patch I_p according to the map and location

3.3 Aging Maps

To avoid penalizing the model for failing to place the bounding boxes with pixel-perfect precision, we blur the aging maps to smooth the edges and compute the discriminator regression loss on downsampled 10×10 maps. This formulation allows packing the information in a more compact and meaningful way than as individual uniform feature maps [10,30,34,35]. Our approach only requires multiple feature maps when there are large overlaps between signs (e.g. forehead pigmentation and forehead wrinkles). Considering an image patch i and aging map patch a, the loss is given in Eq. 2.

$$\mathcal{L}_{Age} = \mathbb{E}_i[\|a - D_{Age}(G(i,a))\|_2] \tag{2}$$

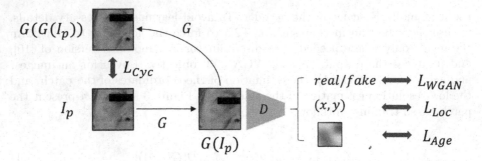

Fig. 4. The discriminator produces the real/fake output, the estimated location of the patch, and the estimated local aging map. The outputs are respectively penalized with the WGAN objective, location, and aging map loss functions. The cycle consistency loss ensures the transformation preserves the key features of the original image

3.4   Location Maps

As in [22], we use two orthogonal gradients as location maps (■, ■) to help the generator apply relevant aging transformations to a given patch. The (x, y) coordinates of the patch could be given to the generator as two numbers instead of linear gradients maps, but doing so would prevent the use of the model on the full-scale image as it would break its fully-convolutional nature. Considering an image patch i and aging map patch a located at coordinates (x, y), the loss is given in Eq. 3.

$$\mathcal{L}_{Loc} = \mathbb{E}_i[\|(x, y) - D_{Loc}(G(i, a))\|_2] \tag{3}$$

3.5   Training

The models are trained with the Adam [21] optimizer with $\beta_1 = 0$, $\beta_2 = 0.99$ and learning rates of 7×10^{-5} for G and 2×10^{-4} for D. Following the two time-scale update rule [17], both models are updated at each step. Additionally, learning rates for both G and D are linearly decayed to zero over the course of the training. To enforce cycle-consistency, we use the perceptual loss [33] with $\lambda_{Cyc} = 100$. For the regression tasks, we use $\lambda_{Loc} = 50$ to predict the (x,y) coordinates of the patch and $\lambda_{Age} = 100$ to estimate the downsampled aging map. The discriminator is penalized with the original gradient penalty presented in [15] with $\lambda_{GP} = 10$. Our complete loss objective function is given in Eq. 4.

$$\mathcal{L} = \mathcal{L}_{WGAN} + \lambda_{Cyc}\mathcal{L}_{Cyc} + \lambda_{Age}\mathcal{L}_{Age} + \lambda_{Loc}\mathcal{L}_{Loc} + \lambda_{GP}\mathcal{L}_{GP} \tag{4}$$

3.6   Inference

For inference, we use exponential moving average [31] over G's parameters. The trained generator can be used directly on the 1024×1024 image no matter the size of the patch used during training thanks to the fully convolutional nature of the network and the use of continuous 2D aging maps. We can either create a target aging map manually or use the face landmarks and target scores to build one.

4   Experiments

4.1   Experimental Setting

Most face aging datasets [9,25,26] suffer from a lack of diversity in terms of phototypes [19], and focus on low-resolution images (up to 250×250 pixels). This isn't sufficient to capture fine details related to skin aging. Moreover, they often fail to normalize the pose and expression of the faces (smiling, frowning, raised eyebrows), which results in accentuated wrinkles unrelated to aging (mostly nasolabial wrinkles, crow's feet wrinkles, forehead wrinkles and wrinkles underneath the eye). Finally, the lack of fine-grained information on the aging signs causes other approaches to capture unwanted correlated features such as the fattening of the face, as observed in datasets such as IMDB-Wiki [26]. These effects can be observed in Fig. 5.

To address these issues, we tested our models on two curated high-resolution datasets, using generated aging maps or uniform aging maps to highlight the rejuvenation/aging.

4.2   Flicker Faces High-Quality Dataset (FFHQ)

To tackle the high-resolution aging problem, we have tested our approach on the FFHQ dataset [20]. To minimize the issues in lighting, pose, and facial expressions, we applied simple heuristics to select a subset of the dataset of better quality. To do so, we extracted facial landmarks from all faces and used them to remove all images where the head was too heavily tilted left, right, up, or down. In addition, we removed all images with an open mouth to limit artificial nasolabial fold and underneath the eye wrinkles. Finally, we used a HOG [12] feature descriptor to remove images with hair covering the face. This selection brings down the dataset from 70k+ to 10k+ images. Due to the extreme diversity of the FFHQ dataset, the remaining images are still far from being perfect, especially in terms of lighting color, direction, and exposure.

To obtain the scores of the individual aging signs on these images, we used aging sign estimation models based on the ResNet [28] architecture that we trained on the dataset described in Sect. 4.3. Finally, we generated the ground truth aging maps using the landmarks as a basis for the coarse bounding-boxes. We trained our model on 256×256 patches randomly selected on the 1024×1024 face.

| | Original | 20-30 | 30-40 | 40-50 | 50-60 | 60+ |

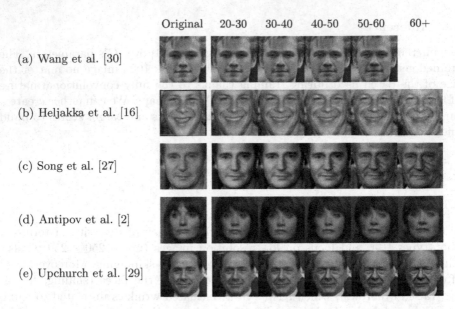

(a) Wang et al. [30]

(b) Heljakka et al. [16]

(c) Song et al. [27]

(d) Antipov et al. [2]

(e) Upchurch et al. [29]

Fig. 5. Previous approaches operate on low-resolution images and suffer from a lack of wrinkles dynamic range, especially for expression wrinkles (a). They are also prone to color shifts and artifacts (b, c, d, e), as well as unwanted correlated features such as the fattening of the face (d), or the addition of glasses (e)

4.3 High-Quality Standardized Dataset

To obtain better performance, we have collected a dataset of 6000 high-resolution (3000 × 3000) images of faces, centered and aligned, spanning most ages (18–80), genders, and origins (African, Caucasian, Chinese, Japanese and Indian). The images were labeled using ethnicity-specific clinical aging sign atlases [4–7,13] and scored on signs covering most of the face (apparent age, forehead wrinkles, nasolabial fold, underneath the eye wrinkles, upper lip wrinkles, wrinkles at the corner of the lips and ptosis of the lower part of the face).

5   Results

5.1 FFHQ

Despite the complexity of the dataset, and without ground truth age values, our patch-based model is able to transform the individual wrinkles on the face in a continuous manner.

Figure 6 displays how the model was able to transform the different wrinkles despite the complexity of the patch-based training, the large variation in lighting in the dataset, and the unbalance between grades of clinical signs/age, with a vast majority of young subjects with few wrinkles. Figure 7 highlights the control we have over the individual signs, allowing aging the face in a controllable way that wouldn't be possible with the only label of the age.

Fig. 6. Rejuvenation (*left*), original (*center*) and aging (*right*) for faces of different age and phototypes from FFHQ dataset using our approach

Fig. 7. Where no sign is defined, we fill the map with the age. This helps the model learn global features like the greying of the hair (*left*). Using individual clinical signs in an aging map allows us to age all signs but keep the appearance of the hair intact (*right*)

5.2 High-Quality Standardized Dataset

On our standardized images, and with better coverage across phototypes and aging signs, our model demonstrates state-of-the-art performance (Fig. 1, Fig. 8), with a high level of detail, realism, and no visible artifacts, color shifts or unwanted correlated features as seen in previous works (Fig. 5). The aging process is successful along the continuous spectrum of age maps, allowing realistic images to be generated for a diverse set of sign severity values (Fig. 9). More examples as well as HD videos are available in the supplementary materials and at https://despoisj.github.io/AgingMapGAN/.

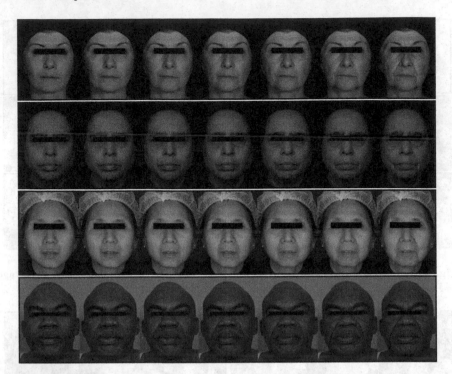

Fig. 8. Faces aged in a continuous manner. No zone is left unchanged, even the forehead or the sagging of lower part of the face. The complementary age information used to fill the gap can be seen on the thinning or greying of the eyebrows. Note: zooming is recommended to see the fine details of the figure

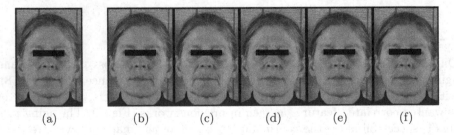

(a)   (b)   (c)   (d)   (e)   (f)

Fig. 9. Same face (a) aged with different aging maps. (b) rejuvenates all signs except for the nasolabial, corner of the lips and underneath the eyes wrinkles on the right part of the face. (c) only ages the bottom of the face and (d) only the top. (e) only ages the wrinkles underneath the eye. (f) ages the face in an asymmetric fashion, namely the right wrinkles underneath the eyes and the left nasolabial fold

5.3   Evaluation Metrics

To be considered successful, the task of face aging requires three criteria to be met: the image must be realistic, the identity of the subject must be preserved, and the face must be aged. These are respectively enforced during training thanks to the WGAN objective function, cycle-consistency loss, and aging map estimation loss. By nature, one single metric couldn't ensure that all criteria are met. For instance, the model could leave the input image without altering it, and still succeed in realism and identity. Contrarily, the model could succeed in aging but fail realism and/or identity. If one model isn't superior to another on every metric, we need to choose a trade-off.

Our experiments on FFHQ and our high-quality standardized dataset never displayed any issue in the preservation of the subject identity. This is a consequence of the use of the attention mechanism that allows the generator to preserve the key facial features of the face. As a result, we chose to focus on the realism and aging criteria for our quantitative evaluation. Because our approach focuses on aging as a combination of aging signs instead of relying solely on age, we don't use the accuracy of the target age as a metric. Instead, we use the Fréchet Inception Distance (FID)[17] to assess the realism of our images, and the Mean Average Error (MAE) for the accuracy of the target aging signs.

To do so, we use half of our dataset as a reference for real images, and the rest as the images to be transformed by our model. The aging maps used to transform these images are chosen randomly from the ground truth labels to ensure a distribution of generated images that follows the original dataset. We estimate the value of individual scores on all generated images using dedicated aging sign estimation models based on the ResNet [28] architecture. As a reference for the FID scores, we compute the FID between both halves of the real image dataset. Note that the size of our dataset prevents us from computing the FID on the recommended 50k+ [17,20], thus leading to the overestimation of the value. This can be seen when computing the FID between real images only, giving a baseline FID of 49.0. The results are presented in Table 1.

Table 1. Fréchet Inception Distance and Mean Average Error for our different models

Method	Patch Size	FID↓	MAE↓
Real Images	–	49.0	–
AMGAN (Ours)	512 × 512	**110.1**	**0.14**
AMGAN (Ours)	256 × 256	110.7	**0.14**
w/o Aging Maps	256 × 256	141.6	0.17
AMGAN (Ours)	128 × 128	112.9	0.17
w/o Location Maps	128 × 128	140.0	0.20

5.4 Comparison Between Age and Clinical Signs

When trained without clinical signs, using only the age to create a uniform aging map, the model still gives convincing results, with low FID and estimated age MAE (Table 2).

By comparing the results with the full aging map approach, however, it appears that some wrinkles don't exhibit their full range of dynamics. This is due to the fact that not all aging signs need to be maximized in order to reach the limit age of the dataset. In fact, the 150 oldest individuals of our standardized dataset (65 to 80 years old) display a median standard deviation of their normalized aging signs of 0.18, highlighting the many possible combinations of aging signs in old people (Supplementary Materials, Fig. 1). For example, signs such as the forehead wrinkles are highly dependant on the facial expressions of the subject and are integral parts of the aging process. This an issue for the age-only model because it only offers one way to age a face.

To the contrary, the faces aged with the aging map offer much more control over the aging process. By controlling each individual sign of aging, we can choose whether to apply these expression wrinkles or not. A natural extension of this benefit is the pigmentation of the skin, which is viewed in some Asian countries as a sign of aging. An age-based model cannot produce aging for these countries without having to re-estimate the age from the local perspective. This doesn't scale, unlike our approach which, once trained with every relevant aging sign, can offer a face aging experience customized to the point of view of different countries, all in a single model and without additional labels.

Table 2. Fréchet Inception Distance and Mean Average Error for our model with clinical signs, and with age only

Method	Patch Size	Control	FID	MAE
AMGAN (Ours)	256 × 256	✓	110.7	0.143
w/o Clinical Signs	256 × 256	✗	101.3	0.116

5.5 Ablation Study

Effect of Patch Size. When training the model for a given target image resolution (1024 × 1024 pixels in our experiments), we can choose the size of the patch used for the training. The bigger the patch, the more context the model will have to perform the aging task. For the same computation power, however, larger patches cause the batch size to be smaller, which hinders the training [8]. We conducted experiment using patches of 128 × 128, 256 × 256 and 512 × 512 pixels. Figure 10 shows that all patch sizes manage to age the high-resolution face but to various degrees of realism. The smallest patch size suffers most from the lack of context and produces results that are inferior to the other two, with visible texture artifacts. The 256 × 256 patch gives convincing results, with minor imperfection only visible when compared to the 512 × 512 patch. These results suggest that we could apply this technique to larger resolutions, such as with patches of 512 × 512 on 2048 × 2048 images.

Patch Size

128 × 128

256 × 256

512 × 512

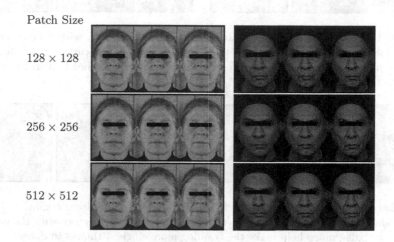

Fig. 10. Results of rejuvenation (*left*) and aging (*right*) for different patch sizes on a 1024 × 1024 image

Location Maps. To see the contribution of the location maps, we compared our model trained with and without them. As expected, the effect of the location maps is more prominent on small patch sizes, where the ambiguity is high. Figure 11 shows how on small patch sizes and in the absence of location information, the model is unable to differentiate similar patches from different parts of the face. It is, therefore, unable to add wrinkles that are coherent with the location, and generates generic diagonal ripples. This effect is less present on larger patch sizes because the location of the patch is less ambiguous.

Spatialization of Information. We compare our proposed aging maps against the baseline method of formatting conditions, namely to give all sign scores as individual uniform feature maps. Since not every sign is present in the patch, especially when the patch size is small, most of the processed information is of no use to the model. The aging maps represent a simple way of only giving the model the labels present in the patch, in addition to their spatial extent and location. Figure 12 highlights the effect of the aging map. On small patches (128 × 128, 256 × 256 pixels), the model struggles to create realistic results. The aging map helps reduce the complexity of the problem.

Fig. 11. Face aged with smallest patch size without (*left*) and with (*right*) location maps, along with the difference with the original image. The location maps eliminate the presence of diagonal texture artifacts, especially on the forehead where they allow horizontal wrinkle to appear

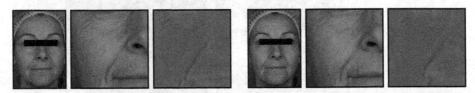

Fig. 12. Face aged with medium patch size with individual uniform condition feature maps (*left*) and proposed aging maps (*right*), along with the difference with the original image. The aging maps help make the training more efficient thanks to denser spatialized information, and produce more realistic aging. The difference highlights the small unrealistic wrinkles for the baseline technique

6   Conclusion

In this paper, we presented the use of clinical signs to create aging maps for face aging. Thanks to this technique, we demonstrated state-of-the-art results on high-resolution images with complete control over the aging process. Our patch-based approach allows conditional generative adversarial networks to be trained on large images while keeping a large batch size. This technique is applicable to various problems and can be used to tackle high-resolution problems with limited computational resources. In the future, the use of longitudinal data following the same person over time would allow a better understanding of the evolution of the aging signs on an individual basis, and therefore better personalizing of face aging factoring lifestyle, environmental and behavioral components.

Acknowledgements. We would like to thank Axel Sala-Martin for his insight on the model architecture and training process, and Robin Kips for many helpful discussions.

References

1. Agustsson, E., Timofte, R., Escalera, S., Baro, X., Guyon, I., Rothe, R.: Apparent and real age estimation in still images with deep residual regressors on appareal database. In: 2017 12th IEEE International Conference on Automatic Face & Gesture Recognition (FG 2017), pp. 87–94. IEEE (2017)

2. Antipov, G., Baccouche, M., Dugelay, J.L.: Face aging with conditional generative adversarial networks. In: 2017 IEEE International Conference on Image Processing (ICIP), pp. 2089–2093. IEEE (2017)

3. Arjovsky, M., Chintala, S., Bottou, L.: Wasserstein GAN. arXiv preprint arXiv:1701.07875 (2017)

4. Bazin, R., Doublet, E.: Skin Aging Atlas, vol. 1. Caucasian Type. MED'COM publishing (2007)

5. Bazin, R., Flament, F.: Skin Aging Atlas, vol. 2. Asian Type (2010)

6. Bazin, R., Flament, F., Giron, F.: Skin Aging Atlas, vol. 3. Afro-American Type. Med'com, Paris (2012)

7. Bazin, R., Flament, F., Rubert, V.: Skin Aging Atlas, vol. 4. Indian Type (2015)

8. Brock, A., Donahue, J., Simonyan, K.: Large scale GAN training for high fidelity natural image synthesis. arXiv preprint arXiv:1809.11096 (2018)

9. Chen, B.-C., Chen, C.-S., Hsu, W.H.: Cross-age reference coding for age-invariant face recognition and retrieval. In: Fleet, D., Pajdla, T., Schiele, B., Tuytelaars, T. (eds.) ECCV 2014. LNCS, vol. 8694, pp. 768–783. Springer, Cham (2014). https://doi.org/10.1007/978-3-319-10599-4_49

10. Choi, Y., et al.: StarGAN: unified generative adversarial networks for multi-domain image-to-image translation. In: Proceedings of the IEEE Conference on Computer Vision and Pattern Recognition, pp. 8789–8797 (2018)

11. Choi, Y., Uh, Y., Yoo, J., Ha, J.W.: Stargan v2: diverse image synthesis for multiple domains. arXiv preprint arXiv:1912.01865 (2019)

12. Dalal, N., Triggs, B.: Histograms of oriented gradients for human detection. In: 2005 IEEE Computer Society Conference on Computer Vision and Pattern Recognition (CVPR 2005), vol. 1, pp. 886–893. IEEE (2005)

13. Flament, F., Bazin, R., Qiu, H.: Skin Aging Atlas, vol. 5, Photo-aging Face & Body (2017)

14. Goodfellow, I., et al.: Generative adversarial nets. In: Advances in Neural Information Processing Systems, pp. 2672–2680 (2014)

15. Gulrajani, I., Ahmed, F., Arjovsky, M., Dumoulin, V., Courville, A.C.: Improved training of Wasserstein GANs. In: Advances in Neural Information Processing Systems, pp. 5767–5777 (2017)

16. Heljakka, A., Solin, A., Kannala, J.: Recursive chaining of reversible image-to-image translators for face aging. In: Blanc-Talon, J., Helbert, D., Philips, W., Popescu, D., Scheunders, P. (eds.) ACIVS 2018. LNCS, vol. 11182, pp. 309–320. Springer, Cham (2018). https://doi.org/10.1007/978-3-030-01449-0_26

17. Heusel, M., Ramsauer, H., Unterthiner, T., Nessler, B., Hochreiter, S.: GANs trained by a two time-scale update rule converge to a local nash equilibrium. In: Advances in Neural Information Processing Systems, pp. 6626–6637 (2017)

18. Isola, P., Zhu, J.Y., Zhou, T., Efros, A.A.: Image-to-image translation with conditional adversarial networks. In: Proceedings of the IEEE Conference on Computer Vision and Pattern Recognition, pp. 1125–1134 (2017)

19. Kärkkäinen, K., Joo, J.: Fairface: face attribute dataset for balanced race, gender, and age. arXiv preprint arXiv:1908.04913 (2019)

20. Karras, T., Laine, S., Aila, T.: A style-based generator architecture for generative adversarial networks. In: Proceedings of the IEEE Conference on Computer Vision and Pattern Recognition, pp. 4401–4410 (2019)

21. Kingma, D.P., Ba, J.: Adam: a method for stochastic optimization. arXiv preprint arXiv:1412.6980 (2014)

22. Liu, R., et al.: An intriguing failing of convolutional neural networks and the coord-conv solution. In: Advances in Neural Information Processing Systems, pp. 9605–9616 (2018)
23. Park, T., Liu, M.Y., Wang, T.C., Zhu, J.Y.: Semantic image synthesis with spatially-adaptive normalization. In: Proceedings of the IEEE Conference on Computer Vision and Pattern Recognition, pp. 2337–2346 (2019)
24. Pumarola, A., Agudo, A., Martinez, A.M., Sanfeliu, A., Moreno-Noguer, F.: GAN-imation: anatomically-aware facial animation from a single image. In: Ferrari, V., Hebert, M., Sminchisescu, C., Weiss, Y. (eds.) ECCV 2018. LNCS, vol. 11214, pp. 835–851. Springer, Cham (2018). https://doi.org/10.1007/978-3-030-01249-6_50
25. Ricanek, K., Tesafaye, T.: Morph: a longitudinal image database of normal adult age-progression. In: 7th International Conference on Automatic Face and Gesture Recognition (FGR 2006), pp. 341–345. IEEE (2006)
26. Rothe, R., Timofte, R., Van Gool, L.: Dex: deep expectation of apparent age from a single image. In: Proceedings of the IEEE International Conference on Computer Vision Workshops, pp. 10–15 (2015)
27. Song, J., Zhang, J., Gao, L., Liu, X., Shen, H.T.: Dual conditional GANs for face aging and rejuvenation. In: IJCAI, pp. 899–905 (2018)
28. Szegedy, C., Ioffe, S., Vanhoucke, V., Alemi, A.A.: Inception-v4, inception-resnet and the impact of residual connections on learning. In: Thirty-first AAAI Conference on Artificial Intelligence (2017)
29. Upchurch, P., et al.: Deep feature interpolation for image content changes. In: Proceedings of the IEEE Conference on Computer Vision and Pattern Recognition, pp. 7064–7073 (2017)
30. Wang, Z., Tang, X., Luo, W., Gao, S.: Face aging with identity-preserved conditional generative adversarial networks. In: Proceedings of the IEEE Conference on Computer Vision and Pattern Recognition, pp. 7939–7947 (2018)
31. Yazici, Y., Foo, C.S., Winkler, S., Yap, K.H., Piliouras, G., Chandrasekhar, V.: The unusual effectiveness of averaging in GAN training. arXiv preprint arXiv:1806.04498 (2018)
32. Zeng, H., Lai, H., Yin, J.: Controllable face aging. arXiv preprint arXiv:1912.09694 (2019)
33. Zhang, R., Isola, P., Efros, A.A., Shechtman, E., Wang, O.: The unreasonable effectiveness of deep features as a perceptual metric. In: Proceedings of the IEEE Conference on Computer Vision and Pattern Recognition, pp. 586–595 (2018)
34. Zhu, H., Huang, Z., Shan, H., Zhang, J.: Look globally, age locally: face aging with an attention mechanism. arXiv preprint arXiv:1910.12771 (2019)
35. Zhu, H., Zhou, Q., Zhang, J., Wang, J.Z.: Facial aging and rejuvenation by conditional multi-adversarial autoencoder with ordinal regression. arXiv preprint arXiv:1804.02740 (2018)
36. Zhu, J.Y., Park, T., Isola, P., Efros, A.A.: Unpaired image-to-image translation using cycle-consistent adversarial networks. In: Proceedings of the IEEE International Conference on Computer Vision, pp. 2223–2232 (2017)

Unconstrained Text Detection in Manga: A New Dataset and Baseline

Julián Del Gobbo[1]([✉])[iD] and Rosana Matuk Herrera[2][iD]

[1] Departamento de Computación, FCEN, Universidad de Buenos Aires,
Buenos Aires, Argentina
jdelgobbo@dc.uba.ar
[2] Departamento de Ciencias Básicas, Universidad Nacional de Luján,
Luján, Argentina
rmatuk@unlu.edu.ar

Abstract. The detection and recognition of unconstrained text is an open problem in research. Text in comic books has unusual styles that raise many challenges for text detection. This work aims to binarize text in a comic genre with highly sophisticated text styles: Japanese manga. To overcome the lack of a manga dataset with text annotations at a pixel level, we create our own. To improve the evaluation and search of an optimal model, in addition to standard metrics in binarization, we implement other special metrics. Using these resources, we designed and evaluated a deep network model, outperforming current methods for text binarization in manga in most metrics.

Keywords: Text-binarization · Text-datasets · Binarization-evaluation · Neural-networks · Japanese-text-detection · Manga

1 Introduction

Manga is a type of Japanese comic book with a huge diversity of text and balloons styles in unconstrained positions (Fig. 1). Japanese is a highly complex language, with three different alphabets and thousands of text characters. It also has about 1200 different onomatopoeia, which frequently appear in manga. Furthermore, characters often look very similar to the art in which they are embedded. These complexities make a text detection method for manga challenging to design.

A translation process of a manga picture consists of detecting the text, erasing it, inpainting the image, and writing the translated text on the image. As it is an intricate process, the translation is usually done manually in manga, and only the most popular mangas are translated. The complexity of the Japanese language hinders the diffusion of manga, and other Japanese artworks, outside of

Electronic supplementary material The online version of this chapter (https://doi.org/10.1007/978-3-030-67070-2_38) contains supplementary material, which is available to authorized users.

A. Bartoli and A. Fusiello (Eds.): ECCV 2020 Workshops, LNCS 12537, pp. 629–646, 2020.
https://doi.org/10.1007/978-3-030-67070-2_38

Fig. 1. Pictures showing the diversity of text styles in manga. (a) The dialogue balloons could have unconstrained shapes and border styles. The text could have any style and fill pattern, and could be written inside or outside the speech balloons. Note also that the frames could have non-rectangular shapes, and the same character could be in multiple frames. (b) Example of manga extract featuring non-text inside speech bubbles. (c) The same text character can have diverse levels of transparency. (d) Text characters could have a fill pattern similar to the background. All images were extracted from the Manga109 dataset [28,29,36]: (a) and (d) "Revery Earth" ©Miyuki Yama, (b) "Everyday Oasakana-chan" ©Kuniki Yuka, (c) "Akkera Kanjinchou" ©Kobayashi Yuki

Japan. Automating the translation would lead to solving the linguistic barrier. In this work, we focus on the first step of the translation process: text detection. To achieve high-quality inpainting of the image, the text detection should be made at a pixel level.

On one side, many works in text detection in comics have taken a balloon detection approach. However, in manga, the text and balloons are also part of the artwork. Thus, balloons could have a multiplicity of shapes and styles. Besides, the text can be outside the dialogue balloons (Figs. 1a,1c,1d), or inside the balloon there could be non-text contents (Fig. 1b), making a balloon detection approach unsuitable for this task. On the other side, most previous works in text detection have taken a box detection approach. However, manga contains texts that are deformed, extremely large, or are drawn on the cartoon characters, which are hard to identify with a single bounding box (Figs. 1a,1c,1d). Thus, we decide to make text segmentation at a pixel level, identifying pixels as either text or background.

This work aims to detect unconstrained text characters in manga at a pixel level. The main contributions of this work are the following:

- The implementation and public release of many metrics for text detection at a pixel level, which others may reutilize, providing an easy way to find better models and compare results (Sect. 3).
- The creation and public release of a new dataset on text segmentation at a pixel level of Japanese manga (Sect. 4). To the best of our knowledge, this is the first dataset of these characteristics in manga.
- A simple and efficient model based on the U-net architecture [39] that outperforms state-of-the-art works on text detection in Japanese manga, with good baseline metrics for future works (Sects. 5 and 6).

Despite the focus in manga, many techniques proposed in this work are general and could be used to do unconstrained text detection in other contexts.

2   Related Work

Speech Balloon Detection. Several works have studied speech balloon detection in comics [14,26,34,38]. While this could be used to detect speech balloons and then consider its insides as text, the problem is that text in manga is not always inside speech balloons. Furthermore, there are a few cases where not everything inside the balloon is text (Fig. 1b).

Bounding Box Detection. Other works in text detection in manga, such as Ogawa et al. [36] and Yanagisawa et al. [49], have focused on text bounding box detection of multiple objects, including text. Wei-Ta Chu and Chih-Chi Yu have also worked on bounding box detection of text [11]. Without restricting to manga or comics, there are many works every year that keep improving either bounding box or polygon text detection, one of the most recent ones being Wang et al. [46]. However, methods trained with rigid word-level bounding boxes exhibit limitations in representing the text region for unconstrained texts. Recently, Baek et al. proposed a method (CRAFT) [4] to detect unconstrained text in scene images, generating non-rigid word-level bounding boxes.

Pixel-level Text Segmentation. There is a long history of text segmentation [30] and image binarization [18,19,37,47] in the document analysis community related to historical manuscripts [35], maps [5], handwritten text [41], documents [32] and more. One of such works that does pixel level segmentation of text in document images is BCDU-net [2]. However, in these works most of the image is text along with a few lines or figures, and the text is more simple than one of manga, which features a lot more context, wide variety of shapes and styles. Outside the document binarization community, there are very few works that do pixel-level segmentation of characters, as there are few datasets available with pixel-level ground truth. One of such works is from Bonechi *et al.* [6]. As numerous datasets provide bounding–box level annotations for text detection, the authors obtained pixel-level text masks for scene images from the available bounding–boxes exploiting a weakly supervised algorithm. However, a dataset with annotated bounding boxes should be provided, and the bounding box app-roach is not suitable for unconstrained text. Some few works that make pixel text segmentation in manga could be found on GitHub. One is called "Text Segmen-tation and Image Inpainting" by yu45020 [50] and the other "SickZil-Machine" by U-Ram Ko [24,25]. Both attempt to generate a text mask in the first step via image segmentation and inpainting with such mask as a second step. In *SickZil-Machine*, the author created pixel-level text masks of the Manga109 dataset, but has not publicly released the labeled dataset. The author neither released the source code of the method but has provided an executable program to run it. In yu45020's work, the source code has been released.

Pixel-level Segmentation. Outside text, there are multiple works that do segmentation of different objects. One of such works is HRNet [42,45], which has top scores in many tasks, including segmentation with cityscapes dataset [13].

Text Erasers. Some authors have explored pixel-level text erasers for scene images. Nakamura *et al.* [33] is one of the first to address this issue using deep neural networks. Newer works (EnsNet) by Zhang *et al.* [51] and (MTRNet) by Tursun *et al.* [43] make use of conditional generative adversarial networks.

3   Evaluation Metrics

Metrics such as recall, precision, and F-measure or F_1 score [10] are widely used to evaluate binary segmentation models in images. These are defined as:

$$Precision = \frac{TP}{TP + FP} \tag{1}$$

$$Recall = \frac{TP}{TP + FN} \tag{2}$$

$$Fmeasure = F_1 = Pixel\,F1 = PF1 = \frac{2\ Recall\ Precision}{Recall + Precision} \tag{3}$$

with TP being pixels that were correctly segmented as text (true positive), FP being pixels that were wrongly segmented as text (false positives) and FN being pixels that were wrongly segmented as background (false negatives). Other standard evaluation measures in document binarization are PSNR and DRD [37]. PSNR is a similarity measure between two images. The higher the value of PSNR, the higher the similarity of the two images. The Distance Reciprocal Distortion Metric (DRD) has been used to measure the visual distortion in binary document images [27]. The lower the DRD, the lower the distortion.

Recall, precision and, F-measure metrics assume that the data is perfectly labeled and allow no compromises on the boundary, which is the part most prone to error. In many tasks, such as segmenting vehicles, this doesn't matter much as the area of a car is very big compared to the area that might be wrongly labeled, so the human error in labeling won't account much to influence metrics. With text, however, this is not the case. Not only are characters usually small, but also the boundary is many times unclear because of artifacts and blurring, as noted in Fig. 2. Another issue is that a large text character can have the same area as 100 small characters, making a model that correctly matches most of its pixels but none of the other 100 characters, as good as one matching the 100 small ones but little of the big one.

Fig. 2. Example of text inside the speech bubble zoomed in. Note that text boundary is unclear and prone to error due to artifacts. Image from "Akkera Kanjinchou" ©Kobayashi Yuki, Manga109 dataset [28,29,36]

Calarasanu *et al.* [7–9] have proposed several metrics to account for these issues. In this work, we have adopted an approach similar to theirs. In addition to the standard pixel metrics, we calculate metrics based on connected components. A connected component in these images is a region of adjacent pixels, considering its 8 neighbors, sharing the same value (see Fig. 3a).

Given a ground truth connected component G_i and its matching detection D_j, its accuracy and coverage are defined as:

$$Acc_i = \frac{Area(G_i \cap D_j)}{Area(D_j)} \qquad (4)$$

$$Cov_i = \frac{Area(G_i \cap D_j)}{Area(G_i)} \qquad (5)$$

To account for multiple detections matching a single ground truth or a single detection matching multiple ground truths, we apply the watershed algorithm to match prediction pixels to a single ground truth, as seen in Fig. 3.

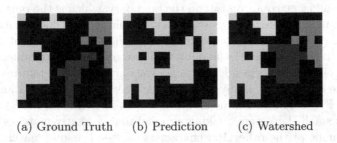

(a) Ground Truth   (b) Prediction   (c) Watershed

Fig. 3. Example of the watershed algorithm matching prediction pixels to ground truth connected components. (a) Masks of five ground truth connected components (labeled in different colors to be distinguished); (b) Predicted text segmentation mask. We marked in red (bottom, right) a predicted connected component with no correspondence to any ground truth connected component; (c) The predicted mask is matched with the ground truth using the watershed algorithm to obtain the evaluation metrics. Five detections matching ground truth connected components are obtained (Color figure online)

We define tp as the number of ground truth connected components that have at least one pixel of detection associated with it. We define fp as the number of detected connected components which had no correspondence to any ground truth (see Fig. 3b).

Given a dataset with m ground truth connected components and d detections, we define the following metrics: quantity recall R_{quant}, quantity precision P_{quant}, quality recall R_{qual}, quality precision P_{qual} and F1 quality $F1_{qual}$:

$$R_{quant} = \frac{tp}{m} \qquad (6)$$

$$P_{quant} = \frac{tp}{tp + fp} \qquad R_{qual} = \frac{\sum_{i=0}^{tp} Cov_i}{tp} \qquad (7)$$

$$P_{qual} = \frac{\sum_{i=0}^{tp} Acc_i}{tp} \qquad (8)$$

$$F1_{qual} = \frac{2\, R_{qual}\, P_{qual}}{R_{qual} + P_{qual}} \qquad (9)$$

Global recall GR, global precision GP, and global F_1 $GF1$ are defined as:

$$GR = R_{quant} R_{qual} = \frac{\sum_{i=0}^{tp} Cov_i}{m} \tag{10}$$

$$GP = P_{quant} P_{qual} = \frac{\sum_{i=0}^{tp} Acc_i}{tp + fp} \tag{11}$$

$$GF1 = \frac{2\ GR\ GP}{GR + GP} \tag{12}$$

We calculate metrics in normal and relaxed mode. Normal mode assumes that the dataset is perfectly labeled. Relaxed mode tries to lessen the effect of wrong boundary labeling (Fig. 4). In normal mode, we calculate the metrics using the segmentation masks of the dataset without modification. In relaxed mode, an eroded version of the ground truth is used to calculate coverage while a dilated version is used to calculate accuracy. In both modes, we consider there is no match to a ground truth component when there is no intersection between the eroded version and prediction, as the eroded version is the most relevant part to detect. For both erosion and dilation, a cross-shaped structuring element is used (connectivity $= 1$).

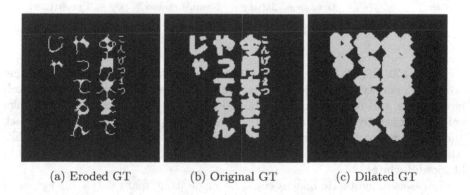

| (a) Eroded GT | (b) Original GT | (c) Dilated GT |

Fig. 4. Example of segmentation masks used in normal mode and relaxed mode metrics. (a) The eroded mask under-segments the ground truth mask. It is used for coverage in relaxed mode; (b) Ground truth mask. It is used in normal mode; (c) The dilated mask over-segments the ground truth. It is used for accuracy in relaxed mode. In relaxed mode, if the network predicts the ground truth of b), it has 100% of accuracy. However, if the prediction is inside the dilated mask of c), it also has 100% of accuracy. Accuracy is measured with Eq. 4.

4   Dataset

There are very few datasets of images with text and their corresponding pixel level mask (Table 1). This is mainly due to the large amount of time required to label them properly. However, most of them correspond to real-world images, which differ greatly from manga, and lack useful context such as speech balloons. Besides, most text in these datasets is in English and manga is in Japanese. Last, in these datasets, the text fonts are not hand-drawn in unrestricted orientations and with artistic styles like in manga.

Table 1. Datasets with pixel-level segmentation masks of text characters

Dataset	Type	Language	Script	Images	Orientation
ICDAR 2013 Scene Text Challenge [23]	Scene	English	Latin	462	Horizontal
ICDAR 2013 Born Digital Challenge [23]	Digital	English	Latin	551	Horizontal
Total-Text (2017)[12]	Scene	English	Latin	1555	Multi-oriented, Curve
DIBCO [37] (2009--2019)	Document	European languages	Latin	136	Horizontal
KAIST[22]	Scene	English, Korean	Latin,Korean	2483	Horizontal
Ours	Document	Japanese	Kanji,Hiragana, Katakana,Latin	900	Unrestricted

Manga109 [28,29] is the largest public manga dataset, providing bounding boxes for many types of objects, including text. However, it does not have pixel-level masks, and not all text has a bounding box. It is composed of 109 manga volumes drawn by professional manga artists in Japan, with all pages in black and white except for the first few pages of each volume. This is because unlike American and European comics which tend to be in color, manga is usually in black and white.

Datasets of synthetic images could be made using manga-style images, such as the images of the Danbooru2019 dataset [1], selecting the images without text, and adding text to them of a particular font and size. However, randomly adding text characters anywhere does not replicate where the text is naturally placed in manga, as much text is inside speech bubbles. Synthetically replicating the speech balloons is not easy either, as they are not always a simple rectangle or ellipse like shape. Besides, text outside speech balloons are part of the artwork, and usually have artistic styles of the author.

Taking into account all these issues, we decided to create our own dataset with pixel-level annotations. We chose to use images from Manga109, as it is a known public dataset, features a wide range of genres and styles, and the manga authors have granted permission to use and publish their works for academic research. To cover as many different styles as possible, few images from many manga volumes are preferable to a lot from few volumes, as long as those few are enough for the network to learn its style. After observing many examples,

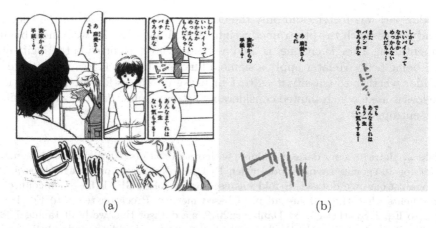

Fig. 5. Example of segmentation mask in our dataset. (a) Original image. Speech text is usually inside balloons and sound effects outside. Note the sound effects, near the stairs, and ripped paper. Image from "Aisazu Niha Irarenai" ©Yoshi Masako, Manga109 dataset [28,29,36]. (b) Corresponding segmentation mask in our dataset. The text inside speech balloons is considered as an easy detection task and labeled with black. Text outside balloons is considered a difficult text detection and labeled with pink. Non-text pixels are labeled with yellow (Color figure online)

we concluded that the first ten images of each manga volume in the Manga109 dataset were a suitable number, as that included the cover of the manga and a few pages of the actual content. Thus we manually annotated with pixel-level text masks the first ten images from 45 different digital mangas, totalizing 450 images. As each manga image in the Manga109 dataset corresponds to 2 pages of a physical manga, we digitally annotated 900 physical pages of mangas.

Instead of a simple binary mask (text and non-text), we label the dataset with 3 classes (Fig. 5, b): non-text, easy text (text inside speech balloons), and hard text (text outside speech balloons). While we still use the binary version for training, we use this separation of difficulties on text characters for a better understanding of model performance in metric evaluation.

In Table 2 we show standard metrics for a U-Net model trained on diverse datasets and tested with our dataset. It is clear that the segmentation of text in manga is greatly improved if the model is trained with our dataset.

5   Methodology

Our text detector model employs a U-net [39] architecture with a pre-trained resnet34 [20] backbone. Despite having been pre-trained with ImageNet, which features images quite different from manga, it has proved to work well. We implemented the model in PyTorch. We used the fastai U-Net model [17] and trained the network with the fastai library [16,21], making use of its one cycle policy, a modified version of the one initially devised by Leslie N. Smith [40]. The encoder part was frozen, and only the decoder part was trained, as the encoder already comes with the pre-trained weights from ImageNet. As we handle binary segmentation, a single channel is used as the last layer to provide the logits of a pixel being text. We later apply a sigmoid function and set 0.5 as a threshold to consider whether to classify it as text or background. As for the loss function, dice loss is used, which showed considerably better results than the simple binary cross-entropy loss.

Table 2. Metrics on our dataset training with other datasets. All trained with resnet34 U-Net for 10 epochs, saving model when PF1 score improved on manga dataset. To test against our own dataset, K-fold was used over 5 folds. GF1 is based on connected components while the rest are all pixel based metrics. Precision refers to Eq. 1 and recall to Eq. 2. Synthetic Text Danbooru2019 is a dataset that we built taking 75929 images without text from the Danbooru2019 [1] dataset and adding randomly Japanese characters from machine fonts.

Dataset	PF1	GF1	Precision	Recall	DRD	PSNR
DIBCO	26.32	13.47	19.09	42.37	74.71	11.64
ICDAR 2013 Scene Text Images	45.86	40.47	39.37	54.91	38.14	14.53
ICDAR 2013 Born-Digital Images	40.90	39.67	51.94	33.73	28.42	16.22
Total-Text	42.49	42.79	47.10	38.70	29.19	15.66
KAIST	45.69	29.17	44.55	46.90	32.64	15.30
Synthetic Text Danbooru2019	57.03	42.83	76.01	45.64	18.88	18.24
Ours	**76.22**	**82.64**	**80.41**	**72.50**	**12.83**	**21.06**

The images of the Manga109 dataset are 1654 width and 1170 height. As they represent sheets of paper from physical books, in almost all cases (with some covers as the exception), the two pages from it have no text in the middle and can be split without affecting text characters. We took advantage of that and cut the images of our dataset in half, so we end up with 900 manga pages to train (see Sect. 4). The only data augmentation used is a 512×800 random crop for training. We tried a few other data augmentations such as flip and warp, but we didn't notice any significant improvement.

We used K-Fold cross-validation with five folds to calculate all metrics, leaving 20% as validation. Between transfer learning, one cycle policy, and a batch size of 4, results are obtained by training for ten epochs, which is completed in less than an hour on a single GeForce GTX 1080 Ti GPU for a single fold.

In the next section, we show how we used our metrics of Sect. 3 to select an optimal loss function and an optimal architecture for the model.

6   Experiments

6.1   Loss Function Selection

Choosing an adequate loss function is a crucial step in the design of a machine learning model. We used our dataset to train a U-net network, which is a model commonly used in segmentation, with different loss functions. Then, we used the metrics of Sect. 3 to measure the performance of the model for each different loss function.

We trained a `fastai resnet18` U-net with each loss function during ten epochs, with 0.001 as the maximum learning rate. After trying different loss functions such as boundary loss, binary cross entropy and focal loss the highest scores in the metrics were obtained by $-log(DiceLoss)$ [31]. Thus, this was the loss function that we choose for further experiments.

6.2   Model Performance

To create a good baseline, we made experiments with different methods and use the metrics to compare their performance for the binarization task of our dataset. The experimental results are shown in Table 3.

Table 3. Performance metrics obtained by similar methods under similar conditions for the task of binarizing our manga dataset. All methods were trained with our `Manga109` labeled dataset except *SickZil-Machine* because the author did not release the source code. The results shown for *SickZil-Machine* are for an executable program provided by the author. However, *SickZil-Machine* was trained by his author with its own `Manga109` dataset in which text was labeled at a pixel level. Precision refers to Eq. 1 and recall to Eq. 2.

Author	Normal						Relaxed	
	PF1	GF1	Precision	Recall	DRD	PSNR	PF1	GF1
BCDU-net [2]	30.24	15.08	40.54	27.32	39.42	14.80	27.38	16.19
yu45020's xception	61.61	62.48	61.25	62.09	20.66	17.77	67.48	79.35
yu45020's mobileNetV2	47.97	39.17	49.43	46.88	28.12	16.12	50.54	52.26
SickZil-Machine	52.07	49.33	41.77	69.15	35.75	14.71	64.66	84.94
HRNet [42,45]	51.64	51.34	43.40	63.85	33.27	15.40	63.36	74.41
fastai Resnet18 U-Net	75.82	83.29	75.53	76.32	14.06	21.35	76.87	87.50
fastai Resnet34 U-Net	**79.36**	**84.92**	**82.26**	**76.71**	**11.15**	**21.91**	80.43	**89.26**

The yu45020's xception [50], the yu45020's mobileNetV2 [50] and the "SickZil-Machine" [24,25] are methods we found on Github that also aim to do pixel-level text segmentation in manga. We trained each one of the yu45020's architectures with our dataset for 10 epochs with all layers unfrozen. For SickZil-Machine the training code is not available so we used their executable to generate the predictions of Table 3.

We also compared against BCDU-net [2], a recent method for segmentation that has shown good results on multiple DIBCO datasets [3]. BCDU-net is a deep auto-encoder-decoder network. This method applies bidirectional convolutional LSTM layers in U-net structure to non-linearly encode both semantic and high-resolution information with non-linearly technique. We chose the BCDU-net implementation that was based on DIBCO [3] and trained it with our dataset in 5 folds, generating 40 random 128 × 128 patches from each image. Each fold was trained for 20 epochs.

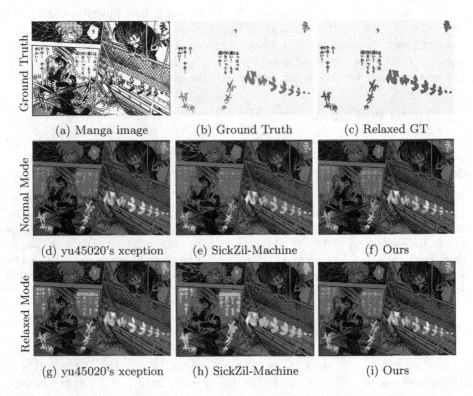

Fig. 6. Segmentation masks obtained by different methods. In red, false positives. In white, missing text. In green, text correctly segmented. (a) Image extracted from "BEMADER_P" ©Hasegawa Yuichi, Manga109 dataset [28,29,36]. (b) Ground Truth. In pink, hard text. In black, easy text. (c) Relaxed Ground Truth. In green, dilated area. In blue, ground truth pixels, that does not belong to the eroded mask. (d, e, f) Normal mode results. (g, h, i) Relaxed mode results. Note that in (h) boundaries between the small letters are lost, but they are still marked as true positives because the pixels are inside the relaxed dilated area (Color figure online)

HRNet [42,45] is a very promising method for visual recognition with state-of-the-art results in many tasks and datasets. The authors show the superiority of the HRNet in a wide range of applications, including human pose estimation, semantic segmentation, and object detection. The configuration that we used

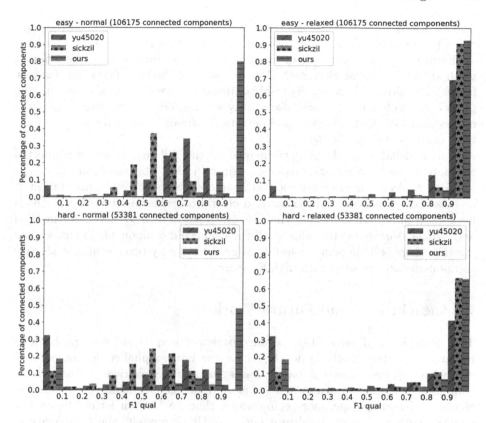

Fig. 7. Histogram of $F1_{qual}$ (see Eq. 9) of the different types of connected components. The first row corresponds with easy text, and the second row corresponds with hard text. The first column corresponds with normal mode, and the second column corresponds with relaxed mode. For easy text, our method predicts most of the connected components with a high $F1_{qual}$ value. In normal mode our method has a much higher percentage of easy and hard connected components predicted with a high $F1_{qual}$ value than the other methods.

was similar to the one provided for the cityscapes segmentation [44]. We trained each fold for 100 epochs each, changing the loss to $-log(DiceLoss)$.

We also experimented with a lot of variations of the U-Net architecture provided with `fastai` library. As shown in Table 3, the best binarization results were achieved by a `fastai` Resnet34 U-Net. For this network, we trained the decoder for 10 epochs, further trained the whole model for 5 epochs, and finally trained with whole images instead of random crops for 3 additional epochs. We kept this network as our baseline model because it achieved the top metric scores.

Last, we also experimented with 23 segmentation models from `qubvel` (Pavel Yakubovskiy)'s library [48], training only the decoder and using the default parameters. However, the `fastai` U-Net network outperformed the models in this library in all metrics for this problem.

Our metrics allow us to find a simple and efficient model, that outperforms the other models especially on normal mode, as shown in Table 3.

Figure 6 shows an example of segmentation masks produced by the different methods. Our segmentation method misses some of the hard texts but has very few false positives (Figs. 6f, 6i). *SickZil-Machine* covers some of those missing texts but also has much more false positives (Figs. 6e, 6h). yu45020's xception misses many of the hard texts, and detects the small letters with less precision than our model (Figs. 6d, 6g).

For a global view of the performance on the different types of connected components and segmentation modes, we draw in Fig. 7 the histograms of $F1_{qual}$ (see Eq. 9). As our method fits the text characters without over-segmentation, it has less false positives, and our method clearly outperforms the other methods for $F1_{qual}$ in normal mode. For the easy text case in relaxed mode, our method and *SickZil-Machine* detect almost all the connected components. Thus, we can see that there is little point in adding more data of easy text, as almost all easy components are detected with high F_1 score.

7   Conclusions and Future Work

The detection and recognition of unconstrained text is an open problem in research. Standard methods developed for the Latin alphabet do not perform well with Japanese, due to Japanese having many more characters: about 2,800 common characters out of a total set of more than 50,000. Besides, each Japanese character is, on average, more complicated than an English letter. Japan is a country with an immense cultural heritage. Unfortunately, the complexity of the Japanese language constitutes a linguistic barrier for accessing its culture. Automatic translation methods would contribute to overcome it.

In this work, we presented a study into unconstrained text segmentation at a pixel level in Japanese manga. We created a dataset manually annotating the text of manga images at a pixel level. Besides, we implemented special and standard metrics to evaluate the binarization task. We show that these tools, together with the `fastai` library, allowed us to find a simple and efficient deep learning model that outperforms in most metrics previous works on the same task. Despite our focus in manga, the techniques proposed in this work could be expanded to do unconstrained Japanese text detection in other contexts. For instance, the text segmentation masks obtained by our method could be useful for Japanese OCR and inpainting in other Japanese graphical documents.

The release of the dataset and metrics provided by this work would also enable other researchers and practitioners to find better models for this problem and compare results. To the best of our knowledge, this would be the first public dataset on text segmentation at a pixel level of Japanese manga.

The annotations of the dataset were made for the use case of text deletion and inpainting. Extending the annotations by grouping the pixels by character so that more detailed recognition-oriented analyses can be performed would significantly enhance the usability and possible applications of this work. The Electrotechnical

Laboratory (ETL) Character Database [15], contains over two hundred thousand images of handwritten Japanese characters. However, it is incomplete as it only features 1004 different Japanese characters. The Manga109 dataset contains also some annotations for text inside speech balloons that we have not used in this work. A future direction to explore is to use the ETL dataset and the text transcriptions of the Manga109 dataset to develop a method for the automatic annotation of the individual characters.

Dataset and Code Availability. Our dataset and the code used in this study is available at the GitHub page https://github.com/juvian/Manga-Text-Segmentation.

References

1. Anonymous, The Danbooru Community, Branwen, G.: Danbooru 2019: a large-scale crowdsourced and tagged anime illustration dataset (2020). https://www.gwern.net/Danbooru2019
2. Azad, R., Asadi-Aghbolaghi, M., Fathy, M., Escalera, S.: Bi-directional convLSTM U-Net with densley connected convolutions. In: ICCV (2019)
3. Azad, R., Asadi-Aghbolaghi, M., Fathy, M., Escalera, S.: DIBCO: document image binarization competition using BCDU-Net to achieve best performance (2019). https://github.com/rezazad68/BCDUnet_DIBCO
4. Baek, Y., Lee, B., Han, D., Yun, S., Lee, H.: Character region awareness for text detection. In: 2019 IEEE/CVF Conference on Computer Vision and Pattern Recognition (CVPR), pp. 9357–9366 (2019)
5. Biswas, S., Mandal, S., Das, A.K., Chanda, B.: Land map images binarization based on distance transform and adaptive threshold. In: 11th IAPR International Workshop on Document Analysis Systems, pp. 334–338 (2014)
6. Bonechi, S., Andreini, P., Bianchini, M., Scarselli, F.: COCO_TS dataset: pixel-level annotations based on weak supervision for scene text segmentation. In: ICANN (2019)
7. Calarasanu, S.: Improvement of a text detection chain and the proposition of a new evaluation protocol for text detection algorithms. Ph.D. thesis, Université Pierre et Marie Curie - Paris 6, Paris, France (2015)
8. Calarasanu, S., Fabrizio, J., Dubuisson, S.: From text detection to text segmentation: a unified evaluation scheme. In: Hua, G., Jégou, H. (eds.) ECCV 2016. LNCS, vol. 9913, pp. 378–394. Springer, Cham (2016). https://doi.org/10.1007/978-3-319-46604-0_28
9. Calarasanu, S., Fabrizio, J., Dubuisson, S.: What is a good evaluation protocol for text localization systems? Concerns, arguments, comparisons and solutions. Image Vis. Comput. **46**, 1–17 (2016)
10. Chinchor, N.: MUC-4 evaluation metrics. In: Proceedings of the 4th Conference on Message Understanding, MUC4 1992, pp. 22–29. Association for Computational Linguistics, USA (1992). https://doi.org/10.3115/1072064.1072067
11. Chu, W.T., Yu, C.C.: Text detection in manga by deep region proposal, classification, and regression. In: 2018 IEEE Visual Communications and Image Processing (VCIP), pp. 1–4 (2018)
12. Ch'ng, C.K., Chan, C.S., Liu, C.: Total-text: towards orientation robustness in scene text detection. Int. J. Doc. Anal. Recogn. (IJDAR) **23**, 31–52 (2020)

13. Cordts, M., et al.: The cityscapes dataset for semantic urban scene understanding. In: Proceedings of the IEEE Conference on Computer Vision and Pattern Recognition (CVPR) (2016)
14. Dubray, D., Laubrock, J.: Deep CNN-based speech balloon detection and segmentation for comic books. In: 2019 International Conference on Document Analysis and Recognition (ICDAR), pp. 1237–1243 (2019)
15. Electrotechnical Laboratory: ETL character database. http://etlcdb.db.aist.go.jp/. Accessed 23 July 2020
16. Fastai: Fastai deep learning library. https://github.com/fastai/fastai. Accessed 10 Feb 2020
17. Fastai: U-net model. https://docs.fast.ai/vision.models.unet.html. Accessed 02 Mar 2020
18. Fletcher, L.A., Kasturi, R.: A robust algorithm for text string separation from mixed text/graphics images. IEEE Trans. Pattern Anal. Mach. Intell. **10**, 910–918 (1988)
19. Gatos, B., Ntirogiannis, K., Pratikakis, I.: ICDAR 2009 document image binarization contest (DIBCO 2009). In: 10th International Conference on Document Analysis and Recognition, pp. 1375–1382 (2009)
20. He, K., Zhang, X., Ren, S., Sun, J.: Deep residual learning for image recognition. In: 2016 IEEE Conference on Computer Vision and Pattern Recognition (CVPR), pp. 770–778 (2015)
21. Howard, J., Gugger, S.: Fastai: a layered API for deep learning. Information **11**(2), 108 (2020). https://doi.org/10.3390/info11020108
22. Jung, J.H., Lee, S.H., Cho, M.S., Kim, J.H.: Touch TT: scene text extractor using touchscreen interface. ETRI J. **33**, 78–88 (2011). https://doi.org/10.4218/etrij.11.1510.0029
23. Karatzas, D., et al.: ICDAR 2013 robust reading competition. In: Proceedings of 12th International Conference on Document Analysis and Recognition, ICDAR 2013, pp. 1484–1493. IEEE Computer Society (2013)
24. Ko, U.R., Cho, H.G.: Sickzil-machine (2019). https://github.com/KUR-creative/SickZil-Machine
25. Ko, U.-R., Cho, H.-G.: SickZil-machine: a deep learning based script text isolation system for comics translation. In: Bai, X., Karatzas, D., Lopresti, D. (eds.) DAS 2020. LNCS, vol. 12116, pp. 413–425. Springer, Cham (2020). https://doi.org/10.1007/978-3-030-57058-3_29
26. Liu, X., Li, C., Zhu, H., Wong, T.-T., Xu, X.: Text-aware balloon extraction from manga. Vis. Comput. **32**(4), 501–511 (2015). https://doi.org/10.1007/s00371-015-1084-0
27. Lu, H., Kot, A., Shi, Y.: Distance-reciprocal distortion measure for binary document images. IEEE Signal Process. Lett. **11**, 228–231 (2004)
28. Manga109: Japanese manga dataset. http://www.manga109.org/en/
29. Matsui, Y., et al.: Sketch-based manga retrieval using manga109 dataset. Multimedia Tools Appl. **76**(20), 21811–21838 (2016). https://doi.org/10.1007/s11042-016-4020-z
30. Mehul, G., Ankita, P., Udeshi Namrata, D., Rahul, G., Sheth, S.: Text-based image segmentation methodology. Procedia Technol. **14**, 465–472 (2014)
31. Milletari, F., Navab, N., Ahmadi, S.: V-net: fully convolutional neural networks for volumetric medical image segmentation. In: 2016 Fourth International Conference on 3D Vision (3DV), pp. 565–571 (2016)

32. Mustafa, W., Kader, M.: Binarization of document images: a comprehensive review. J. Phys. Conf. Ser. **1019**, 012023 (2018). https://doi.org/10.1088/1742-6596/1019/1/012023

33. Nakamura, T., Zhu, A., Yanai, K., Uchida, S.: Scene text eraser. In: 2017 14th IAPR International Conference on Document Analysis and Recognition (ICDAR), vol. 01, pp. 832–837 (2017)

34. Nguyen, N.-V., Rigaud, C., Burie, J.-C.: Comic MTL: optimized multi-task learning for comic book image analysis. Int. J. Doc. Anal. Recogn. (IJDAR) **22**(3), 265–284 (2019). https://doi.org/10.1007/s10032-019-00330-3

35. Ntogas, N., Veintzas, D.: A binarization algorithm for historical manuscripts. ICC **2008**, 41–51 (2008)

36. Ogawa, T., Otsubo, A., Narita, R., Matsui, Y., Yamasaki, T., Aizawa, K.: Object detection for comics using manga109 annotations. ArXiv abs/1803.08670 (2018)

37. Pratikakis, I., Zagoris, K., Karagiannis, X., Tsochatzidis, L., Mondal, T., Marthot-Santaniello, I.: ICDAR 2019 competition on document image binarization (DIBCO 2019). In: 2019 International Conference on Document Analysis and Recognition (ICDAR), pp. 1547–1556 (2019)

38. Rigaud, C., Burie, J.-C., Ogier, J.-M.: Text-independent speech balloon segmentation for comics and manga. In: Lamiroy, B., Dueire Lins, R. (eds.) GREC 2015. LNCS, vol. 9657, pp. 133–147. Springer, Cham (2017). https://doi.org/10.1007/978-3-319-52159-6_10

39. Ronneberger, O., Fischer, P., Brox, T.: U-Net: convolutional networks for biomedical image segmentation. In: Navab, N., Hornegger, J., Wells, W.M., Frangi, A.F. (eds.) MICCAI 2015. LNCS, vol. 9351, pp. 234–241. Springer, Cham (2015). https://doi.org/10.1007/978-3-319-24574-4_28

40. Smith, L.N.: A disciplined approach to neural network hyper-parameters: Part 1 - learning rate, batch size, momentum, and weight decay. ArXiv abs/1803.09820 (2018)

41. Solihin, Y., Leedham, G.: Integral ratio: a new class of global thresholding techniques for handwriting images. IEEE Trans. Pattern Anal. Mach. Intell. **21**, 761–768 (1999)

42. Sun, K., Xiao, B., Liu, D., Wang, J.: Deep high-resolution representation learning for human pose estimation. In: CVPR (2019)

43. Tursun, O., Zeng, R., Denman, S., Sivipalan, S., Sridharan, S., Fookes, C.: MTRNet: a generic scene text eraser. In: 2019 International Conference on Document Analysis and Recognition (ICDAR), pp. 39–44 (2019)

44. Wang, J., et al.: High-resolution networks (HRNets) for Semantic Segmentation. https://github.com/HRNet/HRNet-Semantic-Segmentation

45. Wang, J., et al.: Deep high-resolution representation learning for visual recognition. In: TPAMI (2019)

46. Wang, W., et al.: Shape robust text detection with progressive scale expansion network. In: Proceedings of the IEEE Conference on Computer Vision and Pattern Recognition, pp. 9336–9345 (2019)

47. Wu, V., Manmatha, R., Riseman, E.M.: Finding text in images. In: Proceedings of the Second ACM International Conference on Digital Libraries, DL 1997, pp. 3–12. Association for Computing Machinery, New York (1997). https://doi.org/10.1145/263690.263766

48. Yakubovskiy, P.: Segmentation Models Pytorch (2020). https://github.com/qubvel/segmentation_models.pytorch

49. Yanagisawa, H., Yamashita, T., Watanabe, H.: A study on object detection method from manga images using CNN. In: 2018 International Workshop on Advanced Image Technology (IWAIT), pp. 1–4 (2018)

50. yu45020: Text segmentation and image inpainting (2019). https://github.com/yu45020/Text_Segmentation_Image_Inpainting

51. Zhang, S., Liu, Y., Jin, L., Huang, Y., Lai, S.: EnsNet: ensconce text in the wild. In: AAAI (2018)

Joint Demosaicking and Denoising for CFA and MSFA Images Using a Mosaic-Adaptive Dense Residual Network

Zhihong Pan[1(✉)], Baopu Li[1], Hsuchun Cheng[2], and Yingze Bao[1]

[1] Baidu Research, Sunnyvale, CA 94089, USA
zhihongpan@baidu.com
[2] Baidu Shenzhen R&D, Shenzhen 518000, China

Abstract. Color filter array (CFA) has been a basis for modern photography and recently multispectral filter array (MSFA) has gradually found its wide application. A deep learning network capable of joint demosaicking and denoising for both CFA and MSFA raw images is proposed in this paper. First, a novel dense residual network that includes multiple types of skip connections is introduced to learn features at different resolutions. Then, mosaic adaptive convolution and data augmentation based on mosaic shifting are put forward to fully make use of common characteristics of CFA and MSFA mosaic images. Moreover, an $L1$ loss function normalized by noise standard deviation is suggested to train the deep residual network so it does not rely on an explicit input of known or estimated noise standard deviation. Extensive experiments using simulated and real mosaic images from CFA cameras demonstrate that the proposed mosaic-adaptive dense residual network (MDRN) outperforms other state-of-the-art deep learning algorithms significantly. For simulated MSFA mosaics and real MSFA raw images, it also shows much improved results compared to other methods.

Keywords: Image demosaicking and denoising · Color filter array · Multispectral filter array · Dense residual network

1 Introduction

Since the beginning of modern digital imaging, color filter array (CFA) has been applied in most single-chip digital cameras. It arranges combinations of different color filters on a grid of photosensors to measure lights in different colors. The earliest Bayer filter [3] captures lights in red, green and blue (RGB) channels on a 2×2 grid where the predominant green channel occupies two out of four pixels. More recently, multispectral filter array (MSFA) is widely used to capture a multispectral image (MSI) with one exposure, like the 4×4 MSFA pattern of

Electronic supplementary material The online version of this chapter (https://doi.org/10.1007/978-3-030-67070-2_39) contains supplementary material, which is available to authorized users.

© Springer Nature Switzerland AG 2020
A. Bartoli and A. Fusiello (Eds.): ECCV 2020 Workshops, LNCS 12537, pp. 647–664, 2020.
https://doi.org/10.1007/978-3-030-67070-2_39

IMEC's snapshot spectral camera [12]. It offers more spectral color channels than the three ones in RGB camera, and the narrow bandwidth of these channels and sensing beyond visible lights are beneficial to catch fine color differences for advanced computer vision applications [2,10,11,29,46].

While CFA is convenient to take color images on a single sensor, it only measures one color at each pixel so that it needs a demosaicking process to recover full color at all pixels. The early methods based on nearest neighbor and bilinear interpolation are subjected to significant zippering artifacts along edges and textures with high gradients. To achieve better results, demosaicking methods have been studied comprehensively and efforts before 2008 were summarized in [28]. This topic has since been continuously studied, leading to great methods with impressive results [13,18,51].

The difficulty of demosaicking of raw images increases when camera noise is present. Traditionally, denoising methods are studied on color images after demosaicking. Kalevo and Rantanen [22] first attempted to remove noise on Bayer-matrix raw images. Other works afterwards [1,39,49] further demonstrated the effectiveness of denoising before demosaicking. More recent works have focused on solving the demosaicking and denoising tasks jointly [7,8,18,21,23,25,45] and application of deep learning has led to more impressive methods based on deep neural networks [9,15,19,26,27]. The large mosaic pattern and increased number of spectral channels in MSFA pose more challenges to its raw image processing. Most works [4,20,30–35,41,47] rely on spectral channel correlation to tackle demosaicking task, and deep learning based methods [16,31,38,42] have led to better results. For denoising, either alone or jointly with demosaicking, there is no published method designed particularly for MSFA raw images to our best knowledge.

In this paper, a deep mosaic-adaptive dense residual network (MDRN) applicable to both CFA and MSFA is proposed for joint demosaicking and denoising. A new dense residual network with various skip connections is first proposed to capture and fuse the features at different resolutions. Then, a novel mosaic-stride convolution scheme is further suggested to optimize convolution filter weights adapted to mosaic patterns. Moreover, two new approaches, dynamic data augmentation using varying noise and normalization of loss function by noise standard deviation, are utilized to train the deep residual network for noise level transparency. In the experiments, the proposed network is demonstrated to outperform other state-of-the-art (SOTA) methods of demosaicking-only or joint demosaicking and denoising for both simulated and real CFA mosaic images. It also yields outstanding results on simulated and real MSFA raw mosaic images.

2   Related Works

Joint Demosaicking and Denoising for CFA Image. Joint demosaicking and denoising for CFA has been an active research topic recently. Condat [6,7] proposed a joint method by splitting the image into different frequency channels. Total variation minimization [8] was advanced afterwards to further optimize edge sharpness and chromatic smoothness. Later, Heide et al. [18] designed an end-to-end image processing pipeline for demosaicking and denoising, and Khashabi *et al.* [23] introduced a novel method that can be trained to optimize a user-specific performance metric and to be generalized to non-Bayer mosaic patterns. More recently, Klatzer *et al.* [25] used a sequential energy minimization approach to optimize the joint task at a single noise level.

Gharbi *et al.* [15] proposed the first joint demosaicking and denoising model based a convolutional neural network (CNN). Later Kokkinos *et al.* [26,27] proposed a new iterative demosaicking process using a denoising network trained with deep residual learning [17]. The noise standard deviation σ are included as input in both methods so an accurate estimation of the noise level σ is needed.

MSFA Image Processing. Studies of MSFA raw image processing are relatively rare and most of them focus on demosaicking only. Miao *et al.* [30] first used a binary tree-based edge-sensing (BTES) method to recover secondary bands using information estimated from primary bands. Another 4×4 MSFA with dominant green band was suggested by Monno *et al.* [33,34] to use the dominant band as a guide to demosaick other bands using adaptive kernel upsampling and later residual interpolation. Mihoubi *et al.* [31] came up with a method to estimate a pseudo-panchromatic image (PPI) before recovering the multispectral bands using edge-sensitive PPI difference interpolation (PPID). Experimental results based on IMEC's snapshot spectral camera [12] showed better PSNR performance than earlier methods.

Shinoda *et al.* [42] built the first deep learning based demosaicking model using 3D convolutional layers to minimize the error between the initially demosaicked image using bilinear interpolation and the true MSI image. The trained model shows improvement in PSNR for 30 out of 32 images comparing to PPID [31]. Pan *et al.* [38] proposed a deep residual network (DPI-Net) to recover a deep panchromatic image (DPI) from MSFA raw image and complete demosaicking using DPI as a guide for mosaic residual interpolation (DGRI). It demonstrated better results than other latest methods including PPID [31] and the Shinoda model [42].

Compared to all the related works for CFA and MSFA, our proposed approach differentiates itself in the following aspects: 1) Different from the previous residual network, a new dense residual network is built; 2) A new mosaic-stride convolution is suggested to consider the common features of CFA and MSFA; 3) Some new data augmentation such as mosaic shifting and dynamic noise injection are introduced; 4) A new idea of $L1$ noise normalization is further designed.

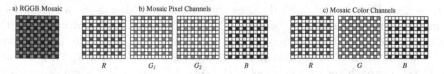

Fig. 1. An example of channel splitting: a *RGGB* mosaic raw could be split into 4 mosaic pixel channels or 3 spectral color channels. (Best viewed in color version) (Color figure online)

3 Problem Formulation

For both CFA and MSFA cameras using single-chip digital imaging, each pixel of the detector can only measure one gray-scale value. To take color images, the pixel sensors are overlaid with tiny color filters which are normally structured in repetitive mosaic patterns. A $w \times h$ rectangular submosaic has $P = w \times h$ pixels, and each is covered by one of C color filters ($C \le P$). One mosaic raw image can be split into P mosaic pixel channels, with each channel subsampling one pixel at a fixed location of each submosaic. It can also be split into C mosaic color channels, with each subsampling pixels belonging to one of C color filters. As shown in Fig. 1, in the case of the well known Bayer mosaic, it has 4 pixel channels corresponding to the $RGGB$ mosaic pattern, and 3 color channels in RGB.

CFA and MSFA cameras are used to reconstruct the latent noise-free color or multispectral image X, which consists of C numbers of 2D images and each corresponds to one of the C spectral color channels. Denote x as the vectorized form of X, x^c is the vectorized form of the 2D image of the cth spectral color channel, where $c \in \{1, 2, \cdots, C\}$.

Denoted as Y, the raw mosaic image is a gray-scale image with repetitive mosaic patterns and it is an observed form of X with the following process:

$$y = Mx + n \tag{1}$$

where $y \in \mathbb{R}^N$ and $x \in \mathbb{R}^{C \cdot N}$ are the vectorized versions of Y and X, M is the matrix representing the subsampling process for raw mosaic, and n is the noise that accounts for all errors introduced in image acquisition, often modeled as signal independent additive white Gaussian noise (AWGN) with zero-mean. Note here N is the number of pixels per spectral color channel. The mosaic subsampling process can also be represented as

$$z = Mx = x^c + m^c, c \in \{1, 2, \cdots, C\}\} \tag{2}$$

where z is the noise-free raw mosaic and m^c is the difference between z and one spectral channel image x^c. m^c can be viewed as an additive signal introduced upon gray-scale image x^c during the mosaic subsampling process. Denoting the denoising and the demosaicking processes $D_n(\cdot)$ and $D_m(\cdot)$ respectively, the denoising-before-demosaicking process could then be expressed as

$$\hat{x} = D_m(D_n(Mx + n)) = D_m(\hat{z}) \tag{3}$$

where $\hat{z} = D_n(x^c + m^c + n)$ denotes the first step of denoising which aims to remove n while preserving m^c. This is challenging as both m^c and n are additive terms that change image signals in the gray scale image x^c in similar fashions.

The joint demosaicking and denoising process is studied here and it is denoted as $D_j(\cdot)$. For each spectral channel c, the subset function $D_j^c(\cdot)$ will separate the combo additive term $m^c + n$ from y to recover the latent image x^c as below,

$$\hat{x}^c = D_j^c(y) = D_j^c(x^c + m^c + n) \tag{4}$$

With all the color channels considered, the goal is to find $\hat{D}_j(\cdot)$ by solving the following optimization problem:

$$\hat{D}_j(\cdot) = \min_{D_j(\cdot)} \sum_{n\in\overline{n}} \sum_{M\in\overline{M}} \sum_{x\in\overline{x}} E(D_j(Mx + n) - x) \tag{5}$$

where $E(\cdot)$ represents an error function, $\overline{n}$, $\overline{M}$ and $\overline{x}$ are the set of all noises, mosaic subsampling processes and latent color or multispectral images respectively. There are multiple options of $E(\cdot)$ available for different optimization strategies. The most common MSE loss is denoted as as $E_{MSE}(r)$ where $r = D_j(Mx + n) - x$ is the residual after joint demosaicking and denoising.

As denoted below, for a given mosaic pattern of $w \times h$, the set of possible M subsampling processes is limited to P unique options, where each M_i starts subsampling x from one pixel channel i.

$$\overline{M} = \{M_i | i \in \{1, 2, \cdots, P\}\} \tag{6}$$

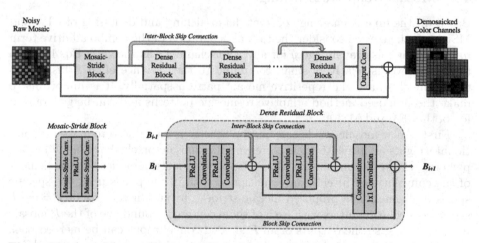

Fig. 2. The deep dense residual network architecture for joint demosaicking and denoising (RGB colors are used to represent different color channels). (Color figure online)

4 Methods

4.1 Deep Dense Residual Network

The key part of our proposed scheme is a deep dense residual network that finds the optimal filter $\hat{D}_j(\cdot)$ in Eq. 5 using deep learning. As depicted in Fig. 2, the network consists of a mosaic-stride block (MSB), a total depth of D dense residual blocks (DRB) and an output convolutional layer. The MSB block includes two mosaic-stride convolution layers, which convert the 1-channel mosaic raw input to a total of F-channels mosaic-adaptive features. For the middle D DRB blocks, each one includes two stages of double layers of convolution and the outputs of two stages are concatenated together before convoluted from $2F$ to F channels. There are two types of skip connections included in each block, the block skip connection (BSC) and inter-block skip connection (IBSC). The BSC is the shortcut between input and output of block B_i, while the IBSC includes two shortcuts from the input of block B_{i-1} to the two stages inside block B_i respectively. The last block is a convolutional layer that transforms all F channels to the estimated C-channel residual image, which is then combined with the input raw to get the jointly demosaicked and denoised output.

Compared to the denoising deep residual network in [27], the proposed network includes multiple dense shortcuts inside and among the residual blocks to combine features of different depths. Another key difference is that the proposed network doesn't need noise level σ as an input. In addition, a mosaic-stride block to extract mosaic-adaptive features is added at the beginning, which will be detailed in the subsequent subsection.

4.2   Mosaic Adaptive Learning

Based on the unique challenge of joint demosaicking and denoising of CFA and MSFA raw image, we consider the task as separation of the combo additive term $m^c + n$ from noisy raw image y for any color channel c as shown in Eq. 4. When the noise level is relatively small compared to the variance of m^c, this combo term will also have the repetitive mosaic pattern spatially. It is important to make the proposed method adaptive to mosaic patterns and can be generalized for both CFA and MSFA.

First, a new mosaic-stride convolution scheme is introduced to make convolutional weights adaptive to their corresponding mosaic pixels. For a $w \times h$ mosaic pattern, when one convolution filter is applied at a stride of $w \times h$, each element of the convolutional filter is only multiplied with image pixels from one specific spectral channel. The proposed mosaic-stride convolution consists of $P = w \times h$ strided convolution filters with each of them centered around one of the P mosaic pixel channels, so the outputs of all P strided convolutions can be merged back to an output image of the same dimension as the input when proper padding is included. With this scheme, each convolutional weight will only be multiplied with pixels from the same mosaic pixel channel. In the case of Bayer mosaic as shown in Fig. 3, some weights will be applied to R pixels only while others only applicable to G_1, G_2 or B respectively. This is in contrast to prior works which often split input to sparse RGB channels and fill missing values with initial interpolation. The subsequent convolutional layer will then process pixels with original values and interpolated values indiscriminately. While for the mosaic-stride convolution, the convolution is applied to pixels with original values only, and each specific filter weight is only applied to pixels from the same mosaic pixel channel. An ablation study is included to show its effectiveness comparing to normal channel-splitting.

Secondly, a mosaic-shifting method is used for training data augmentation. In the example of Bayer mosaic, the original $RGGB$ order can be reordered as

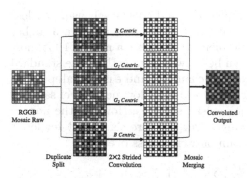

Fig. 3. An example of mosaic-stride convolution: a $RGGB$ mosaic raw is duplicated to 4 sets (highlight colors are used to indicate the central pixels of strided convolution), each duplicate is applied with a convolution at a 2×2 stride, and the resulted set of sparse images with pixels from the same pixel channel are merged together as the convoluted result. (Color figure online)

Table 1. Comparison of PSNR between our demosaick-only models and other SOTA methods for artificial sRGB images. (Results referenced from other publications have the sources marked with *.)

	Kodak	McM	VDP	Moiré
Bilinear	32.9	32.5	25.2	27.6
Condat 2012 [8]	38.3	34.1	29.2	31.5
Zhang [14,50]	40.1	34.2	30.1	32.3
Heide* [18]	40.0	38.6	27.1	34.9
Klatzer* [25]	35.3	30.8	28.0	30.3
Gharbi* [15]	41.2	39.5	34.3	37.0
Henz [19]	41.9	39.5	34.3	36.3
Tan [44]	42.1	-	-	-
Gharbi 2019[b]	41.5	38.7	33.6	36.4
Kokkinos 2019[a]	42.0	39.7	34.5	37.0
MDRN	**42.4**	**39.9**	**35.3**	**38.2**

[a] https://github.com/cig-skoltech/deep_demosaick.
[b] https://github.com/mgharbi/demosaicnet.

$GRBG$ if all color filters on the photosensor are shifted to the left by one pixel. A total of four patterns ($RGGB$, $GRBG$, $GBRG$ and $BGGR$) are possible with mosaic-shifting so four different raw mosaics can be simulated from one RGB image. As noted in Eq. (6), for a mosaic pattern of P mosaic pixels, there are P different ways to subsample the color image x using this shifting. It increases sampling size by P-fold in the $\overline{M}$ space of Eq. (5). This is an effective data augmentation method for MSFA models in particular when training samples are limited.

4.3   Noise Transparency

For joint demosaicking and denoising, most previous works need noise priors, meaning a known or estimated noise level is required at inference. In order to achieve noise transparency at inference, a few data augmentation methods are used in training. First, AWGN noises with a standard deviation of σ randomly chosen from the range of $[0, M_\sigma]$ is added to the noise-free mosaic before used for training. Moreover, to minimize the prediction error at all noise levels, one noise-free mosaic raw image could be augmented to include various noise levels as inputs. As a more efficient alternative, the augmentation can be applied dynamically by changing the added noise before each iteration during training. Both the static and dynamic noise augmentation methods increase sampling in the $\overline{n}$ space of Eq. (5).

However, training the model with samples of mixed noise levels using $L1$ loss can lead to convergence biased towards noisier samples as they have a higher impact on loss values. To alleviate this problem, we propose a novel $L1$ loss normalized by noise standard deviation shown below where σ_n is the noise standard deviation, r_i^c is the residual error for pixel i at channel c and ϵ is a small positive constant. Comparing to $L1$ loss E_{L1}, it reduces loss for low noise-level samples while tolerating some increases in loss for noisier samples. However the impact on PSNR for the corresponding loss changes will be more significant for lower noise-level samples so the performance gain outweighs loss overall.

$$E_{N_\sigma}(r) = \frac{\sum_{c=1}^{C} \sum_{i=1}^{N} |r_i^c|}{N \times C \times (\sigma_n + \epsilon)} \tag{7}$$

5   Experimental Results

A series of experiments using multiple mosaic patterns and datasets were conducted to evaluate and analyze the proposed method. We used Adam optimizer [24] to train our models in PyTorch [40], starting with an initial learning rate of 10^{-3} and multiplied by a ratio of 0.8 for every 20 epochs. All models were trained in floating number where pixel values range from 0 to 1. For RGB images, results were converted back to 8-bit for PSNR calculation. For MSFA multispectral images, to be consistent with prior works [38,43], PSNR was calculated in floating number as below

$$PSNR = -20 \cdot \log_{10} \frac{1}{N} \sum_{i=1}^{N} \sqrt{\frac{1}{C} \sum_{i=1}^{C} (r_i^c)^2} \tag{8}$$

where r is the residual multispectral image after demosaicking, C is the number of spectral channels and N is the number of pixels per channel.

Table 2. Results of PSNR values on MIT validation dataset with (✓) or without (✗) IBSC and MSB.

IBSC	✗	✓	✗	✓
MSB	✗	✗	✓	✓
PSNR	34.68	34.62	35.20	35.37

Table 3. Comparison of PSNR for demosaicking using MDRN models of different depths.

	Kodak	McM	VDP	Moiré	Average
MDRN-12	42.21	39.76	34.83	37.80	38.65
MDRN-20	42.44	39.92	35.31	38.19	38.97
MDRN-40	42.49	40.02	35.43	38.38	39.08

5.1   Ablation Study

To demonstrate the effectiveness of MSB and IBSC, an ablation study of demosaicking simulated mosaic inputs was conducted using MDRN with settings of $D = 12$ and $F = 64$. The baseline model, like other demosaicking models [15, 19, 27, 42], split the input raw mosaic to three color channels and processed with bilinear interpolation before convoluted to a 64-channel output, and then the convoluted outputs are fed into the dense residual blocks without IBSC. It is compared with models with IBSC and BSC added individually or jointly. 64,000 images randomly picked from the training set of the MIT dataset [15] were used to train each model 5×10^4 iterations before comparing PSNR values using the MIT validation dataset. As shown in Table 2, the MSB improves the performance significantly in either case, and the IBSC further improves it when combined with MSB.

Another ablation study was conducted to compare performance of three MDRN models with different depth (number of dense residual blocks D). The models were trained for demosaicking only using the same 64,000 images from the MIT dataset. After fully trained, the models were compared using four datasets, including Kodak [28], McMaster [51], and VDP and Moiré from the MIT dataset [15]. As shown in Table 3, MDRN-20 gains significant improvement from MDRN-12 over all datasets, but further improvement gained from MDRN-40 is marginal comparing to its increase in network depth. As a result, MDRN-20 was used for all CFA related experiments. Other ablation studies related to noise transparency are included in Table 4 and 5.

5.2   Demosaicking Artificial CFA Mosaic

We first compared our model with prior works using simulated mosaic inputs in sRGB color space. The same MDRN-20 model as in the model depth ablation study was used, where $D = 20$, $F = 4$, $K_{MSB} = 5$ and $K_{DRB} = 3$. The latter two parameters are the kernel sizes of MSB and DRB blocks respectively.

As illustrated in the Table 1, the proposed MDRN model improves performance for all four datasets, especially for VDP and Moiré where the PSNR increases by 0.8 and 1.2 respectively. These two were created by Gharbi et al. [15] to evaluate challenging cases that are prone to produce demosaicking artifacts. The results from Kokkinos 2019[1] and Gharbi 2019[2] were generated from their pre-trained models published in GitHub. A few examples from Moiré test set are shown in Fig. 4. For the first example, the Kokkinos one displays Moiré artifacts for half of the image. While both Gharbi's and ours are Moiré free for the whole image, ours recovers the border area better. In the second scene, while the Kokkinos one is the best at reconstructing the blinds pattern, the vertical interference artifacts in our result is minimal compared to the Gharbi's. The third example is an interesting case as there are zipper effects present in the reference image.

---

[1] https://github.com/cig-skoltech/deep_demosaick.
[2] https://github.com/mgharbi/demosaicnet.

(a) Reference   (b) Gharbi 2019 [2]   (c) Kokkinos 2019 [1]   (d) MDRN

Fig. 4. Visual comparison of demosaicking raw mosaics. (Best viewed with zoom in mode to see clearly the difference details) (Color figure online)

Both the Kokkinos model and ours suppress the artifacts effectively, especially along the edge between yellow and black area.

5.3   Joint Demosaicking and Denoising of Artificial CFA Mosaic

Starting from the pre-trained demosaicking model, we further generated three joint models using 12,800 random images from the MIT dataset, starting from E_{L1} loss, then adding dynamic noise (DN) augmentation, and lastly replacing E_{L1} with noise normalized E_{N_σ} loss. For tests, AWGN noises with discrete σ values from 4 to 20 were added to the reference mosaics to generate noisy inputs. Using a single model from each method, the average PSNRs of four datasets were compared at each noise level (including noise-free mosaics) and the results are recorded in Table 4. It shows that our MDRN models outperform other methods consistently at all noise levels, with the PSNR improvement over Gharbi [15] ranging from 0.6 to 1.2 at different noise levels. Among the three MDRN models, the dynamic noise augmentation increases PSNR by $0.1 - 0.2$ at different noise levels when both using E_{L1}. The final model with E_{N_σ} loss has the best performance at noise-free tests and all low-mid noise levels, and is equivalent to E_{L1} loss when σ is 16 or 20. It shows that our joint model is capable of achieving outstanding results with total noise transparency.

For visual comparisons, a few examples from the challenging Moirè test images are shown in Fig. 5. The noise-free reference images are in the first column and the noisy images with noise level at $\sigma = 8$ are shown in the second column. Note that the noisy RGB were subsampled to noisy mosaics before applied with any demosaicking methods. It is shown that both the Gharbi[2] model and our MDRN outperform both FlexISP as in Heide [18] and ADMM as in Tan [45] significantly. In addition, our model is better at removing noises comparing to the Gharbi model for all three examples. For the last one, the Gharbi model loses too many high contrast details that its PSNR is lower even comparing to

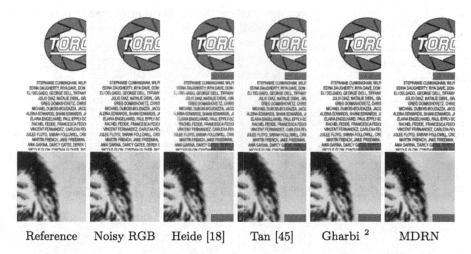

| Reference | Noisy RGB | Heide [18] | Tan [45] | Gharbi [2] | MDRN |

Fig. 5. Visual comparison of joint demosaicking and denoising raw mosaics ($\sigma = 8$).

FlexISP and ADMM (Best viewed with zoom in mode to see clearly the PSNR values in each figure).

5.4 Demosaicking Real CFA Mosaic

Khashabi *et al.* [23] has argued that the demosaicking should be applied on raw linear RGB data with an affine noise model while the PSNR metric should be evaluated in sRGB color space after conversion. They have assembled the MSR dataset from 500 16-bit linear RGB images, each including a noise-free and a noisy version of both mosaic raw and RGB color images. To validate our proposed method, we used the demosaicking only model trained in MIT sRGB dataset for further optimization using the MSR 16-bit linear Panasonic training set. There are 400 images in total, including 200 noise-free and 200 noisy mosaic images from the same 200 ground truth images.

Two joint models were trained using the MSR dataset. The first one utilized 400 MSR training mosaic images in original format. E_{L1} was taken as the loss function since noise statistics are unknown. For the second model, the 200 noise-free mosaic images were augmented dynamically using added AWGN noises and trained with E_{N_σ} loss. Both joint models were trained from the demosaicking only model pre-trained using the MIT sRGB dataset as in previous section. The trained models were then tested using the 200 noise-free and 200 noisy images from the MSR test set respectively, and evaluated in both linear RGB and sRGB color space. The floating point output of the network was used for sRGB conversion before converted to 8-bit for PSNR calculation.

As shown in Table 5, our two models have the best performance in the noisy and noise-free tests respectively. The one trained from 400 original MSR images has much better performance for noise-free images, especially in sRGB.

Table 4. Comparison of PSNR between our MDRN models and other methods for joint demosaicking and denoising of artificial noisy raw mosaics.

Table 5. Comparison of PSNR between our MDRN models and other methods for demosaicking real raw mosaics from the MSR dataset.

σ	0	4	8	12	16	20
Condat 1 [7]	32.4	31.3	29.9	28.7	27.7	26.9
Condat 2 [8]	33.3	32.0	30.4	29.1	28.1	27.3
Gharbi [15]	38.0	34.5	32.3	30.8	29.5	28.5
E_{L1}	38.3	35.5	33.1	31.4	30.2	29.1
E_{L1} + DN	38.5	35.6	33.2	31.5	**30.3**	**29.3**
E_{N_σ} + DN	**38.6**	**35.7**	**33.3**	31.6	30.3	**29.3**

	Noisy		Noise-free	
	RGB	sRGB	RGB	sRGB
Heide* [18]	-	-	40.0	33.8
Khashabi* [23]	37.7	31.4	39.4	32.6
Klatzer [25]	38.7	32.9	40.9	34.6
Gharbi* [15]	38.6	32.6	42.7	35.9
Kokkinos[b]	38.7	33.3	42.8	36.4
Kokkinos[a] Noisy	40.1	34.2	41.9	35.7
Original (E_{L1})	39.4	33.6	**43.1**	**37.3**
+AWGN (E_{N_σ})	**40.4**	**34.9**	42.9	37.1

Its performance in noisy tests is underwhelming, probably due to lack of variations in noises from training samples. The other one trained from 200 noise-free MSR mosaics using dynamic AWGN noise augmentation has significantly better PSNRs in both linRGB and sRGB for noisy tests while keeping the performance degradation in noise-free test minimal. The result demonstrates that the dynamic noise augmentation and E_{N_σ} loss are effective for demosaicking raw images with realistic noises even though the training noises are simulated AWGN. For comparison, the Kokkinos (See footnote 1) models have the second best performances overall. It uses two models which are optimized for the noisy and noise-free tests respectively. The first one needs to specify that no noise-estimation is needed for inference, and the noisy one needs to estimate noise level in advance. On top of that, the Kokkinos models rely on up to 20 iterations of a deep denoising model to get the final result. In summary, our joint model trained from augmented AWGN noises has better results in all tests compared to both Kokkinos models without need of either noise level priors or iterative process during inference.

Two examples of demosaicking noisy MSR 16-bit linear RGB raw images are shown in Fig. 6. The noise-free reference and results from Khashabi [23] and Kokkinos (See footnote 1) are compared with our joint model trained from AWGN augmented MSR images. For the shopfront scene, the Khashabi one has noticeable artifacts on window frames and the Kokkinos one has disfigured letters. Our model has better fidelity in both details. For the outside scene, while the Khashabi one has noisy blue sky and the Kokkinos one does a much better job, our model is the best comparing the reference.

5.5 MSFA Mosaic Results

The joint demosaicking and denoising model for MSFA was first trained using artificial data. Public hyperspectral datasets were used to simulate MSFA raw mosaic images as well as ground-truth multispectral images for model training and testing. The four datasets used in our tests include indoor CAVE

(a) Reference   (b) Khashabi [23]   (c) Kokkinos 2019 [1]   (d) Ours

Fig. 6. Visual comparison of demosaicking noisy MSR mosaics. (Best viewed with zoom in mode to see clearly the difference details)

Table 6. Comparison of PSNR for demosaicking of simulated noisy MSFA raw images.

Noise Level (σ)	0.01	0.02	0.05	0.1	0.2
Denoising + PPID	42.9	40.6	35.3	29.7	23.5
Denoising + DGRI	46.3	42.8	36.1	30.0	23.5
MDRN Joint	**46.9**	**45.1**	**42.0**	**39.3**	**36.1**

dataset [48], the University of Manchester 2015 outdoor dataset [37], and the TokyoTech 31-band and 59-band indoor dataset [36]. Same as previous studies [31,38,42], the specifications from XIMEA's xiSpec camera were used for data simulation. This camera, built from IMEC's MSFA technology [12], uses a 4×4 mosaic pattern with 16 unique spectral color channels whose central wavelengths are $\lambda_i \in \{469, 480, 489, 499, 513, 524, 537, 551, 552, 566, 580, 590, 602, 613, 621, 633\}$ (nm) respectively. The simulated 16-channel ground-truth multispectral images were then subsampled as MSFA raw mosaic images. The two indoor TokyoTech datasets and the Manchester outdoor set were used for training and validation, using mosaic shifting in addition to flipping and rotation for data augmentation. The deep MDRN network was configured as $D=20$, $F=64$ and $K_{MSB}=9$.

As there is no known joint method for MSFA for comparison, we compared our results with denoising-before-demosaicking approaches. There is no previous method published for denoising MSFA raw data either and we modified the latest CFA denoising method by Akiyama et al. [1] for MSFA, using non-local means method [5] in the channel-by-channel denoising. The denoised images were then processed using two state-of-the-art MSFA demosaicking methods, PPID [31] and DGRI [38], respectively. These two methods were compared with our proposed joint method to demosaick noisy MSFA raw images. Random noises of different standard deviations were added to all 31 images of the CAVE dataset and the methods were compared for the average PSNRs at each noise level. As shown in Table 6, using DGRI after denoising improves performance significantly for lower noise levels compared to PPID after denoising. Our joint model exceeds

(a) $\sigma = 0.02$ (b) $\sigma = 0.05$ (c) $\sigma = 0.1$ (d) $\sigma = 0.2$

(e) PSNR = 40.8 (f) PSNR = 37.3 (g) PSNR = 34.1 (h) PSNR = 30.5

Fig. 7. Examples of demosaicking simulated noisy MSFA raw images.

(a) Raw Mosaic (b) Camera Default (c) Demosaick Only (d) Joint

Fig. 8. Examples of demosaicking real MSFA raw images from Spectral Devices' multispectral camera. (Best viewed with zoom in mode to see clearly the difference details)

both by a big margin at all noise levels, up to 12.6 higher in PSNR for $\sigma = 0.2$. Visual examples of demosaicking noisy MSFA raw images are shown in Fig. 7 to demonstrate the effectiveness of our model even when the noise level is very high.

Separate tests were done using real raw images from Spectral Devices' MSC-VIS8-1-A snapshot camera[3]. The 8 unique spectral channels of this multispectral camera, located throughout a 8×8 mosaic pattern, filter lights at central wavelengths of $\lambda_i \in \{474, 495, 526, 546, 578, 597, 621, 640\}$ (nm) respectively. The same public hyperspectral datasets and data simulation process were used to prepare data to build two models, one for demosaicking only trained from noise-free images and one for joint demosaicking and denoising trained from noisy images with noise standard deviation dynamically set between 0 and 0.05. Both models were configured with $D = 20$, $F = 64$, and $K_{MSB} = 17$. Visual results from processing real MSFA camera raw mosaics are shown in Fig. 8. The raw image has a 2048×2048 resolution and the simple default demosaicking method by manufacturer resamples it as $256 \times 256 \times 8$ where 8 is the number of spectral channels. Our model recovers the full resolution $2048 \times 2048 \times 8$ cube. It's shown that the demosaicking only model is good at keeping the sharp edge features and

---

[3] http://spectraldevices.com/products/multispectral-snapshot-cameras.

recovering fine details in the first example, and the joint model keeps the sharp features while losing few details. For the noisy outdoor scene, it shows that the demosaicking model is capable of reconstructing details like the street signs but mosaic artifacts are visible around areas like the street curb. The joint model leads to much better results with suppressed artifacts and corrected white color of the street signs.

6   Conclusions

This paper has presented a new deep mosaic-adaptive dense residual network to jointly demosaick and denoise raw mosaic images. A novel mosaic-stride convolution is proposed for adaptive learning from raw mosaics of CFA or MSFA. Moreover, two new methods, $L1$ loss normalized by noise standard deviation and dynamic noise augmentation, enabled the proposed model to be noise transparent, meaning no known or estimated noise priors are needed like in other methods. In the experiments of CFA, the proposed method has illustrated consistent improvements over other SOTA methods, including joint demosaicking and denoising for both artificial and real CFA mosaics. For MSFA raw images that are simulated or from real snapshot multispectral cameras, comprehensive experiments also demonstrated superior results in terms of PSNR and visual quality as well. All the above results validated that our proposed method works well not only for CFA but also MSFA, representing the good generalization ability of the proposed algorithm. Some new modules such as mosaic-stride convolution and noise normalized L1 loss E_{N_σ} in our scheme may also be applicable to other CNN-based joint demosaicking and denoising models in the future.

References

1. Akiyama, H., Tanaka, M., Okutomi, M.: Pseudo four-channel image denoising for noisy CFA raw data. In: 2015 IEEE International Conference on Image Processing (ICIP), pp. 4778–4782. IEEE (2015)
2. Al-khafaji, S.L., Zhou, J., Zia, A., Liew, A.W.C.: Spectral-spatial scale invariant feature transform for hyperspectral images. IEEE Trans. Image Process. **27**(2), 837–850 (2018)
3. Bayer, B.E.: Color imaging array. United States Patent 3,971,065 (1976)
4. Brauers, J., Aach, T.: A color filter array based multispectral camera. In: Group, G.C. (ed.) 12. Workshop Farbbildverarbeitung. Ilmenau, 5–6 October 2006 (2006)
5. Buades, A., Coll, B., Morel, J.M.: A non-local algorithm for image denoising. In: 2005 IEEE Computer Society Conference on Computer Vision and Pattern Recognition (CVPR 2005), vol. 2, pp. 60–65. IEEE (2005)
6. Condat, L.: A simple, fast and efficient approach to denoisaicking: joint demosaicking and denoising. In: 2010 IEEE International Conference on Image Processing, pp. 905–908. IEEE (2010)
7. Condat, L.: A new color filter array with optimal properties for noiseless and noisy color image acquisition. IEEE Trans. Image Process. **20**(8), 2200–2210 (2011)

8. Condat, L., Mosaddegh, S.: Joint demosaicking and denoising by total variation minimization. In: 2012 19th IEEE International Conference on Image Processing, pp. 2781–2784. IEEE (2012)
9. Dong, W., Yuan, M., Li, X., Shi, G.: Joint demosaicing and denoising with perceptual optimization on a generative adversarial network. arXiv preprint arXiv:1802.04723 (2018)
10. Fotiadou, K., Tsagkatakis, G., Tsakalides, P.: Deep convolutional neural networks for the classification of snapshot mosaic hyperspectral imagery. Electron. Imaging 2017(17), 185–190 (2017)
11. Gao, J., Nuyttens, D., Lootens, P., He, Y., Pieters, J.G.: Recognising weeds in a maize crop using a random forest machine-learning algorithm and near-infrared snapshot mosaic hyperspectral imagery. Biosyst. Eng. 170, 39–50 (2018)
12. Geelen, B., Tack, N., Lambrechts, A.: A compact snapshot multispectral imager with a monolithically integrated per-pixel filter mosaic. In: Advanced Fabrication Technologies for Micro/Nano Optics and Photonics VII, vol. 8974, p. 89740L. International Society for Optics and Photonics (2014)
13. Getreuer, P.: Color demosaicing with contour stencils. In: 2011 17th International Conference on Digital Signal Processing (DSP), pp. 1–6. IEEE (2011)
14. Getreuer, P.: Zhang-Wu directional LMMSE image demosaicking. Image Process. On Line 1, 117–126 (2011)
15. Gharbi, M., Chaurasia, G., Paris, S., Durand, F.: Deep joint demosaicking and denoising. ACM Trans. Graph. (TOG) 35(6), 1–12 (2016). https://doi.org/10.1145/2980179.2982399
16. Habtegebrial, T.A., Reis, G., Stricker, D.: Deep convolutional networks for snapshot hypercpectral demosaicking. In: 2019 10th Workshop on Hyperspectral Image and Signal Processing: Evolution in Remote Sensing. IEEE (2019)
17. He, K., Zhang, X., Ren, S., Sun, J.: Deep residual learning for image recognition. In: Proceedings of the IEEE Conference on Computer Vision and Pattern Recognition, pp. 770–778 (2016)
18. Heide, F., et al.: FlexISP: a flexible camera image processing framework. ACM Trans. Graph. (TOG) 33(6), 231 (2014)
19. Henz, B., Gastal, E.S., Oliveira, M.M.: Deep joint design of color filter arrays and demosaicing. In: Computer Graphics Forum, vol. 37, pp. 389–399. Wiley Online Library (2018). https://doi.org/10.1111/cgf.13370
20. Jaiswal, S.P., Fang, L., Jakhetiya, V., Pang, J., Mueller, K., Au, O.C.: Adaptive multispectral demosaicking based on frequency-domain analysis of spectral correlation. IEEE Trans. Image Process. 26(2), 953–968 (2017). https://doi.org/10.1109/tip.2016.2634120
21. Jeon, G., Dubois, E.: Demosaicking of noisy Bayer-sampled color images with least-squares luma-chroma demultiplexing and noise level estimation. IEEE Trans. Image Process. 22(1), 146–156 (2013)
22. Kalevo, O., Rantanen, H.: Noise reduction techniques for Bayer-matrix images. In: Sensors and Camera Systems for Scientific, Industrial, and Digital Photography Applications III, vol. 4669, pp. 348–359. International Society for Optics and Photonics (2002)
23. Khashabi, D., Nowozin, S., Jancsary, J., Fitzgibbon, A.W.: Joint demosaicing and denoising via learned nonparametric random fields. IEEE Trans. Image Process. 23(12), 4968–4981 (2014)
24. Kingma, D.P., Ba, J.: Adam: a method for stochastic optimization. arXiv preprint arXiv:1412.6980 (2014)

25. Klatzer, T., Hammernik, K., Knobelreiter, P., Pock, T.: Learning joint demosaicing and denoising based on sequential energy minimization. In: 2016 IEEE International Conference on Computational Photography (ICCP), pp. 1–11. IEEE (2016)
26. Kokkinos, F., Lefkimmiatis, S.: Deep image demosaicking using a cascade of convolutional residual denoising networks. In: Ferrari, V., Hebert, M., Sminchisescu, C., Weiss, Y. (eds.) Computer Vision – ECCV 2018. LNCS, vol. 11218, pp. 317–333. Springer, Cham (2018). https://doi.org/10.1007/978-3-030-01264-9_19
27. Kokkinos, F., Lefkimmiatis, S.: Iterative joint image demosaicking and denoising using a residual denoising network. IEEE Trans. Image Process. **28**, 4177–4188 (2019)
28. Li, X., Gunturk, B., Zhang, L.: Image demosaicing: a systematic survey. In: Visual Communications and Image Processing 2008, vol. 6822, p. 68221J. International Society for Optics and Photonics (2008)
29. MacKenzie, L., Choudhary, T., McNaught, A.I., Harvey, A.R.: In vivo oximetry of human bulbar conjunctival and episcleral microvasculature using snapshot multispectral imaging. Exp. Eye Res. **149**, 48–58 (2016)
30. Miao, L., Qi, H., Ramanath, R., Snyder, W.E.: Binary tree-based generic demosaicking algorithm for multispectral filter arrays. IEEE Trans. Image Process. **15**(11), 3550–3558 (2006). https://doi.org/10.1109/tip.2006.877476
31. Mihoubi, S., Losson, O., Mathon, B., Macaire, L.: Multispectral demosaicing using pseudo-panchromatic image. IEEE Trans. Comput. Imaging **3**(4), 982–995 (2017). https://doi.org/10.1109/tci.2017.2691553
32. Monno, Y., Kiku, D., Kikuchi, S., Tanaka, M., Okutomi, M.: Multispectral demosaicking with novel guide image generation and residual interpolation. In: 2014 IEEE International Conference on Image Processing (ICIP), pp. 645–649. IEEE (2014). https://doi.org/10.1109/icip.2014.7025129
33. Monno, Y., Kiku, D., Tanaka, M., Okutomi, M.: Adaptive residual interpolation for color and multispectral image demosaicking. Sensors **17**(12), 2787-1-21 (2017). https://doi.org/10.3390/s17122787
34. Monno, Y., Tanaka, M., Okutomi, M.: Multispectral demosaicking using adaptive kernel upsampling. In: 2011 18th IEEE International Conference on Image Processing, pp. 3157–3160. IEEE (2011). https://doi.org/10.1109/icip.2011.6116337
35. Monno, Y., Tanaka, M., Okutomi, M.: Multispectral demosaicking using guided filter. In: Digital Photography VIII, vol. 8299, pp. 82990O-1-7. International Society for Optics and Photonics (2012)
36. Monno, Y., Teranaka, H., Yoshizaki, K., Tanaka, M., Okutomi, M.: Single-sensor RGB-NIR imaging: high-quality system design and prototype implementation. IEEE Sens. J. **19**(2), 497–507 (2019)
37. Nascimento, S.M., Amano, K., Foster, D.H.: Spatial distributions of local illumination color in natural scenes. Vis. Res. **120**, 39–44 (2016). https://doi.org/10.1016/j.visres.2015.07.005
38. Pan, Z., Li, B., Cheng, H., Bao, Y.: Deep panchromatic image guided residual interpolation for multispectral image demosaicking. In: 2019 10th Workshop on Hyperspectral Image and Signal Processing: Evolution in Remote Sensing. IEEE (2019)
39. Park, S.H., Kim, H.S., Lansel, S., Parmar, M., Wandell, B.A.: A case for denoising before demosaicking color filter array data. In: 2009 Conference Record of the Forty-Third Asilomar Conference on Signals, Systems and Computers, pp. 860–864. IEEE (2009)
40. Paszke, A., et al.: Automatic differentiation in pytorch. In: NIPS-W (2017)

41. Shinoda, K., et al.: Multispectral filter array and demosaicking for pathological images. In: 2015 Asia-Pacific Signal and Information Processing Association Annual Summit and Conference (APSIPA), pp. 697–703. IEEE (2015). https://doi.org/10.1109/apsipa.2015.7415362

42. Shinoda, K., Yoshiba, S., Hasegawa, M.: Deep demosaicking for multispectral filter arrays. arXiv preprint arXiv:1808.08021 (2018)

43. Shrestha, R., Pillay, R., George, S., Hardeberg, J.Y.: Quality evaluation in spectral imaging-quality factors and metrics. JAIC-J. Int. Colour Assoc. **12**, 22–35 (2014)

44. Tan, D.S., Chen, W.Y., Hua, K.L.: DeepDemosaicking: adaptive image demosaicking via multiple deep fully convolutional networks. IEEE Trans. Image Process. **27**(5), 2408–2419 (2018)

45. Tan, H., Zeng, X., Lai, S., Liu, Y., Zhang, M.: Joint demosaicing and denoising of noisy bayer images with ADMM. In: 2017 IEEE International Conference on Image Processing (ICIP), pp. 2951–2955. IEEE (2017)

46. Uemori, T., Ito, A., Moriuchi, Y., Gatto, A., Murayama, J.: Skin-based identification from multispectral image data using CNNs. In: Proceedings of the IEEE Conference on Computer Vision and Pattern Recognition, pp. 12349–12358 (2019)

47. Wang, X., Thomas, J.B., Hardeberg, J.Y., Gouton, P.: Discrete wavelet transform based multispectral filter array demosaicking. In: 2013 Colour and Visual Computing Symposium (CVCS), pp. 1–6. IEEE (2013). https://doi.org/10.1109/cvcs.2013.66262741

48. Yasuma, F., Mitsunaga, T., Iso, D., Nayar, S.K.: Generalized assorted pixel camera: postcapture control of resolution, dynamic range, and spectrum. IEEE Trans. Image Process. **19**(9), 2241–2253 (2010)

49. Zhang, L., Lukac, R., Wu, X., Zhang, D.: PCA-based spatially adaptive denoising of CFA images for single-sensor digital cameras. IEEE Trans. Image Process. **18**(4), 797–812 (2009)

50. Zhang, L., Wu, X.: Color demosaicking via directional linear minimum mean square-error estimation. IEEE Trans. Image Process. **14**(12), 2167–2178 (2005)

51. Zhang, L., Wu, X., Buades, A., Li, X.: Color demosaicking by local directional interpolation and nonlocal adaptive thresholding. J. Electron. Imaging **20**(2), 023016 (2011)

Gated Texture CNN for Efficient and Configurable Image Denoising

Kaito Imai$^{(\boxtimes)}$ and Takamichi Miyata$^{(\boxtimes)}$

Chiba Institute of Technology, Chiba, Japan
s16c3011fm@s.chibakoudai.jp, takamichi.miyata@it-chiba.ac.jp

Abstract. Convolutional neural network (CNN)-based image denoising methods typically estimate the noise component contained in a noisy input image and restore a clean image by subtracting the estimated noise from the input. However, previous denoising methods tend to remove high-frequency information (e.g., textures) from the input. It caused by intermediate feature maps of CNN contains texture information. A straightforward approach to this problem is stacking numerous layers, which leads to a high computational cost. To achieve high performance and computational efficiency, we propose a gated texture CNN (GTCNN), which is designed to carefully exclude the texture information from each intermediate feature map of the CNN by incorporating gating mechanisms. Our GTCNN achieves state-of-the-art performance with 4.8 times fewer parameters than previous state-of-the-art methods. Furthermore, the GTCNN allows us to interactively control the texture strength in the output image without any additional modules, training, or computational costs.

Keywords: Image denoising · Texture gating mechanisms · Interactive modification

1 Introduction

Image denoising, which is one of the fundamental tasks in computer vision, aims to recover an original image from a noisy observation and plays a vital role in a preprocessing step in high-level vision tasks (e.g., image recognition [19,20] and image retrieval [33]). Due to the limitations of computational resources, these real-world applications require an accurate and computationally efficient image denoising algorithm.

Recently, deep convolutional neural networks (CNNs) have been very successful at image denoising. Zhang et al. proposed a denoising CNN (DnCNN) [45], which is a stack of units consisting of a CNN, batch normalization [13],

Electronic supplementary material The online version of this chapter (https://doi.org/10.1007/978-3-030-67070-2_40) contains supplementary material, which is available to authorized users.

© Springer Nature Switzerland AG 2020
A. Bartoli and A. Fusiello (Eds.): ECCV 2020 Workshops, LNCS 12537, pp. 665–681, 2020.
https://doi.org/10.1007/978-3-030-67070-2_40

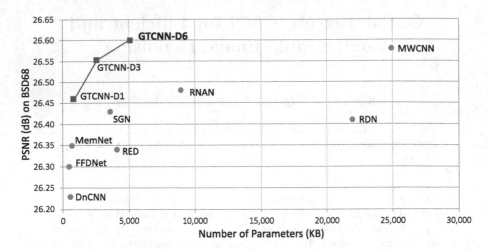

Fig. 1. Model size vs the denoising accuracy (PSNR) with a noise level of $\sigma =$ 50. Our GTCNN significantly outperforms the other methods. In particular, GTCNN-D6 achieves new state-of-the-art denoising performance but is 4.8 times smaller than MWCNN [22] (see Table 1 for more details)

and a rectified linear unit (ReLU) [26], called a CBR unit, with global residual learning. The DnCNN outperforms the previous non-learning-based state-of-the-art methods [4,6,16] and is well suited for parallel computation on GPUs. The great success of DnCNN has inspired much work on CNN-based denoising [2,7,14,17,18,22,24,28,29,34,46,47,49]. These methods employ many layers and a massive number of parameters to achieve a high denoising performance compared with the DnCNN method.

The common problem of these methods is that they tend to remove the high-frequency information (e.g., textures, edge), which has similar properties to the noise, in their denoising process. General CNN-based denoising methods learn to estimate added noise from a noisy observation, which means that the intermediate feature maps (throughout this paper, we simply denote these maps as features) in those CNNs should contain only the noise information. However, these features unintentionally contain texture information, which leads to the removal of textures from noisy observations and worsens the denoising accuracy.

A straightforward approach to this problem is stacking more layers to eliminate the texture information carefully from the features. However, this simple approach suffers from high computational cost and time consumption and makes those denoisers infeasible to real-world applications. For example, one of the state-of-the-art denoising methods, a multilevel wavelet CNN (MWCNN) [22], has 43 times the number of parameters that the DnCNN has [45] (see Fig. 1). Then, the question arises: do we need such extremely deep and complex networks to remove the texture information from the features?

On the other hand, several image inpainting methods [3,21,44] incorporate a gating mechanism to mask the intermediate features based on the user's input.

The gating mechanism allows us to choose which part of the features should be propagated to the next layer. With gating, these methods significantly improve the inpainting results with the user's guide.

Inspired by these results, we propose a novel denoising architecture referred to as a gated texture CNN (GTCNN) that can estimate the texture information contained in the features and remove them by a gating mechanism. We incorporate the gating texture layer (GTL) into the noise stream, as illustrated in Fig. 2. We employ a general denoising architecture for our noise stream to estimate the noise component from the noisy observations. To estimate the texture, we have to capture the information from nearly the entire input image. To capture such information, we use a U-Net-like network [30], which has a wider receptive field than the noise stream, for the proposed GTL.

Our extensive evaluation shows that the proposed GTCNN enables us to scale the model with a good trade-off between accuracy and speed and that it is suitable for resource-limited devices. Figure 1 shows the model size and the performance comparison on the 68-image Berkley Segmentation Dataset (BSD68) [25] with a high level of noise. Our GTCNN-D6 (with a heavyweight configuration) outperforms the state-of-the-art models with 4.8 times fewer parameters than the previous best model [22]. Notably, GTCNN-D1 (with a lightweight configuration) outperforms previously proposed efficient denoising methods [7,24,34,45,47] in terms of the trade-off between the denoising performance, speed, and parameter efficiency.

The experimental results show not only the superior performance but also that our GTCNN model allows users to control the texture strength of the denoising results by tuning a single parameter in the GTL (see Sect. 4.4). Interactive adjustment of the restoration strength is a crucial feature in real-world image processing applications, such as photo editing. Moreover, these results show that our GTCNN can separate noise and textures at the intermediate level. To the best of our knowledge, this is the first study to show that the gate mechanism can separate textures from features. Moreover, this is the first study to determine the architecture that allows users to control the texture strength in image denoising without sacrificing the performance and computational efficiency.

Contributions. Our main contributions are threefold.

1. We show that a simple gating mechanism that removes textures from the intermediate feature maps is effective for image denoising. Our GTCNN achieves state-of-the-art performance in terms of the efficiency and denoising performance.
2. We show that the GTL can effectively separate textures from CNN feature maps.
3. Our GTCNN allows users to interactively and continuously control the texture strength in the denoising results, which suggests that our GTL can remove texture from noise features.

2   Related Work

2.1   CNN-based Image Denoising Methods

Zhang et al. [45] revealed that the combination of batch normalization and a global residual skip connection, which estimates the residuals between the noisy input and the corresponding clean image, plays a key role in CNN-based image denoising methods. Their proposed architecture, DnCNN, clearly outperforms previous, non-learning-based denoising methods such as the block-matching and 3D filtering (BM3D) [4], non-local Bayes [16], and weighted nuclear norm minimization (WNNM) [6] algorithms. The DnCNN algorithm is widely accepted as the baseline for CNN-based denoising methods.

To achieve a high denoising performance, more complex networks [18, 22, 28, 49, 50] have been proposed. A residual dense network (RDN) [50] incorporates densely connected convolutional networks [11] for image restoration. Some methods [18, 49] use a nonlocal (NL) module [41] designed in the neural network. Zhang et al. proposed the residual NL attention network (RNAN) [49], which incorporates NL attention blocks [41] and residual attention learning [38] to capture global information. Liu et al. proposed the MWCNN algorithm [22], which first employs multilevel wavelet pooling to avoid information loss.

These recent CNN-based methods are powerful but lead to high computational costs. For example, MWCNN has 43 times the parameters and is 3.5 times slower than DnCNN. Gu et al. proposed the self-guided network (SGN) [7] for fast image denoising and achieved a better trade-off between the denoising accuracy and runtime by a pixel shuffle operation [31]. However, the SGN needs a large number of parameters to achieve a good trade-off.

2.2   Gating Mechanism

Gating mechanisms were originally proposed and applied to recurrent neural networks in natural language processing [9]. Dauphin et al. incorporated gating mechanisms into CNNs and replaced recurrent neural networks with gated convolutions for language modeling [5].

Gating mechanisms have also been applied to many computer vision problems [3, 10, 35–37, 39, 44] for controlling which information should be passed to the next layer. For example, Yu et al. proposed the use of convolutions with a soft-gating mechanism for user-guided image inpainting to control feature flow in networks [44]. Takikawa et al. incorporated a gating mechanism with multitask learning to extract shape information for more accurate image segmentation [35]. In this paper, we propose using a gating mechanism to remove the texture information from the features for image denoising.

2.3   Interactive Modulation for Denoising Results

CNN-based methods lack the flexibility to control their denoising results. In real-world applications, flexibility is equally essential as denoising accuracy and computational efficiency. Recently, interactive control of denoising output has attracted increasing attention in the image restoration field [8, 32, 40, 42].

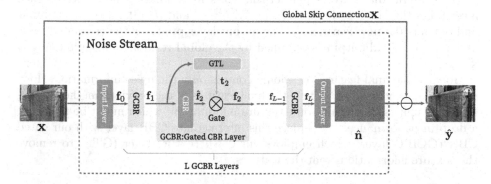

Fig. 2. Overview of the GTCNN architecture. To remove the texture information from the intermediate features, we incorporate our gated texture layer (GTL) into the CBR units with a gating mechanism

Several recent works [8, 32, 40, 42] for interactive modulation proposed incorporating an additional network into the denoising CNN, such as DnCNN, to allow control over the output results. For example, Wang et al. proposed deep network interpolation (DNI), which allows the interpolation of the denoising strength between several networks trained by images with different denoising strengths [42]. However, this network interpolation strategy requires at least several networks for interpolation, which leads to a heavy computational cost that is unacceptable for resource-limited devices. Our GTCNN allows us to continuously control the strength of the texture information in the denoising results without any additional training, modification modules, or postprocessing steps.

3   Gated Texture CNN

First, we introduce a standard noise stream based on the DnCNN, which estimates the added noise of the input image (Sect. 3.1). Then, we describe a novel GTL (Sect. 3.2) and how to modify the strength of the texture component in the denoising results (Sect. 3.3).

3.1   Noise Stream

Let H, W, and C_I be height, width, and number of the channels of the image. A noisy observation image $\mathbf{x} \in \mathbb{R}^{H \times W \times C_I}$ can be modeled as $\mathbf{x} = \mathbf{y} + \mathbf{n}$, where $\mathbf{y}$ refers to the unknown clean image, $\mathbf{n}$ is additive white Gaussian noise.

The purpose of the noise stream is to obtain a $\hat{\mathbf{n}} \in \mathbb{R}^{H \times W \times C_I}$ as the estimate of $\mathbf{n}$ from the input and then obtain a latent clean image $\hat{\mathbf{y}} \in \mathbb{R}^{H \times W \times C_I}$ by subtracting $\hat{\mathbf{n}}$ from $\mathbf{x}$. The noise stream consists of an input/output layer and L intermediate layers, as illustrated in Fig. 2. The input layer converts the noisy input image into the first intermediate features $\mathbf{f}_0 \in \mathbb{R}^{H \times W \times C}$, where C is the number of channels in the feature vectors.

The intermediate layers play crucial roles in estimating noise, where each layer takes the previous features $\mathbf{f}_{l-1} \in \mathbb{R}^{H \times W \times C}$ and $(l = 0, \ldots, L)$ as its input and outputs the new features $\mathbf{f}_l$. The output layer produces the estimated noise image $\hat{\mathbf{n}}$. The final output is obtained by the global residual connection as $\hat{\mathbf{y}} = \mathbf{x} - \hat{\mathbf{n}}$.

Ideally, the final features $\mathbf{f}_L$ should contain only the noise information. However, as we mentioned in Sect. 1, the final features of the previous methods using the CBR units still contain some texture information, which might be the cause a drop in performance. We replace this intermediate CBR layer with our gated CBR (GCBR) layer, which employs our gated texture layer (GTL) to remove the texture information from the features.

3.2   GCBR Layer

Given an intermediate feature map $\mathbf{f}_{l-1}$ as input, the GCBR layer infers the noise features $\mathbf{f}_l \in \mathbb{R}^{H \times W \times C}$ and the texture features $\mathbf{t}_l \in \mathbb{R}^{H \times W \times C}$ in parallel, as illustrated in Fig. 2. Then, the GCBR layer removes the texture information $\mathbf{t}_l$ from the noise features $\hat{\mathbf{f}}_l$ by the gating mechanisms. We define the process of the GCBR layer as $\phi \colon \mathbb{R}^{H \times W \times C} \to \mathbb{R}^{H \times W \times C}$.

The overall GCBR layer process can be summarized as:

$$\phi(\mathbf{f}_{l-1}) = \hat{\mathbf{f}}_l \otimes \mathbf{t}_l, \tag{1}$$

where $\otimes$ denotes Hadamard multiplication. $\hat{\mathbf{f}}_l$ is given by

$$\hat{\mathbf{f}}_l = \theta(\mathbf{f}_{l-1}), \tag{2}$$

where $\theta \colon \mathbb{R}^{H \times W \times C} \to \mathbb{R}^{H \times W \times C}$ is a map corresponding to a CBR layer.

Gated Texture Layer. Our GTL is a crucial component of our GTCNN that estimates texture information from the input features to remove the texture information. We assume that the network, which estimates the texture information from the noise, should have a large receptive field to capture the global context of the scene. We empirically reveal that the large receptive field significantly improves the denoising performance (see Sect. 4.5). From this assumption, we design our GTL based on U-Net [30], as illustrated in Fig. 3. U-Net is an encoder-decoder network with a skip connection between the corresponding layers of the encoder and decoder of the same stage. Note that the layers of each stage are composed of two CBR layers; we call these layers double CBR (DCBR) layers.

The general U-Net decreases the size of the features by a max-pooling operation and increases the number of channels at each stage. The pooling operation enlarges the receptive field and allows us to capture the context. However, increasing the number of channels does not guarantee an improvement in the denoising performance, although it leads to a high computational cost.

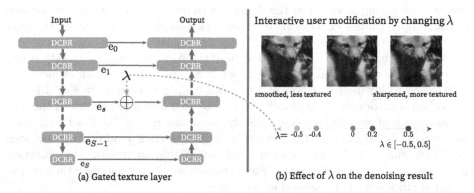

(a) Gated texture layer

(b) Effect of λ on the denoising result

Fig. 3. GTL architecture and how to modulate the texture strength. (a) To capture the global context of the scene, we design our gated texture layer (GTL) based on U-Net [30]. (b) Our GTCNN allows users to interactively and continuously control the texture gating strength by just shifting an output of the skip connection in GTL

We modify our GTL so that it does not increase the number of channels. This modification makes our GTL more computationally efficient than the original U-Net [30], as it has five times fewer parameters then the original U-Net. Furthermore, we found that increasing the depth L of the noise stream above a certain level would make the training procedure numerically unstable. We resolve this issue by placing a 1×1 convolution layer after the last DCBR layer of the decoder. This layer stabilizes the training procedure greatly when using the deep noise stream.

The GTL takes the previous features $\mathbf{f}_{l-1}$ as input and estimates the texture information. The final estimate of the texture information is obtained by:

$$\mathbf{t}_l = \delta(\gamma(\mathbf{f}_{l-1})), \tag{3}$$

where γ is the process of the GTL ($\gamma: \mathbb{R}^{H \times W \times C} \rightarrow \mathbb{R}^{H \times W \times C}$) and δ is the channelwise softmax function. The sigmoid function was commonly employed in previous works that included gating mechanisms [10,35–37,39,44].

We found that the softmax function achieve a better result than the sigmoid function in removing the texture information. We will show the experimental results of the ablation study in Sect. 4.5 to illustrate our findings.

3.3   Modification

For a given input, most CNN-based denoising methods can generate only a single fixed output. In other words, these methods have no flexibility in controlling the denoising results. However, in real-world applications, flexibility is as essential as the denoising accuracy and computational efficiency. Several recent works [8,40,42] incorporated an additional network to the denoising CNN, such as DnCNN, to enable control over the output results. However, there was a trade-off between the flexibility and computational efficiency.

Since our GTCNN is designed to separate the texture information from the noise stream, we can expect that modulating the GTL will allow us to control the texture gating strength in the denoising results. We show that the network output could change continuously by just modulating the output of the skip connection in the GTL.

We define $e_s \in \mathbb{R}^{H \times W \times C}$ as the output of the skip connection of the sth stage. To control the texture gating strength, we just need to perform an elementwise shift e_s by a shifting parameter of $\lambda \in [-0.5, 0.5]$, as illustrated in Fig. 3-b.

When we modulate λ gradually from -0.5 to 0.5 on the inference time, the network output will change continuously, as shown in Fig. 5. A detailed analysis can be found in Sect. 4.5. Note that unlike previous modification methods [8,40,42], this modulation does not need any additional training, modification modules, or postprocessing steps. Furthermore, we do not sacrifice the computational efficiency or the denoising accuracy.

4 Experiments

To thoroughly evaluate the effectiveness of our GTCNN, we first compare our method with the current state-of-the-art denoising methods [7,22,24,34,49,50], which require high computational resources. Then, we also compare our GTCNN with several computationally efficient CNN-based methods [7,24,34,45,47] in terms of the denoising performance in grayscale and color images. Furthermore, we show the configurability of the GTCNN by comparing it with a previous feature modification method [8]. We also performed extensive ablation studies to show the effectiveness of our design choice.

For a fair comparison, we used the authors' official implementations in PyTorch [27] and the pre-trained models to reproduce the results of the comparison methods. If the authors do not provide the pre-trained models, we trained those methods by ourselves. If necessary, we also used some unofficial PyTorch [27] implementations that are linked from the original authors' GitHub repositories. For all the methods, we use the default settings provided by the respective authors. We confirmed that the maximum absolute difference between our reproduced results and the results provided in the original papers is only 0.01 dB.

4.1 Experimental Setup

We use the experimental settings from previous works [7,22,49].

Network Settings. We denote a GTCNN with L intermediate (GCBR) layers as GTCNN-DL. For example, GTCNN-D1 means a GTCNN with only one GCBR layer. In the evaluation, we used GTCNN-D1/D3/D6. Note that

GTCNN-D6 employs a 1×1 convolutional layer after the final DCBR layer of the GTL for stable training, as we mentioned in Sect. 3.2. All the GTCNN models use the same number of stages ($S = 4$) for the GTL.

Table 1. GTCNN performance results. The denoising methods with similar performance on Set12 are grouped together for effective comparisons. Our scaled GTCNN consistently reduced the number of parameters and the runtime. Note that, even in a heavyweight configuration such as GTCNN-D6, the number of parameters and runtime do not increase rapidly

Method	Set12	BSD68	Urban100	Number of parameters	Time [ms]
MemNet [34]	27.39	26.35	26.67	**685**k	169.1
RED [24]	27.35	26.34	26.46	4,100k	41.3
SGN [7]	27.53	26.43	26.96	3,577k	**7.5**
GTCNN-D1 (ours)	**27.56**	**26.46**	**26.97**	851k	12.4
RDN [50]	27.60	26.41	27.40	21,973k	716.8
RNAN [49]	27.67	26.47	**27.65**	8,957k	1,434.9
GTCNN-D3 (ours)	**27.76**	**26.55**	27.50	**2,552**k	**35.3**
MWCNN [22]	27.79	26.58	27.53	24,927k	78.2
GTCNN-D6 (ours)	**27.83**	**26.60**	**27.72**	**5,128**k	**72.7**

Training Settings. We use the 800 standard 2K resolution training images of the DIVerse 2K (DIV2K) dataset [1]. We extracted 192×192 patches from the training images as a training set. The size of the stride is 192. The training set consisted of 55,500 patches. Unlike previous works [7,22,49], we did not perform any data augmentation on the training set (e.g., random flipping).

Our model is trained by the Adam optimizer [15] with a learning rate of 0.001, along with the cosine annealing technique proposed by [23] for adjusting the learning rate. We conducted all the experiments in PyTorch [27].

Evaluation Datasets and Metrics. To compare with the previous denoising algorithms, we use the commonly used BSD68 [25] dataset, which contains 68 images, and the Urban100 dataset [12]. We also use Set12 [45] for the grayscale image denoising experiments.

The denoising results are evaluated with the PSNR. To evaluate the computational efficiency, we provide comparisons on the number of parameters. We also give the runtime for processing a 320×480 image for reference. Note that the runtime is dependent on the computing environment and implementation. As we mentioned before, we used the PyTorch [27] implementations published or introduced by the respective authors for all the comparison methods.

4.2   Comparison with the State-of-the-Art Methods

We performed a comparison with the current state-of-the-art methods, namely, deep residual encoder-decoder (RED) [24], MemNet [34], RNAN [49], RDN [50], SGN [7], and MWCNN [22], with grayscale images under severe noise (σ=50). Table 1 illustrates the parameters and the denoising accuracy of all GTCNN models. Our GTCNN models generally use an order of magnitude fewer parameters than other CNN-based methods and achieve a similar accuracy. In particular, our GTCNN-D6 achieves the state-of-the-art result with 5,128k parameters, which is 4.8 times fewer than the previous best MWCNN model [22]. Notably, our GTCNN models are not only small-sized but also fast. For example, our GTCNN-D3 achieves a comparable accuracy with RNAN [49], but the GTCNN-D3 model is 40.6 times faster and has 2.8 times fewer parameters than the RNAN model. Note that the RNAN algorithm [49] uses NL operations [41], which leads to high computational memory requirements and high time consumption.

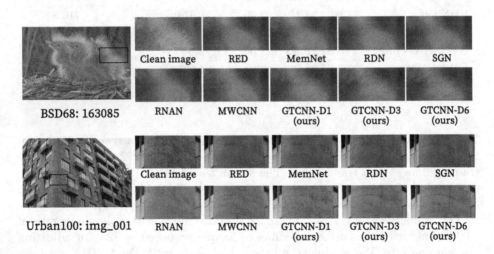

Fig. 4. Grayscale image denoising results with a noise level of $\sigma = 50$

The visual comparisons are shown in Fig. 4. The other methods in the comparison remove details along with the noise, which results in oversmoothing artifacts. Our texture gating strategy can restore sharp textures from noisy input without artifacts.

4.3   Comparison with Computationally Efficient Methods

We compared our GTCNN model with previous methods that have relatively smaller model sizes, such as the DnCNN [45], fast and flexible denoising CNN (FFDNet) [47], RED [24], and SGN [7] models. For these experiments, we use additive white Gaussian noise with standard deviations σ of 30, 50, and 70. We show that the denoising results for the grayscale and color images in Table 2 and Table 3, respectively. We also provide the number of parameters and runtime in Table 4.

These results show that our GTCNN-D1 model outperforms all other methods in terms of the denoising accuracy. The GTCNN-D1 model also achieves a better trade-off between the model size, inference time, and denoising accuracy than the other methods. The GTCNN-D1 model has 4.2 times fewer parameters but also a higher denoising accuracy than the SGN model.

Table 2. Quantitative results from **grayscale** image denoising. The best results are **in bold**

Method	Set12			BSD68			Urban100		
	30	50	70	30	50	70	30	50	70
DnCNN [45]	29.53	27.19	25.52	28.36	26.23	24.90	28.88	26.27	24.36
FFDNet [47]	29.61	27.32	25.81	28.39	26.30	25.04	29.03	26.51	24.86
MemNet [34]	29.63	27.39	25.90	28.43	26.35	25.09	29.10	26.67	25.01
RED [24]	29.70	27.35	25.80	28.50	26.34	25.10	29.18	26.46	24.82
SGN [7]	29.77	27.53	25.90	28.50	26.43	25.17	29.41	26.96	25.29
GTCNN-D1 (ours)	**29.80**	**27.56**	**26.08**	**28.53**	**26.46**	**25.21**	**29.43**	**26.97**	**25.36**

Table 3. Quantitative results from **color** image denoising. The best results are **in bold**

Method	BSD68			Urban100		
	30	50	70	30	50	70
DnCNN [45]	30.40	28.01	26.56	30.28	28.16	26.17
FFDNet [47]	30.31	27.96	26.53	30.53	28.05	26.39
MemNet [34]	28.39	26.33	25.08	28.93	26.53	24.93
RED [24]	28.46	26.35	25.09	29.02	26.40	24.74
SGN [7]	30.45	28.18	26.79	30.75	28.36	26.85
GTCNN-D1 (ours)	**30.51**	**28.24**	**26.83**	**30.90**	**28.53**	**26.90**

4.4 User Modification Comparisons

We demonstrate the effects of the modification of the texture gating strength on the denoising results. We use the GTCNN-D1 model and shift e_2 by λ. The values of the modification parameter λ ranged from -0.5 to 0.5 at an interval of 0.25 for the visual comparison. We also compare the modification results with the previous feature modification method called AdaFM-Net [8]. AdaFM-Net allows us to control the denoising strength by a parameter α. The main component of AdaFM-Net is based on DnCNN [45] and adopts a feature modification layer

Table 4. Comparison of the computational costs. The number of parameters and runtime [ms] for processing a 480 × 320 image are shown for the different methods. All the methods were implemented in PyTorch [27], and the runtime was evaluated on system equipped with an NVIDIA GTX 1080 Ti GPU

Method	DnCNN [45]	FFDNet [47]	MemNet [34]	RED [24]	SGN [7]	GTCNN-D1
Number of Parameters	555k	485k	685k	4,100k	3,915k	851k
Time [ms]	22.3	4.8	169.1	41.3	7.5	12.4

after each convolution layer. To achieve configurable image denoising, AdaFM-Net takes two steps training strategy. In the first step, the entire network is trained with a noise level of $\sigma = 15$. Then, as the second step, the feature modification layers are trained for a noise level of $\sigma = 75$. In our experiment, the interpolation parameter α ranged from 0 to 1 at an interval of 0.25. Note that our GTCNN modifies the texture strength unlike AdaFM-Net, which modifies the denoising strength.

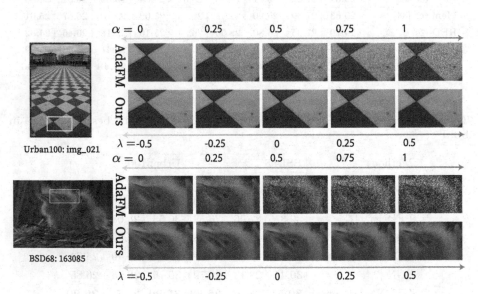

Fig. 5. Comparison of the performance of our gate modulation method and that of AdaFM-Net [8] for a noise level of $\sigma = 70$

Figure 5 shows a few examples of the GTCNN-D1 and AdaFM-Net results. The resulting images show that AdaFM-Net can control the denoising strength, but it also produces some artifacts when the denoising strength is weak. Our GTCNN-D1 model demonstrates a gradual change in the texture strength of the output image with an increase in λ. These results show that modification of our GTCNN-D1 model is more flexible and yields fewer artifacts than AdaFM-Net. Notably, the GTCNN model does not require any additional training, modules, or networks.

4.5   Ablation Studies

In this subsection, we show the effectiveness of our design choice. We first evaluate our gating mechanism and then extensively evaluate the effect of a large receptive field. Furthermore, we perform ablation studies for texture strength modulation. All the denoising results are on BSD68 [25] with a noise level of $\sigma = 50$. Note that for ablation studies, we use a part of the small training set, which consists of 1,600 patches.

Table 5. Comparison of DnCNN models with widely used attention mechanisms. We observe that our simple gating mechanism with a softmax gate surprisingly outperforms recently proposed attention mechanisms [10,41,43,49]

Description	PSNR [dB]	Number of Parameters	Time [ms]
DnCNN (baseline) [45]	25.90	555k	22.3
DnCNN + SE [10]	25.86	564k	28.0
DnCNN + CBAM [43]	26.09	566k	670.8
DnCNN + NL [41]	26.10	566k	14,738.7
DnCNN + RLAB [49]	26.21	5604k	162.1
GTCNN-D1 δ = sigmoid	26.23	851k	12.4
GTCNN-D1 δ = softmax	**26.30**	851k	12.4

Comparison with the Other Modules. To achieve a better trade-off between the denoising performance and computational resources, we compared our GTCNN-D1 model with several attention modules and demonstrate their performance based on image recognition [10,43] and image restoration [2,48,49]. These attention modules are the squeeze and excitation (SE) module [10], the convolutional block attention module (CBAM) [43], the NL module [41], and the residual local attention block (RLAB) [49]. We incorporate these modules into each intermediate layer of a DnCNN [45], which is the baseline denoising method. Note that the NL module [41] is assigned only to one intermediate layer of the baseline to suppress memory consumption; the NL module consumes an enormous amount memory. We also provide the results of the GTCNN-D1 model with a sigmoid gate.

Table 5 clearly shows that only our softmax gate can significantly improve the denoising accuracy with a short runtime and small number of parameters.

Effectiveness of a Large Receptive Field. To show the effectiveness in the global context, we evaluate the denoising results by the GTCNN-D1 model with a different number of stages for the GTL. We denote a GTL with S stages by GTL-BS. For example, GTL-B0 means the GTL without downsampling operations ($S = 0$). We evaluated the six GTLs with different values of S: GTL-B0, GTL-B1, GTL-B2, GTL-B3, GTL-B4, and GTL-B5.

Table 3 shows the performance of all the GTCNN models. The results clearly show that the large receptive field significantly improves the denoising results of the GTCNN model. Notably, GTL-B1 improves the performance of GTL-0 by utilizing only two additional convolution layers with a small spatial resolution. We decided to use GTL-B4 as the default setting of the GTL from this result (Table 6).

Table 6. Effect of the number of stages in the GTL on the performance. We observe that incorporating the global context of the scene significantly boosts the denoising accuracy

Description	PSNR [dB]	Number of Parameters	Time [ms]
GTCNN-D1 with GTL-B0	25.27	186k	8.9
GTCNN-D1 with GTL-B1	26.03	297k	10.9
GTCNN-D1 with GTL-B2	26.24	481k	11.9
GTCNN-D1 with GTL-B3	26.27	666k	12.2
GTCNN-D1 with GTL-B4	26.30	851k	12.4
GTCNN-D1 with GTL-B5	26.31	1,003k	12.7

Analysis of Texture Modulation on the GTL. To control the texture gating strength, we shift the output of the skip connection by λ, as shown in Fig. 3. We modulate each e_0, e_1, ..., e_5 one at a time. The qualitative comparisons are shown in Fig. 6. The results show that our GTCNN-D1 model can control the texture strength in the denoising results without producing artifacts. We can observe that the texture of the denoising results is modulated naturally. Thus, we choose e_2 as the default skip connection to be modulated.

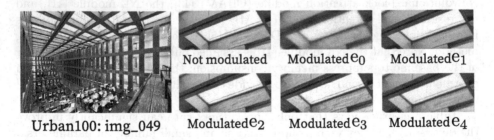

Fig. 6. Results of the modulation by shifting different skip connections. The results show that the GTCNN model can modulate the texture gating strength without artifacts. All the e_s values were shifted by $\lambda = 0.5$

5   Conclusions

Previously proposed denoising methods tend to output smooth results, which are caused by removing the texture information from the input image. To overcome this problem, the previous state-of-the-art methods employ an enormous number of parameters, which leads to high computational costs. In contrast, we proposed a simple yet highly effective gated texture convolutional neural network (GTCNN), which removes texture information from the intermediate feature map. The GTCNN model achieved state-of-the-art performance with an order of magnitude fewer parameters than the previous state-of-the-art methods. Furthermore, the GTCNN model allows us to interactively control the texture strength in the output image without any additional modules, training, or computational cost.

References

1. Agustsson, E., Timofte, R.: NTIRE 2017 challenge on single image super-resolution: dataset and study. In: CVPRW (2017)
2. Anwar, S., Barnes, N.: Real image denoising with feature attention. In: ICCV (2019)
3. Chang, Y.L., Liu, Z.Y., Lee, K.Y., Hsu, W.: Free-form video inpainting with 3D gated convolution and temporal patchGAN. In: ICCV (2019)
4. Dabov, K., Foi, A., Katkovnik, V., Egiazarian, K.: Image denoising by sparse 3-D transform-domain collaborative filtering. TIP **16**(8), 2080–2095 (2007)
5. Dauphin, Y.N., Fan, A., Auli, M., Grangier, D.: Language modeling with gated convolutional networks. In: ICML, vol. 70, pp. 933–941 (2017). JMLR.org
6. Gu, S., Zhang, L., Zuo, W., Feng, X.: Weighted nuclear norm minimization with application to image denoising. In: CVPR (2014)
7. Gu, S., Li, Y., Gool, L.V., Timofte, R.: Self-guided network for fast image denoising. In: ICCV (2019)
8. He, J., Dong, C., Qiao, Y.: Modulating image restoration with continual levels via adaptive feature modification layers. In: CVPR (2019)
9. Hochreiter, S., Schmidhuber, J.: Long short-term memory. Neural Comput. **9**(8), 1735–1780 (1997)
10. Hu, J., Shen, L., Sun, G.: Squeeze-and-excitation networks. In: CVPR (2018)
11. Huang, G., Liu, Z., van der Maaten, L., Weinberger, K.Q.: Densely connected convolutional networks. In: CVPR (2017)
12. Huang, J., Singh, A., Ahuja, N.: Single image super-resolution from transformed self-exemplars. In: CVPR (2015)
13. Ioffe, S., Szegedy, C.: Batch normalization: accelerating deep network training by reducing internal covariate shift. In: ICML, pp. 448–456 (2015). JMLR.org
14. Jia, X., Liu, S., Feng, X., Zhang, L.: FOCNet: a fractional optimal control network for image denoising. In: CVPR (2019)
15. Kingma, D.P., Ba, J.: Adam: a method for stochastic optimization. In: ICLR (2015)
16. Lebrun, M., Buades, A., Morel, J.M.: A nonlocal Bayesian image denoising algorithm. J. Imag. Sci. **6**(3), 1665–1688 (2013)
17. Lefkimmiatis, S.: Universal denoising networks: a novel CNN architecture for image denoising. In: CVPR (2018)

18. Liu, D., Wen, B., Fan, Y., Loy, C.C., Huang, T.S.: Non-local recurrent network for image restoration. In: Bengio, S., Wallach, H., Larochelle, H., Grauman, K., Cesa-Bianchi, N., Garnett, R. (eds.) NeurIPS, pp. 1673–1682. Curran Associates, Inc. (2018)

19. Liu, D., Wen, B., Jiao, J., Liu, X., Wang, Z., Huang, T.S.: Connecting image denoising and high-level vision tasks via deep learning. TIP **29**, 3695–3706 (2020)

20. Liu, D., Wen, B., Liu, X., Huang, T.S.: When image denoising meets high-level vision tasks: a deep learning approach. In: IJCAI, pp. 842–848. International Joint Conferences on Artificial Intelligence Organization, July 2018

21. Liu, G., Reda, F.A., Shih, K.J., Wang, T.-C., Tao, A., Catanzaro, B.: Image inpainting for irregular holes using partial convolutions. In: Ferrari, V., Hebert, M., Sminchisescu, C., Weiss, Y. (eds.) ECCV 2018. LNCS, vol. 11215, pp. 89–105. Springer, Cham (2018). https://doi.org/10.1007/978-3-030-01252-6_6

22. Liu, P., Zhang, H., Lian, W., Zuo, W.: Multi-level wavelet convolutional neural networks. IEEE Access **7**, 74973–74985 (2019)

23. Loshchilov, I., Hutter, F.: SGDR: stochastic gradient descent with warm restarts. In: ICLR (2017)

24. Mao, X.J., Shen, C., Yang, Y.B.: Image restoration using very deep convolutional encoder-decoder networks with symmetric skip connections. In: Lee, D.D., Sugiyama, M., Luxburg, U.V., Guyon, I., Garnett, R. (eds.) NeurIPS, pp. 2802–2810. Curran Associates, Inc. (2016)

25. Martin, D., Fowlkes, C., Tal, D., Malik, J.: A database of human segmented natural images and its application to evaluating segmentation algorithms and measuring ecological statistics. In: ICCV (2001)

26. Nair, V., Hinton, G.E.: Rectified linear units improve restricted Boltzmann machines. In: ICML, pp. 807–814. Omnipress (2010)

27. Paszke, A., et al.: PyTorch: an imperative style, high-performance deep learning library. In: Wallach, H., Larochelle, H., Beygelzimer, A., d Alch e-Buc, F., Fox, E., Garnett, R. (eds.) NeurIPS, pp. 8026–8037. Curran Associates, Inc. (2019)

28. Plötz, T., Roth, S.: Neural nearest neighbors networks. In: Bengio, S., Wallach, H., Larochelle, H., Grauman, K., Cesa-Bianchi, N., Garnett, R. (eds.) NeurIPS, pp. 1087–1098. Curran Associates, Inc. (2018)

29. Remez, T., Litany, O., Giryes, R., Bronstein, A.M.: Class-aware fully convolutional Gaussian and poisson denoising. TIP **27**(11), 5707–5722 (2018)

30. Ronneberger, O., Fischer, P., Brox, T.: U-Net: convolutional networks for biomedical image segmentation. In: Navab, N., Hornegger, J., Wells, W.M., Frangi, A.F. (eds.) MICCAI 2015. LNCS, vol. 9351, pp. 234–241. Springer, Cham (2015). https://doi.org/10.1007/978-3-319-24574-4_28

31. Shi, W., et al.: Real-time single image and video super-resolution using an efficient sub-pixel convolutional neural network. In: CVPR (2016)

32. Shoshan, A., Mechrez, R., Zelnik-Manor, L.: Dynamic-net: Tuning the objective without re-training for synthesis tasks. In: ICCV (2019)

33. Somasundaran, B.V., Soundararajan, R., Biswas, S.: Image denoising for image retrieval by cascading a deep quality assessment network. In: ICIP (2018)

34. Tai, Y., Yang, J., Liu, X., Xu, C.: MemNet: a persistent memory network for image restoration. In: CVPR (2017)

35. Takikawa, T., Acuna, D., Jampani, V., Fidler, S.: Gated-SCNN: gated shape CNNs for semantic segmentation. In: ICCV (2019)

36. Van Den Oord, A., Kalchbrenner, N., Vinyals, O., Espeholt, L., Graves, A., Kavukcuoglu, K.: Conditional image generation with PixelCNN decoders. In: Lee, D.D., Sugiyama, M., Luxburg, U.V., Guyon, I., Garnett, R. (eds.) NeurIPS, pp. 4790–4798. Curran Associates, Inc. (2016)
37. Veit, A., Belongie, S.: Convolutional networks with adaptive inference graphs. In: Ferrari, V., Hebert, M., Sminchisescu, C., Weiss, Y. (eds.) ECCV 2018. LNCS, vol. 11205, pp. 3–18. Springer, Cham (2018). https://doi.org/10.1007/978-3-030-01246-5_1
38. Wang, F., et al.: Residual attention network for image classification. In: CVPR (2017)
39. Wang, H., Wang, Y., Zhang, Q., Xiang, S., Pan, C.: Gated convolutional neural network for semantic segmentation in high-resolution images. Remote Sens. **9**, 446 (2017)
40. Wang, W., Guo, R., Tian, Y., Yang, W.: CFSNet: toward a controllable feature space for image restoration. In: ICCV (2019)
41. Wang, X., Girshick, R., Gupta, A., He, K.: Non-local neural networks. In: CVPR (2018)
42. Wang, X., Yu, K., Dong, C., Tang, X., Loy, C.C.: Deep network interpolation for continuous imagery effect transition. In: CVPR (2019)
43. Woo, S., Park, J., Lee, J.-Y., Kweon, I.S.: CBAM: convolutional block attention module. In: Ferrari, V., Hebert, M., Sminchisescu, C., Weiss, Y. (eds.) ECCV 2018. LNCS, vol. 11211, pp. 3–19. Springer, Cham (2018). https://doi.org/10.1007/978-3-030-01234-2_1
44. Yu, J., Lin, Z., Yang, J., Shen, X., Lu, X., Huang, T.S.: Free-form image inpainting with gated convolution. In: ICCV (2019)
45. Zhang, K., Zuo, W., Chen, Y., Meng, D., Zhang, L.: Beyond a Gaussian denoiser: residual learning of deep CNN for image denoising. TIP **26**(7), 3142–3155 (2017)
46. Zhang, K., Zuo, W., Gu, S., Zhang, L.: Learning deep CNN denoiser prior for image restoration. In: CVPR (2017)
47. Zhang, K., Zuo, W., Zhang, L.: FFDNet: toward a fast and flexible solution for CNN-Based image denoising. TIP **27**(9), 4608–4622 (2018)
48. Zhang, Y., Li, K., Li, K., Wang, L., Zhong, B., Fu, Y.: Image super-resolution using very deep residual channel attention networks. In: Ferrari, V., Hebert, M., Sminchisescu, C., Weiss, Y. (eds.) ECCV 2018. LNCS, vol. 11211, pp. 294–310. Springer, Cham (2018). https://doi.org/10.1007/978-3-030-01234-2_18
49. Zhang, Y., Li, K., Li, K., Zhong, B., Fu, Y.: Residual non-local attention networks for image restoration. In: ICLR (2019)
50. Zhang, Y., Tian, Y., Kong, Y., Zhong, B., Fu, Y.: Residual dense network for image restoration. In: TPAMI (2020)

Quantized Warping and Residual Temporal Integration for Video Super-Resolution on Fast Motions

Konstantinos Karageorgos[(⊠)], Kassiani Zafeirouli[iD],
Konstantinos Konstantoudakis[iD], Anastasios Dimou[iD], and Petros Daras[iD]

Visual Computing Lab, Centre for Research and Technology,
Information Technologies Institute, Hellas, Thessaloniki, Greece
{konstantinkarage,cassie.zaf,
k.konstantoudakis,dimou,daras}@iti.gr
http://vcl.iti.gr

Abstract. In recent years, numerous deep learning approaches to video super resolution have been proposed, increasing the resolution of one frame using information found in neighboring frames. Such methods either warp frames into alignment using optical flow, or else forgo warping and use optical flow as an additional network input. In this work we point out the disadvantages inherent in these two approaches and propose one that inherits the best features of both, warping with the integer part of the flow and using the fractional part as network input. Moreover, an iterative residual super-resolution approach is proposed to incrementally improve quality as more neighboring frames are provided. Incorporating the above in a recurrent architecture, we train, evaluate and compare the proposed network to the SotA, and note its superior performance in faster motion sequences.

Keywords: Super resolution · Motion compensation

1 Introduction

Super resolution (SR) refers to a group of algorithms that aim to upsample a low resolution input (LR) in order to produce a higher resolution (HR) output. The challenge lies in reproducing the missing high frequency details of the input. SR is an ill-posed problem as there is no unique relationship between a LR and a HR image. SR methods can utilize either a single image (SISR), or multiple images (MISR) as an input. Given the abundance of video data streams, it became evident that MISR methods can be used to improve the resolution of a video due to the temporal consistency of successive frames. Video SR methods (VSR) effectively recover high frequency content, using information from neighboring frames.

VSR methods aim to exploit unique information from each one of the neighbouring frames in order to produce a true HR result. For this purpose, the frames,

© Springer Nature Switzerland AG 2020
A. Bartoli and A. Fusiello (Eds.): ECCV 2020 Workshops, LNCS 12537, pp. 682–697, 2020.
https://doi.org/10.1007/978-3-030-67070-2_41

which contain the same content shifted in an arbitrary way, must be accurately registered to the examined one. The biggest challenge here is to account for the inter-frame motion in the sequence. Realistic videos can contain arbitrary motion due to the camera object movement, making the registration a tedious task.

A naive approach to the problem is to concatenate all inputs and let a deep Convolutional Neural Network (CNN) implicitly model the spatial relationship between useful features. Although the increased depth and pooling operations of modern CNNs have quite big effective receptive fields, their convolutional nature remains local. While local correspondences may get captured at higher layers, additional complexity is added to the model making it more difficult to train and generalize. This is especially relevant in faster motion sequences, where object displacements between neighboring frames are larger and a correspondingly wider receptive field is required to capture them.

A common way to alleviate the inter-frame motion is to explicitly compensate this disparity by using warping to spatially align the neighboring images to a common reference location. Despite the intuitive merit of explicit warping, it constitutes a resampling operation using interpolation, which inherently causes blurring, lowered contrast and loss of information, reducing the super-resolution's effectiveness.

Another important parameter of the VSR methods is the strategy used to incorporate information from the neighboring frames, giving rise to different approaches. The number of frames used and the input sequence are important choices that bound the application of the methods proposed in literature. Most recent convolutional methods have to be trained and tested on a fixed number of neighbors, regardless of the early or late fusion scheme used.

This work focuses on improving super-resolution quality on video sequences with larger motions. Towards this goal, we propose a two step approach to neighboring frame registration: to warp neighboring frames only by the integer part of the optical flow, thus avoiding interpolation and the associated quality degradation; and to use the fractional part of the flow as an input to the neural network, letting it model the sub-pixel correspondences. We incorporate this approach into a recurrent residual architecture that fuses information from neighboring frames using a shared reconstruction branch. The resulting network progressively enhances the output quality with each processed input, offering the flexibility to adapt inference speed and quality by using more or less neighboring frames as input.

The contributions of this work can be summarized in the following aspects:

- An explicit quantized motion compensation methodology, that preserves detail at the input level. The proposed method significantly improves the results and the generalization capacity of a baseline network, especially on complex videos with high inter-frame motion.
- An implicit modeling of sub-pixel motions, using the fractional part of the optical flow as an additional input to the network.

 – A recurrent CNN architecture that progressively enhances the produced output with each input frame using residuals is proposed. It can handle frame sequences of arbitrary length, offering unique flexibility.

The proposed methodologies are thoroughly analysed and our claims are firmly supported by extensive experiments and ablation studies.

The rest of this paper is organized as follows: Section 2 discusses recent and relevant advances in deep learning-based SR; Section 3 considers the advantages and disadvantages of different registration strategies and explains the reasoning behind the proposed hybrid approach; The proposed network architecture and its constituent modules are presented in Section 4; Section 5 presents and discusses experimental results, comparisons with state of the art VSR methods, and ablation studies. Lastly, Sect. 6 provides a conclusion.

2   Related Work

Single-Image Super-Resolution: In 2014, for the first time, Dong et al. exploited the power of convolutional neural networks, by proposing SRCNN [2], a lightweight 3-layer convolutional model, to address the single image super resolution (SISR) problem. Later, based on SRCNN, deeper and more complex models, such as VDSR [10] with 20 stacked layers, DRCN [11] and DRRN [19] with recursive leaning and parameters sharing and MemNet [20] with memory block, were introduced and achieved higher reconstruction performance. Inspired by DenseNet [6], Tong et al. suggested SRDenseNet [22], by removing the pooling layers, and the RDN model [26] improved SRDenseNet's performance by exploiting local and global residual skip connections. Yang et al. proposed the Deep Edge Guided Recurrent Residual Network (DEGREE) [25], motivated by the fact that edge features can provide valuable guidance for SISR. Based on the conventional back-projection method [7], Haris et al. proposed DBPN [3], a network with iterative upsampling and downsampling modules. Finally, for more photo-realistic results a combination of generative adversarial networks with perceptual and texture matching losses was used in SRGAN [13] and ENEt [17] models, respectively.

Video Super-Resolution. Most of the deep learning based Video Super Resolution (VSR) approaches address the VSR task by combining a motion estimation module with an image warping module. Kappeler et al. proposed VSRnet [9], a model that exploits the temporal information by jointly processing multiple consecutive frames. The neighboring frames are warped towards the reference frame by a conventional optical flow algorithm before they are fed to the model. Based to this premise, VESPCN [1] introduced a spatial transformer network, in order to efficiently encode motion information between frames. The aforementioned model is jointly trained with a SISR sub-pixel convolution network for fast and accurate reconstruction. Tao et al. [21] used the same motion compensation transformer as in VESPCN to produce the motion field and an SPMC layer for simultaneous sub-pixel motion compensation and resolution enhancement. More recently, Sajjadi [18] proposed an end-to-end recurrent video super resolution model, which exploits the information of the previously inferred super-resolved HR frame to reconstruct the subsequent frame. The flow estimation and the SR network sub-modules are trained simultaneously.

The aforementioned methods have as common core element the image warping module that performs alignment by estimating optical flow information between the reference and its neighboring frames. Unlike this approach, Jo et al. [8] proposed DUF, a network that avoids explicit motion estimation and compensation by generating dynamic upsampling filters. The EDVR architecture [23] follows the logic of implicit alignment, introducing a Pyramid, Cascading and Deformable (PCD) alignment module, where alignment is done in a coarse-to-fine manner without the classic image warping technique. Haris et al. extended the SISR DBPN architecture to video super resolution with the RBPN [4], a recurrent model that treats each neighboring frame as a separate source of information that iteratively refines the HR features through multiple up and down projections. Our work introduces a novel approach to register neighboring frames using a quantized warping method, which models the subpixel displacements, to treat efficiently the flow information. Moreover we employ a recurrent residual reconstruction module to refine the SR output with an arbitrary number of input frames.

3   Optical Flow and Spatial Alignment

In video super resolution, the resolution of a reference frame is increased using information from neighboring frames, which are assumed to depict the same scene at different points in time. In each frame, the same object may occupy a different position, due to its own movement or global camera movement. For this reason, VSR methods must take into consideration the relative displacement of objects in neighboring frames and, explicitly or implicitly, align the information therein with the core information contained in the reference frame. Spatial correspondence between frames is usually expressed with optical flow. Based on optical flow, most deep learning VSR methods either opt for explicit motion compensation, or forgo compensation and use the flow as an additional input, implicitly letting the network compensate. Both approaches, however, have drawbacks.

Explicit motion compensation approaches [1,9,18,21] use optical flow to warp each neighboring frame, producing a warped frame that is spatially aligned with the reference frame. As optical flow values are floating-point, pixel values in the warped frame are calculated by interpolation, based on the original pixels of the neighboring frame. Interpolation, however, degrades image quality by introducing irreversible error, resulting in lowered contrast and blur [12].

No warping approaches [4,8,23], instead, use optical flow as an additional input layer, and let the neural network learn to align information based on this input. This approach, although effective, necessitates a large receptive field in order to capture faster motions, resulting in an increased number of parameters and correspondingly slower training and execution times. Moreover, as the placement of the region of interest within the large receptive field varies, it becomes harder for the network to adapt and focus only in the relevant information.

Driven by the above observations, the present work proposes to split optical flow into an integer and a fractional part, using the former for interpolation-free "quantized" warping, and the latter as an additional input to the network. This approach combines the advantages of both warping and no-warping, retaining a small relative displacement, while avoiding interpolation errors, and making efficient use of all available information.

Figure 1 shows pixel correspondence and information usage in the two approaches mentioned above as well as the proposed approach, showcasing the pros and cons of each with a simplified example. Taking a 5 × 5 pixel area, the example focuses on calculating a new SR value for the green pixel of interest. The corresponding position in the neighboring frame, according to optical flow, lies 1.7 pixels to the right and 1.4 pixels down.

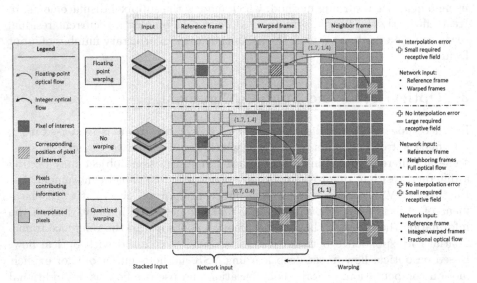

Fig. 1. A visual overview of different approaches to optical flow warping for super resolution. The top row describes floating point warping, where interpolation is used to warp the neighboring frame into exact spatial alignment with the reference. The middle row depicts foregoing warping and alignment, using instead a larger receptive field and the optical flow as an additional input to the network. The bottom row describes the proposed approach, constructing a roughly aligned warped image using only the integer part of the optical flow, and providing the fractional part as an additional network input. The last column summarizes the pros and cons of each approach, along with their network input.

Reference   Neighboring   Floating-point   Quantized
frame   frame   warping   warping

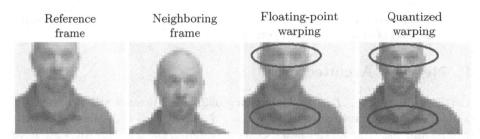

Fig. 2. Illustration of the blurring effect of traditional alignment warping. In the image warped with floating-point optical flow, note the loss of detail in the eyes and the reduced contrast in the shadows of the shirt's collar. Compare with the corresponding regions in the image produced with quantized warping

In floating-point warping, the warped frame is calculated by taking the optical flow vectors and interpolating between pixels. The purple interpolated pixel corresponds exactly to the green pixel of interest. As all information is spatially aligned between referenced and warped frame, the network need not have a large receptive field; in theory, even a 1×1 receptive field could be enough, though usually a somehow wider field is used to also extract information from neighboring pixels. The reference and warped frames are then stacked and used as input to the network.

In the case of no warping, the neighbor frame itself is used as an input, along the reference frame. The optical flow field provides an additional input. Here, the receptive field must be at least as large as the maximum motion vector length. A large number of pixels from the neighboring frame will contribute to the end result, and the network must learn to focus on the most relevant pixels according to the optical flow input.

Finally, in the proposed approach of quantized warping, the warped frame is computed by shifting pixels in the neighbor frame by the integer part of the optical flow vectors. Hence, the spatial correspondence between the reference and warped frame is not perfect, as in floating-point warping, but displacements are confined to the $[0, 1)$ range, for arbitrary large displacements. The minimum required receptive field here is 2×2 pixels, although again this can be widened to extract additional information from neighboring pixels. The network input consists of the reference and warped frames, as well as the fractional part of the optical flow field, which was not used for warping. Therefore, the network must learn to take into account the displacement between the reference and warped frames, but this is now only a sub-pixel displacement. Displacements larger than 1 pixel are offset during the warping phase, allowing the network to compensate for faster motions without a large receptive field.

Figure 2 illustrates floating-point warping's interpolation error in a zoomed detail from a real video sequence. The third image, produced by warping the neighboring frame with the full optical flow, exhibits blur, loss of detail, and reduced contrast. By contrast, the image produced by quantized warping retains the same level of sharpness as the original.

4   Network Architecture

Let $\{I_{t-N}, \ldots, I_t, \ldots, I_{t+N}\}$ be a sequence of $2N+1$ LR consecutive frames. We denote I_t as the reference frame, I_{t+n}, $n \in [-N, N]$, $n \neq 0$ as the neighboring frames and $F_{t->t+n}$ as the flow between I_t and I_{t+n}. The aim of VSR is to reconstruct a HR version of I_t, denoted by I_t^{SR}, by exploiting the information of the neighboring frames.

The proposed network architecture follows a recurrent structure that progressively reconstructs the I_t^{SR} image by adding, in each iteration, extra information from the neighboring frames using the back-projection process [7], inspired by the RBPN [4]. The proposed network comprises 3 processing stages. In the first stage, denoted as Shallow Feature Extraction, features are extracted from the available LR data. Next, in the Back-projection module, the basic processing to produce the respective HR features is performed and, finally, in the Reconstruction stage, the SR image is composed. This procedure is performed repetitively for each new frame used. The overall proposed architecture is depicted in Fig. 3.

Shallow Feature Extraction: The input LR I_t frame is passed through a convolutional layer to extract the initial LR features maps, S_t. Moreover, for each neighboring frame I_{t+n}, the corresponding warped frame I_{t+n}^{WARPED} w.r.t the reference frame is computed based on the proposed 'quantized' warping method. To warp a pixel of the neighboring frame to the reference, only the integer part of the optical flow $F_{t->t+n}$ is used. However, the integer part does not contain the precise displacement information and therefore, for each pixel, we utilize 4 warps with all 4 neighboring pixels in order to fully preserve the subpixel motion information, as shown in Fig. 4. Therefore, for one neighboring frame, 4 warped images are computed that are stacked to produce the corresponding warped frame I_{t+n}^{WARPED}.

Finally, the reference frame I_t, the neighboring warped frame I_{t+n}^{WARPED} and the fractional part of the of pre-computed flow map $F_{t+n}^{fractional}$, that was not used in warping process, are concatenated and given as input to a convolutional layer to produce feature maps M_{t+n}. The S_t and the M_{t+n} feature maps represent the single-scale and the multi-scale information, respectively.

Back-Projection: The back-projection module combines the single and the multi-scale information by projecting the reference features S_t to each neighboring frame's features M_{t+n} in order to capture missing information. It takes as input the S_t and the M_{t+n} feature maps and outputs the refined HR feature maps H_{t+n} and the next LR features S_{t+n}, using convolutional structures. As shown in Fig. 5, the module, first, produces the refined HR H_{t+n} maps through the back projection to particular neighbor frame. Then downscales H_{t+n} to output the next LR features S_{t+n}. The whole process is described as follows:

$$H_{t+N-1}^S = \text{Net}_S(S_{t+N-1}) \tag{1}$$

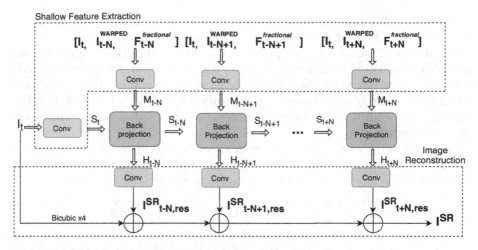

Fig. 3. Illustration of the unfolded architecture of the proposed recurrent network

$$H_{t+N}^M = \mathrm{Net}_M(M_{t+N}) \tag{2}$$

$$H_{t+N_{res}} = \mathrm{Net}_{res}(H_{t+N-1}^S - H_{t+N}^M) \tag{3}$$

$$H_{t+N} = H_{t+N-1}^S + H_{t+N_{res}} \tag{4}$$

$$S_{t+N} = \mathrm{Net}_{downscale}(H_{t+N}), \tag{5}$$

where Net_S, Net_M, Net_{res} and $Net_{downscale}$ are the respective convolutional networks for each task.

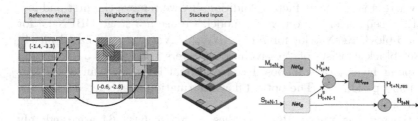

Fig. 4. The 4 warped images that are produced for each neighboring frame using our proposed quantized method

Fig. 5. Back-projection module

Image Reconstruction: In the proposed network, the image reconstruction module follows a temporal integration strategy in order to produce the final super-resolved image I_t^{SR}. A recurrent residual reconstruction process has been developed that progressively enhances the produced I_{t+n}^{SR} at the image level by adding further information from each neighboring frame. This strategy exploits directly and efficiently the extra information from the neighbors and, in the last iteration, outputs a refined, detailed I_t^{SR} image.

Consequently, unlike the majority of VSR approaches that require distinct models for accepting a different number of frames as input, the proposed reconstruction architecture enables the same network, trained on fixed number of frames, to handle frame sequences of arbitrary length. The number of neighboring frames used in the inference phase depends on the desired inference speed and reconstruction quality.

It is evident, though, that the task is characterized by an inherent temporal locality, with the majority of useful information being on frames temporally adjacent to the reference one. The reconstruction process is formulated as:

$$I_t^{SR} = I_t^{bic} + I_{t-N,res}^{SR} + I_{t-N+1,res}^{SR} + \cdots + I_{t+N,res}^{SR} \tag{6}$$

where I_t^{bic} is the bicubic upscaled version of I_t.

This procedure is repeated until all available neighboring frames have been processed.

5   Experimental Results

5.1   Implementation and Training Details

All models are trained with the Vimeo-90k [24] dataset, which consists of 64612 7-frame sequences and contains diverse scenes and motions. For testing we use the standard benchmark datasets including Vid4 [14], and Vimeo-90k-T. The performance of the models is evaluated using the PSNR and SSIM quality metrics, both on the RGB color space and on the Y-channel (luminance) from YCbCr color space. By following [4], we crop $2s$ pixels around image boundary at testing phase, where s is the scale factor. Additionally, we remove the first and last 3 frames of the sequence. For our main model, we use a 3-stage DBPN [3] for Net_S and a 5-block ResNet [5] for Net_M, Net_{res}, $Net_{downscale}$, based on [4]. Each ResNet block consists of 2 convolutional layers with a 3×3 kernel and the up-sampling layer is a transposed convolutional layer with an 8×8 kernel, stride 4 and padding 2. The optical flow information is extracted using the implementation by [15].

During the training phase, RGB patches with size 64×64 are randomly cropped form the LR input images and the mini-batch size is set at 4. The extracted patches are augmented with vertical and horizontal flipping and rotation. The Adam optimizer is used for model's parameter update with $\beta_1 = 0.9$ and $\beta_1 = 0.999$. All proposed models are trained using L_1 norm as loss function with initial learning rate 10^{-4}, which decreases by a factor of 10 every 75 epochs.

5.2   Results on Large Motions and Generalization

We compare our proposed network with the 3 most prominent state-of-the-art methods in VSR, namely DUF [8], RBPN [4] and EDVR [23]. Testing is done on the most challenging and diverse datasets:Vimeo-90k-T and REDS [16].

Table 1. Quantitative evaluation of state-of-the-art VSR methods on Vimeo-90K and REDS dataset. Bold and italic indicate the best and the second best performance (PSNR/SSIM)

Motion type	Bicubic (1 Frame)	DUF [8] (7 Frames)	EDVR [23] (7 Frames)	RBPN [4] (7 Frames)	Proposed (7 Frames)
Vimeo-90k-T (Y)	31.32/0.8684	36.37/0.9387	**37.61/0.9489**	37.16/0.9420	*37.23/0.9445*
REDS (RGB)	26.14/0.7292	28.63/0.8251	*30.49/0.8700*	29.84/0.8538	**30.50/0.8698**

Vimeo-90k-T is a large and commonly used dataset that contains diverse HQ data and a range of motion types. For evaluation on more challenging data, we test with REDS, that consists of high resolution HQ images, with larger and more complex motions. For the following results we trained our model on Vimeo-90k for upscaling x4 and using 6 neighboring frames, 3 past and 3 future ones.

In Table 1, the quantitative evaluation of SoA VSR methods on the most challenging datasets, Vimeo-90k and REDS, is presented. For the results of this table we use networks trained on Vimeo-90k dataset for EDVR, RBPN and the proposed method. First of all, we can see that the proposed method presents a clear improvement over RBPN and DUF on both datasets, with the difference being bigger on REDS. Compared to EDVR, which is the current SoA, the performance of the proposed method is worse on Vimeo-90k but on par on REDS, despite having 8 million parameters less. These results indicate that our model generalizes better on unknown data, irrespective of the training data, and does not suffer from dataset overfitting issues. The fact that our model closes the performance gap with the SoA on the most complex and realistic dataset, indicates that our motion compensation strategy is successful. Qualitatively, the proposed model is capable to recover high frequency details and more accurate textures compared to existing methods, as shown in Fig. 8 on examples obtained from Vimeo-90k, REDS and Vid4.

To further illustrate the merit of our approach, we thoroughly compare our method with RBPN on different Vimeo-90k splits with different motion characteristics. RBPN's architecture is also based on back-projection modules and mainly differs from our model in motion information handling at the input. RBPN uses no warping or any other motion compensation for neighbouring frames. As can be seen on Tables 2 and Fig. 6, the proposed method increasingly outperforms RBPN as the motion magnitude grows larger, with the difference reaching 0.19 db.

5.3   Ablation Studies

In order to validate the additive value of each of our contributions, we implement them one by one and conduct relevant experiments and comparisons. The architectures mentioned throughout this section are smaller versions of the proposed

Table 2. Quantitative comparison between RBPN and the proposed network, on Vimeo90k-T

Dataset	Method		
	RBPN/F7	Proposed/F7	Diff
Vimeo-90k-T (Y)			
Slow	**34.18/0.9200**	**34.18/0.9221**	0.0
Medium	37.28/0.9470	**37.30/0.9496**	0.02
Fast	40.03/0.9600	**40.22/0.9626**	0.19
Avg.	37.16/0.9423	**37.23/0.9447**	0.07

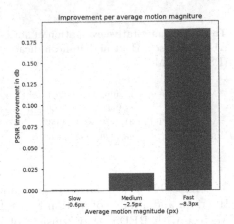

Fig. 6. Improvement over RBPN per motion magnitude

model, to allow for shorter training duration. The total number of parameters is reduced from ≈12 to ≈1.8 million by reducing the ResNet blocks of each back-projection module from 5 to 2, the feature number of de-convolutional layers and DBPN from 64 to 32, as well as reducing the features of each convolutional layer from 256 to 128. If not mentioned explicitly otherwise, the ablation experiments are using 5 input frames in total.

Quantized Warping Effectiveness: To strengthen our claim that the proposed quantized warping process is more suitable for the VSR task than the floating-point warping, we train two separate models with the same structure, parameters and neighbors but with different warping methods at the input level. The one model receives as input the concatenation of the reference frame, the integer warped frame and the fractional optical flow, whereas the other takes as input the concatenation of the reference frame and the floating warped frame. We also compare the above models with a third model, similar to RBPN [4], that uses no warping and relies on implicit motion estimation. The input of this model is a simple concatenation of the reference frame, the neighboring frame and the flow information between them.

Table 3 shows that our quantized warping method outperforms the floating-point one and increases the model's reconstruction performance by 0.44 dB on Vid4 and by more than 1 dB on Vimeo-90k-T, at all motion types. These results show that for the VSR task is more important to maintain the high frequency information of neighboring frames than to achieve a precise motion compensation using a interpolated warping method, which produces blurry input images. Notice that floating point warping causes blur even for motions smaller than 1 pixel, which explains the reduced performance on the slow split.

Table 3. Effect of the warping method on the Vid4 and Vimeo-90k-T datasets for upscaling factor 4

Dataset	Method		
	No warping	Floating-point warping	Proposed quantized warping
Vid4	**26.68/0.801**	26.24/0.786	**26.68/0.801**
Vimeo-90k-T (Y)			
Slow	**33.47/0.9120**	32.90/0.9038	**33.47/0.9120**
Medium	36.48/0.9418	35.30/0.9273	**36.53/0.9423**
Fast	39.26/0.9551	38.16/0.9431	**39.54/0.9580**
Avg.	36.40/0.9363	35.45/0.9247	**36.51/0.9374**

Compared to no warping method, we notice that the two approaches provide similar results for slow motions -Vid4, Vimeo90k-slow- and the effectiveness of our method is more clear at medium and fast motions. These results are expected as for small displacements the network with no warping is capable to focus on the relevant information between the reference and the neighboring frame. However, for faster motions is difficult for the network to capture the larger region of interest and align implicitly the useful information, despite the final large receptive field. Our method provides the network with warped detailed images that make easier and more efficient the reconstruction process.

Usage of Subpixel Motion Information: As described in Sect. 4, our warping method utilizes all 4 neighboring pixels to fully preserve subpixel motion information. Using a simple, nearest-neighbor interpolation, for each neighboring frame is produced only one warped image based on the information of the nearest pixel. This method would result in inputs with lost displacement information, but crisp details. We evaluated the added value of warping the entirety of the neighborhood by training a network using each method. As seen on Table 4, the additional information from all neighboring pixels improves the reconstruction ability of the network.

Table 4. Effect of neighbors per pixel on Vid4 and Vimeo-90k-T datasets

Dataset	Method	
	1 Neighbor	4 Neighbors
Vid4	26.66/0.8005	**26.68/0.8006**
Vimeo-90k-T (avg.)	36.48/0.9374	**36.51/0.9374**

Table 5. Effect of sequence length on Vid4 and Vimeo-90k-T dataset

Dataset	Method	
	Proposed F5	Proposed F7
Vid4	26.68/0.8006	**26.90/0.8104**
Vimeo-90k-T (avg.)	36.51/0.9374	**36.76/0.9402**

Sequence Length: We train our model with video sequences of different lengths to investigate how the number of the neighboring frames affects the reconstruction performance. As shown in Table 5, the model's performance improves with longer sequences, as the network benefits from the extra relevant information. The F7 model, with 3 past and 3 future neighbors outperforms the F5 model, with 2 past and 2 future neighbors, by more than 0.2 dB on both datasets.

Residual Temporal Integration Module: We validate the efficiency and the flexibility of our model to handle arbitrary number of frames. We observed that by training our recurrent model with a fixed number of input frames, its performance sharply deteriorates when presented with inputs of different length. To overcome this, we trained a model with sequences of varying length. As can be seen in Fig. 7, the resulting model achieves more stable performance across a wider range of input lengths.

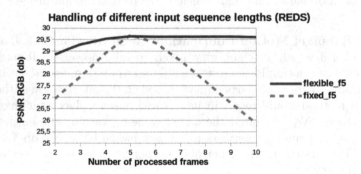

Fig. 7. Performance curves on REDS for models trained using different input lengths (varying between 2–5 frames for the solid-blue, 5 for the dashed-orange). (Color figure online)

Fig. 8. Visual results on REDS and Vimeo-90k. Zoom in to see better visualization

6 Conclusion

In this paper, we propose a quantized warping method and a residual temporal integration module combined to a flexible VSR framework that generates high quality results and outperforms most of the previous approaches on big and complex motions. In an extensive set of experiments, we show that the proposed warping method is more suitable for the VSR task compared to floating-point warping or no warping and boosts the model's performance. The quantized warping method is a general algorithm that could be used to other tasks, which focus more on detailed warped images than precise alignment, beyond VSR. Moreover, the residual temporal integration module allows the network to be flexible to frame sequences with arbitrary length without extra training.

The proposed method is better suited to take advantage of neighboring frames with big displacements, due to rapid motion or temporal frame distance, as it explicitly compensates the relative displacements and lets the network model only the remaining, subpixel displacements. Consequently, it generalizes better across different datasets with diverse motion content, showing performance competitive to the SoA, despite using a significantly smaller network and generic optical flow.

Acknowledgements. This research was funded by the European Commission under contract H2020–787061 ANITA.

References

1. Caballero, J., et al.: Real-time video super-resolution with spatio-temporal networks and motion compensation. In: Proceedings of the IEEE Conference on Computer Vision and Pattern Recognition, pp. 4778–4787 (2017)
2. Dong, C., Loy, C.C., He, K., Tang, X.: Image super-resolution using deep convolutional networks. IEEE Trans. Pattern Anal. Mach. Intell. **38**(2), 295–307 (2015)
3. Haris, M., Shakhnarovich, G., Ukita, N.: Deep back-projection networks for super-resolution. In: Proceedings of the IEEE Conference on Computer Vision and Pattern Recognition, pp. 1664–1673 (2018)
4. Haris, M., Shakhnarovich, G., Ukita, N.: Recurrent back-projection network for video super-resolution. In: Proceedings of the IEEE Conference on Computer Vision and Pattern Recognition, pp. 3897–3906 (2019)
5. He, K., Zhang, X., Ren, S., Sun, J.: Deep residual learning for image recognition. In: Proceedings of the IEEE Conference on Computer Vision and Pattern Recognition, pp. 770–778 (2016)
6. Huang, G., Liu, Z., Van Der Maaten, L., Weinberger, K.Q.: Densely connected convolutional networks. In: Proceedings of the IEEE Conference on Computer Vision and Pattern Recognition, pp. 4700–4708 (2017)
7. Irani, M., Peleg, S.: Improving resolution by image registration. CVGIP Graph. Models Image Process. **53**(3), 231–239 (1991)
8. Jo, Y., Wug Oh, S., Kang, J., Joo Kim, S.: Deep video super-resolution network using dynamic upsampling filters without explicit motion compensation. In: Proceedings of the IEEE Conference on Computer Vision and Pattern Recognition, pp. 3224–3232 (2018)

9. Kappeler, A., Yoo, S., Dai, Q., Katsaggelos, A.K.: Video super-resolution with convolutional neural networks. IEEE Trans. Comput. Imaging **2**(2), 109–122 (2016)
10. Kim, J., Kwon Lee, J., Mu Lee, K.: Accurate image super-resolution using very deep convolutional networks. In: Proceedings of the IEEE Conference on Computer Vision and Pattern Recognition, pp. 1646–1654 (2016)
11. Kim, J., Kwon Lee, J., Mu Lee, K.: Deeply-recursive convolutional network for image super-resolution. In: Proceedings of the IEEE Conference on Computer Vision and Pattern Recognition, pp. 1637–1645 (2016)
12. Konstantoudakis, K., Vrysis, L., Tsipas, N., Dimoulas, C.: Block unshifting high-accuracy motion estimation: a new method adapted to super-resolution enhancement. Sig. Process. Image Commun. **65**, 81–93 (2018)
13. Ledig, C., et al.: Photo-realistic single image super-resolution using a generative adversarial network. In: Proceedings of the IEEE Conference on Computer Vision and Pattern Recognition, pp. 4681–4690 (2017)
14. Liu, C., Sun, D.: A Bayesian approach to adaptive video super resolution. In: CVPR 2011, pp. 209–216. IEEE (2011)
15. Liu, C., et al.: Beyond pixels: exploring new representations and applications for motion analysis. Ph.D. thesis, Massachusetts Institute of Technology (2009)
16. Nah, S., et al.: NTIRE 2019 challenge on video deblurring and super-resolution: dataset and study. In: Proceedings of the IEEE Conference on Computer Vision and Pattern Recognition Workshops (2019)
17. Sajjadi, M.S., Scholkopf, B., Hirsch, M.: EnhanceNet: single image super-resolution through automated texture synthesis. In: Proceedings of the IEEE International Conference on Computer Vision, pp. 4491–4500 (2017)
18. Sajjadi, M.S., Vemulapalli, R., Brown, M.: Frame-recurrent video super-resolution. In: Proceedings of the IEEE Conference on Computer Vision and Pattern Recognition, pp. 6626–6634 (2018)
19. Tai, Y., Yang, J., Liu, X.: Image super-resolution via deep recursive residual network. In: Proceedings of the IEEE Conference on Computer Vision and Pattern Recognition, pp. 3147–3155 (2017)
20. Tai, Y., Yang, J., Liu, X., Xu, C.: MemNet: a persistent memory network for image restoration. In: Proceedings of the IEEE International Conference on Computer Vision, pp. 4539–4547 (2017)
21. Tao, X., Gao, H., Liao, R., Wang, J., Jia, J.: Detail-revealing deep video super-resolution. In: Proceedings of the IEEE International Conference on Computer Vision, pp. 4472–4480 (2017)
22. Tong, T., Li, G., Liu, X., Gao, Q.: Image super-resolution using dense skip connections. In: Proceedings of the IEEE International Conference on Computer Vision, pp. 4799–4807 (2017)
23. Wang, X., Chan, K.C., Yu, K., Dong, C., Change Loy, C.: EDVR: video restoration with enhanced deformable convolutional networks. In: Proceedings of the IEEE Conference on Computer Vision and Pattern Recognition Workshops (2019)
24. Xue, T., Chen, B., Wu, J., Wei, D., Freeman, W.T.: Video enhancement with task-oriented flow. Int. J. Comput. Vis. **127**(8), 1106–1125 (2019)
25. Yang, W., et al.: Deep edge guided recurrent residual learning for image super-resolution. IEEE Trans. Image Process. **26**, 5895–5907 (2017)
26. Zhang, Y., Tian, Y., Kong, Y., Zhong, B., Fu, Y.: Residual dense network for image super-resolution. In: Proceedings of the IEEE Conference on Computer Vision and Pattern Recognition, pp. 2472–2481 (2018)

Pyramidal Edge-Maps and Attention Based Guided Thermal Super-Resolution

Honey Gupta$^{(\boxtimes)}$ and Kaushik Mitra

Computational Imaging Lab, IIT Madras, Chennai, India
hn.gpt1@gmail.com, kmitra@ee.iitm.ac.in

Abstract. Guided super-resolution (GSR) of thermal images using visible range images is challenging because of the difference in the spectral-range between the images. This in turn means that there is significant texture-mismatch between the images, which manifests as blur and ghosting artifacts in the super-resolved thermal image. To tackle this, we propose a novel algorithm for GSR based on pyramidal edge-maps extracted from the visible image. Our proposed network has two sub-networks. The first sub-network super-resolves the low-resolution thermal image while the second obtains edge-maps from the visible image at a growing perceptual scale and integrates them into the super-resolution sub-network with the help of attention-based fusion. Extraction and integration of multi-level edges allows the super-resolution network to process texture-to-object level information progressively, enabling more straightforward identification of overlapping edges between the input images. Extensive experiments show that our model outperforms the state-of-the-art GSR methods, both quantitatively and qualitatively.

Keywords: Guided super-resolution · Thermal image · Hierarchical edge-maps · Attention based fusion · Convolutional neural network

1 Introduction

Thermal imaging has many advantages over traditional visible-range imaging as it works well in extreme visibility conditions. It has found applications in various fields such as firefighting [2], gas leakage detection [39], and automation [5,23,24], but the high cost of thermal sensors has considerably restricted its consumer application. Super-Resolution (SR) techniques can increase its applicability by simulating accurate high-resolution thermal images from measurements captured from the considerably inexpensive low-resolution thermal cameras.

Efficient methods have been proposed to perform super-resolution directly from the low-resolution thermal measurements. These single image SR methods [1,7,22,38,59] either take an iterative approach [59] or use a convolutional neural network (CNN) to learn the upsampling transformation function Ψ, such that

Electronic supplementary material The online version of this chapter (https://doi.org/10.1007/978-3-030-67070-2_42) contains supplementary material, which is available to authorized users.

© Springer Nature Switzerland AG 2020
A. Bartoli and A. Fusiello (Eds.): ECCV 2020 Workshops, LNCS 12537, pp. 698–715, 2020.
https://doi.org/10.1007/978-3-030-67070-2_42

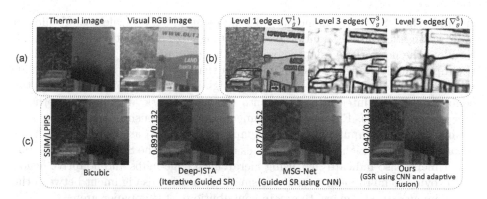

Fig. 1. (a) Texture difference between thermal and visible images. (b) Multi-level edge-maps extracted from the visible image. Finer high-frequency details are present in Level-1 edges, but this level also contains the unwanted edges such as *texts on the back of the truck*, which are absent in Level-5. This antithetical variation of high-frequency information motivates the use of multi-level edge-maps. (c) Due to texture-mismatch, some existing methods such as MSG-Net [20] can produce blurred images. However, with the help of pyramidal edge-maps and adaptive fusion, our method is able to produce better high-frequency details.

$x_h = \Psi(x_l)$. However, if the dimensions of the input thermal image are very small, if *e.g.* the thermal images from a low-end thermal camera FLIR-AX8 have a resolution of 60×80, then single image super-resolution becomes very challenging as the problem becomes highly ill-posed.

Since many low-resolution thermal cameras are accompanied by a high-resolution visible-range camera, a practical solution to get better super-resolved thermal images is to use Guided Super-Resolution (GSR) techniques. A crucial part of super-resolution is to correctly predict the high-frequency details. These high-frequency details are present as edge information in the two images. Since the edges are shared across the modality, estimation of the overlapping edges between the two modalities becomes a crucial task for reconstructing better high-frequency details. Most of the existing guided thermal SR techniques [6,16,31,37,45] estimate high-frequency details implicitly by using CNNs and end-to-end learning. However, the RGB guide image contains fine-texture details that are confined to the visible spectrum. For e.g., the *texts on the back of the truck* in Fig. 1(a) are present only in the visible-range image. Such non-overlapping texture details can cause artifacts when used for guided super-resolution of thermal images. To address this drawback of single RGB guide images, we propose to use hierarchical edge-maps as guide input to our thermal super-resolution network.

We propose a GSR model that takes multi-level edge-maps extracted from the visible image as input instead of a single RGB guide image. Edge-maps at different perceptual scale contain fine-texture to object-level information distinctly, as shown in Fig. 1(b). Due to this property of multi-level edge-maps, they can enhance the GSR performance as edge-maps at different scales could allow a more straightforward estimation of overlapping edge information. Furthermore, to allow the network to adaptively select the appropriate edge information for the input multiple edge-maps, we propose a spatial-attention based fusion module. This module adaptively selects the high-frequency information from the edge-maps before integrating them into the SR network at different depths or receptive-field sizes. Extensive experiments show that using such hierarchical form of guidance input followed by adaptive attention-based integration helps reconstruct better high-frequency details and enhances the SR performance. Our experiments also indicate that using hierarchical edge-maps and adaptive fusion can provide some robustness towards small geometric misalignment between the input images. In summary, the main contributions of this paper are:

- We propose a novel guided super-resolution method that consists of two sub-networks: one for thermal image super-resolution and the other for feature extraction and integration of multi-level edge-maps obtained from the visible image.
- We use hierarchical edge-maps as guidance input and propose a novel fusion module that adaptively selects information from these multi-level edge-maps and integrates them into our SR network with the help of spatial-attention modules.
- We compare our model with existing state-of-the-art GSR methods and show that our method reconstructs more high-frequency details and performs significantly better, both quantitatively and perceptually.

2   Related Works

The high cost of thermal cameras has in the past inspired many research works to aim at thermal image super-resolution. Among the single thermal image super-resolution methods [1,7,22,38], Choi et al. [7] suggested a shallow three-layer convolutional neural network (CNN). Zhang et al. [59] thereafter combined compressive sensing and deep learning techniques to perform infrared super-resolution. Apart from thermal super-resolution methods, multiple methods have been proposed for near-infrared image super-resolution [16,34,45,46,55]. However, the drawback of these methods is that they do not target super-resolution for very low-resolution inputs, which is the case for low-cost thermal cameras. Choi et al. [7] and Lee et al.'s [31] works suggest that using a visible super-resolution method or pre-trained model should perform well in the case of thermal images too. Many deep CNN based single image super-resolution methods, such as [8,10,11,25,30,33,41,47,48,51,57,60,61], have shown great performance on visible images. Most of the recent methods such as RCAN [60] and SAN [8] use self-attention mechanism to produce better reconstructions. But the common concern related to single image methods is that reconstructing HR images solely from low-resolution noisy sensor images can be challenging and a guided approach might perform better.

Among the guided thermal super-resolution methods, Lee *et al.* [31] used brightness information for the visible-range images. Han *et al.* [16] proposed a guided super-resolution method using CNN that extracts features from infrared and visible images and combines them using convolutional layers. Ni *et al.* [37] proposed a method to utilize an edge-map and perform GSR. Almasri *et al.* [1] performed a detailed study of different CNN architectures and up-sampling methods and proposed a network for guided thermal super-resolution. Interestingly, many recent methods for guided super-resolution for depth [12, 14, 18, 27, 32, 40, 52, 54, 56, 62, 63] or hyperspectral [28, 29, 42, 43] images have similar backbone as the thermal guided super-resolution methods. They all use some variation of the Siamese network [4] to simultaneously extract information from both images and merge them to reconstruct the super-resolved image. However, these methods tackle texture-mismatch with the help of implicit or end-to-end learning, which can perform sub-optimally and lead to blurred reconstructions, as shown in Fig. 1(c).

3 Pyramidal Edge-Maps and Attention Based Guided Super-Resolution (PAG-SR)

The guide image belongs to a higher resolution as compared to the input thermal image and has useful high-frequency details that can be fused with the low-resolution thermal image to perform better super-resolution. However, these high-frequency details should be extracted and integrated adaptively according to the input low-resolution thermal image. Non-optimality in feature-extraction can propagate the texture-mismatch, which can further cause artifacts in the reconstructed image. At a first glance, it seems that extracting the object-level edges could be an ideal solution as they are shared across the multispectral images, but as one can observe from Fig. 1(b), there are high-frequency details present in edge-maps at lower levels, *i.e.* levels 1 and 3 that are equally useful. To resolve this conundrum, we use edge-maps extracted at pyramidal levels from the visible image and integrate them with the help of adaptive fusion module using self-attention mechanism. This way, the network can leverage high-frequency information in a hierarchical fashion and adaptively select appropriate features according to the input low-resolution thermal image.

Figure 2 shows the architecture of our proposed method. We denote the low-resolution thermal, the high-resolution visible and ground-truth thermal images as x_l, g_h and x_h, respectively. Our proposed network consists of two sub-networks: one for thermal image super-resolution, denoted as Ψ_x and one for feature extraction and integration of multi-level edge-maps obtained from the visible image, denoted as Ψ_{fus}. Many existing edge-detection methods for single images [35, 53] extract multi-level edges and merge them to obtain object-level edge-map. They extract edges at different perceptual scales by taking output at different layers of the VGG [44] network. Consequently, to obtain edges having visible-range information at different perceptual scales, we used one of these existing methods [35], which provides edge-maps at 5 pyramidal levels. We denote these edge-maps as $\nabla_g = [\nabla_g^1, \nabla_g^2, \ldots, \nabla_g^5]$.

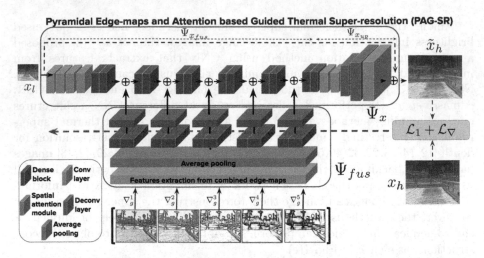

Fig. 2. Our method utilizes hierarchical edge information extracted from the guide visible image and integrates this information into our thermal super-resolution network at different network-depths with the help of feature extraction and self-attention mechanism. We progressively merge information obtained from the guide image and allow the network to adaptively deal with high-frequency information mismatch.

To extract guidance information and fuse it into the super-resolution network, we propose a fusion network and denote it as Ψ_{fus}. As shown in Fig. 2, Ψ_{fus} first contains a convolution layer, which we denote as $\mathbf{C}_{edge}$. The convolution layer takes a concatenate of the multi-level edge-maps as an input and extracts features from these edge-maps collectively. We call these extracted features as edge-features and denote them as $\mathbf{G}_{edges} = \mathbf{C}_{edge} \circledast \nabla_{\mathbf{g}}$. $\mathbf{G}_{edges}$ contains the multi-level high-frequency guidance information from the visible-range image. These edge-features are then passed through an average pooling layer to reach the spatial resolution of $\mathbf{x}_l$. We perform the fusion at the low-resolution scale because our experiments showed that downsampling reduces the edge-mismatch between the input images and leads to better performance as compared to performing fusion in the spatially high-resolution feature-space.

The next part of Ψ_{fus} contains a set of dense [19] and spatial attention blocks [50], which we collectively call as the fusion sub-block. For n edge-maps, we have n sets of fusion sub-blocks, denoted as Ψ_{fus}^{n} that lead to n connections into the thermal super-resolution network. Each fusion sub-block contains a dense-block with 2 convolutional layers for extracting the relevant features from $\mathbf{G}_{edges}$ for that particular connection. Each dense-block is followed by a spatial attention block [50] that adaptively transforms the guidance information and outputs weighted features based on the spatial correlation of different channels in the features. Our spatial-attention block is similar to the one proposed in [50] and its architecture is shown in Fig. 3. The mathematical description of the module can be found in the supplementary paper. We tried different variations of the fusion network Ψ_{fus}, details of which are mentioned in Sect. 4.4.

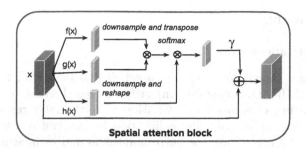

Fig. 3. Architecture of the spatial attention block used in our fusion module. The module adaptively transforms the features according to spatial correlation inside each feature-map and outputs re-scaled features such that the relevant information has a higher activation.

Our thermal image super-resolution sub-network, denoted as Ψ_x, consists of two parts: $\Psi_{x_{fus}}$ and $\Psi_{x_{up}}$, as shown in Fig. 2. The first part of the network, denoted as $\Psi_{x_{fus}}$, is the part that extracts information from the low-resolution thermal image and is merged with Ψ_{fus} to receive the guidance information. $\Psi_{x_{fus}}$ contains convolutional layers having 32 channels, which are followed by dense-blocks [19] of two convolutional layers, each of which again have 32 channels. For n guide edge-maps, $\Psi_{x_{fus}}$ contains $n + 1$ dense-blocks, denoted as $[\mathbf{D}_1, \mathbf{D}_2, \ldots, \mathbf{D}_{n+1}]$. The fusion operation can be summarised as:

$$\mathbf{X}_{n+1} = \mathbf{D}_n(\mathbf{X}_n) + \Psi_{fus}^n(\mathbf{G}_{edges}) \tag{1}$$

where, $\mathbf{X}_n$ and $\mathbf{D}_n$ are n^{th} feature-map and dense-block of Ψ_x, respectively and Ψ_{fus}^n is the nth fusion sub-block, as mentioned in the previous paragraph.

The features from $\Psi_{x_{fus}}$ are fed into $\Psi_{x_{up}}$, which contains convolutional and upsampling layers. For a 2^k super-resolution, $\Psi_{x_{up}}$ contains k deconvolution layers. The output of $\Psi_{x_{up}}$ is $\mathbf{X}_{up} = \Psi_{x_{up}}(\mathbf{X}_{n+1})$. The final deconvolution layer is followed by a convolutional layer and a skip connection from the input image for residual learning. The output can be defined as:

$$\tilde{\mathbf{x}}_h = \mathbf{C} \circledast \mathbf{X}_{up} + \mathbf{x}_{l\uparrow} \equiv \Psi_x(\mathbf{x}_l) \tag{2}$$

Loss Functions. To learn the parameters of Ψ_x, our optimization function contains two loss terms. First is the reconstruction loss $\mathcal{L}_1(\tilde{\mathbf{x}}_h, \mathbf{x}_h) = ||\tilde{\mathbf{x}}_h - \mathbf{x}_h||_1$ for supervised training. The second term is a gradient loss $\mathcal{L}_\nabla(\tilde{\mathbf{x}}_h, \mathbf{x}_h) = ||\nabla(\tilde{\mathbf{x}}_h) - \nabla(\mathbf{x}_h)||_1$ to explicitly penalize loss of high frequency details. Here ∇ is the Laplacian operator that calculates both horizontal and vertical gradients. Hence, our overall loss function is

$$\mathcal{L}(\mathbf{x}_l, \mathbf{x}_h, \Psi_x) = \gamma_1 \mathcal{L}_1(\tilde{\mathbf{x}}_h, \mathbf{x}_h) + \gamma_2 \mathcal{L}_\nabla(\tilde{\mathbf{x}}_h, \mathbf{x}_h) \tag{3}$$

We found the optimal values for γ_1 and γ_2 to be 10 and 1, respectively.

4   Experiments

4.1   Datasets and Setup

We perform experiments on three datasets: FLIR-ADAS [13], CATS [49] and KAIST [21]. FLIR-ADAS contains unrectified stereo thermal and visible-range image pairs having a resolution of 512×640 and 1600×1800, respectively. Since the dataset does not contain any calibration images, we rectified one image pair manually, by identifying the correspondences and estimating the relative transformation matrices. We used this estimated transformations to rectify rest of the images in the dataset. After rectification, both thermal and visible-range images are of resolution 512×640. The CATS dataset contains rectified thermal and visible images, both of dimensions 480×640. This dataset also contains ground-truth disparity maps between the two images, but we observed that the disparity-maps are not accurate and results in artifacts when either of the images is warped using the disparity. Therefore, we used the rectified yet unaligned image pairs for our experiments, similar to the FLIR-ADAS dataset. Hence, both datasets have rectified image pairs (i.e. epipolar lines are horizontal), but they are not pixel-wise aligned. In contrast, the third KAIST dataset contains aligned thermal and visible images of resolution 512×640. This dataset was captured using a beam-splitter based setup and hence it has less practical similarity with the low-resolution thermal cameras. We therefore use this dataset for a smaller set of GSR methods, to present a baseline comparison on aligned thermal and visible images.

To create the low-resolution dataset, we used the blur-downscale degradation model proposed in [57] to simulate the low-resolution images. For the training-set, we down-sample images using blur kernels with $\sigma \in [0, 4]$ at a step of 0.5. For the FLIR-ADAS dataset, our training set contains 43830 image pairs and the test-set contains 1257 pairs. In the CATS dataset, our training set contains 944 image-pairs and the test-set contains 50 pairs. Since CATS training-set is quite small, we used to it fine-tune the models pre-trained on FLIR-ADAS training-set and then tested them on the CATS test-set. For the KAIST dataset, our training-set contains 5581 image-pairs and our test-set contains 964 pairs. We perform experiments for $\times 4$ and $\times 8$ upsampling factors. For both datasets, the input thermal-resolution is close to the resolution of low-cost thermal cameras like FLIR AX8. The $\mathbf{x}_l$ dimensions are 64×80 for FLIR-ADAS and KAIST; and 60×80 for CATS. Hence, for $\times 4$ SR, the guide image and the ground-truth image for FLIR-ADAS and KAIST are of resolution 256×320 and for CATS, they are of resolution 240×320. Similarly, for $\times 8$, the corresponding guide and GT images are of sizes 512×640 and 480×640. For network optimization, we use ADAM optimizer [26] with a learning rate of 1×10^{-4}. The experiments were performed on a Nvidia 2080Ti GPU.

Comparison Details. We compare our method with 9 existing GSR methods: TGV2-L2 [12], FBS [3], Joint-BU [27], Infrared-SR [17], SDF [15], MSF-STI-SR

Table 1. Comparison of existing methods on FLIR-ADAS for ×4 and ×8 SR cases.

Method	G/S	Scale	PSNR	SSIM	MSE	LPIPS
Bicubic	Single	×4	28.37	0.890	0.001652	0.405
RDN [61]	Single	×4	29.28	0.906	0.001441	0.282
RCAN [60]	Single	×4	29.18	0.908	0.001483	0.228
SAN [8]	Single	×4	26.47	0.859	0.002567	0.229
TGV2-L2 [12]	Guided	×4	28.77	0.892	0.001601	0.422
FBS [3]	Guided	×4	25.48	0.787	0.003152	0.387
Joint-BU [27]	Guided	×4	27.77	0.874	0.001855	0.284
Infrared SR [16]	Guided	×4	28.21	0.889	0.001692	0.405
SDF [15]	Guided	×4	28.70	0.875	0.001488	0.321
MSF-SR [1]	Guided	×4	29.21	0.901	0.001447	0.200
MSG-Net [20]	Guided	×4	29.46	0.897	0.001341	0.184
PixTransform [36]	Guided	×4	24.84	0.787	0.003679	0.329
Deep-ISTA [9]	Guided	×4	25.86	0.828	0.028939	0.529
PAG-SR (Ours)	Guided	×4	**29.56**	**0.912**	**0.001309**	**0.147**
RDN [61]	Single	×8	26.80	0.833	0.002314	0.389
RCAN [60]	Single	×8	22.35	0.758	0.006771	0.414
SAN [8]	Single	×8	25.38	0.811	0.003251	0.536
TGV2-L2 [12]	Guided	×8	26.42	0.821	0.002526	0.399
FBS [3]	Guided	×8	25.03	0.770	0.003451	0.476
Joint-BU [27]	Guided	×8	25.61	0.803	0.003006	0.406
Infrared SR [16]	Guided	×8	26.03	0.817	0.002782	0.521
SDF [15]	Guided	×8	26.72	0.819	0.002379	0.363
MSF-SR [1]	Guided	×8	27.92	0.835	0.002350	0.249
MSG-Net [20]	Guided	×8	27.29	0.827	0.002263	0.296
PixTransform [36]	Guided	×8	23.31	0.836	0.005224	0.371
Deep-ISTA [9]	Guided	×8	25.56	0.778	0.030982	0.598
PAG-SR (Ours)	Guided	×8	**28.77**	**0.919**	**0.001581**	**0.214**

[1], MSG-Net [20], Pix-Transform [36] and Deep-ISTA [9]. We also include comparison with a few recent single image SR methods such as RCAN [60], RCAN [60] and SAN [8]. We used the publicly available codes for the existing methods and trained the CNN based single and guided SR methods on the corresponding thermal datasets to perform the comparison. For the CATS dataset, the models pre-trained on FLIR-ADAS dataset were used for fine-tuning. We kept the default settings for most of the methods, except for few filtering based methods such as FBS and Joint-BU, where the weights had to be adjusted to reconstruct better texture-details in the super-resolved images.

Metrics. We use four metrics to quantitatively assess the reconstructions: PSNR, SSIM, Mean-squared Error (MSE) and Perceptual distance (LPIPS) [58]. Among these, PSNR and SSIM are distortion-based metrics and hence, can be biased towards smooth or blurred images. Therefore, we also use LPIPS, a perceptual metric that computes the perceptual distance between the reconstructed and the ground-truth images. A point to note is that since the reconstructed images are thermal measurements, better MSE is also an important factor while comparing the methods.

Table 2. Comparison of guided super-resolution methods on CATS dataset for ×4 and ×8 upsampling cases. *Higher PSNR, SSIM and lower MSE, LPIPS are better.*

Method	G/S	Scale	PSNR	SSIM	MSE	LPIPS
Bicubic	Single	×4	32.19	0.959	0.000744	0.395
RDN [61]	Single	×4	29.41	0.914	0.004811	0.357
RCAN [60]	Single	×4	31.89	<u>0.966</u>	0.000796	0.159
SAN [8]	Single	×4	33.41	0.960	0.000507	**0.141**
TGV2-L2 [12]	Guided	×4	32.17	0.938	0.000741	0.225
FBS [3]	Guided	×4	29.12	0.825	0.035104	0.450
Joint-BU [27]	Guided	×4	31.23	0.953	0.000914	0.233
Infrared SR [16]	Guided	×4	28.27	0.901	0.031501	0.348
SDF [15]	Guided	×4	32.56	0.941	0.000686	0.246
MSF-SR [1]	Guided	×4	29.37	0.830	0.022598	0.415
MSG-Net [20]	Guided	×4	31.56	0.964	0.000789	0.177
PixTransform [36]	Guided	×4	28.48	0.792	0.185427	0.442
Deep-ISTA [9]	Guided	×4	<u>33.72</u>	0.956	<u>0.000488</u>	0.178
PAG-SR (Ours)	Guided	×4	**34.97**	**0.968**	**0.000461**	<u>0.161</u>
Bicubic	Single	×8	31.45	0.958	0.000868	0.413
RDN [61]	Single	×8	<u>33.31</u>	0.956	0.000631	0.392
RCAN [60]	Single	×8	27.63	0.931	0.002296	0.332
SAN [8]	Single	×8	32.17	<u>0.953</u>	0.000615	0.278
TGV2-L2 [12]	Guided	×8	31.55	0.951	0.000846	0.303
FBS [3]	Guided	×8	29.03	0.855	0.035654	0.495
Joint-BU [27]	Guided	×8	30.21	0.950	0.001131	0.314
Infrared SR [16]	Guided	×8	25.23	0.904	0.029725	0.409
SDF [15]	Guided	×8	31.91	0.948	0.000778	0.319
MSF-SR [1]	Guided	×8	27.97	0.811	0.032487	0.418
MSG-Net [20]	Guided	×8	32.83	0.957	0.000622	<u>0.270</u>
PixTransform [36]	Guided	×8	27.79	0.783	0.121195	0.584
Deep-ISTA [9]	Guided	×8	32.51	0.949	<u>0.000595</u>	0.290
PAG-SR (Ours)	Guided	×8	**33.18**	**0.963**	**0.000537**	**0.246**

4.2 Quantitative Comparison

Table 1 and 2 show the results for ×4 and ×8 upsampling factors for FLIR-ADAS and CATS datasets, and Table 3 shows the results for ×4 SR on KAIST dataset. A general trend among the existing methods is that they perform quite well in terms of distortion metrics but poorly in terms of the perceptual metric for the FLIR and CATS datasets. For these datasets, MSG-Net [20] and MSF-SR [1] results are the closest to our method. PixTransform [36] and Deep-ISTA [9] are the most recent methods, yet they perform poorly as compared to the others for the FLIR and CATS datasets, mostly due to edge-mismatch and inability to accommodate the texture difference. For the FLIR-dataset, we observe a small variance in the metric values but for the CATS dataset, the variance is much higher. The reason for this is the higher disparity range or higher misalignment between the input images from the CATS dataset. In contrast, the KAIST dataset has aligned images and hence, the results show much less variance as compared to the other two datasets. For this dataset, Deep-ISTA seems to be the closest to our method in terms of performance.

Our method outperforms the existing methods in terms of distortion as well as perceptual metrics on all three datasets. We observe a significant margin between ours and the existing methods' performances, especially in the case of ×8 SR on FLIR-ADAS dataset. In Table 2, we observe a similar pattern in the metric values. However, an interesting observation is that in the ×4 case for CATS dataset, the single image SR methods perform better than many GSR methods. We believe this could be due to the edge-mismatch caused by the misalignment. For the KAIST dataset, our results are better than the existing methods, which indicates that our method works better for both aligned and misaligned inputs.

Table 3. Comparison of GSR methods on KAIST dataset for ×4 upsampling case.

Method	G/S	Scale	PSNR	SSIM	MSE	LPIPS
SDF [15]	Guided	×4	24.14	0.830	0.005647	0.242
MSF-SR [1]	Guided	×4	25.52	0.855	0.004319	0.274
MSG-Net [20]	Guided	×4	25.61	0.868	0.004031	0.242
PixTransform [36]	Guided	×4	24.85	0.828	0.007692	0.325
Deep-ISTA [9]	Guided	×4	26.12	**0.871**	0.003846	0.273
PAG-SR (Ours)	Guided	×4	**27.98**	0.856	**0.002399**	**0.219**

Robustness Towards Texture-Mismatch and Misalignment. The CATS dataset has higher misalignment which is visualized in the disparity-maps in Fig. 5. Misalignment results in higher texture-mismatch, which consequently reduces the performance of many existing methods. We speculate that usage of edge-maps and attention module in our method provides some form of robustness towards misalignment and hence is the cause of our better performance. To validate this, we experimented with a variant of our network that takes an RGB guide input and does not have the attention block inside the fusion sub-blocks.

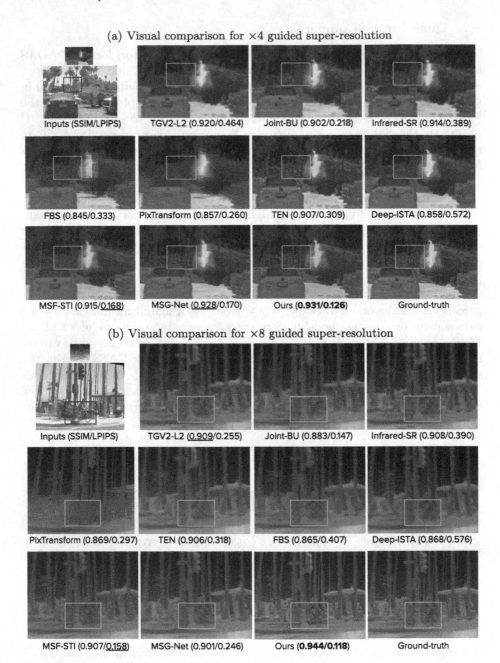

Fig. 4. Visual comparison on sample images from FLIR-ADAS dataset. Our method reconstructs high frequency details more accurately and has less artifacts due to mismatched edges as compared to existing GSR methods, for *e.g.* the ghosting effect of trees in MSF-STI's ×8 reconstruction or blurred edges in most of the other methods. We also achieve higher SSIM and lower perceptual distance (LPIPS) values.

Fig. 5. Visual comparison on images from CATS dataset for ×8 SR.

We found that this model performs lower than our proposed method which has pyramidal edge-maps and attention based fusion. In terms of metrics, the model without edge-maps and attention achieved an SSIM of 0.901 and LPIPS of 0.173 as compared our proposed model's SSIM of 0.912 and LPIPS of 0.147, for ×4 SR on FLIR dataset. This indicates that the edge-maps and attention module contribute towards the performance improvement and hence, are able to tackle texture-mismatch and most probably misalignment as well to a certain extent.

4.3   Qualitative Comparison

We show the qualitative comparison of our method for ×4 and ×8 upsampling rates on FLIR-ADAS dataset in Fig. 4. Most of the existing methods have blurred edges, especially in the case of ×8 SR, which could be either due to very low-resolution of the input thermal images (60×80) or due to texture-mismatch and improper propagation of guidance information. Among the existing methods, MSF-STI, MSG-Net and Joint-BU results are considerably good, yet our method reconstructs high-frequency details more faithfully and has much sharper edges. For *e.g.* in Fig. 4(a), the branches in the red inset for our result are evidently most clear as compared to the other methods. Moreover, ghosting artifacts can be

Table 4. Performance variation with respect to guidance input type: RGB *vs* edge-maps for ×8 super-resolution on FLIR-ADAS dataset.

Integration positions					Input type		PSNR	SSIM	LPIPS
1	2	3	4	5	RGB	Edge-maps			
✓					✓		28.05	0.916	0.249
✓						✓	28.34	0.909	0.222
✓	✓	✓			✓		28.19	0.916	0.243
✓	✓	✓				✓	**28.85**	0.916	0.215
✓	✓	✓	✓	✓	✓		28.14	0.916	0.258
✓	✓	✓	✓	✓		✓	28.77	**0.919**	**0.214**
✓	✓	✓	✓	✓	✓	✓	28.83	0.915	0.221

found in the results from few existing methods, such as MSF-STI's reconstruction for ×8 case in Fig. 4(b). In contrast, our method is able to reconstruct the object structure better for the same image and does not have such artifacts.

Figure 5 shows the ×8 super-resolution results for few samples from the CATS dataset, that has higher misalignment as compared to the FLIR-ADAS dataset. We can observe that the existing guided super-resolution methods show more blur as compared to FLIR-ADAS dataset, mostly due to increased texture-mismatch caused by a higher misalignment. However, our results are overall much sharper than the existing methods, which indicates a comparatively higher robustness towards misalignment, as mentioned in Sect. 4.2.

4.4   Ablation Studies

Usefulness of Edge-Maps. Ideally, the RGB image could be used to extract features/edges in an end-to-end manner. However, estimating the optimal edge-map is very challenging because the SR network will require object-level awareness while extracting features. Using multilevel edge-maps simplifies this task by providing the object-edge information explicitly. To validate this hypothesis, we performed some experiments where we replaced the edge-maps with the visible RGB image for few variants of our model. The experiment was performed for ×8 SR on FLIR-ADAS dataset. Our proposed PAG-SR contains guide information fusion at 5 positions to the thermal super-resolution network. However, since edge-features $\mathbf{G}_{edges}$ contain information from all the edge-maps, these positions can be reduced or expanded. Table 4 summarizes the results for a couple of such variations. When the guide information is fed at position 1, namely after first dense-block or $\mathbf{X}_1$, then RGB performs slightly better than the edge-maps. However, in the case of fusion at 5 positions, the edge-maps perform better than both RGB, RGB combined with edge-maps, and all other variants as well. Thus, we can conclude that using edge-maps as a guidance information and fusing them at multiple-positions is overall a better strategy. We also performed a

Table 5. Performance of different variations of our guidance fusion module.

Edge-features (G_{edges})	Dense block	Attention module	PSNR	SSIM	LPIPS
✗	✗	✗	27.95	0.837	**0.213**
✓	✗	✗	28.15	0.904	0.223
✓	✗	✓	28.39	<u>0.910</u>	<u>0.214</u>
✓	✓	✗	**28.87**	0.907	0.221
✓	✓	✓	<u>28.77</u>	**0.919**	<u>0.214</u>

study to analyze the contribution of different levels of the edge-maps towards performance. The results can be found in Table 1 of the supplementary paper.

Contribution of Different Components of the Fusion Network. To analyze the contribution of different components of our fusion network, we computed the performance of some variants of our fusion network while keeping the SR network constant for ×8 SR on FLIR-ADAS dataset. The results of the experiments are summarized in Table 5. The simplest model is our proposed method without the fusion module and hence contains edge-maps directly added to the SR network. Other variants include either having the dense-blocks or the attention module or neither or both in each fusion sub-block. The results show that having both dense-blocks and attention module helps is achieving better reconstructions. Moreover, Fig. 6 shows a visual comparison of the results from model with and without the fusion block. The model without the fusion module contains many artifacts induced by the edge-mismatch between the input images. Most of such artifacts are eliminated by our fusion network with the help of appropriate selection of edge-information.

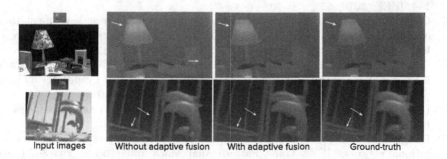

Input images   Without adaptive fusion   With adaptive fusion   Ground-truth

Fig. 6. Comparison of results from our method with and without the fusion module.

5   Conclusion

We proposed a hierarchical edge-maps based guided super-resolution algorithm that tackles edge-mismatch due to spectral-difference between the input low-resolution thermal and high-resolution visible-range images in a systematic and holistic manner. Our method robustly combines multi-level edge information extracted from the visible-range image into our tailored thermal super-resolution network with the help of attention based guidance propagation and consequently produces better high-frequency details. We showed that our results are significantly better both perceptually and quantitatively than the existing state-of-the-art guided super-resolution methods.

References

1. Almasri, F., Debeir, O.: Multimodal sensor fusion in single thermal image super-resolution. In: Carneiro, G., You, S. (eds.) ACCV 2018. LNCS, vol. 11367, pp. 418–433. Springer, Cham (2019). https://doi.org/10.1007/978-3-030-21074-8_34
2. Arrue, B.C., Ollero, A., De Dios, J.M.: An intelligent system for false alarm reduction in infrared forest-fire detection. IEEE Intell. Syst. Appl. 15(3), 64–73 (2000)
3. Barron, J.T., Poole, B.: The fast bilateral solver. In: Leibe, B., Matas, J., Sebe, N., Welling, M. (eds.) ECCV 2016. LNCS, vol. 9907, pp. 617–632. Springer, Cham (2016). https://doi.org/10.1007/978-3-319-46487-9_38
4. Bertinetto, L., Valmadre, J., Henriques, J.F., Vedaldi, A., Torr, P.H.S.: Fully-convolutional Siamese networks for object tracking. In: Hua, G., Jégou, H. (eds.) ECCV 2016. LNCS, vol. 9914, pp. 850–865. Springer, Cham (2016). https://doi.org/10.1007/978-3-319-48881-3_56
5. Borges, P.V.K., Vidas, S.: Practical infrared visual odometry. IEEE Trans. Intell. Transp. Syst. 17(8), 2205–2213 (2016)
6. Chen, X., Zhai, G., Wang, J., Hu, C., Chen, Y.: Color guided thermal image super resolution. In: 2016 Visual Communications and Image Processing (VCIP), pp. 1–4. IEEE (2016)
7. Choi, Y., Kim, N., Hwang, S., Kweon, I.S.: Thermal image enhancement using convolutional neural network. In: 2016 IEEE/RSJ International Conference on Intelligent Robots and Systems (IROS), pp. 223–230. IEEE (2016)
8. Dai, T., Cai, J., Zhang, Y., Xia, S.T., Zhang, L.: Second-order attention network for single image super-resolution. In: Proceedings of the IEEE Conference on Computer Vision and Pattern Recognition, pp. 11065–11074 (2019)
9. Deng, X., Dragotti, P.L.: Deep coupled ISTA network for multi-modal image super-resolution. IEEE Trans. Image Process. 29, 1683–1698 (2019)
10. Dong, C., Loy, C.C., He, K., Tang, X.: Image super-resolution using deep convolutional networks. IEEE Trans. Pattern Anal. Mach. Intell. 38(2), 295–307 (2016)
11. Dong, C., Loy, C.C., Tang, X.: Accelerating the super-resolution convolutional neural network. In: Leibe, B., Matas, J., Sebe, N., Welling, M. (eds.) ECCV 2016. LNCS, vol. 9906, pp. 391–407. Springer, Cham (2016). https://doi.org/10.1007/978-3-319-46475-6_25
12. Ferstl, D., Reinbacher, C., Ranftl, R., Rüther, M., Bischof, H.: Image guided depth upsampling using anisotropic total generalized variation. In: Proceedings of the IEEE International Conference on Computer Vision, pp. 993–1000 (2013)

13. FLIR: Advanced driver assistance systems dataset (2018). https://www.flir.in/oem/adas/
14. Guo, C., Li, C., Guo, J., Cong, R., Fu, H., Han, P.: Hierarchical features driven residual learning for depth map super-resolution. IEEE Trans. Image Process. **28**, 2545–2557 (2018)
15. Ham, B., Cho, M., Ponce, J.: Robust image filtering using joint static and dynamic guidance. In: Proceedings of the IEEE Conference on Computer Vision and Pattern Recognition (CVPR). IEEE (2015)
16. Han, T.Y., Kim, Y.J., Song, B.C.: Convolutional neural network-based infrared image super resolution under low light environment. In: 2017 25th European Signal Processing Conference (EUSIPCO), pp. 803–807, August 2017. https://doi.org/10.23919/EUSIPCO.2017.8081318
17. Han, T.Y., Kim, Y.J., Song, B.C.: Convolutional neural network-based infrared image super resolution under low light environment. In: 2017 25th European Signal Processing Conference (EUSIPCO), pp. 803–807. IEEE (2017)
18. Hayat, K.: Multimedia super-resolution via deep learning: a survey. Digit. Signal Proc. **81**, 198–217 (2018)
19. Huang, G., Liu, Z., Van Der Maaten, L., Weinberger, K.Q.: Densely connected convolutional networks. In: Proceedings of the IEEE Conference on Computer Vision and Pattern Recognition, pp. 4700–4708 (2017)
20. Hui, T.-W., Loy, C.C., Tang, X.: Depth map super-resolution by deep multi-scale guidance. In: Leibe, B., Matas, J., Sebe, N., Welling, M. (eds.) ECCV 2016. LNCS, vol. 9907, pp. 353–369. Springer, Cham (2016). https://doi.org/10.1007/978-3-319-46487-9_22. http://mmlab.ie.cuhk.edu.hk/projects/guidance_SR_depth.html
21. Hwang, S., Park, J., Kim, N., Choi, Y., Kweon, I.S.: Multispectral pedestrian detection: Benchmark dataset and baselines. In: Proceedings of IEEE Conference on Computer Vision and Pattern Recognition (CVPR) (2015)
22. Jones, H., Sirault, X.: Scaling of thermal images at different spatial resolution: the mixed pixel problem. Agronomy **4**(3), 380–396 (2014)
23. Khattak, S., Papachristos, C., Alexis, K.: Marker based thermal-inertial localization for aerial robots in obscurant filled environments. In: Bebis, G., et al. (eds.) ISVC 2018. LNCS, vol. 11241, pp. 565–575. Springer, Cham (2018). https://doi.org/10.1007/978-3-030-03801-4_49
24. Khattak, S., Papchristos, C., Alexis, K.: Keyframe-based direct thermal-inertial odometry. arXiv preprint arXiv:1903.00798 (2019)
25. Kim, J., Kwon Lee, J., Mu Lee, K.: Accurate image super-resolution using very deep convolutional networks. In: Proceedings of the IEEE Conference on Computer Vision and Pattern Recognition, pp. 1646–1654 (2016)
26. Kingma, D.P., Ba, J.: Adam: a method for stochastic optimization. arXiv preprint arXiv:1412.6980 (2014)
27. Kopf, J., Cohen, M.F., Lischinski, D., Uyttendaele, M.: Joint bilateral upsampling. ACM Trans. Graph. (ToG) **26**, 96 (2007)
28. Kwon, H., Tai, Y.W.: RGB-guided hyperspectral image upsampling. In: Proceedings of the IEEE International Conference on Computer Vision, pp. 307–315 (2015)
29. Lahoud, F., Zhou, R., Süsstrunk, S.: Multi-modal spectral image super-resolution. In: Leal-Taixé, L., Roth, S. (eds.) ECCV 2018. LNCS, vol. 11133, pp. 35–50. Springer, Cham (2019). https://doi.org/10.1007/978-3-030-11021-5_3
30. Lai, W.S., Huang, J.B., Ahuja, N., Yang, M.H.: Fast and accurate image super-resolution with deep Laplacian pyramid networks. IEEE Trans. Pattern Anal. Mach. Intell. **41**, 2599–2613 (2018)

31. Lee, K., Lee, J., Lee, J., Hwang, S., Lee, S.: Brightness-based convolutional neural network for thermal image enhancement. IEEE Access **5**, 26867–26879 (2017)

32. Li, Y., Sun, J., Wang, B., Zhao, Y.: Depth super-resolution using joint adaptive weighted least squares and patching gradient. In: 2018 IEEE International Conference on Acoustics, Speech and Signal Processing (ICASSP), pp. 1458–1462. IEEE (2018)

33. Lim, B., Son, S., Kim, H., Nah, S., Mu Lee, K.: Enhanced deep residual networks for single image super-resolution. In: Proceedings of the IEEE Conference on Computer Vision and Pattern Recognition Workshops, pp. 136–144 (2017)

34. Liu, F., Han, P., Wang, Y., Li, X., Bai, L., Shao, X.: Super resolution reconstruction of infrared images based on classified dictionary learning. Infrared Phys. Technol. **90**, 146–155 (2018)

35. Liu, Y., et al.: Richer convolutional features for edge detection. IEEE Trans. Pattern Anal. Mach. Intell. **41**(8), 1939–1946 (2019). https://doi.org/10.1109/TPAMI.2018.2878849

36. Lutio, R.d., D'Aronco, S., Wegner, J.D., Schindler, K.: Guided super-resolution as pixel-to-pixel transformation. In: Proceedings of the IEEE International Conference on Computer Vision, pp. 8829–8837 (2019)

37. Ni, M., Lei, J., Cong, R., Zheng, K., Peng, B., Fan, X.: Color-guided depth map super resolution using convolutional neural network. IEEE Access **5**, 26666–26672 (2017). https://doi.org/10.1109/ACCESS.2017.2773141

38. Panagiotopoulou, A., Anastassopoulos, V.: Super-resolution reconstruction of thermal infrared images. In: Proceedings of the 4th WSEAS International Conference on REMOTE SENSING (2008)

39. Prata, A., Bernardo, C.: Retrieval of volcanic ash particle size, mass and optical depth from a ground-based thermal infrared camera. J. Volcanol. Geoth. Res. **186**(1–2), 91–107 (2009)

40. Riegler, G., Ferstl, D., Rüther, M., Bischof, H.: A deep primal-dual network for guided depth super-resolution. arXiv preprint arXiv:1607.08569 (2016)

41. Sajjadi, M.S., Scholkopf, B., Hirsch, M.: EnhanceNet: single image super-resolution through automated texture synthesis. In: Proceedings of the IEEE International Conference on Computer Vision, pp. 4491–4500 (2017)

42. Shi, Z., Chen, C., Xiong, Z., Liu, D., Zha, Z.-J., Wu, F.: Deep residual attention network for spectral image super-resolution. In: Leal-Taixé, L., Roth, S. (eds.) ECCV 2018. LNCS, vol. 11133, pp. 214–229. Springer, Cham (2019). https://doi.org/10.1007/978-3-030-11021-5_14

43. Shoeiby, M., et al.: PIRM2018 challenge on spectral image super-resolution: methods and results. In: Leal-Taixé, L., Roth, S. (eds.) ECCV 2018. LNCS, vol. 11133, pp. 356–371. Springer, Cham (2019). https://doi.org/10.1007/978-3-030-11021-5_22

44. Simonyan, K., Zisserman, A.: Very deep convolutional networks for large-scale image recognition. arXiv preprint arXiv:1409.1556 (2014)

45. Song, P., Deng, X., Mota, J.F., Deligiannis, N., Dragotti, P.L., Rodrigues, M.R.: Multimodal image super-resolution via joint sparse representations induced by coupled dictionaries. arXiv preprint arXiv:1709.08680 (2017)

46. Sun, C., Lv, J., Li, J., Qiu, R.: A rapid and accurate infrared image super-resolution method based on zoom mechanism. Infrared Phys. Technol. **88**, 228–238 (2018)

47. Tai, Y., Yang, J., Liu, X.: Image super-resolution via deep recursive residual network. In: Proceedings of the IEEE Conference on Computer vision and Pattern Recognition, pp. 3147–3155 (2017)

48. Tai, Y., Yang, J., Liu, X., Xu, C.: MemNet: a persistent memory network for image restoration. In: Proceedings of the IEEE International Conference on Computer Vision, pp. 4539–4547 (2017)
49. Treible, W., et al.: Cats: a color and thermal stereo benchmark. In: Proceedings of the IEEE Conference on Computer Vision and Pattern Recognition, pp. 2961–2969 (2017)
50. Wang, X., Girshick, R., Gupta, A., He, K.: Non-local neural networks. In: Proceedings of the IEEE Conference on Computer Vision and Pattern Recognition, pp. 7794–7803 (2018)
51. Wang, Z., Liu, D., Yang, J., Han, W., Huang, T.: Deep networks for image super-resolution with sparse prior. In: Proceedings of the IEEE International Conference on Computer Vision, pp. 370–378 (2015)
52. Xie, J., Feris, R., Sun, M.T.: Edge-guided single depth image super resolution. IEEE Trans. Image Process. **25**(1), 428–438 (2016)
53. Xie, S., Tu, Z.: Holistically-nested edge detection. In: Proceedings of IEEE International Conference on Computer Vision (2015)
54. Ye, J., Gao, M., Yang, Y., Cao, Q., Yu, Z.: Super-resolution reconstruction of depth image based on edge-selected deep residual network. In: 2019 IEEE 16th International Conference on Networking, Sensing and Control (ICNSC), pp. 121–125. IEEE (2019)
55. Yokoya, N.: Texture-guided multi sensor super resolution for remotely sensed images. Remote Sens. **9**(4), 316 (2017)
56. Yu, S., Lan, H., Jung, C.: Intensity guided depth upsampling using edge sparsity and super-weighted l_0 gradient minimization. IEEE Access **7**, 140553–140565 (2019)
57. Zhang, K., Zuo, W., Zhang, L.: Learning a single convolutional super-resolution network for multiple degradations. In: Proceedings of the IEEE Conference on Computer Vision and Pattern Recognition, pp. 3262–3271 (2018)
58. Zhang, R., Isola, P., Efros, A.A., Shechtman, E., Wang, O.: The unreasonable effectiveness of deep features as a perceptual metric. In: CVPR (2018)
59. Zhang, X., Li, C., Meng, Q., Liu, S., Zhang, Y., Wang, J.: Infrared image super resolution by combining compressive sensing and deep learning. Sensors **18**(8), 2587 (2018)
60. Zhang, Y., Li, K., Li, K., Wang, L., Zhong, B., Fu, Y.: Image super-resolution using very deep residual channel attention networks. In: Ferrari, V., Hebert, M., Sminchisescu, C., Weiss, Y. (eds.) ECCV 2018. LNCS, vol. 11211, pp. 294–310. Springer, Cham (2018). https://doi.org/10.1007/978-3-030-01234-2_18
61. Zhang, Y., Tian, Y., Kong, Y., Zhong, B., Fu, Y.: Residual dense network for image super-resolution. In: CVPR (2018)
62. Zhou, D., Wang, R., Yang, X., Zhang, Q., Wei, X.: Depth image super-resolution reconstruction based on a modified joint trilateral filter. R. Soc. Open Sci. **6**(1), 181074 (2019)
63. Zhou, W., Li, X., Reynolds, D.: Guided deep network for depth map super-resolution: how much can color help? In: 2017 IEEE International Conference on Acoustics, Speech and Signal Processing (ICASSP), pp. 1457–1461. IEEE (2017)

AIM 2020 Challenge on Image Extreme Inpainting

Evangelos Ntavelis[1,2(✉)], Andrés Romero[1], Siavash Bigdeli[2], Radu Timofte[1],
Zheng Hui[3], Xiumei Wang[3], Xinbo Gao[3], Chajin Shin[4], Taeoh Kim[4],
Hanbin Son[4], Sangyoun Lee[4], Chao Li[5], Fu Li[5], Dongliang He[5], Shilei Wen[5],
Errui Ding[5], Mengmeng Bai[6], Shuchen Li[6], Yu Zeng[7], Zhe Lin[8], Jimei Yang[8],
Jianming Zhang[8], Eli Shechtman[8], Huchuan Lu[7], Weijian Zeng[9], Haopeng Ni[9],
Yiyang Cai[9], Chenghua Li[9], Dejia Xu[10], Haoning Wu[10], Yu Han[10],
Uddin S. M. Nadim[11], Hae Woong Jang[11], Soikat Hasan Ahmed[11],
Jungmin Yoon[11], Yong Ju Jung[11], Chu-Tak Li[12], Zhi-Song Liu[12],
Li-Wen Wang[12], Wan-Chi Siu[12], Daniel P. K. Lun[12], Maitreya Suin[13],
Kuldeep Purohit[13], A. N. Rajagopalan[13], Pratik Narang[14], Murari Mandal[15],
and Pranjal Singh Chauhan[14]

[1] Computer Vision Lab, ETH Zürich, Zürich, Switzerland
{entavelis,roandres}@ethz.ch,
siavash.bigdeli@csem.ch, radu.timofte@vision.ee.ethz.ch
[2] CSEM, Neuchâtel, Switzerland
[3] School of Electronic Engineering, Xidian University, Xi'an, China
[4] Image and Video Pattern Recognition Laboratory, School of Electrical
and Electronic Engineering, Yonsei University, Seoul, South Korea
[5] Department of Computer Vision (VIS), Baidu Inc., Beijing, China
[6] Samsung R&D Institute China-Beijing (SRC-Beijing), Beijing, China
[7] Dalian University of Technology, Dalian, China
[8] Adobe, San Jose, USA
[9] Rensselaer Polytechnic Institute, Troy, USA
[10] Peking University, Beijing, China
[11] Computer Vision and Image Processing (CVIP) Lab, Gachon University,
Seongnam, South Korea
[12] Centre for Multimedia Signal Processing, Department of Electronic and
Information Engineering, The Hong Kong Polytechnic University, Hong Kong, China
[13] Indian Institute of Technology Madras, Chennai, India
[14] BITS Pilani, Pilani, India
[15] MNIT Jaipur, Jaipur, India

Abstract. This paper reviews the AIM 2020 challenge on extreme image inpainting. This report focuses on proposed solutions and results for two different tracks on extreme image inpainting: classical image inpainting and semantically guided image inpainting. The goal of track 1 is to

E. Ntavelis (entavelis@ethz.ch, ETH Zurich and CSEM SA), A. Romero, S. Bigdeli, and
R. Timofte are the AIM 2020 challenge organizers, while the other authors participated
in the challenge.
Appendix A contains the authors'teams and affiliations.
AIM webpage: http://www.vision.ee.ethz.ch/aim20/.
Github webpage: https://github.com/vglsd/AIM2020-Image-Inpainting-Challenge.

A. Bartoli and A. Fusiello (Eds.): ECCV 2020 Workshops, LNCS 12537, pp. 716–741, 2020.
https://doi.org/10.1007/978-3-030-67070-2_43

inpaint large part of the image with no supervision. Similarly, the goal of track 2 is to inpaint the image by having access to the entire semantic segmentation map of the input. The challenge had 88 and 74 participants, respectively. 11 and 6 teams competed in the final phase of the challenge, respectively. This report gauges current solutions and set a benchmark for future extreme image inpainting methods.

Keywords: Extreme image inpainting · Image synthesis · Generative modeling

1   Introduction

Image inpainting is the task of recovering regions with some level of corrupted or missing regions. Normally, these regions are the outcome of degradation, artifacts, or they were altered by human intervention such as whitening object removal or image manipulation. The goal of this task is to fill in the missing

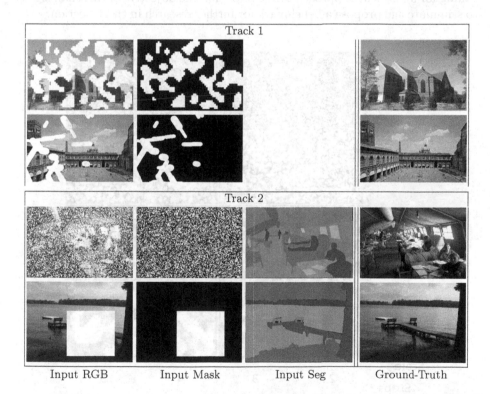

Fig. 1. Visual example of the extreme degraded input images and ground truth images used in the challenge. In both tracks, we automatically degraded each image to simulate different levels of extreme degradation. In Track 1 the aim is to produce realistic images using the Input RGB and Input Mask, and no additional information. Track 2 uses in addition a semantic segmentation map (Input Seg) as condition information for the generation of well defined objects.

pixels of the image, so the generated pixels are harmonious and perceptually plausible looking with the rest of the image.

Since the introduction of Generative Adversarial Networks (GANs) [10], recent efforts on image inpaiting have produced impressive results for replacing objects [32,33], retouching landscapes [4,24], or altering the content of a scene [11,22], either by given weak supervision (semantic segmentation guiding in addition to the binary mask to reconstruct) or no supervision (only using binary reconstruction mask). Interestingly, it is common to assume that the inpainted region is small (*e.g.* squared bounding boxes in general) with respect to the entire image, which leads to expected high perceptual scores.

In our AIM 2020 Challenge on Image Extreme Inpainting, we set the first extreme image inpainting challenge that aims at generating photo-realistic and perceptually appealing inpainted regions. The contestants are called to design a solution that is able to complete images of various sizes, spanning from low to high resolution, where the number of missing pixels is significant with respect to the entire image. Moreover, the masked regions can have a variety of shapes and sizes calling for an intricate approach to the problem. The objective of this challenge is to stimulate and propose a benchmark for further research in this direction.

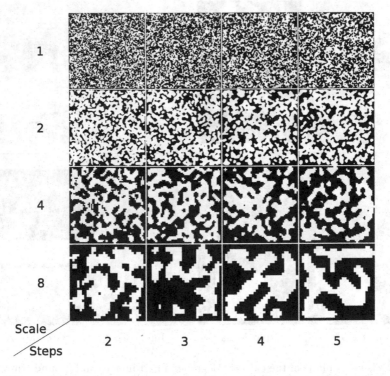

Fig. 2. We use *Cellural Automata* to generate the mask of an image. We apply a median filter at each step of the automaton to change its states. We start with a down-scaled mask size and re-scale after the automaton has reached its final state to create *islands* of different sizes.

This challenge is one of the AIM 2020 associated challenges on: scene relighting and illumination estimation [7], image extreme inpainting [23], learned image signal processing pipeline [13], rendering realistic bokeh [14], real image super-resolution [28], efficient super-resolution [35], video temporal super-resolution [26] and video extreme super-resolution [9].

2   AIM 2020 Challenge

The goals of the AIM 2020 Challenge on Image Extreme Inpainting are: *(i)* to advance towards more challenging conditions for image inpainting methods, *(ii)* to provide a common benchmark, protocol and dataset for image inpainting methods,

Table 1. Technical details of the participants. All teams that participated in Challenge 2 also participated in Challenge 1, and the runtime of using the semantic information is under mild assumptions the same

Team	Runtime (s/img)	GPU	Framework
Rainbow	0.2	TITAN RTX	Pytorch
Yonsei-MVPLab	1.58	RTX 2080Ti	Pytorch
BossGao	10	Tesla V100	Tensorflow
ArtIst	0.32	GTX 1080Ti	Tensorflow
DLUT	36.39^a	Tesla V100	Pytorch
AI-Inpainting	3.54	RTX 2080Ti	Pytorch
qwq	2.5	GTX 1080Ti	Pytorch
CVIP Inpainting	0.57	RTX 2080Ti	Pytorch
DeepInpaintingT1	6.4	RTX 2080Ti	Pytorch
IPCV_IITM	1.2	Titan X	Tensorflow
MultiCog	0.44	K40	Keras

^{a}Participant reported runtime in CPU time.

Table 2. Challenge results for Track 1: Source domain on the final test set

Team	FID↓	LPIPS↓	PSNR↑	SSIM↑	MAE↑
Rainbow	30.69	0.10 ± 0.07	26.71 ± 7.43	0.88 ± 0.09	0.03 ± 0.02
Yonsei-MVPLab	30.71	0.11 ± 0.09	27.25 ± 8.09	0.89 ± 0.09	0.02 ± 0.02
BossGao	31.23	0.11 ± 0.08	26.59 ± 8.37	0.88 ± 0.1	0.03 ± 0.02
ArtIst	33.29	0.12 ± 0.08	26.64 ± 8.55	0.87 ± 0.1	0.03 ± 0.02
DLUT	40.46	0.13 ± 0.09	26.15 ± 8.47	0.87 ± 0.1	0.03 ± 0.02
AiriaBeijingTeam	40.63	0.13 ± 0.08	26.1 ± 6.91	0.87 ± 0.09	0.03 ± 0.02
qwq	41.03	0.19 ± 0.13	25.95 ± 5.86	0.86 ± 0.11	0.03 ± 0.02
CVIP Inpainting Team	44.29	0.16 ± 0.11	26.2 ± 7.59	0.87 ± 0.1	0.03 ± 0.02
DeepInpaintingT1	48.40	0.18 ± 0.11	26.64 ± 7.6	0.87 ± 0.09	0.03 ± 0.02
IPCV_IITM	93.95	0.30 ± 0.27	20.98 ± 7.61	0.68 ± 0.29	0.08 ± 0.08
MultiCog	117.52	0.53 ± 0.18	17.58 ± 2.53	0.62 ± 0.14	0.09 ± 0.04

and *(iii)* to establish current state-of-the-art under extreme conditions. The aim is to obtain a network design/solution capable of producing high quality results with the best perceptual quality and similarity to the reference ground truth.

2.1   Description

In the classical sense, the task of image inpainting aims to reconstruct *damaged* or *missing* areas of an image. The ideal reconstruction provided by an inpainting operation should recreate the original pixels. However, in many cases all the information regarding a present entity in an image, *i.e.* an object, is vanished behind the missing pixels. It is impossible for a model to perfectly reconstruct the missing information without external guidance. Motivated by this problem we created two tracks for the AIM 2020 Extreme Inpainting Challenge: (1) the classical image inpainting track, where no additional information is used, and (2) the semantically guide image inpainting track, where the pixel-level semantic labels of the whole image are provided to drive the generation of the missing pixels.

Table 3. Challenge results for Track 2: Target domain on the final test set

Team	FID↓	LPIPS↓	PSNR↑	SSIM↑	MAE↑
Rainbow	32.60	0.11 ± 0.08	26.77 ± 7.82	0.88 ± 0.1	0.03 ± 0.02
ArtIst	36.00	0.13 ± 0.08	27.11 ± 7.93	0.88 ± 0.09	0.03 ± 0.02
DLUT	43.22	0.14 ± 0.10	25.8 ± 8.1	0.86 ± 0.1	0.03 ± 0.03
qwq	43.38	0.19 ± 0.12	24.74 ± 5.43	0.85 ± 0.1	0.03 ± 0.03
DeepInpaintingT1	44.57	0.18 ± 0.11	26.94 ± 7.09	0.88 ± 0.09	0.03 ± 0.02
AI-Inpainting	45.63	0.15 ± 0.10	25.79 ± 6.68	0.86 ± 0.1	0.03 ± 0.02

Table 4. Results per mask type for three top solutions of Track 1

Team	Mask type	LPIPS↓	PSNR↑	SSIM↑	MAE↑
Rainbow	Box	0.15	22.49	0.82	0.04
	Cellural automata	0.12	25.72	0.89	0.03
	Free-form	0.05	32.44	0.95	0.01
Yonsei-MVPLab	Box	0.17	23.45	0.83	0.03
	Cellural automata	0.13	25.40	0.88	0.03
	Free-form	0.04	33.44	0.95	0.01
BossGao	Box	0.15	22.09	0.81	0.04
	Cellural automata	0.13	25.31	0.87	0.03
	Free-form	0.05	32.94	0.95	0.01
Masked images	Box	0.30	11.47	0.66	0.14
	Cellural automata	0.66	8.21	0.23	0.23
	Free-form	0.25	16.02	0.70	0.07

2.2   Dataset

We use a partition of ADE20k dataset [37] for both tracks of the challenge. The ADE20k is a dataset with a large diversity of contents. A public training and validation set is provided, with each image being fully annotated. The resolution of the images provided in the dataset is highly diverse, and for our challenge, the inpainting must be achieved in the full scale of the image.

We aimed to provide images for both tasks that are drawn from the same distribution. Moreover, for the semantically guided challenge, we decided not to include all the classes and bypass the problem of the distribution's long tail. To achieve this, we selected the union of (1) the most occurring semantic classes per image and (2) the most occurring semantic classes per pixel. Ultimately, we ended up with 51 semantic classes and we filtered the images so that at least 90% of the pixels in a particular image belong to these 51 semantic classes. The resulting training set was 10,330 to be used for both tracks.

In order to create the validation and test set of the challenge, we followed the same procedure as in the training set. We processed the validation set of ADE20k and divided the filtered images into validation and test subset. Each set was divided into three equal numbered parts: (1) images used solely for track 1, (2) images used solely for track 2, and (3) images used for both tracks.

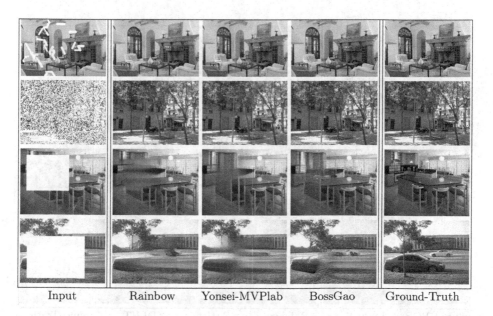

| Input | Rainbow | Yonsei-MVPlab | BossGao | Ground-Truth |

Fig. 3. Qualitative comparison over the top three methods in Track 1. Rainbow and Yonsei-MVPlab team models can successfully interpret the local scene textures and propagate information to the missing regions when the inpainted region is not too extreme. Overall, the results from the rainbow team has fewer visual artifacts. Zoom in for better visual comparisons.

We enriched our test set by mining pictures from the COCO-Stuff dataset [5]. We manually picked 200 images depicting scenes similar to the ones produced by our filtering process on ADE20k. Then, we defined a matching between the class labels of ADE20k and COCO-Stuff and translated the semantic maps accordingly. The additional COCO-Stuff images were divided into three groups similar to ADE20k images.

2.3   Masking the Images

In order to push the boundaries of image inpainting, for this competition we are using three different types of masks: (i) Rectangular masks with width and height between 30–70% of each dimension, (ii) brush strokes randomly drawn [33], and (iii) our own method generated masks based on cellural automata (Fig. 4).

We propose this novel way of masking in order to create a distorted image that has holes distributed across its dimensions, while forming small *islands* of missing pixels that are less trivial to fill compared to just salt and pepper noise. Cellural automata have been utilized in automatic content generation for games [25], but to our knowledge, this is the first time used for mask generation for image inpainting.

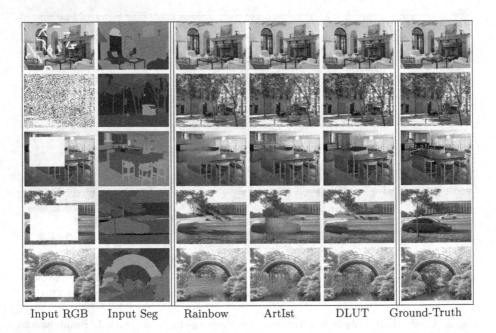

Input RGB   Input Seg   Rainbow   ArtIst   DLUT   Ground-Truth

Fig. 4. Qualitative comparison over the top three methods in Track 2. Semantic labels help the model from ArtIst to better locate object boundaries. Although rainbow team yields better perceptual performance, it is unable to assign consistent object boundaries. We depict the same images as in Fig. 3 for comparison in both tracks.

Our cellural automaton mask is a 2-dimensional grid of pixels having two states: either masked or not. We initialize our grid by randomly assigning a state to each pixel. At each step, every pixel's state is changed based on a majority vote on its neighborhood. We are using a Moor neighborhood: a 3-by-3 square, essentially applying a median filter. To facilitate creating islands of various sizes, we downscale the size of the mask before calculating the states of the automaton and re-scaling to the original size of the image to be masked. When re-scaling, we use the morphological operation of dilation to produce smoother edges. The resulted masks can be found in Fig. 2. To generate each mask, we randomly choose between down-scaling 1, 2, 4 or 8 times, and the number of applied steps (2–5).

2.4   Tracks

Track 1: Image Extreme Inpainting. In this track, we provide only the degraded image with the corresponding mask to fill in the missing pixels. Formally, the aim of this track is to learn a mapping function $\mathbb{G}$ in order to produce a coherent and perceptually looking image $X = \mathbb{G}(X_m, M)$, where X_m and M are the degraded image and the mask image, respectively. See Fig. 1 upper row for a random example of inputs and ground-truth. For this track, only the images are to be used. The use of any other additional information (semantics, object instances) was explicitly not allowed.

Track 2: Image Extreme Inpainting Guided by Pixel-Wise Semantic Labels. Here the task is also to complete the missing pixel information, but using a semantic image as guidance, so the generated image should resemble the same objects and shapes as in the semantic region. It can be formally depicted

Table 5. Results per mask type for three top solutions of Track 2

Team	Mask type	LPIPS↓	PSNR↑	SSIM↑	MAE↑
Rainbow	Box	0.16	22.15	0.81	0.04
	Cellural automata	0.10	26.85	0.90	0.02
	Free-form	0.05	32.84	0.95	0.01
ArtIst	Box	0.16	23.07	0.83	0.03
	Cellural automata	0.16	25.99	0.88	0.03
	Free-Form	0.06	33.08	0.95	0.01
DLUT	Box	0.16	21.70	0.81	0.04
	Cellural automata	0.18	24.49	0.85	0.03
	Free-form	0.07	32.06	0.94	0.02
Masked images	Box	0.32	11.16	0.63	0.14
	Cellural automata	0.65	8.77	0.26	0.22
	Free-form	0.27	15.61	0.69	0.09

as $X = \mathbb{G}(X_m, M, S)$, where S is the semantic map annotation corresponding to the ground-truth X. We depict an example of input images in Fig. 1 bottom row. For the semantic images, we provided a subset of the original ADE20k's semantic classes list, and the new number of classes is 51. The use of any other additional information, *e.g.* object/instance information, was not allowed.

2.5   Challenge Phases

The challenge had three phases: (1) *Development phase*: the participants had access to training inputs and ground-truth, and the input images of the validation set. During this phase, the participants were free to select the number and type of masks described in Sect. 2.3. (2) Validation phase: the participants had the opportunity to compute validation performance using PSNR and SSIM metrics by submitting their results on the server. A validation leaderboard was also available. (3) Final test phase: the participants got access to the test images and had to submit their inpainted images along with the description of the method, code, and model weights for further reproducibility.

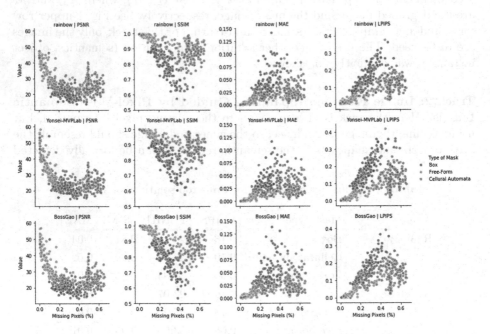

Fig. 5. A visualization of the performance of the top three methods for Track 1 in relation to the percentage of the missing pixels in the input image. Each individual point corresponds to an image of the test set. For PSNR and SSIM larger values are better while for MAE and LPIPS smaller values indicate better performance. For all methods we observe that while *cellural automata* usually remove more pixels than the *box* masks, the latter are difficult to inpaint and consistenly produce worse results for all metrics. The easiest type of mask to inpaint is the Free-Form mask. The missing pixels are less in number and not concentrated as in the *box* case

3   Challenge Results

For more than 150 participants registered on the two tracks combined, 11 teams entered the final phase of Track 1 and submitted results, code/executables, and factsheets. In Track 2, 6 teams entered the final phase. Track 2 participants also participated in Track 1. The Methods of the teams that entered the final phase are described in Sect. 4, the technical details of the teams in Table 1, and the team's affiliation is shown in Sect. 4.11. Table 2 and 3 report the final results of Track 1 and 2 respectively, on the test data of the challenge. Noteworthy, for the top three methods in terms of both perceptual and fidelity metrics, we run a perceptual study to determine the winner of the challenge. Based on our results, Rainbow generated in overall more photo-realistic inpainted images than Yonsei-MVPLab and BossGao in Track 1 and than ArtIst and DLUT in Track 2, hence ranking 1st in both tracks of the first AIM Extreme Inpainting Challenge. We have to note that for Track 1 Yonsei-MVPLab performed better in the fidelity metrics.

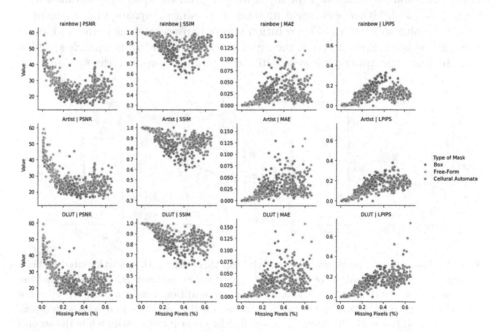

Fig. 6. A visualization of the performance of the top three methods for Track 2 in relation to the percentage of the missing pixels in the input image. Each individual point corresponds to an image of the test set. For PSNR and SSIM larger values are better while for MAE and LPIPS smaller values indicate better performance. We make similar observations with Track 1, as described in Fig. 5

3.1   Architectures and Main Ideas

All the proposed methods are GAN-based solutions. In most cases, a variant of PatchGAN [15] is used for the discriminator, while many generators imitate the structure of recent state-of-the-art architectures with two Stage Architectures, one coarsely inpainting, and the other taking care of the finer details [32,33]. The Edge-Connect approach [21] was also explored. Interestingly, the work of Hui *et al.* [12], the team winning this competition, was also employed by the second-best team of Track 1, Yonsei-MVPLab. The teams that performed the best in the competition propose novel components to their architectures.

3.2   Handling of Extreme Image Sizes

Many of the participants reported that their solution could not handle high-resolution images without prompting an *our of memory* error (OOM). Two approaches were mainly reported to tackle this issue. To circumvent this issue, many contestants downscaled the input images prior to inpainting and up-scaled the results with either a classical method, *e.g.* bilinear upsampling, or using a Super Resolution network. This solution was only used by some teams to handle the big box holes. Alternatively, the input image was divided into patches, which after independent processing were stitched together to produce the final output.

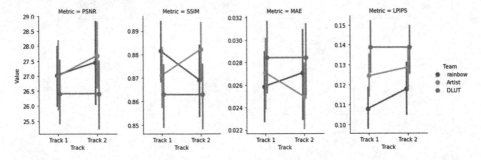

Fig. 7. Point plot of the performance of the top three teams that participated in both tracks, calculated in a subset of the test set shared between them. *DLUT* submitted the same model for both tracks, without utilizing the additional information. We observe that the top two teams produce worse perceptual results (LPIPS) when using semantics. For the second track, the first team is worse for the majority of metrics while the second team is better compared to the results of the first track, indicating that the semantic information can be both beneficial and detrimental to the inpainting task, based on how it is integrated into the network.

3.3   Handling of Different Mask Types

The three different mask types impose different problems and a few of the teams decided to handle them independently. We conducted an analysis on the results of the top three performing teams for each track, which can be found in Table 4 and 5 respectively. As a comparison baseline, we show the metrics results when computed against the input image with holes. For the baseline case, the cellural automata masks remove the most pixels and thus produce the worst results, yet we can see that compared to the massive chunks of information removed from the box masks, cellural automata masks are easier to inpaint. In Fig. 5 and 6 we can observe how the top three teams of each track performed relative to the percentage of missing information.

3.4   The Effect of the Semantic Guidance

In order to be able to fairly compare the results of the two tracks, a subset of their test set was shared. In Fig. 7 we can see how the performance on a variety of metrics differs between the classical inpainting case, where no additional information is used, and the semantically guided case. The results indicate that semantic information can both increase and decrease the performance on the inpainting task, based on how its processing was implemented in the network. Some teams use the same network they used for the first track to produce results for the second one while other trivially incorporate the semantic information in their pipeline. These factors may contribute to counter-intuitive result that many teams produced worse results in the second track.

3.5   Conclusions

The AIM 2020 Challenge on Image Extreme Inpainting gauges the current solutions and proposes a benchmark for the problem of image extreme inpainting. Different methodologies and architectures have been proposed to tackle this problem. Most of these solutions built upon traditional image inpainting methods, which has been qualitative and quantitatively validated in this report that does not necessarily hold for the extreme case. Using semantic information as guidance does not always increase the performance of an image inpainting. We believe that AIM 2020 Challenge on Image Extreme Inpainting could boost research in this challenging direction.

As qualitative and quantitative results show, image extreme inpainting is an unexplored area, where state-of-the-art classical image inpainting methods fail to generalize. Remarkably, the number of missing pixels is not a critical factor for image inpainting, but the type of mask type.

4   Challenge Methods and Teams

4.1   Rainbow

For both task 1 and task 2, Rainbow proposes a one-stage model (see Fig. 8) modified from Hui et al. [12], which utilizes dense combinations of dilated convolutions to obtain larger and more effective receptive fields. To better train the generator, and in addition to the standard VGG feature matching loss, they design a novel self-guided regression loss to dynamically correct low-level features of VGG guided by the current pixel-wise discrepancy map. Besides, they devise a geometrical alignment constraint item to penalize the coordinate center of estimated image high-level features away from the ground-truth. Moreover, for track 2, they add SPADE ResBlock [24] in the decoder to introduce a semantic map for semantic guided image inpainting task.

With self-guided regression loss, geometrical alignment constraint, VGG feature matching loss, discriminator feature matching loss, realness adversarial loss [29], and mean absolute error (MAE) loss, our overall loss function is defined as

$$\mathcal{L}_{total} = \mathcal{L}_{mae} + \lambda \left(\mathcal{L}_{self-guided} + \mathcal{L}_{fm\_vgg} \right) + \eta \mathcal{L}_{fm\_dis} + \mu \mathcal{L}_{real\_adv} + \gamma \mathcal{L}_{align}. \quad (1)$$

Except for $\mathcal{L}_{real\_adv}$, the detailed description of other losses can be found in [12]. Different from the standard GAN, RealnessGAN's discriminator outputs a distribution as the measure of realness.

$$\mathcal{L}_{real\_adv} = \mathbb{E}_{z \sim p_z} \left[\mathcal{D}_{KL} \left(\mathcal{A}_1 \| D \left(G \left(z \right) \right) \right) \right] - \mathbb{E}_{z \sim p_z} \left[\mathcal{D}_{KL} \left(\mathcal{A}_0 \| D \left(G \left(z \right) \right) \right) \right], \quad (2)$$

where $\mathcal{D}_{KL} \left(\cdot \| \cdot \right)$ denotes Kullback-Leibler (KL) divergence. Two virtual ground-truth distributions are needed to stand for the realness distributions of real and fakes images. They refer to these two distributions as $\mathcal{A}_1$ (real) and $\mathcal{A}_0$ (fake). Concretely, $\mathcal{A}_1$ and $\mathcal{A}_0$ are chosen to resemble the shapes of a Gaussian distribution $\mathcal{N} \left(\mathbf{0}, \mathbf{I} \right)$ and a Uniform distribution $\mathcal{U} \left(\mathbf{0}, \mathbf{I} \right)$, respectively.

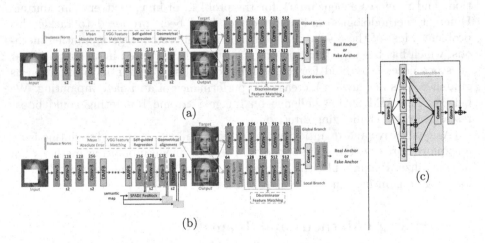

Fig. 8. Overview of Rainbow method. (a) The framework of the solution for classic image inpainting. (b) The framework of the solution for semantic guided image inpainting. (c) The structure of dense multi-scale fusion block (DMFB), "Conv-3-8" indicates 3×3 convolution layer with the dilation rate of 8.

It is set $\lambda = 10$, $\eta = 5$, and $\gamma = 1$ in Eq. 1. The training procedure is optimized using Adam optimizer with $\beta_1 = 0.5$ and $\beta_2 = 0.9$. Learning rate $2e - 4$, and batch size is 16. The training patches are 256×256. For training, given a raw image $\mathbf{I}_{gt}$, a binary image mask $\mathbf{M}$ (value 0 for known pixels and 1 denotes unknown ones). In this way, the input image $\mathbf{I}_{in}$ is obtained from the raw image as $\mathbf{I}_{in} = \mathbf{I}_{gt} \odot (1 - \mathbf{M})$. Our inpainting generator takes $[\mathbf{I}_{in}, \mathbf{M}]$ as input, and produces prediction $\mathbf{I}_{pred}$. The final output image is $\mathbf{I}_{out} = \mathbf{I}_{in} + \mathbf{I}_{pred} \odot \mathbf{M}$. All input and output are linearly scaled to $[-1, 1]$. For arbitrary masks, the random regular regions are cropped and set to the local discriminator.

During the inference stage, our network cannot directly process input ultra-high-resolution images (up to 3872×2592 px) with regular masks. When convolution operation is performed on masked regions, it cannot utilize features on known areas due to the large masked patches and the limited receptive field of the proposed generator. Thus, they downscale the input images and then generate low-resolution painted results. After that, bicubic interpolation is employed to produce high-resolution images. For irregular masks, it can regard as a low-level vision task. Because of the complete image with ultra-high-resolution, they crop it into four overlapped patches and then send them to the generator sequentially for solving the issue of OOM (out of memory).

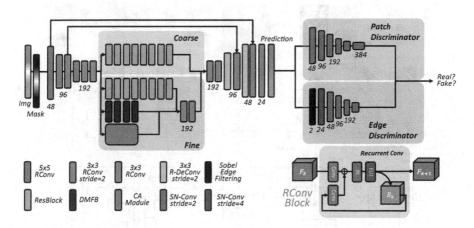

Fig. 9. Overall network structures of Yonsei-MVPLab method. Basic building block is Recurrent Convolution (RConv) that is depicted in the lower-right side.

4.2   Yonsei-MVPLab

This team proposes three novel components for the task of image inpainting: Recurrent Convolution (RConv), Edge Discriminator, and Frequency Guidance Loss. The overall structure is shown in Fig. 9. RConv and R-DeConv indicate Recurrent Convolution and Recurrent Deconvolution, respectively. DMFB and CA Module indicate Multi-scale Fusion Block in [12], and contextual attention module in [32], respectively. They follow the coarse-to-fine two-stage scheme as in similar inpainting algorithms [32,33]. For the coarse route, residual blocks with dilated convolutions used in EdgeConnect [21] are stacked. For the fine route, the same residual blocks and additional parallel blocks: DMFB [12] and CA [32] modules are used.

Like GatedConv [33], Recurrent Convolution is a basic building block for every layer. The recurrent Convolution block is depicted in the lower-right side of Fig. 9. It saves the feature of a coarse route into memory and fusion with the feature from the fine route. It effectively delivers gradients from the last output side of the network to the very first coarse layers via memory. For the discriminator, they modify the patch-based discriminator used in GatedConv [33]. Therefore, a novel discriminator, called Edge Discriminator, is applied after the Sobel edge filter. Sobel edge filter is implemented as convolution without gradient update that extracts horizontal and vertical edges. These edges are passed into the edge discriminator. It is much simple and not depend on the results of the predicted edges as in [21]. For our novel Frequency Guidance Losses, which is inspired by [8], They filter the coarse output using a low-pass filter and the fine output using a high-pass filter. Then compare them with the same filtered ground truth images. For the coarse route, an L1 loss is applied to the low-pass

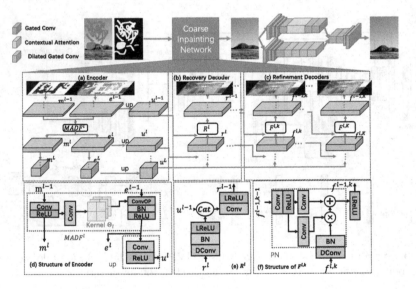

Fig. 10. Two stage framework overview, Image Inpainting With Mask Awareness. Stage 1 fills missing regions coarsely and stage 2 refines the results. In this implementation, they use the exact stage 2 network configuration as DeepFill_v2 [33]. The architecture of the stage 1 network used for block mask is shown in the bottom. $MADF^l$ and R^l are the MADF module and recovery decoder block at l-th level respectively. $F^{l,k}$ represents the k-th refinement decoder block at l-th level. m^l is the l-th mask feature map of the encoder. The convolution operation marked in green in the encoder takes e^{l-1} as input and its kernel for each convolution window is generated from the corresponding region of m^{l-1}.

filtered images, and for the fine route, an L1 loss is applied to the high-pass filtered images only in the hole region.

For some large holes, a selective up-scaling network is used for these images. These images are selected via convolution onto masks. For the up-scaling network, RRDBs in ESRGAN [27] with 48 channels are used after the main network. The hinge loss [19] is employed as the adversarial loss to train the discriminators. For the generator, a total of eight losses are used. For the coarse rouse: l1 loss, adversarial loss, and perceptual loss [16]. For the fine route: style loss, feature matching loss, and two frequency guidance losses. Style loss and feature matching loss are borrowed from those of EdgeConnect [21]. The system is pretrained on Places dataset [36], and then fine-tune on the ADE20K [37] dataset. Training patch size is 256×256 (480×480 for up-scaling network). The learning rate for discriminator is 0.0004, and the learning rate for the generator and up-scaling network is 0.0001. The learning rate is decayed every 25 epochs by half. The entire system is trained for 100 epochs.

4.3 BossGao

In general, BossGao has designed two-stage solutions for extreme image inpainting, as shown in Fig. 10. The first stage tries to recover coarse inpainting results which are relatively smooth for missing regions while keeping the content as semantically similar as possible. Our stage 2 uses the extract framework of Deep-Fill_v2 [33], where gated convolution is designed to assigning soft attention scales to each feature point for adaptively modulation of different regions whose different shapes of valid points. In addition, contextual attention is adopted to leverage valid regions for better hallucination. In this challenge, our proposed image inpainting solution exhibits mask awareness in the following aspects: 1) they develop different networks to handle block mask, brush mask and cellural automata mask, respectively. 2) To handle extreme large block masks, they proposed a novel mask aware dynamic filtering (MADF) coarse inpainting network as stage 1. In MADF, filters for each convolution window are generated from features of the corresponding region of the mask. Furthermore, it is a 7-level downsample-upsample UNet architecture and is capable to generate relatively better coarse results than the coarse inpainting network of DeepFill_v2 because of its larger receptive field. With this solution, block masks can be filled in with much more visually plausible results, especially when the image is of very high resolution and the block mask is relatively large.

The details of stage 1 coarse network for box masks are as follows. The encoder E generates multiple level feature maps. Let denote the finest level feature map as u^1 and the coarsest feature map as u^L, and m^l and e^l are the corresponding feature maps of mask and input generated by the encoder at level l. Let assume a $k \times k$ convolution with stride s will be applied to $e^{l-1} \in R^{H \times W \times C_e^{l-1}}$, and there are $N_H \times N_W$ convolution windows in total. The mask-aware dynamic convolution layer marked in green operates as follows: on $m^{l-1} \in R^{H \times W \times C_m^{l-1}}$, $k \times k$ convolution with stride s and ReLU activation is firstly applied to generate $m^l \in R^{N_H \times N_W \times C_m^l}$, then they utilize 1×1 convolution to generate the kernel tensor $\Theta_l \in R^{N_H \times N_W \times D}$, where D equals $C_e^{l-1} \times k \times k \times C_e^l$. Finally, each of all the $N_H \times N_W$ windows in e^{l-1} is convolved using the kernel reshaped from the corresponding point of Θ_l, $i.e.$, the convolution kernel of the $[n_H, n_W]$-th window in e^{l-1} is reshaped from $\Theta_l[n_H, n_W, :]$. To reduce computational overhead, they choose to apply MADF to extract relatively low dimensional latent features and then map it to a higher dimension. Specifically, C_m^l is set to a relatively small value of 16 and output channel number C_e^l is limited by $\min(128, 16 * 2^l)$ for any l. Then they increase the channels of each e^l by 1×1 convolution with ReLU to produce u^l. Multiple cascaded decoders are used to refine the output step by step.

4.4   ArtIst

This solution proposes a one-stage inpainting solution [3] based on a single UNet architecture consisting of 6 different kinds of layers (operations), where the main contribution is different convolution-based blocks. First, Equilibrium Convolution (EConv) is designed to reduce undesired artifacts in the output image. Second, Mask-wise Convolutions (MGConv) are deployed to reduce the parameters in gated convolutions [33]. Lastly, in order to deal with the large mask challenge, they create a Differentiate Convolution block. A schematic of the architecture is depicted in Fig. 11.

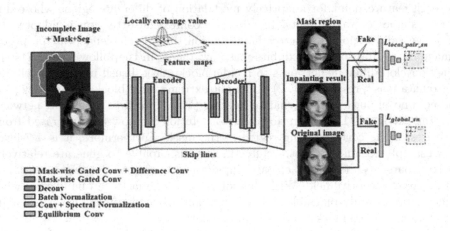

Fig. 11. Overall architecture of the ArtIst approach.

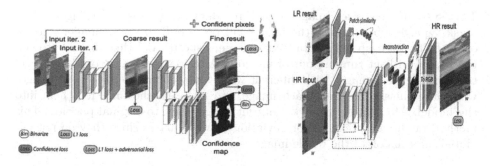

Fig. 12. Overview of DLUT method.

4.5 DLUT

This method is mainly based on the inpainting system proposed by Zeng *et al.* [34]. It is an iterative inpainting model with a guided upsampling module as shown in Fig. 12. Due to the memory limitation, for high-resolution images whose the long side is greater than a threshold, they execute the inpainting system of Zeng *et al.* [34] on 2× downsampled input and then use an external super-resolution model [1][1] to get the inpainted images of the original size.

4.6 AI-Inpainting

The solution is based on Edge-Connect [20], which is mainly focused on small size images. The entire network consists of two sub-modules: an edge part and an in-painting part (see Fig. 13). The edge module uses the masked image to generate the edge of the entire image, and the edge together with the masked image are fed into the inpainting module in order to generate the final result.

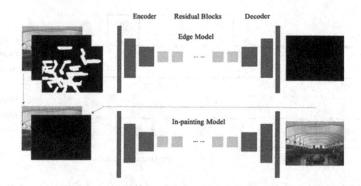

Fig. 13. Overview of AiriaBeijing method. The first module predicts semantic edges, the second uses these edges to estimate the results (zoom-in for better details).

---

[1] https://github.com/tensorlayer/srgan.git.

This system categorizes images into three different groups according to their mask type. For box masks, the image will be resized to three smaller sizes in order to be filled up with details at different aspects, and thus, be able to run the model without running out of memory. After resizing back to original size, they merge three images with different weight into one image. For large images with other masks, they cut each image into many patches and fed them into the model. After all, they put the output images back to original position. This method might cause some color deviation between masks since they do not use global information of the whole image.

4.7   qwq

The proposed solution adopts a AFN network [30] as generator, and a Markovian Discriminator [18] to guide the inpainting process. As shown in Fig. 14, the generator consists of several fractally stacked Attentive Fractal Blocks, which are constructed via progressive feature fusion and channel-wise attention guidance. Shortcuts and residual connections at different scales effectively resolve the vanishing gradients and help the network to learn more key features. The progressive fusion of intermediate features lets the network handle rich information. The discriminator is constructed via stacking several convolution and leaky ReLU layers. The output of the discriminator is designed to be a one-channel confidence map, which penalizes the masked area.

4.8   CVIP Inpainting Team

Following the work of Yu *et al.* [32], this team proposes a model consisting of a two-stage system, namely a coarse network, and a refinement network. Figure 15 shows the proposed solution. In addition to a regular branch, the coarse network uses an attention branch with a novel attention module namely the Global

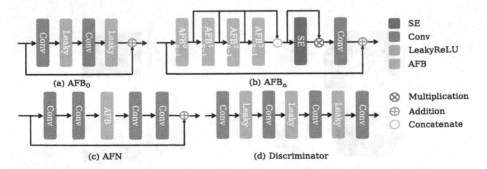

Fig. 14. Architecture of the qwq proposed framework. (a) shows the structure of the basic block AFB_0. (b) shows the hierarchical architecture of AFB_n, where $n \in [1, r]$ is the recursion level of the block. (c) illustrates the structure of AFN, which consists of encoding layers, an AFB_r, and decoding layers from left to right. (d) shows the structure of our discriminator.

Spatial-Channel Attention (GSCA) module, which can capture the structural consistency by calculating global correlation among both spatial and channel features at the global level. For the refinement network, in addition to GSCA, they adopt a recurrent residual attention U-net (RR2U) [2] architecture with major modifications in the architectural level. The recurrent residual attention consists of a multi-stage GRUs [6] that computes the inter-layer feature dependencies.

4.9   DeepInpaintingT1

The proposed model [17] consists of two generators and two discriminators. The overall proposed architecture is displayed in Fig. 16. The first coarse generator G_1 at Coarse Reconstruction Stage (the top left corner) and the second refinement generator G_2 at the Refinement Stage (bottom) constitute the Deep Generative Inpainting Network (DeepGIN) which is used in both training and testing. The two discriminators D_1 and D_2 located within Conditional Multi-Scale Discriminators area (the top right corner) are only used in training as an auxiliary network for generative adversarial training. The generator G_1 is trained to roughly reconstruct the missing regions and gives $\mathbf{I}_{coarse}$. The generator G_2 is trained to exquisitely decorate the coarse prediction with details and textures, and eventually forms the completed image $\mathbf{I}_{out}$. Three main ideas are proposed to accomplish the task of inpainting: i) Spatial Pyramid Dilation ResNet blocks (yellow and green blocks) with various dilation rates to enlarge the receptive fields such that information given by distant spatial locations can be used for both reconstruction and refinement; ii) Multi-Scale Self Attention (orange blocks) to enhance the coherency of the completed image by attending on the self-similarity of the image itself at three different scales;

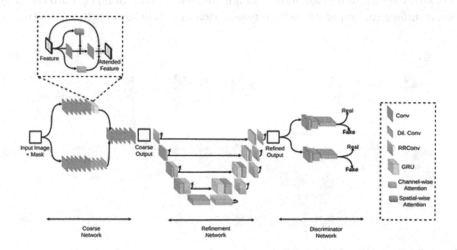

Fig. 15. Overall architecture of the CVIP approach. The model has two stages, namely a coarse network and a refinement network.

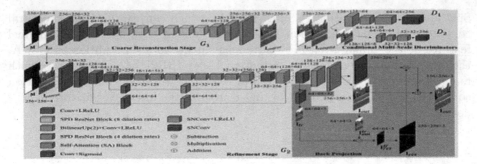

Fig. 16. Overview of DeepInpaintingT1 for extreme image inpainting.

iii) Back Projection strategy (the bottom right shaded area) to encourage better alignment of the generated patterns and the reference ground truth. For the two discriminators (the top right corner), they operate at two input scales, 256×256 and 128×128 respectively, to encourage better details and textures of the locally generated patterns at different scales.

4.10   IPCV_IITM

Team IPCV_IITM proposes a method based on Contextual Residual Aggregation (CRA) network [31]. Although recent deep learning-based in-painting methods are more effective than classic approaches, however, due to memory limitations they can only handle low-resolution inputs, typically smaller than 1K. Meanwhile, the resolution of photos captured with mobile devices increases up to 8K. Naive up-sampling of the low-resolution inpainted result can merely yield a large yet blurry result. Whereas, adding a high-frequency residual image onto the large blurry image can generate a sharp result, rich in details and textures. Motivated

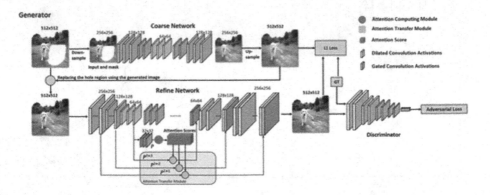

Fig. 17. Overview of IPCV_IITM method. Two models run in parallel to generate results that is evaluated using a discriminator module.

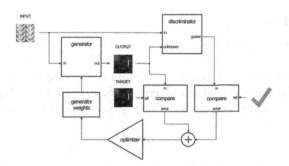

Fig. 18. Overview of MultiCog.

by this, CRA mechanism is employed that can produce high-frequency residuals for missing contents by weighted aggregating residuals from contextual patches, thus only requiring a low-resolution prediction from the network. Figure 17 shows the network design proposed by this team. Since convolutional layers of the neural network only need to operate on low-resolution inputs and outputs, the cost of memory and computing power is thus well suppressed.

4.11 MultiCog

MultiCog uses a Pix2Pix Generative Adversarial Network (GAN) as its core [15]. The main idea here is selecting the two domains as unpainted images and painted images, where the learned mapping function is unpainted to painted. See schematic in Fig. 18.

Acknowledgements. We thank the AIM 2020 sponsors: Huawei, MediaTek, Qualcomm AI Research, NVIDIA, Google and Computer Vision Lab/ETH Zürich.

Appendix A: Teams and affiliations

AIM2020 organizers

Members: Evangelos Ntavelis[1,2] (entavelis@ethz.ch), Siavash Bigdeli[2] (siavash.bigdeli@csem.ch), Andrés Romero[1] (roandres@ethz.ch), Radu Timofte[1] (radu.timofte@vision.ee.ethz.ch). **Affiliations**: [1]Computer Vision Lab, ETH Zürich. [2]CSEM.

Rainbow

Title: Image fine-grained inpainting.
Members: Zheng Hui, Xiumei Wang, Xinbo Gao.
Affiliations: School of Electronic Engineering, Xidian University.

Yonsei-MVPLab

Title: Image Inpainting based on Edge and Frequency Guided Recurrent Convolutions.
Members: Chajin Shin, Taeoh Kim, Hanbin Son, Sangyoun Lee.
Affiliations: Image and Video Pattern Recognition Lab., School of Electrical and Electronic Engineering, Yonsei University, Seoul, South Korea.

BossGao

Title: Image Inpainting With Mask Awareness
Members: Chao Li, Fu Li, Dongliang He, Shilei Wen, Errui Ding
Affiliations: Department of Computer Vision (VIS), Baidu Inc.

ArtIst

Title: Fast Light-Weight Network for Image Inpainting
Members: Mengmeng Bai, Shuchen Li
Affiliations: Samsung R&D Institute China-Beijing (SRC-Beijing)

DLUT

Title: Iterative Confidence Feedback and Guided Upsampling for filling large holes and inpainting high-resolution images
Members: Yu Zeng[1], Zhe Lin[2], Jimei Yang[2], Jianming Zhang[2], Eli Shechtman[2], Huchuan Lu[1]
Affiliations: [1]Dalian University of Technology, [2]Adobe

AI-Inpainting Group

Title: MSEM: Multi-Scale Semantic-Edge Merged Model for Image Inpainting
Members: Weijian Zeng, Haopeng Ni, Yiyang Cai, Chenghua Li
Affiliations: Rensselaer Polytechnic Institute

qwq

Title: Markovian Discriminator guided Attentive Fractal Network
Members: Dejia Xu, Haoning Wu, Yu Han
Affiliations: Peking University

CVIP Inpainting Team

Title: Global Spatial-Channel Attention and Inter-layer GRU-based Image Inpainting
Members: Uddin S. M. Nadim, Hae Woong Jang, Soikat Hasan Ahmed, Jungmin Yoon, and Yong Ju Jung
Affiliations: Computer Vision and Image Processing (CVIP) Lab, Gachon University.

DeepInpaintingT1

Title: Deep Generative Inpainting Network for Extreme Image Inpainting
Members: Chu-Tak Li, Zhi-Song Liu, Li-Wen Wang, Wan-Chi Siu, Daniel P.K. Lun
Affiliations: Centre for Multimedia Signal Processing, Department of Electronic and Information Engineering, The Hong Kong Polytechnic University, Hong Kong

IPCV IITM

Title: Contextual Residual Aggregation Network
Members: Maitreya Suin, Kuldeep Purohit, A. N. Rajagopalan
Affiliations: Indian Institute of Technology Madras, India

MultiCog

Title: Pix2Pix for Image Inpainting
Members: Pratik Narang[1], Murari Mandal[2], Pranjal Singh Chauhan[1]
Affiliations: [1]BITS Pilani, [2]MNIT Jaipur

References

1. A tensorflow implementation of SRGAN. https://github.com/tensorlayer/srgan.git
2. Alom, M.Z., Hasan, M., Yakopcic, C., Taha, T.M., Asari, V.K.: Recurrent residual convolutional neural network based on U-Net (R2U-Net) for medical image segmentation. arXiv preprint arXiv:1802.06955 (2018)
3. Bai, M., Li, S., Fan, J., Zhou, C., Zuo, L., Na, J., Jeong, M.: Fast light-weight network for extreme image inpainting challenge. In: Bartoli, A., Fusiello, A. (eds.) ECCV 2020 Workshops. LNCS, vol. 12537, pp.742–757 (2020)
4. Bau, D., et al.: Semantic photo manipulation with a generative image prior. ACM Trans. Graph. (Proc. ACM SIGGRAPH) **38**(4), 1–11 (2019)
5. Caesar, H., Uijlings, J., Ferrari, V.: Coco-stuff: thing and stuff classes in context. In: CVPR (2018). https://arxiv.org/abs/1612.03716
6. Cho, K., et al.: Learning phrase representations using RNN encoder-decoder for statistical machine translation. arXiv preprint arXiv:1406.1078 (2014)
7. El Helou, M., Zhou, R., Süsstrunk, S., Timofte, R., et al.: AIM 2020: scene relighting and illumination estimation challenge. In: Bartoli, A., Fusiello, A. (eds.) ECCV 2020 Workshops. LNCS, vol. 12537, pp. 499–518 (2020)
8. Fritsche, M., Gu, S., Timofte, R.: Frequency separation for real-world super-resolution. In: 2019 IEEE/CVF International Conference on Computer Vision Workshop (ICCVW), pp. 3599–3608. IEEE (2019)
9. Fuoli, D., Huang, Z., Gu, S., Timofte, R., et al.: AIM 2020 challenge on video extreme super-resolution: methods and results. In: European Conference on Computer Vision Workshops (2020)
10. Goodfellow, I., et al.: Generative adversarial nets. In: Advances in Neural Information Processing Systems, pp. 2672–2680 (2014)

11. Hong, S., Yan, X., Huang, T.E., Lee, H.: Learning hierarchical semantic image manipulation through structured representations. In: Advances in Neural Information Processing Systems, pp. 2713–2723 (2018)
12. Hui, Z., Li, J., Wang, X., Gao, X.: Image fine-grained inpainting. arXiv preprint arXiv:2002.02609 (2020)
13. Ignatov, A., Timofte, R., et al.: AIM 2020 challenge on learned image signal processing pipeline. In: Bartoli, A., Fusiello, A. (eds.) ECCV 2020 Workshops. LNCS, vol. 12537, pp. 152–170 (2020)
14. Ignatov, A., Timofte, R., et al.: AIM 2020 challenge on rendering realistic bokeh. In: Bartoli, A., Fusiello, A. (eds.) ECCV 2020 Workshops. LNCS, vol. 12537, pp. 213–228 (2020)
15. Isola, P., Zhu, J.Y., Zhou, T., Efros, A.A.: Image-to-image translation with conditional adversarial networks (2016)
16. Johnson, J., Alahi, A., Fei-Fei, L.: Perceptual losses for real-time style transfer and super-resolution. In: Leibe, B., Matas, J., Sebe, N., Welling, M. (eds.) ECCV 2016. LNCS, vol. 9906, pp. 694–711. Springer, Cham (2016). https://doi.org/10.1007/978-3-319-46475-6_43
17. Li, C.T., Siu, W.C., Liu, Z.S., Wang, L.W., Lun, D.P.K.: DeepGIN: deep generative inpainting network for extreme image inpainting. In: European Conference on Computer Vision Workshops (2020)
18. Li, C., Wand, M.: Precomputed real-time texture synthesis with Markovian generative adversarial networks. In: Leibe, B., Matas, J., Sebe, N., Welling, M. (eds.) ECCV 2016. LNCS, vol. 9907, pp. 702–716. Springer, Cham (2016). https://doi.org/10.1007/978-3-319-46487-9_43
19. Lim, J.H., Ye, J.C.: Geometric GAN. arXiv preprint arXiv:1705.02894 (2017)
20. Nazeri, K., Ng, E., Joseph, T., Qureshi, F., Ebrahimi, M.: EdgeConnect: structure guided image inpainting using edge prediction. In: The IEEE International Conference on Computer Vision (ICCV) Workshops, October 2019
21. Nazeri, K., Ng, E., Joseph, T., Qureshi, F.Z., Ebrahimi, M.: EdgeConnect: generative image inpainting with adversarial edge learning. arXiv preprint arXiv:1901.00212 (2019)
22. Ntavelis, E., Romero, A., Kastanis, I., Van Gool, L., Timofte, R.: Sesame: semantic editing of scenes by adding, manipulating or erasing objects. In: Proceedings of the European Conference on Computer Vision (ECCV) (2020)
23. Ntavelis, E., Romero, A., Bigdeli, S.A., Timofte, R., et al.: AIM 2020 challenge on image extreme inpainting. In: Bartoli, A., Fusiello, A. (eds.) ECCV 2020 Workshops. LNCS, vol. 12537, pp. 716–741 (2020)
24. Park, T., Liu, M.Y., Wang, T.C., Zhu, J.Y.: Semantic image synthesis with spatially-adaptive normalization. In: CVPR, pp. 2337–2346 (2019)
25. Shaker, N., Liapis, A., Togelius, J., Lopes, R., Bidarra, R.: Constructive generation methods for dungeons and levels. Procedural Content Generation in Games. CSCS, pp. 31–55. Springer, Cham (2016). https://doi.org/10.1007/978-3-319-42716-4_3
26. Son, S., Lee, J., Nah, S., Timofte, R., Lee, K.M., et al.: AIM 2020 challenge on video temporal super-resolution. In: European Conference on Computer Vision Workshops (2020)
27. Wang, X., et al.: ESRGAN: enhanced super-resolution generative adversarial networks. In: Leal-Taixé, L., Roth, S. (eds.) ECCV 2018. LNCS, vol. 11133, pp. 63–79. Springer, Cham (2019). https://doi.org/10.1007/978-3-030-11021-5_5
28. Wei, P., Lu, H., Timofte, R., Lin, L., Zuo, W., et al.: AIM 2020 challenge on real image super-resolution : methods and results. In: Bartoli, A., Fusiello, A. (eds.) ECCV 2020 Workshops. LNCS, vol. 12537, pp. 392–422 (2020)

29. Xiangli, Y., Deng, Y., Dai, B., Loy, C.C., Lin, D.: Real or not real, that is the question. In: ICLR (2020)
30. Xu, D., Chu, Y., Sun, Q.: Moire pattern removal via attentive fractal network. In: The IEEE/CVF Conference on Computer Vision and Pattern Recognition (CVPR) Workshops, June 2020
31. Yi, Z., Tang, Q., Azizi, S., Jang, D., Xu, Z.: Contextual residual aggregation for ultra high-resolution image inpainting. In: Proceedings of the IEEE/CVF Conference on Computer Vision and Pattern Recognition, pp. 7508–7517 (2020)
32. Yu, J., Lin, Z., Yang, J., Shen, X., Lu, X., Huang, T.S.: Generative image inpainting with contextual attention. In: Proceedings of the IEEE Conference on Computer Vision and Pattern Recognition, pp. 5505–5514 (2018)
33. Yu, J., Lin, Z., Yang, J., Shen, X., Lu, X., Huang, T.S.: Free-form image inpainting with gated convolution. In: Proceedings of the IEEE International Conference on Computer Vision, pp. 4471–4480 (2019)
34. Zeng, Y., Lin, Z., Yang, J., Zhang, J., Shechtman, E., Lu, H.: High-resolution image inpainting with iterative confidence feedback and guided upsampling. In: European Conference on Computer Vision. Springer (2020)
35. Zhang, K., Danelljan, M., Li, Y., Timofte, R., et al.: AIM 2020 challenge on efficient super-resolution: Methods and results. In: Bartoli, A., Fusiello, A. (eds.) ECCV 2020 Workshops. LNCS, vol. 12537, pp. 5–40 (2020)
36. Zhou, B., Lapedriza, A., Khosla, A., Oliva, A., Torralba, A.: Places: a 10 million image database for scene recognition. IEEE Trans. Pattern Anal. Mach. Intell. 40(6), 1452–1464 (2017)
37. Zhou, B., Zhao, H., Puig, X., Fidler, S., Barriuso, A., Torralba, A.: Scene parsing through ade20k dataset. In: Proceedings of the IEEE Conference on Computer Vision and Pattern Recognition, pp. 633–641 (2017)

Fast Light-Weight Network for Extreme Image Inpainting Challenge

Mengmeng Bai[1]([✉])[iD], Shuchen Li[1][iD], Jianhua Fan[1][iD], Chenchen Zhou[1][iD], Li Zuo[1][iD], Jaekeun Na[2][iD], and MoonSik Jeong[2][iD]

[1] Samsung Research China - Beijing (SRC-B), Beijing, China
{mengmeng.bai,shuchen.li,jianhua.fan,chen.zhou,li.zuo}@samsung.com
[2] Samsung Electronics - Multimedia Advanced Lab, Suwon, Korea
{worms.na,moonsik.jeong}@samsung.com

Abstract. Image inpainting has a wide range of applications. However, to this challenge existing inpainting models that usually have a large model size can hardly run fast, as memory and supported operations are much limited. In this paper, we propose a novel light-weight inpainting model in which we design three novel operations named Equilibrium Conv Mask-wise Gated Conv, Difference Conv and define a new loss function based on SN-patchGAN. In specific, the incorporation of Equilibrium Conv and Mask-wise Gated Conv not only reduces the model size and improve the efficiency, but also keeps comparative performance. For Difference Conv, it is benefit to handle big mask problem. Moreover, our proposed loss results in a better performance in recovering images with rich textures. Experimental results demonstrate our model is 1.43× speeding up and reduces the size by 2.37× compared with the state-of-the-art model.

Keywords: Inpainting · Fast and light-weight model · Equilibrium convolution · Mask-wise Gated Convolution

1 Introduction

Image inpainting, filling missing pixels, can be applied to facial, removing unwanted objects and completing perspective transformation, etc. However, to extreme image inpainting challenge traditional methods, like Patch Match [2], always result in a weird image due to the insufficient use of semantic information. For CNN approaches, based on gated mechanism, previous researchers have proposed various special convolutions. For all we know Partial Conv [11] firstly applies user defined gated mechanism on inpainting task. Although it has greatly improved performance, the large model size, around 123 Mb, is definitely terrible. With their experience, the authors define fixed rule of gated mechanism

Electronic supplementary material The online version of this chapter (https://doi.org/10.1007/978-3-030-67070-2_44) contains supplementary material, which is available to authorized users.

© Springer Nature Switzerland AG 2020
A. Bartoli and A. Fusiello (Eds.): ECCV 2020 Workshops, LNCS 12537, pp. 742–757, 2020.
https://doi.org/10.1007/978-3-030-67070-2_44

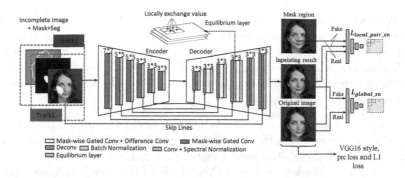

Fig. 1. The overall structure of our inpainting network. For AIM2020 Extreme Image Inpainting Challenge [18] Track1 we only input missing region image and mask. For track2 we add segmentation information.

for Partial Conv, hence it is hard to be designed very efficiently and requires a large number of trainable parameters to meet a good performance. Further, Gated Conv [26] uses a learning gated mechanism to replace fixed user defined one. Concretely, Gated Conv in each layer contains two branches, feature and mask map branch. In the output of each Gated Conv, it uses element-wise multiplication to achieve the soft gated mechanism. Essentially, this is an attentional filtering algorithm. Whereas, each channel mask map makes all previous feature maps as input data, which reduces efficiency. Since different feature maps focus on individual receptive field, if we want to weight calculation for one feature map, we should mainly use the mask map of same receptive field instead of all previous mask maps. Meanwhile, currently more solutions include Contextual Attention mechanism [25], e.g. HiFill [23]. It is benefit to reduce artifacts or blurry textures especially high-resolution images, because when model synthesizes the missing region it borrows contextual patches from known region to fill the hole. But it not only includes huge matrix multiplications, but also has to take a lot of GPU memory to accomplish this operation. Besides, HiFill is too much dependent on Contextual Attention mechanism, it will borrow some disharmonious patches to reconstruct image. Moreover, generally previous networks rely on interpolation method, e.g. nearest-neighbor and bilinear interpolation. Even these methods help reduce strange checkerboard or fish scale pattern of artifacts, they take longer to run compared with Deconvolution (Deconv). Nevertheless when the kernel size of Deconv is not divisible by stride, it has uneven overlap and put more of the metaphorical paint in some places than interpolation methods [15]. At the same time, different kinds of GAN losses are also designed in previous works. Actually GAN loss denotes the distance between original and inpainted dataset distribution, so if the ability of calculating this distance is too strong, like pix2pix pair GAN [5], it tends to make adversarial training more unstable. No matter what inpainting network generates, the results always are identified as fake by discriminator. On the contrary, if discriminator is lack of enough identified ability, Wasserstein GAN [1], global and local GANs [4] and SN-PatchGAN [26], it surely brings back ineffective GAN loss especial for small missing region, which contributes to blur texture or color difference problems. In this paper, aiming at acquiring a fast light-weight inpainting model, we have designed a novel framework which produces high quality restored images, contains fewer trainable parameters and floating point operations (FLOPs). In summary, we make the following contributions:

1. We propose an Equilibrium Convolution (EConv) to address strange checkerboard or fish-scale pattern of artifacts replacing complex interpolation upsampling, which makes our model faster than before.
2. We introduce a Mask-wise Gated Convolution (MGConv) to lighten the previous soft and learning gated mechanism while it keeps same performance, which contributes to our light-weight model size.
3. We design a Difference Convolution (DiffConv) to handle big mask problem.
4. We also present a local pair SN-PatchGAN to further improve effectiveness and enhance training stability.
5. We conduct excessive experiments to validate our design, including rich texture face image cases.

2   Related Work

2.1   Contextual Attention Mechanism

Contextual Attention mechanism utilizes high-level semantic known feature maps patches to reconstruct the missing region. In specific, there are two stages in Contextual Attention, matching and attending. Firstly, with image similarity algorithm it measures the best match for the feature patches of missing pixels from known features patches. In order to run with GPU, the author have to choice cosine similarity metric. However, there are many limitations for user defined image similarity algorithm. For example, even both of images are totally different from a human standpoint, the value of cosine similarity may be very high. Secondly, Contextual Attention reuses known feature maps patches as deconvolution filters to reconstruct missing regions. More recently, HiFill [23], improves it by introducing contextual residual aggregation. But HiFill is too depended on Contextual Attention, it also will borrow unnatural patches to recover image, which is similar with Patch Match [2]. Moreover, the main computational of Contextual Attention comes from attending stage, because there is a huge matrix multiplication. For example, if input data size is 512 * 512 * 3, the input size of this matrix multiplication will be (32, 32, 1024) and (32, 1024, 12288) when the patch size is extracted from image with 3 * 3 size and 1 * 1 stride. Even though we can use Deconv to improve its efficiency, it will cost a lot of GPU memory [25].

2.2   Gated Mechanism

Early CNN-based works only utilize a standard convolution to design inpainting networks. For example Context Encoders [19], Semantic Inpainting [22], Edge

Connect [17] and Globally and Locally Image Completion [4]. Amongst these approaches, they use a standard convolutional network over the corrupted image, using convolutional filter responses conditioned on both valid pixels as well as the substitute values in the masked holes (typically the mean value), which results in the limitation of inpainting performance. To improve performance, Partial Conv [11] makes use of a gated or reweighted mechanism, which allows network to condition output only on known image region. In detail, with a sharing binary mask image in every channel (missing region value is 0, the rest of value is 1), it makes sure output feature maps much depend on the known regions. Among of them, the number 1 indicates that the corresponding feature maps value of this position will be calculated, the 0 denotes that the network will not rely on the corresponding feature map value during convolution. But it is highly hand-crafted. Every channel sharing the same mask map and the rule of updated mask map is defined by user, which definitely limits the flexibility. Therefore, in order to meet a state-of-the-art performance, the trainable parameters of model must be increased, which results in a large model size 123 Mb around. Instead of hard-gating mechanism, Gated Conv [26] utilizes soft mask map automatically updated from data in which there are two convolution branches, namely the feature-extraction and mask-update branch. Gated Conv learns a dynamic feature selection mechanism for each channel and spatial location, while Partial Conv only shares one same mask with every channel. Thanks to this interesting gated mechanism, it not only increases the efficiency of extracting known region, but also reduces many trainable parameters. Nevertheless, Gated Conv contains redundant operations. Intuitively, each feature map should focus on different receptive field, and their corresponding mask map should be relatively independent. If Gated Conv takes all previous mask maps to calculate a new mask, it possibly input some useless mask maps. From this perspective there is also a disadvantage in Gated Conv.

2.3   GAN Loss

Previously, different GAN losses are also added in inpainting works. Without loss of generality, the original image data distribution $P_{original}$ admits a density and $P_{inpainted}$ is the distribution of parameterized density. Essentially GAN loss [9,12,14,16,20] denotes the distance between $P_{original}$ and $P_{inpainted}$. Generated network will asymptotically try to minimize GAN loss or distance. During this processing, if GAN model does not properly meet the requirements of inpainting task, it is impossible to get a good inpainting model. For example, pix2pix pair GAN [5] uses two original images as positive data and makes an original and inpainted image as negative data. Thus the distance of positive and negative data is easy to be calculated with discriminator. Only if the inpainting network generates the same original image, the distance can be minimized. But if we want to use inpainting model to achieve object removing task, this will be an unsuitable loss. To global and local GANs [4], it takes both an image and the missing region image as inputs, but the part of local GAN is merely designed for a rectangular mask with relatively large size, which is unsuitable for free-form mask. To Wasserstein GAN [1] and SN-PatchGAN [26], they just use an original image as positive images and an inpainted image as negative images, which reduces the ability of distance between inpainted data and original data. Such as if the missing region is small, they hardly feedbacks enough loss to inpainting network. In other words, for this case, the distance of original and inpainted data is too short, which means discriminator cannot verify which one is generated by inpainting network.

3   Proposed Method

In this section, we firstly describe our whole framework. Then we introduce EConv and MGConv in detail. Finally, the local pair SN-patchGAN and loss function also are presented.

3.1   Network Design

Our inpainting network is a one-stage U-net architecture designed with EConv, DiffConv and MGConv, as Fig. 1 shows. In encoding stage our inpainting network fully adopts MGConv and Batch Normalization. Besides MGConv and DiffConve in decoding stage, our model contains Deconvolution (Deconv), EConv and Convolution (Conv) as well. Although Deconv contributes to undesired fish-scale or checkerboard artifacts, mainly due to the uneven overlap problem, it requires fewer FLOPs than interpolation methods. Furthermore, our EConv can handle the problem, thus we select Deconv as the up-sampling operation. Moreover DiffConv is able to recover more large missing regions. Meanwhile, our model also concatenates output feature maps to the corresponding feature maps of down-sampling layers with skip links. Additionally, we use a local and global pair SN-PatchGAN to train network, which is not only benefit to stable training but also improves the performance on rich texture images.

3.2   Equilibrium Convolution and Artifacts

As Fig. 2 shows, when 3 * 3 kernel size is not divisible by stride 2, standard Deconv has uneven overlap problem, e.g. dark green and black points. Due to uneven overlap problem stemming from using Deconv as up-sampling method, the inpainting result tends to contain undesired artifacts, such as checkerboard or fish scale, especially in recovering structured texture images. Although early works have adopted to take interpolation methods, e.g. nearest-neighbor or bilinear resize method, as up-sampling method to handle the uneven overlap problem, they obviously require more FLOPs and make model size larger to keep the performance of large missing region. To design a fast inpainting network, we introduce a novel EConv, which can handle the uneven overlap problem and requires fewer FLOPs. Concretely, our EConv randomly exchanges each value of feature maps within every sliding window during the forward propagation

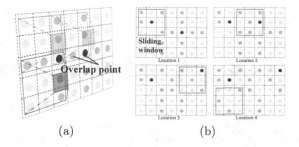

(a)   (b)

Fig. 2. The uneven overlap and EConv. (a) is the illustration of Deconv with stride 2 * 2 and kernel size 3 * 3. Dark green are double counting and black points are counted 4 times. (b) denotes the operations of our EConv. Among, dark green and black points are uneven overlap location in standard Deconv. Top-left of location 1 shows the position up-sampling locations after EConv in the first slid window. The rest of locations show that EConv operation exchanges values in other sliding window regions. (Color figure online)

of training, as Fig. 2 (b) shows. After many training iterations, the weights of EConv are learned from a local position-independent feature map, which reduces the impact of uneven overlap points considerably. In order to improve efficiency, we propose a simple way to implement EConv with a noise mask image. For each input feature map I_x, and noise mask image I_{noise}, we have:

$$EConv(I_x, I_{noise}) = pad_{w_x, h_x}(I_x^{i_1, j_1} \odot I_{noise} + I_x^{i_2, j_2} \odot (1 - I_{noise}))) \quad (1)$$

where $i_1 \in (0, w_x - a), j_1 \in (0, h_x - b), i_2 \in (a, w_x), j_2 \in (b, h_x), w_x$ and w_h are the width and height of I_x, I_{noise} width and height are $w_x - a$ and $h_x - b$. a and b equal to kernel size and both of them must be integers. e.g. if kernel size is 3, the number of arguments is available as a=1 and b=2. I_{noise} is randomly generated, which only contains 0 or 1. $\odot$ denotes the element wise multiplication. $pad_{w_x, h_x}()$ is to implicitly pad the input to the size of (w_x, h_x) as output. Through the Eq. 1, we can easily exchange every value in feature maps locally and randomly. Since this implementation only includes element-wise multiplication, addition and pad operations, it does not increase many computational costs.

3.3 Mask-Wise Gated Convolution

As we mentioned before, the previous methods of gated mechanism, Partial Conv [11] and Gated Conv [26], contain unreasonable or redundant operations. Partial Conv classifies all spatial locations to be either valid or invalid accordingly, because it uses hard-gating mask updated with fixed rules. To remedy the ability of model, it requires a wider and deeper network. Since mask feature maps are regarded as a weight coefficient to determine whether the value of feature maps will be considered or not. Gated Conv resorts to a soft mask updating rule that learning from data, which partly reduces the model size. However it uses all previous feature maps to update every mask map, which contributes to higher

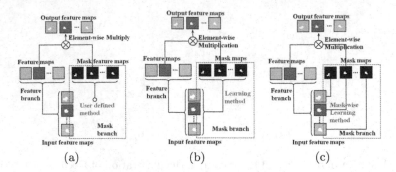

Fig. 3. Gated mechanism Convolution layers. (a) is Partial Conv, (b) is Gated Conv and (c) is our MGConv. The feature branch of MGConv is the same to Gated Conv, and its activation function can be one of normal activations, e.g. ReLU, ELU and LeakyReLU. In the mask branch of MGConv, each channel mask image only requires previous corresponding feature map.

latency and larger model size. Therefore, to lighten trainable parameters, we introduce a novel MGConv, as Fig. 3 shows. The main idea is that each mask image should pay more attention on the feature map of same receptive field rather than all previous feature maps. Further, based on Gated Conv we design MGConv whose parameters are fewer and computational cost less than before.

Specifically, MGConv is composed of two branches: a feature and mask branch. The feature branch is the same as Gated Conv, whereas the mask branch containing pipeline generates a new mask map with the corresponding channel feature map as Fig. 3(c) shows. Thus, each mask map is more concerned about the corresponding previous feature map. In mask branch, we take two kinds of receptive field convolutional kernels to generate two groups of mask feature maps and then combine them to output mask maps. Finally, we use the element-wise multiplication to generate output feature maps.

3.4 Difference Convolution

For big mask problem, if network can not obtain a large receptive field, it is hard to recover a realistic-looking results. Even Dilated Conv [24] can help network improve the performance about big mask with increasing receptive field, it is not supported by every real world device unfortunately. Therefore, we design DiffConv to remedy it. Based on our MGConv, we modify the feature branch. Firstly we use mini U-net structure network to achieve down and up sample, which can increase receptive field like Dilated Conv. Moreover, if model pays more attention on mask region during Decoder stage, it will be benefit to good performance. So we use Element-wise Sub operation to find the mask region difference between input data and the feature maps outputs from mini U-net, and then apply gated mechanism for input data, which is as Fig. 4.

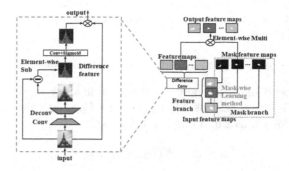

Fig. 4. Difference Convolution. For mini U-net, there two Conv layers in Encoder. First layer kernel size is as Fig. 1 shows. Second is always 3 * 3 with stride 2 * 2. In Decoder, we only use 4 * 4 kernel size Decov to up sample. Conv+sigmoid operation means 3 * 3 kernel size Conv with sigmoid activation.

3.5   Local Pair and Global SN-patchGAN

To better calculate the distance between original image data distribution $P_{original}$ and the distribution $P_{inpainted}$ of inpainting network, we present a local pair SN-patchGAN. Early, SN-patchGAN [26] only requires a complete image as input without the location information of missing region. Thus it likely cannot feedback enough loss especially for small missing region. On the side, pix2pix pair GAN [5] takes a pair data as input, which results that it possesses a much strong ability to distinguish the generated image no matter how the generator updates its weights. Thus we take the pair data of missing region and full image as input to measure quality of the generated image. Among we use a binary mask image to obtain the data of missing region. Finally we apply the hinge loss as an objective function to update discriminator, which is as 2 shows.

$$L_{D\_pair\_SN} = E[max(0, 1 - D_{pair}(I_{gt}, I_m)) + max(0, 1 + D_{pair}(I_o, I_m))] \quad (2)$$

where I_{gt} is the target image, I_m is the target image of mask region, and I_o is the output image of inpainting network. $D_{pair}()$ is the local pair SN-patchGAN. $max()$ denotes the maximization operation. Besides, similar to SN-patchGAN, we also use a global SN-patchGAN to get the global consistent loss of completion image. We take hinge loss to train the global SN-patchGAN too. The objective is expressed as Eq. 3:

$$L_{D\_global\_SN} = E\left(max(0, 1 - D_{global}(I_{gt})) + max(0, 1 + D_{global}(I_{comple}))\right) \quad (3)$$

where, $D_{global}()$ is the global SN-patchGAN, I_{comple} is the complement image.

3.6   Loss Function

For our network, besides the local pair and global SN-patchGAN losses, we also use perceptual style and L1 per-pixel loss which were introduced in Partial

Convolution [11] as total losses to train our inpainting network. The total loss function is as 4 shows.

$$L_{total} = \lambda_1 L_{prc} + \lambda_2 L_{style} + \lambda_3 L_{per\_pixel} + \lambda_4 L_{global} + \lambda_5 L_{pair} \qquad (4)$$

where, L_{prc} and L_{style} are perceptual and style loss come from VGG 16 [21], and $L_{per-pixel}$ is per-pixel loss [6]. L_{global} and L_{pair} are global and local pair SN-patchGAN losses, as Eq. 5 and Eq. 6 shows:

$$L_{global} = E(D_G(I_{output})) + 1 \qquad (5)$$

$$L_{pair} = E(D_{pair}(I_{output}, I_{gt\_mask\_region})) + 1 \qquad (6)$$

4   Experiments

In this section we fully investigate our fast and light-weight inpainting network. We conduct our experiments on Places2 [27], CelebA HQ [7] and FFHQ [8], and train our model with tensorflow v1.8, CUDNN v7.0, CUDA v9.0. All models run on single NVIDIA(R) GTX-1080Ti 12G GPU and Intel(R) Core(TM) i7-7700k CPU @ 4.20 GHz.

Algorithm 1. Equilibrium Convolution

Input:
F_{in}: Input feature maps that are out from Deconv. The shape is(n, h, w, c)
I_{noise}: Input random mask image. The number range is from 0 to 1
Output:
F_{out}: Output feature maps
Begin Algorithm
1:   $F_1 \leftarrow$ crop $F_{in}[:,a:,b:,:]$, $F_2 \leftarrow$ crop $F_{in}[:,:h\text{-}a,:w\text{-}a,:]$
2:   $I_{noise1} \leftarrow$ crop $I_{noise}[:,a:,b:,:]$, $I_{noise2} \leftarrow 1 - I_{noise1}$
3:   $F_3 \leftarrow F_1{}^*I_{noise1} + F_2{}^*I_{noise2}$
4:   $F_{out} \leftarrow$ pad F_3 to original (n,h,w,c) shape with reflection
End

Training Mask. We utilize the irregular mask provided by Edge Connect [17]. This mask image includes lines, circles and ellipses. The width of lines, the radius of circles and the shape of ellipses are randomly generated.

Training Procedure. The training of inpainting network is end to end. We use $\lambda_1 = 0.03$, $\lambda_2 = 60$, $\lambda_3 = 5$, $\lambda_4 = 0.8$, $\lambda_5 = 0.8$ and VGG-16 *pool1*, *pool2* and *pool3* layers for L_{prc} and L_{style} losses. We adopt Adam [10] optimizer with $\beta_1 = 0.5$ and $\beta_2 = 0.9$ to train our model. The learning rate is 0.0001 and batch size is 6. In each training cycle, we train two steps for the generator and one step for discriminators repeatedly.

Equilibrium Convolution Layer. Our model has two EConv before the last up-sampling layer. The first EConv layer has $a = 2$, $b = 1$, the second $a = 0$, $b = 1$ and a padding operation is arranged to preserve the same output size. To assist with reproducibility we provide the detailed experimental settings, which is as Algorithm 1 shows.

4.1   Quantitative Results

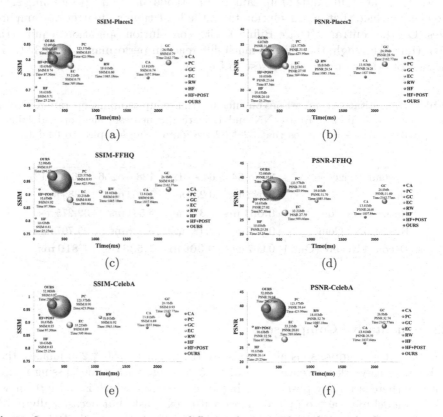

(a)   (b)

(c)   (d)

(e)   (f)

Fig. 5. Quantitative comparison on different dataset. The volume of sphere represents model size. The closer to top-left corner, the faster and better model is.

Fairly, we train all models with 256 * 256, test them with 512 * 512 and use Edge Connect [17] to generate mask. As Fig. 5 shows, each test set contains 1000 images which are randomly selected from valuation set. Both of CA and GC also include a deep coarse-to-fine network, which is benefit to their model size. And GC uses Gated Conv to replace the standard convolution of CA, which further increases FLOPs and model size. PC is designed with user defined gated convolution, so it requires more trainable parameters to achieve a stable result. EC includes ResNet blocks [3] and two stages, hence there are many FLOPs. RW [13] contains complex Region-wise layer, which means more FLOPs. HF [23] is similar to CA and GC, but it prunes the coarse-to-fine network. So the model is light-weight comparing with before. Significantly, in order to improve the model performance on rich texture image, it has to add post processing, named HF+POST. Thus, this total solution takes more running time than HF. Comparing to the best performance PC model, our model is not only 2.37 times smaller, but also 1.43 times faster.

Furthermore, we also compare different up-sampling methods. As Table 1 shows, there are four kinds of up-sampling methods and four up-sampling sizes. We can conclude that deconvolution takes the least time no matter up-sampling sizes. On the contrary, Resize Bilinear with convolution operation requires the most time. Although, there is not much difference in performance from 32 to 64, the rest of others ours is the closest to Deconv.

Table 1. Quantitative comparisons on inference time of up-sampling operation. Deconv and Conv are standard. Resize NN and BN are the nearest-neighbor and bilinear interpolation. $32 \rightarrow 64$ means that 32 * 32 size data is up-sampled to 64 * 64, and so on.

Upsample size	$32 \rightarrow 64$	$64 \rightarrow 128$	$128 \rightarrow 256$	$256 \rightarrow 512$
Deconv	0.042 ms	0.239 ms	1.204 ms	6.289 ms
Resize NN+Conv	**0.061 ms**	2.372 ms	6.541 ms	32.275 ms
Resize BN+Conv	0.075 ms	2.421 ms	6.528 ms	25.707 ms
Deconv+EConv (Ours)	0.067 ms	**0.306 ms**	**1.523 ms**	**7.810 ms**

4.2 Qualitative Comparisons

On qualitative comparisons all models are trained with 256 * 256 images, then each entire network inferences on a 512 * 512 image with same missing region. Notably there is no any post processing for our results, which is as Fig. 6 shows. CA [1] model have a good performance with box mask, but occasionally it will generate artifacts inside the missing region with free-form mask. PC [2] model is the best one, however its model size is too large. GC [3] is trained with SN-patchGAN, which contributes to blurry problem. EC [26] contains two stages, so if there is not a right predict edge result in first stage, it is hard to generate a realistic-looking result. RW [27] only concerns big missing region problem through the region-wise methods, so the model is becoming less sensitive about mask boundary resulting in a sharp. HF+ [4] pay more attention to learn how borrow known image patches to recover missing region, thus it will generate the

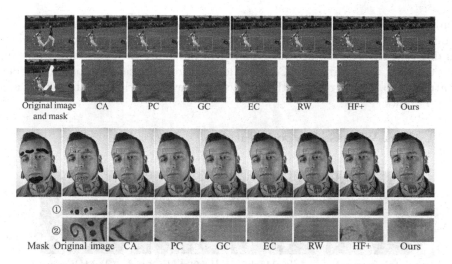

Original image   CA   PC   GC   EC   RW   HF+   Ours
and mask

① ②

Mask Original image   CA   PC   GC   EC   RW   HF+   Ours

Fig. 6. Qualitative result.

unreasonable result that is similar to Patch Match [2]. And when the missing region is large it cannot get enough known patches to reconstruct a highly quality image.

5   Ablation Study

5.1   Equilibrium Convolution

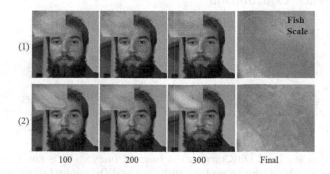

Fig. 7. Ablation study of EConv. (1) is the result with Deconv, (2) is our EConv result. Each column represents different iterations from 100 to 10000.

To solve artifacts that come from uneven overlap problem, we propose EConv layer in term of exchange local feature maps values. Here we provide ablation experiments. We use same inpainting network structure, loss function, datasets and optimization method to train comparative models. If we only take deconvolution as up-sampling methods, the result will appear the uneven overlap problem in different iterations. Since our EConv will randomly exchange local value during training, the weights of EConv are learned from a local position-independent feature map, which reduces the impact of uneven overlap points, which is as Fig. 7 shows.

5.2   Mask-Wise Gated Convolution

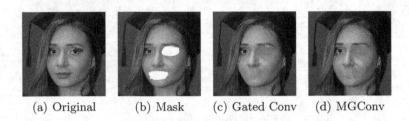

(a) Original   (b) Mask   (c) Gated Conv   (d) MGConv

Fig. 8. Ablation study of MGConv. Test image size is 256 * 256. In order to display more details, we only train the both model within skin region. So the model will only generate skin.

Since MGConv is from Gated Conv [26], we use our MGConv to replace Gated Conv in DeepFillv2 [26] model, than we follow DeepFillv2 step to train the model with Places2 dataset. The new model size reduces to 23.65Mb from original DeepFillv2 26.9 Mb, and the trainable parameters is from 10.5M to 9.5M. As Fig. 8 shows, our MGConv can keep same performance.

5.3   Difference Convolution

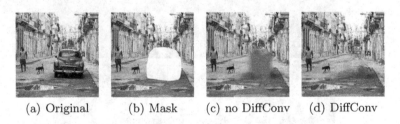

(a) Original   (b) Mask   (c) no DiffConv   (d) DiffConv

Fig. 9. Ablation study of DiffConv. (a) is original image, (b) is the mask, (c) is the model that we use MGConv to replace DiffConv and (b) is our full model

To solve big mask problem, we design DiffConv using mini U-net. To display the DiffConv performance, we replace DiffConv with our MGConv, then we train this model with same hyper-parameters, dataset and so on. Finally, we input same 512 * 512 image with big missing region to obtain each result. The comparison result is as Fig. 9 shows.

5.4   Local Pair SN-patchGAN

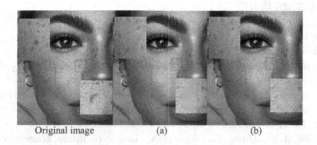

Original image   (a)   (b)

Fig. 10. Ablation study of local pair SN-patchGAN. (a) is the result without local pair SN-patch GAN loss. (b) comes from the model which is trained with full loss.

Our local pair SN-patchGAN takes a pair of images as input, which can offer more missing region loss especially for the small missing region. Meanwhile, unlike the SN-patchGAN [26] which only distinguishes whether real or fake with the local region of the generated image, our method leads to significant results. Because our method not only allows the inpainting network to generate real image, but also gives it a guidance to produce the real target image. We also give ablation experiments with our local pair SN-patchGAN, as Fig. 10 shows. Due to local pair SN-patchGAN, our model generates much richer texture.

6   Conclusions

We have designed a novel light-weight inpainting network, which boosts extreme image inpainting with low latency and light weight consistently. Our model is based on an end-to-end trainable U-net structure. The novel EConv, DiffConv and MGConv are proposed to fast solve uneven overlap, big mask problem and further lighten gated mechanism. The local pair SN-patchGAN improves performance about rich texture images. The analyses quantitatively and qualitatively demonstrate that our model get not only best performance but also requires less runtime. At the same time, we also provide ablation comparison on EConv, MGConv, DiffConv and local pair SN-patchGAN, which shows EConv effectively handles for the artifacts of standard deconvolution uneven overlap problem, DiffConv addresses big mask problem, MGConv keeps same performance with less model size and local pair SN-patchGAN contributes to produce much better texture. In the near future, we will continue to explore its potential to handle various high-resolution images and scenes in the wild.

References

1. Arjovsky, M., Chintala, S., Bottou, L.: Wasserstein GAN. arXiv preprint arXiv:1701.07875 (2017)
2. Darabi, S., Shechtman, E., Barnes, C., Goldman, D.B., Sen, P.: Image melding: combining inconsistent images using patch-based synthesis. ACM Trans. Graph. (TOG) **31**(4), 1–10 (2012)
3. He, K., Zhang, X., Ren, S., Sun, J.: Identity mappings in deep residual networks. In: Leibe, B., Matas, J., Sebe, N., Welling, M. (eds.) ECCV 2016. LNCS, vol. 9908, pp. 630–645. Springer, Cham (2016). https://doi.org/10.1007/978-3-319-46493-0_38
4. Iizuka, S., Simo-Serra, E., Ishikawa, H.: Globally and locally consistent image completion. ACM Trans. Graph. (ToG) **36**(4), 1–14 (2017)
5. Isola, P., Zhu, J.Y., Zhou, T., Efros, A.A.: Image-to-image translation with conditional adversarial networks. In: Proceedings of the IEEE Conference on Computer Vision and Pattern Recognition, pp. 1125–1134 (2017)
6. Jo, Y., Park, J.: SC-FEGAN: face editing generative adversarial network with user's sketch and color. In: Proceedings of the IEEE International Conference on Computer Vision, pp. 1745–1753 (2019)
7. Karras, T., Aila, T., Laine, S., Lehtinen, J.: Progressive growing of GANs for improved quality, stability, and variation. arXiv preprint arXiv:1710.10196 (2017)
8. Karras, T., Laine, S., Aila, T.: A style-based generator architecture for generative adversarial networks. In: Proceedings of the IEEE Conference on Computer Vision and Pattern Recognition, pp. 4401–4410 (2019)
9. Kim, T., Cha, M., Kim, H., Lee, J.K., Kim, J.: Learning to discover cross-domain relations with generative adversarial networks. arXiv preprint arXiv:1703.05192 (2017)
10. Kingma, D.P., Ba, J.: Adam: a method for stochastic optimization. arXiv preprint arXiv:1412.6980 (2014)
11. Liu, G., Reda, F.A., Shih, K.J., Wang, T.-C., Tao, A., Catanzaro, B.: Image inpainting for irregular holes using partial convolutions. In: Ferrari, V., Hebert, M., Sminchisescu, C., Weiss, Y. (eds.) ECCV 2018. LNCS, vol. 11215, pp. 89–105. Springer, Cham (2018). https://doi.org/10.1007/978-3-030-01252-6_6
12. Liu, M.Y., Tuzel, O.: Coupled generative adversarial networks. In: Advances in Neural Information Processing Systems, pp. 469–477 (2016)
13. Ma, Y., Liu, X., Bai, S., Wang, L., He, D., Liu, A.: Coarse-to-fine image inpainting via region-wise convolutions and non-local correlation. In: IJCAI, pp. 3123–3129 (2019)
14. Mao, X., Li, Q., Xie, H., Lau, R.Y., Wang, Z., Paul Smolley, S.: Least squares generative adversarial networks. In: Proceedings of the IEEE International Conference on Computer Vision, pp. 2794–2802 (2017)
15. Mirza, M., Osindero, S.: Conditional generative adversarial nets. arXiv preprint arXiv:1411.1784 (2014)
16. Miyato, T., Kataoka, T., Koyama, M., Yoshida, Y.: Spectral normalization for generative adversarial networks. arXiv preprint arXiv:1802.05957 (2018)
17. Nazeri, K., Ng, E., Joseph, T., Qureshi, F.Z., Ebrahimi, M.: EdgeConnect: generative image inpainting with adversarial edge learning. arXiv preprint arXiv:1901.00212 (2019)
18. Ntavelis, E., Romero, A., Bigdeli, S., Timofte, R., et al.: AIM 2020 challenge on image extreme inpainting. In: European Conference on Computer Vision Workshops (2020)

19. Pathak, D., Krahenbuhl, P., Donahue, J., Darrell, T., Efros, A.A.: Context encoders: feature learning by inpainting. In: Proceedings of the IEEE Conference on Computer Vision and Pattern Recognition, pp. 2536–2544 (2016)
20. Radford, A., Metz, L., Chintala, S.: Unsupervised representation learning with deep convolutional generative adversarial networks. arXiv preprint arXiv:1511.06434 (2015)
21. Simonyan, K., Zisserman, A.: Very deep convolutional networks for large-scale image recognition. arXiv preprint arXiv:1409.1556 (2014)
22. Yeh, R.A., Chen, C., Yian Lim, T., Schwing, A.G., Hasegawa-Johnson, M., Do, M.N.: Semantic image inpainting with deep generative models. In: Proceedings of the IEEE Conference on Computer Vision and Pattern Recognition, pp. 5485–5493 (2017)
23. Yi, Z., Tang, Q., Azizi, S., Jang, D., Xu, Z.: Contextual residual aggregation for ultra high-resolution image inpainting. In: Proceedings of the IEEE/CVF Conference on Computer Vision and Pattern Recognition, pp. 7508–7517 (2020)
24. Yu, F., Koltun, V.: Multi-scale context aggregation by dilated convolutions. In: International Conference on Learning Representations (ICLR) (2016)
25. Yu, J., Lin, Z., Yang, J., Shen, X., Lu, X., Huang, T.S.: Generative image inpainting with contextual attention. In: Proceedings of the IEEE Conference on computer vision and Pattern Recognition, pp. 5505–5514 (2018)
26. Yu, J., Lin, Z., Yang, J., Shen, X., Lu, X., Huang, T.S.: Free-form image inpainting with gated convolution. In: Proceedings of the IEEE International Conference on Computer Vision, pp. 4471–4480 (2019)
27. Zhou, B., Lapedriza, A., Khosla, A., Oliva, A., Torralba, A.: Places: a 10 million image database for scene recognition. IEEE Trans. Pattern Anal. Mach. Intell. **40**, 1452–1464 (2018)

Author Index

Afifi, Mahmoud 499
Ahmed, Soikat Hasan 716
Ahn, Keon-Hee 392
Almasri, Feras 392
Arora, Aditya 392

Bae, Sung-Ho 5, 103
Baek, JaeHyun 152, 202, 392
Bai, Mengmeng 716, 742
Bao, Yingze 647
Beham, M. Parisa 499, 568
Bhaskara, Vineeth 5, 87
Bigdeli, Siavash 716
Bloch, Isabelle 280
Brown, Michael S. 499

Cai, Hengxing 499
Cai, Jie 5
Cai, Yiyang 716
Cani, Marie-Paule 392
Cao, Liang 392
Cao, Zhiguo 213, 245
Chai, Menglei 262
Chauhan, Pranjal Singh 716
Chen, Jun 152, 185
Chen, Liang 5
Chen, Long 5
Chen, Siang 5, 119, 136
Chen, Xueqin 213
Chen, Zhibo 468
Cheng, Hsuchun 647
Cheng, Jian 5, 171, 213, 229, 499, 581
Cheng, Kaihua 392, 453
Choi, Jun-Ho 5, 73, 392
Claesen, Luc 119
Cong, Xiaofeng 392
Crandall, David 312

Dai, Linhui 152, 185
Danelljan, Martin 5
Daras, Petros 682
Das, Sourya Dipta 213
Debeir, Olivier 392

Del Gobbo, Julián 629
Deora, Puneesh 152
Despois, Julien 613
Dimou, Anastasios 682
Ding, Errui 392, 423, 716
Ding, Jiaming 5
Dipta Das, Sourya 499
Dong, Chao 5, 56
Dong, Liping 499, 581
Dutta, Saikat 213

El Helou, Majed 499

Fan, Jianhua 742
Fan, Yanwen 392, 423
Fang, Chen 262
Flament, Frédéric 613
Fushishita, Naoya 596

Gao, Xinbo 5, 716
Gori, Pietro 280
Gu, Jinwei 152
Gu, Shuhang 343
Guan, Wei 392
Guo, Zhenyu 152, 171, 213, 229
Gupta, Honey 698
Gupta, Rajat 392

Han, Junyu 392, 423
Han, Yoseob 392
Han, Yu 716
Hanji, Param 376
Harada, Tatsuya 596
Hayat, Munawar 392
He, Dongliang 716
He, Jingwen 5, 56
He, Xiangyu 5, 171, 581
Ho, Chiu Man 5, 327
Hou, Bingxin 152
Hrishikesh, P. S. 5, 213, 499
Hu, Xueying 152
Hu, Zhongyun 499, 535
Huang, Kai 119, 136

Huang, Xin 499, 535
Hui, Zheng 716
Hwang, Jiwon 5, 103

Ignatov, Andrey 152, 213
Imai, Kaito 665
Ito, Yuichi 152

Jang, Hae Woong 716
Jassal, Akashdeep 499
Jeon, Geun-Woo 5, 73
Jeong, MoonSik 742
Jepson, Allan 5, 87
Jia, Yu 392, 437
Jiang, Bo 171
Jiang, Haitian 119, 136
Jiang, Jiande 5
Jiang, Jun 152
Jiang, Xiaowen 136
Jiang, Zhuolong 499, 581
Jiji, C. V. 5, 213, 499
Jiji, Charangatt Victor 519
Jin, Xin 392, 468
Jung, Yong Ju 716

Kämäräinen, Joni-Kristian 359
Kandula, Praveen 213
Kang, JungHeum 5, 103
Käpylä, Jani 359
Karageorgos, Konstantinos 682
Khan, Fahad Shahbaz 392
Khan, Salman 392
Kim, Byung-Hoon 152, 202, 392
Kim, Jun-Hyuk 5, 73, 392
Kim, Taeoh 716
Kim, Yongwoo 5, 103
Kips, Robin 280
Kneubuehler, Dario 343
Koishekenov, Yeskendir 152
Kong, Xiangtao 5, 56
Kong, Xiangzhen 5
Konstantoudakis, Konstantinos 682
Koskinen, Samu 359
Kuriakose, Melvin 213, 499, 519

Lan, Rushi 5
Lang, Zhiqiang 5
Lee, Jong-Seok 5, 73, 392
Lee, Sangyoun 716
Leng, Cong 5, 152, 171, 213, 229, 499, 581

Levinshtein, Alex 5, 87
Li, Baopu 152, 392, 423, 647
Li, Bowen 119, 136
Li, Chao 716
Li, Chenghua 5, 152, 171, 213, 229, 499, 581, 716
Li, Chengqi 152, 185
Li, Chu-Tak 392, 499, 550, 716
Li, Fu 716
Li, Hao 392
Li, Jing 437
Li, Kai 152
Li, Shuchen 716, 742
Li, Xiaobo 392
Li, Xiaochuan 5
Li, Xin 392, 468
Li, Yaning 499, 535
Li, Yawei 5
Liang, Tian 152, 171
Lin, Jiamin 213, 229
Lin, Liang 392
Lin, Yue 392
Lin, Zhe 716
Liu, Cen 392
Liu, Jianzhao 468
Liu, Jie 5, 41
Liu, Jingtuo 392, 423
Liu, Ming 152
Liu, Sen 392, 468
Liu, Shuai 5
Liu, Xiaohong 5, 152, 185
Liu, Xin 152
Liu, Yuzhong 499
Liu, Zhenbing 5
Liu, Zhi-Song 392, 499, 550, 716
Lu, Hannan 392
Lu, Huchuan 716
Lu, Wen 5
Lun, Daniel P. K. 550, 716
Luo, Xianrui 213, 245
Luo, Xiaotong 5
Luo, Zhipeng 392

Mandal, Murari 716
Mantiuk, Rafał K. 376
Marty, Eric 5
Marty, Steven 5
Matas, Jiri 359
Matuk Herrera, Rosana 629
Meng, Zhaohui 581

Meng, Zibo 5, 327
Micheloni, Christian   5, 392, 484
Minnu, A. L.   213
Mitra, Kaushik 698
Miyata, Takamichi 665
Mukuta, Yusuke 596
Muqeet, Abdul   5, 103

Na, Jaekeun 742
Nadim, Uddin S. M.   716
Nan, Nan 5
Narang, Pratik 716
Nathan, Sabari   499, 568
Ni, Haopeng 716
Nie, Jiangtao 5
Ntavelis, Evangelos 716

Pal, Umapada 152
Pan, Zhihong   152, 392, 423, 647
Pang, Yingxue   392, 468
Panikkasseril Sethumadhavan, Hrishikesh
    519
Peng, Juewen   213, 245
Peng, Yunbo 392
Peng, Zhanglin 152
Perrot, Matthieu   280, 613
Praseeda, S.   213
Purohit, Kuldeep   5, 213, 499, 716
Puthussery, Densen   5, 213, 499, 519

Qian, Ming   213, 229
Qian, Yanlin 359
Qiao, Congyu   213, 229
Qiao, Yu   5, 56
Qu, Yanyun 5

Rajagopalan, A. N.   5, 213, 499, 716
Ren, Jian 262
Ren, Sijie 152
Romero, Andrés 716

Saagara, M. B.   213
Sanjana, A. R.   213
Shah, Nisarg A.   213, 499
Shechtman, Eli 716
Shen, Xiaohui 262
Shen, Yi   392, 437
Shi, Yukai 392
Shin, Chajin 716

Singh, Richa 297
Sinha, Raunak 297
Siu, Wan-Chi   392, 550, 716
Son, Hanbin 716
Song, Joonyoung   152, 202
Suganya, R.   499
Suin, Maitreya   5, 213, 499, 716
Sun, Long 5
Süsstrunk, Sabine 499

Tan, Pengliang 152
Tang, Jie   5, 41
Tejero-de-Pablos, Antonio 596
Timofte, Radu   5, 152, 213, 343, 392, 499,
    716
Tsogkas, Stavros   5, 87
Tulyakov, Sergey 262

Umer, Rao Muhammad   5, 392, 484

Van Gool, Luc 343
Vandamme, Thomas 392
Vasudeva, Bhavya 152
Vatsa, Mayank 297

Wang, Haicheng   5, 87
Wang, Haolin 152
Wang, Li-Wen   392, 499, 550, 716
Wang, Qing   499, 535
Wang, Tengyao 213
Wang, Wenhao 5
Wang, Wenyi 5
Wang, Xiumei 716
Wang, Xuehui 5
Wei, Pengxu 392
Wei, Wei 5
Wen, Shilei 716
Wong, Hulk 213
Wu, Chenhuan   392, 453
Wu, Gangshan   5, 41
Wu, Ge 213
Wu, Guangyang 5
Wu, Haoning   392, 716
Wu, Yaojun   392, 468
Wu, Zijin   213, 245

Xi, Teng   392, 423
Xian, Ke   213, 245
Xie, Tangxin   392, 437

Xiong, Dongliang   5, 119, 136
Xu, Dejia   392, 716
Xu, Kele   499
Xu, Runsheng   327
Xu, Wenjie   5
Xu, Zhenyu   392

Yan, Qiong   5
Yang, Jianchao   262
Yang, Jimei   716
Yang, Subin   5, 103
Yang, Xiaojun   392
Yang, Zhijing   392
Yao, Yuehan   392
Ye, Chen   392
Ye, Hwechul Cho   152
Ye, Jong Chul   152, 202
Yoon, Jungmin   716

Zafeirouli, Kassiani   682
Zaman, Ishtiak   312
Zamir, Syed Waqas   392
Zeng, Bing   437
Zeng, Weijian   716
Zeng, Yu   716
Zha, Lin   5
Zhang, Gang   392, 423

Zhang, Jialiang   392, 437
Zhang, Jiangtao   5
Zhang, Jianming   716
Zhang, Jiawei   152
Zhang, Kai   5
Zhang, Lei   5
Zhang, Ruimao   152
Zhang, Yifan   171
Zhang, Zhilu   152
Zhao, Hengyuan   5, 56
Zhao, Shanshan   5, 392, 499
Zhao, Tongtong   5, 392, 499
Zhao, Yuzhi   5
Zheng, Max   213
Zhong, Fangcheng   376
Zhong, Haoyu   392
Zhou, Bo   392
Zhou, Chenchen   742
Zhou, Ruofan   499
Zhou, Yuanbo   392
Zhu, Yu   5, 152, 171, 499, 581
Zhussip, Magauiya   152
Zou, Jay   213
Zou, Xueyi   392
Zou, Yan   392
Zuo, Li   742
Zuo, Wangmeng   152, 392

Printed in the United States
By Bookmasters